THE HISTORY OF THE JEWISH PEOPLE IN THE AGE OF JESUS CHRIST

THE HISTORY OF THE JEWISH PEOPLE IN THE AGE OF JESUS CHRIST

(175 B.C.–A.D. 135)

BY

EMIL SCHÜRER

A NEW ENGLISH VERSION REVISED AND EDITED BY

GEZA VERMES FERGUS MILLAR

MATTHEW BLACK

Literary Editor
PAMELA VERMES

Organizing Editor
MATTHEW BLACK

VOLUME II

EDINBURGH T. & T. CLARK LTD 59 GEORGE STREET

Revised English Edition

PRINTED IN THE U.K. BY
PAGE BROS. (NORWICH) LTD,
BOUND BY HUNTER & FOULIS LTD, EDINBURGH
FOR

T. & T. CLARK LTD, EDINBURGH

ISBN 0 567 02243 9

LATEST IMPRESSION 1986

Preface

The basic principles underlying the revision of *Geschichte des jüdischen Volkes im Zeitalter Jesu Christi* are set out in the Preface to volume I, where it is also made plain that the editors' intention is to offer students of today an up-to-date compendium to serve as a basis for historical research. In pursuing this task, they have felt free, indeed obliged, already in volume I, to introduce new evidence unavailable to Schürer, and to replace those of his views and opinions which appear untenable in the light of contemporary knowledge.

Both these processes of modernization are even more pronounced in volume II. Sections 22 (languages), 23 I (Hellenistic cities), 24 (priesthood and worship), 27 II (Synagogue), 29 (Messianism), and especially 30 (the Essenes, with fresh appendices on the Therapeutae and the Zealots) include substantial amounts of material yielded by archaeological and manuscript discoveries during the last seven decades. (The bibliographies aim at covering important publications up to the summer of 1977.) Furthermore, in the domain of value judgments, the editors have endeavoured to clear the notorious chapter 28, *Das Leben unter dem Gesetz*—here re-styled as 'Life and the Law'—and the section on the Pharisees (§ 26 I) of the dogmatic prejudices of nineteenth-century theology. A small number of reviewers of volume I have queried the legitimacy of such an approach, but, as most critics know, this is standard policy, in fact the only possible practical method, in the revision of hand-books where the editors play the rôle of co-authors. Those primarily interested in the history of scholarship may still read the original German editions.

Special thanks are due to Dr. Philip Alexander (Manchester University) for revising § 23 II; to Dr. Robert Hayward (Lancaster University) for composing Appendix B to § 30; and to Mr. David Deboys (Wolfson College, Oxford) for compiling the list of abbreviations, and for his considerable assistance in proof-reading. The editors wish also to express their gratitude to the publishers for their help, understanding and patience.

An index to the whole work will appear in volume III.

Preface

Contents

Translators/Revisers*

T. A. Burkill, formerly Professor and Head of the Department of Theology, University of Rhodesia, Salisbury (§ 23.I).

C. H. Cave, Lecturer in Theology, University of Exeter (§ 26–29).

Malcolm C. Doubles, Professor of New Testament, St.Andrews Presbyterian College, Laurinbourg, North Carolina (§ 24–25).

L. Calista Olds, Professor of Religious Studies, Defiance College, Defiance, Ohio (§ 30).

George Ogg, D.D. (1890–1973), (§ 22).

Paul Winter, D.Phil. (1904–1969), (§ 23.II–IV).

* The figures in parentheses appended to the names of Translators/Revisers indicate the sections for which they provided the first draft.

Abbreviations

AAAS	Annales Archéologiques Arabes Syriennes
AAB	Abhandlungen der Deutschen (Preussischen) Akademie der Wissenschaften zu Berlin
AAG	Abhandlungen der Akademie der Wissenschaften in Göttingen
AAM	Abhandlungen der Bayerischen Akademie der Wissenschaften, München
AASOR	Annual of the American Schools of Oriental Research
ADAJ	Annual of the Department of Antiquities of Jordan
AE	Année Épigraphique
AIPhHOS	Annuaire de l'Institut de Philologie et d'Histoire Orientales et Slaves
AJA	American Journal of Archaeology
AJPh	American Journal of Philology
AJSL	American Journal of Semitic Languages and Literatures
ALUOS	Annual of Leeds University Oriental Society
AnglThR	Anglican Theological Review
ARAST	Atti della Reale Accademia delle Scienze di Torino
Arch. f. Pap.	Archiv für Papyrologie
ARW	Archiv für Religionswissenschaft
ASOR Newsletter	American Schools of Oriental Research Newsletter
ASTI	Annual of the Swedish Theological Institute
BA	Biblical Archaeologist
BASOR	Bulletin of the American Schools of Oriental Research
BCH	Bulletin de Correspondance Hellénique
BE	Bulletin Épigraphique, in REG
BGU	Aegyptische Urkunden aus den Staatlichen Museen zu Berlin, Griechische Urkunden
Bibl.	Biblica
BIES	Bulletin of the Israel Exploration Society
BJPES	Bulletin of the Jewish Palestine Exploration Society
BJRL	Bulletin of the John Rylands Library
BMC Arabia	G. F. Hill, *Catalogue of the Greek Coins of Arabia,*

	Mesopotamia and Persia in the British Museum (1922)
BMC Palestine	G. F. Hill, *Catalogue of the Greek Coins of Palestine in the British Museum* (1914)
BMC Phoenicia	G. F. Hill, *Catalogue of the Greek Coins of Phoenicia in the British Museum* (1910)
BMC Roman Republic	H. A. Grueber, *Coins of the Roman Republic in the British Museum* I–III (1910)
BMC Syria	W. Wroth, *Catalogue of the Greek Coins of Galatia, Cappadocia, and Syria in the British Museum* (1899)
BSOAS	Bulletin of the School of Oriental and African Studies
BWAT	Beiträge zur Wissenschaft vom Alten Testament
BZ	Biblische Zeitschrift
BZAW	Zeitschrift für die Alttestamentliche Wissenschaft, Beihefte
CAH	*Cambridge Ancient History*
CBQ	Catholic Biblical Quarterly
CCL	*Corpus Christianorum, series Latina*
CERP	A. H. M. Jones, *Cities of the Eastern Roman Provinces* ([2]1971)
CHB	*Cambridge History of the Bible*
CIG	*Corpus Inscriptionum Graecarum*
CIJ	J.-B. Frey, *Corpus Inscriptionum Iudaicarum*
CIL	*Corpus Inscriptionum Latinarum*
CIRB	I. Struve, *Corpus Inscriptionum Regni Bosporani*
CIS	*Corpus Inscriptionum Semiticarum*
CPh	Classical Philology
CPJ	V. Tcherikover, A. Fuks, M. Stern, *Corpus Papyrorum Judaicarum* I–III
CRAI	Comptes-rendus de l'Académie des Inscriptions et Belles-Lettres
CSEL	*Corpus Scriptorum Ecclesiasticorum Latinorum*
CSHB	*Corpus Scriptorum Historiae Byzantinae*
DB Supp.	*Supplément au Dictionnaire de la Bible*
DJD	*Discoveries in the Judaean Desert*
DSS	G. Vermes, *The Dead Sea Scrolls: Qumran in Perspective*
DSSE	G. Vermes, *The Dead Sea Scrolls in English* ([2]1975)
DThC	*Dictionnaire de la Théologie Catholique*
EAEHL	*Encyclopaedia of Archaeological Excavations in the Holy Land*
EB	*Encyclopaedia Biblica*
EE	Ephemeris Epigraphica
EJ	*Encyclopaedia Judaica* (A–L)
Enc. Jud.	*Encyclopaedia Judaica* (1971)
EThL	Ephemerides Theologicae Lovanienses

ET	Expository Times
ETR	Études théologiques et religieuses
EvTh	Evangelische Theologie
FGrH	F. Jacoby, *Die Fragmente der griechischen Historiker*
FHG	I. Müller, *Fragmenta Historicorum Graecorum*
FIRA[2]	S. Riccobono, *Fontes Iuris Romani Anteiustiniani*
GCS	*Die Griechischen Christlichen Schriftsteller der ersten drei Jahrhunderte*
GGR	*Geographi Graeci Minores*
GLAJJ	M. Stern, *Greek and Latin Authors on Jews and Judaism*
GMVO	H. W. Haussig, *Götter und Mythen im Vorderen Orient* I (1965)
GRM	W. H. Roscher, *Ausführliches Lexicon der griechischen und römischen Mythologie* (1884–1937)
HDB	*Hastings' Dictionary of the Bible*
HERE	*Hastings' Encyclopaedia of Religion and Ethics*
HSCPh	Harvard Studies in Classical Philology
HThR	Harvard Theological Review
HUCA	Hebrew Union College Annual
IB	*The Interpreter's Bible*
ICC	*International Critical Commentary*
IDB	*The Interpreter's Dictionary of the Bible*
IDBS	*The Interpreter's Dictionary of the Bible. Supplementary Volume*
IEJ	Israel Exploration Journal
IG	*Inscriptiones Graecae*
IGLS	*Inscriptions grecques et latines de la Syrie*
IGR	R. Cagnat *et al., Inscriptiones Graecae ad Res Romanas Pertinentes* I, III, IV
IGUR	L. Moretti, *Inscriptiones Graecae Urbis Romae*
ILS	H. Dessau, *Inscriptiones Latinae Selectae*
INB	Israel Numismatic Bulletin
INJ	Israel Numismatic Journal
IOSPE	I. Latyschev, *Inscriptiones Antiquae Orae Septentrionalis Ponti Euxini Graecae et Latinae*
JA	Journal Asiatique
JAC	Jahrbuch für Antike und Christentum
JAOS	Journal of the American Oriental Society
JBL	Journal of Biblical Literature
JBR	Journal of Bible and Religion
JE	*The Jewish Encyclopaedia*
JEA	Journal of Egyptian Archaeology
JHS	Journal of Hellenic Studies
JJS	Journal of Jewish Studies

JNES	Journal of Near Eastern Studies
JOAI	Jahreshefte des Österreichischen Archäologischen Instituts
JPFC	S. Safrai and M. Stern, *The Jewish People in the First Century*
JPOS	Journal of the Palestine Oriental Society
JQR	Jewish Quarterly Review
JR	Journal of Religion
JRS	Journal of Roman Studies
JSJ	Journal for the Study of Judaism in the Persian, Hellenistic and Roman Period
JSS	Journal of Semitic Studies
JThSt	Journal of Theological Studies
JZWL	Jüdische Zeitschrift für Wissenschaft und Leben
KAI	H. Donner and W. Röllig, *Kanaanäische und aramäische Inschriften* ([2]1966–9)
LThK	*Lexicon für Theologie und Kirche*
MAMA	*Monumenta Asiae Minoris Antiqua*
MDPV	Mitteilungen und Nachrichten des Deutschen Palästina-Vereins
MGWJ	Monatsschrift für Geschichte und Wissenschaft des Judentums
MRR	T. R. S. Broughton, *Magistrates of the Roman Republic* I–II
MUSJ	Mélanges de l'Université St. Joseph
NAG	Nachrichten der Akademie der Wissenschaften, Göttingen
NAWG	Nachrichten von der Akademie der Wissenschaften in Göttingen
NGGW	Nachrichten von der (Kgl.) Gesellschaft der Wissenschaften zu Göttingen
NKZ	Neue Kirchliche Zeitschrift
NT	Novum Testamentum
NTSt	New Testament Studies
NZST	Neue Zeitschrift für systematische Theologie
ÖAW	Österreichische Akademie der Wissenschaften
OGIS	W. Dittenberger, *Orientis Graeci Inscriptiones Selectae* I–II
OLZ	Orientalische Literaturzeitung
OTS	Oudtestamentische Studien
OuTW	De Ou Testamentiese Werkgemeenskap in Suid-Africa
PAAJR	Proceedings of the American Academy for Jewish Research
PBJS	G. Vermes, *Post-Biblical Jewish Studies* (1975)

PBSR	Papers of the British School at Rome
PEFA	Palestine Exploration Fund Appeal
PEFQSt	Palestine Exploration Fund Quarterly Statement
PEQ	Palestine Exploration Quarterly
PG	J.-P. Migne, *Patrum Graecorum Cursus Completus*
PL	J.-P. Migne, *Patrum Latinorum Cursus Completus*
PIR[1]	*Prosopographia Imperii Romani*[1]
PIR[2]	*Prosopographia Imperii Romani*[2]
PJB	Palästinajahrbuch
PSI	Papiri della Società Italiana
QDAP	Quarterly of the Department of Antiquities of Palestine
RA	Revue d'assyriologie et d'archéologie orientale
RAC	*Reallexikon für Antike und Christentum*
RB	Revue Biblique
RE	Pauly-Wissowa, *Realencyclopädie der classischen Altertumswissenschaft*
REG	Revue des Études Grecques
REJ	Revue des Études Juives
RES	Répertoire d'épigraphie sémitique I–VII
Rev. arch.	Revue archéologique
RGG	*Die Religion in Geschichte und Gegenwart*
RhM	Rheinisches Musäum
RHPR	Revue d'histoire et de philosophie religieuses
RHR	Revue de l'Histoire des Religions
RIB	*Roman Inscriptions of Britain*
RN	Revue Numismatique
RQ	Revue de Qumrân
RSR	Recherches de Science Religieuse
RThom.	Revue Thomiste
SAB	Sitzungsberichte der Deutschen Akademie der Wissenschaften zu Berlin
SAH	Sitzungsberichte der Heidelberger Akademie der Wissenschaften
SAM	Sitzungsberichte der Bayerischen Akademie der Wissenschaften
SAW	Sitzungsberichte der Österreichischen Akademie der Wissenschaften in Wien
SBFLA	Studii Biblici Franciscani Liber Annuus
Scrip. Hier.	*Scripta Hierosolymitana*
SEG	Supplementum Epigraphicum Graecum
SEHHW	M. Rostovtzeff, *Social and Economic History of the Hellenistic World* (1941)
SHA	Scriptores Historiae Augustae
SIG[3]	W. Dittenberger, *Sylloge Inscriptionum Graecarum*[3]

ST *Studi e Testi*
SThU Schweizerische Theologische Umschau
Strack H. L. Strack, *Introduction to Talmud and Midrash*
Str.-B. H. L. Strack–P. Billerbeck, *Kommentar zum Neuen Testament aus Talmud und Midrasch*
TAPhA Transactions of the American Philological Association
TDNT *Theological Dictionary to the New Testament*
ThLZ Theologische Literaturzeitung
ThStKr Theologische Studien und Kritiken
ThT Theologisch Tijdschrift
ThWNT *Theologisches Wörterbuch zum Neuen Testament*
ThZ Theologische Zeitschrift
TU *Texte und Untersuchungen*
VT Vetus Testamentum
YCS Yale Classical Studies
ZA Zeitschrift für Assyriologie
ZAW Zeitschrift für die Altestamentliche Wissenschaft
ZDMG Zeitschrift der Deutschen Morgenländischen Gesellschaft
ZDPV Zeitschrift der Deutschen Palästina-Vereins
ZNW Zeitschrift für die Neutestamentliche Wissenschaft
ZPE Zeitschrift für Papyrologie und Epigraphik
Zunz L. Zunz, *Die gottesdienstlichen Vorträge der Juden* ([2]1892)
ZWTh Zeitschrift für Wissenschaftliche Theologie

Papyrus Abbreviations

PCZ(en) = *Catalogue géneral des antiquités égyptienne du Musée du Caire*
P. Cairo Zenon or P. Zenon *Zenon Papyri* I–V, ed. C. C. Edgar (1925–40)
P. Col. Zenon = *Zenon Papyri: Business Papers of the Third Century B.C. dealing with Palestine and Egypt* I, ed. W. L. Westermann and E. S. Hasenoehrl (1934); II, ed. W. L. Westermann, C. W. Keyes and H. Liebesny (1940)
P. Nessana = *Excavations at Nessana* III: *Non-literary Papyri* ed. C. J. Kraemer (1958)
P. Ryl. = *Catalogue of the Greek Papyri in the John Rylands Library, Manchester* I–IV (1911–52)
P. Cairo = *Greek Papyri, Catalogue géneral des antiquités égyptiennes du Musée de Caire* X (1903)
P. Lond. = *Greek Papyri in the British Museum* I–VII (1893–1974)
P. Oxy. = *The Oxyrhynchus Papyri* (1898–)
PSI = *Papiri della Società Italiana*

§ 22. THE CULTURAL SETTING

I. Population and Language

In the Greek and Roman period, as in earlier centuries, the Jewish population of Palestine fluctuated considerably both in numbers and extent. From the beginning of the Hellenistic epoch to the time of the Maccabaean uprising, the Jewish element was gradually receding whereas the Greek element was on the advance. A significant change, however, resulted from the Maccabaean revolt and its after-effects: Judaism gained ground intensively and extensively, consolidating itself internally and extending its boundaries in almost every direction.[1]

At the beginning of the Maccabaean period, a compact Jewish population existed only in Judaea proper, i.e. in the region south of Samaria named in 1 Maccabees *Ἰούδα* or *γῆ Ἰούδα* or *Ἰουδαία*.[2] The area occupied by the Jews can be determined with tolerable accuracy for the years 175–135 B.C. The most northerly districts, which were in cultic association with Jerusalem (where the population was therefore not Samaritan but Jewish), were the *νομοί* of Lydda, Ramathaim and Ephraim. Politically, these belonged until 145 B.C. to the province of

1. See G. Hölscher, *Palästina in der persischen und hellenistischen Zeit* (1903); A. Schlatter, *Geschichte Israels von Alexander der Grosse bis Hadrian* ([3]1925); F.-M. Abel, *Géographie de la Palestine II: Géographie politique, les villes* ([2]1938); V. Tcherikover, *Hellenistic Civilization and the Jews* (1959); E. Bickerman, *From Ezra to the last of the Maccabees* (1962). Note also S. K. Eddy, *The King is Dead, Studies in Near Eastern Resistance to Hellenism 334 B.C.–31 B.C.* (1961), especially pp. 183 f.; M. Avi-Yonah, *The Holy Land from the Persian to the Arab Conquests (536 B.C. to A.D. 640): A historical geography* (1966); *idem*, 'Palestina', RE Supp. XIII (1973), cols. 321–454; C. Schneider, *Kulturgeschichte des Hellenismus* I (1967), pp. 864 ff. For the background see the major work by M. Hengel, *Judentum und Hellenismus: Studien zu ihrer Begegnung unter besonderer Berücksichtigung Palästinas biz zur Mitte des 2. Jh. v. Chr.* (1969; [2]1973); English transl., *Judaism and Hellenism* I–II (1974), to which all references will be made. See F. Millar, 'The Background to the Maccabean Revolution: Reflections on Martin Hengel's "Judaism and Hellenism" ', JJS 29 (1978), pp. 1–21.

2. The name *Ἰουδαία* is attested from the beginning of the Hellenistic period: Clearchus in Josephus, *C. Apion.* i 22 (179) = GLAJJ, no. 15: *προσαγορεύεται γὰρ ὃν κατοικοῦσι τόπον Ἰουδαία*; Hecataeus of Abdera in Diodorus xl 3 = Jacoby, FGrH 264 F6 (2) = GLAJJ, no. 11: *εἰς τὴν καλουμένην Ἰουδαίαν*; Manetho in Josephus, *C. Apion.* i 14 (90) = FGrH 609 F8 (90) = GLAJJ, no. 19: *ἐν τῇ νῦν Ἰουδαίᾳ*. For the series of coins of the late Persian and early Hellenistic period giving the official name of the area as יהד (Y[e]hud), or יהדה (Y[e]hudah), see vol. I, p. 603; A. Kindler, 'Silver Coins Bearing the Name of Judea from the Early Hellenistic Period', IEJ 24 (1974), pp. 73–6, and D. Jeselsohn, *ibid.* pp. 77–8.

Samaria, but they were then ceded by Demetrius II to the Jewish High Priest Jonathan because, as is clearly indicated, the population there offered sacrifice in Jerusalem (1 Mac. 11:34). From that time onwards, these districts were always considered to be part of Judaea.[3]

To the east, the Jews no doubt extended as far as the Jordan. Jericho is mentioned among the cities 'in Judaea' which Bacchides fortified and garrisoned with Gentile troops to keep the Jewish population in check (1 Mac. 9:50–2).

To the south, Beth-zur constituted the furthest outpost of Judaism. Judas established a Jewish garrison there to defend the people against Idumaea (1 Mac. 4:61; cf. 6:7, 26). After a few years, however, this garrison was obliged to surrender to the Syrian king and was replaced by a Gentile force (1 Mac. 6:31, 49–50; 2:52). But Simon Maccabee reconquered the city (1 Mac. 11:65–6). South of Beth-zur, on a line from Hebron to Marisa (to be read in 1 Mac. 5:66 instead of Samaria) lived the Gentile sons of Esau, who were repeatedly punished by Judas for ill-treating the Jews among them (1 Mac. 5:2–3, 65–7).[4]

3. For their location see vol. I, p. 182; cf. also I, pp. 140–1.

4. Some sources claim that the settlements of Jews after the Babylonian exile went much further south than Beth-zur, namely as far as Beer-sheba (Neh. 11: 25–30). Note that Aramaic ostraca of the Persian period from there suggest that the population may have included Jews and Arameans as well as Edomites and Arabs, see Y. Aharoni (ed.), *Beer-Sheba* I (1973), pp. 79–82. Southern Judaea was occupied by the Edomites already in the time of Ezekiel, immediately after the conquest of Jerusalem by Nebuchadnezzar (Ezek. 35:10–15; 36:5). As later history shows, they remained there from then on, abandoning their old and more southerly abode in the neighbourhood of Sela (=Petra) to the Nabataeans, who are found there from the end of the fourth century B.C. (see vol. I., App. 2). On the history of the Edomites see E. Meyer, *Die Israeliten und ihre Nachbarstämme* (1906), pp. 328 ff.; F.-M. Abel, *Géog. Pal.* I (1933), pp. 281 ff.; N. Glueck, *The Other Side of Jordan* (1940); DB Supp. s.v. 'Idumée'; J. R. Bartlett, 'The Rise and Fall of the Kingdom of Edom', PEQ 1972, pp. 26–37; C. M. Bennett, s.v. 'Edom', IDBS, pp. 251–2. Jewish territory in the time of Nehemiah, as may be seen from Neh. 3, extended not much farther south than Beth-zur. Accordingly, the list in Neh. 11: 25–30 either refers to the pre-exilic period (so J. Wellhausen, *Zur Israelit. und jüd. Geschichte* (1894), p. 122; A. Schlatter, *Zur Topographie und Geschichte Palästinas* (1893), p. 53), or it is an invention of the chronicler (so E. Meyer, *Die Entstehung des Judentums* (1896), pp. 105–8, 114 ff.; Hölscher, *op. cit.*, pp. 26 f.); cf. Y. Aharoni, *The Land of the Bible* (1967), pp. 355–6, who regards it as implying that these areas still contained some Jewish population. In the Maccabaean period, in any case, only a Jewish diaspora lived beyond Beth-zur (cf. 1 Mac. 5:2–3). The bulk of the population was Edomite. That is attested not only by 1 Mac, 4:61 and 5:65–7, but also by the history of John Hyrcanus. He was the first to conquer and Judaize Adora and Marisa, until then Edomite cities, Josephus *Ant.* xiii 9, 1 (257); *B.J.* i 2, 6 (63). Adora lay just a little south of Beth-zur, Marisa west of Beth-zur. See U. Kahrstedt, *Syrische Territorien in hellenistischer Zeit* (1926), especially pp. 56 ff.; M. Avi-Yonah, *The Holy Land* (1966), p. 37. Note that the name *'Ιδουμαία* is attested in a Zenon papyrus of 259/8 B.C., PCZ 59015, l. 42, which like 59006 and 59537 also mentions Marisa (below).

To the west, the coastal cities with their vast territories reaching far into the interior were wholly Gentile. Most of them, Raphia, Gaza, Anthedon, Ashkelon and Ashdod, remained so. The furthest limit of Judaism to the north-west was provided by Lydda, as already mentioned (1 Mac. 11:34). Nearby lay Adida, fortified by Simon Maccabee (1 Mac. 12:38). South of Adida was Emmaus, the most westerly Jewish city (1 Mac. 9:50). For even Gazara, a short distance west of Emmaus, was at that time still Gentile. But it was precisely to the west that Judaism advanced as early as the Maccabean period. A connection with the coast was of fundamental importance to material prosperity. And this connection was sought and achieved in such a way that the population was also Judaized. Whether Ekron was dealt with in the same manner when Jonathan received it as a gift from Alexander Balas (1 Mac. 10: 88–9) is not known. It is certain, however, that the hitherto Gentile cities of Joppa and Gazara were converted to Judaism by force. Simon set up a Jewish garrison at Joppa (1 Mac. 12:33–4) and soon afterwards drove out its Gentile inhabitants (1 Mac. 13:11). He captured Gazara after a difficult siege and similarly expelled its inhabitants, settling people there who observed the Torah (1 Mac. 13:43–8: *οἵτινες τὸν νόμον ποιοῦσι*).[5] Joppa was the one coastal city to be formally Judaized. But in addition the Jewish element also obtained the upper hand in Jamnia. This does not seem to have happened before 135 B.C.; the books of the Maccabees describe Jamnia as a Gentile city (1 Mac. 5:58; 2 Mac. 12:8 ff., 40) and relate nothing of its permanent occupation by the Jews. But in the time of Philo, the bulk of the population of Jamnia was Jewish.[6]

A considerable expansion of the Jewish element towards the south was made possible by the subjugation of the Idumaeans. John Hyrcanus captured the cities of Adora and Marisa, defeated all the Idumaeans and compelled them to accept circumcision and the Jewish law. From then on, the Idumaeans were Jews, and appeared as such even during the war against the Romans in A.D. 67/68.[7] A Hellenistic colony also inhabited Marisa at the time of its capture by John Hyrcanus. Indeed,

5. On Joppa, see also pp. 110–14 below; on Gazara, vol. I, p. 191. In excavations at Gazara (Gezer), large quantities have been found of handles of earthenware jugs (amphoras) of the same kind as those discovered at Marisa (see n. 8). The Greek stamp which they all bear testifies to their manufacture in Rhodes in the 3rd or 2nd century B.C., and therewith to the introduction of Hellenism even into Gazara before it was Judaized by Simon Maccabee. See R. A. S. Macalister, *The Excavation of Gezer 1902–1905 and 1907–1909* I–III (1912); cf. Abel, *Géog. Pal.* II, pp. 332–3. This is true, however, of almost all sites in Palestine; see Hengel, *op. cit.* II, p. 35, n. 342.

6. Philo *Legat.* 30 (200). Cf. §23.I below.

7. Josephus, *Ant.* xiii 9, 1 (257 f.). Cf. also *B.J.* i 2, 6 (63); *Ant.* xv 7, 9 (254); *B.J.* iv 4, 4 (281). See also vol. I, p. 207.

it appears to have been a fairly important one, for the city was among those subsequently liberated by Pompey from the Jews, which in general happened only in the case of Hellenistic cities.[8] Probably,

8. The excavation in 1902 of some rock-cut tombs has provided remarkable information on the degree of Hellenism in Marisa in around 200 B.C. See the reports of J.-M. Lagrange, 'Deux hypogées Macédo-Sidoniens à Beit-Djebrin', CRAI 1902, pp. 497–505, and J. P. Peters and M. Thiersch, *The Painted Tombs in the Necropolis of Marissa* (1905); C. Watzinger, *Denkmäler Palästinas* II (1935), pp. 17 f.; see also R. A. S. Macalister, 'The erotic graffito in the tomb of Apollophanes of Marissa', PEFQSt 1906, pp. 54–62; 158–9; W. F. Albright, 'Two Cressets from Marisa and the Pillars of Jachim and Boaz', BASOR 85 (1942), p. 18; Tcherikover, *op. cit.*, pp. 105, 115–16; E. R. Goodenough, *Symbols* I (1953), pp. 65 f. The tombs are at Tell Sandahannah south of Beit Jibrin, the Eleutheropolis of the Roman period. As Tell Sandahannah had been shown by Macalister's excavations to have been a city of some significance, there was already reason to suppose that this was the site of the ancient Marisa. According to Eusebius, *Onomast.* (ed. Klostermann, p. 130), Marisa was situated 12 miles from Eleutheropolis; the old name survives in nearby Khirbet Merash. But it is Tell Sandahannah and not Khirbet Merash that should more accurately be regarded as the site of the ancient city. This is confirmed by one of the tomb inscriptions in which Marisa appears as the name of the city (see below). The workmanship of all the burial-places is especially reminiscent of the Egyptian tombs of the period of the Ptolemies. In Tomb I, which probably belongs to the end of the third century B.C., a great frieze of animals is painted on the walls of the principal chamber and above the animals their names are given in Greek: *πάρδαλος*, *πάνθηρος* (*sic*), *ταῦρος* (?), *καμελοπάρδαλος* (?), *γρύψ*, *ῥινόκερως*, *ἐλέφας*, *κροκοδῖλος*, *ἶβις*, *ὀνάγριος* (*sic*), *ὕστριξ* (porcupine), *λύγξ*. On the left of the entrance to this chamber is the painting of a chthonic cock, and on the right, one of three-headed Cerberus. Of the personal names written over the *loculi*, more than half are Greek, and the rest Hellenized Semitic; among the latter, some are Phoenician: *Σεσμαιος*, *Μεερβαλος*, and some Idumaean: *Κοσνατανος*, *Κοσβανος*, from the Idumaean god קס, to be distinguished from *Κοζέ* despite Josephus *Ant.* xv 7, 9 (253); cf. Baudissin s.v. 'Edom', Herzog-Hauck, *Real-Enz.*[3], pp. 166 ff. See T. C. Vriezen, OTS 14 (1965), p. 333; Hengel, *Judaism* II, pp. 44–5, n. 32). The following inscription, however, is of especial importance (*Painted Tombs*, pp. 36 and 38 = OGIS 593): *Ἀπολλοφάνης Σεσμαίου ἄρξας τῶν ἐν Μαρίσῃ Σιδωνίων ἔτη τριάκοντα καὶ τρία*. It is clear from this that a colony of Sidonians of Greek culture lived in Marisa, whose *archon* the deceased had been. The whole burial plot presumably belonged to this colony but, as the Idumaean proper names show, its members also intermarried over the course of time with the natives. In addition to the inscriptions above the *loculi* are others on the walls; thus a certain *Ὀρτας Μακεδών* has perpetuated his memory on the wall in the vicinity of the altar (*Painted Tombs*, p. 56, pl. XX, n. 31); he was probably a visitor to the tombs. In Tomb II there are also some wall-paintings. The personal names are predominantly Greek but some are Phoenician (*Βαδων*, p. 65; *Βαλσαλω*, p. 66; the latter = בעלצלח, which occurs on a Sidonian inscription). A woman called Philotion is designated *Σιδωνία* (p. 66), from which it may be concluded that the majority of those buried in this place were not Sidonians. Tombs III and IV provide little worthy of note. Several of the inscriptions are dated (see the table in *Painted Tombs*, p. 77). Tomb I shows *ZP* = 107 (so Lagrange; Peters regards this as doubtful and is inclined to read *ΞP* = 160), *AOP* = 171, *ΔYP* = 194; in Tomb II, the seven dates range within the limits *EKP* = 125 and *HOP* = 178; in Tomb III occurs *ΘOP* = 179. Assuming, as is very likely, that the Seleucid era was used, 107 (correctly read) = 206/205 B.C.,

Adora was also on the way to being Hellenized. For the city of 'Dora', where, according to an anti-Jewish story reproduced by Apion, Apollo was venerated, cannot have been the Phoenician Dora south of

---

194=119/118 B.C. This last date falls roughly in the period of the capture of Marisa by John Hyrcanus. The numbers *A*, *B*, *E* (1, 2, 5) appearing in Tomb I are striking; it is not likely that these refer to the Pompeian era. Note also the neighbouring tomb published by W. J. Moulton in AJA 19 (1915), pp. 63–70, with the dates 115=198 B.C.; 117 (?)=196 B.C.; 172=141 B.C.; 201 (?)=112 B.C. Cf. Hengel, *Judaism* II, pp. 44–5, n. 32.

It was the excavation of these burial-places that first threw light on the discoveries at Tell Sandahannah. (1) Particularly noteworthy among several fragmentary inscriptions is part of a memorial inscription which, according to the reasonable restoration suggested by Clermont-Ganneau, relates to Arsinoe III Philopator, the sister and consort of Ptolemy IV Philopator (221–205 B.C.): [*Βασίλισσαν 'Αρσ*]*ινόην μεγάλην*/[. . . *Φιλοπάτ*]*ορα τὴν ἐγ βασίλεως*/[*Πτολεμαίου καὶ βασίλισσης* [*Βερενί*/*κης, θεῶν εὐεργέτων*]. See C. Clermont-Ganneau, CRAI 1900, pp. 536–41; *id.* in *Rec. d'arch. or.* IV (1901), pp. 152–6; cf. PEFQSt 1901, pp. 54–8. Facsimile also in F. J. Bliss and R.A.S. Macalister, *Excavations in Palestine* (1902), pp. 68, 69. Another fragment shows the name *Βερενί*[*κη*]. (2) To this same period—the third or second century B.C.—belong the more than 300 amphora handles accumulated at Tell Sandahannah. See Macalister, 'Amphora Handles with Greek Stamps from Tell Sandahannah', PEFQSt (1901), pp. 25–43, 124–43, Supp. pp. 394–7. Cf. also Bliss and Macalister, *Excavations in Palestine*, pp. 52 ff., 131–4. The Greek stamps found on all these handles show that the amphoras of which they are the remnants came from Rhodes. For details see II, 2 below, in the section on trade. (3) Probably to this period—around the second century B.C.—belong also the Greek invocation-oaths (scarified on limestone) accumulated at Tell Sandahannah, cf. Bliss and Macalister, *Excavations in Palestine*, pp. 158–87. R. Wünsch placed them as late as the second century A.D. (*ibid.*, pp. 181 f.). But the character of the script in no way supports this late dating. See the observations of Thiersch, *Painted Tombs*, p. 72, and esp. A. Wilhelm, 'Über die Zeit einiger attischer Fluchtafeln', JÖAI 7 (1904), pp. 105–26. (4) Equally to the pre-Christian period belongs an inscription found in a large *columbarium* (burial-place) at Tell Sandahannah: *Σιμὴ καλὴ δοκεὶ ἐμοὶ Λ. Νικατείδι*. See Macalister, PEFQSt (1901), pp. 11–19; Clermont-Ganneau, *ibid.*, pp. 116–18 and *Rec.* IV, pp. 237–40, pl. 1; facsimile in Bliss and Macalister, *Excavations in Palestine*, p. 245. The inscription can only be understood as a lover's message for which the hidden burial-place was used. An analogous and much longer inscription appears also among those described by Peters and Thiersch in *Painted Tombs*, pp. 56–60; cf. Macalister, 'The erotic graffito etc.', PEFQSt (1906), pp. 54–62. (5) It is of importance finally that among the sixty-one coins brought to light in the excavations at Tell Sandahannah, thirteen are Ptolemaic, nineteen Seleucid, and twenty-five of John Hyrcanus (*Excavations*, p. 68). See now EAEHL s.v. 'Maresha'.

All these finds show that in the period immediately preceding the capture of Marisa by John Hyrcanus Hellenism was well established there. It was because of the remaining Greek element, preserved there even under Jewish domination, that Pompey separated it from the Jewish territory, *Ant.* xiv, 4, 4 (75), *B.J.* i 7, 7 (156), and Gabinius restored it, *Ant.* xiv 5, 3 (88), *B.J.* i 8, 4 (166). As a result of the destruction of the city by the Parthians in 40 B.C., *Ant.* xiv 13, 9 (364), *B.J.* i 13, 9 (269), Hellenism too was brought to an end there.

Ptolemais, since it is described as an Idumaean city, and according to the legend must have been situated not far from Jerusalem. It is much more likely that Adora is meant.[9] Although not mentioned among the cities liberated by Pompey, it was one of those said to have been restored by Gabinius,[10] which may also be seen as evidence that before its capture by John Hyrcanus a proportion of its inhabitants were Greeks.

The capture of Raphia, Gaza and Anthedon by Alexander Jannaeus was not followed by the conversion of these towns to Judaism. Pompey and Gabinius had more success there in restoring Greek culture than in the Idumaean cities just mentioned.

In regard to the extent of the Jewish population during the last few decades before the war of A.D. 70 a great deal is known, since the description of the land given by Josephus in *B.J.* iii 3 (35–58) defines the boundaries of the territories inhabited by Jews.[11] It confirms

9. Josephus *c. Ap.* ii 9 (112–16) = FGrH 616 F4(k) = GLAJJ, no. 172 and commentary on no. 28. Apion drew on the fable of an earlier Hellenistic author named Mnaseas in the mss. According to Niese, the reference is to Mnaseas, a pupil of Eratosthenes (*c.* 200 B.C.), see GLAJJ, pp. 97–101. Although Josephus asserts that there was no Dora in Idumaea, the identity with Adora (which appears as Ἀδώρεον in PCZ 59006, col. iii, of the mid-third century B.C.) can be regarded as certain. Its name in Arabic is still Dura, see Abel, *Géog. Pal.* II, p. 239. R. Marcus, *Josephus* (Loeb) VII, p. 330, note b, suggests that in *c. Ap.* ii 9 (116) Josephus is merely criticizing Mnaseas for saying 'Dora' when he should have said 'Adora'. For the worship of Apollo in Adora note especially an inscription from Memphis in Egypt belonging to the beginning of the second century B.C.; Ἰδουμαῖοι appear to hold their assembly ἐν τῷ ἄνω Ἀπολλωνιείῳ, OGIS 737 = Sammelbuch, no. 681; see U. Rapaport, 'Les Iduméens en Égypte', Rev. Phil. 43 (1969), pp. 73–82.

10. *Ant.* xiv 5, 3 (88); *B.J.* i 8, 4 (166). In *Ant.* xiv 5, 3 (88), Niese followed the best MS reading and restored Ἄδωρα as the name of the town mentioned with Marisa, instead of Δῶρα, found in most codices. In the parallel passage, *B.J.* i 8, 4 (166), the reading Ἀδώρεος (instead of Δώρεος) is guaranteed by two good MSS (and cf. PCZ 59006, n. 9 above). The ease with which corruption was able to slip in is shown by *Ant.* xiii 6, 4 (207), where all the mss. have Δῶρα πόλιν τῆς Ἰδουμαίας, whereas according to 1 Mac. 13:20 the reading should be Ἄδωρα.

11. There can be no doubt, from the whole context, that in the passage referred to this was Josephus's intention. He names the Gentile territories only in order to define the boundaries of the Jewish areas. Galilee is bounded in the west by the territory of Ptolemais, on the north by that of Tyre, on the east by that of Hippos and Gadara, *B.J.* iii 3, 1 (35–40). Peraea is bordered on the north by the territory of Pella, on the east by that of Philadelphia and Gerasa, *B.J.* iii, 3, 3 (47). Also, in the description of Judaea the Gentile cities of the coast are not attributed to Judaea; it is simply said that Judaea is not without the benefits that come from the sea since it extends as far as the coastal lands, *B.J.* iii, 3, 5 (53). Jewish Joppa is not once assigned to Judaea, but the latter is said to extend μέχρις Ἰόπης. But it is very characteristic that after the description of the four Jewish provinces of Galilee, Peraea, Samaria and Judaea, the following are named by way of supplement: (1) the territory of Jamnia and Joppa, because they were the only coastal cities inhabited predominantly by Jews; (2) the provinces belonging to the

everything already learned from the earlier history, and in particular that, of the coastal cities, only Joppa and Jamnia possessed a predominantly Jewish population. Of the villages said by Josephus in *B.J.* iii 3, 5 (51) to form the northern and southern limits of Judaea proper, *'Ανουάθου Βόρκαιος* is probably the modern Berkit, nine miles south of Shechem, and *'Ιαρδά(ν)* is perhaps Tel Arad, sixteen miles south of Hebron.[12] Concerning the division of the region into eleven toparchies, according to his information the most northern of these was Acrabetta. As this place was located considerably further north than Ephraim (see p. 192 below), it may be assumed that since the Maccabaean period Judaism had also spread further towards the north.[13] The two most southerly toparchies were Idumaea and Engeddi. Thus Idumaea was regarded as entirely Jewish, i.e. a land inhabited by Jews. One of the points furthest south was Malatha, which is mentioned as an Idumaean city in the story of the wanderings of Agrippa I.[14]

Whereas in the environs of Judaea only a further spread of the Jewish population had occurred since the time of the Maccabees, Galilee had become an entirely Jewish country for the first time.[15] The restoration of the Jewish community after the exile concerned only Judaea proper. A simultaneous restoration in Galilee, or one that followed soon afterwards, is nowhere attested and even less to be assumed, bearing in mind that before the exile that region was never inhabited by Israelites. גליל הגוים (Isa. 8:23 [E.V. 9:1]) was the most northerly Gentile region of the Israelite kingdom. Elsewhere, it is called simply הגליל, from which *Γαλιλαία*, the name of the region,

---

kingdom of Agrippa—Gamalitis, Gaulanitis, Batanaea and Trachonitis—because the Jewish element there formed a very considerable proportion of the population. It is particularly interesting that Josephus includes Samaria in this description, evidently because he regarded the Samaritans as being essentially Jews, although heterodox.

12. Cf. H. St. J. Thackeray, *Josephus* (Loeb) II, p. 590, notes *b*, *d*.

13. In another passage, *Ant.* xiv 3, 4 (49); *B.J.* i 6, 5 (134), Josephus characterizes Coreae as the northernmost place in Judaea. Its location, as J. Gildemeister, ZDPV 4 (1881), pp. 245 f., determined (cf. vol. I, p. 238), accords with the fact that Acrabattene was the northernmost toparchy of Judaea. Coreae is now identified with Tell Mazar near Kurawa, cf. Abel, *Géog. Pal.* II, p. 301.

14. Josephus *Ant.* xviii 6, 2 (147). According to the *Onomasticon* of Eusebius, Malatha lay 24 Roman miles south of Hebron. Cf. vol. I, p. 443. The Jewish population on the shore of the Dead Sea certainly extended to Masada, as is attested by the events which occurred there during the first war against the Romans, *B.J.* vii 8–9 (252–406).

15. Compare S. Klein, *Galiläa von der Makkabäerzeit bis 67* (1928), pp. 1–21; cf. Hebrew edition, *Galilee*, ed. Y. Elitzur (1967), pp. 9–25; Tcherikover, *Hellenistic Civilisation*, pp. 209–10; Avi-Yonah, *Holy Land*, pp. 66–7.

derives.[16] But in addition to *Γαλιλαία* (1 Mac. 5:14, 17–23, 55; 10:30; 11:63; 12:47, 49), 1 Mac. 5:15 still gives the more precise designation *Γαλιλαία ἀλλοφύλων*. The term Galilee seems by now, in any case, to have included not only the former Gentile district in the neighbourhood of Kedesh (so still in 1 Mac. 11:63), but also the land lying further south as far as the Great Plain south-east of Ptolemais (see especially 1 Mac. 12:47, 49). Accordingly, *Γαλιλαία ἀλλοφύλων* is perhaps a narrower term than *Γαλιλαία*. But even in the whole of Galilee the actual Jewish population can have formed only a slender minority. The earliest indication that the inhabitants of this locality adhered to the cult in Jerusalem in the post-exilic period is given by the Chronicler when he relates that, in the time of Hezekiah, men of Asher, Manasseh and Zebulun humbled themselves and came to Jerusalem (2 Chron. 30:10–11). The district of Zebulun corresponds with tolerable accuracy to what was later known as Lower (Southern) Galilee; the district of Manasseh adjoins it on the south, that of Asher on the north. By applying the conditions of his own age to that of Hezekiah, the Chronicler testifies indirectly that in his time (fourth century B.C.) a proportion of the population of those regions was in cultic communion with Jerusalem. But the number must have been small. This is apparent from the manner in which Simon Maccabee aided the Jews of Galilee harassed by the Gentiles. When news came from Galilee that the Jews there were being persecuted by the Gentiles, it was decided that Simon should bring them help (1 Mac. 5:14–17). He set off for Galilee with three thousand men and defeated the Gentiles (1 Mac. 5:20–22). But the consequence of this was not that he occupied Galilee. On the contrary, he brought the Jews living there, with their wives and children, to Judaea (1 Mac. 5:23). Thus instead of protecting the Jewish population on the spot, he took them all out of Galilee. This is conceivable only if they formed a small minority, indeed no more than a diaspora among the Gentiles.[17] And although the removal of the Jews at that time was not complete, nevertheless the Jewish element in Galilee in the following years was less strongly represented than it had been until then.[18]

16. In the LXX, הגליל is already translated *Γαλιλαία*. The name appears for the first time in Greek in a Zenon papyrus dated 259 B.C., see Avi-Yonah, *Holy Land*, p. 56; CPJ I, no. 2e. According to 1 Kgs. 9:11, Solomon presented twenty cities of *Galil* to Hiram, king of Tyre. In Jos. 20:7; 21:32; 1 Chron. 6:61, Kedesh, situated north west of the Lake of Merom, is described as a city of *Galil*. In 2 Kgs. 15:29, הגלילה is named with Kedesh, Hazor and Gilead among the districts whose population was carried off by Tiglath-Pileser. Isa. 8:23 (=E.V. 9:1) looks back to this when he promises better times for these regions.

17. See vol. I, p. 165.

18. Note however the evidence given by M. Stern, GLAJJ I, p. 225, to show a continuity of Jewish settlement in Galilee in the second century: 1 Mac. 9:2

The Maccabees Jonathan and Simon did not yet occupy Galilee. Not even the conquests of John Hyrcanus extended beyond Samaria. Up to the end of his reign there can therefore have been no Judaizing of Galilee.[19] On the other hand, it is known that Aristobulus I (104–103 B.C.) undertook forcible conversions in northern Palestine. The lost historical work of Strabo, explicitly following Timagenes, records that Aristobulus increased Jewish territory and compelled some of the Ituraeans to adopt circumcision (*δεσμῷ συνάψας τῇ τῶν αἰδοίων περιτομῇ*).[20] Josephus recounts these events similarly (it is not clear whether he had another source in addition to Strabo), saying that he took much Ituraean territory by force and compelled the inhabitants, if they wished to remain there, to be circumcised and live in accordance with Jewish law. The kingdom of the Ituraeans comprised at that time the whole of the region of Mt. Lebanon (see vol. I, App. 1). In the south it extended, as Aristobulus's operations themselves show, to the borders of the Jewish territory. It must therefore have included Galilee (or most of it). For according to the information available, John Hyrcanus did not push his conquests much beyond Samaria.[21] Since the reports cited above do not say that the whole kingdom of the Ituraeans submitted to Aristobulus, but only that he seized part of it, this can only refer to Galilee.[22] But it was this very part that was Judaized at the same time by Aristobulus. The inhabitants were made to submit to circumcision and to accept Judaism. How thoroughly such forced

---

(Jewish inhabitants of Arbel in 160 B.C.); Josephus, *Ant.* xiii 12,1 (322) (Jannaeus educated in Galilee); *Ant.* xiii 12,4 (337) (attack on Jewish town of Asochis on a Sabbath, 102 B.C.).

19. Of the cities known to have been occupied by John Hyrcanus, the most northerly was Scythopolis, *Ant.* xiii 10, 3 (280 f.); *B.J.* I 2, 7 (66). Megillath Taanith §8 may refer to this event: 'On 15 and 16 Sivan the men of Beth-shean and the men of the Plain were driven into exile' (גלו אנשי בית שאן ואנשי בקעתה). By the 'Plain' (בקעתה) is to be understood the great plain north-west of Scythopolis (cf. J. Derenbourg, *Essai*, p. 74; H. Lichtenstein, 'Die Fastenrolle', HUCA 8–9 (1931–2), pp. 288–9. See however M. Avi-Yonah, 'Scythopolis', IEJ 12 (1962), pp. 123 f., on p. 130, who refers the passage to a voluntary departure of the Hellenized inhabitants in the first century B.C.). Thus in so far as an extension of Judaism followed these conquests of John Hyrcanus, it can have affected only the extreme south of Galilee.

20. The passage is given verbatim in Josephus, *Ant.* xiii 11:3 (318–19) = FGrH 91, Strabo, F. 11 = FGrH 88, Timagenes, F. 5 = GLAJJ, nos. 81 and 100.

21. The broad expansion of Ituraean power was made possible at that time by the weakness of the Seleucids. Antiochus IX Cyzicenus (111–95 B.C.) probably resided in Damascus (see the history of Damascus, pp. 127–30 below). But he was unable to prevent the Ituraeans from seizing the whole of Mt. Lebanon and the border districts.

22. Josephus's failure to use the name 'Galilee', otherwise familiar to him, can be explained by his dependence on his Greek sources (Strabo and possibly Nicolaus of Damascus).

conversions were effected is demonstrated by the example of the Idumaeans. There can consequently be very little doubt that the real Judaization of Galilee was essentially the work of Aristobulus I. His reign was admittedly short, and was followed by the stormy years of Alexander Jannaeus. But whatever remained for the task to be completed was made good during the reign of the devout Alexandra.[23]

Josephus, *B.J.* iii 3, 1 (35–40), defines the boundaries of Jewish Galilee during his time as follows. In the west lay the regions of Ptolemais and Carmel; in the south, Samaria and the region of Scythopolis; in the east, the regions of Hippos and Gadara, and then Gaulanitis and the kingdom of Agrippa; in the north, the region of Tyre. He calls the south 'lower Galilee', and the north 'upper Galilee'.[24] Of the villages by which he determines the precise boundaries, several can be accurately located. Exaloth, marking the southern frontier of Galilee, was situated, according to the *Onomasticon* of Eusebius, in the neighbourhood of Tabor, eight Roman miles (south-) east of Sepphoris (Diocaesarea). In Arabic it is still known as Iksal.[25] Chabulon, in the west, in the direction of Akko-Ptolemais, is Kabal, a village on the edge of the plain.[26] Buka in the north, at the boundary with the territory of Tyre, is the village of el-Buqei'a.[27] Galilee reached as far northward as the district of the Lake Merom. One of the most northerly points was Gischala (el-Jish/Gush Ḥalav), on approximately the same line of geographical latitude as the southern tip of Lake Merom (see vol. I, p. 496).

From the time of the Maccabees onwards, the Jewish element was also considerably strengthened east of the Jordan. Alongside the Hellenistic cities founded since the days of Alexander (Hippos, Gadara, Pella, Dium, Gerasa, Philadelphia), at the beginning of the Maccabaean period, mainly uncivilized Gentile tribes inhabited this area.[28] As in

23. Although the Judaizing of Aristobulus I was on the whole successful, it cannot have affected the areas lying to the north or east of Galilee. For there the population, even at a later time, was still Gentile.

24. Besides *B.J.* iii 3, 1 (35) cf. also *B.J.* ii 20, 6 (573); *Vita* 37 (188). The Mishnah also distinguishes between גליל העליון and גליל התחתון (mSheb. 9:2).

25. *Onomast.*, ed. Klostermann (1904), pp. 22, 4 and 28, 23: *Χσαλοὺς ἐν τῇ πεδιάδι παρὰ τὸ ὄρος Θαβώρ, ἀπέχουσα Διοκαισαρείας σημείοις ή πρὸς τὰς ἀνατολάς*; Robinson, *op. cit.* II, 332; W. Oehler, ZDPV 28 (1905), pp. 4–5; G. Dalman, *Sacred Sites and Ways*, E.T., pp. 190 and 196, n. 9; Avi-Yonah, *Map of Roman Palestine* ([2]1940), p. 35.

26. Abel, *Géog. Pal.* II, p. 287; Avi-Yonah, *Map*, p. 33.

27. Abel, *op. cit.*, pp. 154, 261.

28. Named are e.g. the *υἱοὶ 'Αμμών*, 1 Mac, 5:6; cf. 2 Mac. 4:26; 5:7; the *υἱοὶ 'Ιαμβί* (the correct reading in 1 Mac. 9:36–37, cf. vol. I, p. 174); the Moabites and the Gileadites, Josephus, *Ant.* xiii 13, 5 (374); *B.J.* i 4, 3 (89); the Nabataeans, 1 Mac. 5:25; 9:35.

Galilee, the Jews constituted no more than a diaspora among them. The support which they received from the first Maccabees was therefore similar to that given to the Jews of Galilee. Having punished the Ammonites for their hostility to the Jews and captured their city Jazer (1 Mac. 5:6–8, cf. 5:1–2), Judas undertook a military expedition to Gilead, i.e. to the land east of Jordan lying south of Batanaea (Bashan). After various engagements and the conquest of a large number of cities where the Jews had been harassed, he assembled all the Israelites dwelling in Gilead, great and small, with their wives and children and all their belongings, and led them under the protection of his army to Judaea (1 Mac. 5:9–54, cf. especially 5:45; for the particular cities mentioned as inhabited by Israelites see 1 Mac. 5:9, 13, 26–7, 36). The description of the whole undertaking is given even more exhaustively than that of the contemporaneous expedition to Galilee made by Simon, and shows with even greater certainty that it can have had to do only with a Jewish diaspora.

The advance of Judaism east of Jordan seems also to have been promoted by political conquests. John Hyrcanus conquered Medeba, east of the Dead Sea (south of Heshbon).[29] Alexander Jannaeus undertook the subjection of the area on a large scale. He seized most of the Greek cities (Gadara, Pella, Dium and Gerasa); he exacted tribute from the Moabites and Gileadites; he swept away small dynasties ruling over individual cities, such as Demetrius of Gamala and Theodorus of Amathus, by capturing or destroying their towns.[30] At the end of his reign, the whole of the land east of the Jordan, from Lake Merom to the Dead Sea, was under Jewish rule.[31] These conquests were, of course, primarily an exercise of rude force. But once, at the conquest of Pella, Alexander demanded that the subject people should also accept the Jewish customs, *Ant.* xiii 15, 4 (395–7): *ταύτην κατέσκαψεν οὐχ*[32] *ὑποσχομένων τῶν ἐνοικούντων ἐς πάτρια τῶν Ἰουδαίων ἔθη μεταβαλεῖσθαι.* These military victories must therefore have been of great importance for the Judaization of the land, particularly in view of the fact that once the regions were taken, they came under the administration of

29. Josephus, *Ant.* xiii 9, 1 (255); *B.J.* i 2, 6 (63). On its site and history, see vol. I, p. 207.

30. See on Gadara, Josephus, *Ant,* xiii 13, 3 (356); *B.J.* i 4, 2 (86); on Pella, Dium, Gerasa, *Ant.* xiii 15, 3 (393); *B.J.* i 4, 8 (104); on the Moabites and Gileadites, *Ant.* xiii 13, 5 (374); *B.J.* i 4, 3 (89); on Demetrius of Gamala, *Ant.* xiii 15, 3 (394); *B.J.* i 4, 8 (105); on Theodorus of Amathus, *Ant.* xiii 13, 3 and 5 (356 and 374); *B.J.* i 4, 2–3 (86–89).

31. Josephus, *Ant.* xiii 15, 4 (395–7); Georgius Syncellus, *Chronographia,* ed. Dindorf I, pp. 558 f. Cf. vol. I, pp. 226–7.

32. This οὐχ is deleted by Niese because of its absence from the *Codex Palatinus.* It is however given in all the other MSS and its deletion renders the text meaningless.

Alexandra, the friend of the Pharisees. Certainly, in the Hellenistic cities Greek culture was restored by Pompey and Gabinius. Also, not all the subjugated territories were as a rule truly Judaized. But in the immediate neighbourhood of Judaea in particular, the Judaizing must have been effective, for in the Roman-Herodian period a Jewish province of Peraea existed here.[33] When Gabinius divided Jewish territory into five districts, one of the five *synedria* was located at Amathus, obviously for the Jews east of the Jordan, Josephus, *Ant.* xiv 5, 4 (91); *B.J.* i 8, 5 (170). Josephus, *B.J.* iii 3, 3 (46–7), describes the boundaries of Jewish Peraea as follows. To the north lay the region of Pella; to the east, the regions of Gerasa, Philadelphia and Heshbon (to be read in place of the corrupt 'Silbonitis'); to the south, the land of the Moabites, where the southernmost Jewish city was Machaerus.[34] In defining these Gentile territories as the boundaries of Peraea, Josephus intended to indicate that the territory contained within them was a Jewish province inhabited by Jews (see n. 11 above). He remarks also that Peraea, although larger than Galilee, was thinly populated and rugged. That its population was mainly Jewish is confirmed also by other evidence.[35] The name *Περαία* derives from עבר

33. See Avi-Yonah, *Holy Land*, pp. 179–80; cf. vol. I, pp. 268–9.

34. Machaerus is explicitly named by Josephus, *B.J.* iii 3, 3 (46), as the southernmost city of Peraea. That it was Jewish is attested by its stand during the war against the Romans, *B.J.* vii 6, 1–4 (163–209). On its being part of Jewish territory, see also *B.J.* vii 6, 2 (174); *Ant.* xviii 5, 1 (112); Pliny, *NH* v 16/72. The possibility that during the time of Herod Antipas it was temporarily in the possession of the Nabataean king may rest on a textual error in *Ant.* xviii 5, 1 (112); cf. vol. I, pp. 344–5. On the other hand, Medeba, south of Heshbon, belonged at that period to the territory of Aretas IV, as is established by an inscription from the reign of that king found at Medeba, ZA 5 (1890), pp. 289 ff.; 6 (1891), pp. 149 f.; CIS, p. 11 Aram. n. 196; C. Clermont-Ganneau, *Rec. arch. or.* II, pp. 189 ff.; G. A. Cooke, *A Text-book of North-Semitic Inscriptions* (1903), no. 96. On a second copy of the same inscription, also found in Medeba, see Clermont-Ganneau, RA 7 (1906), pp. 415–22 = *Rec. d'arch. or.* VII (1906), pp. 241–7. In accord with this is Ptolemy v 17, 6 = v 16, 4 (ed. Didot, 1901), stating that *Μηδάβα* belonged to the province of Arabia. On Jews in Medeba, see mMikw. 7:1. It should also be noted in connection with the eastern frontier that the Jews of Peraea once quarrelled with the Philadelphians over the boundaries of a village called 'Mia' by Josephus, *Ant.* xx 1, 1 (2). If, as is likely, this is the 'Zia' mentioned by Eusebius, *Onom.* 94, 4, 15 Roman miles west of Philadelphia, then fully half of the land between the Jordan and the city of Philadelphia belonged to the territory of the latter (cf. vol. I, p. 227; see Abel, *Géog. Pal.* II, p. 440). The statement that Ragaba was located in the territory of Gerasa, Josephus, *Ant.* xiii 15, 5 (398), is no objection, for the site of this town is not certain; but cf. Abel, *Géog. Pal.* II, p. 427, identifying it with modern Ragib.

35. Cf. Josephus, *Ant.* xx 1, 1 (1–5) on the boundary dispute of the Jews of Peraea with the Philadelphians; cf. *B.J.* iv 7, 4–6 (419–39) on the participation of the Jews of Peraea in the revolt. The Mishnah, too, assumes Peraea (עבר הירדן) to be inhabited by Jews; see mSheb. 9:2; mBik. 1:10; mTaan. 3:6; mKet. 13:10; mB.B. 3:2; mEdu. 8:7; mMen. 8:3.

הירדן, 'beyond the Jordan' (a term frequently encountered already in the Old Testament), and came to mean both the land east of the Jordan in general, and Jewish territory east of the Jordan in particular.

Thus in the Roman-Herodian period there existed three Jewish provinces: Judaea, Galilee and Peraea. They are often named together (יהודה, גליל, עבר הירדן) both in Josephus and in the Mishnah.[36] Only there was the population mainly Jewish. The more widely drawn boundaries of the Land of Israel (ארץ ישראל) appearing in the Dead Sea Scrolls and rabbinical sources are merely ideal and bear no relation to reality.[37] But even these three provinces were not purely Jewish. After increasing in extent and intensity until the reign of Alexandra, the growth of Judaism came to a standstill, and even went into reverse, under the Romans and Herodians. Pompey, Gabinius and Herod promoted Hellenistic civilization. The Greek cities destroyed by Alexander Jannaeus were re-built, and new cities founded. Herod was instrumental in bringing the splendours of Gentile culture even to the interior of the country. Nevertheless, traditional Judaism was by then so well-established that the set-back was not very significant. Furthermore, Herod's cultural endeavours for the most part spared the religious opinions of the Jews. It can hardly be supposed, therefore, that there were many Gentiles in Judaea even then. They were more numerous in Galilee and Peraea, where the boundaries between Jewish and Gentile populations were of more recent date and consequently also more fluid.[38]

Although the three provinces shared a common religion and nationality, in manners and customs their inhabitants were marked by many differences which, quite apart from the political separation which recurred at various times, imparted a certain independence to the inner life of each region. The Mishnah mentions, for example, slight variations

36. mSheb. 9:2; mKet. 13:10; mB.B. 3:2.

37. Cf. on this subject, P. S. Alexander, *The Toponymy of the Targumim with Special Reference to the Table of the Nations and the Boundaries of the Land of Israel* (Diss. Oxford, 1974), pp. 177–251. For the Dead Sea Scrolls, see IQapGen. 21: 8–20. For a commentary, cf. J. A. Fitzmyer, *The Genesis Apocryphon* ([2]1971), *in loc.*

38. Although the population of Galilee in the Maccabaean period was mainly Gentile, this was certainly not true of Roman-Herodian times (compare n. 14). The Jewish element preponderated even in Tiberias, as is attested by the stand adopted by the city during the revolt against the Romans. But the whole province would have been unable to support the uprising (see §23.I, no. 33), with such resoluteness, had its population not been essentially Jewish. Only one city, Sepphoris, remained on the side of the Romans; but the population there too was mainly Jewish, *B.J.* iii 2, 4 (32): *προθύμως σφᾶς αὐτοὺς ὑπέσχοντο κατὰ τῶν ὁμοφύλων συμμάχους*. Finally, the Gospel accounts indicate that there were synagogues throughout Galilee where the people assembled for worship on the Sabbath. Cf. Vermes, *Jesus the Jew*, pp. 42–57.

in Judaea and Galilee in respect of marriage laws;[39] different customs in the relations between betrothed couples;[40] different weights in Judaea and Galilee.[41] There is even reference to a different observance of Passover: in Judaea, the people worked on 14 Nisan until noon, in Galilee not at all.[42] Since the three provinces were also frequently divided politically, they were regarded as being in certain respects different lands.[43]

In the provinces east of the Lake of Gennesaret, namely, Gaulanitis, Batanaea, Trachonitis and Auranitis (cf. vol. I, pp. 336–8), the population was a mixed one of Jews and Syrians, *B.J.* iii 3, 5 (57). But besides the settled population, bands of nomads, who were the cause of much trouble to the others, lived on these fringes of civilization. The caves of the locality, where they could accumulate stores of water and food and where they and their herds could find shelter in case of an attack, were particularly suited to them. It was therefore very difficult to subdue them. The powerful hand of Herod was the first to introduce a measure of order.[44] With a view to suppressing them permanently, he several times settled foreign colonists there; first, three thousand Idumaeans in Trachonitis,[45] then in Batanaea a military colony of Jews from Babylon to whom he granted the privilege of exemption from taxes.[46] His sons and grandson continued the work. Yet one of

39. mKet. 4:12 (the Galilean marriage deed was identical with that used in Jerusalem but differed from the Judaean type).

40. mYeb. 4:10; mKet. 1:5 (in Judaea it was customary for a young man to eat in his future father-in-law's house before the wedding).

41. mTer. 10:8: 10 zuz in Judaea = 5 selas in Galilee (weight of fish): mKet. 5:9 and mHal. 11:2: 5 selas in Judaea = 10 selas in Galilee (weight of wool).

42. mPes. 4:5. On the ban on work on 14 Nisan (the eve of Passover) see also L. Grünhut ZWTh (1894), pp. 543 ff.; D. Chwolson, *ibid.* (1895), pp. 343 ff.; L. Grünhut, ibid. (1898), pp. 253–66.

43. E.g. in respect of the legal maxim that a wife is not obliged to follow her husband into another country (e.g. from Judaea to Galilee), mKet. 13:10; in respect of the law of prescription (e.g. no Galilean property could validly be acquired through usucaption whilst the owner was absent in Judaea), mB.B. 3:2.

44. *Ant.* xv 10, 1 (342–8). On the caves, cf. also Strabo xvi 2, 20 (756). One cave held four thousand men.

45. *Ant.* xvi 9, 2 (285).

46. *Ant.* xvii 2, 1–3 (23–31). On the history of this colony, cf. also *Vita* 11 (46). See vol. I, pp. 338; 419–20; and G. M. Cohen, 'The Hellenistic Military Colony—A Herodian Example', TAPhA 103 (1972), pp. 83–95. According to *Ant.* xvii 2, 2 (26), these Babylonian Jews founded in Batanaea a village named Bathyra and built several fortresses (*φρούρια*). Bathyra has been identified as Bet Eri, on the northern bank of the Yarmuk, east of Nahr er Rukkad, by A. Schumacher, *Across the Jordan* (1886), p. 52; F. Buhl, *Studien zur Topographie des nördl. Ostjordanlandes* (1894), p. 19; *id.*, *Geographie des alter Palästina*, p. 246; RE III, cols. 138 f.; and Jones, CERP, p. 27. For other views, see G. A. Smith, *The Historical Geography of the Holy Land*, p. 618, n. 1; Abel *Géog. Pal.* II, p. 261 (preferring Basir) and A. Wikgren, *Josephus* (Loeb) VIII, p. 385, n. *b*. Compare J. Neusner, *A*

the two Agrippas still complains in an edict of the brutish way of life (θηριώδης κατάστασις) of the inhabitants, and of their cave dwellings (ἐνφωλεύειν).[47] Herod's cultural enterprises succeeded in the end in introducing the Greek influence into these regions. In the neighbourhood of Canatha (cf. p. 140) are the ruins of a temple which, according to Greek inscriptions discovered there, dates to the time of Herod the Great.[48] A great number of Greek inscriptions of the two Agrippas, especially of Agrippa II, are to be found in the area of the Hauran.[49] In the Roman period, the Greek element gained the ascendancy—superficially at least—in these districts (cf. pp. 41–4 below).

The cities of Samaria and Scythopolis, in the province of Samaria lying between Judaea and Galilee, are to be strictly distinguished from the rest of the country in regard to their population. Alexander the

---

History of the Jews in Babylonia I: The Parthian Period (1965), pp. 38 f. Among the fortresses were the Ecbatana mentioned in *Vita* 11 (54) and the Nineve mentioned by Eusebius, *Onomast.* ed. Klostermann, p. 136, s.v. *Νινευῆ*: ἔστι δὲ καὶ Ἰουδαίων εἰς ἔτι νῦν πόλις Νινευῆ καλουμένη περὶ τὴν Γωνίαν τῆς Ἀραβίας; Jerome, *ibid.*, p. 137: 'est et alia usque hodie civitas Iudaeorum nomine Ninive in angulo Arabiae, quam nunc corrupte [al. correpte] Neneven [Neve?] vocant'. The 'angle' or 'corner' of Arabia is presumably identical with the 'angle' of Batanaea mentioned elsewhere by Eusebius (*Onomast.* ed. Klostermann, p. 18, s.v. *Αὐὼθ Ἰαείρ: ἐν τῇ καλουμένῃ Γωνίᾳ τῆς Βαταναίας*). In his time, Batanaea belonged to the province of Arabia. This Nineve will therefore have been in Batanaea, and may be the Neve of the *Itinerarium Antonini* 196, 5; 198, 8, the *Νευή* of the *Notitiae episcopatuum*, the Nawe of rabbinical and Arabic sources, and the modern Arab Nawa (directly east of the northern tip of the Lake of Gennesaret); perhaps also the *Νοή* mentioned *c.* 259 B.C. in PCZen 59004. See A. Neubauer, *Géographie du Talmud*, p. 245; Schumacher, *Across the Jordan* (1886), pp. 167–80; F. Buhl, *Geogr. d. alten Paläst.*, pp. 247 f.; R. Dussaud, *Topographie historique de la Syrie antique et médiévale* (1927), pp. 341–2; M. Avi Yonah, 'Naveh', Enc. Jud. 12, col. 897; *Gazetteer* s.v. 'Naveh'. This identification becomes very probable if 'Neve' is to be read in Jerome (so one of the mss. collated by Vallarsi, *Hieron. opp.* III, 1, 251; the two Sangallensis manuscripts collated by Klostermann have 'Neve' and 'Neven'). Several seven-branched candlesticks have been found under the ancient ruins of Nawa. (Schumacher, pp. 172–4; L. A. Mayer, A. Reifenberg, BJPES 4 (1936), pl. II, no. 4; R. Amiran, IEJ 6 (1956), p. 243; cf. L. Yarden, *The Tree of Light* (1971), nos. 69, 80, 81.) A Jewish community can also be traced at Tafas in Batanaea, south of Nawa, BCH 21 (1897), p. 47: *Ἰάκωβος καὶ Σεμούηλος . . . τὴν συναγωγὴν οἰκοδόμησαν* = Frey, CIJ, no. 861.

47. The fragments of this edict, unfortunately very scanty, are given by Le Bas-Waddington, *Inscriptions grecques et latines* III, no. 2329 = OGIS 424 = IGR III 1223.

48. Cf. especially the inscription in Le Bas-Waddington III, no. 2364 = OGIS 415 = IGR III 1243.

49. Le Bas-Waddington, III, 2112, 2135, 2211, 2329, 2365, 2413b = OGIS 418, 419, 421, 422, 423, 424. OGIS 425, 426. Cf. PIR² I 131–2, and note especially A. H. M. Jones, 'The Urbanization of the Ituraean Principality', JRS 21 (1931), pp. 265–75.

Great had already settled Macedonian colonists in Samaria. After its destruction by John Hyrcanus, it was re-founded as a Hellenistic city by Gabinius and further enlarged by Herod (for details see p. 162 below). Its population was without doubt overwhelmingly Gentile. The same is true of Scythopolis, which is explicitly mentioned as a Gentile city in the Maccabaean period, and which, after being in the possession of the Jews since the time of John Hyrcanus, was restored as a Hellenistic city by Gabinius. According to *B.J.* ii 18, 3–4 (466–76), a large number of the inhabitants were certainly Jewish. They were nevertheless definitely in the minority. Apart from these two cities, the province of Samaria was presumably mainly inhabited by Samaritans.[50]

50. For a detailed bibliography, cf. L. A. Mayer, *Bibliography of the Samaritans* (1964); see also J. Macdonald, *The Theology of the Samaritans* (1964), pp. 457–63; 'Samaritans', Enc. Jud. 14, cols. 757–8. For general surveys, see A. E. Cowley, s.v. 'Samaritans', EB IV; JE X; J. A. Montgomery, *The Samaritans* (1907); J. E. H. Thomson, *The Samaritans: Their Testimony to the Religion of Israel* (1919); M. Gaster, *The Samaritans: Their History, Doctrines and Literature* (1925); J. W. Lightley, *Jewish Sects and Parties in the Time of Jesus* (1925), pp. 180–265; M. Gaster, *The Samaritan Oral Law and Ancient Traditions* (1932); J. Bowman, 'Importance of Samaritan Researches', ALUOS 1 (1959), pp. 43–54; T. H. Gaster, s.v. 'Samaritans', IDB IV; H. G. Kippenberg, *Garizim und Synagoge* (1971); J. Macdonald, A. Loewenstamm, s.v. 'Samaritans', Enc. Jud. 14, cols. 425–58. R. J. Coggins, *Samaritans and Jews. The origins of Samaritanism reconsidered* (1975). For re-assessments of Samaritan and Jewish history in the light of the Samaria papyri, see F. M. Cross, 'The Discovery of the Samaria Papyri', BA 26 (1963), pp. 110–21; 'Aspects of Samaritan and Jewish History in late Persian and Hellenistic Times', HThR 59 (1966), pp. 201–11; 'Papyri of the Fourth Century B.C. from Dâliyeh', *New Directions in Biblical Archaeology*, ed. D. N. Freedman and J. C. Greenfield (1971), pp. 45–69. On the Samaritan idea of the Messiah, see §29 below. On the Samaritan Pentateuch, see the literature in F. Buhl, *Kanon und Text des A.T.* (1891), pp. 184 ff. [E.T., 1892, p. 184]; see also E. König, s.v. 'Samaritan Pentateuch', HDB, Extra Volume (1904), pp. 68–72; R. E. Moody, 'Samaritan Material at Boston University: The Boston Collection and the "Abisha Scroll" ', Boston University Graduate Journal 10 (1957), pp. 158–60; Kahle, *The Cairo Geniza* (²1959); Eissfeldt, *Introduction*, pp. 694–5. For the text, see J. H. Petermann, K. Vollers, *Pentateuchus Samaritanus* (1872–91); A. F. von Gall, *Der hebräische Pentateuch der Samaritaner* (1918); J. D. Purvis, *The Samaritan Pentateuch and the Origin of the Samaritan Sect* (1968). For Samaritan theology, see J. Bowman, 'Faith in Samaritan Thought', BJRL 40 (1958), pp. 308–15; J. Macdonald, *The Theology of the Samaritans* (1964). The following Samaritan chronicles are extant: T. G. J. Juynboll, *Chronicon samaritanum* (. . . cui titulus est Liber Josuae) (1848); E. Vilmar, *Abulfathi Annales Samaritani* (1865); A. Neubauer, 'Chronique samaritaine', JA 14 (1869), pp. 385–470; O. T. Crane, *The Samaritan Chronicle or the Book of Joshua* (1890); E. N. Adler, M. Seligsohn, 'Une nouvelle chronique samaritaine', REJ 44 (1902), pp. 188–222; 45 (1902), pp. 70–98, 223–54; 46 (1903), pp. 123–46. M. Gaster, 'The Chain of Samaritan High Priests', *Studies and Texts in Folklore* . . . I (1925), pp. 483–502; III (1928), pp. 131–38; *The Asatir. The Samaritan Book of the Secrets of Moses* (1927), Z. Ben Hayyim, Tarbiz 14–15 (1943–44); J. Macdonald, *The Samaritan Chronicle* No. 2 (or Sefer ha-Yamin). From Joshua to Nabuchadnezzar (1969). For the Samaritan liturgy,

As has been said, these are accounted by Josephus as belonging to the Jewish population in the wider sense (cf. n. 11 above). And rightly so. For their essential character can be properly assessed only if the following two facts are borne in mind: (1) that they were a mixed race derived from the intermarriage of earlier Israelite inhabitants with Gentiles, in particular with the Gentile colonists settled there by the Assyrians; (2) that their religion was essentially that of Israel.

Of the colonists from the provinces of Babylon, Cuthah, Avva, Hamath and Sepharvaim settled by the Assyrians in Samaria (2 Kgs. 17:24 ff.), those from Cuthah (כות, כותה 2 Kgs. 17:24, 30) gave to the inhabitants of Samaria their new name of Cuthites (*Κουθαῖοι* in Josephus, *Ant.* ix 14, 3 (288); xi 4, 4 (88); 7, 2 (302); xiii 9, 1 (256) and כותים in rabbinic literature).[51] But it is unlikely that the ancient Israelite population was taken in its entirety from the land, and that it was newly populated solely by these Gentile colonists. A very large percentage of the original population undoubtedly remained there and intermarried with the new immigrants. According to 2 Kgs. 17:24–41, the religion of the resultant mixed race was in the beginning also a combination of the pagan rites brought by the colonists and Israelite provincial worship. But later, Judaism preponderated. For, calumnies apart, according to all that is known of the religion of the Samaritans it was a pure Jewish monotheism. They worshipped one God and honoured Moses as the greatest of the prophets; they observed the rite of circumcision on the eighth day after birth, and kept the Sabbath and the Jewish festivals. Indeed, they accepted the whole of the Torah as divine law. The only difference between them and the Jews was that their centre of worship was not Jerusalem but Mount Gerizim.

How the Samaritan sect came into being is obscure. The most likely hypothesis is that the religious evolution of Judaea affected Samaria also, and that the schism followed the acceptance of the Pentateuch in both areas. This would concur with Josephus's report that the schism occurred shortly before the time of Alexander the Great, when Manasseh, the brother of the High Priest Jaddua, was expelled from Jerusalem for marrying the daughter of the Samaritan Sanballat. Manasseh is said to have started schismatic worship in Samaria by

---

see A. E. Cowley, *The Samaritan Liturgy* I-II (1909). For the most important Samaritan work of Bible exegesis, see J. Macdonald, *Memar Marqah* I–II (1963). S. Lowy, *The Principles of Samaritan Bible Exegesis* (1977). For the language of the Samaritans, see Z. Ben Hayyim, עברית וארמית נוסח שומרון I–IV (1957–67). For the Samaritan calendar, see S. Powels, *Der Kalender der Samaritaner anhand des KITĀB ḤISĀB AS-SININ und anderer Handschriften* (1977).

51. כותים: mBer. 7:1; 8:8; mPea. 2:7; mDem. 3:4, 5:9; 6:1; 7:4; mTer. 3:9; mHal. 4:7; mShek. 1:5; mR. Sh. 2:2; mKet. 3:1; mNed. 3:10; mGit. 1:5; mKid. 4:3; mOhol. 17:3; mToh. 5:8; mNid. 4:1–2; 7:3–5.

building a temple on Gerizim.[52] Until recently however, it has been a source of difficulty that according to Neh. 13:28, the son of a High Priest was expelled from Jerusalem already in the time of Nehemiah for marrying the daughter of Sanballat the Horonite. If these, as seemed plausible, are also the persons named by Josephus, the event has to be dated to about a hundred years earlier than he supposes.[53] However, the recent discovery near Jerusalem of papyri, mainly Aramaic and dating from the first two-thirds of the fourth century, provides a solution, for they record a Sanballat as the father of a mid-fourth century governor of Samaria, who is therefore neither the Sanballat of Josephus nor that of Nehemiah. It thus becomes feasible to suppose a single family in which, as was common in the Persian Empire, the office descended.[54] The beginning of Samaritan separatism may therefore be placed in the late fourth century;[55] moreover from the history of the Samaritan Pentateuch, as seen especially in the light of the Qumran texts, it has been argued that the break was not complete until the first century B.C.[56] Samaritan worship, in any case, existed on Gerizim from, at the latest, the beginning of the Hellenistic period until the time of John Hyrcanus.[57] The destruction of the Gerizim sanctuary by this Hasmonaean ruler in 128 B.C. is likely to have caused deep and lasting resentment among the Samaritans, and to have led to their final alienation from the Jews. In 107 B.C., Hyrcanus attacked again,

52. *Ant.* xi 7, 2 (302–3); 8, 2 ff. (306 ff.).

53. For a full discussion of the conflict between Nehemiah and Josephus, see H. H. Rowley, 'Sanballat and the Samaritan Temple', BJRL 38 (1955), pp. 166–98. Cf. also F. M. Cross, in *New Directions in Biblical Archaeology*, pp. 59 ff.

54. See F. M. Cross, 'The Discovery of the Samaria Papyri', BA 26 (1963), p. 110; 'Aspects of Samaritan and Jewish History in Late Persian and Hellenistic Times', HThR 59 (1966), p. 201; *New Directions in Biblical Arch.* (1971), pp. 59–63; 'A Reconstruction of the Judaean Restoration', JBL 94 (1975), pp. 5–6.

55. Cf. H. H. Rowley, 'The Samaritan Schism in Legend and History', *Israel's Prophetic Heritage*, ed. B. W. Anderson and W. Harrelson (1962), pp. 208–22; R. J. Coggins, *Samaritans and Jews* (1975), p. 163 rejects the concept of a 'schism' and defines the Samaritans as a group within Judaism (pp. 156–61).

56. See Eissfeldt, *Introduction*, pp. 594–5; F. M. Cross, 'The Contribution of the Qumran Discoveries to the Study of the Hebrew Text', IEJ 16 (1966), pp. 81–95; J. D. Purvis, *The Samaritan Pentateuch and the Origins of the Samaritan Sect* (1968), p. 80; Coggins, *op. cit.*, pp. 148–55.

57. The *ἱερὸν Ἀργαριζίν* is also mentioned by Eupolemus, from whose work excerpts are given by Alexander Polyhistor in Eusebius, *Praep. evang.* ix 17, 5 = FGrH 724 F. 1 (5); see Hengel, *Judaism and Hellenism*, pp. 88–92; B. Z. Wachholder, *Eupolemus* (1974), pp. 205–6; cf. vol. III §33; the form also occurs in Josephus *B.J.* i 2, 6 (63). 'Argaris' figures in Pliny, *NH* v 14/68: 'mons Argaris', *Ἀργάριζος* in Damascius quoted by Photius, *Bib.* 242, ed. Bekker, p. 345b; ed. Henri, Budé vol. VI, p. 36. In addition, the Aramaic form *Τουρ Γαριζιν* occurs in the mosaic map at Madaba, see M. Avi Yonah, *The Madaba Mosaic Map* (1954), pl. 6. Under Antiochus Epiphanes it was dedicated, though only temporarily, to *Ζεὺς Ξένιος*, 2 Mac. 5:23; 6:2; Josephus, *Ant.* xii 5, 5 (257–64).

devastating Samaria and probably Shechem as well. Thus when in 64 B.C. Pompey liberated Samaria from the Hasmonaeans, the Samaritan breach with the Jews was complete.[58] But Gerizim remained the holy mountain of the Samaritans, and their place of worship, even after their temple had been destroyed. Also, apart from the Pentateuch, they refused to accept the other sacred writings of the Jewish canon, and, unlike Pharisaic Judaism, rejected as binding any rules beyond those laid down in the Torah. Yet even so, they could justifiably describe themselves as Israelites.

The attitude of Jews towards Samaritans in the inter-Testamental period was always one of hostility: the ancient antagonism of the kingdoms of Judah and Ephraim continued here in a new form. To Ben Sira, 'That foolish people which dwells in Shechem' is as hateful as the Edomites and the Philistines (Ecclus. 50:25–6). The Samaritans responded to these sentiments with equal animosity.[59] Nevertheless, the legal definition of the Samaritans by rabbinic Judaism is not wholly misleading.[60] The Samaritans are never treated purely and simply as foreigners, but as a race of uncertain derivation. Their Israelite extraction cannot be taken as proved, but neither can it be a priori excluded.[61] Their affiliation to the congregation of Israel is accordingly not denied but merely considered doubtful.[62] Inasmuch as their observance of the Torah in regard to tithes and the laws of purity falls short of

58. For its continuing importance, cf. *Ant.* xviii 4, 1 (85); *B.J.* iii 7, 32 (307); Jn. 4:20. After the foundation of Flavia Neapolis, a temple to Zeus stood on Gerizim, and appears on coins of the city from the time of Hadrian, see vol. I, pp. 520–1; the coins, e.g. in F. de Saulcy, *Numismatique de la Terre Sainte*, pl. XIII, n. 1, XIV, n. 2 and n. 3. For recent archaeological traces of both the Samaritan and the Hadrianic temples, see R. J. Bull and G. E. Wright, 'Newly Discovered Temples on Mt. Gerizim in Jordan', HThR 58 (1965), p. 234; R. J. Bull, E. F. Campbell, 'The Sixth Campaign at Balatah (Shechem)', BASOR 190 (1968), pp. 2–41. See *BMC Palestine*, pp. XXVIII–XXX. Following a rebellion of the Samaritans during the reign of the emperor Zeno, their synagogue was converted into a Christian church, see J. E. H. Thomson, *The Samaritans* (1919), pp. 44 f.

59. Lk. 9:52–3; Josephus, *Ant.* xviii 2, 2 (29 f.); xx 6, 1 (118 ff.); *B.J.* ii 12, 3 (232 f.); mR.Sh. 2:2. Galileans travelling to Jerusalem for the festivals were liable to be attacked as they made their way through Samaria, Lk. 9:52–53; *Ant.* xx 6, 1 (118 ff.); *B.J.* ii 12, 3 (232 f.). Some may therefore have preferred the roundabout way through Peraea.

60. See the post Talmudic tractate, *Kutim* (ed. M. Higger), cf. vol. I, p. 90. For the Mishnah passages, see n. 51 above.

61. Cf. on the one hand mShek. 1:5 (Temple offerings are to be accepted only from Israelites, not from Gentiles or even from Samaritans); on the other hand, mBer. 7:1 (when three Israelites have eaten together, they are obliged to prepare themselves formally for prayer; the same also holds good even if one of the three is a Samaritan); mKet. 3:1 (the claim for pecuniary compensation on account of cohabitation with an Israelite virgin holds good also in respect of a Samaritan virgin).

62. mKid. 4:3.

Pharisaic requirements, they are judged by the rabbis to be in many respects on a par with Gentiles.[63] But nowhere are they regarded as idolaters; on the contrary, they are positively distinguished from them.[64] Their Sabbath observance is mentioned from time to time;[65] it is assumed to be at least a possibility that they can recite a correct Israelite grace.[66] Basically, therefore, their observance of the Torah could be compared to that of the Sadducees.[67]

The principal language spoken by Jews in the various regions of Palestine during the final centuries of the pre-Christian era was Aramaic.[68] Aramaic influence on biblical Hebrew, i.e. שפת כנען or

63. Cf. mDem. 7:4; mToh. 5:8; mNid. 4:1–2; 7:3–5.

64. mBer. 7:1; mDem. 3:4; 5:9; 6:1; mTer. 3:9. The allegation that the Samaritans worshipped the image of a dove is unknown to the Mishnah, and first appears in the Talmud (yA.Z. 44d; bHul. 6a). It is possible that the dove was considered sacred from the time of Herod onwards by the Gentile (Greek) habitants of Sebaste. On Herod's doves, see vol. I, p. 310.

65. mNed. 3:10.

66. mBer. 8:8.

67. Cf. mNid. 4:2: 'When the Sadducee women follow the customs of their fathers, they are like the Samaritan women'. Epiphanius, *Haeres.* 14 notes of the Sadducees that τὰ πάντα δὲ ἴσα Σαμαρείταις φυλάττουσιν.

68. Cf. A. Neubauer, 'On the Dialects spoken in Palestine in the Time of Christ', *Studia Biblica* (1885), pp. 39–74; A. Meyer, *Jesu Muttersprache* (1896); G. Dalman, *Die Worte Jesu* (1898, ²1930), pp. 1–10 [E.T. *The Words of Jesus* (1902), pp. 1–12]; R. O. P. Taylor, 'Did Jesus speak Aramaic?' ET 56 (1945), pp. 95–7; H. Birkeland, *The Language of Jesus* [=Hebrew] (1954); M. Black, 'Recovery of the Language of Jesus' NTSt 3 (1957), pp. 305–13; 'Erforschung der Muttersprache Jesu', ThLZ 82 (1957), cols. 653–58; S. Segert, 'Zur Verbreitung des Aramäischen in Palästina zur Zeit Jesu', Arch. Orientalni 25 (1957), pp. 21–37; M. Smith, 'Aramaic Studies and the Study of the New Testament', JBR 26 (1958), pp. 304–13; P. Kahle, 'Das palästinische Pentateuchtargum und das zur Zeit Jesu gesprochene Aramäisch', ZNW 49 (1958), pp. 100–16; E. Y. Kutscher, 'Das zur Zeit Jesu gesprochene Aramäisch', ZNW 51 (1960), pp. 45–54; J. A. Emerton, 'Did Jesus speak Hebrew?', JThSt 12 (1961), pp. 189–202; A. Díez Macho, 'La lengua hablada por Jesucristo', Oriens Antiquus 2 (1963), pp. 95–132; R. H. Gundry, 'The Language Milieu of First Century Palestine', JBL 83 (1964), pp. 404–8; M. Black, *An Aramaic Approach to the Gospels and Acts* (³1967); 'Aramaic Studies and the Language of Jesus', *In Memoriam Paul Kahle* (1968), pp. 17–28; H. P. Rüger, 'Zum Problem der Sprache Jesu', ZNW 59 (1968), pp. 113–22; J. A. Fitzmyer, 'The Languages of Palestine in the First Century A.D.', CBQ 32 (1970), pp. 501–31; J. Barr, 'Which Language did Jesus speak?', BJRL 53 (1970–71), pp. 9–29; M. Delcor, 'Le Targum de Job et l'araméen du temps de Jésus', RScRel 47 (1973), pp. 232–61; A. Díez Macho, 'Arameo del Targum Palestino, substrato arameo de Evangelios y Actos y crítica textual neotestamentaria', *Neophyti 1*, Tomo IV, *Números* (1974), pp. 78*–102*; J. A. Fitzmyer, 'The Contribution of Qumran Aramaic to the Study of the New Testament', NTSt 20 (1974), pp. 382–407; 'Some Notes on Aramaic Epistolography', JBL 93 (1974), pp. 201–25; 'Methodology in the Study of the Aramaic Substratum of Jesus' Sayings in the New Testament', J. Dupont (ed.), *Jésus aux origines de la christologie* (1975), pp. 73–102. C. Rabin, 'Hebrew and Aramaic in

יהודית (Isa. 19:18; 36:11, 13; 2 Kgs. 18:26, 28) came to the fore after the Babylonian exile and is manifest in the scriptural books dating to that period.[69] As the *lingua franca* of the Persian empire,[70] it came progressively to be the common vehicle of communication. Before the epigraphical and manuscript discoveries of the twentieth century, it used to be argued that the transition from Hebrew to Aramaic, and the eventual displacement by the latter of the former, is first attested in the books of Ezra, including untranslated Aramaic documents (Ezr. 4:8–6:18; 7:12–26), and Daniel, which is half in Hebrew (Dan. 1:1–2:4a; 8:1–12:13) and half in Aramaic (Dan. 2:4b–7:18). It was further added that in the Pentateuch and the Prophets, rendered into Greek in the third century B.C., certain biblical words are transliterated not in their Hebrew form but with Aramaic endings (פסח=*πάσχα*, שכר=*σίκερα*, גר=*γιώρας*, etc.). From the presence of Aramaic words in the Greek fragments of 1 Enoch it was also conjectured that Aramaic was the original language of that document (cf. below and vol. III, § 32). Sayings of early Tannaitic teachers, Yose ben Yoezer, Hillel and others,

---

the First Century', *The Jewish People in the First Century*, ed. S. Safrai and M. Stern, II (1976), pp. 1007–90. Note also J. A. Fitzmyer, D. J. Harrington, *A Manual of Palestinian Aramaic Texts* (1978).

69. Cf. E. Kautzsch, *Die Aramäismen im Alten Testament* (1902); A. Kropat, *Die Syntax des Autors der Chronik verglichen mit der seiner Quellen* (1906); R. A. Bowman, 'Aramaeans, Aramaic and the Bible', JNES 7 (1948), pp. 65–90; M. Wagner, *Die lexikalischen und grammatikalischen Aramäismen im alttestamentlischen Hebräisch* (1966); A. Hurvitz, 'The Chronological Significance of "Aramaisms" in Biblical Hebrew', IEJ 18 (1968), pp. 234–40.

70. For Aramaic inscriptions dating to the Persian period, see CIS Pt. II, nos. 108–10 (Asia Minor); 122–55 (Egypt); H. Donner and W. Röllig, *Kananäische und aramäische Inschriften* ([2]1966–69), §F; J. C. L. Gibson, *A Textbook of Syrian Semitic Inscriptions*, II. *Aramaic Inscriptions* (1975), nos. 23–37. For the Aramaic text of the trilingual (Greek, Lycian) text of the fourth century B.C. from Xanthos, Lycia, see A. Dupont-Sommer, CRAI (1974), pp. 132–48. For the Elephantine and other Aramaic papyri, see A. Cowley, *Aramaic Papyri of the Fifth Century B.C.* (1923); E. G. Kraeling, *The Brooklyn Museum Aramaic Papyri* (1953); G. R. Driver, *Aramaic Documents of the Fifth Century* (1957); A. Bresciani, *La lettere aramaiche di Hermopoli*, Mem. d. Acc. Lincei CCCLXII, cl. sc. mor. stor, e fil., ser. VIII v. XII, fasc. 5 (1966); F. M. Cross, 'Papyri of the Fourth Century B.C. from Dâliyeh', *New Directions in Biblical Archaeology* (1971), pp. 45–69. For Aramaic ostraca and inscriptions from Palestine, cf. Y. Aharoni, IEJ 17 (1967), pp. 243–44; 18 (1968), pp. 157–69; L. T. Geraty, HThR 65 (1972), pp. 595–96; BASOR 220 (1975), pp. 55–61. For an evaluation of the position of Aramaic, see F. Altheim, R. Stiehl, 'Aramäisch als Weltsprache', *Die Araber in der alten Welt* I (1964), pp. 181–236. E. Y. Kutscher, 'Aramaic', *Current Trends in Linguistics* 6 (1970), pp. 347–412; Enc. Jud. 3 (1971), cols. 259–87; J. C. Greenfield, 'Standard Literary Aramaic', *Actes du Premier Congrès international de Linguistique sémitique et chamito-sémitique, Paris* 1969 (1974), pp. 280–89. A survey of Aramaic papyri may be found in R. Yaron, 'Aramaica recentiora', *Proc. XIIth Int. Congr. Papyrology* (1970), pp. 537–44. Cf. J. H. Hospers (ed.), *A Basic Bibliography for the Study of the Semitic Languages* I (1973), pp. 283–335.

are given in Aramaic in the Mishnah.[71] Similarly, the Greek New Testament contains a significant number of Aramaic terms: ἀββᾶ (Mk. 14:36), ἀκελδαμάχ (Act. 1:19), γαββαθᾶ (Jn. 19:13), γολγοθᾶ (Mt. 27:33), ἐφφαθά (Mk. 7:34),[72] κορβανᾶς (Josephus, *B.J.* ii 9, 4 (175); Mt. 27:6),[73] μαμωνᾶς (Mt. 6:24), μαρὰν ἀθά (1 Cor. 16:22),[74] Μεσσιάς=משיחא (Jn. 1:41), πάσχα (Mt. 26:17), ῥακά (Mt. 5:22), σατανᾶς (Mt. 16:23), ταλιθὰ κούμ (Mk. 5:41). There are also several Aramaic names (Κηφᾶς, Μάρθα, Ταβιθά)[75] and patronyms introduced by the Aramaic בר (Barabbas, Barjesus, Barnabas, Barsabas, Bartholomew, Bartimaeus). The final cry of Jesus on the cross is given in Aramaic: Ἐλοῒ ἐλοῒ λαμὰ σαβαχθανί (Mk. 15:34). Lastly, it is noteworthy that when Josephus supplies transliterated vernacular phrases for priest, High Priest, sabbath, Passover, Pentecost, etc., they are in Aramaic.[76]

Even on the basis of the evidence available prior to the archaeological finds of this century, a limited survival of Hebrew was admitted, but it was confined to the sphere of worship in the Temple—the לשון הקדש was primarily the language used in the sanctuary, hence the targumic designation לישן בית קודשא—and in the synagogue. During the service, the Bible was read aloud in the 'sacred tongue' before being repeated in the vernacular Aramaic.[77] The Mishnah lists several other liturgical occasions on which Hebrew was compulsory.[78]

71. mEdu, 8:4; mAb. 1:13; 2:6; 5:22–23.

72. For the controversy whether the phrase is in Aramaic or Hebrew, see I. Rabbinowitz, ZNW 53 (1962), pp. 229–38; J. A. Emerton, JThSt 18 (1967), pp. 427–31; I. Rabinowitz, JSS 16 (1971), pp. 151–6; S. Morag, JSS 17 (1972), pp. 198–202. Cf. also vol. I, p. 108.

73. For the *ḳorban* inscription, see below, n. 94.

74. For a recent discussion of this expression, see S. Schulz, 'Maranatha und Kyrios Jesus', ZNW 53 (1962), pp. 125–44; J. A. Emerton, 'Maranatha and Ephphatha', JThSt 18 (1967), pp. 427–31.

75. The accentuation of these words is inconsistent in the editions of the New Testament. Consistency would demand ῥακᾶ, ταλιθᾶ, Ταβιθᾶ.

76. Josephus, *Ant.* iii 7, 1 (151): τοῖς ἱερεῦσι . . . οὓς χαναναίας καλοῦσι . . . τῷ ἀρχιερεῖ, ὃν ἀναραβάχην προσαγορεύουσι. The first is a corruption of כהניא, the second of כהנא רבא. σάββατα, *Ant.* 1, 1 (33); iii 6, 6 (143); 10, 1 (237). πάσχα, *Ant.* ii 14, 6 (313); iii 10, 5 (248); x 4, 5 (70); xi 4, 8 (101); xiv 2, 1 (25); xviii 2, 2 (29); 4, 3 (90); xx 5, 3 (106); *B.J.* ii 1, 3 (10); vi 9, 3 (422); also φάσκα (according to the MSS), *Ant.* ix 13, 3 (271); xvii 9, 3 (213). ἀσαρθά (Hebr. עצרת); *Ant.* iii 10, 6 (252). Cf. also Meyer, *Jesu Muttersprache*, pp. 39–41.

77. Cf. mMeg. 4:4, 6, 10 and §27, pp. 452–3 below.

78. See especially mSot. 7:2: 'The following portions are recited in the sacred tongue only: the section of Scripture at the offering of the first-fruits, the words of ḥaliẓah, the blessings and the curses, the priestly blessing, the words of blessing of the High Priest, the sections read by the King (at the Feast of Tabernacles in the Sabbatical year), the words at the slaughter of a calf (on account of a person having been found murdered) and the discourse delivered by the priest anointed for war when addressing the fighting men'. Cf. 1QM 15:6–16:2 reproducing in Hebrew the speech of הכוהן החרוץ למועד נקם. Cf. P. S. Alexander, 'The

Moreover, mishnaic or rabbinic Hebrew was also the learned language of schools and academies. It is the regular medium in the Mishnah and the Tosefta, and Aramaic the exception. Aramaic did not enter the domain of rabbinic literature until the Amoraim of the third and fourth centuries A.D., by which time it had become the normal vehicle of the Gemara in both Talmuds. The idiom spoken in Galilee survives in the Palestinian Talmud, which, together with Aramaic relics in Genesis Rabbah and the language of the Palestinian Targums, reflects the speech-form of northern Palestine.[79] That there were dialectal differences between Galilee and Judaea may be deduced from references in the New Testament and the Talmud.[80]

The discovery of inscriptions, and the major archaeological finds at Qumran, Masada, Murabba'at and other caves in the Judaean desert, combined with a deeper historical understanding of the position of mishnaic Hebrew and the Greek language (the latter will be discussed in a subsequent section, § 22 II.2) in inter-Testamental Palestine, have considerably improved and clarified ideas concerning the linguistic situation prevailing there between 200 B.C. and A.D. 200.

To begin with, the widespread and predominant use of Aramaic has received definite confirmation. It is seen now as the main literary language of the earlier phase of the post-biblical period.[81] Among the Dead Sea finds, 1 Enoch,[82] the Testament of

---

Rabbinic Lists of Forbidden Targumim', JJS 27 (1976), pp. 177–91. On the other hand, the *Shema'*, the *Shemoneh-'Esreh* (see § 27, appendix), grace at meals, etc., could be recited in either language (mSot. 7:11). All this applies to *oral* recitation. In *writing*, Hebrew was required for the text of the *tephillin* and the *mezuzoth*. Otherwise, even for Scripture, any language was permitted; though according to Rabban Gamaliel, Scripture should be written only in Hebrew and Greek (mMeg. 1:8). According at least to R. Judah, the formula of a bill of divorce was usually in Aramaic (mGit. 9:3), but it could also be in Greek (mGit. 9:8). For an Aramaic *geṭ* from Murabba'at, see J. T. Milik, *DJD* II, pp. 104–9.

79. Cf. G. Dalman, *Grammatik des jüdisch-palästinischen Aramäisch* (²1905); H. Odeberg, *The Aramaic Portions of Bereshit Rabba II: Short Grammar of Galilean Aramaic* (1939); E. Y. Kutscher, 'Studies in Galilean Aramaic' (in Hebrew), Tarbiz 21 (1950), pp. 192–205; 22 (1951), pp. 53–63; 185–92; 23 (1952), pp. 36–60; 'The Language of the Genesis Apocryphon: a Preliminary Study', *Scrip. Hier.* IV (1958), pp. 1–35; *Studies in Galilean Aramaic* [translated from the Hebrew original and annotated . . . by M. Sokoloff] (1976).

80. See Mt. 26:73, Mk. 14:70, and especially bErub. 53b. Cf. G. Dalman, *Die Worte Jesu* (²1930), pp. 63–72 (E. T. *The Words of Jesus* (1902), pp. 80 f.); G. Vermes, *Jesus the Jew* (1973), pp. 52–4.

81. For a list (containing 61 items) of Qumran Aramaic texts, see J. A. Fitzmyer, *art. cit.*, NTSt 20 (1974), pp. 404–6.

82. Cf. J. T. Milik, 'Hénoch au pays des aromates', RB 65 (1958), pp. 70–77; 'Problèmes de la littérature hénochique à la lumière des fragments araméens de Qumrân', HThR 64 (1971), pp. 333–78; *The Books of Enoch, Aramaic Fragments of Qumran Cave 4* (1976).

Levi,[83] the Genesis Apocryphon,[84] as well as the Prayer of Nabonidus,[85] the heavenly Jerusalem compositions,[86] a messianic horoscope[87] and the Targum of Job from Cave XI,[88] are all extant in Aramaic. Another late first century A.D. Aramaic work belonging to the traditional corpus of Jewish literature, the *Megillath Ta'anith*, is to be added to the foregoing list.[89]

More equivocal is the evidence yielded by the large number of ossuary inscriptions discovered during the last hundred years;[90] as they mostly

83. J. T. Milik, 'Le Testament de Lévi en araméen', RB 62 (1955), pp. 394–406. For the Aramaic fragments discovered in the Cairo Geniza, see A. Cowley, R. H. Charles, 'An early Source of the Testament of the Patriarchs?', JQR 19 (1906–7), pp. 566–83; I. Lévi, 'Notes sur le texte araméen du Testament de Lévi récemment découvert', REJ 54 (1907), pp. 166–80; 55 (1907), pp. 285–87; P. Grelot, 'Le Testament araméen de Lévi est-il traduit de l'hébreu?', REJ 14 (1955), pp. 91–99; 'Notes sur le Testament araméen de Lévi', RB 63 (1956), pp. 391–406.

84. N. Avigad, Y. Yadin, *A Genesis Apocryphon* (1956); J. A. Fitzmyer, *The Genesis Apocryphon of Qumran Cave I* (1966, ²1971).

Although the apocryphal Book of Tobit from 4Q is represented both in Hebrew and in Aramaic (cf. J. T. Milik, *Ten Years of Discovery*, pp. 31–32), it cannot be proved which was the original and which the translation. The same comment applies to Daniel. Cf. G. Vermes, 'The Impact of the Dead Sea Scrolls on Jewish Studies during the last twenty five Years', JJS 26 (1975), p. 7.

85. J. T. Milik, 'La prière de Nabonide', RB 63 (1956), pp. 407–11. For another ps.-Danielic fragment, see Fitzmyer, NTSt 20 (1974), pp. 391–4.

86. J. T. Milik, *DJD* III (1962), pp. 184–93. For smaller fragments, see *idem*, *DJD* I (1955), pp. 134–5; M. Baillet, *DJD* III, pp. 84–90; B. Jongeling, 'Publication provisoire d'un fragment provenant de la grotte 11 de Qumrân (11Q Jer nouv ar)', JStJ 1 (1970), pp. 58–64.

87. J. Starcky, 'Un texte messianique araméen de la grotte 4 de Qumrân', *Ecole des langues orientales anciennes . . .: Mélanges du Cinquantenaire* (1964), pp. 51–66.

88. J. P. M. van der Ploeg, A. S. van der Woude, *Le Targum de Job de la grotte 11 de Qumrân* (1971); M. Sokoloff, *The Targum of Job from Qumran Cave XI* (1974); B. Jongeling, C. J. Labuschagne, A. S. van der Woude, *Aramaic Texts from Qumran* I (1976), pp. 1–73. There are also small Targum fragments representing Leviticus and Job found in Cave IV: cf. J. T. Milik, *DJD* VI (1977), nos. 156–7.

89. For a bibliography see vol. I, pp. 114–15.

90. The main collections are: D. Chwolson, *Corpus Inscriptionum Hebraicarum* (1882); S. Klein, *Jüdisch-palästinisches Corpus Inscriptionum (Ossuar-, Grab- und Synagogeninschriften)* (1920); J.-B. Frey, *Corpus Inscriptionum Iudaicarum* II (1952); B. Bagatti, J. T. Milik, *Gli scavi del "Dominus Flevit" I: la necropoli del periodo romano* (1958), pp. 70–109. For individual inscriptions, see C. Clermont-Ganneau, RA 3 (1883), pp. 257–76; *Arch. Res. in Pal.* I (1899), pp. 381–454; R. A. F. Macalister, PEFQSt (1904), pp. 336–43; (1908), pp. 341–42; L.-H. Vincent, RB 16 (1907), pp. 410–14; M. Lidzbarski, PEFQS (1909), p. 73; H. Grimme, OLZ 15 (1912), pp. 529–34; H. Häusler, Das heilige Land 57 (1913), pp. 130–34; G. Dalman, ZDMG 37 (1914), pp. 135–45; M. R. Savignac, RB 34 (1925), pp. 253–66; E. L. Sukenik, JPOS 8 (1928), pp. 113–21; *Jüdische Gräber Jerusalems um Christi Geburt* (1931); JPOS 12 (1932), pp. 22–31; L.-H. Vincent, RB 43 (1934), pp. 564–67; S. Krauss, REJ 97 (1934), pp. 1–34; E. L. Sukenik, Kedem 1 (1942), pp. 61–63; 2 (1945), pp. 23–31; AJA 51 (1947), pp. 351–65; L. Y. Rahmani,

consist solely of names, it often remains uncertain whether they should be classified as Hebrew or Aramaic.[91] There are however several longer Aramaic funerary epigraphs, among them an inscription commemorating the presumed transfer of the remains of Uzziah king of Judah,[92] an epitaph from the Kidron Valley,[93] an ossuary lid with a *ḳorban* inscription,[94] and the Giv'at ha-Mivtar tomb inscription.[95]

The most important new evidence relating to the currency of Aramaic, both as an official (legal) and vernacular idiom, originates from the contracts, archival documents and letters uncovered at Murabba'at, Masada and Naḥal Ḥever.

Murabba'at has yielded an Aramaic acknowledgement of debt dating to the second year of Nero (A.D. 55/56) and an account concerning corn and vegetables;[96] Masada, a letter and an ostracon;[97] and Murabba'at again, various legal texts (deeds of sale, matrimonial and divorce documents) prior to the outbreak of the second Jewish war.[98] Further contracts belong to the Bar Kokhba period and are dated according to the era of the liberation of Israel.[99] There exists also a fragmentary Aramaic report written on an ostracon in which Masada is mentioned.[100]

Among the thirty-five papyri constituting the family archives of Babata the daughter of Simeon, three are in Aramaic and six in Nabataean. Moreover, nine further deeds written in Greek bear Aramaic or Nabataean subscriptions and signatures.[101]

Finally, the majority of the documents dating to the Bar Kokhba

---

Atiqot 3 (1961), pp. 104, 107; N. Avigad, IEJ 12 (1962), p. 1; E. Testa, La terra santa 39 (1963), pp. 36–41; N. Avigad, IEJ 17 (1967), pp. 101–11; J. Naveh, IEJ 20 (1970), pp. 33–37; N. Avigad, IEJ 21 (1971), pp. 185–200; Y. Yadin, IEJ 22 (1972), pp. 235–36; E. S. Rosenthal, IEJ 23 (1973), pp. 72–81; J. Naveh, *ibid.*, pp. 82–91; A. Kloner, V. Tsaferis, J. Naveh, *Jerusalem Revealed, Archaeology in the Holy City* 1968–1974 [Tombs] (1975), pp. 69–74.

91. Cf. J. A. Fitzmyer. 'The Languages of Palestine', CBQ 32 (1970), p. 529.

92. E. L. Sukenik, Tarbiz 2 (1930–1), pp. 288–92; J. N. Epstein, *ibid.*, pp. 293–4; W. F. Albright, BASOR 44 (1931), pp. 8–10.

93. E. L. Sukenik, Tarbiz 6 (1934–5), pp. 190–6.

94. J. T. Milik, SBFLA 7 (1956–7), pp. 232–9; J. A. Fitzmyer, JBL 78 (1959), pp. 60–5; S. Zeitlin, JQR 53 (1962), pp. 160–3; 59 (1968), pp. 133–5; Fitzmyer, *Essays on the Semitic Background of the NT* (1971), pp. 93–101.

95. E. S. Rosenthal, IEJ 23 (1973), pp. 72–81; J. Naveh, *ibid.*, pp. 82–91.

96. J. T. Milik, *DJD* II (1961), Nos. 18 and 8, pp. 100–4, 87–8.

97. Y. Yadin, IEJ 15 (1965), p. 111.

98. Milik, *DJD* II, Nos. 19–21, pp. 104–17.

99. Milik, *DJD* II, Nos. 23, 25–8, 31–5, pp. 121–51.

100. Milik, *DJD* II, No. 72, pp. 172–4.

101. Cf. Y. Yadin, 'The Expedition to the Judean Desert 1961', IEJ 12 (1962), pp. 235–46; *Bar Kokhba* (1971), pp. 222–53. The dates of the papyri range from A.D. 93/4 to 132.

war, discovered in Naḥal Ḥever and listed by Y. Yadin[102]—ten texts out of eighteen—are composed in Aramaic. They include eight letters from Bar Kokhba (Simeon bar Kosiba)[103] and two legal papyri.[104]

Whereas the prominence of Aramaic at every level as the main language of Palestinian Jewry is now solidly backed by evidence, it can also be demonstrated that Hebrew remained alive outside the domain of Jewish liturgy.

It is beyond dispute that biblical Hebrew enjoyed a literary revival during the centuries in question. The language of the Old Testament was imitated by the authors of Ecclesiasticus[105] and Tobit[106] among the Apocrypha; by those of Jubilees[107] and the Testament of Naphtali[108] in the Pseudepigrapha, and in the bulk of the sectarian writings from Qumran.[109] It is equally worthy of note that when independent Jewish (Hasmonaean or revolutionary) authorities issued their own coinage,

102. Yadin, 'Expedition . . . 1960', IEJ 11 (1961), pp. 40–50; 'Expedition . . . 1961', IEJ 12 (1962), pp. 248–57; *Bar Kokhba*, pp. 124–83. Cf. also J. Starcky, 'Un contrat nabatéen sur papyrus', RB 61 (1954), pp. 161–81; J. T. Milik, 'Un contrat juif de l'an 134 après J.-C.', *ibid.* pp. 182–90; 'Deux documents inédits du désert de Juda', Bibl. 38 (1957), pp. 245–68.

103. Cf. Yadin, IEJ 11 (1961), pp. 40–50, Nos. 1, 2, 4, 8, 10, 11, 14, 15.

104. Cf. Yadin, IEJ 12 (1962), p. 249. On the language, see E. Y. Kutscher, 'The Language of the Hebrew and Aramaic Letters of Bar Cochba and his Contemporaries', Leshonenu 25 (1961), pp. 117–33; 26 (1962), pp. 7–23 (in Hebrew). For a full list of Aramaic letters from 600 B.C. to A.D. 200, see J. A. Fitzmyer, 'Some Notes on Aramaic Epistolography', JBL 93 (1974), pp. 201–25, esp. 221–5.

105. For the text discovered in the Cairo Genizah, see S. Schechter, C. Taylor, *The Wisdom of Ben Sira* (1899); I. Lévi, *L'Ecclésiastique ou la sagesse de Jésus, fils de Sira* I-II (1898, 1901); N. Peters, *Der jüngst wiederaufgefundene hebräische Text des Buches Ecclesiasticus* (^{2}1905); M. H. Segal, *Sefer Ben Sira ha-shallem* (^{2}1959); A. Di Lella, *The Hebrew Text of Sirach* (1966). Small fragments from 2Q have been published by M. Baillet, *DJD* III (1962), pp. 75–77. A poem corresponding to Ecclus. 51: 13–20, 30, appears in the Psalms Scroll from cave XI: cf. J. A. Sanders, *DJD* IV (1965), col. xxi, 11–17; xxii, 1; cf. M. Delcor, Textus 6 (1968), pp. 27–47. For the Masada manuscript, see Y. Yadin, *The Ben Sira Scroll from Masada* (1965). Cf. also J. T. Milik, Bibl. 47 (1966), pp. 425–26; P. W. Skehan, JBL 85 (1966), pp. 260–62; J. Strugnell, Eretz Israel 9 (1969/70), pp. 109–19. For a comprehensive edition of all the Hebrew texts, see *The Book of Ben Sira, Text, Concordance and an Analysis of the Vocabulary*, published by the Academy of the Hebrew Language (1973).

106. For a description see J. T. Milik, RB 63 (1956), p. 60; *Ten Years of Discovery*, pp. 31–2; RB 73 (1966), p. 522.

107. J. T. Milik, *DJD* I (1955), pp. 82–4; M. Baillet, *DJD* III (1962), pp. 77–9; J. T. Milik, RB 73 (1966), pp. 94–104; A. S. van der Woude, *Tradition und Glaube –K. G. Kuhn Festschrift* (1971), pp. 128–39; Milik, Bibl. 54 (1973), pp. 77–8.

108. For a description, see Milik, *Ten Years of Discovery*, pp. 34–5.

109. Useful recent lists of published Qumran texts are by J. A. Sanders, 'Palestinian Manuscripts 1947–1972', JJS 24 (1973), pp. 74–83, and J. A. Fitzmyer, *The Dead Sea Scrolls. Major Publications and Tools* (1975). Cf. also G. Vermes, *DSS*, pp. 27–8; 45–86.

they chose Hebrew for the Semitic legends,[110] with a single Aramaic exception for which Alexander Jannaeus was responsible.[111]

No one would argue that biblical Hebrew was spoken in the inter-Testamental era; but what was the status of mishnaic Hebrew? Was it an artificial scholarly idiom resulting from a Hebraization of Aramaic? This opinion, held by many at the turn of the century, is out of favour today.

Contemporary scholarship maintains that a thorough scrutiny of the grammar and vocabulary of mishnaic Hebrew reveals that it is the product of a natural and organic development. The best explanation is offered by those who see in mishnaic Hebrew the vernacular language of the Jews, employed colloquially rather than in writing, possibly already in the biblical period but more probably between 400 B.C. and A.D. 100. It was no doubt used by many as a second language in addition to Aramaic (or Greek).[112] From the first century A.D. onwards, it begins to be attested in writing too, although not in works of literature proper. The most important witnesses are the Copper Scroll (3Q15) from cave III of Qumran,[113] a liturgical calendar (4QMishm) from cave IV,[114] and the legal documents and letters from the Bar Kokhba period found at Murabba'at[115] and Naḥal Ḥever.[116]

It may be inferred from this that before its elevation to the dignity of a scholarly language, mishnaic Hebrew fulfilled the more prosaic role of a means of written communication among patriotic revolu-

110. Cf. vol. I, pp. 603–6.

111. *Ibid.*, p. 604.

112. The pioneering work is that by M. H. Segal, *A Grammar of Mishnaic Hebrew* (1927), pp. 1–20 [The Hebrew edition (1936) is more comprehensive]. See also J. M. Grintz, 'Hebrew as the spoken and written language in the last days of the Second Temple', JBL 79 (1960), pp. 32–47; E. Y. Kutscher, 'Mischnäisches Hebräisch', Rocznik Orientalisczny 28 (1964), pp. 35–48; J. A. Fitzmyer, 'The Languages of Palestine in the First Century A.D.', CBQ 32 (1970), p. 530; E. Ullendorff, 'Is Biblical Hebrew a Language?', BSOAS 34 (1971), pp. 247–49; J. A. Emerton, 'The Problem of Vernacular Hebrew in the First Century A.D. and the Language of Jesus', JThSt 24 (1973), pp. 1–23; C. Rabin, *A Short History of the Hebrew Language* (n.d. [1974]) pp. 38–41; P. Lapide, 'Insights from Qumran into the Languages of Jesus', RQ 8 (1975), pp. 483–501; C. Rabin, 'Hebrew and Aramaic in the First Century', JPFC II (1976), pp. 1017–25. Cf. Kutscher, Enc. Jud. 16, cols. 1590–1607.

113. Cf. J. T. Milik, *DJD* III (1962), pp. 221–35. According to this scholar, the idiom reflects 'un dialecte mishnique, celui de la vallée du Jourdain sans doute': *ibid.*, pp. 222–3.

114. Cf. J. T. Milik, Supp. VT (1957), pp. 24–6; *Ten Years of Discovery*, pp. 41, 107–10. The Hebrew ostraca found in Masada contain only names, and consequently do not mirror linguistic usage. Cf. Y. Yadin, IEJ 15 (1965), pp. 111–2.

115. J. T. Milik, *DJD* II (1961), Nos. 7, 22, 24, 29, 30, 36 (contracts, etc.). Nos. 42–52 (Bar Kokhba letters).

116. Y. Yadin, IEJ 11 (1961), pp. 43–50 (Nos. 5, 7, 9, 12, 13); IEJ 12 (1962), pp. 249–57 (Nos. 44–6).

tionaries during the second uprising against Rome.[117] Needless to say, it is likely to have continued as an oral idiom in bilingual or trilingual Jewish homes.

The final conclusion must be that the principal language, spoken and written, used by Palestinian Jews during the inter-Testamental age was Aramaic. But mishnaic Hebrew served as an additional medium of oral communication. It was later also occasionally employed by scribes at Qumran, and more frequently by those of Simeon bar Kosiba during the A.D. 132–135 war, until it became the official tongue of the Galilean academies in the second half of the second century A.D.[118]

117. Yadin (*Bar Kokhba*, p. 181) remarks that the establishment of Hebrew as the official language may have been brought about by a special decree of Bar Kokhba since 'the earlier documents are written in Aramaic while the later ones are in Hebrew'. However, the available evidence does not altogether bear out this claim, and the complete publication of the finds must be awaited before a definite conclusion can be reached.

118. No new evidence has so far emerged capable of solving the old enigma concerning the equivocal use in Jewish Greek sources of the phrases *Ἑβραϊστί, κατὰ τὴν Ἑβραίων διάλεκτον* and *τῇ πατρίῳ γλώσσῃ* often illustrated by Aramaic words. In the Fourth Gospel *Ἑβραϊστί* refers to *Βηθζαθά* (Jn. 5:2), *Γαββαθά* (Jn. 19:13), *Γολγοθά* (Jn. 19:17) and *ῥαββουνί* (Jn. 20:17). According to Josephus, *Ant.* i 1, 1 (33), *σάββατα* is *κατὰ τὴν Ἑβραίων διάλεκτον*; likewise *ἀσαρθά (Ἑβραῖοι . . . καλοῦσι), Ant.* iii 10, 6 (252). For Philo, the Aramaic *πάσχα* is thus called by the *Ἑβραῖοι . . . πατρίῳ γλώσσῃ*, *Dec.* xxx (159); *Spec. Leg.* ii 27 (145). Yet the same term is said by him elsewhere to be *Χαλδαϊστί*, *V.M.* ii 41 (224), whilst in *Abr.* xii (57) a false Hebrew etymology of *Ἰσραήλ* is explained by the tongue of the *Ἑβραῖοι*. For a discussion of this topic, see A. Meyer, *Jesu Muttersprache* (1896), pp. 39–42. Among the recently discovered documents, the only relevant, but alas inconclusive, passage is contained in a Greek letter despatched by a Sou[mai]os who explains that the message was sent *Ἑληνιστί* (sic) because (?) the desire *(τ[ὸ ὁρ]μὰν)* could not be found to write *Ἑβραεστί* (sic). Cf. B. Lifshitz, 'Papyrus grecs du désert de Juda', Aegyptus 42 (1962), pp. 240–56; cf. Fitzmyer, CBQ 32 (1970), p. 541; Yadin, *Bar Kokhba*, pp. 130–1. G. Howard and J. C. Shelton, IEJ 23 (1973), pp. 101–2, propose to read [*Ἑρ*]*μᾶν*: '[Her]mas could not be found to write . . .' Since Hebrew and Aramaic are both represented among the Semitic texts from the same archive, *Ἑβραεστί* designates either. In regard to the adverb *Χαλδαϊστί*, the original significance of 'Chaldaean', i.e. Babylonian, was still perceived by the LXX translator of Dan. 2:26, who explains Baltasar, the Akkadian surname of Daniel, as being *Χαλδαϊστί*, whereas he renders ארמית in Dan. 2:4 as *Συριστί*. For Philo, however, *Χαλδαϊστί* almost always designates Hebrew. The biblical names *Σάρρα, Abr.* xx (99), *Ἰσαάκ, Abr.* xxvi (201), *Ἰσραήλ, Praem.* vii (44); *Legat.* i (4) are *Χαλδαϊστί*. According to *V.M.* ii 5 (26) the laws of the Jews were written *γλώσσῃ χαλδαϊκῇ*, and Ptolemy Philadelphus ordered the 'Chaldaean' to be translated into Greek, *ibid.* 6 (31), 7 (38–40). Philo's peculiar nomenclature was no doubt necessitated by the fact that in the ordinary usage of Hellenistic Jews *Ἑβραϊστί* meant Aramaic. To describe the language of Scripture, he relies on the association of Israel's ancestors with Mesopotamia. *Μωυσῆς γένος μέν ἐστι Χαλδαῖος*, he writes in *V.M.* i 2 (5) which implies that the tongue of the human author of the Torah was 'Chaldaean'.

II. The Spread of Hellenism

1. *Hellenism in the non-Jewish Regions*

In the Graeco-Roman period, the Jewish region just described was, as in ancient times, surrounded on all sides by Gentile territories. It had reached the Mediterranean coast only at Jamnia and Joppa. Elsewhere, even in the west, it was not the sea that formed the boundary of lands belonging to the Jews, but the Gentile districts of the Philistine and Phoenician cities. These areas, however, were much more fully Hellenized than the Jewish region. No reaction such as the Maccabaean uprising had brought the process of Hellenization to a halt;[1] and besides, polytheism unlike Judaism merged very easily with Hellenism. Thus whereas its advance into the interior of Palestine was impeded by Judaism's religious barriers, here, as in every other place where it had appeared since the time of Alexander the Great, it was able to exercise an overwhelming influence on the native oriental culture. Thus the civilized world, especially in the large cities of the west and east of Palestine, was by and large Hellenized long before the start of the Roman era. Only the lower levels of society and the rural population can be presumed not to have been affected in this way. But besides the border regions, the non-Jewish areas of inner Palestine were dominated by Hellenism also, in particular Scythopolis and the city of Samaria, where Alexander the Great had already settled Macedonian colonists, whilst the Samaritans had their focal point in Shechem.

The penetration of Hellenistic culture shows itself most clearly and comprehensively in religious worship. The indigenous cults, especially in the Philistine and Phoenician cities, in many respects retained their essential character, but they were to a significant extent transformed by Greek elements and blended with them.[2] Moreover, purely Greek cults also gained an entrance and often entirely supplanted those already existing. Unfortunately, the sources do not allow us to distinguish the Greek period proper from that of Rome; most of the material derives from coins, and these chiefly belong to the Roman era. On the whole, however, the picture obtained from them also holds good

1. For the absence of resistençe to Hellenism in Syria see S. K. Eddy, *The King is Dead: Studies in the Near Eastern Resistance to Hellenism* (1961), pp. 148 f.

2. For the survival of the Semitic cults of the Syrian region, see now J. Teixidor, *The Pagan God: Popular Religion in the Greco-Roman Near East* (1977). Note also D. Flusser, 'Paganism in Palestine', JPFC II (1976), pp. 1065–1100.

for the pre-Roman period, for which, furthermore, there is no lack of direct evidence.

On coins of Raphia from the imperial epoch, Apollo and Artemis appear in a purely Greek form;[3] on those of Anthedon, the tutelary goddess of the city is presented as Astarte.[4]

On the cults of Gaza under the Roman empire the fullest evidence comes from the biography of Bishop Porphyry of Gaza written by Mark the Deacon. According to him, there were in Gaza in the time of Porphyry (the end of the fourth century A.D.) eight *δημόσιοι ναοί* of Helios, Aphrodite, Apollo, Persephone (Core) and Hecate, a Heroon, a temple of Tyche and a temple of Marnas.[5] It is clear already from this that the purely Greek cults preponderated, a finding confirmed in general by the coins, which carry the effigies of still more Greek deities.[6] A temple of Apollo in Gaza is mentioned already at the time of the destruction of the city by Alexander Jannaeus, *Ant.* xiii 13, 3 (364). In the Roman epoch, only Marnas, the principal deity of the city was, as his name (מרן/מר=lord) indicates, a Semitic god, although he too was more or less Hellenized.[7]

3. Mionnet, *Description de médailles antiques* V, pp. 551 f., *Suppl.* VIII, pp. 376 f.; F. de Saulcy, *Numismatique* (1874), pp. 237–40, pl. xii, nos. 7–9. *BMC Palestine*, pp. lxxxi–ii; G. Stark, *Gaza*, p. 584.

4. Mionnet, V, pp. 522 f., *Suppl.* VIII, p. 364; de Saulcy, pp. 234–6, pl. xii, nos. 2–4. Cf. *BMC Palestine* xlv–vii; Stark, p. 594.

5. *Marci Diaconi Vita Porphyrii episcopi Gazensis* (ed. Grégoire and Kugener, Budé, 1930), 64: *ἦσαν δὲ ἐν τῇ πόλει ναοὶ εἰδώλων δημόσιοι ὀκτώ, τοῦ τε Ἡλίου καὶ τῆς Ἀφροδίτης καὶ τοῦ Ἀπόλλωνός καὶ τῆς Κόρης καὶ τῆς Ἑκάτης καὶ τὸ λεγόμενον Ἡρῶον [Ἡρωεῖον?] καὶ τὸ τῆς Τύχης τῆς πόλεως, ὃ ἐκάλουν Τυχαῖον, καὶ τὸ Μαρνεῖον, ὃ ἔλεγον εἶναι τοῦ Κρηταγενοὺς Διός, ὃ ἐνόμιζον εἶναι ἐνδοξότερον πάντων τῶν ἱερῶν τῶν ἁπανταχοῦ.* The Marneion is also mentioned frequently elsewhere in this biography; see Budé ed., pp. xi–vii f. Cf. S. A. Cook, *The Religion of Ancient Palestine in the Light of Archaeology* (1930), pp. 180–6.

6. Eckhel, *Doctr. Num.* III, pp. 448 ff.; Mionnet V, pp. 535–49; *Suppl.* VIII, pp. 371–5; de Saulcy, pp. 209–33, pl. xi; Head, *HN*², p. 805; *BMC Palestine*, pp. lxvi ff.; Stark, *Gaza*, pp. 584–9.

7. On Marnas cf. in addition to the passages in Mark the Deacon the following: Stephanus Byz. s.v. *Γάζα·ἔνθεν καὶ τὸ τοῦ Κρηταίου Διὸς παρ'αὐτοῖς εἶναι, ὃν καὶ καθ' ἡμᾶς ἐκάλουν Μαρνᾶν, ἑρμηνευόμενον Κρηταγενῆ;* SHA, *Sev. Alex.* 17; Epiphanius, *Ancoratus* 106, 9. Jerome, *Ep.* 107 *ad Laetam* 2 (PL XXII, col. 870: 'iam Aegyptius Serapis factus est Christianus, Marnas Gazae luget inclusus et eversionem templi iugiter pertimescit'); *id.*, *Vita Hilarionis* 14 and 20 (ed. Oldfather, 1943); *id.*, *Comm. in Isaiam* 7: 1.2–3 (PL XXIV, col. 241=CCL 73, p. 268 'Serapium Alexandriae et Marnae templum Gazae in ecclesias Domini surrexerunt'); Marinus, *Vita Procli* 19 (cf. n. 11 below); Eckhel, *Doctr. Num.* III, pp. 450 f.; Stark, *Gaza*, pp. 576–60; Roscher, GRM II, cols. 2377 ff.; the earliest explicit evidence of the cult of Marnas appears in coins of Hadrian with the inscription *Μαρνα*, see Mionnet V, p. 539; de Saulcy, pp. 216–18, pl. xi, no. 4. Note however the fourth century B.C. coins of Gaza with מ and an ostracon of *c.* 300 B.C. with the name עבדמראן (servant of Maran/Marnas) from near Raphia, reported by D. Flusser, JPFC II, p. 1077. His cult is also found outside Gaza. Cf. the inscrip-

A mixture of indigenous and Greek cults was also followed in Ashkelon. Worship here was principally offered to Ἀφροδίτη οὐρανίη, Astarte Queen of Heaven, mentioned already by Herodotus as the deity of the city and still frequently represented as its tutelary goddess on coins of the period of the empire.[8] Related to her, and at first probably identical with her, is the Atargatis or Derceto worshipped in Ashkelon in the peculiar form of a woman with the tail of a fish. Her Semitic name (עתרעתה composed of עתר=Astarte and עתה) itself indicates that she was a Syrian form of Astarte combined with another deity. This is supported by a Delian inscription identifying her with Aphrodite (Roussel, Launey, *Inscriptions de Délos* 2266: Ἁγνῇ Ἀφροδίτῃ Ἀταργάτι). But from her representation as a fish it is clear that in her the fructifying power of water was especially honoured.[9] Since she was

---

tion from Canatha in Le Bas-Waddington, *Inscriptions* III, no. 2412g (Wetzstein, *Ausgewählte Inschriften* (1864), no. 183): *Διὶ Μάρνᾳ τῷ κυρίῳ*. The late Greek legend that Gaza was called *Μίνῳα* after Minos is also associated with the cult of Marnas as *Ζεὺς Κρηταγενής* (Stephanus Byz. s.v. *Γάζα* and s.v. *Μίνῳα*). Cf. Stark, *Gaza*, pp. 580 f.

8. Herodot. i 105; Pausanias i 14, 7. The coins in Mionnet V, pp. 523–33, *Suppl.* VIII, pp. 365–70; de Saulcy, *Numismatique*, pp. 178–208, pls. ix and x. *BMC Palestine*, pp. xl–viii f. Cf. Stark, *Gaza*, pp. 258 ff., 590 ff. On the Semitic Astarte generally see Roscher, GRM s.v. 'Astarte'; F. Baethgen, *Beiträge zur semitischen Religionsgeschichte* (1888), pp. 31–7; F. Cumont RE II, cols. 1777 f.; W. Baudissin, Herzog-Hauck, RE[3], II, pp. 147–61; S. R. Driver, HDB I, pp. 167–71; J. Gray, IDB I, pp. 255–6; Nötscher, Klauser, RAC I (1950), cols. 806 f.; GMVO s.v. ''Attart, 'Astart, Astarte'. The identity of Aphrodite Urania with the Semitic Astarte is in this instance indubitable. For the general question of the Near Eastern origins of Aphrodite, see M.P. Nilsson, *Gesch. d. gr. Rel.* I ([3]1967), pp. 519 ff. Note the dedications at Delos to 'Astarte Palaistine Aphrodite Ourania', Ph. Bruneau, *Recherches sur les cultes de Délos* (1970), pp. 346–7, and in particular *Ins. de Délos* 2305 erected by a man from Ashkelon and containing the provision, 'It is not lawful to offer any part of a goat, pig or cow'. On Aphrodite cf. also Roscher, GRM I, pp. 390–406; Tümpel, RE I, cols. 2729 ff. (on *Οὐρανία* p. 2774); Preller, *Griechische Mythologie* I (ed. Robert, 1894), pp. 345–85 (on *Οὐρανία* p. 356 f. and index, p. 942); cf. also Pape-Benseler, *Wörterb. der griech. Eigennamen* s.v. *Οὐρανία;* Bruchmann, *Epitheta deorum quae apud poetas Graecos leguntur* (1893), p. 66; M. P. Nilsson, GGR II ([2]1961), pp. 120; 130; 333; 335; W. Burkert, *Griechische Religion* (1977), pp. 238–43.

9. On the worship of Derceto in Ashkelon see especially Diodorus ii 2, 4: *Κατὰ τὴν Συρίαν τοίνυν ἔστι πόλις Ἀσκάλων, καὶ ταύτης οὐκ ἄπωθεν λίμνη μεγάλη καὶ βαθεία πλήρης ἰχθύων. Παρὰ δὲ ταύτην ὑπάρχει τέμενος θεᾶς ἐπιφανοῦς, ἣν ὀνομάζουσιν οἱ Σύροι Δερκετοῦν· αὕτη δὲ τὸ μὲν πρόσωπον ἔχει γυναικός, τὸ δ'ἄλλο σῶμα πᾶν ἰχθύος.* Cf. A. B. Brett, 'The Mint of Ascalon under the Seleucids', *Museum Notes* 4 (1950), pp. 43–54. On the goddess and her worship in general see 2 Mac. 12:26; Strabo xvi 4, 27 (785); Pliny, *NH* v 23/8 (stating that Derceto is the Greek name for Atargatis); Lucian, *De Syra dea* 14; Ovid, *Metam.* iv 44–6. According to euhemeristic legend Atargatis was drowned in Ashkelon (Mnaseas in Athenaeus 346D–E = Müller, FGH III, p. 155, F. 32). For the various forms of the Semitic name of Atargatis used at Palmyra, see especially le comte du Mesnil du Buisson, *Les tessères et les monnaies*

in fact an Aramaic deity, her cult in Ashkelon was probably later than that of the genuinely Philistine Astarte.[10] The coins of Ashkelon from the imperial period also show a god, perhags of Arab origin, named Phanebal, possibly identified with Apollo.[11] According to an inscription from the time of Severus Alexander (A.D. 228) discovered in Egypt (Canobus), Ἡρακλῆς Βῆλος was also worshipped in Ashkelon as θεὸς πάτριος.[12] A statue found in the city represents Isis with her son Horus.[13] Like these, the Ἀσκλήπιος λεοντοῦχος of Ashkelon, for whom Proclus, the Neo-Platonist, composed a hymn, was originally an oriental god.[14] Otherwise, the coins of Ashkeon show also the genuinely Greek deities, Heracles, Poseidon and the Dioscuri.[15] A temple of Apollo is mentioned in the pre-Herodian period; the grandfather of Herod is said to have been a temple attendant there.[16]

Azotus, ancient Ashdod, possessed in the pre-Maccabaean period a temple of the Philistine Dagon, formerly worshipped also in Gaza and

---

de Palmyre (1962), pp. 354–72. The veneration of the dove in Ashkelon was also connected with the worship of Derceto, cf. Philo, *De Provid.* (Loeb IX, p. 501) in Eusebius, *Praep. evang.* viii 14, 64; in the Armenian text of Philo, see 'Philonis Iudaei sermones tres' etc., p. 116; Tibullus i 7, 18: 'alba Palaestino sancta columba Syro'; Lucian, *De Syra dea* 14. See especially J. Six, 'Monnaies d'Hierapolis en Syrie', *NC* N.S. 18 (1878), pp. 103–31 and pl. vi; Mordtmann, 'Mythologische Miszellen', ZDMG 39 (1885), pp. 42 f.; F. Baethegen, *Beiträge zur semitischen Religionsgeschichte* (1888), pp. 68–75, 90; F. Cumont, RE s.v. 'Atargatis' and 'Dea Syria'; M.-J. Lagrange, *Etudes sur les religions sémitiques* ([2]1905), pp. 130 ff.; R. Dussaud, Rev. arch. 4^3 (1904), pp. 226 f. (on the Semitic names) and 240–50 (on the pictorial representations). For the cult of Atargatis at Delos see *Ins. de Délos* nos. 2264–2301; for her description there as 'Hagne Aphrodite Atargatis', see Ph. Bruneau, *Recherches sur les cultes de Délos* (1970), p. 346. See now RAC s.v. 'Atargatis'.

10. So W. Baudissin ThLZ (1897), col. 292.

11. *BMC Palestine*, pp. lix–lxi; H. Seyrig, Syria 47 (1970), pp. 96–7; J. Teixidor, *The Pagan God*, pp. 46–7.

12. IGR I 1092 = Sammelbuch 8452 (from Canobus). A man of Ashkelon erects in the temple of Serapis a statue of his native god Heracles Bel: *Διὶ Ἡ[λίῳ] Μεγά[λῳ] Σεράπιδι ἐν Κα[νώβῳ] θεὸν πάτρι[όν] μου Ἡρ[ακ]λῆ Βῆλον ἀνείκητον M. A. Μάξιμο[ς. . .] Ἀσκαλωνείτη[ς . . .] εὐξάμενος ἀνέθηκ[α]*. Cf. R. Dussaud, Rev. arch. ser. 4, 3 (1904), p. 210.

13. See Savignac, RB (1905), pp. 426–9; cf. J. H. Iliffe, QDAP 5 (1936), pp. 64 ff.; note also that P. Oxy. 1380 records the worship of Isis under various names at Dora, Straton's Tower (see p. 115 below). Ashkelon, Raphia and Gaza. See M. Hengel, *Judaism and Hellenism*, p. 158.

14. Marinus, *Vita Procli* 19: *ἡ τῶν ὕμνιων αὐτοῦ πραγματεία . . . καὶ Μάρναν Γαζαίων ὑμνοῦσα καὶ Ἀσκλήπιον Λεοντοῦχον Ἀσκαλωνίτην καὶ Θεανδρίτην ἄλλον Ἀραβίοις πολυτίμητον θεόν*. Cf. Stark, *Gaza*, pp. 591–3; RE XII, col. 205.

15. See the coins in Mionnet and de Saulcy, *op. cit.* Stark, pp. 589 f.; but cf. *BMC Palestine*, pp. xlviii–lxiv.

16. Eusebius *HE* i 6, 2; 7, 11; see vol. I, p. 234.

Ashkelon.[17] It was destroyed in the capture of Ashdod by Jonathan Maccabaeus and pagan worship in general was extirpated there, 1 Mac. 10:84. Nothing detailed is known concerning its re-establishment during the restoration by Gabinius. At this later period, Azotus also had in any case a considerable Jewish population (see p. 109 below).

In the neighbouring cities of Jamnia and Joppa, the majority of the inhabitants had been Jewish since the age of the Maccabees. Yet Joppa had a role in Greek culture as the scene of the myth of Perseus and Andromeda: it was on the rock of Joppa that Andromeda was exposed to the sea-monster and rescued by Perseus.[18] The myth persisted there even during the period of Jewish predominance. In 58 B.C., the skeleton of the sea-monster, brought by M. Scaurus from Joppa to Rome, was exhibited during the spectacular games given by Scaurus in Rome when he was aedile.[19] Strabo, Mela, Pliny, Josephus, Pausanias, and even Jerome, all testify to the continuance of the myth

17. No reliable evidence exists on the character of Dagon. The name would permit a derivation from דג, fish, or more probably from דגן, corn. The latter etymology is adopted by Philo of Byblos who explains Dagon as the god of agriculture, in Eusebius, *Praep. evang.* i, 10 (36c): *Δαγών, ὅς ἐστι Σίτων;* (37d): *'Ο δὲ Δαγών, ἐπειδὴ εὗρε σίτον καὶ ἄρατρον, ἐκλήθη Ζεὺς 'Αρότριος* = FGrH 790 F 2 (16), (25). It is possible but not likely, that the god worshipped in the cities of the Philistine coast was a god of the sea corresponding to the Phoenician sea-god portrayed on the coins of Aradus as a man with a fishtail (on these coins see E. Babelon, *Catalogue des monnaies grecques de la Bibliothèque nationale. Les Perses Achéménides etc.* (1893), pp. 123–5, 131 f., pl. xxii, nos. 1–9, 23–25; J. Rouvier, *J. Int. arch. num.* 3 (1900), pp. 135–7, pl. vi, nos. 18–24); cf. *BMC Phoenicia*, pp. xvii ff.; J.-P. Rey-Coquais, *Arados et sa pérée aux époques grecque, romaine et byzantine* (1974), p. 324). The worship of Dagon or Dagan was apparently brought to Palestine from Babylonia; and while it was general among the Philistines, it was not confined to them and is well-attested in Ugarit. Dagon appears to have been a god of fertility, and in Palestine and Ugarit to have been eventually dislodged by Baal. See R. A. S. Macalister, *The Philistines. Their History and Civilization* (1914), pp. 99–114; S. A. Cook, *The Religion of Ancient Palestine in the Light of Archaeology* (1930), pp. 170–1; W. F. Albright, *Archaeology and the Religion of Israel* ([3]1953), p. 76; J. Gray, *The Canaanites* (1964), p. 122; R. Dussaud, *Les découvertes de Ras Shamra (Ugarit) et l'Ancien Testament* (1941), pp. 104–6; s.v. 'Dagon', IDB I, p. 756; GMVO I, pp. 49–50 (Mesopotamia); 276–8 (Syria). For the worship of Dagan in Ugarit in the second millennium B.C. see e.g. CAH II, 2 ([2]1975), pp. 136; 139; 153; 155. Cf. R. du Mesnil du Buisson, *Études sur les dieux phéniciens hérités par l'Empire romain* (1970), pp. xv; 46–54.

18. The earliest mention of Joppa as the scene of this event occurs in the fourth century B.C. [Scylax of Caryanda] *Periplus* (Müller, *Geogr. gr. minores* I, p. 79). Cf. generally: Stark, *Gaza*, pp. 255 ff.; 593 f.; RE s.v. 'Andromeda'; Abel, *Hist. Pal.* I, pp. 271–2.

19. Pliny, *NH* ix 4/11: 'Beluae, cui dicebatur exposita fuisse Andromeda ossa Romae apportata ex oppido Iudaeae Ioppe ostendit inter reliqua miracula in aedilitate sua M. Scaurus longitudine pedum XL, altitudine costarum Indicos elephantos excedente, spinae crassitudine sesquipedali'. On Scaurus see vol. I, pp. 244–5.

in that region.[20] The Hellenistic fable according to which Joppa was founded by Cepheus, the father of Andromeda, also points to it.[21] Pliny even speaks of a cult there of the Ceto,[22] and Mela mentions altars bearing the names of Cepheus and his brother Phineus.[23] After Joppa was destroyed as a Jewish city in the revolt of A.D. 66–70, the Gentile cults once more gained the ascendancy there.[24]

In Caesarea, first established as a major city by Herod the Great, we encounter primarily the cult, characteristic of the Roman epoch, of Augustus and Rome. All the provinces, cities and princes competed with one another at that time in attending to this worship, which was indeed prudently rejected by Augustus in Rome but looked on with favour and encouraged in the provinces.[25] It goes without saying that in this matter Herod could not fall behind. If a general observation made by Josephus is to be taken literally, he founded *Caesarea* (*Καισάρεια*, i.e. temples of Caesar) 'in many cities'.[26] Particularly mentioned are those in Samaria, Panias (see below) and our Caesarea. The magnificent temple raised there stood on a hill facing the entrance to the harbour. Inside were two large statues, one of Augustus modelled after Olympian

20. Strabo xvi 2, 28 (759); Mela i 11/64; Pliny *NH* v 13/69; Josephus, *B.J.* iii 9, 3 (420); Pausanias iv 35, 6; Jerome, *Comm. ad Ion.* 1, 3; (PL XXV, col. 1123; CCL lxxvi, 1, p. 383). Most of them mention that traces of Andromeda's chains were pointed out on the rock at Joppa.

21. Stephanus Byz., s.v. *'Ιόπη*.

22. Pliny, *NH* v 13/69: 'Colitur illic fabulosa Ceto'. The name Ceto is merely a Latin version of *κῆτος* (the sea-monster). Cf. Stark, *Gaza*, p. 257. Jonah's fish in the Bible is also called *κῆτος* (Jon. 2:1, LXX; Mt. 12:40).

23. Mela i 11/14: 'ubi Cephea regnasse eo signo accolae adfirmant, quod titulum eius fratrisque Phinei veteres quaedam arae cum religione plurima retinent'.

24. Cf. in general the coins in Mionnet V, p. 499: de Saulcy, *Numismatique*, pp. 176 f. p. ix, nos. 3–4; *BMC Palestine*, pp. xxiv–v.

25. In Tacitus *Ann.* i, 10 Augustus is reproached 'nihil deorum honoribus relictum, cum se templis et effigie numinum per flamines et sacerdotes coli vellet'. Suetonius, *Div. Aug.* 59: 'provinciarum pleraeque super templa et aras ludos quoque quinquennales paene oppidatim constituerunt'. Augustus rejected this cult only in Rome (Suetonius, *Div. Aug.* 52: 'in urbe quidem pertinacissime abstinuit hoc honore'). A temple was first erected to him there by Tiberius (Tacitus, *Ann.* vi, 45; Suetonius, *Calig.* 21). Of the surviving temples to Augustus the most famous is that at Ancyra; see D. Krencker and M. Schede, *Der Tempel in Ankara* (1936), cf. E. Bickermann, 'Die römische Kaiserapotheose', *ARW* 27 (1929), pp. 1–34; L. R. Taylor, *The Divinity of the Roman Emperor* (1931); K. Scott, *The Imperial Cult under the Flavians* (1936); M. P. Charlesworth, 'The Refusal of Divine Honours, an Augustan Formula', PBSR XV (1939), pp. 1–10. Emperor worship was merely a continuation of the divine honours paid to Alexander and his successors; see L. Cerfaux and J. Tondriau, *Un concurrent du Christianisme: le culte des souverains dans la civilisation gréco-romaine* (1957), with full references and bibliography. For the Hellenistic background see Chr. Habricht, *Gottmenschentum und griechische Städte* ([2]1969).

26. *B.J.* i 21, 4 (407). Cf. *Ant.* xv 9, 5 (328).

Zeus, and one of Rome after Hera of Argos, for Augustus permitted worship of himself only in combination with that of Rome.[27]

As for the other cults of Caesarea, the coins display a wide variety. They belong primarily to the second and third centuries, which is very relevant in the case of Caesarea since from the time of Vespasian the Roman element as opposed to the Greek was substantially reinforced by the Roman colony introduced by that emperor, Pliny, *NH* v 14/69; *Dig.* l 15, 8, 7. The deities portrayed on the coin-types of Caesarea include Nike-Victoria, common throughout the Roman world, the distinctive Tyche-Astarte of the town, sometimes in a triad with Dionysus, Demeter and Sarapis, and relatively rarely some of the Olympian deities.[28]

The coins of Dora, attested from the reign of Caligula, bear an image of Zeus with the laurel or of Astarte.[29] Apion in a foolish tale designates Apollo *deus Doriensium*,[30] which Josephus assumes must refer to our Dora. There is, however, considerable reason for supposing that the storyteller had in mind Adora in Idumaea (see p. 5 above).

The worship of Apollo was in any case common in the Philistine cities (cf. Raphia, Gaza, Ashkelon). It was no doubt promoted by Seleucid influence, for Apollo was considered to be the divine ancestor of the Seleucids in the same way that Dionysus was believed to be that of the Ptolemies.[31]

Ancient rites from the time of Elijah (1 Kgs. 18) were still being performed on Carmel in the reign of Vespasian, in the open air with a bare altar, without temple and without a divine image.[32]

27. Suetonius *Div. Aug.* 52: 'templa . . . in nulla tamen provincia nisi communi suo Romaeque nomine recepit'. On the temple in Caesarea see Josephus, *B.J.* i 21, 7 (414); *Ant.* xv 9, 6 (339). Philo too mentions the *Σεβαστεῖον*, see *Leg.* 38/305. The remains of a temple at Caesarea were discovered by Conder and Kitchener, *The Survey of Western Palestine* II, pp. 13 ff., with a plan of the city on p. 15. It is virtually certain that they are of the temple to Augustus. See A. Reifenberg, 'Caesarea: a Study of the Decline of a Town', IEJ 1 (1950), 20; L. I. Levine, *Roman Caesarea; an archaeological-topographical Study*, Qedem 2 (1975), p. 19. See *ibid.*, pp. 19–22 for the Tiberieum and Hadrianeum also attested in the city.

28. See L. Kadman, *The Coins of Caesarea Maritima: Corpus Nummorum Palestinensium* II (1957).

29. Mionnet V, pp. 359–62; *Suppl.* VIII, pp. 258–60; de Saulcy, pp. 142–8, pl. vi, nos. 6–12; Babelon, *Les Perses Achéménides* (1893), pp. 205–7; J. Rouvier, *Journ. int. d'arch. num.* IV (1901), 125. Cf. also Eckhel III, pp. 362 f.; B. V. Head, *HN*², p. 792; *BMC Phoenicia*, pp. lxxiv–vi.

30. Josephus, *C.Ap.* ii 9 (112).

31. Stark, *Gaza*, pp. 568 ff.; Justin. *Epit.* xv 4, 2–3: 'Huius [Seleuci] quoque virtus clara et origo admirabilis fuit: siquidem mater eius Laudice, cum nupta esset Antiocho . . . visa sibi est per quietem ex concubitu Apollonis concepisse'. On inscriptions Apollo is named *ὁ ἀρχηγός* or *ἀρχηγέτης τοῦ γένους*, OGIS 219, 237.

32. Tacitus, *Hist.* ii 78: 'Est Iudaeam inter Suriamque Carmelus: ita vocant montem deumque. Nec simulacrum deo aut templum (sic tradidere maiores), ara

Ancient Ptolemais (Accho) was one of the most flourishing of Hellenistic cities during the period of the Ptolemies and the Seleucids (see pp. 122–4). It may therefore be assumed, even in the absence of specific evidence, that Greek cults penetrated there early. The coinage begins in 174/3 B.C. and continues to A.D. 268; the city became a Roman *colonia* under Claudius or Nero. The types of pre-colonial coinage include Zeus, Tyche, Nike and—infrequently—Perseus. The colonial coinage is very rare until the end of the second century, and then becomes much more common for the last period. Some pre-colonial types are repeated, along with Sarapis, and compound types such as Hades carrying off Persephone.[33] A Hellenistic inscription from near Ptolemais contains also a dedication to Hadad and Atargatis, 'the gods who listen to prayer'.[34] The Mishnah reports an encounter between Rabban Gamaliel II and a Gentile philosopher in the bath of Aphrodite.[35]

In addition to the coastal cities, it was chiefly the eastern regions of Palestine that were Hellenized earliest and most thoroughly. Alexander the Great and the Diadochi probably founded a number of Greek cities there, or Hellenized those already existing. Their prosperity can have been interrupted for only a brief period by the devastation caused by Alexander Jannaeus, for already Pompey, by separating them from Jewish realm, enabled them to develop independently once more. The region was known in the Roman period as the Decapolis (see pp. 125–7 below).

Pliny, *NH* v 18/74 regards Damascus, which had already served Alexander the Great as a citadel, as the foremost of these cities. Its Hellenistic character at that time is also attested by the coins of Alexander minted there (see pp. 127–8). From then on, it became increasingly Hellenized. When the Seleucid empire was split into several parts towards the end of the second century B.C., it was even

---

tantum et reverentia'. Suetonius, *Div. Vesp.* 5: 'Apud Iudaeam Carmeli dei oraculum consulentem' etc. On Carmel as a holy mountain see also [Scylax] in *Geographi gr. minores* ed. C. Müller I, p. 79: [*Κάρμηλος*] *ὄρος ἱερὸν Διός* (from the context the restoration is fairly certain); Iamblichus, *Vita Pythagorae* 3/15: *τοῦ Καρμήλου λόφου (ἱερώτατον δὲ τῶν ἄλλων ὀρῶν ἠπίσταντο αὐτὸ καὶ πολλοῖς ἄβατον).* W. Baudissin, *Studien zur semitischen Religionsgeschichte* II, pp. 234 f. For a fragment of a Phoenician inscription found on Carmel see C. Clermont-Ganneau, *Archives des missions scientifiques*, ser. 3 XI (1885), p. 173. The fragment contains merely a few names. See now M. Avi-Yonah, 'Mount Carmel and the God of Baalbek', IEJ 2 (1952), pp. 118–24; cf. Syria 29 (1952), pp. 384–6, and J. Teixidor, *The Pagan God*, pp. 55–9.

33. See L. Kadman, *The Coins of Akko Ptolemais: Corpus Nummorum Palaestinensium* ser. 1, vol. IV (1961). See the criticisms by H. Seyrig, 'Antiquités syriennes 80: divinités de Ptolemaïs', Syria 39 (1962), p. 193.

34. M. Avi-Yonah 'Syrian Gods at Ptolemais-Accho', IEJ 19 (1959), pp. 1–12; Teixidor, *op. cit.*, pp. 53–4.

35. mA.Z. 3:4.

for a while the capital of one of these kingdoms. Accordingly, for the most part the dated autonomous coins of Damascus, which reach to the beginning of the Roman empire, show purely Greek deities: Artemis, Athene, Nike, Tyche, Helios and Dionysus.[36] On imperial coins proper, portraits and emblems of deities figure relatively seldom. The image of Silenus, which is frequent on coins of the third century, has no connection with a religious cult, but is a sign that as a Roman colony (from the reign of Philip the Arabian) the city possessed the *ius Italicum*.[37] Dionysus appears several times.[38] The Hellenistic legend associating him with the founding of Damascus also points to the cult of this god.[39] His worship there and in other cities of eastern Palestine may be attributable to Arab influence, for the principal god of the Arabs was thought of by the Greeks as Dionysus.[40]

On the few Greek inscriptions surviving in Damascus and its neighbourhood, Zeus is mentioned more frequently.[41]

In many cities of the Decapolis, particularly in Canatha, Gerasa and Philadelphia, the magnificent temple ruins of the Roman period still testify to the former splendour of Hellenistic worship there.[42] But as far as most of these places are concerned, little is known of the cults individually. Zeus, Athene and the θειοὶ σωτῆρες appear on inscriptions from Canatha.[43] Apollo and Artemis are portrayed on an altar found there.[44] Likewise in Canatha, a stone has been discovered with a Nabataean inscription and the image of a bull as an offering presented

36. F. de Saulcy, *Numismatique*, pp. 30–3. Artemis: nos. 2. 3. 7. 8. 14. 16. 21. Athene: nos. 2. 8. 14. 15. Nike: nos. 11. 12. 22. 23. Tyche: nos. 17. 18. Helios: nos. 3. 21. Dionysos: nos. 24. 25. Most of them also in Mionnet V, pp. 283 f.; *Suppl.* VIII, pp. 193 f. Cf. *BMC Syria*, pp. lxxiv–v.

37. Mommsen, *Staatsrecht* III, 1, pp. 809 f. The coins in Mionnet V, pp. 285–97, nos. 61. 62. 68. 69. 72. 77. 85; *Suppl.* VIII, pp. 195–206, nos. 34. 35. 48; de Saulcy, pp. 35–56; *BMC Syria*, pp. lxxiv–v; Head, *HN*², p. 784.

38. Mionnet, nos. 80. 88.

39. Stephanus Byz., s.v. *Δαμασκός*.

40. Herodot. iii, 8; Arrian, *Anab.* vii, 20; Strabo xvi 1, 11 (741); Origen, *C. Cels.* v, 37; Hesych. *Lex.* s.v. *Δουσάρης*, cf. *RAC* s.v. 'Baal' 54. Dusares.

41. Le Bas-Waddington, *Inscriptions* III, nos. 1879. 2549. 2550: *Διὸς Κεραυνίου;* CIG 4520 = Waddington no. 2557a: *Διὶ [μεγ]ίστῳ 'Ηλιοπολείτῃ τῷ Κυρίῳ;* OGIS 607. For the temple of Jupiter Damascenus, built in the third century A.D., see C. Watzinger, K. Walzinger, *Damaskus, die antike Stadt* (1921), pp. 3–42.

42. See the bibliography to § 23.I.

43. Le Bas-Waddington, *Inscriptions* III, nos. 2339 and 2340: *Διὶ μεγίστῳ*, no. 2345: *'Αθηνᾷ Γοζμαίῃ*, no. 2343: *θεοῖς σωτῆρσι*. For illustrations of the ruins of the temple of Zeus see H. C. Butler, *Syria: Publications of the Princeton University Archaeological Expeditions to Syria in* 1904 *and* 1909, *II: Architecture: A. Southern Syria* (1919), pp. 346–54. See especially D. Sourdel, *Les cultes du Hauran* (1952), pp. 23, 71.

44. C. Clermont-Ganneau, JA. ser. 8 19 (1892), p. 109; R. Dussaud, Rev. arch. ser. 4 (1904), pp. 234 f.

to Tyche (Gad).[45] In Scythopolis, Dionysus must have been especially revered since the city was also known as Nysa,[46] the mythological name of the place where Dionysus was reared by the nymphs.[47] The name Scythopolis was also traced mythologically to Dionysus (see p. 143 below). Moreover, the coins of Scythopolis emphasize this god, together with Zeus and Tyche/Astarte.[48] On the coins of Gadara, the god shown more frequently is Zeus, with Heracles, Tyche/Astarte and several other deities.[49] We now have fairly abundant material relating to the deities of Gerasa, though dating mainly to the second century A.D. or later.[50] The city's principal divinity was Artemis, described on coins of Gerasa as the *Τύχη Γεράσων*.[51] The great temple, significant remains of which have been preserved, was consecrated to her.[52] She is also frequently encountered in dedicatory inscriptions.[53] With her, however, were other genuinely Greek deities such as Olympian Zeus,[54] Poseidon,[55] Apollo,[56] and Nemesis,[57] as well as the Egyptian divine pair, Serapis and Isis,[58] and an 'Arabian god'.[59] In Suf, north-west of

45. See Clermont-Ganneau, *Rec. d'arch. or.* II, pp. 108–16, and CRAI 1898, pp. 597–605 = *Rec.* III, pp. 75–82; RES I, n. 53. *Publications of an American archaeological Expedition to Syria*, Part II (1904), p. 414: Part IV (1905), pp. 93 f.; Sourdel, *Cultes du Hauran*, p. 52.

46. Pliny, *NH* v 18/74: 'Scythopolim antea Nysam'. Stephanus Byz. s.v. *Σκυθόπολις, Παλαιστίνης πόλις, ἣ Νύσσης* [l. *Νύσσα*] *Κοίλης Συρίας*. On coins *Νυσ*[*σαιων* ?] *Σκυθο*[*πολιτῶν*] is frequent, see p. 144 below. See M. Avi-Yonah, 'Scythopolis', IEJ 12 (1962), pp. 123–34; D. Flusser, JPFC II, pp. 1065–71, 1083–5; A. Ovadiah, 'Greek Religions in Beth Shean/Scythopolis in the Graeco-Roman Period', Eretz Israel 12 (1975), pp. 116–24 (Hebrew).

47. A number of cities claimed to be the true Nysa. See Stephanus Byz. s.v. *(Νῦσαι πόλεις πολλαί)*; Pape-Benseler, *Wörterb. der griech. Eigennamen* s.v.

48. *BMC Palestine*, pp. xxxiv–vii; cf. B. Lifschitz, 'Der Kult des Zeus Akraios und des Zeus Bakchos in Beisan (Skythopolis)', ZDPV 77 (1961), pp. 186–90 and H. Seyrig, 'Note sur les cultes de Scythopolis à l'époque romaine', Syria 39 (1962), pp. 207–11.

49. Mionnet V, pp. 323–8; *Suppl.* VIII, pp. 227–30; de Saulcy, *Numismatique*, pp. 294–303; pl. xv; *BMC Syria* lxxxvi–viii.

50. See *Gerasa: City of the Decapolis*, ed. C. H. Kraeling (1938).

51. Mionnet V, p. 329; *Suppl.* VIII, pp. 230 f.; de Saulcy, p. 384 f., pl. xxii, nos. 1–2; *BMC Arabia*, pp. xxxiii–v. *Τύχη*, followed by the name of the city concerned, occurs elsewhere. See B. V. Head, *HN*[2] (1911), pp. 701, 704, 733, 782 etc. BCH 12 (1888), p. 272; E. Babelon, CRAI 1898, pp. 388–94 *(Τύχη Μηδάβων)*; cf. Nilsson, *Gesch. d. gr. Rel.*[2] II, p. 208.

52. See *Gerasa*, pp. 125–38.

53. *Gerasa*, Ins. no. 27, 28, 32, 43, 50, 62.

54. *Gerasa*, Ins. no. 2–7, 10, 13, 14. Inscriptions 2–6 dating to the first century A.D. mention contributions to the building of the temple of Olympian Zeus.

55. *Gerasa*, Ins. no. 39.

56. *Gerasa*, Ins. no. 38.

57. *Gerasa*, Ins. no. 38.

58. *Gerasa*, Ins. no. 38.

59. *Gerasa*, Ins. no. 19–22. Cf. R. de Vaux, 'Une nouvelle inscription au dieu arabique', Ann. Dep. Ant. Jordan (1951), pp. 23–4.

Gerasa, a votive stone has been found for a Hellenized Baal with local colouring.[60]

In Philadelphia Heracles seems to have been the chief god.[61] There is accordingly mention on coins of the goddess Asteria, the mother of Tyrian Heracles.[62] The *Τύχη Φιλαδελφέων* also appears, and several other deities.[63] Coins of the remaining cities of the Decapolis are few and provide only scanty information.

Apart from the coastal cities and those of the Decapolis, the two particular other cities in which Hellenism gained an early foothold were Samaria and Panias. Alexander the Great is said to have settled Macedonian colonists in Samaria; but in any case it was an important garrison town in the period of the Diadochi (see pp. 160–1 below). The city was razed to the ground by John Hyrcanus. But in the restoration under Gabinus, the Hellenistic cults were doubtless also re-established there. They will have been stimulated still further by the enlargement of the city under Herod the Great, who erected a splendid temple to Augustus here too.[64] Coins attested only from the reign of Domitian

60. Brünnow, MDPV (1898), p. 86; also C. Clermont-Ganneau, *Rec.* V, 1903, p. 15; also PEFQSt, 1902, pp. 15–21 and 135 f.; OGIS 620: *Δὶι ἁγίῳ Βεελκωσωρῳ καὶ Ἡλίῳ*. If instead of the *κ* marked in Brünnow's copy as indistinct we may read a *β*, we could think of a Baal of Bostra, בעל בצר. Yet Clermont-Ganneau, who proposed this reading, himself acknowledged that it is open to not inconsiderable objections (*Rec.* V, p. 21, note; PEFQSt 1902, p. 135). According to a subsequent reading by Brünnow (*Die Provincia Arabia* II, p. 240), '*κ* seems here to be absolutely certain'. Cf. *RAC* s.v. 'Baal' (48).

61. A coin of Marcus Aurelius and L. Verus shows a bust of the youthful Heracles and above it the inscription *Ἡρακλῆς*, see de Saulcy, p. 391, and the illustration in pl. xxii, no. 7. Two others (one of Marcus Aurelius and one of Commodus) show a chariot drawn by four horses and above it *Ἡράκλειον ἅρμα* (de Saulcy, pp. 390, 391; instead of *ἅρμα*, de Saulcy reads with earlier scholars in the one case *ρμα*, in the other *απαλα*; the correct reading is given by *BMC Syria* p. 306, no. 1 and pl. XXXVII). The carriage presumably served to carry a small temple of Heracles in procession on festival days (Eckhel, III, p. 351). R. Dussaud suggested the sun-chariot, cf. Rev. arch., ser. 4 i (1903), p. 368. A *Ἡράκλεον* or *Ἡράκλειον* (temple of Heracles) is mentioned in an inscription from Philadelphia, see Clermont-Ganneau, 'L'Heracleion de Rabbat-Ammon Philadelphie et la déesse Astéria', Rev. arch. sér. 4 6 (1905), pp. 209–15 = *Rec. d'arch. or.* 7 (1906), pp. 147–55; but see F.-M. Abel, RB 5 (1908), pp. 570–3.

62. *Θεὰ Ἀστερία*: de Saulcy, p. 391; *BMC Syria*, pp. lxxxix–xl. On Asteria as the mother of the Tyrian Heracles see Athenaeus 392D; Cicero, *De nat. deorum* iii 16/42 ed. Pease *ad loc.*; GRM and RE s.v. Cf. H. Seyrig, 'Les grands dieux de Tyr à l'époque grecque et romaine', Syria 40 (1963), pp. 19–28.

63. See generally on the coins of Philadelphia Mionnet V, pp. 330–3; *Suppl.* VIII, pp. 232–6; de Saulcy, pp. 386–92, pl. xxii, nos. 3–9; *BMC Syria*, pp. lxxxix–xl, *Arabia*, pp. xxxix–xli.

64. *B.J.* i 21, 2 (403): cf. *Ant.* xv 8, 5 (298). For the archaeological remains see J. W. Crowfoot, K. M. Kenyon, E. L. Sukenik, *Samaria-Sebaste I, The Buildings* (1942), pp. 23 f.

provide information concerning other cults.[65] In the period of the Roman empire, Samaria was gradually overtaken in importance by the newly founded Flavia Neapolis. There, however, the Gentile cults did not flourish until the second century A.D. or later (cf. Vol. I, pp. 520–1).

In Panias, subsequently Caesarea Philippi, the Greek god Pan must have been worshipped in the grotto from the beginning of the Hellenistic period, for already in the time of Antiochus the Great (*c.* 200 B.C.) the locality is referred to as *τὸ Πάνειον* (see pp. 169–70 below). The continuance of his cult into later times is richly attested by coins and inscriptions.[66] In this place too, as in Caesarea Stratonis and Samaria, Herod the Great built a temple to Augustus.[67] On coins, Zeus occurs frequently and other deities only sporadically; but the image of Pan is by far the most prevalent.[68] In the time of Eusebius, a bronze statue stood in Caesarea of a woman kneeling with hands outstretched in supplication to a man standing before her. In Christian circles this was thought to be an statue of Christ and the woman with an issue of blood, but it was obviously a representation of the god of healing.[69]

From the second century A.D., the existence of Hellenistic cults is attested in other cities of Palestine, such as Sepphoris, Tiberias, etc. It may be taken as reasonably certain, however, that they did not gain a hold there until after the war of Vespasian. Until then, these places were mainly, though not exclusively, inhabited by Jews, who would scarcely have tolerated the public performance of pagan worship in their midst.[70]

65. Mionnet V, pp. 513–6; *Suppl.* VIII, pp. 356–9; de Saulcy, *Numismatique*, pp. 275–81, pl. xiv, nos. 4–7. Cf. *BMC Palestine*, pp. xxxvii–xli; note also J. W. Crowfoot, G. M. Crowfoot, *Samaria-Sebaste III. The Objects* (1957), pp. 43–4, 57 (coins), 35–42 (Graeco-Roman inscriptions) and the Introduction, pp. 5 f., 'The Roman Cities and the Cult of the Kore'.

66. The coins in Mionnet V, pp. 311–15, nos. 10. 13. 16. 20. 23; *Suppl.* VIII, pp. 217–20, nos. 6. 7. 8. 10: cf. de Saulcy, pp. 313–24, pl. xviii. Cf. *BMC Syria*, pp. lxxx–ii; Head *HN*², pp. 785–6. See especially the portrayal of Pan with his flute in de Saulcy, pl. xviii, nos. 8. 9. 10. Inscriptions in de Saulcy, *Voyage autour de la Mer Morte*, Atlas (1853), pl. xlix; CIG 4537, 4538; addenda, p. 1179; Le Bas-Waddington, *Inscr.* III, nos. 1891. 1892. 1893; MDPV 1898, pp. 84 f. = Brünnow and Domaszewski, *Die Provincia Arabia* II, p. 249 (reproduction by Brünnow). Cf. Abel, *Géog. Pal.* II, pp. 297–8. On the cult of Pan in general see Roscher, GRM III (1902), cols. 1347–81 (on the cult in Caesarea Panias see col. 1371); on the cult in Panias RE XVIII, cols. 595–8.

67. *Ant.* xv 10, 3 (364); *B.J.* i 21, 3 (404).

68. See n. 66.

69. Eusebius *HE* vii 18. See E. v. Dobschütz, 'Christusbilder', TU, N.F. III (1899), pp. 197 ff.; A. v. Harnack, *Die Mission und die Ausbreitung des Christentums* (⁴1924), pp. 145–6. Cf. RAC s.v. 'Christusbild' (vol. III, col. 4).

70. That there was no pagan temple in Tiberias may also be concluded indirectly from Josephus, *Vita* 12 (65), which reports the destruction of Herod's palace, adorned with pictures of animals, but says nothing of a temple there. For the development of paganism in these cities in the second century see Jones, CERP, pp. 279–80.

In the semi-Gentile districts east of Lake Gennesaret, viz. Trachonitis, Batanaea and Auranitis, the situation was different. There too, the Hellenistic cults probably did not find wide acceptance until the second century A.D. But the work of Hellenization began as early as the appearance on the scene of Herod and his sons, who won these hitherto half-barbarous regions for civilization (see p. 14 above). From then on, Hellenistic religion also found an entry. Surviving inscriptions, of which many remain in those parts, testify to the vitality there of its cults from the second to the fourth century. Nevertheless, the same observation applies here as has been made in regard to the Philistine cities, namely that the indigenous deities survived alongside those of Greece. Some of these were Syrian, and some, as a result of Nabataean penetration, Arabian. Of the Syrian gods, Atargatis is attested during the Maccabaean period in Carnaim in Batanaea, 2 Mac. 12:26.[71] The remains of a temple are preserved in Si'a, in the neighbourhood of Canatha, and among them inscriptions from the Herodian period. This edifice, the oldest part of which was built before Herod occupied the region (23 B.C.), was dedicated to the Syrian Baal (Baalsamin).[72] A small altar to Hadad (τῷ θεῷ 'Αδάδῳ), at one time a principal god of the Syrians, was found at Khabab in Trachonitis.[73] The Syrian deities Ethaos (?) and Azizos appear in Batanaea.[74] On the other hand,

71. Also between Panias and Damascus (Le Bas-Waddington, *Inscr.* III, no. 1890) and in Trachonitis (PEFQSt 1895, p. 141). On Atargatis see GMVO I, pp. 244–5; RAC s.v.

72. For references to the inscriptions see Jones, CERP, p. 284 f. Illustration of the ruins in M. de Vogüé, *Syrie Centrale, Architecture civile et religieuse*, pls. 2 and 3 and pp. 31–8. The Greek inscriptions in Waddington, *Inscriptions*, nos. 2364-2369a; the Aramaic inscriptions in de Vogüé, *Syrie Centrale, Inscriptions sémitiques*, pp. 92–9, and in the CIS II Aram. nos 163–8. More accurate findings have been made by the American expedition, see H. C. Butler, *Architecture and other Arts* (*Part II of the Publications of an American Archaeological Expedition to Syria*), 1904, pp. 322 f., 334–40; E. Littmann, *Semitic Inscriptions*, *ibid.*, pt. IV (1905), pp. 85–90. See also the information by Butler and Littman in Rev. arch. sér. 4, v (1905), pp. 404–12; R. Dussaud, *Les Arabes en Syrie* (1907), pp. 159–65. That the temple was dedicated to Baalsamin (בעל שמין) is evident from the inscription in de Vogüé, p. 93 = CIS II Aram., no. 163 = Littmann, *Semitic Inscr.*, p. 86. See Sourdel, *Les cultes de Hauran*, p. 21. Cf. on Baalsamin generally: W. Baudissin s.v. 'Baal', Herzog-Hauck, RE³ II, p. 331; F. Cumont, RE II, cols. 2839 f.; s.v. 'Balsamen'; M. Lidzbarski, Eph. Sem. Epig. (1902), pp. 243–60; RAC s.v. 'Baal' 23 (Baalschamin); J. Teixidor, *The Pagan God*, chs. 2 and 4.

73. PEFQSt 1895, p. 132 = Dussaud, *Nouv. arch. des miss. scient.* 10 (1902), p. 642. On Hadad generally: Baudissin in Herzog-Hauck, RE³ VII, pp. 287 ff.; Dussaud in RE s.v.; J. Gray, IDB I, pp. 328 f., s.v. 'Baal'. He was also worshipped, with Atargatis, by the Syrian merchants of Delos, see p. 31 above.

74. *Ἔθαος*: Le Bas-Waddington, *Inscr.* III, no. 2209; R. Dussaud, *Les Arabes* (1907), pp. 150 f. and *La pénétration des Arabes* (1955), p. 147, considers *Ἔθαος* to be an Arabian deity; so also *Ἄζειζος*, *ibid.* no. 2314 (= CIG 4617), Sourdel, *Les cultes*, p. 85. See RE II, col. 2644; R. Dussaud 'Azizos et Monimos, parèdres du

Arabian deities are more widely represented, particularly in the eastern areas. Pre-eminent among these was Dusares (Arab. *Dhu-lShara*), whom the Greeks compared to Dionysus. His cult is also attested during the Roman period by the games dedicated to him, the *Ἄκτια Δουσάρια* in Adraa and Bostra.[75] Inscriptions mention other gods besides him, concerning some of which we know only their names.[76] But in that

---

dieu soleil', Rev. arch., sér. 4, 1 (1903), pp. 128–33. Cf. Sourdel, *Les cultes*, pp. 75–6; RAC s.v. 'Baal' 11 (Aziz). Cf. especially H. J. W. Drijvers, 'The cult of Azizos and Monimos at Edessa', *Ex Orbe Religionum: Studia G. Widengren* I (1972), pp. 355–71.

75. *Δουσάρης:* Le Bas-Waddington, *Inscr.* III, nos. 2023. 2312; R. Dussaud, *Nouv. arch. des miss. scient.* 10 (1902), p. 679=OGIS 770 *(τῷ Θεῷ Δουσάρει . . . ἔτους δεκάτου Ἀντωνείνου Καίσαρος);* Dussaud, Rev. Num. sér. 4 8 (1904), pp. 161 f. *(Δουσάρης Θεὸς Ἀδραηνῶν* on coins of Adraa; see *BMC Arabia*, p. xxiii. *Δουσάριος:* Waddington no. 1916. דושרא: de Vogüé, *Syrie Centrale, Inscriptions sémitiques*, pp. 113, 120=CIS II Aram. nos. 160. 190. The *Ἄκτια Δουσάρια* in Mionnet V, pp. 577–85, nos. 5. 6. 18. 32. 33. 34. 36. 37. Also in de Saulcy, pp. 375. 365. 369 f. *BMC Arabia*, pp. xxiii–xxx. The combination דושרא אערא appears on an inscription in Bostra, RB 14 (1905), p. 593, where Dusara, like Zeus, is to be regarded as the universal deity particularised in the local god אערא; cf. C. Clermont-Ganneau, JA sér. 10, 6 (1905), pp. 363–7=*Rec.* VII (1906), pp. 155–9. דושרא also appears frequently on Nabataean inscriptions from other areas. See especially W. Euting, *Nabatäische Inschriften aus Arabien* (1885), no. II l. 5; III ll. 3, 8; IV ll. 3, 7, 8; XI l. 6; XII l. 8; XX l. 8; XXVII l. 12. The same inscriptions also in CIS II Aram. nos. 197–224. Euting *Sinaitische Inschriften* (1891), no. 437 (דושרא), 499 (הימדושרא), 559 (עבדדושרא). The same inscriptions also in the CIS II Aram. nos. 912. 986. 1225. Inscriptions from Petra, the centre of Nabataean power, in CIS II Aram., nos. 350. 443. In a Nabataean deed from the Babata archive, a יהבדשרא בר מנלס appears as a witness. Cf. Y. Yadin, IEJ 12 (1962), p. 238. At Miletus *Διὶ Δου[σαρει]:* SAW 1906, pp. 260 f. At Puteoli: J. Gildemeister, ZDMG 23 (1869), p. 151=CIS II Aram., no. 157. Latin inscriptions also on the pedestals of several votive offerings found in Puteoli: *Dusari sacrum*, CIL X 1556. Cf. Tertullian, *Apol.* 24: 'Unicuique etiam provinciae et civitati suus deus est, ut Syriae Astartes, ut Arabiae Dusares'. Hesych. *Lex.* s.v. *Δουσάρην τὸν Διόνυσον Ναβαταῖοι*, GRM, art. 'Dusares'; cf. RE s.v. 'Dusares'. R. Dussaud, 'Le culte de Dusares d'après les monnaies d'Adraa et de Bostra', Rev. Num., sér. 4, 8 (1904), pp. 160–73. E. Meyer, *Die Israeliten und ihre Nachbarstämme* (1906), pp. 267 ff. R. Dussaud, *Les Arabes en Syrie* (1907), pp. 166–8; RAC I, 1087–8 ('Baal' no. 54); cf. H. W. Hausing (ed.), *Wörterbuch der Mythologie I: Götter und Mythen im vorderen Orient* (1965), pp. 433–4.

76. *Θεανδρίτης* or *Θεάνδριος* in Waddington nos. 2046. 2374a (CIG 4609, Addenda, p. 1181) 2481; Damascius, *Vita Isidori* in Photius, *Bibliotheca*, cod. 242, p. 347b (Budé ed. VI, p. 41): *Ἔγνω δὲ ἐνταῦθα* (in Bostra) *τὸν Θεανδρίτην ἀρρενωτὸν* (read *ἀρρενωτιὸν) ὄντα θεόν, καὶ τὸν ἄθηλυν βίον ἐμπνέοντα ταῖς ψυχαῖς.* Marinus, *Vita Procli* 19 (cf. note 11 above); compare ILS 4349 (Pannonia); 'Dis patris (*sic*) Manalph et Theandris'. M. C. Fossey, JA sér. 9, 11 (1898), pp. 314, assumes that Theandrites= Dusara; cf. GMVO I, p. 471, no. 2. *Οὐασαιάθου* (?): Waddington, nos. 2374. 2374a; *Μαλειχάθου* (?), PEFQSt 1895, p. 136=IGR III 1111. אלת, Allath (female deity): M. de Vogüé, *Syrie Centrale, Inscr. sémit.*, pp. 100. 107. 119=CIS II Aram. nos. 170. 182, 185; cf. 183. Cf. also Euting, *Nabatäische Inschriften*, no. III 1. 4= CIS II Aram., no. 198. In Herodotus *Ἄλιττα* (i, 131) or *Ἀλιλάτ* (iii, 8). Arab. *al-Lât*,

period the Greek deities predominated, the god most frequently encountered by far being Zeus in various forms,[77] and after him Dionysus, Cronus, Heracles, Hermes, Ares, Pluto (with Persephone) and Ganymede,[78] and the goddesses, Athene[79] and Tyche,[80] and after them Aphrodite, Nike, Irene, the nymphs and Nereids.[81] The Artemis

---

see J. Wellhausen, *op. cit.*, pp. 25–9. In general see F. Baethgen, *Beiträge zur semit. Religionsgeschichte*, pp. 58–9, 90, 97–104; R. Dussaud, *Nouv. arch. des miss. scient.* 10 (1902), pp. 457 ff. (on *al-Lât* and other Arabic deities). Dussaud, *Les Arabes en Syrie*, pp. 116–39; cf. *Wörterb. Myth.* I, pp. 422–4. See Sourdel, *Les cultes*, pp. 69–74. On north-Arabian deities, see now Teixidor, *The Pagan God*, ch. 3.

77. *Διὶ μεγίστῳ*: Waddington, nos. 2116, 2140. 2289. 2292. 2339. 2340. 2412d (Wetzstein 185); PEFQSt 1901, p. 354=1902, p. 21=Clermont-Ganneau, *Rec.* V, p. 22. *Διὶ μεγίστῳ ὑψίστῳ*: R. Dussaud, *Nouv. arch. des miss. scient.* 10 (1902), p. 640. *Διὶ κυρίῳ*: Waddington, nos. 2290, 2413b (Wetzstein 179), 2413j (CIG 4558); *κυρίου Διός*: Waddington, no, 2288. *Θεοῦ Διός*: *ibid.* 2413k (CIG 4559). *Διός*: Waddington 2211. *Ζεῦ ἀνίκητε*: *ibid.* 2390 (cf. also note 83 below on the sun-god). *Τελείῳ ibid.* 2484. *Διὶ ἱκεσίῳ*, in Fîk: Germer-Durand, RB 8 1899, p. 8. *Διὸς Κεραου(νίου)* between Gadara and Pella: *ibid.* p. 7; the simple *Κεραουνίῳ* (in Batanaea): Waddington 2195; cf. also note 41 above (neighbourhood of Damascus) and the inscription of Agathangelos at Abila in the Decapolis (Waddington 2631: *Διὶ μεγίστῳ Κεραουνίῳ*); H. Usener, 'Keraunos', RhM 60 (1905), pp. 1–30. *'Επικαρπίῳ Διί* (Bostra): Waddington 1907. *Διὶ [Φρα]τρίῳ καὶ Ἥρᾳ θεοῖς πατρῴοις* (Bostra): *ibid.* 1922. *Ζεῦ Σαφαθηνέ* (Bostra): Clermont-Ganneau, *Ét. d'arch. or.* II (1897), pp. 28–32; Brünnow, MDPV 1889, p. 82; R. Dussaud, F. Macler, *Voyage archéologique au Safâ* (1901), p. 192 (photograph); J. Halévy, JA sér. 9, 18 (1901), p. 517; OGIS 627; M. Sartre, AAAS 22 (1972), pp. 167–9.

78. Dionysus: Waddington, no. 2309. Cronus: nos. 2375. 2544. Heracles: nos. 2413c, 2428; see Sourdel, *Les cultes*, pp. 33–7. Hermes: *Rev. arch.* sér. 3, 4 (1884), p. 277=Clermont-Ganneau, *Rec. d'arch. or.* I (1888), p. 19. Ares: R. Dussaud, *Nouv. arch. des miss. scient.* 10 (1902), p. 648. Pluto and Persephone: Waddington, no. 2419. Ganymede: nos. 2097. 2118.

79. Waddington, nos. 2081, 2203a, 2203b, 2216, 2308, 2410, 2453 (=Dussaud, Nouv. arch. 10, p. 644), 2461. Also with local colouring (*'Αθηνᾷ Γοζμαίῃ* at Canatha) no. 2345.

80. Waddington, nos. 2127 ,2176, 2413 f. to 2413i (=CIG nos. 4554 to 4557), 2506, 2512, 2514; RB 14 (1905), p. 605 (a better reading of CIG 4557=Waddington 2413i). In Semitic languages, *Τύχη* as the name of a god is rendered by גד, see P. de Lagarde, *Gesammelte Abhandlungen* (1886) p. 16; J. H. Mordtmann, ZDMG 1877, pp. 99–101; Clermont-Ganneau's discussion of the inscription on the image of a bull at Canatha (CRA I 1898, pp. 597–605=*Rec.* III, p. 75–82, see note 45 above); Herzog- Hauck, RE³ VI (1899), p. 333 (s.v. 'Gad'), and cf. the locality גד יון near Jerusalem mentioned in mZab. 1:5. That Tyche is to be identified with Gad is made certain by a bilingual inscription from Palmyra, Waddington, no. 2588 (cf. Cooke, *North Sem. Inscr.*, no. 112); elsewhere Tyche is identified with Astarte or with a number of other Semitic or Greek deities. For recent discussions see M. P. Nilsson, *Geschichte des gr. Religion* II (²1961), pp. 200–10; Sourdel, *Les cultes*, pp. 49–52; H. Seyrig, 'Temples, cultes et souvenirs historiques de la Décapole', Syria 36 (1959), pp. 60–78; *idem*, 'La "Tyché" de Cesarée de Palestine', Syria 49 (1972), pp. 112–15.

81. Aphrodite: Waddington, no. 2098. Nike: nos. 2099, 2410, 2413, CIG 4558. 2479. Irene: no. 2526. Nymphs and Nereids: R. Dussaud, Nouv. arch. 10, p. 694.

venerated in Batanaea in the time of Antoninus Pius was perhaps a Hellenized moon-goddess, the double-horned Astarte, who was indigenous there;[82] many of these Greek deities were Hellenized native gods. Finally, the religious syncretism of the later imperial epoch led to other eastern deities finding favour side by side with the ancient local ones. Chief among these was the Arabian sun-god, who was worshipped here sometimes under the Semitic name *Αὔμου*, sometimes under the Greek name *Ἥλιος*, and sometimes under both.[83] His cult was still popular enough in the time of Constantine for a handsome temple to be erected to him in Auranitis.[84] Besides the Arabian sun-god, the god Marnas of Gaza is attested, and the Egyptian deities Ammon and Isis.[85]

The periodic festival games were in many instances closely connected with the religious cults. In this sphere also the predominance of Hellenistic customs may be proved by numerous examples. Yet the sources for the Greek period proper are again extremely scanty. We know that Alexander the Great celebrated magnificent games in Tyre.[86] The *πενταετηρικὸς ἀγών* held there is mentioned incidentally in the preliminary account of the Maccabaean uprising, 2 Mac. 4:18–20. We also learn that Antiochus Epiphanes wished to introduce the *Διονύσια* into Jerusalem, 2 Mac. 6:7. But where the properly Hellenistic cities of Palestine are concerned, the celebration of such games in the pre-Roman period is nowhere attested in detail. It is however to be assumed that they took place, bearing in mind the general character of the age.[87] Once the Roman epoch is reached the sources become more informative. As is well known, great importance was attached to public games in the period of the empire: no provincial town of any significance was

82. IGR III 1163.

83. *Αὔμου:* Waddington, nos. 2441, 2455, 2456. *Ἥλιος:* nos. 2165, 2398, 2407, in association with *Σελήνη* no. 2430; *Διὸς ἀνικήτου Ἡλίου Θεοῦ Αὔμου:* nos. 2392, 2394, 2395, similarly 2393 = OGIS 619. The form *θεῷ Αὔμου* (nos. 2455, 2456) cannot mean, 'to the god of Aumos', Aumos being the name of the worshipper (see note 73 above); *Αὔμου* or *Αὖμος* is the name of the god himself, as no. 2393 proves: *Ἥλιον θεὸν Αὔμον*. See Sourdel, *Les cultes*, pp. 53–8. Cf. also on the sun-god, R. Dussaud, 'Notes de mythologie syrienne', Rev. arch., sér. 4, 1–3 (1903–4). See on this Baudissin, ThLZ 1906, p. 294; especially *idem*, s.v. 'Sonne', Herzog-Hauck, RE³, XVIII (1906), pp. 489–521; GMVO I, p. 446 ('Helios'), and note H. Seyrig, 'Le culte du soleil en Syrie à l'époque romaine', Syria 48 (1971), pp. 337–66 (the fundamental study of the monuments of the cult, and its nature).

84. Waddington, no. 2393 = OGIS 619. See Sourdel, *Les cultes*, p. 56.

85. Marnas: Waddington, no. 2412g. Ammon: nos. 2313, 2382, IGR III 1222. Isis: no. 2527 = IGR III 1118.

86. Arrian, *Anab.* II 24, 6; III 6, 1. Cf. Plutarch, *Alex.* 29.

87. Cf. e.g. Stark, *Gaza*, pp. 594 f., C. Schneider, *Kulturgeschichte des Hellenismus* II (1969), pp. 187–205.

without them.[88] As early as the reign of Augustus, the games celebrated in the emperor's honour and connected with his worship were everywhere especially well received.[89] In Palestine also, they were introduced into Caesarea and Jerusalem by Herod the Great. There were nevertheless many others of various kinds. Their popularity in the principal cities of Palestine during the second century A.D. is attested by an inscription from Aphrodisias in Caria in which the council and people of the Aphrodisians record the successes won in many competitions by an Aelius Aurelius Menander. Some of the games listed here also took place in Palestinian cities.[90] On a similar inscription at Laodicea in Syria from the third century A.D., the victor himself transmits his successes to posterity. Here too, several Palestinian cities are again mentioned.[91] Lastly, the anonymous *Expositio totius mundi* of the mid-fourth century A.D. specifies the varieties of sports and contests in which the more important cities of Syria at that time distinguished themselves.[92]

88. Cf. on the games in the Roman period especially L. Friedländer, *Darstellungen aus der Sittengeschichte Roms* II (1920), pp. 1–160. On their organization and varieties: J. Marquardt, *Römische Staatsverwaltung* III (1885), pp. 482 f.; E. Reisch, s.v. 'Agones', RE I, cols. 836–66.

89. Suetonius, *Div. Aug.* 59: 'provinciarum pleraeque super templa et aras ludos quoque quinquennales paene oppidatim constituerunt'. For a summary of the evidence see L. Cerfaux, J. Tondriau, *Un concurrent du Christianisme: le culte des souverains dans la civilisation gréco-romaine* (1957), ch. 9. Note the inscriptions published by J.-P. Rey-Coquais, 'Inscriptions grecques d'Apamée', AAAS 23 (1973), pp. 39–84, showing that the first High Priest of Syria dated to the reign of Augustus.

90. Le Bas-Waddington III, no. 1620b = L. Moretti, *Iscrizioni agonistiche greche* (1953), no. 72. As another (no. 1620a) belonging to it shows, the inscription dates to the time of Marcus Aurelius. The relevant portion runs: *Δαμασκὸν β′ ἀνδρῶν πανκράτιν,/Βηρυτὸν ἀνδρῶν πανκράτιν,/Τύρον ἀνδρῶν πανκράτιν,/Καισάρειαν τὴν Στράτωνος ἀνδρῶν πανκράτιν,/Νέαν πόλιν τῆς Σαμαρίας ἀνδρῶν πανκράτιν, Σκυθόπολιν ἀνδρῶν πανκράτιν, Γάζαν ἀνδρῶν πανκράτιν, Καισάρειαν Πανιάδα β′ ἀνδρῶν πανκράτιν, . . . Φιλαδέλφειαν τῆς Ἀραβίας ἀνδρῶν πανκράτιν.*

91. CIG 4472 = Le Bas-Waddington III, no. 1839 = IGR III 1012 = Moretti, *op. cit.* no. 85. The inscription is dated A.D. 221. It mentions games in Caesarea, Ashkelon and Scythopolis.

92. Originally written in Greek, this work is preserved in two Latin versions, the longer and earlier, *Expositio totius mundi et gentium*, and the shorter and later *Descriptio totius mundi*; see J. Rougé, *Expositio totius mundi et gentium*, Sources Chrétiennes no. 124 (1966). *Expositio* 32 reads: 'quoniam autem oportet et singula earum describere, quid ad singulas civitates delectabile esse potest, et hoc dicere necessarium est; habes ergo Antiochiam quidem in omnibus delectabilibus abundantem, maxime autem circensibus, omnia autem quare? quoniam ibi imperator sedet, necesse est omnia propter eum. ecce similiter Laodicia circenses et Tyrus et Beritus et Caesarea; sed Laodicia mittit aliis civitatibus agitatores optimos, Tyrus et Berytus mimarios, Caesarea pantomimos, Heliopolis choraulas, maxime quod a Libano Musae illis inspirent divinitatem dicendi. Aliquando autem et Gaza habet bonos auditores; dicitur autem habere eam et pammacharios, Ascalon athletas luctatores, Castabala calopectas'.

These and other sources allow the following material to be compiled.[93]

Gaza celebrated a πανήγυρις Ἀδριανή from the reign of Hadrian.[94] A παγκράτιον there is mentioned in the Aphrodisias inscription.[95] In a papyrus from the time of Gallienus (A.D. 259–68) an athlete says: ἐστεφανώθην ἱεροῦ εἰσελαστικοῦ οἰκουμενικοῦ ἀγῶνος ἰσολυ[μπίου ἐν] Γάζᾳ.[96] In the fourth century, the *pammacharii* (= παμμάχοι or παγκρατισταί) of Gaza were the most famous in Syria.[97] The circus games held there are noted by Jerome in his *Life of Hilarion*.[98] In Ashkelon, a ταλαντιαῖος ἀγών is attested in an inscription from Laodicea.[99] Its wrestlers (*athletae luctatores*, see n. 92) were particularly famous.

Caesarea possessed a stone theatre and a vast amphitheatre with a view of the sea built by Herod the Great.[100] A στάδιον is mentioned in the time of Pilate.[101] The city must also have had a circus from the beginning, since a ἵππων δρόμος was celebrated at its dedication by Herod (see below). The theatre has now been excavated; the site of the hippodrome is known but only preliminary excavations have so far been carried out.[102] Since this evidence shows that the four main types of

93. The cities are listed in the same order as the cults above, and as in § 23 I. It should be further noted that generally speaking the following types of games took place: (1) chariot races in the circus (ἱππόδρομος); (2) gladiatorial combat and animal-baiting in the amphitheatre; (3) genuine plays, including pantomime, in the theatre; (4) gymnastic displays, i.e., boxing, wrestling and sprinting, in the stadium (1 Cor, 9:24: οἱ ἐν σταδίῳ τρέχοντες), though these were also occasionally given in the circus (Marquardt III, pp. 504 f.). At the great annual feasts, several of these games were as a rule combined.

94. *Chron. pasch.*, ed. Dindorf I, p. 474.

95. The παγκράτιον is the 'combined contest' of wrestling (πάλη) and boxing (πυγμή) and thus belongs to the class of gymnastics. Cf. E. N. Gardiner, 'The Pankration and Wrestling', JHS 26 (1906), pp. 4–22. See H. A. Harris, *Greek Athletes and Athletics* (1964), pp. 105–9.

96. C. Wessely, *Corpus papyrorum Hermopolitanorum* I (1905), no. 70 (p. 33) corrected by U. Wilcken, Arch. f. Pap. 3 (1904–6), p. 540.

97. See n. 92 above. For Gaza, 'boni auditores' are mentioned in addition to the 'pammacharii', which is certainly due to an error in translation or in the transmission of the text. The conjecture appearing most often is ἀκροάματα.

98. Jerome, *Vita Hilarionis* 20, ed. Oldfather (1943): 'Sed et Italicus eiusdem oppidi municeps, Christianus, adversus Gazensem duumvirum, Marnae idolo deditum, circenses equos nutriebat . . .'.

99. IGR III 1012; L. Moretti, *Iscrizioni agonistiche greche* (1953), no. 85.

100. *Ant.* xv 9, 6 (341); *B.J.* i 21, 8 (415).

101. *Ant.* xviii 3, 1 (57); *B.J.* ii 9, 3 (172).

102. Conder and Kitchener, *The Survey of Western Palestine* II, pp. 13 ff. (with a plan of the city on p. 15). See A. Reifenberg, 'Caesarea. A study in the Decline of a Town', IEJ I (1951); *Scavi di Caesarea Maritima* (1966), especially cap. 4–13 ('Il teatro'); for the hippodrome see L. Levine, *Roman Caesarea: an Archaeological-Topographical Study*, Qedem 2 (1975), pp. 27–9; J. M. Humphreys, 'A Summary of the 1974 Excavations in the Caesarea Hippodrome', BASOR 218 (1975), pp. 1–24.

games were provided for from the start, all of them must in fact have taken place at the dedication by Herod the Great.[103]

From then onwards, they were repeated every four years in honour of the emperor.[104] But they were naturally not the only games held there. Individually, all four types are also attested in later times. 1. In the fourth century A.D., the *ludi circenses* of Caesarea were as famous as those of Antioch, Laodicea, Tyre and Berytus (see n. 92). 2. After the close of the Jewish war, Titus organized gladiatorial contests and animal-baiting in which hundreds of Jewish prisoners of war were sacrificed.[105] The emperor Maximinus exhibited exotic beasts from India and Ethiopia at the celebration of his birthday.[106] 3. In the reign of Agrippa I there is mention of games in the theatre.[107] In the fourth century, the *pantomimi* of Caesarea were the most celebrated in Syria (see n. 92). Eusebius's remark concerning the games of Maximinus no doubt also relates to the pantomime shows.[108] 4. The Aphrodisias inscription alludes to a παγκράτιον, and the Laodicea inscription to a boxing contest.[109]

Ptolemais possessed a gymnasium erected by Herod the Great.[110]

Damascus possessed a gymnasium and a theatre, also built by Herod (see Josephus, *loc. cit.*). A παγκράτιον in the same place is attested by the Aphrodisias inscription (see n. 90), and a 'long race' by an inscription from Tralles (Δαμασκὸν ἀνδρῶν δόλιχον).[111] The σεβάσμια (games in honour of the emperor) celebrated there appear on coins from Macrinus onwards.[112]

In Gadara, the ruins of two theatres, and of a third at Emmatha

103. *Ant.* xvi 5, 1 (137): κατηγγέλκει μὲν γὰρ ἀγῶνα μουσικῆς καὶ γυμνικῶν ἀθλημάτων, παρεσκευάκει δὲ πολὺ πλῆθος μονομάχων καὶ θηρίων, ἵππων τε δρόμον . . .

104. The games were celebrated κατὰ πενταετηρίδα, *Ant.* xvi 5, 1 (138), and are therefore known as πενταετηρικοὶ ἀγῶνες, *B.J.* i 21, 8 (415). But according to our method of reckoning, they took place every four years. The same formulae are used of all four yearly games—Olympic, Actian etc.

105. *B.J.* vii 3, 1 (37–40).

106. Eusebius, *De mart. Pal.* vi 1–2.

107. *Ant.* xix 7, 4 (333); 8, 2 (344). On the games in honour of the emperor Claudius which are mentioned in the latter passage see vol. I, p. 453.

108. *Mart. Pal.* vi 2: ἀνδρῶν ἐντέχνοις τισὶ σωμασκίαις παραδόξους ψυχαγωγίας τοῖς ὁρῶσιν ἐνδεικνυμένων.

109. This πύγμη took place on the occasion of the Σεουήρειος Οἰκουμενικὸς Πυθικός (*scil.* ἀγών), i.e. the Pythian games dedicated to the emperor Septimius Severus.

110. *B.J.* i 21, 11 (422).

111. BCH 28 (1904), p. 88=L. Moretti, *Iscrizioni agonistiche greche* (1953), no. 78.

112. Mionnet V, pp. 291 ff.; *Suppl.* VIII, pp. 198 ff.; de Saulcy, pp. 42 ff.; *BMC Syria*, p. lxxxv. Also on the inscriptions: IG II/III 3169=Moretti, no. 90; CIL XIV, 474=ILS 5233. Cf. Clermont-Ganneau, *Rec. d'arch. or.* IV (1901), pp. 302 ff.

nearby, remain to this day.[113] A *ναυμαχία* there may be attested on a coin of Marcus Aurelius.[114]

Canatha, besides the ruins of a temple, has a small theatre hewn out of the rock described in an inscription as *θεατροειδὲς ᾠδεῖον*.[115]

In Scythopolis, traces survive of a hippodrome and the ruins of a theatre.[116] The Aphrodisias inscription mentions a *παγκράτιον* there, and the Laodicea inscription, a *ταλαντιαῖος ἀγών*.[117]

In Gerasa, the magnificent ruins include those of a hippodrome and two theatres.[118] A small theatre outside the city belongs to the late second or early third century; a sixth-century inscription found there refers to the festival of [*M*]*αειουμᾶς*. It apparently provided for shows of the same name, which were of ill-repute because of their licentiousness.[119]

Philadelphia (Amman) possesses the ruins of a theatre and an *odeum* (a small covered theatre).[120] A *παγκράτιον* there is mentioned in the Aphrodisias inscription.

In Caesarea Panias, Titus presented a 'variety of spectacles' (*παντοίας θεωρίας*) after the end of the Jewish war, particularly gladiatorial contests and animal-baitings, for which Jewish prisoners of war were used.[121] It is listed in the Aphrodisias inscription. For the games in the Jewish cities of Jerusalem, Jericho, Tarichea and Tiberias, see the next section.

In addition to the cults and the games, a third indication of the

113. Cf. the bibliography on p. 132 below. The most accurate description of the two theatres is given by C. E. Schumacher, *Northern 'Ajlûn* (1890), pp. 49–60. On the theatre at Emmatha, see L. Steuernagel, ZDPV 49 (1926), pp. 132 f.; E. Frézouls, 'Les Théatres romains de Syrie', Ann. arch. de la Syrie 2 (1952), pp. 46–100, on pp. 79 f.

114. On this see especially Eckhel, *Doctr. Num.* III, pp. 348 ff., also Mionnet V, p. 326, no. 38; de Saulcy, p. 299; cf. however, *BMC Syria*, p. lxxxvii.

115. Le Bas-Waddington III, no. 2341. On the building itself cf. bibliography on p. 140, and now Frézouls, *op. cit.* (n. 113), pp. 61 f.

116. See especially Conder and Kitchener, *The Survey of Western Palestine* II, pp. 106 (plan of the hippodrome) and 107 (plan of the theatre). According to Conder (II, p. 106), the theatre is the best preserved specimen of Roman work in Western Palestine. See A. Rowe, *The Topography and History of Beth-Shan* (1930), pp. 2, 41 and pl. 7.

117. On *ταλαντιαῖος ἀγών*, see n. 99 above.

118. See *Gerasa*, pp. 11 f., 85 ff. (on the hippodrome).

119. For the festival theatre see *Gerasa*, pp. 159 ff. The inscription in *Gerasa*, Ins. no. 279.

120. See the bibliography on pp. 155–6 below. Cf. Conder, *The Survey of Eastern Palestine* I (1889), pp. 35 ff.; R. E. Brünnow and A. v. Domaszewski, *Die Provincia Arabia* II, pp. 216–20; H. C. Butler, *Syria: Publications of the Princeton University Archaeological Expeditions to Syria in* 1904–5 *and* 1909 *II: Architecture; A: Southern Syria* (1919), pp. 34–62. Cf. S. K. Tell, 'Notes on the Archaeology of Amman', ADAJ 14 (1969), pp. 28–33.

121. *B.J.* vii 2, 1 (37 f.).

impact of Hellenism on many of these cities is to be seen in the men they produced with a reputation in Greek literature.[122] On the coast, Ashkelon was particularly outstanding in this respect. Stephanus Byzantinus (s.v. Ἀσκάλων) records no less than four Stoic philosophers —Antiochus, Sosus, Antibius and Eubius—as originating from that city. Antiochus is the only one of whom anything is known. A contemporary of Lucullus and a tutor of Cicero, he lived in the first century B.C. His system, moreover, is not strictly speaking Stoic but eclectic.[123] Sosus is certainly the person after whom Antiochus, his fellow-countryman, named one of his works, so Sosus was not the younger of the two.[124] Stephanus Byzantinus names Ptolemaeus and Dorotheus as grammarians from Ashkelon, and Apollonius and Artemidorus as historians. These last two are unknown but Dorotheus is quoted elsewhere, in particular by Porphyry. He probably lived in the time of Augustus and Tiberius.[125] Next to the philosopher Antiochus, the best known is the grammarian Ptolemaeus.[126] If, as Stephanus Byzantinus states, he was Ἀριστάρχου γνώριμος, he would belong to the second century B.C., but it is more likely that he lived considerably later, at around the beginning of the Christian era.[127]

Of the cities of the Decapolis, Damascus, Gadara and Gerasa are especially conspicuous as the birthplaces of illustrious men. From Damascus came Nicolaus, a contemporary of Herod, famous as a historian and a philosopher (see vol. I, pp. 28–32). From Gadara came the Epicurean Philodemus, a contemporary of Cicero, numerous fragments of whose writings have become known through the rolls found in Herculaneum.[128] The epigrammatic poet Meleager, who likewise lived in the first half of the first century B.C., was also born in

122. Compare the discussion by M. Hengel, *Judaism and Hellenism*, pp. 83–8, 'Greek Literature and Philosophy in Palestine'.

123. Cf. on Antiochus: E. Zeller, *Die Philosophie der Griechen* III. 1 (⁵1923), pp. 618–33; G. Susemihl, *Geschichte der griechischen Literatur in der Alexandrinerzeit* II (1892), pp. 284–91; RE I, col. 2493; Christ-Schmid-Stählin, *Gesch. gr. Lit.* II (⁶1920), p. 342; G. Luck, *Der Akademiker Antiochus* (Diss. Bern, 1953).

124. W. Theiler, *Forschungen zum Neuplatonismus* (1966), pp. 21–3, 73, 82, 124, 148, 273; A. A. Long, *Hellenistic Philosophy* (1974), pp. 222–9. According to the *Index Stoic. Herculan.* 75, 1, he was a pupil of Panaetius. See Zeller, *op. cit.*, p. 589, n. 3; Susemihl II, p. 244. On the dating of Sosus see E. Rohde, RhM 34 (1879), p. 565 = *Kleine Schriften* I, p. 369.

125. See RE s.v. 'Dorotheos' (20).

126. M. Baege, *De Ptolemaeo Ascalonita* (1882); Susemihl, *op. cit.* II, pp. 156–8; RE s.v. 'Ptolemaios' (79).

127. Cf. on the dating of Ptolemaeus, M. Baege, *De Ptolemaio Ascalonita* (1882), pp. 2–6.

128. On Philodemus: E. Zeller, *op. cit.*, p. 386, n. 2; F. Susemihl, *op. cit.* II, pp. 267–78; 571, 689; *Philodemi volumina rhetorica*, ed. Sudhaus, I–II (1892–6); RE s.v. 'Philodemus' (5); cf. O. Murray, 'Philodemus on the Good King according to Homer', JRS (1965), pp. 161–82.

Gadara. About one hundred and thirty of his epigrams are preserved in the Greek Anthology; he was also the first to arrange a collection of Greek epigrams, thereby laying the foundation of our Anthology.[129] The Cynic and satirical poet, Menippus of Gadara, called *ὁ σπουδογέλοιος*,[130] lived in the third century B.C. The end of the first century B.C. saw the appearance of the rhetorician Theodorus of Gadara, tutor to the future Emperor Tiberius.[131] These four are already brought together by Strabo, who, however, confuses our Gadara with Gadara = Gazara in Philistia.[132] The Cynic Oenomaus of Gadara lived in the reign of Hadrian,[133] and in the third century A.D., the rhetorician Apsines of Gadara.[134]

According to Stephanus Byzantinus (s.v. *Γέρασα*), Ariston (*ῥήτωρ ἀστεῖος*), Cerycus (*σοφιστής*) and Plato (*νομικὸς ῥήτωρ*) came from Gerasa, all three being otherwise unknown. The Neo-Pythagoraean philosopher and mathematician Nicomachus of Gerasa lived around A.D. 100.[135]

That these cities were really considered Greek by Greek men of letters is also apparent from the Hellenistic legends relating to their beginnings expressed in the geographical lexicon of Stephanus Byzantinus. Their foundation was traced to Greek gods and heroes, partly by means of etymological speculation, and partly in order to endow them with the aura of a Greek origin; in many instances the local patriotism of native writers may have played a role in this.[136] The relevant article in Stephanus Byzantinus yields the following information.

129. On Meleager: Susemihl, *op. cit.* I, pp. 46 f.; II, pp. 555–7; RE s.v. 'Meleagros' (7); see A. F. S. Gow, D. L. Page, *The Greek Anthology, Hellenistic Epigrams* I (1965), pp. 214–53; II, pp. 591–680.

130. On Menippus: E. Wildenow, *De Menippo Cynico* (1881); R. Helm, *Lukian und Menipp* (1906); RE s.v. 'Menippos' (10). Against the theory that Menippus lived in the first century B.C., Susemihl I, p. 44, n. 138. Since Menippus went from Gadara as a slave to Pontus, he is of course in himself no evidence of the flowering of Hellenism in Gadara in the third century B.C.

131. Susemihl II, pp. 507–11; RE s.v. 'Theodoros' (89); G. W. Bowersock, *Augustus and the Greek World* (1965), p. 35.

132. Strabo xvi 2, 29 (758). On Gadara = Gazara see vol. I, p. 191. According to the context, this is what is meant in Strabo. But since that Gadara was a Jewish city from the time of the Maccabees, it was certainly not the birthplace of the Greek writer, but the Hellenistic Gadara east of the Jordan.

133. On Oenomaus: Zeller, *op. cit.*, pp. 797–8; RE s.v. 'Oenomaos' (5); D. R. Dudley, *A History of Cynicism* (1937), pp. 162–70. Rabbinic literature mentions a pagan philosopher, Abnimos ha-Gardi (אבנימוס הגרדי), who was in contact with R. Meir and is therefore presumed to have lived towards the middle of the second century A.D. (cf. bHag. 15b; Gen. R. 65:19, ed. Theodor, p. 734); W. Bacher, *Die Agada der Tannaiten* II, pp. 31 f.; JE IX, p. 386 and Enc. Jud. 12, cols. 1331–2; s.v. 'Oenomaus'.

134. On Apsines: RE s.v. 'Apsines'. See F. Millar, JRS 59 (1969), p. 16.

135. On Nicomachus: RE s.v. 'Nikomachos' (21); T. L. Heath, *A History of Greek Mathematics* I (1921), pp. 97–112.

136. For this significant motif in Greek historiography see E. Bickerman, 'Origines Gentium', CPh 47 (1952), pp. 65–81.

Raphia is so named *ἀπὸ τῆς ἱστορίας τῆς περὶ τὸν Διόνυσον*.

Gaza was also known as Aza, from Azon the son of Heracles. But some say it was founded by Zeus: *καὶ ἐν αὐτῇ ἀπολιπεῖν τὴν ἰδιάν γάζαν*. It was also called *Ἰώνη*, from Io, and *Μίνῳα*, from Minos.

Regarding Ashkelon, Stephanus quotes the Lydian Xanthus, who was probably a contemporary of Herodotus.[137] In the fourth book of his *Lydiaca*, Stephanus mentions *Τάνταλος καὶ Ἄσκαλος παῖδες* <*Τ*>*υμεναίου*. Ascalus is said to have been sent as a general to Syria by the Lydian king Aciamus and to have founded a city there bearing his own name.

Joppa was named after Jope, the daughter of Aeolus and consort of Cepheus, who founded the city and reigned over it.

Dora was founded, according to some, by Dorus the son of Poseidon: so Claudius Iolaos(?) in the third book of his *Phoenicica*.[138]

Similarly from Claudius Iolaos(?), from the first book of the *Phoenicica*, Stephanus Byzantinus draws the following material regarding Accho (Ptolemais). When Heracles questioned the Delphic oracle about how to heal the wounds caused him by the hydra, he was advised to travel eastwards until he came to a stream that produced a herb resembling the hydra. If he broke off some of this, he would be cured. Heracles found the plant described by the oracle; its heads when cut off grew again like the hydra's. And he was healed and called the city *Ἄκη* (Healing).

Damascus is so named because Ascus, one of the giants, and Lycurgus bound Dionysus and threw him into a river. Hermes delivered him and flayed Ascus (hence Damascus = *δέρμα Ἄσκου*).[139] But others say that Damascus, a son of Hermes and the nymph Halimede, came from Arcadia to Syria and founded a city bearing his own name. Yet others say that Damascus is the name of a man who cut with an axe the vines planted by Dionysus and was punished by him for doing so. (The passage is unclear because of two lacunae.)

No legend concerning the foundation of Scythopolis is provided by Stephanus Byzantinus, but Pliny *NH* v 18/74 writes that the city had its name from the Scythians whom Dionysus settled there to protect the grave of his nurse.[140]

137. *Testimonia* and fragments in Jacoby, FGrH 765; cf. L. Pearson, *Early Ionian Historians* (1939), pp. 109–51.

138. On Claudius Iolaus (?) (also Iulos, Iulies, Iullus) see Müller, FHG IV, pp. 362–4; RE s.v. 'Claudius' (97); fragments (without commentary) in Jacoby FGrH 788. The passages mentioned are F.2 and F.1.

139. Stephanus Byz. s.v. *Δαμασκός*. The legend presupposes the form *Δαρμασκός*, corresponding to the Hebrew דרמשק, 1 Chron. 18:5; 2 Chron. 28:5. In rabbinic texts the name is spelt דרמסק, דרמסקוס, דורמסקוס. A Rabbi Yose דורמסקית, son of a Damascene woman, is mentioned in mYad. 4:3 and elsewhere; see Bacher, *Die Agada der Tannaiten* II^2, pp. 389–94.

140. See M. Avi-Yonah, 'Scythopolis', IEJ 13 (1963), pp. 123–34; D. Flusser, JPFC II, pp. 1066–9.

In the case of other Hellenistic cities where the names show clearly that they were established in the Hellenistic or Herodian period, no mythological foundation-legends could arise.

2. *Hellenism in the Jewish Regions*[141]

Hellenism in its religious aspect was driven out of the Jewish region proper by the Maccabaean uprising and it was not until after the defeat of the Jewish nation in the wars of Vespasian and Hadrian that the Romans forced an entry for the pagan cults. This is not to imply that in those earlier times the Jews remained untouched by Hellenism. It was a civilizing power which extended into every branch of life. It shaped the organization of the constitution, the administration of justice and government, public institutions, art and learning, commerce and industry, the customs of daily life down to fashion and dress, and thereby set the stamp of the Greek spirit on the whole of existence. Hellenistic culture cannot of course be identified with the Greek culture of the classical period. The significance of the former lay rather in the fact that by accommodating the serviceable elements of every foreign civilization within its orbit it developed into a world civilization. But this world civilization itself then became a whole in which the Greek element provided the dominant tone. Into this stream of Hellenistic culture the Jews were also drawn, slowly and with reluctance, but irresistibly. For although religious fervour managed to keep out of Israel pagan cults and everything associated with them, it could not permanently prevent Hellenistic culture from impinging on the remaining areas of life. The several stages can no longer be traced. But bearing in mind that the small Jewish territory was surrounded on almost all sides by Hellenistic regions with which, for the sake of trade, it was obliged to be in constant contact, and remembering also that basically the Maccabaean revolt was directed against pagan worship and not against Hellenism in general, and that the character of the later Hasmonaean dynasty was itself largely Hellenistic (they employed foreign mercenaries, struck Greek coins, assumed Greek names, etc.)[142] and that some of them, such as Aristobulus I, directly patronized Hellenism—when all this is considered, it can certainly be assumed that, in spite of the Maccabaean uprising, Hellenism penetrated Palestine to a not inconsiderable extent already before the Roman period.[143] Subsequently, its further advance was promoted by the

141. For what follows compare especially M. Hengel, *Judaism and Hellenism* (1974) and V. Tcherikover, *Hellenistic Civilization and the Jews* (1959).

142. For the Hellenism of the Hasmonaean dynasty see the penetrating essay by E. Bickerman, *From Ezra to the Last of the Maccabees* (1962).

143. In the time of Hyrcanus I Athenians went to Judaea not only on diplomatic missions *(κατὰ πρεσβείαν)* but also on private business *(κατ' ἰδίαν πρόφασιν)*.

Romans and the Herodians, and it then acquired the Latin element particularly noticeable from the end of the first century A.D. For this later period (the first half of the second century A.D.), the Mishnah contains a great deal of material clearly illustrating the influence of Hellenism on every aspect of life. Numerous Greek and Latin loan-words in the Hebrew of the Mishnah show that it was Hellenistic culture that gained the ascendancy in Palestine also. A series of examples may serve to demonstrate this in some detail.[144]

It was of course primarily in the spheres of the political constitution and military matters, together with foreign institutions, that foreign terms became current. The governor of a province was a **הגמון** (*ἡγεμών*), a province, **הגמוניא** (*ἡγεμωνία*), the municipal authorities of a city, **ארכי** (*ἀρχή*).[145] The military are described as **לגיונות** (*legiones*); an army, as **אסטרטיא** (*στρατία*); war, as **פולמוס** (*πόλεμος*); wages, as **אפסניא** (*ὀψώνιον*); a helmet, as **קסדא** (*cassida*); a shield, as **תריס** (*θυρεός*).[146]

Since Hyrcanus showed himself well-disposed to them, the Athenians decided to honour him by setting up a bronze statue of him and bestowing on him a golden crown, Josephus, *Ant.* xiv 8, 5 (151–5). The decision was made *ἐπὶ Ἀγαθοκλέους ἄρχοντος*. The year is 106/5 B.C., see W. B. Dinsmoor, *The Archons of Athens in the Hellenistic Age* (1931), pp. 276–7; *idem*, *The Athenian Archon List in the Light of Recent Discoveries* (1939), p. 200; cf. W. K. Pritchett and B. D. Meritt, *The Chronology of Hellenistic Athens* (1940), p. xxxiv. Inscriptional evidence from Athens makes the archon date certain. It therefore becomes unavoidable to emend the description of Hyrcanus in the text of the decree of the Athenian people *Ὑρκανὸς Ἀλεξάνδρου ἀρχιερεὺς καὶ ἐθνάρχης τῶν Ἰουδαίων*, by omitting the words *Ἀλεξάνδρου* and *ἐθνάρχης τῶν Ἰουδαίων*, which would refer to Hyrcanus II, not Hyrcanus I.

144. For Greek and Latin loan-words, see e.g. S. Krauss, *Griechische und lateinische Lehnwörter im Talmud, Midrasch und Targum* I–II (1897–9) (a very full but sometimes unreliable collection; vol. II, 623–53 provides a subject index); A. Schlatter, 'Verkanntes Griechisch', *Beiträge zur Förderung christlicher Theologie* 4 (1900), pp. 47–84. See also S. Lieberman, *Greek in Jewish Palestine* (1942); *idem*, *Hellenism in Jewish Palestine* ([2]1965); J. N. Sevenster, *Do You know Greek? How Much Greek Could the First Christians Have Known?* (1968), pp. 38–61. A list of Greek and Latin loan-words in the Targum to the Former Prophets may be found in A. Tal, *The Language of the Targum of the Former Prophets and its Position within the Aramaic Dialects* (1975), pp. 175–86. For more recent general contributions, see J. A. Fitzmyer, 'The Languages of Palestine', CBQ 32 (1970), pp. 501–31 (especially pp. 507–18); Hengel, *Judaism and Hellenism*, pp. 58–65; G. Mussies, 'Greek in Palestine and the Diaspora', JPFC II, pp. 1040–64. For comparative material note M. G. Bertinelli Angeli, *Nomenclatura pubblica e sacra di Roma nelle epigrafi semitiche* (1970), on Latin official terms as transliterated or translated. For the evidence offered by the finds in the Judaean desert, see below, p. 78.

145. הגמון, mEdu, 7:7; הגמוניא, mGit. 1:1; ארכי, mKid. 4:5. Others in Krauss, *Lehnwörter* II, pp. 628 f.

146. לגיונות: mKel. 29:6; mOhol. 18:10; אסטרטיא: mKid. 4:5. פולמוס: mSot 9:14; mPar. 8:9. אפסניא: mSan, 2:4. קסדא: mShab. 6:2; mKel. 9:8. תריס: mShab. 6:4; mSot. 6:8; mAboth 4:11. Cf. Krauss, *Lehnwörter* II, pp. 631 f. See also

In judicial affairs, Jewish traditions in the main held firm. The law which God had given to his people through Moses concerned not only sacred transactions but also matters of civil law and the organization of the judicature. On essential points, the Old Testament was therefore the criterion here. Nevertheless, Greek terms and institutions are encountered in this context too. The court of justice is usually referred to as בית דין, but occasionally also as סנהדרין (*συνέδριον*); the presiding judges, as פרהדרין (*πρόεδροι*);[147] the prosecutor, as קטיגור (*κατήγορος*); the defence, as פרקליט (*παράκλητος*); a pledge, as אפותיקי (*ὑποθήκη*); a testament, as דיתיקי (*διαθήκη*); and a guardian or steward, as אפיטרופוס (*ἐπίτροπος*).[148] Indeed, even for a specifically Jewish legal institution introduced in the time of Hillel, namely the declaration before a court of law that, notwithstanding the sabbatical year, a person reserved the right to demand at any time the repayment of a loan, the Greek expressiou פרוזבול (*προσβολή*) was used.[149]

Of the other public institutions, the games again enter first into consideration. Pharisaic Judaism had always prohibited the pagan type of games. Philo admittedly records that he was once present at an *ἀγὼν παγκρατιαστῶν*, and on another occasion at a performance of one of the tragedies of Euripides.[150] But conduct that the cultured Alexandrian felt able to indulge in was not the norm for the strictly law-abiding Palestinians. Already in the Maccabaean period the construction of a gymnasium in Jerusalem, and resort to it by Jews, is mentioned as one of the principal abominations of the prevailing Hellenism, 1 Mac. 1:14–15; 2 Mac. 4:9–17. And this remained the standpoint of mainstream Judaism.[151] Even Josephus describes the theatre and amphi-

---

Nabataean military titles such as *στρατηγός* and הפרכא (=*ἔπαρχος* or *ἵππαρχος* or *ὕπαρχος*?); אפרתגא: CIS nos. 160, 161, 169, 195, 196, 214, 224, 235, 238. הפרכא: *ibid*. nos. 173, 207, 214, 221.

147. פרהדרין can=*πάρεδροι* or =*πρόεδροι*. The latter is to be considered as correct, for on the bilingual Palmyra tariff בפלהדרותא is parallel to *ἐπὶ προέδρου*. See OGIS 629, 1.4; CIS II 3913, 1.1.

148. סנהדרין: mSot. 9:11; mKid. 4:5; mSanh. 1:5–6; 4:3; mSheb. 2:2; mMid. 5:4. Particularly frequent in the Palestinian Targums, see Levy, *Chald. Wörterb.* s.v.; Krauss II, pp. 401 f. פרהדרין: mYom, 1:1. קטיגור and פרקליט: mAb. 4:11; *κατήγωρ* in this Semitic form also in Rev. 12:10. אפותיקי mGit. 4:4. דיתיקי: mM.K. 3:3; mB.M. 1:7; mB.B. 8:6; Krauss II, p. 197. אפיטרופוס: mSheb. 10:6. mBik. 1:5; mPes. 8:1; mGit. 5:4; mB.K. 4:4, 7; mB.B. 3:3; mSheb. 7:8. אפיטרופא; (administratrix): mKet. 9:4, 6. Cf. Krauss II, 630 f.

149. פרוזבול: mPeah 3:6; mSheb 10:3–7; mM.K. 3:3; mKet 9:9; mGit. 4:3; mUkz. 5:10. For the institution, see below, p. 366.

150. *Quod omnis probus* 5 (26) and 20 (141).

151. mA.Z. 1:7: 'No-one may sell to the Gentiles any beasts, lion or anything else harmful. No-one may help them to build a basilica, a scaffold, stadium or platform (for a tribunal)'. Cf. generally L. Löw, *Die Lebensalter in der jüdischen Literatur* (1875), pp. 291–300 [*Gesammelte Schriften* IV (1898), pp. 108 ff.]; W.

theatre as 'alien to Jewish custom'.[152] Despite this theoretical rejection, Judaism was nevertheless unable to prevent the pageantry of the pagan games from developing in the Holy Land itself from the Herodian period onwards and it should not be assumed that the mass of the Jewish population did not frequent them. In Jerusalem, Herod built a theatre and an amphitheatre, and introduced, as in Caesarea, four-yearly games in honour of Caesar.[153] The implication must be that a stadium and a hippodrome existed there as well, and in fact the latter is once explicitly mentioned.[154] Jericho, where Herod appears to have resided frequently, possessed a theatre, an amphitheatre and a hippodrome.[155] There is occasional mention of a stadium in Tiberias.[156] Even an insignificant town such as Tarichea had a hippodrome.[157]

Public baths and public hostelries were other institutions pointing to the influence of Hellenism. The baths were known by the Hebrew term מרחץ, but the title of the bath-master, בלן (*βαλανεύς*), indicates their Greek origin.[158] In the case of the public inns, their Greek name פונדקי (*πανδοκεῖον* or *πανδοχεῖον*) also reveals that they were a product of the Hellenistic period.[159]

Bacher, *Die Agada der Tannaiten* and *Die Agada der palästinensischen Amoräer* (see the index s.v. 'Theater'); S. Krauss, art. 'Circus', JE IV, pp. 103 f.; S. Krauss, *Talmudisches Archäologie* III (1912), pp. 115–21; note now H. A. Harris, *Greek Athletics and the Jews* (1976).

152. *Ant.* xv 8, 1 (268): *θέατρον . . . ἀμφιθέατρον, περίοπτα μὲν ἄμφω τῇ πολυτελείᾳ, τοῦ δὲ κατὰ τοὺς Ἰουδαίους ἔθους ἀλλότρια· χρησίς τε γὰρ αὐτῶν καὶ θεαμάτων τοιούτων ἐπίδειξις οὐ παραδέδοται.* The Jews saw in the games a *φανερὰ κατάλυσις τῶν τιμωμένων παρ' αὐτοῖς ἐθῶν.*

153. *Ant.* xv 8, 1 (268). The sites of the theatre and amphitheatre remain unknown, see L. H. Vincent and M. A. Stève, *Jérusalem de l'Ancien Testament* II (1956), pp. 708–9. The games in Jerusalem included, as in Caesarea, all four kinds —gymnastic and musical games, chariot-racing and the baiting of animals. See the detailed description in Josephus, *loc. cit.*

154. *Ant.* xvii 10, 2 (255); *B.J.* ii 3, 1 (44).

155. Theatre: *Ant.* xvii 6, 3 (161), Amphitheatre: *Ant.* xvii 8, 2 (194); *B.J.* i 33, 8 (666). Hippodrome (circus): *Ant.* xvii 6, 5 (178); *B.J.* i 33, 6 (659). See J. L. Kelso, D. C. Baramki, *Excavations at New Testament Jericho and Khirbet en-Nitla*, Ann. Am. Sch. Or. Res. 29–30 (1955); and J. B. Pritchard, *The Excavation at Herodian Jericho, 1951*, Ann. Am. Sch. Or. Res. 32–3 (1958), for the excavation of a Herodian building, possibly a palaestra or gymnasium.

156. *B.J.* ii 21, 6 (618); iii 10, 10 (539); *Vita* 17 (92), 64 (331).

157. *B.J.* ii 21, 3 (599); *Vita* 27 (132), 28 (138).

158. בלן mKel. 17:1; mZab. 4:2. See further Krauss II, p. 634. On the baths as a pagan institution but permitted to the Jews, cf. especially mA.Z. 1:7; 3:4. On their distribution and equipment see J. Marquardt, *Das Privatleben der Römer* I (1879), pp. 262 ff.; RE s.v. 'Aquae' and 'Bäder'; R. Ginouvès, *Balaneutikè: recherches sur le bain dans l'antiquité grecque* (1962).

159. פונדקי: mYeb. 16:7; mGit. 8:9; mKid. 4:12; mEdu. 4:7; mA.Z. 2:1. פונדקית (the hostess) mDem. 3:5; mYeb. 16:7. Foreign travellers are אכסניא or אכסנאין (*ξένοι*) mDem. 3:1; mHul. 8:2. פונדקי also occurs not infrequently in the

Architecture in general, especially that of public buildings, was an important aspect of Hellenization.[160] In the Hellenistic cities in the environs of Palestine this is of course obvious. All had their *ναοί, θέατρα, γυμνάσια, ἐξέδρας, στοαί, ἀγοραί, ὑδάτων εἰσαγωγαί, βαλανεῖα, κρῆναι* and *περίστυλα* in the Greek style.[161] But particularly from the time of Herod onward, it may safely be assumed that the Greek style predominated also in Palestine proper. When Herod constructed for himself a magnificent palace in Jerusalem, he undoubtedly adopted for it the Graeco-Roman style.[162] The same is true of the other palaces and monuments in Jerusalem and elsewhere of that period. There are

---

Targums: see the Lexica. For further material, see Krauss II, p. 428; *Talm. Arch.* II, p. 327. A *δημόσιον* or *κοινὸν πανδοχῖον* is mentioned in two Hauran inscriptions: Le Bas-Waddington, *Inscriptions* III, nos. 2462, 2463=PEFQSt 1895, pp. 148, 147. The word also occurs in Lk. 10:34. Cf. RE s.v. *πανδοκεῖον*.

160. See e.g. F. de Saulcy, *Histoire de l'art judaïque* (1858); Conder, 'Notes on architecture in Palestine', PEFQSt, 1878, pp. 29–40; *Syrian Stone-Lore or the monumental History of Palestine* (1886); H. C. Butler, *Architecture and other Arts Publications of an American archaeological Expedition to Syria in 1899–1900* II (1904), pp. 310–422 (important for the history of building in the region of the Hauran in the Herodian-Roman period). For a full and up-to-date survey of the architectural remains of Graeco-Roman Palestine, see G. Foerster, 'Art and Architecture in Palestine', JPFC II, pp. 971–1006; note also *Jerusalem Revealed: Archaeology in the Holy City 1968–1974* (1975). Note especially the Graeco-Roman character of the city foundations of Herod (Caesarea, Sebaste) and the Graeco-Roman (if exotic) style of his royal palaces at Masada and Herodium. See n. 162 below. On the building of dwelling-houses cf. especially A. Rosenzweig, *Das Wohnhaus in der Mišnah* (1907).

161. See especially the survey of the buildings of Herod in *B.J.* i 21, 11 (422–5). On Gaza, cf. Stark, *Gaza*, pp. 598 ff. On Berytus, the buildings of the two Agrippas, see *Ant.* xix 7, 5 (335–7) and xx 9, 4 (211 f.). The Hauran inscriptions provide a rich collection of Greek names for buildings and their parts, see J.-B. Chabot, *Index alphabétique et analytique des inscriptions grecques et latines de la Syrie publiées par Waddington* (1897). In the *Expositio totius mundi* (on the editions of which see n. 92 above), the *tetrapyla* at Caesarea and Bostra are highly spoken of, but they belong to a later time (Caesarea §26, Bostra §38). The טטרפלין at Caesarea is also mentioned in tOhol. 18:13. Cf. Krauss II, p. 262; JQR 14 (1902), p. 745; *Talm. Arch.* II, p. 228. On the public buildings of typical Greek cities see W. Liebenam, *Städteverwaltung im römischen Kaiserreiche* (1900), pp. 134–64; A. H. M. Jones, *The Greek City* (1940), esp. pp. 277–9; R. Martin, *L'urbanisme dans la Grèce antique* (^{2}1974); R. W. Wycherley, *How the Greeks Built Cities* (^{2}1976).

162. See the description of Herod's palace in Jerusalem in *B.J.* v 4, 4 (172–83). For other examples of Herodian architecture see e.g. S. Marie Aline de Sion, *La forteresse Antonia à Jérusalem et la question du Prétoire* (1956); L.-H. Vincent, M. A. Stève, *Jérusalem de l'Ancien Testament* (1956), pp. 704–14; on Masada, described by Josephus, *B.J.* vii 8, 3–5 (280–303), see Y. Yadin, *Masada, Herod's Fortress and the Zealots' Last Stand* (1966), a popular account, full report to follow; on Herodium, described by Josephus, *B.J.* i 20,10 (419–21), see V. Corbo, 'L'Herodion di Gebal Fureidis', LASBF 13 (1962–3), pp. 219–77; EAEHL II, s.v. 'Herodium'. Cf. G. Harder, 'Herodes-Burgen und Herodes-Städte im Jordangraben', ZDPV 78 (1962), pp. 49–63.

in any case known to have been not only stadia in Palestine[163] (as must be assumed from what has been said of the games), but also basilicas,[164] colonnades,[165] vestibules,[166] tribunes,[167] dining-halls[168] and other buildings of the Graeco-Roman type. The Greek style of architecture was adopted even for the Temple at Jerusalem. In the Temple itself (the ναός) Herod did not of course dare to abandon the traditional forms, but in the inner forecourt the Greek pattern was followed. Inside the gates were forecourts (ἐξέδραι), and between them, colonnades (στοαί) ran along on the inner side of the walls.[169] The gate on the eastern side of the forecourt had leaves of Corinthian bronze which were even more costly than those plated with silver and gold.[170] The colonnades

163. אצטדין *(στάδιον)* mB.K. 4:4; mA.Z. 1:7; Krauss II, p. 119; *Talm. Arch.* III, p. 119.

164. בסילקי *(βασιλική)* mA.Z. 1:7; mTohor. 6:8; Krauss II, p. 161; *Talm. Arch.* I, p. 218; II, p. 366.

165. איצטבא *(στοά)* mShek. 8:4; mSuk. 4:4; mOhol. 18:9; mTohor. 6:10; Krauss II, p. 117; *Talm. Arch.* I, p. 223.

166. אכסדרה *(ἐξέδρα)* mMaas. 3:6; mErub. 8:3; mSot. 8:3; mTam. 1:3; mMid. 1:5; mOhol. 6:2; Krauss II, pp. 44 f.; *Talm. Arch.* I, pp. 52, 335. The ἐξέδρα is an open vestibule before the door of the house; see especially mOhol. 2, implying a covered space enclosed by three walls. On epitaphs at Palmyra, אכסדרא (exedra) denotes the vestibule or room of a burial chamber, see G. A. Cooke, *Text-book of North-semitic Inscriptions* (1903), nos. 143–4; M. Lidzbarski, Eph. f. sem. Epig. II, 2 (1906), pp. 269–76.

167. בימא *(βῆμα)* mSot. 7:8; mA.Z. 1:7; Krauss II, p. 150; *Talm. Arch.*, p. 318.

168. טריקלין *(τρίκλινος)* mErub. 6:6; mB.B. 6:4; mAb. 4:16; mMid. 1:6; Krauss II, p. 274; *Talm. Arch.* I, pp. 49, 362; III, pp. 37, 45.

169. The ἐξέδραι of the temple forecourt are mentioned by this name (אכסדרא) in the Mishnah also (mTam. 1:3; mMid. 1:5). Cf. on them *B.J.* v 5, 3 (201–6); also v 1, 5 (38); vi 2, 7 (150 f.); 4, 1 (220–8); *Ant.* xx 8, 11 (191 f.). On the στοαί of the inner forecourt see *B.J.* v 5, 2 (200); vi 5, 2 (293) (where they are definitely distinguished from those of the outer court).

170. *B.J.* v 5, 3 (201); on this gate cf. also *B.J.* ii 17, 3 (411); vi 5, 3 (293–5). In all probability it was identical with the θύρα ὡραία mentioned in Act. 3:2 and certainly the 'Gate of Nicanor' mentioned in the Mishnah (mMid. 1:4; 2:3, 6; mShek. 6:3; mYom. 3:10; mSot. 1:5; mNeg. 14:8), for in the same way that the χαλκῆ πύλη is described as the eastern gate by Josephus, *B.J.* ii 17, 3 (411) and vi 5, 3 (293), so the gate of Nicanor is also given as the eastern gate in the Mishnah (mMid. 1:4; 2:6=mShek, 6:3); and it is likewise said of it that its bronze shone (mMid. 2:3), whereas all the other gates of the forecourt were plated with gold, *B.J.* v 5, 3 (201). In Josephus, and also in the Tosefta (tYom. 2:4) and in the Talmud (bYom. 38a), the bronze of the Nicanor gate is characterized as 'Corinthian', קלנטיא. The gold and silver covering of the other gates had been donated by 'Alexander the father of Tiberius', the alabarch Alexander of Alexandria, *B.J.* v 5, 3 (205). A noteworthy complement to this statement is provided by an ossuary found in Jerusalem. Its inscription runs: 'Οστᾶ τῶν τοῦ Νεικάνορος Ἀλεξανδρέως ποιήσαντος τὰς θύρας נקנר אלכסא; OGIS 599=Frey CIJ 1256. The plural no doubt denotes the two leaves of the gate; it could also be explained from the fact that Nicanor's gate had two side doors (mMid. 2:6=mShek. 6:3). Thus in the same way that the gold and silver covering of the remaining gates was donated

(*στοαί*) surrounding the outer forecourt on all four sides were entirely in the Greek style. They were mainly double (*διπλαῖ*),[171] but those on the southern side were the most magnificent. In the shape of a basilica (*βασίλειος στοά*), they consisted of four rows of immense Corinthian pillars, one hundred and sixty-two in all, forming a three-aisled hall, the middle aisle being broader by one half than each of the two side aisles, and twice as high.[172]

Needless to say, all this is no proof that the Greek style of architecture predominated also on the ordinary domestic level; on this point, more evidence is now appearing.[173] Occasionally, we find that the Phoenician and Egyptian styles were known too in Palestine.[174]

Pictorial art, because of the Jewish rejection of images of men and beasts, was current in first century Palestine in only the most limited forms; the Herodians ventured only in isolated cases to defy Jewish opinion, as for example when Herod the Great placed a golden eagle in the Temple, or when Herod Antipas introduced pictures of animals into his palace at Tiberias.[175] Representations of animals appear also in the

---

by the Alexandrian alabarch Alexander, so the bronze gate was given by an Alexandrian named Nicanor. According to mMid. 2:3 and mYom. 3:10 miracles were associated with the gates of Nicanor. Rabbinic writings (tYom. 2:14; yYom. 41a; bYom. 38a) explain that when Nicanor brought the gates from Alexandria, the sailors cast one of them into the sea in a storm. Nicanor then clutched hold of the remaining one, declaring that if they threw it into the water too, he would go down with it. Whereupon the storm quietened. The other gate came ashore miraculously. Cf. generally Schürer on the *θύρα ὡραία* of Acts 3:2 in ZNW (1906), pp. 51–68.

171. *B.J.* v 5, 2 (190). Cf. also *B.J.* vi 3, 1 (185) and elsewhere; Philo, *Spec. Leg.* i 13 (71). The *στοαί* are given this Greek designation also in the Mishnah (mShek. 8:4; mSuk. 4:4).

172. *Ant.* xv 11, 5 (410–20). For the Temple of Herod see L. H. Vincent and M.-A. Stève, *Jérusalem de l'Ancien Testament* II (1956), pp. 432–70.

173. For preliminary reports of excavations of private houses in Jerusalem from the late Hellenistic and early Roman periods, see *Jerusalem Revealed*, pp. 45–51. For streets of the Herodian period, B. Mazar, *The Mountain of the Lord* (1975), pp. 204 ff.

174. Tyrian courtyards to houses are mentioned in mMaas. 3:5; Tyrian and Egyptian windows in mB.B. 3:6. Tyrian houses were particularly large and beautiful, see Ezek. 26:12; Strabo xvi 2, 23 (757); Josephus, *B.J.* ii 18, 9 (504).

175. The eagle in the temple: *Ant.* xvii 6, 2 (151); *B.J.* i 33, 2 (650). Figures of animals in the palace at Tiberias: *Vita* 12 (65). Figures of beasts admittedly occur occasionally in the Diaspora as ornamentation. Thus in the floor mosaic of the synagogue at Hammam-Lif in North Africa (illustrations in Rev. Arch. 3rd ser. 3 (1884), pls. VII–XI and REJ 13 (1886), pp. 48–9; cf. E. R. Goodenough, *Jewish Symbols in the Greco-Roman Period* II (1953), pp. 89 f.; III, figs. 887–95, 817–906, 913–21, and in the Jewish catacomb in the Vigna Randanini (now Vigna San Sebastiano) in Rome; see H. J. Leon, *The Jews of Ancient Rome* (1960, pp. 51, 70–1, 195 ff.). For eagle and lions in the synagogue of Sardis, see G. M. A. Hanfmann, BASOR 170 (1963), pp. 1–65. Cf. generally D. Kaufmann, REJ 13

remarkable ruins of Arâq el-Emîr north-west of Heshbon. These remains are obviously identical with the castle of Tyre in the vicinity of Heshbon mentioned by Josephus, the building of which he ascribes to the Tobiad Hyrcanus in the reign of Seleucus IV, *Ant.* xii 4, 11 (228 ff.), a date confirmed by the results of excavation.[176] (The use of representational art was nevertheless extremely restricted up to the end of the first century A.D.[177] There was however a substantial change in the second and third centuries. In this period there is significant evidence, not least from tombs and synagogues, of the acceptance of representational forms, including those of the human figure. With this went a more lenient attitude on the part of the rabbis, who, in effect, drew the line only at the actual worship of images, especially those of the emperor.)[178]

(1907), pp. 50–2; *id.* 'Art in the Synagogue', JQR 9 (1897), pp. 254–69. M. Steinschneider, JQR 15 (1903), pp. 326 f. K. Kohler, art. 'Art, attitude of Judaism toward', JE II, pp. 141–3 (see also nn. 177–8 below). For a general survey of ancient Jewish art, see R. Wischnitzer, 'Jewish Pictorial Art in the Late Classical Period' and S. Appelbaum, 'The Minor Arts of the Talmudic Period', in C. Roth (ed.), *Jewish Art: An Illustrated History* (1971), pp. 83–101. Cf. also M. Barasch (ed.), *Studies in Art*, Scrip. Hier. XXIV (1972).

176. For Arâq el-Emîr see Conder, *The Survey of Eastern Palestine* I (1889), pp. 65–87; H. C. Butler, *Publications of the Princeton University Archaeological Expedition to Syria in* 1904–5 *and* 1909 *II: Architecture A: Southern Syria* (1919), pp. 1–25; P. W. Lapp, 'The 1961 Excavations at 'Arâq el-Emîr', Ann. Dep. Ant. Jordan 6–7 (1962), pp. 80–9; *idem*, 'The Second and Third Campaigns at 'Arâq el-Emîr', BASOR 171 (1963), pp. 8–39; M. J. B. Brett, 'The Qasr el-Abd: a Proposed Reconstruction', *ibid.* pp. 39–45; D. K. Hill, 'The Animal Fountain of 'Arâq el-Emîr', *ibid.* pp. 45–55; P. W. Lapp, 'The 1962 Excavation at Arâq el-Emîr', Ann. Dep. Ant. Jordan 10–11 (1965–6), pp. 37–42. Cf. B. Mazar, 'The Tobiads', IEJ 7 (1957), pp. 137–45, 229–38.

177. For the derivative motifs in use in this period see M. Avi-Yonah, *Oriental Art in Roman Palestine* (1961), ch. 1, 'The Art of the Jews until the Destruction of the Second Temple'.

178. A few references to recent work on these questions may be given. The fullest collection of the evidence is E. R. Goodenough, *Jewish Symbols in the Greco-Roman Period* vol. I–XII (1953–65). Vol. I contains the archaeological evidence from Palestine: Vol. IV, pp. 2–44, discusses the evidence in the light of rabbinic prohibitions. The author's conclusions, summarised in vol. XII, are highly controversial; see e.g. E. J. Bickerman, 'Symbolism in the Dura Synagogue: A Review Article', HThR 58 (1956), pp. 127–51. Note also *Excavations at Dura-Europas. Final Report VIII. 1: The Synagogue* (1956) by C. H. Kraeling; see pp. 340–5, 'The Paintings and the Prohibition of Images'; E. E. Urbach, 'The Rabbinical Laws of Idolatry in the Second and Third Centuries in the Light of Archaeological and Historical Facts', IEJ 9 (1959), pp. 149–65; B. Kanael, *Die Kunst der Synagogen* (1961); J. Gutmann, 'The Second Commandment and the Image of God', HUCA 32 (1961), pp. 161–74; E. R. Goodenough, 'The Rabbis and Jewish Art in the Greco-Roman Period', *ibid.*, pp. 269–79; M. Avi-Yonah, 'L'hellénisme juif', *8e cong. int. d'arch. class. 1963* (1965), pp. 611–15; J. M. Baumgarten, 'Art in the Synagogue: some Talmudic Views', Judaism 19 (1970), pp. 196–206; J. Neusner, *Early Rabbinic Judaism* (1975), Part 3: 'Art', pp. 139–215.

Greek music was doubtless performed at festivals in Jerusalem and elsewhere.[179] Already the Aramaic Book of Daniel uses the transliterated names of Greek musical instruments, the *κίθαρις*, *ψαλτήριον* and *συμφωνία*, as does the Mishnah.[180]

In regard to games of amusement and chance, the throwing of dice, קוביא (*κυβεία*), was, as the name indicates, brought to Palestine by the Greeks. It was condemned by Jewish law.[181]

In matters connected with writing, the influence of the Greek and Roman period is evident in the terms for pen קלמוס (*κάλαμος*) and writer לבלר (*librarius*). Abbreviation of a word to its initial letter alone is called נותריקון (*notaricum*).[182]

The influence of Hellenism was most marked in the sphere of trade and industry and in that of the necessities of daily life. As a result of Phoenician and Greek commerce, lands along the coasts of the Mediterranean Sea had already become involved in a brisk interchange of commodities.[183] But whereas in earlier times the effect had been an exchange both of objects of trade and of cultural influences (most notably the adoption and adaptation of the Phoenician alphabet by

179. Herod offered rewards *τοῖς ἐν τῇ μουσικῇ διαγινομένοις καὶ θυμελικοῖς καλουμένοις . . . καὶ διεσπούδαστο πάντας τοὺς ἐπισημοτάτους ἐλθεῖν ἐπὶ τὴν ἅμιλλαν*, *Ant.* xv 8, 1 (270).

180. Dan. 3:5, 10, 15. סמפוניא appears also in mKel. 11:6; 16:8 On Jewish music in general, see A. Z. Idelsohn, *Jewish Music in its Historical Development* (1929); E. Werner s.v. 'Jewish Music', in G. Grove, *Dict. of Music* ([3]1952–4); s.v. 'Music', IDB (1962); cf. also p. 288, n. 83 below.

181. קוביא: mShab. 22:2; mR.Sh, 1:8; mSanh. 3:3; mSheb. 7:4. See generally: L. Löw, *Die Lebensalter in der jüd. Literatur*, pp. 323 ff.; RE, s.v. 'alea'; Krauss, *Talm. Arch.* III, pp. 110–13.

182. קלמוס: mShab. 1:3; 8:5; Krauss II, p. 506; *Talm. Arch.* III, p. 155. לבלר: mPea. 2:6; mShab. 1:3; mGit. 3:1; Krauss II, p. 303; *Talm. Arch.* II, p. 263; III, pp. 159, 169. The form *λιβλάριος* for *librarius* also occurs on Egyptian papyri, see S. Daris, *Il lessico latino nel greco d'Egitto* (1971), p. 69. נוטריקון: mShab. 12:5; Krauss II, p. 356; *Talm. Arch.* III, pp. 172–3; Bacher, *Die exegetische Terminologie der jüdischen Traditionsliteratur* (1905) I, pp. 125–28; II, 124. JE I, pp. 39–42 (s.v. 'Abbreviations'); IX, pp. 339 f. (s.v. 'Notarikon'). On Greek expressions relating to writing see Krauss II, p. 643; S. Lieberman, *Hellenism in Jewish Palestine* (1950), pp. 69–75. 'Notarikon', Enc. Jud. 12, cols. 1231–2.

183. On the trade of the Phoenicians see especially the classic work of J. Movers, *Die Phönizier* II. 3 (1856). E. Meyer, *Geschichte des Altertums* II (1893), pp. 141–54; K. J. Beloch, 'Die Phöniker am ägäischen Meer', RhM 1894, pp. 111–32; see also G. Contenau, *La civilisation phénicienne* (1949): R. D. Barnett, 'Phoenicia and the Ivory Trade', Archaeology 9 (1956); D. Harder, *The Phoenicians* (1962); S. Moscati, *Il mondo dei Fenici* (1966) = *The World of the Phoenicians* (1968). Note however that archaeological evidence shows the importance of Greek trade in both Syria and the West from the eighth century B.C. onwards; see J. J. Dunbabin, *The Greeks and their Eastern Neighbours* (1957); J. Boardman. *The Greeks Overseas* (1964; [2]1973). For Greek finds in Palestine in the OldTestament period see Hengel, *Judaism and Hellenism*, pp. 32–5.

the Greeks), the dominating impact in the Hellenistic period was Greek. This is seen clearly even in the trade and commerce of Jewish Palestine.[184] It not only took Jews out into the world, but also brought Greek merchants into Palestine.

The import of Greek vases into Palestine began as early as the sixth century B.C. In the Hellenistic period Palestine was part of a wider largely unified market characterized by substantial imports, notably wine-jars from Rhodes and other islands, and by local imitations of peculiarly Hellenistic types. A further increase in the volume of imported pottery appears to coincide with the Roman conquest in the middle of the first century B.C.[185] As early as the time of Pericles, Athenian merchant-ships were carrying cargo to Phoenicia and Egypt.[186] The fact that the Phoenician coins of Gaza were minted on the Athenian standard suggests that the city was in commercial contact with Greece in pre-Alexandrian times. Trading relations existed between Athens and Akko already in the age of Isaeus and Demosthenes (see p. 121). It is therefore not surprising that later (in the time of Hyrcanus II), Athenian merchants also came to Judaea (see n. 143 above).

The most vivid evidence, however, for Greek commercial and agricultural activity in Palestine comes from the Ptolemaic period in the form of the Zenon papyri. The relevant documents from Zenon's

184. On Jewish trade see especially L. Herzfeld, *Handelsgeschichte des Juden des Altertums* (1879); W. H. Bennett, s.v. 'Trade and Commerce', HDB IV, pp. 802–6; G. A. Smith, s.v. 'Trade and Commerce' EB IV cols. 5145–99; G. Alon, *Tolᵉdot ha-Yᵉhudim be'Ereẓ Yisra'el bi-tᵉḳufat ha-Mishnah wᵉha-Talmud* I (^{4}1967), pp. 25–52; Krauss, *Talm. Arch.* II, pp. 248–315; D. Sperber, *Roman Palestine 200–400. Money and Prices* (1974); A. Ben David, *Talmudische Ökonomie* (1974); S. Appelbaum, 'Economic Life in Palestine', and 'The Social and Economic Status of the Jews in the Diaspora', JPFC II (1976), pp. 631–727. For a general survey on the basis of articles in Enc. Jud., see N. Gross (ed.), *Economic History of the Jews* (1975). For the wider economic background in the Hellenistic period see the great work of M. Rostovtzeff, *Social and Economic History of the Hellenistic World* (1941).

185. For the pattern of pottery finds in this period see the sketch and bibliography by R. Amiran, *Ancient Pottery of Ereẓ-Yisra'el* (1959), and especially P. W. Lapp, *Palestinian Ceramic Chronology 200 B.C.–A.D. 70* (1961), esp. pp. 221–9 (Appendix A—Economic and Cultural Implications). It should be noted that pottery datings are acutely controversial, and that the volume and pattern of known finds is constantly altering. For a valuable and up-to-date survey see now P. Borinard in DB Supp. VIII (1972), cols. 136–240, s.v. 'Poterie palestinienne'. For the period covered by rabbinic writings, see Y. Brand, *Ceramics in Talmudic Literature* (1953) [Hebrew].

186. Thuc. ii 69, 1: *τὸν πλοῦν τῶν ὁλκάδων τῶν ἀπὸ Φασήλιδος καὶ Φοινίκης καὶ τῆς ἐκεῖθεν ἠπείρου;* viii 35, 2: *τὰς ἀπ' Αἰγύπτου ὁλκάδας προσβαλούσας.* Cf. generally on the international trade of Athens in the time of Pericles, E. Meyer, *Geschichte des Altertums* IV (1901), pp. 53 ff. Cf. F. M. Heichelheim, *Wirtschaftsgeschichte des Altertums* (1938), pp. 320 f.

journey through Palestine in 260–58 B.C. as representative of Apollonius, the *dioiketes* of Egypt, reveal for instance the export of grain from Palestine to Egypt; the development of an estate with 80,000 vines at Beth-Anath in Galilee; the purchase of slaves; and the export to Egypt of foodstuffs and manufactured goods such as furnishings.[187] By the Roman period the Greek influence on the customs of the Jewish people had become very considerable. Terms relating to the mercantile class were already partly Greek. Indeed an ostracon of the third century B.C. from Khirbet el-Kôm (between Hebron and Lachish) now shows κάπηλος (merchant, or perhaps 'moneylender') transliterated as קפילס.[188] A grain-merchant is סיטון (σιτώνης), a sole agent מנפול (μονοπώλης), a retailer פלטר (πρατήρ).[189] A merchant's account-book is פנקס (πίναξ).[190]

The whole monetary system of Palestine was in part Phoenician-Hellenistic, and in part Greek or Roman.[191] The coinage standard of the silver coins minted in the Hellenistic cities of Palestine and Phoenicia from the reign of Alexander the Great, and in some cases before his time,[192] was by turns Attic (the *tetradrachm* of approximately 17 grammes) and Phoenician-Hellenistic (1 *shekel* = 1 *tetradrachm* of approximately 14.55 grammes; half-*shekel* of approximately 7 gram-

187. See V. Tcherikower (Tcherikover), 'Palestine under the Ptolemies (a contribution to the study of the Zenon papyri)', Mizraim 4–5 (1937), pp. 9–90; *idem, Hellenistic Civilisation and the Jews* (1959), pp. 60–71; Hengel, *Judaism and Hellenism*, pp. 35–47.

188. L. T. Geraty, 'The Khirbet el-Kôm Bilingual Ostracon', BASOR 220 (1975), pp. 55–61. The fact that the man in question is lending money does not, however, make it obligatory to translate *kapelos* as moneylender.

189. סיטון: mDem. 2:4; 5:6; mB.B. 5:10; mKel. 12:1; Krauss II, pp. 381 f. מנפול: mDem. 5:4; Krauss II, p. 344. פלטר: mDem. 5:4; mA.Z. 4:9; Krauss II, p. 458; *Talm. Arch.* I, p. 93; II, pp. 349, 365. For further Greek expressions used in commerce see Krauss II, pp. 634 f.; *Talm. Arch.* II, pp. 349–82.

190. פנקס: mShab. 12:4; mSheb. 7:1, 5; mAb. 3:16; mKel. 17:17; 24:7; Krauss II, pp. 466 f.; *Talm. Arch.* I, p. 204; II, pp. 99, 349, 371, 411; III, pp. 144, 160, 180, 208. Such account-books consisted of two tablets bound together which could be opened and shut.

191. On the Jewish monetary system see in addition to the classic works of Eckhel, Mionnet, de Saulcy and Madden, B. V. Head, *Historia Numorum* (²1911); *BMC Palestine*; A. Reifenberg, *Ancient Jewish Coins* (²1947); *idem, Israel's History in Coins from the Maccabees to the Roman Conquest* (1953); cf. *International Numismatic Convention: The Patterns of Monetary Development in Phoenicia and Palestine in Antiquity* (ed. Kindler, 1967); L. A. Mayer, *A Bibliography of Jewish Numismatics* (1966); Y. Meshorer, *Jewish Coins of the Second Temple Period* (1967); D. Sperber, *Roman Palestine 200–400. Money and Prizes* (1974). Cf. vol. I, pp. 9–11, 602.

192. See P. Naster, 'Le développement des monneyages phéniciens avant Alexandre d'après les Trésors', *Int. Num. Conv.: the Patterns of Monetary Development in Phoenicia and Palestine in Antiquity, 1963* (1967), pp. 3–24; A. Kindler, 'The Greco-Phoenician Coins Struck in Palestine in the Time of the Persian Empire', INJ (1963), pp. 2–6.

mes). Alexander minted on the Attic standard, the Ptolemies on the Phoenician, the Seleucids at first on the Attic, and then on occasions from 162 B.C. onwards, and continuously from the time of Alexander Balas, on the Phoenician.[193] The latter standard is perhaps also to be assumed in the Books of the Maccabees where the reckoning is in *drachms* and talents.[194] This same Phoenician-Hellenistic silver money continued to predominate in the wholesale trade in Palestine even during the Hasmonaean period, since the Hasmonaeans probably minted only copper money.[195] These coins bore a Hebrew legend, though the later Hasmonaeans added a legend in Greek. In the Roman-Herodian period, all the coins current in Palestine or minted there bore a Greek (or Greek and Latin) legend. As far as the coinage standard was concerned, there may have been a tendency for the Roman administration to make the Roman standard valid throughout the empire.[196] This is clearer in Palestine than in many other regions. The Herodians were not entitled to mint silver coins (see vol. I, p. 317); they struck copper, and occasionally bronze coins which, though not minted to consistent weights, effectively corresponded with variations in the case of each ruler, to the Roman *as*, *semis*, and *quadrans*. Only the smallest of the small coins of Palestine (*peruṭah*=1/8 *as*) was quite alien to the Roman

193. See T. Reinach, *Les monnaies juives* (1887), pp. 13–15; E. T. Newell, *The Dated Alexander Coinage of Sidon and Ake* (1916); E. Babelon, *Catalogue des monnaies grecques, Les rois de Syrie* (1890), pp. cxxv, clxxxiii; and especially E. J. Bikerman, *Institutions des Séleucides* (1938), pp. 210 ff.; cf. O. Mørkholm, 'The Monetary System of the Seleucid Kings until 129 B.C.', *Int. Num. Conv.* 1963 (see n. 186), pp. 75–87. For a discussion of the metrology of the Tyrian shekel and half-shekel, see A. Ben-David, *Jerusalem und Tyros: ein Beitrag zur palästinischen Münz- und Wirtschaftsgeschichte (126 a.c.–57 p.c.)* (1969), pp. 9–16.

194. *Drachmae:* 2 Mac. 4:19, 10:20, 12:43; Talents: 1 Mac. 11:28. 13:16, 19, 15:31, 35; 2 Mac. 3:11, 4:8, 24, 5:21, 8:10 f. The Hebrew talent amounted to 3,000 shekels, i.e., 12,000 *drachmae* in Phoenician currency. Josephus, in his statements regarding Herod's will, equates one talent with 10,000 'silver pieces', as is evident from a comparison of *Ant.* xvii 6, 1 (146), 8, 1 (189–90) and 11, 5 (321–3). In doing so, he presumably bases his reckoning on the Attic *drachma*, since 10,000 Attic *drachmae* equal approximately 12,000 Phoenician. So F. Hultsch, 'Das hebräische Talent bei Josephus', Klio 2 (1902), pp. 70–2. On the various *drachmae*, see *id.* RE V, cols. 1613–33; also 'Didrachmon', V, cols. 433–6.

195. The view that Simon Maccabee minted silver shekels and half-shekels is now abandoned, see vol. I, p. 603. Note also R. S. Hanson, 'Towards a Chronology of the Hasmonaean Coins', BASOR 216 (1974), pp. 21–3. A hoard of 561 Tyrian silver coins has been discovered at Qumran dating to the end of the second and first centuries B.C., the most recent belonging to the year 118 of Tyre (9/8 B.C.). Cf. R. de Vaux, *Archaeology and the Dead Sea Scrolls* (1973), p. 34 and n. 1. Cf. A. Kindler, 'The Mint of Tyre—The Major Source of Silver Coins in Palestine', *E. Sukenik Memorial Volume* (1967), pp. 318–24 (Hebrew).

196. Compare the advice which Dio (52, 30, 9) puts into the mouth of Maecenas (referring to provincials): *μήτε δὲ νομίσματα ἢ καὶ σταθμὰ ἢ μέτρα ἰδίᾳ τις αὐτῶν ἐχέτω, ἀλλὰ τοῖς ἡμετέροις καὶ ἐκεῖνοι πάντες χρήσθωσαν.*

system.[197] The situation remained the same under the governors. Thus gold coins (*aurei*) and silver coins (*denarii*) minted abroad were current in Palestine, and with them copper money minted in the land itself. A rescript of Germanicus (from the time when he held supreme command in the East A.D. 17–19) cited in the Palmyra tariff expressly prescribes the Italic monetary standard for the payment of tolls.[198] The Palestinian coinage conformed to this standard as early as the reign of Herod I. Furthermore, Roman designations of coins were already in the first century A.D. more common in Palestine than the Greek and Hebrew designations still also in use. This emerges from the following compilation of material from the Mishnah, the New Testament[199] and the Murabba'at caves.

197. See J. Meyshan, 'The Monetary Pattern of the Herodian Coinage', *Int. Num. Conv.* 1963 (see n. 186), pp. 220–6; cf., however, B. Oestreicher, 'The Denominations of Ancient Jewish Coins', INJ 1 (1963), pp. 7–12.

198. Tab. iva II. 42 ff.: *καὶ Γερμανικοῦ Καίσαρος διὰ τῆς πρὸς Στατείλι[ον ἐπισ]τολῆς διασαφήσαντος, ὅτι δεῖ πρὸς ἀσσάριον ἰτα[λικὸν] τὰ τέλη λογεύεσθαι.* See H. Dessau, Hermes 19 (1884), pp. 519 f.; for the text see Cooke, *Text-Book of North-Semitic Inscriptions* (1903), no. 147, p. 319; Greek text in Dittenberger, OGIS 629 and IGR III, 1056; CIS II 3913. Dittenberger wrongly reads *πρὸς ἀσσάριον πά[ντα] τὰ τέλη*. The reading and restoration *ἰτα[λικὸν]* is quite certain, since in the Aramaic parallel text איטלק is preserved. The Palmyra tariff nevertheless permits local small coins for amounts under one *denarius*.

199. A list of Greek and Latin names of coins occurring in rabbinic literature is given in Krauss II, pp. 635 f.; *Talm. Arch.* II, pp. 404–9. On the coins mentioned in the New Testament see F. Madden, *Coins of the Jews*, pp. 289–310; H. Hamburger, s.v. 'Money', IDB III, pp. 423–35, esp. p. 428. For the Murabba'at caves, see the various indices in DJD II. On the Roman monetary system see J. Marquardt, *Römische Staatsverwaltung* II (1876), pp. 3–75; F. Hultsch, *Griechische und römische Metrologie* ([2]1882); E. A. Sydenham, *The Coinage of the Roman Republic* (1952); R. Thomsen, *Early Roman Coinage* I–III (1957–1961); M. H. Crawford, *Roman Republican Coinage* I–II (1974), especially pp. 621–32; H. M. V. Sutherland, *Roman Coins* (1974). The clearest tabulations of the values of Roman gold, silver and bronze coinage under the Empire is given by V. Picozzi, *La monetazione imperiale romana* (1966), part I.

The following list gives the various coins mentioned in rabbinic literature:

Gold

1 *minah*	= 4 gold *denars* = 100 *denars*
1 gold *denar*	= 25 *denars*

Silver

1 *sela'*	= 1 *sheḳel* of the Sanctuary = 2 (common) *sheḳels* = 4 *denars*
1 *sheḳel*	= 2 *denars* or *zuz*
1 *zuz*	= 2 *tropaics* = 5 *aspers* = 6 *maahs* = 8 *tresith* = 12 *pondions*
1 *maah*	= 2 *pondions*

Copper

1 *tresith*	= 1½ *pondions* = 3 *issars*
1 *issar*	= ½ *pondion* = 8 *peruṭah*
1 *peruṭah*	= smallest unit

1 *zuz*	= 2 *tropaics* = 5 *aspers* = 6 *maahs* = 8 *tresith* = 12 *pondions* = 24 *issars* = 196 *peruṭah*

1. The only gold coin circulating in Palestine was the Roman *aureus* of twenty-five *denarii*, frequently referred to in the Mishnah as 'the gold *denarius*' (דינר זהב).[200]

2. The current silver coin was the *denarius* (δηνάριον), the most frequently mentioned of all coins in the New Testament (Mt. 18:28; 20:2 ff.; 22:19; Mk. 6:37; 12:15; 14:5; Lk. 7:41; 10:35; 20:24; Jn. 6-7; 12:5; Rev. 6:6). That this Roman designation was common is also evident from the Mishnah, where the term דינר is almost more frequent than the equivalent Semitic זוז.[201] As the value of the *denarius* was equal to that of an Attic *drachma*, reckoning was still made in *drachmas* as well, but this method was no longer usual.[202]

3. Of the copper coins, the 2-*as* piece, or *dupondius* (in Hebrew פונדיון) is often alluded to.[203] A *dupondius* is also meant by Jesus in Lk. 12:6, where the Vulgate correctly translates ἀσσαρίων δύο by *dipondio*.

200. דינר זהב: mM.Sh. 2:7, 4:9; mShek. 6:6; mNaz. 5:2; mB.K. 4:1; mSheb. 6:3; mMeil. 6:4. On the Roman *aureus*, see Marquardt II, pp. 25 f.; Hultsch, pp. 308 ff. That the דינר זהב equalled 25 *denarii* is evident e.g. from mKet. 10:4; mB.K. 4:1. On a Palmyrene inscription of A.D. 193 appears χρυσᾶ παλαιὰ δηνάρ‹ι›α (Waddington, *Inscr. de la Syrie*, no. 2596 = IGR III 1050).

201. דינר: e.g. mPea. 8:8; mDam. 2:5; mMaas.Sh. 2:9; mShek. 2:4; mBez. 3:7; mKet. 5:7; 6:3, 4, 10:2; mKid. 1:1; 2:2; mB.M. 4:5; mArakh, 6:2, 5, and elsewhere; Krauss II, pp. 207 f. δηνάρια occurs on inscriptions in Batanaea and Trachonitis (Waddington, nos. 2095, 2341, 2537a; more frequently, only the sign * is used in these inscriptions, as also in DJD II, no. 114 verso: * ν′ = 50 *denarii*). The Palmyra tariff also reckons throughout in *denarii*. זוז: mPea 8:8–9; mYom. 3:7; mKet. 1:5; 6:5; 9:8; mGit. 7:5; mKid. 3:2; mB.K. 4:1; 8:6; mB.B. 10:2. זוז as a basic monetary unit is common in the Hebrew and Aramaic deeds discovered in the Judaean Desert. DJD II, no. 18, 4; 20, 5; 22 I, 4; 30, 21 (88 zuz = 22 sela's); 32, 2–4. Cf. also the Khirbet el-Kôm Aramaic-Greek ostracon dating to ca. 277 B.C., line 3. In the Greek text, *drachma* is indicated by the symbol ⊦: L. T. Geraty, BASOR 220 (1975), p. 55. The following Semitic symbols for coins are conjecturally identified by J. T. Milik: כ = כרש = *sela'* or *tetradrachma*; ר = רבע = *denar/zuz*; ם = מעה = 1/6 of *denar:* DJD II, p. 90. For *denarion* in Greek Murabba'at texts, see DJD II, no. 114; 116, 12; 121, 3. Under Nero the weight of the *aureus* and *denarius* was reduced, see Sutherland, *Roman Coins*, p. 159. Hence the Mishnah (mKel. 17:12) mentions a סלע נרונית (1 *sela'* = 1 *tetradrachma* or 4 *denarii*). For the use of סלע at Murabba'at, see DJD II, no. 23, 5; 30:21; 31:5, 2 (?); 46, 8 (?).

202. δραχμή: Lk. 15:8f.; Josephus, *Vita* 44 (224). Both passages may nevertheless refer to *drachmae* in Tyrian currency; cf. n. 210 below; cf. also possibly the [δραχμ]ὰς χιλίας Σύρας on an inscription in the Hauran, Waddington, no. 1994. The reckoning is also by *drachmae* in inscriptions from Gerasa, see *Gerasa*, Ins. nos. 2, 3 [4], 5, 6, 17, [49], 52. Note also that in DJD II, nos. 115, ll. 5, 6, 12 and 118 verso, ll. 9, 12 the symbol ∠ is interpreted as δραχμή.

203. פונדיון: mPea. 8:7; mSheb. 8:4; mMaas.Sh. 4:8; mErub. 8:2; mB.M. 4:5; mB.B. 5:9; mSheb. 6:3; mKel. 17:12 (in the last passage explicitly as an Italic *pondion*, פונדיון איטלקי); Krauss II, p. 427. From mB.B. 5:9 it is clear that a *pondion* equalled two *asses*, as is also noted in the Talmud (yKid. 58d; bKid. 12a). The *pondion* was thus without doubt the Roman *dupondius*. Cf. on the *dupondius*, RE V, cols. 1843–6.

4. The most common copper coin was the *as*, in early Latin *assarius*, after which ἀσσάριον in Greek (Mt. 10:29; Lk. 12:6), אסר in Hebrew, and sometimes explicitly 'the Italic *as*', אסר איטלקי.[204] Originally, it amounted to one-tenth of a *denarius*, but subsequently to only one-sixteenth.[205]

5. The smallest copper coin was the פרוטה (*peruṭah*), equal only to an eighth of an *as*.[206] Unknown to the Roman monetary system, its name is Semitic. It is however identical with the λέπτον appearing in the New Testament (Mk. 12:42; Lk. 12:59; 21:2), which according to Mk. 12:42 amounted to half a *quadrans*, i.e. to an eighth of an *as*. Coins of this value in fact exist from the late Hasmonaean era, and also some from the Herodian-Roman period.[207] It is nevertheless remarkable that both the Mishnah and the New Testament reckon only by this smallest part of the *as*, and not by the Roman *semis* (½ *as*) and *quadrans* (¼ *as*), although the latter were also being minted at that time in Palestine, though in lesser quantities than the *peruṭah*.[208] It would seem that reckoning by the *peruṭah* originated in pre-Roman times but remained customary even after the introduction of the Roman currency.[209]

Coins minted in the Phoenician cities, particularly in Tyre, which still circulated in Palestine when minting on this standard no longer took place there, were not on the standard of the Roman currency.[210]

204. אסר איטלקי mKid. 1:1; mEdu. 4:7; mHul. 3:2; mMikw. 9:5. אסר איטלקן also occurs twice in the Aramaic text of the Palmyra tariff, tab. IIc, ll. 9 and 35 (CIS II 3913). Greek ἀσσάριον ἰταλικόν (see n. 198 above). On אסר in general, e.g. mPea. 8:1; mSheb. 8:4; mMaas. 2:5, 6; mMaas.Sh. 4:3, 8; mErub. 7:10; mB.M. 4:5; mB.B. 5:9; Krauss II, pp. 37 f.; *Talm. Arch.* II, p. 407.

205. See Crawford, *Roman Republican Coinage*, pp. 612–15.

206. פרוטה: mKid. 1:1; 2:1, 6; mB.K. 9:5, 6, 7; mB.M. 4:7, 8; mShebu, 6:1, 3; mEdu. 4:7. That it amounted to 1/8 *as* is stated in mKid. 1:1; mEdu. 4:7.

207. See Madden, *History of Jewish Coinage*, pp. 296–302; and n. 197 above.

208. The *semis* and the *quadrans* are not mentioned in the Mishnah; they appear first in the Jerusalem and Babylonian Talmuds. The *quadrans* (κοδράντης) is referred to twice in the N.T., but in one passage (Mk. 12:42) the words ὅ ἐστιν κοδράντης seem to be an elucidation added by the evangelist, and in the other (Mt. 5:26), the term κοδράντης was probably substituted by the evangelist for the λέπτον provided by Luke's source (12:59). The Gospel sources thus mention only the λέπτον, in the same way that the Mishnah mentions only the פרוטה. Cf. J. Meyshan, 'What is a Prutah?', *Sukenik Memorial Volume* (1967), pp. 325–6 (Hebrew). Cf. Krauss, *Talm. Arch.* II, p. 408. For currency in the late period note D. Sperber, *Roman Palestine 200–400*: *Money and Prices* (1974).

209. There is sporadic mention in the Mishnah of טרפעיק = τροπαϊκόν = ½ *denarius* or *quinarius* (mKet. 5:7) and טריסית = *tressis* = 3 *as* (*tripondius*) (mShebu, 6:3). These too belonged to the Roman monetary system. The meaning of אספר (mMaas.Sh. 2:9, mEdu. 1:10), which likewise occurs once, is uncertain. Cf. on all three Krauss II, pp. 278, 273 f., 293; *Talm. Arch.* II, p. 408.

210. The coins of the Phoenician currency are somewhat lighter than the Roman (which correspond to the Attic standard), see F. Hultsch, *Griechische und römische Metrologie*, pp. 594 ff., and nn. 192, 193. A νόμισμα Τύριον worth 4 *drachmae* is

What applies to money, the medium of commerce, applies also to the objects of commerce.[211] Here, too, Greek and Roman names and items are encountered at every turn.[212] At the same time, it should not be overlooked that Palestine, rich in natural produces, made her own large contribution to international trade: the products of her agriculture and

---

mentioned by Josephus, *B.J.* ii 21, 2 (592); cf. *Vita* 13 (75). For the phrase *ἀργυρίου τ[υ]ρί[ου]*, see DJD II, no. 114, 10 (cf. p. 242) and *Γσ' οἵ εἰσιν τυρίοι V* [200 *drachmae* = 50 Tyrian shekels, see *ibid.* no. 115, 5. The *δίδραχμον* (Mt. 17:24) and the *στατήρ* (= 4 *drachmae*, Mt. 17:27) are also coins of this currency, cf. DJD II, no. 114, 11; the Temple tribute was paid in the Tyrian currency, (כסף צורי) as in general were the taxes derived from the Bible, mBekh. 8:7; tKet. (12) 13:4; cf. צורין מאה (100 Tyrians) in the marriage contract of Babata, in Yadin IEJ (1962), p. 244. Thus the hoard of Tyrian *shekels* and half-shekels, with some *denarii* (4,500 silver coins in all), discovered in Mt. Carmel in 1960, is interpreted as being a consignment of dues for the Temple intercepted en route in A.D. 67, see L. Kadman, 'Temple Dues and Currency in Ancient Palestine in the Light of Recently Discovered Coin-Hoards', INB 1 (1962), pp. 9–11. See also vol. I, p. 11, and A. Ben-David, *Jerusalem und Tyros* (1969). For the Tyrian silver coins found at Qumran see n. 195 above. When Josephus in *B.J.* ii 21, 2 (592) values the *νόμισμα Τύριον* at 4 Attic *drachmae* (as he does the Hebrew *shekel* in *Ant.* iii 8, 2 (194), this is probably no more than an approximate evaluation in contrast to the Egyptian *drachmae* of that time (from the time of Tiberius *tetradrachmae* were minted in Egypt out of billon, an alloy of copper and silver with the former preponderating), which were equated in value to the *denarius*, so that a billon *drachma* possessed perhaps only a quarter of the value of a silver-*drachma*, see F. Hultsch, RE V, col. 1630; strictly speaking the Tyrian *tetradrachma* was somewhat lighter than the Attic (Hultsch, pp. 595 f.).

211. With the various products listed below, compare now the uniquely preserved collection of objects, dating from the early A.D. 130s, found in the 'Cave of Letters'. See Y. Yadin, *The Finds from the Bar Kokhba Period in the Cave of Letters* (1963). The finds listed are metal utensils, glassware, pottery, jewellery, seal-impressions, wooden and bone objects, basketry, leather objects, and textiles.

212. On the commercial commodities of antiquity see especially J. Marquardt, *Das Privatleben der Römer* II (1882). K. F. Hermann and H. Blümner, *Lehrbuch der griechischen Privataltertümer* (1882); *idem*, *Die gewerbliche Tätigkeit der Völker des klassischen Altertums* (1869). See also M. Rostevtzeff, *Social and Economic History of the Roman Empire*, ed. P. M. Frazer (1957); T. Frank, *Economic Survey of Ancient Rome* I–V (1933–40); M. Rostovtzeff, *Social and Economic History of the Hellenistic World* I–III (1941); F. Heichelheim, *An Ancient Economic History* I–III (1958–70). For the rabbinic evidence, see S. Krauss, *Talm. Arch.* II, pp. 249–315. On production techniques, see H. Blümner, *Technologie und Terminologie der Gewerbe und Künste bei Griechen und Römern* I–IV (1875–87); P. Rieger, *Versuch einer Technologie und Terminologie der Handwerke in der Mischnah I. Teil: Spinnen, Färben, Weben, Walken* (1894). See R. J. Forbes, *Studies in Ancient Technology* I–IX (1956–71); C. Singer, E. J. Holmyard, A. R. Hall, T. I. Williams (eds.), *A History of Technology II: The Mediterranean Civilisations and the Middle Ages, c. 700 B.C. to c. A.D. 1500* (1956); D. E. Strong, D. Brown, *Roman Crafts* (1976). *Edictum Diocletiani de pretiis rerum* is in particular a rich source of information concerning commodities. See *Der Maximaltariff des Diocletian*, ed. Mommsen with notes by Blümner (1893). Cf. Blümner, s.v. 'Edictum Diocletiani'

industry were exported into every land and gained some general fame.[213] But whether commodities were produced in the country or imported from outside, they all bore the stamp of the dominant Hellenistic civilization; the native commodities resulted from its requirements, and the goods imported from abroad were precisely those which were in fashion everywhere else.[214] Examples from the spheres of food and drink, clothing and furniture may illustrate this.

Among foreign comestibles in Palestine, we know for example of Babylonian כותח (a mixture of soured milk, bread crumbs and salt), Median beer (שכר), Edomite vinegar (חומץ) and Egyptian *zythos* (זיתום).[215]

RE V, cols, 1948–57; cf. T. Frank, *Economic Survey* V, pp. 310–421; S. Lauffer, *Diokletians Preisedikt* (1971); M. Giacchero, *Edictum Diocletiani et collegarum de pretiis rerum venalium* (1974).

213. On the commercial commodities of Palestine, see J. Movers, *Die Phönizier* II. 3 (1856), pp. 200–35; L. Herzfeld, *Handelsgeschichte der Juden*, pp. 88–117; H. Blümner, *Die gewerbliche Tätigkeit* etc., pp. 24–7; H. Vogelstein, *Die Landwirtschaft in Palästina zur Zeit der Mischnah I. Teil: Der Getreidebau* (1894); F. Goldmann, *Der Ölbau in Palästina zur Zeit der Misnah* (1907). Cf. F. M. Heichelheim, 'Roman Syria' in T. Frank, *Economic Survey* IV, pp. 121–257; M. Avi-Yonah, *The Holy land from the Persian to the Arab Conquest (536 B.C. to A.D. 640): A Historical Geography* (1960), Pt. III, ch. 2, 'Economic Geography'. See Krauss, *Talm. Arch.* II, pp. 148–247; M. Avi-Yonah, *Trade, Industry and Crafts in Palestine in Antiquity* (1937); J. Felicks, *The Agriculture of Eretz Israel in the Period of the Mishnah and the Talmud* (1963). A summary of the chief commodities in the fourth century A.D. is given in the *Expositio totius mundi* ed. Rougé (see n. 92 above), ch. 29: 'Ascalon et Gaza, civitates eminentes et in negotio bullientes et habundantes omnibus, mittunt omni [negotio] Syriae et Aegypto vinum optimum . . . 31: In linteamina sunt hae: Scythopolis, Laodicia, Byblus, Tyrus, Berytus, quae linteamen omni orbi terrarum emittunt et sunt eminentes in omni habundantia; similiter autem et Sarepta et Caesarea et Neapolis quomodo et Lydda purpurem alithinam. Omnes autem praedictae civitates gloriosae et fructiferae in frumento, vino et oleo; †hi et omnibus bonis abundant.† Nicolaum itaque palmulam in Palaestinae regione, loco, qui sic vocatur Jericho, similiter et Damascenam, et alteram palmulam minorem et psittacium et omne genus pomorum habent'. The linen industry in Scythopolis was especially famous. In the *Edictum Diocl.* 26–8, among the various kinds of linen wares those of Scythopolis are listed first as the most costly. See also yKid. 62c: כלי פשתן הדקים הבאין מבית שאן; Movers II, 3, pp. 217 f.; Herzfeld, p. 107; Marquardt, *Das Privatleben der Römer* II, p. 466; Blümner, *Die Gewerbliche Tätigkeit*, p. 25; Krauss, *Talm. Arch.* I, pp. 136–42. The Mishnah also assumes that Galilee's principal industry was the production of linen, whereas that of Judaea was predominantly the production of wool (mB.K. 10:9). Hence the wool-market in Jerusalem, mErub. 10:9; Josephus, *B.J.* v. 8, 1 (331).

214. On imported articles see also Herzfeld, *Handelsgeschichte*, pp. 117–29.

215. In mPes. 3:1 all four are mentioned as examples of food made from cereals which have undergone fermentation. On the Egyptian ζῦθος or ζῦτος (a kind of beer), in Hebr. זיתוס, not זיתום, see J. Levy, *Neuhebräisches Wörterbuch* s.v.; cf. Theophrastus, *de caus. plant.* vi 11, 2; Diodorus i 34, 10; Pliny *NH* xxii 82/164; Strabo xvii 2, 5 (824); *Digest* xxxiii 6, 9; *Edict. Diocletiani* 2, 1. 12; Jerome, *Comm. in Ies.* 7:19; (PL XXIV, col. 253; CCL lxxiii, p. 280); Krauss II, p. 247;

Among Egyptian products besides *zythos* were fish,[216] mustard, pumpkins, beans and lentils.[217] Cilician groats[218] were also eaten in Palestine, and Bithynian cheese, [219] Greek pumpkins,[220] Greek and Roman hyssop[221] and Spanish colias.[222] From abroad came also, as their foreign names indicate, asparagus, lupines (a variety of coarse beans) and Persian nuts.[223] The salting of fish was practised in Palestine,

---

Talm. Arch. II, p. 224; Marquardt, *Privatleben der Römer* II, p. 444; Hermann and Blümner, *Griech. Privataltert.*, p. 235; V. Hehn, *Kulturpflanzen und Haustier* ([3]1877), pp. 126 f.; RE s.v. 'Bier'; EB s.v. 'Wine and Strong Drink'; U. Wilcken, *Griechische Ostraka aus Ägypten und Nubien* I (1890), pp. 369–73. For papyrological references see F. Preisigke, *Wörterbuch* I (1925), and *Supp.* I (1971) s.vv. *ζυτηρά, ζυτοποιία, ζυτοπωλεῖον, ζῦτος*. See C. Préaux, *L'économie royale des Lagides* (1939), pp. 152–8; R. J. Forbes, *Studies in Ancient Technology* III (1955), pp. 125–30. Cf. also Isa. 19:10 LXX.

216. mMakhsh. 6:3. The reference is to pickled fish *(ταρίχη)*, which was produced in quantity in various places in Egypt and was exported in considerable quantities; Blümner, *Die gewerbliche Tätigkeit etc.*, pp. 14 and 17; J. Newman, *Agricultural Life of the Jews in Babylonia* (1932), pp. 136–40; M. Schwabe, *S. Krauss Jubilee Volume* (1936), pp. 80–6. Numerous places on the Egyptian coast had the name *Ταριχέαι* from this industry (Stephanus Byz. s.v.). See generally on its wide distribution Marquardt, *Privatleben der Römer* II, pp. 420 ff.; J. André, *L'alimentation et la cuisine de Rome* (1961), pp. 111–6; cf. M. Ponsich, M. Tarradell, *Garum et industries antiques de salaison dans la Mediterranée occidentale* (1965).

217. Mustard (חרדל) mKil. 1:2. Pumpkin (דלעת) mKil. 1, 2, 5. Beans (פול) mKil. 1:2; 2:11; 3:4; mSheb. 2:8, 9; 9:7; mShab. 9:7; mNed. 7:1, 2. Cf. Pliny, *NH* xviii 30/120–2. Lentils (עדשים) mMaas. 5:8; mKel. 17:8; Jerome, *Com. in Ezech.* 9: 30, 15 (PL XXV col. 289; CCL 75, p. 422): 'unde et poeta Pelusiacam appellat lentem, non quo ibi genus hoc leguminis gignatur, vel maxime, sed quo e Thebaida et omni Aegypto per rivum Nili illuc plurimum deferatur'. The 'poeta' to whom Jerome refers is Vergil, *Georg.* i, l. 228. Cf. also Pliny, *NH* xvi 76/201; Marquardt II, p. 410. The cultivation of lentils in Egypt is very ancient, see V. Hehn, *Kulturpflanzen und Haustiere*[3], p. 188; I. Löw, *Flora der Juden* II, pp. 442–52. Cf. V. F. Hartmann, *L'agriculture dans l'ancienne Egypte* (1923); J. André, *L'alimentation*, ch. 1.

218. גריס קיליקי: mMaas. 5:8; mKel. 17:12; mNeg. 6:1.

219. גבינה ותנייקי: mA.Z. 2:4 (to be read thus instead of the corrupt גבינה בית אונייקי). For the various spellings, see Jastrow, *Dict.* s.vv. In Tg. Neof. Gen. 10:2 the main text reads וביטינא, whilst the marginal variant is ויטינייא. Bithynian cheese is also mentioned in Pliny, *NH* xi 97/241: 'trans maria vero Bithynus fere in gloria est'.

220. דלעת יונית: mKil. 1:5, 2:11; mOrl. 3:7; mOhol. 8:1.

221. אזוב יון and אזוב רומי mNeg. 14:6; mPar. 11:7. The first also in mShab. 14:3.

222. קולייס האספנן: mShab. 22:2; mMakhsh. 6:3; Krauss II, p. 506. *Colias* is a species of tunny (cf. Pliny, *NH* xxxii 53/146; Marquardt II, p. 422, and the lexica). It was of course put on the market salted, as was the famed Spanish *τάριχος*. Cf. Marquardt II, p. 421; Blümner, pp. 130, 135 and n. 216 above.

223. Asparagus (אספרגוס, *ἀσπάραγος*). In the only passage in which it occurs in the Mishnah, mNed. 6:10, the term does not denote real asparagus, but shoots resembling asparagus of various plants. See Löw, *REJ* 16 (18), p. 156. Lupines (תורמוס, *θέρμος=lupinus termis*) mShab. 18:1; mMakhsh. 4:6; mT.Y. 1:4. Persian

as is suggested by the name *Ταριχεαί*, a town on the Lake of Gennesaret, and by the frequent mention of brine (*muries*) in the Mishnah.[224] Here too, the foreign names would suggest that the custom was imported from abroad.

Clothing materials mentioned, and garments of foreign origin,[225] include Pelusian and Indian linen and cotton fabrics,[226] Cilician felt cloth,[227] the *sagum* (סגום), the *dalmatica* (דלמטיקיון), the *paragaudion* (פרגוד), the *stola* (אצטלית),[228] the sweat-rag (סודרין, *σουδάριον*),[229]

---

nuts (אספרסקי, *Περσική*) mKil. 1:4; Maas. 1:2. In both passages, as the context shows, the reference is not to peaches but Persian nuts, on which cf. Marquardt II, p. 411. For more on the Greek names of plants in rabbinic literature see Krauss II, pp. 626 f.

224. On *Ταριχέαι* see especially Strabo xvi 2, 45 (764). It is first mentioned in connexion with Cassius, Josephus, *Ant.* xiv 7, 3 (120); *B.J.* i 8, 9 (180); Cicero, *ad Fam.* xii, 11). מורייס: mTer. 11:1; mYom. 8:3; mNed. 6:4; mAZ. 2:4; mKel. 10:5; Krauss II, p. 329. See Avi-Yonah, *Gazetteer of Roman Palestine* (1976), p. 99.

225. Cf. also the list of Greek and Latin names in Krauss II, pp. 641–3; *Talm. Arch.* I, pp. 127–207; see also A. Rosenzweig, *Kleidung und Schmuck im biblischen und talmudischen Schrifttum* (1905).

226. According to mYom. 3:7, the garments worn by the High Priest on the Day of Atonement were made of both materials. In the morning he wore פילוסין, in the afternoon הנדווין (it is impossible to know from these names whether they were made of linen or cotton). Cf. Krauss, *Talm. Arch.* I, p. 131. The fine Pelusian linen cloth was famous, see Pliny, *NH* xix 1/14: 'Aegyptio lino minimum firmitatis, plurimum lucri. Quattuor ibi genera: Taniticum ac Pelusiacum, Buticum, Tentyriticum'; Movers II, pp. 3, 318; H. Blümner, *Die gewerbliche Tätigkeit*, pp. 6 ff., especially p. 16. Cf. A. H. M. Jones, 'The Cloth Industry under the Roman Empire', *The Roman Economy* (1974), ch. 18; E. Wipszycka, *L'industrie textile dans l'Egypte romaine* (1965). Indian materials (*ὀθόνιον Ἰνδικόν, ὀθόνη Ἰνδική, σινδόνος Ἰνδικαί*) are also often mentioned as articles of commerce in the *Periplus maris Erythraei* (6, 31, 41, 48, 63). These references seem to be cotton cloths, see Marquardt II, pp. 472 f. Cf. E. H. Warmington, *The Commerce between the Roman Empire and India* ([2]1974), pp. 210–12.

227. קילקי: mKel. 29:1. Cilicium was a felt prepared from goats' hair which was used for varied purposes (coarse overcoats, curtains, covers, etc.). See Marquardt II, p. 463; H. Blümner, p. 30; RE s.v. Thus if Paul of Tarsus was a *σκηνοποιός* (Act. 18:13) in Cilicia, this was closely connected with the chief industry of his native place. In the Mishnah קילקי means simply a 'compact mass', e.g. of matted hair on the beard, chest, etc. (mMikw. 9:2).

228. סגום: mKel. 29:1; mOhol. 11:3, 15:1; mNeg. 11:11; mMikw. 7:6; Krauss II, p. 371. דלמטיקיון: mKil. 9:7. פרגוד: mShek. 3:2; mKel. 29:1; Krauss II, p. 477. אצטלית: mYom. 7:1; mGit. 7:5. On these articles of dress see Marquardt II, pp. 548 f., 563 f., 556 f.; cf. L. M. Wilson, *The Clothing of the Ancient Romans* (1938), pp. 104–9; 152–61; 117–18. The *sagum* was a cloak that left the arms free and was therefore worn particularly by soldiers and manual workers. The other three were different kinds of undergarments. The *dalmatica* is mentioned also by Epiphanius in *Panar.* 15, where he speaks of the clothing of the scribes.

229. סודרין: mShab. 3:3; mYom. 6:8; mSanh. 6:1; mTam. 7:3; mKel. 29:1; Krauss II, pp. 373 f.; *Talm. Arch.* I, p. 166, II, p. 243. In the New Testament, see Lk. 19:20; Jn. 11:44; 20:7; Act. 19:12.

the felt hat (פליון, πιλίον), felt socks (אמפליא, ἐμπίλια), sandals, (סנדל), including a special kind known as 'Laodicean' (סנדל לדיקי).[230] In addition, a number of technical expressions relating to industry also point to the influence of Greek prototypes. A spun thread is a נימא (νῆμα), a particular device on the loom, קירוס (καῖρος),[231] a tanner, a בורסי (βυρσεύς).[232] In regard to raw materials, hemp for example (קנבוס, κάνναβος, κάνναβις) first came to Palestine through the Greeks.[233]

Household utensils of foreign origin, particularly Greek and Roman objects, were extremely numerous.[234] Among those deriving from Egypt were the Egyptian basket, the Egyptian ladder and an Egyptian rope.[235] A Tyrian ladder[236] is also referred to, and Sidonian dishes or basins.[237] Among Greek and Roman furniture were the bench (ספסל, *subsellium*), the armchair (קתדרא, καθέδρα), the curtain (וילון, *velum*), the looking-glass (אספקלריא, *specularia*) and the Corinthian candle-

230. פליון: mKel. 29:1; mNid. 8:1; Krauss II, p. 448. אמפליא: mYeb. 12:1; mKel. 27:6; Krauss II, p. 62. (Cf. Marquardt II, p. 486; Waddington, p. 164.) סנדל: e.g. mShab. 6:2, 5, 10:3, 15:2; mShek. 3:2; mBez. 1:10; mMeg. 4:8; mYeb. 12:1; mArakh. 6:5; Krauss II, pp. 399 f. A sandalmaker is called סנדלר: mYeb. 12:5; mKet. 5:4; mAb. 4:11; mKel. 5:5. See on sandals generally Marquardt II, pp. 577 f.; Hermann and Blümner, *Griechische Privataltertümer*, pp. 181, 196; Krauss, *Talm. Arch.* I, pp. 175–85. Note also the sandals discovered in the Cave of Letters, and elsewhere in the Judaean Desert, Y. Yadin, *The Finds from the Bar Kokhba Period in the Cave of Letters* (1963), pp. 165–8.

231. נימא: mErub. 10:13; mShek. 8:5; mKel. 19:1; 29:1; mNeg. 11:10; Krauss II, p. 359. קירוס: mShab. 13:2; mKel. 21:1; Krauss II, p. 520. Cf. on καῖρος, H. Blümner, *Technologie und Terminologie der Gewerbe und Künste* I, pp. 126 ff. Generally: P. Rieger, *Versuch einer Technologie und Terminologie der Handwerke in der Mischnah. I. Spinnen, Färben, Weben, Walken* (1894).

232. בורסי: mKet. 7:10; Krauss II, p. 146. בורסקי (tannery): mShab. 1:2; mMeg. 3:2; mB.B. 2:9; Krauss II, p. 147; *id.*, Byz. Zeitschr. 2 (1893), pp. 516–18.

233. קנבוס: mKil. 5:8, 9:1, 7; mNeg. 11:2: Krauss II, pp. 551 f. On the geographical diffusion of hemp-growing see V. Hehn, *Kulturpflanzen u. Haustiere*³, pp. 168 f.; R. J. Forbes, *Studies in Ancient Technology* IV (1956), pp. 58–60; H. Godwin, 'The Ancient Cultivation of Hemp', Antiquity 41 (1967), pp. 42–8, 137–8.

234. Krauss II, pp. 637 f., 639 f.

235. Basket (כפיפה): mShab. 20:2; mSot. 2:1, 3:1; mKel. 26:1. Also in mT.Y. 4:2 כפיפה should be read instead of כפישה. Ladder (סלם): mB.B. 3:6; mZab .3:1, 3; 4:3. Rope (חבל): mSot. 1:6.

236. mB.B. 3:6; mZab. 3:3.

237. mKel. 4:3 קוסים; cf. the biblical קסת. The reference is probably to glass vessels, the best-known product of Sidon in the Roman period, Pliny, *NH* v 19/76: 'Sidon artifex vitri'. See Herman and Blümner, *Griechische Privataltertümer*, pp. 437 f.; Marquardt, *Privatleben* II, p. 726. Krauss, *Talm. Arch.* II, pp. 285–7. See D. B. Harden, 'Ancient Glass', Antiquity 7 (1933), pp. 419–28; F. Neuburg, *Ancient Glass* (1962); J. Price, 'Glass', in D. E. Strong and D. Brown, *Roman Crafts* (1976), ch. 9. Note especially the finds of glass from the Cave of Letters, Yadin, *Finds from the Bar Kokhba Period in the Cave of Letters* (1963), ch. 5.

stick.[238] Requirements for eating and drinking included the salver (טבולא, *tabula*), the plate (אסקוטלא, *scutella*), the bowl (פילי, φιάλη) and the table-napkin (מפה, *mappa*).[239] The commonest designation for containers of every kind is תיק, θήκη.[240] Particular kinds of hollow receptacles were the basket (קופה, *cupa*), the wine-cask (פיטס, πίθος),[241] the box (גלוסקמא, γλωσσόκομον), the chest (קמטרא, κάμπτρα), the small box (קפסא, *capsa*) and the bag (מרצוף, μαρσύπιον).[242]

These examples by no means exhaust the stock of Greek and Latin words appearing in the Mishnah.[243] They nevertheless suffice to convey a vivid impression of the extent to which western manners and customs were adopted, even in Palestine, in the second century A.D. But Greek influence extended still further. Greek words are encountered in the

238. ספסל: mShab. 23:5; mB.B. 4:6; mSanh. 2:1; mKel. 2:3, 22:3; mMikw. 5:2; mZab. 3:3; 4:4; Krauss II, pp. 408 f., *Talm. Arch.* I, pp. 60–1. Cf. Marquardt II, p. 704. קתדרא: mKet. 5:5; mKel. 4:3, 22:3, 24:2; Krauss II, p. 572; *Talm. Arch.* I, pp. 60–1; Marquardt II, p. 705. וילון mKel. 20:6, 24:13; Krauss II, pp. 235 f.; *Talm. Arch.* I, p. 39. אספקלריא: mKel. 30:2; Krauss II, p. 93; *Talm. Arch.* I, pp. 43, 68, 399. Corinthian candlesticks in the possession of King Agrippa, Josephus, *Vita* 13 (68). They were made of Corinthian bronze, like the Nicanor gate in the forecourt of the Temple in Jerusalem (cf. n. 170 above). The valuable Corinthian utensils were so much the mode that in the imperial court at Rome a slave specially entrusted with their care was known as *a Corinthiis* or *Corinthiarius*. See RE s.v. 'a Corinthiis' and 'Corinthium aes'. On the 'Iudaica vela' with its pictures of monstrous animals, made in the time of the poet Claudian *c.* A.D. 400, probably in Alexandria, see Th. Birt, RhM 45 (1890), pp. 491–3. For furniture in general, G. M. A. Richter, *Ancient Furniture: A History of Greek, Etruscan and Roman Furniture* (1926).

239. טבלא: mShab. 21:3; mBez. 1:8; mM.K. 3:7; mEdu. 3:9 (טבלא also means a marble slab in the floor: mSot. 2:2; mMid. 1:9, 3:3, or a plate with illustrations mR.Sh. 2:8); Krauss II, p. 254. אסקוטלא: mM.K. 3:7; mKel. 30:1. פילי: mSot. 2:2; Krauss II, pp. 443 f.; Marquardt II, p. 632. מפה: mBer. 8:3; Marquardt II, p. 469.

240. תיק: mShab. 16:1; mKel. 16:7–8; Krauss II, p. 588; *Talm. Arch.* I, pp. 60, 197, II, pp. 264–5; III, pp. 155, 158, 195.

241. קופה (a round hollow vessel, cask, basket): mPea 8:7; mDem. 2:5; mShab. 8:2; 10:2, 18:1; mShek. 3:2; mBez. 4:1; mKet. 6:4; mKel. 16:3; 17:1; 28:6; mOhol. 6:2; mTohor. 9:1, 4; mMik. 6:5; 10:5; mMakhsh. 4:6; 6:3; Krauss II, p. 516; *Talm. Arch.* II, pp. 109, 134, 217, 271, 304, 352, 386, 416. פיטס (more correctly פיתס): mB.M. 4:12; mB.B. 6:2; mKel. 3:6; Krauss II, pp. 440 f.; *Talm. Arch.* I, pp. 89–90; II, pp. 236, 293; 445, 626 f.; Hermann and Blümner, *Privataltertümer*, p. 162.

242. גלוסקמא: mGit. 3:3; mB.B. 1:8; mMeil. 6:1; mOhol. 9:15. According to the last passage a coffin could have the shape of a γλοσσόκομον or a κάμπτρα. The LXX (2 Chron. 24:8, 10, 11) writes γλοσσόκομον for ארון. Cf. Krauss, *Talm. Arch.* II, pp. 76–9. In the New Testament (Jn. 12:6, 13:29), γλοσσόκομον is a money-box. See generally the material in Krauss II, pp. 175 f., 213, and the lexica. קמטרא: mKel. 16:7; mOhol. 9:15. Cf. Krauss, *Talm. Arch.* I, pp. 67, 398, 524; קפסא: mKel. 16:7; Krauss II, p. 517 f.; Marquardt II, 705 f. מרצוף: mShab. 8:5; mKel. 20:1; Krauss II, p. 353; *Talm. Arch.* II, p. 125.

243. Many others are attested in targumic Aramaic but because of the well-known problem of dating it is simpler to rely on the Mishnah.

Mishnah even where there is no question of western products and concepts. Air is termed אויר (ἀήρ),[244] a shape, טיפס (τύπος), a sample or pattern, דוגמא (δεῖγμα).[245] An ignorant, or inexpert person, an ordinary individual as opposed to a priest or a nobleman, is known as הדיוט (ἰδιώτης), a dwarf, as ננס (νάννος), a robber, as ליסטים (λῃστής), assassins, as סיקרים (*sicarii*).[246] For the notion 'weak' or 'ill', the Greek expression אסטניס (ἀσθενής) is used, for 'sloping downward' קטפרס (καταφερής).[247] Among the numerous Greek borrowings in targumic Aramaic such words occur as בסיס (βάσις), גלף (γλύφω), כרז (κηρύττω), נימוס (νόμος), טקס (τάξις), etc.[248]

The use of Greek and Latin personal names was also fairly frequent, even among the common people and the Pharisees and rabbis. Not only were Hellenophile aristocratic High Priests called Jason and Menelaus (during the Maccabaean period), and Boethus and Theophilus (during the Herodian era), and not only did Hasmonaean and Herodian princes carry the names of Alexander, Aristobulus, Antigonus, Herod, Archelaus, Philip, Antipas and Agrippa; ordinary people too, for instance two of the apostles of Jesus, were known as Andrew and Philip. In the circles of the rabbinic masters we find Antigonus of Sokho, R. Dosthai (=Dositheus), R. Hanina ben Dosa, R. Dosa ben Archinos (not Harkinas), R. Hananiah ben Antigonus, R. Tarphon (=Tryphon), R. Papias, R. Simon ben Menasia (=Mnaseas) and Symmachus. Latin names also soon began to be adopted. The John

244. אויר: mShab. 11:3; mHag. 1:8; mKet. 13:7; mGit. 8:3; mKin. 2:1; mKel. 1:1; 2:1, 8; 3:4 and elsewhere; mOhol. 3:3, 4:1; mZab. 5:9; Krauss II, pp. 17 f.

245. טופס e.g. the form of the loaf (mDem. 5:3–4) or the form in which the loaf was baked (mMen. 9:1) or the container for the tefillin (mKel. 16:7) or the form for a bill of divorce (mGit. 3:2; 9:5). See also Krauss II, pp. 215, 258. דוגמא (mShab. 10:1): a sample of seeds. See also Krauss II, p. 187.

246. הדיוט very often, in very different connections; e.g. of a layman as opposed to a professional craftsman (mM.K. 1:8, 10), or of a private individual as opposed to a prince or official (mNed. 5:5; mSanh. 10:2; mGit. 1:5); also, of an ordinary priest as distinguished from the High Priest (mYeb. 2:4; 6:2, 3, 5; 7:1; 9:1–3). Cf. also Krauss II, pp. 220 f. ננס: mBekh. 7:6, and in the proper name שמעון בן ננס, mBik. 3:9; mShab. 16:5 and elsewhere; also of animals (mPar. 2:2) and objects (mTam. 3:5; mMid. 3:5). Cf. also Krauss II, pp. 364 f. לסטס, usually in the plur. ליסטים: mBer. 1:3; mPea 2:7–8; mShab. 2:5; mPes. 3:7; mNaz. 6:3; mB.K. 6:1; 10:2; Krauss II, pp. 315 f., M. Hengel, *Die Zeloten* (1961, ²1976), pp. 35–42. סיקרים: mMakhsh. 1:6. Common in the incorrect form סיקריקון as a sing.: mBik. 1:2; 2:3; mGit. 5:6; Krauss II, pp. 392 f. Cf. also vol. I, p. 483; Hengel, *Zeloten*, pp. 51–4.

247. איסטניס: mBer. 2:6; mYom. 3:5. קטפרס: mOhol. 3:3; mTohor. 8: 8–9. Further details in Krauss II, pp. 651 f.

248. Cf. the examples collected by E. Brederek in *Theol. Stud. u. Krit.* (1901), pp. 376 f.; cf. especially G. Dalman, *Neuhebr. u. Aram. Wörterb.* and S. Lieberman, *Greek in Jewish Palestine* (1942). M. Zuckermandel, *Tosephta* (1880) contains a *Glossar* (pp. xxxxix–lxliv) indicating Greek loan-words.

Mark mentioned in the New Testament was, according to Act. 12:12, a Palestinian; so too was Joseph Barsabas surnamed Justus (Act. 1:23). Josephus mentions, in addition to the well-known Justus of Tiberias, a Niger from Peraea.[249]

Notwithstanding all this, it should not be supposed that the Greek language was itself current among the common people of Palestine. The number of individual Greek words that found their way into Hebrew and Aramaic was great, but this is no proof of the people's knowledge of Greek. Indeed, it is probable that the lower levels of Palestinian society had either no more than a limited acquaintance with it or none at all.[250] When the apostle Paul wished to be heard by the people in Jerusalem, he spoke Aramaic, or possibly Hebrew (*τῇ Ἑβραΐδι διαλέκτῳ*, Act. 21:40; 22:2). Again, when Titus, during the siege of Jerusalem, repeatedly called on the besieged to surrender, this was always done in Aramaic, whether Josephus was entrusted with the speech or whether Titus

249. Cf. in general L. Zunz, *Namen der Juden*, *Gesammelte Schriften* II, pp. 1–82; Hamburger, *Real-Enzyklop. für Bibel und Talmud* II, s.v. 'Namen'. For a full list of the Greek and Latin names in rabbinic literature see Krauss II, pp. 647–50. For Greek and Latin names borne by Jews in Palestine see e.g. Frey, CIJ II, nos. 903, 922, 926–7, 929, 934 etc.; cf. also M. Schwabe, B. Lifshitz, *Beth Shearim* II: *the Greek Inscriptions* (1967), pp. viii–ix.

Papyri from the Bar Kokhba period indicate that Greek/Latin names were quite common. They are listed in alphabetical order.

אוטרפלוס (Eutrapelos): קלבס בר א׳, appearing also in Greek as *Κ[λέο]πος Εὐτραπέλ[ο]υ* (DJD II, no. 29 recto, 10; 11; verso 1–2).
[או]פרניס ? (Euphronios): א׳ בן אלעזר (no. 46, 2–3).
ארצטון (Ariston): יהוסף בן א׳ (no. 42, 3).
גבניס (Gabinius): יוסף בר ג׳ (no. 28 II, 2).
דוסתס (Dosthes/Dositheus): ד׳ בר אלעזר (no. 30, 1 ff.); . . . ד׳ בן (no. 39, 2).
דיונטס (Dionytas?): (no. 30, l. 36).
הרדיס (Herodes): (no. 77).
נקלס ? (Nicolaus): נ׳ בן יהונת[ן] (no. 24 D, 20).
נקסן (Nikeus/Nikias): יהוסף בר נ׳ (no. 19 I, 3).
קלבוס (Kleopos): cf. אוטרפלוס.
קלופו (Kleopas): . . . (no. 33, 5).
[תד]טיון (Theodotion): (no. 10 I, 4).
Ἀλεξαῖος (IEJ 11 (1961), p. 55).
Ἀλεξᾶς (DJD II, no. 103, 4).
Αὐρήλιος (no. 116, 7).
Γάϊος (IEJ 11 (1961), p. 55).
Γόργος (DJD II, no. 90 a, 4).
Εὐτράπελος (no. 29 verso, 1).
Κ[λέο]πος (*ibid.*).
Μάϊορ (no. 91 I, 6).
Νεικάνωρ (no. 120 b, 4).
Πανδείον (no. 91 II, 4).
Σατορν[εῖνος] (no. 114, 8).
Σέανος Σεα[νου] (IEJ 11 (1961), p. 55).

250. For the use of Aramaic and Hebrew in Palestine see pp. 20–28 above.

addressed them in his own name through an interpreter.[251] Any knowledge of Greek that the people might have possessed was therefore incomplete.[252] On the other hand, it is probable that a rough familiarity with it was fairly widespread and that the more highly educated used it without difficulty.[253] The Hellenized regions not only bordered Palestine on almost all sides but also existed within it (Samaria, Scythopolis). Continuous contact with them was unavoidable. It is inconceivable that in the long run some knowledge of Greek should not have spread into Palestine as well. Furthermore, both before and after the Hasmonaean period the land was governed by men whose education was Greek, first by the Ptolemies and the Seleucids, and then by the Romans and the Herodians; indeed Greek culture was even promoted by some of the Hasmonaeans. But the foreign rulers brought at the same time certain elements of Greek culture into the country. We know in particular that Herod surrounded himself with Greek *literati* (vol. I, pp. 310–11). Foreign troops were stationed in the

251. *τῇ πατρίῳ γλώσσῃ*: *B.J.* v 9, 2 (361); *ἑβραΐζων*: vi 2, 1 (96). Interpreter: *B.J.* vi 6, 2 (327). If it sometimes seems that Titus speaks directly to the people, *B.J.* v 9, 2 (360); vi 2, 4 (124), it is clear from the latter passage that this is not so: Josephus has to interpret his address, *B.J.* vi 2, 5 (129).

252. Indirect evidence of a lack of general bilingualism appears in mid-fourth century reports (by which time the use of Greek in Palestine had spread): (1) R. Yohanan, who taught in Sepphoris and Tiberias in the third century A.D., (W. Bacher, *Die Agada der palästinensischen Amoräer* I (1892), p. 220) is said to have permitted girls to study Greek. The inference is that it was not the language of the people. (2) In the Christian community at Scythopolis in the reign of Diocletian a person was entrusted, like the *targeman* or *meturgeman* of the synagogue, with the task of translating, during public worship, 'Greek into Aramaic', obviously for the benefit of those who were ignorant of Greek (Euseb., *De mart. Pal.* 'long recension' Syriac text ed. and trans. Violet, TU 14, 4 (1896), p. 4). It should be borne in mind that Scythopolis was a Hellenistic city, yet the Gentile Christian peasants of its neighbourhood continued to speak Aramaic/Syriac. (3) For the Christian community in Jerusalem in the late fourth century the same is attested in an account of a pilgrimage, CSEL vol. XXXVIII; *Ethérie, Journal de voyage* (Sources Chrétiennes, no. 21), ed. Pétré (1957); O. Prinz, *Itinerariam Egeriae* (*Peregrinatio Aetheriae*) ([5]1960), of towards the end of the fourth century. See ch. 47, 3, 'Et quoniam in ea provincia pars populi et grece et siriste novit, pars etiam alia per se grece, aliqua etiam pars tantum siriste: itaque quoniam episcopus, licet siriste noverit, tamen semper graece loquitur et nunquam siriste, itaque ergo stat semper presbyter, qui episcopo graece dicente siriste interpretatur, ut omnes audiant, quae exponuntur'. (4) In Gaza, another Greek city, a local boy speaks in around A.D. 400 *τῇ Σύρων φωνῇ*. His mother asserts, *μηδὲ αὐτὴν μηδὲ τὸ αὐτῆς τέκνον εἰδέναι Ἑλληνιστί* (Mark the Deacon, *Vita Porphyrii episcopi Gazensis* 66–8, Budé text, ed. H. Grégoire, M.-A. Kugener, 1930). Cf. G. Mussies, 'Greek in Palestine and the Diaspora', JPFC II (1976), p. 1041.

253. A variety of archaeological and documentary evidence confirms that Greek was known and used in Palestine. (1) On ossuaries, while most inscriptions are in Hebrew (cf. p. 24, n. 90) or Aramaic, Greek is common. See the conclusions of E. R. Goodenough, *Jewish Symbols* I, p. 111; cf. e.g. N. Avigad, 'A Depository

country. Herod even had Thracian, German and Gallic mercenaries.[254] The festival games which he gave in Jerusalem brought into the Holy City not only foreign performers but also spectators.[255] The greatest influx of foreigners occurred, however, at the time of the main Jewish annual feast-days. The thousands of Jews who on these occasions journeyed to Jerusalem from all parts of the world were largely Hellenistic in speech and education. Also, it was not only Greek Jews who came to offer sacrifice and worship in the Temple, but real Greeks as well, i.e. proselytes (cf. Jn. 12:20 ff.). Considerable numbers of them came to Jerusalem every year on pilgrimage. Again, many of the Jews who had received a Greek education abroad settled permanently in Jerusalem and formed their own communities there. Thus the Acts of the Apostles reports the existence in Jerusalem of a synagogue of freedmen (*Λιβερτίνων*, cf. TDNT IV, s.v.), Cyrenians, Alexandrians, Cilicians and Asians, though it is unsure whether one community is referred to or five (Act. 6:9. Cf. 9:29).[256] In Galilee, the larger towns probably held a proportion of Greek inhabitants. This is certain of

---

of Inscribed Ossuaries in the Kidron Valley', IEJ 12 (1962), pp. 1–12; P. B. Bagatti, J. T. Milik, *Gli Scavi del "Dominus Flevit" (Monte Oliveto—Gerusalemme) I: la necropoli del periodo romano* (1958), pp. 70 ff. (7 Hebrew, 11 Aramaic and 11 Greek epitaphs); N. Avigad, 'Jewish Rock-Cut Tombs in Jerusalem and the Judaean Hill Country', Eretz Israel 8 (1967), pp. 119–42 (16 tombs, 4 including Greek inscriptions); cf. the tomb of the first century B.C. in Jerusalem, with several Aramaic and one Greek inscription, L. Y. Rahmani, 'Jason's Tomb', IEJ 17 (1967), pp. 61–100 (and cf. *ibid.* pp. 101 ff. and 112 ff.). (2) A Greek letter from Masada concerning the supply of liquids and vegetables. Not yet published; noted in IEJ 15 (1965), p. 110. (3) Documents from the period of Bar Kokhba. These comprise (a) Biblical texts in Greek; see B. Lifshitz, 'The Greek Documents from the Cave of Horror', IEJ 12 (1962), pp. 201–7; (b) Fragmentary documents, mainly accounts, which may date from the period of the Revolt, or earlier, P. Benoit, J. T. Milik, R. de Vaux, *Discoveries in the Judaean Desert II: Les grottes de Murabba'at* (1961), nos. 89–103; cf. the re-marriage contract of A.D. 124, no. 115; and (c) letters in Greek dating to the war itself; see B. Lifshitz, 'Papyrus grecs du désert de Juda', Aegyptus 42 (1962), pp. 240–56. (4) For a later period, the Greek inscriptions of the synagogue of Beth-Shearim; see M. Schwabe, B. Lifshitz, *Beth-She'arim II: The Greek Inscriptions* (1967) (Hebrew with English summary). Cf. A. Díez Macho, 'La lengua hablada por Jesucristo', Oriens Antiquus II (1963), pp. 95 ff., and J. N. Sevenster, *Do you Know Greek? How Much Greek Could the Early Jewish Christians Have Known?* (1968).

254. *Ant.* xvii 8, 3 (198).

255. *Ant.* xv 8, 1 (267 ff.).

256. A synagogue of the Alexandrians in Jerusalem is also mentioned in tMeg. (2) 3:6; yMeg. 73d; bMeg. 26a reads instead טורסיים or טרסיים or תרסיים, which is explained by modern scholars as 'Tarsians', i.e. Cilicians. Cf. Jastrow, *Dict.* s.v. Rashi, however, interpreted it as 'copper-smiths'. Cf. Str.-B. II, pp. 663–4. For the exegesis of Act. 6:9, see E. Haenchen, *The Acts of the Apostles, in loc.*

Tiberias,[257] to say nothing of the mainly non-Jewish Caesarea Philippi.

With such a strong penetration by Greek elements of the interior of Palestine, a rough knowledge of the language must have been not uncommon there either. And in fact, various items of evidence point to this. Whereas the coins of the Hasmonaeans still bear legends in Greek and Hebrew, those of the Herodians and the Romans, even for the Jewish region proper, carry a Greek legend only.[258] The statement in the Mishnah that even in the Temple certain vessels were marked with Greek letters, is certainly supported there at least by one authority (R. Ishmael), whilst according to the main tradition the letters were Hebrew.[259] Furthermore, the Mishnaic decision that bills of divorce might be also written in Greek,[260] and that the Bible might be used in the Greek translation also,[261] may originally have been intended for the Jewish Diaspora outside Palestine. On the other hand, the report that during the war of Quietus men were forbidden to teach Greek to their sons[262] presupposes that until then this was done, even in the circles of rabbinic Judaism.[263] Similarly, only a certain familiarity with Greek can explain the fact that the names of Greek letters are often used in the Mishnah to illustrate certain figures, e.g. כי to illustrate the figure *X*, or גמא to illustrate *Γ*.[264]

257. Josephus, *Vita* 12 (67). According to an unpublished paper by J. Strange, 'New Evidence for the Language of Galilee/Golan: 1st–5th Centuries', reported by E. M. Meyers, 'Galilean Regionalism as a Factor in Historical Reconstruction', BASOR 221 (1976), pp. 93–101 (esp. p. 97), seventeen sites along the western shores of Lake Tiberias and in the southern half of Lower Galilee have produced Greek inscriptions. Upper Galilee (with the exception of Qazyon: cf. CIJ II, no. 972) and Gaulanitis have revealed only few Greek inscriptions. But most of these documents belong to the period subsequent to the post-Hadrianic demographic changes.

258. One cannot however conclude from the story of the tribute-money in the New Testament (Mt. 22:19 ff., Mk. 12:15 f., Lk. 20:24) that the Greek legend on coins minted in Palestine was generally intelligible since this money was probably a Roman *denarius* with a Latin inscription (see p. 65 above).

259. mShek. 3:2.

260. mGit. 9:8.

261. mMeg. 1:8. The recitation of the *Shema'* in Greek (אלניסטין) is mentioned in ySot. 21b in connection with the synagogue of Caesarea in the fourth century A.D. The בית הכנסת של לעוזות no doubt refers to a Greek-speaking synagogue in Palestine (tMeg. 4:13).

262. mSot. 9:14. See Lieberman, *Hellenism in Jewish Palestine* (1950), pp. 100–14.

263. Cf. generally on the attitude of rabbinic Judaism to Greek education, W. Bacher, *Die Agada der Tannaiten* II, subject index under 'Griechisch'; cf. Lieberman *op. cit.* (previous note), *passim*. R. Simeon ben Gamaliel is said (bB.K. 83a) to have spoken of 1,000 pupils in his father's house, 500 studying Torah and 500 Greek wisdom (חכמה יונית). Judah the Patriarch in his turn seems to have preferred Greek to Aramaic. 'Why', he asked, 'should one use the Syrian language in Ereẓ Israel? Use either the sacred tongue or Greek' (bGit. 49b).

264. כי: mMen. 6:3; mKel. 20:7. גמא: mMid. 3:1; mKel. 28:7.

Moreover, recent research has shown that the rabbis possessed an undeniable but limited knowledge of Greek culture. 'They probably did not read Plato', writes S. Lieberman, 'and certainly not the pre-Socratic philosophers. Their main interest was centered on Gentile legal studies and their methods of rhetoric.'[265]

The evidence emerging from the manuscript discoveries in the Judaean Desert largely confirms the conclusions reached so far. Concerning Greek loan-words it should be noted that, although there has so far been no trace of them in literary works written in either Hebrew or Aramaic, documents representing the ordinary vernacular attest their presence clearly. The Copper Scroll (3Q15), whose language is characterized as Mishnaic Hebrew (cf. above, p. 27), contains the following borrowed terms: **אכסדרא** (11:3) = *ἐξέδρα* (see above, n. 161); **פריסטלין** (1:7) = *περιστύλιον/περίστυλον*; **לאה** (11:14) = *ἀλόη* (according to Milik); **אסתר[ין]** = *στατήρ* (cf. above, n. 203).[266] Aramaic papyri from Murabba'at and Naḥal Ḥever include further Greek words: **נמסא** = *νόμος* (DJD II, no. 21, 11); **אספליא** = *ἀσφάλεια*; **סיף** = *ξίφος*;[267] **אפ[טרפא]** = *ἐπίτροπος*;[268] **רהומיא** = *'Ρωμαῖοι*;[269] **הפטות** = *ὑπατεία*; **אוטוקרטור** = *αὐτοκράτωρ*; **קסר** = *Καίσαρ*; **סבסטס** = *Σεβαστός*; **הפרכיה** = *ἐπαρχεία*.[270]

More significantly, the various caves have revealed a notable amount of non-biblical Greek texts.[271] Although a few of these are fragments of an apparently literary nature, but too damaged to be identifiable,[272] most of the documents are legal, commercial or epistolary/administrative. A large number of fragmentary accounts and deeds relate mainly

265. S. Lieberman, 'How much Greek in Jewish Palestine?', *Texts and Studies* (1974), pp. 216–34, especially pp. 228. Cf. also *idem, Hellenism in Jewish Palestine* (1950), especially pp. 47–82, 100–14; *Greek in Jewish Palestine* (²1965), pp. 15–28, 144–60; D. Daube, 'Rabbinic Methods of Interpretation and Hellenistic Rhetoric', HUCA 22 (1949), 239–64; H. A. Fischel, *Rabbinic Literature and Greco-Roman Philosophy: A Study of Epicurea and Rhetorica in Early Midrashic Writings* (1973); see also the collection of papers by various authors *Essays in Greco-Roman and related Talmudic Literature* selected with a Prolegomenon by H. A. Fischel (1977).

266. Cf. J. T. Milik, DJD III, pp. 246–7, 248, 251, 253.

267. Cf. Y. Yadin, IEJ 11 (1961), pp. 41–2.

268. H. J. Polotsky, 'Three Greek Documents from the Family Archive of Babata', *E. L. Sukenik Memorial Volume* (1967), p. 50 (Hebrew).

269. Y. Yadin, IEJ 11 (1961), p. 46.

270. Yadin, IEJ 12 (1962), p. 242. The full formula in an Aramaic deed of gift reads: **על הפטות ליקיס קטוליס סורס תינינותא ומרקס אורליס אנטונינס שנת תלת לאוטוקרטור טרינס הדרינס סבסטס ועל מנין הפרכיה די בעשרין וארבעה בתמוז שנת עשר וחמש** ('In the consulship of Lucius Catilius Severus for the second time and Marcus Aurelius Antoninus, in the third yeard of the Emperor Caesar Traianus Hadrianus Augustus and according to the era of this Province (Arabia) on 24 Tammuz of the year 15' [=13 July A.D. 120]).

271. For Greek biblical material found at Qumran, consult J. A. Fitzmyer, *The Dead Sea Scrolls. Major Publications and Tools for Study* (1975), pp. 11–51.

272. Cf. DJD II, nos. 108–12 containing terms such as *φύσις, νόμος, παιδεία*.

to the sale of grains and vegetables,[273] but there is also an acknowledgement of debt,[274] a marriage contract,[275] a re-marriage deed,[276] and a further group of seventeen Greek, and nine Greek/Aramaic, pieces from the Babata archive.[277] Furthermore, fragments from Naḥal Ẓe'elim and Naḥal Mishmar show Greek lists of names, whilst the Naḥal Ḥever papyri include two (unpublished) Greek letters (nos. 3 and 6), the first addressed to the leaders of Engedi, Jonathan and Masabala, and the second sent by Ananos to Jonathan mentioning *Σιμνων Χοσιβα*.[278] Finally, the letter despatched by *Σουμαιος* to Jonathan son of Baianos and to Masabala deserves special notice because of the explanation given there of why the message was actually written in Greek.[279]

These new papyri and the increased number of Greek—mainly funerary—inscriptions discovered in Palestine have persuaded some scholars that bilingualism was widespread in Jewish Palestine in the first century A.D., and that it is quite proper to ask whether Jesus and his immediate disciples could speak Greek.[280]

Relying on sources prior to the demographic changes which ensued from the unsuccessful second revolution led by Bar Kokhba, this survey may be concluded as follows.

In the first century A.D., familiarity with the Greek language may be taken as certain in Jerusalem, with its educated classes and its immigrants from the Diaspora, and also among Jews living in the Hellenistic cities of Palestine. Elsewhere, only a superficial acquaintance with spoken basic Greek may be assumed. Only two Palestinian Jews of the first century are known to have sought literary fame in the Graeco-

273. Cf. DJD II, nos. 89–107.

274. DJD II, no. 114.

275. DJD II, no. 116.

276. DJD II, no. 115 dated to A.D. 124, i.e. the seventh year of Hadrian.

277. Cf. Yadin, IEJ 12 (1962), pp. 235–48; Polotsky, *art. cit.* [in n. 268], pp. 258–62.

278. Cf. B. Lifshitz, IEJ 11 (1961), pp. 53–62; Yadin, *ibid.*, pp. 42, 44.

279. Cf. Lifshitz, Aegyptus 42 (1962), pp. 240–56. The reading offered there is: *Ἐγράφη δ[ὲ] Ἑλληνιστὶ διὰ τ[ὸ ὁρ]μὰν μὴ εὑρηθ[ῆ]ναι Ἑβραεστὶ γ[ρά]ψασθαι.* For a better reconstruction, cf. above, p. 28, n. 118. Lifshitz is followed by J. N. Sevenster, *Do you know Greek?* (1968), p. 172, and J. A. Fitzmyer, CBQ 32 (1970), pp. 513–15, both in his (doubtful) decipherment and in his exegesis, viz. that the writer, possibly Simeon ben Kosiba himself, was completely bilingual and opted for one language or the other according to his mood. Yadin suggests a more sensible meaning (though without linguistic justification): 'The letter is written in Greek as we have no-one who knows Hebrew' (*Bar-Kokhba*, p. 130)—i.e., only a Greek, but no Hebrew or Aramaic, scribe is available. This would imply that the addressees could read Greek or obtain the services of an interpreter.

280. See in particular J. N. Sevenster, *op. cit.*, pp. 176–91. Note the subtitle: 'How much Greek could the First Century Jewish Christians have known?'. Cf. also Hengel, *Judaism and Hellenism* I, pp. 103–6.

Roman world, Justus of Tiberias, whose expertise is recognized even by his arch-enemy Josephus,[281] and Josephus himself, a native Aramaic speaker, who recorded the manner in which he attempted to master Greek.[282] Apart from these two authors, the Greek linguistic achievement of Jews in first century Palestine is of a rather low level: the average ossuary inscription requires no more than an elementary knowledge of the language. Letters written in Greek exist only from the second century A.D., and the sample is too small to justify any statistical inference.[283]

When the Romans came to power, the Latin language and culture was added to the Greek.[284] Yet in Palestine, as in the eastern provinces in general, Latin made no major inroads until the later period of the empire. In the earlier centuries, Roman officials used the Greek language exclusively in their dealings with the provincials. It was only for official documents, inscriptions and the like, that Latin was additionally used, from as early as the time of Julius Caesar. Thus, for example, Caesar commanded the Sidonians to erect a bronze tablet in Sidon recording in Greek and Latin his decree appointing the Jewish High Priest Hyrcanus II, *Ant.* xiv 10, 2 (191). Another official document dating to the same time was to be erected in the same way in Greek and Latin in the temples at Sidon, Tyre and Ashkelon, *Ant.* xiv 10, 3 (197). Antonius ordered the Tyrians to display in a public place, in Greek and Latin, a decree issued by him, *Ant.* xiv 12, 5 (319). In the Temple at Jerusalem, on the enclosure (*δρύφακτος*) beyond which Gentiles were forbidden to proceed further into the sanctuary, tablets (*στῆλαι*) were mounted at various points announcing the ban, some in Greek and some in Latin, *B.J.* v 5, 3 (193); vi 2, 4 (125). The *titulus* on the cross of Jesus was also rendered in Hebrew, Greek and Latin, Jn. 19:20. But the spread of Latin in Palestine in the early period of Roman rule did not extend far beyond official uses of this kind.[285]

281. Cf. *Vita* 9 (40), and Tessa Rajak, 'Justus of Tiberias', Class. Quart. 23 (1973), p. 345. For Justus of Tiberias, see vol. I, pp. 34–7.

282. *Ant.* xx 12, 1 (263): he was a keen student of grammar, prose and poetry, but spoke Greek with an accent.

283. For a criticism of Sevenster's thesis, see D. M. Lewis's review of *Do you know Greek?* in JThSt n.s. 20 (1969), pp. 583–88.

284. Cf. on this L. Hahn, *Rom und Romanismus im griechischen Osten, mit besonderer Berücksichtigung der Sprache, bis auf die Zeit Hadrians* (1906); J. A. Fitzmyer, 'The Language of Palestine', CBQ 32 (1970), pp. 504–7.

285. Note however the famous Latin inscription of Pontius Pilate from Caesarea (vol. I, p. 358), dating to A.D. 26–36; and the earliest Roman milestone from Judaea, inscribed in Latin in A.D. 69, B. H. Isaac and I. Roll, 'A Milestone of A.D. 69 from Judaea', JRS 66 (1976), pp. 15–19.

III. The Position of Judaism in regard to Paganism

The more vigorous and persistent the pressure of paganism on Palestine, the more energetic was the resistance offered by Judaism. The advance of pagan culture could not be prevented, but the watchful religious authorities guarded against everything that might offend against the law. Extreme vigilance in this connection was for Judaism a matter of life and death. Yet the punctiliousness with which it parried the threat to itself—and overcame it—also increased its dangers. For the Jew was in almost daily contact with pagan affairs, whether with persons, or with the commodities and objects which found their way into Palestine by way of trade and commerce. Thus the greater the subtlety with which cases of direct or indirect defilement through Gentile ways were settled, the more frequent was the risk of such defilement.

Two points in particular were not to be lost sight of in the struggle against paganism: idolatry, and the Gentile non-observance of the Levitical laws of purity. In respect to both, the Pharisees and rabbis proceeded with extreme scrupulousness.

1. In order to avoid anything even seeming to approach idolatry, they stressed above all in the first century A.D., the Mosaic prohibition of images (Exod. 20:4 f.; Dt. 4:16 ff.; 27:15).[1] The Jew should be ready to suffer all things rather than allow a statue of Caligula into the Temple at Jerusalem.[2] In fact, he should have nothing to do with any pictorial representations at all, such as the trophies in the theatre in the time of

1. Cf. J. B. Frey, 'La question des images chez les Juifs à lumière des récentes découvertes', Bibl. 15 (1934), pp. 265–300; W. Zimmerli, 'Das zweite Gebot', *Festschrift Bertholet* (1950); S. Lieberman, *Hellenism in Jewish Palestine* (1950) ['Rabbinic Polemics against Idolatry' (pp. 115–27); 'Heathen Idolatrous Rites' (pp. 128–38); 'Three Abrogations of Johanan the High Priest' (pp. 139–43); 'Heathen Pre-Sacrificial Rites' (pp. 144–6). 'The Consecration of a Victim in Heathen Rites' (pp. 147–52); 'Blemishes in Sacrifice' (pp. 153–63)]; K. H. Bernhardt, *Gott und Bild* (1956); H. H. Rowley, *Faith of Israel* (1956), pp. 74 ff.; J. Hempel, *Das Bild in Bibel und Gottesdienst* (1957); J. Gray, IDB s.vv. 'Idol' and 'Idolatry'. See above, p. 59, n. 178. Note also D. Flusser, JPFC II, pp. 1088–1100 and E. E. Urbach, 'The Rabbinical Laws of Idolatry in the Second and Third Centuries in the Light of Archaeological and Historical Facts', IEJ 9 (1959), pp. 149–65; 229–45.

2. *Ant.* xviii 8 (257–309); *B.J.* ii 10 (184–203).

Herod[3] or the eagle at the gate of the Temple.[4] When Pilate marched his troops into Jerusalem with portraits of the emperor, the people rose in uproar.[5] Vitellius took his troops by a detour from Antioch against Petra solely in order that Judaea might not be defiled by the imperial images.[6] And on the outbreak of war, there was nothing more pressing to do in Tiberias than destroy the palace of Antipas because it was decorated with pictures of animals.[7] The circulation of silver coins bearing the emperor's effigy (Mt. 22:19 ff. and parallels) could not be prevented, for no silver money was minted in the land itself (see p. 63 above). But out of consideration for Jewish scruples the copper coins struck in Palestine were without an image of Caesar (though some coins of Agrippa I, presumed to have been minted at Caesarea, showed both himself and his son).[8] Rabban Gamaliel II's argument justifying his visit to the baths of Aphrodite at Akko (Ptolemais), that the image of Aphrodite was there for the adornment of the bath and not the bath for Aphrodite, seems not to have been generally recognized at that time.[9] And although in the Jewish Diaspora, use was sometimes made of representations of animals for decorative purposes (see pp. 58–9 above), it was not until the second and third centuries that a somewhat more permissive attitude gained ground in Palestine.

To obviate the risk of any encouragement of idolatry, direct or indirect, or of incurring any contact with it, the Israelite was forbidden, for three days preceding a pagan festival (according to R. Ishmael, for three days afterwards also), to transact any business with Gentiles; he was neither to lend nor to borrow, and neither to pay them nor to be paid by them.[10] On the feast-day itself, he was not to frequent the city at all.[11] Everything with even a possible connection with idolatry was forbidden. Pagan wine might be offered in libation. It was therefore not

3. *Ant.* xv 8 1–2 (267–79).

4. *Ant.* xvii 6, 2 (149–54); *B.J.* i 33, 2 (648–50).

5. *Ant.* xviii 3, 1 (55–9); *B.J.* ii 9, 2–3 (169–74).

6. *Ant.* xviii 5, 3 (121–2). For details regarding the image of Caesar see vol. I, pp. 379–81.

7. *Vita* 12 (62–7).

8. On the types of Herodian and procuratorial coins see Madden, *History of Jewish Coinage*, pp. 134–153; de Saulcy, *Numismatique de la Terre Sainte*, pp. 69 ff. pl. III and IV; Madden, *Coins of the Jews* (1881), pp. 170–187; Reifenberg, *Ancient Jewish Coins* ([2]1947), pp. 18–28; J. Meyshan, 'The Coins of the Herodian Dynasty', *The Dating and Meaning of Ancient Jewish Coins and Symbols* (Pub. Israel Num. Soc., 1958), pp. 29–41; *idem*, 'An Unknown Portrait Coin of Agrippa I', INJ 4 (1963), pp. 66–7; Y. Meshorer, *Jewish Coins of the Second Temple Period* (1968), pp. 64–87, 102–6.

9. mA.Z. 3:4. Cf. G. Vermes, *PBJS*, p. 77.

10. mA.Z. 1: 1–2. For Qumran legislation prohibiting the selling of 'clean' animals or birds, or agricultural produce and wine to Gentiles, see CD 12:9–10.

11. mA.Z. 1:4.

only prohibited as drink; no profit of any kind was to be derived from it.[12] 'If wood has been taken from an *Asherah* (a pagan grove), it is forbidden to benefit from it. If an oven has been heated with it, if it is new it must be broken up, but if it is old, it must be left to go cold. If bread has been baked with it, it is forbidden to benefit from it. If this bread has been mixed with other bread, it is forbidden to benefit from any of it. . . . If a shuttle has been made of such a tree, it is forbidden to benefit from it in any way. If a garment has been woven with it, it is forbidden to benefit from it at all. If this garment has been mixed with others, and these others with others again, it is forbidden to benefit from any of them.'[13]

2. The separation of Judaism from paganism was further intensified by the notion that Gentiles were unclean because they did not observe the purity laws. Certain contacts with them were thought to defile. Their houses and all their belongings, in so far as they were susceptible to ritual uncleanness, were regarded as 'impure'. The statement in Acts that a Jew may not associate with Gentiles (Act. 10:28: ἀθέμιτόν ἐστιν ἀνδρὶ Ἰουδαίῳ κολλᾶσθαι ἢ προσέρχεσθαι ἀλλοφύλῳ), does not mean that such an association was forbidden, but that each such association was a cause of defilement; Gentile possessions needed to be purified before they were used by Jews.[14] 'If a man buys utensils from a Gentile, those which it is customary to purify by dipping, he must dip; those which are to be scalded, he must scald; those which are to be made white-hot in the fire, he must heat in the fire; spits and grills must be made white-hot in the fire, but a knife has only to be rubbed and it is clean.'[15] Apart from this impurity to which many things were susceptible through use on the part of Gentiles, a quantity of Gentile objects could not be used by Israelites because Jewish laws had not been observed in the course of their production. For one or other of these reasons, many of the most ordinary foods were forbidden to Jews if they came from Gentiles and they were allowed only to profit

12. mA.Z. 2:3. Cf. Enc. Jud. 16, cols. 538–40, s.v. 'Wine'.

13. mA.Z. 3:9.

14. Cf. F. Weber, *System der altsynagogalen palästinischen Theologie* (1880), pp. 68 ff.; J. Neusner, *The Idea of Purity in Ancient Judaism* (1973); *A History of the Mishnaic Law of Purities* (a commentary on Seder Tohoroth in Mishnah and Tosefta) I–XXII (1974–7). More particularly, cf. mOhol. 18:7. Cf. Neusner, *Purities* IV, pp. 340–1. See E. Schürer, *Über φαγῶν τὸ πάσχα Jn.* 18, 28 (1883), pp. 23 f.; D. Chwolson, *Das letzte Passamahl Christi und der Tag seines Todes* (1892), pp. 55–9. See, however A. Büchler, *Der galiläische Am-haareṣ* (1906), p. 114, n. 1, arguing that the rules applied only to Jews visiting the Temple or participating in sacrifice. For the transfer of cultic rules to everyday life, see Neusner, *Idea of Purity, passim.*

15. mA.Z. 5:12.

from them (by buying and selling): thus for example milk milked by a Gentile unless a Jew had witnessed the milking, and also Gentile bread and oil.[16] No law-abiding Jew would partake of Gentile fare (Dan. 1:8; Jud. 10:5; Tob. 1:10 f.) or eat at a Gentile table (Jub. 22:16; Act. 11:3; Gal. 2:12). The Jews were 'separati epulis' (Tacitus, *Hist.* v 5).[17] Consequently, Israelites travelling in Gentile countries were in a very difficult position. If they wished to obey the law strictly, they had to confine themselves to eating raw vegetables and fruits, as for instance some priests, friends of Josephus, who were brought as prisoners to Rome and supported themselves there on figs and nuts.[18]

To all these reasons, which made contact with Gentiles and life with them in the holy land a heavy burden for observant Jews, must be added yet another: they felt that the rule of aliens in the land of Israel constituted a glaring contrast between the ideal and reality. The land was the property of the chosen people. Only Israelites could own territory there. Even the renting of houses and fields to Gentiles was, according to the rabbis, prohibited.[19] Yet Gentiles had taken possession of the whole country. Thus, on the one hand, Gentile customs exerted a strong influence, and on the other, a very stout dividing-wall was erected against them. To the extent that the essential task of the latter was to defend Judaism against pagan religion, it achieved its end. It did not, however, check Graeco-Roman culture, which although the rabbis resisted it, was nevertheless over the course of time quietly assimilated by the Jews.

16. mA.Z. 2:6. Concerning oil, see also Josephus, *Ant.* xii 3, 1 (120); *B.J.* ii 21, 2 (591 f.); *Vita* 13 (74–6). On motives see bA.Z. 35b–37b. Milk, for example, was forbidden because it might include the milk of an unclean animal; oil, because it might have contracted defilement from unclean vessels (so at least according to one authority, Shemuel).

17. Cf. generally A. Wiener, *Die jüdischen Speisegesetze nach ihren verschiedenen Gesichtspunkten, zum ersten male wissenschaftlich-methodisch geordnet und kritisch beleuchtet* (1895); A. H. R. Kennedy, s.v. 'Meals', EB III, pp. 2989–3002; K. Kohler, s.v. 'Dietary Laws', JE IV pp. 596–600; S. H. Dresner, *The Jewish Dietary Laws* ([2]1966); Enc. Jud. 6, cols. 26–45, s.v. 'Dietary Laws'.

18. *Vita* 3 (14).

19. mA.Z. 1:8. The letting of fields was forbidden even more strictly than the letting of houses, for it resulted in the non-payment of tithe for the produce of the soil. See bA.Z. 21a.

§ 23. POLITICAL INSTITUTIONS

I. The Hellenistic Cities

General Bibliography

Stark, G., *Gaza und die philistäische Küste* (1852).

Kuhn, E., *Die städtische und bürgerliche Verfassung des römischen Reichs bis auf die Zeiten Justinians* I–II (1864–5).

Saulcy, F. de, *Numismatique de la Terre Sainte. Description des monnaies autonomes et impériales de la Palestine et de l'Arabie Pétrée* (1874).

Droysen, J. G., *Geschichte des Hellenismus* I–III ([2]1877–8).

Head, B. V., *Historia Numorum, a Manual of Greek Numismatics* (1887, [2]1911), pp. 662–81.

Kuhn, E., *Über die Entstehung der Städte der Alten: Komenverfassung und Synoikismos* (1878) (especially pp. 422–34).

Marquardt, J., *Römische Staatsverwaltung* I ([2]1881).

Mommsen, Th., *Römisches Staatsrecht* III ([3]1887), pp. 590–832.

Mommsen, Th., 'Die römische Provinzialautonomie: Ein Fragment', Hermes 39 (1904), pp. 321–6=*Ges. Schr.* V, pp. 552–6.

Niese, B., *Geschichte der griechischen und makedonischen Staaten seit der Schlacht bei Chäronea* I–II (1893–1903).

Liebenam, W., *Städteverwaltung im römischen Kaiserreiche* (1900).

Schwartz, E., 'Die Ären von Gerasa und Eleutheropolis', NGGW phil.-hist. Kl. (1906), pp. 340–95.

Hill, G. F., *Catalogue of the Greek Coins of Palestine (Galilee, Samaria, and Judaea)* (1914) = *BMC Palestine.*

Beloch, K. J., *Griechische Geschichte* IV. 1–2 ([2]1925–7).

Kahrstedt, U., *Syrische Territorien in hellenistischer Zeit* (1926).

Tscherikower, V., *Die hellenistischen Städtegründungen von Alexander dem Grossen bis auf die Römerzeit,* Philologus Supp. XIX.1 (1927).

Abel, F.-M., *Géographie de la Palestine* I; *Géographie physique et historique;* II; *Géographie politique: les villes* (1933–8) [*Géog. Pal.*].

Avi-Yonah, M., *Map of Roman Palestine* ([2]1940).

Jones, A. H. M., *Cities of the Eastern Roman Provinces* (1937, [2]1971), ch. 10.

Jones, A. H. M., *The Greek City from Alexander to Justinian* (1940).

Rostovtzeff, M., *Social and Economic History of the Hellenistic World* (1941; [2]1953).

Rostovtzeff., M., *Social and Economic History of the Roman Empire* (1926; [2]1957, ed. P. M. Fraser).

Grollenberg, L. H., *Atlas of the Bible* (1956).

Wright, G. E. and F. V. Filson, *The Westminster Historical Atlas of the Bible* (1956).

Tcherikover, *Hellenistic Civilization and the Jews* (1959).

Finegan, J., *Light from the Ancient Past: The Archaeological Background of the Hebrew-Christian Religion* ([2]1959).

Smith, G. A., *The Historical Geography of the Holy Land,* ed. H. H. Rowley (1967).

Avi-Yonah, M., *The Holy Land from the Persian to the Arab Conquests (536 B.C. to A.D. 640): A Historical Geography* (1966) (*Holy Land*).

Schneider, C., *Kulturgeschichte des Hellenismus* I (1967), pp. 864–901.

Vogel, E. K., 'Bibliography of Holy Land Sites', HUCA 42 (1971), pp. 1–96 (repr. separately, 1974) ('Bibliography').
Hengel, M., *Judentum und Hellenismus: Studien zu ihrer Begegnung unter besonder Berücksichtigung Palästinas bis zur Mitte des 2. Jh. v. Chr.* (1969, ²1973) = *Judaism and Hellenism* I–II (1974).
Avi-Yonah, M., 'Palaestina', RE Supp. XIII (1973), cols. 321–454.
Avi-Yonah, M. (ed.), *Encyclopaedia of Archaeological Excavations in the Holy Land* I (1975), II (1976), III (1977) (EAEHL).
Avi-Yonah, M., *Gazetteer of Roman Palestine*, Qedem 5 (1976) ('Gazetteer')
Segal, A. (ed.), *Ancient Sites in the Holy Land in the Classical Period* (1978).

The independent organization of city communities was of fundamental importance in Palestinian political life during the Hellenistic period. This was in itself no novelty; the large cities on the Philistine and Phoenician coasts had from early times been the centres of political life there. Nevertheless, the extension of Hellenistic rule and civilization to this area marks a turning-point in this respect too. On the one hand, it substantially transformed the existing communities; on the other, it led to the foundation of numerous new ones, and in general made the city communities the basis of the political organization of the country in a much more radical way. Wherever Hellenism penetrated—especially on the Philistine coast and on the eastern boundaries of Palestine beyond the Jordan—the country districts were grouped around specific cities as their political centres. Each such community formed a more or less independent unit in charge of its own internal affairs and its dependence on the rulers of Syria or Egypt consisted only in the recognition of their military supremacy and the payment of tribute or certain other taxes. At the head of this Greek type of city was a council of several hundred members which may be envisaged as resembling the Athenian council (βουλή), i.e., 'as a committee of the people that changed annually, and was elected or chosen by lot from the *phylae*' (Marquardt).[1] It formed the ruling authority, not only of the city itself, but also of all the villages and towns belonging to its often extensive territory.[2] The

1. The council of Gaza, for example, consisted of five hundred members, Josephus, *Ant.* xiii 13, 3 (364); that of Tiberias, six hundred, *B.J.* ii 21, 9 (641). Cf. generally, E. Kuhn, *Die städtische und bürgerliche Verfassung* II, p. 354; W. Liebenam, *Städteverwaltung im römischen Kaisserreiche*, pp. 229–30.

2. The attachment to these towns of territories of greater or lesser extent will be illustrated below. On the constitution of Hellenistic cities, see the General Bibliography above, and I. Lévy, 'Études sur la vie municipale de l'Asie Mineure sous les Antonins', REG 8 (1895), pp. 203–50; 12 (1899), pp. 255–89; 14 (1901), pp. 350–71. On the organization and development of the Greek πόλις generally, see J. Burckhardt, *Griechische Kulturgeschichte* I (1898), pp. 55–332; A. H. M. Jones, *The Greek City* (1940). On the constitution of Athens, which provided the pattern for the Hellenistic cities of the East, see G. Busolt, H. Swoboda, *Griechische Staatskunde* II (³1926), pp. 758–1210; on its council see P. J. Rhodes, *The Athenian Boule* (1972); on its later constitution see D. J. Geagan, *The Athenian Constitution after Sulla*, Hesperia Supp. XII (1967).

entire Philistine and Phoenician coast was divided in this way into a number of city communities, some of them of considerable importance. Later, the Hellenistic cities in the east and north-east of Palestine will be considered, as well as the Hellenized towns of the interior such as Samaria and Scythopolis and the cities founded by Herod and his sons, the populations of which were largely non-Jewish.

For all their independence, these cities of course shared on the whole the political fate of the rest of Palestine. During the time of the Diadochi, overall political control changed frequently.[3] In about 319 B.C., Ptolemy Lagus took possession of Syria and Phoenicia. By the following year he had already lost the greater part to Eumenes. And in 315 B.C. Antigonus wrested Palestine from him also, by his conquest of Iope and Gaza. Three years later (312 B.C.), Ptolemy regained the country, but in the same year had to cede it to Antigonus once more, who then held it for ten years (311–01 B.C.) until his death in battle at Ipsus.[4] Almost immediately after this battle in 301 B.C., Ptolemy re-conquered southern Syria as far as the region of Sidon (Diodorus xx 113). On the partition of Antigonus's kingdom, the whole of Syria was awarded to Seleucus. But Ptolemy did not hand over the territory he possessed and Seleucus did not use force to establish his claim (Diodorus xxi 1, 5). So from then on, Ptolemy remained in actual possession of Palestine and southern Phoenicia.[5] In 296 B.C., Samaria was conquered by Demetrius Poliorcetes (Jerome, *Chron.*, ed. Helm, p. 128; cf. p. 161 below). But by 295 B.C., he had lost all his non-Greek territories. Damascus too must have been Ptolemaic for some time, since it was conquered by Antiochus I (Polyaenus iv 15; cf. pp. 127–8 below).[6] The possibility nevertheless remains that it was only transiently Ptolemaic during the war of 274/73 B.C. (so Beloch, *loc. cit.*; cf. Tcherikover,

3. For details, see J. G. Droysen, *Geschichte des Hellenismus* II–III; G. Stark, *Gaza und die philistäische Küste*, pp. 347–67; K. J. Beloch, *Griechische Geschichte* IV.1 (^{2}1925), pts. iii and vi; IV.2 (1927), pp. 321 ff.; V. Tcherikover, *Hellenistic Civilisation and the Jews* (1959), pp. 39 ff.; E. Will, *Histoire politique du monde hellénistique* I (1966), pt. i; H. Bengtson, *Griechische Geschichte* (^{4}1969), pp. 369 ff.

4. See U. Köhler, 'Das asiatische Reich des Antigonos', SAB 1898, especially p. 832. Cf. C. Wehrli, *Antigone et Démétrius* (1968).

5. So Tcherikover, *op. cit.* pp. 53 ff., discussing contrary opinions; cf. RE s.v. 'Ptolemaios' (18), XXIII.2, col. 1624. Tyre and Sidon, which after the battle of Ipsus were held by Demetrius Poliorcetes, the son of Antigonus (Plutarch, *Dem.* 32), probably came under Ptolemaic rule from about 296 B.C. Philocles, the king of Sidon, commanded the fleet of Ptolemy; see SIG^3 390–1. For this view see now R. S. Bagnall, *The Administration of the Ptolemaic Possessions outside Egypt* (1976), p. 11.

6. On Samaria and Damascus, see also Beloch, *Gr. Gesch.* IV.2, pp. 322–3. Whether the capture of Damascus by Antiochus took place during the First Syrian War or somewhat later, may be left undecided here. Tcherikover, Mizraim 4–5 (1937), pp. 34–7, argues that it was an established Ptolemaic possession, temporarily captured by Antiochus; so also Bagnall, *op. cit.* p. 12.

Mizraim 4–5 (1937), p. 35). In general, however, it may safely be assumed that Ptolemy II Philadelphus (285–47 B.C.) inherited Palestine and southern Phoenicia from his father and did not obtain possession of these lands by means of the so-called First Syrian War with Antiochus I (274–73 B.C.).[7] The city era of Tyre, attested by inscriptions as dating from 274 B.C., cannot therefore be based on the definitive seizure of Phoenicia by Ptolemy II. It is probably connected with the Syrian War, when Ptolemy will have granted autonomy to this important town in order to gain its favour.[8]

The boundaries of the Ptolemaic domain around the middle of the third century B.C. have been much debated. During the war between Ptolemy III Euergetes and Seleucus II Callinicus, if the Armenian version of Eusebius' *Chronicle* may be trusted, the cities of Damascus and Orthosias were beseiged by Ptolemy but not taken; they were relieved by Seleucus when, once more victorious, he pushed southwards in 242/41 B.C. (Eusebius, *Chron.* ed. Schoene I, 251, cf. Jacoby, FGrH 260 F. 32 (8) [German trans.]; cf. below p. 128). If this is correct, they belonged both before and afterwards to the territory of the Seleucids. Since Orthosias lies somewhat to the south of the Eleutherus, the boundary is not to be looked for on the River Eleutherus, as is often

7. The dating of this war is based on a cuneiform inscription, namely in year 38 of the Seleucid era according to the Babylonian reckoning, i.e. 274/3 B.C., 273 B.C. being the main year of the war. See C. F. Lehmann-Haupt, ZA 6 (1891), pp. 234 ff. (text of the inscription), 7 (1892), pp. 226 ff., especially p. 232; U. Köhler, SAB 1895, p. 969; Lehmann-Haupt, Klio 3 (1903), pp. 496–512; Beloch, *Gr. Gesch.*, IV.2, pp. 497 ff. See especially W. Otto, *Beiträge zur Seleukidengeschichte des 3. Jahrhunderts v. Chr.*, SAM 34.1 (1928), pp. 1–42.

8. The dating of the era of Tyre from 274 B.C. becomes evident from two inscriptions. (a) According to one (at Oumm el-'Amed; see E. Renan, *Mission de Phénicie*, pp. 711–25=CIS I, no. 7= G. A. Cooke, *Text-book of North-Semitic Inscriptions* (1903), no. 9=M. Dunand, R. Duru, *Oumm el 'Amed* (1962), p. 181, no. 1=KAI, no. 18), the era began 37 years later than the Seleucid era, which would give 275 or 274 B.C. (b) On the other (found at Ma'ṣūb; see C. Clermont-Ganneau, RA 5 (1885), pp. 380–4=Clermont-Ganneau, *Recueil d'archéol. orientale* I (1888), pp. 81–6=Cooke, *North-Semitic Inscriptions*, no. 10=KAI no. 19), the 26th year of Ptolemy III Euergetes, i.e. 222/221 B.C., is equated with the 53rd year of the era of Tyre, which would give 274/3 B.C. as the starting point. The same era may also be used on Ptolemaic coins minted in Tyre (thus M.J.P. Six, 'L'ère de Tyr', NC 6 (1886), pp. 97–113). K. J. Beloch (Arch. f. Papyrusforschung 2 (1903), p. 235, cf. *Gr. Gesch.* IV.2, p. 328) conjectured that the basis for the era lay in the abolition of the monarchy at Tyre by Ptolemy Philadelphus. Lehmann-Haupt, Klio 3 (1902–3), pp. 519 f., objected that it would have been imprudent in view of the impending campaign to offend the city with such an enactment: it is more likely that Philadelphus restored self-government to the city at that time. The latter was certainly the main factor, but the abolition of the monarchy would have been compatible with it. It was not necessarily an offence against the Tyrians; it depends on whether they were content with their king, if such a person still existed.

supposed, but south of Orthosias, between that city and Tripolis.[9]

Ptolemaic domination of Palestine lasted for fully a century. Admittedly, Antiochus III the Great occupied the land from 219–17 B.C., but he was obliged to relinquish it after his defeat at Raphia. After the death of Ptolemy IV Philopator, he nevertheless invaded Palestine for a second time and at the victory at Panias in 200 B.C. the issue was decided permanently in favour of the Seleucids. From then on, Palestine and the whole Philistine-Phoenician coast belonged to the kingdom of Syria.[10]

The supremacy of the Ptolemies, like that of the Seleucids, was chiefly manifested in two matters: in the appointment of military governors (*στρατηγοί*) in the regions subject to them, and in the imposition of regular taxes. Josephus, in his story of the tax-farmer Josephus and his son Hyrcanus, *Ant.* xii 4 (154 ff.), provides a vivid picture of the taxation system as it was organized in the later period of Ptolemaic rule, one that despite its fictitious details faithfully reflects the institutions themselves. It shows that the taxes were not collected by the political authorities but were leased out to great contractors who were made responsible for tax collection in the individual cities.[11] How high and

9. For the river Eleutherus as a boundary see Stark, *Gaza*, p. 371; Kuhn, *Die städtische und bürgerl. Verfassung des röm. Reichs* II, pp. 128 f. (where it is noted that Strabo, xvi 2, 12 (753), describes the Eleutherus as the frontier between *Σελευκίς* and Phoenicia; note also Ptolemy, *Geog.* v 15, 4). But that Orthosias was Seleucid is shown not only by the war of 242–1 B.C., but also by Polybius's account of the invasion of Antiochus the Great, v 68, 7–8. So also was Aradus, see H. Seyrig, Syria 28 (1951), pp. 206–20. Calamus near Tripolis was hostile to Antiochus; Tripolis will therefore have been Ptolemaic. This is confirmed by papyrus evidence from the middle of the third century, which shows the following places to have been Ptolemaic: Tripolis—PSI 495 (258/7); Berytus—P. Cairo Zenon I 59016 (259); Sidon—P. Cairo Zenon 52951; the Plain of Massyas (or some part of it)—P. Cairo Zenon 59063 (257). The most doubt attaches to Damascus. As noted above, Eusebius's *Chronicle* records that it was beseiged by Ptolemy Euergetes. But if the Plain of Massyas was in Ptolemaic hands, Damascus must have been isolated from the Seleucid possessions. Furthermore, P. Cairo Zenon 59006 (*c.* 259), mentioning a gift or payment to one Dionysius 'from Damascus', suggests but does not prove that the city was then Ptolemaic. See Beloch, *Gr. Gesch.*[2] IV.2, pp. 330 f.; W. Otto, *Beiträge zur Seleukidengeschichte des 3. Jahrhunderts v. Chr.*, SAM 34 (1928), pp. 39 f.; V. Tcherikover, Mizraim 4–5 (1937), pp. 32 f.

10. For details, see Stark, *Gaza*, pp. 375–406, 423 f.; Wilcken, RE s.v. 'Antiochus III'; B. Niese, *Geschichte der griech. und makedon. Staaten* II (1899). pp. 373 f., 577 f.; E. R. Bevan, *The House of Seleucus* (1902), I, pp. 311 ff., II, pp. 29–38. For the date of the battle of Panias see M. Holleaux, 'La chronologie de la cinquième guerre de Syrie', Klio 8 (1908), pp. 267–81 = *Études d'épigraphie et d'histoire grecque* III (1942), pp. 317–35. This date, as opposed to 198 B.C., is decisively confirmed by an inscription found *c.* 7 km north-west of Scythopolis, V. H. Landau, 'A Greek Inscription found near Hefzibah', IEJ 16 (1966), pp. 54–70, cf. BE 1967, no. 627.

11. On the farming out of taxes in Egypt and the Hellenistic states generally, see G. Lumbroso, *Recherches sur l'économie politique de l'Égypte sous les Lagides*

various these taxes were under Seleucid domination is shown by the allusions in 1 Mac. 10:29–30; 11:34–5; 13:15, 37, 39; 2 Mac. 14:4. Cf. *Ant.* xii 3, 3 (142 ff.) and (under Roman rule), *Ant.* xiv 10, 6 (202 ff.).[12]

Towards the end of the second century B.C., the Seleucid kingdom exhibited signs of increasing dissolution. The central authority was so weakened by continual changes of sovereignty that a host of independent political entities were able to establish themselves on the borders of the empire. Thus during this period not only the Jews obtained and established complete autonomy, but a number of larger cities, which had often played a part of their own in the wars between

---

(1870), pp. 320–9; E. Ziebarth, *Das griechische Vereinswesen* (1896), pp. 19–26; U. Wilcken, *Griechische Ostraka* I (1899), pp. 515–55; L. Préaux, *L'économie politique des Lagides* (1939). On the exploitation of Palestine and Coele Syria in the 250s, as revealed by the Zenon papyri, see V. Tcherikover, 'Palestine under the Ptolemies', Mizraim 4–5 (1937), pp. 9–90; cf. CPJ I, pp. 115–30; Hengel, *Judaism and Hellenism*, pp. 18–23. See also R. S. Bagnall, *The Administration of the Ptolemaic Possessions Overseas* (1976), ch. 2. For the interpretation of Josephus, *Ant.* xii 4 (154–236), cf. Stark, *op. cit.*, pp. 412–23; J. Wellhausen, *Israelitische und jüdische Geschichte* ([3]1907), pp. 240–3; M. Holleaux, REJ 39 (1899), pp. 161–76= *Études* III (1942), pp. 337–42 on *Ant.* xii 4 (155) ed. Niese: ἀμφοτέρους τοὺς βασιλέας =Ptolemy V and his wife Cleopatra; H. Willrich, *Juden und Griechen vor der makkabäischen Erhebung* (1895), pp. 91 ff.; A. Büchler, *Die Tobiaden und die Oniaden* (1899), pp. 74–91. E. Meyer, *Ursprung und Anfänge des Christentums* II (1921), pp. 128–36; A. Momigliano, 'I Tobiadi nella preistoria del moto maccabaico', ARAST 67 (1932), pp. 165–200. Josephus's account is novelettish in character, and as it stands presupposes an impossible situation. The wife of the King Ptolemy who appears in the story is always called Cleopatra, *Ant.* xii 4, 3 (167); 4, 5 (185); 4, 8 (204); 4, 9 (217). An Egyptian Cleopatra first appears with the marriage of Ptolemy V to Cleopatra, the daughter of Antiochus the Great, in 193–2 B.C. This marriage is mentioned at the beginning of the narrative, *Ant.* xii 4, 1 (154), and it is accordingly assumed that the tax-farming of Joseph, which lasted 22 years, *Ant.* xii 4, 6 (186); 4, 10 (224), occurred in the time of Ptolemy V, i.e. after 193 B.C. (the king's epithet, *Εὐεργέτης*, *Ant.* xii 4, 1 (158) is missing in a few of the good MSS and may be a later gloss). At this time, Palestine and its neighbouring territories were no longer in the power of the Ptolemies. It is true that Polybius xxviii 20, 9; Josephus, *Ant.* xii 4, 1 (154); Appian, *Syr.* 5/18; Eusebius, *Chron.*, ed. Schoene, II, p. 124; Jerome, *In Dan.* 11:17 (CCL LXXVI, p. 911), all say that Coele Syria had been given to Ptolemy V by Antiochus the Great as a dowry for Cleopatra. But this must at best have been a promise that was never fulfilled. From the reliable data supplied by Polybius it emerges with certainty that Coele Syria and Phoenicia remained in the possession of the Syrian king after the battle of Panias (xxviii 1, 2–3; 17, 8–9; cf. vol. I, p. 138). Ptolemy V could therefore not have sent tax-farmers there, as Josephus supposes. So, decisively, M. Holleaux, *Études* III, pp. 337–55. The alternative possibility is that Josephus has misplaced a story which belongs in the Ptolemaic period proper, and that the name 'Euergetes' is not a gloss but an original reference to Ptolemy III Euergetes (246–21). See Tcherikover, *Hellenistic Civilisation*, pp. 126–42; Hengel, *Judaism and Hellenism* I, pp. 268–9.

12. On Ptolemaic taxation, see preceding note. On Seleucid taxation, see E. Bikerman, *Institutions des Séleucides* (1938).

Syria and Egypt, also made themselves independent and, as a token of this, began a new time-reckoning. Hence Tyre has an era dating from 126 B.C.; Sidon, from 111 B.C.; Ascalon, from 104 B.C.; and Berytus, from 81 B.C.[13] In other cities, individual 'tyrants' succeeded in seizing power. Towards the end of the second and early in the first century B.C. a tyrant called Zeno Cotylas appeared in Philadelphia, his son Theodorus in Amathus on the Jordan, Zoilus in Straton's Tower and Dora, and Demetrius in Gamala.[14] And it is in general attested that the Romans on their invasion of Syria found numerous independent princes there.[15]

The strengthening of Jewish power was fateful at that time for the cities in the neighbourhood of Palestine. The earlier Maccabees, and subsequently John Hyrcanus, subjugated several of them. But Alexander Jannaeus in particular set out to conquer on a large scale. By the end of his reign, the following places had been subjugated by the Jews: all the coastal cities from Raphia to Carmel with the single exception of Ascalon; almost all the cities of the region east of Jordan; and needless to say the cities of the interior, such as Samaria and Scythopolis, as far north as Lake Merom.[16]

With the conquest of Syria by Pompey, the independence of all the small states that had detached themselves from the Seleucid empire ended at a stroke. But for the autonomous cities the only result was that they established with the Romans the same relationship of voluntary dependence that they formerly maintained with the Seleucids. For those cities, however, which had fallen to the Jews, the Roman invasion meant deliverance from a hated domination. For Pompey re-separated from the Jewish domain all those cities that had submitted to the Jews from the time of the Maccabees and restored to them their freedom.[17] Josephus names these places 'liberated' by Pompey—which naturally had to acknowledge Roman supremacy—as Gaza, Azotus, Jamnia, Joppa, Straton's Tower, Dora, Samaria,

13. See Abel, *Hist. Pal.* I, pp. 215–16; Jones, CERP², p. 253. On the era of Berytus, cf. J. Rouvier, 'L'ère de Béryte' in Journal int. d'archéologie numismatique 2 (1899), pp. 12–16; H. Seyrig, Syria 27 (1950), p. 38, connects this era with the control of Syria by Tigranes of Armenia.

14. Stark, *op. cit.*, pp. 478 f.; Kuhn, *op. cit.* II, p. 162.

15. Josephus speaks quite generally of *μόναρχοι*, *Ant.* xiii 16, 5 (427). Appian, *Syr.* 50/254 testifies that Pompey *τῶν ὑπὸ τοῖς Σελευκίδαις γενομένων ἐθνῶν τοῖς μὲν ἐπέστησεν οἰκείους βασιλέας ἢ δυνάτας*, which Pompey was nevertheless certainly not the first to create. Pliny, *NH* v 23/82, mentions 17 'tetrarchias in regna descriptas barbaris nominibus'.

16. Josephus, *Ant.* xiii 15, 4 (395–7). See vol. I, pp. 219–28.

17. On Roman grants of freedom to the cities of conquered regions, cf. Kuhn, *op. cit.* II, pp. 15–19; Jones, *Greek City*, ch. vii; R. Bernhardt, *Imperium und Eleutheria: die römische Politik gegenüber den freien Städten des griechischen Ostens* (Diss. Berlin, 1971).

Scythopolis, Hippus, Gadara, Pella and Dium.[18] But the list is incomplete; still other cities possessed a Pompeian era, i.e. a new calendar beginning with the liberation, which many of them retained until late into the imperial age.

Another benefactor of many of these centres was the proconsul Gabinius who in 57–55 B.C. rebuilt Raphia, Gaza, Anthedon, Azotus, Jamnia, Apollonia, Dora, Samaria and Scythopolis, some of which had been entirely destroyed by the Jews.[19]

Yet misfortune fell on these places too through the Roman civil wars which drained the provinces, and through the arbitrary rule of Antonius in the east. The latter presented Cleopatra with the entire Philistine-Phoenician coast from the borders of Egypt to the Eleutherus, with the sole exception of Tyre and Sidon.[20]

Even when a quieter period was established by Augustus after the downfall of Antonius and Cleopatra, whose power had come to an end in 31 B.C., many of these cities underwent several more changes of overlord.[21] Apart from Ascalon, Augustus granted to Herod all the coastal cities from Gaza to Straton's Tower, together with the inland towns of Samaria, Hippus and Gadara.[22] After Herod's death, these places once again experienced various fates. Gaza, Hippus and Gadara were placed under the direct supremacy of the Roman legate of Syria (on Anthedon, see p. 104 below); Azotus and Jamnia together with Phasaelis, which was built by Herod, were given to his sister Salome; Joppa, Straton's Tower and Samaria fell with the remainder of Judaea to Archelaus.[23] The towns belonging to Salome went after her death to the Empress Livia.[24] And when Livia died, they apparently passed into the private possession of her son Tiberius, which explains the existence of an imperial ἐπίτροπος in Jamnia in his time.[25] After the deposition of

18. *Ant.* xiv 4, 4 (75); *B.J.* i 7, 7 (156). See vol. I, p. 240.

19. *Ant.* xiv 5, 3 (88); *B.J.* i 8, 4 (166); Jones, CERP², p. 257.

20. *Ant.* xv 4, 1 (95); *B.J.* i 18, 5 (361); see vol. I, p. 298.

21. For the successive territorial realignments of this period see e.g. G. E. Wright and F. V. Filson, *The Westminster Historical Atlas*, pp. 77 ff.

22. *Ant.* xv 7, 3 (217); *B.J.* i 20, 3 (396). Of the coastal towns, Josephus names only Gaza, Anthedon, Joppa and Straton's Tower. But Azotus and Jamnia, which passed after Herod's death to his sister Salome, must also have come into the possession of Herod at that time.

23. *Ant.* xvii 11, 4–5 (317–23); *B.J.* ii 6, 3 (93–100).

24. *Ant.* xviii 2, 2 (31); *B.J.* ii 9, 1 (167). Azotus is not expressly named but was certainly included.

25. *Ant.* xviii 6, 3 (158); Philo, *Leg.* 30 (199–202). Cf. J. Marquardt, *Römische Staatsverwaltung* II, pp. 248 f.; H.-G. Pflaum, *Carrières procuratoriennes* (1960), no. 9. On imperial private possessions generally, see O. Hirschfeld, 'Der Grundbesitz der römischen Kaiser in den ersten drei Jahrhunderten', *Kleine Schriften* (1913), pp. 516–75; *idem, Die kaiserlichen Verwaltungsbeamten bis auf Diokletian* (²1905), pp. 18–29; on their administration, pp. 121 ff.

Archelaus, the cities bestowed on him came, with the rest of his territory, under the rule of Roman governors of equestrian rank (*praefecti*); from A.D. 41–44 they then passed to King Agrippa I; and after his death, they reverted once more to Roman governors (now called *procuratores*). Yet these frequent changes of government meant little more for all the cities concerned than that taxes had to be paid now to one, now to another overlord. For although the authority of the various overlords made itself felt sometimes more forcefully and sometimes less so, on the whole they managed their internal affairs independently.

Finally, it was of importance for the development of communal life that Herod and his sons refounded a large number of cities such as Caesarea (=Straton's Tower), Sebaste (=Samaria), Antipatris, Phasaelis, Caesarea Philippi, Julias, Sepphoris, Livias and Tiberias.

The kind of dependence on Roman power experienced by these cities varied both in name and in substance.[26] The Roman Empire included free as well as subject communities. The former (*civitates liberae*, ἐλεύθεραι) possessed their own judicature and financial administration and might also be free from taxation proper; if so, they were αὐτόνομοι καὶ φόρον ἀτελεῖς (Appian, *BC* i 102/475).[27] The two privileges of autonomy and immunity were in principle separable, but naturally often went together. Their dependence on Rome consisted essentially in the loss of their right to wage war and make alliances, and in the obligation to offer certain services, particularly military assistance. Depending on whether this relationship was regulated by a treaty with Rome or not, a distinction was made between *civitates foederatae* and those that were *sine foedere immunes ac liberae*; though this distinction is foreign to Greek political terminology, which includes both categories under the title αὐτόνομοι.[28] All the free cities were regarded as not strictly part of the province.[29] The subject towns (ὑπήκοοι) belonging to

26. On the following, cf. Kuhn, *op. cit.* II, pp. 14–41; Marquardt, *op. cit.* I, pp. 71–86, 396; Mommsen, *op. cit.* III, 1, pp. 645–764; L. Mitteis, *Reichsrecht und Volksrecht in den östlichen Provinzen des römischen Kaiserreichs* (1891), pp. 83–110; W. Henze, *De civitatibus liberis quae fuerunt in provinciis populi Romani* (Diss. Berlin, 1892). Also, Stark, *Gaza*, pp. 522–5; Liebenam, *Städteverwaltung im römischen Kaiserreiche*, pp. 463 ff.; Jones, *Greek City*, ch. vii; Bernhardt, *Imperium u. Eleutheria* (n. 17 above).

27. See Marquardt, *op. cit.* I, pp. 78 f., 84 f.; Mommsen, *op. cit.* III, 1, pp. 655 ff., 681 ff.; see A. H. M. Jones, 'Civitates liberae et immunes in the East', *Anatolian Studies presented to W. H. Buckler* (1939), pp. 103–17.

28. Mommsen, *op. cit.* III, 1, pp. 654, 657 ff. Tyre is called in Latin 'foederata' (CIL X, 1601=Kaibel, IG XIV, n. 831), in Greek αὐτόνομος (CIG 5853=Kaibel IG XIV, 830=IGR I, 421).

29. Mommsen, *op. cit.* III, 1, p. 688. The phrase 'exempt from the *formula* of the province (τύπος τῆς ἐπαρχείας)' appears in two documents from the new archive concerned with the privileges of Aphrodisias in Caria. For a preliminary discussion

the province are to be distinguished from these others, the specific difference being that they were all taxed by the Romans; they were ὑποτελεῖς, *stipendiariae*. They had lost their autonomy de jure; the Roman authorities could interfere at will in regard to legislation, the administration of justice and government. But in fact, the subject communities continued in large measure to exercise their own legislative, judicial and administrative powers.[30]

According to Josephus, the Hellenistic cities in Palestine and its environment were made free by Pompey.[31] But this only means that he liberated them from Jewish domination. It discloses nothing whatever of their relationship to Rome. And most of them were certainly not *liberae* in the technical sense, but subject cities. For Josephus asserts at the same time that Pompey incorporated them into the province of Syria.[32] It is emphasized as something special that Ascalon was an *oppidum liberum*.[33] Otherwise, coins and inscriptions, some of them admittedly dating to the later imperial period, describe the following as αὐτόνομοι: Gaza, Dora, Ptolemais (at the time of the Seleucids), Gadara, Abila, Capitolias, Diocaesarea (formerly Sepphoris). It is by no means clear, however, whether this means in each case that there had been a specific grant of 'freedom'; and even in cities for which such a thing is attested, it is evident that the exemptions and privileges conferred could vary considerably and would be set out in detail in each case.[34] Conditions in any case changed frequently, and it must not be assumed that what is attested of one particular time holds good for the whole period of Roman rule.

Some of the Palestinian cities (the four coastal towns of Gaza, Ascalon, Dora and Ptolemais, and four towns of the Decapolis, Hippus, Gadara, Abila and Scythopolis) bear on coins and elsewhere the title ἱερὰ καὶ ἄσυλος. The bestowal upon whole cities of the right of sanctuary,

---

see J. M. Reynolds, 'Aphrodisias, a Free and Federate City', *Akt. VI Int. Kong. Gr. u. lat. Epigr.* (1973), pp. 115–22.

30. Mommsen, *op. cit.* III, 1, pp. 744–51; Mitteis, *loc. cit.*; also Kuhn, *op. cit.* II, pp. 34 ff.; Jones, *op. cit.*, ch. vii–viii; D. Nörr, *Imperium und Polis in der hohen Prinzipatszeit* (1966). Note also the introductory chapters and collection of documents in F. F. Abbott and A. C. Johnson, *Municipal Administration in the Roman Empire* (1926). As most of the more explicit evidence comes from Asia Minor, note D. Magie, *Roman Rule in Asia Minor to the End of the Third Century after Christ* I–II (1950).

31. *Ant.* xiv 4, 4 (76): ἀφῆκεν ἐλευθέρας; *B.J.* i 7, 7 (156): ἠλευθέρωσε.

32. *Ant.* xiv 4, 4 (76): προσένειμεν τῇ ἐπαρχίᾳ; *B.J.* i 7, 7 (157): κατέταξεν εἰς τὴν Συριακὴν ἐπαρχίαν.

33. Pliny, *NH* v, 13/68.

34. See Jones, *op. cit.* (n. 27 above). For an example of a Roman law granting a range of specific privileges to a free city, see the *Lex Antonia de Termessibus*, ILS 38 = Riccobono, FIRA² I, no. 11.

in origin a privilege associated with temples, is first attested in the time of Seleucus II Callinicus (246–26 B.C.).[35] Basically, it meant that the city was not obliged to hand over anyone who took refuge there.[36]

The duty to offer military service applied to the 'free' cities also; indeed it was part of the concept of confederation. Originally, the military assistance required of confederates differed from that imposed upon subject peoples and communities; the former had to provide auxiliary troops (Cic. *fam.* xv 4, 3: 'populorum liberorum regumque sociorum auxilia voluntaria') whereas the latter could be directly ordered to institute levies. But these differences, too, became increasingly blurred. For the Palestinian cities, the obligation to offer military service in one form or another is in general beyond question. From A.D. 44–67, a garrison was stationed at Caesarea of five cohorts and a wing of cavalry formed for the most part of Caesareans and Sebastenians (inhabitants of the towns of Caesarea and Sebaste and their respective districts); but without doubt these were units originally formed by Herod.[37] Josephus speaks quite generally, in connection with the campaign of Cestius Gallus against Jerusalem, of the auxiliaries furnished by 'the cities'.[38] From the time of Vespasian onwards, a number of regular auxiliary cohorts are encountered which take their names from Palestinian and Phoenician cities, even from those recognized as 'free'; it is possible, but not certain, that they originated from units provided by these cities in the earlier period.[39] The differences of

35. Grant to Aradus: Strabo, xvi 2, 14 (754); to Symrna: CIG 3137 = Dittenberger, OGIS, 229, l.12: *τό τε ἱερὸν τῆς Στρατονικίδος Ἀφροδίτης ἄσυλον εἶναι καὶ τὴν πόλιν ἡμῶν ἱερὰν καὶ ἄσυλον*. See C. B. Welles, *Royal Correspondence in the Hellenistic Era* (1934), nos. 25–8. Other examples in Dittenberger, *op. cit.* II, p. 636, index, s.v. *ἄσυλος*. See A. Heuss, *Stadt und Herrscher des Hellenismus*, Klio, Beiheft 39 (1937), pp. 145–54.

36. On Aradus, Strabo, *loc. cit.* has: *ὥστ' ἐξεῖναι δέχεσθαι τοὺς καταφεύγοντας ἐκ τῆς βασιλείας παρ' αὐτοὺς καὶ μὴ ἐκδιδόναι ἄκοντας· μὴ μέντοι μηδ' ἐκπλεῖν ἐᾶν ἄνευ τοῦ ἐπιτρέψαι βασιλέα*. On the right of temple sanctuary, see P. Stengel, s.v. 'Asylon' in RE II, cols. 1881 ff.; Mommsen, *Römisches Strafrecht* (1899), pp. 458 ff.; E. Schlesinger, *Die griechische Asylie* (Diss. Giessen, 1933). For *asylia* in Roman Asia Minor see Magie, *op. cit.* (n. 30), index s.v.

37. *Ant.* xix 9, 1–2 (357, 365); xx 6, 1 (122); *B.J.* ii 12, 5 (236); iii 4, 2 (66); and especially *Ant.* xx 8, 7 (176): *μέγα δὲ φρονοῦντες ἐπὶ τῷ τοὺς πλείστους τῶν ὑπὸ Ῥωμαίοις ἐκεῖ στρατευομένων Καισαρεῖς εἶναι καὶ Σεβαστηνούς*. See vol. I, pp. 363–5.

38. *B.J.* ii 18, 9 (502): *πλεῖστοι δὲ καὶ ἐκ τῶν πόλεων ἐπίκουροι συνελέγησαν, ἐμπειρίᾳ μὲν ἡττώμενοι τῶν στρατιωτῶν, ταῖς δὲ προθυμίαις καὶ τῷ κατὰ Ἰουδαίων μισεῖ τὸ λεῖπον ἐν ταῖς ἐπιστήμαις ἀναπληροῦντες*. Berytus, which in any case occupied a special position as a Roman colony, provided 1500 auxiliary troops for the army of Varus in 4 B.C.; *Ant.* xvii 10, 9 (287); *B.J.* ii 5, 1 (67).

39. On inscriptions: 'cohortes (and alae) Ascalonitarum, Canathenorum, Damascenorum, Sebastenorum, Tyriorum'. See RE s.v. 'ala' and 'cohors'; G. L. Cheesman, *The Auxilia of the Roman Imperial Army* (1914).

organization that existed at the beginning of the imperial period became less and less marked.

Since they were frequently, and perhaps as the standard rule, tax-exempt, the Roman colonies occupied a distinctive position among the cities of the Roman Empire.[40] Such settlements had existed in Palestine and Phoenicia from the time of Augustus. The oldest were Berytus, Heliopolis (both founded by Augustus), Ptolemais (by Claudius) and Caesarea (by Vespasian). All the colonies of the earlier imperial period were military; they consisted of discharged soldiers to whom land was given as a reward for their services, and in such a way that the award was always made to a large number simultaneously and in one place. To begin with, the lands required were simply confiscated from their owners. Later (from the time of Augustus), it was usual to offer compensation, or else the veterans were presented with property already belonging to the state. The colonists either formed a new community side by side with the old one or merged with the older community, in which case the latter received in its entirety the rights and constitution of a colony. Thus the plantation of a colony gradually developed into a benefit to the town whereas previously it had been an imposition. But in the course of the first century, the association of veterans with colonization seems gradually to have become less common. It virtually ceased after the reign of Hadrian. Only Septimius Severus, it seems, returned to the custom of settling veterans; otherwise all the post-Hadrianic foundations of colonies are of a purely fictitious nature. It is simply a matter of bestowing the name and rights of a colony as the highest form of political privilege, primarily upon municipalities, but also on towns with non-Roman populations and on non-urban communities.[41]

The rights of colonies varied.[42] The most favoured were those with the full *ius Italicum*, which seems to have carried with it exemption from poll- and land-taxes.[43] Of *coloniae* in Palestine, Ptolemais had nothing except the title (*Dig.* l 15, 1, 3); Caesarea received exemption from the poll-tax from Vespasian, and from the land-tax from Titus (l 15, 8, 7); Aelia Capitolina seems to have had a similar exemption, but neither had the full *ius Italicum* (l 15, 1, 6; 8, 7).

40. See E. Kornemann, RE s.v. 'colonia'; F. Vittinghoff, *Römische Kolonisation und Bürgerschaftspolitik unter Caesar und Augustus*, AAM 1951. 4; E. T. Salmon, *Roman Colonisation under the Republic* (1969), especially ch. ix; A. N. Sherwin-White, *The Roman Citizenship* ([2]1973).

41. Kornemann, *op. cit.*, col. 566.

42. Kornemann, *op. cit.*, cols. 578–83.

43. On the *ius Italicum*, see Marquardt, *Römische Staatsverwaltung* I, pp. 89 ff. and the literature quoted there; Mommsen, *Römisches Staatsrecht* III, 1, pp. 807–10; A. von Premerstein, RE s.v. 'Ius Italicum'; Sherwin-White, *op. cit.*, pp. 316–22. In the period up to A.D. 135 the term appears only in Pliny, *NH* iii 3/25 and 21/139.

The Augustan system of establishing military colonies was imitated, incidentally, by Herod.[44]

The position of cities temporarily subject to Herodian princes was not essentially different from those under immediate Roman rule. But in certain instances the power of the Herodian princes was more directly felt; note the complaints of Gadara against Herod, made before Augustus in 20 B.C., *Ant.* xv 10, 3 (354–9), and the embassies of the Greek cities in 4 B.C. requesting an end to Herodian rule (see vol. I, pp. 331–5). To secure their sovereignty they had, in some of the cities at least, their own governors; thus Herod the Great had an *ἄρχων* in Idumaea and Gaza,[45] Agrippa I a *στρατηγός* in Caesarea[46] and an *ἔπαρχος* in Tiberias,[47] and Agrippa II a representative (*τοῦ τὴν δυναστείαν διοικοῦντος*) in Caesarea Philippi[48] and an *ἔπαρχος* in Gamala.[49] Just such a governor was also (probably) the *ἐθνάρχης* of King Aretas in Damascus, 2 Cor. 11:32.[50]

The Cities

1. Raphia, *'Ραφία* (written thus on coins), rabbinic רפיח,[51] may still be traced in the ruins of Tell Rafaḥ, situated at a short distance from

44. *Ant.* xv 8, 5 (294). See A. Schalit, *König Herodes*, pp. 173–84, 365. See below, Samaria, Gaba, Heshbon.

45. *Ant.* xv 7, 9 (254).

46. *Ant.* xix 7, 4 (333).

47. Josephus, *Vita* 9 (33): whether there is question here of Agrippa I or II is uncertain.

48. *Vita* 13 (74). Cf. Kuhn, *op. cit.* II, p. 346.

49. *Vita* 11 (46).

50. The title *ἐθνάρχης* for such governors is unusual and is to be explained by the conditions peculiar to the Nabataean kingdom. There, where there were still few towns, organization was predominantly according to tribes. At the head of a tribe or a complex of tribes stood a sheikh (tribal chief; Greek: *ἐθνάρχης*). Traces of such a constitution appear in the Greek inscriptions of the Hauran area from Roman times; cf. especially Le Bas-Waddington, *Inscriptions*, no. 2196 = Dittenberger, OGIS 616: *'Αδριανοῦ τοῦ καὶ Σοαίδου Μαλέχου ἐθνάρχου, στρατηγοῦ νομάδων*. Cf. *Syria* IIIA: *Greek and Latin Inscriptions* (1921), no. 675. The *φυλαί* are frequently mentioned here, Le Bas-Waddington, n. 2173b, 2210, 2220, 2224, 2265, 2287 = IGR III 1298 = *Syria* IIIA, no. 664, 2308, 2309, 2310, 2393, 2396, 2397 = *Syria* IIIA, no. 765[11], 2427, 2431, 2439, 2483; *Syria* IIIA no, 694, 760, 786[3]. An *Αννηλος Σαμεθου παναρετε εθναρχα* appears on an epitaph at Jize, between Adraa and Bostra, ZDPV 20 (1897), p. 135. For the tribal structure of this area see A. H. M. Jones, 'The Urbanization of the Ituraean Principality', JRS 21 (1931), pp. 265–75. Damascus too may have been under such an *ἐθνάρχης*. Where the *ἐθνάρχης* had at the same time a military command, he was called *στρατηγός*, אסרטגא; cf. above p. 53 and Josephus, *Ant.* xviii 5, 1 (112); cf. vol. I, pp. 581–2.

51. ySheb. 36c, and (according to a variant reading) tSheb. 4:11; Tg. Onk. Dt. 2:23 (Tg. Ps.-Jon. *in loc.*: רפיע). Cf. A. Neubauer, *Géographie du Talmud* (1868), p. 21; A. Berliner, *Targum Onkelos* (1884) II, p. 219; P. S. Alexander, *The Toponymy of the Targumim* (Diss. Oxford, 1974), pp. 227–8.

the sea on a flat harbourless shore,[52] and for that reason regarded by Pliny and Ptolemy as an inland town.[53] It was the Syrian city nearest to Egypt.[54] Apart from cuneiform inscriptions, it is first mentioned historically in connection with the campaign of Antigonus against Egypt in 306 B.C., when Antigonus's fleet under the command of his son Demetrius was destroyed by a storm off its shore.[55] It then became famous chiefly through the victory gained there in 217 B.C. by the unwarlike Ptolemy IV Philopator over Antiochus the Great, which resulted in the latter's loss of Palestine and Phoenicia.[56] In 193 B.C., the marriage was celebrated there of Ptolemy V Epiphanes to Cleopatra, daughter of Antiochus the Great.[57] Raphia was conquered at the beginning of the first century B.C. by Alexander Jannaeus, Josephus, *Ant.* xiii 13, 3 (357); *B.J.* i 4, 2 (87); cf. *Ant.* xiii 15, 4 (395); it was then like the neighbouring cities separated by Pompey from the Jewish realm and was subsequently rebuilt by Gabinius, *Ant.* xiv 5, 3 (88); *B.J.* i 8, 4 (166). However, coins of Raphia minted in the imperial epoch (from Marcus Aurelius and Commodus to Philip the Arabian) have an era commencing earlier than the refoundation by Gabinius (57 B.C.?).[58] It seems never to have been in the possession of the Herodian princes.

2. Gaza, *Γάζα*, Hebrew עזה,[59] was the ancient and important city of the Philistines frequently mentioned in the Old Testament. In the

52. Diodorus xx 74 calls Raphia *δυσπροσόρμιστον καὶ τεναγώδη*.

53. Pliny, *NH* v 13/68; Ptolemy (ed. Nobbe) v 16, 6 = (ed. Didot I, 2) v 15, 5. Cf. Strabo xvi 2, 31 (759); *Itinerarium Antonini*, Cuntz I ([2]1929), p. 21; Sozomenus, *HE* vii 15; Hierocles, *Synecdemus* (ed. Burckhardt) 719, 8. See Guérin, *Judée*, pp. 233–5; *BMC Palestine*, pp. lxxi–iii; 171–4; T. Wiegand, *Sinai* (1920), p. 36; Abel. *Géog. Pal.* I, p. 310; II, pp. 431–2; M. Avi-Yonah, *Holy Land*, pp. 70, 151; see Y. Aharoni, *The Land of the Bible* (1967), *passim* for earlier sources. Along with many other Palestinian cities (see below *ad locc.*), it is mentioned in an itinerary preserved on papyrus, and dating to A.D. 317–23, *P. Ryl.* 627 ll.236–7, 314; 630–8, l.436; 638, ll.21–2.

54. Polybius v 80, 3: *πρώτη τῶν κατὰ Κοίλην Συρίαν πόλεων ὡς πρὸς τὴν Αἴγυπτον;* Josephus, *B.J.* iv 11, 5 (662): *ἔστι δὲ ἡ πόλις αὕτη Συρίας ἀρχή*. Note the inscription from near Raphia dating to A.D. 233 with the words *ἀπὸ ὅρων Συρίας Παλαι[στ(ίνης)]*, D. Barag, IEJ 23 (1973), pp. 50–2.

55. Diodorus xx 74; J. Droysen, *Gesch. des Hellenismus*[2] II, 2, p. 147; Stark, *Gaza*, p. 358.

56. The battle is fully described in Polybius, v 82–6, with Walbank, *Commentary on Polybius, ad loc.* Cf. B. Niese, *Gesch. der griech. und makedon. Staaten* II, pp. 380–2; Beloch, *Gr. Gesch.* ([2]1925) IV.1, pp. 694–6; E. Will, *Histoire politique du monde hellénistique* II (1967), pp. 30–2.

57. Livy xxxv 13, 4. On the date of this marriage (194/193 B.C.), see RE XXIII.2 (1959), col. 1697.

58. *BMC Palestine*, p. lxxxii.

59. On the Hebrew form, cf. Stephanus Byz. s.v. *Γάζα· ἐκλήθη καὶ Ἄζα· καὶ μέχρι νῦν Σύροι Ἄζαν αὐτὴν καλοῦσιν*. On a Latin inscription from the second century A.D.

Amarna Tablets it is named Hazati or Azzati, in Egyptian Gadatu.[60] Herodotus knows it as *Κάδυτις* and observes that it was not much smaller than Sardis.[61] The city seems to have been engaged in trade with Greece already in the period of Persian supremacy, as surviving coins suggest.[62] In the time of Alexander the Great it was, next to Tyre, the greatest fortress on the Phoenician-Philistine coast. Alexander conquered it only after a troublesome two months' siege in 332 B.C.[63] From then on, it became more and more a Greek city.[64] The struggles of Ptolemy Lagus with the other Diadochi for the possession of Coele Syria naturally affected Gaza above all. In 315 B.C., it was conquered by Antigonus.[65] In 312 B.C., it again fell into the hands of Ptolemy as a

---

(a list of veterans of the *leg. III Aug.*) the form *Gazza* also occurs, CIL VIII, 18084, l.22. For general accounts of Gaza see especially K. Stark, *Gaza und die philistäische Küste* (1852); M. A. Meyer, *A History of the City of Gaza* (1907); RE s.v. 'Gaza' (1), VII (1912), cols. 880–6; Abel, *Géog. Pal.* II, pp. 327–8; RAC s.v. 'Gaza' (1972). For excavations, see Vogel, 'Bibliography' s.v.; EAEHL I, s.v. (1974); Avi-Yonah, 'Gazetteer', s.v.

60. See *The Tell el-Amarna Tablets*, ed. S. A. B. Mercer and F. H. Hallock (1939) II, p. 719 (Hazati); p. 735 (Azzati). Cf. Aharoni, *Land of the Bible* (1967), *passim*.

61. Herodotus ii 159, 2; iii 5, 2: *Σαρδίων οὐ πολλῷ ἐλάσσονος*; iii 5 describes *Κάδυτις* as a city of *Σύροι Παλαιστῖνοι* near the Egyptian border. Here the identification with Gaza can hardly be doubted. But ii 159 also states that Cadytis was captured by Pharaoh Necho, which according to Jer. 47:1 was in fact the case in regard to Gaza. Cf. Th. Reinach, CRAI 1895, 360–6. In general, cf. Abel, *Hist Pal.* I, p. 54 etc.; II, pp. 327–8. Avi-Yonah, *Holy Land*, especially pp. 150–1; IDB s.v. and 'Gazetteer', s.v.

62. On these coins, cf. the basic discussion by J. P. Six, 'Observations sur les monnaies phéniciennes' in NC, N.S., 17 (1877), pp. 177–241 (on Gaza, pp. 221–39); also E. Babelon, *Catalogue des monnaies grecques de la Bibliothèque Nationale, Les Perses Achéménides, Cypre et Phénicie* (1893), pp. LVI ff., 47 ff. *BMC Palestine*, pp. lxxxiii–ix; pp. 176–83 ('Philisto-Arabian and Egypto-Arabian Series'); cf. U. Rappaport, 'Gaza and Ascalon in the Persian and Hellenistic Period in relation to their Coins', IEJ 20 (1970), pp. 75–80. The coins have partly Phoenician, partly Greek inscriptions. The name of the city (עז or עזה) is discernible on several of them. Their most interesting feature, however, is that they were minted according to an Athenian standard with Athenian (or Greek) types. Avi-Yonah, *Holy Land*, p. 31 and Rappaport, *loc. cit.*, suggest that Gaza was the outlet for the trade of the Arabs in the interior.

63. On the two-months' siege, see Diodorus xvii 48, 7 and Josephus, *Ant.* xi 8, 3–4 (325). Cf. also in particular Arrian ii 26–7; Curtius iv 6, 7–30; Plutarch, *Alex.* 25; Polybius xvi 22a (40), see Walbank *ad loc.*; Droysen, *Gesch. d. Hellenismus*² I. 1, pp. 297–301; Stark, *Gaza*, pp. 236–44; Niese, *Gesch. der griechischen und makedonischen Staaten* I (1893), p. 82.

64. It is explicitly described as a *πόλις Ἑλληνίς* by Josephus, *Ant.* xvii 11, 4 (320); *B.J.* ii 6, 3 (97).

65. Diodorus xix 59, 2; Droysen, *op. cit.* II 2, p. 11; Stark, *op. cit.*, pp. 1–350; Niese, *op. cit.* I, pp. 275 f.

result of his victory there over Demetrius the son of Antigonus.[66] In the same year, however, he renounced possession of Coele Syria and on his retreat razed the most important fortresses, Gaza among them.[67] From 311–01 B.C., Gaza like the rest of Palestine was in the possession of Antigonus, and from then on, probably continuously in that of Ptolemy Lagus and his successors (see p. 87 above). Coins exist of Ptolemy II and III minted in Gaza. The dated coins of Ptolemy II Philadelphus with the monogram of Gaza extend from the twenty-third to the thirty-seventh year of his reign (=263–49 B.C.).[68] In this period Ptolemaic possession of Gaza is illustrated by the Zenon papyri. It chiefly appears as a centre of trade; it is worth noting also that a 'supervisor of the perfumes' was established there.[69] From 218–17 B.C., Gaza with the rest of Palestine was held by Antiochus the Great.[70] Coele Syria came permanently under the dominion of the Seleucids through the victory of Antiochus at Panias (200 B.C.). The city had previously been captured after a difficult siege, apparently in 201 B.C., of which passing mention is made by Polybius.[71] The rule of the Seleucids is attested by, among other things, coins of Demetrius I Soter, Demetrius II Nicator, and perhaps Antiochus VII Sidetes minted at Gaza.[72] For a time the inhabitants appear to have known themselves as *Σελευκεῖς ἐν Γάζῃ* or *Σελευκεῖς Γαζαῖοι* or *δῆμος Σελ[ευκεων?] τῶν ἐν Γάζῃ*.[73] During the conflicts in the Syrian kingdom between Demetrius II Nicator and Antiochus VI or rather Tryphon (145–3 B.C.), Gaza,

66. Diodorus xix 84, 8. On the battle, see Droysen, *op. cit.* II 2, pp. 42 ff.; Stark, *op. cit.*, pp. 351–4; Niese, *op. cit.* I, pp. 295 ff.; Beloch, *Gr. Gesch.* ([2]1925) IV. 1, pp. 129–30, pp. 132 f.

67. Diodorus xix 93, 7: *κατέσκαψε τὰς ἀξιολογωτάτας τῶν κεκρατημένων πόλεων, Ἄκην μὲν τῆς Φοινίκης Συρίας, Ἰόππην δὲ καὶ Σαμάρειαν καὶ Γάζαν τῆς Συρίας*. Cf. Stark, *op. cit.*, pp. 355 f.; Niese, *op. cit.* I, p. 300.

68. R. S. Poole, *BMC: The Ptolemies, Kings of Egypt* (1883), pp. 35, 49; J. N. Svoronos, 'Les monnaies de Ptolémée II qui portent dates', Rev. Belg. Num. (1901), pp. 263–98, 387–412; (Gaza), 285 f. For the most complete account, *idem*, *Τὰ νομίσματα τοῦ κράτους τῶν Πτολεμαίων* (1904), II, pp. 123–4 (Ptolemy II); p. 165 (Ptolemy III); cf. *BMC Palestine*, p. lxvii.

69. P. Cairo Zen. (59001); 59006 (the 'harbour of Gaza'); 59009; 59093 (merchandise brought from Gaza to Tyre); PSI 322; 616; 628 *(ὁ ἐπὶ τῆς λιβανωτικῆς)*; P. Col. Zen. 2. See especially V. Tscherikover, Mizraim 4–5 (1937), pp. 9–90.

70. Polybius, v 80: cf. Stark, *Gaza*, pp. 382–5.

71. Polybius xvi 18, 2; xvi 22a (40); xxix 12 (6a), 8. See Walbank, *Commentary*, *ad loc.*; cf. Stark, *Gaza*, pp. 404 f.

72. P. Gardner, *BMC: Seleucid Kings of Syria* (1878), p. 47; S. Ben-Dor, 'Some New Seleucid Coins', PEQ 78 (1946/7), pp. 43–8; 80 (1948/9), pp. 59–63. The much greater number of Seleucid coins at Ascalon is striking. This city was obviously more important at that time than Gaza, as is also clear from the trade connections; p. 108 below on Ascalon, and cf. Rappoport *op. cit.* (n. 62 above).

73. F. de Saulcy, *Numismatique de la Terre Sainte*, pp. 211 f. *Σελ.* probably= *Σελευκεῖς*, see *Catalogue of Greek Coins in the Hunterian Collection*, ed. G. Macdonald, (1905), p. 282; *BMC Palestine*, pp. lxix; 143.

because it would not ally itself to the party of Antiochus, was besieged by Jonathan Maccabaeus acting in connivance with him and its environs were devastated. It then capitulated, and as a pledge of its adherence to Antiochus handed over hostages to Jonathan.[74] In regard to the constitution of Gaza in this period, it is said to have had a council of five hundred members.[75] In around 96 B.C., it fell with the neighbouring cities of Raphia and Anthedon into the hands of Alexander Jannaeus. Alexander conquered it after a siege lasting one year, though its fall was finally achieved by treachery, and abandoned the town and its inhabitants to destruction, Josephus, *Ant.* xiii, 13, 3 (358 ff.); *B.J.* i 4, 2 (87); cf. *Ant.* xiii 15, 4 (395); Stark, *Gaza*, pp. 499 ff. When Pompey vanquished Syria, Gaza—insofar as it existed at all—also obtained its freedom, *Ant.* xiv 4, 4 (76); *B.J.* i 7, 7 (156). The reconstructed city therefore began a new era from his time (61 B.C.).[76] The rebuilding itself did not take place until the time of Gabinius, *Ant.* xiv 5, 3 (88); but the ancient site of Gaza was probably abandoned at that time and the new city founded somewhat further to the south.[77] In 30 B.C., Gaza came under the domination of Herod the Great, *Ant.* xv 7, 3 (217); *B.J.* i 20, 3 (396). After his death, it was once more annexed to the province of Syria, *Ant.* xvii 11, 4 (320); *B.J.* ii 6, 3 (97). The fact that the imperial coins of Gaza do not begin until after the death of Herod the Great is consistent with this. The oldest coins known

74. 1 Mac. 11:61–2; Josephus, *Ant.* xiii 5, 5 (153); Stark, *Gaza*, p. 492. No conquest of Gaza took place in the Maccabean period; in 1 Mac. 13:43–48, Gazara should be read, see Abel, *ad loc.*

75. Josephus, *Ant.* xiii 13, 3 (364).

76. On the era of Gaza, cf. L. Ideler, *Handbuch der Chronologie* I, pp. 474 f.; Stark, *Gaza*, pp. 513–15; E. Schürer, 'Der Kalender und die Ära von Gaza', AAB (1896), pp. 1065–87. For the coins, see de Saulcy, *Numismatique de la Terre Sainte*, pp. 209–33, pl. XI; Head, *NH*², p. 805; *BMC Palestine*, p. lxvii. The Christian tomb inscriptions collected by J. Germer-Durand and C. Clermont-Ganneau are important in this connection, as are some papyri from Nessana, see n. 86 below. The *Chronicon paschale* (ed. Dindorf I, p. 352) records under Olymp. 179, 4= 61 B.C.: *'Εντεῦθεν Γαζαῖοι τοὺς ἑαυτῶν χρόνους ἀριθμοῦσιν*; and the epitaphs mentioned also point to 61 B.C. as marking the beginning of the era.

77. On the distinction between Old and New Gaza, cf. especially Stark, *Gaza*, pp. 352 f., 509–13; G. A. Smith, *Historical Geography*, p. 186 and n. 3. The town near which Ptolemy Lagus defeated Demetrius Poliorcetes in 312 B.C. is named Old Gaza by Diodorus and Porphyry; see Diodorus xix 80, 5 *(τὴν παλαιὰν Γάζαν)*, Porphyry in the fragment in Eusebius, *Chron.*, ed. Schoene I, cols. 249–50 (according to the Armenian: *veterem Gazam*, the Greek in Syncellus: *Παλαίγαζαν*, or as A. v. Gutschmid reads, *Παλαίγαζην*). It is to this Old Gaza that Strabo refers when he reports that Gaza was destroyed by Alexander and had since lain waste; see Strabo xvi 2, 30 (759): *κατεσπασμένη δ'ὑπὸ 'Αλεξάνδρου καὶ μένουσα ἔρημος*. The observation in Acts 8:26: *αὕτη ἐστὶν ἔρημος* is perhaps not relevant for the *αὕτη* there may refer to *ὁδός*; but see Smith, *loc. cit.* Strabo is admittedly mistaken in that he seems to know nothing of New Gaza. His observation may be based on the statement of an older geographer in whose time New Gaza did not exist. But a

are two of Augustus dating to 63 and 66 of the era of Gaza.[78] In the reign of Claudius, Gaza is spoken of as an important city by the geographer Mela.[79] In A.D. 66 it was attacked and laid waste by the Jewish revolutionaries, Josephus, *B.J.* ii 18, 1 (460). But this can only have been a partial devastation. So strong a fortress can never have been really destroyed by a small group of rebels. In addition, coins from years 130, 132, 135 (=A.D. 69/70, 71/72, 74/75) testify to the continuing prosperity of the city.[80] On a lead weight appears the inscription *L δξρ ἀγορανομοῦντος Δικαίου* (year 164 of the era of Gaza= A.D. 103/4).[81] Special tokens of favour appear to have been bestowed on the city by Hadrian during his stay in Palestine in A.D. 129/30.[82] On an

---

New Gaza, somewhat to the south of Old Gaza, is in particular attested by an anonymous geographical fragment (*Ἀποσπάσματά τινα γεωγραφικά*, ed. Hudson [in the appendix to his edition of Dionysius Periegetes, *Geographiae vet. scriptores Graeci minores* IV (1717)], p. 39: *μετὰ τὰ Ῥινοκόρουρα ἡ νέα Γάζα κεῖται πόλις οὖσα καὶ αὐτή, εἶθ' ἡ ἔρημος Γάζα, εἶτα ἡ Ἀσκάλων πόλις*, and by Jerome (*Onomast.*, ed. Klostermann, 63): 'antiquae civitatis locum vix fundamentorum praebere vestigia, hanc autem quae nunc cernitur, in alio loco pro illa, quae corruit, aedificatam'). But if the difference between Old and New Gaza is beyond doubt, it may also be assumed as most probable that the foundation of New Gaza is to be traced to Gabinius. For the complete destruction of Old Gaza did not occur, as Strabo seems to assume, at its conquest by Alexander the Great, but was due to Alexander Jannaeus. Both Old and New Gaza lay twenty stadia inland (see on Old Gaza, Arrian ii 26; on New Gaza, Sozomenus, *HE* v 3, 6–9; erroneously Strabo, xvi 2, 30 (759), seven stades; Antoninus Martyr, 33: one Roman mile); cf. however Smith, *loc. cit.*, arguing that the new city could have been on the site of the port (Maiumas, see below), supported by *BMC Palestine*, p. lxviii, noting that Maiumas on the Madaba mosaic map (only) is also called Neapolis. It is preferable to distinguish from both the port of Gaza, which remained the same in each case, *Γαζαίων λιμήν*—Strabo xvi 2, 30 (759); Ptolemy v 16, 2=Didot ed. (I. 2, 1901), v 15, 2. This port was raised to the status of a city under the name of *Κωνστάντια* by Constantine the Great (Eusebius, *VC* iv 38; Sozomenus *HE* ii 5, 7–8), but lost this name, together with the rights of a city, through Julian, and was afterwards called only *Μαϊουμᾶς* (=seaport town): see Sozomenus *HE* v 3, 6–9; *Marci Diaconi Vita Porphyrii*, 57 (Budé ed., by H. Grégoire and M.-A. Kugener, 1930); Jerome, *Vita Hilarionis* 3 (PL XXIII, col. 30); R. Raabe, *Petrus der Iberer* (1895), pp. 50–9; Antonius Martyr, *Itin.* 33/ *de locis sanctis* 33 (CCL clxxv, pp. 145/169); Stark, *Gaza*, p. 513; Kuhn, *op. cit.* II, p. 363; Guérin, *Judée* II, pp. 219–21; Thomsen, *Loca sancta*, p. 86.

78. F. de Saulcy, *op. cit.*, p. 213.

79. Mela i 11: 'in Palaestina est ingens et munita admodum Gaza'; cf. Pliny, *NH* v 12/65; 14/68; vi 32/144; xii 32/64 (on the overland spice trade).

80. F. de Saulcy, *op. cit.*, 214; cf. *BMC Palestine*, p. 145.

81. Reported by Clermont-Ganneau, PEFQSt, 1893, pp. 305 f.=*Archaeological Researches in Palestine* II, p. 399. On a similar lead weight, see Clermont-Ganneau, CRAI, 1898, pp. 606–9=*Recueil d'archéol. orientale* III, pp. 82–6. It bears the year number 86, which according to the era of Gaza=A.D. 25/26. But the character of the script suggests an earlier date.

82. For Hadrian's visit see vol. I, p. 541. The coins of Hadrian's time have a new Hadrianic era as well as the usual city era. Also, *Chronicon paschale* (ed.

inscription from the time of Gordian (A.D. 238–44) it is described as ἱερὰ καὶ ἄσυλος καὶ αὐτόνομος.[83] It must subsequently have become a Roman colony.[84] Eusebius refers to it as a πόλις ἐπίσημος.[85] And this it remained up to and beyond the moment of the Arab conquest in the seventh century.[86] The independence of these great cities is perhaps most strikingly shown by the fact that Gaza, as well as Ascalon, Tyre and Sidon, had its own calendar.[87] But Greek culture did not penetrate through to every level of the population. In around A.D. 400, the humbler people were still speaking Syriac (see p. 75 above).

Dindorf, p. 474) mentions a πανήγυρις Ἀδριανή celebrated from the time of Hadrian; see generally, Stark, *Gaza*, p. 550. Note the inscription of M. Aelius Menander) a famous pancratiast of the mid-second century, who had been victorious *int. al.* in the pancration at Gaza, Le Bas-Waddington, *Inscriptions*, no. 1620=L. Moretti, *Iscrizioni agonistiche greche* (1953), no. 72.

83. CIG 5892=IG XIV 926=IGR I 387. Cf. Stark, *Gaza*, pp. 554 f. On the title, see above p. 94.

84. Le Bas-Waddington, *Inscriptions*, no. 1904: Κολωνίας Γάζης. The mention of a *Gazensis duumvir* by Jerome, *Vita Hilarionis*, 20 (PL XXIII, col. 36) also points to a Roman colonial constitution; cf. Marquardt, *Röm. Staatsverwaltung* I, p. 429. On the *duoviri* generally, see W. Liebenam in RE V, cols. 1804–41. The date of the acquisition of the title *colonia* is uncertain. The period between Gordian and Constantine is suggested in the detailed discussion by W. Kubitschek, *Zur Geschichte von Städten des römischen Kaiserreiches*, SAW 177.4 (1916), on pp. 31–40.

85. Eusebius, *Onomast.*, ed. Klostermann, p. 62; note the references to Gaza in papyri relating to a journey made in A.D. 317–23, *P. Ryl.* 627, ll. 237–8, 264; 628, ll.12–13; 638, ll.22–3.

86. Antoninus Martyr (about A.D. 570), *Itinerarium* or *De locis sanctis*, 33 (ed. Gildemeister, 1889; CCL clxxv, 1965): 'Gaza autem civitas splendida deliciosa, homines honestissimi omni liberalitate decori, amatores peregrinorum'. For Christian Gaza see especially the Budé ed. of Marcus Diaconus' Life of Porphyry, H. Grégoire, M.-A. Kugener, *Marc le Diacre, vie de Porphyre évêque de Gaza* (1930), and RAC s.v. 'Gaza'. Note also the reflections of the importance of Gaza in the Nessana papyri of the sixth and seventh centuries, C. J. Kraemer, *Excavations at Nessana* Vol. III: *Non-literary Papyri* (1958), index s.v. on p. 341. Note A. Ovadiah, 'Les mosaïstes de Gaza dans l'Antiquité chrétienne', RB 82 (1975), pp. 552–7.

87. See generally L. Ideler, *Handbuch der Chronologie* I, pp. 410 f., 434 f., 438 f.; E. Schwartz, NGG (1906), pp. 342–5; Stark, *Gaza*, pp. 517 f. Valuable material on the calendar and era of Gaza is provided by the Christian epitaphs found there from the sixth century A.D. (Cf. C. Clermont-Ganneau, *Archaeological Researches in Palestine* II (1896), pp. 400–29). They confirm throughout the information derived from the Hemerologium romanum, from MSS. in Florence and Leiden, see W. Kubitschek, *Die Kalenderbücher von Florenz, Rom und Leyden*, AAW LVII.3 (1915), and in general A. E. Samuel, *Greek and Roman Chronology* (1972), pp. 171–8. Calendars of Gaza and Askalon on p. 177. The Christian epitaphs use the Gazan era, starting in autumn 61 B.C., the Gazan calendar of 12 Macedonian months with extra days at the end of the year, starting on August 29, and also the 15-year indiction cycle starting in autumn A.D. 312. So also do a number of the papyri from Nessana (n. 86 above); see e.g. P. Nessana 45 (A.D. 602), cf. 55 (A.D. 682).

3. Anthedon, *'Ανθηδών*, though erroneously designated by Pliny as an inland town, was situated by the sea;[88] according to Sozomenus, it lay only 20 stades from Gaza, probably in a northerly (north-westerly) direction.[89] It is clear from its name that it was a Hellenistic foundation. The city is first mentioned in the period of Alexander Jannaeus, who conquered it at about the same time as Raphia, Josephus, *Ant.* xiii 13, 3 (357); *B.J.* i 4, 2 (87); cf. *Ant.* xiii 15, 4 (395). Like all the coastal towns, it will have been taken from the Jews by Pompey. Gabinius rebuilt it, *Ant.* xiv 5, 3 (88); *B.J.* i 8, 4 (164). Augustus presented it to Herod, *Ant.* xv 7, 3 (217); *B.J.* i 20, 3 (396), who restored it and named it Agrippias or Agrippeion in honour of M. Agrippa, *Ant.* xiii 13, 3 (357); *B.J.* i 4, 2 (87), 21 8 (416). It was not explicitly mentioned in the partition of Herod's kingdom. It is therefore uncertain whether, like the neighbouring Gaza, it was annexed to Syria, or whether it was transferred to Archelaus, like Joppa and Caesarea. In the latter case, it would have shared the fate of the rest of Judaea, coming under Roman governors after the deposition of Archelaus, and under King Agrippa from A.D. 41–4. The alleged existence of a coin of Anthedon bearing the name of Agrippa would provide evidence of the second event if the reading were certain.

At the onset of the Jewish war, Anthedon was attacked and partly destroyed by the revolutionaries, *B.J.* ii 18, 1 (460).

The name Agrippias never became established; not only Josephus, but also all later authors, call it Anthedon.[90] On coins, too, the name Anthedon predominates and the occurrence of Agrippias is uncertain.[91]

88. Pliny, *NH* v 13/68: 'intus Anthedon'. But from the unanimous testimony of all other authors it may be taken as certain that it was located on the coast; see Josephus, *Ant.* xiii 15, 4 (396); xviii 6, 3 (158); *B.J.* i 21, 8 (416); Ptolemy v 16, 2=Didot ed. (I.2, 1901) v 15, 2; Stephanus Byz., s.v.; Sozomenus, *HE* v 9, 7–8. Cf. generally, RE I, col. 2360 s.v.; *BMC Palestine*, pp. xlv–vii; 103; Abel, *Géog. Pal.*, pp. 244–5.

89. Sozomenus, *HE* v 9, 7. Following Josephus, *Ant.* xiii 15, 4 (396). Anthedon used sometimes to be placed south of Gaza. But most of the Josephus passages speak of it as lying north of Gaza, *Ant.* xv 7, 3 (217); *B.J.* i 4, 2 (87); 20, 3 (396); ii 18, 1 (460); so too Pliny, *NH* v 13/68. Decisive is the statement of Theodosius that it lay between Gaza and Ascalon: see Theodosius, *De situ terrae sanctae*, ed. Geyer, *Itinera Hierosolymitana* (1898), p. 138=CCL clxxv, p. 166: 'inter Ascalonam et Gazam civitates duas, id est Antedona et Maioma'. For a report of the site see W. J. Phythian-Adams, PEFQSt 1923, pp. 14–17.

90. So Pliny, Ptolemy, Stephanus Byz., Sozomenus in the passages cited; Hierocles, *Synecd.*, p. 44; the Acts of the Councils in R. Le Quien, *Oriens christianus* III (1740), p. 631.

91. F. de Saulcy, *Numismatique de la Terre Sainte*, pp. 234–6, pl. XII, no. 1–4; *BMC Palestine*, p. xlvi. Jones, CERP², p. 449, suggests that Anthedon represents the Semitic 'Ain Teda. Its present name is Khirbet Teda, see Avi-Yonah, *Holy Land*, p. 100; Enc. Jud. 3, col. 37.

4. Ascalon, Ἀσκαλών, Hebrew אשקלון, was like Gaza an important city of the Philistines; it is repeatedly mentioned in the Amarna Tablets[92] and in the Old Testament, and was known to Herodotus.[93] Today it lies close to the sea; Ptolemy also refers to it as a coastal town.[94] The results of excavations leave no doubt as to the identification. Nonetheless, writers of the sixth century A.D. distinguish 'Ascalon' and 'Maiuma Ascalonis' (port of Ascalon),[95] and it used to be suggested that the Arab village el-Mejdel (Migdal-Gad) rests on the site of the ancient city.[96]

In the Persian period, Ascalon belonged to Tyre.[97] Coins of Alexander

92. See *The Tell el-Amarna Tablets*, ed. Mercer and Hallock (1939), pp. 710, 719, 893, 896; Y. Aharoni, *The Land of the Bible* (1967), *passim*.

93. Herodotus, i 105. See generally RE s.v. 'Askalon'; G. A. Smith, *Historical Geography of the Holy Land*, pp. 189–92; Vigouroux, DB I, cols. 1060–9. W. J. Phythian-Adams, 'History of Askalon', PEFQSt 1921, pp. 76–90; *BMC Palestine*, pp. xlviii–lxiv; DB Supp. I, cols, 621–8; Abel, *Géog. Pal.* II, pp. 252–3; U. Rappoport, 'Gaza and Ascalon in the Persian and Hellenistic Periods in Relation to their Coins', IEJ 20 (1970), pp. 75–80; EAEHL I, pp. 121–30. For rabbinic material, see A. Büchler, 'Der Patriarch R. Jehuda I. und die griechisch-römischen Städte Palästinas', JQR 13 (1901), pp. 683–740 [E.T. *Studies in Jewish History* (1956), pp. 179–244]; P. S. Alexander, *The Toponymy of Targumim* . . . (Oxford Diss. 1974), pp. 237–46.

94. Ptolemy, v 16, 2=ed. Didot (1, 2, 1901) v 15, 2.

95. Antoninus Martyr, 33; ed. Geyer, *Itinera Hierosol*, p. 180; CCL clxxv, pp. 145 (cf. Itinerarium, p. 169, 'Maioma Ascalonites'): 'Ascalona . . . civitas Maioma Ascalonitis'. In A.D. 518 a bishop of Ascalon and a bishop of Maiuma Ascalonis are mentioned as contemporaries; see R. Le Quien, *Oriens christ.* III (1740), pp. 601–2; Kuhn, *op. cit.* II, p. 363.

96. Thus Clermont-Ganneau, CRAI, 1895, pp. 380 f., and especially *Études d'archéologie orientale* II (1897), pp. 2–9, on the basis of a passage in the Biography of Petrus of Iberia, ed. R. Raabe (1895), Syriac text, p. 77; German translation, p. 75. A place is mentioned here called פאלאא or פלאא, 10 stadia from Ascalon. Clermont-Ganneau read this as Peleia (the dove) and identified it with the place-name Hamâmé (Arabic=the dove). According to this theory the site of ancient Ascalon would not be the modern town of that name, which is over a mile from Hamâmé, but el-Mejdel. However, excavations, including those of the council-chamber *(βουλευτήριον)*, leave no doubt as to the identification, see EAEHL s.v. and Vogel, 'Bibliography' s.v. Note especially D. G. Hogarth, 'Greek Inscriptions from Askalon', PEFQSt (1922), pp. 22–3=SEG I, nos. 552–4. Two are dedications by council and people, and the third reads *Αὐξ. Ἀσκάλ[ων], Αὐξ. Ῥώμη*.

97. Ps.-Scylax in *Geographi graeci minores* (ed. Müller), p. 79: *Ἀσκάλων πόλις Τυρίων καὶ βασίλεια*. J. Mövers, *Die Phönizier* II. 2, pp. 177 f., referred this statement exclusively to the harbour of Ascalon (Maiuma Ascalonis), which he considered to have been a Tyrian foundation. But it is far more likely that during the Persian period (to which the statements of Ps.-Scylax refer) Ascalon was under the rule of the Tyrians, just as Joppa and Dora were under that of the Sidonians (see below, on Joppa and Dora). Thus also A. von Gutschmid, *Kleine Schriften* II (1890), p. 77, and G. Hölscher, *Palästina in der persischen und hellenistischen Zeit* (1903), pp. 15 f., who assumes that Ascalon was given to the Tyrians by the Persian king. Tyrian possession of Ascalon is generally accepted, see e.g. K.

the Great may have been minted there, but the attribution is highly questionable.[98] During the third century B.C., it came, together with the whole of Palestine and Phoenicia, under the rule of the Ptolemies and therefore had to pay them annual tribute.[99] With Antiochus III, the city became subject to the Seleucids, as is also attested by Seleucid coins from this city dating from Antiochus III to Antiochus IX.[100] Ascalon was able to protect itself against the increasing Jewish power by prudent concessions. Jonathan Maccabaeus marched twice against the city, but on each occasion he was pacified by a respectful welcome on the part of the inhabitants.[101] Ascalon is also the only coastal town to have remained unmolested by Alexander Jannaeus. In 104/3 B.C., it seems to have gained its independence and began a new era of its own which it continued to use even in the Roman imperial period.[102] The Romans subsequently seem to have acknowledged its independence, formally at least.[103] The coins attesting the era from 104/3 B.C., usually have the inscription Ἀσκαλωνιτῶν ἱερᾶς ἀσύλου, while some add *αὐτο(νόμου)* or *αὐτονό(μου)* as an assertion of the independence of the city. Some of the autonomous coins bear either (a) the head of one of the later Ptolemies, or (b) the head of Antonius, or (c) the head of the last Cleopatra. They mark the town's respect for the Egyptian rulers of the

---

Galling, *Studien zur Geschichte Israels im persischen Zeitalter* (1964), pp. 200–1; Rappoport, *op. cit.* (in n. 93).

98. *BMC Palestine*, p. iii.

99. For Josephus's account, *Ant.* xii 4, 5 (181), the original version of which probably belongs to this period, see p. 89 above. It is not mentioned in the surviving papyri of the Zenon archive. But note the reference to its harbour in the *Letter of Aristeas* (ed. Wendland) 115, set in the reign of Ptolemy Philadelphus (285–46 B.C.).

100. See A. B. Brett, 'The Mint of Ascalon under the Seleucids', Am. Num. Soc., Mus. Notes 4 (1950), pp. 43–54; cf. O. Mørkholm, *Antiochus IV of Syria* (1966), p. 127.

101. 1 Mac. 10:86 and 11:60; cf. Stark, *Gaza*, pp. 490 f., 492.

102. On the era from 104/3, see *Chron. pascale*, on Ol. 169, 1 = 104/3 B.C. (ed. Dindorf, I, p. 346): Ἀσκαλωνῖται τοὺς ἑαυτῶν χρόνους ἐντεῦθεν ἀριθμοῦσιν. Jerome, *Chron. ad ann. Abrah.* 2295 (in Eusebius, *Chron.*, ed. Schoene II, p. 185, ed. Helm, p. 223): the 2nd year of Probus (A.D. 277) = 380 of the era of Ascalon. Cf. Ideler, *Handbuch der Chronologie* I, pp. 473 f.; Stark, *Gaza*, pp. 475 f. A papyrus found in Egypt concerning the purchase of a slave in Ascalon (reported by Wilcken in Hermes 19 (1884), pp. 417–31 = BGU 316) confirms earlier data on the era of that city. The document is dated according to the consuls for A.D. 359, Fl. Eusebius and Fl. Hypatius, from the 12 October of that year; it also bears the date (ll. 3–4) ἔτους δευτέρου ἑξηκοστοῦ τετρακοσιοστο[ῦ τοῦ μ]ηνὸς Γορπαίου δι'. The year 462 of the era of Ascalon is in fact A.D. 358/9; and the month of Gorpiaios is the last month of the Ascalonian year, roughly corresponding to October. For further details on the calendar of Ascalon, see L. Ideler, *Handbuch der Chronologie* I ([2]1883), pp. 410 f., 438 f.; Mommsen, Hermes, *loc. cit.*, pp. 420 f.; E. Schwartz, NGG (1906), pp. 342–5; A. E. Samuel, *Greek and Roman Chronology* (1972), p. 177.

103. Pliny, *NH* v 13/68: 'oppidum Ascalo liberum'.

time, perhaps as a result of the intervention of Ptolemy X Lathyrus against Alexander Jannaeus in 103 B.C., and later for the queen to whom Antonius eventually granted most of the Philistine-Phoenician coast as her own property (see above, p. 92).[104] Ascalon, however, is never mentioned as being attached to Syria by Pompey, presented to Cleopatra or incorporated in Herod's kingdom, though Herod probably adorned it with public buildings.[105] He also appears to have possessed a palace there, which after his death passed to his sister Salome.[106] In view of the ancient enmity between Jews and Ascalonites the outbreak of the war in A.D. 66 was fateful for both parties. First, Ascalon was destroyed by the Jews,[107] whereupon the Ascalonites massacred the two and a half thousand Jews living in their city.[108] Finally, the rebels attacked yet again, but this was easily repulsed by the local Roman garrison.[109] Ascalon retained its freedom in the later period of the Caesars, though auxiliary units of Ascalonites are attested as having been in existence at that time;[110] in the fourth century, the city was a Roman colony.[111] It remained for long a flourishing Greek city, famed for its religious cults and festival games.[112] Various individuals renowned in Greek literature were natives of the town,[113] in particular the

104. For the dating of the coinage of Ascalon with portraits of the late Ptolemies and Cleopatra, see A. B. Brett, 'A New Cleopatra Tetradrachm of Ascalon', AJA 41 (1937), pp. 452–63; de Saulcy, *Numismatique de la Terre Sainte*, p. 190, no. 9, reports a coin of Ascalon with a double era-reckoning, 56 and 102. If the latter relates to the era of 104/3, the former will give 58/7, a possible era of Gabinius. But subsequent examples do not seem to have been reported.

105. Josephus, *B.J.* i 21, 11 (422). For the archaeological remains of Ascalon, see EAEHL s.v.

106. Josephus, *Ant.* xvii 11, 5 (321): *B.J.* ii 6, 3 (98). Cf. Stark, *Gaza*, p. 542. On the question whether Herod came from Ascalon, see vol. I, p. 234, n. 3.

107. Josephus, *B.J.* ii 18, 1 (460).

108. Josephus, *B.J.* ii 18, 5 (477).

109. Josephus, *B.J.* iii 2, 1–3 (9–28). On the hostility of the Ascalonites towards the Jews, see also Philo, *Legat.* 30 (205).

110. (1) *Cohors I Ascalonitanorum*, CIL III 600 = ILS 2724, probably under Hadrian. (2) [*Coh. I?*] *Ascalonitana*, of the time of Tiberius, CIL IX 3664. (3) *Coh. I Ascalonit(anorum) sag(ittariorum)*, as a part of the Syrian army on discharge diplomas of A.D. 88 and 157, CIL XVI 35; 106; AE 1939 126.

111. Papyrus document from A.D. 359 (n. 102, above), 11, 2–3: *ἐν κολωνίᾳ Ἀσκ[άλωνι] τῇ πιστῇ καὶ ἐλευθέρᾳ*. See W. Kubitschek, *Zur Geschichte von Städten des römischen Kaiserreiches* SAW 177.4 (1916), pp. 97–112, explaining the anomalous retention of *ἐλευθέρα* as a product of local pride in the city's history.

112. Note the boxer of the early third century A.D. who was victorious at Ascalon, IGR III 1012 = L. Moretti, *Iscrizioni agonistiche greche* (1953), no. 85.

113. Stephanus Byz. s.v., lists four philosophers, two grammarians and two historians from Ascalon: and the catalogue is not complete, see above, p. 49. On Stephanus' list see Hengel, *Judaism and Hellenism*, pp. 86–7. An actor from Ascalon named Apelles at the court of Caligula is mentioned in Philo, *Leg.* 30 (203–6).

prominent philosopher of the first century B.C., Antiochus of Ascalon. Despite its Hellenistic civilization, however, the humbler members of the population seem to have retained Aramaic culture and nomenclature.[114]

Much information on the importance of Ascalon as a trading city in the Hellenistic period emerges from inscriptions. Merchants from Ascalon are attested in Athens by the third century B.C., and later also in Delos, Rhodes, and Puteoli.[115] In the fourth century A.D., it was one of the most flourishing cities in Palestine and is still mentioned in the sixth and seventh centuries.[116]

5. Azotus, *Ἄζωτος* or Ashdod (Hebrew אשדוד), like Gaza and Ascalon, was an ancient Philistine city frequently mentioned in the Old Testament and known to Herodotus.[117] Ptolemy refers to it as a coastal town,[118] and in the works of Josephus it appears sometimes as a coastal and sometimes as an inland city.[119] The latter description is more accurate as it lay, like the Arab village of Isdud, about three miles from the sea, which is why in Christian times *Ἄζωτος παράλιος*,

114. A soldier of the 8th praetorian cohort from Ascalon, and with a genuine Semitic name, appears on an inscription in Rome. CIG 6416 = IG XIV 1661 = IGR I 266 = Moretti, IGUR 590: *Ἰαμοὺρ Ἀσάμου Σύρος Ἀσκαλωνείτης Παλαιστείνῃ, ἀδελφὸς Ἀντωνείνου, στρατιώτης χόρ(της) η΄ πρ(αιτωρίας)*. The name Yamur is also found on a Nabataean inscription (in the form יעמרו = CIS, P.II, Aram. no. 195) and frequently in Arabic. The Greek *Ἰάμαρος* appears on inscriptions in the Hauran (*Nouvelles archives des missions scientifiques* 10 (1902), pp. 685 f., nos. 126, 131, 132). Against the reading proposed by Clermont-Ganneau, *Rec. d'arch. or.* III, pp. 347 f.: *Ἰαμούρας Ἄμου*, see M. Lidzbarski, *Eph. sem. Epig.* I, p. 216.

115. Athens: Grave-relief of Antipatros of Ascalon, CIS I, no. 115 = Cooke, *Hand-book of North-Semitic Inscriptions*, no. 32 = IG II² 8388 (early third century B.C.); cf. also 8389–90; and an Ascalonite in a list of ephebes in 100/99 B.C., IG II² 1028, l.148. Delos: see P. Bruneau, *Recherches sur les cultes de Délos* (1970), p. 474; Rhodes: IG XII 118; A. Maiuri, *Nuova silloge epigrafica di Rodi e Cos* (1925), nos. 161–2, 175, Puteoli: CIL X 1746.

116. See Ammianus Marcellinus xiv 8, 11, and the papyrus references of A.D. 317–23 (*P. Ryl.* 627–8; 630; 638), and an allusion in *P. Nessana* 160 (sixth and seventh century). For its churches see EAEHL s.v. Cf. 'Gazetteer', s.v. 'Ascalon'.

117. Herodotus ii 157. See Guérin, *Judée* II, pp. 70–8; for Ashdod in the biblical period see Y. Aharoni, *The Land of the Bible* (1967), *passim*; Abel, *Géog. Pal.* II, pp. 253–4; Avi-Yonah, *Holy Land*, pp. 149–50. Note the spelling *Ἀσζωτ(ίς)* on an epitaph in Rhodes, IG XII 406. Cf. *BMC Palestine*, pp. lxiv–v, noting that no coins can be surely attributed to Azotus. For excavations of the site of (inland) Ashdod, mainly concerned with the pre-Hellenistic period, see M. Dothan, D. N. Freedman, *Ashdod* I–III (1967–71) ('Atiqot, Eng. ser. 7, 9–10); cf. EAEHL s.v.

118. Ptolemy v 16, 2 = ed. Didot (I. 2, 1901), v 15, 2.

119. As a coastal town: *Ant.* xiii 15, 4 (395); as an inland town; *Ant.* xiv 4, 4 (75); *B.J.* i 7, 7 (156). Cf. Kuhn, *op. cit.* II, pp. 362, 364.

the harbour, is distinguished from Ἄζωτος μεσόγειος.[120] The territory of Azotus is mentioned several times in Maccabees but no certain indication is given as to its size.[121] Nothing is known in detail of the fate of the city under the Ptolemies and Seleucids. At the time of the Maccabaean rising, it was unable to hold its own against Jewish supremacy. Judas destroyed its altars and images (1 Mac. 5:68). But Jonathan burned down the entire city, including its temple of Dagon (1 Mac. 10:84; 11:4). At the time of Alexander Jannaeus, Azotus, or rather its ruins, formed part of Jewish territory, Josephus, *Ant.* xiii 15, 4 (395). Pompey separated it once more, and granted it freedom, *Ant.* xiv 4, 4 (75); *B.J.* i 7, 7 (156). But it was left for Gabinius to restore it, *Ant.* xiv 5, 3 (88); *B.J.* i 8, 4 (166). Together with the other coastal cities, it presumably came under Herod's dominion in 30 B.C., and after his death passed to his sister Salome, *Ant.* xvii 8, 1 (189); *B.J.* ii 6, 3 (98). Whether it then, like Jamnia, became the possession of the Empress Livia after Salome died, is not quite certain because Azotus is not explicitly named, *Ant.* xviii 2, 2 (31); *B.J.* ii 9, 1 (167). The city probably contained a considerable proportion of Jewish inhabitants, which would account for Vespasian feeling obliged to establish a garrison there during the war, *B.J.* iv 3, 2 (130). No coins of Azotus from the Roman period have come to light.

6. Jamnia, Ἰάμνεα, in the Old Testament Yavneh, יבנה (2 Chron. 26:6), under which name it appears frequently in rabbinic literature.[122] Jamnia like Azotus is also sometimes described by Josephus as a coastal town and sometimes as an inland city.[123] It lay at a considerable distance from the sea, but possessed a harbour. The two are correctly distinguished by Pliny and Ptolemy.[124] It is expressly attested that

120. Hierocles, *Synecdemus*, ed. Parthey (1866), p. 43. Also on the mosaic map of Madaba Ἄζωτος πάραλο[ς] appears next to Ἀσδω[δ ἡ νῦν καὶ Ἄζωτος]; see M. Avi-Yonah, *The Madaba Mosaic Map* (1954), p. 70.

121. 1 Mac. 14:34; 16:10. Cf. Aristeas 117: τὴν Ἀζωτίων χώραν. For its territory as attested in late-Roman sources, see Avi-Yonah, *Holy Land*, pp. 149–50.

122. mShek. 1:4; mR.Sh. 2:8–9; 4:1–2; mKet. 4:6; mSanh. 11:4; mEdu. 2:4; mAb. 4:4; mBekh. 4:5; 6:8; mKel. 5:4; mPar. 7:6. For the Tosefta passages, see the index to Zuckermandel's edition. Cf. A. Neubauer, *La Géographie du Talmud* (1868), pp. 73–6; S. Klein (ed.), *Sefer ha-Yishuv* I (1939), pp. 74–7; G. Alon, *Studies in Jewish History* I ([2]1967), pp. 219–52 (Hebrew); [E.T. *Jews, Judaism* . . . pp. 269–313].

123. As a coastal town: *Ant.* xiii 15, 4 (395). As an inland town: *Ant.* xiv 4, 4 (75); *B.J.* i 7, 7 (156); cf. Kuhn, *op. cit.* II, pp. 362 f.

124. Pliny, *NH* v 13/68: 'Iamneae duae, altera intus'; Ptolemy v 16, 2 = ed. Didot (I, 2, 1901) v 15, 2: Ἰαμνιτῶν λιμήν; v 16, 6 = Didot, v 15, 5: Ἰάμνια. See generally: Guérin, *Judée* II, pp. 53–65; Clermont-Ganneau, *Archaeological Researches in Palestine* II (1896), pp. 167–84; DB s.v. 'Jamnia'; Abel, *Géog. Pal.*, pp. 352–3; Avi-Yonah, *Holy Land*, p. 147; Enc. Jud. 9, cols. 1176–8; 'Gazetteer' s.v. 'Jamnia'.

Jamnia possessed a territory of its own.[125] According to Strabo, it was once so thickly populated that the city and its neighbourhood could provide forty thousand fighting men.[126] At the time of the Maccabees, Jamnia—according to 2 Mac.—was attacked by Judas and its harbour, together with the fleet, set on fire.[127] Nevertheless the town itself did not fall into Jewish hands either then, or, as Josephus asserts, under Simon.[128] It did not become part of Jewish territory until the time of Alexander Jannaeus, *Ant.* xiii 15, 4 (395). Pompey separated it from the Jewish realm, *Ant.* xiv 4, 4 (75); *B.J.* i 7, 7 (156). Gabinius rebuilt it, *B.J.* i 8, 4 (166). Like Azotus, Jamnia must also have belonged to Herod since it was bequeathed by him to his sister Salome, *Ant.* xvii 8, 1 (189); 11, 5 (321); *B.J.* ii 6, 3 (98). From Salome it passed to the Empress Livia, *Ant.* xviii 2, 2 (31); *B.J.* ii 9, 1 (167); after her death it seems to have become a private possession of Tiberius, *Ant.* xviii 6, 3 (158); (see above, p. 92). The population was then a mixed one of Jews and Gentiles, but with the Jewish element preponderating.[129] This would explain why Vespasian was twice compelled to garrison the city,[130] and why, soon after the destruction of Jerusalem, Jamnia became a centre of Jewish learning.[131]

7. Joppa, *'Ιόπη* or *'Ιόππη*,[132] (Hebrew יפו),[133] the present-day Jaffa (now adjoining Tel-Aviv), appears already in the Amarna Tablets as

125. Josephus, *B.J.* iii 3, 5 (56); *'Ιάμνεια καὶ 'Ιόπη τῶν περιοίκων ἀφηγοῦνται.*

126. Strabo, xvi 2, 28 (759). Admittedly, Strabo mistakenly calls Jamnia a *κώμη* here.

127. 2 Mac. 12, 8 f., 40. Cf. Stark, *Gaza*, p. 487.

128. Josephus, *Ant.* xiii 6, 7 (215); *B.J.* i 2, 2 (50). See on the other hand, 1 Mac. 10:69; 15:40.

129. Philo, *Legat.* 30 (200–3): *[ταύτην] μιγάδες οἰκοῦσιν, οἱ πλείους μὲν 'Ιουδαῖοι, ἕτεροι δέ τινες ἀλλόφυλοι παρεισφθαρέντες ἀπὸ τῶν πλησιοχώρων, οἱ τοῖς τρόπον τινὰ αὐθιγενέσιν ὄντες μέτοικοι κακὰ καὶ πράγματα παρέχουσιν, ἀεί τι παραλύοντες τῶν πατρίων 'Ιουδαίοις.* By assigining to the Jews the role of natives, and to the Gentiles that of *metoikoi*, Philo of course reverses the true situation. For Jamnia was a predominantly Gentile city even in the Maccabaean period. The Jewish element did not increase until later.

130. Josephus, *B.J.* iv 3, 2 (130); 8, 1 (444).

131. Cf. vol. I, pp. 525–6.

132. The orthography varies. In the texts of Greek and Roman authors, the editors tend to prefer the form *'Ιόπη* required by Greek grammarians (see J. Mövers, *Phönizier* II, 2, p. 176, n. 74) and attested by the usage of poets (Alexander Ephesius in Stephanus Byz, ed. Meineke, p. 255: *Δῶρός τ' ἀγχιαλός τ' 'Ιόπη προύχουσα θαλάσσης;* also Dionysius Perieg., in Müller, *Geogr. gr. min.* II, p. 160: *οἵτ' 'Ιόπην καὶ Γάζαν 'Ελαΐδα τ' ἐνναίουσι*). The biblical manuscripts, on the other hand, seem always to have *'Ιόππη*, whether in the Greek Old or the New Testament (so 1 Mac. and Acts). The Josephus manuscripts also normally have *'Ιόππη*; see Niese's ed. and A. Schalit, *Namenwörterbuch zu Flavius Josephus* (1968), p. 61. The few coins that have come to light sometimes show one form and sometimes the other. On inscriptions *'Ιόππη* occurs (OGIS 602 = Frey, CIJ no. 953) and *'Ιοπίτ(ης)*, IG II^2

Iapu.[134] Its special importance resided in its having possessed relatively the best harbour on the Palestinian coast.[135] It was therefore at almost all times the main port of disembarkation for commerce with the interior of Judaea, and with the growth of trade in later times its possession was a matter of vital importance for the Jews.

In the Persian period, during the reign of the Sidonian king Eshmunazar, Joppa was granted to the Sidonians by the 'Lord of kings', i.e., the Persian ruler.[136] To the Greeks it was chiefly known as the scene of the myth of Perseus and Andromeda and is mentioned by Ps.-Scylax even before the age of Alexander (see above, p. 33). In the period of the Diadochi it seems to have been an important strongpoint. When Antigonus took Coele Syria from Ptolemy Lagus in 315 B.C., he was obliged to capture Joppa and other places by force.[137] And when three years later (312 B.C.) Ptolemy Lagus thought that he could not hold the reconquered territory against Antigonus, he razed Joppa as he withdrew, regarding it as one of the more important fortresses.[138] A number of coins exist of Ptolemy II and III minted in Joppa. The dated coins of Ptolemy II with the monogram of Joppa range from the twenty-third to the thirty-ninth year of his reign (263–47 B.C.); those of Ptolemy III, from the second to the sixth year of his reign (245–41 B.C.).[139] In Maccabaean times, the efforts of the Jews were above

---

8938 and SEG XXV 275 (Athens); *Εἰοπιτῶν*, in SEG VIII 140 (Jerusalem); *Ἰόπη* on papyri, PSI 406; P. Cairo Zen. 14, P. Lond, 2086, all mid-third century B.C. The Greek *Ἰόπη* is related to יפו as *Ἄκη* is to עכו. But it might also derive from יפי, the form of the name given on the inscription of Eshmunazar; see Cooke, *Text-book of North-Semitic Inscriptions* (1903), no. 5 = KAI no. 44.

133. Jos. 19:46; Jon. 1:3; 2 Chr. 2:15; Ezr. 3:7; mNed. 3:6; tDem. 1:11; tYom. 2:4. Cf. A. Neubauer, *La géographie du Talmud*, pp. 81–2; Enc. Jud. 9, cols. 1250–1.

134. *The Tell el-Amarna Tablets*, ed. Mercer and Hallock II (1939), pp. 457, 893.

135. Josephus, *B.J.* iii 9, 3 (421) admittedly describes the harbour as dangerous, but it must have been relatively the best. According to Diodorus i 31, 2 there was only one safe harbour *(ἀσφαλῆ λιμένα)* from Paraetonium in Libya to Joppa in Coele Syria, namely, the Pharos of Alexandria. Strabo xvi 2, 28 (759), also emphasizes the importance of Joppa as a port for Judea; cf. 1 Mac. 14:5. In general see Guérin, *Judée* I, pp. 1–22; *BMC Palestine*, pp. xxiv–v; S. Tolkowsky, *The Gateway of Palestine: a History of Jaffa* (1924); Abel, *Géog. Pal.* II, pp. 355–6; Avi-Yonah, *Holy Land*, p. 147; for excavations see Vogel, 'Bibliography' s.v. 'Jaffa'; EAEHL s.v. 'Jaffa'; 'Gazetteer' s.v. 'Joppa', and the sketch by J. Kaplan, 'Jaffa's History revealed by the Spade', Archaeology 17 (1964), pp. 270–6 = *Archaeological Discoveries in the Holy Land* (1967), pp. 113–8.

136. See the inscription of Eshmunazar; the standard text is CIS I, 9–20, ll.18–20 = Cooke, *Text-book of North-Semitic Inscriptions* no. 5 = KAI no. 14.

137. Diodorus xix 59, 2.

138. Diodorus xix 93, 7.

139. *BMC Ptolemies, Kings of Egypt*, pp. 32, 34, 35, 42, 49, 54; J. N. Svoronos, 'Les monnaies de Ptolemée II, qui portent dates' in Rev. Belge. de Num. (1901),

all directed towards gaining possession of the city. Judas Maccabaeus, if the report is at all trustworthy, only destroyed the harbour and fleet by fire during a night attack (2 Mac. 12:3–7). Jonathan, too, did not definitively conquer the city in 147 or 146 B.C., but as an ally of Alexander Balas merely expelled the garrison of Demetrius II (1 Mac. 10:75–6). But a few years later, when Jonathan fought in alliance with Tryphon against Demetrius II and the inhabitants threatened to bring in troops of Demetrius, Simon, the brother of Jonathan, established a Jewish garrison there (1 Mac. 12:33, 34) and soon afterwards forced the Gentile inhabitants to vacate the city (1 Mac. 13:11: *ἐξέβαλε τοὺς ὄντας ἐν αὐτῇ*).[140] Thus the seizure and Judaizing of Joppa, which remained with little interruption in Jewish possession until the time of Pompey, dates from then. Simon improved the harbour and fortified the town (1 Mac. 14:5, 34). When the energetic Antiochus VII Sidetes endeavoured to reduce the power of the Jews, Joppa became a major bone of contention. Even while Antiochus was battling with Tryphon, he demanded from Simon the surrender of the city (1 Mac. 15:28–30) or the payment of a large indemnity (15:31). Simon, however, declared himself ready to pay only a considerably smaller amount (1 Mac. 15:35). Since some years later, at the beginning of the reign of John Hyrcanus, the whole of Palestine was conquered by Antiochus and even Jerusalem was besieged, it is probable that Joppa too had already been taken by him. Nevertheless, when peace was concluded he contented himself with the payment of a tribute for the city, *Ant.* xiii 8, 3 (246).[141] It therefore remained a Jewish domain and in the course of time even the tribute ceased to be paid. The possession of Joppa by Alexander Jannaeus is attested explicitly, *Ant.* xiii 15, 4 (395).[142] But this coastal city too was

---

pp. 263 ff., 387 ff. (Joppa: pp. 282–5); the most complete: *idem*, *Τὰ νομίσματα τοῦ κράτους τῶν Πτολεμαίων* II (1904), pp. 119–121 (Ptolemy II); p. 164 (Ptolemy III). Note the inscription in honour of Ptolemy IV Philopator and his wife Berenice found in Joppa, B. Lifshitz, ZDPV 78 (1962), pp. 82–4=SEG XX 467.

140. Josephus, *Ant.* xiii 6, 4 (202), correctly renders *τοὺς ὄντας ἐν αὐτῇ* as *τοὺς οἰκήτορας*. Cf. Stark, *Gaza*, pp. 493 f.; cf. Abel on 1 Mac. 13:11. A similar procedure was adopted against Gazara, 1 Mac. 13: 47–8; 14:34.

141. The seizure of Joppa by an Antiochus is also presupposed in two decrees issued by the Roman senate, the second of which commands him to surrender it, Josephus, *Ant.* xiii 9, 2 (261); xiv 10, 22 (249). Perhaps this explains the unexpected mildness of Antiochus in the conditions of the peace. However, it is not certain that Antiochus Sidetes is meant; cf. vol. I, pp. 204–5.

142. Jannaeus' conquest of Joppa is reflected in the hoard of 851 of his coins discovered there in 1949. The continuation of the use on many of them of the anchor motif, combined with the fact that this type is found predominantly in the coastal region, has suggested that these coins may actually have been minted there by Jannaeus. See A. Kindler, 'The Jaffa Hoard of Alexander Jannaeus', IEJ 4 (1954), pp. 170–85. Minting in Jaffa is not accepted in the review by B. Kanael, Jahrb. f. Num. u. Geldg. 17 (1967), p. 170.

taken by Pompey from the Jews, who were thereby once again completely cut off from the sea, *Ant.* xiv 4, 4 (76); *B.J.* i 7, 7 (156). Of the favours granted by Caesar, one of the most valuable was the restoration of Joppa to the Jews, *Ant.* xiv 10, 6 (205).[143] Whether Herod possessed Joppa from the start is not quite clear. From 34–30 B.C., in any case, it belonged to Cleopatra, as did all the coastal towns (see vol. I, pp. 288–9), and from then on, to Herod, *Ant.* xv 7, 3 (217); *B.J.* i 20, 3 (396).[144] It then remained united to Judaea proper and in consequence passed to Archelaus after Herod's death, *Ant.* xvii 11, 4 (319); *B.J.* ii 6, 3 (97). After the deposition of Archelaus it came under the Roman governors.[145] Because of its predominantly Jewish population, Joppa at the start of the war of A.D. 66 was a revolutionary centre. It was promptly destroyed by Cestius Gallus, *B.J.* ii 18, 10 (508), but was soon refortified, only to be conquered a second time by Vespasian, *B.J.* iii 9, 2–4 (414–27). Subsequently, it probably became once more a predominantly Gentile town, though a considerable number of Jewish epitaphs derive from there.[146] A coin shows that it was also called Flavia, a name which it must have received between A.D. 70 and

143. See vol. I, p. 274.

144. As Joppa was again Jewish from the time of Caesar, and as it is stated that Herod conquered it when he acceded to his kingdom, *Ant.* xiv 15, 1 (397); *B.J.* i 15, 3–4 (290 ff.), it would appear that the city was his from the beginning of his reign, and that after the short interregnum of Cleopatra he regained it in 30 B.C. The only difficulty is that in the territorial enlargement of 30 B.C. Joppa is named, not as one of the areas restored to him, but expressly as among the towns newly assigned to him.

145. Evidence for the existence of a Greek *βουλή* in Joppa at that time would be provided if the inscription allegedly found in Jaffa (Joppa) (see K. R. Lepsius, *Denkmäler aus Ägypten und Äthiopien* XII, Sheet 100, *Inscr. Gr.*, no. 589: *Ἡ βουλὴ καὶ ὁ δῆμος Λούκιον Ποπίλλιον Βάλβον πρεσβυτὴν Τιβερίου Κλαυδίου Καίσαρος Σεβαστοῦ Γερμανικοῦ τὸν πάτρωνα τῆς πόλεως)* really belonged there. But in fact, the site of its discovery is unknown. The French scholars who accompanied Napoleon's army to Egypt in 1798 saw it in Damietta at Phatne on the old mouth of the Nile; (*Description de l'Égypte, etc., publiée par ordre du gouvernement, Antiquités*, Tables, v, tab. 56, n. 27); W. R. Hamilton did the same a few years later, *Remarks on Several Parts of Turkey* I, *Aegyptiaca* (1809), p. 385; and also Viscount Valentia, *Voyages and Travels to India, Ceylon, etc.* III (1809), p. 419; cf. 416; similarly, J. K. Bailie, *Fasciculus inscriptionum graecarum potissimum ex Galatia Lycia Syria et Aegypto* III (1849), p. 115; cf. CIG III 4529, 4697b and Addenda, p. 1175. These travellers were told that it had been brought to Damietta from Syria (Valentia) or specifically from Berytus (Hamilton and Bailie). Lepsius probably saw it in Damietta as well; he copied it in 1845, about the same time as Bailie, *Denkmäler aus Ägypten und Äthiopien*, text, ed. Naville and Sethe I (1897), p. 224. The information in Lepsius's book of plates must therefore be based on an error, and it is misleading when Cagnat gives the inscription under 'Joppa' (IGR III 1209). Also, it cannot have come from Berytus, since this was a Roman colony from the time of Augustus, whereas the city whose authorities placed the inscription was evidently not a colony.

146. For Jewish epitaphs from Joppa/Jaffa see Frey, CIJ II, nos. 892–960.

96.[147] Despite its close association with Judaea, Joppa seems to have been a Greek city proper.[148] Few specimens of its coinage have been preserved.[149]

8. Apollonia, Ἀπολλωνία. An Apollonia between Joppa and Caesarea is mentioned by geographers up to the later imperial period.[150] This place appears only twice in recorded history: during the reign of Alexander Jannaeus when it belonged to Jewish territory, Josephus, *Ant*. xiii 15, 4 (395), and at the time of Gabinius, who had it restored, *B.J.* i 8, 4 (166). From the distance given in the Peutinger Table (22 Roman miles from Caesarea) it must have lain on the site of Tel Arshaf (Arsūf).[151] This is confirmed by the name itself, for the Phoenician god רשף (Rešeph), from whom Arsūf derived its name, corresponds to the Greek Apollo.[152] Stark's conjecture that it is identical with Σώζουσα is supported by the circumstance that in Cyrenaica an Apollonia and a Sozousa were also probably one and the same town.

147. T. H. Darricarrère, 'Sur une monnaie inédite de Joppé' in RA 43 (1882), pp. 74–5. The coin is from the time of Elagabalus and bears the inscription: ʼΙΟΠΠΗΣ ΦΛΑΥΙΑΣ.

148. This is suggested by the way in which Josephus, *B.J.* iii 3, 5 (56), mentions Joppa as distinct from Judaea proper: μεθ' ἃς Ἰάμνεια καὶ Ἰόπη τῶν περιοίκων ἀφηγοῦνται. Also in *B.J.* iii 9, 4 (430), the κῶμαι and πολίχναι τῆς Ἰόπης are mentioned.

149. F. de Saulcy, *Numismatique de la Terre Sainte*, p. 176 f., pl. IX, n. 3–4; Darricarrère, *loc. cit.*, *BMC Palestine*, pp. xxiv–v; 44.

150. Pliny, *NH* v 13/69; Ptolemy v, 16, 2=ed. Didot (I 2, 1901), v 15, 2; *Tabula Peutingeriana* Segm. IX (ed. K. Miller, 1916); *Geographus Ravennas*, ed. Pinder et Parthey (1860), pp. 83, 356; *Guidonis Geogr*. in the above-named edition of *Geogr. Ravenn.*, p. 524; ed. J. Schnetz (1940), pp. 25, 90, 133; Stephanus Byz., s.v. Ἀπολλωνία enumerates 25 towns bearing this name, among them no. 12: περὶ τὴν Κοίλην Συρίαν; no. 13: κατὰ Ἰόπην (this being the one now in question); no. 20: Συρίας κατὰ Ἀπάμειαν.

151. See generally: RE II, col. 117; Kuhn, *op. cit.* II, p. 362; Guérin, *Samarie* II, pp. 375–82; Conder and Kitchener, *The Survey of Western Palestine, Memoirs* II, pp. 135, 137–40 (with plan); de Saulcy, *Numismatique*, pp. 110 f., pl. VI, n. 1–2; Abel, *Géog. Pal.* II, p. 247; Avi-Yonah, *Holy Land*, p. 147 *et passim*; B. Lifshitz, ZDPV 78 (1962), pp. 85–8.

152. On a bilingual inscription at Idalion in Cyprus (CIS no. 89) לרשף מכל appears in the Semitic text, τῷ Ἀπόλωνι τῷ Ἀμυκλοῖ in the Greek. On two inscriptions at Tamassos in Cyprus, reported by W. Euting, SAB 1887, pp. 115–23, see Cooke, *Text-book*, n. 30=KAI no. 41. לרשף on one side corresponds to Ἀπείλωνι or Ἀπόλωνι on the other. The identity of the names Apollonia and Arsūf was first recognized by Clermont-Ganneau, RA n. 5 32 (1876), pp. 374–5; cf. Th. Nöldeke, ZDMG (1888), p. 473. On the god רשף, see also the observations in CIS no. 10; Clermont-Ganneau, *Recueil d'archéologie orientale* I (1888), pp. 176–82; G. F. Hill, *A History of Cyprus* I (1940), pp. 87–8; S. Moscati, *I Fenici e Cartagine* (1972), p. 528; Hengel, *Judaism and Hellenism* ch. iv, n. 27; for *Rešeph*, see GMVO I, pp. 305–6. Among the Jews, Resheph was the name of a demon (Jerome, *In Hab.* 3:5, ed. Vallarsi VI, p. 641; bBer, 5a, אין רשף אלא מזיקין; Rashi on Dt. 32:24 (ed. Berliner, p. 354) and Job 5:17; M. Schwab, *Vocabulaire de l'angélologie* (1897), p. 250).

Sozousa would thus be the city of Apollo *Σωτήρ*.[153] The existence and tenacious retention of the Semitic name Arsūf make it questionable whether Apollonia had its original establishment in the Greek period. In any case it cannot have been founded by the early Seleucids[154] since they were not in possession of the Palestinian coast (see above, p. 87).

9. Straton's Tower, *Στράτωνος πύργος*, later Caesarea.[155] The Greek name of the city might suggest that it was founded during the Hellenistic period, perhaps as a fortress named after a Ptolemaic general. But it is now generally accepted that it was first established in the Persian period by a Sidonian king named Straton, either Straton I (375/4–61) or II (343/2–32).[156] The earliest reference to it under this name is provided by a papyrus giving the intinerary pursued in 259 B.C. by Zenon, an agent of the Ptolemaic *dioiketes*, who evidently landed there before proceeding to Jerusalem and elsewhere.[157] The first geographical author to mention it is Artemidorus in about 100 B.C.[158]

153. *Σώζουσα* in Hierocles, *Synecdemus* 719, 5 (ed. Parthey, p. 44; ed. Buckhardt, p. 41). Cf. Stark, *Gaza*, p. 452. On Sozousa in Cyrenaica, see Jones, CERP², p. 362. Cf. also Apollonia-Sozopolis in Pisidia, *ibid.* p. 139, and another in Thrace, p. 24 (both called 'Sozopolis' only in the Christian period).

154. So Stark, *loc. cit.*

155. See *BMC Palestine*, pp. xvi–xxiii; 12–42; L. Haefeli, *Caesarea am Meer* (1923); Abel, *Géog. Pal.* II, pp. 296–7; A. Reifenberg, 'Caesarea: A Study in the Decline of a Town', IEJ (1950), pp. 20–32; L. Levine, *Caesarea under Roman Rule* (1975). There are no coins of Straton's Tower; for those of Caesarea see L. Kadman, *The Coins of Caesarea Maritima* (1957), and note L. Levine, 'Some Observations on the Coins of Caesarea Maritima', IEJ 22 (1972), pp. 131–40. For the very extensive remains of the city, see especially A. Frova *et al.*, *Scavi di Caesarea Maritima* (1965); EAEHL s.v. and the thorough study by L. Levine, *Roman Caesarea: an Archaeological-Topographical Study*, Qedem 2 (1975). On the hippodrome, note also J. M. Humphreys, 'A Summary of the 1974 Excavations in the Caesarea Hippodrome'; BASOR 218 (1975), pp. 1–24, with J. A. Riley, *ibid.*, pp. 25–63, on the pottery. For the Mithraeum, see L. M. Hopfe, 'The Caesarea Mithraeum: a Preliminary Announcement', BA 38 (1975), pp. 2–10. Note also BASOR Supp. 19, The Joint Expedition to Caesarea Maritima, vol. I, *Studies in the History of Caesarea Maritima* (1975), ed. D. N. Freedman; and J. Ringel, *Césarée de Palestine, étude historique et archéologique* (1975).

156. In Justinian's *Novella* 103 *praef.*, it is said of Caesarea: *Καίτο γε ἀρχαία τέ ἐστι καὶ ἀεὶ σεμνή, ἡνίκα τε αὐτὴν Στράτων ἱδρύσατο πρῶτος, ὅς ἐξ Ἑλλάδος ἀναστὰς γέγονεν αὐτῆς οἰκιστής, ἡνίκα τε Οὐεσπασιανὸς ... εἰς τὴν τῶν Καισάρων αὐτὴν ὠνόμασε προσηγορίαν.* The worthlessness of this statement is apparent already from the gross mistake in regard to Vespasian. There was a Straton's Island in the Red Sea off the Abyssinian coast, Strabo xvi 4, 8 (770). For the foundation see L. Levine, 'A propos de la fondation de la Tour de Straton', RB 80 (1973), pp. 73–81.

157. P. Cairo Zen. 59004=CPJ I, no. 2; see also, V. Tscherikower, 'Palestine under the Ptolemies', Mizraim 4–5 (1937), pp. 9–10.

158. Artemidorus in Stephanus Byz., s.v. *Δῶρος;* see RE s.v. 'Artemidorus' (27). The latest geographer to refer to Straton's Tower by that name alone is Strabo xvi 8, 27 (758).

It also appears in recorded history at that time in connection with Aristobulus I in 104 B.C., *Ant.* xiii 11, 2 (312). At the beginning of the reign of Alexander Jannaeus, a 'tyrant' called Zoilus was lord of Straton's Tower and Dora, *Ant.* xiii, 12, 2 (324), but he was captured by Ptolemy Lathyrus and his city handed over to Alexander Jannaeus, *Ant.* xiii 12, 4 (334–5).[159] Straton's Tower is therefore named among the towns belonging to Alexander, *Ant.* xiii 15, 4 (395). It obtained its freedom through Pompey, *Ant.* xiv 4, 4 (76), *B.J.* i 7, 7 (156); and it was granted to Herod by Augustus, *Ant.* xv 7, 3 (217); *B.J.* i 20, 3 (396). The particular importance of the city dates from that time. Herod rebuilt it on a most magnificent scale and furnished it with an ingenious breakwater and an excellent harbour, *Ant.* xv 9, 6 (331–7); xvi 5, 1 (136); *B.J.* 1 21, 5–8 (408–14).[160] He called the town *Καισάρεια* in honour of the emperor, and the harbour *Σεβαστὸς λιμήν*.[161] Hence on the coinage of Agrippa I from A.D. 42/3 and 43/4, and on Caesarean coins from the reign of Nero, is inscribed *Καισάρια ἡ πρὸς Σεβαστῷ λιμένι*.[162] The form *Καισάρεια Σεβαστή* is used once by Josephus.[163] Otherwise the town is called *Καισάρεια Στράτωνος* to distinguish it from other Caesareas,[164] and in later times *Καισάρεια τῆς Παλαιστίνης*.[165] It quickly became prosperous and was for long one of the major cities of Palestine.[166] After Herod's death, it passed with the rest of Judaea into the hands of Archelaus, *Ant.* xvii 11, 4 (320); *B.J.* ii 6, 3 (97). From then on, it remained united with Judaea. It consequently came

159. For full details, including a discussion of the probable reference to this event in Megillat Ta'anit on 14th Sivan, and a fifth century scholion, see L. I. Levine, 'The Hasmonean Conquest of Strato's Tower', IEJ 24 (1974), pp. 62–9.

160. Besides the principal passages mentioned, cf. Josephus, *Ant.* xv 8, 5 (293); Pliny, *NH* v 13/69. On the date of its construction, see vol. I, pp. 291, 293. On its constitution and political position, cf. also Kuhn, *Die städtische und bürgerliche Verfassung* II, pp. 347–50.

161. On the latter, see *Ant.* xvii 5, 1 (87); *B.J.* i 31, 3 (613); cf. Levine, *Roman Caesarea*, pp. 13–18.

162. On these coins, see de Saulcy, *Numismatique de la Terre Sainte*, pp. 116 f.; *BMC Palestine*, pp. xvii–xviii; Kadman, *op. cit.*, pp. 29, 98–100.

163. Josephus, *Ant.* xvi 5, 1 (136); cf. Philo, *Legat.* 38 (305): *Καισάρειαν, ἐπώνυμον τοῦ προπάππου Σεβαστήν*. The designation *Αὐγοῦστα Καισάρεια* on an inscription from Laodicea iu Syria, CIG 4472 = Le Bas-Waddington, *Inscriptions* III, no. 1839 = IGLS IV 1265 = L. Moretti, *Iscrizioni agonistiche greche*, no. 85, is an abbreviation of *colonia prima Flavia Augusta Caesarea*, the official title of Caesarea as a colony from the time of Vespasian onwards; see below, p. 118 and Kuhn, *op. cit.* II, p. 349.

164. Ptolemy v 16, 2 (= ed. Didot, v 15, 2); viii 20, 14; Clement, *Homil.* i 15, 20; xiii 7; *Recogn.* i 12; CIL XVI 15. Cf. the inscription of *c.* A.D. 165 from Aphrodisias, Le Bas-Waddington, *Inscriptions* III 1620 = L. Moretti, *Iscrizioni agonistiche greche*, no. 72: *Καισάρειαν τὴν Στράτωνος*.

165. E.g. Eusebius, *Onomast.*, ed. Klostermann, pp. 2, 78; *De mart. Pal.* i 2.

166. Josephus, *B.J.* iii 9, 1 (409); Clement, *Recogn.* i 12; Apollonius of Tyana *Ep.* xi (in *Epistolographi graeci*, ed. Hercher, 1873, Didot); *Expositio totius mundi* (ed. Rougé) 26; 31; 32; Ammianus xiv 8, 11.

under the Roman prefects after the deposition of Archelaus, then under Agrippa I, and later under the Roman procurators. Agrippa I minted coins in Caesarea.[167] His στρατηγός there is occasionally mentioned, *Ant.* xix 7, 4 (333). As is known, he himself died there (see vol. I, pp. 452–3). He was however hated by the Caesareans because of his Judaizing tendencies, *Ant.* xix 9, 1 (356). The Roman *praefecti* and procurators, both before and after the reign of Agrippa, resided in Caesarea (see vol. I, p. 361), which explains why Tacitus was able to refer to the city as 'Iudaeae caput' (*Hist.* ii 78). It was also the main garrison for the forces under the command of the governors, troops drawn, moreover, predominantly from the locality (see vol. I, pp. 363–5). As the population was chiefly Gentile, *B.J.* iii 9, 1 (409), yet included a considerable Jewish element, disputes easily arose, especially since both parties enjoyed equal civic rights and were therefore called on to manage the city's affairs together.[168] Neither the Jews nor the Gentiles were satisfied with this situation. Each party claimed exclusive rights to citizenship. Towards the end of Felix's term of office the quarrel erupted in violence, whereupon Nero, whose *ab epistulis* had been bribed by the Gentile party, deprived the Jews of their rights and in A.D. 61 declared the Gentiles to be sole masters of the city, *Ant.* xx 8, 7 (173–8) and 9 (182–4); *B.J.* ii 13, 7 (266–70); 14, 4–5 (284–92).[169] At the outbreak of the war in A.D. 66, the Jews as a minority fell victim to the fury of the Gentile mob. All twenty-thousand Jewish inhabitants are said by Josephus to have been massacred within an hour, *B.J.* ii 18, 1 (457); vii 8, 7 (362).[170] Under Vespasian, Caesarea was transformed

167. See n. 162 above, and Y. Meshorer, *Jewish Coins of the Second Temple Period* (1967), p. 79.

168. From the context, the ἄνδρες οἱ κατ' ἐξοχὴν τῆς πόλεως in Acts 25:23 are to be regarded as Gentiles. But this does not mean that the Jews had no share in the government; it merely corresponds to the preponderance of the Gentile element attested by Josephus. It must of course be borne in mind that at the time of Festus, when the events recounted in Acts 25:23 occurred, the Jews were excluded from civil rights (see below). But these events took place at the very beginning of Festus's period of office, whereas Nero's rescript decreeing the exclusion has to be dated somewhat later.

169. It might appear from *B.J.* ii 14, 4 (284) that Nero's rescript was not issued before A.D. 66. But as it was promulgated under the influence of Pallas, *Ant.* xx 8, 9 (182), who died in A.D. 62 (Tacitus, *Ann.* xiv 65), it can scarcely be dated later than A.D. 61. Cf. vol. I, pp. 465–7. For an earlier chronology, dating the arrival of Festus to A.D. 56, see now M. T. Griffin, *Seneca* (1976), pp. 449–52.

170. At least from the early third century, however, a substantial Jewish community was established there. See Levine, *Caesarea under Roman Rule* ch. 5; note also N. R. M. de Lange, *Origen and the Jews* (1976). For Jewish funerary inscriptions see, e.g. Frey, CIJ II, no. 1, pp. 886–90; B. Lifshitz RB, 68 (1961), pp. 114 f.; 71 (1964), pp. 384–7; 72 (1965), pp. 98–107; 74 (1967), p. 50; A. Negev, RB 78 (1971), pp. 247–50; and for an ἀρχισ(υνάγωγος) καὶ φροντιστής there, RB 67 (1960), p. 60.

into a Roman colony, though without the full *ius Italicum*.[171] On coins and inscriptions it bears the title *col(onia) prima Fl(avia) Aug(usta) Caesariensis* or *Caesarea*.[172] To this was added, from the time of Severus Alexander, the title *metropolis*, or as it is given more fully on coins after Decius, *metropolis pr. S. Pal.* (=*provinciae Syriae Palaestinae*).[173]

10. Dora, *Δῶρα*, in Polybius *Δοῦρα*, elsewhere also *Δῶρος*, in Pliny, *Dorum*,[174] Hebrew דור or דאר,[175] an old Phoenician settlement at eight to nine Roman miles north of Caesarea,[176] was known to the

171. Pliny, *NH* v 13/69: 'Stratonis turris, eadem Caesarea, ab Herode rege condita, nunc colonia prima Flavia a Vespasiano imperatore deducta'; *Digest.* l 15, 8, 7 (from Paulus): 'Divus Vespasianus Caesarienses colonos fecit non adiecto, ut et iuris Italici essent, sed tributum his remisit capitis; sed divus Titus etiam solum immune factum interpretatus est'; *ibid.*, l 15, 1, 6 (from Ulpian): 'In Palaestina duae fuerunt coloniae, Caesariensis et Aelia Capitolina, sed neutra ius Italicum habet'. On the *ius Italicum*, see the literature quoted on p. 96.

172. See Kadman, *op. cit.*, for the coins, and for inscriptions, e.g. CIL III 12082; AE 1964 188. Note also the Greek expression *ΚΟΛ(ΩΝ) ΚΑΙΣΑΡΕΥΣ* on an inscription from Mt. Carmel, M. Avi-Yonah, IEJ 2 (1952), pp. 118–24=AE 1952, 206.

173. *BMC Palestine*, pp. 27 ff.; Kadman, *op. cit.*, pp. 24; 46–7. Note the wooden tablet of A.D. 509 with *ἀπὸ τῆς Καισαραίων μητροπόλεως ἐπαρχείας*, SB 5941. Note also the early fourth century references to Caesarea in *P. Ryl.* 627–8 etc., and in the sixth and seventh centuries, *P. Nessana* 36; 37; 74.

174. The form *Δῶρος* occurs especially in older authors but is also preferred by Stephanus Byz.; *Δῶρα* was afterwards used exclusively. (1) *Δῶρος* is found in Ps.-Scylax (fourth century B.C.); Apollodorus (*c.* 140 B.C.); Alexander of Ephesus, see RE s.v. 'Alexander' (86); Charax (the three last-named in Stephanus Byz., s.v. *Δῶρος*); to this series belongs also Pliny, *NH* v 19/75: 'Dorum'; (2) *Δῶρα* or *Δωρά*, besides 1 Mac., in Artemidorus (*c.* 100 B.C.); Claudius Iolaus (both in Stephanus Byz., see Jacoby, FGrH 788 F2); Josephus (constantly); on coins of Caligula, Trajan, Elagabal (in de Saulcy, *Numismatique de la Terre Sainte*, pp. 142–8); Ptolemy (v 15, 5=ed. Didot, v 14, 3), Clement, *Recogn.* iv 1; Eusebius (*Onom.*, ed. Klostermann, p. 78); Jerome (*ibid.*, p. 79); Hierocles (*Synecdemus* 718, 2); the lists of bishops (Le Quien, *Oriens christ.*, pp. 574 ff.); *Ravenna Geographer* (ed. Pinder et Parthey, pp. 89, 357); to this group belong also Polybius (v 66, 1: *Δῶρα*) and the *Tabula Peutingeriana*. ('*Thora*'). Cf. also n. 194 below. 1 Mac. uses *Δωρᾶ* as an undeclined proper name, but elsewhere it is treated as a neuter plural (Josephus usually; Eusebius (*op. cit.*, p. 130), the list of bishops); though sometimes also as a fem. sing.: Josephus, *Ant.* xiii 7, 2 (223) and according to a few manuscripts, Clement, *Recogn.* iv 1).

175. דור, Jos. 11:2; 12:23; Jg. 1:27; 1 Chron. 7:29; דאר, Jos. 17:11; 1 Kg. 4:11. Similarly on the Eshmunazar inscription, see above, n. 132. It is uncertain whether נפת דור (Jos. 12:23; 1 Kg. 4:11) or נפות דור (Jos. 11:2), is distinguished from the city of דור. Solomon is said to have possessed only the former (1 Kg. 4:11). See G. Dahl, *Materials for the History of Dor* (1931); W. L. Reed, s.v., IDB I (1962), p. 864; Y. Aharoni, *The Land of the Bible* (1967), index s.v.; M. Avi-Yonah, Enc. Jud. 6, col. 172; 'Gazetteer' s.v. 'Dora'; EAEHL I, s.v. 'Dor'.

176. The foundation by the Phoenicians is narrated by Claudius Iolaus in Stephanus Byz., s.v. *Δῶρος* (=Jacoby FGrH 788 F.2). Josephus also calls Dora a

Greeks from ancient times. It is mentioned already in the geography of Hecataeus of Miletus in about 500 B.C.[177] The city has sometimes been thought to have paid tribute to the Athenians when they dominated much of the Mediterranean during the fifth century B.C.[178] In the reign of the Sidonian king Eshmunazar it was given to the Sidonians by the Persian 'Lord of kings'.[179] Ps.-Scylax, whose description refers to the Persian period, therefore rightly describes Dora as a city of the Sidonians.[180]

Although not large,[181] Dora was a strong and important fortress because of its favourable position. Antiochus the Great besieged it without success at the time of his first attack on Coele Syria in 219 B.C.[182] Eighty years later (139 B.C.), Tryphon was surrounded there by Antiochus Sidetes and his powerful army, with similar results. The siege

---

πόλις τῆς Φοινίκης, *Vita* 8 (31); *C. Ap.* ii 9 (116). The distance from Caesarea: 8 Roman miles according to *Tabula Peutingeriana*; 9 according to Eusebius (*Onom.*, ed. Klostermann, p. 78, 136) and Jerome (*ibid.*, p. 79, 137); according to Artemidorus (Stephanus Byz. s.v.) Dora lay *ἐπὶ χερσονησοειδοῦς τόπου*. Cf. generally: G. Dahl, *Materials for the History of Dor* (1931); Abel, *Géog. Pal.* II, p. 308; EAEHL I, s.v.

177. Hecataeus in Stephanus Byz., s.v. *Δῶρος* (=Jacoby, FGrH 1 F.275): *μετὰ δὲ ἡ πάλαι Δῶρος, νῦν δὲ Δῶρα καλεῖται*. This is of course unlikely to be an exact quotation from Hecataeus for it affirms a change in designation not otherwise attested until Polybius, in the middle of the second century (see above, n. 174); so it is probable that there has been an interpolation in the copy used by Stephanus.

178. A town by the name of *Δῶρος* paid tribute jointly with the towns of Caria to Athens (Stephanus Byz., s.v. *Δῶρος · Κρατερὸς ἐν τῷ περὶ ψηφισμάτων τρίτῳ 'Καρικὸς φόρος · Δῶρος, Φασηλῖται'* = Jacoby, FGrH 342 F.1; on Craterus, see F. Susemihl, *Gesch. der griech. Literatur* I, pp. 599 ff. and Jacoby's commentary *ad. loc.*). Since however a Carian town of this name is unknown, and since the power of the Athenians extended at least to Cyprus, it has been argued, e.g. by B. D. Merritt, H. T. Wade-Gery and M. F. McGregor, *The Athenian Tribute Lists* I (1939), pp. 154, 483, that the reference is to this Dor. But it is correctly pointed out by V. Tcherikover, *Hellenistic Civilisation and the Jews* (1959), p. 92 and n. 15, that there is no evidence that Athenian rule extended to the Syrian-Palestine coast, and that Pliny, *NH* v 27/92 attests 'Doron' in Cilicia, not far from Phaselis. Cf. R. Meiggs, *The Athenian Empire* (1972), pp. 420–1, returning to the identification with this Dor.

179. See the inscription of Eshmunazar, ll. 18–20; cf. n. 136 above.

180. Ps.-Scylax in *Geographi graeci minores*, ed. C. Müller, I, p. 79: *Δῶρος πόλις Σιδονίων*. On Scylax, see, e.g. A. von Gutschmid, *Kleine Schriften* IV, pp. 139 ff.; K. Galling, 'Die Syrische-palästinische Küste nach der Beschreibung bei Pseudo-Skylax', *Studien zur Geschichte Israels im persischen Zeitalter* (1964), pp. 185–210.

181. Artemidorus: *πολισμάτιον;* Claudius Iolaus: *βραχεῖα πολίχνη* (both in Stephanus Byz.); Clement, *Recogn.* iv 1: 'breve oppidum'.

182. Polybius v 66, 1.

ended only with the flight of Tryphon.[183] Some decades later, Dora is found to be in the hands of the tyrant Zoilus, *Ant.* xiii 12, 2 (324),[184] who was afterwards overthrown by Alexander Jannaeus, *Ant.* xiii 12, 4 (334–5). It must, therefore, have belonged subsequently to Jewish territory but was again separated from it by Pompey, *Ant.* xiv 4, 4 (76); *B.J.* i 7, 7 (156). Like many other towns, Dora introduced from then on a new calendar which it continued to use on coins of the imperial era.[185] It is not named among the cities restored by Gabinius, for in *Ant.* xiv 5, 3 (88) *"Αδωρα* should probably be read rather than *Δῶρα*, though this is given in the majority of manuscripts and modern editions (see p. 5 above). After Pompey, the city remained under direct Roman rule and therefore never belonged to Herod (whose territory on the coast extended no farther north than Caesarea). On coins of the imperial period it is described as *ἱερὰ ἄσυλος αὐτόνομος ναυαρχίς*.[186] The existence of a Jewish community in Dora is attested by an incident during the reign of King Agrippa I: a number of young people erected an image of the emperor in the Jewish synagogue, and it needed the energetic intervention of Petronius the governor, in a letter addressed to the city authorities (*Δωριτῶν τοῖς πρώτοις*), to ensure that the Jews should enjoy the religious freedom pledged to them, *Ant.* xix 6, 3 (300–11). In the later imperial period Dora seems to have declined.[187] Yet Christian bishops of the city are mentioned up to the seventh century.[188]

183. 1 Mac. 15: 11–37; Josephus, *Ant.* xiii 7, 2 (223). Earlier numismatists thought they might assign to this period a coin of Tryphon allegedly minted in Dora (Stark, *Gaza*, p. 477). But it is now accepted that it belongs rather to Ascalon (de Saulcy, *Mémoire sur les monnaies datées des Séleucides*, p. 42; E. Babelon, *Catalogue des monnaies grecques de la Bibliothèque nationale, Les rois de Syrie*, pp. cxxxix f., 137. *BMC Phoenicia*, p. lxxiv).

184. Note that the name *Ζωιαλ* (read *Ζωιλα* or *Ζωιλλ.*) occurs on a Dora epitaph of the year 233 of the era of Dora, i.e., about A.D. 170; see Clermont-Ganneau, *Rec. d'arch. or.* V (1903), pp. 285–8.

185. The starting-point of the era cannot be determined exactly, but it is that of Pompey (63 B.C.?), not of Gabinius (as de Saulcy suggested despite misgivings); an era of Gabinius could not have begun earlier than the autumn of 58 B.C., whereas the coins of Trajan do not permit so late a starting-point. So, with some doubts, Kubitschek in RE I, cols. 649–50, s.v. 'Aera'. Cf. Ideler, *Handb. der Chronologie* I, p. 459; and for the coins, see de Saulcy, *Numismatique de la Terre Sainte*, p. 142–8, 405; pl. VI, n. 6–12; J. Rouvier, Journal international d'archéologie numismatique 4 (1901), pp. 125–31; *BMC Phoenicia*, pp. lxxv; 113–18; cf. H. Seyrig, Syria 27 (1950), pp. 51–2.

186. See de Saulcy, *op. cit.*; Rouvier, *op. cit.* On the title, see above, p. 94. All four titles (*ἱερὰ ἄσυλος αὐτόνομος ναυαρχίς*) were used by Tripolis (OGIS 587), Laodicea ad Mare (OGIS 603) and Tyre (OGIS 595).

187. See Jerome, *Onomast.*, ed. Klostermann, p. 79: 'Dora . . . nunc deserta'; *ibid.*, p. 137: 'Dor autem est oppidum iam desertum'; and his *Ep.* 108, 8: 'ruinas Dor, urbis quondam potentissimae'.

188. Le Quien, *Oriens Christianus* II, pp. 574–9.

11. Ptolemais, *Πτολεμαΐς*.[189] The original name was Acco, עכו (Jg. 1:31), Acca in the Amarna Tablets,[190] *Ἄκη* in Greek. It was known to the Greeks by this name already in pre-Hellenistic times.[191] It was here that the army of Artaxerxes Mnemon assembled in 374 B.C. for the campaign against Egypt.[192] In the time of Isaeus and Demosthenes, trading contracts existed between Athens and Akē (see n. 191). In the age of Alexander the Great, Akē must have been an important city for very many of its coins figure among those of Alexander minted in Phoenicia. They bear the name of Alexander in Greek, that of the town in Phoenician characters (*Ἀλεξάνδρου*, עך, sometimes עכא), and the

189. For a description of the site, see Josephus, *B.J.* ii 10, 2 (188–91). Cf. J. Rouvier, 'Ptolemais-Acé, ses noms et ses ères sous les Seleucides et la domination romaine', RB 8 (1899), pp. 393–408; Abel, *Géog. Pal.* II, pp. 235–7; RE XXIII (1959), cols, 1883–6 s.v. 'Ptolemais' (9); EAEHL I, pp. 14–23; 'Gazetteer' s.v. 'Ptolemais'. For the coins, see especially nn. 193 and 201. Note also M. Avi-Yonah, 'Syrian Gods at Ptolemais-Accho', IEJ 9 (1959), pp. 1–12; Y. H. Landau, 'A Greek Inscription from Acre', IEJ 11 (1961), pp. 118–26; H. Seyrig, 'Divinités de Ptolemaïs', Syria 39 (1962), pp. 193–207.

190. See *The Tell el-Amarna Tablets*, ed. Mercer and Hallock II (1939), p. 892. For the biblical references, Y. Aharoni, *The Land of the Bible* (1967), *passim.*

191. For the name in pre-Hellenistic texts, see Ps.-Scylax in *Geogr. gr. min.*, ed. Müller, I, p. 79; Isaeus, *Orat.* iv, 7 (depending on an emendation); Demosthenes, *Orat.* 41 24 (where for *Θρᾴκην*, read *Ἄκην*; so Valesius on the basis of the gloss in Harpocration, *Lex.*, s.v. *Ἄκη*). For later texts, Diodorus xv 41, 3; xix 93, 7; Herodas, *Mimiambi*, ii 16, and references in n. 192. Both the old and the new names are given by Strabo (see n. 192); Pliny, *NH* v 7/75; Charax in Stephanus Byz., s.v. *Δῶρος*; Claudius Iolaus in Stephanus Byz., s.v. *Ἄκη* = FGrH 788 F.1; Stephanus Byz., *ibid.* and s.v. *Πτολεμαΐς*; Harpocration, *Lex.* (ed. Dindorf) s.v. *Ἄκη· πόλις αὕτη ἐν Φοινίκῃ· Δημοσθένης ἐν τῷ πρὸς Κάλιππον. Ἣν Νικάνωρ ὁ περὶ μετονομασιῶν γεγραφὼς καὶ Καλλίμαχος ἐν τοῖς ὑπομνήμασι τὴν νῦν Πτολεμαΐδα καλουμένην φασὶν εἶναι. Δημήτριος δὲ ἰδίως τὴν ἀκρόπολιν τῆς Πτολεμαΐδος πρότερον Ἄκην ὠνομάσθαι φησίν.* Cf. Kuhn, *op. cit.* II, p. 331. Callimachus is the celebrated poet who lived under Ptolemy II Philadelphus. On his historico-geographical writings, see F. Susemihl, *Gesch. der griech. Literatur* I, pp. 366 f.; P. M. Fraser, *Ptolemaic Alexandria* (1972), ch. 11. On Demetrius of Magnesia, a contemporary of Cicero, see Susemihl, *ibid.* I, p. 507. The articles on *Ἄκη* in the *Etymologicum magnum* and in the Suda are drawn from Harpocration. On the earlier history of Akē, cf. especially the fragment from Menander in Josephus, *Ant.* ix, 14, 2 = FGrH 783 F.4; also A. von Gutschmid, *Kleine Schriften* II, p. 66 (instead of *Ἄκη* most of the MSS here show *Ἄρκη*, which can hardly be correct since Arca lies too far to the north).

192. Diodorus xv 41, 3; Pompeius Trogus, *Prol. libri x*. This is referred to also by Polyaenus iii 9, 56; Cornelius Nepos, *Vita Datames* xiv 5, 5. Cf. Strabo, xvi 2, 25 (758): *Εἶθ' ἡ Πτολεμαΐς ἐστι μεγάλη πόλις ἣν Ἄκην ὠνόμαζον πρότερον, ᾗ ἐρχῶντο ὁρμητηρίῳ πρὸς τὴν Αἴγυπτον οἱ Πέρσαι.* On Egyptian-Persian relations in the fourth century generally, see W. Judeich, *Kleinasiatische Studien* (1892), 144 ff.; A. T. Olmstead, *History of the Persian Empire* (1948), ch. 28–30; F. K. Kienitz, *Die politische Geschichte Ägyptens vom 7. bis 4. Jahrhundert vor der Zeitwende* (1953); E. Bresciani in H. Bengtson, *The Greeks and the Persians* (1965), pp. 333–53.

year of an era beginning with Alexander the Great. As elsewhere, these coins continued to be issued long after Alexander's death.[193] Akē is said to have been razed to the ground in the year 312 B.C. by Ptolemy Lagus when he withdrew from the newly conquered Coele Syria before Antigonus.[194] It is very unlikely that Seleucus I was ever in possession of Akē since his domination of the Phoenician coast can hardly have extended so far south (see above, p. 87). Akē received from Ptolemy II the name *Πτολεμαΐς*, which from then on became the style most generally used;[195] one of the Zenon papyri shows conclusively that it was current by 259 B.C.[196] Nevertheless, its original name of Acco was maintained without interruption, and indeed later superseded the Greek name once more.[197] In the restoration carried out by Ptolemy II, the city must also have been extensively enlarged; this must be the meaning of the report of Demetrius of Magnesia to the effect that only the acropolis of Ptolemais was formerly known as Akē (see n. 191). The dated coins of Ptolemy II, minted in Ptolemais, range from the twenty-fifth to the thirty-eighth year of his reign = 261–48 B.C., those of Ptolemy III from the second to the fifth year of his reign = 245–42 B.C.; only undated coins of Ptolemy IV are known.[198] In the Seleucid period, Ptolemais again figures as one of the major cities of the Phoenician-Philistine coast. The initial conquest of this region by Antiochus the Great in 219 B.C. was greatly facilitated by the surrender to him of Tyre

193. See E. T. Newell, *The Dated Alexander Coinage of Sidon and Ake* (1916), pp. 39–68, arguing that the era used on these coins is a local one, and that the series goes down to 307 B.C. For Phoenician elements in Ake, see now M. Dothan, 'A sign of Tanit from Tell Akko', IEJ 24 (1974), pp. 44–9.

194. Diodorus xix 93, 7. Cf. above, nn. 67 and 138. The continuation of the coinage (cf. previous note) clearly suggests that the destruction was not complete.

195. The re-foundation (and re-naming) is expressly attributed to Ptolemy II in the Letter of Aristeas 115: *Πτολεμαΐδα τὴν ὑπὸ τοῦ βασιλέως ἐκτισμένην*. This is certainly correct. The poet Callimachus, living under Ptolemy II, already knows the new name of the city (thus the entry in the *Lexicon* of Harpocration; see above, n. 191). That Ptolemy II Philadelphus founded cities in Palestine is demonstrated by the example of Philadelphia (see below). Referring to 219–17 B.C., Polybius mentions Ptolemas under this name (Polybius, v 61–2; 71, 1.2) Moreover, coins minted by Ptolemy II show the Greek monogram of Ptolemais; see J. N. Svoronos, 'Les monnaies de Ptolemée II qui portent dates', Revue belge de numismatique (1901), pp. 280–2; *BMC Phoenicia*, p. lxxviii; B. V. Head, *Historia Numorum* (²1911), pp. 793–4.

196. P. Cairo Zen. 59004 = CPJ I, no. 2a. Cf. P. Cairo Zen. 59008 (?259 B.C.); 59698 ?; PSI 495 (258/7 B.C.); 366 (250/49 B.C.); 403; 612; 616; *P. Lond.* 1931 (258); probably 2022.

197. The name עכו occurs also in rabbinic literature; see mNed. 3:6; mGit. 1:2; 7:7; mAZ 3:4; mOhol. 18:9. For relevant passages of the Tosefta, see the index to Zuckermandel's edition; A. Neubauer, *Géographie du Talmud*, pp. 231–2. 4QpIsa 5–6, 1.11 on Isa. 10:32 mentions בקעת עכו (cf. DJD IV, no. 161, p. 12).

198. Svoronos, *Τὰ νομίσματα τοῦ κράτους τῶν Πτολεμαίων* (1904) II, pp. 113–16 (Ptolemy II); p. 163 (Ptolemy III); p. 192 (Ptolemy IV).

and Ptolemais by the Ptolemaic general Theodotus.[199] In 218/17 B.C., Antiochus wintered in Ptolemais.[200] After the definitive occupation of Phoenicia by the Seleucids following the battle of Panion in 200 B.C., Ptolemais was especially favoured by them. On coins, particularly from the times of Antiochus IV and VII but also from the Roman period, its inhabitants are described as *Ἀντιοχεῖς οἱ ἐν Πτολεμαΐδι*, sometimes with the addition *ἱερὰ ἄσυλος*, or *ἱερὰ αὐτόνομος*.[201] The privilege of calling themselves *Ἀντιοχεῖς* was a favour coveted by many other cities, such as, for example, Jerusalem when it was dominated by the Hellenizing party.[202] Coins of the Seleucid kings minted in Ptolemais are extant from the reigns of Seleucus IV (187–75 B.C.) and especially from Antiochus IV (175–64 B.C.) to Antiochus XII. [203] The city was favoured as a place of residence by the kings during their temporary stays in those parts (1 Mac. 10:56–60; 11:22, 24). It was consistently hostile to the Jews. Already at the beginning of the Maccabaean rising it was Ptolemais, Tyre and Sidon in particular that fought against the Jews in revolt against Syrian sovereignty (1 Mac. 5:15 ff.). Also Jonathan was treacherously taken prisoner there by Tryphon (1 Mac. 12:45 ff.). After the accession of Alexander Jannaeus in 104 B.C. when the Seleucids had already lost all control in the south of their kingdom, three neighbouring powers contended for the possession of Ptolemais.

199. Polybius v 61–2. Cf. Stark, *Gaza*, pp. 375 ff.; Niese, *Gesch. der griech. und makedon. Staaten* II, pp. 374 f.

200. Polybius v 71, 13.

201. For the coins see *BMC Phoenicia*, pp. lxxvii–lxxxvii; 128–38; L. Kadman, *The Coins of Akko Ptolemais* (1961), with the important review-article by H. Seyrig 'Le monnayage de Ptolemais en Phénicie', RN N.S. 4 (1962), pp. 25–50. The *ἀσυλία* of the city may date from 120/19 B.C., see Seyrig, pp. 28–9.

202. The official designation of the citizens as *Ἀντιοχεῖς* was, for example, desired by the Hellenizing party in Jerusalem, see 2 Mac. 4:9. Jason promised large sums if the inhabitants of Jerusalem were permitted to register themselves as *Ἀντιοχεῖς: τοὺς ἐν Ἱεροσολύμοις Ἀντιοχεῖς ἀναγράψαι*; cf. 4:19. He sent to the games of Heracles at Tyre *θεωροὺς ὡς ἀπὸ Ἱεροσολύμων Ἀντιοχεῖς ὄντας*. Similarly, the citizens of Adana in Cilicia called themselves *Ἀντιοχεῖς οἱ πρὸς τῷ Σάρῳ*; those of Tarsus, *Ἀντιοχεῖς οἱ πρὸς τῷ Κύδνῳ*; those of Edessa, *Ἀντιοχεῖς οἱ ἐπὶ Καλλιρόῃ*; those of Hippus, *Ἀντιοχεῖς οἱ πρὸς Ἵππῳ*; those of Gerasa, *Ἀντιοχεῖς οἱ πρὸς τῷ Χρυσορόᾳ*. To the same category belong the designations *Σελευκεῖς*, *Ἐπιφανεῖς* and *Πομπηιεῖς*, *Γαβινιεῖς*, *Κλαυδιεῖς*. The designation *Ἀντιοχεῖς* therefore had nothing to do with the town of Antioch (the capital of Syria) and the rights of its citizens, but is derived directly from the name of the king. *Ἀντιοχεῖς* are those loyal to the monarch. In so describing oneself, one paid homage to the king; but it was also a mark of favour on the part of the king if he permitted its use. Cf. generally, E. Babelon, *Catalogue etc. Les rois de Syrie* (1890), pp. ci–civ; 77–81; RN (1898), p. 186; G. F. Hill, *Historical Greek Coins* (1906), pp. 143–5. See in general V. Tscherikower, *Die hellenistischen Städtegründungen* (1927), pp. 165–81.

203. For Seleucid minting in Ptolemais, see E. T. Newell, *Late Seleucid Mints in Ake-Ptolemais and Damascus* (1939); A. B. Brett, 'Seleucid Coins of Ake-Ptolemais in Phoenicia', Am. Num. Soc., Mus. Notes 1 (1945), pp. 17–35.

Alexander Jannaeus intended to capture it. He was prevented from carrying out his plan by Ptolemy Lathyrus, the ruler of Cyprus, who himself occupied the city by force, *Ant.* xiii 12, 2–6 (324 ff.). It was however quickly taken from him by his mother Cleopatra, the queen of Egypt, *Ant.* xiii 13, 1–2 (348 ff.). That Ptolemais in around 90 B.C. and somewhat later was nevertheless still subject to the Seleucids used to be deduced from coins of Philip and Antiochus XII, but is no longer accepted.[204] The power of the Armenian king Tigranes, who in 83 B.C. overthrew the Seleucid kingdom, evidently did not extend over the southernmost parts. For in around 70 B.C., Ptolemais was under the dominion, or at any rate the influence, of Cleopatra Selene, a daughter of the Cleopatra already mentioned and sister of Ptolemy Lathyrus. Selene was once the wife of her brother Ptolemy Lathyrus, but through her subsequent marriages with Antiochus VIII Grypus, Antiochus IX Cyzicenus and Antiochus X Eusebes, became a Syrian queen.[205] She appears to have retained a small dominion in the southernmost part of Syria.[206] At her instigation, Ptolemais closed its gates against Tigranes when he pressed southwards in around 70 B.C. It was captured by him, but as quickly liberated when he found himself obliged to retreat in face of a Roman attack on his own kingdom, *Ant.* xiii 16, 4 (421); *B.J.* i 5, 3 (116). Ptolemais may have gained some favour from Caesar in 47 B.C. when he regulated Syrian affairs for some of its coins from the imperial period show a Caesarian era, calculated from 48 B.C., and probably established in 47 and (like that of Laodicea) backdated to the

204. So Newell, *op. cit.* (n. 203), pp. 35–40, and L. Kadman, *The Coins of Akko Ptolemais* (1961), pp. 20–1, implicitly rejecting the earlier ascription to Philip and Antiochus XII of minting there; cf. E. Babelon, *Catalogue etc., Les rois de Syrie* (1890), pp. 204, 209; J. Rouvier, Journal international d'archéologie numismatique 4 (1901), pp. 206 f.

205. Selene, soon after the death of her father, Ptolemy Physcon (117/16 B.C.) and at the instigation of her mother, married her brother, Ptolemy Lathyrus (Justin, *Hist.* xxxix 3, 2). Likewise at the instigation of her mother, she later married the Syrian king Antiochus VIII Grypus, a confederate at that time of Cleopatra (Justin, *Hist.* xxxix 4, 1–4). According to Appian, *Syr.* 69/366, Selene was also the wife of Antiochus IX Cyzicenus and of his son Antiochus X Eusebes. In regard to Antiochus IX (d. 95 B.C.) a difficulty arises in that he survived Antiochus VIII (d. 96 B.C.) by about only one year; yet Appian expressly states that Selene was the consort of the three Syrian kings. When Ptolemais was captured by Tigranes, she appears to have been taken prisoner, for Tigranes had her executed soon afterwards at Seleucia on the Euphrates, Strabo xvi, 2, 3 (749). On Selene generally, see Kuhn, *Beiträge zur Gesch. der Seleukiden* (1891), pp. 21, 42; M. L. Strack, *Die Dynastie der Ptolemäer* (1897), p. 201, and the genealogy at the end; A. Bouché-Leclercq, *Histoire des Séleucides* (1913), pp. 30–4; RE s.v. 'Kleopatra' (22).

206. Josephus writes, *Ant.* xiii 16, 4 (420): *βασίλισσα γὰρ Σελήνη ἡ καὶ Κλεοπάτρα καλουμένη τῶν ἐν Συρίᾳ κατῆρχεν* (the reading *κατῆρχεν* is poorly attested; but the *κατεχέιν* adopted by Niese is grammatically impossible).

previous autumn.[207] The coins with the legend *Πτολεμαίεων ἱερᾶς καὶ ἀσύλου* (or the like) probably belong to this period also (shortly after Caesar). Under Claudius in A.D. 51/2, coins show the city with the name *Γερμανικεῖς*, probably after Claudius himself, whose names included Germanicus, rather than after Germanicus or Gaius.[208] Claudius also settled a colony of veterans in Ptolemais, evidently at the very end of his reign, since the Greek coins continue up to A.D. 52/3. The city was then called *colonia Ptolemais*, with the full title thereafter of *Colonia Claudia Stabilis Germanica Felix Ptolemais*, though it did not possess the privileges of a colony.[209] On the outbreak of the first Jewish war, the two thousand Jews in Ptolemais were massacred by its inhabitants, *B.J.* ii 18, 5 (477). The territory of Ptolemais is mentioned by Josephus as the western boundary of Galilee, *B.J.* iii 3, 1 (35); cf. *Vita* 24 (118). The formula *Πτολεμαΐδα καὶ τὴν προσκυροῦσαν αὐτῇ*, viz. *χώραν* (1 Mac. 10:39) is characteristic.

Like the great coastal towns, those of the so-called Decapolis also belong to the category of independent Greek cities. The term *ἡ Δεκάπολις* is first encountered during the Roman period[210] and most of the cities of the Decapolis owed their independent political status to Pompey.

207. For the Caesarian era, see Rouvier, *op. cit.* (n. 189); *BMC Phoenicia*, p. lxxxi. See especially H. Seyrig, Syria 31 (1954), p. 74, and for the era of Laodicea, 27 (1950), pp. 26–32.

208. *BMC Phoenicia*, pp. lxxix, lxxxii; W. Kubitschek, 'Zur Geschichte von Städten des römischen Kaiserreiches', SAW 177.4 (1916), p. 81; cf. Kadman, *op. cit.* (n. 201), p. 23; Seyrig, RN 4 (1962), p. 39.

209. Pliny, v 19/75: 'colonia Claudi Caesaris Ptolemais quae quondam Acce'; cf. xxxvi 26/190; *Digest.* l 15, 1, 3 (from Ulpian): 'Ptolemaeensium enim colonia, quae inter Phoenicen et Palaestinam sita est, nihil praeter nomen coloniae habet'. Note AE 1907 194 (A.D. 56): '(Nero) [viam] ab Antiochea [fecit ad n]ovam colon[ia]m [Ptolemai]da'; and M. Avi-Yonah, QDAP 12 (1946), pp. 85–6, (=AE 1948 142): 'Imp. Ner. Caes. col. Ptol. veter. vici Nea Com(e) et Gedru'. On the numismatic evidence, see de Saulcy, *op. cit.*, pp. 153–69, 405 f., pl. VIII, n. 2–11; *BMC Phoenicia*, pp. lxxxii–iii; W. Kubitschek, *op. cit.*, pp. 82–94; Kadman, *op. cit.*, pp. 110 f.; Seyrig, *op. cit.*, pp. 43–5.

210. Mt. 4:25; Mk. 5:20; 7:31; Pliny, *NH* v 6/74; Josephus, *B.J.* iii 9, 7 (446); *Vita* 65 (341), 74 (410); Ptolemy v 15, 22; CIG 4501=Le Bas et Waddington, *Inscr.*, no. 2631=OGIS 631 (inscription of the time of Hadrian; cf. below on Abila); Eusebius, *Onomast.*, ed. Klostermann, p. 80; Epiphanius, *Haer.* 29, 7; *De mens.* 15; Stephanus Byz., s.v. *Γέρασα* (the extant text here has *τεσσαρεσκαιδεκαπόλεως*, for which however Meineke rightly reads *δεκαπόλεως*). Cf. in general, van Kasteren, DB s.v. 'Décapole'; RE s.v. 'Dekapolis' (2); G. Hölscher, *Palästina in der persischen und hellenistischen Zeit* (1903), pp. 97 f.; E. Schwartz, NGG (1906), pp. 365–76; Abel, *Géog. Pal.* II, pp. 145–6; H. Bietenhard, 'Die Dekapolis von Pompeius bis Trajan', ZDPV 79 (1963), pp. 24–58. For a clear statement of the argument that 'Decapolis' is merely a geographical term, see S. Thomas Parker, 'The Decapolis Reviewed', JBL 94 (1975), pp. 437–41. Note also H. Seyrig, 'Temples, cultes et souvenirs historiques de la Décapole', Syria 36 (1959), pp. 60–78.

They were primarily the Greek cities of the territory east of the Jordan which were subjugated by Alexander Jannaeus and later freed from Jewish rule by Pompey. It has often been supposed that they formed a kind of confederacy consisting originally of ten cities, whence the appellation 'Decapolis', a name retained even after the number was increased through the addition of other cities. But the evidence offers no clear support for the idea of a league or confederacy, and it is better to see 'Decapolis' simply as a loose geographical term. On their liberation by Pompey, almost all these towns adopted a calendar of their own customarily known as the Pompeian era. This is not to be taken to refer to a uniform era, but to a complex of local eras beginning at various times between 64 and 61 B.C.[211] The list of cities given as belonging to the Decapolis is not always the same, as Piny, our chief authority, observes in *NH* v 16/74: 'Decapolitana regio a numero oppidorum, in quo non omnes eadem observant, plurimum tamen Damascum . . . Philadelphiam, Rhaphanam . . . Scythopolim . . . Gadara . . . Hippon, Dion, Pellam . . . Galasam (read: Garasam=Gerasam), Canatham'. Ptolemy v 15, 22–3 (Didot ed. v 14, 18) appears to give the Decapolis a much wider radius. He lists in this section all the cities mentioned by Pliny except Raphana, but mentions also nine more, among them Heliopolis and Abila Lysaniae in the Lebanon. But the heading of the section presented in the majority of the manuscripts, *Κοίλης Συρίας Δεκαπόλεως*, is oddly ambiguous. (For *Δεκαπόλεως* several manuscripts have *δὲ καὶ πόλεως*, which is the same; the insertion of *καί* after *Συρίας* is a conjectural restoration; see the apparatus criticus in the Didot ed. I, 2 (1901), begun by C. Müller and continued by Fischer). So it may be

211. Schwartz, *loc. cit.*, for this reason opposed the expression 'Pompeian era'. But there is general agreement in using it for city eras whose epochs vary by a year or two, going back to 64, 63 or even 66 or 61 B.C. See A. E. Samuel, *Greek and Roman Chronology* (1972), p. 247. Schwartz also rejected (correctly) the conjecture that these cities formed a sort of federation. He supposed that they were founded by the first Seleucids, who looked on them 'as a great fortress of the Syrian kingdom against the Egyptian rivals' (*ibid.*, p. 375). On this view, 'Decapolis' was perhaps originally the name of a province of the Seleucid kingdom in the third century B.C. (*ibid.*, pp. 372–5). On the other hand, since the whole of the area west of the Jordan belonged to the Ptolemies from the beginning of the third century B.C. (see above, p. 87), it is very unlikely that the power of the Seleucids east of the Jordan extended at that time to Gerasa and Philadelphia, or that the Scythopolis area belonged to them (as it certainly did not immediately before the conquest of 200 B.C., see p. 144 below). Damascus was fought for repeatedly in the third century (see above, pp. 87–8). Whatever lay to the south of it will have been Ptolemaic. The cities of the Decapolis (apart from Damascus) were certainly Ptolemaic in the second half of the third century B.C., for they were captured by Antiochus the Great. Philadelphia, as the name testifies, was ruled already by Ptolemy II. The existence of a Seleucid province 'Decapolis' is in consequence very questionable, the more so since the name is not traceable before the Roman period.

preferable to follow the minority of manuscripts in which *Δεκαπόλεως* does not appear. Alternatively, the restoration *Κοίλης Συρίας καὶ Δεκαπόλεως* may be correct, for neither term had any clearly established definition. The cities of the Decapolis are also elsewhere designated as towns of *Κοίλη Συρία* (in Stephanus Byzantinus: Scythopolis, Pella, Dium, Gerasa; on coins, Gadara, Abila, Philadelphia; see below on the individual cities). Accordingly, Ptolemy should be ignored in regard to the extent of the Decapolis, and Pliny alone should be relied on. With the exception of Scythopolis, all the cities lay east of Jordan. The inclusion of Damascus, far to the north, is striking. Also, it employed not the Pompeian but the Seleucid era.[212] Pliny's evidence, however, definitely shows that it can be counted as belonging to the Decapolis. The fact that 'Decapolis' seems to have been a geographical rather than a legal or constitutional expression explains why it could continue to be used (Ptolemy, *loc. cit.*; Epiphanius, *Pan.* 29, 7; *De mens.* 15; OGIS 631) after some of the cities included in it, Gerasa and Philadelphia, were joined to the province of Arabia, established in A.D. 106.

12. Damascus, *Δαμασκός*, Hebrew דמשק in the Amarna Letters, Dimasqa, Dumaasqa, Timaasqi.[213] From the varied history of this town, attention need be drawn here only to what is relevant to its constitution during the Hellenistic and Roman periods.[214] The rule of Alexander the Great over Damascus is attested not only by literary evidence, but also by coins of his minted there.[215] In the third century B.C. it is uncertain whether Damascus, like Phoenicia and Palestine, belonged to the Ptolemies or to the Seleucids. Ptolemy II Philadelphus must have possessed Damascus in around 274 B.C., whether he seized it or inherited it from Ptolemy I (on this, see above, p. 87). But the city was then captured by Antiochus I (280–61). It may then have remained in the possession of the Seleucids but a Zenon papyrus of

212. So Hölscher, *op. cit.*, p. 97.

213. *The Tell el-Amarna Tablets*, ed. Mercer and Hallock (1939), I, p. 223; II, p. 895; see Y. Aharoni, *The Land of the Bible* (1967).

214. See generally, G. Le Strange, *Palestine under the Moslems* (1890), pp. 224–73; DB II, pp. 1213–31; RE IV, cols. 2042 ff., JE IV (1903), cols. 415–20; E. Schwartz, NGG (1906), 366–9; J. Sauvaget, *Esquisse d'une histoire de la ville de Damas* (1937); Abel, *Géog. Pal.* II, pp. 301–2; C. Watzinger, K. Wulzinger, *Damascus: die antike Stadt* (1921); DB Supp., s.v. 'Damas' (1934); LThK, s.v. 'Damaskos' (1959). On the use of the Seleucid era there, and the dating (to the first century A.D.) of the temple of Jupiter Damascenus, note especially H. Seyrig, Syria 27 (1950), pp. 34–7.

215. Curtius iii 13, 4; iv 1, 4; Arrian, *Anab.* ii 11, 9–10; 15, 1. For the coins, see L. Müller, *Numismatique d'Alexandre le Grand*, pp. 287 f., pl. nos. 1338–46. Cf. G. Kleiner, *Alexanders Reichsmünzen* (1949); A. R. Bellinger, *Essays on the Coinage of Alexander the Great* (1963).

about 259 B.C. strongly suggests that it was Ptolemaic.[216] However, during the great invasion of the Seleucid kingdom by Ptolemy III in 246 B.C., when all Syria was lost for some years to Seleucus II, Damascus besieged, was nevertheless not taken. Seleucus relieved it in 242/41 as he pressed victoriously southwards.[217] Indirectly, the city's adherence to the Seleucid kingdom is also confirmed by the fact that in the detailed account given by Polybius (v 61–71) of the conquest of Phoenicia and Palestine by Antiochus the Great, mention is made of the occupation of the most important Phoenician and Palestinian cities but none at all of Damascus. When as a result of the strife between the brothers Antiochus VIII Grypus and Antiochus IX Cyzicenus, Syria was divided in 111 B.C., and Antiochus Cyzicenus established himself in the southern part,[218] Damascus presumably became the capital of his small kingdom. In any case, in around 95–85 B.C. it was repeatedly the capital of a kingdom of Coele Syria detached from that of Syria, first under Demetrius Eucaerus, a son of Antiochus Grypus, Josephus, *Ant.* xiii 13, 4 (370), then under Antiochus XII, likewise a son of Grypus, *Ant. xiii* 15, 1 (387). Antiochus XII fell in battle before the king of Nabataea, and Damascus then came under the latter's rule, *Ant.* xiii 15, 1–2 (387–92); *B.J.* i 4, 7–8 (99–102).[219] Subsequently, the city was in

216. Polyaenus, *Strat.* iv 15: *Ἀντίοχος Σελεύκου· Ἀντίοχος βουλόμενος κρατῆσαι Δαμασκοῦ, ἣν ἐφύλασσε Δίων Πλολεμαίου στρατηγός, ἐπήγγειλε τῇ στρατιᾷ καὶ τῇ χώρᾳ πάσῃ Περσικὴν ἑορτὴν . . . καὶ ἀπροσδοκήτως ἐπιφανεῖς αἱρεῖ Δαμασκόν, Δίωνος οὐ δυνηθέντος ἀντισχεῖν Ἀντιόχῳ παρόντι.* Cf. J. Droysen, *Gesch. des Hellenismus* II, 1, pp. 256, 274; K. B. Stark, *Gaza*, pp. 366–7, B. Niese, *Gesch. der griech. und makedon. Staaten* II, pp. 127 f.; E. R. Bevan, *The House of Seleucus* I, p. 234; G. Hölscher, *Palästina in der pers. u. hell. Zeit*, p. 8; Beloch and Tcherikover, *op. cit.*, p. 87 above; U. Kahrstedt, *Syrische Territorien* (1926), p. 23. On the relevance of the papyrus, P. Cairo Zen. 59006, see R. S. Bagnall, *Administration of the Ptolemaic Possessions outside Egypt* (1976), p. 12.

217. Eusebius, *Chron.*, ed. Schoene I, p. 251: 'Ptolomaeus autem, qui et Triphon, partes (regiones) Syriorum occupavit: quae vero apud (ad contra) Damaskum et Orthosiam obsessio fiebat, finem accepit (accipiebat) centesimae tricesimae quartae olompiadis anno tertio, quum Seleukus eo descendisset (descenderit)'. German translation in Jacoby, FGrH 260 F 32 (8) (242/141 B.C.). Cf. B. Niese, *Gesch. der griech. und makedon. Staaten* II, pp. 145 ff.; E. R. Bevan, *The House of Seleucus* I, pp. 181 ff.; G. Corradi, 'Note sulla guerra tra Tolemeo Evergete e Seleuco Callinico', *Atti della R. Accademia delle scienze di Torino* 40 (1905), pp. 805–26; with Eusebius, Corradi dates the siege of Damascus to 242/1 B.C.

218. Eusebius, *Chron.*, ed. Schoene I, p. 260.

219. The name of the Arabian king who defeated Antiochus XII is not given, *Ant.* xiii 15, 1 (387); *B.J.* i 4, 7 (101). But it is stated immediately afterwards that Damascus came under the domination of Aretas, *Ant.* xiii 15, 2 (392); *B.J.* i 4, 8 (103). It is therefore unlikely that two different people were involved (the former a predecessor of the latter), as Gutschmid supposed, see vol. I, p. 578. For coins of Aretas III in Damascus see E. T. Newell, *Late Seleucid Mints in Ake-Ptolemais and Damascus* (1939), pp. 92–4; Y. Meshorer, *Nabataean Coins* (1975), pp. 12–15, and cat. nos. 5–8.

the power of Tigranes of Armenia during his fourteen-year reign in Syria; coins of Damascus attest his rule there in 72–69 B.C. (vol. I, p. 135). But in the time of Alexandra, at around this moment, her son Aristobulus undertook a military expedition to Damascus, ostensibly to protect it from Ptolemy Mennaei, who cannot in the context be a foreign ruler, *Ant.* xiii 16, 3 (418); *B.J.* i 5, 3 (115). Moreover, an autonomous coin of Damascus exists from the year 243 of the Seleucid era = 70/69 B.C. (de Saulcy, *op. cit.*, p. 31, no. 9; Newell, *op. cit.*, p. 100). When Pompey advanced into Asia, in southern Syria his legates occupied Damascus before all else, *Ant.* xiv 2, 3 (29); *B.J.* i 6, 2 (127). From then on, it formed part of the Roman province of Syria.[220] The time of Cassius (44–42 B.C.) found a Roman commander, Fabius, in the city, *Ant.* xiv 11, 7 (295); 12, 1 (297); *B.J.* i 12, 1–2 (236). During the reign of Antonius, coins were minted there bearing the image of Cleopatra.[221] The life of Damascus in this and the following period is illustrated by the description by Nicolaus of Damascus (vol. I, pp. 28–32) of the role of his father Antipater, rich and well-trained in rhetoric, who held offices in the city, served on embassies, and defended Damascus' interests before the neighbouring dynasts (FGrH 90 F. 131). Roman imperial coins of Damascus exist already from the time of Augustus and Tiberius; nevertheless (as at Ascalon) other autonomous coins also derive from the same period. On both, the Seleucid era is used, which thus remained dominant in Damascus.[222] There are no coins of Caligula and Claudius, though some exist from Nero onwards. This, combined with the fact that when Paul fled from the city (probably in the time of Caligula)—Damascus was apparently under an ethnarch of the Arabian king Aretas IV (2 Cor. 11:32)—seems to indicate that at that time it belonged temporarily to the king of Nabataea, whether he seized it by force or obtained it by imperial

220. Jerome, *Comment. in Isa.* 17 (CCL lxxiii, 1): 'Alii aestimant de Romana captivitate praedici, quoniam et Iudaeorum captus est populus, et Damascus, cui imperabat Areta, similem sustinuit servitutem'. The view of Marquardt, *Röm. Staatsverwaltung* I, p. 405 and Mommsen, *Röm. Gesch.* V, pp. 476 f. that Damascus remained under the rule of the Arabian kings until A.D. 106, is supported only by 2 Cor. 11:32, and is not certain (see below).

221. F. de Saulcy, *Numismatique de la Terre Sainte*, p. 34; J. N. Svonoros, *Τὰ νομίσματα τοῦ κράτους τῶν Πτολεμαίων* II (1904), p. 315; IV (1908), cols. 387–8, giving the datings 36, 35 and 32 B.C.

222. For the era see H. Seyrig, Syria 27 (1950), pp. 34–7, noting that it also appears on Damascus inscriptions, e.g. SEG VII, pp. 230, 237–8; 242–3, 245. Note that Damascus used the 'Babylonian' Seleucid era (see vol. I, p. 126) beginning in spring 311 B.C.; the spring New Year is attested by Simplicius, *Com. in Arist. Phys.* 226b 34 (*Com. in Ar. Gr.* X, p. 875). See L. Ideler, *Handbuch der Chronologie* I, pp. 413, 437. For the 'Year of Damascus' on inscriptions see Clermont-Ganneau, *Rec. arch. or.* I, pp. 8 f.: E. Schwartz, NGG (1906), pp. 341, 353, 367, 385.

favour.[223] The existence of a Jewish community in Damascus is known already from the New Testament, Act. 9:2; 2 Cor. 11:32. Its size may be deduced from the report that the number of Jews slain there at the outbreak of the revolution was ten thousand, *B.J.* ii 20, 2 (561), or even eighteen thousand according to another statement, *B.J.* vii 8, 7 (368). From the last decades of the first century onwards, Damascene troops were to be found already in the remoter provinces of the Roman empire: the *cohors I Flavia Damascenorum milliaria* was stationed from at least A.D. 90 to 134 in Germania Superior.[224] As the coins testify, after Hadrian the city bore the title *μητρόπολις*, and after Severus Alexander it was a colony.[225]

During the reign of Tiberius, a boundary dispute is recorded between the Damascenes and the Sidonians, *Ant.* xviii 6, 3 (153), which is chiefly interesting because it demonstrates how extensive these city territories were: the territory of Damascus must have adjoined that of Sidon.

Although Damascus was an inland town, its merchants travelled widely. Already in the second century B.C., Damascenes appear with Sidonians and Tyrians on inscriptions from Delos.[226]

13. Hippus, *Ἵππος*, is properly the name of a mountain or hill of that name on which the town stood.[227] It is presumably identical with the Aramaic Susitha, סוסיתא, frequently mentioned in rabbinic sources

223. The latter is more probable: H. Willrich, III (1903), p. 229; cf. vol. I, pp. 581–2. On the title *ἐθνάρχης*, see above, p. 97.

224. A military diploma of A.D. 90 found at Mainz (CIL XVI 36), one of 116 at Wiesbaden (XVI 62), and another at Neckarburken (XVI 80). An *ἔπαρχος σπείρης πρώτης Δαμασκηνῶν* occurs on certain Egyptian documents of A.D. 135 (BGU nos. 73; 136). A few years later, in 139, this *coh. I Damascenorum* (to be distinguished from the *coh. I Flavia Dam.*) was stationed in Palestine (military diploma of 22nd November 139, CIL XVI 87). For further material on both cohorts, see RE IV, cols. 279 f. s.v. 'cohors'.

225. On the title *μητρόπολις*, see Kuhn, *op. cit.*, p. 192; Marquardt, *op. cit.* I, p. 430. For the coins of Damascus with this title, see *BMC Syria*, pp. 283–6, and for its coins in Latin with the COL(ONIA) DAMAS(CUS) METR(OPOLIS), pp. 286–8. Note also the inscription from Damascus, SEG VII no. 224, with [*Δαμασ*]*κό*[*ς*] *Ἀ*[*ραβι*]*ῶν μητρόπολις*.

226. For persons from Damascus on an ephebic list from Delos of 117/16 B.C. see P. Roussel, *Délos colonie Athénienne* (1916), p. 86; for dedications made there to Hagne Aphrodite by Damascenes, p. 268. For private inscriptions of Damascenes in Athens, IG II/III^2 8466–70.

227. Ptolemy, v 15, 8 = Didot ed. (I. 2, 1901) v 14 6. In general, cf. RE s.v. 'Hippos' (4), VIII (1912), cols. 1913–14; R. Dussaud, *Topographie historique de la Syrie antique et mediévale* (1927), pp. 388–9; Ḥadashot Archeologiot 6 (1957), 30–3; EAEHL s.v. 'Hippos' summarizing the results of the excavations of 1950–2, for which no detailed report is available; Abel, *Géog. Pal.* II, pp. 471–2; Avi-Yonah, *Holy Land*, pp. 169–70; 'Gazetteer' s.v. 'Hippos'.

as a Gentile town of Palestine,[228] and with the Susiye of Arabic geographers.[229] It was sited according to Pliny on the eastern shore of Lake Gennesareth;[230] according to Josephus, only thirty stadia from Tiberias;[231] according to Eusebius and Jerome, in the neighbourhood of a village or castle called Apheka.[232] From these data it is now accepted that the ruins of Qal'at el-Ḥuṣn on a hill on the eastern shore of Lake Gennesaret mark the actual site of ancient Hippus; a village named Fik,[233] which must be identical with the ancient Apheka, lies a short distance away. It was of course a mistake to think that the name el-Ḥuṣn (allegedly 'horse') is the same as Hippus; el-Ḥuṣn—a common place-name in Syria—means 'fortress'.[234] Nevertheless, the identification is certainly correct, for the ancient name is preserved in the ruins of Susiye, between el-Ḥuṣn and Fik.[235]

Little is known of the history of Hippus. Alexander Jannaeus conquered it.[236] It was liberated by Pompey, *Ant.* xiv 4, 4 (75); *B.J.* i 7, 7 (156). Subsequently, it is listed as one of the cities of the Decapolis (Pliny, *NH* v 18/74; on Ptolemy, see above, p. 126). It was bestowed by Augustus upon Herod, *Ant.* xv 7, 3 (217); *B.J.* i 20, 3 (396), but on Herod's death it was again detached from the Jewish realm, *Ant.* xvii 11,4 (320); *B.J.* ii 6, 3 (97). In this connection it is explicitly described as a Greek city (*loc. cit.*). On the outbreak of the first revolution, the territory of Hippus, like that of Gadara, was devastated by the Jews under the leadership of Justus of Tiberias, *B.J.* ii 18, 1 (459); *Vita* 9

228. In tOhol. 18:4, Susitha is referred to along with Ascalon as an example of a Gentile town 'surrounded' by the land of Israel. It is often mentioned elsewhere in conjunction with Tiberias: A. Neubauer, *Géographie du Talmud*, pp. 238–40; A. Schlatter, *Zur Topographie und Geschichte Palästinas* (1893), pp. 306 f.

229. C. Clermont-Ganneau, 'Où était Hippos de la Décapole?', RA N.S 29 (1875), pp. 362–9; K. Furrer, ZDPV 2 (1879), p. 74; G. Le Strange, *Palestine under the Moslems*, pp. 472, 540.

230. Pliny, *NH* v 15/71: 'in lacum . . . Genesaram . . . amoenis circumsaeptum oppidis, ab oriente Iuliade et Hippo'.

231. Josephus, *Vita* 65 (349). The information given here is admittedly very schematic: Hippus 30 stadia from Tiberias, Gadara 60 stadia, Scythopolis 120. Such figures betray a tendency to shorten the distances as much as possible, and so should not be taken as strictly accurate. Moreover, it also appears from Josephus that the territory of Hippus lay by the lake opposite Tarichea, *Vita* 31 (151–3), in the neighbourhood of Gadara, *Vita* 9 (42).

232. Eusebius, *Onomast.*, ed. Klostermann, p. 22; Jerome, *ibid.*, p. 23.

233. For a description of the site, see Dalman, *Sacred Sites and Ways* (1935), pp. 169–71; cf. Avi-Yonah, 'Gazetteer', s.v. 'Apheca'.

234. See C. Clermont-Ganneau, *loc. cit.*, p. 364; H. Guthe, ZDPV 9 (1886), 334, note.

235. First demonstrated by G. Schumacher, ZDPV 9 (1886), pp. 324, 349 f., and since then generally accepted.

236. Syncellus, ed. Dindorf, I p. 559, from a source independent of Josephus; see vol. I, pp. 219–28.

(42). The inhabitants of Hippus retaliated by killing or imprisoning the Jews resident there, *B.J.* ii 18, 5 (478). In Christian times Hippus was an episcopal see.[237] The name of the town has until now appeared on only a few coins (from the reigns of Nero and Domitian). But others with the legend *'Αντιοχέων τῶν πρὸς Ἵπ(πῳ) τῆς ἱερ(ὰς) κ(αὶ) ἀσύλου* have rightly been assigned to Hippus by numismatists. As is to be expected, they have the Pompeian era calculated from 64 B.C. Most of them bear the image of a horse; they also represent the Tyche of the city, and some portray Zeus Antesios.[238] On a Gadarene epitaph found in Saffure, south-east of Susiye, Hippus is called *σοφή*, perhaps as being a town of Greek culture (see below, n. 255). The ruins of el-Ḥusn have also revealed an epitaph in Greek verse.[239] The town appears for the first time on a Latin inscription in the discharge-diploma dated to A.D. 105 granted to 'M(arco) Spedio M.f. Corbuloni Hippo', H. G. Pflaum, Syria 44 (1967), pp. 339–62 = AE 1968, 513. Unpublished milestones are reported from the road leading to Damascus (Dalman, *op. cit.*, p. 183).

The territory of Hippus is mentioned in *Vita* 9 (42), 31 (153); *B.J.* iii 3, 1 (37). The most instructive is *Vita* 9 (42): *ἐμπίπρησι τάς τε Γαδαρηνῶν καὶ Ἱππηνῶν κώμας, αἳ δὴ μεθόριοι τῆς Τιβεριάδος καὶ τῆς τῶν Σκυθοπολιτῶν γῆς ἐτύγχανον κεῖμεναι.* This passage shows that the combined territories of these four cities were so large as to form a coherent whole.[240]

14. Gadara, *Γάδαρα*. The location of Gadara on the site of the ruins of the Um el-Qeis, south-east of Lake Gennesaret, was determined by Seetzen as early as 1806 and has long been regarded as settled.[241] The

237. Epiphanius, *Haer.* 73, 26; Le Quien, *Oriens christianus* III, pp. 710 f.; Hierocles, *Synecd.*, ed. Parthey, p. 44; cf. p. 144 (*Notit. episcopat.*). For the four churches excavated on the site, see A. Ovadiah, *Corpus of the Byzantine Churches of the Holy Land* (1970), pp. 174–8.

238. For the coins, see *BMC Syria*, pp. lxxxiii–iv; B. V. Head, *Historia Numorum* (²1911), p. 786; H. Seyrig, Syria 34 (1959), pp. 70–1, 78–9.

239. J. Germer-Durand, 'Nouvelle exploration épigraphique de Gérasa', RB 8 (1899), pp. 539, no. 31 (p. 24).

240. See Avi-Yonah, *Holy Land*, pp. 169–70.

241. J. G. Seetzen, *Reisen durch Syrien*, ed. Kruse (1854–9) I, pp. 368 ff.; IV, pp. 188 ff.; G. Schumacher, *Northern Ajlun* (1890), pp. 46–80 (the most accurate description of the ruins, with plan and map of the surrounding area); *idem*, ZDPV 22 (1899), pp. 181 (on the progressive destruction of the ruins); G. A. Smith, PEFQSt (1901), p. 341. On the baths at el-Ḥammeh near Gadara, see Dechent, ZDPV 7 (1884), pp. 187–96; Schumacher, ZDPV 9 (1886), pp. 294–301; Nötling, ZDPV 10 (1887), pp. 59–88; Kasteren, ZDPV 11 (1888), pp. 239–41. For both, cf. also G. Schumacher, C. Steurnagel, *Der 'Adschlun* (1927), pp. 504–18, and see Vogel, 'Bibliography' s.v. 'Hammat-Gader'. For a detailed survey of the region S. Mittmann, *Beiträge zur Siedlungsgeschichte des nördlichen Ostjordanlandes* (1970). For its history, see Kuhn, *op. cit.* II, pp. 365 f., 371. In general, Abel,

main evidence is provided by the warm springs, for which Gadara was famous and which are still found in those parts.[242] Their source is on the northern bank of the Sheriat el-Mandur or Yarmuk; on the southern side, about three kilometres from the springs, are the ruins of the city, situated on a lofty ridge. The Sheriat el-Mandur is therefore identical with the Hieromices, which according to Pliny flowed past Gadara.[243] According to the *Itinerarium Antonini* (197–8), Gadara lay sixteen Roman miles from both Capitolias and Scythopolis; Roman milestones remain from both roads, as well as from that leading from Gadara to Tiberias.[244]

By the time of Antiochus the Great, Gadara was already an important fortress. It was conquered by Antiochus during his first invasion of Palestine in 218 B.C.,[245] and also when he took final possession of the country after his victory at Panias in 200 B.C.[246] Alexander Jannaeus subdued the city but only after a siege that lasted ten months, *Ant.* xiii 13, 3 (356); *B.J.* i 4, 2 (86). Under him and his successors it therefore belonged to the Jewish territory, *Ant.* xiii 15, 4 (396), but was again

---

Géog. Pal. II, p. 323; Avi-Yonah, *Holy Land*, p. 174. For the synagogue at el-Hammeh see E. L. Sukenik, *The Ancient Synagogue of el-Hammeh* (*Hammath-by-Gadara*) (1935); EAEHL II s.v. 'Ḥammat Gader'. Note also N. Lux, 'Der Mosaikfussboden eines spätantiken Bades in *umm qes*', ZDPV 82 (1966), pp. 64–70, and S. Mittmann, *ibid.*, pp. 71–3.

242. On its location, cf. Eusebius *Onomast.*, ed. Klostermann, p. 74: *Γάδαρα· πόλις πέραν τοῦ Ἰορδάνου, ἀντικρὺ Σκυθοπόλεως καὶ Τιβεριάδος πρὸς ἀνατολαῖς ἐν τῷ ὄρει, οὗ πρὸς ταῖς ὑπωρείαις τὰ τῶν θερμῶν ὑδάτων λουτρὰ παράκειται*. *Ibid.*, p. 22: *Ἀιμάθ ... κώμη πλησίον Γαδάρων ἐστὶν Ἐμμαθᾶ, ἔνθα τὰ τῶν θερμῶν ὑδάτων θερμὰ λουτρά*. On the baths, see also Epiphanius, *Haer.* 30, 7; Antoninus Martyr, *Itin.* 7 (CCL clxxv, p. 132, cf. p. 159) and Eunapius, *Vit. Soph.* 459 (who declares them to have been the most important after those of Baiae). Also Origen, *Com. on John* 6: 41 (24) (GCS *Origenes* IV, p. 150 f.): *Γάδαρα γὰρ πόλις μέν ἐστι τῆς Ἰουδαίας, περὶ ἣν τὰ διαβόητα θερμὰ τυγχάνει*. The place where the springs are situated also occurs in the Talmud under the name חמתה. See the passages in Levy, *Neuhebr. Wörterb.* II, pp. 69 f.

243. Pliny, *NH* v 18/74: 'Gadara Hieromice praefluente'. The form *Hieromax* derives from the incorrect reading *Hieromace*. That *Hieromices* is to be assumed as the nominative is proved by the occurrence elsewhere of the forms *Heromicas* (Tab. Peuting.) and *Ieromisus* (*Geogr. Ravennas*, ed. Pinder et Parthey, p. 85). The correct Greek form, *Ἱερομύκης*, is now attested in documentary form on a coin of Adraa, see A. Spijkerman, 'Yarmouk-Coins of Adraa Arabiae', SBFLA 21 (1971), pp. 327–30. The native name is ירמוך; see mPar. 8:10, 10, and Arab geographers, G. Le Strange, *Palestine under the Moslems*, pp. 54 f. Cedrenus, ed. Bekker, I, p. 746 has *τοῦ ποταμοῦ Ἱερομοχθᾶ*.

244. See Mittmann, *op. cit.*, pp. 133–50.

245. Polybius v 71, 3; see Walbank *ad. loc.*, and B. Niese, *Gesch. der griech. und makedon. Staaten* II, p. 378. Polybius says of Gadara on this occasion: *ἃ δόκει τῶν κατ' ἐκείνους τοὺς τόπους ὀχυρότητι διαφέρειν*.

246. Polybius xvi 39, 3 (see Walbank *ad. loc.*) = Josephus, *Ant.* xii 3, 3 (136). Cf. B. Niese, *op. cit.* II, p. 579.

separated from it by Pompey, *Ant.* xiv 4, 4 (75); *B.J.* i 7, 7 (155 f.). Out of regard for his freedman, Demetrius of Gadara, Pompey then rebuilt the city, which had been devastated by the Jews (perhaps under Alexander Jannaeus).[247] From then on, it formed part of the Decapolis (Pliny, *NH* v 18/74; cf. p. 126). Hence on the numerous coins of the city dating from Augustus to Gordian, the Pompeian era is always used, 64/63 B.C. in the case of Gadara. The refoundation by Pompey is also perpetuated on coins from Antoninus Pius to Gordian by the legend, *Πομπηιέων Γαδαρέων*.[248] It is incorrect to consider this Gadara as the seat of one of the five Jewish councils established by Gabinius (see vol. I, p. 268). In the year 30 B.C. Augustus bestowed it on Herod, *Ant.* xv 7, 3 (217); *B.J.* i 20, 3 (396). The city was, however, very dissatisfied with his rule. As early as 23–21 B.C., several Gadarenes laid complaints against him to M. Agrippa whilst he was staying in Mytilene, *Ant.* xv 10, 2 (351). The charges were repeated in 20 B.C., when Augustus visited Syria in person, *Ant.* xv 10, 3 (354). In both cases, the complainants were dismissed.[249] Following Herod's death, Gadara was detached from the kingdom and became part of the province of Syria, *Ant.* xvii 11, 4 (320), *B.J.* ii 6, 3 (97). At the beginning of the first revolt, its territory, together with that of neighbouring Hippus, was devastated by the Jews under the leadership of Justus of Tiberias, *B.J.* ii 18, 1 (459); *Vita* 9 (42). The Gadarenes and the people of Hippus avenged themselves by slaughtering or imprisoning the Jews living in their towns, *B.J.* ii 18, 5 (478).

The Gadara which Josephus describes as *μητρόπολις τῆς Περαίας*, and which requested a Roman garrison from Vespasian in the later period of the war, *B.J.* iv 7, 3–4 (410–39) cannot be this Gadara, but must be the Gadara or Gadora in Peraea.[250] Its coins, especially from the

247. Demetrius accompanied Pompey on his campaigns in the east and brought back enormous booty. See RE s.v. 'Demetrius' (50) and S. Treggiari, *Roman Freedmen during the Late Republic* (1969), pp. 184–5.

248. On the coins and era see *BMC Syria*, pp. lxxxvi–viii, 304–5; B. V. Head, *Historia Numorum* (²1911), p. 787. For the argument that an anonymous issue with *I. A. ΡΩΜΗΣ* (year 1 of Rome) should be attributed to Gadara, see H. Seyrig, Syria 36 (1959), pp. 72–6. See also Y. Meshorer, 'Coins of the City of Gadara struck in commemoration of a local Naumachia', *Sefunim* (1966), pp. 28–31 (speculative).

249. Mionnet, *Médailles* V, p. 323, and Suppl. VIII, p. 227, and de Saulcy, *Numismatique*, p. 295, describe coins of Gadara with the head of Augustus and dated to the year 44 of the city (20 B.C.) which de Saulcy interprets as minted by Herod in gratitude for Augustus' judgement. They do not seem to have been described or discussed since.

250. Since in the subsequent course of the operations, *B.J.* iv 7, 4–6 (419 ff.), only southern Peraean localities are named, A. Schlatter, *Zur Topographie und Geschichte Palästinas* (1893), pp. 44–51, assumed the existence of a Jewish Gadara in those regions; so also H. Guthe, Mitteilungen und Nachrichten des DPV (1896),

Antonine period, show the legend ἱ(ερὰ) ἄ(συλος) α(ὐτόνομος) γ(. . .) Κοί(λης) Συρ(ίας); the restorations are entirely hypothetical.[251] According to an inscription discovered by Renan, it was a Roman colony during the later imperial period.[252] The statement of Stephanus Byzantinus (s.v.) that it was also known as Ἀντιόχεια and Σελεύκεια is quite isolated, and probably refers to temporary official designations and not to names in common usage. There is abundant evidence that in pre-Christian times Gadara was a flourishing Hellenistic city. Josephus calls it at the time of Herod's death a πόλις Ἑλληνίς, *Ant.* xvii 11, 4 (320); *B.J.* ii 6, 3 (97). Strabo mentions as renowned natives of Gadara Philodemus the Epicurean, the poet Meleager, Menippus the cynic and satirist and Theodorus the orator. To these must be added from a later period, Oenomaus the cynic and the orator Apsines.[253] Meleager says of himself that he was born in 'an Attic fatherland among Syrians—Gadara'.[254] On an epitaph of a Gadarene named Apion, found in Saffure, south-east of Susiyyah (Hippus), Gadara is called χρηστομούσια.[255] Epitaphs of

---

pp. 5–10; F. Buhl, *Geographie des alten Palästina* (1896), pp. 255, 263. Nevertheless, μητρόπολις points to an important Greek city. From *Vita* 15 (82) it might appear that Josephus, as commander of Galilee, once took possession of Gadara by force. But instead of Γαδαρεῖς, which almost all the MSS. have, either Γαβαρεῖς or Γαραβεῖς should certainly be read; cf. *Vita* 25 (123), 45 (229), 47 (242); in 15 (82) one MS. has Γαραβεῖς. In *B.J.* iii 7, 1 (132), also Γαβαρέων or Γαβάρων should be read in place of Γαδαρέων. See A. Schalit, *Namenwörterbuch*, s.vv. Γαδαρεῖς, Γάραβα. Finally, in *Ant.* xiii 13, 5 (375), either the text is corrupt or another Gadara is meant. The reading is very uncertain.

251. For these legends, see Mionnet, *Médailles* III, pp. 325–6; *Suppl.* VIII, pp. 229–30; de Saulcy, *Numismatique*, pp. 299–303. Cf. *BMC Syria*, p. 305. The adjective ἱερά is however applied to Gadara in an epigram of Meleager, *Anth. Pal.* VII, 419 (Gow and Page, *The Greek Anthology: Hellenistic Epigrams*, Meleager iv). Stephanus Byz., s.v., describes Gadara as a city of Coele Syria.

252. E. Renan, *Mission de Phénicie*, p. 191 = CIL III 181 = 6697 (epitaph at Byblos): 'col(onia) Valen(tia) Gadara'. Cf. J. Jeremias, ZDPV 55 (1932), pp. 78–9. For a man from Gadara, named M. Calpurnius Germanus, in a list of veterans of II Traiana discharged in A.D. 157, see AE 1969/70, 633 vi.

253. On all these men, cf. pp. 49–50 above.

254. *Anth. Pal.* VII 417 (transl. Gow and Page, *The Greek Anthology: Hellenistic Epigrams*, Meleager ii, cf. iii and iv):

Νᾶσος ἐμὰ θρέπτειρα Τύρος πάτρα δέ με τεκνοῖ
Ἀτθὶς ἐν Ἀσσυρίοις ναιομένα Γάδαρα

255. C. Clermont-Ganneau, *Études d'archéologie orientale* II (1897), p. 142. Another, apparently less accurate, copy was published in PEFQSt (1897), pp. 188 f. (where Nazareth is given as the site of discovery). The first four lines run:

ἦν μου πατὴρ Κοίντος, ἦν μήτηρ Φιλοῦς.
τ(ὸ) δ' οὔνομ' ἐστὶν Ἀπείων, πατρὶς δὲ μου
καὶ πᾶσι κοινῆς Γάδαρα χρηστομούσια·
σοφῆς δ' ἀφ' Ἵππου ἐστὶν ἡ μήτηρ Φιλοῦς.

Cf. the metrical charm on a papyrus ascribed to a 'Syrian Gadarene woman' *(Σύρας Γαδαρηνῆς)*, P. Maas, JHS 62 (1942), pp. 33–8. For χρηστομουσία (with this

Gadarenes have also been found in Athens.[256]

The territory of Gadara formed the eastern boundary of Galilee, *B.J.* iii 3, 1 (37). On its extent, cf. *Vita* 9 (42) and above, p. 132. That it reached as far as Lake Gennesaret is not to be concluded from Mt. 8:28 alone (the reading is very uncertain), but also from the coins, which often portray a ship. One of them (a coin of Marcus Aurelius) even mentions a *ναυμα(χία)*.[257]

15. Abila, *Ἄβιλα*. The place-name Abel (אבל) or Abila is very common in Palestine. Eusebius knows of no less than three places of this name celebrated for viticulture: (1) a village in southern Peraea, six Roman miles from Philadelphia; (2) a *πόλις ἐπίσημος* twelve miles east of Gadara; (3) a place between Damascus and Paneas.[258] Of these, the second is the locality which concerns us here. Its site on the south bank of the Sheriat el-Mandur was, like that of Gadara, discovered by Seetzen.[259] Pliny does not include it among the cities of the Decapolis, yet its membership is attested by an inscription from the reign of Hadrian.[260] An *Ἄβιδα*, certainly this *Ἄβιλα*, is also listed by Ptolemy among the cities of the Decapolis.[261] It first appears in recorded history

---

accentuation), Clermont-Ganneau, *Rec. d'arch. or.* II (1898), p. 399, proposed the interpretation 'aux belles mosaïques'; but a more likely meaning is, 'ville lettrée', a city that cultivates poetry and rhetoric. (So P. Perdrizet, RA 35 (1899), 49–50.) For Greek inscriptions from Gadara see CIG 4660 = Guérin, *Galilée* I, p. 303 = Clermont-Ganneau, *Rec. arch. or.* I, p. 21, no. 37; cf. nos. 38–40; Mittmann, *op. cit.*, pp. 124–9; cf. F. Zougadine, 'A Dated Greek Inscription from Gadara-Um Queis', ADAJ 8 (1973), p. 78.

256. IG II/III² 8448a–8449.

257. See n. 248 above.

258. Euseb., *Onomast.*, ed. Klostermann, p. 32: *Ἄβελ ἀμπελώνων· ἔνθα ἐπολέμησεν Ἰεφθαέ. γῆς υἱῶν Ἀμμών καὶ ἔστιν εἰς ἐτὶ νῦν κώμη ἀμπελοφόρος Ἀβελὰ ἀπὸ ϛʹ σημείων Φιλαδελφίας, καὶ ἄλλη πόλις ἐπίσημος Ἀβελὰ οἰνοφόρος καλουμένη, διεστῶσα Γαδάρων σημείοις ιβʹ τοῖς πρὸς ἀνατολαῖς, καὶ τρίτη τις αὐτὴ Ἀβελὰ τῆς Φοινίκης μεταξὺ Δαμασκοῦ καὶ Πανεάδος*. On the third see vol. I, pp. 567–9.

259. J. G. Seetzen, *Reisen durch Syrien* (ed. Kruse) I, pp. 371; IV, pp. 190 f. G. Schumacher, 'Abila of the Decapolis' (suppl. to PEFQSt, July 1889), gives the most accurate description. In general, cf. Abel, *Géog. Pal.* II, pp. 234–5. Avi-Yonah, *Holy Land*, p. 175. See also G. Schumacher, C. Steuernagel, *Der 'Adschlun* (1927), pp. 536–8 = ZDPV 49 (1926), pp. 152–4; N. Glueck, *Explorations in Eastern Palestine* IV (AASOR XXV–VIII, 1951), pp. 125–6.

260. CIG 4501 = Le Bas-Waddington, *Inscriptions* III. 2, no. 2631 = OGIS 631 = IGR III 1057 (inscription found in Taiyibeh, north-east of Palmyra, now in the British Museum, dated 445 *aer. Sel.* = A.D. 133/134): *Ἀγαθάνγελος Ἀβιληνὸς τῆς Δεκαπόλεως*. For the Palmyrene parallel text with the name אגתגלס but with no place of origin, see CIS II 3912.

261. Ptolemy v 15, 22. The Codex of Vatopedi also has *Ἄβιδα*; see *Géographie de Ptolemée, reproduction photolithogr. du manuscrit grec du monastère de Vatopedi* (1867), p. lvii, l, 4. In the Didot edition (I. 2, 1901), v 14, 18. Müller and Fischer have restored *Ἄβιλα*.

at the time of Antiochus the Great, who in both his first and second conquest of Palestine (218 and 200 B.C.) captured Abila and neighbouring Gadara.[262] It seems in general to have frequently shared Gadara's fate. Like the latter, Abila too was conquered by Alexander Jannaeus;[263] both were re-established as Greek cities by Pompey. For the coins of Abila showing the Pompeian era are rightly ascribed to this Abila. Again, the titles of the town are exactly the same as those of Gadara: ἱ(ερὰ) ἄ(συλος) α(ὐτονομος) γ(. . .) Κοί(λης) Συρ(ίας) Coins of the second century A.D. show that the city was also known as Σελεύκεια, its inhabitants as Σελευκεῖς Ἀβιληνοί.[264] In Nero's reign it may have been this Abila that was granted to Agrippa II.[265] In the sixth century A.D., there is mention of Christian bishops of Abila, almost certainly the Abila discussed here.[266]

16. Raphana, not to be confused with Syrian Ῥαφάνεια in Cassiotis, is mentioned only by Pliny, *NH* v 18/74.[267] It is probably identical with the Ῥαφών of 1 Mac. 5:37 = Josephus, *Ant.* xii 8, 4 (342),[268] which according to the context of the story (cf. 5:43) lay not far from Ḳarnaim. The site of the latter place is not certain, but is likely to be Seih Sa'al, fifteen kilometres west of er-Râfi (Raphana?).[269]

262. Polybius v 71, 2 (see Walbank, *ad loc.*) and xvi 39, 3 = Josephus, *Ant.* xii 3, 3 (136).

263. Syncellus, ed. Dindorf, I, p. 559. Cf. above, n. 236.

264. On the coins, see Mionnet, *Médailles* V, p. 318; *Suppl.* VIII, pp. 223–4; de Saulcy, *Numismatique*, pp. 308–12; cf. *BMC Syria*, p. lxxxiii; Head, *Historia Numorum*², p. 786; H. Herzfelder, 'Contribution à la numismatique de la Décapole', RN 39 (1936), pp. 285–95, on pp. 291 f.; H. Seyrig, Syria 36 (1959), pp. 61–2; W. Kellner, 'Commodus-Münzen aus der Dekapolis', Schweiz. Münzbl. 20 (1970), pp. 1–3.

265. *B.J.* ii 13, 2 (252): (Nero) προστίθησιν . . . Ἄβελα μὲν καὶ Ἰουλιάδα κατὰ τὴν Περαίαν. In the parallel passage, *Ant.* xx 8, 4 (159), Josephus does not mention Abila. Moreover, *Ant.* xii 3, 3 (136) is the only other passage in which he certainly refers to this Abila. *Ant.* iv 8, 1 (176), v 1, 4 (4), and *B.J.* iv 7, 6 (438), allude to another Abila near to the Jordan, facing Jericho and not far from Julias-Livias, which is not identical with any of the three places of the same name mentioned by Eusebius. In view of the conjunction of Abila and Livias in *B.J.* ii 13, 2 (252), it may have been this Abila that was granted to Agrippa II; cf. vol. I, p. 473. Cf. Avi-Yonah, *Holy Land*, p. 96 on the Peraean Abila.

266. R. Le Quien, *Oriens christianus* III, pp. 702 f. Cf. Hierocles, *Synecd.*, ed. Parthey, p. 44; *ibid.*, p. 144 (*Notit. episcopat.*).

267. On the Syrian Raphaneia, see Josephus, *B.J.* vii 1, 3 (18); 5, 1 (97); Ptolemy v 15, 16 = Didot ed. (I. 2, 1901) v 14, 12; *Tab. Peuting.*, Hierocles, ed. Parthey, p. 41. See RE s.v. 'Raphana' (1).

268. On Raphana see Abel, *Géog. Pal.*, p. 432; on Karnaim, see Avi-Yonah, *Holy Land*, p. 168; D. Sourdel, *Les cultes du Hauran à l'époque romaine* (1952), pp. 41–2.

269. See Abel on 1 Mac. 5:43; H. Bietenhard, ZDPV 79 (1963), p. 29. The Masoretic text of Gen. 14:5 mentions an 'Ashtaroth-Ḳarnaim, which has been identified with 'Ashtaroth, the city of Og, king of Bashan, and with the Karnaim of 1 Mac.

As Ptolemy does not cite Raphana among the cities of the Decapolis, he probably lists it under another name. No definite identification can be advanced, but the one most frequently suggested is Capitolias, mentioned in Ptolemy v 15, 22 and frequently elsewhere from the second century A.D. This however is better identified with Bet Ras on the road between Gadara and Adraa.[270]

17. Kanata? Waddington attempted to prove, on the basis of inscriptions, the existence of a town of this name as distinct from Kanatha=Kanawât.[271] On an inscription found at el-Afine (on the western incline of the Hauran, north-east of Bostra) an *ἀγωγὸς ὑδάτων εἰσφερομένω[ν] εἰς Κάν[α]τα* is mentioned, built by Cornelius Palma, governor of Syria during the reign of Trajan.[272] This aqueduct cannot have led to Kanawât, since it lies higher than el-Afine and has in any case plentiful water of its own.[273] Waddington argued that the Kanata of the aqueduct is more likely to have been the present-day Kerak (in the plain, directly west of es-Suweda), for an inscription found there by Wetzstein reads: *Διῒ μεγίστ(ω) Κανατηνῶν ὁ* (*δῆμος*?).[274] Other inscriptions also testify to the former Greek culture of this locality.[275] One mentions a *βουλευτής* (without indicating of which place).[276] On another from the middle of the third century A.D., the

270. For the identification of Raphana and Capitolias see A. H. M. Jones, CERP², ch. 10, n. 45. According to *Tab. Peuting.*, Capitolias lay 16 Roman miles from Adraa, and the latter only 6 Roman miles from Ashtaroth (Eusebius, *Onomast.*, ed. Klostermann, p. 12). But the *Tabula* also shows that Capitolias was situated east of Adraa, on the road to Gadara, 13 Roman miles away. The *Itinerarium Antonini* (196; 198) places it 16 Roman miles from Gadara and 36 from Neve. On Capitolias, see vol. I, p. 521, n. 40; cf. Mittmann, *op. cit.*, pp. 133–4; 169–73 (inscriptions); H. Seyrig, Syria 36 (1959), pp. 62–8 (cults).

271. Le Bas-Waddington, *Inscriptions* III, comments on nos. 2296, 2329, 2412d.

272. Le Bas-Waddington, *op. cit.*, III, no. 2296=OGIS 618=IGR III 1291. For further inscriptions of the same aqueduct see also M. Dunand, 'Kanata et Kanatha', Syria 11 (1930), pp. 272–9=SEG VII 969, 977; cf. also SEG VII 1143, 1148; AE 1933, 146.

273. Cf. the map of the Hauran area in ZDPV 12 (1889); H. C. Butler, *Princeton University Archaeological Expedition to Syria 1904–5, 1909*, II A, 7 (1919), map at p. 403; cf. the sketch-map by A. H. M. Jones, 'The Urbanisation of the Ituraean Principality', JRS 21 (1931), pp. 265–75, pl. xxxi.

274. J. C. Wetzstein, *Ausgewählte griechische und lateinische Inschriften* (1863), no. 185=Le Bas-Waddington, *Inscriptions*, no. 2412d=Dussaud et Macler, *Voyage archéologique* (1901), p. 198. It may well be correct to read *Κανατηνῷ Νο*[......], as proposed by Sourdel, *op. cit.*, p. 22.

275. Wetzstein, *op. cit.*, nos. 183–186=Le Bas-Waddington, *op. cit.*, nos. 2412d–2412g, and cf. Jones and Sourdel, *op. cit.*

276. Wetzstein, *op. cit.*, no. 184=Le Bas-Waddington, *op. cit.*, no. 2412e. Cf. Jones, *op. cit.*, p. 273, n. 1.

term κώμη is used, apparently of the location where Kerak now lies.[277] If according to this, Kanata = Kerak is to be distinguished from Kanatha = Kanawât, it is probably the second that is also meant on an inscription naming a γαίης ἐγ Κανάτων ἀνὴρ ἀγαθός τε σαόφρων,[278] and on coins with the legend Καvατηνῶν.[279] The coins have the Pompeian era; only those from the reigns of Claudius and Domitian are definitely ascertainable. That the date on an inscription found at Kerak from the middle of the third century A.D. is reckoned according to the era of the province of Arabia (from A.D. 106) would therefore give rise to no difficulties.[280]

Nevertheless, despite the reasons adduced by Waddington, the distinction Kanata = Kerak and Kanatha = Kanawât is not tenable. Above all, and as Mordtmann pointed out, the difference in the orthography is without significance, since τ and θ are interchangeable in the spelling of other names too.[281] In addition, it happens that in the immediate vicinity of Kerak, namely in Dêr-Ḥulêf, Seetzen read on an inscription the words Καναθηνῶ[ν ἡ] πόλις ἔκτισεν.[282] If only one πόλις is concerned, it is clear that it must be the one whose extensive remains are to be found at Kanawât (see below). Furthermore, there are no remains at Kerak that would suggest an important urban centre;[283] nor is there any unambiguous epigraphic evidence for a πόλις there. It therefore seems best to conclude that there was one πόλις, at Kanawât, whose name, Kanatha, was spelled in various ways in Greek inscriptions (see below). When a number of inscriptions from the area show aqueducts built to bring water—for irrigation—'to Kanata' (εἰς Κάνατα),[284] this must either mean 'to the territory of Kanatha', which is possible,[285] or, more probably, that Kanata was the name of a village on the site of Kerak.

277. Wetzstein, *op. cit.*, n. 186 = Le Bas-Waddington, *op. cit.*, n. 2412 f. For the significance of the term, see G. M. Harper, 'Village Administration in the Roman Province of Syria', YCS 1 (1928), pp. 103–68.

278. C. Clermont-Ganneau, *Rec. Arch. Or.* I (1888), p. 7 = C. Fossey, BCH 21 (1897), p. 55.

279. Mionnet, *Médailles* V, p. 321; *Suppl.* VIII, p. 225; de Saulcy, *Numismatique*, pp. 399 ff.; *BMC Syria*, pp. xxxiv–v, 302; Head, *Historia numorum*², p. 786.

280. Wetzstein, *op. cit.*, no. 186 = Le Bas-Waddington, *op. cit.*, no. 2412 f (and also Waddington's comments).

281. J. H. Mordtmann, *Archäol.-epigr. Mitteilungen aus Österreich-Ungarn* VIII, p. 183.

282. J. G. Seetzen, *Reisen durch Syrien* I (1854), p. 64 = CIG 4613 = Le Bas-Waddington, *op. cit.*, no. 2331a. The inscription was not, as is incorrectly stated in CIG and Waddington, found by Seetzen in Kanawât, but in Dêr Ḥulêf (as is plain from the context in Seetzen I, p. 64; cf. also the Kruse's remarks in Seetzen's *Reisen* IV, p. 40). But Dêr Ḥulêf is not far from Kerak.

283. So Dunand, Syria 11 (1930), p. 277.

284. See Dunand, *op. cit.*

285. So Sourdel, *op. cit.*, p. 13, n. 6. The distance from Kanawât to Kerak is 25 km. Such a size for a city territory is by no means uncommon (cf. the remarks

18. Kanatha. On the western slopes of the Hauran range lies Kanawât, the ruins of which are among the most important east of the Jordan.[286] Numerous inscriptions and the well-preserved remains of temples and other public buildings prove that a considerable city once stood here; and indeed, both ruins and inscriptions point to the first centuries of the Roman imperial epoch. The ruins have been frequently described since Seetzen's first fleeting visit. The most complete collection of the inscriptions remains that of Waddington.[287] The form of the name, above all, suggests that it is here that one should look for the 'Kanatha', 'Kanotha' or sometimes 'Kanautha' mentioned on inscriptions and in literary works.[288] But in addition, the data concerning Kanatha—probably all, but certainly some of them—relate to Kanawât.[289] In the

---

at the end of the articles on Damascus, Hippus, Scythopolis, Gerasa, Philadelphia, Sebaste). The existence of several *cohortes Canathenorum* suggests that Kanatha may have possessed an extensive territory.

286. See especially J. G. Seetzen, *Reisen durch Syrien*, ed. Kruse, I, pp. 78–80; IV, pp. 40–1, 51–5; M. de Vogüé, *Syrie Centrale, Architecture civile et religieuse* I (1865), pp. 59 f.; H. C. Butler, *American Arch. Exped. to Syria 1899–1900 II; Architecture and Other Arts* (1903), pp. 351–61; 402–5, 407–8; R. E. Brünnow, A. von Domaszewski, *Die Provincia Arabia* III (1909), pp. 107–44; H. C. Butler, *Princeton Univ. Exped. to Syria 1904–5, 1909* IIA (1919), pp. 346–54.

287. Le Bas-Waddington, *Inscriptions* III, nos. 2329–63; cf. CIG 4612–15; IGR III 1223–6. Subsequent publications are noted below. See especially the bibliography of epigraphical publications from the Hauran in D. Sourdel, *Les cultes du Hauran à l'époque romaine* (1952), pp. v–ix.

288. An *Αὐρηλία 'Ασχόνη Καναυθηνή* on an inscription at Bostra (IGR III 1334). A *βουλευτής πολίτης τε Κανωθαί[ω]ν ἐπ[ὶ] Συρίης* on an inscription found in the neighbourhood of Trevoux in France (see below, n. 297). This man is described after his native town as *'Αθειληνός;* the village of Atil still exists in the neighbourhood of Kanawât. An *"Αραψ πόλεως Σεπτιμίας Κάνωθα* on the island of Thasos, IGR I 839, revised by M. Launey, BCH 58 (1934), pp. 495–500, see L. Robert, *Hellenica* II (1946), pp. 43–50. Note also *Κανωθηνίς* on an inscription from Shuhba in the Hauran, AE 1933, p. 161. 'Kanotha' is used in Hierocles, ed. Parthey, p. 46 *(Κανοθά); Notitia episcopat., ibid.*, p. 92 *(Κανοθάς);* Acts of the Council of Chalcedon, R. Le Quien, *Oriens christ.* II, p. 867 (genitive *Κανώθας).* On the name Kanawât, see J. G. Wetzstein, *Reisebericht über Hauran und die Trachonen* (1860), pp. 77 f.

289. The Peutinger Table shows a road from Damascus leading southwards through Aenos to 'Chanata'. Aenos is probably Phaena = Mismie. But 'Chanata' can only be Kanawât, since the Roman road still visible from Damascus to Bostra passes very near to Kanawât. Also, the data on distances agree (from Aenos to Chanata, 37 Roman miles; the distance on the map from Mismie to Kanawât, 33 Roman miles). A *cohors prima Flavia Canathenorum* is known from several inscriptions (CIL VIII 2394–5; *diplomata* of the mid-second century, CIL XVI 94, 117, 118, 121, 183. Cf. also AE 1969/70 465; tile of the *coh. I Can.* in the region of Regensburg and Straubing in CIL III 6001, 11992; cf. RE IV, col. 267). A city in whose territory a cohort could be raised must have been a very significant one, which once again points necessarily to Kanawât. Eusebius, *Onomast.*, ed. Klostermann, p. 112, mentions: *Κανάθ, κώμη τῆς 'Αραβίας εἰς ἔτι [νῦν Καναθὰ] καλουμένη . . . κεῖται δὲ εἰς ἔτι καὶ νῦν ἐν Τραχῶνι πλησίον Βόστρων.* This might however be a

Old Testament, a קנת east of the Jordan is mentioned twice (Num. 32:42; 1 Chron. 2:23), and it figures similarly in a rabbinic discussion of borders of Palestine.[290] This too may be identified with Kanawât.[291]

Apart from the Old Testament passages, the history of Kanatha cannot be traced beyond the time of Pompey; its coins have the Pompeian era,[292] and Pliny, v 18/74 (for Ptolemy, see above, p. 126) includes it among the cities of the Decapolis. On the coins of Commodus the inhabitants are described as *Γαβειν(ιεῖς) Καναθ(ηνοί)*: the town seems therefore to have been restored by Gabinius. Herod experienced a mortifying defeat at Kanatha in a battle against the Nabataeans.[293] According to inscriptions found in Kanawât and the neighbouring regions, the city may have belonged to Herod; it was certainly in the possession of Agrippa II.[294] The inscriptions furnish some information on the civic constitution: *βουλευταί* are often mentioned,[295] and a *πρόεδρος* and an *ἀγορανόμος*, each once.[296] Of particular interest is a Graeco-Latin epitaph, found in 1862 near Trévoux in France (Département de l'Ain, not far from Lyons), of a Syrian merchant described in the Greek text as *βουλευτὴς πολίτης τε Κανωθαί[ω]ν ἐπ[ὶ] Συρίης*, and in Latin as *decurio Septimianus Canotha*.[297] The latter style is explained by

---

reference to the hypothetical village of Kanata discussed above, n. 279. But Stephanus Byz., *Lex.* s.v. *Κάναθα · πόλις πρὸς τῇ Βόστρᾳ Ἀραβίας*, clearly alludes to the city of Kanatha. The other data on Kanatha correspond: Pliny, *NH* v 18/74; Ptolemy v 15, 23 (Didot ed. V 14, 18); Josephus, *B.J.* i 19, 2 (366) = *Ant.* xv 5, 1 (112). The form 'Kanatha' also appears on coins (see below) and inscriptions (Le Bas-Waddington, *op. cit.*, no. 2216: *Καναθηνὸς βουλευτής*, cf. AE 1936, 152: *Καναθηνοί*. On the inscription in Seetzen, *op. cit.* I, p. 64 = CIG 4613, see above, n. 280). On one occasion also *Κεναθηνός* (Le Bas-Waddington, *op. cit.*, no. 2343). On Kanatha see DB II, cols. 121–9; Enc. Jud. 10, cols. 905–6, s.v. 'Kenath'. The site has never been excavated, and no detailed descriptions have succeeded those published early in this century.

290. ySheb. 36c; tSheb. 4:11; Sifre Dt. 51. Cf. A. Neubauer, *Géographie du Talmud*, pp. 10 ff., 20; H. Hildesheimer, *Beiträge zur Geographie Palästinas* (1886), Introduction and pp. 49–51; S. Lieberman, *Tosephta Ki-Fshuṭah, in loc.*

291. See A. Schalit, *König Herodes* (1969), pp. 697–8.

292. See de Saulcy, *Numismatique*, pp. 399–401, pl. xxiii, no. 10; especially J. C. Reichardt, 'Die Münzen Kanathas', Wiener Numismatische Zeitschrift (1880), pp. 68–72; *BMC Syria*, pp. lxxxiv–v; 302; Head, *Historia Numorum*², p. 786. Cf. H. Seyrig, Syria 36 (1959), p. 61.

293. *B.J.* i 19, 2 (366 ff.). In the parallel passage, *Ant.* xv 5, 1 (112), the place is called *Κανά* in some MSS, but Niese reads *Κάνατα* on good authority.

294. Herod: Le Bas-Waddington, *op. cit.*, no. 2364 = OGIS 415 (from Si'a; see vol. I, p. 296, n. 24); Agrippa II: *ibid.*, nos. 2329 = OGIS 424, 2365 = OGIS 419 (Si'a). See vol. I, pp. 471–83.

295. Le Bas-Waddington, *op. cit.*, nos. 2216, 2339 (= Wetzstein, no. 188). On CIG 4613, which also mentions a *βουλευτής*, see above, n. 289.

296. *Πρόεδρος*, CIG 4614 = Le Bas-Waddington, *op. cit.*, no. 2341; *ἀγορανόμος*, CIG 4612 = Le Bas-Waddington, no. 2330.

297. IG XIV 2532 = CIL XIII 2448 = IGR I 25 = ILS 7529.

the inscription from Thasos which reads *Ἄραψ πόλεως Σεπτιμίας Κάνωθα*.[298] The city had evidently acquired the title 'Septimia' during the reign of Severus (A.D. 193–211). There is nothing to show that any change of status was granted at the same time. The term 'Arab' is not to be taken as meaning that the city then belonged to the province of Arabia, and the expression 'in Syria' of the former inscription would naturally imply that it belonged to Syria. As noted above (n. 298), the village (*κώμη*) of 'Kanatha' (*Κανάθ*) which Eusebius describes as part of Arabia[299] might reasonably be taken to be the village Kanata at Kerak. A Christian bishop of Kanotha was present at the Councils of Ephesus (A.D. 449), Chalcedon (451) and Constantinople (459).[300]

19. Scythopolis, *Σκυθόπολις*, one of the major centres of Hellenism in Palestine, was the only city of the Decapolis that lay west of the Jordan.[301] Its ancient name was Beth-Shean, בית שאן or בית שן. In the Septuagint and Maccabees it appears as *Βηθσάν* or *Βαιθσάν* (1 Mac. 5:52; 12:40 f.),[302] also contracted to *Βαίσων* and *Βασάν*.[303] It occurs already in the Amarna Letters under the name *Bîtsuani*.[304] The ancient name was preserved at all times alongside the Greek;[305] indeed it

298. IGR I 839, revised by M. Launey, BCH 58 (1934), pp. 495–500; see especially L. Robert, *Hellenica* II (1946), pp. 43–50.

299. *Onomast.*, ed. Klostermann, p. 112, see n. 289 above.

300. R. Le Quien, *Oriens christianus* II, p. 867.

301. See generally, Kuhn, *op. cit.* II, p. 371; Guérin, *Samarie* I, pp. 284–99; Conder and Kitchener, *The Survey of Western Palestine, Memoirs* II, pp. 83, 101–14 (with plans); G. Le Strange, *Palestine under the Moslems*, pp. 410 f.; I. Benzinger, ZDPV 14 (1891), pp. 71 f.; G. A. Smith, *Historical Geography of the Holy Land*, pp. 357–64; DB s.v. 'Bethshan'; DB Supp. I, cols. 950–6; III, cols. 421–6; A. Rowe, *History and Topography of Beth-Shan* (1930); P. Thomsen, *Loca sancta*, pp. 106 f.; Abel, *Géog. Pal.* II, pp. 280–1; Tcherikover, *Hellenistic Civilisation*, pp. 102–3; M. Avi-Yonah, 'Scythopolis', IEJ 12 (1962), pp. 123–34; Avi-Yonah, *Holy Land*, pp. 138–40; EAEHL I, s.v. 'Beth-Shean'; B. Lifschitz, 'Scythopolis: L'histoire, les institutions et les cultes de la ville à l'époque hellénistic et impériale', *Aufstieg und Niedergang der röm. Welt*, ed. H. Temporini, II.8 (1978), pp. 262–92.

302. In the Old Testament, Jos. 17:11, 16; Jg. 1:26; 1 Sam. 31:10, 12; 2 Sam. 21:12; 1 Kg. 4:12; 1 Chr. 7:29. See A. Aharoni, *The Land of the Bible* (1967) *passim*. For a brief archaeological survey relating to this period, see H. O. Thompson, 'Tell el-Husn – Biblical Beth-shan', BA 30 (1907), pp. 110–35. On the identity of Beth-Shean and Scythopolis, cf. Josephus, *Ant.* v 1, 22 (84); vi 14, 8 (374); xii 8, 5 (348); xiii 6, 1 (188); the LXX gloss at Jg. 1:27; Eusebius, *Onomast.*, ed. Klostermann, p. 54; Stephanus Byz. and Syncellus (see next note).

303. Stephanus Byz., s.v. *Σκυθόπολις· Παλαιστίνης πόλις ἢ Νύσσης* (read *Νύσσα*) *Κοίλης Συρίας, Σκυθῶν πόλις, πρότερον Βαίσαν λεγομένη ὑπὸ τῶν βαρβάρων*. Syncellus, ed. Dindorf I, p. 559: *Βασὰν τὴν νῦν Σκυθόπολιν* (in the history of Alexander Jannaeus). Also, I, p. 405 (in the passage cited in note 308 below).

304. *The Tell el-Amarna Tablets*, ed. Mercer and Hallock (1939), II, pp. 718 f.

305. בית שאן in mA.Z. 1:4; 4:12. For the adjective בישני cf. mPea. 7:1. Cf. A. Neubauer, *Géographie du Talmud*, 174 f.; A. Büchler, JQR 13 (1901), pp. 683–740;

eventually superseded it again. The tell of Beth-Shean has been extensively excavated, producing mainly finds of the Iron Age and earlier. Limited excavations have been carried out in the Graeco-Roman city and its cemeteries. The name *Σκυθόπολις* is certainly not to be derived from the Hebrew סכות since the old name of the town was not Sukkoth but Beth Shean.[306] Nor is there any sound basis for the derivation from the god Sikkuth (Am. 5:26). The name having also been written *Σκυθῶν πόλις*,[307] Syncellus supposed that Scythians settled there in their great invasion of Palestine in the seventh century B.C., and that this accounts for the place being called 'Scythians' City'.[308] The theory has also been advanced, unconvincingly, that the name relates to hypothetical 'Scythian' units serving in the Ptolemaic army.

Studies in Jewish History (1956), pp. 179–244. The form בשני = *Σκυθοπολίτης* appears on some ossuary inscriptions in Jerusalem, probably from the last century before the destruction of Jerusalem; see M. Lidzbarski, Ephemeris für semitische Epigraphik II. 2 (1906), pp. 191–7 = CIJ 1372–4.

306. For the biblical Sukkoth and its possible site, see N. Glueck, BASOR 90 (1943), pp. 14–19. Jerome, *Quaest. hebr. in Genesin*, remarks on Succoth, Gen. 33:17 (CCL lxxii, pp. 41–2): 'Est autem usque hodie civitas trans Iordanem hoc vocabulo inter partes Scythopoleos'. But Beth-Shean cannot have received its new name from a town across the Jordan.

307. *Σκυθῶν πόλις*: Jud. 3:11; 2 Mac. 12:29; LXX at Jg. 1:27; Polybius v 70, 4; Aristides, ed. Dindorf, II, p. 470 = *Or.* XV Keil, 82. Milestones of the Roman period, however, show that the official description was *Σκυθόπολις*, AE 1948, 154–5; 1966, 497.

308. Syncell., ed. Dindorf, I, p. 405: *Σκύθαι τὴν Παλαιστίνην κατέδραμον καὶ τὴν Βασὰν κατέσχον τῆς ἐξ αὐτῶν κληθεῖσαν Σκυθόπολιν.* On the Scythian (or Cimmerian) invasion, see especially Herodotus I 105; Eusebius, *Chron.*, ed. Schoene II, pp. 88 f.; A. von Gutschmid, *Kleine Schriften* III (1892), pp. 430 ff.; G. Hölscher, *Palästina in der persischen und hellenistischen Zeit* (1903), pp. 43–6 (who explains Scythopolis as 'town of the Scythians'): K. Bittel, *Grundzüge der Vor- und Frühgeschichte Kleinasiens* ([2]1950), pp. 90–3; A. Malamat, IEJ 1 (1950), pp. 154–9. Pliny and his successor Solinus also derive the name from the Scythians, but from those whom the god Dionysius settled there to protect the grave of his nurse; Pliny v 18/74: 'Scythopolim, antea Nysam, a Libero Patre sepulta nutrice ibi Scythis deductis'; Solinus, ed. Mommsen, c. 36: 'Liber Pater cum humo nutricem tradidisset, condidit hoc oppidum, ut sepulturae titulum etiam urbis moenibus amplaret. Incolae deerant: e comitibus suis Scythas delegit, quos ut animi firmaret ad promptam resistendi violentiam, praemium loci nomen dedit'. For another and equally mythological derivation from the Scythians, see Malalas, ed. Dindorf, p. 140, and Cedrenus, ed. Bekker, I, p. 237. Pseudo-Hegesippus, *De bello Iudaico*, reproducing Josephus, *B.J.* iii 9, 1 (411 f.), adds his own note on Scythopolis (Hegesippus III 19): 'ideoque memorata urbs Dianae Scythicae consecrata, tamquam ab Scythis condita, et appellata civitas Scytharum ut Massilia Graecorum'. Stephanus Byz. also explains the name by *Σκυθῶν πόλις* (see above, n. 303). For the view that it derived from Scythians in Ptolemaic service, see M. Avi-Yonah, IEJ 12 (1962), p. 127. A. H. M. Jones, CERP[2], p. 240, compares the names of Egyptian metropoleis of the Ptolemaic period such as Gynaecopolis or Crocodilopolis.

But in fact, no satisfactory explanation can be offered. On the name Nysa, by which Scythopolis was also known according to Pliny, Stephanus Byzantinus and the coins, see above, p. 38.

The city appears under its Greek name Scythopolis in the third century B.C., when it was tributary to the Ptolemies.[309] When Antiochus the Great invaded Palestine in 218 B.C., it surrendered to him voluntarily.[310] Nevertheless, like the rest of Palestine, it did not come under permanent Syrian rule until 200 B.C. In the time of the Maccabees, Scythopolis is referred to as a Gentile city, but not as one hostile to the Jews (2 Mac. 12:29–31). Towards the end of the second century (about 107 B.C.) it came under Jewish rule. The weak Antiochus IX Cyzicenus was unable to withstand the advance of John Hyrcanus; indeed his general, Epicrates, treacherously surrendered Scythopolis to the Jews, *Ant.* xiii 10, 3 (280) [*B.J.* i 2, 7 (64 ff.) gives a different account].[311] For this reason it passed into the possession of Alexander Jannaeus, *Ant.* xiii 15, 4 (396). The city was made once again separated from the Jewish realm by Pompey, *Ant.* xiv 4, 4 (75), *B.J.* i 7, 7 (156), and was restored by Gabinius, *Ant.* xiv 5, 3 (88), *B.J.* i 8, 4 (166). From then on, it remained independent. Neither Herod nor his successors ever governed the city. Besides Pliny, *NH* v 18/74 (for Ptolemy see above, p. 126), Josephus too describes it as belonging to the Decapolis and even as being one of its major towns, *B.J.* iii 9, 7 (446): ἡ δ' ἐστὶ μεγίστη τῆς Δεκαπόλεως. Scythopolis used the Pompeian era beginning in autumn 64 B.C., as is shown most clearly by an inscription of A.D. 519 dated to the year 585 of the city. The belief that it also used the Caesarian era has been proved unfounded. The city titles, especially on the coins of Gordian, are ἱερὰ ἄσ(υλος).[312] When at the outbreak of the first war in A.D. 66 the rebels attacked the territory of Scythopolis, *B.J.* ii 18, 1 (458), the Jewish inhabitants found themselves obliged in the interest of their own safety to fight on the side of the Gentiles against their compatriots. Afterwards, however, the Jews were enticed into the sacred grove and massacred by the Gentiles—allegedly thirteen thousand people in all, *B.J.* ii 18, 3–4 (466–76); vii 8, 7 (363); *Vita* 6

309. Josephus, *Ant.* xii 4, 5 (183); cf. above, p. 89. The attribution of coins of Alexander the Great with the letters Σχ to Scythopolis (see L. Müller, *Numismatique d'Alexandre le Grand*, pp. 304–5, pl. 1429, 1464) is no longer accepted, see *BMC Palestine*, p. xxxiv.

310. Polybius v 70, 4–5, see Walbank, *ad. loc.*; Stark, *Gaza*, p. 381; Niese, *Gesch. der griech. und makedon. Staaten* II, p. 378.

311. On the chronology, cf. vol. I, p. 210.

312. On the coinage and era, see de Saulcy, *Numismatique*, p. 287–90, pl. XIV, n. 8–13; E. Schwartz, NGG 1906, pp. 358 f.; *BMC Palestine*, pp. xxxiv–vii, 75–7; S. Ben-Dor, 'Concerning the Era of Nysa-Scythopolis', PEQ 76 (1944), pp. 152–6; 77 (1945), pp. 47–8; H. Seyrig, 'L'ère de Scythopolis', RN N.S. 6 (1964), pp. 65–7 (disproving the Caesarian era).

(26). Josephus's remark, in connection with the Jewish war, that Scythopolis was at that time obedient to King Agrippa, *Vita* 65 (349), τῆς ὑπηκόου βασιλεῖ, is definitely not to be understood as signifying that it belonged to his territory, but simply that Scythopolis was on the side of Agrippa and the Romans.[313]

The territory of Scythopolis must have been very extensive. On the occasion of the city's capture, together with Philoteria (a town on Lake Gennesaret possibly to be identified with Beth Yeraḥ), by Antiochus the Great in 218 B.C., Polybius observes that the territories subject to these two places could easily provide for the upkeep of the whole army.[314] It is not certain, however, whether Polybius is referring to territories in the technical sense of an area belonging to a city. For the later period the evidence is clearer. According to Josephus, *Vita* 9 (42), the territory of Scythopolis bordered on that of Gadara (see above, p. 132). The same territory is also mentioned in *B.J.* iv 8, 2 (453).

The subsequent history of Scythopolis, which continued for centuries to prosper and flourish cannot be pursued here.[315] On its cults, rites, games and products, cf. above, pp. 38, 48, 68, n. 213.

20. Pella, Πέλλα. Josephus describes the territory of Pella as forming the northern boundary of Peraea.[316] According to Eusebius, the biblical Jabesh lay only six Roman miles away, on the road from Pella to Gerasa.[317] Now since Gerasa is situated south of the Wadi Jabis, Pella must have lain a little to the north of it. It has therefore long been established that the important ruins of Tabagat Faḥil on a terrace above the Jordan valley almost opposite Scythopolis (in a south-easterly direction) mark the site of the ancient Pella. This is confirmed by

313. There is no reason to deduce from this that Scythopolis actually belonged to the kingdom of Agrippa II, on which see vol. I, pp. 471–83.

314. Polybius v 70, 5: εὐθαρσῶς ἔσχε πρὸς τὰς μελλούσας ἐπιβολὰς διὰ τὸ τὴν ὑποτεταγμένην χώραν ταῖς πόλεσι ταύταις ῥαδίως δύνασθαι παντὶ τῷ στρατοπέδῳ χορηγεῖν καὶ δαψιλῆ παρασκευάζειν τὰ κατεπείγοντα πρὸς τὴν χρείαν. See Walbank, *ad loc.* For the territory of Scythopolis in the Roman period, see Avi-Yonah, *Holy Land*, pp. 138–40.

315. For the extensive late-Roman finds from Scythopolis, see Vogel, 'Bibliography' s.v. 'Bethshan' and EAEHL I, s.v. 'Beth-Shean'. Note that it appears in a Greek papyrus of A.D. 685, *P. Nessana* 74.

316. *B.J.* iii 3, 3 (47); Peraea is here the Jewish province of Peraea, excluding therefore the cities of the Decapolis (cf. above, p. 6). Peraea as a geographical concept could be taken as extending much further north to include, for example, Gadara, *B.J.* iv 7, 3 (413).

317. Eusebius, *Onomast.*, ed. Klostermann, p. 32: ἡ δὲ Ἰάβις ἐπέκεινα τοῦ Ἰορδάνου νῦν ἐστι μεγίστη πόλις, Πέλλης διεστῶσα σημείοις ς′ ἀνιόντων ἐπὶ Γερασάν. Similarly, *ibid.*, p. 110 (where Jabis is more correctly termed a κώμη). See Mittmann, *op. cit.*, pp. 152–9, for the remaining traces of this road and its milestones, and p. 147 for a milestone marked ἀπὸ Πελλῶν, with the distance.

Eusebius,[318] who notes that Ammathus lay twenty-one Roman miles south of Pella, which corresponds to the distance between the modern Amatha and Faḥil.[319] The site of Faḥil is also borne out by Pliny's allusion to Pella as 'aquis divitem'.[320] The warm springs of Faḥil, חמתא דפחל, are also mentioned occasionally in the Jerusalem Talmud.[321] Presumably, Faḥil is the original Semitic name; 'Pella' may have been chosen by the Greeks because of the similarity of sound.[322] The name Pella was in any case borrowed from the well-known Macedonian town of the same name. Since the latter was the birth-place of Alexander the Great, it has been suggested that this Pella, like the neighbouring Dium, was founded by Alexander himself, as a gloss on the text of Stephanus Byzantinus reports.[323] But in view of the uncertainty of this notice, it remains possible that Pella was founded by one of the Diadochi, perhaps Antigonus, who kept a firm hold of Palestine for some ten years (311 to 301 B.C.; see above, p. 87).[324] According to another

318. Eusebius, *Onomast.*, ed. Klostermann, p. 22.

319. See generally, Guérin, *Galilée* I, pp. 288–92; S. Merrill, *East of the Jordan* (1881), pp. 442–7; G. Schumacher, *Pella* (1888) contains a good description of the site and ruins, with map. See now R. H. Smith, *Pella of the Decapolis I: The 1967 Season of the College of Wooster Expedition to Pella* (1973), and his preliminary reports: 'The 1967 Excavations at Pella of the Decapolis', ADAJ 14 (1969), pp. 5–10; 'Pella of the Decapolis', Archaeology 21 (1968), pp. 134–7; Illustrated London News, March 16, 1968, pp. 26–7. See EAEHL II, s.v. 'Fahil'. On its history, see Droysen, *Hellenismus* III. 2, pp. 204 f.; Kuhn, *op. cit* II, p. 370; RE s.v. 'Pella' (4); Abel, *Géog. Pal.* II, pp. 405–6; Avi-Yonah, *Holy Land*, p. 175, and most fully, DB Supp. VII (1961–6) s.v. 'Pella' (J.-M. Fenasse).

320. Pliny, *NH* v 18/74; also, Schumacher, *op. cit.*, pp. 31 ff.

321. ySheb. 36c bottom: R. Zeira went to חמתא דפחל; cf. A. Neubauer, *Géographie du Talmud*, p. 274. On *Faḥl* in the Arab geographers, see G. Le Strange, *Palestine under the Moslems*, p. 439; A.-S. Marmardji, *Textes géographiques arabes sur la Palestine* (1951), pp. 158-9.

322. So also Th. Nöldeke, ZDMG (1885), p. 336.

323. Stephanus Byz., ed. Meineke, s.v. *Δῖον· πόλις . . . Κοίλης Συρίας, κτίσμα Ἀλεξάνδρου, καὶ Πέλλα*. The words *καὶ Πέλλα* are presumably a gloss introduced by a learned reader who wished thereby to say that Pella, like Dium, was a foundation of Alexander the Great. The reading *ἡ καὶ Πέλλα* is an erroneous emendation by an earlier editor; cf. Droysen, *op. cit.* III. 2, pp. 204 f.

324. K. J. Beloch, Archiv f. Papyrusforschung 2 (1903), p. 233=*Griech. Geschichte*, IV. 2 (^{2}1927), pp. 325–6, is inclined to take this view. A Syrian Pella is also mentioned among the foundations of Seleucus I in Appian, *Syr.* 57/296–8, and Eusebius, *Chron.*, ed. Schoene, II, p. 116 f. (according to the Latin text of Jerome: 'Seleucus Antiochiam Laodiciam Seleuciam Apamiam Edessam Beroeam et Pellam urbes condidit'; so also Syncellus, ed. Dindorf, I, p. 520, and the Armenian text of Eusebius, in which only Seleucia is missing). But this Pella probably refers to the town of Apamea on the Orontes, which was first called Apamea by its founder Seleucus I and afterwards Pella, which name it subsequently lost (see especially Pausanias Damascenus in Malalas, ed. Dindorf, p. 203=Müller, FHG IV, p. 470=Dindorf, *Historici graeci minores* I, p. 160; also Strabo, xvi 2, 10 (752); Stephanus Byz. s.v. *Ἀπάμεια;* in Diodorus xxi 20

passage in Stephanus Byzantinus, this Pella was also known as *Βοῦτις*. Stephanus is also the only source for the statement that Pella was called 'Berenike', a name which it will have acquired in the Ptolemaic period.[325]

Pella is first mentioned in connection with the conquest of Palestine by Antiochus the Great in 218 B.C., when the king, after taking Atabyrion (Tabor), turned towards the land east of the Jordan and seized Pella, Camoun and Gephroun.[326] Alexander Jannaeus conquered and destroyed the city because it would not adopt 'Jewish customs', *B.J.* i 4, 8 (104); *Ant.* xiii 15, 4 (397).[327] It was detached from the Jewish realm by Pompey, *Ant.* xiv 4, 4 (75), *B.J.* i 7, 7 (156). That it was part of the Decapolis is attested by Eusebius and Epiphanius, as well as by Pliny.[328] The few surviving coins use, as might be expected, the Pompeian era. They are attested from the reigns of Domitian to Elagabal, one coin from the latter period bearing the legend *Φιλιπ(πέων) Πελλη(νῶν) τ(ῶν) π(ρὸς) Νυμφ(αίῳ) Κοι(λῆς) Συ(ρίας)*. The description 'Philippian' may go back to L. Marcius Philippus, proconsul of Syria in 61–60 B.C. 'Nymphaeum' must refer to a fountain-house there; as noted above, Pella had abundant springs.[329] Josephus includes Pella among the chief towns of the eleven toparchies of Judaea, *B.J.* iii 3, 5 (55), but this mistake must be ascribed either to the author himself or to an error in the received text (see the Loeb text, *ad. loc.*). At the onset of the rebellion, during which the Christian community from Jerusalem

---

Apamea appears under the name of Pella. The lists in Appian and Eusebius mention Pella along with Apamea as though they were two different cities, but this mistake came about because the change of name was regarded as a second foundation and treated accordingly in the lists of city-foundations. There is no question of Pella (in the Decapolis) having been founded by Seleucus I.

325. Stephanus Byz. s.v. *Πέλλα · πόλις . . . Κοίλης Συρίας, ἡ Βοῦτις λεγομένη. Idem*, s.v. *Βερενῖκαι πολεῖς . . . ἔστι καὶ ἄλλη περὶ Συρίαν, ἣν Πέλλαν καλοῦσι.* See Tcherikover, *Hellenistic Civilisation*, p. 99.

326. Polybius v 70, 12; see Walbank, *ad loc.*

327. In the latter passage, too, *Ant.* xiii 15, 4 (397), the reference is certainly to this Pella and not to another Moabite place of the same name. Josephus only mentions Pella right at the end, after enumerating the Moabite towns, merely because he wishes to append a special observation. In Niese's edition of Josephus the text of *Ant.* xiii 15, 4 (397) has become unintelligible through the omission of *οὐχ* before *ὑποσχομένων*.

328. Pliny, *NH* v 18/74. (On Ptolemy, see above, p. 126.) Eusebius *Onomast.*, ed. Klostermann, p. 80; Epiphanius, *Haer.*, 29, 7; *De mens.* 15.

329. For the coins, see de Saulcy, *Numismatique*, pp. 291–3, pl. XVI, n. 8; K. Regling, 'Nachlese zu den Münzen von Sinope und Pella', Num. Zeitschr. 42 (1904), pp. 15–18; W. Kubitschek, 'Münzen von Pella in Palästina', *ibid.*, pp. 25–32; H. Herzfelder, 'Contribution à la numismatique de la Décapole', RN 39 (1936), pp. 285–95; H. Seyrig, Syria 36 (1959), pp. 69–70; A. Spijkerman, 'An Unknown Coin-Type of Pella Decapoleos', SBFLA 20 (1970), pp. 353–8.

is said to have found refuge there,[330] Pella was attacked by the insurgent Jews, *B.J.* ii 18, 1 (458). Christian bishops of Pella are mentioned in the fifth and sixth centuries A.D.[331]

21. Dium, *Δίον*. Among the towns of this name, seven of which are recorded by Stephanus Byzantinus, the Dium in Macedonia at the foot of Mt. Olympus is the best known. It is therefore supposed from the notice of Stephanus Byzantinus that, like Pella (see above, p. 146), this Dium (in Coele Syria) was founded by Alexander the Great.[332] According to the astronomical calculations of Ptolemy v 15, 23 = Didot edition v 14, 18, Dium lay near Pella, $\frac{1}{6}$ of a degree east of it and $\frac{1}{6}$ of a degree north (thus C. Müller in the Didot edition, though the figures given in the tradition vary). This accords with Josephus's information concerning the route of Pompey's march, namely that the Jewish king Aristobulus accompanied him on his expedition from Damascus against the Nabataeans as far as Dium. Here Aristobulus suddenly parted from Pompey and as a result the latter also wheeled about towards the west and came by way of Pella and Scythopolis to Judaea.[333] There is thus no reason to reject Ptolemy's data and look for Dium further to the north.[334]

Little is known of the history of Dium. It was conquered by

330. Eusebius, *HE* iii 5, 2–3; Epiphanius, *Haer.* 29, 7; *De mens.* 15. See S. G. F. Brandon, *The Fall of Jerusalem and the Christian Church* (1951), pp. 168–73. Contra (defending the authenticity of the reported flight), S. Sowers, 'The Circumstances and Recollection of the Pella Flight', ThZ 26 (1970), pp. 305–20. Note also R. H. Smith, 'A Sarcophagus from Pella: New Light on the Earliest Christianity', Archaeology 26 (1973), pp. 250–6.

331. R. Le Quien, *Oriens christianus* III, pp. 698 f.

332. Stephanus Byz. also remarks on our Dium: *ἧς τὸ ὕδωρ νοσερόν*, and quotes the following epigram: *νᾶμα τὸ Διηνὸν γλυκερὸν ποτόν, ἤνιδε πίῃς/παύσει μὲν δίψης, εὐθὺ δὲ καὶ βιότου*.

333. Josephus, *Ant.* xiv 3, 3–4 (46 ff.); *B.J.* i 6, 4 (132). In both passages, Dium has only come into the text through Dindorf's emendations. The older editions have *Ant.* xiv 3, 3 (47); *εἰς Δήλιον πόλιν*, and *B.J.* i 6, 4 (132) *ἀπὸ Διοσπόλεως*. In the best manuscript (*cod. Pal.*) the first passage reads *εἰς Δεῖλον πόλιν*, and in *B.J.* the manuscripts vary between *ἀπὸ Διὸς ἡλίου πόλεως* and *ἀπὸ Διοσπόλεως*; one (*cod. Bodl.*, not considered by Niese) has *ἀπὸ Δίου πόλεως* (according to Bernard and Hudson). In view of the nature of this manuscript otherwise (see Niese, vol. VI, proleg. p.L.), it is uncertain whether this is based on an ancient tradition or is merely a conjecture on the part of a copyist. There can however be no doubt whatever concerning the correctness of the emendation (*Διὸς ἡλίου* arose from *Διὸς ἢ Δίου*).

334. E. Schwartz, NGG (1906), pp. 359–61, was inclined to look for Dium on the site of Tell-el-Ash'ari, east of the Lake of Gennesaret, where according to an inscription found there (IGR III 1164) an ancient city must have stood that used the Pompeian era (unless the stone has been displaced). On Tell-el-Ash'ari, see ZDPV 20 (1897), p. 167, and Schumacher's map, *ibid.*, sect. b 6. For other possibilities cf. Abel, *Géog. Pal.* II, pp. 306 f.; H. Bietenhard, ZDPV 79 (1963) p. 27.

Alexander Jannaeus, *Ant.* xiii 15, 3 (393),[335] liberated by Pompey, *Ant.* xiv 4, 4 (75), and on that account belonged to the Decapolis, Pliny, *NH* V 18/74; on Ptolemy, see above, p. 126. The coins of Dium with the legend *Δειηνῶν* have the Pompeian era; they are attested only from the reigns of Caracalla, Geta, and in one case of Elagabal.[336] The *Δία* mentioned by Hierocles and others is without doubt identical with this Dium.[337]

22. Gerasa, *Γέρασα*. The Semitic form גרשו (Garshu) is now attested on a Nabataean inscription.[338] The well-known ruins of Jerash are the most important of the region east of the Jordan and, together with those of Palmyra, Baalbek and Petra, of Syria in general. Considerable vestiges remain of public buildings, notably of the hippodrome, theatres, triumphal arch, temples of Zeus and Artemis, the city wall with gates and towers, the 'forum', and the three main streets, with tetrapylons where two streets running east-west intersect the main street leading north-south. The principal edifices belong to first and second centuries A.D. Knowledge of the inscriptions was for a long time very incomplete. They were not investigated systematically (insofar as this is possible without excavation) until 1895. Extensive excavation was conducted later between 1928 and 1934; the report of the excavations includes a complete collection of the inscriptions known up to that time.[339]

'Garasa'[340] occurs in one or two instances in addition to 'Gerasa'.[341]

335. Syncellus, ed. Dindorf, I 559 mentions among the acquisitions of Alexander Jannaeus *Λίαν*, which without doubt should be read *Δίαν*, as in all the MSS of Josephus, *Ant.* xiii 15, (393). Cf. H. Gelzer, *Julius Africanus* I, p. 257.

336. See de Saulcy, *Numismatique*, pp. 378–83, pl. XIX, nos. 8–9; *BMC Syria*, pp. lxxxv–vi, 303; *BMC Arabia*, pp. xxxi–ii, 28; H. Seyrig, Syria 36 (1959), pp. 68, 77 (with the coin of Elagabal). For the report of a coin-hoard from Migdal with new coins of various cities in the region, including Dium, see Ḥadashot Archeologiot 48–9 (Jan. 1974), p. 41.

337. Hierocles, *Synecd.*, ed. Parthey, p. 45; *Notitia episcopat. ibid.*, p. 92. Also in Josephus, *Ant.* xiii 15, 3 (393), the MSS have *Δίαν*. On Syncellus, cf. above, n. 335.

338. J. Starcky, RB 72 (1965), pp. 95–7.

339. For the inscriptions see C. B. Welles in C. H. Kraeling, *Gerasa: City of the Decapolis* (1938), pp. 355–494. This volume should be noted as by far the most complete account of any of the cities described here. For inscriptions note also B. Lifshitz, ZDPV 79 (1963), p. 91 and 82 (1966), pp. 58–9.

340. A 'Surus Garasenus' on a *diploma* of A.D. 71 from Pompeii, CIL XVI 15; possibly also CIL III 6958. In Pliny, *NH* v 18/74, the list of cities of the Decapolis, 'Galasa' should perhaps be emended to 'Garasa' rather than 'Gerasa'.

341. For its history, see Kuhn, *op. cit.* II, pp. 370, 383 and especially Kraeling, *Gerasa*, pp. 27–69. For subsequent bibliography note Vogel, 'Bibliography', s.v. 'Jerash'; Avi-Yonah, 'Gazetteer', s.v. 'Gerasa I'; EAEHL II s.v. 'Gerasa'. For a brief account and description see G. Lankester Harding, *The Antiquities of Jordan* ([2]1967), ch. iv. Note also the brilliant exposition by M. I. Rostovtzeff, *Caravan Cities* (1932), ch. 3.

The derivation of the name from the *γέροντες* (veterans) of Alexander the Great who may have settled there is of course merely an etymological speculation.[342] Nevertheless, the tradition that Gerasa was founded as a Hellenistic city by Alexander is clearly attested by a coin of the city from the reign of Commodus; the fact that a statue of Perdiccas was erected there as late as the first century B.C. may suggest a tradition that he had founded the city on Alexander's orders.[343] It certainly existed as a city by 143/2 B.C., when the expression 'of the Antiochenes by the Chrysorhoas' (see below) appears on a lead weight dated to the year 170 of the Seleucid era.[344] The city is first mentioned in a narrative context during the reign of Alexander Jannaeus, when it was dominated by a certain Theodorus (a son of the tyrant Zeno Cotylas of Philadelphia). Alexander Jannaeus conquered it towards the end of his reign after an arduous siege.[345] He died whilst besieging the fortress of Ragaba 'in the district of Gerasa' (*ἐν τοῦ Γερασηνῶν ὅροις*).[346] Gerasa was undoubtedly also liberated by Pompey, for it was subsequently listed among the cities of the Decapolis and used the Pompeian era.[347] On the outbreak of the revolution, it was attacked by the rebels, *B.J.* ii 18, 1 (458); the Jews living in the town were, however, spared by the non-Jewish inhabitants, *B.J.* ii 18, 5 (480). The Gerasa which was conquered and destroyed by Lucius Annius at the command of Vespasian, *B.J.* iv 9, 1 (487), cannot have been this Gerasa because as a Greek city it would certainly have been friendly towards Rome.[348]

342. See the passages from Iamblichus and the *Etymolog. magnum* cited by J. G. Droysen, *Hellenismus* III. 2, pp. 202 f.; cf. Kraeling, *op. cit.*, p. 28; Tcherikover, *Hellenistic Civilisation*, p. 100.

343. See H. Seyrig, 'Alexandre le Grand, fondateur de Gérasa', Syria 42 (1965), pp. 25–8. The coin reads *Ἀλέξ(ανδρος) Μακ(εδὼν) κτί(στης) Γεράσων*. For the statue of Perdiccas, see *Gerasa*, p. 423, no. 137.

344. For the inscription, see *Gerasa*, p. 461, no. 251, re-read by H. Seyrig, 'Notes on Syrian Coins', Numismatic Notes and Monographs 119 (1950), p. 33, n. 45.

345. *B.J.* i 4, 8 (104). In the parallel passage, *Ant.* xiii 15, 3 (393), *Ἔσσαν* appears in place of *Γέρασαν*. Bearing in mind that the context undoubtedly requires the same city, that the text of *B.J.* as a whole is more reliable than that of *Ant.*, and finally since the existence of a city named Essa is uncertain (see Neubauer, *Géographie*, p. 38), the reading of *B.J.* is the version to be accepted.

346. *Ant.* xiii 15, 5 (398). Ragaba can hardly be the *Ἐργά* of Eusebius, *Onomast.*, ed. Klostermann, p. 16; it lay 15 Roman miles west of Gerasa and was therefore presumably under the rule of Alexander Jannaeus before Gerasa was conquered.

347. Stephanus Byz., s.v. *Γέρασα· πόλις τῆς Κοίλης Συρίας, τῆς Δεκαπόλεως* (such is also the reading accepted by Meineke, instead of the traditional *τεσσαρακαιδεκαπόλεως*). For Ptolemy, see above, p. 126. For the era of Gerasa, note also the inscriptions from the theatre dated to the year 153 of the era (A.D. 90/1) and naming the *legatus* of Syria (A. Buccius) Lappius Maximus, Newsletter ASOR 4 (Oct. 1974), p. 2 = AE 1973, 558.

348. For possible identifications of this 'Gerasa', see Schalit, *Namenwörterbuch zu Flavius Josephus* s.v. 'Gerasa 2'.

In the second century A.D., Gerasa was still known as 'Antiochia on the Chrysorhoas', and its inhabitants as 'Antiochenes by the Chrysorhoas, the former Gerasenes', an appellation deriving from the Seleucid period (see above). This is attested both by a number of inscriptions and two coin-types. The inscriptions from Gerasa with this title date between the reigns of Trajan and the early third century; a dedication from Pergamum to C. Antius Aulus Iulius Quadratus, *legatus* of Syria in A.D. 102–4, by the 'Antiochenes by the Chrysorhoas' will date to before his second consulship in 105;[349] an epitaph consisting of four distichs, to the later imperial period.[350] The two coins have the inscription *'Αντιοχέων τῶ(ν) πρ(ὸς) Χρ(υσορόᾳ) τῶ(ν) πρ(ότερον) Γε(ρασηνῶν)*. Both types belong to the period of Marcus Aurelius (one has the likeness of Marcus Aurelius with a corresponding inscription, the other of Lucius Verus with a corresponding inscription).[351] The Chrysorhoas can, of course, only be the Wadi Jerash that flows through Gerasa, and not the Nahr Barada, also called Chrysorhoas, that runs from the Lebanon to Damascus.[352]

Inscriptions have yielded a mass of material relating to the civic constitution of Gerasa. The phrase, 'council and people' (*ἡ βουλὴ καὶ ὁ δῆμος*) occurs on a number from the first and second centuries.[353] From the time of Hadrian, the more frequent expression seems to have been simply *ἡ πόλις*. Numerous offices are mentioned on two inscriptions, in particular on one from the first century A.D.,[354] and on another from

349. For this title see *Gerasa*, p. 401, nos. 56/7 (115) and 58 (130); p. 426, no. 147 (179–80?); p. 406, no. 69 (190 or 191); p. 428, 153 (209–11). Note also the Latin inscription p. 390, no. 30, a dedication by the *equites singulares* of Hadrian who wintered there in 129/30: 'Antioch[i]ae ad Chrysorhoan quae et Gerasa hiera et asylo(s) et autonomos'. For the dedication at Pergamum, see *Inschriften v. Pergamon* II (1895), p. 301, no. 437=IGR IV 374: *'Αντιοχέων τῶν [πρὸς τ]ῷ Χρυσορόᾳ ἡ [β]ουλὴ καὶ ὁ δῆμ[ος]*. For Quadratus see PIR² I 507.

350. *Gerasa*, p. 456, no. 232.

351. For the coins, see *BMC* Arabia, pp. xxxiii–v; 31–2; see now A. Spijkerman, 'A List of the Coins of Gerasa Decapoleos', SBFLA 25 (1975), pp. 73–84. For finds of coins from Gerasa, see A. R. Bellinger, 'Coins from Jerash', NNM 81 (1938), summarized in *Gerasa*, pp. 497–503.

352. The name Chrysorhoas is attested for the Nahr Barada by Strabo xvi 2, 16 (755); Pliny, *NH* v 18/74; Ptolemy, v 15, 9 (Didot ed., v 14, 7). But it is also frequent elsewhere; see RE s.v. 'Chrysorrhoas'.

353. Pergamene inscription from the reign of Trajan (see above, note 349). Inscription from Jerash in honour of Trajan, IGR III 1346=*Gerasa*, p. 424, no. 141; cf. p. 438, no. 181 (A.D. 117) and p. 382, no. 15 (143). For the *γραμματεὺς βουλῆς καὶ δήμου* see nos. 45–6 (66/7) (see below).

354. OGIS 621=IGR III 1376=*Gerasa*, p. 395, no. 45: *[ἐπὶ τ]ῆς ἀρχῆς 'Απολλωνίο[υ 'Ηφαι<σ>]τίωνος προέδρου καὶ... Δημητρίου δεκαπρ(ώτου) [διὰ β]ίου πόλεως καὶ 'Αντιόχ[ου 'Αρίστ]ωνος ἀρχόντων καὶ Ξέρ[ξου Χ]αιρέου γραμματέ[ως]* (cf. no. 46). The date is given as 129 of the Gerasene era, so 66/7, see below, n. 358. *ἀρχόντων* refers to the three men already named, the first of whom was also called *πρόεδρος*, the second *δεκάπρωτος διὰ βίου*.

259.[355] There are also further individual items of evidence. The material is listed briefly together with that from the two inscriptions already mentioned.[356] At some time in the early third century, perhaps under Caracalla or, more likely, Elagabal, Gerasa may have become a *colonia* with the title *Colonia Aurelia Antoniniana*.[357]

On the era employed in Gerasa, the coins so far discovered provide no clear evidence. The epigraphic material is more plentiful. The usual era of Gerasa, like that of almost all the towns of the Decapolis, was Pompeian. Clermont-Ganneau's conjecture that this was so has been confirmed by the evidence of the inscriptions.[358] It can now be taken as certain that the Pompeian era (or more properly, as it was referred to locally, 'the era of the city') from 62 B.C. (autumn) was the only one in use in this period. It is attested up to A.D. 611.[359] Since from Trajan

355. *Gerasa*, p. 408, no. 74: *ἔτους ακτʹ Ξάνθικου γκʹ · ἐπὶ γραμματίας Μάρωνος Ἀββίβου καὶ συναρχίας αὐτοῦ Γάμου ἄρχοντος καὶ Μαλχαίου καὶ διοικητῶν Ἐριννίου καὶ Ἀρίστωνος καὶ τῶν πέντε . . .*

356. *πρόεδρος*: nos. 45–6, 73, 190
πρῶτος τῆς πόλεως: 188
δεκάπρωτος: 45–6
γραμματεύς: 45–6, 181?
διοικητής: 74
οἱ πέντε: 74
ἀγορανόμος (ἀγορανομοῦντος): 53, 134, 188
γυμνασιάρχης: OGIS 662 = *Gerasa*, p. 375, no. 4; cf. nos. 3 and ?192
ἐπιμελητής: nos. 40, 46, 114, 146, 150–2, 154–9, 161, 168, 172, 186
ξυστάρχης: no. 172

357. This depends on two restored inscriptions, *Gerasa*, p. 437, no. 179: '[coloniae Aur(eliae)] Antoninianae'; p. 442, no. 191: *[πά]τρωνα τῆς κ[ολω]νείας*. But note that in the inscription of A.D. 259 (n. 355 above) the city appears still to have a Greek constitution.

358. C. Clermont-Ganneau, *Études d'archéologie orientale* I (1895), p. 142; *Rec. d'arch. or.* II, pp. 17 f.; G. Kubitschek, 'Die Ären von Medaba und von Gerasa', Mitt. Geogr. Ges. Wien 43 (1900), pp. 368–73; on Gerasa, pp. 369–73; E. Schwartz, 'Die Ären von Gerasa und Eleutheropolis', NGG 1906, pp. 340–95; on Gerasa, pp. 361–5. Kubitschek and Schwartz consistently assumed the Pompeian era. Dittenberger did the same, except in the case of the inscription to be discussed in n. 359. For a full examination of the inscriptions see C. C. McCown, 'The Calendar and Era of Gerasa', TAPhA 64 (1933), pp. 81–8; cf. *Gerasa*, p. 358.

359. McCown, *op. cit.*, discusses the alternative eras that have been proposed. In particular, earlier readings of *Gerasa*, p. 395, no. 45 (see above) gave *ἔτους θκρʹ [ἀπὸ τῆ]ς Σεβαστῆς Εἰρήν[ης]*, hence a supposed era from Actium, 31 B.C. But the era of Actium was never designated so; it is an era *τῆς νίκης*, not *τῆς εἰρήνης*. Dittenberger, OGIS 621, took 9 B.C. to be the starting point, when the great Altar of Peace on the Campus Martius was consecrated. Both eras would be quite exceptional for Gerasa. Kubitschek (*op. cit.*, p. 370) and Schwartz (*op. cit.*, p. 362) therefore proposed the reading *[ὑπὲρ τῆ]ς Σεβαστῆς εἰρήν[ης]*, and suggested that the year *θκρʹ* (129) related to the Pompeian era = 66/67. This reading is now confirmed by the duplicate, no. 46. It may also be relevant that when during Nero's reign the Armenian king Tiridates paid homage in A.D. 66 to the Emperor in Rome (Cassius Dio lxiii 1–7; cf. Tacitus, *Ann.* xv 29; xvi 23; Pliny, *NH* xxx 16 f.), the temple

onwards Gerasa was part of the province of Arabia (see below), one might expect it to have used the era of that province. Indeed some, scholars have felt obliged to assume on palaeographical grounds its employment for a few dates. But a simultaneous use sometimes of one, and sometimes of the other era, with no further indication, is most unlikely. And the Pompeian, or city, era is just as certain for the second and third centuries as it is for the Byzantine period, up to the early seventh century.[360]

Like all the cities of the Decapolis, Gerasa belonged originally to the province of Syria. The inscription from Pergamum (see above, n. 349) attests this for the earlier part of the reign of Trajan; and even the geographer Ptolemy, who wrote under Antoninus Pius (and already knew of the founding of Aelia by Hadrian) reckoned Gerasa as being part, like the rest of the Decapolis, of the province of Syria.[361] For this, however, he must have followed earlier information, since the inscriptions prove that already under Trajan, Gerasa belonged to the province of Arabia, and probably did so from the moment of its establishment in 106.[362] Of the known governors of Arabia,[363] the following are attested in relation to Gerasa: (1) C. Claudius Severus, 107–115;[364] (2) Ti. Iulius

---

of Janus was closed (Suetonius, *Nero*, 13–14), and that the Arval brothers, presumably on the same occasion, sacrificed a cow for peace in A.D. 66. See H. Henzen, *Acta fratrum Arvalium*, p. 85; CIL VI 2044, p. 12; G. Wissowa, *Religion und Kultus der Römer* (1902), p. 277. The inscriptions from Gerasa dating to A.D. 66/67, of which only the beginning is preserved, must therefore also have related to a dedication by the city authorities on the feast of *Σεβαστῇ εἰρήνῃ* (the same expression also occurs in the Greek text of the *Monumentum Ancyranum*, in connexion with the great Altar of Peace on the Campus Martius; see Mommsen, *Res gestae divi Augusti*, ed. 2, p. 49). Cf. Welles's commentary, *Gerasa*, p. 396.

360. It is now accepted that the era of the province of Arabia (106, not 105) was not used in Gerasa, see McCown, *op. cit.*, p. 29.

361. Ptolemy v 15, 23 = Didot ed. (I. 2; Paris, 1901), v 14, 18; cf. above, p. 126. On Ptolemy's dates, see RE s.v. 'Ptolemaios' (66).

362. This was shown by A. von Domaszewski, CIL III, p. 2315, preamble to n. 14156. See also R. E. Brünnow and A. von Domaszewski, *Die Provincia Arabia* III (1909), pp. 264–8 (on Gerasa, p. 265). Earlier, much too late a date was suggested for the assignment of Gerasa to the province of Arabia. J. Marquardt, *Römische Staatsverwaltung* I, p. 433, was inclined to place this measure in around A.D. 295. Rohden, *De Palaestina et Arabia* (1885), p. 11, attempted to demonstrate that it occurred under Septimius Severus (193–211). C. Clermont-Ganneau recognized correctly that Gerasa belonged to Arabia already in A.D. 162, *Et. d'arch. or.* II (1897), pp. 85–6, 88–9. See now G. W. Bowersock, 'The Annexation and Original Garrison of Arabia', ZPE 5 (1970), pp. 37–47, especially pp. 37–9.

363. For a recent list of all the known governors of Arabia see G. W. Bowersock, 'A Report on Arabia Provincia', JRS 61 (1971), pp. 219–42, on pp. 235–6.

364. C. Claudius Severus constructed at the command of Trajan in A.D. 111 a new road from the Syrian border to the Red Sea: 'Traianus . . . trib. pot. XV . . .

Iulianus Alexander, *c.* 125, see now M. Sartre, ADAJ 21 (1976), pp. 105–8; (3) C. Allius Fuscianus, perhaps before 140, see *Gerasa*, p. 433, nos. 165–7, PIR² A 544 and Bowersock, JRS 61 (1971), p. 235; (4) L. Aemilius Carus, 142/3;[365] (5) L. Attidius Cornelianus, attested as *legatus* of Arabia, and suffect consul in 150;[366] (6) P. Iulius Geminius Marcianus, between 162 and 166[367] (several inscriptions from Gerasa attest his name);[368] (7) Q. Antistius Adventus, likewise under Marcus Aurelius, A.D. 166–167.[369]

In the fourth century A.D., Gerasa was one of the most important

---

redacta in formam provinciae Arabia viam novam a finibus Syriae usque ad mare rubrum aperuit et stravit per C. Claudium Severum leg. Aug. pr. pr.'. Similarly, in differing states of preservation, on various milestones on the road from Petra to Philadelphia, CIL III 14149, [19, 21, 30]; see vol. I, p. 586. See Brünnow and von Domaszewski, *op. cit.* II, pp. 83–6, III, p. 287. Full references to the inscriptions of Claudius Severus in PIR² C 1023. Severus, of course, carried out this project as governor of Arabia. In the following year, A.D. 112, he also improved the road northwest to Gerasa: 'Traianus . . . trib. potest. XVI . . . refecit per C. Claudium Severum leg. Aug. pr. pr.'. Similarly on 3 milestones with the numbers IIII, VI and VII, in Suf northwest of Gerasa, where they were evidently brought from the surrounding area, Brünnow and Domaszewski, *op. cit.* II, p. 240 = CIL III 14176³; cf. 14176²; for a full list of milestones of Claudius Severus with distances measured from Gerasa, see *Gerasa*, pp. 462–3 (nos. 252–7). Note also the inscription, *Gerasa*, p. 401, no. 56/7, a dedication to Trajan of 115 mentioning Claudius Severus as *legatus*. There can therefore be no possible doubt that Gerasa belonged to Arabia in the governorship of Severus. For late milestones on the road to Adora, note S. Mittmann, 'The Roman Road from Gerasa to Adora', ADAJ 10–11 (1965–6), pp. 65–87, and *idem*, *Beiträge zur Siedlungs- und Territorialgeschichte des nördlichen Ostjordanlandes* (1970), pt. 4 (Roman roads from Gerasa to Pella, Philadelphia and possibly Bostra); note p. 157, a milestone of Claudius Severus.

365. L. Aemilius Carus has long been known as a governor of Arabia; see below, on Philadelphia, n. 388. That Gerasa also formed part of this territory in the time of Antoninus Pius is evident from a reference to him as governor on an inscription of 143, *Gerasa*, p. 382, no. 15. See PIR² A 338.

366. *Gerasa*, p. 402, no. 60; p. 432, no. 163. He is given as *legatus* of Syria on a military diploma of 156/7 found in Bulgaria, CIL XVI 106. He was defeated by the Parthians at the beginning of the reign of Marcus Aurelius, *SHA*, *Vita Marci* 8, but was still governor of Syria in 162, CIL III 6658. See PIR² A 1341.

367. CIL III 96 (Bostra); VIII 7050–2 (Cirta); PIR² I 340. For milestones with his name and the date 162 on the road from Petra to Philadelphia see CIL III 14149[23, 32, 41]; Brünnow and Domaszewski, *Die Provincia Arabia* I (1904), pp. 37, 82, 85; from Philadelphia to Bostra: II, pp. 312–23; from Philadelphia to Gerasa, CIL III 14173; 14175³ = *Gerasa*, p. 463, no. 257; 14175² = *ibid.* no. 259; 14177 = no. 258.

368. *Gerasa*, pp. 380–1, nos. 11–12; p. 405, no. 645.

369. He is attested as governor of Arabia by an inscription from Bostra (CIL III 92). For the date 166/7 see PIR² A 754. See *Gerasa*, pp. 433–4, no. 168: *Κρισπῖναν σύμβιον Κ(οἰντου) Ἀντιστίου Ἀδουέντου ὑπάτου ἡ πόλις*. For later governors attested on inscriptions from Gerasa, see *Gerasa*, pp. 591–2.

cities of the province of Arabia.[370] Its territory was so extensive that Jerome could say that what was formerly Gilead was now called Gerasa.[371]

Stephanus Byzantinus mentions famous men of Gerasa.[372] The names of certain Christian bishops are also known.[373]

On its cults and festivals, see above, pp. 38, 48.

23. Philadelphia, *Φιλαδέλφεια*, the ancient capital of the Ammonites, called in the Old Testament רבת בני עמון, Rabbah of the Ammonites (the chief city of the Ammonites), or in a shortened form רבה, Rabbah.[374] In one of the Zenon papyri of 259 B.C. (PSI 616) this name is still used (*Ῥαββαταμμάνοις*), and it is employed also by Polybius;[375] in Eusebius, Jerome and Stephanus Byzantinus, it appears as Amman and Ammana.[376] The location of the city is clearly attested by the extensive ruins to be found in present-day Amman, and by an increasing number of inscriptions discovered there (see below). Like those of Kanatha and Gerasa, the ruins belong to the Roman period.[377] The city will have

370. Ammianus Marcellinus xiv 8, 13: 'Haec quoque civitates habet inter oppida quaedam ingentes Bostram et Gerasam atque Philadelphiam murorum firmitate cautissimas'. Cf. Eusebius, *Onomast.*, ed. Klostermann, p. 64: *Γέρασα, πόλις ἐπίσημος τῆς Ἀραβίας*. For the history of the city in the late Roman period see *Gerasa*, pp. 56–9, and note the extensive remains of churches and other buildings of the Christian period, *ibid.*, pp. 171–296.

371. Jerome, *Com. in Abd.* 19 (PL XXV, col. 1114): 'Beniamin autem . . . cunctam possidebit Arabiam, quae prius vocabatur Galaad et nunc Gerasa nuncupatur'. Also, a late Midrash (M. Shemuel, ed. Buber, ch. 13) states that גרש is Gilead. On the territory of Gerasa see Avi-Yonah, *Holy Land*, pp. 175–7.

372. Stephanus Byz., s.v. *Γέρασα ἐξ αὐτῆς Ἀρίστων ῥήτωρ ἀστεῖός ἐστιν . . . καὶ Κήρυκος σοφιστὴς καὶ Πλάτων νομικὸς ῥήτωρ*. To these must be added the neo-Pythagorean philosopher and mathematician Nicomachus of Gerasa, second century A.D. Cf. above, p. 50.

373. Epiphanius, *Haer.* 73, 26. R. le Quien, *Oriens christ.* II, cols. 859 f. A. v. Harnack, *Die Mission und Ausbreitung des Christentums* II ([4]1924), p. 702.

374. Dt. 3:11; Jos. 13:25; 2 Sam. 11:1; 12:26–29; 17:27; Jer. 49:2–3; Ezek. 21:25; 25:5; Am. 1:14; 1 Chron. 20:1. On the identity of Rabbah of the Ammonites with Philadelphia, see below, notes 376 and 378. For Rabbath-Ammon in the biblical period see Y. Aharoni, *The Land of the Bible* (1967), index s.v. Note also the fragmentary inscription of perhaps the seventh-sixth century B.C. from the theatre at Amman, with the words Ben Ammi (בן עמי), ADAJ 12–13 (1967–8), pp. 65–7.

375. Polybius v 71, 4: *Ῥαββατάμανα*. See Walbank *ad loc.* So also Stephanus Byz., s.v. *Ῥαββατάμμανα, πόλις τῆς ὀρεινῆς Ἀραβίας*.

376. Eusebius, *Onomast.*, ed. Klostermann, p. 16: *Ἀμμᾶν ἡ νῦν Φιλαδελφία, πόλις ἐπίσημος τῆς Ἀραβίας*. *Ibid.*, p. 24: *Ἀμμών . . . αὕτη ἐστιν Ἀμμᾶν ἡ καὶ Φιλαδελφία πόλις ἐπίσημος τῆς Ἀραβίας*. Cf. *ibid.*, p. 146: *Ῥαββάθ* [*cod.* *Ῥαββά*] *πόλις βασιλείας Ἀμμών, αὕτη ἐστὶ Φιλαδελφία*. Jerome, *In Naum* 3:8–12 (CCL lxxvi A, pp. 564–5): 'Ammana, quae nunc vocatur Philadelphia'. Stephanus Byz., see below, n. 378.

377. See Conder, *The Survey of Eastern Palestine* I (1889), pp. 19–64 (exhaustive description of the ruins with accurate plan). Illustrations: Brünnow and Doma-

received the name *Φιλαδέλφεια* from Ptolemy II Philadelphus, to whom its Hellenization is to be attributed.[378]

In the time of Antiochus the Great, it was a fortified place. He attempted to take it by storm in 218 B.C., but it did not fall into his hands until a prisoner showed him the underground passage down which the inhabitants passed to draw water. Antiochus blocked this way and thus forced the town to surrender.[379] In around 135 B.C. (at the time of the death of Simon Maccabaeus), Philadelphia was in the power of a certain Zeno Cotylas, *Ant.* xiii, 8, 1 (235); *B.J.* i 2, 4 (60). It was not conquered by Alexander Jannaeus, though he occupied Gerasa to the north and Heshbon to the south. It therefore does not appear among the cities separated by Pompey from the Jewish region. Nevertheless, it was subsequently listed by him among the cities of the Decapolis[380] and for that reason used the Pompeian era.[381] Herod fought in the

---

szewski, *Die Provincia Arabia* II (1905), pp. 216–20 (p. 216 for older bibliography). For a full survey of the ruins as at the beginning of this century, see H. C. Butler, *Pub. Princeton Univ. Arch. Exped. Syria 1904–05* II A (1907), pp. 34–62. For excavations since the establishment of the kingdom of Jordan see ADAJ 1 (1951), pp. 7–16; 14 (1969), pp. 28–33 (bibliography), 15 (1970), pp. 11–15; 18 (1973), pp. 17–35: note especially A. Hadidi, 'The Excavations of the Roman Forum at Amman (Philadelphia), 1904–67', ADAJ 19 (1974), pp. 71–91 (with bibliography and survey of earlier excavations). See also Vogel, 'Bibliography', s.v. 'Ammân'. For its history, see Kuhn, *op. cit.*, II, pp. 383 f.; G. Le Strange, *Palestine under the Moslems*, pp. 391–3; EB and IDB, s.v. 'Rabbah'; Thomsen, *Loca sancta*, p. 113; RE s.v. 'Philadelphia' (3); Abel, *Géog, Pal.* II, pp. 424–5; Avi-Yonah, *Holy Land*, p. 177. For a brief account see G. Lankester Harding, *The Antiquities of Jordan* ([2]1967), pp. 61–70.

378. Stephanus Byz., s.v. *Φιλαδέλφεια . . . τῆς Συρίας ἐπιφανὴς πόλις, ἡ πρότερον Ἄμμανα, εἶτ' Ἀστάρτη, εἶτα Φιλαδέλφεια ἀπὸ Πτολεμαίου τοῦ Φιλαδέλφου.* Jerome, *In Hiezech.* 25 (CCL lxxv p. 335): 'Rabbath, quae hodie a rege Aegypti Ptolemaeo cognomento Philadelpho, qui Arabiam tenuit cum Iudaea, Philadelphia nuncupata est'. C. L. Müller, *Numismatique d'Alexandre le Grand* (1855), p. 309, pl. nos. 1473 ff., attributed certain coins of Alexander the Great with the letters *Φ*, to our Philadelphia, but although it is possible that coins bearing the name of Alexander were still being minted even in the time of Ptolemy II, this interpretation is doubtful. If one must go back to Ptolemy II, one can also think of Philoteria (Polybius v 70) for instance.

379. Polybius v 71, 4–11. Conder's surveys in north Amman led to the discovery of a passage possibly identical with that mentioned by Polybius; see Athenaeum (1883), no. 2905, p. 832: 'The discovery at Ammân'. Cf. also PEFQSt (1882), p. 109, and especially Conder, *The Survey of Eastern Palestine* I (1889), p. 34.

380. Pliny, *NH* v 18/74. On Ptolemy, see above, p. 126.

381. *Chron. Paschale* (ed. Dindorf I, p. 351) *ad Olymp.* 179, 2= 63 B.C.: *Φιλαδελφεῖς ἐντεῦθεν ἀριθμοῦσι τοὺς ἑαυτῶν χρόνους.* The era is also frequently found on coins: see on these, de Saulcy, *Numismatique*, pp. 386–92, pl. XXII, nos. 3–9; *BMC Syria*, pp. lxxxix–xci; 306; *BMC Arabia*, pp. xxxix–xli, 37–41; see also A. Alt, 'Inschriftliches zu den Ären von Scythopolis und Philadelphia', ZDPV 55 (1932), pp. 128–34, on pp. 152–4.

environs of Philadelphia against the Arabs.[382] In A.D. 44, a bloody conflict took place between the Jews of Peraea and the Philadelphians over the boundaries of a village given as Mia in the present text of Josephus, but probably Zia, *Ant.* xx 1, 1 (2).[383] Roman soldiers from Philadelphia are mentioned from about A.D. 69.[384] At the outbreak of the revolution, Philadelphia was attacked by the Jews, *B.J.* ii 18, 1 (458).

Like Gerasa, Philadelphia was presumed by the geographer Ptolemy, writing under Antoninus Pius, to have been part of the province of Syria, and indeed of Coele Syria (Ptolemy v 15, 22–3 = Didot edition v 14, 18; cf. above, p. 126). This accords with the fact that in Stephanus Byzantinus, and on coins, the cities of the Decapolis as such are defined as belonging to Coele Syria (in Stephanus, Scythopolis, Pella, Dium, Gerasa; on coins, Abila until Caracalla, Gadara until Elagabalus). But coins of Philadelphia with the inscription *Φιλαδελφέων Κοίλης Συρίας* continue to the time of Severus Alexander.[385] In the cases of Abila and Gadara, the addition *Κοι. Συρ.* is also correct in the official Roman sense, for since Syria was divided under Septimius Severus into Syria Phoenice and Syria Coele (the latter comprising northern and inland Syria with the capital Antiochia),[386] the towns of the Decapolis may very well have remained in Syria Coele despite their southern location. Philadelphia, however, certainly belonged to the province of Arabia from the time of Trajan. The reasons advanced above in this respect for Gerasa (pp. 153–4) are valid also for Philadelphia, lying further to the south. Under Trajan, a new road was built from Bostra to Petra by the governor C. Claudius Severus in A.D. 111 to connect these two highly important towns of the newly founded province of Arabia with each other and with the Red Sea. But this road passed through Philadelphia.

382. *B.J.* i 19, 5 (380); in the parallel passage, *Ant.* xv 5, 4 (148), Philadelphia is not mentioned.

383. A village called Zia, 15 Roman miles west of Philadelphia, is mentioned by Eusebius, *Onomast.*, ed. Klostermann, p. 94: *καὶ ἔστι νῦν Ζία κώμη ὡς ἀπὸ ιε′ σημείων Φιλαδελφίας ἐπὶ δυσμάς.*

384. A 'Proculus Rabili f(ilius)' from Philadelphia served in the *cohors II Italica civium Romanorum* stationed in Syria in about A.D. 70. It seems likely from the fact that his tombstone was found in Carnuntum (on the Danube below Vienna) that he was among the troops led by Mucianus from Syria to the west at the end of 69, CIL III 13483a. Similarly, AE 1953, 74, a 'Domitius Domitii f.' from Philadelphia on a diploma of 88 from Morocco. An 'M. Ulpius C. fil.' from Philadelphia appears in a list of A.D. 194 (CIL III 6580). This is probably also a reference to our Philadelphia (Mommsen, *Ephem. epigr.*, V, p. 206); possibly also AE 1949, 198 (Drobeta).

385. See n. 378. Note also the inscription from the forum of Amman dating to A.D. 189: *Φιλαδελφέων τῶν κατὰ Κοίλην Συρίαν ἡ πόλις;* F. Zayadine, ADAJ 14 (1969) pp. 34–5; Syria 48 (1971), pp. 385–9; AE 1972, 673.

386. Marquardt, *Römische Staatsverwaltung* I, p. 423.

It must therefore also have belonged to Arabia. This has to be assumed in any case for the reason that Gerasa, lying to the north, was already part of Arabia. In addition, we have direct proof of Philadelphia's attachment to Arabia at the time of Antoninus Pius, namely, a votive-stone found there with the inscription, *I.O.M. Conservatori L. Aemilius Carus leg. Aug. pr. pr.*[387] L. Aemilius Carus is known to have been governor of Arabia under Antoninus Pius.[388] It is therefore officially correct that in an inscription from the time of Marcus Aurelius Philadelphia is described as *Φιλαδέλφεια τῆς Ἀραβίας*.[389] That it was nevertheless named *Φιλ. Κοίλης Συρίας* on coins from the reign of Hadrian to that of Severus Alexander, is a striking example of the retention of an established geographical usage in preference to the official terminology of the Roman provinces. The use of the local era instead of the era of the province is to be understood similarly. The same conclusion is arrived at here concerning Ptolemy's statement as in the case of Gerasa (see above, p. 153).

In the fourth century, Philadelphia was one of the most important cities of the province of Arabia.[390]

Josephus mentions the region of Philadelphia (*Φιλαδελφινή*) as forming the eastern frontier of Peraea, *B.J.* iii 3,3 (47). If it is correct to assume that Josephus, *Ant.* xx 1, 1 (2) should read 'Zia', Philadelphian territory will have extended to about 15 Roman miles west of the city; i.e. of the land lying between itself and the Jordan, fully half will have been Philadelphian territory.

There is no doubt whatever that all the cities so far reviewed constituted independent political communities which, after the time of Pompey at least, were never merged internally with Jewish territory to form a unified organization, but were at the very most united with it

387. CIL III 14149[1]. On Carus' governorship see p. 154 above.

388. It is now to be taken as established that Philadelphia belonged to the new province from its inception in 106, for it lay directly on the road built by Claudius Severus from Bostra to the gulf of Aqaba. See Brünnow and von Domaszewski, *Die Provincia Arabia* III (1909), pp. 264–5. The road from Gerasa to Philadelphia also dates back at least to the reign of Hadrian; see S. Mittmann, *Beiträge zur Siedlungs- und Territorialgeschichte der Ostjordanländer* (1970), pp. 159–62. See in general G. W. Bowersock in JRS 61 (1971), pp. 236–42. It is not however formally documented before the milestone of Aemilius Carus, see previous note. But note the coin hoard including 310 Trajanic drachmae, probably struck at Bostra in A.D. 111–15, found near Amman, W. E. Metcalf, 'The Tell Kalak Hoard and Trajan's Arabian Mint', Am. Num. Soc., Mus. Notes 20 (1975), pp. 34–108.

389. Le Bas-Waddington, *Inscriptions* III, no. 1620b. Cf. above, p. 45, n. 90.

390. Ammianus Marcellinus xiv 8, 13; see above, n. 370; also the passages from Eusebius cited in n. 376. For Christian Philadelphia see B. Bagatti, 'Le antiche chiese di Filadelphia-'Amman (Transgiordania)', SBFLA 23 (1973), pp. 261–85.

externally under the same ruler. In almost all of them, the inhabitants were predominantly pagan, and from the third century B.C. became increasingly Hellenized. It was only in Joppa and Jamnia, and perhaps Azotus, that, from the Maccabaean period, the Jewish element gained the ascendancy. But even these cities, with their respective territories, were independent political units both before and after that time.

To the same category belong also, as Kuhn correctly assumed,[391] the cities founded by Herod and his sons. In many of them the population was mainly Jewish. But even where this was so, the constitution was nevertheless Hellenistic in character, as is shown in particular by the example of Tiberias. In most of them, however, the Gentile population will have preponderated. It must therefore not be assumed that they were incorporated into the organization of the Jewish realm; they occupied within it an independent position similar to that of the older Hellenistic cities. Indeed in Galilee, the Jewish land, which was admittedly interspersed with Gentile elements, seems on the contrary to have been subordinate to the newly-built capitals—first Sepphoris, then Tiberias, then Sepphoris again (see nos. 31 and 33).

Among the cities built by Herod, the two most important were Sebaste (=Samaria) and Caesarea (for the latter, see above). Gaba in Galilee, and Heshbon (Esebonitis) in Peraea, *Ant.* xv 8, 5 (294) were of less significance, but these too are to be regarded as predominantly pagan towns since at the outbreak of the revolution they were attacked by the Jews, as were Ptolemais and Caesarea, Gerasa and Philadelphia, *B.J.* ii 18, 1 (458–60). There remain to be mentioned, as cities founded by Herod, Antipatris and Phasaelis;[392] Cypros, which is named together with the Phasaelis, was simply a citadel near Jericho and not a πόλις, *B.J.* i 21, 9 (417); *Ant.* xvi 5, 2 (143). The same applies also to the fortresses of Alexandrium, Herodium, Hyrcania, Masada and Machaerus.[393]

Of Herod's sons, Archelaus founded only the village (κώμη) of Archelais.[394] Philip, on the other hand, built Caesarea (=Panias) and

391. *Die städtische und bürgerliche Verfassung des röm. Reichs*, pp. 346–8.

392. See G. Hassler, 'Herodes-Burgen und Herodes-Städte in Jordangraben, ZDPV 78 (1962), pp. 49–63.

393. On Alexandrium, Hyrcania, Machaerus and Masada, see vol. I, pp. 307–8 and 511–12. The excavations at Masada (1963–5) have so far been reported only in preliminary or popular form: cf. vol. I, p. 511, n. 137. Note also O. Plöger, 'Die Makkabäischen Burgen', ZDPV 71 (1955), pp. 141–72, and (for Machaerus and its region) W. Schottroff, ZDPV 82 (1966), pp. 163–208. See A. Strobel, 'Machaerus', *Bibel und Qumran: Festschrift H. Bardtke* (1968), pp. 198–225; *idem*, ADAJ 19 1974), pp. 101–27.

394. Cf. Josephus, *Ant.* xvii 13, 1 (340); xviii 2, 2 (31); Pliny, *NH* xiii 4/44; Ptolemy, v 16, 7=Didot ed. (I, 2, 1901), v 15, 5. For the Archelais in the mosaic map of Madaba, see A. Schulten, AAG *Phil.-hist. Kl.*, N.F., IV 2 (1900), p. 6; M. Avi-Yonah, *The Madaba Mosaic Map* ([2]1940), pp. 27, 36. According to the

Julias (=Bethsaida), and Herod Antipas, the cities of Sepphoris, Julias (=Livias) and Tiberias. Thus ten cities remain to be considered.[395]

24. Samaria=Sebaste.[396] The Hellenization of the town of Samaria (Hebrew שמרון) was the work of Alexander the Great. During Alexander's stay in Egypt (332–1 B.C.), the Samaritans had assassinated Andromachus, his commander in Coele Syria. When, therefore, Alexander returned from Egypt (331 B.C.), he punished the offenders and planted Macedonian colonists in Samaria.[397] The Chronicle of Eusebius refers also to a re-foundation by Perdiccas,[398] which he could have carried out during his campaign against Egypt, shortly before his death (321 B.C.). But since a re-foundation so soon after the colonization by Alexander the Great is unlikely, it may be that the two are identical, and that Perdiccas acted on the orders of Alexander.[399] The aftermath of this episode seems to be reflected in the discovery in 1962, in a cave in the Wadi Dâliyeh, of some two hundred skeletons, with Tyrian and

---

tabula Peutingeriana, Archelais lay on the road from Jericho to Scythopolis, 12 Roman miles from Jericho and 24 from Scythopolis. One of these figures, probably the second, is too low; see vol. I, p. 355, n. 12. Cf. also J. Guérin, *Samarie* I, pp. 235–8; Conder and Kitchener, *The Survey of Western Palestine* II, pp. 387, 395 f.; G. A. Smith, *Historical Geography*, p. 354; A. Alt, PJB 27 (1931), p. 46; Abel, *Géog. Pal.* II, p. 249.

395. For a detailed historical survey, see A. H. M. Jones, 'The Urbanisation of Palestine', JRS 21 (1931), pp. 78–85.

396. Cf. generally, J. Guérin, *Samarie* II, pp. 188–210; Conder and Kitchener, *The Survey of Western Palestine* II, pp. 160 f., pp. 211–15 (with plan); G. A. Reisner, C. S. Fisher, A. G. Lyon, *Harvard Excavations at Samaria* I–II (1924); J. W. Crowfoot, K. M. Kenyon, E. L. Sukenik, *Samaria-Sebaste* I, *The Buildings at Samaria* (1942); Abel, *Géog. Pal.* II, pp. 443–6; note also A. Parrot, *Samarie, capitale du royaume d'Israël* (1955); M. T. Petrozzi, *Samaria* (1973) (bibliography, historical sketch and archaeological guide). Cf. also *Eretz Shomron* (Israel Exploration Society, 1973) (in Hebrew).

397. Curtius Rufus iv 8: 'Oneravit hunc dolorem nuntius mortis Andromachi, quem praefecerat Syriae: vivum Samaritae cremaverant. Ad cuius interitum vindicandum, quanta maxime celeritate potuit, contendit, advenientique sunt traditi tanti sceleris auctores'; Eusebius, *Chron.*, ed. Schoene II, p. 114 (ad. ann. Abr. 1680, following the Armenian): 'Andromachum regionum illarum procuratorem constituit quem incolae urbis Samaritarum interfecerunt: quos Alexander ab Egipto reversus punivit: capta urbe Macedonas ut ibi habitarent collocavit'. So too Syncellus, ed. Dindorf I, p. 496: *τὴν Σαμάρειαν πόλιν ἑλὼν Ἀλέξανδρος Μακεδόνας ἐν αὐτῇ κατῴκισεν.*

398. For the text see n. 404 below.

399. E.g. J. Willrich, *Juden und Griechen vor der makkabäischen Erhebung* (1895), pp. 16–18. For a discussion and subsequent bibliography see R. Marcus in Loeb *Josephus* VI, App. C. Tcherikover, *Hellenistic Civilization*, pp. 103–4, prefers the view that city status was given by Perdiccas in 323–1 B.C. But see H. Seyrig, Syria 42 (1965), pp. 27–8.

other coins, and Aramaic seals and papyri dating to the last years of the Persian Empire.[400] The wider effects of the colonization are very uncertain. For Josephus, *Ant.* xi 8, 1–7 (302–47) also reports that the Samaritans gained the favour of Alexander and that it was by his permission that they now established their separate temple on Mt. Gerizim, which was to be destroyed by John Hyrcanus in 128 B.C., *Ant.* xiii 9, 1 (255–6). Traces of what appears to have been the podium of this temple have been discovered under the foundations of the Hadrianic temple of Zeus Hypsistos.[401] At the same time, there are indications of the reoccupation and fortification of Shechem (Tell Balâtah) from the early Hellenistic period to the second century B.C.[402] It is Shechem that Josephus, *Ant.* xi 8, 6 (340) identifies as the chief city of the Samaritan apostates, and those who worshipped there described themselves to Antiochus Epiphanes as 'the Sidonians in Shechem' (*τῶν ἐν Σικίμοις Σιδωνίων*), *Ant.* xii 5, 5 (257). It is Shechem that Josephus, *B.J.* i 2, 6 (63), *Ant.* xiii 9, 1 (255) asserts to have been destroyed at the same time as the temple on Mt. Gerizim. None the less, Samaritan worship, and specifically attachment to the mountain, *Ant.* xviii 4, 1–2 (85–9), continued. There are thus many uncertainties as to the relations between the successive Greek cities of Samaria and Sebaste and the surrounding population, and as to whether the area formed a true political and administrative unit.

As in ancient times, the city of Samaria was still an important fortress. It was for this reason razed by Ptolemy Lagus in 312 B.C., when he surrendered to Antigonus the region of Coele Syria which he had recently conquered.[403] Some fifteen years later (around 296 B.C.), Samaria, which had no doubt been restored in the meanwhile, was once again laid waste by Demetrius Poliorcetes in his struggle against Ptolemy Lagus.[404] From then on, no specific evidence exists concerning

400. The finds have not yet been published. For reports and very important preliminary discussions, see F. M. Cross, 'The Discovery of the Samaria Papyri', BA 26 (1963), pp. 110–21; 'Aspects of Samaritan and Jewish History in Late Persian and Hellenistic Times', HThR 59 (1966), pp. 201–11; 'Papyri of the Fourth Century B.C. from Dâliyeh', in D. N. Freedman and J. C. Greenfield (ed.), *New Directions in Biblical Archaeology* (1971), pp. 45–69.

401. See R. J. Bull, G. E. Wright, 'Newly Discovered Temples on Mt. Gerizim in Jordan', HThR 58 (1965), pp. 234–7; 'The Excavation of Tell en Râs on Mt. Gerizim', BA 31 (1968), pp. 58–72.

402. G. E. Wright, 'The Samaritans and Shechem', HThR 55 (1962), pp.357–62.

403. Diodorus xix 93, 7. Cf. above, notes 68 (Gaza), 132 (Joppa), 181 (Ptolemais).

404. Eusebius, *Chron.*, ed. Schoene II, p. 118 (*ad Ol.* 121, 1 = 296 B.C., following the Armenian): 'Demetrius rex Asianorum, Poliorcêtes appellatus, Samaritanorum urbem a Perdica constructam (s. incolis frequentatam) totam cepit'. The same passage according to Jerome (Schoene II, p. 119; ed. Helm, pp. 127–8): 'Demetrius rex Asiae cognomento Poliorcetes Samaritanorum urbem vastat quam Perdicca

the history of the city. Polybius reports that Antiochus the Great occupied the territory of Samaria during his first and second conquests of Palestine (218 and 200 B.C.),[405] but the fate of the city is not considered. It is of interest that the region of Samaria, under the Ptolemies as well as under the Seleucids, constituted like Judaea a province of its own which was divided into several districts, *νομοί*.[406] Towards the end of the second century B.C., when the Seleucids were no longer able to prevent the encroachment of the Jews, Samaria, following Shechem, fell victim to the Jewish policy of conquest. Already under John Hyrcanus (around 107 B.C.), the city, which was at that time a *πόλις ὀχυρωτάτη*, was conquered by his sons Antigonus and Aristobulus after a year's siege, and entirely abandoned to destruction, *Ant.* xiii 10, 2–3 (275–83); *B.J.* i 2, 7 (64–5).[407] Alexander Jannaeus occupied the city or its ruins, *Ant.* xiii 15, 4 (396). It was detached from the Jewish realm by Pompey and from then on was never again organically bound to it, *Ant.* xiv 4, 4 (75); *B.J.* i 7, 7 (156). Its reconstruction was the work of Gabinius, *Ant.* xiv 5, 3 (88); *B.J.* i 8, 4 (166). The inhabitants may on this account also have been called 'Gabinians' (*Γαβινεῖς*).[408] Augustus granted the city to Herod, *Ant.* xv 7, 3 (217); *B.J.* i 20, 3 (396). Not till then did it regain its prosperity. Whereas it had formerly been a strong but comparatively small town, it was considerably enlarged by Herod, so that with a circumference of twenty stadia it was not inferior to the most important cities. Herod settled six thousand colonists there, some of them disbanded soldiers, and some, people from the surrounding area. The colonists received excellent estates. In addition, the fortifications were renewed and extended. Finally, with the erection of a temple to Augustus and other magnificent edifices, the city also acquired the splendours of modern culture.[409] Herod named the restored city *Σεβαστή*, *Ant.* xv 8, 5 (392); *B.J.* i 21,

---

ante construxerat'. Syncellus, ed. Dindorf, I, p. 519: *Δημήτριος ὁ Πολιορκητὴς τὴν πόλιν Σαμαρέων ἐπόρθησεν*. So too I, p. 522. For evidence of rebuilding, probably in this period, see Crowfoot, Kenyon, Sukenik, *Samaria-Sebaste* I (1942), pp. 117–18 (a round tower, possibly of the late fourth century).

405. Polybius v 71, 11; xvi 39, 3 = Josephus *Ant.*, xii 3, 3 (136).

406. See generally *Ant.* xii 4, 1 (154); 4 (175); 1 Mac. 10:30, 38; 11:28, 34; cf. Abel, *Géog. Pal.* II, pp. 134–5.

407. On the chronology, cf. vol. I, p. 210. For a fort built in the second century B.C. and apparently breached after the Jewish conquest, see *Samaria-Sebaste* I, pp. 28–31.

408. This is attested only by Cedrenus, ed. Bekker I, p. 323: *τὴν τῶν Γαβινίων* (read *Γαβινιέων*) *πόλιν τὴν ποτε Σαμάρειαν* (Herod) *ἐπικτίσας Σεβαστὴν αὐτὴν προσηγόρευσε*. Admittedly, Cedrenus here confuses Herod the Great with Herod Antipas, and the latter with Agrippa I.

409. For the substantial remains of Herodian and later Sebaste, see especially Reisner, Fisher, Lyon, *Harvard Excavations in Samaria* I (1924), pp. 167–223; *Samaria-Sebaste* I (1942), pp. 51–91.

2 (403); Strabo xvi 2, 34 (760), in honour of the emperor, who had recently assumed the title of Augustus. Its coins have the inscription *Σεβαστηνῶν* or *Σεβαστηνῶν Συρ(ίας)* and a special era commencing with the year of its restoration, probably 25 B.C.[410] The city is also mentioned in rabbinic literature under the new name Sebaste (סבסטי).[411] Josephus's statement that Herod granted it an 'excellent constitution', *ἐξαίρετον εὐνομίαν*, *B.J.* i 21, 2 (403), leaves us little the wiser. It is however, possible that the Samaritan region was subordinated to the city of Sebaste, as Galilee was subject to Sepphoris (and Tiberias), and Judaea to Jerusalem. At the time of the unrest among the Samaritans under Pilate, there is mention of a 'council of Samaritans', *Σαμαρέων ἡ βουλή*, which tends to suggest a united political organization of the territory, *Ant.* xviii 4, 2 (88).[412] Sebastenian soldiers served in the army of Herod, and supported the Romans against the Jews in the conflicts which broke out in Jerusalem after Herod's death, *B.J.* ii 3, 4 (52); 4, 2–3 (57 ff.); *Ant.* xvii 10, 3 (266). In the subsequent partition of Palestine, Sebaste, together with the rest of Samaria, passed to Archelaus, *Ant.* xvii 11, 4 (320); *B.J.* ii 6, 3 (96), and after his banishment, to Roman *praefecti*, and then temporarily to Agrippa I, and once again to the procurators. During this last period, Sebastenian soldiers were a main element of the Roman troops stationed in Judaea (see vol. I, pp. 363–5). At the outbreak of the revolution, Sebaste was attacked by the Jews, *B.J.* ii 18, 1 (460). With its predominantly pagan population, the city doubtless remained on the side of the Romans, as it had done already during the disturbances following the death of Herod, *Ant.* xvii 10, 9 (289); *B.J.* ii 5, 1 (69). The native Samaritans in the neighbourhood of Shechem (see above), on the other hand, adopted a quite different attitude. Assembling on Mt. Gerizim, they planned rebellion, but were slaughtered by a detachment sent by Vespasian, *B.J.* iii 7, 32 (307–15).

Under Septimius Severus, Sebaste became a Roman colony.[413] But it

410. For the coins, see *BMC Palestine*, pp. xxxvii–xli, 78–81. On the date, see vol. I, p. 290, n. 9.

411. mArakh. 3:2 (the 'pleasure gardens of Sebaste') פרדסות סבסטי are here adduced as an example of especially valuable property. Cf. Neubauer, *Géographie du Talmud*, pp. 171 f.; Krauss, *Lehnwörter* II, p. 370.

412. It could however be a reference simply to the council of the Greek city of Samaria, whose territory *(χώρα)* at this time included the area in which the Samaritan population lived. But see Avi-Yonah, *Holy Land*, e.g. map on p. 92, who appears to assume that the Samaritan area was not in the territory of Sebaste; so also *idem* in Safrai and Stern (ed.) *The Jewish People in the First Century* I (1974), pp. 99–100. In that case, the allusion could be to a common council of Samaritans distinct from the *boule* of the city of Sebaste.

413. *Digest* L 15, 1, 7 (Ulpian): 'Divus quoque Severus in Sebastenam civitatem coloniam deduxit'. On coins, COL. L. SEP. SEBASTE. For the coins, see n. 410 above.

then declined in importance before the growing prosperity of Neapolis:[414] Eusebius merely refers to it as a 'small city'.[415] Nevertheless, its territory was extensive enough to include, for example, Dothaim, twelve Roman miles to the north.[416]

25. Gaba, *Γάβα* or *Γαβά*. The name, which corresponds to the Hebrew גבע or גבעה (=hill), is not infrequent as a place-name in Palestine, but the Gaba we are concerned with lay, according to the clear description given by Josephus, adjacent to Carmel, in the great Plain, in the neighbourhood of the region of Ptolemais and the borders of Galilee, and therefore on the north-eastern slopes of Carmel; see especially *B.J.* iii 3, 1 (35–6) and *Vita* 24 (114–18). Herod settled a colony of retired cavalry-men there, on which account the city was also known as *πόλις ἱππέων*, *B.J.* iii 3, 1 (36); *Ant.* xv 8, 5 (294).[417] It is obvious from the way in which the town is mentioned in the two passages, *B.J.* iii 3, 1 (35–6) and *Vita* 24 (118), that it did not belong to the territory of Galilee. Since its population was chiefly pagan, it was attacked by the Jews at the start of the great rebellion, *B.J.* ii 18, 1 (459), and in return took an active part in the struggle against them, *Vita* 24 (115–18).

The city is probably the 'Geba' on Carmel referred to by Pliny.[418] No agreement has been reached on its precise location.[419] A 'Gabe'

414. Ammianus Marcellinus xiv 8, 11, names Neapolis but not Sebaste among the most important towns of Palestine.

415. Eusebius, *Onomast.*, ed. Klostermann, p. 154: *Σεβαστήν, τὴν νῦν πολίχνην τῆς Παλαιστίνης*. Cf. Stephanus Byz., s.v. *Σεβαστή . . . ἔστι δὲ καὶ ἐν τῇ Σαμαρειτίδι πολίχνιον*.

416. Eusebius, *Onomast.*, ed. Klostermann, p. 76: *Δωθαείμ διαμένει ἐν ὁρίοις Σεβαστῆς, ἀπέχει δὲ αὐτῆς σημείοις ιβ' ἐπὶ τὰ βόρεια μέρη*. Cf. Avi-Yonah, *Holy Land*, pp. 161–3.

417. The latter passage, *Ant.*, xv 8, 5 (294), according to the traditional text reads: *ἔν τε τῷ μεγάλῳ πεδίῳ, τῶν ἐπιλέκτων ἱππέων περὶ αὐτὸν ἀποκληρώσας, χωρίον συνέκτισεν ἐπί τε τῇ Γαλιλαίᾳ Γάβα καλούμενον καὶ τῇ Περαίᾳ τὴν Ἐσεβωνῖτιν*. It might be supposed from this that Herod founded three colonies: (1) an unknown place in the Great Plain; (2) a place called Gaba in Galilee; (3) Esebonitis in Peraea. However, the first two are certainly identical; the *τε* after *ἐπί* must be omitted, and the meaning of *ἐπὶ τῇ Γαλιλαίᾳ* is, as the whole context shows, 'for the domination of Galilee'. This also confirms the view that Gaba lay on the eastern slope of Carmel. Moreover, the reading here, as well as in *B.J.* iii 3, 1 (36), fluctuates between *Γάβα* and *Γάβαλα;* but the former is preferable.

418. Pliny, *NH* v 19/75.

419. See E. Kuhn, *Die städt. u. bürgerl. Verf.* II, pp. 320, 350 f., and *Über die Entstehung der Städte der Alten*, p. 424; A. Schlatter, *Zur Topographie und Geschichte Palästinas* (1893), pp. 292–4; ZDPV 19 (1896), p. 227. Cf. A. Alt, 'Die Reiterstadt Gaba', ZDPV 62 (1939), pp. 3–21; Abel, *Geog. Pal.* II, pp. 321–2; B. Maisler, 'Beth She'arim, Gaba and Harosheth of the Peoples', HUCA 24 (1952–3), pp. 75–84; Avi-Yonah, *Holy Land*, pp. 140–1; cf. Schalit, *König Herodes*, p. 363.

sixteen Roman miles from Caesarea is mentioned by Eusebius, but this distance is too short for a site north-east of Carmel.[420] It is even less probable that the coins with the inscription *Κλαυδι(έων) Φιλιπ(πέων) Γαβηνῶν* relate to our Gaba. These titles suggest rather a Gaba belonging to the territory of the tetrach Philip,[421] and this could be the 'Gabe' said by Pliny to have been close to Caesarea Panias. On the other hand, it is perhaps more likely that the name 'Philippeioi' derives from L. Marcius Philippus, proconsul of Syria in 61–60 B.C. (vol. I, p. 245), the date from which the era of this city seems to begin.[422] Finally, the identification of the *Γάβαι* in *Palaestina secunda*, mentioned by Hierocles, must remain in doubt.[423]

Guérin thought he had discovered our Gaba in the village of Sheikh Ibreikh on a hill near Carmel, but while the situation corresponds admirably to Josephus's topographical statements, the identification cannot be correct.[424]

26. Esbon or Hesbon, Hebrew חשבון, in the LXX and Eusebius *Ἐσεβών*, later *Ἐσβοῦς*. According to Eusebius, the city lay twenty Roman miles east of the Jordan, opposite Jericho.[425] This description agrees precisely with the site of the modern Heshban, east of the Jordan, on the same degree of latitude as the northern extremity of the Dead Sea, where extensive ruins are still to be found.[426]

420. Euseb., *Onomast.*, Klostermann, p. 70: καὶ ἔστι πολίχνη Γαβὲ καλουμένη ὡς ἀπὸ σημείων ις' τῆς Καισαρείας et alia villa Gabatha in finibus Diocaesareae παρακειμένη τῷ μεγάλῳ πεδίῳ τῆς Λεγεῶνος. The words in Latin translation interpolated from Jerome will have dropped from the Eusebius text through homoioteleuton. Their omission made it seem that the small town of Gabe lay 16 Roman miles from Caesarea, and at the same time in the Great Plain of Legeon (Megiddo), which is impossible.

421. For these coins, see de Saulcy, *Numismatique*, pp. 339–43, pl. XIX, n. 1–7; *BMC Syria*, pp. lxxxii–iii, 300. They have an era beginning in 61 B.C., see A. Alt, *Kleine Schriften* II, p. 425.

422. Pliny, *NH* v 18/74. Cf. E. Schwartz, NGG (1906), p. 370. For the suggestion about L. Marcius Philippus, see A. H. M. Jones, JRS 25 (1935), p. 230, followed by H. Herzfelder, RN 39 (1936), p. 288, and H. Seyrig, Syria 36 (1959), p. 69, n. 1.

423. Hierocles, *Synecd.*, ed. Parthey, p. 44.

424. Guérin, *Galilée* I, pp. 395–7. *The Survey of Western Palestine* I, pp. 343–51. But this identification is ruled out by Avi-Yonah, *Holy Land*, pp. 140–1. Sheikh Abreikh however is Beth She'arim, well known as an important necropolis of the 3rd and 4th centuries. See EAEHL I, s.v.

425. Eusebius, *Onomast.*, ed. Klostermann, p. 84: Ἐσεβών . . . καλεῖται δὲ νῦν Ἐσβοῦς, ἐπίσημος πόλις τῆς Ἀραβίας, ἐν ὄρεσι τοῖς ἀντικρὺ τῆς Ἱεριχοῦς κειμένη, ὡς ἀπὸ σημείων κ' τοῦ Ἰορδάνου.

426. For earlier accounts, see de Saulcy, *Voyage en Terre Sainte* (1865) I, pp. 279 ff. (with a plan of the ruins); Conder, *The Survey of Eastern Palestine* I (1889), pp. 104–9. On its history, see E. Kuhn, *Die städtische und bürgerl. Verf.* II,

Hesbon is frequently alluded to as the capital of an Amorite kingdom.[427] By contrast, in Isaiah and Jeremiah it appears as a Moabite town.[428] It is also described as such by Josephus, even at the time of Alexander Jannaeus, through whose conquests it was amalgamated with the Jewish realm, *Ant.* xiii 15, 4 (397); Syncellus I, p. 558. Its later history cannot be traced with accuracy. It was occupied in any case by Herod the Great, who re-fortified it for the domination of Peraea and established a military colony there, *Ant.* xv 8, 5 (294).[429] The territory of Esbon is said by Josephus to have formed the eastern boundary of Peraea, so it did not belong to Jewish Peraea, *B.J.* iii 3, 3 (47).[430] When the Jewish war broke out, it was assaulted by the rebels, *B.J.* ii 18, 1 (458). On the establishment of the province of Arabia in A.D. 106, Esbon, or Esbus as it was now called, will have been included in it from the beginning. For already Ptolemy assigns it to Arabia.[431] The few coins that have come to light belong to Elagabalus, and possibly also to Caracalla, and show that the city was then known as Aurelia Esbus.[432] In the time of Eusebius it was a place of importance. Christian bishops of Esbus (Esbundorum, Ἐσβουντίων) are mentioned in the fourth and fifth centuries.[433]

---

pp. 337, 386 f. See also Abel, *Géog. Pal.* II, pp. 348–9. For a brief history of the site and a preliminary report of excavations, see S. H. Horn, 'The 1968 Heshbon Expedition', BA 32 (1969), pp. 26–41. For further reports see ADAJ 12–13 (1968), pp. 51–2; 17 (1972), pp. 15–22; 19 (1974), pp. 151–6.

427. Num. 21:26 ff.; Dt. 1:4; 2:24 ff.; 3:2 ff.; 4:46; Jos. 9:10; 12:2 ff.; 13:10, 21; Jg. 11:19 ff. Cf. also Jud. 5:15.

428. Isa. 15:4; 16:8, 9; Jer. 48:2, 34, 45; 49:3. See Y. Aharoni, *The Land of the Bible* (1967), index s.v.

429. This is certainly how the passage cited in n. 372 should be understood. But note that A. H. M. Jones, JRS 25 (1935), p. 230, denies that it was the Heshbon settled by Herod, on the grounds that it was subsequently part of the province of Arabia. The form Ἐσεβωνῖτις designates the *district* of Esbon. The town itself is Ἐσεβών. Sometimes Σεβωνῖτις occurs instead of Ἐσεβωνῖτις, *B.J.* II 18, 1 (458); iii 3, 3 (47); see the following note.

430. Ἐσεβωνῖτις or Σεβωνῖτις, not Σιλβωνῖτις, should be read here, as in *B.J.* ii 18, 1 (458); cf. Schalit, *Namenwörterbuch* s.v. Ἐσεβωνῖτις.

431. Ptolemy v 17, 6 = Didot ed. (I. 2, 1901), v 16, 4. The town is here named Ἐσβοῦτα (so also the Codex of Vatopedi; see *Géographie de Ptolémée* (1867), p. lvii; also the Didot edition) which, however, is properly the accusative form of Ἔσβους.

432. F. de Saulcy, *Numismatique*, pp. 393 f., pl. XXIII, n. 5–7; *BMC Arabia*, pp. xxxiii, 29–30.

433. See n. 380 above. Eusebius also frequently mentions the town elsewhere in the *Onomasticon*; see Klostermann's index, p. 196, s.v. Cf. R. Le Quien, *Oriens christianus* II, p. 863; *Patrum Nicaenorum nomina*, ed. Gelzer, *et al.*, 1898 (Scriptores sacri et profani, fasc. 2), index, s.v. Cf. A. von Harnack, *Die Mission und Ausbreitung des Christentums* II ([4]1924), pp. 201–2.

27. Antipatris, Ἀντιπατρίς.[434] The town was situated in the neighbourhood of a village called *Καφαρσαβᾶ*[435] or *Χαβαρσαβᾶ*,[436] and also *Καπερσαβίνη*.[437] The form *Καφαρσαβᾶ* strongly suggests that the place is identical with the rabbinic כפר סבא[438] and contemporary Kfar Saba, north-east of Jaffa. The site of the latter does not, however, exactly tally with the information concerning Antipatris, namely that it lay 150 stadia from Joppa,[439] at the entrance to the hill country[440] on the main road from Caesarea to Lydda.[441] But according to Eusebius, *Onomast.*, ed. Klostermann, p. 68, Antipatris was six Roman miles south of Galgulis, which is apparently identical with the locality of Jaljûliye, a few miles south-east of Kfar Saba. This would mean that Antipatris is to be looked for about eight miles south of Kfar Saba, in a well-watered neighbourhood, whereas Kfar Saba itself stands on arid soil.[442]

434. See J. Guérin, *Samarie* II, pp. 357–67; Conder and Kitchener, *The Survey of Western Palestine* II, pp. 134, 258–62; also RE s.v. 'Antipatris'; also Abel, *Géog. Pal.* II, pp. 245–6; Avi-Yonah, *Holy Land*, pp. 145–7.

435. Josephus, *Ant.* xvi 5, 2 (142–3).

436. *Ant.* xiii 15, 1 (390) according to most manuscripts; the Latin translation has *Cafarsaba*; Niese reads, with *cod. Pal.* *Χαβερσαβᾶ*. Cf. Schalit, *Namenwörterbuch*, s.v. *Καφαρσαβᾶ*.

437. Such is undoubtedly the reading, not *καὶ Περσαβίνη*, in the passage of the *Chronicon paschale*, ed. Dindorf I, p. 367: ὁ αὐτὸς δὲ καὶ Ἀνθηδόνα ἐπικτίσας Ἀγρίππειαν ἐκάλεσεν ἔτι δὲ καὶ Περσαβίνην εἰς ὄνομα Ἀντιπάτρου τοῦ ἰδίου πάτρος. The parallel passage in Syncellus, ed. Dindorf I, p. 595, reads: ἔτι τε Παρσανάβαν εἰς τιμὴν Ἀντιπάτρου τοῦ πατρὸς αὐτοῦ Ἀντιπατρίδα ὠνόμασε.

438. tNid. 8:5; bNid. 62a; yDem. 22c. Cf. A.-S. Marmardji, *Textes géographiques arabes sur la Palestine* (1951), p. 174.

439. *Ant.* xiii 15, 1 (390). Niese reads 160 following the *cod. Pal.*, though this is unsupported by other manuscripts.

440. *B.J.* i 4, 7 (99).

441. The *Itinerarium Burdigalense* 600, 4 (in Geyer, *Itinera Hierosolymitana*, p. 25, CCL clxxv, pp. 20–1) gives the distance from Caesarea to Antipatris as XXVI Roman miles, from Antipatris to Lydda, as X Roman miles; on the figures see F.-M. Abel, RB 1923, p. 354. It is attested elsewhere that Antipatris was located on the road from Caesarea to Lydda and Jerusalem; see Act. 23:31; Josephus, *B.J.* ii 19, 1 (515) and 9 (554); iv 8, 1 (443–4); Jerome, *Peregrinatio Paulae = Ep.* 108 *ad Eustochium* 8. A papyrus of A.D. 307–24, P. Ryl. 627, ll. 240–3, now gives 11 miles from Lydda to Antipatris, 17 from Antipatris to 'the Allage' (presumably = *mutatio*, stopping-place), and 16 from there to Caesarea.

442. Antipatris is now normally located at or near Tell Apheq or Rosh ha 'Ayin in the plain of Sharon; if so, it may well be the place called *Πηγαί* (Springs) mentioned in a Zenon payrus of the mid-third century B.C., PSI 406. See Abel, *Géog. Pal.* II, p. 246; Vogel, 'Bibliography', s.v. 'Apheq' and EAEHL I, s.v. 'Aphek'. But no clear evidence of the Herodian city has been revealed. *BMC Palestine*, pp. xv–xvi and 11, presents one very dubious coin of Antipatris. If this approximate location is correct, only one of Josephus' statements is accurate, that Antipatris was founded 'in the plain of Kapharsaba', *Ant.* xvi 5, 2 (142): ἐν τῷ πεδίῳ τῷ λεγομένῳ Καφαρσαβᾶ. The other, that Chabarsaba 'is now called Antipatris', is misleading, *Ant.* xiii 15, 1 (390): Χαβαρσαβᾶ, ἣ νῦν Ἀντιπατρὶς καλεῖται.

There, in a watered and wooded plain, Herod founded a new city which he named Antipatris in honour of his father Antipater, *Ant.* xvi 5, 2 (142–3); *B.J.* i 21, 9 (417). It appears in rabbinic literature under this name, אנטיפטרס,[443] as well as in the writings of Ptolemy, Eusebius and Stephanus Byzantinus.[444] By the fourth century A.D. it had declined considerably: the *Itinerarium Burdigalense* refers to it merely as a *mutatio* (stopping-place), not as a *civitas*; Jerome designates it as *semirutum oppidulum*.[445] Yet a bishop of Antipatris still appears in the Acts of the Council of Chalcedon (A.D. 451).[446] Its existence in these later times is also attested elsewhere.[447] In fact, it is still mentioned in the eighth century A.D. as a town inhabited by Christians.[448]

28. Phasaelis, *Φασαηλίς*,[449] was founded by Herod in honour of his brother Phasael in the Jordan valley north of Jericho, in a region hitherto unplanted but fertile which he thus acquired for cultivation, *Ant.* xvi 5, 2 (145); *B.J.* i 21, 9 (417). After his death, the city with its valuable palm plantations passed into the possession of his sister Salome, *Ant.* xvii 8, 1 (189); 11, 5 (321); *B.J.* ii 6, 3 (98), and after her death into that of the empress Livia, *Ant.* xviii 2, 2 (31); *B.J.* ii 9, 1 (16). Pliny, too, refers to the excellent dates obtained from its palm trees.[450] The city is in addition mentioned by Ptolemy, Stephanus Byzantinus and the geographer of Ravenna.[451] Its name is preserved in the modern Khirbet Fasayil, in a fertile district on the edge of the Jordan plain.

443. mGit. 7:7; bGit. 76a; Neubauer, *Géographie du Talmud*, 86–90; Krauss, *Lehnwörter* II, pp. 70, 599; Enc. Jud. 3, col. 78.

444. Ptolemy, v 16, 6=Didot ed. (I 2, 1901), v 15, 5; Eusebius, *Onomast.*, pp. 68, 72; Stephanus Byz., s.v.

445. See the passages cited above, n. 441.

446. R. Le Quien, *Oriens christianus* III, pp. 579 f.

447. Hierocles, *Synecd.*, ed. Parthey, p. 43; the *Notitia episcopat.*, *ibid.*, p. 143.

448. Theophanes, *Chronographia*, ad ann. A.D. 743 (Bonn ed. I, p. 658).

449. See J. Guérin, *Samarie* I, pp. 228–32; Conder and Kitchener, *The Survey of Western Palestine* II, pp. 388, 392 f. and the large English chart, sheet XV; Abel, *Géog. Pal.* II, pp. 408–9; N. Glueck, *Explorations in Eastern Palestine*, AASOR 25/8 (1945–9), pp. 414–15); RE s.v. 'Phasaelis'; L. Mowry, 'Settlements in the Jericho Valley in the Roman Period', BA 15 (1952), pp. 26–42, on pp. 31–2; G. Harder, 'Herodes-Burgen und Herodes-Städte im Jordangraben', ZDPV 78 (1962), pp. 49–63, on pp. 54–60; Thomsen, *Loca sancta*, 113; Avi-Yonah, *Holy Land*, pp. 100, 164.

450. Pliny, *NH* xiii 4/44: 'sed ut copia ibi atque fertilitas, ita nobilitas in Iudaea, nec in tota, sed Hiericunte maxume, quamquam laudatae et Archelaide et Phaselide atque Liviade, gentis eiusdem convallibus'.

451. Ptolemy, v 16, 7=Didot ed. (I 2, 1901), v 15, 5; Stephanus Byz., s.v.; *Georgraphus Ravennas*, ed. Pinder et Parthey (1860), p. 84. The town is also mentioned in the Middle Ages (in Burchardus and Marinus Sanutus); see the passages in Guérin, *Samarie* I, pp. 231 f.

The stream flowing from there to the Jordan is known as Wadi Fasayil.[452]

29. Caesarea Panias.[453] *Τὸ Πάνειον* means the grotto dedicated to Pan at the source of the Jordan.[454] Polybius is the first to mention it by this name in connection with Antiochus the Great, who gained a decisive victory there in 200 B.C. over the Egyptian general Scopas, as a result of which the whole of Palestine fell into his hands.[455] From this early reference alone, the inference is that the place was Hellenized in the third century B.C. The population of the region was in any case, as its later history shows, chiefly non-Jewish.

In the early years of Herod's reign, the region of Panias belonged to a certain Zenodorus. After his death in 20 B.C., Augustus granted it to Herod (see vol. I, p. 291), who built a magnificent temple to Augustus in the neighbourhood of the grotto of Pan, *Ant.* xv 10, 3 (363); *B.J.* i 21, 3 (404). The place which stood there was originally called *Πανιάς* or *Πανεάς*, like the region.[456] But it was the tetrarch Philip, the son of Herod, who first made it into a handsome city. He laid it out and called it *Καισάρεια* in honour of Augustus, *Ant.* xviii 2, 1 (28); *B.J.* ii 9, 1 (168).

452. See especially the sketch-map in Hassler, *op. cit.*

453. See E. Kuhn, *op. cit.* II, p. 334; J. Guérin, *Galilée* II, pp. 308–23; Conder and Kitchener, *The Survey of Western Palestine* I, p. 95, 109–13, 125–8; RE III, cols 1290 f. On the history of the town in the Middle Ages, see Gildemeister, ZDPV 10 (1887), pp. 188 f.; C. Clermont-Ganneau, *Rec. d'arch, or.* I (1888), pp. 242–61; M. van Berchem, 'Le château de Bâniâs et ses inscriptions', JA, 8e Série, 12 (1888), pp. 440–70; 'Inscription arabe de Banias', RB (1903), pp. 421–4; G. Le Strange, *Palestine under the Moslems*, p. 418 f. On the topography of the neighbourhood, see Schumacher's map of Golan in ZDPV 9 (1886). For views of the Pan grotto, see *Oxford Bible Atlas* (²1974), p. 114. For inscriptions, CIG nos. 4537–9, *Addenda*, 1179; J. K. Bailie, *Fasciculus inscr. graec.* III, *potissimum ex Galatia Lycia Syria etc.* (1849), pp. 130–3; F. de Saulcy, *Voyage autour de la Mer Morte, Atlas* (1853), pl. XLIX; Le Bas-Waddington, *Inscriptions* III, nos. 1891–4; IGR III 1108–9; Brünnow and Domaszewski, *Die Provincia Arabia* II, p. 249. See also Abel, *Géog. Pal.* II, pp. 297–8; Avi-Yonah, *Holy Land*, pp. 164–7; G. Hölscher, RE s.v. 'Panias', XVIII (1949), cols. 594–600 (the fullest account).

454. The Paneion is described as a grotto (*σπήλαιον, ἄντρον*) in Josephus, *Ant.* xv 10, 3 (364); *B.J.* i 21, 3 (404–6); iii 10, 7 (509): *δοκεῖ μὲν Ἰορδάνου πηγὴ τὸ Πάνειον;* Stephanus Byz., s.v. *Πανία*. The mountain nearby was called by the same name as the grotto, Eusebius, *HE* vii 17: *ἐν ταῖς ὑπορείαις τοῦ καλουμένου Πανείου ὄρους πηγαῖς*. (*τὸ Πάνειον* is in fact an adjective requiring as a complement either *ἄντρον* or *ὄρος*).

455. Polybius xvi 18, 2 (see Walbank *ad loc.*); xxviii 1, 3.

456. *Πανιάς* or *Πανεάς* is properly an adjective, the fem. of *Πάνειος* (as *ἀγριάς, λευκάς, ὀρειάς* are the poetic feminines of *ἄγριος, λευκός, ὄρειος*). The same word therefore serves to designate both the region (where *χώρα* is the complement, as in *Ant.* xv 10, 3 (360); *B.J.* ii 9, 1 (168); Pliny, *NH* v 18/74; 'Panias in qua Caesarea'), and the town or locality, where *πόλις* or *κώμη* is the complement, as in *Ant.* xviii 2, 1 (28).

The foundation occurred right at the beginning of Philip's reign, for the coins of the town have an era that probably starts in 3 B.C., or at the latest 2 B.C.[457] After the death of Philip, his territory was administered for a few years by the Romans. It subsequently passed to Agrippa I, then again to the Roman procurators, and finally, from A.D. 53, to Agrippa II, who enlarged Caesarea and re-named it *Νερωνίας* in honour of Nero, *Ant.* xx 9, 4 (211), a designation occasionally found on coins.[458] That the town was still predominantly non-Jewish can be seen from Josephus, *Vita* 13 (74). Hence both Titus and Vespasian spent their days of rest there during the Jewish war, amidst games and other festivities.[459]

The name Neronias seems never to have become generally accepted. In the first century A.D., our Caesarea was usually designated *Καισάρεια ἡ Φιλίππου*[460] to distinguish it from other Caesareas; its official name on coins, especially of the second century, is *Καισ(άρεια) Σεβ(αστὴ) ἱερ(ὰ) καὶ ἄσυλ(ος) ὑπὸ Πανείῳ*.[461] Otherwise, it is usually referred to from the second century onward as *Καισάρεια Πανιάς*, and on coins of the third century this name predominates.[462] From the fourth century, the name Caesarea disappears entirely and the city from then on becomes once more simply *Πανεάς*.[463] This name seems in any case always to have

457. See F. de Saulcy, *Numismatique*, pp. 313–24, pl. XVIII. *BMC Syria*, pl. lxxx-ii, 298–9; *BMC Palestine*, p. 239; see H. Seyrig, Num. Chron. 10 (1950), pp. 286–7. The statement in the Chronicle of Eusebius, which dates the foundation to the time of Tiberius, is without value; see below, re Tiberias. Following Eusebius, also Jerome in the *Chronicle* and *Comm. in Mt.* 16:13 (see below, n. 463).

458. Y. Meshorer, *Jewish Coins of the Second Temple Period* (1967), pp. 85–7; see vol. I, p. 473.

459. Josephus, *B.J.* iii 9, 7 (444); vii 2, 1 (23–4).

460. Mt. 16:13; Mk. 8:27; Josephus, *Ant.* xx 9, 4 (211); *B.J.* iii 9, 7 (443); vii 2, 1 (23); *Vita* 13 (74).

461. See F. de Saulcy, *Numismatique*, cf. above, n. 457.

462. Ptolemy v 15, 21 (Didot ed. v 14, 17); viii 20, 12 *(Καισάρεια Πανιάς)*; CIG 4750=OGIS 687= SB 8257=H. and E. Bernand, *Les inscriptions grecques et latines du colosse de Memnon* (1960), no. 69; CIG 4921=SB 8418=E. Bernand, *Les inscriptions grecques et latines de Philae* II, no. 170), both with *Καισαρείας Πανιάδος*; Le Bas-Waddington, *Inscriptions* III, no. 1620b=L. Moretti, *Iscrizioni agonistiche greche* (1953), no. 72 (from Aphrodisias in Caria, *c.* A.D. 165 commemorating an athlete who twice won the *pankration* there): *Καισάρειαν Πανιάδα*; *Tabula Peutingeriana* ('Caesareapaneas'); *Geographus Ravennas*, ed. Pinder et Parthey, p. 85; also, the coins in de Saulcy, *Numismatique*, pp. 317, 322 f.

463. See especially AE 1936, 129, a third century milestone on the road 'a Tyro metropoli Paneam'. Eusebius, who frequently mentions the town in the *Onomasticon*, always calls it *Πανεάς* (see the index in Klostermann's ed.). And this in general is its name in patristic literature; see e.g. Eusebius, HE vii 17–18; Jerome, *Com. in Esaiam* (CCL lxxiiiA, p. 479); ('in confinio Caesareae Philippi, quae nunc vocatur Paneas'); *in Hiezech.* 27: 19 (CCL lxxv, p. 374): ('ubi hodie Paneas, quae quondam Caesarea Philippi vocabatur'); and in Mt. 16:13 (CCL

remained current among the native population[464] and is the one mainly used (in the form פניים) in rabbinic literature.[465] The view that Caesarea became a Roman colony under Elagabalus can now be regarded as disproved.[466]

In the reference to the 'villages of Caesarea Philippi' (*αἱ κῶμαι Καισαρείας τῆς Φιλίππου*) in the New Testament (Mk. 8:27), the genitive does not of course signify merely a 'spatial relationship' of the villages to the city, but that the villages belonged to and were subject to it. Like each of these cities, Caesarea possessed and governed a territory of its own. The site of the city, which is not open to doubt, remains to be excavated.

30. ?Julias, formerly Bethsaida.[467] On the site of a village called Bethsaida, north of Lake Gennesaret, Philip founded a new city which he named Ἰουλιάς in honour of Julia, the daughter of Augustus, *Ant.* xviii 2, 1 (28); *B.J.* ii 9, 1 (168). Its location east of the Jordan, a short distance from its outflow into Lake Gennesaret, is established beyond

---

lxxvii, p. 139): ('in honorem Tiberii [sic.] Caesaris Caesaream, quae nunc Paneas dicitur, construxit'); Sozom. *HE* v 21; Philostorgius vii 3 (cf. also Müller, FHG IV, p. 546); Cyril of Scythopolis, *Vita Sabae* 24; Malalas, ed. Dindorf, p. 237; Photius, *Bib.* 271 (ed. Bekker, p. 505); The Acts of the Councils (in R. Le Quien, *Oriens christianus* II, p. 831); *Patrum Nicaenorum nomina*, ed. Gelzer etc. (1898), index, s.v.; the Christian itineraries in Geyer, *Itinera Hierosolymitana*, p. 128, 16 (Eucherius), 138 (Theodosius), 268 (Adammanus) cf. CCL clxxv, Index s.v. 'Paneas'; Hierocles, *Synecd.*, ed. Parthey, p. 43. On the alleged statue of Christ at Paneas, see above p. 40. Cf. A. von Harnack, *Die Mission und Ausbreitung des Christentums* I ([4]1924), pp. 145–6.

464. Cf. Eusebius, *HE* vii 17: *ἐπὶ τῆς Φιλίππου Καισάρειας, ἣν Πανεάδα Φοίνικες προσαγορεύουσι.*

465. mPar. 8:11; tBekh. 7:4 (in both passages the 'Cave of Panias', מערת פניים, is mentioned); J. Levy, *Chald. Wörterb.* II, pp. 273 f.; Neubauer, *Géographie du Talmud*, pp. 236–8; Krauss, *Lehnwörter* II, p. 463; Avi-Yonah, *Holy Land*, pp. 150–2.

466. K. Regling, Zeitschr. für Numism. 24 (1904), pp. 133 f., assigned a coin with the inscription 'Aur. Alexandros Caisar' (i.e. Severus Alexander as Caesar, A.D. 221 or 222) and 'Col. Cesaria Itur.', on account of the addition 'Itur.', to our Caesarea Panias. But it is certainly a coin of Caesarea ad Libanum, ancient Arka, the birthplace of Severus Alexander; cf. vol. I, p. 478, and J. Starcky, 'Arca du Liban', Les Cahiers de l'Orient 10 (1971–2), pp. 103–13. Regling himself drew attention to the affinity of the coin with those of Orthosias, located in the neighbourhood of Arka. For confirmation of this view, see *BMC Phoenicia*, p. lxxiii, and cf. H. Seyrig, 'Une monnaie de Césarée du Liban', Syria 36 (1959), pp. 39–43.

467. See Kuhn, *op. cit.* II, p. 352; Guérin, *Galilée* I, pp. 329–38; Abel, *Géog. Pal.* II, pp. 279–80; Avi-Yonah, *Holy Land*, pp. 96, 105. It is normally identified with Tell el 'Araj, northeast of the outflow of the Jordan into Lake Gennesaret, see Avi-Yonah, 'Gazetteer', pp. 40–1.

doubt by the repeated and consistent statements of Josephus.[468] If it is correct that the town was named after Julia, its foundation must also have taken place close to the beginning of Philip's reign, for Julia was banished by Augustus in 2 B.C. to the island of Pandateria.[469] It is inconceivable that Philip would subsequently have named a town after her.[470]

Of the later history of the town, it is known only that Nero bestowed it on Agrippa II, *Ant.* xx 8, 4 (159); *B.J.* ii 13, 2 (252). It is also mentioned by Pliny, Ptolemy and the geographer of Ravenna.[471]

From the way Josephus writes of it, *Ant.* xviii 2, 1 (28), it might seem that Philip merely altered the name of the village Bethsaida to Julias, and that the new place was also only a *κώμη*.[472] In another passage, however, *Ant.* xx 8, 4 (159), he distinguishes Julias as a *πόλις* from the surrounding villages. It was therefore a *πόλις* proper from the time of its re-foundation. That there is no trace of it ever having minted coins, may, however, suggest the opposite.[473]

Whether the Bethsaida of the New Testament was identical with the place under discussion, may be left undebated here.[474]

31. Sepphoris, *Σέπφωρις*.[475] The Semitic rendering of this place-name varies between צפורין and צפורי. The first is possibly the older, and the second, the abbreviated form.[476] The Greek and Latin *Σεπφουρίν*,

468. See especially *B.J.* iii 10, 7 (515) and *Ant.* xviii 2, 1 (28) (on Lake Gennesaret); *Vita* 72 (399) (close to the Jordan); *Ant.* xx 8, 4 (159) and *B.J.* ii 13, 2 (252) (in Peraea). Also, Pliny, *NH* v 15/71, mentions Julias on the eastern shore of Lake Gennesaret.

469. Velleius ii 100, 3; Dio lv 10, 4. Cf. Suetonius, *Aug.* 65; Tacitus, *Ann.* i 53. See PIR² I 634.

470. The Chronicle of Eusebius erroneously places the foundation of Julias in the time of Tiberius; see below, on Tiberias.

471. Pliny *HN* v 15/71; Ptolemy v 16, 4 = Didot ed. (I. 2, 1901), v 15, 3; *Geogr. Ravennas*, ed. Pinder et Parthey, p. 85.

472. *Ant.* xviii 2, 1 (28): *κώμην δὲ Βηθσαϊδὰ πρὸς λιμνῇ τῇ Γεννησαρετίδι, πόλεως παρασχὼν ἀξίωμα πλήθει τε οἰκητόρων καὶ τῇ ἄλλῃ δυνάμει, Ἰουλίᾳ θυγατρὶ τῇ Καίσαρος ὁμώνυμον ἐκάλεσεν.*

473. So A. H. M. Jones, JRS 21 (1931), p. 80.

474. For the identity: G. A. Smith, *Historical Geography of the Holy Land*, pp. 457 f.; F. Buhl, *Geogr. des alten Palästina*, p. 242. Against the identity: HDB I, pp. 282–3, see G. Schille, ZDPV 73 (1957), p. 142. P. Baldi, SBFLA (1959/60), pp. 120–46; Avi-Yonah, s.v. 'Beth-Saida', IDB I, pp. 396–7; *Holy Land*, p. 105.

475. See Kuhn, *op. cit.* II, p. 372; R. Guérin, *Galilée* I, pp. 369–76; Conder and Kitchener, *The Survey of Western Palestine* I, pp. 279 f., 330–8; RE s.v. 'Sepphoris', II A (1923), cols. 1546–9; L. Waterman, *Preliminary Report of the University of Michigan Excavations at Sepphoris, Palestine, 1931* (1937); for its history see S. Yeivin, *ibid.*, pp. 17 ff., 'Historical and Archaeological Notes'; Abel, *Géog. Pal.* I, pp. 305 f.; Avi-Yonah, *Holy Land*, pp. 135–8.

476. The place finds no mention in the Old Testament but appears frequently in rabbinical literature. In the Mishnah it is found in the following four places:

Saphorim, Safforine, correspond to צפורין,[477] and *Σαπφουρεί*, Sepori, Sabure, to צפורי.[478] Josephus constantly employs the Graecized form, *Σέπφωρις*.[479] On coins, the inhabitants are named *Σεπφωρηνοί*.[480]

The earliest mention of Sepphoris appears in Josephus at the beginning of the reign of Alexander Jannaeus, when Ptolemy Lathyrus made an unsuccessful attempt to take Sepphoris by force, *Ant.* xiii 12, 5 (338). When, in around 57–55 B.C., Gabinius divided the Jewish realm into five 'synedria', he transferred the 'synedrium' of Galilee to Sepphoris, *Ant.* xiv 5, 4 (91); *B.J.* i 8, 5 (170).[481] It must already at that time, therefore, have been the most important city in Galilee. It is also referred to as a garrison town during the conquest of Palestine by Herod the Great, who was able to capture it without difficulty only because the troops of Antigonus had evacuated the place, *Ant.* xiv 15, 4 (414); *B.J.* i 16, 2 (304). Sepphoris appears to have been a centre of the rebellion that followed Herod's death. Varus dispatched a division of his army there, set fire to the city and sold the inhabitants into slavery, *Ant.* xvii 10, 9 (289); *B.J.* ii 5, 1 (68). With this, it reached the most important turning-point in its history. From being a Jewish city, it became loyalist, presumably with a mixed population. Herod Antipas, into whose possession it then passed, rebuilt it and made of it an 'ornament of all Galilee', *Ant.* xviii 2, 1 (27): *πρόσχημα τοῦ Γαλιλαίου παντός*.[482] In the revolution of A.D. 66–70, the population seems to have

---

mKid. 4:5; mB.M. 8:8; mB.B. 6:7; mArakh. 9:6; it figures very often in the Tosefta (see Zuckermandel's index). Cf. Neubauer, *Géographie du Talmud*, pp. 191–5; Bacher, *Die Agada der palästinensischen Amoräer* III, index, s.v. 'Sepphoris'; JE XI, pp. 198–200. The orthography fluctuates between צפורין (or צפורים, ציפורין) and צפורי (or ציפורי), resembling the variation between the forms *Modein*, *Modeim* and *Modei*. The plural form may in both cases be the original.

477. *Σεπφουρίν:* Epiphanius, *Haer.* 30, 11; 'Saphorim': Jerome, *Praef. in Ionam* (CCL lxxvi, p. 378); 'Safforine': Jerome, *Onomast.*, ed. Klostermann, p. 17, p. 14. In Jn. 11:54, the Greek and Latin text of Codex D has the addition *Σαμφουριν*, Sapfurim, after *χώραν*. Here also, as the form of the name shows, it is certainly Sephoris that is intended.

478. *Σαπφουρεί:* Ptolemy v 16, 4 = Didot ed. (I. 2, 1901), v 15, 3 (the form *Σαπφουρεῖ* without addition is decisively attested, among others, also by the Codex of Vatopedi; see *Géographie de Ptolemée* (1867), p. lvii); 'Sapori', *Geographus Ravennas*, ed. Pinder et Parthey, p. 85; 'Sabure', *Notitia dignitatum*, ed. Seeck, p. 73.

479. Only in *Ant.* xiv 5, 4 (91) is the tradition very uncertain. Among others, the forms *Σαφούροις*, *Σαπφόροις*, *Σαμφώροις*, *Σεπφώροις*, are found (see Niese). Cf. Schalit, *Namenwörterbuch*, p. 110.

480. See de Saulcy, *Numismatique*, p. 325 f., pl. XVII, n. 1–4; *BMC Palestine*, pp. xi–xiii, 1–4.

481. Cf. vol. I, pp. 268–9.

482. The surviving remains, not all to be attributed to the initial phase, include a theatre, an aqueduct and a later Christian basilica, see Waterman, *op. cit.*, pp. 1–16.

been predominantly Jewish, but none the less supported the Roman operations against the rebels.[483] The Mishnah may be referring to this change in a passage in which the '*old* government of Sepphoris' is assumed to have been a purely Jewish one.[484] On its reconstruction by Herod Antipas, Sepphoris may have been promoted to the rank of capital of Galilee.[485] Yet the same prince subsequently bestowed this dignity on the newly-built city of Tiberias and subordinated Sepphoris to it.[486] And so it remained until, under Nero, Tiberias was separated

483. That it was, however, still predominantly Jewish is evident especially from *B.J.* iii 2, 4 (32): *προθύμως σφᾶς αὐτοὺς ὑπέσχοντο κατὰ τῶν ὁμοφύλων συμμάχους.*

484. mKid. 4:5. We read here that any person is to be reckoned an Israelite who can prove his descent from a priest or Levite who actually ministered as such, or from a member of the Sanhedrin: indeed, any person whose ancestors are known to have been public officials or almoners and in particular, according to Rabbi Yose, anyone מי שהיה חתום בארכי הישנה של ציפורין. In explanation of this difficult passage, it should be noted that חתום, properly 'sealed', is here equivalent to, 'confirmed, acknowledged, accredited by documents' (cf. the use of *σφραγίζω* in Jn. 3:33; 6:27). On the evidence of the best MSS, the word which follows חתום in the common text, should be deleted. ארכי=*ἀρχή* (not='archive', as Krauss thought). Accordingly, two interpretations are possible. Either (1) 'Anyone who (in respect of his ancestors) was acknowledged in the old Sepphoris government as one of its members'. The presupposition would then be that all the members of the old government of Sepphoris were pure-blooded Israelites. Or (2) 'Anyone who was acknowledged *by* the old government of Sepphoris', viz., as a pure-blooded Israelite. In this case, too, the old government of Sepphoris would be assumed to have consisted of purely Israelite officials. The first explanation seems preferable in the light of the context. It is of course uncertain when the ancient purely Jewish government of Sepphoris was replaced by a mixed or pagan administration. It may possibly have been in the reign of Hadrian when many changes took place in consequence of the Jewish insurrection. It was, in addition, at about that time that Sepphoris received the new name of Diocaesarea (see below). It appears probable, however, that Sepphoris ceased to be a purely Jewish city from the time of its re-foundation by Herod Antipas. Also, the example of Tiberias shows that the constitutions of the cities founded by Herod Antipas were not organized in accordance with Jewish standards. Josephus even asserts, in regard to the whole of Galilee, that it was through him that a Jewish type of administration was first introduced there, *B.J.* ii 20, 5 (570–1). Coins of Sepphoris, bearing the image of Trajan should also be mentioned.

485. Josephus observes in *Ant.* xviii 2, 1 (27): *ἦγεν* [or *ἤγαγεν*] *αὐτὴν αὐτοκρατίδα.* This may mean that self-government was granted–*αὐτοκρατίδα = αὐτόνομον).* But it may be that the rest of Galilee was still, or once again, subordinated to it. The explanation of *αὐτοκρατίς* as 'capital' can hardly be conceded, and a secure interpretation of the passage is made all the more difficult because the reading varies. Dindorf proposes *ἀνῆκεν αὐτὴν αὐτοκράτορι*, and Niese reads *ἠγόρευεν αὐτὴν Αὐτοκρατίδα.* It is indeed frequently taken as in Loeb ed. *ad loc.* that he gave it the appellation *Αὐτοκρατωρίς* formed from the Greek equivalent of imperator=emperor. If this is correct, nothing can be deduced about its relation to the surrounding area.

486. *Vita* 9 (37): Justus said of Tiberias, *ὡς ἡ πόλις ἐστὶν ἀεὶ τῆς Γαλιλαίας, ἄρξειεν δὲ ἐπί γε τῶν Ἡρώδου χρόνων τοῦ τετράρχου καὶ κτίστου γενομένου, βουληθέντος αὐτοῦ τὴν Σεπφωριτῶν πόλιν τῇ Τιβεριέων ὑπακούειν*

from Galilee and granted to Agrippa II, as a result of which Sepphoris became once again the region's capital.[487] It may have been then that it received the name Eirenopolis Neronias Sepphoris. [488] Thus these two cities alternately occupied the same position in regard to Galilee as did Jerusalem in relation to Judaea (see below, pp. 197–8).

Sepphoris at that time constituted the most significant fortress in Galilee, [489] and after Tiberias, the largest city in the province.[490] It was therefore of the greatest importance, on the outbreak of the Jewish war, that it did not support the insurrection but from the beginning remained on the side of the Romans. When Cestius Gallus marched against Jerusalem, Sepphoris adopted a friendly attitude towards him;[491] and it remained loyally pro-Roman during the winter of A.D. 66/67, when Josephus was organizing the revolt in Galilee.[492] He therefore took it by force, and in so doing was unable to prevent it from being plundered by his Galilean troops.[493] In consequence, Cestius Gallus sent a garrison to the oppressed city which repulsed Josephus when he forced a second entrance.[494] Soon afterwards Vespasian arrived

487. *Vita* 9 (38): *ἄρξαι γὰρ εὐθὺς τὴν μὲν Σέπφωριν, ἐπειδὴ Ῥωμαίοις ὑπήκουσε, τῆς Γαλιλαίας.*

488. For the identification of a small series of coins whose fragmentary legends can be combined to give the reading *ΕΙΡΗΝΟΠΟΛΙ ΝΕΡΩΝΙΑ ΣΕΠ(ΦΩΡΙΣ)*, see H. Seyrig, 'Eirenopolis-Neronias-Sepphoris', NC 10 (1950), pp. 284–9.

489. *B.J.* ii 18, 11 (511): *ἡ καρτερωτάτη τῆς Γαλιλίας πόλις Σέπφωρις*; cf. *B.J.* iii 2, 4 (34). The *ἀκρόπολις* is mentioned in *Vita* 67 (376); cf. mArakh 9:6: **קצרה הישנה של ציפורין**, 'the old citadel of Sepphoris'; tShab. 13:9: **קצטרא שבציפורי**.

490. *Vita* 65 (346): *τῶν ἐν τῇ Γαλιλαίᾳ πόλεων αἱ μέγισται Σέπφωρις καὶ Τιβεριάς.* *Vita* 45 (232): *εἰς Σέπφωριν μέγιστην τῶν ἐν τῇ Γαλιλαίᾳ πόλιν.* *B.J.* iii 2, 4 (34): *μεγίστην μὲν οὖσαν τῆς Γαλιλαίας πόλιν ἐρυμνοτάτῳ δ' ἐπιτετειχισμένην χωρίῳ.* According to *Vita* 25 (123), Tiberias, Sepphoris and Gabara were the three largest towns of Galilee.

491. *B.J.* ii 18, 11 (511).

492. Josephus, *Vita* 8 (30), 22 (104), 25 (124), 45 (232), 65 (346). Two passages in *B.J.* admittedly seem to contradict this. According to *B.J.* ii 20, 6 (574), Josephus left the fortification of their city to the Sepphorites themselves, since he found them in any case 'ready for war' *(προθύμους ἐπὶ τὸν πόλεμον)* i.e., against the Romans. Also, according to *B.J.* ii 21, 7 (629), at the outbreak of the conflict between Josephus and the more fanatical war party, Sepphoris supported the latter. The true significance of these two points emerges, however, from the more specific statements contained in the *Vita*. The Sepphorites only pretended to be ready for the cause of the revolution in order to keep the whole revolutionary party at arm's length; they fortified their city, not against, but for the Romans; see especially *Vita* 65 (347). And as they were without Roman protection for a considerable time during the winter of 66/67, they were obliged to tack between the two opposing revolutionary parties and where possible adopt a seemingly friendly position towards both, see *Vita* 25 (124), and especially *Vita* 45 (232). It is in the context of this situation that *B.J.* ii 21, 7 (629) is to be understood.

493. *Vita* 67 (373–80).

494. *Vita* 71 (394–7). The remark in *Vita* 15 (82), *δὶς μὲν κατὰ κράτος ἑλὼν Σεπφωρίτας,* refers to this dual capture of Sepphoris.

in Galilee with his army, and Sepphoris requested and received from him yet another Roman garrison.[495]

Information concerning the subsequent history of the city is no more than fragmentary. On coins of Trajan, its inhabitants are still described as *Σεπφωρηνοί*. A little later, however, it was given the name Diocaesarea, which appears on coins from the time of Antoninus Pius. Its official designation on coins is, *Διοκαι(σάρεια) ἱερὰ ἄσ(υλος) καὶ αὐτό(νομος)*.[496] Diocaesarea remained the prevailing name among Greek authors.[497] Yet the original appellation continued to exist; indeed in the end it ousted the later one.[498]

The territory of Diocaesarea was so extensive that it included, for example, the village of Dabira on Mount Tabor.[499]

32. Julias or Livias.[500] The Old Testament mentions a town called Beth-haram (בית הרם or בית הרן) east of the Jordan, in the territory of the Amorite king of Heshbon, Jos. 13:27; Num. 32:37. In the Jerusalem Talmud, בית רמתא is given as a more recent name of

495. *Vita* 74 (411); *B.J.* iii 2, 4 (31); 4, 1 (61). The earlier garrison sent by Cestius Gallus had in the meantime either been withdrawn or was now replaced or strengthened by the troops of Vespasian.

496. See de Saulcy, *Numismatique*, pp. 325–30, pl. XVII, n. 1–7; *BMC Palestine*, pp. xi–xiii, 1–4. On the identity of Sepphoris and Diocaesarea, see Epiphanius *Haer.* 30, 11, Jerome, *Onomast.*, ed. Klostermann, pp. 17, 13 f., and his *Prologus in Ionam* (CCL lxxvi, p. 378); Hegesippus, *De bello Iud.* i 30, 7.

497. Eusebius in *Onomast.* names the town exclusively *Διοκαισάρεια* (see the index in Klostermann). Cf. also, besides the literature cited in the preceding note, Socrates, *HE* ii 33; Sozomenus, *HE* iv 7; Theophanes, *Chronographia*, Bonn ed. I, p. 61; Cedrenus, ed. Bekker, I, p. 524; R. Le Quien, *Oriens christ.* III, p. 714.

498. On the continued use of the name of Sepphoris, see above, nn. 476–8. For the later Sepphoris note A. Büchler, *The Political and Social Leaders of the Jewish Community of Sepphoris in the Second and Third Centuries* (1909); 'The Minim of Sepphoris and Tiberias in the Second and Third Centuries', *Studies in Jewish History* (1956), pp. 245–74; M. Avi-Yonah, 'A Sixth-Century Inscription from Sepphoris', IEJ 11 (1961), pp. 184–7.

499. Eusebius, *Onomast.*, p. 78: *Δαβειρά . . . ἐν τῷ ὄρει Θαβώρ ἐν ὁρίοις Διοκαισαρείας*. Gabatha, the modern Gevat (Jebata), about 7–8 Roman miles from Diocaesarea, also belonged to its territory; see above, n. 477; for its territory see Avi-Yonah, *Holy Land*, pp. 135–9.

500. See E. Kuhn, *Die städtische und bürgerl. Verfassung* II, pp. 352 f.; *Über die Entstehung der Städte der Alten* (1878), p. 426; *The Survey of Eastern Palestine, Memoirs etc.* I, by Conder (1889), pp. 238 f.; Thomsen, *Loca sancta*, 83 f.; N. Glueck, BASOR 91 (1943), pp. 20–1; *Explorations in Eastern Palestine* IV, AASOR XXV–VIII (1951), pp. 38–91; Abel, *Géog. Pal.* II, p. 273; G. Hassler, ZDPV 78 (1962), pp. 60–3; Avi-Yonah, *Holy Land*, pp. 96, 105. M. Donner and H. Cüpper, ZDPV 83 (1967), pp. 22–3 suggest that this region is portrayed on the Madaba mosaic map (pl. II–III Avi-Yonah). Cf. also Enc. Jud. 4, col. 736.

this Beth-haram,[501] and Eusebius and Jerome likewise identify the biblical Beth-haram with the place known by them as *Βηθραμφθά* or *Bethramtha.*[502] The latter is in any case identical with *Βηθαράματος*, where Herod the Great possessed a palace that was destroyed during the insurrection after his death.[503] This Bethramphtha was then rebuilt and fortified by Herod Antipas, and named Julias in honour of the wife of Augustus, Josephus, *Ant.* xviii 2, 1 (27); *B.J.* ii 9, 1 (168). Eusebius and others give the name as Livias instead of Julias,[504] and the town is also frequently referred to elsewhere as Livias.[505] Since the wife of Augustus was really called Livia, and was only admitted into the *gens Iulia* in virtue of her husband's will, and therefore bore the name Julia only after his death,[506] it seems that Livias was the older of the two names and that this was later changed to Julias. But as in the cases of Caesarea Philippi and Neronias, the new official name was unable to supplant the original one. Josephus alone uses the official designation Julias. He still writes of the town as Julias during the time

501. ySheb. 38d (on mSheb. 9:2). Peraea is here divided into three parts in accordance with its physical characteristics: mountains, plain, valley (הר, שפלה, עמק). In the mountains lie, for example, Machaerus; in the plain, Heshbon; in the valley, בית הרן and בית נמרה ; בית רמתה and בית נמרין are then given as the newer names of the two latter places. In the Tosefta (tSheb. 7:11) both towns are called בית נמרה רמתא. Has בית been omitted here before רמתא? Or was it known simply as רמתא?

502. Eusebius, *Onomast.*, ed. Klostermann, pp. 48–9.

503. *B.J.* ii 4, 2 (59). In the parallel passage, *Ant.* xvii 10, 6 (277), the name is corrupt. Instead of *ἐν Ἀμάθοις* or *ἐν Ἀμμαθοῖς* as the traditional text has it, the reading should be either *ἐν Ἀραμαθοῖς* (with the omission of 'Beth') or *ἐν Βηθαραμαθοῖς*.

504. Eusebius, *Onomast.*, ed. Klostermann, p. 48: *Βηθραμφθά . . . αὐτὴ δέ ἐστιν ἡ νῦν καλουμένη Λιβιάς;* Jerome, *ibid.*, p. 49: 'Bethramtha . . . ab Herode in honorem Augusti Libias cognominata'; Eusebius, *Chron.*, ed. Schoene II, pp. 148–9: 'Herodes Tiberiadem condidit et Liviadem' (according to Jerome and the Armenian); Syncellus, ed. Dindorf, I, p. 605: *Ἡρώδης ἔκτισε Τιβεριάδα εἰς ὄνομα Τιβερίου Καίσαρος· ὁ αὐτὸς Λιβιάδα.* The identity of Livias with Josephus' Betharamphtha-Julias is thus beyond reasonable doubt. See now H. W. Hoehner, *Herod Antipas* (1972), pp. 87–91.

505. Pliny, *NH* xiii 4/44; Ptolemy v 16, 9=Didot ed. (I 2, 1901), v 15, 6 (*Λιβιάς* following the most important MSS. authorities, also the cod. of Vatopedi among others); Eusebius in *Onomast.*, frequently; Hierocles, *Synecd.*, ed. Parthey, p. 44; the *Notitia episcopat, ibid.*, p. 144; the Acts of the Councils (Le Quien, *Oriens christ.* III, pp. 655 f.); *Vita S. Ioannis Silentiarii* 18; *Geographus Ravennas*, ed. Pinder et Parthey, p. 84 ('Leviada', as nominative); Gregory of Tours, *De gloria martyr.* I 18; H. Raabe, *Petrus der Iberer* (1895), pp. 81 f.; cf. CCL clxxvi, Indices, p. 370.

506. On the will of Augustus, see Tacitus, *Ann.* I 8: 'Livia in familiam Iuliam nomenque Augustum adsumebatur'. The name Julia for Livia among writers (e.g., Tacitus, *Ann.* i 14; V 1; Suetonius, *Calig.* 16; Dio lvi 46, 1; Pliny, *NH* x 55/154; Josephus (frequently) and on coins and inscriptions; see PIR² L 301. For Palestinian coins of Julia, see de Saulcy, *Numismatique*, pp. 73–6; *BMC Palestine*, pp. 251–8.

of the Jewish war, when it was occupied by Placidus, one of Vespasian's generals.[507]

The most accurate description of the location of the city is given by Theodosius, the sixth-century Palestinian pilgrim, and after him by Gregory of Tours, according to whom it lay beyond the Jordan, opposite Jericho, twelve Roman miles from that town, in the neighbourhood of warm springs.[508] Eusebius concurs with this, siting the city opposite Jericho on the road to Heshbon.[509]

The dates of Julias are praised by Theodosius and similarly by Pliny.[510]

33. Tiberias, *Τιβεριάς*.[511] The most important of the foundations of Herod Antipas was the new capital which he built on the western shore of Lake Gennesaret and named *Τιβεριάς* in honour of the emperor Tiberius. Situated in the neighbourhood of renowned warm springs, it lay 'in the best region of Galilee' (*τοῖς κρατίστοις . . . τῆς Γαλιλαιάς*), *Ant.* xviii 2, 3 (36); *B.J.* ii 9, 1 (168); cf. vol. I, p. 342.[512] Its construction

507. *B.J.* iv 7, 6 (438): 8, 2 (454). The city is not otherwise mentioned by Josephus. *Ant.* xx 8, 4 (159); *B.J.* ii 13, 2 (252) certainly have Julias = Bethsaida in mind; and *Ant.* xiv 1, 4 (18), should read (with the *cod. Pal.*) *Λιββά* instead of *Λιβιάς;* it is the place called in *Ant.* xiii 15, 4 (397) *Λεμβά*. Cf. Niese's ed. and A. Schalit, *Eretz Israel* 1 (1951), pp. 104–21, especially p. 117.

508. Theodosius in Geyer, *De situ terrae sanctae* 19 (*Itinera Hierosolymitana*, CSEL XXXIX, p. 145 = CCL clxxv, p. 121): 'Civitas Leviada trans Jordanen, habens de Hiericho milia XII . . . ibi aquae calidae sunt, ubi Moyses lavit, et in ipsas aquas calidas leprosi curantur'; Gregory of Tours, *De gloria martyrum* i 18: 'Sunt autem et ad Levidam [al. Leviadem] civitatem aquae calidae, . . . ubi similiter leprosi mundantur; est autem ab Hiericho duodecim millia'.

509. Eusebius, *Onomast.*, ed. Klostermann, pp. 12, 16, 48. Cf. *Vita S. Ioannis Silentiarii* 18. The evidence accords with the site of Tell er-Râme on the south side of the Wadi Hesban, almost exactly midway between Jericho and Heshbon (see especially the accurate map in *The Survey of Eastern Palestine* I (1889) and the text, pp. 238 f.). Cf. G. Hassler, *op. cit.*, in n. 449. Beth-ramtha = Livias is therefore certainly to be located here. *The Survey of Eastern Palestine*, pp. 101, 229–30; cf. N. Glueck, AASOR XXV–VIII (1951), pp. 378–9.

510. Pliny, *NH* xiii 4/44 (n. 505 above); Theodosius, *loc. cit.*: 'ibi habet dactalum Nicolaum maiorem'. Cf. vol. I, p. 298, n. 36.

511. See Guérin, *Galilée* I, pp. 250–64; Conder and Kitchener, *The Survey of Western Palestine* I, pp. 361 f., 379, 418–420; Marmardji, *Textes géographiques arabes*, pp. 127–33; Abel, *Géog. Pal.* II, pp. 483–4; Avi-Yonah, 'The Foundation of Tiberias', IEJ 1 (1950), pp. 160–9; H. W. Hoehner, *Herodes Antipas* (1972), pp. 91–100; T. Rajak, 'Justus of Tiberias', CQ 23 (1973), pp. 345–68, especially 346–51. For a useful brief account of the city, its history and remains, and of its topography and the warm springs, see A. Kindler, *The Coins of Tiberias* (1961), pp. 14–34.

512. On the warm springs, see Pliny, *NH* v 15/71: 'Tiberiade aquis calidis salubri'; Josephus, *Ant.* xviii 2, 3 (36); *B.J.* ii 21, 6 (614); iv 1, 3 (11); *Vita* 16 (85); mShab. 3:4; 22:5; mNeg. 9:1; mMaksh. 6:7; tShab. 12:13; Antoninus Martyr 7, in

appears to have taken place considerably later than that of Sepphoris and Livias, for whereas Josephus mentions the building of these two cities at the very beginning of the reign of Herod Antipas, he does not allude to the foundation of Tiberias until after Pilate's assumption of office, which began in A.D. 26, *Ant.* xviii 2, 1–3 (26 ff.). This would suggest that Tiberias came into being in around A.D. 26. Eusebius in his Chronicle definitely dates the foundation to the fourteenth year of Tiberias, but this statement is chronologically useless.[513] However, the era of the town as shown on coins of Trajan indicate that it will have been founded between A.D. 17 and 20.[514] The population of Tiberias was very mixed. To collect inhabitants for the new city, Herod Antipas was obliged to settle a veritable *colluvies hominum* there, partly by compulsion (see vol. I, p. 342). Their attitude during the great revolt showed, however, that they were mainly Jewish. On the other hand, the constitution was entirely Hellenistic:[515] the city was ruled by a council (βουλή) of six hundred members,[516] at the head of which stood

---

Geyer, *Itinera Hieros.*, p. 163=CCL clxxv, p. 132: 'in civitatem Tiberiada, in qua sunt thermae . . . salsae'. Modern Tiberias lies some 2 km. north of the springs and there is no reason to assume that the ancient city stood elsewhere. For a clear account of the topography of the area, see J. Finegan, *The Archaeology of the New Testament* (1969), pp. 44–5. The site of the springs was known as Ἀμμαθοῦς (such should certainly be the reading of *Ant.* xviii, 2, 3 (36), and probably also *B.J.* iv, 1, 3 (11); cf. Hebrew חמתה, yErub. 22d; tErub. 7:2. For excavations at the springs of Hamath, see Vogel, 'Bibliography', s.v. They include a synagogue which in its earlier form may have been in use as such in the first century A.D.

513. Eusebius, *Chron.*, ed. Schoene II, pp. 146–9, reports the building of new cities by the sons of Herod in the following order: Philip founded Caesarea and Julias; Herod Antipas, Tiberias and Livias. All the foundations are dated to the time of Tiberius; Sepphoris is passed over in complete silence. It is beyond doubt that Eusebius' statements are derived entirely from Josephus, *B.J.* ii 9, 1 (167–8), since the foundations are listed there in exactly the same sequence, i.e., after the accession of Tiberius, and with the same neglect of Sepphoris. The data supplied by Eusebius are consequently not only without independent value, but are derived from the relatively inexact report of Josephus in *B.J.*, and ignore his more accurate account in *Ant.* xviii 2, 1–3 (26–8).

514. For the coins, see de Saulcy, *Numismatique*, pp. 333–8, pl. XVII, n. 9–14; *BMC Palestine*, pp. xiii–xv, 5–10; Avi-Yonah, IEJ 1 (1950), pp. 178–9; A. Spijkerman, 'Some Rare Jewish Coins', SBFLA 15 (1962–3), pp. 303–4. A more precise dating to A.D. 18, as suggested by Avi-Yonah, is speculative. Note also A. Kindler, 'The Coins of Tiberias in the Roman Period' in *The Book of Tiberias* (Heb.), ed. O. Avissar (1973), pp. 50–9.

515. Compare Kuhn, *Die städtische und bürgerl. Verfassung* II, pp. 353 f.; *Über die Entstehung der Städte der Alten*, pp. 427 f.; A. H. M. Jones, *The Greek City* (1940).

516. *B.J.* ii 21, 9 (641); cf. generally, *Vita* 12 (64), 34 (169), 55 (284), 58 (300), 61 (313), 68 (381).

an ἄρχων[517] and a committee of the δέκα πρῶτοι[518] and in addition *hyparchoi*[519] and an *agoranomos*.[520] It was also raised to the status of capital of Galilee, Sepphoris itself being subordinated to it (see above, pp. 174–5). Coins of Tiberias minted in the time of Herod Antipas bear the simple inscription, Τιβεριάς.[521]

Following the deposition of Herod Antipas, Tiberias passed into the possession of Agrippa I. A coin of this period also has the inscription Τιβεριέων.[522] When Agrippa died, the city came under the authority of the Roman procurators of Judaea. It must at the same time have received new political privileges, or at least experienced a favour of some kind, from the emperor Claudius, for on coins of Trajan and Hadrian the inhabitants describe themselves as Τιβεριεῖς Κλαυδιεῖς.[523] The city maintained its position as capital of Galilee uninterruptedly until the reign of Nero, Josephus, *Vita* 9 (37 f.). It was then (probably

517. *Vita* 27 (134), 53 (271), 54 (278), 57 (294); *B.J.* ii 21, 3 (599). A Jesus son of Sapphias is mentioned here as *archon* of Tiberias during the time of the revolt. One of his functions was to preside at meetings of the council, *Vita* 58 (300).

518. *Vita* 13 (69), 57 (296); *B.J.* ii 21, 9 (639) = *Vita* 33 (168). See especially *Vita* 13 (69): τοὺς τῆς βουλῆς πρώτους δέκα; *Vita* 57 (296): τοὺς δέκα πρώτους Τιβεριέων. On these δέκα πρῶτοι, so frequently found in Hellenistic communities, see E. Kuhn, *op. cit.* I, p. 55; J. Marquardt, *Röm. Staatsverwaltung* (1881) I, pp. 213 f.; W. Liebenam, *Städteverwaltung im römischen Kaiserreiche* (1900), 552 f.; RE IV, cols. 2417 ff.; O. Seeck, 'Decemprimat und Dekaprotie', Klio (1901), pp. 147–87; E. G. Turner, 'Δεκάπρωτοι', JEA 22 (1936), pp. 7–19; A. H. M. Jones, *The Greek City* (1940), p. 139. They were not the ten oldest or most respected members of the council, but a changing committee of such people, with definite official functions, as is shown by the frequent formula δεκαπρωτεύσας. Their chief role was the collection of taxes, for the payment of which they were answerable with their private property, see *Digest.* l 4, 1, 1: 'Munerum civilium quaedam sunt patrimonii, alia personarum. Patrimonii sunt munera rei vehicularis, item navicularis, decemprimatus: ab istis enim periculo ipsorum exactiones sollemnium celebrantur'; *Digest.* l 4, 18, 26: 'Mixta munera decaprotiae et icosaprotiae, ut Herennius Modestinus . . . decrevit: nam decaproti et icosaproti tributa exigentes et corporale ministerium gerunt et pro omnibus defunctorum (?) fiscalia detrimenta resarciunt'. The connexion between the *dekaprotoi* and the collection of tribute is now conclusively proved by an inscription from Iotape in Cilicia—[δεκαπρω]-τεύσαντος πλειστά[κις] ἐπὶ τῆ[ς εἰσαγω]γῆς τῶν κυριακῶν φόρων, cf. AE 1965, 318. It is worth noting that Josephus during his administration of Galilee delivered certain valuables of King Agrippa to the *decem primi* at Tiberias, and made them responsible for their safe-keeping, *Vita* 13 (69), 57 (296).

519. *B.J.* ii 21, 6 (615): τοῖς κατὰ τὴν πόλιν ὑπάρχοις.

520. *Ant.* xviii 6, 2 (149). On the office of ἀγορανόμος, see Stephanus Byz., s.v.; RE I, cols. 884 f.; N. Liebenam, *Städteverwaltung im röm. Kaiserreiche*, pp. 362 ff., 539–42. Jones, *The Greek City*, pp. 188, 215–17, 230, 240, 255. Rabbinic sources are also familiar with the office of אגרונימוס (Krauss, *Lehnwörter* II, pp. 11 f.).

521. See Y. Meshorer, *Jewish Coins of the Second Temple Period* (1967), pp. 133–4.

522. F. W. Madden, *History*, p. 110; *Coins of the Jews*, p. 138.

523. Cf. n. 514.

in A.D. 61) granted to Agrippa II and thereby separated from Galilee, *Ant.* xx 8, 4 (159); *B.J.* ii 13, 2 (252); *Vita* 9 (38).[524] It therefore formed part of the territory of Agrippa II when the war broke out in 66. The attitude of its inhabitants towards the conflict was very varied: some wished to remain on the side of Agrippa and the Romans, whereas others—the mass of those without property—supported the revolution. Others still, took up a position of caution, *Vita* 9 (32 ff.); cf. also *Vita* 12 (66), where the revolutionary party is called ἡ τῶν ναυτῶν καὶ τῶν ἀπόρων στάσις. The revolutionary party definitely predominated and the rest had consequently to comply with them. One of their leaders was Jesus, son of Sapphias, the then *archon* of the city.[525] Yet even after the victory of the revolutionary element, one section of the population maintained contact with Agrippa and repeatedly, though vainly, begged for his support.[526] When Vespasian had subjugated the greater part of Galilee and pressed forward as far as Tiberias, the city dared offer no resistance; it voluntarily opened its gates, and begged for mercy, which was granted out of regard for Agrippa. Vespasian allowed his soldiers to enter Tiberias but spared the city and restored it to Agrippa.[527] It is uncertain whether Agrippa held it until his death. Tiberias then, either in A.D. 85/6 or 92/3 (the probable time of his death), or possibly 100, when later evidence suggests that he died, came once more under direct Roman rule,[528] as is attested by extant coins, mostly from the reigns of Trajan and Hadrian. Eusebius describes it as a πόλις ἐπίσημος.[529] In the third and fourth centuries A.D., it was a centre of rabbinic scholarship and is therefore frequently mentioned in Talmudic literature.[530] But from the second century it also had pagan temples, an Ἀδριάνειον, for example, that was a ναὸς μέγιστος.[531] As for its commercial importance in the second century, this is attested by two inscriptions found in Rome, according to which the merchants of Tiberias had their own *statio* (guild and guild-hall) in the imperial capital.[532]

524. For the date, see vol. I, p. 473.

525. Josephus, *Vita* 12 (66), 27 (134), 53 (271), 54 (278), 57 (294); *B.J.* ii 21, 3 (599); iii 9, 7–8 (455–61). For the conflicts of attitude in Tiberias at this time, see especially T. Rajak, 'Justus of Tiberias', CQ 23 (1973), pp. 345–68.

526. *B.J.* ii 21, 8–10 (630–40); *Vita* 32–4 (155–73), 68–70 (381–93).

527. *B.J.* iii 9, 7–8 (445–61).

528. For these questions see vol. I, pp. 480–2.

529. *Onomast.*, ed. Klostermann, p. 16.

530. A. Neubauer, *Géographie du Talmud*, pp. 208–14; W. Bacher, *Die Agada der paläst. Amoräer* III (1899), index, s.v. 'Tiberias'; S. Krauss, *Lehnwörter* II, pp. 255 f., S. Klein, *Sefer ha-Yishuv* (1939), s.v. JE XII, pp. 142–3; Enc. Jud. 15, cols. 1130–3.

531. Epiphanius, *Haer.* 30, 12.

532. IGR I 132=1384=Moretti, IGUR I 82: *Στατίων [Τιβε]ριέων τῶν καὶ Κλ[α]υδιοπολιτῶν Συρίᾳ Παλε[σ]τείνῃ*. The restoration [Τιβε]ριέων is certainly correct. Cf. L. Robert, BE 1939, no. 13. The inscription belongs at the earliest to the middle

In this period and subsequently, it was also a major centre of Jewish life.[533]

Of some of these places, such as Antipatris, Phasaelis, Julias and Livias, it cannot be determined with certainty whether they really belonged to the category of independent cities possessing the formal constitution of a Greek *polis*.[534] Any town may be accepted as a *polis* which issued its own coinage.[535] But actual minting was in many cases surprisingly discontinuous, and our knowledge of it is also subject to the vagueness of the evidence. A more satisfactory criterion would be the possession of a defined territory (χώρα); but here too the evidence is incomplete and of very varying dates.[536] It may well be that not all of these towns were true *poleis*, but that some were incorporated in a subordinate role in the general organization of the area. It has however been necessary to include them here because some, at least, of the cities founded by Herod and his sons did belong to the above category. On the other hand, it is possible that the number of self-governing *poleis* is not exhausted by the towns enumerated.[537] This list is consequently not to be regarded as definitive.[538]

For the Roman imperial period, a further number of formally constituted *poleis* should be given, but they have been deliberately omitted because they did not acquire that status until later (at the

---

of the second century A.D., and before A.D. 194. IGR I 111=IGUR I 83: Ἰαμῆνος Ἰωήνου υἱὸς Τιβεριεὺς τῇ στατίωνι. The 'stationes municipiorum' near the Forum in Rome are mentioned also by Pliny, *NH* xvi 86/236; Suetonius, *Nero* 37. See especially L. Robert, *Hellenica* VII (1949), pp. 202–5; L. Moretti, 'Sulle stationes municipiorum del Foro Romano', Athenaeum 36 (1958), pp. 106–16. Note also a Jewish Τιβεριεύς from Rome, CIJ I 502, another from Carthage, Robert, BE 1955=SEG XVIII, 775, and another from Tenaros, CIJ I 1256.

533. See especially M. Avi-Yonah, *The Jews of Palestine* (1976), Index, s.v.

534. On the concept of the foundation of a Greek *polis*, see V. Tscherikower, *Die hellenistischen Städtegründungen von Alexander bis auf die Römerzeit*, Philologus Supp. XIX 1 (1927), pp. 112–37; cf. G. M. Cohen, *The Seleucid Colonies: Studies in Founding, Administration and Organization*, Historia Einzelschrift 30 (1978), esp. pp. 83–6.

535. For the importance of this criterion see A. H. M. Jones, 'The Hellenisation of Palestine', JRS 21 (1931), pp. 78–85.

536. For the Hellenistic period see U. Kahrstedt, *Syrische Territorien im hellenistischen Zeit*, AAG XIX.2 (1926); for the Roman, Avi-Yonah, *Holy Land*, pp. 127–80.

537. Even if we could finally define the number of *poleis* at any one time, and the extent of their territories, we still have no clear conception of their administrative relationship to the toparchies listed by Josephus and Pliny the Elder. See below, pp. 190–4.

538. For instance, it may be that at least in the earlier period Philoteria on Lake Gennesaret, mentioned by Polybius v 70, 3–4, constituted a *polis*. It is identified with the site Beth Yerah, where there are substantial remains from the Graeco-Roman period, see EAEHL, s.v. 'Beth Yerah'.

earliest, from A.D. 70). Such was the case, in particular, with Flavia Neapolis (founded in about A.D. 72/3), Capitolias in the Decapolis (in about A.D. 97–98), Diospolis=Lydda, Eleutheropolis (both under Septimius Severus), Nicopolis=Emmaus (under Elagabalus), and communities belonging to the province of Arabia, such as Bostra, Adraa and others. Aelia Capitolina (=Jerusalem) was also a full *polis* in the period after Hadrian. Indeed, even in the period of the Second Temple, while it would not be correct to characterize it as a *polis* in the strict sense, it not only exhibited many of the architectural features of a Greek city,[539] but possessed many institutions closely resembling those of a *polis*.[540] On Neapolis and Capitolias, see vol. I, p. 520–1.

No more material exists concerning the position of the Jews in these predominantly Gentile communities than has already been presented in connection with the places in question. The history of Caesarea (no. 9) is especially instructive. Until the reign of Nero, Gentiles and Jews possessed equal civic rights there (*ἰσοπολιτεία*), *Ant.* xx 8, 7 (173) and 9 (183), and were thus equally qualified to vote and to stand for election to the city council. As this necessarily led to all sorts of trouble, each party attempted to change the situation. Each wished to obtain control. There were thus three possibilities: (1) equality; (2) exclusion of Jews from civic privileges; (3) exclusion of Gentiles from civic privileges. All of these, without doubt, actually occurred. However, in the ancient Philistine and Phoenician cities, the Jews hardly possessed civic rights. They lived there in their thousands, but as inhabitants they were merely tolerated. Indeed, proof of the tension that existed between them and the Gentile townspeople is best seen in the bloody persecution of the Jews in many of these cities that followed the outbreak of the revolution, as in Ascalon, Ptolemais and Tyre. In other places, Gentiles and Jews may have enjoyed equal rights, as for instance in Jamnia and Joppa, where Jews had outnumbered Gentiles since the Maccabaean period. Whether Gentiles were excluded from civic rights in any of the towns named hitherto is very doubtful; it is not probable even in Sepphoris and Tiberias. In any case, the third possibility is represented by Jerusalem, and in general by the towns of the strictly Jewish territory. Further particulars cannot be given because of the lack of material; it must suffice to have determined the general state of affairs. On the organization of the Jewish communities in these cities, see § 27.II and § 31.II.

539. See vol. I, pp. 304–5, and now the popular account of extensive excavations in the Old City since 1967, *Jerusalem Revealed: Archaeology in the Holy City, 1968–74* (1975); see also B. Mazar, *The Mountain of the Lord* (1975). No detailed report of these excavations has yet been published.

540. See especially, V. A. Tcherikover, 'Was Jerusalem a "Polis"?', IEJ 14 (1964), pp. 61–78.

II. The Jewish Region*

Bibliography

Momigliano, A., *Ricerche sull' organizzazione della Giudea sotto il dominio romano. Ann. della r. Scuola Normale Superiore di Pisa*, ser. i, vol. III (1934—XII), pp. 54–80, repr. Amsterdam (1967).

Schalit, A., *Ha-mishṭar ha-Roma'i be-'Ereẓ Yisra'el* (1937).

Jones, A. H. M., *Cities of the Eastern Roman Provinces* (1937; [2]1971), Ch. X.

Abel, F.-M., *Géographie de la Palestine* II (1938), pp. 141–60.

Vaux, R. de, *Ancient Israel: Its Life and Institutions* (1961), pp. 137–8, 152–5.

Sherwin-White, A.N., *Roman Society and Roman Law in the New Testament* (1965), pp. 127–43.

Avi-Yonah, M., *The Holy Land: From the Persian to the Arab Conquests* (1966), pp. 52–107.

Schalit, A., *König Herodes* (1969), pp. 183–223.

Jeremias, J., *Jerusalem in the Time of Jesus* (1969).

Safrai, S., and Stern, M. (eds.), *The Jewish People in the First Century* I (1974), ch. 6, 'The Province of Judaea' (M. Stern); ch. 7, 'Jewish Self-Government' (S. Safrai).

See also the bibliography, vol. I, pp. 243–4.

Jewish territory proper—leaving aside Samaria—consisted of the three districts of Judaea, Galilee and Peraea, with the exception of those parts of the country that belonged to the Greek cities (see § 22.I). The Gentile inhabitants of this region, if there were any, formed no more than a minority, and it may be assumed that the city councils established in these parts were composed exclusively of Jews. For without doubt, the Jewish towns also had their representative communal bodies to whom the management of local affairs was entrusted. From time immemorial in Israel, 'the elders of the city', **זקני העיר**, are spoken of as the local authorities (see Deut. 19:12, 21:2 ff., 22:15 ff., 25:7 ff.; Jos. 20:4; Jg. 8:14; Ruth 4:2 ff.; 1 Sam. 11:3, 16:4, 30:26 ff.; 1 Kgs 21:8, 11). Their number is almost never given but must have been fairly large. In Succoth, for instance, there were seventy-seven elders (Jg. 8:14). They represented the community in every respect and consequently exercised judicial functions as well (see, e.g., Deut. 22:15 ff.). But in addition to these, there is also specific mention of 'judges' (**שפטים**) and 'officers' (**שטרים**): both classes are named in Deut. 16:18. 2 Chron. 19:5 ff. relates how Jehoshaphat appointed 'judges in the land, throughout all the cities of Judah, city by city'.

* This section has been revised by Dr. P. S. Alexander (University of Manchester).

Since the judges are explicitly referred to together with the elders (Deut. 21:2; Ezr. 10:14), the two groups are clearly distinct from each other, but probably only to the extent that the judges were elders specially charged with the administration of justice. Similarly, the officers must also have been elders, and were doubtless the real executives of the community. This local organization persisted without substantial change into the post-exilic era. Thus in the Persian and Greek periods also, the 'elders' of a city are frequently spoken of (Ezr. 10:14; Judith 6:16, 21; 7:23; 8:10; 10:6; 13:12). For the Roman period, there is evidence of the existence of local councils, for example in the statement of Josephus that Albinus, out of greed, set free for a monetary reward certain persons who had been imprisoned for robbery by their local council (*βουλή*).[1] This shows that it was the *βουλή* itself which exercised the functions of both police and judiciary. It is nevertheless possible, particularly in the larger towns, that other special courts existed in addition to the *βουλή*. Local Sanhedrins must also be alluded to in Mk. 13:9=Mt. 10:17, where it is said that the faithful will be handed over *εἰς συνέδρια*. To the same category belongs the *συνέδριον* mentioned in Mt. 5:22, while the *πρεσβύτεροι τῶν Ἰουδαίων* who met Jesus at Capernaum (Lk. 7:3) were presumably also members of the local council.[2] However, it is the Mishnah above all which throughout presupposes the existence of local courts in the Jewish districts.[3] Josephus alludes to 'village clerks' in the time of Herod.[4]

1. *B.J.* ii 14, 1 (273): *καὶ τοὺς ἐπὶ λῃστείᾳ δεδεμένους ὑπὸ τῆς παρ' ἑκάστοις βουλῆς ἢ τῶν προτέρων ἐπιτρόπων ἀπελύτρου τοῖς συγγενέσι.*

2. Cf. the *πρεσβύτεροι τῆς κώμης* in Egypt; F. Preisigke, *Wörterbuch* III, p. 147; M. Strack, 'Die Müllerinnung in Alexandrien', ZNW 4 (1903), pp. 213–34; H. Hauschildt, '*Πρεσβύτεροι* in Aegypten im I-III Jahrh. n. Chr.', *ibid.*, pp. 235–42. See L. Mitteis and U. Wilcken, *Grundzüge u. Chrestomathie der Papyruskunde* I. 1 (1912), pp. 43, 84, 217; A. Tomsin, 'Etude sur les *presbuteroi* des villages de la *chôra* égyptienne', Bull. Cl. lett. sc. mor. Acad. roy. Belg. 38 (1952), pp. 95–130; 467–532. For an excellent collection and discussion of comparative evidence from inscriptions of the Syrian region relating to the organizational structure of villages, see G. M. Harper, 'Village Administration in the Province of Syria', YCS 1 (1928), pp. 103–68.

3. Note, for example, the *prosbul* (פרוסבול, פרוזבול) formula: 'I affirm to you, such-a-one and such-a-one, *the judges in such-a-place*, that, touching any debt due to me, I will collect it whensoever I will' (mSheb. 10:4). On the meaning of the word *prosbul* see below, p. 366. According to mSheb. 10:3, the *prosbul* was instituted by Hillel; J. Neusner, *The Rabbinic Traditions about the Pharisees before 70* I (1971), pp. 217–20 has analysed this tradition. Further references to local courts are found in mSot. 1:3; mSanh. 11:4. Among the enactments of Ezra, bB.K. 82a lists the establishment of local courts, which were to meet on Mondays and Thursdays, i.e. on the two market-days.

4. *Ant.* xvi 7, 3 (203): *κωμογραμματεῖς*; *B.J.* i 24, 3 (479): *κωμῶν γραμματεῖς*. For the *κωμογραμματεύς* in Egypt, see Preisigke, *Wörterbuch* III, p. 130; *idem*, RE XI, cols. 1281–84 s.v. 'Komogrammateus'. See also Harper, *op. cit.*, in n. 2. Jones, CERP[2],

As far as the size of the local courts is concerned, it has been estimated from the Mishnah that the smallest was composed of only three persons. But this is based on a misunderstanding. For the relevant passages merely enumerate issues and undertakings for decisions on which, and for the performance of which, no more than three persons were needed. Thus three were considered sufficient for cases involved with money, or with robbery and assault, or with the award of damages;[5] for condemning a wrongdoer to be scouraged; for determining the date of the new moon and to intercalate the year;[6] similarly, for the laying on of hands (on a sin-offering sacrificed in the name of the community), or for the breaking of the heifer's neck (because of someone found murdered). Other cases within the competence of three were those connected with *ḥaliẓah,* and with the refusal of a girl to marry the man chosen for her by her mother or brothers; with the redemption of fruit-trees during the first four years of their growth; with the redemption of the second tithe the value of which had not previously been established; and also with the re-purchase of consecrated objects.[7] But nowhere is there mention of local courts with only three magistrates on the bench. The correct interpretation of the Mishnah is made clear by the passage that reads: 'Law-suits concerned with money (דיני

---

chap. X, argues that, broadly speaking, Palestine was administered by Herod and the Roman procurators according to the Ptolemaic system (elements of which could have survived from the time when the Ptolemies controlled the area; for Ptolemaic Palestine see Rostovtzeff SEHHW I pp. 346 ff., and V. Tscherikower, 'Palestine under the Ptolemies', Mizraim 4–5 (1937), pp. 9 ff.). The basic unit was the *κώμη,* which was administered by a *κωμογραμματεύς* appointed by the central government. The *κώμαι* were grouped into *τοπαρχίαι,* each of which was controlled by a *στρατηγός* and run from one of the villages, which was promoted to 'district capital' (*μητρόπολις*). Avi-Yonah further suggests that, at least in the time of Herod the Great, the toparchies were in turn grouped into five *μερίδες,* each under a *μεριδάρχης, Ant.* xv 7, 3 (217); cf. *Ant.* xii 5, 5 (261–4), 1 Mac. 10:65); these were Judaea proper, Idumaea, Samaria, Galilee and Peraea (*Holy Land*, p. 98; *Atlas of Israel* (1970) IX/7). The *μερίς* as an administrative region embracing several toparchies is attested in the Arsinoite nome in Egypt; see E. Kiessling, RE XV, col. 1028. The parallels with Egypt are valuable since the documentation for that area (in contrast to Palestine) is so rich. For the administration of Egypt see F. Preisigke, *Städtisches Beamtenwesen im römischen Aegypten* (1903); P. Jouguet, *La vie municipale dans l'Égypte romaine* (1911); L. Mitteis and U. Wilcken, *Grundzüge u. Chrestomathie der Papyruskunde* I/1 (1912), pp. 8–11, 34–43; E. R. Bevan, *A History of Egypt under the Ptolemaic Dynasty* (1927), pp. 132 ff.; M. Rostovtzeff, CAH VII, pp. 116–26; W. Schubart, *Verfassung und Verwaltung des Ptolemäerreiches* (1937); J. David Thomas, *The Epistrategos in Ptolemaic and Roman Egypt* I: *The Ptolemaic Epistrategos* (1974). See now R. S. Bagnall, *The Administration of the Ptolemaic Possessions outside Egypt* (1976).

5. mSanh. 1:1.
6. mSanh. 1:2; cf. mR.H. 2:9; 3:1.
7. mSanh. 1:3; cf. mYeb. 13:1–2.

ממונות) are decided by three judges. Each party chooses a judge, and then both parties together choose a third. So R. Meir rules. But the Sages say: the two judges choose the third'.[8] The truth of the matter is that the smallest local courts consisted of seven magistrates. For it is safe to assume that Josephus's statement, that Moses decreed that 'seven men should bear rule in every city . . . and that two men of the tribe of Levi should be assigned to each court as subordinate officers (*ὑπηρέται*)', is a description of the situation of Josephus's own time, since this direction does not appear in the Pentateuch.[9] This is corroborated by the fact that Josephus himself, when he wished to introduce a model constitution for the Jews in Galilee, set up a tribunal of seven magistrates in every town.[10] One might of course argue that such a statement suggests that an arrangement of this nature did not exist in Galilee prior to the revolution. But Josephus's boast that he was the first to create this ideal Jewish constitution must be taken with a grain of salt: what he did was to take steps to enforce it. The Talmud, too, mentions 'the seven foremost men of the town' (שבעה טובי העיר) as the authority in charge, in particular, of the community's financial affairs.[11] Josephus's assertion that two Levites were to be co-opted to the local courts as *ὑπηρέται* (see above, n. 9) is not without its analogies in the Old Testament.[12] According

8. mSanh. 3:1.

9. *Ant.* iv 8, 14 (214): *ἀρχέτωσαν δὲ καθ' ἑκάστην πόλιν ἄνδρες ἑπτά . . . ἑκάστῃ δὲ ἀρχῇ δύο ἄνδρες ὑπηρέται διδόσθωσαν ἐκ τῆς Λευιτῶν φυλῆς.* Again, in recounting the law regarding deposits (Exod. 22:6 ff.), Josephus presupposes the existence of courts with seven judges, *Ant.* iv 8, 38 (287): *εἰ δὲ μηδὲν ἐπίβουλον δρῶν ὁ πιστευθεὶς ἀπολέσειεν, ἀφικόμενος ἐπὶ τοὺς ἑπτὰ κριτὰς ὀμνύτω τὸν θεόν κ τ λ.*

10. *B.J.* ii 20, 5 (571): *ἑπτὰ δὲ ἐν ἑκάστῃ πόλει δικαστὰς* [*κατέστησεν*]. These courts of seven judges dealt only with minor cases and not with *τὰ μείζω πράγματα καὶ τὰς φονικὰς δίκας*, the adjudication of which was reserved for the council of seventy which Josephus established.

According to CD 10:4–6, the court of the 'Damascus' community consisted of six Israelite judges and four further magistrates chosen from the sons of Levi and Aaron. A similar tribunal of ten appears in mMeg. 4:3; mSanh. 1:3. For a court of twelve judges (two priests and ten laymen), see 4Q159 2–4, ll. 3–4 (DJD V, p. 8). For an Essene court of one hundred see *B.J.* ii 8, 9 (145).

11. bMeg. 26a: 'Raba said: This rule (of the Mishnah regarding the sale of synagogues and their furniture) was meant to apply only to those cases in which the seven leading men of the town (שבעה טובי העיר) have not disposed of them by public sale'; cf. bMeg. 26b: 'Rabina was in possession of the ground of a dismantled synagogue. He applied to R. Ashi to know whether he could plant seeds there. R. Ashi replied: Go and buy it from the seven leading men of the town in the assembly of the townspeople (משבעה טובי העיר במעמד אנשי העיר) and then you may sow it'. See further, J. Neusner, *A History of the Jews in Babylonia* V (1970), pp. 263–4.

12. Deut. 21:5; 1 Chron. 23:4; 26:29; cf. Deut. 16:18. See R. de Vaux, *Ancient Israel: Its Life and Institutions* (1961), p. 154.

to the Mishnah, certain special cases demanded the inclusion of the priests on the panel of judges.[13]

In the more populous towns, the local tribunals seem to have been composed of twenty-three members. The Mishnah observes that a lower Sanhedrin (סנהדרין קטנה) should consist of twenty-three and that such a court may be established in every town with a population of at least a hundred and twenty, or according to R. Nehemiah two hundred and thirty, adult males so that each judge may correspond to a chief of ten (Exod. 18:21 f.).[14] Here too, there is no guarantee that reality corresponded in any way to these regulations but since there is no obvious biblical basis for a court of twenty-three (note the extreme difficulty with which the rabbis read it into Scripture—mSanh. 1:6), it is reasonable to suppose that it represents a real institution. According to the Mishnah, courts of twenty-three were also competent to adjudicate major cases of criminal law (דיני נפשות).[15] Mt. 5:21–22 lends some support to this statement, for it may be read as implying that the trial and condemnation of murderers did not fall exclusively within the jurisdiction of the Great Sanhedrin.

As in the Greek cities, so in the Jewish areas the villages were subordinated to the towns and the smaller towns to the larger. The distinction between a town (עיר) and a village (חצר or sometimes כפר) is presupposed throughout the Old Testament, the former being as a rule a walled settlement, and the latter an open one (see especially Lev. 25:29–31); though the towns themselves are also distinguished as walled and unwalled (Deut. 3:5; Esth. 9:19). Josephus and the New Testament also always differentiate between a *πόλις* and a *κώμη*. One passage of the New Testament mentions *κωμοπόλεις* in Palestine (Mk. 1:38), i.e. towns which, in respect of their constitution, had only the status of a village.[16] The Mishnah consistently distinguishes between

13. See mSanh. 1:3: 'Property pledged as security for vows of valuation, if movable property, must be sold before three judges (R. Judah says: One of them must be a priest); and if pieces of land, before nine and a priest; and similarly for the valuation vow of men'; cf. mKet. 1:5; tSanh. 4:7; Sifre Deut. §153. On the judicial functions of the priests in the biblical period see R. de Vaux, *Ancient Israel*, p. 154.

14. mSanh. 1:6; see S. Krauss, *Sanhedrin-Makkot* (1933), pp. 92–3.

15. mSanh. 1:4. On Jewish courts see, *Enziklopedia Talmudith* III, p. 150, s.v. בית דין; H. H. Cohn, Enc. Jud. 4, col. 719, s.v., 'Beth Din and Judges'; further J. Juster, *Les Juifs dans l'empire romain* II (1914), pp. 94–106, 127–52; S. Assaf, *Battei ha-din ve-sidreihem 'aḥarei ḥaṭimat ha-talmud* (1924). M. Avi-Yonah, *Holy Land*, p. 99 suggests that 'a court of three sat in each village, a court of seven in a toparchy, of twenty-three in a *meris*, and the great Sanhedrin of seventy-one was at the head of the whole system'. This is pure conjecture.

16. See A. N. Sherwin-White, *Roman Society and Roman Law in the New Testament* (1965), pp. 127 ff. On the terms *κώμη*, *πόλις* and *κωμόπολις* see J.

three concepts: a large city (כרך), a town (עיר) and a village (כפר). The difference between the two first seems to have been a matter of size, for even an ordinary town (עיר) could have been walled, and usually was so.[17]

The subordination of villages to towns is frequently indicated already in the Old Testament. In the town-lists of the Book of Joshua, particularly in chapters 15 and 19, allusion is often made to 'the cities and their villages' (הערים וחצריהן). Elsewhere, there is mention of a 'city and its daughters' (בנותיה) (Num. 21:25, 32; 32:42; Jos. 15:45–7; 17:11; Jg. 11:26; Neh. 11:25 ff.; 1 Chron. 2:23; 5:16; 7:28 f.; 8:12; 18:1; 2 Chron. 13:19; 28:18; Ezek. 16:46 ff.; 26:6; 30:18). Correspondingly, the chief town of a district is designated 'mother' (2 Sam. 20;19). It is abundantly clear, in any case, that the villages were everywhere dependent on the towns. Very probably, the same relationship obtained between the smaller and larger towns, for the term 'daughter' is frequently applied to the former as well as to villages; in several instances this is beyond doubt (Num. 21:25; Jos. 15:45–47; 1 Chron. 2:23). These facts of the situation as it is known to have been in Old Testament times may be assumed for later ages as well (see especially 1 Mac. 5:8: τὴν Ἰαζὴρ καὶ τὰς θυγατέρας αὐτῆς; *ibid*. 5:65: τὴν Χεβρὼν καὶ τὰς θυγατέρας αὐτῆς). Peculiar to Transjordan, and in particular to the region of Trachonitis, is the occurrence of 'capital villages' (μητροκωμίαι), i.e. villages with the status of a 'capital town' (μητρόπολις).[18] Thus Phaena, the modern Mismiye, is called μητροκωμία τοῦ Τράχωνος.[19]

Marquardt, *Römische Staatsverwaltung* I ([2]1881), pp. 3–20; F. F. Abbott and A. C. Johnson, *Municipal Administration in the Roman Empire* (1926), pp. 21 ff.; G. McL. Harper, 'Village administration in the Roman Province of Syria', Yale Classical Studies 1 (1928), pp. 143 ff.; A. H. M. Jones, *The Greek City* (1940), *passim*. The term κωμόπολις is found in Strabo xii 2, 6 (p. 537); xii 3, 31 (p. 557); xii 6, 1 (p. 568), and in Byzantine writers; see the Lexica, including *Thes. Ling. Lat.* s.v. 'comopolis'.

17. mMeg. 1:1; 2:3; mKet. 13:10; mKid. 2:3; mB.M. 4:6; 8:6; mArakh. 6:5. For a 'walled *town*' cf. the expression עיר חומה in mArakh. 9:3 ff.; mKel. 1:7. See further Str.-B. II, p. 3 (to Mk. 1:38) = also the '*Arukh* (ed. Kohut), and the Lexica of Levy and Jastrow s.v. For a discussion of the terms see J. Rabbinowitz, *Mishnah Megillah* (1931), pp. 38; 40; L. Tetzner, *Die Mischna: Megilla* (1968), pp. 17–21.

18. See E. Kuhn, *Die städtische und bürgerliche Verfassung des römischen Reichs* II (1865), pp. 380 ff.; J. Marquardt, *Römische Staatsverwaltung* I ([2]1881), p. 427, n. 1; Jones, CERP[2], pp. 282 ff. See also the Lexica, including *Thes. Ling. Lat.* s.v. 'metrocomia'.

19. CIG 4551 = Les Bas-Waddington, *Inscr.* III, no. 2524 = OGIS 609 = IGR III 1119. The inscription dates from the time of Commodus, or of Severus Alexander, probably the latter (see OGIS, *loc. cit.*). On Phaena, see G. Hölscher, RE XIX, col. 1562, s.v. Brunnow and von Domaszewski, *Die Provincia Arabia* III, p. 277; R. Dussaud, *Topographie historique de la Syrie*, p. 376 and map II A/1. Inscriptions: Le Bas-Waddington, *Ins.* 2524–37.

Other *μητροκωμίαι* in this region were Borecath, present-day Breike, to the south of Trachonitis, towards the Hauran;[20] Acraba, west of Trachonitis (=modern ʻAḳraba, appox. 11 miles east of El Quneitra);[21] Bacathos, called by Epiphanius *μητροκωμίαν τῆς Ἀραβίας τῆς Φιλαδελφίας*; and Sûr in Trachonitis, described in an inscription of A.D. 326 as a *μητροκωμία*.[22] It should be borne in mind, however, that these documents date only from between the second and the fourth centuries A.D. Moreover, the population of the area, though mixed, was predominantly Gentile.

Specific data are available concerning the subordination of certain rural areas to some of the larger towns. Thus in the reorganization by Gabinius, the country was divided into five regions, each of which was placed under the control of a *συνέδριον* or *σύνοδος*. The *συνέδρια* were located (1) at Jerusalem (for central Judaea); (2) at Jericho (for the Jordan valley); (3) at Amathus (for Peraea); (4) at Sepphoris (for Galilee); and (5) at (?)Adora (for Idumaea).[23] This arrangement did not last for long; but in later times also, under the Herodian tetrarchs that is to say, Galilee was again governed from a single capital city, either Sepphoris or Tiberias (see § 23. I, nos. 31, 33). This is an interesting case of a Jewish province being subordinated to a city not itself purely Jewish.[24]

Also to be considered is the evidence for the division of the country into toparchies. According to Josephus, Judaea was divided into the following eleven *κληρουχίαι* or *τοπαρχίαι*: (1) Jerusalem; (2) Gophna; (3) Acrabatta; (4) Thamna; (5) Lydda; (6) Ammaus; (7) Pelle; (8)

20. Le Bas-Waddington, III 2396. See Benzinger, RE III, col. 730 s.v. ʻBorechath'; Dussaud, *Topographie*, p. 372.

21. Dussaud, *Nouvelles archives des missions scientifiques* 10 (1902), p. 700= OGIS 769=IGR III, 1112=Y. Aharoni, ʻThree New Boundary Stones from the Western Golan', ʻAtiqot 1 (1955), p. 112 no. 9: Diocletian and his co-regents *λίθον διορίζοντα ὅρους μητροκωμίας Ἀκράβης καὶ Ἄσιχων στηριχθῆναι ἐκέλευσαν, φροντίδι Λουκίου καὶ Ἀ[κακίου κ]ηνσιτόρ[ων]* (Aharoni's reconstruction). For a similar inscription relating to the regulation of the borders in the time of Diocletian, see OGIS 612=IGR III, 1252. For a third, badly mutilated, from Jermana SE of Damascus (see Dussaud, *Topographie* map IV A/2), see Jalabert, ʻInscr. gr. et lat. de Syrie', Mélanges de la Faculté Orientale de l'Université de Beyrouth 1 (1906), pp. 150 f.=Aharoni, ʻAtiqot 1 (1955), p. 111, no. 7. For ʻAqraba, see Dussaud, *Topographie*, pp. 327, 341 and map I, D2.

22. Epiphanius, *Anacephal.* i 249 (ed. Dindorf)=*Bakatha* in Epiphanius, *Adv. haer.* II 543 (ed. Dindorf). The place has not been identified; see I. Benzinger, RE II, col. 2782 s.v. ʻBakatha'. For Sûr, see *Syria. Pub. Princeton University Arch. Exped. Syria 1904–5, 1909* III A (1921), no. 397[2]; cf. Harper, *op. cit.*, p. 130.

23. *Ant.* xiv 5, 4 (91); *B.J.* i 8, 5 (170); see further vol. I pp. 268–9; cf. also p. 204 below.

24. The relationship was really one of subordination, since Josephus speaks emphatically of *ἄρχειν* and *ὑπακούειν*; see above pp. 174–5 and nn. 48–67.

Idumaea; (9) Engaddi; (10) Herodium; (11) Jericho. At the end of this list of towns, and apparently distinct from them, Josephus mentions Jamnia (Yavneh) and Joppa (Jaffa) as having 'jurisdiction over their surrounding districts'.[25] Elsewhere, however, in connection with Salome's bequest to Livia, he refers to Jamnia as a toparchy.[26] Pliny also provides a list of Judaean toparchies similar to that of Josephus, but whereas it includes those enumerated above under 2, 3, 4, 5, 6, 10 and 11, it adds to them the following three: Iopica (=Joppa), Betholethephene and Orine.[27] The naming of Orine in place of Jerusalem makes no material difference since *ἡ ὀρεινή* is the Judaean uplands, and according to Pliny's own statement this region included Jerusalem. It corresponds to the הר המלך in Rabbinic texts.[28] Pliny's 'Betholethephene' and Josephus's 'Pelle' are one and the same place, the former representing its native, and the latter its Greek name. It is not to be confused with the more famous 'Pella' in Peraea.[29] Josephus himself speaks on another occasion of a 'toparchy of Bethleptenpha', which must be the same as Pliny's 'Betholethephene'.[30] Pliny does not mention Josephus's toparchies of Idumaea and Engaddi, probably because he does not regard them as belonging strictly to Judaea. Thus the only substantial difference between Josephus and Pliny is reduced

25. *B.J.* iii 3, 5 (54–5): *μερίζεται δὲ εἰς ἕνδεκα κληρουχίας, ὧν ἄρχει μὲν ὡς βασίλειον τὰ Ἱεροσόλυμα, προανίσχουσα τῆς περιοίκου πάσης, ὥσπερ ἡ κεφαλὴ σώματος, αἱ λοιπαὶ δὲ μετ' αὐτὴν διῄρηνται τὰς τοπαρχίας, Γόφνα δευτέρα, καὶ μετ' αὐτὴν Ἀκραβαττά, Θαμνὰ πρὸς ταύταις καὶ Λύδδα καὶ Ἀμμαοῦς καὶ Πέλλη καὶ Ἰδουμαία καὶ Ἐγγαδδαὶ καὶ Ἡρώδειον καὶ Ἰεριχοῦς· μεθ' ἃς Ἰάμνεια καὶ Ἰόππη τῶν περιοίκων ἀφηγοῦνται.*

26. *Ant.* xviii 2, 2 (31): *Ἰαμνειάν τε . . . καὶ τὴν τοπαρχίαν πᾶσαν*; *B.J.* ii 9, 1 (167): *τήν τε αὐτῆς τοπαρχίαν καὶ Ἰαμνειάν.*

27. Pliny, *NH* v 14/70: 'relinqua Iudaea dividitur in toparchias decem quo dicemus in ordine: Hiericuntem palmetis consitam, fontibus riguam, Emmaum, Lyddam, Iopicam, Acrabatenam, Gophaniticam, Thamniticam, Betholethephenen, Orinen, in qua fuere Hierosolyma longe clarissima urbium orientis non Iudaeae modo, Herodium cum oppido inlustri eiusdem nominis'. For the textual variants see D. Detlefsen, *Die geographischen Bücher der Naturalis Historia des C. Plinius Secundus* (1904).

28. Cf. Josephus, *Ant.* xii 1, 1 (7): *ἀπό τε τῆς ὀρεινῆς Ἰουδαίας καὶ τῶν περὶ Ἱεροσόλυμα τόπον*; Lk. 1:39, 65. The expression is found frequently in the LXX, particularly in Judith (see Hatch-Redpath, *Concordance* s.v.). For הר המלך, see mSheb. 9: 2–3; tSheb. 7:10–11; bBer. 44a.

29. See Abel, *Géog. Pal.* II, pp. 153, 277; E. Honigmann, RE XIX, col. 350.

30. *B.J.* iv 8, 1 (445): *τὴν Βεθλεπτηνφῶν τοπαρχίαν.* There are many variants of the name: *Βεθλεπτημφων, Βετελεπτηφων, Βεθλεπτηφων*, 'Bethlepton' (see Niese's apparatus, and Schalit, *Namenwörterbuch*, p. 20). So too in the text of Pliny: 'Bertholethephenen', 'Betholtthephenen', 'Betolethenepenen'. Note, however, that 'Bethleptephenen' is merely a conjecture of Harduin (see Detlefsen's apparatus). The first element of the name = Semitic בית; the second element has rather too many consonants: the /n/ or /m/ before the /p/ and the /p/ before the /t/ are the most likely intrusions. Consequently, the original form of the name was probably *Bethletepha*.

to the question of whether the former is correct in classing Jamnia, and the latter Joppa, as toparchies of Judaea.

The toparchies of Judaea may, then, be grouped as follows: in the centre (1) Jerusalem; to the north (2) Gophna[31] and (3) Acrabatta;[32] to the northwest (4) Thamna[33] (5) Lydda[34] and (6) (?) Joppa;[35] to the west

31. According to the *Tab. Peut.*, Gophna lay on the road leading from Jerusalem to Neapolis (Sichem), 16 Roman miles north of Jerusalem (see Miller, *Itineraria Romana*, p. 833 s.v. '*Cofna*'), or according to Eusebius, *Onom.*, ed. Klostermann, p. 168, 16) 15 Roman miles: *Γοφνά . . . ἀπέχουσα Αἰλίας σημείοις ιε' κατὰ τὴν ὁδὸν τὴν εἰς Νεάπολιν ἄγουσαν*). In the time of Cassius it was a place of some importance: its inhabitants were sold by him into slavery because they did not pay the war-tax which he imposed on them (*Ant.* xiv 11, 2 (275); *B.J.* i 11, 2 (222); see further vol. I, p. 277). The *Γοφνιτικὴ τοπαρχία* is mentioned by Josephus elsewhere, *B.J.* ii 20, 4 (568); cf. also *B.J.* v 2, 1 (50); vi 2, 2 (115). In Ptolemy v 16, 7 (=Didot edition I/2 (1901), v 15, 5) the form of the name is *Γούφνα;* cf. also Eusebius, *Onom.*, ed. Klostermann, p. 74, 2); Jerome: 'Gufna'; but on the Madeba Map, *Γοφνα* (Avi-Yonah, *Madaba Mosaic Map* (1954), no. 46). In Rabbinic texts, בית גופנין, גופנא (tOhol. 18:16; yTaan. 69a; bBer. 44a). Modern *Jifna* (*Atlas of Israel*, I/11, 15K). See, Abel, *Géog. Pal.* II, p. 339; Avi-Yonah, *Map of Rom. Pal.*, p. 11; *idem*, Enc. Jud. 7, col. 691.

32. Acrabatta was still further north than Gophna, 9 Roman miles south-east of Neapolis (=Sichem: Eusebius, *Onom.*, ed. Klostermann, p. 14): *'Ακραββείν . . . κώμη δέ ἐστιν μόγις* (l. *μεγίστη*) *διεστῶσα Νέας πόλεως σημείοις θ')*. According to mM.Sh. 5:2 עקרבת] (v.l. עקרבה) was a day's journey to the north of Jerusalem, just as Lydda was to the west, which is very close to the mark. In the Book of Jubilees 29:14 the place is spoken of (Ethiopic, *Aqrabet*; Lat. Acrabin) together with Bethsean and Dothain. The *'Ακραβατηνὴ τοπαρχία* is found frequently elsewhere in Josephus and Eusebius, Josephus, *B.J.* ii 12, 4 (235); 20, 4 (568); 22, 2 (652); iii 3, 4 (48); iv 9, 3; 4 (504–11); Eusebius, *Onom.*, ed. Klostermann, pp. 14, 86, 108, 156, 160). Present-day 'Aqraba (*Atlas of Israel*, I/11, 13L). See further: Conder and Kitchener, *Survey of Western Palestine* II, pp. 386, 389 f.; Guérin, *Samarie* II, pp. 3–5; Abel, *Géog. Pal.* II, p. 339; Avi-Yonah, *Map of Rom. Pal.*, p. 24 (where the name of the town is erroneously given as *Acrabbein*). It should not be confused with a range of hills bearing a similar name in the south of Judaea (Num. 34:4; Jos. 15:3; Jg. 1:36; Eusebius, *Onom.*, p. 14), from which the *'Ακραβαττίνη* mentioned in 1 Mac. 5:3=Josephus, *Ant.* xii 8, 1 (328) is usually derived; see G. Hölscher, *Palästina in der persischen und hellenistischen Zeit* (1903), p. 69; *idem*, ZDPV 29 (1906), p. 133 f.; Abel, *Les Livres des Maccabées* (1949), p. 89. The 'ascent of עקרבים' in Num. 34:4 is identified by Tg. Ps.-Jonathan with the 'ascent of עקרבית' (so both the editio princeps and BM MS 27031, contra Ginsburger's edition).

33. Thamna is undoubtedly the ancient תמנת סרח or תמנת חרס in the hill-country of Ephraim where Joshua was buried (Jos. 19:50; 24:30; Jg. 2:9). Eusebius frequently mentions the place as a large village in the territory of Diospolis (=Lydda), see especially *Onom.*, ed. Klostermann, p. 96: *Θαμνά . . . διαμένει κώμη μεγάλη ἐν ὁρίοις Διοσπόλεως*, and remarks that the tomb of Joshua was still shown there in his day (p. 70: *δείκνυται δὲ ἐπίσημον εἰς ἔτι νῦν αὐτοῦ τὸ μνῆμα πλησίον Θαμνὰ κώμης*, *ibid.*, p. 100: *Θαμναθσαρά . . . αὕτη ἐστι Θαμνά . . . ἐν ᾗ εἰς ἔτι νῦν δείκνυται τὸ τοῦ 'Ιησοῦ μνῆμα*). So too Jerome in his description of the pilgrimage of St. Paula, *Epist.* 108 *ad Eustochium* 13: 'Sepulcra quoque in monte Ephraim Iesus filii Nave et Eleazari filii Aaron sacerdotis e regione venerata est, quorum alter

(7) Emmaus[36] and (8) (?) Jamnia;[37] to the southwest (9) Bethletepha;[38]

---

conditus est in Tamnathsare a septentrionale parte monte Gaas'). Modern Khirbet Tibneh, about 7½ miles WNW of Jifna. The traditional tomb of Joshua is still shown there. See Guérin, *Samarie* II, pp. 89–104; Abel, *Géog. Pal.* II, p. 481; *idem*, RB 34 (1925), pp. 209 ff.; Avi-Yonah, *Map of Rom. Pal.*, p. 16; *idem*, Enc. Jud. 15, col. 1147. In the time of Cassius, Thamna suffered the same fate as Gophna, Josephus, *Ant.* xiv 11, 2 (275); cf. *B.J.* i 11, 2 (222). The toparchy of Thamna is mentioned by Josephus and Eusebius elsewhere, *B.J.* ii 20, 4 (567); iv 8, 1 (444); Eusebius, *Onom.*, ed. Klostermann, pp. 24, 56. Cf. also Ptolemy v 16, 8 (=Didot edition v 15, 5). There are several other places named תמנה or תמנתה to be distinguished from our Thamna: (1) תמנה/תמנתה on the border between the tribes of Dan and Judah (Jos. 15:10; 19:43; Jg. 14:1 ff.; 2 Chron. 28:18). This was formerly located at Kh. Tibnah, approx. 4 km SW of Beth Shemesh (=Ḥ. Timna, *Atlas of Israel* (1970) I/11, 18G); see Robinson, *Biblical Researches* II, p. 343; Conder and Kitchener, *op. cit.* II, pp. 417, 441; Abel, *Géog. Pal.* II, p. 481, but rather is it probably to be identified with Tell el-Batashi, approx. 7.5 km NW of Beth Shemesh in the middle of Naḥal Sorek (=Tel Batash, *Atlas of Israel* I/11, 17G); see Y. Aharoni, PEFQSt 90 (1958), pp. 27 ff.; Y. Kaplan, Eretz Israel 5 (1959), pp. 9 ff.; B. Mazar, IEJ 10 (1960), p. 66. (2) תמנה in the hill country of Judah (Gen. 38:12–14; Jos. 15:57). (3) Which תמנה is meant by the *Θαμναθά* in 1 Mac. 9:50 cannot be determined with certainty.

34. Lydda (Hebr. לד; later called *Diospolis*), the well-known town on the road from Joppa (Jaffa) to Jerusalem, is mentioned also in *B.J.* ii 20, 1 (567) as one of the toparchies of Judaea. On one occasion Josephus characterizes it as a *κώμη* ... *πόλεως τὸ μέγεθος οὐκ ἀποδέουσα*, *Ant.* xx 6, 2 (130). On its history cf. especially 1 Mac. 11:34; Josephus, *Ant.* xiv 10, 6 (208); 11, 2 (275); *B.J.* ii 19, 1 (515); iv 8, 1 (444); cf. i 11, 2 (222). See Abel, *Géog. Pal.* II, p. 370; Avi-Yonah, *Map of Rom. Pal.*, p. 15.

35. Greek *'Ιόππη;* Hebr. יפו; see further above §23. I, n. 132.

36. Emmaus or Ammaus (later Nicopolis) is the modern 'Imwas (*Atlas of Israel* I/11, 17G), approx. 16 km SSE of Lydda. Because of its position at the foot of the hill-country it was a place of some military importance, and is mentioned frequently as such already in the Maccabean period (1 Mac. 3:40, 57; 4:3; 9:50). For its later history see especially *Ant.* xiv 11, 2 (275); *B.J.* i 11, 2 (222); *Ant.* xvii 10, 9 (191); *B.J.* ii 5, 1 (69); iv 8, 1 (444). It is mentioned also in *B.J.* ii 20, 4 (567) as a Jewish toparchy. In Rabbinic texts it is called אמאום (mArakh. 2:4; mKer. 3:7; see further, A. Neubauer, *Géogr. du Talmud*, pp. 100–2). It is found in Ptolemy v 16, 7 (=Didot edition, I/2 (1901), v 15, 5) as *'Εμμαοῦς*. It is to be distinguished from the Emmaus near Jerusalem mentioned in *B.J.* vii 6, 6 (217) and Lk. 24:13 (see above vol. I, pp. 512–13). See Robinson, *Biblical Researches* II, p. 254; III, pp. 146–50; Abel, *Géog. Pal.* II, p. 314; L. H. Vincent and F.-M. Abel, *Emmaüs, sa basilique et son histoire* (1932); G. Dalman, *Sacred Sites and Ways* (1935), pp. 226–32; Avi-Yonah, *Map Rom. Pal.*, p. 17; *idem*, Enc. Jud. 6, col. 726.

37. Greek *'Ιάμνεια;* ; Hebr. יבנה; see above §23 I, n. 124.

38. Probably the modern Beith Nettîf (=Ḥ. Bet Nāṭif, *Atlas of Israel* I/11, 18G). This is in the right position, since to judge from the context in Josephus, *B.J.* iv 8, 1 (445) Bethletepha lay between Emmaus and Idumaea. It is probably not to be identified with the biblical נטפה (Ezr. 2:22; Neh. 7:26 cf. נטפתי 2 Sam. 23:28; 29; 2 Kgs. 25:23; Jer. 40:8; Neh. 12:28; 1 Chron. 2:54; 9:16; 11:30; 27:13, 15) as this is better located at Kh. Bedd Falūḥ, approx, 5½ km south of Bethlehem (see Abel, *Géog. Pal.* II, p. 399; Aharoni, *Land of the Bible*, p. 382; Avi-Yonah, Enc. Jud. 12, col. 1001). The rabbinic בית נטפה (mSheb. 9:5) and נטפה (mPea.

to the south (10) Idumaea;[39] to the south-east (11) Engaddi[40] and (12) Herodium;[41] and to the east (13) Jericho.[42] Outside Judaea, Josephus mentions two toparchies in Peraea—Julias and Abila, and two in Galilee—Taricheae and Tiberias.[43]

7:1–2) refer to a third place, viz., Kh. el-Nāṭif, approx. 14 km WNW of Tiberias (=Ḥ. Bet Netofa, *Atlas of Israel* I/10, 6L); see Avi-Yonah, Enc. Jud. 4, col. 752. On Beit Nettîf=Bethletepha, see A. Schlatter, *Zur Topographie und Gesch. Palästinas* (1893), p. 354; Abel, *Géog. Pal.* II, p. 277; Avi-Yonah, *Map Rom. Pal.*, p. 21; *idem.* Enc. Jud. 4, col. 747.

39. Idumaea was Judaized by John Hyrcanus, *Ant.* xiii 9, 1 (257); xv 7, 9 (254); *B.J.* i 2, 6 (63); hence the Idumaeans acted like Jews in the Jewish revolt, *B.J.* iv 4, 14 (270). Cf. also *B.J.* ii 20, 4 (566). The toparchy was probably administered from Beth Guvrin, בית גוברין (tOhol. 18:16)=*Βαιτογαβρεί/Βαιτογαβρά* (Ptolemy, v 16, 6)='Betogabri' (*Tab. Peut.*; see Miller, *Itin. Rom.*, p. 836 s.v.); later Eleutheropolis; modern Beit Jibrin (=Beth Guvrin, *Atlas of Israel* I/10, 19G); see I. Benzinger RE V, col. 2353 s.v. 'Eleutheropolis'; Abel, *Géog. Pal.* II, p. 272; Avi-Yonah, *Map of Rom. Pal.*, p. 20; *idem*, Enc. Jud. 4, col. 731.

40. Engaddi, the ancient עין גדי (Jos. 15:62; 1 Sam. 24:1 ff.; Ezek. 47:10; Cant. 1:14; 2 Chron. 20:2), on the western shore of the Dead Sea (Josephus, *Ant.* ix 1, 2 (7) *'Εγγαδδὶ πόλιν κειμένην πρὸς τῇ 'Ασφαλτίδι λίμνῃ;* Eusebius, *Onom.* (ed. Klostermann, p. 86): *καὶ νῦν ἔστι κώμη μεγίστη 'Ιουδαίων 'Εγγάδδι παρακειμένη τῇ νεκρᾷ θαλάσσῃ).* Josephus calls it a *πολίχνη* in *B.J.* iv 7, 2 (402). In Ptolemy v 16, 8 (= Didot edition I/2 (1901) v 15, 5) it is given as *'Εγγάδδα*. Modern 'Ain Jidi (=En Gedi, *Atlas of Israel* I/11, 21L). Famous for its palm and balsam groves: see Pliny v 17/73: 'Infra hos (scil. Essenos) Engada oppidum fuit, secundum ab Hierosolymis fertilitate palmetorumque nemoribus, nunc alterum bustum'. Ecclus. 24:14 *(ὡς φοῖνιξ . . . ἐν Αἰγγαδοις);* Jerome, *Epist.* 108 *ad Eustochium* 11=Tobler, *Palaestinae Descriptiones* (1869), p. 20: 'contemplata est balsami vineas in Engaddi' (Tobler emends the text unnecessarily). On palms and balsam, see vol. I, p. 298, n. 36). For En-Gedi, see Abel, *Géog. Pal.* II, p. 316; Avi-Yonah, *Map of Rom. Pal.*, p. 21; B. Mazar, T. Dothan, I. Dunayevsky, *En-Gedi: the first and second seasons of excavations, 1961–62*, 'Atiqot, Eng. ser. 5 (1966); B. Mazar in *Archaeology and O.T. Study*, ed. by D. Winton-Thomas (1967), pp. 223 ff.; *idem.* Enc. Jud. 6, cols. 741 ff. EAEHL II, s.v. 'En-Gedi'.

41. Herodium was an important fortress built by Herod the Great in the south of Judaea and used as his mausoleum, 60 stadia from Jerusalem, *Ant.* xiv 13, 9 (360); xv 9, 4 (324); *B.J.* i 13, 8 (265); 21, 10 (419); modern Jebel el-Fureidis: see vol. I, p. 307, n. 64. For further archaeological literature, see Vogel, 'Bibliography', s.v. 'Herodium'; E. Netzer, IEJ 22 (1972), pp. 247–9; A. Segal, 'Herodium', IEJ 23 (1973), pp. 27–9; EAEHL II, s.v.

42. Jericho was the most important town in the east of Judaea and was therefore chosen at the time of Gabinius as the seat of one of the five *συνέδρια*, *Ant.* xiv 5, 4 (91); *B.J.* i 8, 5 (170). It is mentioned as a district of Judaea also in *B.J.* ii 20, 4 (567). Cf. further *B.J.* iv 8, 2 (451); 9, 1 (486). Roman Jericho was at Tulūl Abu el-'Alayiq, a short distance to the SW of Tell es-Sultan (=the biblical Jericho). See vol. I, pp. 298–300, and for bibliography of excavations, Vogel, 'Bibliography', s.v. 'Jericho', and EAEHL II, s.v.

43. *B.J.* ii 13, 2 (252): *τέτταρας πόλεις . . . σὺν ταῖς τοπαρχίαις "Αβιλα μὲν καὶ 'Ιουλιάδα κατὰ τὴν Περαίαν, Ταριχαίας δὲ καὶ Τιβεριάδα τῆς Γαλιλαίας.* Cf. *Ant.* xx 8, 4 (159): *'Ιουλιάδα πόλιν τῆς Περαίας καὶ κώμας τὰς περὶ αὐτὴν τεσσαρεσκαίδεκα.* These four toparchies cannot be the sum total of the administrative subdivisions of Peraea and

This arrangement was presumably made chiefly for administrative reasons, and may have been relevant to the collection of revenue. Whether the same districts also served for judicial circuits, it is impossible to say. The organization known from the accounts of Josephus and Pliny probably dates only from the Roman period.[44] A similar one

---

Galilee. In the case of Peraea we should add Gadara, which is described as the capital of Peraea in *B.J.* iv 7, 3 (413), and Amathus. The latter was the seat of one of Gabinius's *συνέδρια*, Josephus, *Ant.* xiv 5, 4 (91); *B.J.* i 8, 5 (170). Moreover, in the troubles that followed the death of Herod, we learn from *Ant.* xvii 10, 6 (277) that the 'government buildings' there (? *τὰ βασίλεια*) were burned down. Thus the Peraean toparchies were as follows (from north to south): (1) Amathus = modern Tell 'Ammatā, situated a short distance to the east of the Jordan, where W. Rājeb (= W. Rājib, *Atlas of Israel* I/11, 12N) enters the plain of the Jordan. See W. F. Albright, AASOR 6 (1924–5), p. 44; N. Glueck, AASOR 25–8 (1945–9) pt. I, pp. 300–1. Eusebius, *Onom.*, ed. Klostermann, p. 22, locates it 21 Roman miles south of Pella (*'Αμμαθοῦς κώμη ἐν τῇ Περαίᾳ τῇ κατωτέρᾳ, Πέλλων διεστῶσα σημείοις κα' εἰς νότον*). See further Abel, *Géog. Pal.* II, p. 242. (2) Gadara = modern Tell Jadūr, very close to es-Salṭ (*Atlas of Israel* I/11, 140). It is called *Γάδωρα* in Ptolemy v 14, 18. See further Abel, *Géog. Pal.* II, p. 324. (3) Abila = Kh. el-Kefrein, approx. 1½ km WSW of el-Kefrein (= Kafrein, *Atlas of Israel* I/11, 170). See Albright, AASOR 6 (1924–5), p. 49; Glueck, AASOR 25–8 (1945–9), pt. I, pp. 376–8. Cf. Josephus, *Ant.* v 1, 1 (4); *B.J.* iv 7, 6 (438). (4) Julias (formerly Livias) = בית רמתה (ySheb. 38d) = בית הרם (Jos. 13:27), בית הרן (Num. 32:36). Located at modern Tell er-Rāmeh, approx. 2½ km S of Kh. el-Kefrein. See Albright, AASOR 6 (1924–5), p. 49; Abel, *Géog. Pal.* II, p. 273; Glueck, AASOR 25–8 (1945–9), pt. I, pp. 389–91. See further above pp. 176–8. For a map of Peraea, see *Atlas of Israel* IX/7. For Galilee, we may add to Taricheae and Tiberias, Sepphoris, which was for some time capital of the region, Josephus, *Vita* 9 (37–8); cf. 37 (188), and probably also Gabara *(Γάβαρα)*, which is referred to by Josephus as an important Galilean town, see *B.J.* ii 21, 7 (629); *Vita* 40 (203), and (by emendation) *B.J.* iii 7, 1 (132). Thus the toparchies of Galilee were: (A) For Upper Galilee: none known. (B) For Lower Galilee: in the east (1) Tiberias (see above §23 I, n. 511), and (2) Taricheae. The latter lay on the Sea of Galilee, to the north of Tiberias, Josephus, *B.J.* iii 9, 7 ff. (443 ff.). Its position is marked by the present-day ruin of Majdal, to the SE of Migdal (*Atlas of Israel* I/10, 6M). See Albright, AASOR 2–3 (1921–2), pp. 29 ff.; Abel, *Géog. Pal.* II, p. 476 ff.; Avi-Yonah, *Map Rom. Pal.*, p. 37; *idem*, Enc. Jud. 11, col. 685. In western Galilee: (3) Sepphoris (Diocaesarea); see above, pp. 172–6; and (4) Gabara. This name should be emended to *Garaba* (*Γάραβα*) = *'Αραβά* in Eusebius, *Onom.*, ed. Klostermann, p. 16: *κώμη καλουμένη 'Αραβὰ ἐν ὁρίοις Διοκαισαρείας*. It is marked by the modern Arab village of 'Arrābat al-Baṭṭūf) (*Atlas of Israel* I/10, 5L). See further Abel, *Géog. Pal.* II, p. 322; Avi-Yonah, *Map of Rom. Pal.*, p. 33. On the whole subject of the toparchies of Peraea and Galilee see Avi-Yonah, *Holy Land*, pp. 96–7; Jones, CERP², pp. 273–4.

44. On the division of the Roman provinces into administrative districts (*conventus*), see Marquardt, *Römische Staatsverwaltung* I (²1881), p. 500 f.; C. Habicht, JRS 65 (1975), pp. 64–91 (on the province of Asia); G. P. Burton, 'Proconsuls, Assizes and the Administration of Justice', *ibid.*, pp. 91–106. Whether the division of large provinces governed by senators is relevant to the division of Judaea into toparchies is not clear.

nevertheless existed already during that of Greek domination. At the time of Jonathan, in the year 145 B.C., three districts of Samaria, namely Aphaerema, Lydda and Ramathaim, are said to have been ceded by Demetrius II to Jonathan and thus joined to Judaea (1 Mac. 11:34; cf. 10:30, 38; 11:28, 57).[45] These districts are described as *τοπαρχίαι* (1 Mac. 11:28) or *νομοί* (10:30, 38; 11:34, 57) and must have been of approximately the same extent as the toparchies of the Roman era. But the toparchies in existence in the Roman period cannot have been identical to those in Jonathan's time, since the extent of Judaea to the south and the north was then considerably less than in Roman times (cf. above, pp. 1–7).[46] On the other hand, incontestable evidence exists for the presence of the Roman sub-divisions as early as the time of Cassius (43 B.C.). The latter sold the inhabitants of Gophna, Emmaus, Lydda and Thamna as slaves because they did not pay the tax imposed by him.[47] All these four towns are mentioned by Josephus and Pliny as capitals of toparchies. It seems that they ranked as such already in the time of Cassius. The promotion of Herodium to be the main town of a toparchy must have taken place later, but the toparchy itself may have been pre-Herodian.

The sources are remarkably indefinite concerning the constitutional position of the main towns, which are sometimes described as *πόλεις* and sometimes as *κῶμαι*. It is of little significance that Eusebius calls the places in question for the most part *κῶμαι*, for conditions had changed considerably by the time he wrote.[48] But Josephus himself lacks consistency. For example, he speaks of Emmaus as the *μητρόπολις* of its district, and obviously, therefore, of the toparchy as well;[49] on the other hand, he describes Lydda simply as a *κώμη*, apparently speaking very precisely (see above, n. 34). It must therefore be presumed that, in the proper Graeco-Roman sense of the word, none of the places in question was a *πόλις*, i.e. not cities with Greek constitutions. It was only because of Jewish popular usage that they were spoken of as

45. See vol. I, p. 182.

46. In the passages cited from 1 Mac. *τοπαρχία* means the same as *νομός*. In Egypt however a toparchy was a subdivision of a nome; see Strabo xvii 1, 3 (p. 787): *πάλιν δ' οἱ νομοὶ τομὰς ἄλλας ἔσχον εἰς γὰρ τοπαρχίας οἱ πλεῖστοι διῄρηντο καὶ αὗται δ' εἰς ἄλλας τομάς*. Further, n. 4 above.

47. See vol. I, p. 277.

48. The names of several of the toparchies (*'Ακραβαττηνή, Θαμνατική*) persisted till the time of Eusebius, but the constitution itself had been altered essentially by the establishment of new, independent 'civitates' such as Diospolis and Nicopolis. As a result, Thamna, for example, no longer ranked as the capital of a toparchy, but was reduced to a *κώμη μεγάλη ἐν ὁρίοις Διοσπόλεως* (see n. 33 above) and became subordinate to Lydda-Diospolis.

49. *B.J.* iv 8, 1 (445).

πόλεις, 'cities'. It might be more exact to call them κωμοπόλεις (see above, n. 16), or when viewed in relation to their respective toparchies, μητροκωμίαι (see above, nn. 18–22).

One town alone in Judaea proper, namely Jerusalem, may have enjoyed the rank of πόλις in the strict Graeco-Roman sense. All the rest of Judaea was subordinated to it, and it ruled over this area ὡς βασίλειον (see above, n. 25). Its relation to Judaea was consequently similar to that in which the Greek cities stood to their respective territories.[50] This is further implied in the manner of address used in imperial edicts to the Jews which ran as follows: Ἱεροσολυμιτῶν ἄρχουσι βουλῇ δήμῳ, Ἰουδαίων παντὶ ἔθνει—terms very similar to those employed in letters addressed to Greek cities, in which the city and its council was the ruler and hence representative of the whole district.[51] It seems likely that the council of Jerusalem (the Sanhedrin) was also responsible for the collection of taxes throughout the whole of Judaea.[52] The Mishnah preserves a recollection that the 'elders' of Jerusalem exercised authority over the whole of Judaea.[53] On the other hand, from the

50. Cf. E. Kuhn, *Die städtische und bürgerl. Verfassung* II, pp. 342–5. But see V. Tcherikover, 'Was Jerusalem a "Polis"?', IEJ 14 (1964), pp. 61 ff., who argues against this view. In *Ant.* xvii 11, 4 (320)—a passage dealing with the settlement after Herod's death—Joppa is listed as one of the πόλεις which Augustus made subject to Archelaus. The others were, Straton's Tower, Sebaste, and Jerusalem.

51. *Ant.* xx 1, 2 (11); cf. the similar form of address in the edicts cited in *Ant.* xiv 10 (185 ff.) (Σιδωνίων ἄρχουσι βουλῇ δήμῳ, Ἐφησίων βουλῇ καὶ ἄρχουσι καὶ δήμῳ, etc.); xiv 12, 4–5 (314–22); xvi 6 (160 ff.). See further F. F. Abbott and A. C. Johnson, *Municipal Administration in the Roman Empire* (1926), nos. 30, 35, 36, 54, 68, 71, 75, 76, 80, 82, 83 etc.

52. When, after the first convulsions of revolt, a more peaceful policy was adopted for a brief period, the magistrates and members of the Council of Jerusalem dispersed among the villages to collect the arrears of tribute, *B.J.* ii 17, 1 (405): εἰς δὲ τὰς κώμας οἵ τε ἄρχοντες καὶ οἱ βουλευταὶ μερισθέντες τοὺς φόρους συνέλεγεν. These were speedily gathered and amounted to 40 talents. However, immediately afterwards, Agrippa sent ἄρχοντες and δυνατοί to Florus in Caesarea with the request that he should appoint from their number tribute-collectors *for the country* (*ibid.* ἵνα ἐκεῖνος ἐξ αὐτῶν ἀποδείξῃ τοὺς τὴν χώραν φορολογήσοντας). Since this happened after the taxes of the city-territory (and consequently also of the toparchy of Jerusalem) had been collected, it may be implied that by χώρα the whole of Judaea is meant. For the Roman practice of using city councils to collect Roman taxes see J. Marquardt, *Römische Staatsverwaltung* I (²1881), p. 501; O. Hirschfeld, *Die kaiserlichen Verwaltungsbeamten bis auf Diokletian* (²1905), pp. 73 ff.; F. F. Abbott and A. C. Johnson, *Municipal Administration in the Roman Empire* (1926), pp. 117 ff.; A. H. M. Jones, *The Greek City* (1940), pp. 138–40; 151–4; RE VIIA (1948), cols. 65–8.

53. mTaan. 3:6, 'The elders once went down from Jerusalem to their towns (ירדו הזקנים מירושלים לעריהם) and decreed a fast, because in Ashkelon (באשקלון) there appeared blight the extent of an oven's mouth'. The implication of this text is that the towns of Judaea were subject to the authority of the 'elders' of Jerusalem. Though Ashkelon was not administratively within the territory of Judaea, it was regarded as being Land of Israel by the religious authorities

time at least of the death of Herod the Great, the civil jurisdiction of the Sanhedrin of Jerusalem no longer reached beyond Judaea proper. From then on, Galilee and Peraea formed separate administrative districts. It would be quite wrong to conclude from the fact that the rebellion in Galilee was directed from Jerusalem that this area fell within the jurisdiction of the Great Sanhedrin in peace time as well, for the circumstances were obviously exceptional. It was only in earlier times, particularly under the Hasmonaeans, that the whole of the Jewish territory constituted a real political unity (see below, pp. 203–4). Nonetheless it is possible that in the administration of Jewish law the Sanhedrin in Jerusalem exercised a *de facto* authority (e.g. in the sending of Paul to Damascus to effect arrests, Act. 9:1) which took no account of formal administrative, or even provincial, divisions.

Since the Council of Jerusalem can hardly have handled all the minutiae of the administration of justice by itself it is *a priori* probable that one or more other lower courts of justice existed in the city besides the Great Sanhedrin. According to a tradition contained in the Mishnah, these numbered three.[54]

in the first century A.D. It was first excluded from the Land by the boundary-formula of R. Judah ben Elai in the mid-second century A.D. (mGit. 1:2).

54. mSanh. 11:2 lays down the proper procedure to be followed when an 'elder' (זקן) disagreed on a fundamental point of law with the other members of his local court. The dispute was to be referred to the three courts (בתי דינין) in Jerusalem. First it was submitted to the court that sat at the gate of the Temple Mount (על פתח הר הבית). If this court could not resolve it, the case was passed on to the second court, which sat at the gate of the Temple Court (על פתח העזרה). If this court, too, was unsuccessful, the matter was submitted finally to the supreme court (בית דין הגדול) which met in the *Lishkath ha-gazith* (בלשכת הגזית; see below, p. 224). On the interpretation of this text see S. Krauss, *Sanhedrin-Makkot* (1933), pp. 287 ff.

III. The Great Sanhedrin in Jerusalem

Bibliography

Geiger, A., *Urschrift und Übersetzungen der Bibel* (1857), pp. 114–21.

Derenbourg, J., *Essai sur l'histoire et la géographie de la Palestine* (1867), pp. 83–94, 465–68.

Wellhausen, J., *Pharisäer und Sadducäer* (1874), pp. 26–43.

Jelski, I., *Die innere Einrichtung des grossen Synedrions zu Jerusalem und ihre Fortsetzung im späteren palästinensischen Lehrhause bis zur Zeit des R. Jehuda ha-Nasi* (1894).

Kuenen, A., 'Über die Zusammensetzung des Sanhedrin', *Gesammelte Schriften zur biblischen Wissenschaft* (1894), pp. 49–81.

Bacher, W., 'Sanhedrin', HDB IV (1902), pp. 397–402.

Büchler, A., *Das Synedrion in Jerusalem und das grosse Beth-Din in der Quaderkammer des jerusalemischen Tempels* (1902). [A pioneering, but controversial work, arguing that there were two institutions.]

Lauterbach, J. Z., 'Sanhedrin', JE XI (1905), pp. 41–4.

Hölscher, G., *Sanhedrin und Makkot* (1910).

Juster, J., *Les Juifs dans l'empire romain* (1914) I, pp. 400–02; II, pp. 132–45. [Argues in favour of the Sanhedrin's capital jurisdiction before A.D. 70.]

Danby, H., 'The Bearing of the Rabbinical Criminal Code on the Jewish Trial Narratives in the Gospels', JThSt 21 (1919–20), pp. 51–76.

Moore, G. F., *Judaism in the First Three Centuries of the Christian Era* III (1930), pp. 32–4.

Lietzmann, H., 'Der Prozess Jesu', SPAW 14 (1931), pp. 313–22.

Lietzmann, H., 'Bemerkungen zum Processe Jesu', ZNW 30 (1931), pp. 211–15; 31 (1932), pp. 78–89.

Lietzmann, H., *Kleine Schriften* II (1959), pp. 251–76.

Krauss, S., *Sanhedrin-Makkot* (1933).

Bickermann, E., 'Utilitas Crucis', RHR 112 (1935), pp. 169–241.

Bickermann, E., על הסנהדרין, Zion 4 (1938), pp. 356–66.

Zeitlin, S., *Who crucified Jesus?* (1942, [2]1964).

Benoit, P., 'Jésus devant le Sanhédrin', Angelicum 20 (1943), pp. 143–65. [*Exégèse et théologie* I (1961), pp. 290–311.]

Wolfson, H. A., 'Synedrion in Greek Jewish Literature and Philo', JQR 36 (1945–6), pp. 303–06.

Zeitlin, S., 'The Political Synedrion and the Religious Sanhedrin', JQR 36 (1945–46), pp. 109–40.

Zeitlin, S., 'Synedrion in Greek Literature, the Gospels and the Institution of the Sanhedrin', JQR 37 (1946–7), pp. 189–98.

Jeremias, J., 'Zur Geschichtlichkeit des Verhörs Jesu vor dem hohen Rat', ZNW 43 (1950–1), pp. 145–50.

Hoenig, S. B., *The Great Sanhedrin* (1953).

Burkill, T. A., 'The Competence of the Sanhedrin', Vigiliae Christianae 10 (1956), pp. 80–96.

Burkill, T. A., 'The Trial of Jesus', *ibid.* 12 (1958), pp. 1–18.

Blinzler, J., *Der Prozess Jesu* ([3]1960). [A detailed, conservative study.]

Blinzler, J., 'Das Synedrium in Jerusalem und die Strafprozessordnung der Mischna', ZNW 52 (1961), pp. 54–65.

Winter, P., *On the Trial of Jesus* (1961). [A standard work on the subject arguing in favour of the competence of the Sanhedrin in capital cases. The second posthumous edition (1974) contains supplementary material and some addenda by the editors, T. A. Burkill and G. Vermes.]

Mantel, H., *Studies in the History of the Sanhedrin* (1961). [A thorough survey of the sources from a conservative Jewish point of view.]

Burkill, T. A., 'Sanhedrin' IDB IV (1962), pp. 214–18.

Sherwin-White, A. N., *Roman Society and Roman Law in the New Testament* (1963).

Lohse, E., '*Synedrion*', TWNT VII (1964), pp. 863–69=TDNT VII (1971), pp. 860–71.

Tcherikover, V. A., 'Was Jerusalem a "Polis"?', IEJ 14 (1964), pp. 61–78.

Zeitlin, S., *The Rise and Fall of the Judean State* II (1967), pp. 385–94.

Efron, Y., הסנהדרין בחזון ובמציאות של הבית השני [The Sanhedrin as an Ideal and as Reality in the Period of the Second Temple], *DORON sive Commentationes de antiquitate classica docto viro Benzioni Katz . . . dedicatae* (1967), pp. 167–204. [For an English summary see Immanuel 2 (1973), pp. 44–9.]

Brandon, S. G. F., *The Trial of Jesus of Nazareth* (1968).

Jeremias, J., *Jerusalem in the Time of Jesus* (1969), pp. 222–32.

Burkill, T. A., 'The Condemnation of Jesus: A Critique of Sherwin-White's Thesis', NT 12 (1970), pp. 321–42.

Bammel, E., 'Ex illa itaque die concilium fecerunt . . .', *The Trial of Jesus*, ed. E. Bammel (1970), pp. 11–40.

Catchpole, D. R., 'The Problem of the Historicity of the Sanhedrin', *ibid.*, pp. 47–65.

Catchpole, D. R., *The Trial of Jesus. A Study in the Gospels and Jewish Historiography from 1770 to the Present Day* (1971).

Mantel, H., 'Sanhedrin', Enc. Jud. 14 (1971), cols. 836–9.

Safrai, S., 'Jewish Self-Government', *The Jewish People in the First Century*, ed. by S. Safrai and M. Stern, I (1974), pp. 379–400.

Bammel, E., 'Die Blutsgerichtbarkeit der römischen Provinz Judäa', JJS 25 (1974), pp. 35–49.

Rivkin, E., 'Beth Din, Boulé, Sanhedrin: A Tragedy of Errors', HUCA 46 (1975), pp. 181–99.

Baumgarten, J. A., 'The Duodecimal Courts of Qumran, Revelation and the Sanhedrin', JBL 95 (1976), pp. 59–78.

Mantel, H., 'Sanhedrin', IDBS (1976), pp. 784–6.

Catchpole, D. R., 'Trial of Jesus', *ibid.*, pp. 917–9.

1. *History of the Sanhedrin*

An aristocratic council, with its seat in Jerusalem and endowed with total or quasi total power in matters of government and jurisdiction over the Jewish people, is first definitely attested in the Greek era. It is true that rabbinic exegesis sees in the council of the seventy elders given to Moses in accordance with his wish (Num. 11:16) the 'Sanhedrin' of that age, and assumes that the institution was continually in existence from Moses to talmudic times. But for the first thousand years of this period no trace of it is to be found. The 'elders' occasionally mentioned in the Bible as the people's representatives (e.g. 1 Kgs. 8:1; 20:7; 2 Kgs. 23:1; Ezek. 14:1; 20:1) were not organized as a court like the later Sanhedrin. Also, the supreme tribunal in Jerusalem presupposed by the deuteronomic legislation (Deut. 17: 8 ff.; 19:16 ff.), the institution of which is traced by the Chronicler to Jehoshaphat (2 Chron. 19:8), was merely a court of law with exclusively judicial functions; it was not a senate that governed or had any essential share in government, as was the Sanhedrin in the Graeco-Roman period.[1]

It is not until the Persian era that one may with any probability assume the existence or gradual development of a court resembling that of the later Sanhedrin. Conditions were then substantially identical with those prevailing in the Graeco-Roman period; the Jews formed themselves into a self-governing community under foreign domination. Communal affairs required some kind of communal direction by the representatives or leaders of the people. The 'elders' usually appear as such in the book of Ezra (Ezr. 5:5, 9; 6:7, 14; 10:8), and as חורים or סגנים, nobles or dignitaries, in Nehemiah (Neh. 2:16; 4:8; 13; 5:7; 7:5). Nothing further is said concerning their number and organization. Since in Ezr. 2:2 = Neh. 7:7 twelve men are named as leaders of the exiles, it is likely that in early post-exilic days twelve clan chiefs headed the community.[2] On the other hand, Neh. 5:17 mentions one hundred and fifty Jewish dignitaries (סגנים).[3] In any case, the later organization was distinguished from the earlier by the fact that—before as well as immediately after the exile—the tribes and clans were largely independent, and therefore a common direction existed only insofar as the heads of the clans decided on a joint action, whereas

1. This is certainly how Josephus envisages it when, following the analogy of later conditions, he designates that court of justice ἡ γερουσία, *Ant.* iv 8, 14 (218).

2. Cf. H. E. Ryle, *The Books of Ezra and Nehemiah* (1897), p. 18; W. Rudolph, *Esra und Nehemiah* (1949), p. 19; H. Schneider, *Die Bücher Esra und Nehemia* (1959), pp. 92–3; K. Galling, 'Serubabel und der Wiederaufbau des Tempels in Jerusalem', *Verbannung und Heimkehr—Festschrift für Wilhelm Rudolph* (1961), pp. 76, 96; L. H. Brockington, *Ezra, Nehemia and Esther* (1969), pp. 52–4. Government by twelve tribal leaders corresponding to the Mosaic organization of Israel is strongly advocated by the conservative legislation of the Qumran Community, cf. 1QS 8:1–4; 1QSa 1:27–9; 1QM 2:2–3. 'The sect was divided symbolically into twelve tribes. As in the New Testament, where the twelve apostles are the new tribal chiefs and the Letter of James is addressed to the "twelve tribes of the dispersion", so among the Community the tribal system corresponded to an ideal. Thus the supreme Council in the pre-Messianic age appears to have been formed by twelve laymen and three Priests.' See G. Vermes, *DSSE*, pp. 17–18; cf. *DSS*, pp. 88, 91–2.

3. It should be recalled, however, that E. Meyer, *Die Entstehung des Judentums* (1896), considered the twelve men in Ezr. 2:2 = Neh. 7:7 not as high officials, but as leaders of the homebound exiles on their desert journey (p. 193). Cf. S. Mowinckel, *Studien zu dem Buche Esra-Nehemia* I (1964), pp. 64–5.

later, the whole community was placed under a central authority proper. The latter resulted from a closer bond between heads of clans, both priestly and lay.[4]

Moreover, the fact that the end of Persian rule meant the end of the appointment of a 'governor' (see vol. I, p. 603) nominated by the king must have given greater importance to the aristocratic council.[4a]

One general consideration argues for the existence of such an authority in the form of an aristocratic council already in the Persian period. Wherever entirely new Hellenistic city constitutions were established, these were at least formally democratic, with an assembly (*ἐκκλησία*) as well as a council (*βουλή*). In Judaea, however, there existed in the Greek period an aristocratic council, a *γερουσία*. This is highly likely to have originated in pre-Hellenistic, i.e. Persian times. It may have undergone certain changes but was essentially pre-Hellenistic in character.

The decisive authority in this supreme court lay without doubt in the hands of the priests. Hecataeus of Abdera, a contemporary of Alexander the Great and Ptolemy I Lagus, gives the following remarkable description of the Jewish constitution in a surviving fragment of his *Aegyptiaca*: 'He (Moses) selected the men of most refinement and with the greatest ability to head the entire nation, and appointed them priests (*τούτους ἱερεῖς ἀπέδειξε*). . . . These same men he appointed to be judges in all major disputes (*δικαστὰς τῶν μεγίστων κρίσεων*), and entrusted to them the guardianship of the laws and customs. For this reason the Jews never have a king, and authority over the people is regularly vested in whichever priest is regarded as superior to his colleagues in wisdom and virtue (*τὴν δὲ τοῦ πλήθους προστασίαν δίδοσθαι διὰ παντὸς τῷ δοκοῦντι τῶν ἱερέων φρονήσει καὶ ἀρετῇ προέχειν*). They call this man the High Priest (*ἀρχιερέα*), and believe him to be a messenger to them of God's commandments'.[5]

4. The same mode of central government, echoing an archaic model, is manifest throughout the Qumran documents. 'They . . . shall unite . . . under the authority of the sons of Zadok, the Priests . . ., and of the multitude of the men of the Community' (1QS 5:2–3). 'These are the men who shall be called to the Council of the Community . . . the tribal chiefs and all the Judges and officers, the chiefs of Thousands . . . these are . . . the members of the assembly summoned to the Council of the Community in Israel before the sons of Zadok, the Priests' (1QSa 1:27–2:3).

4a. See Hengel, *Judaism and Hellenism* II, p. 21, n. 178. But see A. Kindler, IEJ 24 (1974), pp. 73–6, and D. Jeselsohn, *ibid.*, pp. 77–8.

5. Hecataeus, in Diodorus xl, 3 (preserved in Photius, *Cod.* 244; for the text, see F. Jacoby, FGrH III A 264, F. 6 and especially Stern, GLAJJ I, p. 26; cf. translation and commentary on pp. 28, 31. On the question of authenticity, see Stern, pp. 23–4, and vol. III, §33 of this work. Hecataeus appears not to regard the office of High Priest as hereditary (cf. also *Letter of Aristeas*, §98: *ὁ κριθεὶς ἄξιος*). In fact, as a general rule it passed in the Greek period from father to son. Cf. Stern, *op. cit.*, p. 31.

The first mention of the Jewish *γερουσία* occurs in Josephus in the time of Antiochus the Great (223–187 B.C.).[6] Its aristocratic character is suggested by the title itself.[7] Its powers must have been fairly extensive. For the Hellenistic kings left considerable freedom to the cities in internal affairs and were content as long as taxes were paid and their sovereignty acknowledged. At the head of the Jewish state, and therefore of the *Gerousia*, stood the hereditary High Priest. These two together directed the country's internal affairs.

As a result of the Maccabaean uprising, the old high-priestly dynasty was ousted and replaced by the new—and from Simon onwards equally hereditary—High Priesthood of the Hasmonaeans. The old *Gerousia* must also have undergone a substantial transformation through the removal of its Hellenophile elements. But the institution itself continued, even side by side and under Hasmonaean princes and High Priests; for these too dared not push the Jerusalem nobility entirely to one side. There is in consequence mention of the *Gerousia* during the time of Judas (2 Mac. 1:10; 4:44; 11:27; cf. 1 Mac. 7:33, *πρεσβύτεροι τοῦ λαοῦ*); of Jonathan (1 Mac. 12:6, *γερουσία τοῦ ἔθνους*; 11:23, *οἱ πρεσβύτεροι Ἰσραήλ*; 12:35, *οἱ πρεσβύτεροι τοῦ λαοῦ*); and of Simon (1 Mac. 13:36; 14:20, 28).[8] Its existence is assumed also in the Book of Judith which dates probably to the same period (Jud. 4:8; 11:14; 15:8). The assumption of the royal title by the Hasmonaean princes, and in particular the autocratic rule of Alexander Jannaeus, mark an advance towards pure monarchic rule, as was very sharply emphasized by the Jewish embassy which complained to Pompey on precisely this account.[9] Yet the old *Gerousia*

6. *Ant.* xii 3, 3 (138). On the question of the authenticity of this letter see especially E. Bickermann, 'La charte séleucide de Jérusalem', REJ 100 (1935), p. 4, and Loeb *Josephus*, vol. VII, App. D. Concerning a possible reference to the *Gerousia* in Ecclus. 33:27 (Gr. 30:27), see Hengel, *Judaism and Hellenism* II, p. 21, n.176.

7. A *γερουσία* always denotes a non-democratic body. The Council of Sparta in particular is described as such, and so too were those in the Doric states generally. See RE VII, 1264–8; for the Hellenistic and Roman periods (when, however, they exercised no general powers), A. H. M. Jones, *The Greek City* (1940), pp. 225–6; J. H. Oliver, *The Sacred Gerusia*, Hesperia Supp. VI (1941).

8. It is interesting to compare 1 Mac. 12:6 with 1 Mac. 14:20. It deals with the correspondence between the Jews and the Spartans. In the former passage, 1 Mac. 12:6 = *Ant.* xiii 5, 8 (166), the Jews are represented as taking the initiative: *Ἰωνάθαν ἀρχιερεὺς καὶ ἡ γερουσία τοῦ ἔθνους καὶ οἱ ἱερεῖς καὶ ὁ λοιπὸς δῆμος τῶν Ἰουδαίων.* The Spartans' reply runs as follows (1 Mac. 14:20): *Σίμωνι ἱερεῖ μεγάλῳ καὶ τοῖς πρεσβυτέροις καὶ τοῖς ἱερεῦσι καὶ τῷ λοιπῷ δήμῳ τῶν Ἰουδαίων.* Observe (1) that *ἡ γερουσία* and *οἱ πρεσβύτεροι* are identical; (2) that in both cases the classification is of four categories: High Priest, *Gerousia*, priests, people.

9. Diodorus xl 2 = Stern, GLAJJ I, pp. 185–7: *ἀπεφήναντο τοὺς προγόνους ἑαυτῶν ἀφεστηκότας τοῦ ἱεροῦ πεπρεσβευκέναι πρὸς τὴν σύγκλητον, καὶ παρειληφέναι τὴν προστασίαν τῶν Ἰουδαίων ἐλευθέρων καὶ αὐτονόμων, οὐ βασιλέως χρηματίζοντος ἀλλ' ἀρχιερέως <τοῦ> προεστηκότος τοῦ ἔθνους. τούτους δὲ νῦν δυναστεύειν καταλελυκότας τοὺς πατρίους νόμους*

still asserted itself. There is in any case explicit reference during the reign of Alexandra to τῶν Ἰουδαίων οἱ πρεσβύτεροι.[10] From then on, increasing numbers of scribes also entered the *Gerousia*. For the transfer of power to the Pharisees cannot have taken place without a corresponding reformation of the *Gerousia*. Thereafter, the constitution of the Sanhedrin represented a compromise between the nobility on the one hand—lay and priestly—and Pharisaic learning on the other.[11]

In the reorganization set in train by Pompey, the monarchy was abolished. The High Priest was nevertheless given the προστασία τοῦ ἔθνους, *Ant.* xx 10, 4 (244) and, to begin with, the position of the *Gerousia* was therefore also not substantially altered.[12] On the other hand, the prevailing system was seriously affected when Gabinius (57–55 B.C.) divided the Jewish territory into five σύνοδοι, *B.J.* i 8, 5 (170) or συνέδρια, *Ant.* xiv 5, 4 (91). As three of the five *synedria* (Jerusalem, Gazara and Jericho) were situated in Judaea proper, the sphere of influence of the council in Jerusalem, if it retained anything of its previous character, covered only about a third of Judaea itself. But this measure probably meant more than a simple limitation of jurisdiction, for it is described by Josephus as a thorough transformation of the political situation: though it is not made quite clear whether the five areas were fiscal or judicial (*conventus iuridici*) districts, or both at once.[13]

The rearrangement for which Gabinius was responsible lasted not longer than about ten years. In 47 B.C. Caesar reappointed Hyrcanus II ethnarch of the Jews (cf. vol. I, p. 271), and from an episode belonging to that period, namely that the young Herod had to answer before the

---

καὶ καταδεδουλῶσθαι τοὺς πολίτας ἀδίκως· μισθοφόρων καὶ πλήθει καὶ αἰκίαις καὶ πολλοῖς φόνοις ἀσεβέσι περιπεποιῆσθαι τὴν βασιλείαν. Cf. *Ant.* xiv 3, 2 (58).

10. *Ant.* xiii 16, 5 (428). In Tyre and Sidon, for example, a senate may also have operated—side by side with the king—up to and including the Persian period. See F. C. Movers, *Die Phönizier* II, 1 (1849), pp. 529–42; E. Kuhn, *Die städtische und bürgerl. Verfassung* II (1865), p. 117; A. von Gutschmid, *Kleine Schriften* II (1889), p. 72; but cf. S. Moscati, *I Fenici e Cartagine* (1972), ch. 3, especially pp. 657 f.

11. On the history of the *Gerousia* under the Hasmonaean princes, see J. Wellhausen, *Israelitische und jüdische Geschichte* ([9]1958), pp. 267–71; E. Lohse, 'Synedrion', TDNT VII, pp. 862–3.

12. In the Psalms of Solomon, which were mainly composed in the time of Pompey, the author refers to any person or party he dislikes as ἵνα τί σὺ βέβηλε κάθησαι ἐν συνεδρίῳ ὁσίων (Pss. of Sol. 4:1). Since it is clear from the context that συνέδριον is understood to mean a court of justice, it may possibly refer to the *Gerousia*. But in view of the ambiguity of the expression and of the impossibility of fixing a more exact date to the composition of the Psalm, little historical information is to be gleaned from this passage. Any light to be obtained from it must come from circumstances already known to us.

13. Cf. vol. I, pp. 268–9.

συνέδριον in Jerusalem for his actions in Galilee, *Ant.* xiv 9, 3–5 (165–79), it emerges that the competence of the council in Jerusalem reached once more as far as Galilee. It should be emphasized that the term συνέδριον is used here for the first time, and henceforward repeatedly, to denote the Jerusalem council. Since it is not usually applied to Greek city councils, the usage is somewhat peculiar, but is probably to be explained by the fact that the Jerusalem council was primarily regarded as a court of law (בית דין). Indeed, this is the sense given to συνέδριον in later Greek usage.[14]

Herod the Great began his reign by executing all the members of the Sanhedrin, *Ant.* xiv 9, 4 (175), πάντας ἀπέκτεινε τοὺς ἐν τῷ συνεδρίῳ. Whether 'all' is to be taken literally remains an open question. Elsewhere, it is stated instead that he executed forty-five of the most prominent supporters of Antigonus, *Ant.* xv 1, 2 (5), ἀπέκτεινε δὲ

14. Hesychius, *Lexicon* s.v. defines συνέδριον precisely by the term δικαστήριον (court of justice). In the Septuagint of Prov. 22:10, συνέδριον = דין. Cf. also Pss. of Sol. 4:1. Again, in the New Testament, συνέδριον means simply 'court of justice' (Mt. 10:17, Mk. 13:9); similarly in the Mishnah (see especially mSanh. 1:5, סנהדרין לשבטים = courts for the tribes, and 1:6; סנהדרין קטנה = an inferior court of justice). Stephanus in his *Thesaurus.*, s.v. correctly observes: 'praecipue ita vocatur consessus iudicum'. It is true that in itself συνέδριον is a very general term and may be applied to any 'assembly' or corporate body, e.g. the Roman senate, see H. J. Mason, *Greek Terms for Roman Institutions* (1974), p. 89. Also, in many Greek cities the members of the city council are occasionally called οἱ συνέδροι, e.g. TDNT VII, p. 861, in Dyme in Achaia (Dittenberger, SIG³ 684); so also in Akraephia in Boetia (IG VII 4138, cf. parallels listed in BCH 14 (1890), pp. 17 f.). For this use of the term elsewhere see RE IVA, cols. 1345–6. But the expression is comparatively seldom used for city councils, for which, as is known, the designations βουλή and γερουσία predominate. It is used more often to denote representative assemblies composed of deputies from various constituencies; see RE IV A, pp. 1333–45; J. A. O. Larsen, *Representative Government in Greek and Roman History* (1955); *Greek Federal States* (1968). So we have for example, the συνέδριον of the Phoenicians, which usually met in Tripolis (Diodorus xvi 41); the κοινὸν συνέδριον of ancient Lycia, which was composed of representatives from twenty-three towns, Strabo, xiv 3, 3 (664–5); the συνέδριον κοινόν of the province of Asia (Aristides, *Or.* xxvi Dindorf, xli Keil, 103); the assemblies of the Achaian, Phocian, and Boeotian federation (Pausanias vii 16, 9). For this reason too we find σύνεδροι and βουλευταί mentioned separately on an inscription at Balbura in Pisidia, IGR III 473. Moreover, the *senatores* of the four Macedonian districts, who according to Livy were called *synedri* (45, 32, 1) were not city councillors, but deputies representing an entire *regio* (see Larsen, *Greek Federal States*, pp. 295 f.). As the term in question is first used in relation to Judaea in the time of Gabinius, and is later applied to the council of Jerusalem as well, one might be inclined to suppose that it had been introduced in connection with the Gabinian measures of reform, and that it continued to be used in changed conditions. But in view of the fact that the term is otherwise generally used, even in Hebrew, in the sense of a 'court of justice', this explanation can only be a hypothesis. Cf. A. D. Momigliano, *Ricerche sull' organizzazione della Giudea sotto il dominio romano (63 a.c.–70 d.c.)*, Ann. Sc. Norm. Sup. Pisa II 2, 3 (1934) (repr. 1967), p. 6.

τεσσαράκοντα πέντε τοὺς πρώτους ἐκ τῆς αἱρέσεως Ἀντιγόνου. Be this as it may, the purpose of the measure was either to eliminate the old nobility hostile to him, or so to intimidate them that they would ally themselves to the new ruler. It was of these submissive elements, among whom were also a number of Pharisees who saw in the despot's government a well-deserved divine punishment, that the new Sanhedrin was formed. For there is explicit evidence of its existence under Herod insofar as the 'council' (συνέδριον) before which the elderly Hyrcanus was charged can only have been the Sanhedrin.[15]

After Herod's death Archelaus was awarded only part of his father's realm, the provinces of Judaea and Samaria. With this, the competence of the Sanhedrin was undoubtedly also restricted to Judaea proper (cf. above p. 198). The same state of affairs prevailed under the Roman governors. However, during their administration the country's internal affairs were handled by the Sanhedrin to a greater extent than under Herod and Archelaus. Josephus indicates this specifically when he observes that after the death of Herod and Archelaus, 'the constitution of the state was aristocratic' (ἀριστοκρατία . . . ἦν ἡ πολιτεία) under the leadership of the High Priests.[16] He consequently regards the aristocratic senate of Jerusalem as the real governing institution in contrast to the previous monarchic rule of the Herodians.

In the New Testament the συνέδριον of Jerusalem also frequently appears as the supreme Jewish court, in particular as the supreme Jewish court of justice (Mt. 5:22, 26, 59; Mk. 14:55; 15:1; Lk. 22:66; Jn. 11:47; Act. 4:15; 5:21 ff.; 6:12 ff. 22:30; 23:1 ff.; 24:20). In place of συνέδριον, expressions πρεσβυτέριον (Lk. 22:66; Act. 22:5) and γερουσία (Act. 5:21) are also used.[17] A member of this body, Joseph of Arimathea, is called βουλευτής in Mk. 15:43=Lk. 23:20. Josephus designates the supreme court of Jerusalem the συνέδριον [18] or

15. *Ant.* xv 6, 2 (173). Cf. A. Schalit, *König Herodes* (1969), pp. 43–8.

16. *Ant.* xx 10, 5 (251). As throughout the whole section it is strictly the High Priests who are involved (and of whom only one was in office at a time), it follows that the word ἀρχιερεῖς is to be taken as the categorical plural, so that the meaning would be that the προστασία τοῦ ἔθνους was in the hands of the then High Priest.

17. A striking feature of the last-mentioned passage (Act. 5:21) is the formula τὸ συνέδριον καὶ πᾶσαν τὴν γερουσίαν τῶν υἱῶν Ἰσραήλ. As there can be no question of the identity of the two concepts συνέδριον and γερουσία, only two possibilities exist: either καί is to be taken as explanatory, or it must be assumed that the author wrongly held that the Sanhedrin was of a less comprehensive character than the *Gerousia* ('the Sanhedrin and all the elders of the people together'). The wording would suggest the latter. Cf. however, E. Haenchen, *The Acts of the Apostles, in loc.*

18. See *Ant.* xiv 9, 3 (167); 9, 4, (168, 170–72, 175); 9, 5 (177–78, 180); xv 6, 2 (173), xx 9, 1 (200); *Vita* 12 (62). The latter passage reads: τὸ συνέδριον τῶν Ἱεροσολυμιτῶν. Cf. Lohse, TDNT VII, pp. 861–2. It is possible that the supreme Sanhedrin is intended in *Ant.* xx 9, 6 (216–8) also; cf. L. H. Feldman's note *a, b*, in *Josephus* (Loeb) IX, pp. 504–5.

βουλή,[19] or refers to the court and people under the comprehensive title of 'the community' (*τὸ κοινόν*).[20] In the Mishnah the supreme court of law is known as 'the Great Tribunal' (בית דין הגדול),[21] or 'the Great Sanhedrin' (סנהדרין גדולה),[22] and also as 'the Sanhedrin of Seventy-one' (סנהדרין של שבעים ואחד)[23] or simply 'the Sanhedrin' (סנהדרין).[24]

This terminological diversity lies at the basis of the theory first elaborated by A. Büchler,[25] and adopted with or without modifications by a number of scholars,[26] according to which 'the Great Tribunal', 'the Great Sanhedrin' and 'the Sanhedrin of Seventy-one' allude in rabbinic documents to an institution concerned exclusively with religious matters, Temple worship and the interpretation of religious law. It was dominated either by the Sadducees or the Pharisees. The *συνέδριον* of the Greek sources (consisting essentially of priests) is to be distinguished from this body. It was a council involved with Temple matters as well as with politics. Finally, distinct from both, the *βουλή* was the administrative institution of the city of Jerusalem and its inhabitants.[27]

19. *B.J.* ii 15, 6 (331) *τούς τε ἀρχιερεῖς καὶ τὴν βουλήν*. *B.J.* ii 16, 2 (336) *Ἰουδαίων οἵ τε ἀρχιερεῖς ἅμα τοῖς δυνατοῖς καὶ ἡ βουλή*. *B.J.* ii 17, 1 (405) *οἱ ἄρχοντες καὶ βουλευταί*. Cf. *Ant.* xx 1, 2 (11); *B.J.* v 13, 1 (532). The place of assembly is called *βουλή* in *B.J.* v 4, 2 (144); *βουλευτήριον* in *B.J.* vi 6, 3 (354).

20. *Vita* 12 12 (65); 13 (72); 38 (190); 46 (254); 52 (267); 60 (309); 65 (341); 70 (393). On Josephus's usage see especially V. A. Tcherikover, IEJ 14 (1964), pp. 61–75, especially 67–73.

21. mSot. 1:4; 9:1. mGit. 6:7; mSanh. 11:2, 4; mHor. 1:5. In most of these passages the phrase, 'that is in Jerusalem' (שבירושלים), is added.

22. mSanh. 1:6; mMid. 5:4. As the term סנהדרין is borrowed from the Greek, so in Palmyrene inscriptions we read: בולא ודמוס = *ἡ βουλὴ καὶ ὁ δῆμος*. See e.g. C. Dunant, *Le sanctuaire de Baalshamin à Palmyre* III*: les inscriptions* (1971), nos. 44B; 45B; 48B; C. F. Jean, J. Hoftijzer, *Dictionnaire des inscriptions sémitiques de l'Ouest* (1965), pp. 33, 59.

23. mShebu. 2:2.

24. mSot. 9:11; mKid. 4:5; mSanh. 4:3. The word סנהדרין (with various meanings) also occurs frequently, especially in the Targums. See J. Levy, *Chald. Wörterb.*, s.v.; S. Krauss, *Griechische und lateinische Lehnwörter im Talmud* II (1899), pp. 401–2.

25. *Das Synedrion in Jerusalem* (1902), pp. 193–4, 227, 232.

26. J. Z. Lauterbach, 'Sanhedrin', JE XI, pp. 41–4. (The Great Sanhedrin = *Gerousia* = political body, presided over by the High Priest; the other, the Great *Beth Din* = a religious assembly.) S. Zeitlin, *Who crucified Jesus?* ([4]1964), pp. 68–83 (political Sanhedrin and Great *Beth Din*; the former lost its capital jurisdiction in A.D. 6, but the letter retained it in the religious domain until A.D. 70). H. Mantel, *Studies in the History of the Sanhedrin* (1961), pp. 61–101 (a detailed survey of the two Sanhedrins thesis, approved by the author). See also E. Rivkin, 'Beth Din, Boulé, Sanhedrin', HUCA 46 (1975), pp. 181–99.

27. The three Sanhedrins hypothesis advanced by A. Geiger, 'Mechilta und Sifre', JZWL 4 (1866), pp. 117–8, and adopted by J. Derenbourg, *Essai*, pp. 90–3, is based on the assumption that separate courts existed for priests, Levites and Israelites. Each consisted of twenty-three members. Matters of

Although the thesis of two or three Sanhedrins offers at first sight a satisfactory solution to the conflict between Greek and rabbinic sources, it is not without serious weaknesses. There is no valid reason to distinguish with Büchler between סנהדרין and *συνέδριον* (both the terms and their semantic contents are identical). Neither is it permissible in the light of the sources to define *βουλή* as a judicial, and *συνέδριον* as a governmental institution. Büchler and his followers assume that the situation described in the Mishnah—a bench of experts deciding on points of rabbinic law—applies also to the Sanhedrin during the era of the Second Temple.[28] But this hypothesis is far from being solidly established.

Two further points are to be borne in mind. (1) The 'Sanhedrin of Seventy-one' of the Mishnah is described as possessing powers belonging not to a college of religious experts, but to a body at the same time judicial, administrative and governmental. It judges the High Priest (but not the king who is above the court), it decides on boundary changes and declares war.[29] (2) Neither the Greek sources (Josephus, Philo and the New Testament) nor the rabbinic, seem to be aware of a plurality of institutions. Such a plurality is attested only in the conjectures advanced by modern scholars with a view to defending the historicity of all the rabbinic data. In the light of these considerations the only legitimate conclusion is that if by 'the Great Sanhedrin' is meant a body officially recognized by the occupying power and endowed with competence in judicial and administrative matters and in legal exegesis, this was a single institution under the presidency of the High Priest (in the absence of a king). Any other theory creates more difficulties than it resolves.[30]

---

general concern were discussed by the three jointly under the presidency and vice-presidency of the High Priest—the *Nasi*—and the *Ab Beth Din*, forming a court of seventy-one judges. Cf. Mantel, *op. cit.*, pp. 58–60.

28. The principal difficulty arises from the apparent lack of awareness on the part of the Tannaim of the plurality of religious parties in the Second Temple era, entailing multiple orthodoxies as well as unavoidable reciprocal toleration. Each no doubt possessed its own court/academy which elaborated its particular brand of *halakhah*. The rabbinic heirs of the Pharisees, who emerged as the sole recognized authority after A.D. 70, envisaged the situation preceding the end of the Jewish state as essentially identical with the new regime, and claimed that the *Sanhedrin*-Senate, like the academy/*Beth Din*, was under the only legitimate leadership of the *Zugoth* followed by the dynasty of Hillel and his successors.

29. mSanh. 1:5.

30. Cf. also S. Safrai, 'Jewish Self-Government', *The Jewish People in the First Century* I, pp. 381–2. Once more the situation described by the Dead Sea Scrolls may be illuminating. The Community was governed by a 'council' composed of priests and lay leaders. This single body dealt with administration, authoritative teachings and the dispensation of justice, and was expected to conduct the final

After the destruction of Jerusalem in A.D. 70, the Sanhedrin ceased to exist in its previous form. The relatively large degree of self-government hitherto exercised by the Jewish people could no longer be allowed after so violent an insurrection. With the fall of the Jewish capital city, the Jewish court was also brought to an end: the Romans now took over the powers of government directly into their own hands. The Jewish people soon created for themselves a new centre in the so-called court (בית דין) of Yavneh.[31] But this court/academy was essentially different from the old Sanhedrin; instead of a political senate, it was a tribunal whose decisions were at first of only theoretical significance. And although this new institution also soon acquired considerable authority over the Jews and exercised jurisdiction over them, partly with Roman consent and partly without it,[32] rabbinic Judaism was nevertheless fully aware that the old Sanhedrin had ceased to exist.[33]

---

war. It was also a legislative body and hoped, as soon as the Community had gained the leadership of the nation, to impose its legal doctrine on the whole people of Israel. Cf. G. Vermes, *DSSE*, pp. 16–23, and *DSS*, pp. 87–115.

31. See especially mR. Sh. 2:8–9; 4:1–2; mSanh. 11:4; cf. also mBekh. 4:5; 6:8; mKel. 5:4; mPar. 7:6. Cf. vol. I, pp. 514–28. This centre of rabbinic Judaism was transferred in the second century A.D. to Galilee. Its seats were at Usha, Beth Shearim, Sepphoris and Tiberias. Cf. Mantel, *op. cit.*, pp. 140–74. See M. Avi-Yonah, *The Jews of Palestine. A Political History from the Bar Kokhba War to the Arab Conquest* (1976), pp. 15–25.

32. Origen, *Epist. ad Africanum* 14 (PG XI, cols. 82–4): *Καὶ νῦν γοῦν Ῥωμαίων βασιλευόντων καὶ Ἰουδαίων τὸ δίδραχμον αὐτοῖς τελούντων, ὅσα συγχωροῦντος Καίσαρος ὁ ἐθνάρχης παρ' αὐτοῖς δύναται, ὡς μηδὲν διαφέρειν βασιλεύοντος τοῦ ἔθνους, ἴσμεν οἱ πεπειραμένοι. Γίνεται δὲ καὶ κριτήρια λεληθότως κατὰ τὸν νόμον, καὶ καταδικάζονταί τινες τὴν ἐπὶ τῷ θανάτῳ, οὔτε μετὰ τῆς πάντη εἰς τοῦτο παρρησίας, οὔτε μετὰ τοῦ λανθάνειν τὸν βασιλεύοντα. Καὶ τοῦτο ἐν τῇ χώρᾳ τοῦ ἔθνους πολὺν διατρίψαντες χρόνον μεμαθήκαμεν καὶ πεπληροφορήμεθα.* See J. Juster, *Les Juifs* II, p. 151. Cf. Th. Mommsen, *Römisches Strafrecht* (1899), p. 120 ('The Jewish procedure for capital charges provides the most remarkable proof of the toleration even of institutions running counter to Roman ordinances during the time of imperial rule'). Origen himself had contact with a Patriarch Iullos *('Ἰούλλῳ τῷ πατριάρχῃ)* from whom he had received instruction on exegetical questions (*Selecta in Psalmos*, Preface, PG XII, col. 1056). The name is given as 'Huillus' in Jerome (*Contra Rufinum* i, 13, PL XXIII, cols. 407–8: 'certe etiam Origenes Patriarchen Huillum qui temporibus eius fuit nominat . . . secundum Huilli expositionem'). The individual in question is identified as Hillel, brother of the Patriarch Judah II (H. Graetz, MGWJ (1881), pp. 433 ff.; M. Avi-Yonah, *The Jews of Palestine* (1976), p. 150) or as Judah II himself (cf. W. Bacher, JE VII, p. 338). N. R. M. de Lange argues, however, that Ioullos was the head of the Jewish Community of Alexandria (*Origen and the Jews* (1976), pp. 23–5). On Jewish jurisdiction after A.D. 70, see J. Juster, *Les Juifs* II, pp. 90–106, 108–9, 112–5, 151–2.

33. mSot. 9:11: 'Since the Sanhedrin ceased (משבטלה סנהדרין) all singing ceased at the wedding feasts; as it is written, 'They shall not drink wine with a song. . . ." (Isa. 24:9)'.

2. *The Composition of the Sanhedrin*

The Mishnah and the Talmud represent the Great Sanhedrin, by analogy with later rabbinical courts of justice, as a council composed exclusively of scholars. This was certainly never the case until the destruction of Jerusalem. From the unanimous testimony of Josephus and the New Testament, it is quite clear that the high-priestly aristocracy, supported by distinguished laymen, stood at the head of the Sanhedrin until the end. All the changes of the time were therefore unable to destroy the original nature of the Sanhedrin—which was that of a representation of the nobility, not a council of scholars. But the growing influence of the Pharisees could not in the long run fail to affect its composition; the more they gained in prestige, the more the priestly aristocracy was obliged to allow them a place. The process no doubt began under Alexandra and made particular advances under Herod. For the latter's ruthless treatment of the old nobility must necessarily have been to the Pharisees' advantage. Thus the Sanhedrin of the Roman period consisted in a mixture of aristocratic—priestly and lay—Sadducees and learned Pharisees. Such is the context in which the data surviving in the ancient sources must be viewed.

According to the Mishnah, the number of members was seventy-one, after the model, obviously, of the council of elders constituted in the time of Moses (Num. 11:16).[34] From the two statements in *Ant.* xiv 9, 4 (175)—(that Herod killed all the members of the Sanhedrin on his accession to the throne) and *Ant.* xv 1, 2 (5)—that he killed forty-five of the most prominent members of the supporters of Antigonus—one might be inclined to deduce that the number of members was forty-five. But the term 'all' (πάντας) is assuredly not to be taken literally. On the other hand, there is much to support the count of seventy-one. The colony of Babylonian Jews in Batanaea was represented by seventy distinguished men.[35] When Josephus organized the uprising in Galilee,

34. mSanh. 1:6: 'The Great Sanhedrin consisted of 71 members'. Cf. mSanh. 1:5; 2:4. 'The Sanhedrin of 71' is also mentioned in mShebu. 2:2. In several other passages we read of 72 elders (mZeb. 1:3; mYad. 3:5; 4:2). But these have nothing to do with the present matter. (In all three passages, R. Simeon ben Azai appeals to traditions he received 'from the mouth of the seventy-two elders on the day when they appointed R. Eleazar ben Azariah head of the school'. There is therefore no question here of the Great Sanhedrin but of the academy of Yavneh and the deposition of Gamaliel II. Cf. R. Goldenberg, 'The Deposition of Rabban Gamaliel II', JJS 23 (1972), pp. 167–90. Equally irrelevant are the supposed seventy-two translators (six from each of the twelve tribes), of the Hebrew Bible into Greek. Cf. Letter of Aristeas (ed. Wendland), § 46–51. Why the seventy-two should have produced the version of the seventy is yet another matter. Cf. also B. M. Metzger, 'Seventy or Seventy-two Disciples?', NTSt 5 (1958–9), pp. 299–306.

35. *B.J.* ii 18, 6 (482); *Vita* 11 (56).

he placed seventy elders in charge of the administration of the province.[36] Similarly, after suppressing the existing authorities, the Zealots in Jerusalem established a tribunal of seventy members.[37] In Alexandria too, the council of elders is said to have consisted of seventy-one members.[38] This number would therefore seem to have been accepted as the normal one for a Jewish supreme court of justice. Hence the traditions of the Mishnah are in themselves quite probable.[39]

Nothing whatever is known of how appointments to it were made. But from the aristocratic character of this body, it may be presumed that the members were not changed yearly and elected by the people, as in the case of the democratic councils of the Greek cities, but held office for a longer period, perhaps for life, and that new members were appointed either by the existing members or by the supreme political authorities (Herod and the Romans). The Mishnah, too, suggests that vacancies were filled by co-option, in that it considers rabbinical learning as the sole test of a candidate's eligibility.[40] One requirement of Jewish law, anyway, will probably have been observed in the Great Sanhedrin also: namely, that only Israelites of legitimate descent should qualify as judges.[41] Admission took place through the ceremony of the laying on of hands (סמיכת ידים), as in the 'ordination' of Joshua by Moses (Num. 27:18–23, Deut. 34:9).[42]

36. *B.J.* ii 20, 5 (570); cf. *Vita* 14 (79). See vol. I, pp. 489–90.

37. *B.J.* iv 5, 4 (336).

38. tSuk. 4:6: '71 golden chairs were there (in the great synagogue at Alexandria) corresponding to the 71 elders'.

39. On the number seventy in general, see Num. 11:16; Jg. 9:2 (seventy sons of Jerubbaal); 2 Kgs. 10:1 (seventy sons of Ahab). M. Steinschneider, ZDMG 4 (1850), pp. 145–70; 57 (1903), pp. 474–507.

40. mSanh. 4:4.

41. It may be taken for granted that the Sanhedrin was composed exclusively of Jews. However, the Mishnah stipulates further: 'Every man is qualified to try non-capital cases. But only priests, Levites and Israelites who may give their daughters in marriage into the priesthood are qualified to try capital cases' (mSanh. 4:2). These are the first three of the ten classes listed in mKid. 4:1. They are distinguished from, for instance, the *mamzer* (bastard) and the חרור, the emancipated slave, who were not allowed to marry into the priestly stock. The Mishnah seems to presuppose that every member of the Sanhedrin should be of legitimate Israelite descent and that this needed no further confirmation (mKid. 4:5). As the demands of the priesthood and Pharisaism coincided on this point, it is probable that this rule was strictly followed.

42. The verb סמך (to lay on hands) means in the Mishnah 'to install as a judge' (mSanh. 4:4). The ceremony is therefore comparatively very ancient. According to Deut. 34:9, the laying on of hands effected a transmission of the spirit from one to the other, while in Num. 27: 18–23, it obviously has to do with a transfer of office. This was surely the prevailing idea in rabbinical usage also. The laying on of hands was originally performed by individual teachers, but the privilege was later retained either for the Patriarch alone, or in conjunction with his court (ySanh. 19a). The actual rite of the laying on of hands seems to have been discontinued in

In regard to the several categories of members of the Sanhedrin, both the New Testament and Josephus are agreed that the ἀρχιερεῖς were the real leading personalities. In almost every instance in which the New Testament enumerates the several categories, the ἀρχιερεῖς are mentioned first.[43] Sometimes *οἱ ἄρχοντες* is substituted as an alternative.[44] This is in particular the case with Josephus, who designates the supreme authorities in Jerusalem either by combining ἀρχιερεῖς with δυνατοί, γνώριμοι, and βουλή,[45] or by selecting ἄρχοντες instead of the former expression,[46] but never so that ἀρχιερεῖς appears with ἄρχοντες.

---

the second century A.D.—the term used thereafter was מנוי = appointment—and ordination itself came to an end at least with the extinction of the Patriarchate in A.D. 425, and possibly earlier. 'When the ceremony of ordination became an official prerogative of the Patriarch, the custom of laying on of hands . . . lost its significance and was abolished' (J. Z. Lauterbach, 'Ordination', JE IX, p. 429). Its disappearance is attributed by some scholars to the adverse effect of the adoption of the rule by Christians, cf. Lauterbach, JE IX, p. 429. See also L. Löw, *Gesammelte Schriften* IV (1898), p. 215. Cf. generally on the rabbinic סמיכה, A. Epstein, 'Ordination et autorisation', REJ 46 (1903), pp. 197–211. J. Z. Lauterbach, 'Ordination', JE IX (1905), pp. 428–30. J. Coppens, *L'imposition des mains et les rites connexes dans le Nouveau Testament et dans l'église ancienne* (1925); J. Newman, *Semikhah (Ordination): A Study of its Origin, History and Function* (1950); E. Lohse, *Die Ordination im Spätjudentum und N.T.* (1951); D. Daube, 'The Laying on of Hands', *The New Testament and Rabbinic Judaism* (1956), pp. 224–46; H. Mantel, *Studies in the History of the Sanhedrin* (1961), pp. 38, 206–21; *idem*, 'Ordination and Appointment in the Period of the Temple', HThR 57 (1964), pp. 325–46; S. Zeitlin, 'The Semikah Controversy between the School of Shammai and Hillel', JQR 56 (1966), pp. 240–4, A Rofe, 'Semikhah', Enc. Jud. 14 (1971), cols. 1140–7.

43. The following formulae occur: (1) ἀρχιερεῖς, γραμματεῖς and πρεσβύτεροι (or with the two latter in reverse order): Mt. 27:41; Mk. 11:27; 14:43, 53; 15:1. (2) ἀρχιερεῖς and γραμματεῖς Mt. 2:4; 20:18; 21:15; Mk. 10:33; 11:18; 14:1; 15:31; Lk. 22:2; 66; 23:10. (3) ἀρχιερεῖς and πρεσβύτεροι Mt. 21:33; 26:3; 47; 27:1, 3, 12, 20; 28: 11–12; Act. 4:23; 23:14; 25:15. (4) οἱ ἀρχιερεῖς καὶ τὸ συνέδριον ὅλον Mt. 26:59; Mk. 14:55; Act. 22:30. Thus as a rule the ἀρχιερεῖς are mentioned first. The instances in which this is not the case (Mt. 16:21; Mk. 8:31 = Lk. 9:22; Lk. 20:19) or in which they are omitted altogether (Mt. 28:57; Act. 6:12) are extremely rare.

44. See especially Act. 4:5, 8 (ἄρχοντες, πρεσβύτεροι and γραμματεῖς) compared with 4:23 (ἀρχιερεῖς and πρεσβύτεροι). On a few occasions οἱ ἀρχιερεῖς καὶ οἱ ἄρχοντες also occur together (Lk. 23:13; 24:20).

45. *B.J.* ii 14, 8 (301): οἵ τε ἀρχιερεῖς καὶ δυνατοὶ τό τε γνωριμώτατον τῆς πόλεως. *B.J.* ii 15, 2 (316): οἱ δυνατοὶ σὺν τοῖς ἀρχιερεῦσι. *B.J.* ii 15, 3 (318): τοὺς ἀρχιερεῖς σὺν τοῖς γνωρίμοις. *B.J.* ii 15, 6 (331): τούς τε ἀρχιερεῖς καὶ τὴν βουλήν. *B.J.* ii 16, 2 (336): οἵ τε ἀρχιερεῖς ἅμα τοῖς δυνατοῖς καὶ ἡ βουλή. *B.J.* ii, 17, 2 (410): τῶν τε ἀρχιερέων καὶ τῶν γνωρίμων. *B.J.* ii, 17, 3 (411): οἱ δυνατοὶ τοῖς ἀρχιερεῦσιν καὶ τοῖς τῶν Φαρισαίων γνωρίμοις. *B.J.* ii 17, 5 (422): οἱ δυνατοὶ σὺν τοῖς ἀρχιερεῦσι. *B.J.* ii 17, 6 (428): τῶν δυνατῶν καὶ τῶν ἀρχιερέων.

46. *B.J.* ii 16, 1 (333): οἱ τῶν Ἱεροσολύμων ἄρχοντες. *B.J.* ii 17, 1 (405): οἵ τε ἄρχοντες καὶ οἱ βουλευταί. *B.J.* ii 17, 1 (407): τοὺς ἄρχοντας ἅμα τοῖς δυνατοῖς. *B.J.* ii 21, 7 (627): οἱ δυνατοὶ καὶ τῶν ἀρχόντων τινές.

On the other hand, the ἀρχιερεῖς often stand alone as the leading personalities in the Sanhedrin.[47] However difficult it now is to determine the exact significance of this term (see below, pp. 233–6), there can at all events be no doubt that they were the most prominent representatives of the priesthood. The conduct of affairs therefore still remained in their hands. But the γραμματεῖς, the professional lawyers, also exercised a considerable influence in the Sanhedrin. Other members belonging to neither of these two special categories were known simply as πρεσβύτεροι, a general designation applicable to both priests and laymen (on these two categories, see the New Testament passages quoted in n. 43).

Now since the ἀρχιερεῖς belonged predominantly, if not exclusively, to the party of the Sadducees,[48] and the γραμματεῖς just as predominantly to that of the Pharisees, it follows that Sadducees and Pharisees alike sat in the Sanhedrin (especially during the Roman-Herodian period, the only one of which anything precise is known). This is also confirmed by explicit literary evidence.[49] In practice, the Pharisees exercised considerable influence during this time, and according to Josephus, their demands were met by the Sadducees, albeit unwillingly, because otherwise the people would not have tolerated them.[50] But whether the Sanhedrin was really dominated by Pharisaism is still under debate.[51]

A remark made by Josephus may be construed as pointing to the existence of an organization peculiar to the Hellenistic-Roman period. He writes that when differences once arose between the Jewish authorities and the procurator Festus about alterations in the Temple buildings, the Jews, with Festus's agreement, sent 'the ten foremost men and the High Priest Ismael and the treasurer Helcias' as envoys to Nero, *Ant.* xx 8, 11 (194): τοὺς πρώτους δέκα καὶ Ἰσμάηλον τὸν ἀρχιερέα καὶ Ἑλκίαν τὸν γαζοφύλακα. If by πρῶτοι δέκα is meant, not the ten most distinguished persons in general, but men holding a specific official position, this would allude to the committee of δέκα πρῶτοι so

47. E.g. *B.J.* ii 15, 3 (322); 16, 3 (342); v 1, 5 (36); vi 9, 3 (422).

48. Act. 5:17; Josephus, *Ant.* xx 9, 1 (199).

49. For the Sadducees, see Act. 4:1 ff.; 5:17; 23:6; Josephus, *Ant.* xx 9, 1 (199). For the Pharisees, see Act. 5:34; 23:6. Cf. Josephus, *B.J.* ii 17, 3 (411); *Vita* 38 (191); 39 (197).

50. *Ant.* xviii 1, 4 (17): 'For whenever they (the Sadducees) assume office, they submit though unwittingly and perforce, to the formulas of the Pharisees, since otherwise the masses would not tolerate them'.

51. Cf. below, pp. 388–403. The link between High Priests and Pharisees so frequently referred to in the New Testament (Mt 21:45; 27:62; Jn. 47:32, 45; 1:47, 57; 18.3) corresponds to the actual state of affairs. This is also the case with Josephus, *B.J.* ii 17, 3 (411): συνελθόντες . . . οἱ δυνατοὶ τοῖς ἀρχιερεῦσιν εἰς ταὐτὸ καὶ τοῖς τῶν Φαρισαίων γνωρίμοις. Cf. also *Vita* 38 (191); 39 (197).

frequently encountered in Greek cities, as is clearly attested in, for example, the constitution of Gerasa and Tiberias (see above, pp. 152, 180). This would be characteristic evidence of the interaction of Jewish and Hellenistic-Roman influences on the organization of the Sanhedrin at that time.[52]

Another sign of this is the לשכת פלהדרין or לשכת פרהדרין mentioned in mYom. 1:1.[53] This לשכה was a hall or chamber in the outer courtyard of the Temple (cf. mYom. 1:5) where the High Priest spent the last seven days before the Day of Atonement. Since בפלהדרותא is parallel with ἐπὶ προέδρου in the bilingual customs tariff of Palmyra (see above, p. 54), here also פלהדרין = πρoέδροι, and as at Palmyra the use of this *terminus technicus* may be seen as proof of Greek influence on the organization of the Sanhedrin.[54] If it is correct that the same hall was also called לשכת בלווטין, 'Hall of the βουλευταί',[55] this would merely serve to confirm the theory concerning Greek influence: πρoέδροι is the more limited idea, βουλευταί the larger. The hall must have been named sometimes one way, sometimes the other. However, cf. below, n. 89.

It should finally be mentioned that Josephus calls the secretary of the court—entirely in the Greek fashion—γραμματεὺς τῆς βουλῆς.[56]

52. 'Ten foremost men' are also met with in the ancient Phoenician cities, as in Carthage (Justin xviii 6, 1: 'decem Poenorum principibus') and Marathus (Diodorus xxxiii 5, 2: τῶν πρεσβυτάτων τοὺς ἐπιφανεστάτους παρὰ τουτοῖς δέκα) cf. A. von Gutschmid, *Kleine Schriften* II (1889), p. 72. Yet these parallels are less obvious than the δέκα πρῶτοι attested in Greek cities in the Imperial period, such as may safely be asserted to have existed in Gerasa and Tiberias. The δέκα πρῶτοι of the city also appear on the bilingual customs tariff of Palmyra (col. I, line 8); see the literature above, p. 64, and vol. I, p. 373. For the δεκάπρωτοι see Jones, *The Greek City* (1940), 139, and for their introductions into Egypt in the Imperial period, E. G. Turner, JEA 32 (1936), pp. 7–19. Their role in the collection of tribute is clearly attested, most recently in an inscription from Iotape, Cilicia, cf. G. E. Bean and T. B. Mitford, *Journeys in Rough Cilicia in* 1962 *and* 1963 (1965), no. 29a.

53. The latter is the correct form given in Cod. de Rossi 138, Cod. Kaufmann, Cod. Munich 95, etc. Cf. J. Meinhold, *Joma* (1913), p. 75.

54. On the πρόεδροι in Greek cities, see RE XXIII.2 (1959), cols. 2303–5. They occur frequently in the Greek cities of Palestine and Syria, e.g. in Gerasa (see above, p. 64); Ascalon (IGR III 1210); Bostra (IGR III 1325 = *Syria* III.A (1921), no. 571, cf. no. 569; Philippopolis in Batanaea (Waddington, *Inscr.*, no. 2072), Kanatha (IGR III 1235), Adraa: IGR III 1286; 1287 = OGIS 615 and 614 also in Tyre, OGIS 595.

55. tYom. 1:1; yYom. 38c; bYom. 8b, J. Levy, *Neuhebr. Wörterb.* I, p. 199 IV, p. 103. A. Büchler, *Das Synedrion*, p. 25. S. Lieberman, *Tosefta ki-Fshuṭah* IV (1962), pp. 717–8.

56. *B.J.* v. 13, 1 (532). On the γραμματεὺς τῆς βουλῆς in Greek cities, see W. Liebenam, *Städteverwaltung im römischen Kaiserreiche* (1900), p. 289; 551; RE VII (1912), cols. 1740–70.

In regard to the presidency of the Sanhedrin, rabbinic tradition, which on the whole identifies the institution as a council of scholars, assumes that the heads of the Pharisaic schools were regularly also Presidents of the Sanhedrin. These heads are enumerated in pairs in the Mishnah tractate Aboth chap. 1 from around the middle of the second century B.C. to about the time of Jesus (see below § 25). And it is also stated, though not in Aboth but in another section of the Mishnah, that the first of each pair was *Nasi* (נשיא), and the second, *Ab-beth-din* (אב בית דין); i.e., according to the employment later of both titles, President and Vice-President of the Sanhedrin.[57] The heads of schools who follow these 'pairs' (זוגות), namely Gamaliel I and his son Simon, are also represented by later tradition as having been Presidents of the Sanhedrin. In all this there is nothing historical.[58] The unanimous testimony of Josephus and the New Testament is that the High Priest was always President of the Sanhedrin. From the nature of things, this was only to be expected. From the beginning of the Greek period, the High Priest was at the same time head of the nation. The Hasmonaean High Priests were simultaneously princes, and even kings. In regard to the Roman period, Josephus expressly indicates that the High Priests were also the political heads of the nation, *Ant.* xx 10, 5 (251): *τὴν προστασίαν τοῦ ἔθνους οἱ ἀρχιερεῖς ἐπεπίστευντο.* In his theoretical descriptions of the Jewish constitution, he invariably speaks of the High Priest as the supreme judge, *C.Ap.* ii 23 (194): The High Priest *φυλάξει τοὺς νόμους, δικάσει περὶ τῶν ἀμφισβητουμένων, κολάσει τοὺς ἐλεγχθέντας ἐπ' ἀδίκου. Ant.* iv, 8, 14 (218): Moses is said to have ordained that if the local courts were unable to decide a case, they should go to Jerusalem, *καὶ συνελθόντες ὅ τε ἀρχιερεὺς καὶ ὁ προφήτης καὶ ἡ γερουσία τὸ δοκοῦν ἀποφαινέστωσαν.* From these statements it must be

57. mHag. 2:2: 'Yose ben Yoezer says: It is not permitted to lay on hands on Feast Days. Yose ben Yohanan allows it. Joshua ben Perahiah decided in the negative, Nittai (or Mattai) in the affirmative, Judah ben Tabbai in the negative, Simeon ben Shetaḥ in the affirmative. Shemaiah in the affirmative, Abtalion in the negative. Hillel and Menahem did not differ in their opinions; when Menahem went out and Shammai came in. Shammai declared himself in the negative, and Hillel in the affirmative. Of these men, the first were always Presidents and the others Vice-Presidents' (הראשונים היו נשיאים ושניהם אבות בית דין). It should be observed that the identification of the *Zugoth* as Presidents and Vice-Presidents of the Sanhedrin is purely incidental, and seems to be aimed at making sense of the mention of teachers two by two.

58. See already A. Geiger, *Urschrift* (1857), p. 116. (The *Zugoth* were the heads of the Pharisaic party; the Tannaim transformed them into the leaders of the Sanhedrin.) W. Bacher, 'Sanhedrin', HDB IV (1902), pp. 400–1; G. F. Moore, *Judaism* I, p. 45, n. 3. For a detailed survey of views, ending with a traditional conclusion, see Mantel, *Studies in the History of the Sanhedrin*, pp. 1–18. For the inconsequential character of the statement in mHag. 2:2, see S. Lieberman, *Tosefta ki-Fshuṭah*, Part V, *Seder Mo'ed* (1962), p. 1297.

concluded that the High Priest acted as President of the Sanhedrin. But there exists in addition the most positive evidence to this effect. Already in the decree declaring the rank of High Priest and prince to be hereditary in the family of Simon Maccabee it was prescribed that no man should be allowed 'to contradict his (Simon's) orders or to convene any assembly in the land without his permission'.[59] In the few cases where Josephus actually refers to sessions of the Sanhedrin, the High Priests are invariably Presidents. Thus in 47 B.C. it was Hyrcanus II,[60] in A.D. 62, the younger Ananus.[61] Likewise, in the New Testament the ἀρχιερεύς appears throughout as the presiding personage.[62] Whenever the President is named, it is the reigning High Priest, Caiaphas at the time of Jesus (Mt. 26:3, 57), and Ananus in the time of Paul (Act. 23:2; 24:1). The trial of Jesus before Annas (Jn. 18), who at that time was of course no longer in office, is no argument to the contrary. For there are indications that this cannot have been a formal trial (cf. p. 225). It matters equally little that Ananus (or Annas) the Younger appears at head of affairs[63] during the war, long after he had been deposed.[64] For this was due to a special popular decree enacted at the outbreak of the revolution.[65] The sole passage that might be interpreted as arguing against the view advanced here is Act. 4:6, where Annas (an ex-High Priest) is said to be President of the Sanhedrin. But the case is the same for this passage as for the parallel text of Lk. 3:2. In both, Annas is mentioned *before* Caiaphas as though he were the High Priest, which he certainly no longer was. Hence just as it is illegitimate to deduce from Luke 3:2 that this was so, it also does not follow from Act. 4:6 that he was President of the Sanhedrin, which would contradict Mt. 26: 56–66. The fact is that in both instances there is a certain amount of inaccuracy. In accord with the hypothesis that the High Priest was President (πρόεδρος, see p. 214) is the tradition that he was obliged to spend the seven days preceding the Day of Atonement in the hall or chamber of the πρόεδροι (פרהדרין). This was in fact his official chamber as distinct from his private residence. That the persons named in rabbinic documents were not Presidents of the Sanhedrin is further evident from the fact that those same men, when mentioned in the New Testament or by Josephus, are always ordinary members: thus Shemaiah (Sameas) in the time of Hyrcanus II,[66] Gamaliel I in the time

59. 1 Mac 14:44.
60. *Ant.* xiv 9, 3–5 (165–77).
61. *Ant.* xx 9, 1 (200).
62. Cf. Act. 5:17 ff.; 7:1; 9:1–2; 22:5; 23:2, 4: 24:1.
63. *Ant.* xx 9, 1 (200).
64. *B.J.* ii, 20, 3 (564); 22, 1 (648); iv 3, 7 (151)—5, 2 (325); *Vita* 38 (193–4); 39 (195–6); 44 (216); 60 (309).
65. *B.J.* ii 20, 3 (563–4).
66. *Ant.* xiv 9, 4 (172–6).

of the Apostles (Act. 5:34, cf. 5:27), and Simon ben Gamaliel in the time of the First Jewish War.[67]

The rabbinic tradition in question is therefore at variance with all the certain historical facts. Furthermore, it is itself of late origin. The one Mishnaic passage in which it occurs, mHag. 2:2, is entirely isolated. Everywhere else, the heads of schools are spoken of simply as heads of schools. It is therefore quite possible that this passage did not find its way into the text of the Mishnah until later.[68]

The titles *Nasi* and *Ab-beth-din* for the President and Vice-President of the Sanhedrin would also seem foreign to the period of the Mishnah.[69] It is true that both *termini* occur there, but *Nasi* always refers to the actual head of state, especially the king, as is expressly asserted on one occasion;[70] and *Ab-beth-din* can hardly be taken to mean anything other than President of the supreme court of justice (and hence of the Sanhedrin). The title *Rosh-beth-din* is given precisely the same significance.[71] It is not until the post-Mishnaic age that the titles *Nasi* and *Ab-beth-din* are so to speak downgraded and transferred to President and Vice-President respectively.[72]

Finally, the so-called מופלא, who on the basis of certain talmudic passages is also frequently mentioned by scholars as a special functionary of the court, was no such thing, but simply the most 'prominent', i.e. most learned, of its ordinary members.[73]

67. *Vita* 38 (191–4); 39 (195–6).

68. Later interpolations in the text of the Mishnah may also be detected elsewhere, for example, at *Aboth* 5:21. Cf. K. Marti, G. Beer, *'Abot* (1927), p. 153. In many MSS and editions the text of mSot. 9:15 is amplified from the Tosefta and the Jerusalem Talmud. Cf. H. Bietenhard, *Soṭa* (1956), pp. 15–17. We may therefore assume that Hagigah 2:2 also was originally transferred from post-Mishnaic sources into the Mishnah text. But it is to be noted that a shorter version of the same passage, omitting the individual names, is also to be found in tHagigah 2:8. I. Jelski, *Die innere Einrichtung des grossen Synedrions zu Jerusalem*, pp. 37–42, does not consider the whole passage, but the decisive words ('Each of the former was a President, and the others chief judges') to be an interpolation in that he recognizes that they stand in complete isolation in the Mishnah.

69. נשיא: mTaan. 2:1; mNed. 5:5; mHor. 2:5–7; 3:1–3 and elsewhere—אב בית דין: mTaan. 2:1; mEdu. 5:6.

70. mHor. 3:3.

71. mR.Sh. 2:7; 4:4.

72. The first rabbinical President of the Sanhedrin to whom the title *Nasi* is applied in the Mishnah is Judah *ha-Nasi* at the end of the second century A.D. (mAb. 2:2). Apart from mHag. 2:2, none of the rabbis who occupied this position before R. Judah is known by the designation *Nasi*. It may therefore be assumed that the title came into use towards the end of the Mishnaic age (cf. Mantel, *Studies*, pp. 39–41). For various theories assigning the first introduction of the title during the first century A.D. (Gamaliel II or Yohanan ben Zakkai, or Hillel), if not earlier, see Mantel, *op. cit.*, pp. 7–39.

73. The expression מופלא של בית דין occurs only once in the Mishnah, mHor. 1:4. This passage determines what is to be done if, in the absence of the מופלא

In sum, it may be held as certain that in the age of Jesus it was always the reigning High Priest, and indeed the High Priest as such, who presided over the Sanhedrin.

3. *The Competence of the Sanhedrin*

As has already been observed (p. 198), the civil authority of the Great Sanhedrin in the time of Jesus was restricted to the eleven toparchies of Judaea proper. It consequently had no judicial authority at all over Jesus whilst he remained in Galilee. He came directly under its jurisdiction only in Judaea. In a sense, of course the Sanhedrin exercised such jurisdiction over all the Jewish communities throughout the world, and in that sense over Galilee too. A measure of moral weight was attached to its decrees throughout the entire domain of traditional Judaism. If Acts is to be believed, the leaders of the community of Damascus in neighbouring Syria were instructed by the High Priest and his council to expel the Christians living amongst them (Act. 9:2; 22:5; 26:12). At the same time, the extent to which Jews outside Judaea were willing to obey the orders of the Sanhedrin always depended on how far they were favourably disposed towards it. It was only within the limits of Judaea proper that it exercised direct power.

Regarding the Sanhedrin's sphere of competence, it would be wholly wrong to define it as a spiritual or theological tribunal in contrast to the secular authority of the Romans. The truth is rather that, as opposed to the foreign domination of the Romans, it constituted the supreme indigenous tribunal which the Romans, here as almost everywhere else, allowed to continue as before, whilst imposing certain limitations on its competence. It was therefore the forum for every judicial decision and every administrative measure which could either not be dealt with by the lesser local courts or was reserved to the Roman governor himself.

The Sanhedrin was above all the final tribunal for decisions on questions connected with the Jewish law: not in the sense that it was possible to appeal against the decisions of the lower courts, but that where the latter could not agree, people could go before the Jerusalem Sanhedrin.[74] But once an issue was decided, the provincial judges of the lower courts were obliged on pain of death to adhere to the Sanhedrin's ruling.[75] According to the theory later recorded in the Mishnah, the following cases fell within the competence of the supreme court: 'A tribe (charged with idolatry) or a false prophet or a High

---

של בית דין i.e. the most distinguished and most eminent member of the council, the court should arrive at an erroneous decision. Cf. Mantel, *op. cit.*, pp. 135–9.

74. *Ant.* iv 8, 14 (218); mSanh. 11:2 (see the passage above, p. 198).

75. mSanh. 11:2.

Priest may not be tried except by the court of Seventy-One. A war of conquest may not be waged except by the decision of the court of Seventy-One. The city (of Jerusalem) or the courts of the Temple may not be enlarged except by the decision of the court of Seventy-One. Sanhedrins for the several tribes may not be established except by command of the court of Seventy-One. A city may be not proclaimed an Apostate City except by the decision of the court of Seventy-One.'[76] The High Priest could therefore be tried by the Sanhedrin.[77] The king by contrast, was not subject to its authority; neither could he become one of its members.[78] All these regulations appear to be purely theoretical, not an expression of real circumstances, but only a recollection of the past, as well perhaps as pious wishes of the Tannaitic masters. Of more value are the facts gleaned from the pages of the New Testament: that Jesus is said to have stood before the Sanhedrin on account of blasphemy (Mt. 26:65; Jn. 19:7); that Peter and John were charged before the Sanhedrin with seduction of the people (Act. 4–5), Stephen with blasphemy (Act. 6:13 ff.) and Paul with breaking the law (Act. 23).[79]

Of particular interest is the question of how far the Sanhedrin's competence was limited by the authority of the Roman governors.[80]

76. mSanh. 1:5. Cf. m. Sanh. 2:4: 'The king may not send forth (the people) on a war of conquest except by the decision of the court of Seventy-One'.

77. See mSanh. 2:1.

78. mSanh. 2:2. See, however, n. 76.

79. Concerning the unreliable nature of the Gospel accounts of the trial of Jesus by the Sanhedrin in general, and the charge of blasphemy, in particular, see P. Winter, *On the Trial of Jesus* ([2]1974), especially pp. 27–43. Cf. also G. Vermes, *Jesus the Jew*, pp. 35–7, 234.

80. For works relating to Judaea, and more specifically to the trial and execution of Jesus, see the bibliography on pp. 199–200. As regards the wider background, namely the question of whether there was in the first century a general rule prohibiting the carrying out of executions except by Roman governors, general uncertainty prevails. Even as regards the governors themselves there are considerable difficulties in defining the nature and limits of their judicial powers in relation to Roman citizens and non-citizens. For recent discussions see, e.g. A. N. Sherwin-White, *Roman Society and Roman Law* (1963); P. D. A. Garnsey, 'The *Lex Iulia* and Appeal under the Empire', JRS 56 (1966), p. 167; 'The Criminal Jurisdiction of Governors', JRS 58 (1968), p. 51.

As regards local communities, much will have depended in this period on their status and location. Recent examination of the evidence from Italy shows a substantial degree of independent criminal jurisdiction in the first century, see W. Simshäuser, *Iuridici und Munizipalgerichtsbarkeit in Italien* (1973), with M. W. Frederiksen in JRS 65 (1975), pp. 191–3; note especially the reference to condemnation by a local *iudicium publicum* in ILS 6085 (Heraclea, later first century B.C.); moreover the penalties available in the *colonia* of Puteoli included, for both slaves and free men, death by crucifixion, AE 1971 88, no. ii, ll. 8–14.

Although Judaea at the time of the prefects and procurators was not an autonomous but a subject community (see above, p. 93; cf. also § 17), the Sanhedrin still enjoyed a comparatively high degree of independence. Not only did it exercise civil jurisdiction according to Jewish law (which

---

Note also that Agennius Urbicus, writing probably in the second century, states that cities generally have 'loca (suburbana) noxiorum poenis destinata' (*Corp. agrim. rom.* I.I, ed. Thulin, p. 47).

The *coloniae* and *municipia* of the Latin West similarly enjoyed a degree of local criminal jurisdiction; see Simshäuser, *op. cit.*; A. Torrent, *La 'iurisdictio' de los magistrados municipales* (1970). Note the criminal *iudicium* which could be held by a *duovir* (chief magistrate) in the *colonia* of Urso in Spain (ILS 6087, para. 102); in the *municipium* of Malaga under Domitian a duumvir or aedile could impose a fine, but actions on behalf of the town for restitution of more than a certain (but unspecified) amount probably had to go to the proconsul (ILS 6089, paras. 66, 69).

The Eastern provinces contained a few cities enjoying the rank of *colonia* (e.g. Berytus, see vol. I, p. 323), but were otherwise made up of Greek *poleis*, some enjoying 'freedom' (*eleutheria*), a few a treaty-relationship with Rome, and a few immunity from Roman taxation. In the case of the free cities at least, a local criminal jurisdiction, including the death penalty, was retained, though progressively affected by recourse to, or interference by, the Roman governors or the Emperor; see J. Colin, *Les villes libres de l'Orient gréco-romain* (1965), and R. Bernhardt, *Imperium und Eleutheria* (Diss. Hamburg, 1971), pp. 229–40. As regards the ordinary *poleis*, the limits of their jurisdiction and its relation to that of the governor, are not clearly attested. See in general L. Mitteis, *Reichsrecht und Volksrecht in den östlichen Provinzen des römischen Kaiserreichs* (1891), pp. 90 f.; D. Nörr, *Imperium und Polis in der hohen Prinzipatszeit* (1966), especially pp. 30–4. The evidence is very slight, but it can be taken that, just as Acts 16: 19–40 shows the magistrates of the *colonia* of Philippi imposing a beating and imprisonment, so those of the *poleis* could exert at least fines, imprisonment and beating (e.g. OGIS 515, from Mylasa: beating and imprisonment of slaves, fining of free men).

A few items of evidence suggest the possibility of death sentences being passed by the authorities in Greek cities. Plutarch, *Cimon* I reveals that the council of Chaeroneia passed such a sentence in the 70s B.C.; Dio of Prusa, *Or.* xxxi 82, addressing the Rhodians, shows that they could exercise the death penalty (but the city may then have been 'free'); and in the second century Apuleius, *Met.* iii 2 f. provides a fictional account of a murder trial taking place in a city in Thessaly; *Dig.* xlviii 3, 6 shows that under Hadrian city authorities conducted criminal trials of bandits, without making explicit what penalty was involved.

On the other hand Augustus in the fourth Cyrene edict of 7/6 B.C. (SEG IX, no. 8) states clearly that capital cases are reserved for the governor, who will judge them himself or appoint a jury. It must also be significant, at least for the second century and after, that all the Christian martyrdoms recorded from the provinces took place before the governor, and not before city officials.

The evidence thus tends to suggest that, if the Sanhedrin exercised an accepted capital jurisdiction in the first century, this was an exception rather than the rule for a local authority in a province. But the official structure of Judaea was in any case anomalous (see V. A. Tcherikover, 'Was Jerusalem a Polis?', IEJ 14 (1964), pp. 61–78) and the evidence from elsewhere is not such as to rule out conclusively the possibility that the Sanhedrin might have had these powers.

is obvious for otherwise a Jewish court of justice would be inconceivable), but it also participated to a large extent in the administration of criminal justice. It possessed an independent police force, and consequently the right to make arrests.[81] It could also judge non-capital cases (Act. 4:5–23; 5:21–40). Whether it was competent to order and execute a capital sentence prescribed by Jewish law without confirmation by the Roman governor is still hotly debated. Scholars who deny that it had such powers point not only to the explicit statement in Jn. 18:31 (ἥμιν οὐκ ἔξεστιν ἀποκτεῖναι οὐδένα)[82] but also to the general tenor of the account in the Synoptics and to reminiscences preserved in rabbinic writings.[83] Those, on the other hand, who maintain that the Sanhedrin was competent to try cases entailing the death penalty and entitled to execute a convicted criminal,[83a] cite: (1) Philo's extract from a letter to Agrippa I asserting that entry into the Holy of Holies by a

81. According to Mt. 26:47=Mk. 14:43, Jesus was arrested by the Jewish police. The Fourth Gospel alone seems to imply that it was a Roman tribune (officer) with his cohort who seized him. (Jn. 18:3, 12.) Cf. Act. 7:3; 5:17–18. See P. Winter, *Trial* ([2]1974), pp. 60–9.

82. Scholars who hold Jn 18:31 to be historically reliable, associate it with the establishment in A.D. 6 of a direct Roman administration of Judaea. The governor possed the power to execute—μέχρι τοῦ κτείνειν *B.J.* ii 8, 1 (117),—a fact interpreted to signify that although Jewish law continued to be administered by the Jewish courts, supreme judicial power was vested in the prefect/procurator. This is thought to have included his consent to any capital sentence pronounced by the Sanhedrin. For a recent statement of the case see E. Lohse, TDNT VII, p. 865; E. Bammel, 'Blutgerichtsbarkeit in der römischen Provinz Judäa', JJS 25 (1974), pp. 35–49. On the judicial authority of the Roman governor, see vol. I, pp. 367–70. On the meaning of Jn. 18:31, see P. Winter, *Trial* (1974), pp. 110–30. Apart from it being inappropriate that Jews should instruct Pilate in Roman law, the statement need not be taken in an absolute sense. Already in antiquity Augustine and John Chrysostom connect the dictum with the Passover, during which no execution could lawfully take place: 'Non sibi licere interficere quemdam propter diei festi sanctitatem' (Augustine, *In Johannis Evangelium*, Tract, cxiv 4, CCL xxxvi, p. 641); κατὰ τὸν καιρὸν ἐκεῖνόν φασιν (Chrysost. *In Ioannem Hom.* lxxxiii 4, PG LIX, col. 452). Note that in the Fourth Gospel the episode occurs on the day preceding the Feast (Jn. 18:28), and that according to mSanh. 4:1, capital cases may not be tried by a Jewish court on the eve of a sabbath or festival.

83. ySanh, 18a, 24b. 'The right to try capital cases was taken from Israel (ביטלו דיני נפשות) forty years before the destruction of the Temple'. Similarly, bSanh. 41a; bA.Z 8b. Cf. Str.-B, I, pp. 1026–7. The validity of the saying was defended by J. Lehmann, REJ 37 (1898), pp. 12–20. On the other hand, Lohse (TDNT VII, p. 866) and others regard it as a round figure alluding to the beginning of direct rule by the Romans.

83a. The most powerful advocate of this case was J. Juster: 'Des témoignages circonstanciés, sûrs, émanant non seulement du Talmud, mais, ce qui plus est, de Philon et de Josèphe, nous montrent le Sanhédrin exerçant la juridiction capitale librement, je veux dire en se réunissant seul, ordonnant seul l'arrestation des coupables, prononçant et faisant exécuter les sentences de mort, en matière religieuse.' *Les Juifs* II (1914), pp. 138–42; cf. pp. 127–45. See also Winter, *Trial* ([2]1974), pp. 12–20, 97–130.

Jew, or even a priest, or even the High Priest, when not expressly ordered, constituted a crime punishable by 'death without appeal';[84] (2) literary and epigraphic evidence indicating that a non-Jew, even a Roman citizen, was to be put to death if apprehended in the inner Temple court;[85] (3) the trial and stoning of Stephen;[86] (4) the trial before the Sanhedrin of Paul;[87] (5) the trial and stoning of James the brother of Jesus;[88] (6) the execution by burning of a priest's daughter convicted of adultery.[89]

Neither theory can be effectively proved. The Johannine statement is unparalleled. The talmudic view that the Sanhedrin had lost its capital jurisdiction forty years before the destruction of the Temple is a late and uncertain interpretation of an obscure and otherwise unattested episode, viz. that the high court had to evacuate its traditional seat, the Hall of the Hewn Stone, and move to the Bazaar. On the other hand, Philo's mention of the High Priest's capital guilt is purely theoretical; the threat to the Gentile to prevent him from entering the forbidden area of the Temple, can be seen as legalized lynching.[89a] Similarly, the execution of Stephen is claimed to be illegal popular justice.[90] Lastly, it can always be claimed that none of the arguments advanced in favour of the competence of the Sanhedrin exclude of themselves the eventual need for Roman confirmation of a death sentence. It would be a mistake however to assume, on the basis of a statement in Josephus, that the Sanhedrin was not allowed to meet without the consent of the governor.[91] The words concerned may mean

84. *Legat.* 39 (307).

85. Josephus, *B.J.* v 5, 2 (194); *Ant.* xvii 11, 5 (417); C. Clermont-Ganneau, 'Une stèle du Temple de Jérusalem', RA 13 (1872), pp. 214–34, 290–6; J. H. Iliffe, QDAP 6 (1936), pp. 1–3 (a second copy); Frey, CIJ 1400: *Μηθένα ἀλλογενῆ εἰσπορεύεσθαι ἐντὸς τοῦ περὶ ἱερὸν τρυφάκτου καὶ περιβόλου. ὃς δ'ἂν λήφθῃ ἑαυτοῦ αἴτιος ἔσται διὰ τὸ ἐξακολουθεῖν θάνατον.* ('No foreigner is to enter within the forecourt and the balustrade around the sanctuary. Whoever is caught will have himself to blame for his subsequent death.') Cf. Philo, *Legat.* 31 (212). In the speech placed on the lips of Titus in *B.J.* vi 2, 4 (126), explicit reference is made to Jewish capital jurisdiction over Roman citizens in this particular case.

86. Act. 7:54–8:2.

87. Act. 23:26.

88. Josephus, *Ant.* xx 9, 1 (200).

89. mSanh. 7:2. Scholars who deny that the Sanhedrin possessed capital jurisdiction under Roman prefects and procurators assign this story to the reign of Agrippa I. Cf. J. Jeremias, ZNW 43 (1950–1), p. 146; E. Lohse, TDNT VII, p. 865.

89a. See especially E. J. Bickerman, 'The Warning Inscription of Herod's Temple', JQR 37 (1946/7), pp. 387–405 (interpreting the inscription as a warning to any foreigner that he could be summarily killed if found there).

90. E. Lohse, TDNT VII, p. 866.

91. *Ant.* xx 9, 1 (202): *οὐκ ἐξὸν ἦν Ἀνάνῳ χωρὶς τῆς ἐκείνου γνώμης καθίσαι συνέδριον.* It is equally unwarranted to deduce from this that the High Priest and the

only that the High Priest had not the right to hold a sovereign court in the absence, and without the agreement, of the procurator.[92] Nor are we to conclude that the Jewish authorities were required to hand over every offender in the first instance to the Romans. This is no doubt what they did, if at any time it seemed to them expedient.[93] But it does not necessarily follow that they were bound to do so.

Accordingly, whilst the Sanhedrin was left to enjoy a tolerably extensive jurisdiction, its most serious restriction was that the Roman authorities could at any time take the initiative themselves and proceed independently, as in fact they did when they suspected a political offence, e.g. when Paul was arrested (Act. 22:30; 23:15; 20:28).

4. *Time and Place of Sessions*

The local courts usually sat on the second and fifth days of the week (Monday and Thursday),[94] but there is no evidence that this was also the practice of the Great Sanhedrin. On days of festival (יום טוב) there were no proceedings, still less on the Sabbath.[95] Also, since a capital sentence in criminal cases could not be pronounced till the day following the trial, such cases were not heard on the eve of a Sabbath or feast day.[96] Whether all these procedural details recorded in the Mishnah are traceable to the time of Jesus cannot be positively demonstrated, except that the ban on holding court on the Sabbath is attested also by Philo.[97]

The meeting-place in which the Great Sanhedrin (the βουλή) usually assembled was situated, according to Josephus, *B.J.* v 4, 2 (144), close to the so-called Xystus, to the east of it in the direction of the Temple

---

Sanhedrin were deprived of capital jurisdiction during the era of the procurators, as F. Büchel has argued: 'Noch einmal: Zur Blutgerichtsbarkeit des Synedrions', ZNW 33 (1934), p. 86.

92. An alternative view is that χωρὶς τῆς ἐκείνου γνώμης (202) may refer to Agrippa II, who is mentioned just previously, who immediately after (203) deposes Ananus, and who in *Ant.* xx 9, 6 (216–8) himself convenes the Sanhedrin.

93. During the feast of Tabernacles in A.D. 62, under Albinus, for example, the Jewish ἄρχοντες handed over to the procurator a certain Jesus bar Ananias whose behaviour seemed to them dangerous *B.J.* vi, 5, 3 (300–5). The man had uttered prophetic cries on the city. After the authorities had delivered him to Albinus, he was flogged and interrogated and then released as a lunatic.

94. mKet. 1:1.

95. mBez. 5:2. Philo also mentions δικάζειν among the things forbidden on the Sabbath, *Migr. Abr.* 16 (91). For a similar prohibition at Qumran cf. CD 10:18 (אל ישפוט על הון ובצע).

96. mSanh. 4:1. Cf. p. 221, n. 82 above.

97. The importance of this is shown also by the Edict of Augustus which released Jews from the obligation to appear before a court on the Sabbath, *Ant.* xvi, 6, 2 (163); 6, 4 (168). Cf. J. Juster, *Les Juifs* II, pp. 121–2.

Mount. Since *B.J.* ii 16, 3 (344) states that a bridge led directly from the Xystus to the Temple Mount,[98] the βουλή was probably located on the western boundary of the Temple Mount itself. It must in any case have stood outside the upper city. For according to *B.J.* vi 6, 3 (354) the βουλευτήριον (=βουλή) was destroyed by the Romans even before they had seized the upper city. The Mishnah repeatedly calls the seat of the Great Sanhedrin לשכת הגזית [99] and since firstly, its statements cannot refer to any other period than that of Josephus, and secondly, Josephus undoubtedly understands by βουλή the meeting-place of the Great Sanhedrin, the לשכת הגזית must necessarily be identical with Josephus's βουλή. Presumably, therefore, the expression לשכת הגזית did *not* signify (as has commonly been supposed) that that hall was built of hewn stones (גזית)—which would not be a distinctive characteristic—but that it stood beside the Xystus (for גזית=ξυστός, cf. the LXX to 1 Chron. 22:2; Am. 5:11). To distinguish it from the other halls (לשכות) of the Temple site, it was called, from its situation, 'the Hall beside the Xystus'. The Mishnah admittedly represents it as located inside the inner forecourt.[100] But taking into account the unreliability, and to some extent inaccuracy, of its information elsewhere regarding the topography of the Temple, its evidence forms no adequate counter-weight to the conclusion arrived at here, especially as it is in itself unlikely that a chamber in the inner forecourt should have been used for anything but ritual purposes.[101] The talmudic statement that forty

98. Note that recent excavations have shown that only one bridge, 'Wilson's Arch', led from the Temple Mount across the Tyropoion to the Upper City. For a preliminary report see B. Mazar in *Jerusalem Revealed: Archaeology in the Holy City 1968–74* (1975), pp. 25–30; *The Mountain of the Lord* (1975), pp. 132–4; 217–20. There is therefore no doubt as to the approximate location of the council-chamber.

99. mSanh. 11:2; mMid. 5:4; cf. mPea. 2:6; mEdu. 7:4. According to bYom. 25a, the *Lishkath ha-Gazith* was 'like a great basilica'. (כמין בסלקי גדולה.)

100. See especially mMid. 5:4; mSanh. 11:2. In bYom. 25a it is stated in greater detail that the לשכת הגזית stood half within and half without the forecourt. mPea. 2:6, and mEdu. 7:4 provide no pointer to the location of the building; neither does mTam. 2:5; 4:3. For although according to these last two passages the priests were in the habit of repairing to the לשכת הגזית during the intervals between the various parts of the service for the purpose of casting lots and reciting the *Shema'*, it does not necessarily follow that the building was situated in the forecourt. Büchler maintains that this was so because the priests would not have left the inner forecourt in their vestments (*Das Synedrion in Jerusalem*, pp. 11–14). But he himself cites examples of priests, under certain circumstances, wearing their vestments even outside the Temple forecourt (p. 14, n. 11).

101. The לשכת פלהדרין or better, לשכת פרהדרין (hall or room of the πρόεδροι) mentioned in mYom. 1:1 is, according to the context (cf. 1:5), to be looked for outside the forecourt. If, as tradition will have it, it was really also called 'the hall of the βουλευταί', (see above, p. 214), this would point to the location of the βουλή. In fact, what is implied is not the identity but only the close association of the 'hall of the πρόεδροι' with the 'hall of the βουλευταί'. The special chamber

years before the destruction of the Temple the Sanhedrin either moved or was expelled (גלתה) from the *Lishkath ha-Gazith*, and that from then on its sessions took place in the *ḥanuyoth* or a *ḥanuth* (a bazaar), lacks historical reliability.[102] Not only is it not echoed in the pages of the Mishnah, but the latter appears to presuppose that the Sanhedrin met in the *Lishkath ha-Gazith* right to the last before the destruction of the Temple. In fact, the tradition concerning the loss of capital jurisdiction by the Sanhedrin, as well as that concerning the transfer of its meetings to the 'Bazaars' or a 'Bazaar'—both apparently forty years before the destruction of the Temple—are without serious support.[103]

As for the Gospel references (Mk. 14:53 ff.; Mt. 26:57 ff.) to a meeting of the Sanhedrin, or of members of the Sanhedrin, in the palace of the High Priest, quite apart from any other consideration of authenticity, these may be explained by the simple fact that the session took place at night when the gates of the Temple Mount were closed.[104]

5. *Judicial procedure*

The Mishnah contains no account of the procedures of the Great Sanhedrin or Sanhedrin of Seventy-One, but those of the lesser Sanhedrins or Sanhedrins of Twenty-Three, which according to the same source were also empowered to try capital cases, are set out in minute detail.[105] Again, although it is impossible to demonstrate that these procedural rules correspond on every point to those observed before A.D. 70, they are unlikely to be the inventions pure and simple of the Tannaim. The reasonable assumption is that trials before the

---

for the πρόεδροι will have been situated near the hall of assembly of the βουλευταί. Thus mYom. 1:1 may provide some confirmation to the hypotheses advanced here.

102. bShab. 15a; bR.Sh. 31a; bSanh. 41a; bA.Z. 8b.

103. Cf. mB.K. 2:2; 6:6; mB.M. 2:4; 4:11; mB.B. 2:3. For the plural חנויות, cf. mTaan. 1:6; mB.M. 8:6; mA.Z. 1:4; mToh. 6:3. A shopkeeper is called חנוני. In another Talmud passage, bR.Sh. 31a, the Sanhedrin is said to have moved from the *ḥanuth* to Jerusalem, implying that the former was situated outside the city, but it is impossible to verify these statements.

104. mMid. 1:1. There is no other evidence of any meeting of the Sanhedrin having been held in the High Priest's palace. Lk 22:54 ff. and Jn. 18:13 ff. refer only to a preliminary investigation before the High Priest. As for Mt. 26:3, the place of meeting is a later addition by the evangelist, cf. Mk. 14:1; Lk. 22:2. For a fuller discussion of the question see P. Winter, *Trial* ([2]1974), pp. 27–43. Note also that, if we follow mSanh. 4:1, this could not have been a meeting of the Sanhedrin as a court, for trials could not be held except during hours of daylight.

105. mSanh. 4–5. On the forms of judicial procedure in the Bible, see Z. W. Falk, *Hebrew Law in Biblical Times* (1964), pp. 67–72. For the rules in force in the post-biblical era, see *idem, Introduction to Jewish Law in the Second Commonwealth* I (1972), pp. 98–112.

Great Sanhedrin were conducted on similar or identical lines, but lack of evidence forbids any more positive conclusion.

According to the Mishnaic description of the Lesser Sanhedrin, the members of the court sat in a semi-circle (כחצי גורן עגולה, literally, like the half of a circular threshing floor) so that they could see one another. Before them stood the two clerks of the court, one on the right hand and one on the left, and these wrote down the speeches pleading for acquittal and conviction.[106] In front of them were three rows of students, each in his own place.[107] The accused was required to show humility, to wear his hair long and to be dressed in a black garment.[108] In cases involving a capital sentence, special forms of procedure were prescribed for the conduct of the trial and the pronouncement of judgement. In such instances, the hearing was to begin with the argument for the defence, and this was to be followed by the argument for the prosecution.[109] No one who had spoken for the accused could afterwards speak to his disadvantage, though the reverse was permissible.[110] The students in attendance were permitted to speak only for and not against the accused, whereas on other occasions not involving a capital sentence they could do both.[111] Sentence of acquittal was to be pronounced on the day of the trial itself, but one of conviction, not until the day after.[112] Voting, for which each man stood,[113] began 'from the side', מן הצד, i.e. with the junior member of the court, whereas in certain non-capital cases, when the court was faced with difficult points of law relating to cleanness and uncleanness, it was the practice to begin with the most experienced member.[114] A simple majority was sufficient for sentence of acquittal; for condemnation a majority of at least two was required.[115] Thus if twelve of the twenty-three judges voted for acquittal and eleven for conviction, the accused went free. But if twelve were for conviction and eleven for acquittal, the number of judges had to be increased by two, and this process continued until an acquittal was secured or the majority required for a conviction was reached. The maximum arrived at hereby was seventy-one.[116]

106. mSanh. 4:3.
107. mSanh. 4:4.
108. Josephus, *Ant.* xiv 9, 4 (172).
109. mSanh. 4:1.
110. mSanh. 4:1; 5:5.
111. mSanh. 4:1; 5:4.
112. mSanh. 4:1; 5:5.
113. mSanh. 5:5.
114. mSanh. 4:2.
115. mSanh. 4:1.
116. mSanh. 5:5.

IV. The High Priests

Bibliography

Schürer, E., 'Die ἀρχιερεῖς im Neuen Testamente', *Studien und Kritiken* (1872), pp. 593–657.

Graetz, H., *Geschichte der Juden* III (⁴1888), pp. 720–52.

Büchler, A., *Die Priester und der Cultus im letzten Jahrzehnt des jerusalemischen Tempels* (1895).

Bevan, E. R., *Jerusalem under the High Priests* (1904).

Hölscher, G., *Der Sadducäismus* (1906), pp. 37–84.

Hölscher, G., *Die Hohenpriesterliste bei Josephus und die evangelische Chronologie* (1940).

Alon, G., *Studies in Jewish History in the Times of the Second Temple, the Mishna and the Talmud* I (1957, ²1967), pp. 48–76 (Hebrew). [E.T. *Jews, Judaism and the Classical World* (1977), pp. 48–77 (On the History of the High Priesthood at the end of the Second Temple Period)].

Vaux, R. de, *Ancient Israel* (1961), pp. 397–403.

Smallwood, E. M., 'High Priests and Politics in Roman Palestine', JThSt n.s. 13 (1962), pp. 14–34.

Schrenk, G., 'ἀρχιερεύς', TDNT III (1965), pp. 265–83.

Jeremias, J., *Jerusalem in the Time of Jesus* (1969), pp. 147–82, 377–8.

Le Moyne, J., *Les Sadducéens* (1972), pp. 249–83 [Doctrinal divergences between Sadducees and Pharisees regarding the High Priest].

Safrai, S., Stern, M., *The Jewish People in the First Century* I (1974), pp. 400–4.

The salient characteristic of the Jewish constitution in the post-exilic era is that the High Priest was also the political leader of the nation. At the beginning of the Persian rule, this was not yet the case.[1] But it indisputably became so from the second half of that period until the Roman-Herodian domination. The High Priests of the pre-Maccabaean as well as of the Hasmonaean age were not merely priests but also princes. And although their power was curbed, on the one hand by the Greek overlords, and on the other by the Jewish *Gerousia*, it was nevertheless strongly consolidated by the principle of life-tenure and inheritability. The priestly kingship of the later Hasmonaeans represented the climax of priestly power.[2] From the appearance of the

1. J. Wellhausen, *Israelitische und jüdische Geschichte* (⁴1901), pp. 193–4; (⁹1958), pp. 181–2; A. Cody, *A History of the Old Testament Priesthood* (1969), pp. 175–7.

2. Priests who were simultaneously kings or princes are also attested in the neighbourhood of Palestine. In an inscription on his sarcophagus, discovered in 1887 and dating to *c.* 300 B.C., Tabnith king of Sidon refers to himself as 'I, Tabnith, priest of Ashtart, king of the Sidonians, son of Eshmunazar, priest of

Romans, and even more under the government of the Herodians, much of their authority was of course lost. The Hasmonaean dynasty was overthrown and indeed extinguished. Life-tenure and inheritability were cancelled. Both Herod and the Romans deposed and appointed High Priests at will. Added to this was the steady increase in power of Pharisaism and rabbinic learning. Yet even in face of the combination of all these factors, the High Priesthood nevertheless managed to retain a large part of its authority until the destruction of the Temple. The High Priest still presided over the Sanhedrin, and hence over the civil affairs of the nation. It was still from among a few privileged families that the High Priest was almost always chosen. Thus, although no longer a monarchic dynasty, they were still an influential aristocracy under the sovereignty of the Romans and the Herodians.

As the succession of High Priests until the fall of the Hasmonaeans has been dealt with in the previous volume, only a list of Pontiffs of Herodian-Roman times is given here. Josephus says that they numbered twenty-eight,[3] and the following twenty-eight names are arrived at by collating his various accounts.[4]

Ashtart, king of the Sidonians'. Cf. G. A. Cooke, *A Text-Book of North-Semitic Inscriptions* (1903), pp. 26–7; H. Donner, W. Röllig, *Kanaanäische und aramäische Inschriften* ([2]1966–9) I, pp. 2–3; II, pp. 17–19. The rulers of Chalcis (Ptolemy, Zenodorus and Lysanias) describe themselves on their coins as ἀρχιερεῖς and τετράρχαι; cf. vol. I, pp. 564–6. For priest-princes in Asia Minor, see R. Hennig, *Symbolae ad Asiae minoris reges sacerdotes Polemonemque I Ponti regem* (1893); D. Magie, *Roman Rule in Asia Minor* (1950); for a family with 'royal' honours at Apamea in Syria, one of whom was the first High Priest of the province, under Augustus, see J.-P. Rey-Coquais, Ann. Arch. Arab. Syr. 23 (1973), pp. 39–79.

3. *Ant.* xx 10, 5 (250). Note, however, A. Kindler, 'Silver Coins bearing the Name of Judea from the Early Hellenistic Period', IEJ 24 (1974), pp. 73–6; F. Millar, JJS 29 (1978), pp. 7–8 (with reference to Ezechias); F. M. Cross, 'A Reconstruction of the Judean Restoration', JBL 94 (1975), pp. 4–18.

4. The list of these High Priests was compiled by various Byzantine writers on the basis of Josephus's accounts, i.e. by (1) the Christian Josephus, *Hypomnesticum* or *Liber memorialis* (PG CVI), and (2) Nicephorus of Constantinople in *Chronographia compendiaria* (or more exactly by the reviser of this work), cf. C. G. de Boor, *Nicephori Constantinopolitensis opuscula* (1880), pp. 110–12. Also Zonaras, who reproduces almost integrally the passages concerning the High Priests in his excerpts from Josephus (*Annales* v 12–vi 17). For rabbinic lists, see A. Büchler, 'Die Schauplätze des Barkochbakrieges und die auf diesen bezogenen jüdischen Nachrichten', JQR 16 (1904), pp. 175–7. Josephus's section on the High Priests at the time of Jesus, *Ant.* xviii 2, 2 (34–5), is quoted by Eusebius, *HE* i 10, 4–6 and *Demonstr. evang.* viii 2, 100; cf. *Chronicon paschale* (ed. L. Dindorf) I, p. 417. For a detailed discussion, see E. Schürer, *Stud. u. Krit.* (1872), pp. 597–607. A complete list of High Priests from 200 B.C. to A.D. 70, with suggested dates, may be found in J. Jeremias, *Jerusalem*, pp. 377–8.

(a) *Appointed by Herod the Great (37–4 B.C.)*

1. Ananel (37–36 B.C.) a Babylonian of inferior priestly origin, *Ant.* xv 2, 4 (22); 3, 1 (40). Rabbinic tradition represents him as an Egyptian.[5]

2. Aristobulus the last Hasmonaean (35 B.C.), *Ant.* xv 3, 1 (41); 3, 3 (51–6); cf. xx 10, 5 (247–9). Ananel for the second time (34 B.C.–?), *Ant.* xv 3, 3 (56).

3. Jesus son of Phiabi, *Ant.* xv 9, 3 (322).[6]

4. Simon son of Boethus, or according to other accounts Boethus himself, but in any case Herod's father-in-law and the father of the second Mariamme (*c.* 24–5 B.C.), *Ant.* xv 9, 3 (320–2); xvii 4, 2 (78); cf. xviii 5, 1 (109); xix 6, 2 (297). The family originated from Alexandria, *Ant.* xv 9, 3 (320).

5. Matthias son of Theophilus (5–4 B.C.), *Ant.* xvii 4, 2 (78); 6, 4 (164–6).

6. Joseph son of Ellem, *Ant.* xvii 6, 4 (166).[7]

7. Joazar son of Boethus (4 B.C.), *Ant.* xvii 6, 4 (164).

(b) *Appointed by Archelaus (4 B.C.–A.D. 6)*

8. Eleazar son of Boethus (4 B.C.–?), *Ant.* xvii 3, 1 (339).

5. mPar. 3:5 lists the High Priests under whom in conformity with Num. 19 a red heifer was burned. In the post-Hasmonaean period this occurred to the following three: (1) Elihoenai son of ha-Ḳoph or ha-Ḳayyaph, (2) Ḥanamel the Egyptian and (3) Ismael ben Phiabi. Ḥanamel the Egyptian is probably Josephus's Ananel. The form of the name is certainly as incorrect as is the statement concerning the country of origin. The chronological order is also likely to be inexact, for Elihoenai, named at the head of the list, can be only Elionaeus son of Cantheras (No. 19). 'Egyptian' is moreover a synonym for 'Alexandrian', which other High Priests of the time of Herod actually were, namely the sons of Boethus, *Ant.* xv 9, 3 (320–2). A general reference to Babylonian priests figures in mMen. 11:7.

6. The patronym Phiabi appears also for Nos. 11 and 22. The spelling varies. In *Ant.* xv 9, 3 (322) the manuscripts read τὸν τοῦ Φοαβιτος/Φοβιτος/Φοβητος (likewise Zonaras, *Annal.* v 16); Josephus, *Hypomnest.*, ὁ τοῦ Φαυβῆ. In two further instances, *Ant.* xviii 2, 2 (35) and xx 8, 8 (179) the very correctly written Cod. Ambrosianus has Φιαβι, a reading supported also by the Latin version (though in the first case it gives 'Iabi'). This is no doubt the best reading. It is confirmed furthermore by mSot. 9:15 and mPar. 3:15, as well as by tMen. 13:21 and tPar. 3:6, which all have פיאבי.

7. It is questionable whether this Joseph is to be counted as a High Priest since he officiated only once, replacing the then unclean Matthias. However, he was *de facto* High Priest for at least one day, and is probably included in Josephus's list because otherwise the number twenty-eight cannot be obtained. The Christian Josephus (*Hypomnest.* 2) does likewise. Rabbinic literature also frequently mentions the same episode: cf. yMeg. 72a; yYom. 38d; yHor. 47d; bMeg. 9b; bYom. 12b; bHor. 12b. Cf. J. Derenbourg, *Essai sur l'histoire et la géographie de la Palestine* (1867), p. 160, n. 1; S. Lieberman, *Tosefta Ki-Fshuṭah*, Part IV, *Order Mo'ed* (1962), pp. 723–4. The name of the High Priest is יוסף בן אילם, Joseph son of the Mute.

9. Jesus son of *Σεέ*, *Ant.* xvii 3, 1 (341).[8] Joazar for a second time, *Ant.* xviii 1, 1 (3); 2, 1 (26).

(c) *Appointed by Quirinius* (*A.D. 6*)

10. Ananus or Annas son of Sethi (A.D. 6–15), *Ant.* xviii 2, 1 (26); 2, 2 (34); cf. xx 9, 1 (197); *B.J.* v 12, 2 (506). See Lk. 3:2; Jn. 18:13–24; Act. 4:6.[9]

(d) *Appointed by Valerius Gratus* (*A.D. 15–26*)

11. Ismael son of Phiabi (*c.* A.D. 15–16), *Ant.* xviii 2, 2 (34).[10]
12. Eleazar son of Ananus (*c.* A.D. 16–17), *Ant.* xviii 2, 2 (34).
13. Simon son of Camithus (*c.* A.D. 17–18), *Ant.* xviii 2, 2 (34).[11]
14. Joseph surnamed Caiaphas (*c.* A.D. 18–36), *Ant.* xviii 2, 2 (35); 4, 3 (95). Cf. Mt. 26:3, 57; Lk. 3:2; Jn. 11:49; 18:13, 14, 24, 28; Act. 4:6. According to Jn. 18:13, Joseph was the son-in-law of Annas = Ananus.[12]

(e) *Appointed by Vitellius* (*A.D. 35–9*)

15. Jonathan son of Ananus (A.D. 36–7), *Ant.* xviii 4, 3 (95); 5, 3 (123). Cf. xix 6, 4 (313). After playing an important part in public life during the time of Cumanus (A.D. 50–2), *B.J.* ii 12, 5–6 (240–3), Jonathan was later murdered at the instigation of the Procurator Felix, *B.J.* ii 13, 3 (256); *Ant.* xx 8, 5 (163). See Vol. I, pp. 459–60.
16. Theophilus son of Ananus (A.D. 37–?), *Ant.* xviii 5, 3 (123).

8. In the best manuscripts for *Ant.* xvii 13, 1 (341) he is called *Ἰησοῦς ὁ Σεέ*; Josephus, *Hypomnest.* *Ἰησοῦς ὁ τοῦ Σεέ*; Nicephorus *Ἰησοῦς Ὡσηέ*; Zonaras, *Annal.* vi 2 *παῖς Σεέ*.

9. The father's name is given in *Ant.* xviii 2, 1 (26) as *Σεθί* or *Σέθ*. The former reading is better attested.

10. Eusebius, *HE* i 10, 4 and Zonaras, *Annal.* vi 3 spell the patronym *Φαβι*; Eusebius in *Demonst. evang.* viii 2, 100 as *Φήβα*; Josephus, *Hypomnest.* as *Βιαφῆ*, and the *Chron. pasch.* (ed. Dindorf) I, p. 417, as *Βιαφεί*. The most reliable manuscripts of Josephus give *Φιαβι*, which is no doubt the correct reading (cf. n. 6 above).

11. Rabbinic literature refers to him as שמעון בן קמחית, cf. tNid. 5:3; yYom. 38d; yMeg. 72a; yHor. 47d; bYom. 47a; bNid. 33b, etc. Cf. J. Le Moyne, *Les Sadducéens* (1972), pp. 280–1. Josephus, Eusebius (*HE*) and Zonaras give the father's name as *Κάμιθος* against *Κάθιμος* (*Demonst. evang.*), *Κάθημος* (*Hypomnest.*) and *Καμαθεί* (*Chron. pasch.* I, 408, 417).

12. The epithet Caiaphas equals קייפא or קייף and not כיפא (Cephas). See n. 5 above. Cf. Derenbourg, *op. cit.*, p. 215, n. 2; G. Dalman, *Grammatik des jüd.-pal. Aramäisch* ([2]1905), p. 161.

(f) *Appointed by Agrippa I (A.D. 41–4)*

17. Simon Cantheras son of Boethus (A.D. 41–?), *Ant.* xix 6, 2 (297); 6, 4 (313).[13]

18. Matthias son of Ananus, *Ant.* xix 6, 4 (316).

19. Elionaeus son of Cantheras, *Ant.* xix 8, 1 (342).[14]

(g) *Appointed by Herod of Chalcis (A.D. 44–8)*[15]

20. Joseph son of Camei or Camydus, *Ant.* xx 1, 3 (16); 5, 2 (103).[16]

21. Ananias son of Nedebaeus (*c.* A.D. 47–59), *Ant.* xx 5, 2 (103). Cf. xx 6, 2 (131); *B.J.* ii 12, 6 (243); Act. 23:2; 24:1. As a result of his wealth, Ananias remained an influential man even after his deposition, but was unpopular on account of his greed, *Ant.* xx 9, 2–4 (206–13). He was murdered by the revolutionaries at the beginning of the war, *B.J.* ii 17, 6 (429); 17, 9 (441–2).[17]

(h) *Appointed by Agrippa II (A.D. 50–?92/3)*

22. Ismael son of Phiabi (*c.* A.D. 59–61), *Ant.* xx 8, 8 (179); 8, 11 (194–5). He is probably identical with the person whose execution in Cyrene is mentioned in *B.J.* vi 2, 2 (114).[18]

13. Cf. H. Graetz, MGWJ 30 (1881), pp. 97–112; *Geschichte der Juden* III ([4]1888), pp. 739–46. Κανθηρᾶς is probably a Hebraized form of *Κάνθαρος*. However see now B. Mazar, *The Mountain of the Lord* (1975), p. 85 (a stone weight marked כר קתרס).

14. The name of the father is variously spelt in the Greek manuscripts, but the Latin version and the reviser of the Cod. Ambrosianus attest Cantheras, a reading supported by the parallel of No. 17. *Ant.* xx 1, 3 (16) mentions also the deposition of the High Priest 'surnamed Cantheras'. Cf. L. H. Feldman, *Josephus* (Loeb) IX, p. 398, note b. mPar. 3:5 describes him as אליועיני בן הקייף cf. n. 5 above. For the name Elionaeus (Elihoenai), see Ezr. 8:4; 10:22, 27; 1 Chron. 3:23; 4:36; 7:8; 26:3.

15. The High Priest Ismael, who according to *Ant.* iii 15, 3 (320) held office at the time of the great famine under Claudius (*c.* A.D. 44), may also have belonged to this period. Since, however, he is not mentioned in Josephus's historical account of the epoch, the incidental reference may be due to a fault of memory. Cf. J. Jeremias, *Jerusalem*, pp. 142–3.

16. The patronym appears as *Καμεί*, *Ant.* xx 1, 3 (16) = Zonaras, *Annal.* vi 12, or *Κάμη* (*Hypomnest.*), or as *Καμυδος*, *Καμοιδι*, *Κεμεδι*, *Κεμεδη*; see the variants in *Ant.* xx 5, 2 (103), but no doubt identical with Camithus.

17. Concerning his gluttony, see bPes. 57a; cf. Derenbourg, *op. cit.*, p. 234. The name of his father was not *Νεβεδαῖος*, but *Νεδεβαῖος*, modelled on Nedebiah in 1 Chron. 3:18.

18. For the rabbinic traditions concerning ישמעאל בן פיאבי, see mPar. 3:5; mSot. 9:15; the latter passage also refers to the High Priest of this name, cf. H. Bietenhard, *Soṭa* (1956), pp. 169–70. See also tYom. 1:21; tMen. 13:21. Cf. Derenbourg, *op. cit.*, pp. 232–5; Lieberman, *Tosefta Ki-Fshuṭah*, Part IV (1962), pp. 749–50. The name of Ismael's father is often given in a corrupt form; פיאבי or פי אבי is the correct spelling. See above n. 6.

23. Joseph Cabi[19] son of the High Priest Simon (A.D. 61–2), *Ant.* xx 8, 11 (196). Cf. *B.J.* vi 2, 2 (114).

24. Ananus son of Ananus (A.D. 62 for three months), *Ant.* xx 9, 1 (197–203). One of the leading personalities during the first phase of the War, Ananus was later assassinated by the rebels, *B.J.* ii 20, 3 (563); 22, 1–2 (648–53); iv 3, 7 (151)–5, 2 (325). *Vita* 38 (193–4); 39 (195–6); 44 (216); 60 (309).

25. Jesus son of Damnaeus (*c.* A.D. 62–3), *Ant.* xx 9, 1 (203); 9, 4 (213). Cf. *B.J.* vi 2, 2 (114).

26. Jesus son of Gamaliel (*c.* A.D. 63–4), *Ant.* xx 9, 4 (213); 9, 7 (222). During the Jewish War Jesus is often mentioned together with Ananus and shared his fate, *B.J.* iv 3, 9 (160); 4, 6 (238); 5, 2 (316); *Vita* 38 (193); 41 (204). According to rabbinic tradition, Jesus's wife Martha came from the house of Boethus.[20]

27. Matthias son of Theophilus (A.D. 65–?), *Ant.* xx 9, 7 (223). Cf. *B.J.* vi 2, 2 (114).[21]

(i) *Appointed by the people during the War* (*A.D. 67/68*)

28. Phannias, also Phanni or Phanasos, son of Samuel, of humble origin, *B.J.* iv 3, 8 (155); *Ant.* xx 10, 1 (227).[22]

With the High Priests constantly changing, there was always a considerable number of them no longer in office. These too nevertheless occupied an important and influential position, as may be demonstrated in respect of at least some of them.[23] It is clear from the New Testament that the elder Ananus or Annas (No. 10) enjoyed great esteem even as a

19. The epithet is written *Καβί* in *Ant.* xx 8, 11 (196), *Δεκαβί*, (i.e. δὲ *Καβί*) in Zonaras, *Annal.* vi 17, but *Κάμης* in *Hypomnest.* The latter would correspond to Camithos.

20. 'If a man is betrothed to a widow and is afterwards appointed High Priest, he may marry her. It happened that Joshua son of Gamla was betrothed to Martha daughter of Boethus and married her after the king had appointed him High Priest' (mYeb. 6:4). This Joshua son of Gamla is probably identical with Ben Gamla who, according to mYom. 3:9, substituted golden lots for those made of box-wood which were used over the two goats on the Day of Atonement. For rabbinic references (bYom. 18a; bYeb. 61a, etc.), see Derenbourg, *op. cit.*, pp. 248–9; J. Jeremias, *Jerusalem*, pp. 155–7. Concerning his contribution to education, see below p. 419.

21. Cf. Graetz, *Geschichte der Juden* III (^{4}1888), pp. 750–1.

22. For references in rabbinic literature, see S. Lieberman, *Tosefta Ki-Fshuṭah*, Part IV, p. 728, on tYom. 1:6. Cf. also Derenbourg, *op. cit.*, p. 269. In Hebrew his name appears as פינחס or פנחס (Phineas). Josephus offers various forms: *Φαννίας, Φάνι τις, Φάννι τις, Φαννίτης*, *B.J.* iv 3, 8 (155); Ps.-Hegesippus: Phanes or Phanis; *Ant.* xx 10, 1 (227) *Φάνασος, Φήνασος*, Finasus, *Φιννέεσος*.

23. Cf. Schürer, *Stud. u. Krit.* (1872), pp. 619 ff.

deposed High Priest. The same remark applies to his son Jonathan (No. 15), who in A.D. 52, some fifteen years after he had retired, led a delegation to Ummidius Quadratus the governor of Syria and was sent by him to Rome to answer for the unrest prevailing in Judaea. When the affair was settled in favour of the Jews, he begged the Emperor to despatch Felix as the new procurator. As the latter's administration led to general dissatisfaction, Jonathan ventured to remind him of his duties and paid for this with his life. Another High Priest, Ananias son of Nedebaeus (No. 21), reigned almost as a despot in Jerusalem after his deposition. The younger Ananus (No. 24) and Jesus son of Gamaliel (No. 26) stood at the head of affairs in the early stages of the War in spite of the fact that they no longer held the office of High Priest. It therefore appears that removal from office in no way condemned these men to political inactivity. Rather is it that the office conferred on its bearer an indelible stamp in virtue of which he retained, even in retirement, a large part of the rights and duties belonging to the officiating High Priest,[24] including of course the title, ἀρχιερεύς, accorded in Josephus to all the deposed High Priests. Consequently, when in the New Testament ἀρχιερεῖς appear at the head of the Sanhedrin, these are to be understood as former High Priests as well as the one currently in office.[25]

Sometimes, on the other hand, persons are designated as ἀρχιερεῖς who do not figure in the foregoing list. Act. 4:6 speaks of 'Annas the High Priest and Caiaphas, and John, and Alexander, and those who were of the high priestly stock' (ἐκ γένους ἀρχιερατικοῦ). In Act. 19:14, there is mention of a Jewish High Priest called Sceva and his seven

24. Cf. mHor. 3:1–4. See in particular 3:4: 'A High Priest in office differs from a former High Priest only in regard to the bullock offered on the Day of Atonement and the Tenth of the Ephah. Both are equal in respect of the service on the Day of Atonement and are subject to the commandments to marry a virgin; both are forbidden to marry a widow; neither may contract uncleanness because of their (deceased) near kin, or unbind their hair or rend their garments, and the death of either of them permits one guilty of manslaughter to return home.' Compare also mMeg. 1:9 and mMak. 2:6.

25. Schürer's historical interpretation of the plural ἀρχιερεῖς has exercised a considerable influence on subsequent scholarship and is still given as the first alternative in the most widely used New Testament dictionary, Bauer-Arndt-Gingrich, *A Greek-English Lexicon of the New Testament* (1957), p. 112. His argument will be reproduced intact and followed by an assessment in the light of recent criticism.

For evidence from Josephus, see *B.J.* ii 12, 6 (243): *τοὺς ἀρχιερεῖς Ἰωνάθην καὶ Ἀνανίαν*. *Vita* 38 (193): *τοὺς ἀρχιερεῖς Ἄνανον καὶ Ἰησοῦν τὸν τοῦ Γαμαλᾶ*. *B.J.* iv 3, 7 (151): *ὁ γεραίτατος τῶν ἀρχιερέων Ἄνανος*. *B.J.* iv 4, 3 (238): *ὁ μετ' Ἄνανον γεραίτατος τῶν ἀρχιερέων Ἰησοῦς*. *B.J.* iv 3, 9 (160): *οἱ δοκιμώτατοι τῶν ἀρχιερέων Γαμαλᾶ, μὲν υἱὸς Ἰησοῦς, Ἀνάνου δὲ Ἄνανος*. In the last three instances ἀρχιερεῖς must be understood of deposed High Priests in the strict sense as the term applies to Ananus and Jesus.

sons. Josephus names a Jesus son of Sapphias *τῶν ἀρχιερέων ἕνα*;[26] a Simon *ἐξ ἀρχιερέων*, who was still a young man at the time of the War and cannot therefore have been Simon Cantheras (No. 17);[27] and finally, a Matthias son of Boethus *τὸν ἀρχιερέα* or *ἐκ τῶν ἀρχιερέων*.[28] Rabbinic literature, too, knows of several High Priests unmentioned in the list.[29] The following comments may help to explain this fact.

Apropos of the riotous election of Phannias (Phinehas) to the High Priesthood, Josephus notes that the Zealots had thereby abrogated 'the claims of those families from which the High Priests had always been drawn'.[30] The High Priesthood was thus regarded as the prerogative of a few families, which indeed the above list confirms: nos. 3, 11, 22 belong to the family of Phiabi; 4, 7, 8, 17, 19, 26 to that of Boethus; 10, 12, 14, 15, 16, 18, 24, 27 to that of Ananus or Annas; 13, 20, 23 to that of Camith. Apart from Ananel, who was of lowly Babylonian origin (No. 1), Aristobulus the last Hasmonaean (No. 2) and Phannias the High Priest of the revolutionary period (No. 28), only five remain—5, 6, 9, 21, 25—who cannot be proved to have belonged to one or other of those families, though they may have done so. With this limitation of the High Priesthood to a few families, and taking into consideration the high prestige with which the office was invested, the mere fact of belonging to one of the privileged families must have conferred a particular distinction. This explains why Josephus, when naming the aristocrats among those who went over to the Romans, lists in addition to the *ἀρχιερεῖς* the 'sons of the High Priests' (*υἱοὶ τῶν ἀρχιερέων*).[31] In the Mishnah, 'sons of the High Priests' (בני כהנים גדולים) are on one occasion introduced as legal authorities in matrimonial issues without even mentioning their names because as sons of High Priests they were men of distinction and authority.[32] On another occasion it is related that letters bearing unusually large seals had arrived from abroad addressed 'to the sons of the High Priests' (לבני כהנים גדולים),[33] from which it may be concluded that they were respected even outside Palestine. But it was not prestige alone that they enjoyed. Members of the high priestly families occupied a really privileged position. According to Act. 4:6, those who were of high priestly stock, *ὅσοι ἦσαν ἐκ γένους ἀρχιερατικοῦ*, possessed a seat and a vote in the Sanhedrin, and by *γένος ἀρχιερατικόν* can be meant none other than the privileged families.

26. *B.J.* ii 20, 4 (566).
27. *Vita* 39 (197).
28. *B.J.* iv 9, 11 (574); v 13, 1 (527); vi 2, 2 (114).
29. See *Stud. u. Krit.* (1872), p. 639.
30. *B.J.* iv 3, 6 (148).
31. *B.J.* vi 2, 2 (114).
32. mKet. 13: 1–2.
33. mOhol. 17:5.

If, then, the members of these families held such a favoured position, it is conceivable that the name ἀρχιερεῖς was assigned to them in a wider sense. That this was so may be deduced, not only from all that has been said here, but also from the passage of Josephus already quoted in which he reports the secession of two High Priests and eight sons of High Priests to the Romans, and subsequently includes both categories under the common title of ἀρχιερεῖς.[34]

Accordingly, the ἀρχιερεῖς who appear in the New Testament as well as in Josephus[35] as leading personalities are firstly, High Priests in the strict sense, i.e. the High Priest in office and his predecessors, and secondly, members of the noble families from which the High Priests were selected. Under Roman rule, these men were at the head of the Sanhedrin and of internal government in general. The majority of them were without doubt Sadducees, although in practice they at times complied, albeit unwillingly, with Pharisaic demands. (See above, p. 213.)

The chief critic of this theory is Joachim Jeremias.[36] According to him, the two main proof-texts, *B.J.* 2, 2 (144) and Act. 4:6, are not altogether convincing. The reference to High Priests at the end of the first may concern only Joseph and Jesus, two previous holders of the office, and the persons of high priestly stock of Act. 4:6 may have been members of the Sanhedrin, not 'by virtue of their family background' but 'rather by virtue of their office'.[37] As for the two Mishnah passages, Jeremias claims that בני כהנים גדולים means, not 'sons of the High Priests', but simply 'High Priests'. 'The term "son of" denotes not descent, but membership of a class.'[38] He shrewdly appeals to the

34. *B.J.* vi 2, 2 (114): *Ὧν ἦσαν ἀρχιερεῖς μὲν Ἰώσηπός τε καὶ Ἰησοῦς, υἱοὶ δ' ἀρχιερέων τρεῖς μὲν Ἰσμαήλου τοῦ καρατομηθέντος ἐν Κυρήνῃ, καὶ τέσσαρες Ματθίου, καὶ εἷς ἑτέρου Ματθίου, διαδρὰς μετὰ τὴν τοῦ πατρὸς ἀπώλειαν, ὃν ὁ τοῦ Γιώρα Σίμων ἀπέκτεινε σὺν τρισὶν υἱοῖς, ὡς προείρηται. Πολλοὶ δὲ καὶ τῶν ἄλλων εὐγενῶν τοῖς ἀρχιερεῦσι συμμετεβάλλοντο.* For the use of the title in pagan cults, see C. G. Brandis, RE II, cols. 471–83, s.v. *ἀρχιερεύς.*

35. Especially in *B.J.* ii 14–17 (271–456).

36. J. Jeremias, *Jerusalem zur Zeit Jesu* (1929), II, B 1, pp. 34 ff. His latest view, presented here, appears in the English edition, *Jerusalem in the Time of Jesus* (1969), pp. 175–81. It concludes as follows: the captain of the Temple was second to the High Priest and headed the chief priests. Next to him came the leader of the weekly course of priests, and the leaders of the four to nine daily courses. There were also seven Temple overseers, among them four chief Levites and three Temple treasurers. 'The chief priests permanently employed at the Temple formed a definite body who had jurisdiction over the priesthood and whose members had seats and votes on the council' (*ibid.*, p. 180). Jeremias's thesis has been adopted by G. Schrenk, TDNT III, p. 271, n. 37; G. Alon, *Studies in Jewish History* I ([2]1967), p. 61, n. 41 (Hebrew), *et al.*

37. *Op. cit.*, p. 176.

38. *Op. cit.*, p. 177.

parallel of the Qumran War Rule which, in addition to the 'Chief Priest' (כוהן הראש), mentions also twelve 'chief priests' (ראשי הכהנים).[39] In brief, ἀρχιερεῖς does not signify merely present or past occupants of the pontifical role and their sons, but more generally, priests 'of higher rank than the majority'[40], i.e. the priestly aristocracy.

Jeremias is doubtless correct in pointing out that the Hebrew expression, 'sons of the High Priests', may designate representatives of a social class, though it would be difficult, to say the least, to argue that the genealogical meaning is necessarily excluded. He is also justified in emphasizing that if the phrase were taken literally, and all the sons of all the High Priests had been members of the Sanhedrin by birthright, there would have scarcely been room for anyone else in a legislative-judicial body of seventy-one members.[41]

Nevertheless, the real difference between the two theories may be smaller than Jeremias and his followers believe. For if allowance is made for the somewhat elastic terminology in all the sources, and if we bear in mind also that, in an institution *de jure* dynastic, the principal offices were more than likely to have been assigned to the close relations of the office-holder—and Jeremias himself admits that there was high-priestly nepotism[42]—priestly aristocracy on the one hand and present and past High Priests and their heirs on the other are bound to have been substantially the same.

39. 1QM 2:1 (*DSSE*, p. 125). For the phrase ראשי הכהנים, see Neh. 12:7= ἄρχοντες τῶν ἱερέων, 2 Esd. 22:7.

40. *Op. cit.*, p. 178.

41. *Op. cit.*, p. 176–7.

42. *Op. cit.*, p. 181.

§ 24. PRIESTHOOD AND TEMPLE WORSHIP

Bibliography

For a full nineteenth-century bibliography on the priesthood, see W. W. Baudissin, *Geschichte des alttestamentlichen Priesterthums* (1889), pp. xi–xv. For more recent material, see TWNT III (1937), pp. 257 f.; TDNT III (1965), pp. 257 f.; IDB III (1962), p. 889, IV (1962), pp. 159, 560; Enc. Jud. 13, cols. 1090–1; 15, cols. 987–8.

Wellhausen, J., *Prolegomena zur Geschichte Israels* ([5]1899), pp. 15–165. [E.T. [2]1885.]

Baudissin, W. W., *Die Geschichte des alttestamentlichen Priesterthums* (1889).

Büchler, A., *Die Priester und der Cultus im letzten Jahrzehnt des jerusalemischen Tempels* (1895).

Hoonacker, A. van, *Le sacerdoce lévitique dans la loi et dans l'histoire des Hébreux* (1899).

Baudissin, W. W., art. 'Priests and Levites', HDB IV (1902), pp. 67–97.

Harper, A., *The Priestly Element in the Old Testament* (1909).

Schmitz, O., *Die Opferschauung des späteren Judentums und die Opferaussagen des Neuen Testaments* (1910).

Vincent, L. H., Abel, F. M., *Jérusalem antique et nouvelle* I–II (1914–22).

Eissfeldt, O., *Erstlinge und Zehnte im A. T.* (1917).

Loisy, A., *Essai historique sur le sacrifice* (1920).

Hölscher, G., art. 'Levi', RE XI (1922), cols. 2155 ff.

Pfister, F., art. 'Kultus', RE XI (1922), cols 2180 ff.

Gray, G. B., *Sacrifice in the Old Testament* (1925), pp. 179–270; repr. with a Prolegomenon by B. A. Levine (1971).

Wendel, C., *Das Opfer in der altisraelitischen Religion* (1927).

Löhr, M., *Das Räuchopfer im Alten Testament* (1927).

Jeremias, J., *Jerusalem zur Zeit Jesu* (1929), II, B, 1, pp. 2–87 ([2]1958).

Moore, G. F., *Judaism in the First Centuries of the Christian Era* I–III (1927–30).

Elbogen, I., *Der jüdische Gottesdienst in seiner geschichtlichen Entwicklung* ([3]1931).

Idelsohn, A. Z., *Jewish Liturgy* (1932).

Watzinger, C., *Denkmäler Palästinas* I–II (1933–5).

Bonsirven, J., *Le judaïsme palestinien au temps de Jésus-Christ* I–II (1934–5).

Guignebert, C., *Le monde juif vers le temps de Jésus* (1935); E.T. *The Jewish World in the Time of Jesus* (1939), pp. 50–61.

Welch, A. C., *Prophet and Priest in Old Israel* (1936).

Oesterley, W. O. E., *Sacrifice in Ancient Israel* (1938).

Hooke, S. H., *Prophets and Priests* (1938).

Pedersen, J., *Israel, Its Life and Culture* III/IV (1940), pp. 150–97, 299–465.

Bertholet, C., *Der Sinn des kultischen Opfers* (1942).

Rowley, H. H., 'The Meaning of Sacrifice in the O.T.', BJRL 33 (1950), pp. 74–110.

Simons, J., *Jerusalem in the Old Testament* (1952), especially pp. 344–436.

Mowinckel, S., *Religion och Kultus* (1953).

Vincent, F.-M., 'Le temple hérodien d'après la Mishna', RB 61 (1954), pp. 5–35, 398–418.

Kraus, H. J., *Gottesdienst in Israel* (1954); E. T. *Worship in Israel* (1966).

M. Avi-Yonah, 'The Second Temple', *Sepher Yerushalayim* (1956), pp. 392–418 (Hebrew).

Herbert, A. S., *Worship in Ancient Israel* (1959).
Vaux, R. de, *Ancient Israel* (1961), pp. 331–475.
Abba, R., art. 'Priests and Levites', IDB III, pp. 876–89.
Gaster, T. H., art. 'Sacrifice', IDB IV, pp. 147–59.
Stinespring, W. F., art. 'Temple', IDB IV, pp. 423–60.
Vaux, R. de, *Studies in Old Testament Sacrifice* (1964).
Clements, R. E., *God and Temple* (1965).
Gunneweg, A. H. J., *Leviten und Priester* (1965).
Rowley, H. H., *Worship in Ancient Israel: Its Forms and Meaning* (1967).
Jeremias, J., *Jerusalem in the Time of Jesus* (1969), pp. 147–221.
Cody, A., *A History of Old Testament Priesthood* (1969).
Haran, M., Stern, M., 'Priest and Priesthood', Enc. Jud. 13, cols. 1069–88.
Porten, B., Avi-Yonah, M., Safrai, S., 'Temple (Second Temple)', Enc. Jud. 15, cols. 955–84.
Falk, Z. W., *Introduction to Jewish Law of the Second Commonwealth* I (1972), pp. 58–69.
Fohrer, G., *History of Israelite Religion* (1972).
Levine, B. A., *In the Presence of the Lord—A Study of Cult and Some Cultic Terms in Ancient Israel* (1974) [*Shelamim* sacrifice; sacrifices of expiation].
Milgrom, J., *Cult and Conscience* (1976).
Safrai, S. and Stern, M., *The Jewish People in the First Century* II (1977): 'The Priesthood and other Classes' (M. Stern), pp. 561–630; 'The Temple' (S. Safrai), pp. 865–907.
Haran, M., *Temples and Temple Service in Ancient Israel* (1978).

See also Str.-B. II, pp. 55–68; III, pp. 696–700; IV, pp. 150, 238, 244–5, 351, 646, 664; Schrenk, G., '*Hieros*', TDNT III, pp. 221–83; Neusner, J., *History of the Mishnaic Law of Purities* I–XXII (1974–77).

For special studies concerning priesthood and Temple at Qumran see:

Betz, O., 'Le ministère cultuel dans la secte de Qumrân et dans le Christianisme', *Recherches Bibliques* IV (1959), pp. 163–202.
Cullmann, O., 'L'opposition contre le Temple de Jérusalem', NTSt 5 (1959), pp. 157–73.
Jaubert, A., *La notion de l'alliance dans le judaïsme* (1963), pp. 145–50.
Delcor, M., 'Le vocabulaire juridique, cultuel et mystique de l' "initiation" dans la secte de Qumrân', *Qumran-Probleme*, ed. H. Bardtke (1963), pp. 109–34.
Gärtner, B., *The Temple and the Community in Qumran and the New Testament* (1965).
Liver, J., 'The "Sons of Zadok the Priests" in the Dead Sea Sect', RQ 6 (1967), pp. 3–30.
Klinzing, G., *Die Umdeutung des Kultus in der Qumrangemeinde und im Neuen Testament* (1971).
Neusner, J., *Early Rabbinic Judaism* (1975), pp. 34–49.
Vermes, G., *PBJS*, pp. 83–5; *DSS*, pp. 180–2, 192–3, 215.

I. The Priesthood as a Class

The internal development of Israel after the exile was essentially determined by two equally influential groups: the priests and the scribes. In the first post-exilic centuries until well into the Hellenistic period the priests were dominant. They organized the new community;

it was from them that the Torah emanated; in their hands lay the leadership of the community, not only in spiritual but also in material affairs. Whereas, however, they were originally themselves the expert interpreters of the Torah, gradually an independent order of Torah scholars and teachers came into being alongside of them. And these were to increase in prestige and influence as zeal for the Torah cooled among the priests whilst among the people it was growing in value and significance. This was especially true following the Maccabaean wars of independence. From then on, the scribes took more and more control of the nation's spiritual guidance. The predominance of the priests was followed by that of the scribes. This must not, however, be understood to imply that the priests lost all their influence. Politically and socially their precedence was unchanged. The scribes, it is true, were the nation's teachers. But by virtue of their political position, of the powerful resources at their command, and finally and above all, of their religious position—that they alone could offer sacrifice and that their mediation was therefore necessary for the fulfilment of every individual's religious duties—the priests continued to hold an extraordinary significance in the life of the Jewish people.[1]

In the main, this significance was grounded precisely in the fact that they formed a closed circle with the exclusive right to sacrifice. According to the legislation of the Pentateuch, accepted as unconditionally binding from the time of Ezra and Nehemiah, only the 'sons of Aaron' could take part in the sacrificial worship.[2] The priesthood was thus a community the boundaries of which were irremovable since they were laid down for ever by natural descent. No one not belonging to this group by birth could be admitted to it; and no one belonging to it through legitimate birth could be excluded from it. And this group was in possession of the highest conceivable privilege: that of presenting to God all the offerings of the nation and of each individual. This circumstance alone was bound to have invested the priesthood with immense importance, especially since civil life in its entirety was bound up in every kind of way with the religious cult.[3]

1. W. Eichrodt, *Theology of the Old Testament* (E.T. 1961) I, pp. 395–402.

2. See especially Ex. 28–9, Lev. 8–10, Num. 16–18. For further details, cf. W. W. Baudissin, *Die Geschichte des alttestamentl. Priesterthums* (1889), pp. 22–5; R. de Vaux, *Ancient Israel* (1961), pp. 345–57, 372–405.

3. For example, many points relating to marriage laws and to the treatment of persons suspected of suffering from certain illnesses could only be resolved by reference to the priests; see Num. 5:11–31 (procedure in the case of a woman suspected of adultery); Lev. 13-14; Dt. 24:8, 9 (procedure in the case of leprosy). The Qumran community considered the priestly privilege to be absolute in the latter case; even if the priest was ignorant or simple or needed expert guidance, the actual incarceration of the leper was reserved to him alone. Cf. CD 13:2–7; G. Vermes, *DSS*, p. 98.

Moreover, since the Deuteronomic legislation of the time of Josiah, all the temples outside Jerusalem had been declared unlawful and the whole cult concentrated in the one sanctuary of Jerusalem.[4] Thus all the sacrificial offerings from every corner of the land flowed into this centre, which thereby became a source of wealth and power for the priesthood officiating there. Such a concentration also had the effect of welding the priesthood into a closely-knit and compact unity.

The primary requirement of a priest was, in consequence, evidence of his genealogical descent. This was of the greatest moment. Whoever was unable to produce it had no title to recognition of his priestly rights. Already at the time of the first return of the exiles under Zerubbabel certain priestly families, unable to present their family trees, were expelled from the priesthood.[5] On the other hand, Josephus asserts that he found his lineage recorded 'in the public archives'.[6] Because of their importance to the community, family registers thus had the character of public records.

To preserve the purity and dignity of the priesthood, certain rules also existed in respect of marriage. According to the law in Lev. 21:7–8, a priest may not marry a prostitute, or a girl no longer a virgin, or a divorced woman: only a virgin or a widow therefore, and only those, needless to say, who were of Israelite descent.[7] A caste-like limitation of marriage to the daughters of priests is, however, not required. These directions continued to be adhered to in later times and were defined even more sharply.[8] Thus a *haluzah*, i.e. a widow not taken by her brother-in-law in leviratic marriage (relieved from it, as it were), was

4. For the relationship between Josiah and Deuteronomy, see J. Pedersen, *Israel, Its Life and Culture* (1940) III/IV, pp. 179 f.; G. von Rad, *Studies in Deuteronomy* (1953), pp. 17 ff. For a summary of scholarly opinion, cf. H. H. Rowley, 'The Prophet Jeremiah and the Book of Deuteronomy', *From Moses to Qumran* (1963), pp. 187–209. For the latest discussion, see M. Weinfeld, *Deuteronomy and the Deuteronomic School* (1972), where the deuteronomic composition is assigned to scribal circles at work from before the time of Josiah until after the fall of Judah (cf. p. 9).

5. Ezr. 2:61–3 = Neh. 7: 63–5.

6. *Vita* 1 (6): τὴν μὲν οὖν τοῦ γένους ἡμῶν διαδοχήν, ὡς ἐν ταῖς δημοσίαις δέλτοις ἀναγεγραμμένην εὗρον, οὕτως παρατίθεμαι. In *Vita* 1 (4–6), Josephus traces his family tree to the time of John Hyrcanus, giving the year of birth of each of his ancestors. For the problems arising from this genealogy, see vol. I, pp. 45–6, and J. Jeremias, *Jerusalem in the Time of Jesus* (1969), p. 214, n. 212.

7. Josephus, *C.Ap.* i 7 (31): δεῖ γὰρ τὸν μετέχοντα τῆς ἱεροσύνης ἐξ ὁμοεθνοῦς γυναικὸς παιδοποιεῖσθαι.

8. See in general, Philo, *Spec. Leg.* i (101–11). Josephus, *Ant.* iii 12, 2 (276–9). For the rabbinic regulations, see P. Grünbaum, *Die Priestergesetze bei Flavius Josephus* (1887), pp. 15–25; B.-Z. Schereschewsky, Enc. Jud. 11, cols. 1052–3.

also to be counted as divorced.[9] A woman taken captive in war was forbidden to a priest in case she might have been raped.[10] If a priest was without children, he was not permitted to marry a widow who was barren.[11] No proselyte or freed slave-woman could ever become his wife, and the daughter of a proselyte or a freed slave-woman only when the mother was an Israelite.[12]

For the High Priest, the rules were even stricter. He could not even marry a widow, but only a virgin (Lev. 21:13–15). This regulation, too, continued to be maintained and was later defined even more precisely.[13] When Philo states that the High Priest might marry only a virgin from a priestly family,[14] this corresponds neither to the text of Leviticus, nor to the later legal opinion, which both permit him to marry any Israelite virgin. Philo may have arrived at this idea from the wording of the Septuagint,[15] or from the custom as it actually was, or from both together.

Ezekiel's demand (44:22) that a priest should marry only a virgin or

9. mSot. 4:1; 8:3; mMak. 3:1. Tg. Ps.-Jon., Neof. and Sifra to Lev. 21:7. Cf. also bKid. 77a; bYeb. 92a.

10. Josephus, *Ant.* iii 12, 2 (276); *C.Ap.* i 7 (35); *Ant.* xiii, 10, 5 (292) (story of John Hyrcanus). According to mKet. 2:9, even priests' wives found in a town captured by the enemy were prohibited any further sexual intercourse with their husbands unless witnesses could testify to their integrity.

11. mYeb. 6:5.

12. No female proselyte or freed-woman, mYeb. 6:5. Concerning the daughters, see mBik. 1:5: 'R. Eliezer b. Jacob says: A daughter of a proselyte may not marry a priest unless her mother is of Israel'. The same is applicable to the daughters of freed slaves. Even in the tenth generation it is lawful only where the mother is of Israelite origin. mKid. 4:7: 'R. Eliezer b. Jacob says: If an Israelite has married a proselyte woman, his daughter may marry into the priestly class; and if a proselyte has married an Israelite woman, his daughter may marry into the priestly class; but if a proselyte has married a proselyte woman, his daughter is not so qualified. A proselyte is equal to a freed slave: even to the tenth generation, until the mother is an Israelite woman. R. Yose says: Even if a proselyte has married a proselyte woman, his daughter may marry into the priestly class'.

13. Philo, *Spec. Leg.* i (101–4). Josephus, *Ant.* iii 12, 2 (277). mYeb. 6:4: 'A High Priest may not marry a widow, whether she became a widow after betrothal or after marriage; and he may not marry one that is *bogereth* ('ripe for childbearing', i.e. aged twelve years and six months). But R. Eliezer and R. Simeon declare a *bogereth* to be eligible. He may not marry one who has lost her virginity accidentally.' According to Philo, *Spec. Leg.* i (107), the High Priest was on no account to marry a woman previously betrothed. Cf. B. Ritter, *Philo und die Halacha* (1879), p. 72; I. Heinemann, *Philons griechische und jüdische Bildung* (1932), pp. 59–62; P. Grünbaum, *op. cit.* (in n. 8 above), pp. 26–30.

14. *Spec. Leg.* i (110): 'The High Priest must not propose marriage save to one who is not only a virgin but a priestess descended from priests (*ἀλλὰ καὶ ἱέρειαν ἐξ ἱερέων*).

15. In the LXX, Lev. 21:13 reads as follows: *οὗτος γυναῖκα παρθένον ἐκ τοῦ γένους αὐτοῦ λήψεται*, where the words *ἐκ τοῦ γένους αὐτοῦ* are not found in the Hebrew text. B. Ritter, *Philo und die Halacha*, pp. 72 f.

a priest's widow was not incorporated into the law as it developed later.

Because of the great importance attached to the observance of these rules, when a priest married he was naturally obliged to scrutinize his wife's lineage very closely. Josephus describes at length the care with which this was done.[16] The Mishnah determines how far back the scrutiny was to go,[17] and in what situations it might be dispensed with.[18]

The idea underlying these regulations concerning marriage is that the priesthood should be a holy order. The same idea finds expression in still further regulations. Since, according to the Torah (Num. 19), any contact with a corpse, and even entry into a house containing a corpse, renders unclean, priests were forbidden to approach the dead or to take part in funeral ceremonies. This prohibition was absolute in the case of the High Priest, and for the other priests was lifted only in respect of their nearest relations—parents, children, brothers and sisters (Lev. 21:1–4, 11–12; Ezek. 44:25–7). It seems that a priest was not even permitted to mourn the death of his wife. Or, although not explicitly

16. *C.Ap.* i 7 (31). From what is said here it must be assumed that many families were in possession of genealogical records. Compare in addition the copious lists in the Books of Ezra and Nehemiah. Irrespective of their historical reliability, the New Testament genealogies presuppose that knowledge of one's ancestors was not exceptional. Cf. Mt. 1:1–16; Lk. 2:36, 3:23–38; Rom. 11:1; Phil. 3:5. Also mYeb. 4:13; mTaan. 4:5; Eusebius *HE* i 7 = Iul. African. *Epist. ad Aristidem*, ed. M. J. Routh, *Reliquiae sacrae* II, pp. 228 ff., and W. Reichardt, TU 34, 3 (1909). See also A. von Harnack, *Gesch. der altchristl. Literatur* (1893) I, p. 512 f. Heirs of David are claimed to have been found in the time of Vespasian, Domitian and Trajan according to Eusebius, *HE* iii, 12, 19–20, 32; cf. G. Vermes, *Jesus the Jew* (1973), p. 157; E. L. Curtis, 'Genealogy', HDB II, pp. 121–37; S. A. Cook, 'Genealogies' EB II, cols. 1657–66; R. Kittel, *Geschichte des Volkes Israel* ([2]1929) III, pp. 396–7; H. H. Schaeder, *Esra der Schreiber* (1930), pp. 15 ff.; S. Klein, 'A Genealogical Record found in Jerusalem', Zion 4 (1938/9), pp. 30–50, 177–8; A. L. Allrik, 'The Lists of Zerubbabel (Neh. 7 and Ezra 2) and the Hebrew Numeral Notation', BASOR 136 (1954), pp. 21–7; K. Galling, 'The "Gola-list" according to Ezra 2/Neh. 7', JBL 70 (1951), pp. 149–58; *idem*, 'Von Nabonid zu Darius', ZDPV 69 (1953), pp. 42–64; 70 (1954), pp. 4–32; W. Rudolph, *Esra und Nehemia* (1949), pp. xxiii–xxiv, 173–4; J. M. Myers, *Ezra-Nehemiah, Anchor Bible* (1965), pp. 151, 175, 204, 223–45; J. Jeremias, *Jerusalem in the Time of Jesus* (1969), pp. 275–97; I. Ta-Shma, 'Genealogy', Enc. Jud. 7, cols. 379–83.

17. mKid. 4:4: 'Whoever wishes to marry a woman of priestly stock, he must trace her family back through four mothers (on each side); that is to say through her mother, mother's mother, mother's father's mother, and the latter's mother; also her father's mother, and the latter's mother, her father's father's mother, and the latter's mother. In the case of a woman of Levitical or Israelite descent, he must trace the line back to one further mother'.

18. mKid. 4:5: 'They do not search from the altar and beyond, from the platform and beyond, and from the Sanhedrin and beyond; and all whose fathers are known to have been public officers or almoners may marry into the priestly class and none need trace their descent'. Serving priests and Levites and members of the Sanhedrin are presumed to have proved their genealogical fitness.

stated, should it be taken for granted that she was included among the exceptions?[19]

In no circumstances was a priest to participate in mourning customs involving disfigurement, such as shaving the head or lacerating the skin (Lev. 21:5–6; cf. Ezek. 44:20). The High Priest was not even allowed to uncover his head or rend his garments (Lev. 21:10; cf. 10:6–7).

It was also part of the holiness of the priest that he should be without physical blemish.[20] If he suffered from any kind of bodily defect, he could not officiate, even though he was a 'son of Aaron'. Leviticus (21:16–23) already lists such defects in considerable detail. But here too, a later age was ingeniously specific. It has been reckoned that a total of one hundred and forty-two physical defects could disqualify a man from the priesthood.[21] But the same priests who for these reasons could not perform their duties nevertheless shared in the emoluments.[22]

Nothing is laid down in the Torah concerning the age at which a priest was to be admitted to office. Possibly it was the same for priests as for Levites. Yet even this is not given consistently in the Old Testament.[23] Rabbinic tradition asserts that a priest was qualified for office as soon as the first signs of manhood were apparent, but that in fact he was not admitted until he was twenty years old.[24]

19. According to the usual interpretation of the text of Lev. 21:4, mourning for a wife was expressly forbidden. Although both text and interpretation are in this instance questionable it is nevertheless a fact that the wife is not included among the exceptions. Nor is she named by Philo, *Spec. Leg.* i (112), or Josephus, *Ant.* iii 12, 2 (277). The Rabbis, on the other hand, regard שארו of Lev. 21:2 as alluding to her, and understand 21:4 to refer to mouring for an illegitimate wife. See Targ. Ps.-Jon. and Sifra *in loc.* Maimonides, *Hilkhoth Ebel* II, 7 [E.T. *The Commandments* (1966, II), sec. 166 on priests, sec. 168 on High Priest]. Cf. E. Neufeld, *Ancient Hebrew Marriage Laws* (1944), pp. 23–55.

20. The exclusion of persons afflicted with a physical blemish from holding office in the Qumran community is justified by the presence among them of the Angels of holiness. Cf. 1QSa 2:5–9.

21. Cf. 'Blemish', JE III, pp. 241–2; Enc. Jud. 4, cols. 1081–4. See in general, Philo, *Spec. Leg.* i (80–1); Josephus, *Ant.* iii 12, 2 (276–7); mBekh. 7. It was customary to name a priest after his infirmity. Thus among the ancestors of Josephus are Simon 'the Stutterer', and Matthias 'the Hump-back', *Vita* 1 (3–4). Among the High Priests is listed a Joseph son of 'the Mute' (בן אילם); cf. above, p. 229.

22. Lev. 21:22; Philo, *Spec. Leg.* i (117); Josephus, *Ant.* iii 12, 2 (278); *B.J.* v 5, 7 (228); mZeb. 12:1; mMen. 12:10.

23. Thirty years old: Num. 4:3, 23, 30, 35, 39, 43, 47; 1 Chron. 23:3. Twenty-five years old: Num. 8:23–6. Twenty years old: Ezr. 3:8, 1 Chron. 23:24, 27, 2 Chron. 31:17. Cf. W. W. Baudissin, *Die Geschichte des alttest. Priestertums*, pp. 167–8.

24. See bHul. 24b. In general, cf. P. Grünbaum, *Die Priestergesetze bei Flavius Josephus* (1887), pp. 34–6. Two passages from the Dead Sea Scrolls provide additional information. 1QSa 1:8–15 associates the following ages with the as-

Whoever met all these requirements, and had been examined and accepted by the Sanhedrin in regard to his fitness,[25] was sanctified for office by a special act of consecration. This solemn act, according to Exod. 29 = Lev. 8, consisted of: (i) a purificatory bath; (ii) the donning of the sacred vestments; (iii) a succession of sacrifices accompanied by still further special ceremonies: certain parts of the ordinand's body were smeared with blood, and his person and garments were sprinkled with blood and oil. Another rite was that of the 'filling of the hands', i.e. the laying of certain portions of the sacrifice on the hands of the priest in order to indicate his future priestly duties and privileges. Other passages (Exod. 28:41; 30:30; 40:12–15; Lev. 7:36; 10:7; Num. 3:3) mention also anointing, which the principal passage represents as a distinguishing mark for the High Priest alone.[26] The whole ceremony lasted seven days (Exod. 29:35 ff.; Lev. 8:33 ff.). How in detail this act of consecration was performed in later times is uncertain.[27] It is probable that anointing remained a distinction reserved to the High Priest.[28]

---

sumption of lay offices: twenty-year olds become full members of the congregation; at twenty-five they may take their place among the 'foundations' of the sect; at thirty they qualify for higher office. CD 14:6–9 specifies that 'the Priest who enrols the Congregation' and 'the Guardian of all the camps' may exercise these leading functions between the ages of thirty and sixty, and thirty and fifty, respectively. Consequently, at Qumran the age of thirty was the lower limit at which a man could hold major priestly offices. Cf. Vermes, *DSS*, pp. 97–8, 104.

The same socio-legal requirement seems to be reflected in the Lucan representation of Jesus—and implicitly of John the Baptist, the son of a priest—as aged 'about thirty years' at the start of his public life (Lk. 3:23).

25. mMid. 5:4.

26. Cf. R. de Vaux, *Ancient Israel* (1961), pp. 346–8. On the assumption of priestly office, see E. Lohse, *Die Ordination im Spätjudentum und im N.T.* (1951); M. Noth, *Amt und Berufung im Alten Testament* (1958). On anointing, see H. Weinel, 'משיח und seine Derivate' ZAW 18 (1898), pp. 1–82; J. Wellhausen, 'Zwei Rechtsriten bei den Hebräern' ARW 7 (1904), pp. 33–9; W. Robertson Smith, *Lectures on the Religion of the Semites* (^{3}1927), pp. 233, 383–6; D. Lys, 'L'onction dans la Bible', Études Théologiques et Religieuses 29 (1954), pp. 3 ff.; J. Morgenstern, 'A Chapter in the History of the High-Priesthood', AJSL 55 (1938), 187 f., 196 f.; E. Kutsch, *Salbung als Rechtsakt*, BZAW 87 (1963). See in general 'Anointing', JE I, pp. 611–13; Enc. Jud. 3, cols, 27–31; IDB I, pp. 138–9.

27. No additional light is thrown upon the subject by Philo, *Vita Mosis* ii (141–58) and Josephus, *Ant.* iii 8, 6 (206–7), as they only reproduce Ex. 29 = Lev. 8.

28. Cf. R. de Vaux, *Ancient Israel* (1961), p. 400. But in the latter days of the Second Temple even the High Priest does not appear always to have been anointed since the Mishnah distinguishes anointed High Priests from those consecrated through investment with the sacred garments. See in particular mHor. 3:4; mMak. 2:6. There is in any case no truth in the tradition based on bHor. 11b that anointing had been discontinued since the exile. The Alexandrian Aristobulus mentioned in 2 Mac. 1:10 was 'from the order of anointed priests' (*ὄντι ἀπὸ τοῦ τῶν χριστῶν ἱερέων γένους*). Dan. 9:26 speaks of an 'Anointed', which probably refers to

The number of priests was so great that it was impossible for all of them to officiate at the same time. A strict rotation had therefore to be observed. To this end, the whole priesthood was divided into twenty-four families or courses.[29] On the origin of these, and their organization, rabbinic tradition has the following to say:[30]

> 'Four courses (משמרות) returned from the exile: Jedaiah, Harim Pashur, and Immer. . . . The prophets among them then arose and made twenty-four lots and cast them in an urn. And Jedaiah came and drew five lots, thus making six including himself. And Harim came and drew five lots, thus making six including himself. And Pashur came and drew five lots, thus making six including himself. And Immer came and drew five lots, thus making six including himself. . . . And heads of the courses (ראשי משמרות) were appointed. And the courses were divided into fathers' houses (בתי אבות). And there were courses of five, six, seven, eight, or nine fathers' houses. In a course of five houses, three had one day each, and two, two days of service each; in a course of six houses, five had one day each, and one, two days of service; of seven, each had one day; of eight, six had one day each, two together had one day; of nine, five had one day each, four together had two days.'

---

the High Priest Onias III; cf. J. A. Montgomery, *The Book of Daniel* (1927), p. 381. Thus at that time anointing was still current and the Hasmonaean priest-kings would have hardly discontinued its practice. It is more likely to have been abolished in the Herodian-Roman period. In addition to anointed High Priests, rabbinic tradition refers also to the משוח מלחמה, i.e. a priest anointed as a war leader (cf. mSot. 8:1; bYom. 72b, 73a. Cf. Y. Yadin, *The Scroll of the War of the Sons of Light against the Sons of Darkness* (1962), pp. 208–9. If it is permissible to draw a historical conclusion from the War Rule of Qumran, 1QM 9:9, in referring to the 'oil of the priestly anointing' (שמן משיחת כהונתם) of the seven priestly trumpeters, implies that the rite was still practised in general, and not only in connection with the High Priest. For a metaphorical use of 'to anoint', see Vermes, *Jesus the Jew*, pp. 158–9.

29. See D. Sperber, 'Mishmarot and Ma'amadot', Enc. Jud. 12, cols. 89–93. J. Liver, פרקים בתולדות הכהונה והלוייה (1968), pp. 35–52; M. Avi-Yonah, 'A List of Priestly Courses from Caesarea', IEJ 12 (1962), pp. 137–42. E. J. Vardaman, 'Introduction to the Caesarea Inscription of the twenty-four Priestly Courses', *Studies in Memory of H. Trentham* (1964), pp. 42–5; M. Avi-Yonah, 'The Caesarean Inscription of the twenty-four Priestly Courses', *ibid.* pp. 46–57.

30. yTaan. 68a. Cf. also tTaan. 2:1–2; bArakh. 12b. The Qumran sect divided its priesthood into twenty-six courses or משמרות, each destined to serve twice a week during the year (the sectarian calendar calculated fifty-two weeks to the year: cf. vol. I, p. 600). See 1QM 2:2; Y. Yadin, *The Scroll of the War* . . ., pp. 204–6; P. Winter, 'The Twenty-Six Priestly Courses', VT 6 (1956), pp. 215–17; G. Vermes, *Discovery* . . ., pp. 212–13; S. Talmon, 'The Calendar Reckoning of the Sect from the Judaean Desert', Scrip. Hier. 4 (1958), pp. 169–70. On the as yet unpublished 4Q Mishmarot see J. T. Milik, *Ten Years of Discovery in the Wilderness of Judaea* (1959), pp. 41, 107–10, 152. See Str.-B. II, pp. 55–68.

This information concerning the origin, or according to the Talmud the restoration, of the twenty-four courses does not constitute an independent tradition but is based merely on inferences drawn from other known facts. Yet it is essentially accurate. Four priestly families returned from the exile with Zerubbabel and Joshua: the children of Jedaiah, Immer, Pashur, and Harim, a total of four thousand two hundred and eighty-nine.[31]

These four families still constituted the entire priesthood at Ezra's arrival, as is evident from Ezra 10:18–22.[32] At the same time, there is mention as early as the period of Zerubbabel and Joshua of twenty-two priestly divisions with as many 'heads' (Neh. 12:1–7). And these same divisions are found again under Joshua's successor, the High Priest Joiakim (Neh. 12:12–21).[33] The four families were therefore clearly subdivided into twenty-two units. Essentially the same situation is still encountered in the time of Ezra. To the four priestly families already in the land, Ezra, with his band of returning exiles, added two more (Ezra 8:2).[34] But the number of divisions soon became the same as in the time of Zerubbabel, i.e. twenty-one, as may be seen in the list given in Neh. 10:3–9. However, of the names found in the latter,

31. Ezr. 2:36–9; Neh. 7:39–42. The accuracy of the alleged numbers for the time of Zerubbabel is widely questioned. Cf. K. Galling, 'The "Gola-List" according to Ezra 2/Nehemiah 7', JBL 70 (1951), pp. 149–58; *idem*. 'Von Nabonidus zu Darius', ZDPV 69 (1953), pp. 42–64, 70 (1954), pp. 4–32; A. L. Allrik, 'The Lists of Zerubbabel (Nehemiah vii and Ezra ii) and the Hebrew Numeral Notation', BASOR 136 (1954), pp. 21–7. It should also be borne in mind that Hecataeus of Abdera at the beginning of the Hellenistic period, gives the number of Jewish priests as only fifteen hundred in all, Josephus, *C.Ap*. i 22 (188): *καίτοι [φησίν,] οἱ πάντες ἱερεῖς τῶν Ἰουδαίων οἱ τὴν δεκάτην τῶν γινομένων λαμβάνοντες καὶ τὰ κοινὰ διοικοῦντες περὶ χιλίους μάλιστα καὶ πεντακοσίους εἰσίν*. Should the women and children be understood as also included in the biblical figure of four thousand two hundred and eighty-nine? A. Büchler, *Die Priester und der Cultus* (1895), pp. 47 ff. argues that Hecataeus had in mind only those living in Jerusalem. The opinion that the lists are to be regarded as a survey of the population of Judah in the time of Ezra or Nehemiah has been advanced by Wellhausen, Kosters, Hölscher, Pfeiffer, Albright, Ahlemann, Bright, etc. For the view that the lists are genuine, cf. O. Eissfeldt, *The Old Testament: An Introduction* (1965), pp. 550–1 and the literature cited there. For the whole issue, see also J. Jeremias, *Jerusalem in the Time of Jesus* (1969), pp. 200–1 and M. Stern, GLAJJ I, p. 42.

32. For a recent discussion of the chronology of Ezra-Nehemiah with copious bibliography, see J. A. Emerton, 'Did Ezra go to Jerusalem in 428 B.C.?' JThSt 17 (1966), pp. 1–19. [The date 398 B.C. is seen as more probable than 428 or the traditional 458 B.C.]

33. Only one name from the first list is missing from the second (Hattush). The remaining twenty-one names are identical, as is clearly evident notwithstanding the numerous inaccuracies of the text. W. Rudolph, *Esra und Nehemia* (1949), pp. 192–3.

34. Gershom and Daniel mentioned here are the names of priestly families; see Rudolph, *op. cit.*, pp. 79 f.

only fourteen appear in the two earlier lists; all the rest are different (Neh. 12:1–7, 12–21). Hence, many changes took place in the meanwhile in the organization of the divisions, changes necessitated by the additional priestly families brought in by Ezra, but perhaps also by other circumstances. Nevertheless, in the new arrangement the number of divisions remained the same as before, and in the main continued to do so in the years that followed. In the age of the Chronicler, who traces back the conditions of his own day to that of David, the number of divisions amounts to twenty-four (1 Chr. 24:7–18). It is true that hardly more than one-third of the earlier lists is re-encountered in his register. Consequently, unless the Chronicler's names for the time of David are in part fictitious, further important alterations must have taken place. It is certain, however, that from then on, the division into twenty-four courses remained unchanged. For Josephus explicitly attests that they existed in his day,[35] and some of the names are even occasionally mentioned (Joiarib: 1 Mac. 2:1, 14:29; Abia: Lk. 1:5).[36] Surprisingly, in a passage from his *Against Apion*—admittedly extant in Latin only—Josephus speaks of four tribes or divisions ('tribus') of priests.[37] One might be inclined to see in this a reference to the four clans who returned with Zerubbabel, and to assume that he ascribes to them Temple service by rotation, but only in general terms. Otherwise this is a textual corruption and should read twenty-four instead of four. It is no contradiction of this interpretation that each division is said by him to amount to more than five thousand. For the Levites (who were also divided into twenty-four courses so that each course of priests had a corresponding course of Levites) are probably included in this number, and perhaps the women and children as well. Besides, Josephus's numbers, as is well known, must be treated with caution.

35. *Ant.* vii 14, 7 (366): διέμεινεν οὗτος ὁ μερισμὸς ἄχρι τῆς σήμερον ἡμέρας. *Vita* 1 (2): ἐμοὶ δ' οὐ μόνον ἐξ ἱερέων ἐστὶν τὸ γένος, ἀλλὰ καὶ ἐκ τῆς πρώτης ἐφημερίδος τῶν εἰκοσι-τεσσάρων, πολλὴ δὲ κἀν τούτῳ διαφορά, καὶ τῶν ἐν ταύτῃ δὲ φυλῶν ἐκ τῆς ἀρίστης. Cf. also mTaan. 4:2; mSuk. 5:6–8.

36. Joiarib and Jedaiah are also mentioned, mB.K. 9:12. The course of Joiarib is said to have been the one officiating when the Temple was destroyed, bTaan. 29a. Cf. Derenbourg, *Essai*, p. 291. The course of Bilga is mentioned in mSuk. 5:8, the proper names *Βελγᾶς* and *Δαλαῖος* in Josephus, *B.J.* vi 5, 1 (280) (Bilga is the fifteenth course, Delaiah the twenty-third.) A family called Ḥezir (חזיר), presumably the priestly family of that name (1 Chron. 24:15), is mentioned in a tomb inscription dating to around the Herodian period discovered by M. de Vogüé (Rev. archéol. N.S. 9 (1864), pp. 200–9.) Cf. also S A. Cooke, *Text-book of North-Semitic Inscriptions* (1903), no. 148; CIJ no. 1394. For a second mention of the same family name, see CIJ no. 1395. N. Avigad, מצבות קדומות בנח קדרון (1954), pp. 37–78.

37. *C.Ap.* ii 8 (108), 'Licet enim sint tribus quattuor sacerdotum, et harum tribuum singulae habeant hominum plus quam quinque milia, fit tamen obseruatio particulariter per dies certos; et his transactis alii succedentes ad sacrificia ueniunt . . .'

In a Qumran liturgical calendar, the names of the priestly courses designate the week of the year during which they were to officiate:

> 'On Tuesday in (the week of) Maaziah: the Passover. On Sunday in (the week of) Jeda[iah]: the waving of the First Sheaf. On Thursday in (the week of) Seorim: the [Second] Passover. On Sunday in (the week of) Jeshna: the feast of Weeks. [On] Wednesday in (the week of) Maaziah: the Day of Memorial (New Year). [On] Friday in (the week of) Joiarib: the Day of Atonement. [On Wednesday in (the week of) Jeda]iah: the feast of Tabernacles'.

Elsewhere, reference is made also to Jehezekel.[38]

Palestinian liturgical poems dating to the sixth and seventh centuries A.D. indicate the Galilean bases of the twenty-four priestly courses.[39] The existence of a similar list in the third/fourth century A.D. is attested by three fragments of an inscription engraved on marble and discovered at Caesarea. The reconstructed lines read:

> 'The 17th course Hezir: *Mamliaḥ.*
> The 18th course Aphses: *Nazareth.*
> The 19th course Pethahiah: *Akhlah Arab*
> The 20th course Jehezel: *Migdal Nunaya.*'[40]

Each of the twenty-four main divisions was further subdivided.

The number of these subdivisions varied from five to nine for each main division—assuming, that is to say, that the Talmudic tradition cited above (p. 245) is reliable. The main divisions are given either the general designation מחלקות (divisions; thus 1 Chron. 28:13, 21; 2 Chron. 8:14, 23:8, 31:2, 15–16); or in so far as they were composed of one family, בית אבות (fathers' houses; thus 1 Chron. 24:4, 6); or in so far as they were responsible for the Temple service, משמרות (watches; thus Neh. 13:30; 2 Chron. 31:16). The subdivisions, which are attested only

38. Cf. J. T. Milik, 'Le travail d'édition des manuscrits du désert de Juda', *Volume du Congrès—Strasbourg 1956*, Suppl. VT 4 (1957), p. 25. The extracts from 4Q Mishmarot are given in transliteration:

*b*3 [*b*] *m'wzyh hpsḥ*
[*b*1] *byd'*[*yh*] *hnp h*[*'mr*]
*b*5 *bs'rym hpsḥ* [*hšny*]
*b*1 *byšw' ḥg hšbw'ym*
[*b*]4 *bm'zyh ywm hzkrwn*
[*b*]6 *bywyryb ywm hkpwrym*
[*b*4 *byd'*]*yh ḥg hswkwt*

Cf. also Milik, *Ten Years of Discovery* . . ., pp. 108–9.

39. Cf. I. Rabin's discussion in P. Kahle, *Masoreten des Westens* I (1930), pp. 81–7; 1*–59*, א–כא. See S. Klein, *Galilee*, ed. Y. Elitzur (1967), pp. 64–5.

40. Cf. M. Avi-Yonah, 'A List of Priestly Courses from Caesarea', IEJ 12 (1962), pp. 137–9. The editor notes (p. 139, n. 6) that this is the earliest Jewish, and the only epigraphic, reference to Nazareth.

in post-biblical literature, are called בתי אבות. Indeed it had become usual to distinguish between the two by designating the main division משמר and the subdivision, בית אב.[41] This distinction is not necessarily founded on the significance of the words themselves. For in the same way that משמר can be any serving division, so בית אב can be any family group, large or small.[42] Thus, as has been observed, the Chronicler still refers to the main divisions as בית אברת (shortened into אבות in Neh. 12:12). But later, a strong distinction is made, in the manner indicated. In Greek, a main division is called *πατρία* or *ἐφημερία* or *ἐφημερίς* and a subdivision, *φυλή*.[43]

The courses as well as the subdivisions were each presided over by a head. In the Old Testament, those of the main units are called שרים (princes)[44] or ראשים (heads).[45] Later, the second designation (ראש המשמר) seems to have been the one commonly adopted, and ראש בית אב for the head of a subdivision.[46] In addition, 'elders' are met with, זקני כהנים[47] and זקני בית אב.[48]

The prestige of the different courses was by no means the same. Despite a formal equality in the regular rotation of service, those from which the High Priest or other influential officials were selected must themselves have gained in influence. It is therefore quite safe to believe Josephus when he asserts that it was of great advantage to belong to the first of the twenty-four courses,[49] i.e. that of Joiarib, from which

41. This distinction is particularly evident in mTaan. 2:6, 7. See also the passage quoted above, p. 245; yHor. 48b; and tHor. 2:10 where it is stated that the ראש המשמר ranks higher than the ראש בית אב. משמר is also encountered mSuk. 5:6–8, mTaan. 4:2 and mTam. 5:1, in the sense of 'course', or 'division for a week's service'. Cf. also mBik. 3:12; mYeb. 11:7; mB.K. 9:12; mTem. 3:4 and mPar. 3:11. בית אב, on the other hand, occurs in the sense of a sub-division or division for one day's service in mYom. 3:9; 4:1; mTam. 1:1; mMid. 1:8. The Qumran War Rule mentions twenty-six משמרות of priests, Levites and lay Israelites serving in the Temple of Jerusalem (1QM 2:2–4).

42. See S. R. Driver's note on Ex. 6:14 in *The Book of Exodus* (1911), p. 46.

43. *πατρία*, Josephus, *Ant.* vii 14, 7 (366); *πατριαί*, *Ant.* vii 14, 7 (364); *ἐφημερία*, Lk. 1:5, 8; *ἐφημερίς* and *φυλή*, Josephus, *Vita* 1 (2). Mention is made of a *φυλὴ Ἐνιαχείμ* in Josephus, *B.J.* iv 3, 8 (155).

44. שרי הכהנים, Ezr. 8:24, 29, 10:5; 2 Chron. 36:14. שרי קדש, 1 Chron. 24:5. That these שרים are identical with ראשי אבות is especially clear in 1 Chron. 15:4–12, where both expressions are used to denote the heads of the Levitical courses.

45. ראשים לבית אבות, 1 Chron. 24:4. ראשי האבות, Neh. 12:12; 1 Chron. 24:6. Cf. also Neh. 11:13, 12:7.

46. Both expressions figure in tHor. 2:10; yHor. 48b. The former appears also in yTaan. 68a; the latter in mYom. 3:9; 4:1.

47. mYom. 1:5.

48. mTam. 1:1; mMid. 1:8.

49. *Vita* 1 (2): *πολλὴ δὲ κἀν τούτῳ διαφορά* = 'there is a great advantage also in this'.

the Hasmonaean High Priests and princes had come.[50] Particularly influential circles also developed within the individual courses. The families which lived in Jerusalem will have known how to secure the most important of the Temple offices, those which endowed their holders with great authority. But in the Roman period in particular, the privileged families from which the High Priests were taken (see above, p. 234) formed themselves into a distinguished aristocracy greatly superior to the other priests. The social difference was so marked that towards the end of the period before the destruction of the Temple the High Priests are even said to have snatched the tithes from the other priests by force so that they starved.[51] As a result, the political mood varied so widely that at the outbreak of the revolution the serving priests joined the revolt while the High Priests did everything in their power to allay the storm.[52]

The 'Levites', as second rank ministers, are to be carefully distinguished from the priests proper.[53] The difference between them is

50. It has been argued that the list in Chronicles (1 Chron. 24:7–18) was not redacted until the Hasmonaean period. It is in any case very striking that the course of Joiarib, to which the Hasmonaeans belonged, is here moved to the top, whereas in the lists of Neh. 12:1–7, 12–21 it occupies a somewhat subordinate place, and is completely missing from the list in Neh. 10:3–9. J. Köberle, 'Priestertum in A.T.', Herzog-Hauck, *Real-Enz.* 16 ([3]1905), p. 40: 'The primacy of the course of Joiarib is probably connected with the rise to power of the Maccabees, who were of that house; 1 Chron. 24 must therefore be seen as material set in Maccabaean times'); A. Jaubert, 'Le calendrier des Jubilés,' VT 7 (1957), 35–61, especially pp. 44–5; P. Winter, 'Twenty-six Priestly Courses', VT 6 (1956), pp. 215–17; M. Avi-Yonah, 'A List of Priestly Courses from Caesarea', IEJ 12 (1962), pp. 137–42; R. H. Pfeiffer (with reservations), *Introduction to the Old Testament* (1948), p. 794; A. Lods, *Histoire de la littérature hébraïque et juive* (1950), p. 637; O. Eissfeldt, *The Old Testament: An Introduction* (1965), p. 540. For criticism of this view, see R. Kittel, *Die Bücher der Chronik* (1902), p. 89; J. M. Myers, *I Chronicles* (Anchor Bible) (1965), p. 165: 'The discovery of a fragment of Chronicles at Qumran renders a Maccabean date virtually impossible for any part of Chronicles'. Nevertheless, the Qumran evidence would be compelling only if the verse in question were attested in a scroll representing the Masoretic type of tradition.

51. Josephus, *Ant.* xx 8, 8 (180–1); 9, 2 (206–7). Cf. S. W. Baron, *A Social and Religious History of the Jews* I ([2]1952), pp. 272–3; J. Jeremias, *Jerusalem* . . . (1969), pp. 38, 106, 108.

52. *B.J.* ii 17, 2–4 (408–21).

53. See in general: W. W. Baudissin, *Die Geschichte des alttestamentlichen Priesterthums* (1889), pp. 28–36, 67–77, 79–84; A. Büchler, *Die Priester und der Cultus im letzten Jahrzehnt des jerusalemischen Tempels* (1895), pp. 118–59; 'Zur Geschichte der Tempelmusik und der Tempelpsalmen', ZAW 19 (1899), pp. 96–133, 329–44; G. A. Barton, 'Levites', JE VIII, pp. 49–50; H. P. Smith, 'Priest, Priesthood (Hebrew)', HERE X, pp. 307–11. E. Auerbach, 'Levi', EJ X, cols. 833–7. L. Steinberger, *Der Bedeutungswechsel des Wortes Levit* (1935); A. C. Welch, *Post-Exilic Judaism* (1935), 217–41; M. Gertner, 'The Masorah and the Levites',

still unknown in Deuteronomy, where the 'Levites' are entitled to participate in priestly service: 'priests' and 'Levites' are simply synonyms (see especially Dt. 18:5, 21:5 and generally, 17:9, 18; 18:1; 24:8; 27:9). The two are first distinguished in Ezekiel; though it is likely that this prophet was drawing on traditions in practice in the pre-exilic monarchy.[54] According to the Deuteronomic legislation all the sanctuaries outside Jerusalem were suppressed. But the 'Levites' officiating there—the priests that is to say—were not deprived of their priestly rights; they were merely required to perform these functions exclusively in Jerusalem. But this position could not last for long. The Jerusalem priesthood cannot have welcomed such an immigration of colleagues from the provinces. In addition, the latter had been guilty, to a larger extent than the priests of Jerusalem, of mixing the cult of the God of Israel with the worship of alien gods. Ezekiel therefore now draws the consequences from the Deuteronomic position: he forbids the provincial Levites from officiating at sacrificial worship altogether. This is to be the exclusive privilege of Levites of the house of Zadok, i.e. the Jerusalem priesthood. Only the sons of Zadok may from now on 'offer fat and blood before God' at the altar and enter the inner sanctuary. To the other Levites were assigned the less important offices of guard service, slaughter of the sacrificial animals, etc. This had the additional advantage that the Gentile Temple servants, who until then had been employed to carry out the more menial tasks, could be excluded from the sanctuary altogether (see in general, Ezek. 44:6–16).

The order initiated by Ezekiel was the one which in all essential respects prevailed. The distinction established by him between priests, the 'sons of Aaron', and the remaining Levites is taken as fixed already in the Priestly Code. Only the former have the right to minister at the

---

VT X (1960), 241–72. R. Abba, 'Priests and Levites', IDB III, pp. 876–89; R. de Vaux, *Ancient Israel* (1961), pp. 358–71; 390–4; J. Jeremias, *Jerusalem* . . . (1969), pp. 207–13; A. Cody, *A History of Old Testament Priesthood* (1969), pp. 146–74. On the regular distinction between priests and Levites in Deuteronomy, cf. T. J. Meek, *Hebrew Origins* (1936), pp. 119 ff.; G. T. Manley, *The Book of the Law* (1957), pp. 104–7; J. A. Emerton, 'Priest and Levite in Deuteronomy', VT 12 (1962), 129–38; for the argument that Levite and priest is nowhere equivalent, see Baudissin, 'Priests', in HDB IV, p. 70b. In all the Qumran documents the Levites always come second to the priests, whether it is merely a question of order of precedence ('the Priests shall enter first . . . then the Levites; and thirdly all the people': 1QS 2:11; cf. CD 14:3–5), or explicitly a question of authority ('the sons of Levi shall hold office . . . under the authority of the sons of Aaron': 1QS 1:22). Apart from their liturgical functions, the Levites' duties consisted in administration in association with the lay leaders (1QS 1:21, 2:1; cf. 1 Chron. 26: 30–32) and probably teaching. See G. Vermes, *DSSE*, pp. 16–25; G. Driver, *The Judaean Scrolls* (1965), pp. 61–5.

54. See in general, J. Pedersen, *Israel* III/IV, p. 181; J. Bright, *History*², pp. 162–3; R. de Vaux, *Ancient Israel*, p. 364 ff.

altar and in the sanctuary (Num. 18:7). The 'Levites', by contrast, are merely assistants of the sons of Aaron 'in all the service of the tabernacle' (Num. 18:4). Accordingly, they can and must support the priests in the great variety of Temple duties and offices: in the administration of the priestly dues and property, in the presentation and preparation of the many requirements of sacrificial worship, etc. (for further details, see Part III). The slaughter and preparation of the sacrificial victims is their responsibility, in Ezekiel as later in Chronicles.[55] They are debarred only from what takes place on the altar or within the sanctuary (Num. 18:3; see in general, Num. 3:5–13 and 18:1–7).[56]

55. 2 Chron. 29:34; 35:11. It may well be concluded from these passages that the Levites were only summoned to act as slaughterers when great numbers of victims had to be dealt with. Cf. R. H. Pfeiffer, *Introduction to the Old Testament*, pp. 791–2; on the functions of the Levites, cf. W. Rudolph, *Esra und Nehemia* (1949), pp. 91 f. As a rule, this too was the task of the priests. But legally, it was permitted even to laymen, and was in effect carried out by them at Passover because of the overwhelming numbers, as appears from the clear testimony of Philo and the Mishnah: cf. Philo, *Vita Mosis* ii (224); *Decal.* 30 (159); *Spec. Leg.* ii 27 (145). mPes. 5:6: 'An Israelite slaughtered his (own) offering and the priest caught the blood'. See Z. Fränkel, *Ueber den Einfluss der palästinischen Exegese auf die alexandrinische Hermeneutik* (1851), p. 134; B. Ritter, *Philo und die Halacha*, pp. 110 ff. A. Büchler, *Die Priester und der Cultus* (1895), pp. 137–40. Ritter is correct in understanding the act of *θύειν*, which Philo attributes to the laity at the Passover, as alluding only to the slaughter, and not to the bringing of the offering to the altar.

56. The genealogical derivation of the priests from Aaron is above all merely a dogmatic postulate from which nothing whatever can be inferred with regard to the actual state of affairs during the post-exilic period. It is true, however, that the concept of the 'Sons of Aaron' in the Priestly Code is a wider one than that of the 'Sons of Zadok' in Ezekiel: cf. Baudissin, *Geschichte des alttestamentl. Priesterthums*, pp. 107 ff. On the 'sons of Zadok', cf. J. Le Moyne, *Les Sadducéens* (1972), pp. 63–7; J. Liver, 'The "Sons of Zadok the Priests" in the Dead Sea Sect', RQ 6 (1967), pp. 3–30. The former include the two lines of Eleazar and Ithamar, on the basis that of the four sons of Aaron, Exod. 6:23, two (Nadab and Abihu) were eliminated Lev. 10:1–2. But the 'sons of Zadok' represent only the line of Eleazar (1 Chron. 5:30–41); on the problems arising a propos of Zadok's lineage, cf. S. R. Driver, *Notes on the Hebrew Books of Samuel* (²1913), p. 283, on 2 Sam. 8:17; R. de Vaux, *Ancient Israel* (1961), p. 372–4. Thus the Priestly Code does not venture to make out the latter to be those solely entitled but finds it necessary to enlarge the circle somewhat. In point of fact, among the priests of the new communities after the exile we also find some from the line of Ithamar (Ezr. 8:2, 1 Chron. 24); even at Qumran, where the Zadokites ruled, the legitimacy of Ithamar's line was recognized, 1 QM 17:3. In the main, therefore, Ezekiel's theory prevailed, but not in every particular; see J. Wellhausen, *Die Pharisäer und die Sadducäer*, p. 48; in another passage, however, which although perhaps secondary is related to the Priestly Code (Num. 25:10 ff.), only Phinehas, the son of Eleazar and father of the Zadokite line, is promised eternal priesthood. Hence this fragment wholly represents Ezekiel's standpoint. See de Vaux, *Ancient Israel*, pp. 394–7. Also worthy of note is the view advanced by Jesus ben Sira. He traces back to the 'Covenant' with Phinehas the claim of his descendants to the 'High Priesthood'

Like the priests, the Levites formed a closed circle based on family descent. Their ancestry was now traced back to Levi, one of the twelve patriarchs of Israel (Exod. 6:17–25; Num. 3:14–39, 4:34–49, 26:57–62; 1 Chron. 5:27–6:66 and ch. 23). Thus here, also, it was birth that decided the claim to participation in the rights and duties of the community. The 'priests' stood to them in the relation of a privileged family vis-à-vis the tribe in general. For Aaron, the patriarch of the priests, was a great-grandson of Levi (Exod. 6:17 ff.).

How flexible and fluid these genealogical theories were, is particularly clear in the history of the Levites itself. In the post-exilic period, 'Levites' in the sense already described were still strictly distinguished from the Temple singers, door-keepers, and Temple servants (Nethinim, originally, at all events, slaves). This continued to be the case not only during the time of Zerubbabel, but also in that of Nehemiah and Ezra (see especially Ezra 2:40–58 = Neh. 7:43–60; also Ezra 2:70; 7:7, 24; 10:23–4; Neh. 7:1, 73, 10:29, 40; 12:44–7; 13:5, 10). But little by little the Temple singers and door-keepers came to be included among the 'Levites'. The affiliation of the Temple singers to the Levites is presupposed in the revision of several parts of the Book of Nehemiah.[57]

(כהונה גדולה), Ecclus. 45:23–4 and 50:24 (in Hebrew) and praises God for choosing 'the sons of Zadok to be priests' (*ibid.* 51:12 extant only in Hebrew: בוחר בבני צדוק לכהן). On the subject of Aaron and the Aaronites in general, see L. Ginzberg, *Legends of the Jews* II, pp. 331–6, 347–52, III, pp. 119–24, 320–30; M. Guttmann, *Mafteaḥ Hatalmud* II (1919), pp. 37–55; T. J. Meek, 'Aaronites and Zadokites', AJSL 45 (1929), pp. 149–66; K. Möhlenbrink, 'Die levitischen Überlieferungen des AT', ZAW 52 (1934), pp. 184–231; J. Morgenstern, 'A Chapter in the History of the High Priesthood', AJSL 55 (1938), pp. 1–24, 360–77; C. F. North, 'Aaron', IDB I, pp. 1 f. The distinction between 'sons of Zadok' and 'sons of Aaron' appears to have been obscured in the Qumran documents, where the two titles are used synonymously. In the Community Rule, the members 'shall unite, with respect to the Law and possessions, under the rule of the *sons of Zadok*, the Priests, Keepers of the Covenant' (1QS 5:2). Those seeking admission to the sect were to 'return . . . to every commandment of the law of Moses in accordance with all that has been revealed of it to the *sons of Zadok*, the Keepers of the Covenant' (*ibid.* 5:8–9). On the other hand, the candidate was to be examined 'with respect to his understanding and practice of the Law under the authority of the *sons of Aaron*' (1QS 5:4). 'The *sons of Aaron* alone shall command in matters of justice and property (1QS 9:7). The same interchangeability is attested in the Messianic Rule. The chiefs of the Israelite laity are said to be '[under the authority] of the *sons of* [*Aar*]*on* the Priests' (1QSa 1:15–16; cf. 1:23; 2:13), or 'under the authority of the *sons of Zadok*, the Priests' (1 QSa 1:24; cf. 1:2; 2:3). On the allegorical use of 'sons of Zadok' in the 'Zadokite' Document or Damascus Rule (CD 3:21–4:4) see J. Liver, *art. cit.*, RQ 6 (1967), pp. 8–12.

57. Neh. 11:15–19, 22, 23; 12:8–9, 24–25, 27–29. Here, the Temple singers are classed throughout as Levites, but not the door-keepers. Neh. 11 and 12 must therefore have been transmitted in a revised form representing an intermediate stage between the standpoint of the oldest sources of the Book of Nehemiah and that of the author of Chronicles. See Baudissin, *op. cit.*, pp. 143 f.

Later, the door-keepers were accorded this honour: the Chronicler deliberately numbers both categories among the Levites and traces their ancestry, too, back to Levi.[58] The Temple singers rose still higher in rank shortly before the destruction of the sanctuary, when King Agrippa II, with the consent of the Sanhedrin, permitted them to wear linen robes similar to those worn by the priests.[59]

Of the occupation of 'Levites' who were neither Temple singers nor door-keepers little more is known than has already been said (cf. p. 252). They were the priests' assistants in their various services.[60]

The Levites, like the priests, were divided into courses of service. But their history is even more obscure than that of the priests. Only very few of them returned from the exile with Zerubbabel and Joshua; seventy-four in all, plus one hundred and twenty-eight Temple singers and one hundred and thirty-nine door-keepers (Ezra 2:40–2; the numbers given in the parallel text Neh. 7:43–5 differ somewhat from these). Ezra brought altogether only thirty-eight 'Levites' with him, and these only after pressing expostulations on his part (Ezra 8:15–20). This disinclination to return was due to the subordinate position allotted to them. But it may safely be assumed that the number that returned was soon enlarged from among those who had remained in the land. For far fewer 'Levites', who lived scattered throughout the country, must have been deported than 'priests'—which at that time meant the Jerusalem priesthood. Thus in the list of Levites and Temple singers at the time of Zerubbabel and Joshua (Neh. 12:8), several more families are mentioned than in the record of those who returned with Zerubbabel (Ezr. 2:40 f.; Neh. 7:43 f.).[61] A list from the period of Ezra and Nehemiah already enumerates seventeen families of Levites in the

58. On the affiliation of the Temple singers to the Levites, see 1 Chron. 15:16 ff.; 23: 3–5; 2 Chron. 29:25, etc. On the door-keepers see 1 Chron. 9:26; 15:18, 23, 24; 23:3–5. On the descent from Levi of the three families of Temple singers—Heman, Asaph, and Ethan, see 1 Chron. 6:16–32; but also of the door-keepers, partly in any case, through Obed Edom, see 1 Chron. 15:18. In Chronicles also, the *Nethinim* are still distinct from the Levites, 1 Chron. 9:2. On the institution of Temple slavery, see I. Mendelsohn, *Slavery in the Ancient Near East* (1949), pp. 99–106. In general, J. Köberle, *Die Tempelsänger* (1899); A. Büchler, ZAW (1899), pp. 96–133; S. Mowinckel, *The Psalms in Israel's Worship* II (1962), pp. 79–84; E. Gerson-Kiwi, 'Musique dans la Bible', DB Supp. V, pp. 1411 ff.; E. Werner, 'Music' in IDB III, pp. 457–69; B. Bayer, H. Avenary, 'Music', Enc. Jud. 12, cols. 559 ff. On temple-singers in the Near East, see Mowinckel, *op. cit.*, p. 80, nn. 3, 4 and 5.

59. Josephus, *Ant.* xx 9, 6 (216–17).

60. It should not be concluded from the paucity of detailed information that this entire category did not exist at all in the time of the Chronicler.

61. See J. M. Myers, *Ezra-Nehemiah* (Anchor Bible), pp. 18–22, 146 f.

stricter sense of the word (Neh. 10:10–14).[62] Another, also probably dating to Nehemiah,[63] gives the number of Levites residing in Jerusalem alone, including of course the Temple singers, as two hundred and eighty-four (Neh. 11:15–18). Presumably, the number of those living outside the city, in the towns and villages of Judaea, was considerably larger (Neh. 11:20, 36).[64]

At the time of the Chronicler, it seems that the Levites as well as the priests were divided into twenty-four courses. This writer, who classes Temple singers and door-keepers as Levites, nevertheless differentiates between the three leading groups: Levites for the Temple service generally, Temple singers and door-keepers (see for example 1 Chron. 23:3–5). For the first group, he gives in 1 Chron, 23:6–24 a list of fathers' houses (בית אבות) which, if a few are corrected, probably amount to twenty-four.[65] The Temple singers are expressly divided into twenty-four courses (1 Chron. 25). In post-biblical times this division of the Levites is attested as firmly established, and indeed in such a way that each course of priests had its corresponding course of Levites.[66]

62. M. Noth, *The History of Israel* ([2]1960), p. 329, and J. Bright, *A History of Israel* ([2]1972), pp. 396 ff., consider this list as possibly a later interpolation.

63. On the dating of this list, see F. Bertholet, *Die Bücher Esra und Nehemia* (1902), p. 82; W. Rudolph, *Esra und Nehemia* (1949), p. 185.

64. The number of priests living in Jerusalem is given in this same list as 1,192 (Neh. 11:10–14), while the total number is estimated at around 6,000 (according to Ezr. 2:36–39 and 8:2; see p. 246 above). It may be assumed that the proportion of Levites in the provinces compared to those living in Jerusalem was even greater. There must, in any case, have been more 'Levites' than Temple singers and door-keepers. For when the author of Chronicles reckons that in David's time there were 24,000 Levites proper, 4,000 Temple singers and 4,000 door-keepers (1 Chron. 23:4–5), the relative proportions must have corresponded approximately to the reality existing in his own day, however greatly the numbers themselves were exaggerated.

65. See K. Möhlenbrink, *art. cit.* ZAW (1934), pp. 184 ff. Nine fathers' houses to the family of Gershom, nine to that of Kohat, and probably six to that of Merari—if, that is to say, the three missing houses of Shoham, Zakkur and Ibri are added to 1 Chron. 24:26–7 and the duplicated name of Mahi is erased from 23:23. For other attemps to reach the number twenty-four: M. Berlin, 'Notes on genealogies of the tribe of Levi', JQR 12 (1900), pp. 291–8. The reconstruction of the number twenty-four in our genealogy is considered inadmissible by I. Benzinger, *Die Bücher der Chronik* (1901), p. 68, and R. Kittel, *Die Bücher der Chronik* (1902), p. 86. That the whole chapter reflects a fluctuating situation when the ranks of the Levites were depleted is argued by W. Rudolph, *Esra und Nehemia* (1949), pp. 155 ff. See also A. C. Welch, *Post-Exilic Judaism* (1935), pp. 81–96. For the twenty-six Levitical divisions at Qumran, see n. 41 above.

66. Josephus, *Ant.* vii 14, 7 (367): *ἐποίησε δὲ καὶ τῆς Ληουίτιδος εἴκοσι μέρη καὶ τέσσαρα καὶ κληρωσαμένων κατὰ τὸν αὐτὸν ἀνέβησαν τρόπον ταῖς τῶν ἱερέων ἐφημερίσιν ἐπὶ ἡμέρας ὀκτώ.* mTaan. 4:2: 'Therefore the First Prophets ordained twenty-four courses (משמרות) and for every course there was a *Ma'amad* (מעמד) in Jerusalem of priests, Levites and Israelites. When the time came for a course to go up, the

As in the case of the priests, each division of Levites was also presided over by a head (ראשים)[67] (שרים).[68]

Very little reliable information is available concerning the places of residence of the priests and Levites for the legislation relating to forty-eight Levitical cities remains largely a theory (Num. 35, Jos. 21).[69] Certainly, in the reorganization of the community only some of the priests and Levites were given residence in Jerusalem itself; the remainder were dispersed among the towns and villages of Judaea, most of them probably not far from the centre. In the list of Neh. 11:10–19 already mentioned, the number of priests living in Jerusalem is given as one thousand one hundred and ninety-two;[70] of Levites and Temple singers, two hundred and eighty-four; and of door-keepers, one hundred and seventy-two. But the sum total of the priests amounted to around five times that number, if not more (see above n. 61); and in the case of the other categories, the relative number of those living in the provinces may have been greater still. In any case, the fact that priests as well as Levites lived in the villages and towns of Judaea is attested repeatedly and positively.[71] But as far as the details are concerned, nothing more is known.[72]

---

priests and the Levites went up to Jerusalem, but the Israelites assembled in [the synagogues of] their own towns and read the Story of the Creation . . .'.

67. Cf. Neh. 12:22–3; 1 Chron. 9:33–4; 15:12; 23:24; 24:6, 31. The divisions whose heads are discussed in these passages are, of course, separate and distinct from each other. For Qumran, see 1QS 2:2–3.

68. Cf. 1 Chron. 15.4–12; 2 Chron. 35:9; 1QSa 2:1.

69. On the Levitical cities see H. M. Nicolsky, 'Asylrecht in Israel', ZAW 48 (1920), pp. 146–75; W. F. Albright, *Archaeology and the Religion of Israel* (^{2}1946), pp. 121–5; *idem*, 'The List of Levitic Cities', *Louis Ginzberg Jubilee Volume* (1945), pp. 49–73; A. Alt, *Kleine Schriften* II (1953), pp. 258 ff., 294 ff., 310 ff., and M. Noth, *Das Buch Josua* (1953), 127 ff. Y. Kaufmann, *Sepher Yehoshua'* (1959), pp. 270–82; B. Mazar, 'The Cities of the Priests and Levites', *Congress Volume*, Suppl. VII to VT, (1960), pp. 193–205; R. de Vaux, *Ancient Israel* (1961), pp. 366–7; M. Haran, JBL 80 (1961), pp. 45 ff., 156 ff.; M. Greenberg, JAOS 88 (1968), pp. 59 ff.; 'Levitical Cities', Enc. Jud. 11, cols. 136–8; B. Z. Luria, ערי הכהנים בימי בית שני, HUCA 44 (1973), pp. 1–19 (Hebrew Section).

70. The parallel passage, 1 Chron. 9:10–13, puts it at a somewhat higher figure.

71. Ezr. 2:70; Neh. 7:73; 11:3, 20, 36; 2 Chron. 31:15, 19.

72. A number of places where Temple singers had settled are mentioned in Neh. 12:27–9. The Maccabees came from Modein (1 Mac. 2:1). The priest Zacharias lived in the hills of Judah (Lk. 1:39). According to Origen, Bethphage was a priests' village. *Comment. in Matt.* (PG XVI, c. 17; Lommatzsch X, p. 532): *ἑρμηνεύεσθαι δέ φαμεν τὴν Βηθφαγὴ μὲν οἶκον σιαγόνων* (*ἥτις τῶν ἱερέων ἦν χωρίον*). Compare also in general: A. Büchler, *Die Priester und der Cultus im letzten Jahrzehnt des jerusalemischen Tempels* (1895), pp. 159 ff.

II. The Priestly Dues

Until the time of the exile, the emoluments which the priests received for their livelihood from the people were very modest and even irregular. After the exile, they increased enormously. This one fact indicates in a particularly striking manner the considerable gain in power and prestige which the priesthood won for itself through the reorganization of affairs after the exile,[1] an advancement which was no doubt as much the cause of the loftier pretensions as they were a consequence of an augmented material income. The later scribes and rabbis, who were not always favourably disposed towards the priests, were unable to change this situation since the priestly law had long since become divine law. Indeed, it was for this very reason that the scribes contributed still further to the growth of the priestly income. Since it was believed that a man earned divine approval in proportion to his accurate observance of the precepts of the Torah, the commandments were almost always interpreted in a sense favourable to the priests. The singular consequence was that an age that had already begun to regard the priests with distrust nevertheless collaborated in the consolidation and heightening of priestly power.

In pre-exilic times there were no real emoluments as such, none, that is to say, unassociated with sacrifice and purely in the nature of a tax. They were offered to priests only on the occasion of sacrifices and in connection with them.[2] A man brought the choicest produce of his fields and the first-born of his cattle to God. Of this, one part was burned on the altar and another part went to the priest, but most of it went to the benefit of the offerer himself to be consumed as a joyful sacrificial meal. When the earliest (J) legislation requires the finest produce of the field and the first-born of the cattle to be brought before the Lord (first-fruits of the field, Exod. 22:28; 23:19; 34:26; first-born of the cattle, Exod. 13:11–16; 22:29; 34:19–20) this is the sense in which it is to be understood.[3] The related laws of Deuteronomy are

1. A correct insight into these matters has been made possible through Pentateuch criticism since J. Wellhausen, *Geschichte Israels* I, pp. 156–64 = *Prolegomena*, 5th ed., pp. 149–56. For subsequent developments see C. R. North, 'Pentateuchal Criticism', *The Old Testament and Modern Study* (ed. H. H. Rowley), 1951, pp. 48–83, O. Eissfeldt, *Introduction* (1965), pp. 155–241.

2. R. de Vaux, *Ancient Israel* (1961), pp. 379–82.

3. The more subtle question as to whether Exod. 13:11–16 and 34:19–20 are part of the J document or were inserted by another hand may be left open. For

absolutely clear and unequivocal. This book knows nothing of the offering of tithe or first-born to the priests. The tithe of the fruits of the field was of course to be set apart and brought to the sanctuary in Jerusalem. It was not however given to the priest but consumed by the worshipper; the priests—i.e. the Levites—and the poor received it only once in every three years (Dt. 14:22–9; 26:12–15; cf. also 12:6; 11:17–19). It was the same with the first-born. These too, namely the male first-born of the cattle and sheep, were to be brought to the sanctuary in Jerusalem, but they were to be consumed there by their owners in sacrificial meals (Dt. 15:19–23; cf. also 12:6, 17–19; 14:23). Of all this, the priests received only certain portions: only the ראשית, the best, of the produce of the fields (Dt. 18:4; 26:1–11), and only the shoulders, cheek and stomach of the sacrificed beasts (Dt. 18:3). Apart from this, there is mention of only one further gift, the first of the sheep-shearing (Dt. 18:4).

Ezekiel's demands serve to confirm these remarks (44:28–30). He too, who was himself a priest and certainly favoured rather than discouraged the priestly claims, knows as yet nothing of any payment of tithe or offering of first-born to the priests. His claims are admittedly already somewhat higher than those of Deuteronomy, but move on the whole along the same lines. Whereas Deuteronomy assigns only a few portions of the sacrificed beast to the priests, Ezekiel requires that they should receive the whole of the sin-offerings, guilt-offerings (which are unknown to Deuteronomy) and grain-offerings (Ezek. 44:29), as well as every 'devoted thing' (44:29); and finally the ראשית, the best of the first-fruits, of offerings of every sort, and of dough (44:30).[4]

Considerably heavier than any of the claims described so far are, however, those of the Priestly Code, which in its review of priestly dues (Num. 18:8–32) concurs in many respects with Ezekiel but at the same time introduces as a most important innovation the offering of the tithe and the first-born. Like Ezekiel, the Priestly Code allots to the priests sin-offerings, guilt-offerings and grain-offerings, or any rate the greater part of the latter (Num. 18:9–10; for fuller details, see Lev. 1–7). Of sacrifices from which the worshipper was at liberty to prepare a sacrificial meal (the so-called זבחי שלמים), the priests were to receive the breast and the right shoulder (Lev. 7.30–4): considerably better portions therefore than those assigned to them by Deuteronomy. Again,

the latter view, see M. Noth, *Exodus, A Commentary* (1962), pp. 101 ff. For the former view, see G. Beer-K. Galling, *Exodus* (1939), pp. 160 f. The verses are assigned to the source L by O. Eissfeldt, *Hexateuch-Synopse* ([2]1962), pp. 270*–1*, 274*–5*, 31–7, 55–8.

4. For a review of the question of Ezekiel's place between Deuteronomy and the Priestly Code, see H. H. Rowley, 'The Book of Ezekiel in Modern Study', BJRL 36 (1953), pp. 146–90.

as in Ezekiel, so also in the Priestly Code, the priests were to get all the devoted things (Num. 18:14) and the best, the ***reshith***, of the produce of the soil: oil, wine, and grain (Num. 18:12). But a due of yet another sort was added to the ***reshith***, that of the first-fruits, **בכורים** (Num. 18:13). And finally, as the most essential revenue, exceeding everything imposed heretofore, came the tithe (Num. 18:20–32) and the first-born (Num. 18:15–18). The tithe nevertheless belonged in the first instance to the 'Levites', who in turn were to give a tenth part of it to the priests. The tribute of dough to the priests, which is missing from the chief source on the subject, is also mentioned in the Priestly Code but in another passage (Num. 15:17–21).

In the time of Nehemiah, these regulations were already fully enforced. Neh. 10:36–40 records that the following dues were handed over: the first fruits or *bikkurim* (10:36); the best of the produce of the soil, which here as in the Priestly Code is clearly distinguished from the first-fruits as well as from the tithe (10:38); the tithe, as in the Priestly Code (10:38–40); the first-born (10:37); and the tribute of dough (10:38)[5]

Here tithe always means only the tithe of the fruits of field and tree. But in one passage of the Priestly Code a tithe of cattle is demanded in addition (Lev. 27:32–3). Presumably, this wholly isolated requirement does not belong to the original Priestly Code.[6] In the time of the Chronicler, the tithe of cattle seems actually to have been exacted; or else it was one of his ideals (2 Chron. 31:6). In post-biblical times the entire passage (Lev. 27:30–3) was understood as referring to the tithe prescribed by Deuteronomy.

The legal prescriptions of Deuteronomy and the Priestly Code not only formed a whole in the literary sense but were combined with one another in practice. Thus the law in its later development raised still further the already high dues laid down in the Priestly Code. To the Levitical tithe of the Priestly Code was now joined, simply as a 'second tithe', the tithe prescribed in Deuteronomy which its owner was to consume before God. The contradictory instructions of the Priestly Code and Deuteronomy in regard to the portions of the sacrificial beasts to be given to the priests were now reconciled by understanding the first to allude only to sacrificed animals, and the second to animals slaughtered for profane use: according to Lev. 7:30–4, the priests were

5. Cf. 'First-Fruits', EJ V, pp. 398–400; Enc. Jud. 6, cols. 1312–16. A noteworthy innovation in the Priestly Code is the introduction of the tithe and the first-born as a tax due to ministers of the cult. The Talmud legitimizes the transfer of the tithes to the priests by explaining that Ezra took them from the Levites because so few were willing to return (bHul. 131b, bKet. 26a, bYeb. 86ab); cf. G. F. Moore, *Judaism* II, pp. 70–1.

6. See J. Wellhausen, *Geschichte Israels* I, p. 162 = *Prolegomena*, 5th ed., p. 155; M. Noth, *Leviticus, A Commentary* (1965), pp. 202 ff., especially pp. 207–8; O. Eissfeldt, *Introduction* (1965), p. 189.

to receive the breast and the right shoulder of the former, and according to Dt. 18:3, a foreleg, the cheeks and stomach of the latter. Finally, to all the imposts of the Priestly Code was added the other tribute prescribed in Deuteronomy (18:4), that of the fleece. This process of amalgamation resulted in the following list of priestly dues, one that may be regarded as having been fully valid in the age of Jesus.[7]

I. Of the sacrifices, the priestly share was:

(1) Sin-offerings in their entirety, as a rule at least, since a few special kinds were required to be burnt outside the camp.[8]
(2) Guilt-offerings, also in their entirety.[9] In both cases only the fat was burnt on the altar; the meat belonged to the priests.
(3) Of grain-offerings by far the greater part inasmuch as only a remnant was laid on the altar whereas the rest went to the priests.[10]

All these types occurred frequently, especially the grain-offerings, which could not only be offered independently but were a necessary supplement to most animal sacrifices.[11]

7. Philo already provides a synopsis in his treatise *Spec. Leg.* i 27–32 (131–59); cf. also B. Ritter, *Philo und die Halacha* (1879), pp. 114–26, and S. Belkin, *Philo and the Oral Law* (1940), pp. 76 ff.; G. Alon, *Jews, Judaism and the Classical World*, pp. 89 ff. See also Josephus in the main passage on the subject, *Ant.* iv 4, 4 (69–75), with which iii 9, 1–4 (224–36) (sacrificial offerings) and iv, 8, 22 (241) (firstlings), may be compared. As the result of an artificial system of reckoning, the rabbis represent the priestly dues as numbering 24 in all; see tHal. 2: 7–9; yHal. 60b; bB.K. 110b; bHul. 133b. Several of the 24 in question are already enumerated in mHal. 4:9. For the Talmudic passages, see J. Pedersen, *Israel* III/IV, pp. 299–375. Interesting parallels may be found in the sacrificial tariffs preserved in Phoenician inscriptions from Marseilles CIS I, no. 165; S. A. Cooke, *Text-book of North-Semitic Inscriptions*, no. 42; H. Donner and W. Röllig, *Kanaanäische und aramäische Inschriften*, no. 69, and Carthage CIS I, nos. 167–70; Cooke, *op. cit.*, no. 43; Donner and Röllig, KAI, no. 74.

8. Lev. 5:13; 6:19, 22 f.; Num. 18:9, 10; Ezek. 44:29; Josephus, *Ant.* iii 9, 3 (230–2); Sifra to Lev. 6:19 ff. (ed. Weiss 32a). Concerning sin- and guilt-offerings generally, see Lev. 4–7; M. Seligsohn, J. Z. Lauterbach, 'Sacrifice', JE X, pp. 615–25; P. Schötz, *Schuld- und Sündopfer im AT* (1930); L. Moraldi, *Espiazione sacrificiale e riti espiatori nell' ambiente biblico* (1956); T. H. Gaster, 'Sacrifice', IDB IV, pp. 147–59; R. de Vaux, *Studies in Old Testament Sacrifice* (1964), pp. 91 ff.; H. H. Rowley, *Worship in Ancient Israel* (1967), pp. 126–31; A. Rothkoff, 'Sacrifice', Enc. Jud. 14, cols. 599–616.

9. Lev. 7:6–7; Num. 18:9–10; Ezek. 44:29; Josephus, *Ant.* iii 9, 3 (231); Sifra to Lev. 7:6–7 (ed. Weiss 33b).

10. Lev. 2:3, 10; 6:9–11; 7:9–10, 14; 10:12–13; Num. 18:9–10; Ezek. 44:29; Josephus, *Ant.* iii 9, 4 (235): *τὴν δὲ λοιπὴν οἱ ἱερεῖς πρὸς τροφὴν λαμβάνουσιν ἢ ἑψηθεῖσαν ἐλαίῳ γὰρ συμπεφύραται ἢ γενομένων ἄρτων.* On the grain-offerings generally, see Lev. 2 and 6:7–11. Cf. also Gaster, IDB IV, pp. 150 f.; R. de Vaux, *Ancient Israel*, pp. 421–2, 430–1.

11. Some idea of the frequency of many of these sacrifices may be obtained by reading the laws on ritual defilement and its removal (Lev. 11–15; Num. 19). For

(4) The twelve loaves of showbread belong also to the same category: placed fresh in the Temple every week, those taken away belonged to the priests.[12]

All these four classes of dues were 'most holy', and as such, were to be consumed only in a holy place, i.e. only in the inner forecourt, and only by the priests themselves (not by their relatives).[13]

The regulations were not so stringent in respect of the sacrificial imposts on thank-offerings and burnt-offerings.

(5) Of זבחי שלמים, i.e. offerings to be consumed by the offerer himself, known as 'thank-offerings' but more properly 'communion sacrifice', the priests received two parts: the breast and right shoulder. These could be eaten in any 'pure place', outside the sanctuary therefore, not only by the priests but also by all those belonging to the priestly class, including wives and daughters.[14]

(6) The *burnt offerings*, which were entirely consumed on the altar were the least rewarding to the priests. But even so, the hides went to them; and considering the frequent burnt-offerings, Philo was certainly correct when he rated this due as a handsome one also.[15]

---

example, every woman after childbirth had to offer a lamb as a burnt-offering and a dove as a sin-offering, or if she were without means, two doves as burnt-offering and sin-offering, Lev. 12:1–8; Lk. 2:24. In general, see J. Pedersen, *Israel* III/IV, especially pp. 348–53.

12. Lev. 24:5–9; see also Josephus, *Ant.* iii 10, 7 (255–6); Mt. 12:4; Mk. 2:26; Lk. 6:4. On the method of distribution, see mSuk. 5:7–8 (the retiring course of service received one half and the incoming course the other).

13. Num. 18:10 and the passages cited in the preceding notes; also Josephus, *Ant.* iv 4, 4 (74–5).

14. Lev. 7:30–4; 10: 14–15; Sifra to Lev. 7:30–4 (ed. Weiss 39ab). Philo, *Spec. Leg.* i 29 (145): *παντὸς γὰρ ἱερείου προστέτακται δύο τοῖς ἱερεῦσιν ἀπὸ δυεῖν δίδοσθαι μελῶν, βραχίονα μὲν ἀπὸ χειρὸς δεξιᾶς, ἀπὸ δὲ τοῦ στήθους ὅσον πῖον.* Josephus, *Ant.* ii 9, 2 (229) *τὸ δὲ στῆθος καὶ τὴν κνήμην τὴν δεξιὰν τοῖς ἱερεῦσι παρασχόντες.* On thank-offerings generally, see Lev. 3 and 7:11–21, 28–34. A. Bertholet, 'Zum Verständniss der ATlichen Opfergedanken', JBL 49 (1930), pp. 218–33; T. H. Gaster, 'Sacrifices and Offerings, OT', IDB, IV, 147 ff.; H. H. Rowley, *Worship in Ancient Israel* (1967), pp. 122–5.

15. Lev. 7:8; Sifra on Lev. 7:8 (ed. Weiss 53b); mZeb. 12: 2–4; tZeb. 3:7–15. Philo, *Spec. Leg.* i 30 (151): *'Εφ' ἅπασι μέντοι καὶ τὰς τῶν ὁλοκαυτωμάτων, ἀμύθητα δὲ ταῦτ' ἐστί, δορὰς πρόσταττει τοὺς ὑπηρετοῦντας ταῖς θυσίαις ἱερεῖς λαμβάνειν, οὐ βραχεῖαν ἀλλ' ἐν τοῖς μάλιστα πολυχρήματον δωρέαν.* Josephus, *Ant.* iii 9, 1 (227). B. Ritter, *Philo und die Halacha*, p. 126. Among the Greeks also the hide of the sacrificed animals belonged to the priests; likewise according to the first sacrificial tariff from Carthage (CIS I, no. 167; Cooke, no. 43; KAI no. 74; whereas according to that of Marseilles, which also derives from Carthage (CIS I, no. 165; Cooke, no. 42; KAI no. 69), it belonged to the offerer. Cf. J. B. Pritchard, *Ancient Near Eastern Texts Relating to the O.T.* ([2]1955), pp. 502 ff. On burnt-offerings generally, see Lev. 1:3–17; W. B. Stevenson, 'Hebrew 'olah and zebach Sacrifices', *Festschrift*

II. Substantial though these sacrificial imposts were, they still formed only the lesser part of the priestly revenues; indeed they benefited only the ministering priests. The real bulk derived from dues paid independently of the sacrifices, dues therefore purely in the nature of a tax for the priesthood. These were in part connected with the produce of the soil and in part with the breeding of cattle, and were discharged either in kind, or in money to an equivalent value. Dues from the produce of the soil were of four kinds and were to be set apart in the following order:[16]

(1) The first-fruits, בכורים. These were offered from the so-called 'seven kinds', i.e. the seven principal crops of Palestine listed in Deuteronomy (8:8): wheat, barley, grapes, figs, pomegranates, olives and honey. Those who lived near Jerusalem brought fresh fruit and those from the provinces brought it dried. The people went in procession to make their offering in what is described by Philo and the Mishnah as a joyous festival. The country people gathered in the principal towns and to the music of pipes travelled from there to Zion in happy columns. At their head went the ox destined for the communion sacrifice, its horns gilded and crowned with olive branches. In Jerusalem the leading priests went out to meet the procession. The people laid wreaths on the baskets containing the first-fruits and carried them on their shoulders up to the Temple Mount as far as the forecourt. Even the most distinguished did this, including King Agrippa himself. When the procession entered the court, the Levites welcomed it with the singing of Psalm 30. Each man then handed over his basket to the priest whilst reciting Dt. 26:5–10, and it was laid beside the altar.[17]

(2) Next came the so-called *terumah*. Distinct from the first-fruits, the offering of which was invested with more of a symbolical-religious significance and to that extent does not entirely belong to the same category, the *terumah* (תרומה) was in the nature of a payment made to the priests purely in kind. By *terumah* in its

---

Bertholet (1950), pp. 109–18; L. Rost, 'Erwägungen zum israelitischen Brandopfer', BZAW 77 (1958), pp. 177–83; R. de Vaux, *Studies in Old Testament Sacrifice* (1964), pp. 27–51.

16. On the correct order, mTer. 5:6–7.

17. See in general, Num. 18:13; Neh. 10:36; also Exod. 23:19, 34:26; Dt. 26:1–11; Josephus, *Ant*. iv 8, 22 (241). In the Mishnah, the entire tractate Bikkurim is devoted to the subject of first-fruits. Cf. especially mBik. 1:3 (on the 'seven kinds' to be offered) and 3:1–9 (description of the festive procession). Philo deals with this matter in *Spec. Leg*. ii 29 (162–75). J. A. MacCullock, 'Firstfruits', in HERE VI, pp. 41 f.; O. Eissfeldt, *Erstlinge und Zehnte im AT* (1917); A. Wendel, *Das Opfer in der altisraelitischen Religion* (1927), pp. 99, 174 ff.; H. H. Guthrie, Jr., 'Tithe', IDB IV, pp. 654 ff.

narrower sense (for in its broader sense *terumah* is every 'heave', i.e. every offering brought to the sanctuary) rabbinic Judaism understands the offering of the best of the fruits of field and tree to the priests. This due related not only to the 'seven kinds' but to every sort of fruit of field and tree. Here, too, the most important were wheat, wine and oil. The due was not to be discharged according to measure, weight or number.[18] It was to amount to an average one-fiftieth of a person's income: one-fortieth was considered generous and one-sixtieth mean.[19] Whatever was set apart for *terumah* could only be eaten by priests.[20]

(3) After the separation of these two dues, there now followed the setting apart of the most important and greatest due of all, that of the tithe. The Gospels make clear how scrupulously the laws of tithe were observed: even the most valueless objects were tithed, such as mint, dill and cummin (Mt. 23:23, Lk. 11:42). The principle laid down in the Mishnah in this respect reads: 'Whatsoever serves for food and is tended and grows out of the soil is liable to tithe'.[21] The yield from this tax must have been considerable. Yet for the most part it was intended not so much for the priests as for the ministers of second rank, the Levites. The tithe went first of all to them, and they in turn gave the priests one tenth of it.[22]

18. mTer. 1:7.

19. mTer. 4:3. Cf. Jerome, *Comment. in Ezech.* 45:13–14 (CCL lxxv, p. 682): 'At vero primitiva quae de frugibus offerebant, non erant speciali numero definita, sed offerentium arbitrio derelicta. Traditionemque accepimus Hebraeorum non lege praeceptam, sed magistrorum arbitrio incolitam: qui plurimum, quadragesimam partem dabat sacerdotibus, qui minimum, sexagesimam: inter quadragesimam et sexagesimam licebat offerre quodcumque voluissent'.

20. See in general, Num. 18:12; Neh. 10:38. For the rabbinic regulations, see the tractate Terumoth. Philo, *Spec. Leg.* i 27 (134): *προστάττει καὶ ἀπὸ τῆς ἄλλης κτήσεως ἀπάρχεσθαι, καθ' ἑκάστην μὲν ληνὸν οἶνον, καθ' ἑκάστην δὲ ἅλωνα σῖτον καὶ κριθήν. 'Ομοίως δὲ ἐξ ἐλαιῶν ἔλαιον καὶ ἀπὸ τῶν ἄλλων ἀκροδρύων ἡμέρους καρπούς.* Josephus, *Ant.* iv 4, 4 (70): *ἔτι δὲ ἀπαρχὰς τὸν λαὸν δίκαιον τῷ θεῷ πάντων τῶν τῆς γῆς φυομένων καρπῶν ἐπιφέρειν.* G. B. Gray, *Numbers* (1903), pp. 227–9; S. Belkin, *Philo and the Oral Law* (1940), pp. 67 ff.; A. Vincent, 'Les rites de balancement (tenoûphâh) et de prélèvement dans le sacrifice de communion de l'Ancien Testament', in *Mélanges Syriens offerts à M. R. Dussaud* I (1939), pp. 267–72; H. H. Rowley, *Worship in Ancient Israel* (1967), p. 126.

21. mMaas. 1:1. For details, see mMaas. 4:5–6; 5:8; on the tithing of dill (*ἄνηθον*, שבת) see mMaas. 4:5; on that of cummin (*κύμινον*, כמון), mDem. 2:1.

22. See in general, Num. 18:20–32; Neh. 10:38–40; Philo, *Virt.* 18 (95); *Spec. Leg.* i 82 (156–7); the tithe is also probably meant in *Spec. Leg.* i 28 (141–2); Josephus, *Ant.* iv 4, 3–4 (68–9); the Mishnah tractate Maaseroth. B. Ritter, *Philo und die Halacha*, pp. 122–4; A. Büchler, 'Die priesterlichen Zehnten und die römischen Steuern in den Erlassen Caesars', *Steinschneider-Festschrift* I (1896), pp. 91–109; [E.T. 'The Priestly Dues . . .', *Studies in Jewish History* (1956), pp. 1–23]; O. Eissfeldt, *Erstlinge und Zehnte im AT* (1917); W. R. Smith, *The Religion*

After deducting this Levitical tithe, the owner had yet another tenth of his income, the so-called second tithe, to set apart. But this, together with several other offerings of a similar nature, was used for sacrificial meals for himself in Jerusalem. They were therefore not for the benefit of the priests at all and do not in consequence belong here.[23]

---

of the Semites (1927), pp. 244 ff.; A. Wendel, *Das Opfer in der altisraelitischen Religion* (1927), pp. 99, 174 ff.; S. Belkin, *Philo and the Oral Law*, pp. 67 ff.; J. Pedersen, *Israel* III/IV (1940), 307–13; R. de Vaux, *Ancient Israel*, pp. 140–1, 380–2, 403–5; H. H. Guthrie, Jr., 'Tithe' in IDB, iv, 654 f.; M. Wischnitzer, 'Tithe', Enc. Jud. 15, cols. 1156–62.

23. To the category of imposts consumed in Jerusalem by the owner himself belong: (1) The *'second tithe'* according to Dt. 14:22–6; Lev. 27:30–1 was also understood in this sense. Cf. Tob. 1:7; Josephus, *Ant.* iv 8, 8 (205). The Book of Jubilees, 32:10–14 considers the second tithe in detail and the Mishnah devotes to it the whole of tractate Ma'aser Sheni. Cf. D. J. Bornstein, 'Ma'aser Sheni', Enc. Jud. 11, cols. 652–4; J. M. Powis Smith, 'The Deuteronomic Tithe', AJT 18 (1914), pp. 119–26; S. R. Driver, *Deuteronomy*, pp. 166–73; Ch. Albeck, *Das Buch der Jubiläen und die Halacha* (1930), pp. 30–2. Those living at a distance from Jerusalem could convert the second tithe into money, adding one-fifth to its value (Lev. 27:31; mM. Sh. 4:3). But this money was to be spent exclusively on the purchase of foods, drinks and ointments to be consumed or used in Jerusalem (Dt. 14:26; mM. Sh. 2:1). W. T. McCree, 'The Covenantal Meal in the OT', JBL 45 (1926), 120–38; E. Bammel, *Das heilige Mahl im Glauben der Völker* (1950). (2) The *cattle-tithe*. The one passage in the Pentateuch requiring cattle to be tithed, viz. Lev. 27:32–3, was understood by later legislation in the sense of the 'second tithe', so the tithed beast was also used for the festival meal. See mZeb. 5:8; cf. the commentaries of Bartenora and Maimonides on mBekh. 9:1. Admittedly, Philo seems to include the cattle tithe among the priestly dues, *Virt.* 18 (95). *Spec. Leg.* i 28 (141) (where the tithe is probably meant). So also Tob. 1:6 according to the recension preserved in Codex Sinaiticus. Cf. J. Jeremias, *Jerusalem* . . ., p. 135, n. 27. The Book of Jubilees clearly awards the cattle tithe to the priests, who are to eat it 'before God' (32:15; cf. also 13:26; 32:2, 8). For further details see mBekh. 9:1–8; mM. Sh. 1:2; mShek. 1:7, 3:1, 8:8; mR. Sh. 1:1; mHag. 1:4; mZeb. 5:8, 10:3; mMen. 9:6; mHul. 1:7. Cf. R. de Vaux, *Ancient Israel* (1961), pp. 404–5; J. Jeremias, *Jerusalem* . . ., pp. 134–6. (3) The *yield of four-year old trees and vines*. According to Lev. 19:23–5, the fruits of newly-planted trees (and vines) were not to be gathered during the first three years, but in the fourth year they were to be consecrated to God. Not until the fifth year were they to be at the free disposal of their owner. The Book of Jubilees defines more precisely that the first fruits of the fourth year are to be brought to the altar, and that the rest is to be eaten by 'the servants of the House of God' (Jub. 7:36; cf. R. H. Charles, *The Book of Jubilees*, 1902, pp. 64 ff.). Later, however, the prescription was understood to mean that the produce of the fourth year was, like the second tithe, to be consumed by the owner himself in Jerusalem. See especially, Josephus, *Ant.* iv 8, 19 (227): *τῷ δὲ τετάρτῳ τρυγάτῳ πᾶν τὸ γενόμενον, τότε γὰρ ὥριον εἶναι, καὶ συναγαγὼν εἰς τὴν ἱερὰν πόλιν κομιζέτω, καὶ σὺν τῇ δεκάτῃ τοῦ ἄλλου καρποῦ μετὰ τῶν φίλων εὐωχούμενος ἀναλισκέτω καὶ μετ᾽ὀρφανῶν καὶ χηρευουσῶν γυναικῶν*. Comp. also Philo, *Virt.* 29 (150), mPea. 7:7; mM. Sh. 5:1–5; mOrl. throughout; mEdu. 4:5. A. Geiger, *Urschrift und Übersetzungen der Bibel* (1857), pp. 181 ff. A. Schwarz, *Die Controversen der Schammaiten und Hilleliten* I (1893), pp. 45–8; J. Jeremias, *Jerusalem* . . ., pp. 137–8. (4) Finally, belonging to those offerings which did *not*

(4) The last due from the produce of the soil was the so-called *ḥallah* (חלה) i.e., the offering of dough (*ἀπαρχὴ τοῦ φυράματος*, Rom. 11:16). According to the Mishnah, five varieties of grain were subject to this due: wheat, barley, spelt, oats, and rye (?).[24] The due was to be discharged not in the form of meal but as dough.[25] For a private citizen it amounted to one twenty-fourth, and for bakers one forty-eighth of the whole.[26]

Offerings of livestock formed the second leading category of regular dues. These were of three kinds.

(1) The most important was the handing-over of the first-born male (i.e. the first-born whenever it happened to be a male). The Torah links the precepts on this to ordinances relating to first-born children. The earlier legislation (J and D) already prescribes that the male first-born of cattle were to be consecrated to God, i.e. used for sacrifice and the sacrificial meal (Exod. 13:11–16, 22:28–9, 34:19–20, Dt. 15:19–23). The priestly legislation makes of this a priestly due (Exod. 13:1–2; Lev. 27:26–7; Num. 18:15–18; Neh. 10:37). To the first-born of cattle, both add the first-born of men, who are equally regarded as belonging to God and therefore in need of redemption. For besides having to distinguish between clean and unclean animals,

---

fall to the priests, were the *offerings to the poor*, namely: (a) corn growing at the margins of the fields at harvest time and gleanings, Lev. 19:9–10, 23:22; Dt. 24: 19–22. Josephus, *Ant.* iv, 8, 21 (231); Philo, *Virt.* 17 (90–1); mPea throughout. (b) The so-called *third tithe* or *poor tithe*. According to the ordinance (Dt. 14:28–9, 26:12) on which this tithe is based one would expect the poor tithe to alternate with the second tithe. For Deuteronomy prescribes that the tithe which was otherwise to be consumed by the owner himself before God was to be assigned in the third year to the poor. So also LXX of Dt. 26:12: (*ἐν τῷ ἔτει τῷ τρίτῳ*) *τὸ δεύτερον ἐπιδέκατον δώσεις τῷ Λευίτῃ καὶ τῷ προσηλύτῳ καὶ τῷ ὀρφανῷ καὶ τῇ χήρᾳ*. The later practice however was to add the poor tithe to the second tithe every third year (more exactly, twice in seven years, the Sabbatical year being omitted). See Tob. 1:7–8. Josephus, *Ant.* iv 8, 22 (240); mPea. 8:2–9; mDem. 4:3–4; mM. Sh. 5:6, 9–10; mYad. 4:3. Palestinian Targums to Dt. 14:28–9; 26:12. Jerome, *Com. in Ezech.* 45: 13–14 (CCL lxxv, p. 682).

24. mHal. 1:1. The meaning of the two words (שבולת שועל and שפון), usually translated 'oats' and 'rye', is unclear: שפון = *σίφων, σιφώνιον*, in particular, probably means some kind of oats.

25. mHal. 2:5.

26. mHal. 2:7. See in general, Num. 15:17–21; Neh. 10:38; Ezek. 44:30. Philo, *Spec. Leg.* i 27 (132): *κελεύει γὰρ τοὺς σιτοπονοῦντας ἀπὸ παντὸς στέατός τε καὶ φυράματος ἄρτον ἀφαιρεῖν ἀπαρχὴν εἰς ἱερέων χρῆσιν;* Josephus, *Ant.* iv 4, 4 (71): *τούς τε πέττοντας τὸν σῖτον καὶ ἀρτοποιουμένους τῶν πεμμάτων αὐτοῖς τινα χορηγεῖν*. Mishnah tractate Ḥallah; Sifra to Num. 15:17 ff. (ed. Weiss 77b–78a); 'Hallah', Enc. Jud. 7, cols. 1193–6; Targum Ps.-Jonathan to Num. 15:20–1; G. Dalman, *Arbeit und Sitte in Palästina* IV, p. 52. On a difference between Shammai and Hillel: mEdu. 1:2; A. Schwarz, *Die Controversen der Schammaite und Hilleliten* I (1893), pp. 26–9.

the following more specific regulations existed in respect of the first-born.[27] (a) The first-born of livestock clean and fit for sacrifice, i.e. oxen, sheep and goats, were to be given in kind. If without blemish, they were to be treated as sacrifices: the blood was to be sprinkled on the altar and the fat burned on it.[28] The meat was to be eaten by anyone belonging to the priestly class, women included, anywhere in Jerusalem (Num. 18:17–18; Neh. 10:37; Exod. 22:29, 34:19; Dt. 15:19–20).[29] If the animal was blemished, it still belonged to the priests but was to be treated as profane food (Dt. 15:21–3).[30] (b) The first-born of unclean livestock—in particular according to Philo the horse, the ass and the camel, and here as always only the first-born male—was to be redeemed with the payment of money in accordance with the valuation made by the priests plus one-fifth (Num. 18:15; Neh. 10:37; Lev. 27:27). An ass was to be redeemed with the payment of a sheep (Exod. 13:13, 34:20). Josephus writes that redemption was effected by means of a fixed tax of one and a half shekels for each beast. (c) The first-born son, i.e. the first child of a woman if it was a boy, was to be 'redeemed' at the age of one month with the payment of five shekels (Num. 18:15–16; cf. Num. 3:44 ff.; Neh. 10:37; Exod. 13:13; 22:28; 34:20). It was not necessary to present the boy in the Temple, as is usually supposed from Lk. 2:22 f.[31] As is explicitly observed there, the shekels in question were those of the Tyrian currency.[32] This tax was imposed on rich and poor alike.[33]

27. Subsequent practice amalgamated the enactments of J and D with those of P, and interpreted them according to the standard of the latter.

28. Hence the Mishnah designates the first-born also as 'holy' but only in the second degree, קדשים קלים, like the Passover lamb and the cattle tithe, mZeb. 5:8.

29. In Dt. 15:20, the 'thou' is construed as addressed to the priests and not (as was the original meaning) to the Israelites.

30. In such cases the meat could be sold by the priests to non-priests as well and could be eaten by them; see mBekh. 5:1, cf. Danby's notes.

31. Against this, see L. Löw, *Die Lebensalter in der jüdischen Literatur* (1875), pp. 110 ff.

32. mBekh. 8:7; cf. p. 66, n. 210. A shekel in Phoenician (=early Hebrew) currency of the Tyrian variety, minted between 126 B.C. and A.D. 56, had an average weight of 14.2 grams of good silver. Cf. A. Kindler, 'Shekel' Enc. Jud. 14, cols. 1347–8; for the use of the Tyrian coins, see vol. I, p. 11 and p. 66 above. Consequently 5 shekels would be equivalent to 71 grams (cca 2½ oz of silver). The older legislation (Exod. 13:13; 34:20) doubtless envisages redemption not through money, but through a sacrificial victim. On the 'ransom' at Qumran, see below, p. 271, n. 52.

33. See in general, Philo, *Spec. Leg.* i 27 (135–6, 139): *Τρίτον ἐστὶ γέρας τὰ πρωτότοκα ἀρρενικὰ καὶ πάντα τῶν χερσαίων ὅσα πρὸς ὑπηρεσίας καὶ χρῆσιν ἀνθρώπων. Ταῦτα γὰρ κελεύει διαδίδοσθαι τοῖς ἱερωμένοις ἀνθρώποις. βοῶν μὲν καὶ προβάτων καὶ αἰγῶν αὐτὰ τὰ ἔκγονα, μόσχους καὶ κριοὺς καὶ χιμάρρους, ἐπειδὴ καθαρὰ καὶ πρὸς ἐδωδὴν καὶ πρὸς θυσίας ἐστί τε καὶ νενόμισται· λύτρα δὲ κατατιθέναι τῶν ἄλλων ἵππων καὶ ὄνων καὶ καμήλων*

(2) Of the flesh of everything slaughtered, the priests were to receive three portions: the foreleg, the two cheeks and the stomach. This is the sense in which Dt. 18:3 in particular was understood, as applying therefore to animals slaughtered for profane use and not to beasts of sacrifice. The ordinance was also accepted by later interpreters as applying only to animals fit for sacrifice—oxen, sheep and goats.[34]
(3) A due was also to be handed to the priests from the proceeds of the sheep-shearing, though only if a person possessed several sheep—according to the school of Shammai, two, but according to that of Hillel, five. The due was to amount to five Judaean (=ten Galilean) *sela*.[35]

III. In addition to the regular dues, countless further irregular and extraordinary offerings went to the priesthood. Strictly speaking, this

---

καὶ τῶν παραπλησίων μὴ μειοῦντας τὴν ἀξίαν. Ἔστι δὲ καὶ ταῦτα παμπληθῆ . . . [Τὴν] δὲ τῶν πρωτοτόκων υἱῶν [καθιέρωσιν], ὡς ὑπὲρ τοῦ μήτε γονεῖς τέκνων μήτε τέκνα γονέων διαζεύγνυσθαι, τιμᾶται τὴν ἀπαρχὴν ἀργυρίῳ ῥητῷ, προστάξας ἴσον εἰσφέρειν καὶ πένητα καὶ) πλούσιον. Compare also *Virt.* 18 (95). Josephus, *Ant.* iv, 4, 4 (70–1): *τῶν τετραπόδων δὲ τῶν εἰς τὰς θυσίας νενομισμένων τὸ γεννηθὲν πρῶτον, ἂν ἄρσεν ᾖ καταθῦσαι παρασχεῖν τοῖς ἱερεῦσιν, ὥστε αὐτοὺς πανοικὶ σιτεῖσθαι ἐν τῇ ἱερᾷ πόλει· τῶν δ' οὐ νενομισμένων ἐσθίειν παρ' αὐτοῖς κατὰ τοὺς πατρίους νόμους τοὺς δεσπότας· [τῶν τικτομένων] σίκλον καὶ ἥμισυ αὐτοῖς ἀναφέρειν, ἀνθρώπου δὲ προτοτόκου πέντε σίκλους.* Cf. the tractate Bekhoroth in the Mishnah. Z. Fränkel, *Über den Einfluss der palästinischen Exegese etc.* (1851), pp. 98f. (on the LXX rendering of Exod. 13:13 and 34:20). B. Ritter, *Philo und die Halacha*, pp. 118–22, 136 f.; L. Löw, *Die Lebensalter in der jüd. Literatur* (1875), pp. 110–18, 390–2; G. B. Gray, *Sacrifice in the OT* (1925), pp. 33–6, 86–93; G. Beer, *Exodus* (1939) on Exod. 13:1–2, 13 and 34:20; J. J. Stamm, *Erlösen und Vergebung im AT* (1940); S. Belkin, *Philo and the Oral Law* (1940), pp. 68–9; J. Pedersen, *Israel* I/II (1946), pp. 193, 258–9, 399; A. Kirchgässner, *Erlösung und Sünde im NT* (1950); I. Mendelsohn, 'On the Preferential Status of the Eldest Son', BASOR 156 (1959), pp. 38–9; V. H. Kooy, 'First-Born', IDB (1962), ii, 270 ff.; B.-Z. Schereschewsky, 'Firstborn', Enc. Jud. 6, cols. 1306–12.

34. See in general besides Dt. 18:3, Philo, *Spec. Leg.* i 29 (147): *Ἀπὸ δὲ τῶν ἔξω τοῦ βωμοῦ θυομένων ἕνεκα κρεωφαγίας τρία προστέτακται τῷ ἱέρεῖ δίδοσθαι, βραχίονα καὶ σιαγόνα καὶ τὸ καλούμενον ἤνυστρον.* Josephus, *Ant.* iv 4, 4 (74): *εἶναι δὲ καὶ τοῖς κατ' οἶκον θύουσιν εὐωχίας ἕνεκα τῆς αὐτῶν ἀλλὰ μὴ θρησκείας ἀνάγκην κομίζειν τοῖς ἱερεῦσιν ἔνυστρόν τε καὶ χελύνιον καὶ τὸν δεξιὸν βραχίονα τοῦ θύματος.* See H. St. J. Thackeray's comment in *Josephus* (Loeb) IV, p. 512, n. 6; cf. mHul. 10; bHul. 130a–4b; Sifre to Dt. 18:3 (ed. Horovitz-Finkelstein, §165, pp. 214–5). Jerome, *Epist.* 64 *ad Fabiolam* 2: 'caeterum et alia tria, exceptis primitiis hostiarum, et de privato et de macello publico, ubi non religio sed victus necessitas est, sacerdotibus membra tribuuntur, brachium, maxilla et venter'. The Emperor Julian in Cyril, *Adv. Iulianum*, 306 F.: *Ἰουδαῖοι καὶ νῦν ἔτι . . . τὸν δεξιὸν ὦμον διδόασιν ἀπαρχὰς τοῖς ἱερεῦσιν.* See B. Ritter, *Philo und die Halacha*, pp. 124 f. J. Wellhausen, *Gesch. Israels* I, pp. 158 f.=*Prolegomena* 5th ed., p. 151; S. Belkin, *Philo and the Oral Law*, p. 68.

35. See in general, Dt. 18:4; Tob. 1:6. Josephus, *Ant.* iv 4, 4 (71): *εἶναι δὲ ἀπαρχὰς αὐτοῖς καὶ τῆς προβάτων κουρᾶς.* Sifre to Dt. 18:4 (ed. Horovitz-Finkelstein §166, pp. 275–6); Philo, *Virt.* 18 (95) erroneously includes this due among the tithes.

category includes the numerous sacrifices offered for a variety of reasons (see pp. 260–1 above), but to these may be added the following:

(1) Votive offerings which could be of many sorts. A person could consecrate himself or others to the sanctuary. In such a case, it was the rule to effect redemption in exchange for money: fifty shekels for a man, thirty for a woman. But animals, houses and parcels of land could also be consecrated to the sanctuary. If these were animals acceptable for sacrifice, they were to be surrendered in kind. With unclean animals, houses and land, redemption could equally be effected with money on certain conditions fixed in detail in the Torah.[36]

(2) The anathema, a votive offering entailing irredeemable consecration to the sanctuary. Anything consecrated to the sanctuary in this form (as anathema, חרם) fell to it—i.e. to the priests—in kind, whether it was man, beast, or landed property.[37]

(3) Lastly, reparation for goods stolen or otherwise unlawfully acquired. Where it was impossible to return them to their rightful owner, they belonged to the priests.[38]

In regard to the last two instances, the Bible clearly states that they were to belong to the priests personally. The votive offerings, by contrast, appear as a rule to have been utilized for cultic purposes in general.[39] Yet Josephus certainly mentions among the priestly dues the ransom money of fifty and thirty shekels respectively where a

36. See in general, Lev. 27; Dt. 23:22–4. Josephus, *Ant.* iv 4, 4 (71); Mt. 15:5; Mk. 7:11. G. F. Moore, EB IV, 'Vows', 'Votive offerings'. On vows at Qumran, see CD 16:13–16. On Mt. 15:5 and Mk. 7:11, see Str.-B. I, p. 711. A. Wendel, *Das israelitisch-jüdische Gelübde* (1932); S. Belkin, 'Dissolution of Oaths and the Problem of Anti-Social Oaths in the Gospels', JBL 45 (1936), pp. 227–34; S. Lieberman, *Greek in Jewish Palestine* ([2]1965), pp. 115–43, 197–200; R. de Vaux, *Ancient Israel* (1961), pp. 417, 465–6. In IDB the following articles: H. H. Guthrie, Jr., 'Corban' (I, p. 681), T. H. Gaster, 'Sacrifices and Offerings' (IV, especially p. 149) and G. H. Davies, 'Vows' (IV, pp. 792 f.). M. Black, *An Aramaic Approach* ([3]1967), p. 139. On the validity of vows in the case of women, see Num. 30; the tractate Nedarim in the Mishnah, and at Qumran, CD 16:10–12.

37. See Lev. 27:28; Num. 18:14; Ezek. 44:29. See C. H. W. Brekelmans, *De Ḥerem in het Oude Testament* (1959); M. Greenberg, 'Herem', Enc. Jud. 8, cols. 344–50.

38. Num. 5:5–8; CD 9:13–16.

39. mShek. 4:6–8: 'If a man consecrates his possessions . . . and there are cattle among them, male or female, fit for the altar, according to R. Eliezer: the males shall be sold for a burnt-offering and the females for a thank-offering to those who need them, and the money together with the remaining possessions shall fall to the fund for the Temple maintenance. Rabbi Joshua says: The males shall be sacrificed as burnt offerings, the females sold to those who need thank-offerings, and burnt-offerings shall be made with the money; the remaining possessions shall fall to the fund for the Temple maintenance. If a man con-

person had consecrated himself to God.[40] And the rabbis reckoned among the twenty-four priestly dues, besides the anathema and the reparation, the inherited field presented as a votive offering (Lev. 27: 16–21).[41]

It is impossible to determine with any certainty to what extent Jews in the diaspora contributed to all these dues.[42] The imposts on produce of the soil (*bikkurim, terumah,* tithe) disappear de facto for the meaning of the relevant ordinances of the Torah is not that land in general is liable to taxation but only the soil of the Holy Land (though certain exceptions were ordained by later casuists in regard to neighbouring territories).[43] In many particulars the views of the experts wavered concerning the obligations of the diaspora. A large part of them was no doubt discharged and because of its massive size formed a rich source of priestly prosperity.

It is also no longer possible to obtain any clear idea how these offerings were made or of what sort they were. Many dues, such as *ḥallah* and the three portions of meat after slaughter, could not be preserved for long so dispatching them to Jerusalem was out of the question. But in places where there were priests, they were given to them directly.[44] Insofar as it was feasible, however, administration of

---

secrates his possessions and there are things among them fit for the altar—wine, oil, flour or birds—according to R. Eleazar, they shall be sold to those who need that kind of sacrifice and with the money burnt-offerings shall be made; the remaining possessions shall fall to the fund for the Temple maintenance.'

40. *Ant.* iv 4, 4 (73).

41. Cf. the rabbinical references in n. 7 above.

42. See mHal. 4:7–11; mYad. 4:3; mHul. 10:1 (the three portions of the slaughtered animals to be given outside Palestine as within). Cicero, *pro Flacco* 28/66–9; Philo, *Spec. Leg.* i 14 (77); *Legat.* 23 (156); 40 (312–16); Josephus, *Ant.* xiv 7, 2 (111–13); xvi 6, 2–7 (162–73); xviii 9, 1 (312); Epiphanius, *Haer.* xxx 11. Cyril. *Adv. Iulian.* p. 306A. The passages from Philo and Josephus refer above all to the didrachma tax but not to this alone; see *Ant.* xviii 9, 1 (312): *τό τε δίδραχμον . . . καὶ ὁπόσα δὲ ἄλλα ἀναθήματα.* Cf. G. Hoennicke, *Das Judenchristentum im ersten und zweiten Jahrhundert* (1908), pp. 27 ff.; J. Juster, *Les Juifs dans l'empire romain* I (1914), pp. 377 ff.; E. Bickerman, 'Héliodore au temple du Jérusalem', AIPhHOS 7 (1939–44), p. 14; J. R. Harris, 'Hadrian's Decree of Expulsion of the Jews from Jerusalem', HThR 19 (1926), pp. 199–206; S. Safrai, 'Relations between the Diaspora and the Land of Israel' in JPFC I (1974), pp. 188–91.

43. Concerning the inhabitants of Syria, compare mDem. 6:11; mSheb. 6:2, 5–6; mMaas. 5:5; mHal. 4:7, 11; mOrl. 3:9; mA.Z. 1:8; mOhol. 18:7. A. Büchler, *Der galiläische Am-ha-Areṣ des zweiten Jahrhunderts* (1906), pp. 255–74. J. Juster, *Les Juifs . . .* I, (1914), pp. 377–88; L. Finkelstein, *The Pharisees* ([3]1962), pp. 754–61; M. Stern, 'The Jewish Diaspora' in JPFC I, pp. 137–42; B. Z. Luria, *Ha-Yehudim be-Suryah* (1975).

44. It is said in mTer. 2:4 with the reference to the *terumah*: 'Where there is a priest, *terumah* is to be given from the best; but where there is no priest, from that which lasts long'. According to mHal. 4:8–9, *ḥallah*, anathema, first-born, re-

the dues was centralized in Jerusalem. They were brought there, and from thence were distributed among the priests.[45] This priestly central administration extended also to the tithes, which were in reality not handed over to the Levites at all but were received and administered by the priests.[46]

Entitlement to enjoy the priestly revenues was not exclusive to the priests themselves but extended to their relations. Only the 'most holy' was to be consumed by the priests alone (see above, pp. 260–1). Otherwise, all the revenues went to the benefit of those belonging to the priest's household—his wife, daughters and slaves. Hired workmen and daughters married to non-priests were not included. But the gifts were always to be consumed in a state of ritual purity.[47]

With regard to the priests, no distinction was made between those who really officiated and those debarred from service because of some physical defect. When it was the turn of their course to officiate, the latter could participate even in the 'most holy'.[48]

All the dues listed so far constituted the priests' personal income. From these must now be distinguished imposts directly intended for the maintenance of public worship. The most important was the half-

---

demption money for first-born sons, redemption money for the first-born of an ass, shoulder, cheeks and stomach (on the occasion of slaughter for profane use), the due from the sheep-shearing, among others, could be given to 'any priest'. Hence *terumah*, the tithe, and the first-born were to be paid even after the destruction of the Temple, mBik. 2:3; mShek. 8:8.

45. See especially, 2 Chron. 31:11–19; Neh. 12:44; 13:5; Mal. 3:10. Philo, *Spec. Leg.* i 30 (152): *Ὑπὲρ δὲ τοῦ μηδένα τῶν διδόντων ὀνειδίζειν τοῖς λαμβάνουσι, κελεύει τὰς ἀπαρχὰς εἰς τὸ ἱερὸν κομίζεσθαι πρότερον, εἶτ' ἐνθένδε τοὺς ἱερεῖς λαμβάνειν.*

46. See Josephus, *Vita* 12 (63); 15 (80); *Ant.* xx 8, 8 (181); 9, 2 (206–7). J. Wellhausen, *Geschichte Israels* I, pp. 171 f. = *Prolegomena* (5th ed.), p. 164; B. Ritter, *Philo und die Halacha*, pp. 123 f.; S. Belkin, *Philo and the Oral Law* (1940), pp. 72–8; S. W. Baron, *A Social and Religious and Religious History of the Jews* I (^{2}1952), pp. 272 f., 413 f. In the time of Nehemiah, the tithe was still paid to the Levites precisely in accordance with the Priestly Code, and only the tithe of the tithe was handed over by the latter to the Temple treasury; yet both operations took place under the supervision of the priests (Neh. 10: 38–9). The Mishnah appears to take it for granted that the correct procedure was for the priests and the Levites each to receive their respective share directly from the owner: mM. Sh. 5:6.

47. Lev. 22:1–16. Philo, *Spec. Leg.* i 24 (119)–27 (113); Josephus, *Ant.* iv 4, 4 (75): *πάντων δὲ τῶν τοῖς ἱερεῦσι τελουμένων κοινωνεῖν διέταξε καὶ τοὺς οἰκέτας καὶ θυγατέρας καὶ γυναῖκας ἔξω τῶν ὑπὲρ ἁμαρτημάτων ἐπιφερομένων θυσιῶν· ταύτας γὰρ ἐν τῷ ἱερῷ μόνοι δαπανῶσιν οἱ ἄρρενες τῶν ἱερέων αὐθημερόν.* mTer. 6:2; 7:2. Sifra to Lev. 22:10 ff (ed. Weiss 97a).

48. Lev. 21:22. Philo, *Spec. Leg.* i 27 (131); Josephus, *Ant.* iii 12, 2 (278); *B.J.* v 5, 7 (228); mZeb. 12:1; mMen. 13:10.

shekel or didrachma tax.[49] A levy of this sort did not exist before the exile because until then the expenses of public sacrifice were defrayed by the king (Ezek. 45:17 ff., LXX 46:13–15).[50] But it was paid already in the time of Nehemiah, though it then amounted to a third of a shekel (Neh. 10:33–4). The increase to half a shekel can only have been introduced after Nehemiah. The relevant passage in the Pentateuch in which the half-shekel valuation tax is prescribed (Exod. 30:11–16) should therefore be regarded as a later addition to the Priestly Code.[51] The actual payment of this tax in the time of Jesus is reliably attested.[52]

49. W. W. Baudissin, *Geschichte des alttestamentlichen Priesterthums*, p. 220; A. Schwartz, 'Die Schatzkammer des Tempels in Jerusalem', MGWJ 63 (1919), pp. 234 f.; J. Wellhausen, *Die Pharisäer und die Sadducäer* (²1924), p. 70; B. W. Bacon, *Studies in Matthew* (1930), 228 ff.; E. Klostermann, *Matthäusevangelium*, on Mt. 17:24; J. Liver, 'The Ransom of the Half-Shekel', *Y. Kaufmann Jubilee Volume*, ed. M. Haran (1960), pp. 54–67 (Hebrew); L. Finkelstein, *The Pharisees* (³1962), pp. 281–2; J. Liver, 'The Half-Shekel Offering in Biblical and Postbiblical Literature', HThR 56 (1963), pp. 173–98. However, the tax does appear to have been paid by Egyptian Jewry as argued by A. Tcherikover, *Ha-Yehudim be-Miṣrayim* (²1963), pp. 109 ff.; for the contrary view, cf. S. L. Wallace, *Taxation in Egypt from Augustus to Diocletian* (1938), pp. 174 ff. In general, see S. W. Baron, *A Social and Religious History of the Jews*, I, p. 394, n. 11; H. Hamburger, in IDB, 'Didrachma', 'Piece of Money', 'Money, Coins'; S. Safrai, 'Temple', Enc. Jud. 15, cols. 979–82; *idem*, JPFC II, pp. 880–1.

50. On the significance of the disappearance of the king for the priesthood, cf. J. Pedersen, *Israel* III/IV, pp. 168 ff. R. de Vaux, *Ancient Israel*, p. 379.

51. F. Nau, 'Le denier du culte juif à Eléphantine au 5e s. av. J.-C.', ROChr 17 (1912), pp. 100–4. M. Noth, *Exodus*, p. 236; R. de Vaux, *Ancient Israel*, p. 403. Exod. 30:11–16 speaks of a due paid once only, viz., on the occasion of the numbering of the people in the time of Moses (Num. 1). But without a doubt this was indirectly intended to furnish a legal basis for the exaction of a regular half-shekel tax. The Chronicler also understood it in this sense (2 Chron. 24:4–10). Doubts over such annual payments before the Maccabean age have been voiced by E. Bikermann, 'Héliodore au temple de Jérusalem', AIPhHOS 7 (1939–44), pp. 14 f.

52. Mt. 17:24; Josephus, *Ant.* xviii 9, 1 (312); *B.J.* vii 6, 6 (218); the tractate Shekalim in the Mishnah. A Qumran fragment known as 4Q Ordinances (4 Q 159), cf. J. M. Allegro, A. A. Anderson, *DJD* V (1968), pp. 6–9, throws new light on Exod. 30:11–16: 'Concerning . . . the money of valuation that a man gives as ransom for his life, it shall be half [a shekel . . .]. He shall give it once in his life' (Cf. Vermes, *DSSE*, p. 249.) 'Thus instead of considering it as a unique event belonging to the Mosaic age, or as a yearly occurrence after Nehemiah affecting Jewish men from twenty years old, the Dead Sea sect interpreted the rule as applying to every male Israelite on reaching his twentieth birthday. The substitution by the Qumran sect of a single contribution instead of a yearly payment was not motivated by leniency. It was a compromise solution to a dilemma. Having withdrawn from the sanctuary of Jerusalem because of their condemnation of the existing form of Temple worship, and being obliged to choose therefore between faithfulness to their convictions and obedience to the written law, the sectaries adopted a peculiar exegesis and decided to follow the letter of the Bible and pay a single instalment of ransom money. If this indirectly contributed to the Temple treasure, such was not their intention.' Vermes, 'The Qumran Interpretation of Scripture in its Historical Setting', ALUOS 6 (1969), p. 89 [*PBJS*, p. 42],

It was to be paid by every male Israelite of twenty years and over, whether rich or poor,[53] and as in the case of all the sacred dues, the money was to be of the ancient Hebrew or Tyrian (Phoenician) currency.[54] The time set for payment was the month of Adar (February-March),[55] and it was carried out in such a way that the contributions were first collected within the community and then delivered to Jerusalem on its behalf.[56]

This tax was chiefly utilized to defray the expenses of the daily burnt-offering and of all the sacrifices in general made in the name of the people, as well as for other daily purposes.[57]

After the destruction of Jerusalem, the didrachma had for a long time to be paid to the temple of Jupiter Capitolinus in Rome.[58] The 'calumnia fisci Iudaici' was abolished under Nerva but the tax itself was never repealed.[59]

---

cf. also J. Liver, *art. cit.*, HThR 56 (1963), pp. 173–98; L. Moraldi, *I Manoscritti di Qumrān* (1971), pp. 655–6.

53. Exod. 30:14–15. Philo, *Spec. Leg.* i 14 (77): *Προστέτακται γὰρ ἀνὰ πᾶν ἔτος ἀπαρχὴν εἰσφέρειν ἀπὸ εἰκοσαετοῦς ἀρξαμένους.*

54. tKet. 13:3: 'All money spoken of in the Torah is Tyrian money (כסף צורי)'. In effect, surviving Hebrew shekels tally with coins of the Phoenician currency. A half-shekel therefore equals two Tyrian drachmas. Cf. above pp. 66 and 266. In New Testament times, only the Roman currency, which corresponded to the Attic standard, was minted in Palestine; see in general above pp. 62–6. None the less it is clear that Tyrian shekels continued to be used, see especially L. Kadman, 'Temple Dues and Currency in Ancient Palestine', *Cong. int. de Num., Roma 1961* II (1965), pp. 69–76. In paying the sacred dues it was consequently very often necessary to resort to the money-changers. See M. Lambert, 'Les changeurs et la monnaie en Palestine etc.', REJ 51 (1906), pp. 217–44; 52 (1906), pp. 24–42; W. F. Albright, 'The Judicial Reform of Jehoshaphat', *Alexander Marx Jubilee Volume* (1950), pp. 61–82. F.-M. Abel, *Histoire de la Palestine* I (1952), pp. 424 ff. R. de Vaux, *Ancient Israel* (1961), pp. 203–9.

55. mShek. 1:1, 3.

56. mShek. 2:1. Cf. Mt. 17:24.

57. Neh. 10:33–4. mShek. 4:1–3.

58. Josephus, *B.J.* vii 6, 6 (218). Dio lxvi 7, 2. Cf. Suetonius, *Domitian.* 12: 'Iudaicus fiscus acerbissime actus est'. Martial (ed. Friedlander), vii. 55. O. Hirschfeld, *Die kaiserlichen Verwaltungsbeamten bis auf Diocletian* ([2]1905), p. 73. J. Juster, *Les Juifs* II, pp. 282 ff. and the evidence cited there. I. A. F. Bruce, 'Nerva and the *Fiscus Iudaicus*', PEQ 96 (1964), 34–46. On the relationship of this tax to the rebellion in Gaul and Germany, cf. Tacitus, *Hist.*, especially iv 54. Comp. S. W. Baron, *A Social and Religious History of the Jews* II ([2]1952), pp. 105 ff., 373; C. Jullian, *Histoire de la Gaule* IV, pp. 199 ff.; U. Bianchi, 'Disegno storico del culto capitolino', Atti, Accademia Naz. dei Lincei, 8th ser., II, pp. 349–415.

59. Its abolition is attested by a coin from the reign of Nerva inscribed with the words 'fisci Indaici calumnia sublata', *BMC Roman Empire* III, pp. xlvii–viii and p. 15, no. 88.This refers to the denunciation in the interest of *fiscus Iudaicus* which Nerva forbad (see below, § 31, II, 2). Dio lxviii, 1. The tax itself was still being paid at a later time; cf. Appian *Syr.* 50 and especially Origen's *Epist. ad*

Besides the half-shekel tax, yet another regular due was paid to the Temple, namely an annual offering of wood for the altar of burnt-offering.[60] It was laid down as early as the time of Nehemiah that priests, Levites and the people should at certain times of the year supply wood for the altar, all of them according to their 'fathers' houses', the sequence of which was to be determined by lot (Neh. 10:35; 13:31). Later, the 'wood-offering' mostly fell on the 15th of Ab, which for this reason acquired a certain festive character.[61] But it was also supplied by certain families on other days.[62] Every sort of wood was permissible except that of olive and vine.[63]

African. 14 (ed. Lommatzsch, XVII, p. 44): *καὶ νῦν γοῦν Ῥωμαίων βασιλευόντων, καὶ Ἰουδαίων τὸ δίδραχμον αὐτοῖς τελούντων.* The rabbis for their part decided that the half-shekel tax was not an obligation if no Temple existed (mShek. 8:8). Cf. M. S. Ginsburg, 'Fiscus Judaicus', JQR 21 (1930), pp. 281–91; I. A. F. Bruce, 'Nerva and the *Fiscus Iudaicus*', PEQ 96 (1964), pp. 34–46.

60. On this see H. Graetz, *Geschichte der Juden*, III[4], pp. 571 and 707 f.; J. Derenbourg, *Histoire de la Palestine*, p. 109, n. 2; C. C. Torrey, *Ezra Studies*, p. 277; L. E. Brown, *Early Judaism* (1920), p. 193; L. W. Batten, *Ezra and Nehemiah* (1913), pp. 377–8; W. Rudolph, *Esra und Nehemia* (1949), p. 180; R. de Vaux, *Ancient Israel* (1961), p. 403; J. Jeremias, *Jerusalem in the Time of Jesus* (1969), p. 227. Cf. A. C. Welch, *Post-Exilic Judaism* (1935), p. 80, where it is suggested that the three deliveries of wood, first-fruits of the soil and firstlings of men and animals were all decided by lot.

61. Meg. Taan. §11, ed. Lichtenstein, HUCA 8–9 (1931–2), pp. 268–71, 331–2; Josephus, *B.J.* ii 17, 6 (425): *τῆς τῶν ξυλοφορίων ἑορτῆς οὔσης, ἐν ᾗ πᾶσιν ἔθος ἦν ὕλην τῷ βωμῷ προσφέρειν.* As Josephus in *B.J.* ii 17, 7 (430) calls the day following it the 15th of the casting of lots (= Ab), the implication is that the offering of wood took place on the 14th of Ab. But according to the rabbis, there can be no doubt that the 15th of Ab was the principal day; see Meg. Taan. §11 (*loc. cit.*); mTaan. 4:5, 8; in general also, mTaan. 4:4; mMeg. 1:3; yTaan. 68b–69c; yMeg. 70c; bTaan. 28a–31a.

62. mTaan. 4:5: 'The times for the wood-offering of the priests and the people were on nine appointed days: (1) on the 1st of Nisan by the sons of Araḥ son of Judah (cf. Ezr. 2:5; Neh. 7:10); (2) on the 20th of Tammuz by the sons of David son of Judah (cf. Ezr. 8:2); (3) on the 5th of Ab by the sons of Parosh son of Judah (cf. Ezr. 2:3; 8:3; 10:25; Neh. 3:25; 7:8; 10:15); (4) on the 7th of the same month by the sons of Jonadab son of Rechab (cf. 2 Kgs. 10:15, 23; Jer. 35:8; 1 Chron. 2:55); (5) on the 10th of the same month by the sons of Senaah son of Benjamin (cf. Ezr. 2:35; Neh. 3:3; 7:38); (6) on the 15th of the same month by the sons of Zattu son of Judah together with the priests and Levites and all whose tribal descent was in doubt and the sons of the pestle-smugglers and the sons of the fig-pressers (cf. Ezr. 2:8; 10:27; Neh. 7:13; 10:15; on the meaning of 'pestle-smugglers' and 'fig-pressers', see H. Danby, *The Mishnah* (1933), p. 200, n. 9); (7) on the 20th of the same month by the sons of Pahath Moab son of Judah (cf. Ezr. 2:6; 8:4; 10:30; Neh. 3:11; 7:11; 10:15); (8) on the 20th of Elul by the sons of Adin son of Judah (cf. Ezr. 2:15, 8:6; Neh. 7:20, 10:17); (9) on the 1st of Tebet no *ma'amad* assembled because the *Hallel*, an additional offering and a wood-offering (by the sons of Parosh) were appointed for that day' (cf. Num. 28:11 ff.).

63. mTam. 2:3. For a list limited to twelve kinds of trees, see Jub. 21:12–15; T. Levi 9:12. Cf. R. H. Charles, *The Book of Jubilees* (1902), pp. 134 f.; *Apocrypha and Pseudepigrapha* II, pp. 44, 310.

Great wealth must finally have flowed into the Temple from voluntary donations. It has already been mentioned that most of the votive-offerings were probably not given to the priests personally but were used to defray the expenses of public worship (see above, p. 268). This was certainly the case with votive-offerings made for particular purposes and with voluntary gifts not specifically dedicated on the basis of a vow.[64] Very often, individual objects were presented for use in worship or as Temple ornaments.[65] For example, it was possible to make gifts of gold in the form of individual leaves, grapes or berries for the enlargement of the golden vine over the Temple portal;[66] the rich Alabarch, Alexander of Alexandria, provided the gold and silver cladding for the gates of the forecourt.[67] Even distinguished Gentiles sometimes presented gifts to the Temple (see below, pp. 309–13). But the usual custom was to donate money, and in this respect even the mite of poor widows was not unwelcome (Mk. 12:41–4; Lk. 21:1–4). In the Temple treasury were thirteen trumpet-shaped coffers into which money intended for particular liturgical purposes was dropped. No fewer than six of these contained 'voluntary gifts' pure and simple, without further definition, and all of them, according to the Mishnah anyway, were used for burnt-offerings (the meat being destined 'to God', and only the hide to the priests).[68]

64. For a formal distinction between vows (נדרים) and voluntary donations (נדבות) see mMeg. 1:6.

65. See in general, Josephus, *B.J.* v. 13, 6 (563–4); mYom. 3:10.

66. mMid. 3:8.

67. Josephus, *B.J.* v 5, 3 (205).

68. mShek. 6:5, 6.

III. The Priestly Offices

The great number of priests, their abundant wealth and the multiplicity of their functions, demanded also a wide distribution of offices. It has already been demonstrated in § 24.I that the entire priesthood was divided into twenty-four courses, each forming a unified body presided over by heads and elders. But apart from this social structure of the whole order, the many cultic functions and rules necessitated a system of special offices. Among these, during the last centuries at least of the Temple's existence, two were outstanding.

1. The first was that of the High Priest (כהן גדול, ἀρχιερεύς; in Aramaic: כהנא רבא, see above, p. 22, n. 76).[1] The chief feature of his position was the conjunction in one person of a political and a priestly dignity. Not only was he the supreme officer in the field of religion who alone had the right to perform certain cultic acts of the highest ritual significance, such as the offering of the sacrifice on the Day of Atonement; he was at the same time the political leader of the nation, the head of state, in so far, that is, as it was not under the domination of foreign overlords. In the days of national independence, the hereditary Hasmonaean High Priests were simultaneously princes and kings; later, the High Priests were Presidents of the Sanhedrin as well as the supreme representatives of the nation *vis-à-vis* the Romans even in political matters (for details, see § 23.IV, pp. 227–36). One consequence of the High Priest's distinguished social position was that he officiated as a priest only on

1. J. Wellhausen, *Geschichte Israels* I, pp. 153–6 = *Prolegomena*, 5th ed., pp. 145–9; W. W. Baudissin, *Geschichte des alttestamentlichen Priesterthums*, pp. 26–8, 88 f., 127–30, 140–2, 214, 251–3, 289 f.; E. G. Hirsch, 'High Priest', EJ VI, pp. 389–93; Str.-B. III, pp. 696–700 (cf. also II, pp. 56, 626, 634 f.); G. Schrenk, TDNT, s.vv. 'ἱερός', and esp. 'ἀρχιερεύς'; J. Gabriel, *Untersuchungen über das alttestamentliche Hohepriestertum* (1933); J. Morgenstern, 'A Chapter in the History of the High Priesthood', AJSL 55 (1938), pp. 16–24, 183–97, 360–77; F. Stummer, 'Gedanken über die Stellung des Hohenpriesters in der alttestamentlichen Gemeinde', in *Episcopus, Festgabe Faulhaber* (1949), pp. 19–49; E. Cothenet, 'Onction', in DB Supp. VI (1959), pp. 701–32; R. Abba, 'Priests and Levites' in IDB III, pp. 876–89, especially 886 f.; J. Juster, *Les Juifs dans l'empire romain* I, pp. 391–400, especially in relation to the Roman Diaspora; J. Pedersen, *Israel* III/IV (1940), pp. 189–97; R. de Vaux, *Ancient Israel*, pp. 397–403; J. Jeremias, *Jerusalem in the Time of Jesus* (1969), pp. 147–82; A. Cody, *A History of Old Testament Priesthood* (1969), especially pp. 175–80; I. Gafni, 'High Priest', Enc. Jud. 8, cols. 470–4.

festive occasions. By law, he was obliged to do so only on the Day of Atonement, when he presented the great sin-offering of the nation to God (Lev. 16); according to later practice, he also offered the daily sacrifice during the week preceding the Day of Atonement.[2] Otherwise, he was completely free to sacrifice whenever he wished.[3] According to the testimony of Josephus, he did this as a rule every Sabbath day and on the feasts of New Moon and New Year.[4] These sacrifices which he offered as the representative of the people and in their name are not to be confused with the daily grain-offering which he was required to offer as his own sacrifice (Lev. 6:12–16). But here it was not so much a question of officiating himself (which as a rule he seldom did) as of defraying the costs.[5]

The uniqueness of his position also found expression in the special purity and holiness required of him (see pp. 241, 242–3 above) as well as in the magnificent vestments worn in the performance of his priestly duties.[6] Only on the Day of Atonement when he entered the Holy of Holies did he wear a simple white garment, which was nevertheless also made of the most costly Pelusian and Indian linen (or cotton?).[7]

2. mYom. 1:2.
3. mYom. 1:2; mTam. 7:3.
4. *B.J.* v 5, 7 (230): *ὁ δὲ ἀρχιερεὺς ἀνῄει μὲν σὺν αὐτοῖς, ἀλλ' οὐκ ἀεί, ταῖς δ' ἑβδομάσι καὶ νουμηνίαις καὶ εἴ τις ἑορτὴ πάτριος ἢ πανήγυρις ἦν πάνδημος ἀγομένη δι' ἔτους.* The description of the High Priestly functions of Simon II in Ecclus. 50:11–21 is surely not to be understood as referring only to the Day of Atonement since the ceremony depicted here is the customary daily sacrifice, whereas only 50:5 alludes to the Day of Atonement. The Hasmonaean princes and kings had also discharged the priestly functions. See Josephus, *Ant.* xiii 10, 3 (282): John Hyrcanus; xiii, 13, 5 (372): Alexander Jannaeus.
5. Josephus, *Ant.* iii 10, 7 (257). For a fuller treatment, see below, pp. 301–2.
6. This splendid attire is described by biblical and post-biblical sources with special vividness. See Exod. 28 and 30; Ecclus. 45:6–13, 50:5 ff.; Aristeas (ed. Wendland) 96–9; Philo, *Vita Mosis* ii 23 (109–26, 135); *Spec. Leg.* i 16 (82)–17 (97); Josephus, *Ant.* iii 7, 4–7 (159–87) and *B.J.* v 5, 7 (231–6); mYom. 7:5. Jerome, *Epist.* 64 *ad Fabiolam*, 10–18. Cf. W. Nowak, *Lehrbuch der hebräischen Archäologie* (1894), pp. 116 ff.; J. Gabriel, *Untersuchungen über das altestamentliche Hohepriestertum* (1933), pp. 25–90; J. Pedersen, *Israel* III/IV (1940), pp. 222–4; K. Elliger, VT 8 (1958), pp. 19–35; M. Haran, HUCA 36 (1965), pp. 191–226; 'Priestly Vestments', Enc. Jud. 13, cols. 1063–9; J. Jeremias, *Jerusalem* . . . (1969), pp. 148–9; P. Grünbaum, *Die Priestergesetze bei Flavius Josephus* (1887), pp. 37–55. During the Roman period a serious political dispute arose about custody of the High Priest's vestments, see Josephus, *Ant.* xv 11, 4 (408); xviii 4, 3, (93); xx 1, 1–2 (6–7); cf. P. Winter, *On the Trial of Jesus* ([2]1974), pp. 20–6. When Jerusalem was conquered, this attire fell into the hands of the Romans, *B.J.* vi 8, 3 (389).
7. Lev. 16:4. mYom. 3:7 (on the materials mentioned here, see above p. 70. Cf. also section IV on the priestly apparel in general). Josephus, *B.J.* v 5, 7 (236): *ταύτην μὲν οὖν τὴν ἐσθῆτα οὐκ ἐφόρει χρόνιον, λιτοτέραν δ' ἀνελάμβανεν ὁπότε δὲ εἰσίοι εἰς τὸ ἄδυτον.* The High Priest wore the linen robes (בגדי לבן) only for the

2. Next to the high priest in rank was the סָגָן or סֶגֶן, in Aramaic סְגַן, concerning whose official duties the rabbinical authorities are anything but clear. The Talmud suggests that he was the High Priest's representative, with the particular task of replacing him when he was prevented from exercising his ministry because of ritual defilement;[8] this view has been adopted by modern scholars also.[9] But it is undoubtedly incorrect. None of the passages of the Mishnah mentioning the *sagan* give any additional information about his official position. They merely indicate that he stood next to the High Priest in rank. When the High Priest drew the lot for the two he-goats on the Day of Atonement, the *sagan* stood at his right hand and the head of the officiating priestly course (ראש בית אב) on his left.[10] When the High Priest had occasion to read the Scriptures, the president of the synagogue handed the scroll to the *sagan*, and he in turn gave it to the High Priest.[11] When the High Priest wished to offer the daily sacrifice, the *sagan* was again found at his side.[12] It cannot, however, be concluded from all this that the *sagan* was meant to be a deputy for the High Priest when he was prevented from officiating himself. And such an inference would be quite wrong. For the Mishnah says the following concerning this matter: 'Seven days before the Day of Atonement, . . . another priest (כהן אחר) is appointed to represent the High Priest in case an accident should prevent him from officiating at one of the services'.[13] This would have been superfluous if there had been a permanent vicar of the High Priest.

The true position of the *sagan* becomes quite clear when one examines the LXX rendering of the term סגנים in the Old Testament. It is

---

activities special to the Day of Atonement. For the others, he dressed in his gorgeous vestments (בגדי זהב), Lev. 16:23–24, on the Day of Atonement as well as on any other occasion. For further details see mYom. 3:4, 6; 7:1, 3–4; cf. also Josephus, *Ant.* xviii 4, 3 (94): when the Romans had the robes in their custody, they handed them over to the Jews *τρισὶν ἑορταῖς ἑκάστου ἔτους καὶ κατὰ τὴν νηστείαν*, i.e. on the Day of Atonement.

8. bYom. 39a.

9. J. Levy, *Chaldäisches Wörterbuch*, s.v.; *Neuhebräisches Wörterbuch*, s.v.; A. Büchler, *Die Priester und der Cultus im letzten Jahrzehnt des jerusalemischen Tempels* (1895), pp. 103–18. On the סגנים in the Old Testament, consult the dictionaries of Gesenius-Buhl, Brown, Driver, Briggs, and Köhler-Baumgartner, s.v. E. Bickermann, 'The Historical Foundations of Post-Biblical Judaism', *The Jews* (ed. L. Finkelstein, 1949), p. 71, notes that the term סגן indicates the native leader of a deported group and is often found in Aramaic documents from Phrygia, Caria, etc., as well as in cuneiform records from Babylonia.

10. mYom. 3:9; 4:1.

11. mYom. 7:1; mSot. 7:7–8.

12. mTam. 7:3.

13. mYom. 1:1.

translated, in effect, almost constantly as *στρατηγός*.[14] Thus the *sagan* is none other than the *στρατηγὸς τοῦ ἱεροῦ*, the captain of the temple often mentioned in the Greek sources, in the New Testament as well as Josephus.[15] He had supreme charge of order in and around the Temple. And the importance of this position was such that it is quite comprehensible that it should have been regarded as next to the High Priest in rank.[15a]

Besides the *sagan* or *στρατηγός* in the singular, there were also סגנים-*στρατηγοί* in the plural. When the processions of country people came to Jerusalem with the first-fruits, the leading priests went to meet them, namely the פחות, סגנים and גזברים.[16] The first two of these categories are called in Luke *οἱ ἀρχιερεῖς καὶ στρατηγοί* (Lk. 22:4, 52).[17] The meaning of *ἀρχιερεῖς* has already been discussed on pp. 233–5 above. But the סגנים or *στρατηγοί* are, in kind anyway, the same as the *sagan* or *στρατηγός*, but of a lower rank—i.e., also heads of the temple police but subordinate to the supreme *στρατηγός*.[18]

In the lists of the priestly ranks given in several passages of the rabbinic writings, the heads of the courses of service are named as being next in importance to the High Priest and the *sagan*, the heads of the twenty-four divisions (ראש המשמר) in the first place, and secondly

14. So Jer. 51:23, 28, 57; Ezek. 23:6, 12, 23; Ezr. 9:2; Neh. 2:16; 4:8; 12:40; 13:11; Dan. 3:2, 27; 6:8. Occasionally, *ἄρχοντες* is substituted for it: (Isa. 41:25; Neh. 4:13, 5:7, 7:5) and once *σατράπαι* (Dan. 2:48).

15. Act. 4:1: *ὁ στρατηγὸς τοῦ ἱεροῦ*; cf. also Act. 5:24, 26. Josephus, *Ant.* xx 6, 2 (131): *Ἀνανίαν τὸν ἀρχιερέα καὶ τὸν στρατηγὸν Ἄνανον*. *B.J.* vi 5, 3 (294): *οἱ τοῦ ἱεροῦ φύλακες ἤγγειλαν τῷ στρατηγῷ*. *Ant.* xx 9, 3 (208): *τὸν γραμματέα τοῦ στρατηγοῦντος Ἐλεαζάρου*. *B.J.* ii 17, 2 (409): *Ἐλεάζαρος υἱὸς Ἀνανίου τοῦ ἀρχιερέως, νεανίας θρασύτατος, στρατηγῶν τότε*. In several of these latter passages it is possible that Josephus refers not to the chief *στρατηγός*, but to subordinate *στρατηγοί*. On the other hand, it can be argued, on the basis of yYom. 41a, that the High Priest, before acceding to his office, held that of the *sagan*: in other words, that this function was usually the privilege of the High Priests' sons. In the Josephus quotations both Ananus and Eleazar are sons of the High Priest Ananias. Cf. also, J. Jeremias, *Jerusalem*, pp. 160–3; TDNT VII, s.v. '*στρατηγός*'.

15a. The priestly hierarchy of the Qumran sect designates the *sagan* by the biblical title of 'Deputy' (משנה): cf. 2 Kgs. 23:4; 25:18; Jer. 52:24. The War Rule lists among those who are to officiate at the daily burnt offerings, the High Priest (כוהן הראש), his Deputy (משנהו) and the twelve chief priests (ראשי הכוהנים). See 1QM 2:1–2; cf. Y. Yadin, *The Scroll of the War of the Sons of Light against the Sons of Darkness* (1962), pp. 202–8, especially p. 207, n. 6.

16. mBik. 3:3.

17. The פחות and סגנים are often linked in the Old Testament also (Jer. 51:23, 28, 57; Ezek. 23:6, 12, 23). The LXX usually translates this as *ἡγεμόνες* (or *ἡγούμενοι*) *καὶ στρατηγοί*, once (Jer. 51:57) as *ἄρχοντες καὶ στρατηγοί*. In mBik. 3:3, where priests are discussed, the פחות can hardly be anything other than the *ἀρχιερεῖς*, for the *ἄρχοντες* among the *ἱερεῖς* are in effect the *ἀρχιερεῖς*.

18. Rabbi Hananiah סגן הכהנים often mentioned in the Mishnah was presumably a סגן of this kind. See p. 371 below.

the heads of the subdivisions (ראש בית אב).[19] The liturgical office of these heads is unspecified, except in the Qumran community in regard to worship in the eschatological Temple.[19a]

The cultic offices other than that of the High Priest and the *sagan* still remaining to be mentioned have to do partly with the administration of the Temple assets, partly with policing the Temple, and partly with the cultic activities themselves.[20]

I. A very important function was the administration of the vast Temple treasure. In this respect, the Temple of Jerusalem was not different from other famous temples of the ancient world.[21] Cuneiform documents testify to the riches of the temples in Babylonia and Assyria and to the punctiliousness with which their receipts and outgoings were recorded.[22] Particularly rich inscriptional evidence exists on the administration of the estate of the temple at Delos. A vast treasure was accumulated there, and the financial administration was conducted in a remarkably detailed manner.[23] In Arsinoe, in Egypt,

19. See especially tHor. 2:10, yHor. 48b.

19a. 'They shall rank the Chief Priests below the High Priest and his vicar. And the twelve Chief Priests shall minister at the daily sacrifice before God, whereas the twenty-six leaders of the priestly divisions shall minister in their divisions. Below them in perpetual ministry, shall be the chiefs of the Levites to the number of twelve. . . . The leaders of their divisions shall minister each in his place. . . . These are the men who shall attend at holocausts and sacrifices. . . .' (1QM 2:1–5; Vermes, *DSSE*, pp. 125–6.)

20. Cf. H. H. Rowley, *Worship in Ancient Israel* (1965). In general see also the literature on the Levites cited on p. 250, n. 53.

21. For the argument that a temple as a rule had a treasury administration separate from the financial administration of the city, see H. Swoboda, 'Über griechische Schatzverwaltung', Wiener Studien 10 (1888), pp. 278–307; 11 (1889), pp. 65–87. See L. Ziehen, RE VIA (1937), cols. 1–7, s.v. θησαυρός.

22. O. Weber, *Die Literatur der Babylonier und Assyrer* (1907), pp. 260–2: records of the Temple treasuries; H. Torczyner, *Altbabylonische Tempelrechnungen* (1913); A. Falkenstein, 'La cité-temple sumérienne', Cahiers de l'histoire mondiale 1 (1953/4), pp. 790–5.

23. Part of the inscribed documents concerning the temple at Delos refer to the time of Athenian domination (fifth-fourth century B.C.), while part refer to the time during which the island was independent (end of the fourth to the middle of the second century B.C.). (1) In the time of Athenian domination, the accounts of the amphictyony were rendered every four years. These were inscribed on two marble slabs, of which one was kept in Athens, the other in Delos, see IG I² 377 = R. Meiggs and D. M. Lewis, *Greek Historical Inscriptions*, no. 62 = *Inscriptions de Délos, période de l'amphictyonie attico-délienne* (1972), ed. J. Coupry, no. 89; see M. N. Tod, *Greek Historical Inscriptions* II (1948), no. 125; Coupry, *op. cit.*, nos. 90–133. (2) During the period of the island's independence the accounts of the ἱεροποιοί were rendered every year and were likewise inscribed on marble slabs (cf. T. Homolle, BCH 6 (1882), pp. 1–167 (accounts from 180 B.C.); 14 (1890), pp. 389–511; 15 (1891), pp. 113–68 (accounts from 279 B.C.); 27 (1903), pp. 62–103 (accounts from 250 B.C.). Cf. Homolle, *Les archives de l'intendance*

a similar kind of papyrus document has been found from the year A.D. 215. 'The receipts and expenditures for several months of the Temple of Jupiter Capitolinus in Arsinoe have been preserved, which must have been carefully drawn up by the High Priest himself as a statement of accounts to be delivered to the city assembly.'[24] It must be assumed that as far as wealth of possessions is concerned the situation in the Temple at Jerusalem was similar. Certainly, the Jewish Temple possessed no land. But enormous quantities of valuable objects of every kind poured into the sacred treasuries in the form of dues and donations. Even the vessels needed for sacrificial worship were of great worth: there was an abundance of the gold and silver basins, bowls, pitchers, pans and similar vessels required to catch and sprinkle the blood and to make offerings of incense, grain and drink.[25] There were stocks of curtains and priests' garments, and of the materials necessary for making them.[26] There were in particular large supplies of such products as flour and oil for the grain-offerings, wine for the drink-offerings, fragrant substances for the incense; and in addition, there were the dues contributed to the priests.[27] But above all, in the

---

sacrée à Délos, 315–166 av. J.C.=Bibl. éc. fr. d'Ath. et de Rome 49 (1887). See *Inscriptions de Délos*, nos. 290–498; RE s.v. 'Delos'. See P. Roussel, *Délos, colonie athénienne* (1916); W. A. Laidlaw, *A History of Delos* (1933). The French excavations are fully published in *Exploration archéologique de Délos*, Éc. fr. d'Ath. (1909–).

24. U. Wilcken, 'Arsinoitische Tempelrechnungen aus dem J. 215 n. Chr.', Hermes 20 (1885), pp. 430–76. See above in regard to the Egyptian temple: W. Otto, *Priester und Tempel im hellenistischen Ägypten* I (1905), pp. 258–405: 'Besitz und Einnahmen der Tempel'. On the Jewish Tax in Arsinoe, cf. Tcherikover and Fuks, CPJ II, pp. 204–8.

25. According to a list of doubtful authenticity (Ezr. 1:9–11) the returning exiles in the time of Cyrus brought back with them from Babylon 30 gold and 1,000 silver basins, 29 knives, 30 gold and 410 silver bowls, in all 5,400 gold and silver vessels (the Greek Esdras gives different numbers). According to the authentic account originating with Ezra himself (Ezr. 8:26–7) the exiles returning with him brought: 650 talents of silver, silver vessels to the value of 100 talents, 100 talents of gold, 20 golden bowls to the value of 1,000 darics, 2 vessels of fine bronze. See W. Rudolph, *Esra und Nehemia*, p. 82; cf. K. Galling, 'Das Protokoll über die Rückgabe des Tempelgeräte', *Studien zur Geschichte Israels* (1964), pp. 78–88. Cf. also 1 Mac. 1:21–3; Josephus, *Ant.* xiv 4, 4 (72); *B.J.* i 7, 6 (152); v 13, 6 (562); vi 5, 2 (282); vi 8, 3 (387; 391); mYom. 3:10; 4:4. According to mTam. 3:4, 93 gold and silver utensils were required for the daily service; according to mHag. 3:8, all these were available in three sets. For further details see Exod. 25:29, 38; 27:3; 37:16, 23; 38:3; Num. 4:7, 9, 14. On royal gifts to temples, see K. Galling, 'Beiträge zur biblischen Landes- und Altertumskunde', ZDPV 68 (1950), p. 139.

26. *B.J.* vi 5, 2 (282); vi 8, 3 (390).

27. Neh. 12:44; 13:5, 9, 12; 1 Chron. 9:29. Josephus, *B.J.* v 13, 6 (562); vi 8, 3 (390); *Ant.* xiv 4, 4 (72); *B.J.* i 7, 6 (152). Salt was also required in large quantities: Ezr. 6:9; 7:22; Mk. 9:49; Josephus, *Ant.* xii 3, 3 (140); hence a salt-chamber in the Temple forecourt, mMid. 5:3. Cf. 'Salt', Enc. Jud. 14, cols. 710–11.

Treasuries of the Temple lay huge sums of money, which not infrequently tempted the greed of foreign potentates and yet were always speedily replaced.[28] Finally, to the money belonging to the sanctuary were added funds deposited there by private individuals; for it was the custom to entrust private money to the keeping of the Temple, where because of the holiness of the place people knew it was most secure.[29]

All these monies and objects of value were kept in separate treasure-chambers (γαζοφυλάκια) in the inner forecourt of the Temple and needed not only to be constantly guarded but also, because of the continuous influx and outflow, carefully administered.[30]

The treasurers charged with this administration were known as γαζοφύλακες in Greek[31] and גזברים in Hebrew.[32] Theirs was the management not only of the Temple money but of the possessions in general belonging to the categories mentioned. They had the safe-keeping of the sacred vessels,[33] the curtains and the priestly vestments;[34] they

28. Plunder attempted by Heliodorus (2 Mac. 3); by Antiochus Epiphanes (1 Mac. 1:21–3). Pompey leaves the treasury intact, *Ant.* xiv 4, 4 (72); *B.J.* i 7, 6 (152–3); plunder by Crassus, *Ant.* xiv 7, 1 (105); *B.J.* i 8, 8 (179), of 2,000 talents; similarly Sabinus after the death of Herod, *Ant.* xvii 10, 2 (264); *B.J.* ii 3, 3 (50); Pilate, *Ant.* xviii 3, 2 (60); *B.J.* ii 9, 4 (175); Florus, *B.J.* ii 14, 6 (293). On the ἱερὸς θησαυρός in general, cf. also Mt. 27:6; Josephus, *B.J.* v 5, 1 (187); *Ant.* xx 9, 7 (220).

29. 2 Mac. 3:10–12:15. Josephus, *B.J.* vi 5, 2 (282); cf. also J. Jeremias, *Jerusalem* . . ., p. 56. This often occurred in pagan temples also. See in general, J. Marquardt, *Römische Staatsverwaltung* (1878) III, p. 210. K. F. Hermann, H. Blümner, *Lehrb. der griechischen Privataltertümer* (1882), pp. 456 f.; R. Bogaert, *Banques et banquiers dans les cités grecques* (1968).

30. On the γαζοφυλάκια, see especially Josephus, *B.J.* v 5, 2 (200); vi 5, 2 (282); *Ant.* xix 6, 1 (294); Neh. 12:44; 13:5, 9, 12–13; 2 Mac. 3:6, 24, 28, 40; 4:42; 5:18. Mention of γαζοφυλάκιον in the New Testament refers not to a treasure-chamber but treasury box (Mk. 12:41, 43; Lk. 21:1; probably also Jn. 8:20). According to mShek. 6:5, there were 13 money chests in the Temple made in the form of trumpets; cf. Str.-B. II, pp. 37–41. For the identification of the contents of the Copper Scroll from Qumran (3Q15) as real or fictional Temple treasure, see J. M. Allegro, *The Treasure of the Copper Scroll* (1960), pp. 56–62; J. T. Milik, *DJD* III (1962), pp. 275–84; G. Vermes, *DSSE* ([2]1975), pp. 271–3.

31. *Ant.* xv 11, 4 (408); xviii 4, 3 (93): the γαζοφύλακες had custody of the high priest's garments. *Ant.* xx 8, 11 (194): Ἰσμάηλον τὸν ἀρχιερέα καὶ Ἑλκίαν τὸν γαζοφύλακα, they were sent on an embassy to Rome. *B.J.* vi 8, 3 (390): ὁ γαζοφύλαξ τοῦ ἱεροῦ Φινέας surrendered the priests' garments to the Romans. Cf. also *Ant.* xiv 7, 1 (106–7): ὁ τῶν θησαυρῶν (*al.* χρημάτων) φύλαξ ἱερεύς, Ἐλεάζαρος ὄνομα . . . πεπιστευμένος τὴν τῶν καταπετασμάτων τοῦ ναοῦ φυλακήν, in the time of Crassus.

32. mPea. 1:6; 2:8; 4:8; mHal. 3:3–4; mBik. 3:3; mShek. 2:1; 5:2, 6; mMen. 8:2, 7; mMeil. 3:8. The term also occurs in the Old Testament Ezr. 1:8; 7:21. Cf. also J. Levy, *Chaldäisches Wörterbuch* s.v.; *Neuhebr. Wörterbuch*, s.v.; E. Meyer, *Die Entstehung des Judentums* (1896), p. 24; M. Jastrow, *Dictionary*, s.v.; S. Lieberman, *Tosefta ki-Fshuṭah* Part IV, *Order Mo'ed* (1962), pp. 692–3; J. Jeremias, *Jerusalem* . . ., pp. 166–7.

33. mShek. 5:6; 1 Chron. 9:28.

34. Josephus, *Ant.* xiv 7, 1 (106–7); xv 11, 4 (408); xviii 4, 3 (93); *B.J.* vi 8, 3 (390).

received the flour for the grain-offerings and the wine for the drink-offerings;[35] they accepted those things that had been sanctified (i.e. presented to the Temple) and released them on payment of their redemption;[36] they purchased wood[37] and collected the half-shekel tax.[38]

Needless to say, there were also gradations of rank among the treasurers. From the Old Testament it would appear that all these offices were performed by the Levites.[39] This may indeed have been the case in regard to the humbler posts but the more important were certainly in the hands of the priests. In Josephus, the γαζοφύλαξ (probably the chief of his class) appears next to the High Priest as one of the most prominent of the Temple officers.[40] Elsewhere also, the גזברים are usually reckoned among the holders of the higher Temple posts.[41]

When the Mishnah declares that there must be at least three *gizbarim* in the Temple,[42] it doubtless has in mind only the chief treasurers and not the whole personnel necessary for the administration of the treasury.

The *amarkelin* (אמרכלין) also probably belong to the category of officers of the treasury. Mention of them on one occasion in the Mishnah without any indication of their functions[43] led to rabbinical speculations concerning them later, partly on the basis of etymological puns.[44] The

35. mMen. 8:2, 7.
36. mPea. 1:6; 2:8; 4:8; mHal. 3:3–4.
37. mMeil. 3:8.
38. mShek. 2:1.
39. 1 Chron. 9:28–9; 26:20–8; 2 Chron. 31:11–19. In Neh. 13:13 a priest is head of the treasurers.
40. *Ant.* xx 8, 11 (194); cf. n. 31 above.
41. mBik. 3:3 (see above, p. 278); in the lists of the various ranks of priests in tHor. 2:10 the גזברים also take precedence over ordinary priests and the latter over the Levites. In the famous rabbinical lament over the decline of the High Priests, the גזברים appear, as in Josephus, next to the High Priests: 'They are High Priests and their sons are גזברים and their sons-in-law אמרכלין'. tMen. 13:21; bPes. 57a. Derenbourg, *Essai*, p. 232, n. 1; J. Jeremias, *Jerusalem* . . ., pp. 195–6.
42. mShek. 5:2.
43. mShek. 5:2.
44. In tShek. 2:15 it is stated that they had the seven keys of the seven gates of the forecourt, but this is merely a conjecture founded upon a remark in the Mishnah to the effect that there had to be at least seven *amarkelin*. The word is explained etymologically either by מר כל (lord of all) or by אמר כל (he who says, i.e. commands, all). See in general, J. Levy, *Chaldäisches Wörterbuch* and *Neuhebr. Wörterbuch*, s.v.; A. Büchler, *Die Priester und der Cultus* (1895), p. 94 ff.; K. Kohler, 'Amarkol', JE I, pp. 485 ff.; H. Mantel, *Studies in the History of the Sanhedrin* (1961), pp. 42–3; S. Liebermann, *Tosefta ki-Fshuṭah* Part IV, p. 693. A different theory concerning the precise function of the *amarkelin* has been advanced by J. Jeremias (*Jerusalem* . . ., pp. 165–74). He argues that the reference to the keys implies that these officers 'held the keys of power of supervision over the Temple', i.e. that they were the Temple overseers. He finds confirmation of

word is of Persian origin and means an 'accountant'.[45] It entered imperial Aramaic and is attested in the form of המרכר in documents dating to the fifth century B.C.[46] In the Targum of Jonathan, for example, on 2 Kgs. 12:10 and 22:4, אמרכליא is substituted for the Hebrew שמרי הסף, 'gate-keepers', a reference to the priestly treasurers. It is true that it also occurs elsewhere in the Targums in the wider sense of prefects in general.[47] But in view of the original meaning of the term, and since the priestly אמרכלין are usually named together with the גזברין,[48] it may be regarded as certain that they also belonged to the category of treasurers. It is possible that they were minor officials;[49] but perhaps *gizbarim* were distinguished from *amarkelin* in that the former were concerned with the receipt and custody of the treasures, and the latter with the distribution among the priests of the priestly dues.[50]

Besides these two, the Jerusalem Talmud mentions the קתולקין (καθολικοί), of whom however the Mishnah knows nothing.[51]

Although the administration of the treasury lay essentially in the hands of the priests, in Roman times there seems nevertheless to have

---

his hypothesis in an analysis of tShek. 2:14 and mShek. 5:1–2, two lists of serving Temple officers. This is perfectly tenable. The chief argument against it springs from the quasi automatic coupling in rabbinic literature of the terms *amarkelim-gizbarin* (cf. mShek. 5:2; tYom. 1:6; bPes. 57a, etc. cited by Jeremias himself, p. 166) whereas for the association of treasurers with *seganim* he quotes only mBik. 3:3 (*ibid.*).

45. F. Perles, *Etymologische Studien* (1871), p. 106; G. R. Driver, *Aramaic Documents of the Fifth Century B.C.* ([2]1965), p. 75.

46. Cf. A. Cowley, *Aramaic Papyri of the Fifth Century B.C.* (1923), no. 26, pp. 89–90 (incorrectly spelt as המדכריא); Driver, *op. cit.*, letters 8, 9, 10, pp. 30–3. See especially, J. C. Greenfield, 'Hamarakara>'Amarkal', *W. B. Henning Memorial Volume* (1970), pp. 180–6.

47. J. Levy, *Chaldäisches Wörterbuch*, s.v. and Jastrow, *Dictionary*, s.v. In Tg. Onk. and Ps.-Jon. to Num. 3:32 and Ps.-Jon. to Num. 34:18 the term is used to render נשיא.

48. Besides mShek. 5:3, so also in the list of the ranks of the priests, 2:10, and in the lamentation of tMen. 13:21. (See n. 41 above).

49. In the list of priestly grades in tHor. 2:10 the *amarkelin* are ranked higher than the *gizbarin*. But this can hardly be correct. See, on the other hand, mShek. 5:2; tMen. 13:21. In mBik. 3:3, the *gizbarin* are included among the prominent members of the priesthood while the *amarkelin* are again not mentioned at all.

50. In Chronicles (2 Chron. 31:11–19) there is a clear distinction between officers whose task it was to receive the priestly dues and those who distributed them. In mShek. 5:2 we read: 'Not less than 3 treasurers (*gizbarin*) were engaged, and not less than 7 *amarkelin*.' A comparison of this statement with another relating to the collection and distribution of money for the poor (mPea. 8:7: 'The collection is by two, the distribution by three.'), would suggest that the *gizbarim* and *amarkelin* stood in the same relation to each other as the collectors and distributors of the money for the poor.

51. yShek. 49a. Cf. J. Jeremias, *Jerusalem* . . ., p. 161, n. 45.

been a certain amount of political supervision. It is observed in any case of Herod of Chalcis that besides the right to name High Priests, he had also received τὴν ἐξουσίαν τοῦ νεὼ καὶ τῶν ἱερῶν χρημάτων.[52] This authority was probably exercised before him by the procurators and after him by Agrippa II.[53] As in the administration of the treasury, so in the completion of the Temple buildings the priestly and political powers worked together.[54]

II. Police duties, which demanded a very large personnel, were performed mostly by Levites. In earlier times, until those of Ezra and Nehemiah, the 'gate-keepers' (שערים) were not Levites at all but of a lower rank; the Chronicler is the first to count them as Levites (see p. 253 above). In the inner forecourt, law and order was the care of the priests themselves.

Chronicles, followed by Philo and the Mishnah, provide more detailed information concerning the organization of these officials.[55] Chronicles counts in all twenty-four watchmen under four chiefs, posted according to the four points of the compass (1 Chron. 26: 12–18; also 9:17, 24–7). Its statements relate to the Temple of Zerubbabel. Under Herod, the area of the Temple esplanade or so-called outer forecourt was greatly enlarged so that it now formed a vast quadrangle with its longer side running from north to south. Inside this large area lay yet another rectangular space enclosed by strong walls with its longer side running from west to east: this was the inner forecourt or 'forecourt' proper. Access to this forecourt was gained by mounting a flight of steps around the base of which ran a railing indicating the limit beyond which no Gentile might pass. Any non-Jew who overstepped this boundary and set foot in the inner forecourt was punished with death and the Roman authorities respected Jewish opinions in this regard even to the point of permitting the penal sentence to be applied to Roman citizens.[56] Warnings were fixed to the railings at

52. Josephus, *Ant.* xx 1, 3 (15).

53. *Ant.* xx 9, 7 (223).

54. Cf. especially *B.J.* v 1, 5 (36): a structural alteration of the Temple was decided 'by the people and the chief priests' and completed by King Agrippa II; on the same subject, see also *Ant.* xv 11, 3 (391). On the unilateral decision of the priests to erect a wall blocking a view of the Temple from the royal dining-hall, and on the resulting conflict between them and the political authorities (Agrippa and Festus), see *Ant.* xx 8, 11 (191–4).

55. See in general, 'Temple, Administration of', JE XII, p. 81; F. D. Gealy, 'Captain of the Temple', IBD I, pp. 535–6; TDNT VII s.v. 'στρατηγός'; W. Rudolph, *Esra und Nehemia*, pp. 91, 174 ff. J. M. Myers, *I Chronicles* (Anchor Bible), pp. 176–8.

56. See in general, Josephus, *Ant.* xv 11, 5 (417); *B.J.* v 5, 2 (194); vi 2, 4 (124–8); *C.Ap.* ii 8 (103). Philo, *Legat.* 31 (212); mMid. 2:3; mKel. 1:8. It was in consequence of an alleged violation of this ban committed by St. Paul, when he

regular intervals announcing the ban, and the penalty for infringing it, in Greek and Latin.[57] For the Israelites too, access to the outer and inner forecourts was subject to certain restrictions, particularly in regard to the various degrees of ritual impurity.[58]

---

took Trophimus into the inner forecourt, that the riot began which led to the apostle's arrest (Acts 21:28); see pp. 221–2 above. The stipulation that no foreigner could enter the περίβολος of the Temple at Jerusalem was already authorized by Antiochus the Great, *Ant.* xii 3, 4 (145).

57. One complete and two fragmentary inscriptions have been found, the full text in 1871 and the larger of the fragments in 1935. The former was discovered by C. Clermont-Ganneau and published in RA, N.S. 28 (1872), pp. 214–34, 290–6, pl. X; the latter by J. H. Iliffe, '*Θανατός* Inscription from Herod's Temple', QDAP 6 (1936), pp. 1–3. On the former, see J. Derenbourg, JA 20 (1872), pp. 178–95; Th. Mommsen, *Römische Geschichte* V, p. 513; H. Graetz, *Gesch. der Juden* III⁴, p. 225. A. Bertholet, *Die Stellung der Israeliten und der Juden zu den Fremden* (1896), p. 311 f.; Dittenberger, OGIS 598. (Derenbourg and Graetz understood the penalty as a threatened judgment of God). On the larger of the fragments, see E. J. Bickermann, 'Warning Inscription of Herod's Temple', JQR 37 (1946/7), pp. 387–405, with comments by S. Zeitlin, *ibid.* 38 (1947/8), 111–16. Also F. J. Hollis, *The Archaeology of Herod's Temple* (1934), pp. 147 ff.; J. B. Frey, CIJ II, no. 1400, pp. 328–30; A. Schalit, *König Herodes* (1969), p. 383–4 and n. 815; P. Winter, *On the Trial of Jesus* (²1974), pp. 18–19. For a photographic reproduction see CIJ II, p. 329 or Schalit, *König Herodes*, Pl. VII. Examples of similar prohibitions in Greek temples are given in Bickermann's article in JQR 37 (1946/7), p. 390; note also P. M. Fraser, Samothrace II. 1 (1960), on nos. 62–3. The inscription reads:

ΜΗΘΕΝΑ ΑΛΛΟΓΕΝΗ ΕΙΣΠΟ
ΡΕΥΕΣΘΑΙ ΕΝΤΟΣ ΤΟΥ ΠΕ
ΡΙ ΤΟ ΙΕΡΟΝ ΤΡΥΦΑΚΤΟΥ ΚΑΙ
ΠΕΡΙΒΟΛΟΥ ΟΣ Δ ΑΝ ΛΗ
ΦΘΗ ΕΑΥΤΩΙ ΑΙΤΙΟΣ ΕΣ
ΤΑΙ ΔΙΑ ΤΟ ΕΞΑΚΟΛΟΥ
ΘΕΙΝ ΘΑΝΑΤΟΝ

58. mKel. 1:8: 'The Temple Mount (see mMid. 2:1) is holier (than the rest of the city), for no men or women with a flux (זבים וזבות), no menstruating and no recently confined women may enter there (on the latter, cf. Lev. 12; Jub. 3:9–14). The חיל (i.e. the space within the railing) is holier for no Gentiles or such as have become unclean through a corpse may enter there. The forecourt of the women is holier for none of "this day's immersed" (who have bathed because of an uncleanness, lasting until the evening) may enter there . . . the forecourt of the Israelites is holier for no "un-atoned" (who because of some offence has not yet offered the prescribed sacrifice) may enter there. . . . The forecourt of the priests is holier, for no Israelites may enter there except when it is necessary for the laying on of hands, slaughtering and waving.' Cf. J. Neusner, *A History of the Mishnaic Law of Purities* I (1974), pp. 37–40. The forecourt of the women, the forecourt of the Israelites and the forecourt of the priests are parts of the inner forecourt (on this, see below Section IV). These subtle regulations of the Mishnah are not entirely in accord with the parallel information given by Josephus, *B.J.* v 5, 6 (227): γονορροίοις μὲν δὴ καὶ λεπροῖς ἡ πόλις ὅλη, τὸ δ' ἱερὸν γυναικῶν ἐμμήνοις ἀπεκέκλειστο, παρελθεῖν δὲ ταύταις οὐδὲ καθαραῖς ἐξῆν ὃν προείπαμεν ὅρον. ἀνδρῶν δ' οἱ μὴ καθάπαν ἡγνευκότες εἴργοντο τῆς ἔνδον αὐλῆς, καὶ τῶν ἱερέων πάλιν οἱ καθαρεύοντες εἴργοντο. *C.Ap.* ii 8 (103): 'In exteriorem (porticum) itaque ingredi licebat omnibus

According to Philo, guards were stationed at the gates of the outer and inner forecourts to attend to the enforcement of this order. In addition, watchmen patrolled day and night to make sure that nothing unseemly occurred.[59] The Mishnah asserts that (during the night) the Levites served as watchmen in twenty-one places and the priests in three. Some of the Levitical watchmen stood at the gates and corners of the outer forecourt (on the inside), and some at the gates and corners of the inner forecourt (on the outside); the priestly guards were in the inner forecourt.[60] A Temple captain made the rounds at night to ensure that the sentries were awake.[61] This Temple captain was called **איש הר הבית**. There is also an occasional reference to an **איש הבירה**.[62] As the language of the Mishnah has no other word to denote the outer Temple esplanade, even when it distinguishes it from the inner forecourt, than **הר הבית**,[63] **איש הר הבית** must refer to the Temple captain with responsibility for order in the outer forecourt, whereas the **איש הבירה** was in charge of the Temple itself. For the **בירה** cannot be the Antonia Fortress, which was under a Roman *φρούραρχος*,[64] but only the Temple.[65] These two groups of officers must therefore be identical with the **סגנים** or *στρατηγοί* already discussed.

The closing and opening of all the gates of the forecourts, which were shut at night, was also part of the duties of those in charge of security. Here too an officer was appointed to superintend the closing of the gates.[66] According to Josephus, two hundred men were required for this each time,[67] twenty for the heavy bronze gate in the east of the forecourt alone.[68] The gate of the Temple itself is said to have creaked

---

etiam alienigenis; mulieres tantummodo menstruatae transire prohibebantur. In secunda vero porticu cuncti Iudaei ingrediebantur eorumque coniuges, cum essent ab omni pollutione mundae; in tertia masculi Iudaeorum mundi existentes atque purificati, in quartam autem sacerdotes stolis induti sacerdotalibus.' Concerning similar divisions in regard to a pagan temple, see E. Miller, RA, 3e série, 2 (1883), pp. 181–4.

59. Philo, *Spec. Leg.* i 62 (156): *Τούτων οἱ μὲν ἐπὶ θύραις ἵδρυνται παρ' αὐταῖς ταῖς εἰσόδοις πυλωροί. οἱ δὲ εἴσω κατὰ τὸ πρόναον ὑπὲρ τοῦ μή τινα ὧν οὐ θέμις ἑκόντα ἢ ἄκοντα ἐπιβῆναι· οἱ δε ἐν κύκλῳ περινοστοῦσιν, ἐν μέρει διακληρωσάμενοι νύκτα καὶ ἡμέραν, ἡμεροφύλακες καὶ νυκτοφύλακες.* According to Josephus, *Ant.* xviii 2, 2 (30), the watch was intensified after the occasion during the time of Coponius (A.D. 6–9) when Samaritans scattered human bones in the Temple.

60. mMid. 1:1; mTam. 1:1.

61. mMid. 1:2.

62. mOrl. 2:12.

63. E.g., mBik. 3:4; mPes. 5:5–10; mShek. 7:2–3; mSanh. 11:2.

64. Josephus, *Ant.* xv 11, 4 (408); xviii 4, 3 (95).

65. So also 1 Chron. 29:1, 19; mPes. 3:8; 7:8; mZeb. 12:5; mTam. 1; mMid. 1:9; mPar. 3:1.

66. m.Shek. 5:1.

67. *C.Ap.* ii 9 (119).

68. *B.J.* vi 5, 3 (293). On this door, see above pp. 57–8.

so loudly when it was opened that the sound could be heard as far away as Jericho.[69] The elders of the priestly course on watch in the forecourt had custody of the keys.[70] When the priestly courses changed, the retiring course handed them over to the course coming on duty.[71] As the morning sacrifice was offered at daybreak, the gates had to be open before that time. At Passover, they were open by midnight.[72]

III. Acts of worship proper, i.e. sacrifice and everything associated with it, were in the main performed by the entire priesthood, the twenty-four courses of which succeeded each other weekly (see below, pp. 292–3). Nevertheless for certain functions permanent officers were required here too. An idea of the variety of these functions is provided by a passage from the Mishnah in which are enumerated, in an admittedly confused and unsystematic arrangement, the names of those who at a certain period (clearly in the last years before the destruction of the Temple) held the most important cultic offices.[73] From this it appears for example that a special officer presided 'over the lots' (No. 3) with the daily task of determining by lottery which parts of the service were to be assigned to the various priests.[74] There was another officer 'over the seals' (No. 1), and yet another 'over the drink-offerings' (No. 2). For to simplify matters, 'seals' or tokens were

69. mTam. 3:8.

70. mMid. 1:8-9; mTam. 1:1.

71. *C.Ap.* ii 8 (108).

72. Josephus, *Ant.* xviii 2, 2 (29). During the Feast of Weeks, the officiating priests entered the court by night, *B.J.* vi 5, 3 (299). Cf. also mYom. 1:8.

73. mShek. 5:1: 'These are the officers who served in the Temple: 1. Yoḥanan son of Pinḥas was over the seals; 2. Aḥiah was over the drink-offerings; 3. Mattithiah son of Samuel was over the lots; 4. Petaḥiah was over the bird-offerings; 5. the son of Aḥiah was over bowel-sickness; 6. Neḥuniah was the ditcher; 7. Gabini was the herald; 8. the son of Geber was over the closing of the gates; 9. the son of Bebai was over the wicks (?); 10. the son of Arza was over the cymbal; 11. Hygros son of Levi was over the singing; 12. the house of Garmu was over the preparation of the shewbread; 13. the house of Abtinas was over the preparation of the incense; 14. Eleazar was over the curtains; 15. Pinḥas was over the garments.' The parallel text in tShek. 2:14 presents many variations. Cf. S. Lieberman, *Tosefta Ki-Fshuṭah*, Part IV, pp. 691–2. For both Mishnah and Tosephta, see J. Jeremias, *Jerusalem . . .*, pp. 167–72.

74. On this casting of lots see mYom. 2:2–4; mTam. 1:2; 3:1; 5:2. The Mattithiah son of Samuel mentioned as the officer over the lots appears also in mYom. 3:1 and mTam. 3:2 as the guarantor of certain practices in the Temple. A. Büchler, 'Die Verlösung der Dienstgeschäfte', *Recueil des travaux rédigés en mémoire du jubilé scientifique de M. Chwolson* (1899), pp. 1–8, thought that the casting of lots for the assignment of cultic duties was not introduced until the last three decades before the destruction of the Temple. [Cf. A. Büchler, *Studies in Jewish History* (1956), pp. 24–31]; R. Press, 'Das Ordal im Alten Testament', ZAW 51 (1933), pp. 227–31; F. J. Foakes-Jackson and K. Lake, *The Beginnings of Christianity*, Part I (1933), p. 15; 'Lots', Enc. Jud. 11, cols 510–13.

issued, in exchange for which the corresponding drink-offering could be obtained. A token was first of all bought from the officer 'over the seals', it was given to the officer 'over the drink-offerings', and the drink-offering required for the purpose intended was handed over.[75] The same method was adopted in regard to bird-offerings. The money for these was placed in a coffer and it was the business of the officer 'over the bird-offerings' (No. 4) to spend it speedily and properly.[76] Many sacrifices were of a kind that needed for their preparation a certain skill reserved to particular families. Thus the house of Garmu prepared the shewbread and that of Abtinas (No. 13) the incense.[77] An officer also conducted the Temple singers (No. 11).[78] Yet another sounded the cymbal (צלצל) as a sign to the Levites to begin the singing (No. 10).[79] There were in addition a Temple physician (No. 5), a well-master (No. 6) and a herald whose voice was so powerful that it could be heard as far away as Jericho (No. 7).[80] As the curtains in the Temple needed to be renewed from time to time,[81] an officer was appointed specially to make them and to see to their storage (No. 14). Finally, a special officer was given charge of the priestly vestments (No. 15).[82]

The sacred musicians, whose function was to accompany the daily burnt-offering and other solemn activities with singing and string-music,[83] constituted a very numerous order of cultic officers. They are

75. mShek. 5:3–5.

76. The money was dropped into one of the 13 trumpet-shaped coffers which stood in the Temple; see n. 30, p. 281 above.

77. In mYom. 3:11 both families are reproached for not wishing to share their skill with others. A chamber in the inner forecourt was named בית אבטינס after the family of Abtinas (=Greek *Εὔθυνος*), mYom. 1:5; mTam. 1:1; mMid. 1:1. Compare in general also 1 Chron. 9:30–2; 23:29.

78. On this official, see also mYom. 3:1.

79. Cf. mTam. 7:3.

80. mTam. 3:8.

81. mShek. 8:5.

82. The priests' vestments were kept in the forecourt (Ezek. 42:14). The master of the wardrobe, Pinḥas, is also mentioned in mMid. 1:4 and Josephus, *B.J.* vi 8, 3 (390). It is not quite clear whether his duty was concerned simply with the safe-keeping of the garments or whether he also had to see to the making of new ones.

83. On these officers and the Temple music generally, see H. Graetz, 'Die Tempelpsalmen', MGWJ (1878), pp. 217–22; 'Die musikalischen Instrumente im jerusalemischen Tempel und der musikalische Chor der Leviten', *ibid.* (1881), pp. 241–59; J. Wellhausen, *The Book of Psalms* (1898), pp. 217 ff. A. Büchler, 'Zur Geschichte der Tempelmusik und der Tempelpsalmen', ZAW 19 (1899), pp. 96–133, 329–44; 20 (1900), pp. 97–135. [Cf. A. Büchler, *Studies in Jewish History* (1956), pp. 44–63]; 'Music', HDB III, pp. 456–63; EB III (1902), col. 3225 ff.; H. Gressmann, *Musik und Musikinstrumente im A.T.* (1903); E. Gerson-Kiwi, 'Musique dans la Bible', DB Supp. V, cols. 1411 ff.; E. Werner, 'Music' and 'Musical Instruments', IBD III, pp. 457–76; H. Gese, 'Zur Geschichte der Kultsänger im zweiten Temple', *Abraham unser Vater* (Festschrift für O. Michel) (1963), pp. 222–34; H. H. Rowley, *Worship in Ancient Israel* (1967),

called in Hebrew משררים (frequently so in Ezra and Nehemiah), in Greek ψαλτῳδοί, ἱεροψάλται, ὑμνῳδοί, κιθαρισταί τε καὶ ὑμνῳδοί.[84] Their membership was genealogically exclusive and was distinguished from that of the Levites even till the time of Ezra and Nehemiah, though later they were counted as the Levites (see above, p. 253).[85] They were divided into three families, the houses of Heman, Asaph, and Ethan or Jeduthun (1 Chron. 6:16–32, 15:16–19, 25, 1–31; 2 Chron. 5:12),[86] and again distributed as a whole into twenty-four courses of service (1 Chron. 25).

Their principal task was to sing. Music came into consideration only as an accompaniment to the singing. The instruments used were chiefly the following three:[87] (1) the cymbals (מצלתים, κύμβαλα), an instrument of percussion similar to that which sounded the signal for the singing to start (צלצל).[88] As the dual form indicates, it consisted of two large brass plates[89] which made a loud noise when struck together. A somewhat more harmonious accompaniment to the singing was provided by (2) the harp (נבל, νάβλα) and (3) the lyre (כנור, κινύρα). Both were stringed instruments, the νάβλα having twelve strings according to Josephus, the κινύρα ten.[90] The νάβλα was played with the hand, the κινύρα according to Josephus with the plectrum (in earlier biblical times the כנור too was played with the hand).[91] According to the Mishnah, the number of נבלים employed in the Temple choir was never less than two or more

---

pp. 176–212. For parallels with the ancient Near East, see M. Wegner, *Die Musikinstrumente das Alten Orients* (1950); for Greek Music, cf. K. v. Jan, *Die griechischen Saiteninstrumente* (1882), pp. 30 f.; M. Wegner, *Das Musikleben der Griechen* (1949); *Musikgeschichte in Bildern* 2: *Musik des Altertums* 4: *Griechenland* (1963).

84. ψαλτῳδοί or according to another reading ψαλμῳδοί, Ecclus. 47:9; 50:18. ἱεροψάλται, Josephus, *Ant.* xii 3, 3 (142); ὑμνῳδοί, *Ant.* xx 9, 6 (216); κιθαρισταί τε καὶ ὑμνῳδοί, *B.J.* ii 15, 4 (321). It should not be deduced from this latter passage that the instrumentalists and the singers belong to different categories. Both come μετὰ τῶν ὀργάνων. 'They who play on the stringed instrument and sing' are consequently the same persons. Cf. 1 Chron. 15:16 המשררים בכלי שיר; see also 1 Chron. 23:5.

85. The Mishnah also always describes the Temple singers as 'Levites': mBik. 3:4; mSuk. 5:4; mR.Sh. 4:4; mArakh. 2:6; mTam. 1:3–4.

86. The only family mentioned among the exiles who returned with Zerubbabel and Joshua is that of Asaph, Ezr. 2:41; Neh. 7:44.

87. See Neh. 12:27; 1 Chron. 13:8; 15:16–22; 15:28; 16:5; 2 Chron. 5:12; 29:25; 1 Mac. 4:54; 13:51; Josephus, *Ant.* vii 12, 3 (306); mSuk. 5:4; mArakh, 2:3–6; mMid. 2:6.

88. Cf. p. 288 above. In the principal source concerning the musical instruments, mArakh. 2:3–6, מצלתים are not mentioned at all, but only the צלצל. Cf. E. Werner, 'Musical Instruments', IDB III, p. 470.

89. 1 Chron. 15:19; Josephus, *Ant.* vii 12, 3 (306).

90. *Ant.* vii 12, 3 (306). On both instruments, see E. Werner, IDB III, pp. 474–5.

91. 1 Sam. 16:23; 18:10; 19:9.

than six, while at least nine כנורות were required and their number might be increased indefinitely.[92] It is possible to conclude from this that the כנור was the dominant and leading instrument and that the נבל served more as an accompaniment.

Besides these three instruments, flutes—or more exactly clarinets (חלילים)—were used at the great yearly festivals of Passover, Pentecost, and the Feast of Tabernacles.[93]

Whereas all these instruments were played by the Levites (only in regard to the חלילים is the tradition unclear), the blowing of the trumpets (חצוצרות) was the business of the priests. This took place in particular at the presentation of the daily burnt-offering as well as on other festive occasions.[94] The beginning and end of the Sabbath was also announced by the priests with trumpet blasts from the Temple roof.[95]

The Dead Sea Scrolls, especially the War Rule, include a considerable amount of direct or figurative musical references. Of the instruments mentioned above, reference is made to the נבל in the inscription of the standard of the Ten, 'Praised be God on the ten-stringed harp' (1QM 4:4–5); נבל and כנור together figuratively (1QS 10:10; 1QH 11:23–4): to כנור also metaphorically (1QH 5:30–1; 11:22). The trumpets (חצוצרות) and their various uses are fully described in the War Rule, especially 1QM 2:15–3:11; 7:8–9:9; 16:2–17:15. Even the tones of the different signals are specified (8:5–14).[96] As in the Bible, they are in the hands of the priests, six of them precisely. The ram's horn (שפר) is not specifically connected in the Bible with the Temple, except probably in 2 Chron. 5:14. In the eschatological liturgy of the War Rule seven Levites blow on seven rams' horns (1QM 7:13; cf. 8:9, 11, 15; 16:6–7; 17:13).[97]

In the time of Zerubbabel, Ezra and Nehemiah, the humbler duties were carried out by Temple slaves (נתינים).[98] It is true that in the later

92. mArakh. 2:3, 5.

93. On their use, see in particular mArakh. 2:3–4. Cf. H. Avenary, 'Flutes for a Bride or a Dead Man—The Symbolism of the Flute according to Hebrew Sources', Orbis Musicae 1 (1971), pp. 11–24.

94. See in general, Num. 10:1–10; Ezr. 3:10; Neh. 12:35; 1 Chron. 15:24, 16:6; 2 Chron. 5:12; 7:6; 29:26–8; Ecclus. 50:16; Josephus, *Ant.* iii 12, 6 (294); mSuk. 5:4–5; mR.Sh. 3:3–4; mTam. 7:3. E. Werner, IDB III, pp. 472–3.

95. Josephus, *B.J.* iv 9, 12 (582); mSuk. 5:5.

96. See Y. Yadin, *The Scroll of the War of the Sons of Light*, pp. 101–4. Cf. also H. Avenary, 'Pseudo-Jerome Writings and Qumran Tradition', RQ 4 (1963), pp. 3–6; J. Carmignac, *ibid.* pp. 9–10.

97. For the use of the horn in general, cf. 'Shofar', Enc. Jud. 14, cols. 1442–7. For the use of the trumpets see Y. Yadin, *op. cit.*, pp. 87–113. For the problem of music in general, see E. Werner, 'Musical Aspects of the Dead Sea Scrolls', Musical Quarterly 43 (1957), pp. 21–37.

98. Ezr. 2:43, 58, 70; 7:7, 20; 8:17, 20; Neh. 3:26, 31; 7:46, 60, 73; 10:29; 11:3, 21; 1 Chron. 9:2. Cf. 'Nethinim', HDB III, pp. 519 f.; EB III, pp. 3397 ff.; J. Pedersen,

literature נתינים are still mentioned occasionally in legal discussions,[99] but it is no longer possible to state with certainty how they were employed. 'Servants' (חזנים) next appear in their place;[100] Philo even describes the cleaning and sweeping of the Temple, together with the watch-duties, as the business of the *νεωκόροι*, i.e. the Levites.[101]

The growing sons of the priests (פרחי כהונה) were also employed for much of the daily work.[102]

Israel III/IV (1940), p. 183. G. Henton Davies, 'Nethinim', IBD III, 541; A. Cody, *A History of the Priesthood* (1969), p. 168; B. A. Levine, 'Gibeonites and Nethinim', Enc. Jud. 7, cols. 552–4; 'Later Sources on the Netînîm', *Orient and Occident—Essays presented to C. H. Gordon*, ed. H. H. Hoffner, Jr. (1973), pp. 101–7. [The Talmudic Netînîm were Jews whose behaviour met with rabbinic disapproval. They may have descended from Hellenizing families (p. 107).] For a similar meaning of *min*, cf. Vermes, *PBJS*, pp. 176–7.

99. For example, mYeb. 2:4; mKid. 4:1; mMak. 3:1; mHor. 3:8.

100. mSuk. 4:4; mTam. 5:3. Cf. also mSot. 7:7–8; mYom. 7:1.

101. Philo, *Spec. Leg.* i 32 (156): *Ἕτεροι δὲ τὰς στοὰς καὶ τὰ ἐν ὑπαίθρῳ κοροῦντες τὸν φορυτὸν ἐκκομίζουσιν, ἐπιμελόμενοι καθαρότητος.*

102. mYom. 1:7; mSuk. 5:2; mSanh. 9:6; mTam. 1:1; mMid. 1:8; 3:8.

IV. Daily Worship

The daily sacrificial worship was celebrated by the twenty-four priestly courses in rotation (see pp. 245–9 above), each serving for a week at a time. The change-over took place on the Sabbath, the retiring course offering the morning sacrifice and the extra Sabbath sacrifices (according to Num. 28:9, 10), and the incoming priests offering the evening sacrifice.[1] On the three great festivals of Passover, the Feast of Weeks and the Feast of Tabernacles, all twenty-four courses officiated together.[2]

Attempts made by New Testament scholars to ascertain chronologically the service week of the course of Abiah for the year of Jesus' birth (Lk. 1:5) are without any historical foundation.[3]

Every weekly course was sub-divided into some five to nine groups, each of which served on an average for one day. If these numbered less than seven, some served twice; if more than seven, two divisions officiated together on some days (see p. 245 above). But only a fraction of the priests belonging to a day's sub-division could be appointed by lot to any real participation in the regular daily public worship.

Like the priests, the Levites were also divided into twenty-four courses (see p. 255) which succeeded one another week by week.[4]

Finally, in uniformity with these twenty-four priestly and Levitical courses, the nation itself was divided into twenty-four משמרות, each of

1. See especially tSuk. 4:24–5; also mSuk. 5:7–8; mTam. 5:1. Cf. also 2 Chron. 23:4, 8 (which, unlike the parallel text 2 Kgs. 11:5, 9, clearly concerns the priestly courses). Josephus, *Ant.* vii 14, 7 (365): *διέταξέ τε μίαν πατριὰν διακονεῖσθαι τῷ θεῷ ἐπὶ ἡμέρας ὀκτώ ἀπὸ σαββάτου ἐπὶ σάββατον. C.Ap.* ii 8 (108) probably also relates to the change-over of the weekly (not daily) courses: 'alii succedentes ad sacrificia veniunt et congregati in templum mediante die a praecedentibus claves templi et ad numerum omnia vasa percipiunt'.

2. See mSuk. 5:6–8.

3. The calculations rest partly on completely unproven assumptions, and partly on the rabbinical tradition that the course of Joiarib was in service on the day of the destruction of the Temple. See bTaan. 29a; *Seder Olam* (ed. A. Neubauer, *Mediaeval Jewish Chronicles* II (1895), p. 66, and B. Ratner, *Seder Olam Rabba* (1897), pp. 147 ff.). This tradition is suspect because it is based on the dogmatic claim that the time-table of the second destruction was an exact repetition of the first, following the prophetic interval of seventy weeks of years. For a modern discussion see P. Winter, 'The Cultural Background of the Narratives in Luke I and II', JQR 45 (1954), 160–5.

4. 1 Chron. 9:25; 2 Chron. 23:4, 8. Josephus, *Ant.* vii 14, 7 (367); mTaan. 4:2.

which was to serve in weekly rotation as the people's representative before God when the daily sacrifice was offered.[5] The course in service was known as the מעמד or standing body. Unlike the priests and Levites, however, the Israelites were not obliged to go up to Jerusalem *en masse* when their turn came. They assembled instead in their local synagogues for prayer and Bible reading and probably only a delegation actually went up to Jerusalem to be present while the sacrifice was offered. This delegation was then the מעמד in the real sense, in that it 'stood by' while the sacrifice was offered.[6]

The officiating priests wore during the service special vestments consisting of the following four articles: 1. מכנסים, short trousers made of byssus (probably not of cotton but fine white linen). 2. Over these, the כתנת, a long coat reaching to the feet, rather close-fitting and with narrow sleeves, also made of byssus. 3. This coat was held together in the region of the chest by a girdle, אבנט, also mainly of byssus but interwoven with purple, scarlet and blue ornaments. It provided therefore the only colour in the otherwise completely white priestly raiment. 4. The מגבעה, a kind of cap or turban, served as a head-covering.[7]

5. G. F. Moore, *Judaism* II, 12–13. I. Elbogen, *Der jüdische Gottesdienst* ([3]1931), pp. 127 ff.; D. Sperber, 'Mishmarot and Ma'amadot', Enc. Jud. 12, cols. 89–93.

6. See especially mTaan. 4:1–4. The main passage, mTaan. 4:2, reads: 'The first prophets ordained twenty-four courses (משמרות). For every course there was a *ma'amad* (standing body) in Jerusalem composed of priests, Levites and Israelites. When the time came for a course to go up, the priests and the Levites went up to Jerusalem and the Israelites of the same course assembled in (the synagogues of) their towns and read the story of the Creation . . .'. The wording of this passage contains a contradiction in that the entire *ma'amad* is said to be in Jerusalem yet the Israelites assembled only in the synagogues of their towns. The parallel passage of tTaan. 4:3 probably gives the correct sense in that to 'Israelites of the same course' is added: 'who were unable to go up to Jerusalem'. The meaning therefore is that priests and Levites belonging to a course of service and capable of serving were obliged to go up, but Israelites prevented from so doing could stay at home, provided that some of them really did travel to Jerusalem. It is consequently presumed without further ado in mTam. 5:6 that 'the chief of the *ma'amad*' ראש מעמד, was present in Jerusalem. The Qumran War Rule lays down a similar regulation after introducing a suitable change, viz. 26 instead of 24 courses: 'Below them (the Levites) shall be the chiefs of the tribes together with the (52) heads of family of the congregation. They shall attend daily at the gates of the Sanctuary, whereas the leaders of the divisions with their numbered men shall attend at their appointed times' (1QM 2:3–4). mBik. 3:2 associates the מעמד with a geographically defined area and assumed that the meeting took place in the district capital. Cf. however mTaan. 2:7.

7. On the priestly vestments see Ezek. 44:17–19; Exod. 28: 40–3; 39:27–9, and especially the detailed description in Josephus, *Ant.* iii 7, 1–3 (151–8). For a briefer account, see Philo, *Vita Mosis* ii 28 (45): χιτῶνας λινοῦς, ζώνας τε καὶ περισκελῆ. *Spec. Leg.* i 16 (83): ἡ δὲ ἐσθής ἐστι χιτὼν λινοῦς καὶ περίζωμα. Josephus, *Ant.* xx 9, 6 (216): λινῆν στολήν. Aristeas (ed. Wendland 87) τῶν ἱερέων κεκαλυμμένων μέχρι τῶν σφυρῶν βυσσίνοις χιτῶσιν. The fullest description of the 'battle raiment' of the

Shoes are nowhere mentioned and it may be regarded as certain that the priests officiated barefoot.[8]

As the white raiment was symbolic of purity, sobriety and ritual cleanness was demanded of the serving priests. During their turn of office they were allowed no wine or other intoxicating drinks.[9] No-one who was not ritually clean was permitted to enter the forecourt for worship. Indeed, even those who were, were required without exception to take a ritual bath before entering on the services of the day.[10]

---

priests appears in the War Rule of Qumran: 'They shall be clothed in vestments of white cloth of flax (byssus, שש), in a fine linen tunic (כתונת בד) and fine linen breeches (מכנסי בד); and they shall be girdled with fine cloth of flax (byssus) embroidered with blue, purple and scarlet thread (אבנט בד שש משזור תכלת וארגמן ותולעת שני), a many-coloured design worked by a craftsman and on their heads they shall wear mitred turbans (פרי מגבעות). These shall be battle raiments; they shall not take them into the Sanctuary' (1QM 7:9–10; Vermes, *DSSE*, p. 133; Y. Yadin, *The Scroll of the War . . .*, pp. 217–20). The literature on this subject is the same as that on the garments of the High Priest, see above, p. 276. On the question of whether *byssus* = linen rather than cotton, see among others, S. R. Driver, *Exodus* (1911), p. 265; 'Linen', EB III, cols. 2799–2801; S. Krauss, *Talmudische Archäologie* I (1910), pp. 138 ff.; K. Galling, *Biblisches Reallexikon* (²1977), p. 326; A. G. Barrois, *Manuel d'archéologie biblique* I, p. 469; F. Olck, 'Byssus' RE III, cols. 1108–1114; G. Widengren, *Sakrales Königtum im Alten Testament und im Judentum* (1955), pp. 26 ff.; R. J. Forbes, *Studies in Ancient Technology* IV (1956); L. Bellinger, 'Cloth', IDB I, pp. 650–5; J. M. Myers, 'Linen', IBD III, pp. 134–5. Since the ancients did not always strictly distinguish between linen and cotton, it is quite possible that in some circumstances cotton was also used for the priestly vestments, for example the fine Indian fabric which the High Priest wore in the afternoon of the Day of Atonement was probably made of cotton, see above, p. 276. On the other hand it may safely be assumed that as a rule linen was used. According to the mKil. 9:1, only flax פשתים, and sheep's wool, צמר, were employed, the latter for the colourful ornamentation of the girdle. Josephus observes that the priests and the priests alone were permitted to wear material composed of linen and cotton mixed, *Ant.* iv 8, 11 (208): μηδεὶς δ' ἐξ ὑμῶν κλωστὴν ἐξ ἐρίου καὶ λίνου στολὴν φορείτο· τοῖς γὰρ ἱερεῦσι μόνοις ταύτην ἀποδεδεῖχθαι. The priests' attire was therefore expressly excluded from the prohibition of Lev. 19:19 and Dt. 22:11.

8. On services in the synagogue see mMeg. 4:8: 'Whoever says, I will not pray in coloured raiment, he may not do so in white raiment either. Whoever will not do so in sandals, he may not do so barefoot either'. The meaning is: it is not permitted to presume to wear priestly garments in synagogal worship. On the other hand, Yohanan ben Zakkai is said to have ordered in respect of the priestly blessing that, even after the destruction of the Temple it was only to be pronounced by the priests barefoot (bR.Sh. 31b; bSot. 40b; J. Derenbourg, *Essai*, p. 305, n. 3; J. Neusner, *A Life of Yohanan ben Zakkai* (²1970), p. 212).

9. Lev. 10:8–11; Ezek. 44:21; Hecataeus in Josephus, *C.Ap.* i 22 (199): τὸ παράπαν οἶνον οὐ πίνοντες ἐν τῷ ἱερῷ = Stern, GLAJJ I, no. 63; Philo, *Spec. Leg.* i 18, (98–100); Josephus, *Ant.* iii 12, 2 (279); *B.J.* v 5, 7 (229). mTaan. 2:7; yTaan. 65d; Sifra to Lev. 10:9 (ed. Weiss 46ab).

10. mYom. 3:3: 'None may enter the forecourt for worship, even though he be clean, until he has immersed himself'. Cf. mTam. 1:2; Jub. 21:16; T. Levi 9:11: καὶ πρὸ τοῦ εἰσελθεῖν εἰς τὰ ἅγια λούου καὶ ἐν τῷ θύειν νίπτου· καὶ ἀπαρτίζων πάλιν τὴν

Furthermore, they were also obliged to wash their hands and feet in the bronze basin (כיור) which stood in the open between the Temple and the altar of burnt-offering.[11]

The great quantities of sacrifices offered daily[12] belonged to the two categories of public and private sacrifices.[13] The first were offered in the name of the people and were paid for out of the dues discharged by them, particularly the half-shekel tax. The second were the concern of private individuals and could be offered for a wide variety of motives, some of them voluntary, and others, for one reason or another, obligatory. Both were again of various kinds according to the content and purpose of the offering, viz.:

1. burnt-offerings, the essence of which was that the sacrificed beast was burnt whole on the altar;

2. sin- and guilt-offerings, when only the fat was burned on the altar while the meat went to the priests;

3. communion sacrifices (זבחי שלמים) or peace-offerings, when likewise only the fat went to the altar while the meat was used by the worshipper himself for a joyful sacrificial feast.[14]

θυσίαν νίπτου. A bath had also to be taken after excreting, mYom. 3:2. On the location of the bath, see mTam. 1:1; mMid, 1:9.

11. Exod. 30:17–21, 40:30–2; mTam. 1:4; 2:1. Philo, *Vita Mosis* ii 27 (138): πόδας μάλιστα καὶ χεῖρας ἀπονιπτόμενοι. Jub. 21:16. Also in the passage cited in the preceding note, T. Levi 9:11, the νίπτεσθαι is mentioned together with the λούεσθαι. On the כיור itself, see also Exod. 38:8; mMid. 3:6; mYom. 3:10; mTam. 3:8. I. Benzinger, *Hebräische Archäologie* (³1927), plate xiv: 2, 3, C. Watzinger, *Denkmäler Palästinas* (1933), pp. 105–6; W. F. Albright, *Archaeology and the Religion of Israel* (²1946), pp. 152–4; J. L. Kelso, *The Ceramic Vocabulary of the Old Testament* (1948), p. 20; P. L. Garber, 'Laver', IDB III, p. 76–7. On the ritual of handwashing, cf. L. Finkelstein, *The Pharisees*, pp. 273–7, 718–9.

12. On sacrificial worship in general, see J. Wellhausen, *Geschichte Israels* I, pp. 53–84 = *Prolegomena*, 5th ed., pp. 54–81. F. Pfister, 'Kultus', RE XI, cols. 2180 ff. G. B. Gray, *Sacrifice in the Old Testament* (1925), pp. 179–270; J. Pedersen, *Israel* III/IV (1940), pp. 299–375; H. H. Rowley, 'The Meaning of Sacrifice in the Old Testament', BJRL 33 (1950), pp. 74–110 [*From Moses to Qumran* (1963), pp. 67–107]; R. Rendtorff, *Studien zur Geschichte des Opfers im alten Israel* (1953); T. H. Gaster, 'Sacrifice', IDB IV, pp. 147–59; R. de Vaux, *Ancient Israel*, pp. 415–32, 440–56; *Studies in O.T. Sacrifice* (1964); H. H. Rowley, *Worship in Ancient Israel* (1967), pp. 111–43; 'Sacrifice', Enc. Jud. 14, cols. 599–616. See also the standard works on the archaeology and theology of the Old Testament.

13. Philo, *Spec. Leg.* i 35 (168): Ἐπεὶ δὲ τῶν θυσιῶν αἱ μέν εἰσιν ὑπὲρ ἅπαντος τοῦ ἔθνους, εἰ δὲ δεῖ τὸ ἀληθὲς εἰπεῖν ὑπὲρ ἅπαντος ἀνθρώπων γένους, αἱ δὲ ὑπὲρ ἑκάστου τῶν ἱερουργεῖν ἀξιούντων, λεκτέον πρότερον περὶ τῶν κοινῶν. Josephus, *Ant.* iii 9, 1 (224): δύο μὲν γὰρ εἰσιν ἱερουργίαι, τούτων δ' ἡ μὲν ὑπὸ τῶν ἰδιωτῶν ἑτέρα δ' ὑπὸ τοῦ δήμου συντελούμεναι κ.τ.λ.

14. In the main source on sacrifice, Lev. 1–7, five kinds are mentioned: 1. the burnt-offering; 2. the grain-offering; 3. the peace-offering; 4. the sin-offering; 5. the

Needless to say, the numerous private offerings formed the bulk of the sacrifices. Nevertheless, in this description of the regular daily worship only public sacrifice is taken into consideration, especially the most important of them all: the community's daily burnt-offering.

A few preliminary topographical remarks seem to be called for at this point.[15] The inner forecourt where all the cultic activities were carried out was divided by a wall into a western and an eastern half. The latter was called 'the forecourt of the women', not because women alone were admitted there, but because women could enter as well.[16] The beautiful gate to the east of this forecourt, with its artistically worked bronze leaves (*ἡ θύρα ἡ λεγομένη ὡραία*, Act. 3:2), afforded the main entrance to the forecourt (cf. above, pp. 57–8), which is why beggars used to sit there (Act. 3:2). The western section of the forecourt was accessible only to male Israelites; and there stood the Temple proper. Relatively speaking not large, it was nevertheless a magnificent building. The interior, into which presumably little daylight penetrated, consisted of a spacious ante-chamber and a room only half as big beyond it. The latter was the 'Holy of Holies' into which no-one set foot except once a year, when the High Priest entered on the Day of Atonement. In the ante-chamber (the eastern room) were the three sacred vessels, the punctilious handling of which was one of the main parts of the priestly ministry: 1. in the centre, the golden altar of incense (מזבח הזהב), also called 'the inner altar' (מזבח הפנימי), on which incense was offered daily, morning and evening;[17] 2. south of this, the golden seven-branched

guilt-offering. But the grain-offering is not on a level with animal sacrifices and for the most part occurs only as a supplement to them, as does the drink-offering. The sin- and guilt-offerings are admittedly different, yet they are so closely related that they may be regarded as one kind. In regard to animal sacrifice, and this was by far the most important, three main types are therefore to be distinguished, as is done in Philo, *Spec. Leg.* i 36 (194), and Josephus, *Ant.* iii 9, 1–3 (224–32). All three types appeared in private and in public sacrifices alike, though the peace-offering was a rare event in public sacrifice, occurring regularly only on the Feast of Weeks (Lev. 23:19, otherwise on special occasions (see 'Peace Offering', JE IX, p. 566; 'Sacrifice', Enc. Jud. 14, cols. 603–4). The meat of the public peace-offerings belonged to the priests (Lev. 23:20). On these generally, see mPes. 7:4; mZeb. 5:5; mMen. 5:7; mMeil. 2:5. Burnt-offerings and sin-offerings offered in the name of community were very frequent; see the list of these for feast days in Num. 28–9. On burnt-offerings see L. Rost, 'Erwägungen zum israelitischen Brandopfer', *Von Ugarit und Qumran* [O. Eissfeldt Festschrift] (1958), pp. 177–83.

15. For the sources and literature on the Temple of Herod, see vol. I, pp. 308–9, n. 71.

16. See Josephus, *C.Ap.* ii 8 (104): 'in secunda vero porticu (by which the women's court is meant) cuncti Iudaei ingrediebantur eorumque coniuges'.

17. On the daily incense-offering, see Exod. 30: 7–8. On the preparation of the incense, Exod. 30:34–8. On the altar of incense, Exod. 30:1–10, 34:25–9. 1 Mac.

candelabrum (מנורה) which was to be kept continuously burning;[18]

1:21; 4:49. Philo, *Vita Mosis* ii, 21 (101); *Spec. Leg.* i 35 (171); Josephus, *Ant.* iii 6, 8 (147); *B.J.* v 5, 5 (216). M. Löhr, *Das Räuchopfer im Alten Testament* (1927); A. Vincent, *La religion des judéo-araméens d'Éléphantine* (1937), pp. 212–23; M. Haran, 'The Censor Incense and Tamid Incense', Tarbiz 26 (1956), pp. 115–25; 'The Use of Incense in the Ancient Israelite Ritual', VT 10 (1960), pp. 113–29; R. de Vaux, *Ancient Israel* (1961), pp. 319, 411; H. H. Rowley, *Worship in Ancient Israel* (1967), pp. 84 ff.; J. Milgrom, 'Altar', Enc. Jud. 2, cols. 765–7. On the meaning of זהב as incense, cf. G. Ryckmans, 'De l'or (?), de l'encens et de la myrrhe', RB 58 (1951), pp. 372–6; R. de Langhe, 'Het gonden altaar in de Israëlitische eredienst', Mededelingen van de Koninklijke Vlaamse Academie, Klasse de Letteren 14, nr. 6 (1952), pp. 3–23; *Studia Biblica et Orientalia* I (1959), pp. 342–60=Bibl. 40 (1959), pp. 476–94. מזבח הזהב: mYom. 5:5, 7; mHag. 3:8; mZeb. 5:2; mMen. 3:6; 4:4. מזבח הפנימי: mYom. 2:3; 5:5; mZeb. 4:2; mMeil. 3:4; mTam. 3:6, 9; 5:1. The existence of the altar of incense in the Second Temple is unanimously attested from the time of the Maccabees down to Josephus and the Mishnah. It is true that besides the candelabrum Hecataeus of Abdera in Josephus, *C.Ap.* i 22 (198), mentions only a golden *βωμός* inside the Temple, which can as easily refer to the shewbread table as to the altar of incense. And the altar of incense is not listed among the objects found in the Temple by Pompey, *Ant.* xiv 4, 4 (72). But in a parallel passage, *B.J.* i 7, 6 (152), there is allusion to the candelabrum, the table, and also to *θυμιατήρια*, which can mean the altar of incense. And taking into account the rest of the evidence, there can be no doubt of the altar's existence in Pompey's time, for its non-appearance among the booty taken by Titus, *B.J.* vii 5, 5 (218), may be explained by its limited value. It is less certain that it existed at the time of Hecataeus (third century B.C.).

18. On the care of the *menorah* see Exod. 27:20–21; 30:7–8; Lev. 24:1–4; Num. 8:1–4; 2 Chron. 13:11. From the biblical texts it seems that the lamps were only to be lit in the evening so that they burned during the night. Thus also Philo, *Spec. Leg.* i 54 (296). On the other hand, according to Josephus, *Ant.* iii 8, 3 (199), three of the seven lamps burned by day, and by night all seven; according to the Mishnah, one by day, by night all seven, mTam. 3:9; 64:1; likewise Sifra on Lev. 24:1–4 (ed. Weiss 103ab), and Sifre on Num. 8:1–4 (§59-61, ed. Horovitz, pp. 57–9). Cf. also Hecataeus in Josephus, *C.Ap.* i 22 (199): *ἐπὶ τούτων φῶς ἐστιν ἀναπόσβεστον καὶ τὰς νύκτας καὶ τὰς ἡμέρας*. Diodorus, xxxiv–v 1, 4=FGrH 87 F.109=Stern, GLAJJ I, no. 63: *τὸν δὲ ἀθάνατον λεγόμενον παρ' αὐτοῖς λύχνον καὶ καόμενον ἀδιαλείπτως ἐν τῷ ναῳ*. On the *menorah* itself see Exod. 25:31–40; 37:17–24; 1 Mac. 1:21; 4:49. Philo, *Vita Mosis* ii 21 (102–3); Josephus, *Ant.* iii 6, 7 (145–6); *B.J.* v 5, 5 (217); vii 5, 5 (149): mMen. 3:7; 4:4; 9:3; mTam. 3:6, 9; 6:1. 'Menorah', JE VIII, pp. 493 ff.; K. Galling, *Biblisches Reallexicon* (^{2}1977), pp. 200–1; W. F. Robin, *The Story of the Lamp* (1939); R. F. Funk and I. Ben-Dor, 'Lamp', IDB III, pp. 63–4; L. E. Toombs, 'Lampstand', IDB III, pp. 64–6; H. Strauss, 'Menorah', Enc. Jud. II, cols. 1355–67; L. Yarden, *The Tree of Light* (1971). A representation of the lamps is preserved on the reliefs of the Arch of Titus in Rome (see vol. I, p. 510; cf. W. Eltester, 'Der siebenarmige Leuchter am Titusbogen', *Festschrift J. Jeremias* (1960), pp. 62–76; Enc. Jud. II, cols. 1363–66). For representations on tombs and in synagogues both in Palestine and the Diaspora see the plates in Yarden, *op. cit.*, and figures 1–12 in Enc. Jud. 11, cols. 1355–63. A Herodian *menorah* engraved on plaster was discovered during the 1969 excavations of the Old City of Jerusalem. Cf. N. Avigad, Qadmoniot 3 (1970), pp. 28–9; Enc. Jud. 11, col. 1358, fig. 19. Cf. also N. Avigad, in *Jerusalem Revealed: Archaeology in the Holy City 1968–1974* (1975), pp. 47–9. The earliest record is

3. north of the altar, the golden table of the shewbread on which twelve fresh loaves were placed on each Sabbath day.[19]

The front of the Temple faced towards the east. Before it and in the open was the great altar of burnt-offering, or 'the altar', on which with the exception of the offering of incense all the acts of sacrifice were performed. It was a tall square construction of large dimensions, thirty-two square cubits at the base according to the measurements given in the Mishnah (whereas for example the interior of the Temple was only twenty cubits wide). It tapered towards the top in several steps so that the upper level still measured twenty-four square cubits.[20] The whole edifice was built of unhewn stones untouched by tools.[21] On

---

probably that provided by coins of Mattathias Antigonus depicting a *menorah* with a triangular base, dating to around 37 B.C. Y. Meshorer, *Jewish Coins of the Second Temple Period* (1967). nos. 36 and 36A, see Pl. V. On the location of the *menorah* south of the altar, see Exod. 26:35, 40:24. On the *menorah* as a Jewish symbol, see A.-M. Goldberg, 'Der siebenarmige Leuchter', ZDMG 117 (1967), pp. 232–46.

19. On the care of the table of shewbread see Lev. 24:5–9. Philo, *Spec. Leg.* i 35 (172–6); Josephus, *Ant.* iii 10, 7 (255–7). On the table of shewbread itself, see Exod. 25:23–30; 37:10–16; 1 Mac. 1:22, 4:49; Philo, *Vita Mosis* ii 22 (104); Josephus, *Ant.* iii 6, 6 (139–41); *B.J.* v 5, 5 (216); vii 5, 5 (148); mMen. 9:5–7. Cf. also the description of the table allegedly given to the Temple at Jerusalem by Ptolemy Philadelphus in Aristeas (ed. Wendland 52–72); Josephus, *Ant.* xii 2, 7–8 (57–63). Cf. A. R. S. Kennedy, 'Shewbread', HDB IV, pp. 495–7. A representation of the table is also found in the reliefs of the Arch of Titus. Cf. H. Holzinger, 'Der Schaubrodtisch des Titusbogens', ZAW 21 (1901), pp. 341 f. On the placing of the table north of the altar of incense, see Exod. 26:35; 40:22. J. Pedersen, *Israel* III/IV, p. 312, n. 1, p. 474, n. 3; R. de Vaux, *Ancient Israel*, p. 422. H. F. Beck, 'Bread of the Presence', IDB I, p. 464. See E. R. Goodenough, *Jewish Symbols* V (1956), pp. 62–95 and plates.

20. Cf. especially the descriptions in mMid. 3:1–4 and Josephus, *B.J.* v 5, 6 (225); *Ant.* iv 8, 5 (200–1); see also Hecataeus in Josephus, *C.Ap.* i 22 (198) = Stern, GLAJJ I, no. 12; Aristeas (ed. Wendland 87); 1 Mac. 4:44–7; Philo, *Spec. Leg.* i 51 (274–6). Measurements also in Ezek. 43: 13–17. Cf. further, 'Altar', JE I, pp. 464–9; RE I, cols. 1640–91 for parallels in the Gentile cults; K. Galling, *Der Altar in den Kulturen des Alten Orients* (1925); W. F. Albright, 'The Babylonian Temple-tower and the Altar of Burnt-Offering', JBL 39 (1920), 137–42; *Archaeology and the Religion of Israel* ([2]1946), pp. 150 ff. G. B. Gray, *Sacrifice in the Old Testament* (1925), pp. 96–178. L. H. Vincent, 'L'autel des holocaustes et le caractère du Temple d'Ezéchiel', *Mélanges Paul Peeters, Analecta Bollandiana* 67 (1949), pp. 7–20. K. Galling, 'Altar', IDB I, pp. 96–100; R. de Vaux, *Ancient Israel*, pp. 410–13.

21. Hecataeus in Josephus, *C.Ap.* i 22 (198) = Stern, GLAJJ I, no. 12: *ἀτμήτων συλλέκτων ἀργῶν λίθων*. 1 Mac. 4:47. Philo, *Spec. Leg.* i 51 (274): *ἐκ λίθων λογάδων καὶ ἀτμήτων*. Josephus, *Ant.* iv 8, 5 (200–1); *B.J.* v 5, 6 (225); mMid. 3:4. The oldest and most primitive altars were undoubtedly constructed of rough stones or even of piles of earth and in the J legislation are still presumed to be customary (Exod. 20: 24–6; cf. Dt. 27:5–6). Solomon, however, built a bronze altar in Jerusalem (1 Kgs. 8:64; 9:25; 2 Kg. 16:14–15; 2 Chron. 4:1). The Priestly Code intends to

the south side, a gradual ascent formed also of unhewn stone led to the altar. The fire on this altar was never permitted to die, not even at night.[22]

Between the Temple and the altar, equally in the open air, stood the bronze basin (כיור) already mentioned in which the priests washed their hands and feet before engaging in worship.

North of the altar, and still in the open, was the slaughter area; fixed to the ground were rings to which the animals were tied when they were slaughtered. Nearby were pillars on which to hang them when they were dead and marble tables where they were skinned and their entrails washed.[23]

The Temple, including the altar and the slaughter area, was surrounded by an enclosure within which as a rule only the priests were allowed, the ordinary Israelites entering only 'when it was necessary for the laying on of hands, slaughtering and waving' (תנופה).[24]

The most important part of regular worship was the daily burnt-offering of the people, the עלת התמיד, or simply התמיד, 'the perpetual one'.[25] The custom of offering regular daily sacrifice is relatively very ancient. In detail, however, its performance varied from age to age, not only insofar as its cost was borne by the kings before the exile (Ezek. 45:17 and 46:13–15 according to LXX), whereas it was later discharged by the people, but also in its actual nature.[26] In the time of Ahaz only

---

portray the whole Sanctuary as a portable one, and with this end in view constructs an altar of burnt-offering made of wood and covered with bronze (Exod. 27:1–8; 38:1–7; Num. 17:1–5). Such an altar can hardly have existed. The post-exilic practice reverted rather to the older legal ordinances, Exod. 20: 25; Dt. 27:5–6. Cf. generally, J. Wellhausen, *Geschichte* I, pp. 30, 38 f. *Prolegomena*, 5th ed., pp. 29 f., 37 f.; R. de Vaux, *Ancient Israel*, pp. 408–13.

22. Lev. 6:6; Philo, *Spec. Leg.* i 52 (285); Josephus, *B.J.* ii 17, 6 (425); cf. also 2 Mac. 1:18–36.

23. mMid. 3:5; 5:2; mTam. 3:5; mShek. 6:4. Lev. 1:11 prescribes that the slaughter of the burnt-offerings is to take place north of the altar. But sin and-guilt-offerings are to be slaughtered in the same place (Lev. 4:24, 29, 33; 6:18; 7:2; 14:13). This regulation is omitted only in the case of peace-offerings. For further details concerning the various places at which sacrificial victims were slaughtered, see mZeb. 5.

24. See mKel. 1:8. On the enclosure see especially Josephus, *B.J.* v 5, 6 (226); *Ant.* viii 3, 9 (95); xiii 13, 5 (373).

25. עלת התמיד: Num. 28:10, 15, 24, 31; 29:16, 19, 22, 25 ,28, 31, 34, 38; Ezr. 3:5; Neh. 10:34. התמיד: Dan. 8:11–13; 11:31; 12:11. mPes. 5:1; mYom. 7:3; mTaan. 4:6; mMen. 4:4. The tractate Tamid takes its name from this.

26. J. Wellhausen, *Geschichte* I, pp. 81–2 = *Prolegomena*, 5th ed., pp. 78 f.; A. C. Welch, *Post-Exilic Judaism* (1935), pp. 284–90; Ch. Tschernowitz, *Toledoth Ha-Halakah* I/2 (1936), 260 f.; L. Finkelstein, *The Pharisees*, pp. 282–3, 854–5.

a burnt-offering was presented in the morning and only a grain-offering in the evening (2 Kgs. 16:15). This practice was fixed so firmly that the times of the day were determined by it. To speak of 'when the grain-offering is brought' was equivalent to saying, 'towards evening' (1 Kgs. 18:29, 36). Indeed, this way of denoting the time became so established that it continued to be used long after burnt-offerings were sacrificed in the evening as well (Ezr. 9:4, 5; Dan. 9:21).[27] Such was not yet the practice, it seems, in the age of Ezekiel. Yet already in his day there was an extension of the older custom since according to him a burnt-offering and a grain-offering were to be made in the morning (Ezek. 46:13–15). The Priestly Code, by contrast, prescribes that a burnt-offering and a grain-offering be presented in both morning and evening, and a drink-offering with each (Ex. 29:38–42; Num. 28:3–8). The Chronicler, too, assumes that the daily sacrifice in the form of a burnt-offering made twice a day is one of long standing (1 Chron. 15; 40; 2 Chron. 8:11, 31:3). It was the true heart and centre of the entire sacrificial worship. In no circumstances could it be dispensed with. In A.D. 70, when Jerusalem had for long been besieged by the Romans and famine was at its peak, the daily sacrifice was nevertheless regularly offered, and it counted as one of the heaviest of blows when, on the 17th of Tammuz, it had at last to be discontinued.[28]

The more detailed stipulations contained in the Priestly Code concerning the *Tamid* are as follows (Ex. 29:38–42; Num. 28:3–8).[29] In the morning and in the evening a year-old ram without blemish was to be sacrificed as a burnt-offering, and on both occasions the ordinanaces relating to burnt-offerings in general, i.e. Lev. 1:10–23 and 6:1–6, were to be observed. Each sacrifice was to be accompanied by a grain-offering and a drink-offering since the Priestly Code lays down that an additional offering of grain and drink is to accompany all burnt-offerings without exception (Num. 15:1–16). The grain-offering in the case of a lamb consisted of one-tenth of an ephah (2.2 litres) of fine flour (סלת) mixed (בלול, i.e. not baked) with a quarter of a hin (0.9 litres) of pure oil; the drink-offering was of a quarter of a hin of wine. The hour for the morning sacrifice was break of day, that for the evening sacrifice, at dusk, in accordance with the biblical definition, בין הערבים. Later it

27. In the Mishnah the time of the *minḥah* (the grain-offering) is still equivalent to the afternoon; e.g. mBer. 4:1; mPes. 10:1; mR.Sh. 4:4; mMeg. 3:6; 4:1. Even today, *minḥah* is the afternoon prayer.

28. Josephus, *B.J.* vi 2, 1 (94–5); mTaan. 4:6. Likewise in the persecution under Antiochus Epiphanes the discontinuation of the *tamid* was viewed as the greatest calamity (Dan. 8:11–13; 11:31; 12:11).

29. E. König, *Theologie des A.T.* (1923), pp. 87 ff. R. H. Pfeiffer, *Introduction*, pp. 253–69. J. Hempel, 'Priesterkodex', RE XXII (1954), cols. 1943–67. R. de Vaux, *Studies in O.T. Sacrifice* (1964), pp. 27–36. For further details see the treatise mTamid; cf. below, n. 42.

became usual to offer the evening sacrifice in the afternoon, at about three o'clock.[30]

The daily grain-offering of the High Priest was also always presented in conjunction with the daily burnt-offering of the people. According to Lev. 6:12–16, the High Priest was to bring every day (תמיד)[31] in the morning and in the evening a grain-offering different both in its nature and preparation from the grain-offering of the people that supplemented the burnt-offering. It consisted altogether of only one-tenth of an ephah of flour, half of which was offered in the morning and half in the evening; and it was not only mixed with oil, but after this was done, was baked on a flat pan (מחבת). When they were cooked, the cakes were broken into pieces, sprinkled with oil, and thus offered (Lev. 6:14; cf. Lev. 2:5–6).[32] Because of this method of preparation it was known in later times as חביתים, 'flat cakes', and appears under this name directly or indirectly in Chronicles,[33] and particularly in the Mishnah.[34]

As the offering of this sacrifice was the duty of the High Priest, it is

30. Philo and Josephus in their main references to *tamid*, merely repeat the biblical time rulings (Philo, *Spec. Leg.* i 35 (169): *Καθ' ἑκάστην μὲν οὖν ἡμέραν δύο ἀμνοὺς ἀνάγειν διείρηται, τὸν μὲν ἅμα τῇ ἕῳ, τὸν δὲ δείλης ἑσπέρας.* Josephus, *Ant.* iii 10, 1 (237): *ἐκ δὲ τοῦ δημοσίου ἀναλώματος νόμος ἐστὶν ἄρνα καθ' ἑκάστην ἡμέραν σφάζεσθαι τῶν αὐτοετῶν ἀρχομένης τε ἡμέρας καὶ ληγούσης*). The actual practice in later times is made clear in *Ant.* xiv 4, 3 (65): *δὶς τῆς ἡμέρας πρωΐ τε καὶ περὶ ἐνάτην ὥραν ἱερουργούντων ἐπὶ τοῦ βωμοῦ.* This agrees exactly with mPes. 5:1, which states that the evening sacrifice was usually slaughtered at about thirty minutes after the eighth hour and offered an hour later (i.e. at 2.30 and 3.30 p.m.). Cf. also Josephus, *C.Ap.* ii 8 (105): 'mane etenim aperto templo opportebat facientes traditas hostias introire et meridie rursus, dum clauderetur templum'. Thus it was also the custom to go to the Temple to pray at about the ninth hour (3.00 p.m.). (Act. 3:1; 10:3, 30). See generally, Str.-B. II, pp. 696–8; R. de Vaux, *Ancient Israel*, p. 469.

31. The words, 'on the day of his anointing', Lev. 6:13, cannot be reconciled with this, and in effect the statement is omitted in the New English Bible. R. H. Pfeiffer, *Introduction*, p. 254. M. Noth, *Leviticus* (1967), pp. 55–7, considers the text to be a conflation of two different sets of instructions.

32. On the preparation, cf. also Philo, *Spec. Leg.* i 47 (256); Josephus, *Ant.* iii 10, 7 (255–7); mMen. 11:3. It entailed לשה, kneading, and אפיה, baking. J. Pedersen, *Israel*, III/IV, pp. 349 ff. N. H. Snaith, 'Sacrifices in the O.T.', VT 7 (1957), pp. 308–17. R. de Vaux, *Ancient Israel*, pp. 416 ff.

33. 1 Chron. 9:31. The LXX interprets מעשה חביתים by *τὰ ἔργα τῆς θυσίας τοῦ τηγάνου τοῦ μεγάλου ἱερέως.* But the Chronicler probably means by this not only the grain-offering of the High Priest but also the baked grain-offering in general; cf. Brown-Driver-Briggs, *Lexicon*, s.v. The reference is not limited to the High Priest.

34. mTam. 1:3; 3:1; 4:3; mYom. 2:3; 3:4; mMen. 4:5; 11:3; mMid. 1:4. From mTam. 3:1, 4:3, mYom. 2:3, it is clear that the High Priest's grain-offering was presented between the grain-offering of the people and the drink-offering. Cf. in general the detailed description of daily worship in the tractate Tamid.

possible to speak of his daily sacrifice.[35] But he offered it only in the sense that the people offered the daily burnt-offering. He caused it, that is to say, to be offered in his name and at his expense.[36] In no way was it necessary for him to officiate himself. It is known from Josephus that the High Priest officiated as a rule on the Sabbaths and feast days (see above, p. 276, n. 4). On the remaining days of the year, the High Priest's grain offering as well as the sacrifice of the people were made by whichever priests were serving: when lots were cast over the various duties of the day, one of them was always to determine who should present the חביתין, i.e. the High Priest's grain-offering.[37] In fact, since the Bible describes this sacrifice as a sacrifice of 'Aaron and his sons' (Lev. 6:13), it could also be conceived of as a sacrifice which the priests offered for themselves.[38]

In addition to these sacrifices, it was the daily duty of the priests to attend to the altar of incense and the candelabrum inside the Temple. An offering of incense had to be made every morning and evening (Ex. 30:7, 8), the morning offering preceding, and the evening offering following, that of the burnt-offering, so that the latter was as it were set within a frame of incense-offerings.[39]

35. Ecclus. 45:14. 'His grain-offerings shall be burned whole, twice every day continually.' Philo, *Spec. Leg.* iii 23 (131): *εὐχὰς δὲ καὶ θυσίας τελῶν καθ' ἑκάστην ἡμέραν.* The well-known passage in Heb. 7:27 is probably also to be explained on this basis; though this daily grain-offering by the High Priest is of course not a sin-offering, as might appear in Hebrews. Cf. Str.-B. III, pp. 696–700.

36. Josephus, *Ant.* iii 10, 7 (257): *θύει δὲ ὁ ἱερεὺς* (=the High Priest) *ἐκ τῶν ἰδίων ἀναλωμάτων, καὶ δὶς ἑκάστης ἡμέρας τοῦτο ποιεῖ, ἄλευρον ἐλαίῳ μεμαγμένον καὶ πεπηγὸς ὀπτήσει βραχείᾳ, καὶ εἷς μέν ἐστιν ἀσσάρων τοῦ ἀλεύρου, τούτου δὲ τὸ μὲν ἥμισυ τὸ πρωῒ τὸ δ' ἕτερον δείλης ἐπιφέρει τῷ πυρί.* When a High Priest died, the grain-offering was to be made at the expense of the people until his successor assumed office; according to R. Judah b. Elai, the heirs bore the cost (mShek. 7:6).

37. mTam. 3:1; 4:3; mYom. 2:3. Strictly speaking, these passages are not concerned with the sacrifice itself but only with bringing the sacrificial elements to the altar steps. But according to mTam. 5:2 and mYom. 2:4–5, the same number of priests were appointed to offer the sacrifice (placing it on the altar) as were charged with bringing it to the altar, namely 9, to correspond with the 9 sacrificial elements, among which in the passages referred to (mTam. 3:1, 4:3, mYom. 2:3) the חביתין are explicitly mentioned. There can therefore be no doubt that the actual offering of the חביתין was performed as a rule by an ordinary priest.

38. Philo, *Quis rerum div. heres*, 36 (174): *Ἀλλὰ καὶ τὰς ἐνδελεχεῖς θυσίας ὁρᾷς εἰς ἴσα διῃρημένας, ἥν τε ὑπὲρ αὐτῶν ἀνάγουσιν οἱ ἱερεῖς διὰ τῆς σεμιδάλεως, καὶ τὴν ὑπὲρ τοῦ ἔθνους τῶν δυοῖν ἀμνῶν, οὓς ἀναφέρειν διείρηται.* *Spec. Leg.* i 47 (256): *Σεμίδαλις γὰρ ἡ ἐνδελεχὴς αὐτῶν θυσία μέτρου ἱεροῦ τὸ δέκατον καθ' ἑκάστην ἡμέραν, οὗ τὸ μὲν ἥμισυ πρωΐας, τὸ δὲ ἥμισυ δείλης προσάγεται ταγηνισθὲν ἐν ἐλαίῳ, μηδενὸς εἰς βρῶσιν ὑπολειφθέντος.*

39. Philo, *Spec. Leg.* i 35 (171): *δὶς δὲ καθ' ἑκάστην ἡμέραν ἐπιθυμιᾶται τὰ πάντων εὐωδέστατα θυμιαμάτων εἴσω τοῦ καταπετάσματος, ἀνίσχοντος ἡλίου καὶ δυομένου, πρό τε τῆς ἑωθινῆς θυσίας καὶ μετὰ τὴν ἑσπερινήν.* *Spec. Leg.* i 51 (276): *οὐ γὰρ ἐφίεται τὴν ὁλόκαυτον θυσίαν ἔξω προσαγαγεῖν, πρὶν ἔνδον περὶ βαθὺν ὄρθρον ἐπιθυμίασαι.* Even more

The candelabrum had also to be attended to morning and evening. In the morning the lamps were cleaned and provided with fresh oil, and one or several (three, according to Josephus) were left burning all day. In the evening, the remaining lamps were lit as all seven were to burn during the night (see especially Ex. 30:7–8; 2 Chron. 8:11; and in general pp. 296–7 above).

Lastly, music and singing contributed to the beauty of divine worship. When the burnt-offering was presented, the Levites joined in with song and string music and two priests blew silver trumpets (2 Chron. 29:26–8; Num. 10: 1–2, 10). Meanwhile, the people too assembled for prayer in the Temple. Whenever the priests sounded their trumpets in the intervals between the singing, the people threw themselves down in adoration.[40] For each day of the week a psalm was set for the Levites to sing: Ps. 24 for Sunday, Ps. 48 for Monday, Ps. 82 for Tuesday, Ps. 94 for Wednesday, Ps. 81 for Thursday, Ps. 93 for Friday and Ps. 92 for the Sabbath.[41]

---

precise is the statement in mYom. 3:5: 'The morning incense was offered between (the sprinkling of) the blood and (the offering of) the parts; the evening incense between (the offering of) the parts and the drink-offerings'.

40. On the assembly of the people in the Temple for prayer see Lk. 1:10 and Act. 3:1. For the more precise information of mTamid, see below. The hours for prayers were: 1. early morning at the time of the morning sacrifice; 2. the ninth hour of the day (3.00 p.m.); 3. in the evening at sunset. See mBer. 1:1 ff.; 4:1. Cf. J. Doller, *Das Gebet im AT* (1914); I. Elbogen, *Der jüdische Gottesdienst in seiner geschichtlichen Entwicklung* ([3]1931), pp. 27–60; A. Z. Idelsohn, *Jewish Liturgy* (1932); A. Cronbach, 'Worship in NT Times, Jewish', IDB IV, pp. 895–903. On Jewish prayer during the first centuries of the Christian era, see J. Heinemann, *Prayer in the Talmud. Forms and Patterns* (1977). On Christian prayer periods see A. V. Harnack's note on *Διδαχή* viii 3 (*Texte und Untersuchungen* II 1–2, p. 27); Foakes-Jackson and Lake, *The Beginnings of Christianity* IV (1933), pp. 10–11, 191. Str.-B. IV, pp. 208–49; C. W. Dugmore, *The Influence of the Synagogue upon the Divine Office* (1944), pp. 59–70.

41. mTam. 7:4. A. Graetz, 'Die Tempelpsalmen', MGWJ (1878), pp. 217–22; A. Büchler, 'Zum Vortrage und Umfange der Tempelpsalmen', ZAW (1900), pp. 97–114. For five of these psalms a statement of the day involved is also correctly given in the LXX: Ps. 24 (23) *τῆς μιᾶς σαββάτου*; Ps. 48 (47) *δευτέρᾳ σαββάτου ἡ γῆ*; Ps. 94 (93) *τετράδι σαββάτου*; Ps. 93 (92) *εἰς τὴν ἡμέραν τοῦ προσαββάτου ὅτε κατῴκισται*; Ps. 92 (91) *εἰς τὴν ἡμέραν τοῦ σαββάτου*. To these should be added Vet. Lat. Ps. 81: 'quinta Sabbati', which also must stem from a Greek model. In the case of the Sabbath psalm the statement has also found its way into the Masoretic text. According to Jewish opinion, the parallel with the six days of creation influenced the selection of the psalms (see bR.Sh. 31a; Soferim 18:1). But for most of them such a parallel is simply not to be found. This view was obviously arrived at because the Scripture readings of the מעמדות (see above, p. 293) were so arranged that the whole story of the creation was read consecutively in the course of the week (mTaan. 4:3: on Sunday they read the first day of Creation, on Monday the second, on Tuesday the third, etc.). Besides the psalms for the days of the week, there were, of course, many others for the various Temple occasions.

The form of Temple worship described here is that portrayed so enthusiastically by Ben Sira (Ecclus. 50:11–21). A very detailed account evidently based on reliable tradition is given in the Mishnah tractate *Tamid*, the essence of which may supplement the foregoing remarks.[42]

The serving priests slept in a chamber in the inner forecourt. Early in the morning, before sunrise, the officer charged with determining by lots the duties of the day first of all caused them to be thrown to decide who was to attend to the ashes of the altar of burnt-offering. Those who wished to do so will have taken the prescribed bath already before the officer's arrival. Lots were then cast among them for this task. The man chosen went immediately about his business in a darkness lit only by the glow of the altar fire. He washed his hands and feet in the bronze basin standing between the Temple and the altar, ascended the altar and swept up the ashes with a silver pan. While he was doing so, the priests preparing the baked grain-offering (of the High Priest) also attended to their task.[43]

Fresh wood was now brought to the altar, and while it burned, the priests, after washing their hands and feet in the basin, went down to the *lishkath ha-gazith* (on this see above, pp. 224–5), where a further casting of lots took place.[44]

The officer now cast to determine 1. who should act as slaughterer, 2. who should sprinkle the blood on the altar; 3. who should clean the ashes from the inner altar; 4. who should clean the lamps; and further, who should bring the pieces of the sacrificial victim to the altar steps, namely, who should carry 5. the head and one hind leg; 6. the two forelegs; 7. the tail and the other hind leg; 8. the breast and neck; 9. the two sides; 10. the entrails; 11. who should carry the fine flour; 12. the baked grain-offering (of the High Priest); 13. the wine.[45]

They then went out to see whether it was yet daybreak, and at the first sign of dawn in the sky fetched a lamb from the lamb-shed and the ninety-three sacred utensils from the utensil-room. The lamb destined to be sacrificed was given a drink from a golden bowl and led to the slaughter place north of the altar.[46]

For example, the so-called *hallel* was always sung on high feast days, i.e. according to the common view, Ps. 113–18; but tradition varies on what is to be understood by the *hallel*; see J. Levy, *Neuhebräisches Wörterbuch* s.v.; A. Büchler, 'Die Hallelpsalmen im Tempel', ZAW (1900), pp. 114–35; L. Cohen, 'Hallel', JE VI, pp. 176–8. Str.-B. I (1922), pp. 845 ff.; I. Elbogen, *Der jüdische Gottesdienst* (³1931), pp. 136–8, 495–6; E. Lohse, 'Hallel', RGG III (1959), col. 38. J. Hempel, 'Hallel' and 'Hallelujah', IDB II, pp. 513–15; 'Hallel', Enc. Jud. 7, cols 1197–9.

42. For a critical edition with commentary, see O. Holtzmann, *Tamid* (1928).

43. mTam. 1:1–4. Cf. mYom. 1:8; 2:1–2.

44. mTam. 2:1–5.

45. mTam. 3:1; mYom. 2:3.

46. mTam. 3:2–5. Cf. mYom. 3:1–2.

In the meantime, the two priests whose duty it was to clean the altar of incense and the candelabrum went to the Temple, the former with a golden pail (טני) and the latter with a golden pitcher (כוז). Opening the great Temple gate, they entered and attended to the cleaning of the altar of incense and the candelabrum. In the case of the latter task, if the two lamps farthest east were still burning they were left untouched and only the remaining lamps were cleaned. But if the two most easterly lamps had gone out, they were cleaned and relit first, before the others. The two priests left the utensils they had been using behind them in the Temple when they departed.[47]

While these two were thus occupied, the lamb was killed on the slaughter site by the priest appointed and its blood was caught by another and sprinkled on the altar. It was then skinned and its carcase divided. Each of the appointed priests received the piece due to him. The entrails were washed on marble tables on the slaughter site. The individual pieces of the animal were divided among six priests altogether. A seventh had the flour offering, an eighth the baked grain-offering (of the High Priest), a ninth the wine for the drink-offering. All this was first of all laid on the lower half of the western side of the steps to the altar and supplied with salt,[48] whereupon the priests went once more to *lishkath ha-gazith* to recite the Shema'.

This done, lots were again cast. Firstly a lot was cast for the incense-offering among those who had never performed this duty,[49] and subsequently to determine who should bring the individual sacrificial elements to the altar (according to R. Eliezer ben Jacob the same priests did this as carried them to the altar steps). Those on whom no lot fell on this occasion were free to go, and removed their sacred garments.[50]

The priest selected to bring the incense-offering now took a lidded

47. mTam. 3:6–9. For an exegesis of mTam. 3:6, cf. H. Graetz, MGWJ (188), pp. 289 ff.; O. Holtzmann, *Tamid*, pp. 44–5.

48. mTam. 4:1–3. On the place where the pieces were laid, see also mShek. 8:8. According to mShek. 6:4, a marble table for this purpose stood to the west of the altar steps. On the salting of the sacrificial pieces, see Lev. 2:13; Ezek. 43:24; Josephus, *Ant.* iii 9, 1 (227); Jub. 21:11; T. Levi 9:14: *καὶ πᾶσαν θυσίαν ἅλατι ἁλιεῖς.* Following Lev. 2:13, many manuscripts of Mk. 9:49 have the addition *καὶ πᾶσα θυσία ἁλὶ ἁλιθήσεται.* The consumption of salt was so considerable that the Temple forecourt had its own salt-chamber; cf. above, p. 280, n. 27.

49. The offering of the incense was considered the most solemn moment of the entire service. See Philo, *Spec. Leg.* i 51 (275): *Ὅσῳ γὰρ, οἶμαι, λίθων μὲν ἀμείνον χρυσὸς, τὰ δὲ ἐν ἀδύτοις τῶν ἐκτὸς ἁγιώτερα, τοσούτῳ κρείττων ἡ διὰ τῶν ἐπιθυμιωμένων εὐχαριστία τῆς διὰ τῶν ἐναίμων.* Hence it was above all when they were offering incense that revelations were experienced by the priests; thus John Hyrcanus, Josephus, *Ant.* xiii 10, 3 (282), and Zacharias, Lk. 1:9–20.

50. mTam. 5:3; cf. mYom. 2:4–5.

golden pan (כף) containing a smaller pan (בזך) with the incense.[51] A second priest fetched coals from the altar of burnt-offering in a silver ladle (מחתה) and emptied them into a golden ladle.[52] The two then went into the Temple. One of them poured the coals from his fire-pan onto the altar of incense, prostrated himself in adoration and retired. The other priest took the small pan with the incense out of the larger pan, handed the latter to a third priest and poured the incense out of the pan onto the coals on the altar so that the smoke ascended. Then he also prostrated himself and retired. The two who had attended to the cleaning of the altar of incense and the candelabrum had already re-entered before these others, the first to fetch his golden pail (the טני), and the second likewise to fetch his כוז, but also to clean the more easterly of the lamps still uncleaned, while the other was left burning so that the rest could be lit from it in the evening. If it had gone out, it too was cleaned and lit from the fire on the altar of burnt-offering.[53]

The five priests who had been busy inside the Temple then mounted the steps in front of the sanctuary with their five golden utensils and pronounced the priestly blessing (Num. 6:22 ff.) on the people; and in so doing, they uttered the divine Name as it is written, that is to say יהוה, not אדוני.[54]

51. It is apparent from mTam. 7:2 that the lid belonged not to the בזך but to the כף; as also from the assumption that some incense could fall out of the well-fitted בזך into the כף, mTam. 6:3.

52. mTam. 5:4–5. On the silver and gold ladles and on the incense itself, cf. also mYom. 4:4.

53. mTam. 6:1–3. According to this description from the Mishnah only *one* of the seven lamps of the *menorah* burned during the day, the middle one of the three easterly lamps. On the other hand, according to the weightier testimony of Josephus, three lamps burned in the day-time. On the whole problem of which, and how many, lamps burned by day, see above, p. 297.

54. mTam. 7:2. Cf. mSot. 7:6 (see below, p. 453, n. 137). Outside the Temple, according to the passages cited, not even the priests were allowed to pronounce the sacred Name. This fact is obviously already presupposed by Ecclus. 50:20. Philo too observes that the Name of God may be heard and uttered only in the Sanctuary (ἐν ἁγίοις), *Vita Mosis* ii 23 (114); further B. Ritter, *Philo und die Halachah*, p. 131; W. L. Knox, *Some Hellenistic Elements in Primitive Christianity* (1944), p. 48; and Josephus relates that Moses prayed God to communicate his Name to him also, so that when he offered sacrifice, he might beg Him by name to be present, *Ant.* ii 12, 4 (275–6): *ἵνα θύων ἐξ ὀνόματος αὐτὸν παρεῖναι τοῖς ἱεροῖς παρακαλῇ. Καὶ ὁ θεὸς αὐτῷ σημαίνει τὴν αὐτοῦ προσηγοριάν.* It was as a mark of special solemnity that the High Priest, on the Day of Atonement and during the confession of sins, pronounced the holy Name of God (mYom. 6:2; mTam. 3:8). On the ineffability of the Name see also mSanh. 10:1; A. Geiger, *Urschrift und Übersetzungen der Bibel*, p. 261 ff.; B. Jacob, *Im Namen Gottes* (1903), pp. 164–76; W. Bousset, *Die Religion des Judentums* ([3]1926), pp. 349–50; W. Bacher, JE XI, p. 264; G. Dalman, *Worte Jesu* ([2]1930), pp. 146–55; A. Marmorstein, *The Old Rabbinic Doctrine of God* I (1927), pp. 17–40; H. Gunkel, 'Yahve', RGG III[2], pp. 9 ff.; W. von Baudissin, *Kyrios* III, p. 63 f.; G. F. Moore, *Judaism* I, pp. 424–9. M.

Next the presentation of the burnt-offering took place. The appointed priests took the pieces of the sacrificial animal lying at the altar steps and after laying hands on them, threw them onto the altar.[55] When the High Priest wished to officiate, he had the priests hand the pieces to him (cf. Ecclus. 1:12), laid his hands on them and threw them onto the altar. Lastly, the two grain-offerings (of the people and of the High Priest) were presented, together with the drink-offering. When the priest bent to pour out the drink-offering, a sign was given to the Levites to begin singing. They broke into song, and at every pause in the singing two priests blew on silver trumpets; and with every blast of the trumpets the people prostrated themselves in adoration.[56]

The evening worship was very similar to that of the morning. In the former, however, the incense-offering was made after, rather than before, the burnt-offering; and the lamps of the candelabrum were not cleaned in the evening but lit (see above, p. 303).

These two daily public sacrifices constituted the kernel of all the Temple ceremonies. They were also offered in the manner described on all Sabbaths and feast-days. Sabbaths and feast-days were however distinguished by the addition to the usual *Tamid* of other public sacrifices. On the Sabbath, the supplement consisted of two one-year-old rams offered as burnt-offerings, together with two-tenths of an ephah of fine flour as a grain-offering and a corresponding amount as a drink-offering. The Sabbath sacrifice was therefore equivalent to the daily morning and evening sacrifices taken together.[57] The additions on

---

Buber, *Moses* (1946), pp. 39–55 [*Werke* II (1964), pp. 47–66]; *Kingship of God* (1967), pp. 99–107 [*Werke* II (1964), pp. 608–26]; cf. P. Vermes, 'Buber's Understanding of of the Divine Name related to Bible, Targum and Midrash', JJS 24 (1973), pp. 147–66; E. E. Urbach, *The Sages* (1969), pp. 103–14 (Hebrew); 'God, Names of', Enc. Jud. 7, cols. 880–4. For a bibliography, see G. Fohrer, *History of Israelite Religion* (1973), pp. 75–9.

55. The casting demanded particular skill, praised already in Aristeas (ed. Wendland 93).

56. mTam. 7:3; cf. Ecclus. 50:11–21. The Mishnah tractate Tamid is rather summary toward the end. It only describes the offering of sacrifice in those cases in which the High Priest himself officiated. Moreover, the presentation of the two grain-offerings is not explicitly alluded to at all. From the sequence in which they are mentioned elsewhere, mTam. 3:1; 4:3, there can be no doubt that we have inserted them in their correct place. The High Priest's grain-offering was therefore not offered before the public sacrifice, as might appear from Heb. 7:27, but after it.

57. Num. 28:9–10; Philo, *Spec. Leg.* i 35 (170): *Ταῖς δὲ ἑβδόμαις διπλασιάζει τὸν τῶν ἱερείων ἀριθμόν.* Josephus, *Ant.* iii 10, 1 (237): *κατὰ δὲ ἑβδόμην ἡμέραν, ἥτις σάββατα καλεῖται, δύο σφάττουσι, τὸν αὐτὸν τρόπον ἱερουργοῦντες.* The prescriptions in Ezek. 46:4–5 are essentially different. However, the main distinction between pre-exilic and post-exilic times for festival sacrifices as well as for the *tamid*, was

feast-days were much larger. On the seven days of Passover, for example, the daily burnt-offering comprised two bullocks, a ram and seven lambs, together with the corresponding grain- and drink-offerings, and besides all this a male goat as a sin-offering (Num. 28:16–25). On the Feast of Weeks, which lasted only one day, the same sacrifices were offered as on each day of Passover (Num. 28:26–31). On the Feast of Tabernacles, which as a celebration of the end of the harvest called for special thanks, the number of sacrifices was still greater. On the first day of the festival thirteen bullocks, two rams and fourteen lambs were sacrificed as a burnt-offering, together with the corresponding grain- and drink-offerings, and in addition a male goat as a sin-offering; and the same sacrifices were made on each of the following six feast-days, except that the number of bullocks offered was reduced every day by one (Num. 29:12–34). Similar supplementary sacrifices, some larger and some smaller, were prescribed for the remaining festivals of New Moon, New Year and the Day of Atonement (see in general, Num. 28–29). And to these offerings, intended merely to indicate in general the festive nature of the day, were added special sacrifices relating to the particular significance of the feast (cf. Lev. 16 and 23).[58]

Many though these public sacrifices were, their number was insignificant compared to private sacrifices. It was this huge quantity, so great as to be almost unbelievable, that gave the Temple cult its peculiar stamp. Day after day, masses of victims were slaughtered there and burnt, and in spite of the thousands of priests, when one of the great festivals came round the multitude of sacrifices was so great that they could hardly cope with them.[59] But the Israelites regarded the accurate performance of this liturgy as an essential means of assuring divine mercy for themselves.

---

that prior to the exile it was the king who had to bear the costs, whereas afterwards the people defrayed them. See especially Ezek. 45:17, and generally Ezek. 45:18–46:15.

58. A description of feast-day sacrifices according to Num. 28–9 and Lev. 16 and 23 is given by Philo in *Spec. Leg.* i 35 (180–9).

59. Aristeas (ed. Wendland 88): *Πολλαὶ γὰρ μυριάδες κτηνῶν προσάγονται κατὰ τὰς τῶν ἑορτῶν ἡμέρας.* Philo, *Vita Mosis* ii 31 (159): *Πολλῶν δὲ κατὰ τὸ ἀναγκαῖον ἀναγομένων θυσιῶν καθ' ἑκάστην ἡμέραν, καὶ διαφερόντως ἐν πανηγύρεσι καὶ ἑορταῖς ὑπέρ τε ἰδίᾳ ἑκάστου καὶ κοινῇ ὑπὲρ ἁπάντων διὰ μυρίας καὶ οὐχὶ αὐτὰς αἰτίας κ.τ.λ.* Cf. the numbers in 1 Kgs. 8:63; 1 Chron. 29:21; 2 Chron. 29:32 f.; 30:24; 35:7–9.

APPENDIX

Gentile Participation in Worship at Jerusalem

It is a well-attested fact that despite the rigid barrier erected between Jews and Gentiles in regard to religious matters, Gentiles participated in Temple worship at Jerusalem. By Gentiles is meant here not the great crowd of proselytes, i.e. people who to some degree also accepted the Jewish religion and for this reason demonstrated their respect for the God of Israel by offering sacrifices, but real Gentiles who, whilst sacrificing in Jerusalem, wished in no way to make thereby a confession of faith in the *superstitio Iudaica*. This fact can only be understood by remembering how superficial in the practice of everyday life the originally very close connection between faith and worship often turns out to be. In the period under consideration this was particularly the case in the Graeco-Roman world. To offer sacrifice at some famous sanctuary was very often no more than an expression of a piety that had become cosmopolitan, an act of courtesy towards the nation or city concerned by no means intended as an adherence to a particular religion. Since this happened in other celebrated sanctuaries, why not in Jerusalem also? And for their part, the Jews and their priests had no reason to reject the reverence shown to their God, even if it was only an act of politeness. The actual offering of the sacrifice was after all the business of the priests; they had to attend to the correct performance of the rites. The question of who was responsible for the cost was relatively of no consequence. In any case, there was no religious objection to accepting a gift from one who did not otherwise observe the Torah. Thus the Old Testament already assumes that a sacrifice may be offered by an unconverted Gentile (בן נכר).[60] In the prayer which Solomon is said to have uttered at the dedication of the Temple, the king asks that God may also hear 'the stranger (הנכרי) who is not of the people of Israel' when he comes from a distant land and prays in this temple. 'For they shall hear of Thy great name and of Thy strong hand and of Thine outstretched arm.'[61] Later Judaism specified

60. Lev. 22:25. It is stated here that blemished animals may not be accepted even from Gentiles, which of course presupposes that in the ordinary course of events Gentile sacrifices was lawful.

61. 1 Kgs. 8:41–43; reproduced by Josephus, *Ant.* viii 4, 3 (116): *ἀλλὰ κἂν ἀπὸ περάτων τῆς οἰκουμένης τινὲς ἀφίκωνται, κἂν ὁποθενδηποτοῦν προστρεπόμενοι καὶ τυχεῖν τινὸς ἀγαθοῦ λιπαροῦντες, δὸς αὐτοῖς ἐπήκοος γενόμενος*. Also cf. A. Bertholet, *Die Stellung der Israeliten und Juden zu Fremden* (1896), p. 127 f., 293 f.; 'Sacrifice', Enc. Jud. 14, col. 612.

exactly which kinds of sacrifices could and could not be accepted even from Gentiles: sacrifices offered by reason of a vow or as voluntary offerings (all נדרים and נדבות) were acceptable, but those of an obligatory nature such as sin- and guilt-offerings, fowl-offerings by men or women suffering from a discharge, and by women after child-birth, were not.[62] Accordingly, the sacrifices permitted to Gentiles were burnt-offerings, grain-offerings and drink-offerings.[63] The special legal precepts referring to these offerings therefore frequently take into account the sacrifices of Gentiles.[64]

The fact that sacrifice was offered by and for Gentiles is nowhere better attested than by Josephus, who writes that on the outbreak of the revolution in A.D. 66 one of the first acts was to declare that no more sacrifices were acceptable from Gentiles.[65] The conservative opposition pointed out that 'all our forefathers received sacrifices from Gentiles', and that Jerusalem would acquire a reputation for ungodliness if Jews were the only people to refuse foreigners the opportunity to offer sacrifice.[66] Some noteworthy cases of this kind are known from history. When it is recounted that Alexander the Great sacrificed in Jerusalem,[67] the truth of this event stands or falls by the (very improbable) historicity of his visit to that city. But the story as such proves that from the point of view of Judaism such an act was found to be quite in order. Ptolemy III is likewise said to have offered sacrifice in Jerusalem.[68] Antiochus VII Sidetes, even while engaged in open warfare with the Jews and laying siege to Jerusalem, sent sacrifices into the city for the Feast of Tabernacles, presumably to obtain the favour of the God of his enemy, while the Jews for their part gladly accepted them as a sign of the king's piety.[69] When Herod's distinguished patron Marcus Agrippa came to Jerusalem in 15 B.C., he sacrificed a hecatomb there, a burnt-offering of one hundred oxen.[70] Again, Josephus writes of Vitellius that he went to Jerusalem at Passover in A.D. 37 to sacrifice

62. mShek. 1:5.

63. Not peace-offerings because they could only be eaten in a state of ritual purity (Lev. 7:20–21).

64. mShek. 7:6; mZeb. 4:5; mMen. 5:3, 5, 6; 6:1; 9:8. Cf. 'Sacrifice', Enc. Jud. 14, col. 612.

65. *B.J.* ii 17, 2–4 (408–21).

66. *B.J.* ii 17, 4 (417): *ὅτι πάντες οἱ πρόγονοι τὰς παρὰ τῶν αλλογενῶν θωσίας ἀπεδέχοντο*. *B.J.* ii 17, 3 (414): *καταψηφίσασθαι τῆς πόλεως ἀσέβειαν, εἰ παρὰ μόνοις Ἰουδαίοις οὔτε θύσει τις ἀλλότριος οὔτε προσκυνήσει*. See C. Roth, 'The Debate on the Loyal Sacrifices in A.D. 66', HThR 53 (1960), pp. 93–7.

67. Josephus, *Ant.* xi 8, 5 (329–30).

68. Josephus, *C.Ap.* ii 5 (48).

69. *Ant.* xiii 8, 2 (242–3).

70. *Ant.* xvi 2, 1 (14). Sacrifices of this size were not unusual in the Temple at Jerusalem. See Ezr. 6:17; Josephus, *Ant.* xv 11, 6 (422); Philo, *Legat.* 45 (356); Sibyll. III, 576, 626.

to God.[71] The frequency of such acts of courtesy or cosmopolitan piety may be judged from the fact that Augustus expressly praised his grandson Gaius Caesar for not having stopped to worship in Jerusalem on his way from Egypt to Syria.[72] Tertullian can in consequence say with justice that the Romans once honoured the God of the Jews with sacrifices and their Temple with votive offerings.[73] And Josephus is not alluding merely to proselytes when he names the altar in Jerusalem, 'the altar venerated by all Greeks and barbarians',[74] and says of the place where the Temple stood that it is 'worshipped by all the world and honoured for its renown by strangers at the ends of the earth'.[75]

To this category of sacrifices offered for Gentiles and in their name should be added sacrifices presented for the Gentile authorities. Darius, like the Israelite kings who before the exile bore the costs of public sacrifice, ordered that they should be defrayed out of state funds, with the proviso that prayers should be said 'for the life of the king and his sons' (Ezr. 6:9–10).[76] Antiochus the Great provided large contributions from the same sources for the Temple cult, from which it must be inferred that sacrifice was offered regularly for the king.[77] Aristeas (ed. Wendland, 45) has the High Priest Eleazar assure Ptolemy Philadelphus in his letter that he has offered sacrifices *ὑπὲρ σοῦ καὶ τῆς ἀδελφῆς καὶ τῶν τέκνων καὶ τῶν φίλων*. A sacrifice for the king (*ὁλοκαύτωσις προσφερομένη ὑπὲρ τοῦ βασιλέως*) is definitely attested during the period of the Maccabaean movement (1 Mac. 7:33). So even at that time, when a large part of the nation was waging war against the Syrian kings, the priests were offering sacrifices presumably instituted by the kings themselves. Under the Romans, this sacrifice for the Gentile authorities was the sole form under which Judaism could furnish an equivalent to the cult of Augustus and Rome practised elsewhere in the provinces. According to the clear testimony of Philo, Augustus himself commanded that for all time to come, two lambs and a steer should be

71. *Ant.* xviii 5, 3 (122).

72. Suetonius, *Div. Aug.* 93: 'Gaium nepotem, quod Iudaeam praetervehens apud Hierosolyma non supplicasset, conlaudavit'.

73. Tertullian, *Apol.* 26: 'cuius (Iudaeae) et deum victimis et templum donis et gentem foederibus aliquamdiu Romani honorastis'.

74. *B.J.* v 1, 3 (17): *τὸν Ἕλλησι πᾶσι καὶ βαρβάροις σεβάσμιον βωμόν.*

75. *B.J.* iv 4, 3 (262): *ὁ δ' ὑπὸ τῆς οἰκουμένης προσκυνούμενος χῶρος καὶ τοῖς ἀπὸ περάτων γῆς ἀλλοφύλοις ἀκοῇ τετιμημένος.*

76. The authenticity of this edict of Darius (who refers in it to an older decree by Cyrus) is disputed. E. Meyer, *Die Entstehung des Judenthums*, pp. 50–2; R. de Vaux, 'Les décrets de Cyrus et de Darius sur la reconstruction du Temple', *RB* 46 (1937), pp. 29–57.

77. Josephus, *Ant.* 3, 3 (140).

sacrificed daily at the expense of the emperor.[78] The Jews expressly referred to this sacrifice 'for the Emperor and the Roman people' at the time of Caligula, when their loyalty was questioned because they opposed the erection of the Emperor's statue in the Temple at Jerusalem.[79] And it was offered regularly until the outbreak of the revolution in A.D. 66.[80] Philo asserts that it was not only a sacrifice *for* the Emperor but instituted *by* him, a step which Augustus, in spite of his instinctive antipathy to Judaism, may well have felt obliged to take from political considerations. Josephus, admittedly, maintains that the cost was borne by the Jewish people.[81] The real situation was probably similar to that of the Persian period, when the expenses were covered by Jewish taxes falling to the treasury.[82] On special occasions t would appear that very handsome sacrifices were offered for the Emperor at public expense; thus, for example, a hecatomb was sacrificed three times under Caligula, the first on his accession to the throne, the second on his recovery from a severe illness, and the third at the beginning of his campaign in Germany.[83]

Besides sacrifices, Gentiles very frequently brought votive offerings to the Temple in Jerusalem. For example, Aristeas describes in full detail the splendid gifts presented by Ptolemy Philadelphus when he invited the Jewish High Priest to send him men capable of translating the law of the Jews into Greek: twenty golden and thirty silver bowls,

78. Philo, *Legat.* 23 (157): *προστάξας καὶ δι' αἰῶνος ἀνάγεσθαι θυσίας ἐνδελεχεῖς ὁλοκαύτους καθ' ἑκάστην ἡμέραν ἐκ τῶν ἰδίων προσόδων, ἀπαρχὴν τῷ ὑψίστῳ θεῷ, αἳ καὶ μέχρι τοῦ νῦν ἐπιτελοῦνται καὶ εἰς ἅπαν ἐπιτελεσθήσονται.* Almost identical is also *Legat.* 40 (317), which has the added remark *ἄρνες εἰσὶ δύο καὶ ταῦρος τὰ ἱερεῖα, οἷς Καῖσαρ ἐφαίδρυνε τὸν βωμόν.* Cf. J. Juster, *Les Juifs dans l'empire romain* I, pp. 346 ff.

79. Josephus, *B.J.* ii 10, 4 (197): *'Ιουδαῖοι περὶ μὲν Καίσαρος καὶ τοῦ δήμου τῶν 'Ρωμαίων δίς τῆς ἡμέρας θύειν ἔφασαν.* From the final words it will be seen that, like the public sacrifices, the daily sacrifice for the Emperor was offered partly in the morning and partly in the evening.

80. *B.J.* ii 17, 2–4 (408–21).

81. Josephus, *C.Ap.* ii 6 (77): 'facimus autem pro eis (scil. imperatoribus et populo Romano) continua sacrificia et non solum cotidianis diebus ex impensa communi omnium Iudaeorum talia celebramus, verum cum nullas alias hostias ex communi neque pro filiis peragamus, solis imperatoribus hunc honorem praecipuum pariter exhibemus, quem hominum nulli persolvimus'.

82. Thus E. Meyer, *Die Entstehung des Judenthums*, pp. 53 f.

83. Philo, *Legat.* 45 (356); on sacrifice offered on accession to the throne, see also 32 (232). Sacrifice and prayer for Gentile authorities are generally recommended: Jer. 29:7; Bar. 1:10–11; mAb. 3:2: 'R. Hanina the prefect of the priests said: Pray for the peace of the empire' (המלכות, meaning the Gentile authorities). For Christian prayer for the government, cf. 1 Tim. 2:1–2; Letter of Clement 61; Polycarp 12:3; Tertullian. *Apologet.* c. 30 and 39; Origen, *C. Celsum* viii, 73; *Acts of Apollonius* c. 6; *Acts of Cyprian* 1, 2 (both in Gebhardt, *Ausgewählte Märtyrerakten*, 1902); *Acts of Dionysius*, Eusebius, *HE* vii 11, 8. See Harnack, *The Mission and Expansion of Christianity* (1961), pp. 258 ff.; J. W. Swain, 'Gamaliel's Speech and Caligula's Statue', HThR 37 (1944), pp. 341–9.

five pitchers and an elaborately worked golden table.[84] Even if this story is no more than a legend, it faithfully reflects the custom of the time. For it is many times attested elsewhere that the Ptolemaic rulers often gave votive presents to the Temple at Jerusalem.[85] Nor was it otherwise in the Roman period. When Sosius in conjunction with Herod conquered Jerusalem, he offered a golden crown.[86] Marcus Agrippa, in the visit already mentioned, also made votive offerings to the Temple.[87] Among the sacred vessels melted down by John of Gischala during the siege, were costly gifts presented by the Emperor Augustus, his wife Julia, and other Roman Emperors.[88] Altogether it was not unusual for Romans to dedicate gifts to the Temple.[89]

In a sense, therefore, even the exclusive Temple of Jerusalem became cosmopolitan; in common with the renowned sanctuaries of the Gentiles, it received the homage of the whole world.

84. Aristeas (ed. Wendland 42, 51–82); see Josephus, *Ant.* xii 2, 5–9 (40–77).
85. 2 Mac. 3:2, 5:16; Josephus, *Ant.* xiii 3, 4 (74–9); *C.Ap.* ii 5 (48–9).
86. *Ant.* xiv 16, 4 (488).
87. Philo, *Legat.* 37 (297).
88. Josephus, *B.J.* v 13, 6 (562–3): *ἀπέσχετο δὲ οὐδὲ τῶν ὑπὸ τοῦ Σεβαστοῦ καὶ τῆς γυναικὸς αὐτοῦ πεμφθέντων ἀκρατοφόρων. οἱ μέν γὰρ Ῥωμαίων βασιλεῖς ἐτίμησάν τε καὶ προσεκόσμησαν τὸ ἱερὸν ἀεί.* According to Philo, Augustus and almost his entire household adorned the Temple with gifts, *Legat.* 23 (157): *μονον οὐ πανοίκιος ἀναθημάτων πολυτελείαις τὸ ἱερὸν ἡμῶν ἐκόσμησε.* The letter of Agrippa I to Caligula reads, Philo, *Leg.* 40 (319): *ἡ προμάμμη σου Ἰουλία Σεβαστὴ κατεκόσμησε τὸν νεὼν χρυσαῖς φίαλαις καὶ σπονδείοις καὶ ἄλλων ἀναθημάτων πολυτελεστάτων πλήθει.*
89. *B.J.* iv 3, 10 (181); cf. ii 17, 3 (412–13).

§ 25. TORAH SCHOLARSHIP

I. The Canonicity of Scripture[1]

For the religious life of the Jews during the period under discussion, the first and most decisive principle was that the Torah, which regulated not only the priestly service but the whole life of the nation in all its aspects, was acknowledged as having been given by God. Every one of its demands being a claim by God on his people, a scrupulous observance of these laws was a religious duty, indeed the highest, and in some sense the only, religious duty. The whole piety of the Israelite was primarily directed towards obeying in all its details, and with zeal and love, the God-given Torah.

It is possible to determine almost to the day and the hour when this self-commitment was first made. It dates to an event the epoch-

1. See the literature on the history of the Old Testament canon by R. H. Pfeiffer, s.v. 'Canon of the Old Testament', IDB (1962) I, pp. 498–520 (bibl.: pp. 519–20); O. Eissfeldt, *The Old Testament. An Introduction* (1965), pp. 551, 770, and Enc. Jud. 4, col. 836. In addition, cf. 'βίβλιον', 'γράφω, γράφη' in TDNT I; F. Buhl, *Kanon und Text des Alten Testaments* (1891); H. E. Ryle, *The Canon of the Old Testament* (²1909); H. B. Swete, *An Introduction to the Old Testament in Greek* (1914, ²1968); S. Zeitlin, *An Historical Study of the Canonization of the Hebrew Scriptures* (1933); J. P. Audet, 'A Hebrew-Aramaic List of Books of the Old Testament in Greek Transcription', JThSt NS 1 (1956), pp. 135–54; M. L. Margolis, *The Hebrew Scriptures in the Making* (³1948); G. E. Flack, B. M. Metzger, *et al.*, *The Text, Canon and Principal Versions of the Bible* (1956). See further, P. Katz, 'The OT Canon in Palestine and Alexandria', ZNW 49 (1958), pp. 223 ff.; A. C. Sundberg, 'The OT in the Early Church. A Study in Canon', HThR 51 (1958), pp. 205–26; A. Jepsen, 'Zur Kanongeschichte des AT', ZAW 71 (1959), pp. 114–36; F. Hesse, 'Das AT als Kanon', NZST 3 (1961), pp. 315–27; P. Leenhardt, ' "Sola Scriptura" ou Écriture et tradition', ETR 36 (1961), pp. 5–46; A. Lods, 'Tradition et Canon des Écritures', ETR 36 (1961), pp. 47–59; F. Michaeli, 'A propos du Canon de l'AT', ETR 36 (1961), pp. 61–8; W. D. Davies, *Christian Origins and Judaism* (1962); H. Eybers, 'Some Light on the Canon of the Qumran Sect', OuTW (1962/3), pp. 1–14; A. Lacoque, 'L'insertion du Cantique des Cantiques dans le Canon', RHPR 42 (1962), pp. 38–44; H. W. Robinson, *Inspiration and Revelation* (²1962); B. J. Roberts, 'The Old Testament Canon: A Suggestion', BJRL 46 (1963/4), pp. 164–78; O. Eissfeldt, *Introduction* (1965), pp. 559–71; A. Mirsky, 'The Schools . . .', *Essays presented to I. Brodie* (1967), pp. 291–99; A. C. Sundberg, 'The "Old Testament": a Christian Canon', CBQ 30 (1968), pp. 143–55; G. W. Anderson, 'Canonical and Non-Canonical', CHB I (1970), pp. 113–59; J. A. Sanders, *Torah and Canon* (1972); H. A. Orlinsky, *Essays in Biblical Culture and Bible Translation* (1974), pp. 257–86; S. Z. Leiman, *The Canonization of Hebrew Scripture: The Talmudic and Midrashic Evidence* (1976); D. N. Freedman, s.v. 'Canon of the OT', IDBS (1976), pp. 130–6; J. Blenkinsopp, *Prophecy and Canon* (1977); G. Vermes, *DSS*, pp. 202–3.

making significance of which is also stressed in the Book of Nehemiah; namely the occasion when Ezra read the Torah (תורה) to the people and they solemnly bound themselves to it (Neh. 8–10). It is of course uncertain whether Ezra's Torah was the entire Pentateuch or only the Priestly Code, though the first hypothesis, advanced by Wellhausen, is still generally in favour.[2] But in either case, the basic significance of the event remains the same: the Priestly Code appearing under the name of Moses was recognized by the people as the Torah of God and hence as a binding rule of life, i.e. as canonical. For it is in the very nature of the Torah that acceptance of it *eo ipso* involves acceptance of its binding and normative dignity.[3]

As a result of the acknowledgement of the divine origin of the Torah, the book containing it also soon became sacrosanct and inspired. This idea certainly achieved general currency long before the beginning of the Christian era. According to the Book of Jubilees, the whole Torah in all its detail is recorded on heavenly tablets (3:10, 31; 4:5, 32; 6:17, 29, 31, 35; 15:25, 16; 28 f.; 18:19; 28:6; 30:9; 32:10, 15; 33:10; 39:6; 49:8; 50:13). The Torah of Moses is merely a copy of the heavenly original. Belief in the divine origin of the Torah now becomes the condition determining membership of the chosen people and consequently participation in the promises given to them. 'Whoever asserts that the Torah is not from heaven (אין תורה מן השמים), he has no share in the world to come.'[4] As time passed, this opinion was expressed with increasing seriousness and rigorousness. 'Whoever says that the whole Torah is from heaven except this verse, for God did not utter it, but Moses from his own mouth (מפי עצמו), he is one (of whom it is written),

2. Cf. J. Wellhausen, *Israelitische und jüdische Geschichte* (⁹1958), p. 167: 'Ezra made the Priestly Code into law, not of itself, however, but as a component of the Pentateuch'. Against Wellhausen: E. Meyer, *Die Entstehung des Judenthums* (1896), pp. 206–16; K. Budde, *Der Kanon des A.T.*, p. 31; K. Stade, *Biblische Theologie des A.T.* (1905), § 144, 145. In support of Wellhausen: H. H. Schraeder, *Esra der Schreiber* (1930), pp. 63 ff.; W. F. Albright, *From Abraham to Ezra* (1963), pp. 94–5; H. Cazelles, 'La mission d'Esdras', VT 4 (1954), pp. 113–40; E. Sellin, *Geschichte* II, 140 ff.; J. Bright, *A History of Israel* (²1972), pp. 391–2; O. Eissfeldt, *The Old Testament, An Introduction* (1965), pp. 556–7; J. M. Myers, *Ezra-Nehemiah* (*Anchor Bible*, 1965), p. lix; G. Fohrer, *History of Israelite Religion* (1973), p. 358. For the view that Ezra's law was an assemblage of pre-exilic laws with some added passages, cf. G. von Rad, *Das Geschichtsbild des chronistischen Werkes* (1930), pp. 38 ff.; W. Rudolph, *Esra und Nehemia* (1949), p. 169; M. Noth, *Überlieferungsgeschichtliche Studien* (1943) I, p. 100; [E.T.] *The Laws in the Pentateuch* (1967), pp. 75–6 (especially p. 3, n. 2); *History of Israel* (²1960), pp. 333–5.

3. Cf. J. Wellhausen, *Geschichte Israels* I, 2 f., 425 f. = *Prolegomena zur Geschichte Israels* (⁵1899), pp. 2 f., 414 f.; M. Noth, *The Laws in the Pentateuch* (1967), pp. 103 ff.

4. mSanh. 10:1.

For he has despised the word of God' (Num. 15:31).[5] So the whole Pentateuch was now viewed as having been dictated by God and prompted by the Spirit of God.[6] Even the last eight verses of Deuteronomy recounting the death of Moses were written by Moses himself in virtue of a divine revelation.[7] But in the end, the theory that God dictated the Torah was itself not enough. The book was said to have been handed to Moses by God already completed, and the only remaining argument turned on whether Moses had received it all at once or scroll by scroll (מגלה מגלה).[8]

Further writings of Israelite antiquity which followed the Torah acquired a similar authority; viz. the writings of the prophets and works devoted to the earlier (pre-exilic) history of Israel. They were respected and used as a valuable legacy of the past long before their canonization was contemplated. But gradually, they took their place beside the Torah as a second category of 'sacred Scriptures', and as people became accustomed to their connection with the Torah, so the latter's specific dignity, i.e., its legally binding and therefore canonic authority, was transferred to them also. They too came to be seen as documents in which God's will is revealed in a manner absolutely binding. Finally, at a still later stage, this corpus of the 'Prophets' (נביאים) was joined by a third collection of 'Writings' (כתובים) which little by little moved into the same category of canonic Scriptures. The origin of these two collections is not known. The earliest testimony to their collocation with the Torah is the prologue to the book of Jesus ben Sira (second century B.C.).[9] But it cannot be deduced from this source that the third collection was by then already made. In the New Testament, the two-part formula still prevails: ὁ νόμος καὶ οἱ προφῆται (Mt. 5:17; 7:12; 9:13 22:40; Lk. 16:16, 29, 31; 24:27, 44 [here alone with the added ψαλμοί]; Jn. 1:46; Act. 13:15; 24:14; 28:23; Rom. 3:21). It should not of course be

5. bSanh. 99a.

6. See W. Bacher, *Terminologie* I (1899, 1905, repr. 1965), pp. 180–2, see under רוח. K. Kohler, 'Inspiration', JE VI, pp. 607–9. H. Wheeler Robinson, *Inspiration and Revelation in the O.T.* (1944), pp. 211–22; G. W. H. Lampe, 'Inspiration', IDB II (1962), pp. 713–18; M. Noth, *The Laws in the Pentateuch* (1960), especially pp. 85–107; O. Eissfeldt, *Introduction*, pp. 560–1.

7. Philo, *Vita Mosis* ii, 51 (195). Josephus, *Ant.* iv 8, 48 (326). Cf. (J.) I. Israelsohn, 'Les huit derniers versets du Pentateuque', REJ 20 (1890), pp. 304–7; W. Bacher, *Die Agada der Tannaiten* II, pp. 48–9; 259.

8. bGit. 60a. An alternative interpretation attributes the composition of successive scrolls to Moses. Cf. L. Goldschmidt, *Der babylonische Talmud* V (1912), p. 565, n. 381.

9. Prologue of Ecclus: *Πολλῶν καὶ μεγάλων ἡμῖν διὰ τοῦ νόμου καὶ τῶν προφητῶν καὶ τῶν ἄλλων τῶν κατ' αὐτοὺς ἠκολουθηκότων δεδομένων, ὑπὲρ ὧν δέον ἐστὶν ἐπαινεῖν τὸν Ἰσραὴλ παιδείας καὶ σοφίας κ.τ.λ.* For literature on the Prologue see O. Eissfeldt, *Introduction*, p. 596.

concluded from this that the third collection did not as yet exist: in fact, there are good reasons to think that it was closed in the middle of the second century B.C. But it was not felt to be a group possessing independent significance and of the same status as the other two.[10] The earliest evidence for an established form of the canon, very probably the one now extant, is provided by Josephus. He says explicitly that among the Jews only twenty-two books rightly enjoyed confidence (βιβλία . . . δικαίως πεπιστευμένα);[11] none of the others were deemed worthy of equal trust (πίστεως οὐχ ὁμοίας ἠξίωται). True, he does not enumerate them individually, but he very likely means the books of the present canon and them alone. For the Church Fathers, particularly Origen and Jerome, expressly state that the Jews were accustomed to count the books of the then canon so that they amounted to twenty-two.[12] During the deliberations at Yavneh at the end of the

10. The main evidence for a complete canon by *c.* 150 B.C. is provided by the fact that Daniel, dating to *c.* 160 B.C., is the last work to enter the Hebrew Bible. See also S. Z. Leiman, *Canonization*, pp. 131–5. Whether the Aramaic phrase תלתא ספריא (the Three Books) occurring in a Messianic document from Cave IV (4Q Mess ar 1:5) should be understood as an allusion to a tripartite division of the Bible remains a matter for debate. (Cf. J. Starcky, 'Un texte messianique araméen de la grotte 4 de Qumrân'; *Mémorial du Cinquantenaire de l'École des langues orientales anciennes de l'Institut Catholique de Paris* (1964), pp. 51–6; J. A. Fitzmyer, *Essays on the Semitic Background of the New Testament* (1971), pp. 141–8; Vermes, *DSSE*², p. 270.

11. Instead of δικαίως πεπιστευμένα, Eusebius in his rendering of Josephus (*HE* iii 10) has δικαίως θεῖα πεπιστευμένα. But as θεῖα is missing in both the Greek and the Latin text of Josephus, it was rightly deleted by Niese and Thackeray.

12. Josephus, *C. Ap.* i 8 (38–41): *Οὐ μυριάδες βιβλίων εἰσὶ παρ' ἡμῖν ἀσυμφώνων καὶ μαχομένων. δύο δὲ μόνα πρὸς τοῖς εἴκοσι βιβλία τοῦ παντὸς ἔχοντα χρόνου τὴν ἀναγραφήν, τὰ δικαίως πεπιστευμένα. Καὶ τούτων πέντε μέν ἐστι Μωυσέος, ἃ τούς τε νόμους περιέχει καὶ τὴν ἀπ' ἀνθρωπογονίας παράδοσιν μέχρι τῆς αὐτοῦ τελευτῆς. Οὗτος ὁ χρόνος ἀπολείπει τρισχιλίων ὀλίγων ἐτῶν. 'Απὸ δὲ τῆς Μωυσέος τελευτῆς μέχρι 'Αρταξέρξου τοῦ μετὰ Ξέρξην Περσῶν βασιλέως οἱ μετὰ Μωυσῆν προφῆται τὰ κατ' αὐτοὺς πραχθέντα συνέγραψαν ἐν τρισὶ καὶ δέκα βιβλίοις. Αἱ δὲ λοιπαὶ τέσσαρες ὕμνους εἰς τὸν θεὸν καὶ τοῖς ἀνθρώποις ὑποθήκας τοῦ βίου περιέχουσιν. 'Απὸ δὲ 'Αρταξέρξου μέχρι τοῦ καθ' ἡμᾶς χρόνου γέγραπται μὲν ἕκαστα, πίστεως δ' οὐχ ὁμοίας ἠξίωται τοῖς πρὸ αὐτῶν διὰ τὸ μὴ γενέσθαι τὴν τῶν προφητῶν ἀκριβῆ διαδοχήν.* A similar chronological scheme underlies the baraita in bBB. 14b–15a attributing the biblical books to the following authors: 'Moses wrote his book, the section of Balaam and Job. Joshua wrote his book and (the last) eight verses in the Torah. Samuel wrote his book, Judges and Ruth. David wrote the book of Psalms with the help of ten elders (the first Adam, Melkizedek, Abraham, Moses, Heman, Yeduthun, Asaph, and the three sons of Korah). Jeremiah wrote his book, Kings and Lamentations. Hezekiah and his group wrote Isaiah, Proverbs, Song of Songs and Ecclesiastes. The men of the Great Synagogue wrote Ezekiel, the Twelve, Daniel and the scroll of Esther. Ezra wrote his book and the genealogies of Chronicles down to his own.' (Cf. G. Dalman, *Traditio rabbinorum veterrima de librorum Veteris Testamenti ordine atque origine* (1891); J.-P. Audet, 'Les proverbes d'Isaïe dans la tradition juive ancienne', Cahiers de Théol. et de Philos. 8 (1952), pp. 23–30; O. Eissfeldt, *Introduction*, p. 563. On Josephus's view of the canon, see R. Meyer, 'Bemerkungen zur Kanontheorie des Josephus', *Josephus-Studien*;

first century A.D., where the existence of a canon is already assumed, doubts were raised only in respect of a few of the books, notably the Song of Solomon and the book of Koheleth. Even so, the traditional view prevailed that they 'defile the hands', i.e. that they are to be revered as canonical writings.[13] Of writings other than those forming

---

Festschrift für O. Michel, ed. by O. Betz, R. Haacker and M. Hengel (1974), pp. 285–99. Jerome in his *Prologus galeatus* to the Books of Samuel (ed. Vallarsi IX, pp. 455–6) gives the following enumeration as the one customary among the Jews: (1–5) Pentateuch; (6) Joshua; (7) Judges and Ruth; (8) Samuel; (9) Kings; (10) Isaiah; (11) Jeremiah and Lamentations; (12) Ezekiel; (13) Twelve minor prophets; (14) Job; (15) Psalms; (16) Proverbs; (17) Ecclesiastes; (18) Song of Solomon; (19) Daniel; (20) Chronicles; (21) Ezra and Nehemiah; (22) Esther. The same enumeration but in a somewhat different order (and with the omission of the Twelve Minor Prophets, which can only be an oversight of the copyist) is given by Origen in Eusebius, *HE* vi 25 (where the designation Ἀμμεσφεκωδείμ for the Book of Numbers, which is usually left unexplained, transliterates חמש פקודים, mYom. 7:1; mSot. 7:7; mMen. 4:3). Cf. on the canon of Jerome, H. F. D. Sparks, CHB I (1970), pp. 532–5; on that of Origen see J. P. v. Kasteren, RB (1901), pp. 413–23; M. F. Wiles, CHB I, pp. 455–61. There is little doubt therefore that Josephus also takes this enumeration for granted, and with his 5+13+4=22 books has the present canon in mind. The four books containing 'hymns of praise to God and rules of life for men' are the Psalms and the three books of Solomon. In addition to the count of 22 books, there is in 4 Ezra 14:44–6 mention of 24 (the number 24 is preserved in the Syriac text but also results indirectly from the other texts by subtraction: 94 less 70). This figure is the usual one in later rabbinical literature. But Josephus's statement, which cannot be explained from the collection forming the Greek Bible, testifies to the fact that twenty-two was at that time the prevailing number in Palestine. Cf. G. Hölscher, *Kanonisch und Apokryph*, pp. 25–9; O. Eissfeldt, *Introduction*, p. 569. Otherwise, A. Lods, *Histoire de la littérature hébraïque et juive* (1950), p. 1007; R. E. Pfeiffer, s.v. 'Canon of the O.T.', IDB I, 498–520. The difference here depends upon whether Judges-Ruth and Jeremiah-Lamentations are accepted as being single books or works distinct from one another. That Chronicles formed the conclusion of the canon already in the age of Jesus may be deduced from Mt. 23:35=Lk. 11:51, where the killing of Zechariah, 2 Chron. 24:20–2, is said to be the last murder of a prophet. Actually, the murder of Uriah, Jer. 26:20–3, was later. But according to the canonical sequence the murder related in Chronicles is of course the last.

13. mYad. 3:5: '. . . All Holy Scriptures render the hands unclean. The Song of Songs and Ecclesiastes render the hands unclean. R. Judah says: The Song of Songs renders the hands unclean but concerning Ecclesiastes there is dissension. R. Yose says: Ecclesiastes does not render the hands unclean and concerning the Song of Songs there is dissension. R. Simeon says: Ecclesiastes is one of the points concerning which the school of Shammai adopts the more lenient and the school of Hillel the more stringent ruling. R. Simeon b. Azzai says: I have heard as a tradition from the seventy-two elders that on the day when they made R. Eleazar b. Azariah head of the academy it was decided that the Song of Songs and Ecclesiastes both render the hands unclean. R. Akiba says: God forbid! Never has any man in Israel disputed concerning the Song of Songs (that he should say) it does not render the hands unclean, for all the ages are not worth the day on which the Song of Songs was given to Israel; for all the Writings are holy, but the Song of Songs is the holy of holies. And if anything was in dispute, the dispute

the present canon, it cannot be shown that they were ever accepted as canonical by the Jews of Palestine, though the book of Jesus ben Sira was esteemed so highly that it is sometimes cited as part of the writings with the introductory formula דכתיב.[14] Only the Hellenistic Jews combined a certain number of other writings with those of the Hebrew canon. But their canon was never completed.

Despite the collocation of the Prophets and the Writings with the Torah, at no time were they placed on the same footing: the Torah has always occupied the higher place. In it is set down, in writing and in full, the original revelation given to Israel. The Prophets and the Writings merely hand down the message still further. For this reason they are described as 'tradition' (קבלה, Aramaic אשלמתא) and cited as such.[15] It

---

concerned Ecclesiastes alone. R. Yohanan b. Joshua, the son of R. Akiba's father-in-law, says: According to the words of Ben Azzai so did they dispute and so did they decide.' mEdu. 5:3: 'R. Simeon (variant: Ishmael) reports three opinions in which the school of Shammai follow the more lenient and the school of Hillel the more stringent ruling. According to the school of Shammai the book of Ecclesiastes does not render the hands unclean. And the school of Hillel says: It renders the hands unclean.' Jerome, *Comment. in Ecclesiast.* 12:13 (ed. Vallarsi III, p. 496): 'Aiunt Hebraei quum inter caetera scripta Salomonis quae antiquata sunt nec in memoria duraverunt et hic liber obliterandus videretur eo quod vanas Dei assereret creaturas et totum putaret esse pro nihilo et cibum et potum et delicias transeuntes praeferret omnibus, ex hoc uno capitulo meruisse auctoritatem, ut in divinorum voluminum numero poneretur.' See W. Bacher, *Tannaiten* I, pp. 20 f., II, p. 493; A. Schwarz, *Die Erleichterungen der Schammaiten und die Erschwerungen der Hilleliten* (also under the title, *Die Controversen der Schammaiten und Hilleliten* I) (1893), pp. 90–1; G. Hölscher, *Kanonisch und Apokryph*, pp. 31–5; G. F. Moore, *Judaism* I, pp. 242–6; J. Hempel, *Die althebräische Literatur* (1930), pp. 191–2; W. Rudolph, 'Das Hohe Lied im Kanon', ZAW 59 (1941), pp. 189–99; P. Benoit, 'Rabbi Aqiba ben Joseph, sage et héros du judaïsme', RB 54 (1947), pp. 54–89. According to Rab, reported in bShab. 30b, Ecclesiastes was finally accorded canonical status because '. . . it begins with words of Torah and ends with words of Torah'. For the eventual decision concerning the status of the Song of Songs, cf. tYad. 2:14, ARN A chs. 1, 36 (ed. Schechter, pp. 2, 108), and especially tSanh. 12:10 (paralleled by bSanh. 101a): 'Whoever sings the Song of Songs with an unsteady voice in the taverns and treats it as a secular song, has no share in the world to come.' S. Z. Leiman introduces a distinction between canonicity and inspiration. It is not the canonical, but the inspired character of Ecclesiastes, etc. was questioned at Jamnia. Cf. *The Canonization of Hebrew Scripture* (1976), pp. 127–8. On the meaning of the expression, 'to defile the hands', see below, n. 18.

14. bBK. 92b. Cf. Zunz, pp. 107–8. Cf. generally the literature on Ecclesiasticus in vol. III, § 32, and O. Eissfeldt, *Introduction*, p. 596; see especially C. Roth, 'Ecclesiasticus in the Synagogue Services', JBL 71 (1952), pp. 171–8.

15. Cf. mTaan. 2:1 (citing Joel 2:13); tNid. 4:10 (citing Job 10:10–11): Sifre Num. 112, ed. Horovitz, p. 120 (citing Ps. 50:21); 139, ed. Horovitz, p. 186 (citing Song of Solomon 1:7); yHal. 57b (citing Isaiah 28:16). Recent interpreters of rabbinic texts render the word קבלה as 'protest' (see H. Danby, *The Mishnah*, p. 195, n. 12), but such a translation fits only certain passages. Cf. in general

was also prescribed that because of its greater value a Torah scroll might be purchased with the proceeds from a sale of other biblical books, but not *vice versa*.[16]

Nevertheless, in general the Prophets and the Writings participate in the qualities of the Torah. They all are 'holy Scriptures' (כתבי הקדש)[17] and they all render the hands unclean.[18] They are all cited with

---

Zunz, p. 46 and n.b.; C. Taylor, *Sayings of the Jewish Fathers* ([2]1897); repr. with a Proleg. by J. Goldin, 1969), pp. 106–8; L. Blau, *Zur Einleitung in die Heilige Schrift* (1894), pp. 24 ff.; W. Bacher, *Terminologie* (1899), pp. 165–6; *Pal. Amoräer* I (1892), pp. 164, 500; Moore, *Judaism* I, p. 87, n. 3 and pp. 239–40.

16. mMeg. 3:1.

17. mShab. 16:1; mErub. 10:3; mB.B. 1:6; mSanh. 10:6; mPar. 10:3; mYad. 3:2, 5; 4:6. L. Blau, *op. cit.*, pp. 12–16.

18. mEdu. 5:3; mKel. 15:6; mYad. 3:2, 4, 5; 4:5, 6. The meaning of this is nowhere explained and can only be deduced from the following individual passages. mYad. 3:2: '. . . the one hand can render the other unclean. So R. Joshua. But the sages say: Whatever suffers second-grade uncleanness cannot convey second-grade uncleanness to anything else. He said to them, But do not the Holy Scriptures, which suffer second-grade uncleanness, render the hands unclean?' mYad. 3:3: 'The straps of phylacteries (while still joined) with the phylacteries render the hands unclean.' mYad. 3:5: 'If the writing in a scroll were erased yet eighty-five letters still remained, as many as in the paragraph "And it came to pass when the ark set forward" (Num. 10:35 f.) . . . it still renders the hands unclean. A (single) written sheet (in a biblical scroll) on which are written eighty-five letters . . . . renders the hands unclean.' 4:5: 'The (Aramaic) targum that is in Ezra and Daniel renders the hands unclean. If an (Aramaic) targum is written in Hebrew, or if a Hebrew (Scripture) is written in an (Aramaic) targum or in Hebrew (i.e. archaic) script, it does not render the hands unclean. (The Holy Scriptures) render the hands unclean only if they are written in (square) Assyrian characters on leather and with ink.' mYad. 4:6: 'The Sadducees say, We must reprove you, Pharisees, because you say, The Holy Scriptures render the hands unclean (but), "The writings of Hamiras do not render the hands unclean." Rabban Yoḥanan b. Zakkai said, Have we nothing against the Pharisees beyond this? For they say, The bones of an ass are clean and the bones of Yoḥanan the High Priest are unclean. They (the Sadducees) said to him, their uncleanness is according to our love to them, that no man may make spoons of the bones of his father or mother. He said to them, in the case of the Holy Scriptures also, their uncleanness as is our love for them; but the writings of Hamiras which are not loved do not render the hands unclean.' mKel. 15:6: '. . . All scrolls (of Scripture) render the hands unclean except the scroll used in the Temple Court.' There can be no doubt that according to all these texts contact with the Scriptures really had the effect of rendering the hands unclean. They needed subsequently to be cleansed because they had been in touch with holiness. The underlying idea is that of taboo: i.e., the primitive religious concept of something removed from profane use, unapproachable (in Latin 'sacer'). A person involved with such matters must, on his return to profane existence, undergo a ritual of purification. The Bible was regarded similarly. An analogous example is that of the High Priest, who was to take a purificatory bath not only before, but also after the performance of his duties (Lev. 16:4, 24). Cf. W. Robertson Smith, *The Religion of the Semites*, p. 117; K. Budde, *Der Kanon des A.T.*, pp. 3–6; G. Hölscher, *Kanonisch und Apokryph*, pp. 4–5. Further, see R. Otto, *The Idea of the Holy*

essentially the same formula. For although special phrases are sometimes employed for the Torah, the one most commonly used, שנאמר, 'for it is said', is applied without distinction to them all,[19] as is the formula γέγραπται and others like it in the sphere of Hellenism (cf. the New Testament).[20] Indeed, now and then the Prophets and Writings are also cited simply as 'Law' (νόμος).[21] But for the Jew, the books of the Bible are not primarily works of law, or of exhortation and comfort, or of edification and history. They are Torah, a divine instruction, commandment and revelation addressed to Israel.[22]

([2]1950), pp. 50 ff.; Moore, *Judaism* III, Appended n. 9; J. Neusner, *A Life of Yohanan ben Zakkai* ([2]1970), pp. 75–6; *Development of a Legend* (1970), pp. 60–1, 203–4; *Pharisees* I, pp. 161–2, cf. also *idem*, *The Idea of Purity in Ancient Judaism* (1973), p. 105; *A History of the Mishnaic Law of Purities* XIX (1977), *Yadayim, in loc.*

19. E.g., to mention only citations from the Writings: mBer. 7:3 (Ps. 68:27); 9:5 (Ruth 2:4); mPea. 8:9 (Prov. 11:27), mShab. 9:2 (Prov. 30:19); 9:4 (Ps. 109:18); mR.Sh. 1:2 (Ps. 33:15). In all these the citation is introduced with the formula שנאמר. For a list of biblical quotations in the Mishnah, see H. Danby, *The Mishnah* (1933), pp. 807–11; in The Tosefta, see ed. Zuckermandel, pp. xxvi–xxxi. For the citation of Scripture in the Dead Sea Scrolls, see J. A. Fitzmyer, 'The Use of Explicit Old Testament Quotations in Qumran Literature and in the New Testament', *Essays on the Semitic Background of the New Testament* (1971), pp. 3–58.

20. On the citation formulas, see Fitzmyer, *op. cit.*, pp. 7–16. See also B. M. Metzger. 'The Formulas introducing Quotations of Scripture in the N.T. and the Mishnah', JBL 70 (1951), pp. 297–307.

21. Rom. 3:19; 1 Cor. 14:21; Jn. 10:34, 12:34, 15:25. A number of passages from the Prophets and Writings are designated Torah in rabbinic literature: Mekh. on Ex. 15:19 (ed. Lauterbach II, pp. 5–6, 54–5); bErub. 58a; bM.K. 5a; bYeb. 4a; bBekh. 50a; bSanh. 104b; bGit. 36a; bArakh. 11a. Cf. L. Löw, *Gesammelte Schriften* I (1889), p. 310; L. Blau, *op. cit.* (in n. 14 above), pp. 16–17; W. Bacher, *Terminologie* I, p. 197; Moore, *Judaism* I, p. 240; W. D. Davies, 'Law in first-century Judaism', IDB III, pp. 89–95.

22. J. A. Sanders offers a most pertinent definition of Torah in biblical and post-biblical terminology: '. . . it appears that the oldest and most common meaning is something approximate to what we mean by the word *revelation* . . . in the majority of cases the word (Law) is probably used in the broad sense of revelation, that is, authoritative tradition' (*Torah and Canon* (1972), pp. 2–3). In a well-documented study, Monsengwo Pasinya argues that the LXX rendering of Torah as νόμος implies no legalistic bias but is meant to convey the wide overtones of the underlying Hebrew concept. Cf. *La notion de 'nomos' dans le Pentateuque grec* (1973). For an earlier philological survey, see S. H. Blank, 'The LXX Renderings of Old Testament Terms for Law', HUCA 7 (1930), pp. 259–83. The Aramaic substitute for Torah, viz. אוריתא suggests that in the mind of Aramaic-speaking Jews Torah was a source of enlightenment. Cf. the same concept in Ps. Philo, LAB 12:2 ('Moyses . . . legem illuminabit vobis') and the Talmudic dictum, אורה זו תורה (bMeg. 16b). See G. Vermes, 'The Torah is a Light', VT 8 (1958), pp. 436–38.

II. The Torah Scholars and their Work in General

Bibliography

Bacher, W., *Die Agada der Tannaiten* I²–II (1903, 1890); (Index, s.v. Lehrhaus, Lehrer, Schüler).
JE s.v. 'Scribes', XI, pp. 123–6; 'Rabbi', X, pp. 294–5.
Smith, W. Robertson, *The Old Testament in the Jewish Church* (1907), pp. 42–72.
Str.-B. I, pp. 79–82, 691–5; II, pp. 647–61.
Bousset, W., Gressmann, H., *Die Religion des Judentums im neutestamentlichen Zeitalter* (³1926=⁴1966), pp. 171–8.
Moore, G. F., *Judaism* I, pp. 37–47.
Schlatter, A., *Die Theologie des Judentums nach dem Bericht des Josefos* (1932), pp. 199 ff.
Sellin, E., *Israelitische-jüdische Religionsgeschichte* (1933), pp. 140 f.
Guignebert, C., *The Jewish World in the Time of Christ* (1939), pp. 67–73.
Baron, S. W., *The Jewish Community* (1942), especially pp. 126 ff.
Jeremias, J., s.v. 'γραμματεύς', TWNT I, pp. 740–2; TDNT I, pp. 740–2.
Lieberman, S., *Hellenism in Jewish Palestine* (1950), pp. 83–99.
Urbach, E. E., 'The Derasha as a Basis of the Halakah and the Problem of the Soferim', Tarbiz 27 (1958), pp. 166–82 (Hebr.). (On the relationship of the scribes to the Pharisees.)
Meyer, R., *Tradition und Neuschöpfung im antiken Judentum* (1965), pp. 33–45.
Black, M., 'Scribe', IDB IV (1962), pp. 246–8.
Jeremias, J., *Jerusalem in the Time of Jesus* (1969), pp. 232–45, 252–8.
Urbach, E. E., *The Sages, their Concepts and Beliefs* (1969, 1971), especially pp. 1–14 (Hebr.), E.T. (1975), pp. 1–18.
Hengel, M., *Judentum und Hellenismus* (1969, ²1973), pp. 143–52, 242–8. E.T. *Judaism and Hellenism* I (1974), pp. 78–83, 131–8.
Enc. Jud. s.v. 'Soferim' (Y. D. Gilat), 15, cols. 79–81; 'Sages' (E. E. Urbach), 14, cols. 636–55.
Maier, J., *Geschichte der jüdischen Religion* (1972), pp. 69–71.
Baumgarten, J. M., 'The Un-Written Law in the Pre-Rabbinic Period', JSJ 3 (1972), pp. 7–29; 'Form-Criticism and the Oral Law', *ibid.* 5 (1974), pp. 34–40.
Neusner, J., 'The Written Tradition in the Pre-Rabbinic Period', JSJ 4 (1973), pp. 56–65; 'Exegesis and Written Law', *ibid.* 5 (1974), pp. 176–8.
Mantel, H. D., 'The Development of the Oral Law during the Second Temple Period', *Society and Religion in the Second Temple Period*, ed. M. Avi-Yonah and Z. Baras, *World History of the Jewish People* VIII (1977), pp. 41–64, 325–37.

The existence of a law provokes the need for professional knowledge of it and expertise. This requirement makes itself felt in proportion as the law is comprehensive and complicated. Only by dealing with it professionally can familiarity with its details be acquired, and certainty in applying its individual regulations to everyday life. At the time of Ezra and for a considerable period afterwards this was primarily the concern of the priests. Ezra himself was both priest and scribe (סופר). It was in the interest of the priestly cult that the Priestly Code, that very important component of the Pentateuch, was written. Hence the priests were at first both the experts in, and guardians of, the Torah. Gradually this changed however. The higher the Torah rose in the estimation of the people, the more its study and interpretation became an independent exercise. It was the teaching of God. To know and obey it was as much the business of every individual Jew as it was of the priests. Increasingly, therefore, lay Israelites took over the study of the Torah, and side by side with the priests an independent order of 'Torah scholars' or scribes came into being.[1] Just how respected and influential this class of *soferim* was at the beginning of the second century B.C. is made clear in Ecclesiasticus 38:24–39:11. Like the sages of the past, the scribes take precedence in assemblies of the people; they are the judges and the legal experts; they are conversant with the wisdom and maxims of the ancients (Ecclus. 37:33–39:1). The scribe devoted to 'the study of the law of the most High will serve among the great and appear before rulers' (39:1, 4). 'If the great Lord is willing, he will be filled with the spirit of understanding' (39:6). 'He will reveal instruction in his teaching and will glory in the law of the Lord's covenant' (39:8). 'Many will praise his understanding and it will never be blotted out; his memory will not disappear, and his name will live through all generations.' (39:9). 'Nations will declare his wisdom, and the congregation will proclaim his praise' (39:10).

When in Hellenistic times some of the priests of higher rank turned to Gentile culture and more or less neglected the tradition of their fathers, the scribes set a very different example. It was no longer the priests but the scribes who were the zealous guardians of the Torah.

1. The Qumran Community preserved the archaic structure of Jewish society with its absolute priestly predominance. 'Final authority lay in the hands of the Priests. The phrase, "according to the decision of the multitude of the men of their Covenant", occurs whenever there is reference in the scrolls to the acceptance of new members or to the expulsion or punishment of offenders; but it is always coupled with, and preceded by, the obviously more important decision of the "sons of Zadok". In the fields of doctrine, justice and common ownership, it was they who held the reins; newcomers were to "unite with respect to the Law and possession, under the authority of the sons of Zadok" (1QS 5:2) and, with even more emphasis, the "sons of Zadok alone" were to "command in matters of justice and property" and every rule concerning the men of the Community "was to be determined according to their word" (1QS 9:7). There is no indication that the Levites were to be distinguished from the Priests, so it is reasonable to suppose that both clerical classes are envisaged in these general statements.' (G. Vermes, *DSSE*, pp. 18–19). 'Since the sect expressly intended to model its organization as a microcosmic Israel, it followed that, as in Judaism generally, the prime religious duties of worship and instruction were divided between Priests and Levites.' (*Ibid.*, p. 25.) Cf. *DSS*, pp. 87–115.

Consequently, from then on they were also the real teachers of the people, over whose spiritual life they increased their control.

In New Testament times, this process was already complete: the scribes are represented as the undisputed spiritual leaders of the people. Usually, they are alluded to as γραμματεῖς, 'Scripture experts', 'the learned', *homines literati*, to correspond with the Hebrew סופרים.[2] It goes without saying that their occupation was primarily concern with the Torah: significantly, Jewish tradition describes Moses as the scribe (*safra*) par excellence.[3] Besides this general designation, there were also the special νομικοί, 'lawyers' (Mt. 22:35; Lk. 7:30; 10; 25; 11:45 f.; 52; 15:3);[4] and as they not only knew the law but taught it, they are likewise known as νομοδιδάσκαλοι, 'teachers of the law' (Lk. 5:17; Act. 5:34), i.e. of the Torah, for in Jewish-Greek sources, in the Septuagint as well as in the New Testament, νόμος has the same meaning as Torah—instruction, direction, revelation.[5] Josephus calls them πατρίων ἐξηγηταὶ νόμων,[6] or in Hellenistic style σοφισταί[7] and ἱερογραμματεῖς.[8] The term

2. A סופר is a person professionally concerned with books, e.g. also a writer (mShab. 12:5; mNed. 9:2; mGit. 3:1; 7:2; 8:8; 9:8; mB.M. 5:11; mSanh. 4:3; 5:5) or a book-binder (mPes. 3:1). In the Old Testament, a *sofer* is originally an officer dealing with written records, specifically the king's chancellor charged with drafting state documents, but later also a scholar and legal expert. See TDNT I, pp. 740–1 (J. Jeremias). On scribes of the pre-Maccabaean period, see also J. Wellhausen, *Israelitische und jüdische Geschichte* ([9]1958), pp. 199–204; J. Bright, *A History of Israel* ([2]1972), pp. 215 and 439–41. R. de Vaux, *Ancient Israel*, especially pp. 225, 251. The Talmudic etymology of *soferim* as they who count the letters of the Torah (bKid. 30a) is without historical significance. Cf. in general, Bacher, *Terminologie* I, pp. 113–36; H. H. Schaeder, *Esra der Schreiber* (1930), 48 ff.; R. Meyer, *Tradition und Neuschöpfung*, pp. 33–43; M. Hengel, *Judentum und Hellenismus* (1973), pp. 143–8; E.T. I, pp. 78–83.

3. Josephus, *Ant.* xx 11, 2 (264) says of the Jews: μόνοις δὲ σοφίαν μαρτυροῦσιν τοῖς τὰ νόμιμα σαφῶς ἐπισταμένοις καὶ τὴν τῶν ἱερῶν γραμμάτων δύναμιν ἑρμηνεῦσαι δυναμένοις. For Moses, see G. Vermes, *Scripture and Tradition*, pp. 51–2. On חק/מחקק, scribe, see *ibid.*, pp. 52–5. Note that מחקק of the Hebrew Ecclesiasticus 10:5 is rendered in Greek as γραμματεύς.

4. νομικός in later Greek dialects is the technical expression for 'lawyer', *iuris peritus*. Thus also particularly of Roman jurists, Strabo xii 2, 9 (539): οἱ παρὰ Ῥωμαίοις νομικοί, also in *Edictum Diocletiani*, see A. A. F. Rudorff, *Römische Rechtsgeschichte* II, p. 54. See W. Kunkel, *Herkunft und soziale Stellung der römischen Juristen* ([2]1967), pp. 267–70. The term is absent in Mark but occurs several times in Luke, who wishes to characterize Jewish 'scribes' as experts in biblical law. Cf. H. Kleinknecht-W. Gutbrod, *Law* (1962), especially pp. 141–3.

5. Cf. Kleinknecht-Gutbrod, *op. cit.*, pp. 47–9; 67–78. By adopting νόμος as the usual equivalent of Torah, the LXX appears to have implied that the Pentateuch was the legal code of the Jewish diaspora comparable to the laws of the Greek *polis*. Cf. Z. W. Falk, *Introduction to Jewish Law of the Second Commonwealth* (1972), p. 6. See also p. 321 above.

6. *Ant.* xvii 6, 2 (149). Cf. xviii 3, 5 (84).

7. *B.J.* i 33, 2 (648); ii 17, 8, 9 (433, 445).

8. *B.J.* vi 5, 3 (291).

סופר is still to be found in Ecclus. 38:24. In the Mishnah, by contrast, סופרים is applied only to scribes of earlier times who had already become an authority for the age of the Mishnah itself.[9] Contemporary scribes are always referred to as sages (חכמים).

The extraordinary respect which these sages enjoyed among the people finds expression even in the titles given them. The most usual form of address was רבי, 'my lord' (in Greek transliteration ῥαββί, Mt. 23:7 and elsewhere).[10] This reverential appellation nevertheless gradually lost, through frequent use, the pronominal meaning attached to its suffix and came to be employed as a title (Rabbi Joshua, Rabbi Eliezer, Rabbi Akiba).[11] The usage is not attested prior to the New

9. Thus mOrl. 3:9; mYeb. 2:4; 9:3 (mSot. 9:15); mSanh. 11:3; mKel. 13:7; mPar. 11:4–6; mTohor. 4:7, 11; mTeb.Y. 4:6; mYad. 3:2. In all these passages (except mSot. 9:15, which does not belong to the original text of the Mishnah), reference is made to 'the words of the scribes' (דברי סופרים) as distinct from the commandments of the Torah, and in such a way that the former are also regarded as having been authoritative for a long time. Otherwise, the expression סופרים occurs in the Mishnah only in the sense stated above in note 2. In the common text of the *Shemoneh 'Esreh*, God is entreated in the 13th *berakhah* (ברכת צדיקים) to show mercy towards 'the righteous, the pious, and the elders of Israel and the remnant of the *soferim*' (פליטת סופרים). But the last two words are absent from the older versions of the prayer (which also show other variations, too); see I. Elbogen, *Geschichte des Achtzehngebets* (1903), p. 59. *Der jüdische Gottesdienst in seiner geschichtlichen Entwicklung* ([3]1931), p. 52. The Greek γραμματεύς is still found in Jewish epitaphs in Rome from the second to the fourth century A.D.; see H. J. Leon, *The Jews of Ancient Rome* (1960), pp. 183–6. Cf. inscriptions nos. 7, 18, 67, 99, 121, 125, 146, 148, 149, 180, 279, 284, 318, 351, 433, on pp. 265–331.

10. רב in the Old Testament means 'chief' (e.g. of the eunuchs or magicians, Jer. 39:3, 13). In the Mishnah it signifies 'master', e.g. as opposed to slave (mSuk. 2:9; mGit. 4:4, 5; mEdu. 1:13; mAb. 1:3). Subsequently, like the Latin 'magister', it acquired the meaning, 'instructor', 'teacher'. It seems already to be used in this way in a saying attributed to Joshua ben Perahiah, mAb. 1:6. This sense is in any case quite customary in the age of the Mishnah; see mR.Sh. 2:9; mB.M. 2:11; mEdu. 1:3; 8:7; mAb. 4:12; mKer. 6:9; mYad. 4:3. Hence when a teacher is addressed as Rabbi (e.g. mPes. 6:2; mR.Sh. 2:9; mNed. 9:5 mB.K. 8:6; cf. also רבינו mBer. 2:5–7), the meaning is not only 'my master', but also 'my teacher'. For other important persons, e.g. the High Priest, the address אישי is used (mYom. 1:3, 5, 7; 4:1; mTam. 6:3; mPar. 3:8). The interpretation of ῥαββεί by διδάσκαλε (Jn. 1:38) is therefore not incorrect. Cf. also Jerome, *In Mt.* 23:7 (CCL lxxvii, p. 212): 'et vocentur ab hominibus Rabbi, quod Latino sermone magister dicitur'. *Idem, Onomasticon*, ed. Lagarde, p. 63: 'Rabbi magister meus, syrum est'. See also the Greek Onomastica, pp. 175, 30; 197, 26; 204, 26.

11. Like *Monsieur*. On the title of Rabbi in general see Graetz, *Geschichte der Juden* IV, p. 431; Th. Reinach, REJ 48 (1904), pp. 191–6 (inscriptions from Cyprus: εὐχὴ ῥαββὶ Ἀττικοῦ = Frey, CIJ, no. 736); JE X pp. 294–5; G. Dalman, *Die Worte Jesu* ([2]1930), pp. 272–80; S. W. Baron, *A Social and Religious History of the Jews* II (1952), pp. 120 ff.; G. Vermes, *Jesus the Jew* (1973), pp. 115–21, 248–9. It was after A.D. 70, and possibly at Yavneh, that '*Rabbi*' became a title for

Testament era. Hillel and Shammai are never called Rabbi, neither is ῥαββί found in the New Testament except as a form of address. Its use as a title seems to have originated at about the time of Jesus.

רבן, or according to another spelling רבון, is superior to *Rab*. The first form seems to belong more to the Hebrew, the second to the Aramaic usage.[12] Thus *Rabban* is employed in the Mishnah as the title of four prominent scholars of the Mishnaic age (about A.D. 40–150).[13] In the New Testament, on the other hand, ῥαββουνί (*rabbôn* or *rabbûn* followed by a suffix) is a polite form of address directed to Jesus (Mk. 10:51; Jn. 20:16).[14]

In New Testament Greek, Rabbi is rendered as κύριε (Mt. 8:2, 6, 8, 21, 25 and frequently) or διδάσκαλε (Mt. 8:19 and frequently), and in Luke also as ἐπιστάτα (Lk. 5:5; 8:24, 45; 9:33, 49; 7:13).

Still remaining to be included among the styles given to the scribes are πατήρ and καθηγητής (Mt. 23:9, 10). The latter probably=מורה,

---

ordained scholars authorized to teach: cf. A. Büchler, *Die Priester und der Cultus* (1895), 16 ff.; Moore, *Judaism* I, pp. 43 f.; G. Dalman, *Die Worte Jesu*, pp. 272–4; W. D. Davies, *The Setting of the Sermon on the Mount* (1964), p. 298. Besides *Rabbi*, there is the later pronunciation *Rebbi*, e.g. '*duo rebbites*' on an epitaph to Venosa (CIS IX, nos. 648 and 6220; Frey, CIJ I, no. 611; βηρεβι = בירבי, בר רבי on inscriptions from Jaffa and Beth She'arim, Frey, CIJ II, nos. 893, 951, pp. 121, 145; B. Mazar, *Beth She'arim* I ([2]1957), p. 137; N. Avigad, *Beth She'arim* III (1971), no. 16, p. 179). For the spelling Βαραβαι, see M. Schwabe-B. Lifschitz, *Beth She'arim* II (1967), no. 89, p. 30. *Ribbi* (or *Rib*) Ῥιββι (Ῥιβ) appear in *Beth She'arim* II, nos. 41, 42, 202.

12. Both forms appear in the Targums (see J. Levy, *Chaldäisches Wörterbuch*, s.v.) whereas in Hebrew it is almost always רבן. רבון figures only once in the Mishnah, mTaan. 3:8, where the reference is to God. The traditional meaning of Rabban-Rabbi-Rab according to a formulation by the Gaons Sherira and Ḥai (cca. A.D. 1000) is given in *Arukh* s.v. אביי. Cf. A. Kohut, *Aruch Completum* I (1955), pp. 6–7: גדול מרב רבי גדול מרבי רבן ('Rabbi is superior to Rab, Rabban is superior to Rabbi . . .') Cf. tEdu. 3:4.

13. These four are Rabban Gamaliel the Elder, Rabban Yoḥanan ben Zakkai, Rabban Gamaliel II, Rabban Simeon ben Gamaliel II. In the best manuscripts of the Mishnah, they are as a rule given the title רבן. In addition, there is one mention in the Mishnah of Rabban Gamaliel III son of R. Judah ha-Nasi (mAb. 2:2). On the other hand, of two others to whom the title is occasionally applied (Simeon son of Hillel and Simeon son of Gamaliel I, one is not alluded to in the Mishnah at all, and the other (Simeon son of Gamaliel I) is not called Rabban, in the principal passage at least (mAb. 1:17). Nevertheless he is probably the Rabban Simeon ben Gamaliel mentioned in mKer. 1:7 in connexion with the price of sacrificial doves.

14. On the change in pronunciation *rabbōn*, see G. Dalman, *Grammatik des jüdisch-palästinischen Aramäisch* ([2]1905), p. 176, and n. 1. On the vocalization of רבוני as ῥαββουνί (*rabbuni*) in the Targums, cf. M. Black, *An Aramaic Approach* ([3]1967), pp. 23–4, 43–6. For its appearance with this pronunciation in one passage of one Mishnah codex, cf. E. Y. Kutscher, 'Das zur Zeit Jesu gesprochene Aramäisch', ZNW 51 (1960), p. 53.

'teacher',[15] while the former corresponds to the Aramaic אבא, the title of several rabbis in the Mishnah and Tosefta.[16]

The rabbis were held in high esteem. Indeed, their pupils were recommended to revere them even more than their own fathers and mothers. 'Let the honour of your disciple be as dear to you as the honour of your companion, and the honour of your companion as the fear of your teacher, and the fear of your teacher as the fear of Heaven.'[17] 'In the study of the Torah, if a son has acquired much wisdom while sitting before his teacher, his teacher precedes his father, for both he and his father are obliged to honour the teacher.'[18] If a man is in search of property lost by his father and his teacher, the teacher's loss has precedence (i.e. he must be the first to be helped). For his father brought him only into this world, but his teacher who teaches him wisdom brings him into the world to come. But if his father is himself a sage, then his father has precedence. If a man's father and teacher carry burdens, he must first help his teacher and afterwards his father. If his father and teacher are in captivity, he must first ransom his teacher and afterwards his father. But if his father is himself a sage, he must ransom his father first, and afterwards his teacher.[19]

The rabbis in general took precedence everywhere, as is reflected in the polemical language of the Gospels. 'They love the uppermost rooms at feasts, and the chief seats in the synagogues and greetings in the markets, and to be called of men Rabbi, Rabbi' (Mt. 23:6–7; Mk. 12:38–9; Lk. 11:43, 20:46). Even their dress was that of the priesthood and the nobility. They wore *στολάς*, according to Epiphanius, *ἀμπεχόνας* and *δαλματικάς*.[20]

15. On the use of the Aramaic מר, see Dalman, *Die Worte Jesu*, pp. 266–80; G. Vermes, *Jesus the Jew*, pp. 111–22.

16. For *Mōreh* see Dalman, *op. cit.*, p. 276. The best known teacher called Abba was Saul (mPea. 8:5; mKil. 2:3; mShab. 23:3; mShek. 4:2; mBez. 3:8; mAb. 5:8; mMid. 2:5; 5:4, etc.). See also Abba Gorion (mKid. 4:14), Abba Yose ben Ḥanan (mMid. 2:6). For others bearing this title, see Zuckermandel, *Index zur Tosephta*, p. xxxi and Strack, Index III. In JE I pp. 29–35 more than thirty rabbis are called Abba. See in general K. Kohler, 'Abba, father, title of spiritual leader and saint', JQR 13 (1901), pp. 567–80; Str.-B. I (1922), pp. 392–6, 410–18, 918–19; G. Dalman, *Die Worte Jesu*, pp. 150–9, 296–304; S. V. McCasland, 'Abba Father', JBL 72 (1953), pp. 79 ff. On the miracle-working Hasid, Abba Hilkiah, see Vermes, *Jesus the Jew*, pp. 118–21.

17. mAb. 4:12.

18. mKer. 6:9.

19. mB.M. 2:11. Cf. also the treatise Derekh Ereẓ zuṭṭa (see vol. I, pp. 80, 89); Maimonides, *Mishneh Torah: Hilkoth Talmud Torah* 5–6 (ed. M. Hyamson, *The Book of Knowledge*, 1962, pp. 61b–64a); S. W. Baron, *A Social and Religious History of the Jews* II, pp. 278–9.

20. *στολάς*, Mk. 12:38=Lk. 20:46. In addition, Epiphanius, *Haer*. 15: *ἀλλ' ἐπειδὴ στολάς, εἴτ' οὖν ἀμπεχόνας οἱ τοιοῦτοι ἀνεβάλλοντο καὶ δαλματικάς, εἴτ' οὖν κολοβίωνας ἐκ πλαυτυσήμων διὰ πορφύρας ἀλουργοϋφεῖς κατεσκευασμένας* etc. The *στολή* is the attire of

All the activities of the sages, educational as well as judicial, were to be unpaid. 'R. Zadok said: Make them (the words of the Torah) neither into a crown with which to exalt yourself nor into a space with which to dig (a living).' 'For Hillel used to say: Whoever makes use of the crown (of the Torah for secular aims), shall vanish. Thus he who makes a profit from the words of the Torah removes his life from the world.'[21] That a judge may not accept gifts is prescribed already in the Old Testament (Ex. 32:8; Deut. 16:19). The Mishnah likewise states: 'If a man accepts payment for a judicial decision, his judgement is void.'[22]

The rabbis were therefore instructed to obtain their livelihood from other sources. Some were born well-to-do; others practised a trade in addition to studying the Torah. The combination of scholarly and secular activities was specifically recommended by Rabban Gamaliel III, son of R. Judah ha-Nasi: 'Excellent is the study of the Torah combined with worldly business, for effort in both puts sin out of mind. All Torah study without secular labour comes eventually to nothing and causes transgression.'[23] As is known, the apostle Paul followed a trade even when he was a preacher of the Gospel (Act. 18:3, 20:34; 1 Thess. 2:9; 2 Thess. 3:8; 1 Cor. 4:12, 9, 6 ff.; 2 Cor. 11:7 ff.). The same is reported of many rabbis.[24] Needless to say, concern with the Torah was always considered to be more important, and they were warned against setting too much store by secular matters. Ben Sira cautions against an exclusive preoccupation with work and extols the blessing of scholarship (Ecclus. 38:24–39:11). R. Meir said: 'Devote yourself less to business and occupy yourself more with the Torah.'[25] Hillel said: 'Whoever dedicates himself too much to trade will not grow wise.'[26]

The principle of non-remuneration was probably adhered to only in respect of judicial functions; it can hardly have operated among the rabbis in their role as teachers. The Gospel combines Jesus' admonition to the disciples, δωρεὰν ἐλάβετε, δωρεὰν δότε (Mt. 10:8), with the maxim

---

the priests: Philo, *Legat.* 37 (296); Josephus, *Ant.* iii 7, 1 (151) and of the aristocracy (1 Mac. 6:15). On the dalmatic, see above, p. 70.

21. mAb. 4:5; cf. 1:13. Also Derekh Ereẓ zuṭṭa 4:2.

22. mBekh. 4:6.

23. mAb. 2:2.

24. Cf. S. Meyer, *Arbeit und Handwerk im Talmud* (1878), pp. 23–36; Baron, *A Social and Religious History of the Jews* II, pp. 260–79; H. Z. Reines, 'The Support of Scholars in the Talmudic Period', Sinai 4, nos. 106–7, pp. 137–52. For comparative data, see F. V. Filson, 'Christian Teachers in the First Century', JBL 60 (1941), pp. 317–28; J. Jeremias, *Jerusalem in the Time of Jesus*, p. 234; M. Avi-Yonah, *The Jews of Palestine: A Political History from the Bar Kokhba War to the Arab Conquest* (1976), pp. 22–3.

25. mAb. 4:10.

26. mAb. 2:6.

that a labourer is worthy of his hire (Mt. 10:10; Lk. 10:7). Paul expressly refers to this (1 Cor. 19:14) when he claims the right to be maintained by those to whom he preaches the Gospel, even though he rarely made use of it (1 Cor. 9:3–18; 2 Cor. 11:8–9; Phil. 4:10–18. Cf. also Gal. 6:6). It may therefore be assumed that Jewish teachers in general did not always offer instruction free of charge. Indeed, the very exhortations cited above, not to teach Torah for reasons of self-interest, lead to the conclusion that non-remuneration was not the sole rule. The diatribes of the Gospels against the scribes and Pharisees lay special emphasis on greed (Mk. 12:40; Lk. 20:47; 16:14). Yet the only rabbinic attestation of receiving payment appears in a late talmudic anecdote, without any historical worth, according to which Hillel had to hire himself out as a labourer in order to be able to afford the admission fee to the school of Shemaiah and Abtalion.[27]

Until A.D. 70, the activities of the Torah scholars were, of course, mainly centred on Judaea. But it would be a mistake to look for them there alone. Wherever zeal for the Torah was alive, they were indispensable. Consequently, they were to be found in Galilee too, at first sporadically, but after A.D. 140 in large numbers.[28] γραμματεῖς are mentioned frequently in Jewish epitaphs in Rome in the later period of the empire (see n. 7 above); and it was the Babylonian rabbis, the Amoraim of the third to the fifth centuries, who were responsible for the main work of rabbinic Judaism, the Talmud.

After the parting of the ways of the Pharisees and Sadducees, the 'scribes' for the most part adhered to the Pharisees. For the latter were none other than people who acknowledged, as a sacred rule of life to be strictly obeyed, the statutes developed during the course of time by the *soferim*. But in so far as Torah scholars were men 'learned in the law', some of them were bound to be Sadducees. It is after all inconceivable that this party, which acknowledged the written Torah as binding, should have in its midst no professional Bible interpreters. In fact, passages in the New Testament which speak of 'doctors of the law' who were Pharisees (Mk. 2:16; Lk. 5:30; Act. 23.8) imply that there must have been Sadducaean lawyers as well.[29]

27. bYom. 35b. J. Jeremias (*Jerusalem in the Time of Jesus*, p. 112) notes however that the fee was paid, not to the teacher, but to the school janitor.

28. For evidence of Pharisaic presence in Galilee before A.D. 70, see Vermes, *Jesus the Jew*, pp. 56–7. It may well be asked whether some of the 'scribes' mentioned in the Gospels in a Galilean context should be identified as κωμῶν γραμματεῖς or κωμογραμματεῖς, *B.J.* i 24, 3 (479); *Ant.* xvi 7, 3 (203), i.e. village clerks or (perhaps) elementary school teachers rather than experts in the law. Concerning Galilean scholars from the end of the first century A.D. to Hadrianic times, see A. Büchler, *Der galiläische Am-ha'areṣ des zweiten Jahrhunderts* (1906), pp. 274–338.

29. G. Vermes, *Jesus the Jew*, p. 35. The halakhah referred to by R. Eliezer b.

The professional activity of the Torah scholars was concerned primarily with the legal sections of the Torah, and therefore with the administration of justice. In the first instance lawyers, they were responsible (1) for defining and perfecting the legal principles underlying or deriving from the Torah; (2) for teaching them to their pupils; and (3) for helping to administer the law as learned counsellors in the courts of justice.[30]

(1) In regard to the theoretical formation of the law itself, its basic principles were of course thought to be fixed, implicitly or explicitly, in the written Torah. But no legal code is so detailed that it requires no further interpretation. In any case, the directions provided by the law of Moses are in part very general. There was, therefore, wide scope for the work of the Torah scholars. They had to develop, with the help of careful casuistry, the general precepts given in the Torah in such a way as to guarantee that their bias was really understood in accordance with the precepts' full significance and extent. Where the written Torah advances no direct ruling, this had to be made good, either by determining the common law, or by reasoning from other legal regulations already valid. Owing to the assiduity with which this whole operation was carried on in the last centuries B.C., biblical law gradually became a complex and intricate branch of knowledge. And as this law was not fixed in writing but was mainly handed down by word of mouth, continuous study was necessary even to become familiar with it. But knowledge of legal obligations was never more than the basis and prerequisite of the Torah scholar's professional activity. Their real business was to go on developing what was already lawful by continuous methodical work, in ever finer casuistical detail.

As the purpose of this activity was to establish a legal system valid for all, it could not be pursued by scholars working in isolation. There is very little concrete information regarding the consultative process prior to Yavneh, but if it is permissible to consider the methods of the rabbis assembled by Yoḥanan ben Zakkai and Gamaliel II as typical, the experts were in constant communication with each other with the aim of arriving, by way of mutual understanding, at commonly acknowledged results. Thus the whole undertaking of the formation of the law was effected by means of oral discussions. The accepted authorities not only gathered pupils around them in order to instruct

Zadok in mSanh. 7:2, according to which the death penalty by burning is to be applied literally, is described in bSanh. 52b as Sadducee legal practice.

30. This 'three-fold power of the sages' is correctly recognized by F. Weber, *System der altsynagogalen palästinischen Theologie*, pp. 130–43; cf. Moore, *Judaism*, I, pp. 39–43; Jeremias, *Jerusalem*, pp. 235–7.

them in the Torah; they also debated legal questions with them, indeed discussed with them the whole substance of the law. The Mishnah everywhere attests to this procedure.[31]

For such a method to be possible, the heads of schools at least had to live together in certain central places, though many of their disciples were scattered around the country as teachers and specialists in the law. But most of the predominantly creative authorities must have been concentrated in one locality—until A.D. 70 in Jerusalem, and later in the academies of Yavneh, Usha, Tiberias, etc.

The law developed theoretically by the scholars was, to begin with, theory alone. In many respects it remained so, since the actual historical and political circumstances, both before and after A.D. 70, prevented its implementation.[32] In general, however, the work of the scribes was related to real life. And as their reputation grew, so did their theory become, first influential, and later binding. In the century before the destruction of Jerusalem, the views of Pharisaic teachers carried already such weight that the Great Sanhedrin, despite its mixed composition of Pharisees and Sadducees, generally adhered in practice to the legal doctrines of the Pharisees (see above, p. 213). Many matters were in any case of a kind that needed no formal legislation. For the pious observed the religious statutes by reason of a voluntary submission to an authority recognized as legitimate.[33] Thus as soon as the schools were in agreement over them, the statutes developed by the scholars were accepted as binding in practice also. They were in consequence—if not formally recognized, nevertheless in fact—legislators. This is especially true for the period following the destruction of the Temple. By then, a civil court of justice like the former Sanhedrin no longer existed. The rabbinical teachers, with their purely spiritual power, constituted the one remaining authoritative body. Whereas formerly they had in fact established the law, now they were also formally acknowledged as legislators. Their pronouncements sufficed to determine what was valid in law. Whenever any doubt arose on some point, whether a person should behave this way or that, the problem needed only to be brought before the sages for an authoritative

31. E.g. mPea. 6:6; mKil. 3:7; 6:4; mTer. 5:4; mM.Sh. 2:2; mShab. 8:7; mPes. 6:2, 5; mKer. 3:10; mMaksh. 6:8; mYad. 4:3. For a full analysis of the disputes between the schools of Shammai and Hillel, see Neusner, *Pharisees* II, pp. 1–5 and *passim*.

32. mYad. 4:3–4 records an instructive example. Cf. also the obviously theoretical rulings on tribes in mSanh. 1:5; mHor. 1:5.

33. The priests are almost always represented as following the theory of the rabbis. Although the evidence of the Mishnah in areas of conflict between the two groups is not fully reliable, it relates only occasional differences between priestly practice and rabbinical theory; see mShek. 1:3–4; mYom. 6:3; mZeb. 12:4.

decision to be obtained.[34] The standing of the Torah teachers was such that the opinion of a single one of them was sometimes enough to settle the question.[35] As a result of their decrees, new doctrines were laid down even when there was no special reason for them, i.e., new legally valid ordinances, some of which were even at variance with statutes customary until then.[36] Nevertheless, it was always assumed that the opinion of the one was in agreement with that of the majority, and was accepted by them. For it was the majority that had the final word (see below, p. 342). It could therefore happen that the decision of an individual teacher was subsequently corrected,[37] and even that a scholar of distinction was obliged to subordinate his own view to that of a rabbinical 'court of law'.[38]

The legislative powers of the rabbis were so much taken for granted during the time of the Mishnah that it is presumed without further ado that the same was the case before the destruction of Jerusalem. It it said quite ingenuously that Hillel decreed this and that,[39] and that Gamaliel I arrived at such and such a decision.[40] Yet it was not Hillel and Gamaliel I who were the final authorities at that time, but the Great Sanhedrin of Jerusalem. The Mishnah itself asserts that from it proceeded '*torah* (i.e. authoritative teaching) for all Israel'.[41] On the other hand, it is true that the great teachers of the Torah were even then *in fact* the deciding authorities.

(2) The second main task of the Torah scholars was to teach. The ideal of Judaism has always been that every Israelite, or as many of them as possible, should acquire expertise in the Torah. 'Raise many disciples' was already a slogan of the Great Synagogue.[42] The more celebrated of the rabbis therefore gathered around them youths eager to learn—often in large numbers[43]—in order to furnish them with a

34. 'The case came before the sages (חכמים) and they declared it permissible' (or forbidden) is a formula that occurs frequently. See e.g. mKil. 4:9; mEdu. 7:3; mBekh. 5:3.

35. Cf. Rabban Yohanan ben Zakkai (mShab. 16:7; 22:3), Rabban Gamaliel II (mKel. 5:4), R. Akiba (mKil. 7:5; mTer. 4:13; mYeb. 12:5; mNid. 8:3).

36. See for example Rabban Yohanan ben Zakkai (mSuk. 3:12; mR. Sh. 4:1, 3, 4; mSot. 9:9; mMen. 10:5) and R. Akiba (mM.Sh. 5:8; mNaz. 6:1; mSanh. 3:4).

37. A decision by Nahum the Mede was once afterwards amended by 'the sages', mNaz. 5:4.

38. Thus R. Joshua complied with a decision of Rabban Gamaliel II and his court, mR.Sh. 2:9.

39. mSheb. 10:3; mGit. 4:3; mArakh. 9:4; everywhere with the formula התקין, 'he decreed'.

40. mR.Sh. 12:5; mGit. 4:2–3; likewise with the formula התקין.

41. mSanh. 11:2. Cf. especially J. Juster, *Les juifs dans l'empire romain* II, pp. 127–49.

42. mAb. 1:1.

43. Josephus, *B.J.* i 33, 2 (649); cf. bSot. 49b.

thorough knowledge of the complex and extensive 'oral Torah'. The pupils were known as תלמידים or תלמידי חכמים.[44] Instruction consisted in a continuous exercise of the memory. For since the aim was to imprint on the pupil's mind the whole subject, in all its countless details, and since moreover the oral Torah was not to be written down, one lesson could never suffice. The teacher had to repeat his material with his pupils over and over again. Hence in rabbinic usage, 'to repeat' (שנה = δευτεροῦν) is the same as 'to teach' (משנה = teaching).[45] But this repetition did not take the form of a recitation on the part of the teacher alone. The whole proceeding was disputational. The teacher either posed halakhic questions for his students to answer, or he solved them himself. The students were also free to put questions to him.[46] This form of catechetical education has left its stamp on the style of the Mishnah, where the question is frequently asked how this or that subject is to be understood so that the decision may then be given.[47]

All study of the Torah being strictly traditional, the students had only two duties. One was to remember everything faithfully. R. Dosthai said in the name of R. Meir: 'Whoever forgets one word of his instruction in the Torah, he is reckoned as though he had forfeited his life.'[48] The other duty was never to alter the doctrine received. The student was even to express himself in his teacher's words. 'Everyone must reproduce the expressions of his teacher', חייב אדם לומר בלשון רבו.[49] The highest praise of a student was to liken him to 'a plastered cistern which loses not one drop'.[50]

At the time of the Mishnah, and no doubt earlier, Bible study, scholarly disputation and teaching proper took place in special 'Houses

44. mAb. 5:12; mSanh. 11:2. There is mention in particular of the תלמידים of Rabban Yohanan ben Zakkai (mAb. 2:8), Rabban Gamaliel II (mBer. 2:5–7), R. Eliezer (mErub. 2:6), R. Ishmael (mErub. 1:2), R. Akiba (mNid. 8:3), students of the school of Shammai (mOrl. 2:5, 12). For תלמיד חכם, see mPes. 4:5; mYom. 1:6; mSuk. 2:1; mHag. 1:7; mNed. 10:4; mSot. 1:3; mSanh. 4:4; mMak. 2:5; mHor. 3:8; mNeg. 12:5. Cf. Enc. Jud. 15, cols. 746–9. The term חבר for a person who has completed his studies but has not yet obtained a publicly recognized position belongs to a later period. For the Mishnaic use of חבר, see § 26.

45. Cf. Jerome, *Epist.* 121 *ad Algasiam, quaest. X* (CSEL LVI, p. 49): 'Doctores eorum σοφοί hoc est sapientes vocantur. Et si quando certis diebus traditiones suas exponunt discipulis suis, solent dicere: οἱ σοφοὶ δευτερῶσιν, id est sapientes docent traditiones'. For the meaning of שנה and משנה, see vol. I, p. 70.

46. According to Hillel, 'a timid man cannot learn' (mAb. 2:6).

47. E.g. mBer. 1:1–2; mPea. 4:10; 6:8; 7:3, 4; 8:1; mKil. 2:2; 4:1, 2, 3; 6:1, 5; mSheb. 1:1, 2, 5; 2:1; 3:1, 2; 4:4. Questions are very frequently introduced by כיצד (= how?): mBer. 6:1; 7:3; mTer. 4:9; mM.Sh. 4:4; 5:4; mHal. 2:8; mOrl. 2:2; 3:8; mBik. 3:1, 2; mErub. 5:1; 8:1. On Mishnaic literary forms, see Neusner, *Pharisees* III, pp. 5–179; *Purities* XXI (1977).

48. mAb. 3:8.

49. mEdu. 1:3.

50. mAb. 2:8.

of Instruction' (בית מדרש, plur. בתי מרדשות).[51] These are often named in conjunction with synagogues as places which, from the legal point of view, enjoyed certain advantages.[52] In Yavneh, a locality called 'the vineyard' (כרם) is mentioned as a meeting-place of sages; though it should not be concluded from this that כרם was in general the poetic term for a House of Instruction.[53] In Jerusalem, to judge from the New Testament evidence, lessons were also given 'in the Temple' (ἐν τῷ ἱερῷ, Lk. 7:46; Mt. 21:23, 26:55; Mk. 14:49; Lk. 20:1, 21, 37; Jn. 18:20), i.e., in the pillared halls or some other room of the outer forecourt.

During instruction, the students sat on the floor (בקרקע) and the teacher on a raised dais (thus Act. 22:3: παρὰ τοὺς πόδας Γαμαλιήλ; cf. also Lk. 2:46).[54]

(3) The third and final task of the Torah scholars was to take part in the administration of justice. They were professionally expert in the law and their opinion was authoritative. It is true that, in the period under discussion at least, an academic knowledge of the Torah was by no means essential to the office of judge. Anyone could be a judge who had been appointed as such through the confidence of his fellow-citizens. And it is safe to assume that the small local courts were primarily lay courts of arbitration. But clearly, the more a judge excelled in a thorough and sure knowledge of the Torah, the greater the confidence he enjoyed. Where, therefore, Torah scholars were available, they were bound to be selected for judicial office. The New Testament expressly testifies with respect to the Great Sanhedrin of Jerusalem that γραμματεῖς were among its members (cf. above, p. 212).

51. Already Jesus ben Sira assembled his ישיבה (=auditors, Ecclus. 51:29) in his בית מדרש (Ecclus. 51:23). In the Mishnah cf. mBer. 4:2; mDem. 2:3; 7:5; mTer. 11:10*; mShab. 16:1; 18:1; mPes. 4:4*; mBez. 3:5; mAb. 5:14; mMen. 10:9; mYad. 4:3, 4. An asterisk marks the plural form.

52. mTer. 11:10; mPes. 4:4. It is clear from both passages that schools are distinct from the synagogues. On schools in general see K. Kohler, s.v. *Bet ha-midrash* in JE III, pp. 116–18; G. F. Moore, *Judaism* I, 308–19, iii. nn. 89–90; Enc. Jud. 4, cols. 751–2. Cf. also below, pp. 417–22.

53. mKet. 4:6; mEdu. 2:4. In these two passages כרם is a place where scholars in Yavneh used to assemble (R. Eleazar or R. Ishmael lectured on this or that topic before the scholars in the vineyard at Yavneh). Presumably this was a real vineyard, with a house or hall that served as a meeting-place. The traditional explanation of the term is that the students sat in their schools in rows like vines (see already yBer. 7d).

54. According to talmudic tradition, it did not become customary for students to sit on the ground until after the death of Gamaliel I; in earlier times they stood (bMeg. 21a). The legend is, however, simply an interpretation of mSot. 9:15: 'Since Rabban Gamaliel the Elder died, respect for the Torah has vanished'. On the other hand see, besides Lk. 2:46, mAb. 1:4, according to which already Yose ben Yoezer recommended that a man should allow himself to be made dusty at the feet of the sages.

After the fall of the Jewish state in A.D. 70, rabbinic authority gained in importance in this regard also. Recognized as independent legislators, they were now also acknowledged as independent judges. People complied willingly with their judgement, whether decisions were made collectively or individually. For example, it is said of R. Akiba that he once sentenced a man to pay 400 zuz (*denarii*) in compensation to a woman for uncovering her head in the street.[55]

This threefold activity of the scribes as Torah scholars constituted their true and primary occupation. But the Torah is not law alone. A large part of the Pentateuch consists in historical narration. The other biblical writings are almost exclusively either historical or doctrinal in content. However accustomed scholars had become to consider issues primarily from a halakhic point of view, this fact was always borne in mind. Thus whilst subjecting these writings, too, to exhaustive study as Scripture, it was inevitable that the history was spoken of as such, and the doctrine similarly. But the factor common to the treatment of the legal material and these documents was that they were also considered to be one sacred text, one holy composition, which was not only to be studied intensively but which men felt impelled to develop and elaborate. As they amplified the law more and more, so they did the same to sacred history and doctrine, but always in line with the text of Scripture, whose very holiness it was that required such thorough attention. The opinions of later periods had, of course, an important influence on this process of development in so far as history and doctrine were not only expanded but also reshaped in conformity with later ideas. Thus arose the literary genre usually known as haggadah.[56]

Work on haggadah was admittedly not the primary occupation of the teacher of Torah. But as the elaboration of the law, and that of the sacred text according to its historical and religious-ethical content, arose from a related need, so it came about quite naturally that both were carried out by the same men. The sages occupied themselves as a rule with both haggadah and halakhah, though some distinguished themselves more in the one than in the other.

In virtue of their dual expertise in law and haggadah, the Torah

55. mB.K. 8:6. That there were strictly speaking, no recognized rabbinical 'courts of law' in Palestine after A.D. 70, was argued by H. P. Chajes, 'Les juges juifs en Palestine de l'an 70 à l'an 500', *REJ* 39 (1899), pp. 39–52. Also, cf. p. 210 above. For the opposite view, see J. Juster, *Les Juifs dans l'empire romain* II, pp. 94–116. On the existence in Palestine at this time of two kinds of permanent local courts, see G. Alon, *Toledot ha-Yehudim be-Erez Yisrael* I (^{4}1967), pp. 136–44. Cf. also A. Büchler, *The Political and Social Leaders of the Jewish Community of Sepphoris in the Second and Third Centuries* (1909), pp. 21–33; H. Mantel, *Studies in the History of the Sanhedrin* (1961), pp. 223–5.

56. For further details, see pp. 346–55 below.

scholars were well qualified to preach in the synagogues. Preaching was not restricted to specific persons: anybody able to do so could teach there if permitted by the archisynagogus (see p. 435). But in the same way that experts in the law were preferred to the uneducated in the courts, so too the natural superiority of the Scripture expert asserted itself in the synagogues.

Finally, to the legal and historico-doctrinal exegesis and elaboration of Scripture was added a third scholarly concern: care for the biblical text as such. The more the sacred writings increased in authority, the more urgent was the need to preserve them scrupulously and without adulteration. From this preoccupation originated the observations and remarks included in the term Masorah (the computation of verses, words and letters, orthographical notes, critical notes on the text, etc.).[57] Nevertheless most of this work was carried out in a later period. The age under discussion saw, at the very most, only its beginning.[58]

57. On the expression 'Masorah' cf. W. Bacher, *Terminologie* I, pp. 106–9; JE VIII, p. 365. For other discussions cf. G. Dalman, *Studien zur bibl. Theologie* (1889), p. 8; F. Buhl, *Kanon und Text des A.T.* (1891), pp. 95 ff. For the view that the word is a legitimate noun, prouounced *mesorah*, cf. M. Gertner, 'The Masorah and the Levites', VT 10 (1960), pp. 241–72.

58. Cf. on the Masorah: P. E. Kahle, *Masoreten des Ostens*, BWAT 15 (1913); *Masoreten des Westens* I–II (1927/30); L. Lipschütz, *Ben Ascher—Ben Naftali. Der Bibeltext der tiberischen Masoreten* (1937); B. J. Roberts, 'The Emergence of the Tiberian Massoretic Text', JThSt 49 (1948), pp. 8 ff.; P. Kahle, *The Cairo Geniza* ([2]1959); M. Goshen-Gottstein, 'The Rise of the Tiberian Bible Text', *Studies and Texts of the Philip W. Lown Institute of Advanced Judaic Studies* I, ed. A. Altmann, (1963), pp. 79–122; G. E. Weil, *Élie Lévita, humaniste et massorète* (1965); for a review of the entire subject see H. Orlinsky, 'The Massoretic Text: A Critical Evaluation', Prolegomenon to the 1966 reprint of C. D. Ginsburg, *Introduction to the Massoretico-Critical Edition of the Hebrew Bible*; O. Eissfeldt, *Introduction*, pp. 678–93; A. Díez Macho, *Manuscritos hebreos y arameos de la Biblia* (1971); A. Dotan, 'Masorah', Enc. Jud. 16, cols. 1401–82; H. M. Orlinsky (ed.), *Masoretic Studies* I (1974); L. Diez Merino, *La biblia babilonica* (1975); E. J. Revell, *Biblical Texts with Palestinian Pointing and their Accents* (1977). For isolated remarks in the Mishnah see mPes. 9:2 (that there is a dot over the ה in רחקה Num. 9:10); mSot. 5:5 (that לא in Job 13:15 may mean 'to him' or 'not'). Jerome, *Quaest. Heb. in Genesim* comments on Gen. 19:33 (CCL lxxii, p. 24): 'Denique Hebraei, quod sequitur "Et nescivit quum dormisset cum eo et quum surrexisset ab eo" appungunt desuper quasi incredibile.' When R. Akiba, mAb. 3:13, asserts that מסרת is a 'fence around the Torah', he presumably refers to a careful transmission of the biblical text; see W. Bacher, *Terminologie I*, p. 108; L. Finkelstein, 'Maxim of *Anshe Keneset ha-Gedolah*', JBL 59 (1940), pp. 457–63 [*Pharisaism in the Making* (1972), pp. 161–7].

III. Halakhah and Haggadah

Bibliography

Zunz, L., *Die gottesdienstlichen Vorträge der Juden, historisch entwickelt* (1832, ²1892).

Frankel, Z., *Vorstudien zu der Septuaginta* (1841), pp. 162–203, especially pp. 179–91. *Über den Einfluss der palästinischen Exegese auf die alexandrinische Hermeneutik* (1851). *Über palästinische und alexandrinische Schriftforschung* (1854).

Geiger, A., *Urschrift und Übersetzungen der Bibel in ihrer Abhängigkeit von der inneren Entwickelung des Judenthums* (1857).

Siegfried, K., *Philo von Alexandria* (1875), pp. 142 ff., 283 ff. (interrelation between Palestinian and Alexandrian exegesis).

Bacher, W., *Die Agada der babylonischen Amoräer* (1878). *Die Agada der Tannaiten* I: *Von Hillel bis Akiba* (1884, ²1903); II: *Von Akibas Tod bis zum Abschluss der Mischna* (1890). *Die Agada der palästinensischen Amoräer* I: *Vom Abschluss der Mischna bis zum Tode Jochanans* (1892). II: *Die Schüler Jochanans* (1896). III: *Die letzten Amoräer des heiligen Landes* (1899). *Die Agada der Tannaiten und Amoräer*, Bibelstellenregister (1902). *Die exegetische Terminologie der jüdischen Traditionsliteratur* I–II (1899–1905). *Die Proömien der alten jüdischen Homilie* (1913). *Rabbanan. Die Gelehrten der Tradition, Beitrag zur Geschichte der anonymen Agada* (1914).

Mielziner, M., *Introduction to the Talmud* (1894, ⁴1968).

Ginzberg, L., *Die Haggada bei den Kirchenvätern und in der apokryphischen Litteratur* (1900). *The Legends of the Jews* I–VII (1909–14; ¹⁰1954).

Schwarz, A., *Die hermeneutische Antinomie in der talmudischen Litteratur* (1913). *Die hermeneutische Analogie in der talmudischen Litteratur* (1897). *Der hermeneutische Syllogismus in der talmudischen Litteratur* (1901). *Die hermeneutische Induktion in der talmudischen Litteratur* (1909). *Die hermeneutische Quantitätsrelation in der talmudischen Litteratur* (1916). *Der hermeneutische Kontext in der talmudischen Litteratur* (1921).

JE I, pp. 403–11 ('Allegorical Interpretation' by L. Ginzberg); IV, pp. 80–6 ('Church Fathers' by S. Krauss); VIII, pp. 548–50 ('Midrash' by S. Horovitz).

Bousset, W., *Die Religion des Judenthums im neutestamentlichen Zeitalter* (²1906), pp. 176–86; (³1926, ⁴1966), pp. 153–61.

Lauterbach, J. Z., 'Midrash and Mishnah, a study in the early history of the Halakah', JQR 5 (1915), pp. 503–27; 6 (1916), pp. 23–95, 303–23. *Rabbinic Essays* (1951).

Albeck, Ch., *Untersuchungen über die Redaktion der Mischna* (1923). *Untersuchungen über die halachischen Midraschim* (1927).

Moore, G. F., *Judaism* I (1927).

Kasher, M., *Ḥumash Torah Sheᵉlemah, A Talmudic-Midrashic Encyclopaedia of the Pentateuch* (1927–).

Waxman, M., *A History of Jewish Literature* I (1930).

Klausner, J., *Ha-Bait ha-Sheni bi-Gᵉdullatah* (1930), pp. 148–59.

Strack, H. L., *Introduction to the Talmud and Midrash* (1945).

Kaplan, J., *The Redaction of the Babylonian Talmud* (1933).

Rosenblatt, S., *The Interpretation of the Bible in the Mishna* (1935).

Belkin, S., *Philo and the Oral Law* (1939). *Alexandrian Halakah in the Apologetic Literature of the First Century C.E.* (1940)

Heinemann, I., *The Methods of the Aggadah* (1949) [in Hebrew].

Daube, D., 'Rabbinic Methods of Interpretation and Hellenistic Rhetoric', HUCA 22 (1949), pp. 239–64.

Neubauer, J. J., 'Halakah and Halakhic Hermeneutics', Syria II, nos. 128–30, pp. 49–80.

Seeligmann, I. L., 'Voraussetzungen der Midraschexegese', *Congress Volume 1953*, Suppl. to VT I (1953), pp. 150–81.

Doeve, J. V., *Jewish Hermeneutics in the Gospels and Acts* (1954).

Bloch, R., 'Midrash' Suppl. DB V (1955), cols. 1253–80.

Epstein, J. N., *Introduction to Tannaitic Literature* (1959) [Hebrew]. *Introduction to Amoraitic Literature*, ed. E. Z. Melamed (1962) [Hebrew].

Betz, O., *Offenbarung und Schriftforschung in der Qumransekte* (1960).

Vermes, G., *Scripture and Tradition in Judaism. Haggadic Studies* (1961, ²1973).

Wright, A. G., *The Literary Genre Midrash* (1961).

Loewe, R., 'The "Plain" Meaning of Scripture in Early Jewish Exegesis', *Papers of the Institute of Jewish Studies* I (1964), pp. 140–85.

Vermes, G., 'The Qumran Exegesis of Scripture in its Historical Setting', ALOUOS 6 (1969), pp. 85–97 [*PBJS*, pp. 37–49].

Lowy, S., 'Some Aspects of Normative and Sectarian Interpretation of the Scriptures' (*ibid.*, pp. 98–163).

Le Déaut, R., 'A propos d'une définition du midrash', Bibl. 50 (1969), pp. 395–413.

Vermes, G., 'Bible and Midrash: Early Old Testament Exegesis', *The Cambridge History of the Bible* I (1970), pp. 199–231, 592 [*PBJS*, pp. 59–91]

Neusner, J. (ed.), *The Formation of the Babylonian Talmud* (1970). *The Modern Study of the Mishnah* (1973).

Albeck, Ch., *Einführung in die Mischna* (1971).

Heinemann, J., *Sermons in the Talmudic Period* (1970) [in Hebrew].

Enc. Jud. 2, cols. 354–66 ('Aggadah' by M. D. Herr *et al.*); 7 cols. 1156–66 ('Halakhah' by L. Jacobs); 11, cols. 1567–14, 1521–3 ('Midrash' by M. D. Herr).

Heinemann, J., Noy, D. (ed.), *Studies in Aggadah and Folk-Literature*, Scrip. Hier. XXII (1971).

Neusner, J., *The Rabbinic Traditions about the Pharisees before* 70 I–III (1971).

Le Déaut, R., 'Un phénomène spontané de l'herméneutique juive ancienne: le "'targumisme"', Bibl. 52 (1971), pp. 505–25.

Falk, Z. W., *Introduction to Jewish Law of the Second Commonwealth* (1972).

Elon, M., *Jewish Law, History, Sources, Principles*: I. The History and Elements of Jewish Law; II. The Legal Sources of Jewish Laws; III. The Literary Sources of Jewish Law (1973) [in Hebrew].

Komlosh, Y., *The Bible in the Light of the Aramaic Translations* (1973) [in Hebrew].

Ménard, J-E. (ed.), *Exégèse biblique et judaïsme* (1973).

Heinemann, J., *Aggadah and its Development* (1974) [in Hebrew].

Vermes, G., *Post-Biblical Jewish Studies* (1975).

Urbach, E. E., 'Halakhah and History', *Jews, Greeks and Christians—Essays in Honor of W. D. Davies*, ed. R. Hamerton-Kelly and R. Scroggs (1976), pp. 112–28.

Mantel, H. D., 'The Development of the Oral Law during the Second Temple Period', *Society and Religion in the Second Temple Period*, ed. M. Avi-Yonah and Z. Baras, *World History of the Jewish People* VIII (1977), pp. 41–64, 325–37.

1. Halakhah

The theoretical work of the Torah scholars or sages was, as has been observed in the preceding section, essentially of two kinds: (1) to develop and establish the law; and (2) to interpret the historical and religious-doctrinal sections of the Bible. As a result of the first activity, a form of common law took shape side by side with the written Torah called in rabbinical language halakhah (הלכה, literally 'walking'). From the second, a rich variety of historical and ethical ideas came into being usually known collectively as haggadah or aggadah (הגדה or אגדה, literally 'teaching', see pp. 346–55 below).

The basic purpose of both halakhah and haggadah is to enquire into, and elucidate (in Hebrew דרש), the biblical text.[1] 'Enquiry' (מדרש) is here not taken to mean historical exegesis in the modern sense, but a search for new insight on the ground of the existing text. The question asked was not only what the text actually says, but what knowledge could be gained from it by means of logical inferences, the combination of one passage with others, allegorical exegesis, etc. The manner and method of this investigation was relatively more rigorous in the treatment of the legal texts of the Torah than in that of the narrative and doctrinal sections.

Halakhic midrash (that is, the exegetical treatment of legal texts) was concerned in the first instance only with the compass and consequences of the individual commandments. It was necessary to know the cases in practical life to which a precept under consideration was applicable, what its consequences would be, and in general, what was to be done to ensure that it was strictly and punctiliously observed in its entirety. The commandments were therefore divided and subdivided in finest casuistic detail, and the most comprehensive pre-

1. דרש occurs in the Mishnah in the following constructions: (1) 'to investigate or expound a passage or a section of Scripture' (mBer. 1:5; mPes. 10:4; mShek. 1:4; 5:1; mYom. 1:6; mMeg. 2:2; mSot. 5:1–5; 9:15; mSanh. 11:2); (2) with the preposition ב in the same meaning, 'to expound a passage' (mHag. 2:1); (3) 'to discover a teaching or an exposition by investigation'; e.g. את זו דרש מן (this he discovered from such and such a passage' (mYom. 8:9), or without מן (mYeb. 10:3; mHul. 5:5), or in the phrase זה מדרש דרש, 'so-and-so and so-and-so gave this explanation' (mShek. 6:6; mKet. 4:6). The noun formed from דרש is מדרש, 'investigation, explanation, elaboration (mShek. 6:6; mKet. 4:6; mNed. 4:3; mAb. 1:17); also in the expression בית מדרש see above, p. 334, n. 51. It appears already in 2 Chron. 13:22, 24:27; cf. also Ecclus 51:23; 1QS 6:24. On דרש, see W. Bacher, *Die exegetische Terminologie* I, pp. 25–7; II, 41–3; Strack, pp. 6–7, 239–40. On מדרש, see Bacher, *op. cit.* I, pp. 103–5; II, p. 107; S. Zeitlin, 'Midrash: A Historical Study', JQR 44 (1953), pp. 21–36; Renée Bloch, 'Écriture et tradition dans le Judaïsme. Aperçus sur l'origine du Midrash', Cahiers Sioniens 8 (1954), pp. 9–34; M. Gertner, 'Terms of Scriptural Interpretation', Bull. SOAS 25 (1962), pp. 1–27.

cautionary measures were devised to ensure that in their observance no accidental circumstance should occur which might be regarded as impairing their absolutely accurate fulfilment.

The halakhist's task was not, however, limited to an analysis of the text. Various difficulties needed to be solved, some arising from contradictions within the legal code itself, some from the incongruity of the demands of the Torah with the changed conditions of real life, and some deriving in particular from the incompleteness of the written law. To all such problems the Torah scholars had to seek an answer. It was their business to eliminate discrepancies by determining an authoritative interpretation; to point out, in cases where the observance of a commandment was impossible, difficult or inconvenient because of altered circumstances, how it was nevertheless possible to comply with its wording; and finally, especially in all those matters not directly regulated by the written law, to look for a fixed form when the need for it appeared. The last field was an especially inexhaustible source of legal activity. Again and again, questions arose to which the written law or the law prevailing until then supplied no answer, questions which therefore still required to be settled. Essentially, this could be done in two ways: by scholarly deduction from propositions already recognized, and by the establishment of a previously undefined tradition. Also, in so far as it could be formulated, the latter was decisive in itself.

Scholarly exegesis (midrash) was thus by no means the only source for the formation of the legal code. A considerable part of the law later in force has no connection with the Torah at all, but was originally merely custom and habit. Confronted with such and such a situation, one did so and so. Imperceptibly, however, habit developed into a law of habit, or common law. If anything in the legal sphere had been customary for so long that it could be said to have been so from time immemorial, it was common law. It was then not necessary to trace it back to the Torah; ancient custom was binding as such. And confirmation of this common law was also a duty and right of recognized Torah scholars.

From these two sources there arose with the passing of time, and side by side with the Torah, a large number of legal decisions with authority equal to that of the written law. They are all included in the collective concept of halakhah, i.e., common law. For once they had come into effect, the findings of scholarly enquiry were also common law, הלכה.[2] Accordingly, the law in force fell into two main categories:

2. The comprehensive concept of halakhah emerges from the following passages: mPea. 2:6; 4:1–2; mOrl. 3:9; mShab. 1:4; mHag. 1:8; mYeb. 8:3; mNed. 4:3; mEdu. 1:5; 8:7; mAb. 3:11, 18; 5:8; mKer. 3:9; mYad. 4:3. Cf. Bacher, *Die exegetische Terminologie* I, pp. 42–3; II, pp. 53; 6; I. H. Weiss, *Dōr Dōr Wedōreshaw* II (1924), ch. 7; L. Jacobs, Enc. Jud. 7, cols. 1156–66; M. Elon, *Jewish Law,*

the written Torah and halakhah,[3] which until towards the end of the period under discussion was in the main transmitted only orally. Within halakhah itself, however, there are various further categories: (1) individual halakhoth (traditional statutes) traced back expressly to Moses;[4] (2) the great corpus of halakhah pure and simple; (3) certain statutes designated as 'ordinances of the scribes' (**דברי סופרים**).[5] All three were legally binding. But their authority was graded according to the same order, those of the first type being the highest, and those of the third, relatively the lowest. For whereas **הלכה** in general was regarded as having been valid from time immemorial, people believed that the **דברי סופרים** were first introduced by the successors of Ezra.[6] There was in any case a clear awareness during the age of the Mishnah that many traditional statutes were either not grounded in the Torah at all or only slightly connected with it.[7] The common law was nevertheless quite as binding as the written Torah;[8] it was even laid down that to oppose the **דברי סופרים** is a graver offence than to oppose the statutes of the Torah[9] since the former are the authentic interpretation

---

pp. 143–5. 'Jewish customs', דת יהודית (mKet. 7:6), is analogous to דרך ארץ (mKid. 1:10), and is not to be confused with הלכה. The later concept of *minhag* designating a local or otherwise limited 'usus', belongs to the same category. Cf. JE s.v. 'Custom', IV, pp. 395–8; Enc. Jud. 12, cols. 4–26, s.v. 'Minhag'; M. Elon, *Jewish Law* II, pp. 713–25. On דרך ארץ, see Bacher, *Terminologie* I, p. 25, II, pp. 40–1. Enc. Jud. 5, col. 1551.

3. תורה or מקרא (Scripture) is distinguished from הלכה in e.g. mOrl. 3:9; mHag. 1:8; mNed. 4:3. Similarly מקרא from משנה (legal doctrine) in mKid. 1:10. On מקרא see Bacher, *Terminologie* I, pp. 117–21; II, pp. 119–20.

4. Such a הלכה למשה מסיני is mentioned in three Mishnah passages: mPea. 2:6; mEdu. 8:7; mYad. 4:3. Some 50–60 examples in all are to be found in rabbinical literature. See Moore, *Judaism* I, pp. 30, 256–8; III, nn. 19–21; Bacher, *Tradition und Tradenten*, pp. 33–46; Strack, p. 9. Enc. Jud. 7, cols. 1167.

5. mOrl. 3:9; mYeb. 2:4; 9:3; mSanh. 11:3; mPar. 11:4–6; mToh. 4:7, 11; mYad. 3:2; cf. also mKel. 13:7; mBez. 4:6.

6. A lesser authority attached to the 'ordinances of the scribes' than to halakhah: see mOrl. 3:9 (where it is quite unjustifiable to supplement הלכה with למשה מסיני). On the late date of the דברי סופרים, cf. especially mKel. 13:7; Bez. 4:6: דבר חדש חדשו סופרים.

7. Cf. in particular the remarkable passage mHag. 1:8; '(The statute concerning) release from vows is one which is as it were suspended in the air for there is nothing in Scripture to support it. The statutes concerning Sabbath, festival sacrifice and misappropriation (of sacred things by misuse) are like mountains which hang by a hair. For there are few Scripture texts concerning them and many הלכות. By contrast, the civil laws, and laws of purity, impurity and incest, rely entirely on Scripture. They form the essential content of the (written) Torah.'

8. Cf. especially mAb. 3:11; 5:8: 'The sword comes upon the world . . . because of those who teach the Torah not according to the halakhah.' The parallel expression in 3:11 is absent from the best manuscripts (cf. K. Marti–G. Beer, *'Abôt*, pp. 77–8, 191).

9. mSanh. 11:3: חומר בדברי סופרים מדברי תורה. Cf. also Z. W. Falk, *Introduction to Jewish Law*, pp. 10–11; M. Elon, *Jewish Law*, pp. 180, 194–207.

and completion of the latter and therefore the truly decisive authority.[10]

It is of the essence of halakhah that it can never be concluded and brought to a close. The two sources from which it derived are inexhaustible. Continuing scholarly exegesis (midrash) resulted in increasing numbers of new statutes; and as is normal, to these could be added new customs. Once these too had succeeded in becoming common law, they also became halakhah, the scope of which therefore extended indefinitely. But at each stage of its development distinction was made between what was already valid, and what was merely a conclusion arrived at by the rabbis by means of learned reasoning and argument: between הלכה and דין (judgement). Only the former was mandatory; in and of itself, the latter had not yet reached that stage.[11] When a majority of Torah scholars had decided in favour of it, this too would become binding, and from then on part of halakhah. For a majority of men distinguished for their learning constituted the final tribunal.[12] It was therefore an obligation to observe the דברי חכמים.[13] It goes without saying that this principle applied only to cases not already regulated by a valid halakhah. For where a halakhah existed, it was to be followed without question, even if ninety-nine should declare against it and only one for it.[14]

The majority principle also helped to overcome the great difficulty which arose from the parting of the schools of Hillel and Shammai (see below, pp. 365–6). As long as the differences between the two schools were not reconciled, the law-abiding Jew was perplexed to know which one he should support. Here too the majority finally decided, either that the school with the larger following outvoted the other,[15] or that

10. A similar attitude is manifest at Qumran, where any valid observance of the Torah depended on the acceptance of its interpretation by the sons of Zadok the priests: 'Whoever approaches the Council of the Community . . . shall undertake by a binding oath to return . . . to every commandment of the Law of Moses in accordance with all that has been revealed of it to the sons of Zadok' (1QS 5:7–9). 'The sons of Aaron all shall command in matters of justice and property, and every rule concerning the men of the Community shall be determined according to their word' (*ibid.* 9:7). Cf. G. Vermes, *DSSE*, p. 18; 'The Qumran Interpretation of Scripture', ALUOS 6 (1969), p. 87 [=*PBJS*, p. 39]; *DSS*, pp. 90, 95.

11. See especially mYeb. 8:3; mKer. 3:9. On דין, see Bacher, *Terminologie* I, pp. 21–3; II, pp. 37–8. הלכות and מדרש are distinguished from one another in mNed. 4:3 as two subjects of instruction.

12. mShab. 1:4 ff.; mEdu. 1:4–6; 5:7; mMikw. 4:1; mYad. 4:1, 3.

13. mNeg. 9:3; 11:7.

14. mPea. 4:1–2. Cf. however D. Daube, 'One against Ninety-Nine', Niv-Ha-Midrashia (1971), pp. 43–6, arguing that the passage applies to a disagreement between poor men and not between scholars.

15. Thus a few cases are mentioned in which the School of Shammai outvoted the School of Hillel, mShab. 1:4 ff.; mMikw. 4:1.

later scholars resolved the difference by their conclusive judgement.[16]

It might appear from the strictness with which in general the immutability of halakhah was proclaimed, that once valid, it could never be changed. But no rule is without its exception. In effect, not a few laws and customs were altered, either on purely theoretical grounds, or because of changed circumstances, or because an ancient custom led to inconvenience.[17]

However far halakhah departed from the written Torah, the fiction was nevertheless maintained that in essence it was an exposition and restatement of the Torah itself. Formally, the latter was still regarded as the supreme norm from which every legal precept must stem.[18] Halakhah was independently binding even without scriptural support. Its validity did not therefore depend on success in providing evidence from the Bible. Yet for all that, one of the rabbinic arts was to found halakhah on Scripture and thus endow its teachings with an authority to which the rabbis had no hereditary claim.[19] The demand for an adequate substantiation of newly propounded or disputed precepts was even more imperative. These could obtain recognition only by means of methodical midrash, i.e., by being shown to derive from scriptural precepts or other acknowledged rulings. The methods by which such a demonstration was furnished may seem, in part, somewhat strange. It was nevertheless a skill with its own rules and regulations. A distinction was made between the evidence proper (ראיה) and mere innuendo

16. As a rule the Mishnah, after mentioning the differences between the two schools, gives the sages' decision.

17. Such innovations were introduced by e.g. Hillel (mSheb. 10:3; mGit. 4:3; mArakh. 9:4); Rabban Gamaliel I (mR. Sh. 2:5; mGit. 4:2–3); Rabban Yoḥanan ben Zakkai (mSuk. 3:12; mR. Sh. 4:1, 3, 4; mSot. 9:9; mMen. 10:5); R. Akiba (mM.Sh. 5:8; mNaz. 6:1; mSanh. 3:4); generally: mSheb. 4:1; mHal. 4:7; mBik. 3:7; mShek. 7:5; mYom. 2:2; mKet. 5:3; mNed. 11:12; mGit. 5:6; mEdu. 7:2; mTeb.Y. 4:5. Cf. furthermore JE I, pp. 131–3; G. F. Moore, *Judaism* I, pp. 78 ff.; II, pp. 27–8; S. Lieberman, *Hellenism in Jewish Palestine* (1950), pp. 83–99; Ch. Albeck, *Untersuchungen über die Redaktion der Mischna* (1923), p. 5 ff.; Z. W. Falk, 'Binding and Loosing', JJS 25 (1974), pp. 92–100. For Philo's views on halakhah, see B. Ritter, *Philo und die Halacha* (1879); G. Alon, 'Studies in Philonic Halacha', Tarbiz (1933–4), pp. 28–36, 241–6; 6 (1934–5), pp. 30–7, 452–9; S. Belkin, *Philo on the Oral Law* (1939); *Alexandrian Halakah in the Apologetic Literature of the First Century C.E.* (1940); S. Daniel, 'La Halacha de Philon selon le premier livre des "Lois Spéciales" ', *Philon d'Alexandrie. Lyon 11–15 Septembre* 1966 (1967), pp. 221–40; G. Alon, *Jews, Judaism and the Classical World* (1977), pp. 81–137.

18. This holds true in spite of mHag. 1:8, mentioned in n. 7. See Moore, *Judaism* I, p. 99; Urbach, '*Halakhah u-Nebu'ah*', Tarbiz 18 (1946–7), pp. 1–27.

19. That this subsequent scholarly demonstration of the biblical origin of halakhah often drew on commandments of Scripture quite other than those from which the halakhic rulings actually arose is evident from e.g. the classic passage, mShab. 9:1–4. The biblical texts underlying the various tractates of the Mishnah are prefixed to each of them in the Albeck-Yalon edition.

(זכר).[20] For the evidence proper, Hillel drew up seven rules (מדות) which constitute a kind of rabbinical logic.[21] These are: (1) קל וחומר, lightness and heaviness, i.e., inference *a minori ad maius*;[22] (2) גזרה שוה inference *ex analogia*;[23] (3) בנין אב מכתוב אחד, a main proposition from one scriptural passage, viz., the derivation of a legal axiom from a single text; (4) בנין אב משני כתובים, a main proposition from two scriptural passages; (5) כלל ופרט ופרט וכלל, general and particular and particular and general, i.e., a more precise definition of the general by means of the particular, and of the particular by means of the general;[24] (6) כיוצא בו במקום אחר, according to what is similar in another text, i.e., a more precise definition of one passage with the help of another; (7) דבר הלמד מענינו, a matter to be understood from its subject.

These seven rules were later expanded to thirteen by specifying rule 5 in eight different ways and omitting rule 6. R. Ishmael is credited with having drawn up these thirteen *middoth*. Judaism values them so highly for the correct interpretation of the Torah that the so-called Baraita of R. Ishmael has become an integral part of the morning prayer.[25]

20. mShab. 8:7; 9:4; mSanh. 8:2. On ראיה see Bacher, *Die exegetische Terminologie* I, pp. 178–9; II, p. 201. On זכר *ibid.* I, pp. 51–5.

21. See tSanh. 7:11, ARNa 37 (ed. Schechter, p. 110), and the conclusion of the introduction to Sifra (M. Friedmann, *Sifra, die älteste Midrasch zu Leviticus* (1915), p. 27). Cf. H. Graetz, *Geschichte der Juden* III, p. 712; *idem.*, 'Hillel und seine sieben Interpretationsregeln', MGWJ (1851/51), pp. 156–62; Z. Frankel, *Über palästinische und alexandrinische Schriftforschung* (1854), pp. 15–17; Strack, pp. 93–4; see also the relevant articles in Bacher, *Terminologie* I and II; J. Z. Lauterbach, s.v. 'Talmudic Hermeneutics', JE XII, pp. 30–3; Moore, *Judaism* I, pp. 248–9. D. Daube, 'Rabbinic Method of Interpretation and Hellenistic Rhetoric', HUCA 22 (1949), pp. 239–64; S. Lieberman, *Hellenism in Jewish Palestine* (1950), pp. 53–4; J. W. Doeve, *Jewish Hermeneutics in the Synoptic Gospels and Acts* (1954), pp. 65–72; Neusner, *Pharisees* I, pp. 240–2; L. Jacobs, s.v. 'Hermeneutics', Enc. Jud. 8 cols. 366–72.

22. Cf. mBer. 9:5; mSheb. 7:2; mBez. 5:2; mYeb. 8:3; mNaz. 7:4; mSot. 6:3; mB.B. 9:7; mSanh. 6:5; mEdu. 6:2; mAb. 1:5; mZeb. 12:3; mHul. 2:7; 12:5; mBekh. 1:1; mKer. 3:7–10; mNeg. 12:5; mMakhsh. 6:8. See Bacher, *Terminologie* I, pp. 172–4; II, pp. 189–90 and the literature quoted in the preceding note.

23. E.g. mBez. 1:6: 'Dough-offering and gifts are presents to the priest, as also is the heave-offering. As they may not bring the latter to the priest on feast days, so may they not bring the former.' Another example, mArakh. 4:4. Both passages contain the expression גזרה שוה. See A. Schwarz, *Die hermeneutische Analogie in der talmudischen Litteratur* (1897); Bacher, *Terminologie* I, pp. 13–16; II, p. 27.

24. In the thirteen middoth of R. Ishmael (Sifra, ed. Friedmann, pp. 17–23), this figure is particularized in eight different ways, e.g. by the formula כלל ופרט וכלל, general and particular and general, i.e., a more precise definition of two general expressions by means of an intermediate particular one, as in Dt. 14:26, where 'all that your soul desires', the general expression used at the beginning and the end is limited by the words in between, 'oxen, sheep, wine, intoxicating drink'.

25. Cf. e.g. S. Singer, *The Authorised Daily Prayer Book* (1962), pp. 14–15. Attribution of the seven principles to Hillel and of the thirteen to Ishmael is in no

The subjects of the Torah scholars' legal research were essentially supplied by the Torah itself. A considerable proportion were precepts concerning prayers, sacrifices and religious practices in general. For the Torah characteristically considers the whole of life to be a cultic domain, and its prime purpose to proclaim how God is to be honoured: what sacrifices to offer, what festivals to celebrate, how to provide for the priesthood, which religious customs to observe. It was to this content of the Torah that the motive of the zealous scribal endeavours corresponded, namely a desire to ensure by means of a punctilious interpretation of the law that none of God's 'rights' should be injured in the slightest way, but that all of them should be conscientiously observed. Thus the scribes and rabbis developed primarily: (1) precepts relating to sacrifice, types of sacrifice, occasions and manner of sacrifice, besides everything associated with it—the entire sacrificial ritual that is to say; (2) precepts relating to the celebration of festivals, particularly the Sabbaths, but also the yearly feasts of Passover, Weeks, New Year, Tabernacles and the Day of Atonement; (3) precepts relating to dues to be handed over to the Temple and the priesthood, viz., first fruits, heave-offerings, tithes, the first-born, the half-shekel tribute, and relating to vows and voluntary offerings and everything connected with them such as redemption, valuation, misappropriation, etc.; (4) various other religious ordinances, of which by far the greater number have to do with cleanness and uncleanness. Legal decisions in respect of the latter constituted an inexhaustible opportunity for the exercise of rabbinic perspicacity.

However, these primarily religious issues by no means comprised the whole substance of the work carried out by the Torah scholars. As the law of Moses includes also the fundamentals of Israelite criminal and civil law, the demands of everyday life necessitated continuous changes in these matters too. They were of course not all elaborated equally. The laws most thoroughly developed were those of marriage, partly because the need for them was great, and perhaps partly also because marriage has always been closely connected with religion. The remaining spheres of civil law are not treated with quite the same thoroughness in the Mishnah (the tractates Baba Ḳamma, Baba Meẓi'a and Baba Bathra), and criminal law receives even less detailed attention in the tractates Sanhedrin and Makkoth, although both fields are considerably enriched in the Gemara of the two Talmuds. Constitutional law is almost completely neglected. The Torah in any case affords extremely small occasion for developing it, and in addition, an

---

way equivalent to proven authorship. In his surviving exegeses Hillel seems to restrict himself to *ḳol-wa-ḥomer* and *g^ezerah shawah*. Cf. Neusner, *Pharisees* I, p. 241. See also G. G. Porton, *The Traditions of Rabbi Ishmael* II (1977), p. 6.

independent approach to constitutional issues was in practice not required because all such matters were regulated by imperial legislation.[26]

2. Haggadah

Haggadic midrash, i.e., the elaboration of the historical and religious-ethical parts of the Bible, is very different from halakhic midrash. Whereas the latter pre-eminently develops and carries further the material contained in the text itself, haggadah actually supplements and enriches it. It modifies scripture in accordance with the requirements and opinions of a later age. The point of departure, here too, is the biblical text. And here too, we have an elaboration similar to that applied to legal passages: history is rewritten by combining different textual statements, or by completing one text with the aid of another, or by establishing a chronology, etc.; and ethical sections are rewritten by interpreting older teachings in the light of the doctrine of the prophets and their successors. But this more rigorous type of exegetical treatment is nevertheless outweighed by one that is much freer, dealing quite informally with the text and supplementing it with a wide variety of its own ingredients. The historical and moral 'teachings' thus arrived at are known as הגדות or אגדות.[27]

Historical midrash is illustrated very instructively by one of the

26. For details, see the survey of the contents of the Mishnah in § 3 (vol. I, pp. 71–4).

27. The word 'haggadah' or 'aggadah' is explained as story, lesson, communication, from הגיד, to tell, relate and as a 'class of Rabbinic literature which explains the Bible homiletically, homiletics'; cf. Jastrow, *Dictionary*, s.v. אגדה and הגדה; J. Derenbourg, 'Haggada et légende', REJ 9 (1884), pp. 301–4; W. Bacher, 'The Origin of the word Haggada (Agada)', JQR 4 (1892), pp. 406–29; *Die Agada der Tannaiten* I², pp. 451–75; *Die exegetische Terminologie* I, pp. 30–7; II, p. 44. Bacher argues as follows: In Mekhilta and Sifre הגיד is used as a synonym for לִמֵּד. מגיד הכתוב, the passage of Scripture teaches, or usually simply מגיד, it teaches (or, it points out) serves to introduce an inference from a biblical text, both in halakhic and in non-halakhic discussions. In Sifra, on the other hand, מגיד is no longer used, but is replaced by the synonymous מלמד. Hence the former belongs to an older language usage still preserved in the school of Ishmael but abandoned by that of Akiba. On the other hand, the noun הגדה is now limited to the non-halakhic explanations. Accordingly, haggadah is a non-halakhic 'teaching' drawn from a passage of Scripture. In Ned. 4:3, מדרש (exegesis), הלכות (legal teachings) and אגדות (non-legal teachings) are mentioned side by side; Midrash underlies the other two. Cf. on these three concepts, Bacher, REJ 38 (1899), pp. 211–19=*Die Agada der Tannaiten* I², pp. 475–89. On several details of medieval linguistic usage, see Bacher 'Derasch et Haggada', REJ 23 (1891), pp. 311–13. For a historical assessment, see G. Vermes, *Scripture and Tradition in Judaism, Haggadic Studies* (1961, ²1973); 'Bible and Midrash', CHB I, pp. 199–231[=*PBJS*, pp. 59–91³; J. Heineman, *Aggadah and its Development* (1974) [Hebrew].

canonical writings of the Old Testament, the Book of Chronicles. A comparison of its narrative with parallel portions of the older historical books (Samuel and Kings) shows that the Chronicler has added a whole category of information to the history of the Jewish kings of which the older sources contain next to nothing, such as the stories of the many merits acquired, not only by David but by a number of other pious kings, for maintaining and giving more sumptuous shape to the priestly cult. The Chronicler's principal concern is to relate how conscientiously these kings cared for the institutions of worship. It may admittedly be argued that the absence of such reports from Samuel and Kings is not evidence of their inauthenticity and that the Chronicler merely took them from other sources. But the odd feature here is that the institutions themselves, which these kings tended with such distinction, also all belong to the post-exilic period, as may in the main be definitely attested (see § 24). It would therefore appear that the Chronicler rewrote the earlier history from a certain point of view which seemed to him essential; for him, divine worship was central, consequently the theocratic kings must also have been noted for their interest in it. He thereby simultaneously pursued the practical aim of demonstrating the just claim and high worth of those institutions by pointing out how the most illustrious kings had attended to them. The idea that this was a falsification of history presumably never occurred to him. In adjusting it to the needs of his time, he thought he was improving it. His work, or rather the larger work of which Chronicles is probably no more than an excerpt, is therefore quite properly speaking an historical midrash, and is indeed explicitly designated as such (מדרש) by its final editor (2 Chron. 13:22; 24:27).[28]

The method described here of rewriting sacred history continued to flourish in later ages and became more and more colourful. The higher its prestige and importance in the minds of the people, the more exhaustively did the Torah scholars work at it, fixing its details with increasing precision, elaborating it copiously and investing the whole with glory and honour. The stories of the patriarchs and of Moses, in particular, were subjected to rich adornment. The Hellenized Jews were especially active in this kind of rewriting of history. Indeed, one might also suspect that haggadah originated with them were it not for Chronicles, but also for the fact that the whole method of

28. Cf. J. Wellhausen, *Geschichte Israels* I, pp. 236–7. Without reference to the term, but concluding that Chronicles is a homiletical treatment of earlier sources: G. von Rad, 'The Levitical Sermon in I and II Chronicles', in *The Problem of the Hexateuch and Other Essays* (1966). For the argument that Chronicles uses a homiletical source, the 'Midrash of the Kings', cf. O. Eissfeldt, *Introduction*, pp. 532–4.

this type of midrash exactly reflects the spirit of rabbinical Judaism.

The literature retaining relics of haggadic historiography is relatively rich and varied. They appear in the works of the Hellenists Demetrius, Eupolemus, Artapanus (see vol. III, § 33); in Philo and Josephus;[29] in the so-called apocalypses; and in pseudepigraphic literature[30] in general. Much is preserved also in the Qumran texts,[31] in the Targums and in the Talmud, but especially in the midrashim proper, devoted *ex professo* to the exegetical development of biblical texts (cf. vol. I, § 3, pp. 90–9). The most ancient of these are the so-called Book of Jubilees and the Qumran Genesis Apocryphon, both of which may serve as classic models of the haggadic treatment of biblical history. Jubilees reproduces the entire text of the canonical book of Genesis (in the 1 Q apGen manuscript only Gen. 5–15 survives) in such a way that the historical details are not only fixed chronologically but are also enriched in regard to their content and remodelled to suit contemporaneous taste.

The ensuing few examples are given in illustration of this branch of exegetical activity.

The story of the creation is expanded as follows.

> 'Ten things were created on the eve of the Sabbath at dusk: the mouth of the earth (for Korah and his band); the mouth of the well (of Miriam); the mouth of the she-ass (of Balaam); the rainbow; the manna in the wilderness; the rod (of Moses); the *shamir* (a worm which splits stones); the alphabet; the writing-tool; the stone tablets. Some say also the evil spirits, the grave of Moses and the ram of our father Abraham; still others say, the first tongs for the making of future tongs.'[32]

29. On haggadic material in Josephus, see S. Rappaport, *Agada und Exegese bei Flavius Josephus* (1930) and the literature indicated in vol. I, p. 62. On Philo's contacts with Palestinian midrash, see C. Siegfried, *Philo von Alexandria als Ausleger des Alten Testaments* (1875), pp. 142–59; E. Stein, *Philo und der Midrasch* (1931); S. Belkin, 'Philo and the Midrashic Tradition of Palestine', *Horeb* (1958), pp. 1–60 [Hebrew]; S. Sandmel, *Philo's Place in Judaism: A Study of the Conception of Abraham in Jewish Literature* (1971), and § 34 in vol. III.

30. Cf. L. Ginzberg, *The Legends of the Jews* I–VII ([10]1954). See also R. H. Charles, *The Apocrypha and Pseudepigrapha of the Old Testament in English* I–II (1912–13, repr. 1963).

31. Cf. O. Betz, *Offenbarung und Schriftforschung in der Qumransekte* (1960); G. Vermes, *Scripture and Tradition in Judaism* (1961, [2]1973); 'The Qumran Interpretation of Scripture in its Historical Setting', ALUOS 6 (1969), pp. 84–97 [=*PBJS*, pp. 37–49]; S. Lowy, 'Some Aspects of Normative and Sectarian Interpretation of the Scriptures', *ibid.*, pp. 98–163.

32. mAb. 5:6. Cf. Ps.-Jon.Tg. on Num. 22:28 (manna, the well, Moses' staff, the *shamir*, the rainbow, the clouds of glory, the mouth of the earth, the writing of the tables of the covenant, the evil spirits and the mouth of the speaking she-ass). For a detailed comparison of all the recensions, see W. S. Towner, *The Rabbinic*

On the life of Adam, numerous legends came into being, known chiefly from their deposits and further development in Christian and late Jewish literature.[33]

Enoch, who was miraculously conveyed to God in heaven, seemed especially well qualified to reveal heavenly mysteries to men. A book containing such revelations was therefore ascribed to him towards the end of the period of the Second Temple (cf. vol. III, § 32). Later legend praises his piety and describes his ascension.[34] The Hellenist Eupolemus refers to him as the inventor of astrology.[35]

Abraham, the progenitor of Israel, was of course of very special interest for this kind of historical treatment. Hellenized and Palestinian Jews exerted themselves equally on his behalf. Probably as early as the third century B.C., a Jewish Hellenist devoted to him a book ascribed to Hecataeus.[36] According to Artapanus, Abraham instructed King Pharethothes of Egypt in astrology.[37] For rabbinic Judaism, he was a model of Pharisaic piety. He fulfilled the whole of the Torah even before it was given.[38] He withstood, it was reckoned, ten temptations.[39]

'*Enumeration of Scriptural Examples*' (1973), pp. 65–71. For the seven things antedating the creation of the world, viz. the Torah, repentance, the Garden of Eden, Gehenna, the Throne of Glory, the Temple and the name of the Messiah, cf. bPes. 54a.

33. L. S. Wells in R. H. Charles, *The Apocrypha and Pseudepigrapha of the OT in English* II (1913, repr. 1963), pp. 123 ff. K. Kohler, s.v. 'Adam' in JE I, pp. 174–7; L. Ginzberg, s.v. 'Adam, Book of', *ibid.* pp. 179 ff. L. Ginzberg, *The Legends of the Jews* I, pp. 86–107; V, pp. 114–35; A. Altmann, 'Gnostic Background of the Rabbinic Adam Legend', JQR 35 (1945), pp. 371–91; O. Eissfeldt, *Introduction*, pp. 636–7; A.-M. Denis, *Introduction aux pseudépigraphes grecs de l'Ancien Testament* (1970), pp. 3–14; M. E. Stone and J. Licht, Enc. Jud. 2, cols. 245–7. See also § 32 in vol. III.

34. For the place of Enoch in haggadic literature, see L. Ginzberg, *Legends* I, pp. 127–40; the Book of Enoch will be discussed in detail in the light of the Aramaic fragments from Qumran in § 32 in vol. III.

35. Eusebius *Praep. ev.* ix 17. For an up-to-date treatment of the literary problems of the Enoch cycle, see J. T. Milik, 'Problèmes de la littérature hénochique à la lumière des fragments araméens de Qumran', HThR 64 (1971), pp. 333–78 and especially *The Books of Enoch: Aramaic Fragments of Qumran Cave 4* (1976).

36. Josephus, *Ant.* i 7, 2 (159); Clement of Alexandria, *Strom.* v 14, 113. Cf. Stern, GLAJJ I, p. 22.

37. Eusebius *Praep. ev.* ix 18. On Abraham as an astrologer, cf. also Josephus, *Ant.* i 7, 1 (155–6); G. Vermes, *Scripture and Tradition*, pp. 76–83.

38. Apoc. Baruch, ch. 57:1–2; mKid. 4:14. Cf. also mNed. 3:11.

39. mAb. 5:3; Jub. 19:8; ARNa ch. 33 (ed. Schechter, pp. 94–5); PRE 26–31; Tg. Ps.-Jon. Gen. 22:1; B. Beer, *Lebensgemälde biblischer Personen nach Auffassung der jüdischen Sage*, pp. 78, 190–2; R. H. Charles, *The Book of Jubilees* (1902), p. 121; L. Ginzberg, *Die Haggada bei den Kirchenvätern*, p. 117–18; *Legends* V, p. 253, n. 253; mAb. 5:3; C. Taylor, *Sayings of the Jewish Fathers*, p. 94; Marti-Beer, *'Abot*, pp. 119–21; Moore, *Judaism* I, p. 276, III, n. 46.

Because of his righteousness, he received the reward of all the preceding ten generations, which they had lost by their sin.[40]

The greatest lustre of all was attached to the law-giver Moses and his time. In their works intended for Gentile readers, the Hellenists depict him as the father of all science and culture. According to Eupolemus, Moses was the inventor of the alphabet, which passed from him to the Phoenicians and from them to the Greeks. According to Artapanus, the Egyptians owed their whole civilization to Moses.[41] It is therefore somewhat of an understatement when the author of Acts says merely that he was learned in all the wisdom of the Egyptians, though even this exceeds the Old Testament account (Act. 7:22). The history of his life and work is embellished in all sorts of ways, as may be seen in Philo and Josephus.[42] The Egyptian sorcerers vanquished by Moses and Aaron are named: Jannes and Jambres (2 Tim. 3:8).[43] During the travels of the Israelites through the wilderness they were not miraculously provided with water from a rock once only; a water-giving rock accompanied them throughout their entire journey (1 Cor. 10:4).[44] The law was not given to Moses by God himself, but was conveyed to him by his angels

40. mAb. 5:2. See in general B. Beer, *Leben Abrahams nach Auffassung der jüdischen Sage* (1859); K. Kohler, s.v. 'Abraham', JE I, pp. 85–7; L. Ginzberg, JE I, pp. 91 ff.; *The Legends of the Jews* I, pp. 209 ff., 299–306; V, pp. 217, 229–30, 266–7; G. Vermes, *Scripture and Tradition in Judaism*, pp. 67–95; M. Delcor, *The Testament of Abraham* (1973). For the 'binding of Isaac', see Vermes, *Scripture and Tradition*, pp. 193–218; R. Le Déaut, *La nuit pascale* (1963), pp. 122–200; S. Spiegel, *The Last Trial* (1969).

41. Eupolemus: Eusebius, *Praep. ev.* ix 26, 1 = Clement of Alexandria, *Strom.* i 23, 153. Cf. B. Z. Wacholder, *Eupolemus. A Study of Judaeo-Greek Literature* (1974), pp. 71–96. Artapanus: Eusebius, *Praep. ev.*, ix 29. Cf. G. Vermes, 'La figure de Moïse au tournant des deux Testaments', in H. Cazelles *et al.*, *Moïse l'homme de l'Alliance* (1955), pp. 68–9.

42. Philo, *Vita Mosis*; Josephus, *Ant.* ii–iv. Cf. in general B. Beer, *Leben Moses nach Auffassung der jüdischen Sage* (1863); W. Z. Lauterbach, s.v. 'Moses', JE IX, pp. 46–54; J. Jeremias, TDNT IV, pp. 852 ff.; H. J. Schoeps, *Theologie und Geschichte des Judenchristentums* (1949), pp. 87 ff.; B. Botte, G. Vermes and Renée Bloch, *Moïse l'homme de l'Alliance* (1955), pp. 55–167; D. Daube, *The New Testament and Rabbinic Judaism* (1956), pp. 5–12; W. A. Meeks, *The Prophet-King* (1967), pp. 100–46. On Moses in the murals at Dura-Europos, cf. M. Rostovtzeff, *Dura-Europos and its Art* (1938), ch. iii; C. H. Kraeling, *The Excavations at Dura-Europos. Final Report* VIII, 1: *The Synagogue* (1956), especially pp. 349–56. Cf. also Wacholder in n. 41 and J. G. Gager, *Moses in Greco-Roman Paganism* (1972); T. Rajak, 'Moses in Ethiopia: Legend and Literature', JJS 29 (1978), pp. 111–23.

43. Cf. R. Bloch, *art. cit.*, *Moïse l'homme de l'Alliance*, p. 105, n. 21. For 'Jannes (יחנה) and his brother' in CD 5: 19–20, see C. Rabin, *The Zadokite Documents* (1954), p. 21.

44. See Ps.-Philo, *LAB* 10:7; cf. G. Vermes, *art. cit.*, *Moïse l'homme de l'Alliance*, p. 89; M. R. James, *The Biblical Antiquities of Philo*, Proleg. by H. Feldman (1971), pp. xciv, 105–6; C. Perrot et P.-M. Bogeart, *Pseudo-Philon: Les Antiquités bibliques* II (1976), p. 110.

(Act. 7:53; Gal. 3:19; Heb. 21:2).[45] It was part of the perfection of his revelation that it was recorded in seventy different languages on stones erected on Mount Ebal (Deut. 28:2 ff.).[46] Since the two unlucky dates in Israel's history were 17 Tammuz and 9 Ab, the misfortunes of the Mosaic age must also occur on those two days: on 17 Tammuz the stone tablets of the law were broken, and on 9 Ab it was decreed that the generation of Moses was not to enter into the land of Canaan.[47] The marvellous circumstances associated with Moses' death (Deut. 34) also afforded abundant material for the formation of legends.[48] The struggle between the archangel Michael and Satan for his body is mentioned in the New Testament (Jude 9).

The history of the post-Mosaic era is given the same midrashic treatment as Israel's earlier history. To take a few examples from the

45. Cf. Str.-B. on Gal. 3:19; G. Vermes, 'The Decalogue and the Minim', *In Memoriam Paul Kahle* (1968), p. 239 [=*PBJS*, pp. 169–77]. On the ἄγγελοι responsible for the transmission of 'the holiest of our laws' in Josephus, *Ant.* xv 5, 3 (136) interpreted either as angels or as prophets (or priests), cf. R. Marcus, *Josephus* (Loeb) VIII, p. 66, n. a.

46. mSot. 7:5, with reference to Dt. 27:8: באר היטיב, engraving them clearly (therefore intelligibly). The 70 languages correspond to the 70 nations assumed from Gen. 10; see Tg.Ps.-Jon. on Gen. 11:7–8; Dt. 32:8. PRE 24; S. Krauss, 'Die Zahl der biblischen Völkerschaften', ZAW (1899), pp. 1–14; *ibid.* (1900), pp. 38–43 and (1906), pp. 33–48. Cf. also S. Krauss, 'Die biblische Völkertafel im Talmud, Midrasch und Targum', MGWJ 39 (1895), pp. 1–11, 49–63; Moore, *Judaism* I, p. 278, III, n. 49; Enc. Jud. 12, cols. 882–6. An enumeration of the 70 or 72 nations and languages of the world based on Gen. 10 may be found in various Christian chronicles (see A. von Gutschmid, *Kleine Schriften* V (1894), pp. 240–73, 585–717); among others in the chronicle of Hippolytus, for the *Διαμερισμὸς τῆς γῆς* treated by A. v. Gutschmid belongs here, see A. Bauer, *Die Chronik des Hippolytus* (1905), pp. 100–3, 136–40; cf. Hippolytus, *Refutatio* x 30: *ἦσαν δὲ οὗτοι οβ' ἔθνη ὧν καὶ τὰ ὀνόματα ἐκτεθείμεθα ἐν ἑτέραις βίβλοις*. On the various lists, see also Bauer, *loc. cit.*; Moore, *Judaism* I, pp. 227–8; III, n. 2. The appointment of 70 angels in the Book of Enoch as 'shepherds' of the world is based on this assumption concerning the 70 Gentile nations (see vol. III, § 32). On the 70 languages, see also mShek. 5:1 (Mordecai understand 70 languages); *Clementine Homilies* 18, 4: *περιγράψας γλώσσαις ἑβδομήκοντα*, *Clementine Recognitions* ii 42: 'in septuaginta et duas partes divisit totius terrae nationes'. Epiphanius, *Haer.* i 5: *τὰς γλώττας . . . ἀπὸ μιᾶς εἰς ἑβδομήκοντα δύο διένειμεν*. Augustine, *Civ. Dei* xvi 9: 'per septuaginta duas gentes et totidem linguas'. On the number 70 in general: cf. M. Steinschneider, ZDMG 4 (1850), pp. 145–70; 57 (1903), pp. 474–507. On the 70 angels, Moore, *Judaism* II, p. 300. On a relevant Qumran fragment, see Vermes, *DSS*, pp. 204–5.

47. mTaan 4:6; Ps.-Philo (*LAB* 19:7) places the destruction of the Temple on the 17th day of the 4th month (Tammuz), the day Moses broke the tables of the Covenant. Cf. M. R. James, *op. cit.*, pp. 29–31; M. Wadsworth, 'A New Pseudo-Philo', JJS 29 (1978), pp. 187–92.

48. Cf. already Josephus, *Ant.* iv 8, 48 (320–26); cf. Ginzberg, *Legends* III, pp. 448–81; VI, pp. 152–168; R. Bloch, *Moïse l'homme de l'Alliance*, pp. 127–38; M. Wadsworth, 'The Death of Moses and the Riddle of the End of Time in Pseudo-Philo', JJS 28 (1977), pp. 12–19.

New Testament, in the list of David's ancestors in Chronicles and Ruth a certain Salma or Salmon appears, the father of Boaz (1 Chron. 2:11; Ruth 4:20–1). Historical midrash divulges that this Salmon was the husband of Rahab (Mt. 1:5).[49] The drought and famine at the time of Elijah (1 Kings 17) lasted, according to historical midrash, for three and a half years, i.e., half a week of years (Lk. 4:25; Jas. 5:17).[50] Among the martyrs of the old covenant, the author of Hebrews mentions such as were sawn asunder (Heb. 11:37). He means by this Isaiah, of whom Jewish legends make the same report.[51]

As in the case of biblical history, so also the reworking of the moral-doctrinal content of Scripture is of two kinds; it is in part a real reworking of the text as it stands by means of combination, deduction, etc., and in part a free supplementation of the scriptural account with products of the creative imagination.

Each element encroaches imperceptibly on the other. Quite a number of the religious ideas and concepts of later ages sprang from subjecting a biblical passage to an 'enquiry', i.e., from reflection on the written word, from learned reasoning and combinations made on the basis of the text itself. But the imagination was an even richer source of new developments. And whatever was won by one method merged with what was gained by the other. The free creations of phantasy linked up with the results of learned enquiry; in fact, consciously or unconsciously, the former usually followed the same course, and the same direction, as the latter. And once they were firmly established, they were in turn methodically traced back to Scripture by midrash.

This investigative and continuously creative theological activity, extending over the whole field of religion and ethics, gave to the religious ideas of Israel in the inter-Testamental era a stamp of imagination on the one hand and of scholasticism on the other.

49. According to another midrash (bMeg. 14b) Rahab was the wife of Joshua.

50. On Elijah legends generally, cf. L. Ginzberg, *Eine unbekannte jüdische Sekte* (1922), 303 ff. [E.T. *An Unknown Jewish Sect* (1976), pp. 239–56]; R. B. Y. Scott, 'The Expectation of Elijah', The Canadian Journal of Religious Thought 3 (1962), pp. 490–502; Moore, *Judaism* II, pp. 357 ff.; J. Jeremias, TDNT on Elijah (but cf. Giblet, 'Le Messianisme prophétique', *L'Attente du Messie*, p. 112); W. D. Davies, *The Setting of the Sermon on the Mount* (1964), pp. 158 ff.

51. Martyrdom of Isaiah 5 (Charles, *Apocrypha and Pseudepigrapha* II, p. 162); bYeb. 49b; Ginzberg, *Legends* IV, p. 279; VI, pp. 374–5; Justin, *Dial. c. Trypho*, c. 120; Tertullian, *De patientia*, c. 14, *Scorpiace*, c. 8; Hippolytus, *De Christo et Antichristo*, c. 30; Origen, *Epist. ad African.*, c. 9; *Comment. in Matth.* 13:57 and 23:37 (ed. Lommatzsch III, p. 49, IV, pp. 238–9); Commodianus, *Carmen apologeticum*, ll. 509–10 (ed. Ludwig); Priscillianus iii, 60, ed. Schepss, p. 47; Jerome, *Comment. in Isaiam* 57 fin. For Jeremiah, see A. A. Wieder, 'Josiah and Jeremiah: Their Relationship according to Aggadic Sources', *Texts and Responses. Studies presented to N. N. Glatzer*, ed. M. A. Fishbane and P. R. Flohr (1975), pp. 60–72.

The eschatological and apocalyptic trend, nourished by a pessimism arising from successive political crises, from the Maccabees to Bar Kokhba, inevitably moved towards the transcendental in time and space: the future age and the heavenly world. The apocalyptic mind considered this world and the present aeon as having come almost to the brink of extinction and sought to base its hopes and expectations on the new reality of a universe brought into being by means of a final divine intervention. In their interpretation of prophetic sayings, the scriptural exegetes outlined Israel's salvation in a world to come and determined in advance the conditions and circumstances in which it would be realized. But they also concerned themselves with the heavenly world itself and speculated inexhaustibly on the nature and attributes of God and his angels. Philosophical problems were discussed too: e.g., the notions of revelation, divine transcendence, good and evil, etc.

Theosophical thinking was prompted by two sections of the Bible in particular: the story of the creation (מעשה בראשית) and the chariot of Ezekiel (מעשה מרכבה). The interpretation of these two sections entailed dealing with those profounder divine mysteries believed appropriate only to initiates.

> 'The story of the creation may not be expounded before two, and the Chariot not even before one, unless he be a scholar and able to understand by his own discernment.'[52]

These carefully guarded interpretations of the story of creation and of the chariot foreshadow the fully developed theosophic mysticism and esotericism of medieval Kabbalah.[53]

Whilst the exposition and expansion of the law was relatively strictly controlled, much more freedom was permitted in the field of religious speculation. Rules and methods were elastic. In particular, by comparison with the treatment of legal matters one element above all was missing: the principle of a binding tradition. The haggadist was allowed to give free rein to his imagination as long as he remained within the bounds of Judaism. A certain tradition developed here too,

52. mHag. 2:1. Cf. also mMeg. 4:10. Cf. G. Scholem, *Major Trends of Jewish Mysticism* (1955). pp. 40–3; *Kabbalah* (1974), pp. 8–14, 373–6. Jerome, *Prolog. Commentarii in Ezech.*: 'aggrediar Ezechiel prophetam, cuius difficultatem Hebraeorum probat traditio. Nam nisi quis apud eos aetatem sacerdotalis ministerii, id est tricesimum annum impleverit, nec principia Geneseos, nec Canticum Canticorum, nec huius voluminis exordium et finem legere permittitur'. *Idem, Epist.* 53 *ad Paulinum* 8: 'tertius (scil. Ezechiel) principia et finem tantis habet obscuritatibus involuta, ut apud Hebraeos istae partes cum exordio Geneseos ante annos triginta non legantur'.

53. Cf. G. Scholem, *Major Trends*, pp. 40–79; *The Kabbalah and its Symbolism* (1965); s.v. 'Kabbalah', Enc. Jud. 10, cols. 489–653; *Kabbalah* (1974).

of course, but adherence to it was not compulsory.[54] Religious thought was relatively free, whereas behaviour was strictly disciplined. But in the absence of an authoritative tradition, rules can only be spoken of in a loose sense. Thirty-two such *middoth* or hermeneutical principles are ascribed to R. Eliezer son of R. Yose the Galilean.[55] Later Jewish tradition found that Scripture has four meanings indicated by the word פרדס, paradise; (1) פשט, the simple or literal meaning; (2) רמז (allusion), the typical or allegoric meaning; (3) דרש (research), the meaning deduced from research; (4) סוד (mystery), the theosophic meaning.[56]

Midrashic Bible exegesis found its way into the New Testament and ancient Christian literature.[57] With Scripture itself, its particular inter-

54. On haggadic tradition, see G. Vermes, *Scripture and Tradition in Judaism* (1961, ²1973); 'Bible and Midrash', CHB I (1970), pp. 199–231 [=*PBJS*, pp. 59–91]; J. Heinemann, *Aggadah and its Development* (1974) [in Hebrew, containing a full discussion of the history of haggadah from the inter-Testamental era to Pirḳe de-Rabbi Eliezer].

55. See Bacher, *Tannaiten* I, pp. 365–6; II, pp. 293 ff.; JE II, pp. 520–1; Strack, pp. 95–8; H. G. Enelow, *The Mishnah of R. Eliezer, or the Midrash of the Thirty-two Hermeneutic Rules* (1933).

56. The initial letters of these four terms yield the word פרדס. Cf. Bacher, 'L'exégèse biblique dans le Zohar', REJ 22 (1891), pp. 33–46, 219–29; 'Das Merkwort פרדס in der jüdischen Bibelexegese', ZAW 13 (1893), pp. 294–305. Bacher shows that the Zohar (thirteenth century) was the first to point to this four-fold meaning. There is, admittedly, a Talmudic legend to the effect that four sages entered 'Paradise', and only one of them, R. Akiba, came out uninjured (tHag. 2:3, yHag. 77b; bHag. 14b). But 'Paradise', i.e. the place of heavenly mysteries, does not here allude to the fourfold exegesis but to theosophic and cosmogonic speculations deriving from Gen. 1 and Ezek. 1. On the four exegetical notions, see the relevant articles in Bacher, *Terminologie* I and II and E. E. Urbach, 'The Tradition of Merkabah Mysticism in the Tannaitic Period', *Studies in Mysticism and Religion* [Scholem Festschrift] (1967), Hebrew Section, pp. 1–28. On the 4 sages in Paradise, cf. Bacher, *Tannaiten* I, pp. 332–5; A. Néher, 'Le voyage mystique des quatre', RHR 140 (1951), pp. 59–82; G. Scholem, *Jewish Gnosticism, Merkabah Mysticism, and Talmudic Tradition* (1965), pp. 14–19; H. A. Fischel, *Rabbinic Literature and Greco-Roman Philosophy* (1973), pp. 4–34.

57. G. Vermes, *Scripture and Tradition in Judaism* (1961, ²1973), especially pp. 178–227; 'The Qumran Interpretation of Scripture in its Historical Setting', ALUOS 6 (1969), pp. 85–97; 'Bible and Midrash', CHB 1 (1970), pp. 199–231 [=*PBJS*, pp. 37–49; 59–91]; R. Le Déaut, *La nuit pascale* (1963); M. McNamara, *The New Testament and the Palestinian Targum to the Pentateuch* (1966); *Targum and Testament* (1972); B. J. Malina, *The Palestinian Manna Tradition* (1968); J. Luzarraga, *Las tradiciones de la nube en la Biblia y en el judaismo primitivo* (1973); J.-E. Ménard (ed.), *Exégèse biblique et judaïsme* (1973). On the allegorical exposition of Scripture by Philo, see E. Stein, 'Allegorische Exegese des Philo aus Alexandria', ZAW 51 (1929), pp. 1–61; G. Alon, 'Studies in the Halakah of Philo' [Hebr.], Tarbiz, cf. n. 17 above; *Jews, Judaism and the Classical World*, cf. *ibid.* D. Daube, 'Alexandrian Methods of Interpretation and the Rabbis', *Festschrift H. Lewald* (1953), pp. 27–44; R. J. Z. Werblowsky, 'Philo and Zohar', JJS 10 (1959), pp. 25–44, 113–35; I. Christiansen, *Die Technik der allegorischen Auslegungswissenschaft bei Philon von Alexandrien* (1969); R. Hamerton-Kelly, 'Some Techniques of Composition in Philo's Allegorical Commentary with Special

pretations were taken over by Christianity from Judaism. Indeed, many a formulation of New Testament theology is dependent on a Christian adaptation of a Jewish exegetical tradition.

Reference to *De Agricultura*. Study in the Hellenistic Midrash', *Jews, Greeks and Christians* (W. D. Davies Festschrift), ed. R. Hamerton-Kelly and R. Scroggs (1976), pp. 45–56. For a mystical treatment of numbers, see mUkz. 3:12, where the assertion that God will give 310 words to every righteous man as his inheritance is proved by Prov. 8:21, להנחיל אהבי יש, for יש has as its numerical value 310. Among early patristic writers, the author of the *Letter of Barnabas* (ch. 9) proves from Abraham's 318 servants that the Patriarch had already seen the cross of Jesus in spirit, for the number 18 = *IH* = the name Jesus and the number 300 = *T* = the cross. Numerous similar examples are indicated by Bacher in *Tannaiten* I–II, and *Paläst. Amoräer* I–III, Register, s.v. 'Wortdeutung', and *Die exegetische Terminologie* I, pp. 125–8 (s.v. נוטריקון) and II, pp. 27–8 (s.v. גמטריא). Cf. JE V, pp. 589–92 (s.v. 'Gematria') and IX, pp. 339–40 (s.v. 'Notarikon'); Enc. Jud. 7, cols. 369–74 (s.v. 'Gematria') and 12, cols. 1231–2 (s.v. 'Notarikon'). On a fresh explanation of *gemaṭria*, see S. Sambursky, 'On the Origin and Significance of the Term *Gemaṭria*', JJS 29 (1978), pp. 35–8. For an earlier version in Hebrew, see Tarbiz 45 (1976), pp. 268–71.

IV. The Major Torah Scholars

Bibliography

Graetz, H., *Geschichte der Juden* III–IV.

Derenbourg, J., *Essai sur l'histoire et la géographie de la Palestine d'après les Thalmuds et les autres sources rabbiniques*. I: *Histoire de la Palestine depuis Cyrus jusqu'à Adrien* (1867).

Bacher, W., *Die Agada der Tannaiten* I: *Von Hillel bis Akiba* (1884, [2]1903); II: *Von Akibas Tod bis zum Abschluss der Mischna* (1890). *Tradition und Tradenten in den Schulen Palästinas und Babyloniens* (1914, repr. 1966), especially pp. 47–71.

Loeb, I., *La chaîne de la tradition dans le premier chapître des Pirké Abot* (1889), pp. 307–22; *idem*., 'Notes sur le chapitre 1er des Pirké Abot', REJ 19 (1889), pp. 188–201.

Hyman, A., *Tol[e]dot Tanna'im we-'Amora'im* I–III (1901–11).

Weiss, I. H., *Dōr Dōr We-dōr[e]shaw* I–IV (1924).

Moore, G. F., *Judaism* I-III (1927–30).

Strack, H. L., *Introduction to the Talmud and Midrash* (1931).

Finkelstein, L., *The Pharisees, The Sociological Background of their Faith* (1938, [3]1962).

Goldin, J., 'The Period of the Talmud', L. Finkelstein (ed.), *The Jews* (1949), pp. 115–215.

Alon, G., *Tol[e]dot ha-Yehudim be'Erez Yisra'el bi-t[e]ḳufat ha-Mishnah we-ha-Talmud* I–II ([2]1961). *Meḥḳarim b -toledot Yisra'el* I–II (1958) [E.T. *Jews, Judaism and the Classical World* (1977)].

Guttmann, A., *Rabbinic Judaism in the Making* (1970) [Traditional approach].

Neusner, J., *The Rabbinic Traditions about the Pharisees before* 70 I–III (1971). [A historical and analytical survey of traditions relating to Pharisaic teachers of the age of the Second Temple.] *Early Rabbinic Judaism. Historical Studies in Religion, Literature and Art* (1975).

Green, W. S. (ed.), *Persons and Institutions in Early Rabbinic Judaism* (1977).

Very little is known of individual Torah scholars before the age of the Mishnah, i.e., before around A.D. 70. Even in respect of the famous heads of schools, Hillel and Shammai, our information is scanty. The names and order of succession of the most celebrated among them from about the second century B.C. to A.D. 70 have been preserved primarily in the first chapter of the tractate Aboth (or Pirke Aboth), which records an uninterrupted line of the men who, from Moses to the time of the destruction of Jerusalem, were the transmitters of Jewish tradition. The whole chapter reads as follows.[1]

1. For a bibliography see vol. I, pp. 81–2. To the works listed there may be added J. H. Herz, *Sayings of the Fathers with Introduction and Commentary* (1952);

1. 'Moses received the Torah from (God on) Sinai and transmitted it to Joshua, and Joshua to the Elders, and the Elders to the Prophets, and the Prophets transmitted it to the men of the Great Assembly. These laid down three rules: Be deliberate in judgment! Raise many disciples! And make a fence around the Torah! 2. Simeon the Just was one of the last of the Great Assembly. He used to say: The world stands on three things: the Torah, (Temple)- worship and acts of loving-kindness. 3. Antigonus of Sokho received (the Torah) from Simeon the Just. He said: Be not like slaves who serve a master for a reward, but be like those who serve without considering a reward; and may the fear of God ever be with you.

4. Yose ben Yoezer of Zeredah and Yose ben Yohanan of Jerusalem received (the Torah) from him. Yose ben Yoezer of Zeredah said: Let your house be a meeting-house for sages; become dusty from the dust of their feet; and drink in their words thirstily. 5. Yose ben Yohanan of Jerusalem said: Let your house ever be wide open, and let the poor be members of your household. Chatter not too much with women. It is unbecoming with a man's own wife; how much more so with the wife of another. Therefore the sages also say: Whoever chatters too much with a female brings misfortune on himself, is held back from concern with the Torah, and will in the end inherit Gehenna.

6. Joshua ben Perahiah and Nittai (or Mattai) of Arbela received (the Torah) from these. Joshua ben Perahiah said: Provide yourself with a teacher and acquire a fellow-disciple; and judge all men favourably. 7. Nittai of Arbela said: Keep away from a wicked neighbour; do not associate with the godless; and do not doubt that punishment will come.

8. Judah ben Tabbai and Simeon ben Shetah received (the Torah) from these. Judah ben Tabbai said: Do not (as a judge) make yourself into an adviser. When the parties stand before you, see them as though they are both in the wrong. But if they are released and have accepted the sentence, see them both as exonerated. 9. Simeon ben Shetah said: Examine the witnesses diligently but be careful when you interrogate them lest they learn to speak untruth. 10. Shemaiah and Abtalion received (the Torah) from these. Shemaiah said: Love work, hate domination, and do not crowd in among the authorities. 11. Abtalion said: Sages, be careful in your teaching that you may not incur the guilt that leads to exile, and may not be

---

J. Goldin, *The Living Talmud: the Wisdom of the Fathers and its Classical Commentaries* (1957). For textual criticism, see 'Textkritischer Anhang' in K. Marti-G. Beer, *'Abot* (1927), pp. 186–7. See also E. Bickerman, 'La chaîne de la tradition pharisienne', RB 59 (1952), pp. 44–54.

exiled to a place of evil water. For disciples who come after you will drink of it and will die, and the name of Heaven will thereby be profaned.

12. Hillel and Shammai received (the Torah) from these. Hillel said: Be a disciple of Aaron, loving peace, establishing peace; love men and draw them to the Torah. 13. He also used to say: Whoever wishes to make a great name for himself, suffers the loss of his own; whoever does not increase (his knowledge), decreases; but whoever does not learn at all, is worthy of death; whoever makes use of the crown (of the Torah) (for other purposes), perishes. 14. He used to say: If I do not work for myself, who shall do it for me? And if I do it for myself alone, what am I? And if not now, when? 15. Shammai said: Make your study of the Torah a regular occupation; promise little and do much; and receive all men with friendliness.

16. Rabban Gamaliel said: Provide yourself with a teacher and you thus avoid the doubtful. And do not tithe too often by approximation.

17. His son Simeon said: I have grown up among sages since my early youth and have found nothing more beneficial for men than silence. Study is not the most essential, but practice. Whoever makes many words brings sin to pass.

18. Rabban Simeon ben Gamaliel said: The world is established on three things: on justice, on truth and on peace. [As it is written (Zech. 8:16): Render in your gates judgements that are true and make for peace.]

The first to interest us in this list of authorities are the 'men of the Great Assembly' or Great Synagogue (אנשי כנסת הגדולה). They appear here as transmitting tradition between the last prophets and the first Torah scholars known by name. Later Jewish tradition ascribes to them all kinds of legal ordinances.[2] Together with Ezra, they are believed to have 'written' the books of Ezekiel, the Twelve Minor Prophets, Esther, Ezra and Chronicles.[3] In a more modern version traceable to Elia Levita in 1538, they are represented as responsible for the canon of the Old Testament.[4] As none of the sources say who they

2. W. Bacher, 'Synagogue, the great', JE XI, pp. 640–3; J. Z. Lauterbach, 'Sanhedrin', *ibid.*, pp. 41–4; Moore, *Judaism* I, pp. 31 ff.; L. Finkelstein, 'The Maxim of the *Anshe Keneset Ha-Gedolah*', JBL 59 (1940), pp. 455–69 [*Pharisaism in the Making* (1972), pp. 159–73]; E. Bickerman, 'Viri magnae congregationis', RB 55 (1948), pp. 397–402.

3. bBB 15a.

4. Cf. O. Eissfeldt, *The Old Testament. An Introduction* (1966), p. 546. On Elia Levita, see G. E. Weil, *Élie Lévita, humaniste et massorète (1469–1549)*, (1963), pp. 304–5.

actually were, all kinds of theories have been advanced concerning them.[5] But their existence as a formal institution, about which doubts were expressed as early as the eighteenth century,[6] was definitely disproved by A. Kuenen,[7] and has never been revived since. The historical basis of the whole concept lies solely in the story of Neh. 8–10, that at the time of Ezra the Torah was solemnly accepted by a great assembly of the people. This 'great assembly' did in fact play a prominent part in the preservation of the Bible. But once the idea of a 'great assembly' was fixed as an important authority for the preservation of the Torah, a totally unhistorical notion gradually become attached to it in tradition. Instead of an assembly that received the Torah, it was thought of as a council of men who transmitted the Torah further; and thus the gap was filled between the last prophets and the first Torah scholars.[8]

With the concept of the great synagogue dismissed, the statement that Simon the Just was one of its last members also holds no water. Instead, he was one of the two High Priests called Simeon, one of whom, according to Josephus, was surnamed ὁ δίκαιος.[9] It was by reason of his great piety that he was marked out as a transmitter of

5. H. Graetz, 'Die grosse Versammlung', MGWJ (1857), pp. 31–7, 61–70; J. Derenbourg, *Essai*, pp. 29–40; J. Fürst, *Der Kanon des A.T. nach den Überlieferungen in Talmud und Midrasch* (1868), pp. 21–3; D. Hoffmann, 'Über "die Männer der grossen Versammlung"', Magazin für die Wissenschaft des Judenthums 10 (1883), pp. 45–63; S. Krauss, 'The great Synod', JQR 10 (1898), pp. 347–77; H. Englander, 'Men of the Great Synagogue', HUCA Jub. Vol. (1925), pp. 145–69; E. Bickerman, 'Viri Magnae Congregationis', RB 55 (1948), pp. 397–402; L. Finkelstein, *The Pharisees* ([3]1962), pp. 62 ff., 578 ff.; H. Mantel, 'The Nature of the Great Synagogue', HThR 60 (1967), pp. 69–91.

6. Cf. J. E. Rau, *Diatribe de synagoga magna* (1726).

7. A. Kuenen, *Over de mannen der groote synagoge* (1876); 'Über die Männer der grossen Synagoge', *Gesammelte Abhandlungen zur biblischen Wissenschaft*, von Dr. Abraham Kuenen (1894), pp. 125–60; W. Bacher, JE XI, pp. 640–3, attempted to combine Kuenen's conclusions with Jewish tradition. Cf. Moore, *Judaism* I, pp. 29–36; III, pp. 6–15; Finkelstein, 'The Maxim of the *Anshe Keneset Ha-Gedolah*', JBL 59 (1940), pp. 455–69; E. Dhorme, 'Le texte hébreu de 1 'AT', RHhR 35 (1955), pp. 129–44; S. Hoenig, *The Great Sanhedrin* (1953); P. Parker, 'Synagogue, The Great', IDB IV, p. 491; J. Schiffer, 'The Men of the Great Synagogue', W. S. Green (ed.), *Persons and Institutions in Early Rabbinic Judaism* (1977), pp. 257–83.

8. For various contemporary attempts to link biblical and post-biblical tradition, see J. Weingreen, 'The Rabbinic Approach to the Study of the Old Testament', BJRL 34 (1951–2), pp. 168–90; 'Oral Torah and Written Record', *Holy Book and Holy Tradition* (ed. F. F. Bruce and E. G. Rupp, 1968), pp. 54–67; G. Vermes, *Scripture and Tradition*, pp. 173–7; CHB I, pp. 199–201 [*PBJS*, pp. 59–61]; J. Weingreen, *From Bible to Mishna: The Continuity of Tradition* (1976).

9. Josephus, *Ant*. xii 2, 5 (43): ὁ καὶ δίκαιος ἐπικληθεὶς διά τε τὸ πρὸς τὸν θεὸν εὐσεβὲς καὶ τὸ πρὸς τοὺς ὁμοφύλους εὔνουν.

tradition.[10] The only question is whether the High Priest Simeon I is meant (beginning of the third century B.C.) or Simeon II (end of the third century B.C.).[11] According to Josephus, it would have been the former. But Jesus ben Sira 50:1–21 praises a High Priest Simeon for the faithfulness with which he conducted the Temple worship in its ancient splendour. He appears to have lived during the latter's term of office and contrasts it with the High Priesthood of the time in which he wrote. Since his description can only refer to Simeon II, it must be assumed that Josephus attached the epithet 'the Just' to the wrong Simeon.[12]

The earliest Torah scholar of whom tradition has at least preserved the name is Antigonus of Sokho. But otherwise almost nothing is known of him.[13]

Of subsequent Torah scholars also, down to the time of Jesus, the Mishnah preserves but the thinnest of information. This is already

10. He is also mentioned in mPar. 3:5 as one of the High Priests under whom a red heifer was burned. For other traditions see tNaz. 4:7; mSot. 13:6–7. H. Graetz, 'Simon der Gerechte und seine Zeit', MGWJ (1857), pp. 45–56; Derenbourg, *Essai*, pp. 46–7; Bacher, 'Simeon the Just', JE XI, pp. 352–4; R. Smend, *Die Weisheit des Jesus Sirach, erklärt* (1906), pp. xv–xvii; G. F. Moore, 'Simon the Just', *Jewish Studies in Memory of I. Abrahams* (1927), pp. 348–64; *idem.*, *Judaism* I, pp. 34 ff.; III, n. 5; RE III, pp. 162–80 (s.v. 'Σίμων'); W. Foerster, 'Der Ursprung des Pharisäismus', ZNW 34 (1935), pp. 41 f.; L. Finkelstein, 'The Maxim of the *Anshe Keneset Ha-Gedolah*', JBL 59 (1940), pp. 455–69; *The Pharisees* (^{3}1962), pp. 576 ff.; G. Hölscher, 'Die Hohenpriesterliste bei Josephus', SAH (1939); V. Tcherikover, *Hellenistic Civilization and the Jews* (1959), especially pp. 403–4; R. Marcus, *Josephus* (Loeb) (1943), pp. 732–6; J. Goldin, 'The Three Pillars of Simeon the Righteous', PAAJR 27 (1958), pp. 43–58; Enc. Jud. 14 cols. 1566–7; Neusner, *Pharisees* I, pp. 24–59.

11. On the latter, see Josephus, *Ant.* xii 4, 10 (224).

12. The identification, common among contemporary scholars is also implied to some extent in yYom. 43cd; bMen. 109b where Simon is described as the father of Onias, the builder of a Jewish Temple in Egypt. (In fact, he was his grandfather.)

13. Cf. JE I, p. 629; Strack, p. 107; E. J. Bickerman, 'The Maxim of Antigonus of Socho', HThR 44 (1951), pp. 153–65; Enc. Jud. 3, col. 67. Neusner, *Pharisees* I, pp. 60–1. Both recensions of Aboth de-Rabbi Nathan, ch. 5, (ed. Schechter, p. 26), ascribe to Antigonus two pupils, Zadok and Boethus, to whom the Sadducees and Boethusians are traced back. Three places named Sokho (שוכו) occur in the Old Testament: (1) a city in the plain, Shephelah of Judah, Jos. 15:35, 1 Sam. 17:1, 2 Chron. 11:7, 28:18; (2) a city in the Judaean mountains, Jos. 15: 48; (3)a place in the third district of Solomon, 1 Kg. 4:10. The names of the first two survive in Arabic as Khirbet Shuweike. The former lies southwest of Jerusalem, in the direction of Eleutheropolis, and the latter south of Hebron. As the region south of Hebron was Edomite in the second century B.C., the first will have been the home of Antigonus. The third place, located some 10 miles north-west of Samaria, is today identified with Tell er-Ras. Cf. Abel, *Géog. Pal.* II, p. 467; W. F. Stinespring, 'Soco', IDB (1962), IV, p. 395; M. Avi-Yonah, s.v. 'Socoh', Enc. Jud. (1971) 15, cols. 69–70; *Gazetteer*, p. 97.

evident in the apparently schematic arrangement into five pairs. For it can hardly be a historical fact that in every generation only two scholars distinguished themselves. It is more likely that ten names were known, and by coupling those who were approximately contemporary, five pairs were formed, presumably by analogy with the last and most famous pair, Hillel and Shammai.[14] In such circumstances, it is clear that the chronology can be determined only in roughest outline. The surest clues, relatively speaking, are the following.[15] Simeon ben Shetah was a contemporary of Alexander Jannaeus and Alexandra; he therefore lived around 90–70 B.C.[16] Accordingly, the first pair is to be dated to two generations earlier, to around 150 B.C. Hillel, according to Talmudic tradition, flourished one hundred years before the destruction of Jerusalem, i.e., during the time of Herod the Great.[17] Gamaliel I is mentioned in Acts (5:34; 22:3) in around A.D. 30–40, whereas his son Simeon, according to Josephus, was active at the time of the Jewish war in around A.D. 60–70.[18] That a later tradition represented all five pairs as Presidents and Vice-Presidents of the Sanhedrin has already been mentioned (p. 215); it has also been pointed out that this is quite incorrect. In reality, they were merely heads of schools.

The first pair, Yose ben Yoezer and Yose ben Yohanan, appears, apart from mAboth 1:4–5, only seldom in the Mishnah.[19] The second pair, Joshua ben Perahiah and Nittai (or Mattai) of Arbela, is referred

14. In rabbinical literature these ten are simply named 'the pairs' (זוגות), e.g., mPea. 2:6.

15. On the chronology, cf. I. Jelski, *Die innere Einrichtung des grossen Synedrions zu Jerusalem* (1894), pp. 36 ff.; Strack, p. 107 f.; L. Finkelstein, *Akiba* (1936), pp. 294–304; Moore, *Judaism* I, p. 45, n. 3, p. 255; for a defence of the traditional interpretation, H. Mantel, *Studies in the History of the Sanhedrin* (1961), pp. 13–18, 102, 107.

16. This accords with mTaan. 3:8, which states that Simeon ben Shetaḥ was a contemporary of the Onias famous for the power of his prayer, whose death in 65 B.C. is reported by Josephus, *Ant.* xiv 2, 1 (22–4).

17. bShab. 15a. Cf. Jerome, *Com. in Esaiam* 8: 11 ff. (CCL lxxiii, p. 116): 'Sammai igitur et Hellel non multo prius quam Dominus nasceretur orti sunt in Iudaea'.

18. *B.J.* iv 3, 9 (159); *Vita* 38 (190–1), 39 (195–7), 44 (216), 60 (309).

19. Both appear in mHag. 2:2; mSot. 9:9. According to mHag. 2:7, Yose ben Yoezer was a priest and indeed a ḥasid among the priesthood. The remark in mSot. 9:9 that there had been no more אשכולות since the deaths of Yose ben Yoezer and Yose ben Yohanan, is obscure. As the Mishnah itself refers to Micah 7:1, the term is probably to be understood in its usual meaning of grapes, as a metaphor for men in whom spiritual refreshment could be found. Others wish to equate it with *σχολαί*. Cf. R. Loewe, 'Rabbi Joshua ben Ḥananiah: LL.B. or B.Litt.', JJS (1974), pp. 137–54. See in general Derenbourg, pp. 65, 75, 456–60; JE VIII, p. 242; Moore, *Judaism* I, pp. 45 ff.; Strack, p. 107, Neusner, *Pharisees* I, pp. 61–81; Enc. Jud. 16, cols. 853–4; G. G. Porton, 'The Grape-Cluster in Jewish Literature and Art in Late Antiquity', JJS 27 (1976), pp. 159–76.

to even more rarely.[20] Of the third pair, only Simeon ben Shetah has any tangible form, though most of the information is also of a legendary nature.[21] Josephus says nothing of any of these. On the other hand, he seems to allude to the fourth pair, Shemaiah and Abtalion, under the names *Σαμαίας* and *Πολλίων*. He writes that when the young Herod stood accused before the Sanhedrin in 47 B.C. because of his behaviour in Galilee, none of its members except a certain Samaias dared to voice their complaints. Samaias alone spoke up, prophesying to his colleagues that they would all lose their lives through Herod. Ten years later, the prophecy was fulfilled; after his conquest of Jerusalem in 37 B.C., Herod executed all his former accusers.[22] He spared only the Pharisee Pollio and his pupil Samaias (*Πολλίων ὁ Φαρισαῖος καὶ Σαμαίας ὁ τούτου μαθητής*). Indeed, he held them in great favour because when he was besieging one city they advised that he should be permitted to enter. The Samaias mentioned here is expressly identified by Josephus with the earlier Samaias.[23] Finally, Josephus refers to Pollio and Samaias, and again in this order, in yet another passage. Unfortunately, there is no clear indication of the chronology. He reports that the followers of Pollio and Samaias (*οἱ περὶ Πολλίωνα τὸν Φαρισαῖον καὶ Σαμαίαν*) once refused to offer Herod the required oath of allegiance but were not punished because they obtained indulgence for

20. Both figure only in mAb. 1:6–7 and mHag. 2:2. Joshua ben Perahiah is anachronistically depicted as the teacher of Jesus in bSanh. 107b; bSot. 47a; cf. J. Klausner, *Jesus of Nazareth* (1925), pp. 24–7. Instead of Nittai (נתיי or נתאי), good manuscripts have מתיי or מתאי, i.e. Matthew, in both passages, which is perhaps preferable (cf. K. Marti-G.Beer, *Abot* (1927), pp. 18, 186). In the list of the 72 translators in the *Letter of Aristeas*, ed. Wendland (49), a *Ναṭθαίος* also figures, which some textual witnesses show as *Ματθαῖος*. ארבל, the home of Nittai, is the present-day Irbid and lies to the north-west of Tiberias (cf. vol. I, p. 282, n. 6). Ruins of an old synagogue, said by legend to have been built by Nittai, still survive here. Cf. Derenbourg, pp. 93–4; Moore, *Judaism* I, pp. 311, 348; Strack, p. 108; JE VII, p. 295; IX, p. 318; Enc. Jud. 10, cols. 284–5; 12, col. 1187; Neusner, *Pharisees* I, pp. 81–6.

21. On his relations with Alexander Jannaeus and Alexandra, see vol. I, pp. 221–2, 231. Besides mAb. 1:8–9, mHag. 2:2, cf. also mTaan. 3:8, mSanh, 6:4, tHag. 2:8, tKet. 12:1, tSanh. 6:6, 8:3. (For a full analysis of all the passages, including those from Mekhilta, Sifra, Sifre and the Talmuds, see J. Neusner, *Pharisees* I, pp. 86–141.) Cf. Graetz, *Geschichte der Juden* III⁴, pp. 703–8 (nn. 13–14); Derenbourg, pp. 96–111; Schlatter, *Geschichte Israels* (²1906), p. 116 ff.; JE XI, pp. 357–8; Enc. Jud. 14, cols. 1563–5. On his alleged execution of eighty witches in Ashkelon, cf. vol. I, p. 231 and n. 7. See also Moore, *Judaism* III, p. 33; H. Mantel, *Studies in the History of the Sanhedrin*, pp. 9, 81.

22. *Ant.* xiv 9, 4 (175).

23. *Ant.* xv 1, 1 (3). In the sentence referring to the earlier event, the Josephus manuscripts admittedly have *Πολλίων*; only the Epitome and the Latin have *Σαμαίας*. But according to *Ant.* xiv 9, 4 (172–6), the latter is the correct reading, provided that Josephus is not guilty of a slip of the pen in one or other of the two passages.

the sake of Pollio (ἐντροπῆς διὰ τὸν Πολλίωνα τυχόντες).[24] This observation is placed among the events of the eighteenth year of the reign of Herod (=20/19 B.C.). But it is not very clear from the context whether it actually happened in that year. In any case, the two names *Σαμαίας* and *Πολλίων* correspond so strikingly with שמעיה and אבטליון that their identity suggests itself very strongly.[25] The chronology, too, would more or less tally. The one point to arouse misgivings is that Samaias is described as a pupil of Pollio, whereas otherwise Shemaiah always takes precedence over Abtalion. One might therefore be tempted to identify Samaias with Shammai,[26] but then again, it would be strange for Josephus to name him twice with Abtalion and not with his contemporary, Hillel. But if, because of this association, one wishes to identify Pollio and Samaias as Hillel and Shammai,[27] one is faced with the problem of the difference between the names Pollio and Hillel, and with the fact that Samaias is represented as the pupil of Pollio whereas Shammai was Hillel's pupil. On the whole, the association of Samaias and Pollio with Shemaiah and Abtalion seems the most likely.[28]

Of the five pairs, Hillel and Shammai are by far the most famous.[29] Each was the head of a whole school of Torah scholars diverging

24. *Ant.* xv 10, 4 (370).

25. The name Shemaiah, which figures frequently in the Hebrew Bible, especially in Nehemiah and Chronicles, is rendered in the LXX by *Σαμαία, Σαμαίας, Σαμείας, Σεμείας*. The name *Πολλίων* is of course not identical with Abtalion but with the Latin Pollio; but it is well-known that with their Hebrew names Jews often had similar-sounding Greek or Latin names (Jesus and Jason, Saul and Paul, etc.). It should also be noted that A. Schlatter, *Zur Topographie und Geschichte Palästinas* (1893), p. 126, takes Abtalion for the Greek *Εὐθαλίων*. This is phonetically possible, but it is unlikely because *Εὐθαλίων* is not an attested Greek name. The identity of Abtalion with *Πολλίων* may be assumed if the latter is taken to be a form of *Πτολλίων*. Cf. Marti-Beer, *Abot*, pp. 22–3. See also L. H. Feldman, 'The Identity of Pollio the Pharisee in Josephus', JQR 49 (1958–9), pp. 53–62.

26. שמאי or שמיי (apparently only an abbreviation of שמעיה, see Derenbourg, p. 95), can very well be *Σαμαίας*, in Greek, like ינאי *'Ιανναῖος* or *'Ιαννέας*; the manuscripts waver between the forms, *Ant.* xiii 12, 1 (320).

27. Thus, e.g. J. Lehmann, 'Le procès d'Hérode, Saméas et Pollion', REJ 24 (1892), pp. 68–81. Cf. also Moore, *Judaism* I, p. 313, n. 4; A. Schalit, *König Herodes* (1969), pp. 768–71.

28. Cf. on both, besides mAb. 1:10–11 and mHag. 2:2, mEdu. 1:3; 5:6. Derenbourg, pp. 116–18, 149–50, 463–4; A. Schalit, *op. cit.* (1969), pp. 668–71; 'Shemajah', JE XI, p. 268, and 'Abtalion' I, p. 136; S. Zeitlin, 'Sameias and Pollion', Journal of Jewish Lore and Philosophy 1 (1919), pp. 63–7; Neusner, *Pharisees* I, pp. 142–59.

29. H. Graetz III[4], p. 207 ff.; A. Geiger, *Das Judenthum und seine Geschichte* I, pp. 99–107; Derenbourg, pp. 176–92; W. Bacher, *Die Agada der Tannaiten* I[2], pp. 1–11; W. Bacher, 'Hillel', JE VI, pp. 397–400; J. Z. Lauterbach, 'Shammai', JE XI, p. 230–1; Moore, *Judaism* I, pp. 79–82; L. Finkelstein, *Akiba* (1936); A. Kaminka, 'Hillel and his Works', Zion 4 (1938–9), pp. 258–66; 'Hillel's Life and Works', JQR 30 (1939–40), pp. 107–22; I. Sonne, 'The Schools of Shammai and

from each other, if not in principle, nevertheless in a great many individual legal rulings. Both are of outstanding importance to the history of Judaism and Jewish law, for both worked with zeal and perception on a more subtle development of halakhah. It must however not be supposed that their personal lives and works also stand revealed in the clear light of history. Relatively very little is known of them. The Mishnah, the earliest source, mentions both of them scarcely a dozen times.[30] And the accounts provided by the later sources bear almost throughout the stamp of legend. Hillel, who to distinguish him from others was called 'the Elder', הזקן,[31] is said to have been of Davidic descent[32] and to have immigrated from Babylon to Palestine. Because he was poor, he was obliged to hire himself out as a day-labourer to support himself and his family, and also to meet the cost of his instruction. His eagerness to learn was so great that when on one occasion he was unable to pay the entrance fee into the Beth-ha-Midrash, he climbed up to the window to listen to the lesson from there. As it was winter, he became stiff with cold and was found in that condition by his astonished teachers and colleagues.[33] Tradition relates marvels of the erudition which he acquired through such zeal. He understood every language, including those of mountains, hills, valleys, trees, plants, animals wild and tame, and demons.[34] He was in any case the most distinguished Torah teacher of his time; but he was as little President of the Sanhedrin as was any other scholar of that period. His

---

Hillel seen from within', *Louis Ginzberg Memorial Volume* (1945), pp. 275–91; J. Goldin, 'Hillel the Elder', JR 26 (1946), pp. 263–77; 'The Period of the Talmud', *The Jews*, ed. L. Finkelstein (1949), pp. 129–33; A. Guttman, 'Foundations of Rabbinic Judaism', HUCA 23 (1950–1), pp. 452–73; N. N. Glatzer, *Hillel the Elder* (1956); 'Hillel the Elder in the Light of the Dead Sea Scrolls', *The Scrolls and the New Testament* (ed. K. Stendahl, 1957); Neusner, *Pharisees* I, pp. 185–340; S. Zeitlin, 'Hillel and the Hermeneutic Rules', JQR 54 (1963), pp. 161–73; Neusner, *History of the Jews in Babylonia* I (1965), pp. 36–8; E. E. Urbach, *The Sages* I, pp. 576–93.

30. Hillel is mentioned in the Mishnah only in the following passages: mSheb. 10:3; mHag. 2:2; mGit. 4:3; mB.M. 5:9; mEdu. 1:1–4; mAb. 1:12–14; 2:4–7; 4:5; 5:17; mArakh. 9:4; mNid. 1:1. Shammai, only in the following: mM.Sh. 2:4, 9; mOrl. 2:5; mSuk. 2:8; mHag. 2:2; mEdu. 1:1:4, 10, 11; mAb. 1:12, 15; 5:17; mKel. 22, 4; mNid. 1:1.

31. mSheb. 10:3; mArakh. 9:4.

32. yTaan. 4:2, 68a; Gen. R. 98:8 on Gen. 49:10. On the unreliability of the tradition relating to Hillel's Davidic descent, see Israel Lévi, 'L'origine davidique de Hillel', REJ 31 (1895), pp. 202–11, 33, p. 143–4; cf. J. Jeremias, *Jerusalem*, pp. 275–90.

33. bYoma. 35b. Cf. F. Delitzsch, *Jesus und Hillel* ([3]1879), pp. 9–11; Moore, *Judaism* I, p. 313; N. N. Glatzer, *Hillel the Elder* (1956), pp. 24–5; S. Zeitlin, *The Rise and Fall of the Judaean State* II (1969), pp. 105–6.

34. M. Soferim 16:9; cf. F. Delitzsch, *Jesus und Hillel*, p. 8.

main characteristics were kindness and gentleness, of which remarkable examples are related.[35] They are also manifest in the first of the sayings cited above (Aboth 1:12): 'Be a disciple of Aaron, loving peace, establishing peace; love men and draw them to the Torah.'

Shammai, who was severe and likewise called הזקן,[36] was the opposite of the mild Hillel. The Mishnah relates the following example of his rigorous zeal for the literal fulfilment of the law. When his daughter-in-law gave birth to a son on the Feast of Tabernacles, he had the ceiling broken through and the roof over the bed covered with foliage so that the new-born child should also celebrate the festival in accordance with the law.[37]

To the mildness and severity of Hillel and Shammai corresponded the mildness and severity of their two schools. The school of Hillel preferred to decide legal questions leniently, that of Shammai, strictly. The former sought to get away with a minimum, the latter willingly chose the maximum. It is however not possible to describe this as a real difference in principle for both were in agreement that the letter of the law was to be punctiliously fulfilled. There are in consequence not a few instances when the school of Hillel made decisions that were strict, and that of Shammai, decisions that were lenient.[38] But the differences never turned on anything more than minutiae. There is therefore no point in examining the contrast in detail.[39] A few extreme

35. See Delitzsch, *op. cit.*, p. 31 f.; Moore, *Judaism* I, p. 79; II, pp. 196, 274, 342 etc.

36. mOrl. 2:5; mSuk. 2:8.

37. mSuk. 2:8.

38. mEdu. 4:1–12; 5:1–5. Cf. further A. Schwarz, *Die Erleichterungen der Schammaiten und die Erschwerungen der Hilleliten* [also under the title, *Die Controversen der Schammaiten und Hilleliten* I] (1893); Moore, *Judaism* I, pp. 77–86.

39. The following Mishnah passages mention the differences between the two schools: mBer. 1:3; 8:1–8; mPea. 3:1; 6:1, 2, 5; 7:6; mDem. 1:3; 6:6; mKil. 2:6; 4:1, 5; 6:1; mSheb. 1:1; 4:2, 4, 10; 5:4, 8; 8:3; mTer. 1:4; 5:4; mMaas. 4:2; mM.Sh. 2:3, 4, 7, 8, 9; 3:6, 7, 9, 13; 4:8; 5:3, 6. 7; mHal. 1:6; mOrl. 2:4; mShab. 1:4–9; 3:1; 21:3; mErub. 1:2; 6:4; 6; 8:6; mPes. 1:1; 4:5, 8:8; 10:2, 6; mShek. 2:3; 8:6; mSuk. 1:1, 7; 2:7, 3:5, 9; mBez. 1:1–9; 2:1–5; mR.Sh. 1:1; mHag. 1:1–3; 2:3, 4; mYeb. 1:4; 3:1, 5; 4:3; 6:6; 13:1; 15:2, 3; mKet. 5:6; 8:1, 6; mNed. 3:2, 4; mNaz. 2:1, 2; 3:6, 7; 5:1, 2, 3, 5; mSot. 4:2; mGit. 4:5; 8:4, 8, 9; 9:10; mKid. 1:1; mB.M. 3:12; mB.B. 9:8, 9; mEdu. 1:7–14; 4:1–12; 5:1–5; mZeb. 4:1; mHul. 1:2, 8:1; 11:2; mBekh. 5:2; mKer. 1:6; mKel. 9:2; 11:3, 14:2; 18:1; 20:2, 6; 22:4; 26:6; 28:4; 29:8; mOhol. 2:3; 5:1–4; 7:3; 11:1, 3–6, 8; 13:1, 4; 15:8, 18:1, 4, 8; mPar. 12:10; mTohor. 9:1, 5, 7; 10:4; mMikw. 1:5; 4:1; 5:6; 10:6; mNid. 2:4, 6; 4:3; 5:9; 10:1, 4, 6–8; mMakhsh. 1:2–4; 4:4, 5; 5:9; mZab. 1:1–2; mTeb.Y. 1:1; mYad. 3:5; mUkz. 3:6, 8, 11. Beth Shammai only: mBer. 6:5; mDem. 3:1; mKil. 8:5; mTer. 4:3; mOrl. 2:5, 12; mBez. 2:6; mEdu. 3:10; mMikw. 4:5. This list shows that the differences relate mainly to matters dealt with in the first, second, third, and sixth *seder* of the Mishnah, i.e. (1) religious dues; (2) Sabbaths and holy days; (3) marriage laws; (4) laws of purification. Those dealt with in the fourth and sixth *seder* (civil and criminal law and the

examples may suffice to demonstrate their efforts to sanctify everyday life. It was debated whether, and under what circumstances, an egg laid on a festival might be eaten on the same day;[40] whether fringes (*ẓiẓith*) might be attached to a linen garment;[41] whether a ladder might be carried from one dovecot to another on a holy-day, or should only be tilted from one hole to another.[42] In practice, the milder school of Hillel eventually gained the upper hand. Nevertheless, it conceded on many points to the school of Shammai.[43] On others, later generations followed neither Hillel's opinion nor Shammai's.[44]

The name of Hillel is also associated with an institution which, although it contradicted biblical rulings, was in the circumstances certainly beneficial in its results. The legal ordinance that every seven years all debts should be remitted (Deut. 15:1–11) had the unfortunate effect 'that people hesitated to lend each other money', although the Torah itself warns that one should not hold back from lending on that account (Deut. 15:9). The 'judicial proviso' (פרוזבול = προσβολή) was introduced under Hillel's influence to remove this obstacle. Specifically, a creditor was permitted to make a declaration before the court: **מוסר אני לכם איש פלוני ופלוני הדיינים שבמקום פלוני שכל חוב שיש לי שאגבנו כל זמן שארצה** 'I, so-and-so, do deliver to you, the judges of such and such a place, the declaration that I may demand payment of all my outstanding debts at any time I choose.' Such a proviso made before the court safeguarded the creditor during a sabbatical year as well.[45] The

---

laws of sacrifice) are hardly involved at all. The latter, which are not concerned with the religious behaviour of private individuals but are either purely civil or priestly affairs, were not discussed in the schools with the same zeal as the rest. The sacrificial laws had presumably already been developed by the older priestly Torah scholars and lay outside the sphere of direct rabbinic competence. Tosefta deals with the matter similarly to the Mishnah (see the list of passages in the Index to Zuckermandel's edition, p. xxxiii). In the Midrashim (Mekhilta, Sifra and Sifre), the two schools are mentioned but rarely. See the list of passages in D. Hoffmann, *Zur Einleitung in die halachischen Midraschim* (Berlin, Jahresbericht des Rabbiner-Seminars, 1887), p. 84, and especially Neusner, *Pharisees* II, pp. 6–40. Compare also S. Mendelssohn, 'Bet Hillel and Bet Shammai', JE III, pp. 115–16; S. Zeitlin, 'Les écoles de Schammai et de Hillel', REJ 93 (1932), pp. 73–83; 'The Semikhah Controversy between the Schools of Shammai and Hillel', JQR 56 (1965), pp. 240–4; I. Sonne, 'The Schools of Shammai and Hillel seen from within', *L. Ginzberg Jubilee Volume* I (1945), pp. 275–91. L. Ginzberg, *On Jewish Law and Lore* (1962), pp. 88–124; A. Guttmann, *Rabbinic Judaism in the Making* (1970), pp. 59–124.

40. mBez. 1:1; mEdu. 4:1.

41. mEdu. 4:10.

42. mBez. 1:3.

43. mEdu. 1:12–14.

44. E. g. mEdu. 1:1–3. Cf. generally the passages cited in n. 39.

45. Cf. especially mSheb. 10:3–7 (the formula, mSheb. 10:4); introduction by Hillel, mSheb. 10:3; mGit. 4:3; generally, mPea. 3:6; mM.K. 3:3; mKet. 9:9; mUkz.

regular naming of this proviso as פרוזבול has not yet been satisfactorily explained. It is certainly not πρὸς βουλήν, as many have thought, for this would not express its main concept at all. It can hardly be anything but προσβολή. But so far, no instance has been attested of προσβολή being given this meaning in Greek. A possible, but unlikely, conjecture is that it is equivalent to the Latin word 'adiectio' in the sense of 'addition, supplement, clause', for the פרוזבול statement was in fact a supplementary clause to a loan contract.[46]

The son of Hillel is usually said to have been a certain Simeon, the father in his turn of Gamaliel I. However, the existence of this Simeon, and therefore of the whole genealogical relationship, is highly questionable.[47] Indeed, no new historical personality emerges until Gamaliel I,

3:10. S. Krauss, *Griechische und lateinische Lehnwörter im Talmud* II (1899), p. 482; J. H. Greenstone, 'Prosbul', JE X, p. 219–20; Moore, *Judaism* I, pp. 261–2, III, n. 25; Z. W. Falk, *Introduction to Jewish Law of the Second Commonwealth* I (1972), pp. 22, 112; Neusner, *Pharisees* I, pp. 217–24. An Aramaic acknowledgement of debt discovered at Murabba'at, dating to Nero's second year (A.D. 55–6), refers—without using the term *prosbol*—to a similar custom. A certain Absalom son of Hanin declares that he will repay his creditor, Zekhariah son of Yohanan, twenty *zuz* by a certain date. 'And if I have not repaid the sum by that date, it will be returned with one-fifth added, and it will be reimbursed in full even if it is a Shemittah year'. See J. T. Milik, *Discoveries in the Judaean Desert* II (1961), pp. 101–3. Cf. E. Koffmann, *Die Doppelurkunden aus der Wüste Juda* (1968), pp. 80–9.

46. For *adiectio* with the meaning 'addition, supplement, proviso', H. G. Heumann, *Handwörterbuch zu den Quellen des römischen Rechts*, 9th ed., rev. by E. Seckel, 1907, gives the following examples: Gaius, *Inst.* iv, 126–9 (where, e.g., in the case that one comes to an agreement with another: 'ne pecuniam, quam mihi debes, a te peterem', the proviso is recommended: 'si non postea convenit, ut mihi eam pecuniam petere liceret'). *Dig.* xxviii 5, 70; xxx 30, 1–4; 81, 4; 108, 8; cf. *Vocabularium iurisprudentiae romanae* I (1903), col. 219. προσβολή would then have to be a Latinism (literal rendering of *adiectio*). It cannot however be said that *adiectio* in this sense is a prominent technical term in Roman law, and the connection remains speculative. The Jewish פרוזבול seems indeed not to be a proviso in the loan contract itself, but a general reservation for all cases (cf. besides the formula itself, also mSheb. 10:5, '. . . if five borrow from one person, only one *prozbul* is drawn up for them all'). Cf. L. Blau, 'Prosbol im Lichte der griechischen Papyri under der Rechtsgeschichte', *Festschrift zum 50-jährigen Bestehen des Franz Joseph Landesrabbinerschule, Budapest* (1927), pp. 96–151.

47. This Simeon does not appear in the Mishnah at all. He first emerges in the Babylonian Talmud and even here is not described as the son of Hillel but merely as holder of the office of *nasi* between Hillel and Gamaliel I. The complete passage reads (bShab. 15a): הלל ושמעון גמליאל ושמעון נהגו נשיאותן לפני הבית מאה שנה, 'Hillel and Simeon, Gamaliel and Simeon, held the office of *nasi* for a hundred years during the existence of the Temple'. The historical reliability of this late Talmudic statement is more than questionable and the very existence of this Simeon is uncertain. Apart from mShab. 15a, he is not mentioned anywhere else in either Talmud. The historicity of Simeon is reasserted without new evidence by A. Guttmann, *Rabbinic Judaism in the Making* (1970), p. 177.

רבן גמליאל הזקן, as he is called in the Mishnah to distinguish him from Gamaliel II.[48] St. Paul is said to have sat at his feet (Act. 22:3), and it was he who counselled the Sanhedrin to free the accused apostles (Act. 5:34–9). Because of this, Christian legend has made him into a Christian,[49] whilst Jewish tradition honours him as one of the most celebrated teachers. 'From the time that Rabban Gamaliel the Elder died, respect for the Torah (כבוד התורה) ceased; and purity and abstinence (טהרה ופרשות) died at the same time.'[50] It is clear from Acts 5:34 ff. that he was an ordinary member of the Sanhedrin and was no more its President than was Hillel. Much confusion has been caused by attributing to him matters which apply to Gamaliel II, such as the activities in Yavneh, etc.

His son, Simeon, also enjoyed extraordinary fame as Torah scholar.[51] Josephus says of him:[52] *ὁ δὲ Σίμων οὗτος ἦν πόλεως μὲν Ἱεροσολύμων, γένους δὲ σφόδρα λαμπροῦ, τῆς δὲ Φαρισαίων αἱρέσεως, οἳ περὶ τὰ πάτρια νόμιμα δοκοῦσι τῶν ἄλλων ἀκριβείᾳ διαφέρειν. Ἦν δ' οὗτος ἀνὴρ πλήρης*

48. mOrl. 2:12; mR.Sh. 2:5; mYeb. 16:7; mSot. 9:15; mGit. 4:2–3. In all these passages he is explicitly named 'the Elder' (הזקן). Moreover, apart from mAb. 1:16, this elder Gamaliel is probably also meant in mPea. 2:6 and mShek. 6:1 .In all the other passages it is doubtful. In particular, the famous Torah expert, the slave Tabi (טבי), was not in the service of the elder but of the younger Gamaliel (mBer. 2:7; mSuk. 2:1). Only mPes. 7:2, which recounts that Gamaliel ordered Tabi to roast the Passover-offering, appears to allude to Gamaliel I. If this is not a mistake, it must be presumed that Tabi served both Gamaliels, grandfather and grandson (thus Derenbourg, *Histoire*, pp. 480–1), or that there was more than one Tabi. Cf. on Gamaliel I generally: H. Graetz, *Geschichte der Juden* III, pp. 349 ff; A. Büchler, *Das Synedrion in Jerusalem* (1902), pp. 115–31 (defends the opinion that Gamaliel I was President of the supreme *beth-din*); W. Bacher, 'Gamaliel', JE V, pp. 558–60; Str.-B. II, pp. 636–40; M. S. Enslin, 'Paul and Gamaliel', JR 7 (1927), pp. 360–75; J. W. Swain, 'Gamaliel's Speech and Caligula's Statue', HThR 37 (1944), pp. 341–9; Guttmann, *Rabbinic Judaism*, pp. 177–82; Enc. Jud. 7, cols. 295–9; Neusner, *Pharisees* I, pp. 341–76.

49. Ps.-Clement, *Recogn.* i 65 ff. A divinized Gamaliel appears in some of the Gnostic discoveries printed in the Jung Codex and from the Cairo Museum, especially the *Sacred Book of the invisible Great Spirit* and the *Apocalypse of Adam to his son; Seth* for instance, cf. J. Doresse, *The Secret Books of the Egyptian Gnostics* (1960), especially p. 286, n. 73.

50. mSot. 9:15. כבוד התורה = 'respect for the law'; cf. mNed. 9:1: כבוד אביו = 'respect for his father'. Similarly, mAb. 4:2. The meaning therefore is that no one any longer had such a respect for the Torah as had Rabban Gamaliel the Elder.

51. Cf. Josephus, *B.J.* iv 3, 9 (159); *Vita* 9 (38, 39); 10 (44); 11 (60). Derenbourg, pp. 270–2, 474–5; Büchler, *Das Synedrion*, pp. 131–44; J. Z. Lauterbach, JE XI, p. 347; A. Guttmann, *Rabbinic Judaism in the Making* (1970), pp. 182–4; Neusner, *Pharisees* I, pp. 377–88. In the Mishnah, the much-mentioned Rabban Simeon ben Gamaliel is as a rule to be understood as the son of Gamaliel II, especially in mAb. 1:18. Besides mAb. 1:17, only mKer. 1:7 relates perhaps to Simeon son of Gamaliel I.

52. *Vita* 38 (191).

συνέσεως καὶ λογισμοῦ δυνάμενός τε πράγματα κακῶς κείμενα φρονήσει τῇ ἑαυτοῦ διορθώσασθαι. He lived at the time of the Jewish war and during its earlier period (A.D. 66–8) played a prominent role in the conduct of affairs. Nevertheless, he too was never President of the Sanhedrin.

The fall of Jerusalem and destruction of the Jewish community, until then relatively independent, was of far-reaching significance for the further development of Torah learning. The old Sanhedrin headed by Sadducean High Priests now departed the stage for good. The Pharisee Torah teachers, who had in fact exercised the greater influence during the preceding century, became the sole leaders of the people. The political downfall therefore had as a direct result an increase of rabbinic power and an upswing of rabbinic studies.

From this point on, the sources flow more abundantly, since the first codification of Jewish law was undertaken by men still directly associated with the generation which had experienced the city's destruction.

Jamnia, or Yavneh, which had been predominantly inhabited by Jews since the time of the Hasmonaeans, became a centre of scholarship after Jerusalem fell. It is here that the most respected of the surviving scholars seem to have settled.[53] Another was Lydda or Lod.[54] Usha, then Tiberias, did not come into favour as a seat of learning until about the middle of the second century A.D.

The most distinguished master of the first decades following the loss of the Holy City was Rabban Yohanan ben Zakkai.[55] The date of his

53. See in general mShek. 1:4; mR. Sh. 2:8–9; 4:1–2; mKet. 4:6; mSanh. 11:4; mEdu. 2:4; mAb. 4:4; mBekh, 4:5; 6:8; mKel. 5:4; mPar. 7:6.

54. mR. Sh. 1:6; mTaan. 3:9; mB.M. 4:3; mYad. 4:3; Jerome, *Com. in Habac.* 2:17 (CCL lxxvi A, p. 610); A. Neubauer, *Géographie du Talmud* (1868), pp. 76–80; E. Neumann, 'Lydda', JE VIII, pp. 227–8; G. A. Smith, *The Historical Geography of the Holy Land* (1931), pp. 159–62; Abel, *Géog. Pal.* II, p. 370; D. Baly, *The Geography of the Bible* (1957), pp. 135–6; Avi-Yonah, *The Holy Land*, pp. 156–9; *Gazetteer*, p. 75.

55. See H. Graetz, *Geschichte der Juden* IV, pp. 10 ff.; Derenbourg, *Essai*, pp. 266–7, 276–88, 302–18; W. Bacher, *Die Agada der Tannaiten* I², pp. 22–42; 'Johanan b. Zakkai', JE VII, pp. 214–17; A. Büchler, *Synedrion* (1902), pp. 139–44; D. Chwolson, *Beiträge zur Entwicklungsgeschichte des Judenthums* (²1908), pp. 17–19; V. Aptowitzer, 'Besprechungen', MGWJ 52 (1908), pp. 744–5; Moore, *Judaism* I, pp. 83–6; G. Alon, *'Nesi'uto shel R. Yoḥanan b. Zakkai'*, *Meḥkarim* I (1958), pp. 253–73; *'Halikhato shel Rabban Yoḥanan ben Zakkai l*ᵉ*-Yavneh'*, *ibid.*, pp. 219–52; J. Neusner, *A Life of Rabban Yohanan ben Zakkai* (1962, ²1970); *Development of a Legend. Studies on the Traditions concerning Yoḥanan ben Zakkai* (1970); 'The Traditions concerning Yohanan ben Zakkai: Reconsiderations', JJS 24 (1973), pp. 65–73; A. J. Saldarini, 'Johanan ben Zakkai's Escape from Jerusalem', JSJ 6 (1975), pp. 189–204. In the Mishnah he is mentioned in the following passages: mShab. 16:7; 22:3; mShek. 1:4; mSuk. 2:5; 12; mR. Sh. 4:1, 3, 4; mKet. 13:1–2; mSot. 5:2, 5; 9:9, 15; mEdu. 8:3, 7; mAb. 2:8–9; mMen. 10:5;

activities is evident from the fact that he modified several legal rulings and usages 'after the Temple was destroyed'.[56] He appears to have resided chiefly in Yavneh,[57] but Beror Hayil is also named as a scene of his labours.[58] He must in addition have stayed in Arab (ערב), where various legal questions were presented to him for his decision.[59] One of his noteworthy innovations was the abolition of the law (Num. 5:12–31) requiring a wife suspected of adultery to undergo the ordeal of drinking the 'water of bitterness'.[60] He disputed legal questions with the Sadducees:[61] which shows how near he still was to conditions as they existed before Jerusalem was destroyed, for the Sadducees soon afterwards disappeared from history. He was also the vehicle of age-old traditions traced back to Moses himself.[62] Legend recounts of him what Josephus says of himself: that he predicted Vespasian's future elevation to the imperial throne.[63] The Mishnah names as his five pupils, R. Eliezer ben Hyrcanus, R. Joshua ben Hanania, R. Yose the Priest, R. Simeon ben Nathanael, R. Eleazar ben Arakh.[64] The best known and most eminent of these are R. Eliezer and R. Joshua.

---

mKel. 2:2; 17:16; mYad. 4:3, 6. Only as בן זכאי, mSanh. 5:2. For Tosefta references, see the index to Zuckermandel's edition. Passages in the Tannaitic Midrashim, the Talmud, etc., may be seen in J. Neusner, *Development*, pp. 15–184. Cf. now G. Alon, *Jews, Judaism and the Classical World* (1977), pp. 269–343.

56. mSuk. 3:12; mR.Sh. 4:1, 3, 4; mMen. 10:5.

57. mShek. 1:4; mR.Sh. 4:1.

58. bSanh. 32b; tMaas. 2:1 (cf. yDemai 23b; yMaas, 49d); Derenbourg, p. 307. Derenbourg suggested that Yoḥanan ben Zakkai withdrew to Beror Hayil in order to leave command in Yavneh to Gamaliel II (*Histoire*, pp. 306–10). Others advanced the conjecture that Beror Hayil was Yavneh. Graetz, MGWJ (1884), pp. 529–33 (Beror Hayil='Iamnia intus' of Pliny) and S. Krauss, Magazin für die Wissenschaft des Judenthums 20 (1893), pp. 117–22 (ברור=*φρούριον*=army; therefore Beror Ḥayil='military district', by which was meant Yavneh). See J. Neusner, *A Life of Yohanan ben Zakkai* (²1970), pp. 225–6.

59. mShab. 16:17, 22:3. Arab is a town in Galilee not far from Sepphoris; see Derenbourg, *Essai*, p. 318, n. 3; Eusebius, *Onomasticon* (ed. Klostermann, p. 16): *ἔστι δὲ καὶ κώμη καλουμένη Ἀραβὰ ἐν ὁρίοις Διοκαισαρείας καὶ ἀπὸ τριῶν σημείων Σκυθοπόλεως ἄλλη πρὸς δυσμάς*. Cf. Abel. *Géog. Pal.* II, p. 248; M. Avi-Yonah, *The Holy Land* (1966), p. 97; G. Vermes, 'Hanina ben Dosa', JJS 24 (1973), p. 58 [*PBJS*, pp. 206–7]; cf. Schalit, *Namenwörterbuch* s.v. 'Gabara'.

60. mSot. 9:9. Altogether nine decrees (תקנות) introduced by him are enumerated in the Talmud, bR.Sh. 31b; bSot. 40b; Derenbourg, pp. 304 f.; cf. also S. Zeitlin, 'The Takkanot of Rabban Joḥanan ben Zakkai', JQR 54 (1964), pp. 288–310; J. Neusner, *A Life* (²1970), pp. 203–10; *Development of a Legend*, pp. 206–9.

61. mYad. 4:6.

62. mEdu. 8:7; mYad. 4:3. Cf. p. 341, n. 4, above.

63. Lam. R. on Lam. 1:5; Derenbourg, pp. 282 f. Cf. vol. I, p. 494, n. 41.

64. mAb. 2:8–9. According to bBer. 34b, Hanina ben Dosa, the Galilean miracle-worker, was another pupil of Yohanan ben Zakkai. Cf. G. Vermes 'Hanina ben Dosa', JJS 23 (1972), pp. 28–50; 24 (1973), pp. 51–64 [=*PBJS*, pp. 178–214]. In the manuscripts and editions, the abbreviation R.=rabbi, while the title Rabban is usually written in full.

One scholar roughly contemporary with Rabban Yohanan ben Zakkai was R. Zadok[65] (or Zadduk, as it should be pronounced). He is said to have lived before the destruction of the Temple but to have associated nevertheless with Gamaliel II, Joshua and Eliezer. His name in fact frequently appears with theirs in the Mishnah,[66] though some of the passages probably allude to a later R. Zadok.[67]

The first decades after the destruction of the Temple also saw the appearance of the leading Torah scholar, R. Hanina, the 'Captain of the priests' (סגן הכהנים).[68] He relates what his father did in the Temple, and what he himself saw,[69] and indeed acts in the Mishnah almost entirely as a kind of reporter on the details of the priestly cult.[70] Characteristic of him as a leading priest is his call for prayers on behalf of the imperial authorities.[71]

To the same first generation belongs also R. Eliezer ben Jacob.[72] For it is very likely that an older sage of the same name who lived not long after the destruction of the Temple is to be distinguished from the considerably later R. Eliezer ben Jacob quoted rather frequently in the Mishnah.[73] His uncle served as a Levite in the Temple[74] and he himself

65. See Derenbourg, pp. 242–4; Bacher, *Die Agada der Tannaiten* I², pp. 43–6; JE XII, pp. 629–30; Enc. Jud. 16, cols. 915–6. In the Mishnah: mTer. 10:9; mPes. 7:2; mSuk. 2:5; mNed. 9:1; mEdu. 3:8; 7:1–4; mAb. 4:5; mBekh. 1:6; mKel. 12: 4–5; mMikw. 5:5. Regarding mShab. 20:2; 24:5, cf. n. 67 below. For Tosefta references, see the index to Zuckermandel's edition. The pronunciation Zadduk is according to the partially pointed Cod. de Rossi 138. Cf. *Σαδδούκ* in the LXX in Ezekiel, Ezra, and Nehemiah. See also the textual apparatus to *Ant.* xviii 1, 1 (4). Cf. J. Lightstone, 'Sadoq the Yavnean', W. S. Green (ed.), *op. cit.* [p. 359, n. 7], pp. 49–147.

66. With Gamaliel II, mPes. 7:2; with Joshua, mEdu. 7:1 = mBekh. 1:6; with Eliezer, mNed. 9:1.

67. Thus mShab. 20:2; 24:5. Cf. Bacher, *Die Agada der Tannaiten* I², p. 50. If the existence of the second R. Zadok is acknowledged, the question of course arises whether further passages also relate to him.

68. See Derenbourg, pp. 368–70; Bacher, *Die Agada der Tannaiten* I², pp. 51–3; Moore, *Judaism* II, pp. 114–15; S. W. Baron, *The Jewish Community* III, p. 28, Enc. Jud. 7, cols. 1266–7. According to the best authorities the name is not Hanina but Hananiah. Cf. Marti-Beer, *Abot*, p. 62 and the critical apparatus to 3:2 on p. 190. On the office of a priestly סגן, see above, pp. 277–8.

69. mZeb. 9:3; 12:4.

70. See in general, mPes. 1:6; mShek. 4:4; 6:1; mEdu. 2:1–3; mAb. 3:2; mZeb. 9:3; 12:4; mMen. 10:1; mNeg. 1:4; mPar. 3:1.

71. mAb. 3:2.

72. Derenbourg, p. 374–5; Bacher, *Agada der Tannaiten* I², pp. 62–7; Finkelstein, *The Pharisees* (³1962), pp. 731–4; JE V, pp. 115–16; Strack, p. 110; Enc. Jud. 6, col. 624.

73. Thus also Derenbourg, p. 375, n. 3, and Bacher, p. 62. The younger Eliezer ben Jacob was a contemporary of R. Simeon ben Yohai, around A.D. 150 (mPar. 9:2), and speaks in the name of Hananiah ben Hakhinai, who in turn echoes R. Akiba (mKil. 4:8; tNeg. 1:2; tTohor. 11:3).

74. mMid. 1:2.

is frequently appealed to as an informant in the description of the Temple given in the tractate Middoth;[75] later tradition even ascribes the writing of the whole tractate to him.[76] It is no longer possible to determine which passages are connected with the older and which with the younger R. Eliezer ben Jakob. But perhaps the information regarding the cult may be ascribed to the younger of the two.[77]

Rabban Gamaliel II, son of Simeon and grandson of Gamaliel I, the most celebrated scholar of the turn of the century (ca. A.D. 90–110),[78] lived a few decades later than R. Yohanan ben Zakkai. The academy at Yavneh, of which he was the head, was in his day generally recognized as the highest authority in Israel.[79] The most eminent scholars gathered around him there and in this respected circle Gamaliel's judgement was final.[80] Among the sages more closely associated with him, the most outstanding were his appropriate coeval, R. Joshua, and the younger R. Akiba.[81] Gamaliel does not, on the other hand, appear to have been in contact with the likewise contemporary and famous R. Eliezer ben Hyrcanus. There is in any case no sign of such a relationship in the Mishnah; on the contrary, later tradition relates that Eliezer was excommunicated by Gamaliel (see below). Gamaliel once travelled by sea to Rome with Joshua, Akiba and the similarly distinguished R. Eleazar ben Azariah, an event that acquired a certain renown in rabbinical literature.[82]

75. mMid. 1:2, 9; 2:5, 6; 5:4. Cf. mShek. 6:3.

76. bYom. 16a; Derenbourg, p. 374, n. 1.

77. E.g., information concerning priestly marriages (mBik. 1:5; mKid. 4:7); the sacrificial ritual (mMen. 5:6; 9:3; mTam. 5:2); first-born cattle (mBekh. 3:1); sacred singers (mArakh. 2:6); sacrifices of proselytes (mKer. 2:1).

78. H. Graetz, *Geschichte der Juden* IV, pp. 30 ff.; 423 ff.; Derenbourg, pp. 306–13, 319–46; Bacher, *Die Agada der Tannaiten* I², pp. 73–95; JE V, pp. 650–2; B. Z. Bokser, *Pharisaic Judaism in Transition* (1935), pp. 23 ff.; Moore, *Judaism* I, pp. 86–92; Alon, *Toledot* I, pp. 71–192; A. Guttmann, *Rabbinic Judaism in the Making* (1970), pp. 200–21; Enc. Jud. 7, cols, 296–8. The chronology follows from the fact that his younger contemporary, Akiba, played a role in the Bar Kokhba war.

79. mR.Sh. 2:8–9; mKel. 5:4. Cf. Derenbourg, pp. 319–22; Graetz, *Geschichte* II, pp. 330 ff.; Enc. Jud. 9, cols. 1176–8. Gamaliel is once met in Kefar-Othnai (mGit. 1:5) but he seems to have stayed there only temporarily.

80. Thus when it was once necessary to decree, during Gamaliel's absence, whether a year should be a leap-year, this was done with the proviso that Gamaliel should subsequently give his approval (mEdu. 7:7). Cf. also for Gamaliel's authoritative position, the formula 'Rabban Gamaliel and the elders' (mM.Sh. 9; mShab. 16:8; mErub. 10:10).

81. On the relations between Gamaliel, Joshua and Akiba, cf. especially mM.Sh. 5:9; mErub. 4:1; mR.Sh. 2:8–9; mM.Sh. 2:7; mSuk. 3:9; mKer. 3:7–9; mNeg. 7:4. Between Gamaliel and Joshua, mYad. 4:4. Between Gamaliel and Akiba, mR.Sh. 1:6; mYeb. 16:7.

82. mErub. 4:1–2; mM.Sh. 5:9; mShab. 16:8. Derenbourg, pp. 334–40; Bacher, *Die Agada der Tannaiten* I², pp. 79–82. J. Goldin, 'The Period of the Talmud', *The*

Gamaliel is said to have been removed on one occasion from his position as President of the seventy-two elders because of his autocratic behaviour, and to have been replaced by R. Eleazar ben Azariah.[83] But on a show of remorse, Eleazar voluntarily relinquished the office and Gamaliel was quickly reinstated. The promotion of Eleazar by the seventy-two elders to the position of head of the school is attested in the Mishnah.[84]

In his legal rulings, Gamaliel followed the school of Hillel; it is mentioned as an exception that on three points his decision was in accordance with the school of Shammai.[85] In general, he was characterized as much by legal strictness,[86] as by a certain worldliness, and even open-mindedness.[87]

The two most famous contemporaries of Gamaliel were R. Joshua ben Hananiah and R. Eliezer ben Hyrcanus, both pupils of Yohanan ben Zakkai.[88] The two are frequently found debating with each other on legal questions, with the younger Akiba also taking part.[89] Only Joshua seems to have been in contact with Gamaliel. The explanation, according to later tradition, is that Gamaliel excommunicated Eliezer.[90]

R. Joshua was of Levitical descent.[91] He was gentle and yielding by

---

Jews (ed. Finkelstein), pp. 150 ff.; Guttmann, *Rabbinic Judaism*, pp. 218–19; M. D. Herr, Scrip Hier. 22 (1971), pp. 123–50.

83. yBer. 1cd; bBer. 27b; Graetz, *Geschichte der Juden* IV, pp. 35 ff.; Derenbourg, pp. 327–9; R. Goldenberg, 'The Deposition of Rabban Gamaliel II: an Examination of the Sources', JJS 23 (1972), pp. 167–90. Concerning the argument whether Eleazar bore the title of *nasi* or *ab beth din*, see H. Mantel, *Studies in the History of the Sanhedrin* (1961), pp. 119–20.

84. mZeb. 1:3; mYad. 3:5; 4:2.

85. mBez. 2:6; mEdu. 3:10.

86. mBer. 2:5–6. Cf. Ginzberg, *A Commentary on the Palestinian Talmud* I (1941), pp. 159–60.

87. Cf. in addition to the journey to Rome, his dealings with the governor (*hēgemōn*) of Syria (mEdu. 7:7)—for ἡγεμών as a common Greek term for 'governor', see H. J. Mason, *Greek Terms for Roman Institutions* (1974), p. 52—and his visit to the Bath of Aphrodite at Acco despite the presence there of a statue of the goddess (mA.Z. 3:4). Cf. Mantel, *Studies*, p. 23; G. Vermes, CHB I, p. 217 [*PBJS*, p. 77].

88. mAb. 2:8. Cf. mEdu. 8:7; mYad. 4:3.

89. On the relations between Joshua, Eliezer and Akiba cf. especially, mPes. 6:2; mYeb. 8:4; mNed. 10:6; mNaz. 7:4; mEdu. 2:7. Between Joshua and Eliezer, mPes. 6:5; mTaan 1:1; mZeb. 7:4; 8:10: mNaz. 7:4. Between Joshua and Akiba, mPes. 9:6; mSanh. 7:11. Between Eliezer and Akiba, mPea. 7:7; mKer. 3:10: mSheb. 8:9–10.

90. yM.K. 81d; bB.M. 59b. Graetz, *Geschichte der Juden* IV, p. 47; Derenbourg, pp. 324–5; J. Bassfreund, MGWJ 42 (1898), pp. 49–57; Moore, *Judaism* II, p. 250; J. Neusner, *Eliezer ben Hyrcanus—The Tradition and the Man* I, pp. 423–4; II, p. 350.

91. This is evident from mM.Sh. 5:9. Cf. on Joshua in general, Graetz, *Geschichte der Juden* IV, pp. 50 ff., 426 ff.; Derenbourg, pp. 319–46, 416–19; Bacher, *Die*

nature and therefore subordinated himself also to the unbending Gamaliel.[92] 'When R. Joshua died, goodness ceased in the world.'[93] His motto was: 'Envy, evil desire and hatred of humankind put a man out of the world.'[94]

Peki'in, or Beki'in, is given as the site of R. Joshua's labours,[95] but taking into consideration his close relationship with Gamaliel, it is probable that he also lived partly in Yavneh. Among other things, it is said of him that he had various discourses with the Emperor Hadrian on religious topics.[96]

In contrast to the yielding Joshua, R. Eliezer was a stubborn, inflexible person who adhered with great rigour to tradition, which, due to a retentive memory and extensive learning, h emastered as none other.[97] His teacher, Yohanan ben Zakkai, boasted of him that he was like a cistern coated with lime which loses not a single drop.[98] But no argument or representation could move him from what he recognized as tradition. Hence the strained relations with Gamaliel, although he is said to have been his brother-in-law.[99] He lived in Lydda.[100] The view that he inclined towards Christianity, or was even a crypto-Christian, is based on a legend which in fact proves the opposite. According to this, when Eliezer was once brought before a Gentile court he viewed his predicament as God's righteous punishment for having been pleased with the shrewd solution to a legal question imparted to him by a Judaeo-Christian, Jacob of Kefar Sekhaniah, as coming from Jesus.[101]

Agada der Tannaiten I², pp. 123–7; JE VII, pp. 290–2; Strack, p. 111; S. Lieberman, *Greek in Jewish Palestine* (²1965), pp. 16–19; Enc. Jud. 10, cols 279–81.

92. mR.Sh. 2:8–9. Derenbourg, pp. 325–7; Guttmann, *Rabbinic Judaism*, pp. 169–70.

93. mSot. 9:15. Parallel passages in Tosefta and Talmud express in varying ways the thought that after R. Joshua died, 'good counsel' existed no longer. (See Bacher, *Die Agada der Tannaiten* I², p. 156.)

94. mAb. 2:11.

95. פקיעין, bSanh. 32b; tSot. 7:9. בקיעין yHag. 75d. Derenbourg, p. 307. It lay between Lydda and Yavneh, see especially, yHag. 75d; also bHag. 3a. Neubauer, *La géographie du Talmud*, p. 81. Cf. M. Avi-Yonah, *Carta's Atlas of the Period of the Second Temple, the Mishnah and the Talmud* (1966), no. 116 on p. 77.

96. Bacher, *Die Agada der Tannaiten* I², pp. 170–3.

97. See Graetz, *Geschichte der Juden* IV, pp. 43 ff., 425 f.; Derenbourg, pp. 319–46, 366–8; Bacher, *Die Agada der Tannaiten* I², pp. 96–155; JE V, pp. 113–15; Strack, p. 111; A. Guttmann, 'Eliezer b. Hyrcanus—a Shammaite', *I. Goldziher Memorial Volume* (1948–58), pp. 100–10; M. Aberbach, 'Did Rabban Gamaliel impose the Ban on Eliezer b. Hyrcanus?', JQR 54 (1964), pp. 201–7; Enc. Jud. 6, cols. 619–23; J. Neusner, *Eliezer ben Hyrcanus* I, pp. 395–7;II, pp. 294–307, 343–7.

98. mAb. 2:8.

99. bShab. 116a.

100. mYad. 4:3; bSanh. 32b.

101. The legend is found in several recensions: tHul. 2:24 (ed. Zuckermandel, p. 503); bA.Z. 16b; Eccl. R. 1:8; cf. T. R. Herford, *Christianity in Talmud and*

Side by side with these scholars, an honourable position was also occupied by R. Eleazar ben Azariah,[102] a rich and eminent priest whose line went back to Ezra.[103] His wealth was such that it was said that after he died, riches no longer existed among the sages.[104] His association with Gamaliel, Joshua and Akiba, their joint expedition to Rome, his promotion to the presidency by the seventy-two elders and his voluntary resignation from that office, have already been discussed. It is clear from these data alone that he worked in Yavneh, a fact also attested elsewhere.[105] He was also in personal contact with R. Ishmael and R. Tarphon, contemporaries of Akiba.[106]

Another contemporary of Gamaliel and Joshuah was R. Dosa ben Archinos (or Harkhinas).[107] It is recounted in particular of him that he induced Joshua to submit to Gamaliel.[108]

To the later men of this generation belongs also R. Eleazar ben Zadok, the son of the R. Zadok already mentioned.[109] Like his father,

---

Midrash (1903), pp. 137–45, 412–13. In Abodah Zarah, the Judaeo-Christian is called a disciple of ישו הנוצרי; in Midrash Rabbah, of ישו בן פנדרא; in the Tosefta, of ישו בן פנטירי. See in general, Graetz, IV, pp. 47–8; Derenbourg, pp. 357–60; Bacher, *Die Agada der Tannaiten* I^2, pp. 107–8; A. Schlatter, *Die Kirche Jerusalems vom J. 70–130* (1898), pp. 11–14; H. L. Strack, *Jesus die Häretiker und die Christen nach ältesten jüdischen Angaben* (1910), p. 23; H. J. Schoeps, *Theologie und Geschichte des Judenchristentums* (1949), p. 24; M. Simon, *Verus Israel* (^{2}1964), pp. 219–20; Neusner, *Eliezer ben Hyrcanus* II, pp. 330–4, 365–7.

102. See Derenbourg, pp. 327–30; Graetz IV (^{4}1908), pp. 35; Bacher, *Die Agada der Tannaiten* I^2, pp. 212–32; JE V, pp. 978; Strack, p. 111; Moore, *Judaism* I, pp. 86 ff.; Enc. Jud. 6, cols. 586–7; T. Zahavy, *The Traditions of Eleazar ben Azariah* (1977). According to the best authorities, the name does not read Eliezer but Eleazar (in the Cod. de Rossi 138 and in the Cambridge MS usually לעזר). The latter is the prevailing form in Galilean Aramaic and is echoed by the Greek *Λάζαρος*, Lk. 16:20 ff.; Jn. 11:1 ff.; Josephus, *B.J.* v 13, 7 (567). See also *Λαζε* and *Λαζαρ* in M. Schwabe-B. Lifshitz, *Beth She'arim II: the Greek Inscriptions* (1967), pp. 34, 73; cf. G. Vermes, *Jesus the Jew*, pp. 190–1, 261; 'The Present State of the Son of Man Debate', JJS 29 (1978), pp. 128–9.

103. Bacher, *Die Agada der Tannaiten* I^2, p. 212. That he was a priest follows from mM.Sh. 5:9.

104. mSot. 9:15.

105. mKet. 4:6. Some aphorisms of Eleazar in mAb. 3:17.

106. On a dispute between him, Tarphon, Ishmael and Joshua, see mYad. 4:3. Between Eleazar and Ishmael, also tBer. 1:6. Between Eleazar and Akiba, tBer. 4:12; tShab. 3:3.

107. See Derenbourg, pp. 368–9; Enc. Jud. 6, col. 178.

108. mR.Sh. 2:8–9. Cf. mErub. 3:9; mKet. 13:1–2; mEdu. 3:1–6; mAb. 3:10; mHul. 11:2; mOhol. 3:1; mNeg. 1:4.

109. See Derenbourg, pp. 342–4; Bacher, *Die Agada der Tannaiten* I^2, pp. 46–50; JE V, p. 120; Enc. Jud. 6, cols. 600–1. As with R. Zadok, there were probably two scholars with the name of Eleazar ben Zadok, an older and a younger. See Bacher, *Die Agada der Tannaiten* I^2, pp. 49–50; cf. however Derenbourg, p. 262, n. 2, 344, n. 4. The younger speaks in the name of R. Meir (mKil. 7:2), so he did not live until after the middle of the second century.

he too was close to Gamaliel and reports on his decrees and the legal customs of his house.[110]

R. Ishmael occupied an independent position among the scholars of this period.[111] He is admittedly found occasionally in Yavneh;[112] he was also in close communication with his famous contemporaries, Joshua, Eleazar ben Azariah, Tarphon and Akiba.[113] But his usual residence was in southern Palestine on the borders of Edom, in a village called Kefar-'Aziz where Joshua once visited him.[114] In age, he seems to have been nearer to Tarphon and Akiba than to Joshua: he questions Joshua and walks 'after him' like a pupil, whereas he associates with Tarphon and Akiba as with equals.[115] It would be especially interesting if, as tradition has it, his father really were a functioning High Priest. But this is doubtful, though it is likely that he was of priestly descent.[116]

In the history of halakhah, Ishmael represents a trend of his own inasmuch as in contrast to the artificial and arbitrary exegesis of Akiba he holds—speaking very relatively of course—more to the simple and literal meaning of Scripture: 'The Torah speaks the language of men'.[117]

110. tHal. 2:5; tShab. 1:22; tY. Tob 1:22; 2:13; tKid. 1:11.

111. See Graetz, *Geschichte der Juden* IV, pp. 60 ff., 427 ff.; Derenbourg, pp. 386–95; Bacher, *Die Agada der Tannaiten* I², pp. 232–63; M. Petuchowski, *Der Tanna R. Ismael* (1894); JE V, pp. 648–50; Strack, p. 112; S. Zeitlin, JQR 36 (1945–6), pp. 1–11; S. Safrai, Enc. Jud. 9, cols. 83–6; G. G. Porton, *The Traditions of Rabbi Ishmael* I–II (1976–7). On the school of Ishmael, D. Hoffmann, *Zur Einleitung in die halachischen Midrashim* (1887), pp. 5 ff.

112. mEdu. 2:4.

113. Joshua and Ishmael: mKil. 6:4; mA.Z. 2:5; tPar. 10:3. Akiba and Ishmael: mEdu. 2:6; mMikw. 7:1. On a dispute between Tarphon, Eleazar ben Azariah, Ishmael and Joshua, see mYad. 4:3. That Joshua and Ishmael did not live in the same place is apparent from mKil. 6:4; tBekh. 2:12. The same is clear in respect of Akiba from mErub. 1:2; tZab. 1:8 (the pupils of Ishmael report on their master's teaching to Akiba).

114. On the borders of Edom, mKet. 5:8; in Kefar-'Aziz, mKil. 6:4. On Kefar-'Aziz, see Conder and Kitchener, *The Survey of Western Palestine* III, pp. 315, 348–50; Abel, *Géog. Pal.* II, p. 288; Avi-Yonah, *Gazetteer*, p.71. mMikw. 7:1, according to which people from Medaba, the well-known Moabite city, report on Ishmael's teaching, points to activity in Peraea.

115. Cf. the passages cited in n. 113; regarding Joshua, especially mA.Z. 2:5; tPar. 10:3. Bacher, *Die Agada der Tannaiten* I², pp. 232–3.

116. bKet. 105b; bHul. 49a; tHal. 1:10. Cf. Derenbourg, pp. 287 f.; Finkelstein, *The Pharisees*, pp. 181–2.

117. Sifra on Num. 112 (ed. Horovitz, p. 121). Cf. Bacher, *Die Agada der Tannaiten* I², p. 242 f. On the simple exegesis of the Tannaitic period generally, see E. von Dobschütz, *Die einfache Bibelexegese der Tannaim* (1893); J. Weingreen, 'The Rabbinic Approach to the Study of the OT', BJRL 34 (1951–2), pp. 166–90; R. Loewe, 'The "Plain" Meaning of Scripture in Early Jewish Exegesis', *Papers of the Institute of Jewish Studies, London* I (1964), pp. 140–85; G. Vermes, CHB I, pp. 203–20 [*PBJS*, pp. 63–80].

The composition of the thirteen middoth, or exegetical rules, for halakhic exegesis is ascribed to him.[118] Also, a large part if not all, of the exegetical material contained in two of the oldest midrashim (Mekhilta on Exodus and Sifre on Numbers and Deuteronomy), derives from him and his school.[119]

According to legend, Ishmael, like many of his fellow rabbis, died a martyr's death in the war of A.D. 132–5.[120]

Among the scholars who were in contact with Gamaliel, Joshua and Eliezer, but whose relationship with them was rather that of pupils, the most famous by far is R. Akiba ben Joseph.[121] He flourished around A.D. 110–35. His relations with Gamaliel, Joshua and Eliezer have already been discussed (nn. 80, 81 and 88). In influence and reputation he surpassed them all. None of them attracted so many pupils[122] or has been so glorified by tradition. It is however almost impossible to distinguish historical fact from fiction. Not even the scene of his activities is known for certain. According to the Mishnah, it appears to have been Lydda;[123] the Talmud names Bene Berak.[124] Such of his sayings as have been handed down are not only characteristic of his legally strict point of view, but show that he reflected on questions of doctrine and philosophy.[125] Like the ancient Zealots, he combined religious zeal with patriotism. He therefore hailed the revolutionary hero Bar Kokhba as the Messiah,[126] and is said to have suffered martyrdom for the national cause.[127]

R. Akiba's exegetical method was intended to provide scriptural proof for every Jewish usage. Talmudic humour underlines its artificiality in the following anecdote. 'When Moses ascended to heaven, he

118. See above, p. 344. Cf. Derenbourg, pp. 389–91, and Moore, *Judaism* I, pp. 88–9.

119. Cf. Bacher, *Agada der Tannaiten* I², p. 235. On Mekhilta and Sifre, see vol. I, pp. 90–3, and the literature mentioned in n. 111.

120. Graetz, IV, p. 175; Derenbourg, p. 436; see vol. I, p. 552.

121. See Graetz, *Geschichte der Juden* IV, pp. 53 ff., 427 ff.; Derenbourg, pp. 329–31, 395–401; Bacher, *Agada der Tannaiten* I², pp. 263–342; L. Ginzberg, 'Akiba', JE I, pp. 304–10; A. Schlatter, *Geschichte Israels* (²1906), pp. 284–9; Strack, pp. 112–13; L. Finkelstein, *Akiba, Scholar, Saint, and Martyr* (1936, ²1962); Enc. Jud. 2, cols. 488–92.

122. Derenbourg, pp. 395–6.

123. mR.Sh. 1:6.

124. bSanh. 32b; Derenbourg, pp. 307, 395. Also cf. bSanh. 96b, bGit. 57b; A. Neubauer, *La géographie du Talmud*, p. 82. בני ברק also occurs in Jos. 19:45. Eusebius, *Onom.* (ed. Klostermann), p. 54, s.v. *Βαρακαί*, mistakenly locates it in the tribe of Ashdod. Cf. Abel, *Géog. Pal.* II, pp. 263–4.

125. The sayings: mAb. 3:13–16. Among them, 3:15, is הכל צפוי והרשות נתונה, 'Everything is foreseen (by God) but freedom is granted (to man)'.

126. See vol. I, p. 543 and n. 130.

127. Graetz, IV, pp. 176–7; Derenbourg, p. 436; Bacher, *Die Agada der Tannaiten* I², p. 265; cf. vol. I, p. 552.

found the Holy One, blessed be He, sitting and attaching little crowns to the letters (of the Torah). Amazed by this, Moses asked for the meaning of what God was doing and was told: After many generations a man will come called Akiba ben Joseph who will derive heaps and heaps of halakhic rules from each of these decorations.'[128]

To achieve his aim, he adopted the principle that not a single word of the text was superfluous: it is the smallest and apparently unnecessary elements that contain important truths.[129] More valuable than these exegetical skills, and of truly epoch-making significance for the history of Jewish law, was the first codification in the time of Akiba, and probably under his guidance, of the halakhah previously transmitted for the most part by word of mouth. The various legal matters were arranged according to their subject, and the law currently valid was recorded, together with the dissentient opinions of all the most prominent scholars. This work forms the basis the Mishnah of R. Judah ha-Nasi.[130]

One contemporary of Akiba was R. Tarphon, a priestly Torah scholar said to have taken his inherited privileges and duties very seriously, insofar as this was possible after the Temple was destroyed.[131] He lived in Lydda[132] and communicated chiefly with Akiba,[133] though he also participated in a disputation with Eleazar ben Azariah, Ishmael and Joshua.[134] Subsequent tradition represents him, like almost all the

128. bMen. 29b. Cf. Bacher, *Die Agada der Tannaiten* I², p. 263–4; D. Barthélemy, *Les devanciers d'Aquila* (1963), pp. 3–15.

129. Thus e.g. the particle את is said to indicate that in addition to the object mentioned, something else is meant. In the account of the creation, את השמים is used because the sun, moon and stars are included as well, Gen. R. 1:14 (ed. Theodor, p. 12). Cf. Derenbourg, p. 397; Barthélemy, *op. cit.*, pp. 10–15. The proselyte Aquila sought to do justice to this exegetic principle in his Greek version by translating Gen. 1:1 as *σὺν τὸν οὐρανὸν καὶ σὺν τὴν γῆν*. Jerome, *Epist.* 57 *ad Pammachium* 11 3, pours ridicule on a construction of this kind 'quod Graeca et Latina lingua omnino non recipit'. Also cf. on Aquila as pupil of Akiba, Jerome, *Comment. in Esaiam* 8:11 ff. (CCL lxxiii, p. 116): 'Akibas quem magistrum Aquilae proselyti autumant'. Graetz, *Geschichte der Juden* IV, p. 437; see especially Barthélemy, *op. cit.*, pp. 15–21.

130. That an older work from the time of Akiba underlies our Mishnah may be concluded almost with certainty from the contents. That that work was edited by Akiba himself may likewise be accepted as probable from rabbinic tradition (mSanh. 3:4; bSanh. 86a) and from the testimony of Epiphanius, *Haer.* xxxiii 9 (ed. Holl, I, p. 45a). See further, vol. I, p. 77, n. 23. Cf. also Derenbourg, pp. 399-401; Strack, pp. 221, 249; Danby, *The Mishnah* (1933), p. xxi; C. Primus, *Aqiva's Contribution to the Law of Zera'im* (1977).

131. See in general, Derenbourg, pp. 376–83; Bacher, *Die Agada der Tannaiten* I², pp. 342–52; JE XII, pp. 56–7; Strack, p. 113; J. Neusner, 'A Life of Rabbi Tarfon ca. 50–130 C.E.', Judaica 17 (1961), pp. 141–67; Enc. Jud. 15, cols. 810–11.

132. mB.M. 4:3; mTaan. 3:9.

133. mTer. 4:5; 9:2; mNaz. 6:6; mBekh. 4:4; mKer. 5:2–3; tMikw. 1:19; 7:11.

134. mYad. 4:3.

Torah scholars of his time, as a martyr in the Bar Kokhba war.[135] But as this story possesses exactly the same value as the Christian tradition which makes martyrs of all the apostles, he might perhaps be identical with the Tryphon encountered by Justin who said of himself that he had fled Palestine because of the war. But this is by no means likely.[136] He adopted an especially harsh position vis-a-vis Jewish heretics and argued that their Bible scrolls and religious books should not be saved from fire on the Sabbath even though they contained the Tetragrammaton. Likewise, he declared that whereas a Jew might take refuge in a pagan temple, he was not to use the house of a heretic as a place of sanctuary.[137]

Apart from R. Tarphon, other contemporaries of Akiba needing to be mentioned are R. Yohanan ben Nuri, who lived as early as the time of Gamaliel II, Joshua and Eliezer, but is referred to most frequently in connection with Akiba;[138] R. Simeon ben Azzai, or simply Ben Azzai, especially celebrated for his untiring studiousness;[139] R. Yohanan ben

135. Graetz, IV, p. 179; Derenbourg, p. 436; and vol. I, p. 552, n. 173. Cf. also L. Finkelstein, 'The Ten Martyrs', *Essays and Studies in Memory of Linda Miller* (1938), pp. 29–55; Enc. Jud. 15, cols. 1006–8.

136. Justin, *Dialogus cum Tryphone*, c. 1: *εἰμὶ δὲ Ἑβραῖος ἐκ περιτομῆς, φυγὼν τὸν νῦν γενόμενον πόλεμον, ἐν τῇ Ἑλλάδι καὶ τῇ Κορίνθῳ τὰ πολλὰ διάγων*. The names טרפון and *Τρύφων* are identical, for it cannot be proved that the former was a genuinely Semitic name even if this were possible from the form. The time likewise agrees exactly. Yet although Tryphon is seldom attested in Jewish sources, it would be rash to conclude that only one rabbi was known by this name in the middle of the second century A.D. Cf. Strack, p. 309, n. 44. For convincing arguments against the identification, see L. W. Barnard, *Justin Martyr, His Life and Thought* (1967), pp. 24–5.

137. bShab. 116a; yShab. 15c; tShab. 13:5: Derenbourg, pp. 379 f.; Bacher, *Die Agada der Tannaiten* I², p. 351. See especially K. G. Kuhn, 'Gilionim und Sifre minim', *Judentum, Urchristentum, Kirche, Festschrift für J. Jeremias* (1960), pp. 24–61. גליון means the margin of a scroll (*ibid*. pp. 31–2). The term was later used as an anti-Christian pun on the Greek *εὐαγγέλιον*. bShab. 116a: 'The school of R. Meir named them (i.e. the gilyonim) און גליון, the school of R. Yoḥanan עון גליון.' See also the anecdote immediately following in which Imma Shalom, the sister of Rabban Gamaliel, refutes a philosopher's argument from the עון גליון (bShab. 116b). The text quoted there does not figure in the Gospels. Cf. Kuhn, *art. cit.*, p. 32. For older views see JE V, pp. 668–9; T. R. Herford, *Christianity in Talmud and Midrash* (1903), pp. 146–57, 413–14. A Hebrew epitaph found in Jaffa reads: הדא קבורת דיודן בריה דרבי טרפון. (This is the tomb of Yudan son of Rabbi Tarphon). Cf. S. Klein, 'Inschriftliches aus Jaffa', MGWJ 75 (1931), p. 370; Frey, CIJ II (1952), no. 892, p. 120.

138. At the time of Gamaliel: mR.Sh. 2:8. At the time of Joshua: tTaan. 2:5. At the time of Eliezer: tOrl. 1:8; tKel. 6:3–4. In contact with Akiba: mR.Sh. 4:5; mBekh. 6:6; mTem. 1:1; mUkz. 3:5; tPes. 1:10. Cf. Bacher, *Die Agada der Tannaiten* I², pp. 366–8; Strack, p. 113; JE VII, p. 113; Enc. Jud. 10, cols, 147-8.

139. A contemporary of Akiba: mShek. 4:6; mYom. 2:3; mTaan. 4:4; mB.B. 9:10. It was said of him: 'After Ben Azzai died, diligent students were no more (mSot. 9:15). Some of his sayings appear in mAb. 4:2–3.—Cf. Bacher, *Die Agada*

Beroka, who associated with Joshua and Yohanan ben Nuri;[140] R. Yose the Galilean, represented as a contemporary of Eleazar ben Azariah, Tarphon and Akiba;[141] R. Simeon ben Nannos, or simply Ben Nannos, likewise a contemporary of Tarphon and Akiba.[142]

To this same period belongs also Abba Saul, who although he relates a saying of Yohanan ben Zakkai, and is repeatedly cited as an authority on the Temple organization, cannot be older than Akiba since he frequently reports on his sayings also;[143] and further, R. Judah ben Bethera, who is mentioned as a contemporary, on the one hand of Eliezer, and on the other, of R. Meir, and who must therefore have flourished between the two of them, i.e. in the time of Akiba.[144]

The men of the following generation—R. Judah ben Elai, R. Yose ben Halafta, R. Meir and R. Simeon ben Yohai—are mentioned in the Mishnah more frequently than any of those listed so far. But their activities took place in the middle of the second century and consequently fall outside the limits of the period discussed here.

---

der Tannaiten I², pp. 406–22; Strack, p. 114; JE II, pp. 672–3; Enc. Jud. 4, col. 472. Cf. H. A. Fischel, *Rabbinic Literature and Greco-Roman Philosophy* (1973), pp. 90–7, 161–5.

140. With Joshua: tSot. 7:9. With Yoḥanan ben Nuri: tTer. 7:14. Cf. Bacher, *Die Agada der Tannaiten* I², pp. 448–9, JE VII, p. 210; Enc. Jud. 10, col. 143.

141. With these three: yGit. 9:1 (Derenbourg, p. 368). With Akiba and Tarphon: tMikw. 7:11. He also speaks in the name of Yohanan ben Nuri: tOrl. 1:8. Cf. Bacher, *Die Agada der Tannaiten* I², pp. 352–65.

142. See especially tMikw. 7:11. He appears in association with Ishmael in mB.B. 10:8. Mentioned by his full name, Simeon ben Nannos (*νάννος* = the dwarf) in mBik. 3:9; mShab. 16:5; mErub. 10:15; mB.B. 10:8; mMen. 4:3. As Ben Nannos: mKet. 10:5; mGit. 8:10; mB.B. 7:3; 10:8; mShab. 7:5.

143. On a saying of Yohanan ben Zakkai: mAb. 2:8. On the Temple arrangements: mMid. 2:5; 5:4; also mMen. 8:8; 11:5. On sayings of Akiba: tKil. 4:11; tSanh. 12:10. Bacher, *Die Agada der Tannaiten* II, pp. 36–9; Strack, p. 116; JE XI, p. 78; Enc. Jud. 2, col. 40.

144. A contemporary of Eliezer: mNeg. 9:3; 11:7. A contemporary of Meir: tNaz. 5:1. Cf. also for the chronology, mPea. 3:6; mPes. 3:3; mEdu. 8:3; mKel. 2:4; mOhol. 11:7; tYeb. 12:11. Cf. Bacher, *Die Agada der Tannaiten* I², pp. 374–80; Strack, p. 114; JE II, pp. 598–9; Enc. Jud. 10. col. 343.

§ 26. PHARISEES AND SADDUCEES

Bibliography

Geiger, A., *Urschrift und Übersetzungen der Bibel* (1857), pp. 101–58.
Geiger, A., 'Sadduzäer und Pharisäer', JZWL 2 (1863), pp. 11–54.
Derenbourg, J., *Essai sur l'histoire et la géographie de la Palestine* (1867), pp. 75–78, 119–44, 452–6.
Wellhausen, J., *Die Pharisäer und Sadducäer* (1874).
Elbogen, I., *Die Religionsanschaungen der Pharisäer* (1904).
Kohler, K., 'Pharisees', JE IX, pp. 661–6. 'Sadducees', JE X, pp. 630–3.
Hölscher, G., *Der Sadduzäismus* (1906).
Leszynsky, R., *Die Sadduzäer* (1912).
Abrahams, I., *Studies in Pharisaism and the Gospels* I (1917), II (1924).
Herford, R. Travers, *The Pharisees* (1924).
Moore, G. F., *Judaism in the First Three Centuries* I (1927), pp. 56–71 [Rise of the Pharisees].
Strack, H., Billerbeck, P., *Kommentar zum Neuen Testament aus Talmud und Midrasch* IV/1 (1928), pp. 339–52 [Pharisees and Sadducees].
Manson, T. W., 'Sadducee and Pharisee: The Origin and Significance of the Names', BJRL 22 (1938), pp. 144–59.
Lauterbach, J. Z., *Rabbinic Essays* (1951), pp. 23–48 [The Sadducees and Pharisees (1913)]; pp. 51–83 [A Significant Controversy between the Sadducees and the Pharisees (1927)]; pp. 87–159 [The Pharisees and their Teachings (1929)].
Baron, S. W., *A Social and Religious History of the Jews* II ([2]1952), pp. 35–46 [Pharisees and Sadducees].
Bikerman, E., 'La chaîne de la tradition pharisienne', RB 59 (1952), pp. 44–54.
Marcus, R., 'The Pharisees in the Light of Modern Scholarship', Journal of Religion 32 (1952), pp. 153–64.
Marcus, R., 'Pharisees, Essenes and Gnostics', JBL 73 (1954), pp. 155–61.
Rabin, C., *Qumran Studies* (1957) [an attempt at linking the Qumran sect to Pharisaism].
Beilner, W., *Christus und die Pharisäer* (1959).
Alon, G., 'The Attitude of the Pharisees to the Roman Government and the House of Herod', Scrip. Hier. 7 (1961), pp. 53–78.
Finkelstein, L., *The Pharisees: The Sociological Background of their Faith* I–II ([3]1962).
Zeitlin, S., 'The Pharisees: A Historical Study', JQR 52 (1961), pp. 97–129.
Meyer, R., *Tradition und Neuschöpfung im antiken Judentum dargestellt an der Geschichte des Pharisäismus* (1965).
Michel, A., Le Moyne, J., 'Pharisiens', DBSupp VII (1966), cols. 1022–1115.
Zeitlin, S., 'The Origin of the Pharisees Re-affirmed', JQR 59 (1968–9), pp. 255–67.
Jeremias, J., *Jerusalem in the Time of Jesus* (1969), pp. 228–32 [Sadducees]; pp. 246–67 [Pharisees].
Rivkin, E., 'Defining the Pharisees', HUCA 40–1 (1969–70), pp. 205–49.
Flusser, D., *In Memory of Gedaliahu Alon: Essays in Jewish History and Philology* (1970), pp. 133–68.
Guttmann, A., *Rabbinic Judaism in the Making* (1970), pp. 124–75 [Pharisees, Sadducees, Essenes].

Neusner, J., *The Rabbinic Traditions about the Pharisees before* 70 I–III (1971) [A form-critical examination of the rabbinic sources].
Meyer, R., *Σαδδουκαῖος*, TDNT VII (1971), pp. 35–54.
Mansoor, M., 'Pharisees', Enc. Jud. 13, cols. 363–66. 'Sadducees', Enc. Jud. 14, cols. 620–2.
Maier, J., *Geschichte der jüdischen Religion* (1972), pp. 45–8 [Sadducees]; pp. 51–6 [Ḥasidim]; pp. 66–79 [Pharisees].
Le Moyne, J., *Les Sadducéens* (1972) [A comprehensive survey of the sources].
Neusner, J., 'Josephus' Pharisees', *Ex Orbe Religionum* (Widengren Festschrift) I (1972), pp. 224–44.
Neusner, J., *From Politics to Piety: The Emergence of Pharisaic Judaism* (1973).
Bowker, J., *Jesus and the Pharisees* (1973).
Zeitlin, S., *Studies in the Early History of Judaism* II (1974), pp. 259–91 [The Sadducees and the Pharisees (1936)].
Meyer, R., Weiss, H. F., *Φαρισαῖος*, TDNT IX (1974), pp. 11–48.
Finkel, A., *The Pharisees and the Teacher of Nazareth* ([2]1974).
Lightstone, J., 'Sadducees *versus* Pharisees: The Tannaitic Sources', *Christianity, Judaism and other Greco-Roman Cults*, ed. J. Neusner III (1975), pp. 706–17.
Rivkin, E., 'Pharisees', IDBS (1976), pp. 657–63.
Mantel, H. D., 'The Sadducees and the Pharisees', *Society and Religion in the Second Temple Period*, ed. M. Avi-Yonah and Z. Baras, *World History of the Jewish People* VIII (1977), pp. 99–123, 346–51.
Vermes, G., *The Dead Sea Scrolls: Qumran in Perspective* (1977), pp. 118–22, 131–2.

The Evidence from Josephus

B.J. ii 8, 14 (162–6): *Φαρισαῖοι μὲν οἱ μετὰ ἀκριβείας δοκοῦντες ἐξηγεῖσθαι τὰ νόμιμα καὶ τὴν πρώτην ἀπάγοντες αἵρεσιν, εἱμαρμένῃ τε καὶ θεῷ προσάπτουσι πάντα, καὶ τὸ μὲν πράττειν τὰ δίκαια καὶ μὴ κατὰ τὸ πλεῖστον ἐπὶ τοῖς ἀνθρώποις κεῖσθαι, βοηθεῖν δὲ εἰς ἕκαστον καὶ τὴν εἱμαρμένην· ψυχὴν δὲ πᾶσαν μὲν ἄφθαρτον, μεταβαίνειν δὲ εἰς ἕτερον σῶμα τὴν τῶν ἀγαθῶν μόνην, τὰς δὲ τῶν φαύλων ἀϊδίῳ τιμωρίᾳ κολάζεσθαι. Σαδδουκαῖοι δέ, τὸ δεύτερον τάγμα, τὴν μὲν εἱμαρμένην παντάπασιν ἀναιροῦσι, καὶ τὸν θεὸν ἔξω τοῦ δρᾶν τι κακὸν ἢ ἐφορᾶν τίθενται, φασὶ δ' ἐπ' ἀνθρώπων ἐκλογῇ τό τε καλὸν καὶ τὸ κακὸν προκεῖσθαι, καὶ τὸ κατὰ γνώμην ἑκάστῳ τούτων ἑκατέρῳ προσιέναι. Ψυχῆς τε τὴν διαμονὴν καὶ τὰς καθ' Ἅιδου τιμωρίας καὶ τιμὰς ἀναιροῦσι. Καὶ Φαρισαῖοι μὲν φιλάλληλοί τε καὶ τὴν εἰς τὸ κοινὸν ὁμόνοιαν ἀσκοῦντες, Σαδδουκαίων δὲ καὶ πρὸς ἀλλήλους τὸ ἦθος ἀγριώτερον, αἵ τε ἐπιμιξίαι πρὸς τοὺς ὁμοίους ἀπηνεῖς ὡς πρὸς ἀλλοτρίους.*

Ant. xiii 5, 9 (171–3): *Κατὰ δὲ τὸν χρόνον τοῦτον τρεῖς αἱρέσεις τῶν Ἰουδαίων ἦσαν, αἳ περὶ τῶν ἀνθρωπίνων πραγμάτων διαφόρως ὑπελάμβανον· ὧν ἡ μὲν Φαρισαίων ἐλέγετο, ἡ δὲ Σαδδουκαίων, ἡ τρίτη δὲ Ἐσσηνῶν. Οἱ μὲν οὖν Φαρισαῖοι τινὰ καὶ οὐ πάντα τῆς εἱμαρμένης ἔργον εἶναι λέγουσιν, τινὰ δ' ἐφ' ἑαυτοῖς ὑπάρχειν, συμβαίνειν τε καὶ μὴ γίνεσθαι. Τὸ δὲ τῶν Ἐσσηνῶν γένος πάντων τὴν εἱμαρμένην κυρίαν ἀποφαίνεται, καὶ μηδὲν ὃ μὴ κατ' ἐκείνης ψῆφον ἀνθρώποις ἀπαντᾷ. Σαδδουκαῖοι δὲ τὴν μὲν εἱμαρμένην ἀναιροῦσιν, οὐδὲν εἶναι ταύτην ἀξιοῦντες, οὐδὲ κατ' αὐτὴν τὰ ἀνθρώπινα τέλος λαμβάνειν, ἅπαντα δ' ἐφ' ἡμῖν αὐτοῖς τίθενται, ὡς καὶ τῶν ἀγαθῶν αἰτίους ἡμᾶς αὐτοὺς γινομένους καὶ τὰ χείρω παρὰ τὴν ἡμετέραν ἀβουλίαν λαμβάνοντας.*

Ant. xiii 10, 5 (288): [*Οἱ Φαρισαῖοι*] *τοσαύτην ἔχουσι τὴν ἰσχὺν παρὰ τῷ πλήθει ὡς καὶ κατὰ βασιλέως τι λέγοντες καὶ κατ' ἀρχιερέως εὐθὺς πιστεύεσθαι.*

Ant. xiii 10, 6 (294): *Ἄλλως τε καὶ φύσει πρὸς τὰς κολάσεις ἐπιεικῶς ἔχουσιν οἱ Φαρισαῖοι.*

Ant. xiii 10, 6 (297–8): Νόμιμά τινα παρέδοσαν τῷ δήμῳ οἱ Φαρισαῖοι ἐκ πατέρων διαδοχῆς, ἅπερ οὐκ ἀναγέγραπται ἐν τοῖς Μωυσέως νόμοις, καὶ διὰ τοῦτο ταῦτα τὸ Σαδδουκαίων γένος ἐκβάλλει, λέγον ἐκεῖνα δεῖν ἡγεῖσθαι νόμιμα τὰ γεγραμμένα, τὰ δ' ἐκ παραδόσεως τῶν πατέρων μὴ τηρεῖν. Καὶ περὶ τούτων ζητήσεις αὐτοῖς καὶ διαφορὰς γίνεσθαι συνέβαινε μεγάλας, τῶν μὲν Σαδδουκαίων τοὺς εὐπόρους μόνον πειθόντων, τὸ δὲ δημοτικὸν οὐχ ἑπόμενον αὐτοῖς ἐχόντων, τῶν δὲ Φαρισαίων τὸ πλῆθος σύμμαχον ἐχόντων.

Ant. xvii 2, 4 (41): Ἦν γάρ μόριόν τι Ἰουδαϊκῶν ἀνθρώπων ἐπ' ἐξακριβώσει μέγα φρονοῦν τοῦ πατρίου νόμου, οἷς χαίρειν τὸ θεῖον προσποιουμέν[ων]οις ὑπῆκτο ἡ γυναικωνῖτις· Φαρισαῖοι καλοῦνται, βασιλεῖ δυνάμενοι μάλιστα ἀντιπράσσειν, προμηθεῖς, κἀκ τοῦ προύπτου εἰς τὸ πολεμεῖν τε καὶ βλάπτειν ἐπηρμένοι.[1]

Ant. xviii 1, 2–4 (12–15): Ἰουδαίοις φιλοσοφίαι τρεῖς ἦσαν ἐκ τοῦ πάνυ ἀρχαίου τῶν πατρίων, ἥ τε τῶν Ἐσσηνῶν καὶ ἡ τῶν Σαδδουκαίων· τρίτην δὲ ἐφιλοσόφουν οἱ Φαρισαῖοι λεγόμενοι. Καὶ τυγχάνει μέντοι περὶ αὐτῶν ἡμῖν εἰρημένα ἐν τῇ δευτέρᾳ βίβλῳ τοῦ Ἰουδαϊκοῦ πολέμου, μνησθήσομαι δὲ ὅμως καὶ νῦν αὐτῶν ἐπ' ὀλίγον.

Οἵ τε γὰρ Φαρισαῖοι τὴν δίαιταν ἐξευτελίζουσιν, οὐδὲν εἰς τὸ μαλακώτερον ἐνδιδόντες, ὧν τε ὁ λόγος κρίνας παρέδωκεν ἀγαθῶν, ἕπονται τῇ ἡγεμονίᾳ, περιμάχητον ἡγούμενοι τὴν φυλακὴν ὧν ὑπαγορεύειν ἠθέλησε. Τιμῆς γε τοῖς ἡλικίᾳ προήκουσι παραχωροῦσιν, οὐδὲν ἐπ' ἀντιλέξει τῶν εἰσηγηθέντων ταῦτα οἱ[2] θράσει ἐπαιρόμενοι. Πράσσεσθαί τε εἱμαρμένῃ τὰ πάντα ἀξιοῦντες, οὐδὲ τοῦ ἀνθρωπείου τὸ βουλόμενον τῆς ἐπ' αὐτοῖς ὁρμῆς ἀφαιροῦνται, δοκῆσαν τῷ θεῷ κρᾶσιν γενέσθαι καὶ τῷ ἐκείνης βουλευτηρίῳ καὶ τῶν ἀνθρώπων τὸ ἐθελῆσαν[3] προσχωρεῖν μετ' ἀρετῆς ἢ κακίας. Ἀθάνατόν τε ἰσχὺν ταῖς ψυχαῖς πίστις αὐτοῖς εἶναι, καὶ ὑπὸ χθονὸς δικαιώσεις τε καὶ τιμὰς οἷς ἀρετῆς ἢ κακίας ἐπιτήδευσις ἐν τῷ βίῳ γέγονε, καὶ ταῖς μὲν εἱργμὸν ἀΐδιον προτίθεσθαι, ταῖς δὲ ῥᾳστώνην τοῦ ἀναβιοῦν. Καὶ δι' αὐτὰ τοῖς τε δήμοις πιθανώτατοι τυγχάνουσι, καὶ ὁπόσα θεῖα εὐχῶν τε ἔχεται καὶ ἱερῶν ποιήσεως ἐξηγήσει τῇ ἐκείνων τυγχάνουσι πρασσόμενα. Εἰς τοσόνδε ἀρετῆς αὐτοῖς αἱ πόλεις ἐμαρτύρησαν ἐπιτηδεύσει τοῦ ἐπὶ πᾶσι κρείσσονος ἔν τε τῇ διαίτῃ τοῦ βίου καὶ λόγοις.

Σαδδουκαίοις δὲ τὰς ψυχὰς ὁ λόγος συναφανίζει τοῖς σώμασι, φυλακῇ δὲ οὐδαμῶς τινων μεταποίησις αὐτοῖς ἢ τῶν νόμων· πρὸς γὰρ τοὺς διδασκάλους σοφίας, ἣν μετίασιν, ἀμφιλογεῖν ἀρετὴν ἀριθμοῦσιν. Εἰς ὀλίγους δὲ ἄνδρας οὗτος ὁ λόγος ἀφίκετο, τοὺς μέντοι πρώτους τοῖς ἀξιώμασι, πράσσεταί τε ἀπ' αὐτῶν οὐδὲν ὡς εἰπεῖν· ὁπότε γὰρ ἐπ' ἀρχὰς παρέλθοιεν, ἀκουσίως μὲν καὶ κατ' ἀνάγκας, προσχωροῦσι δ' οὖν οἷς ὁ Φαρισαῖος λέγει, διὰ τὸ μὴ ἄλλως ἀνεκτοὺς γενέσθαι τοῖς πλήθεσιν.

Ant. xx 9, 1 (199): αἵρεσιν δὲ μετῄει τὴν Σαδδουκαίων, οἵπερ εἰσὶ περὶ τὰς κρίσεις ὠμοὶ παρὰ πάντας τοὺς Ἰουδαίους, καθὼς ἤδη δεδηλώκαμεν.

Vita 2 (12): ἠρξάμην πολιτεύεσθαι τῇ Φαρισαίων αἱρέσει κατακολουθῶν, ἣ παραπλήσιός ἐστι τῇ παρ' Ἕλλησι Στωικῇ λεγομένῃ.

Vita 38 (191): τῆς δὲ Φαρισαίων αἱρέσεως, οἳ περὶ τὰ πάτρια νόμιμα δοκοῦσι τῶν ἄλλων ἀκριβείᾳ διαφέρειν.

1. This hostility towards the Pharisees is obviously not the work of Josephus's pen. The words are copied by him from Nicolaus of Damascus (cf. Derenbourg, p. 123 n). They are valuable as a corrective to Josephus's flattering picture. The textual tradition is uncertain.
2. The words ταῦτα οἱ, missing in the *Epitome*, should probably be deleted.
3. Thus the *Epitome*, no doubt accurately. The codices have τῷ ἐθελήσαντι or τῷ θελήσαντι.

The Evidence of the Mishnah

(a) *Pharisees and Sadducees*

mYad. 4:6: 'The Sadducees say: We must reprove you, Pharisees, because you say, The Holy Scriptures render the hands unclean, (but) the writings of Hamiras[4] do not render the hands unclean. Rabban Yohanan ben Zakkai said: Have we nothing else against the Pharisees beyond this? For they also say: The bones of an ass are clean and the bones of Yohanan the High Priest are unclean. They (the Sadducees) said to him: Their uncleanness is according to our love for them, that no man makes spoons of the bones of his father or mother. He said to them: In the case of the Holy Scriptures also, their uncleanness is according to our love for them; but the writings of Hamiras which are not loved do not render the hands unclean.'

mYad. 4:7: 'The Sadducees say: We must reprove you, Pharisees, that you declare the streaming (when pouring liquid from a clean into an unclean vessel) to be clean. The Pharisees answered, We must reprove you, Sadducees, that you declare a conduit from a burial-ground to be clean. The Sadducees said further: We must reprove you, Pharisees, for you say, If my ox or my ass cause damage, I owe compensation, and if my slave or my maid-servant cause damage, I am free. If I have to pay compensation for ox or ass, to which I have no legal obligations, how shall I not owe compensation for my slave or maid-servant to whom I have legal obligations? They (the Pharisees) answered: Not the same can apply in regard to ox or ass which have no understanding as in regard to slave or maid-servant, who have understanding. For if I make him angry, he may go and set fire to another man's field, and oblige me to make restitution.'

mYad. 4:8: 'A Galilean heretic[5] said: I reprove you, Pharisees, that you write in a bill of divorce the name of the ruler together

4. The reading המירס is suggested. For the variants, see G. Lisowsky, *Jadajim* (1956), p. 91. For a discussion, see *ibid.*, p. 74, and especially S. Lieberman, *Hellenism in Jewish Palestine* (1950), pp. 105–14; M. Hengel, *Judaism and Hellenism* I, p. 75; II, p. 52.

5. According to the best evidence (Geniza fragment, Codex Kaufmann, ed. princ. of the Mishnah 1492; cf. Lisowsky, *op. cit.* pp. 79, 91) here and in the following, instead of צדוקי גלילי read מן גלילי, possibly a Galilean Zealot. See M.

with that of Moses. The Pharisees answered: We reprove you, Galilean heretic, that you write the name of the ruler and the Name (of God) on one page, and moreover, the first above and the Name below. As it is written, *Pharaoh said, Who is YHWH that I should hearken to his voice and let Israel go*? (Exod. 5:2)'.

mHag. 2:7: 'The garments of an *'am-ha'areẓ* are *midras* (i.e. defiled by pressure) for the Pharisees; those of the Pharisees are *midras* for them who eat the heave-offering; those of the latter are *midras* for them who eat holy things; and those of the latter are *midras* for them who sprinkle the water of sin-offering.'[6]

mSot. 3:4: 'R. Joshua used to say: A foolish ḥasid, a clever wicked man, a Pharisee woman and the plagues of the Pharisees, these destroy the world'.[7]

mErub. 6:2: 'Rabban Gamaliel relates: A Sadducee once lived with us in a *maboi* (a street cordoned off to facilitate freer movement on the Sabbath) in Jerusalem. My father said to us, Bring quickly all the vessels into the *maboi* before the Sadducee brings something there and makes it unlawful for you. R. Judah quotes the saying differently: Whatever you have to do in the *maboi*, do it quickly, before the Sadducee brings something there and makes it unlawful for you.'[8]

Hengel, *Die Zeloten* ([2]1976), pp. 57–61; G. Vermes, *Jesus the Jew* (1973), pp. 45–6. For a hypothetical Zadok the Galilean, see E. Rivkin, 'Defining the Pharisees: The Tannaitic Sources', HUCA 40–1 (1969–70), p. 211.

6. On the significance of the *'am ha-'areẓ* (עם הארץ), see below. 'Those who eat the heave-offering' (*terumah*) are the priests and their relations; 'those who eat holy things' are the officiating priests. Each category stands one degree higher in holiness and purity than the one that precedes it, whose clothes are therefore unclean (*midras*) to it and not allowed. Cf. Levy, *Neuhebr. Wörterb.* s.v. מדרס, III, pp. 33–4. Cf. Rivkin, *art. cit.* HUCA 40–1 (1969–70), pp. 206–7; Neusner, *Pharisees* I, pp. 63–4.

7. For a commentary, see H. Bietenhard, *Soṭa* (1956), pp. 72–3. bSot. 22a gives various explanations for 'Pharisee woman', the first being that it is a girl who devotes herself to prayer or fasting, i.e. an ascetic. For the 'plagues of the Pharisees', see bSot. 22b; Rivkin, *art. cit.*, HUCA 40–1 (1969–70), pp. 240–1.

8. The explanation of this difficult Mishnah passage is controversial. The general rule to be assumed from the special cases cited is that several Jews living communally in one courtyard or in one street could declare the area in which they laid up food for the Sabbath to be a private domain. It was then lawful to carry things in and out of the area on the Sabbath, whereas it was forbidden in a public domain. The establishment of common tenure by depositing food was nevertheless

mMak. 1:6: 'False witnesses will be executed only when judgement has fallen on those whom they have accused. For the Sadducees say: Only after he (the convicted person) has been executed; as it is written, *Life for life* (Dt. 19:21). But the sages said to them: Is it not also written, *Then you shall do unto him as he had planned to do to his brother* (Dt. 19:19)? Behold, his brother is still alive.'[9]

mPar. 3:7: 'The priest who burned the red heifer was intentionally made unclean on account of the Sadducees, that they might not say, Let the heifer be prepared only by those rendered clean through the setting of the sun.'

mNid. 4:2: 'When they walk in the ways of their fathers, the daughters of the Sadducees are as Samaritan women. When they walk in the way of Israel, they are as Israelite women. R. Yose says: Until it is proved that they walk in the ways of their fathers, they are all regarded as Israelite women.'

(b) *Ḥaver and 'am-ha'areẓ*

mDem. 2:3: 'Whoever undertakes to be a *ḥaver* (חבר) sells to an *'am-ha'areẓ* neither fresh fruit nor dried, buys from him no fresh fruit, does not enter his house as guest, and does not accept him as guest if he wears his own garments. R. Judah says: Nor must he rear sheep or goats,[10] nor be frivolous with vows and jokes, nor defile himself through the dead. He must busy himself in the school. But they said to him: All this does not come to the main point.'[11]

mDem. 6:6: 'The school of Shammai says: No olives are to be sold except to a *ḥaver*. The school of Hillel says: Also to one who always pays tithes. The scrupulous of the school of Hillel conformed in this to the school of Shammai.

---

allowed only when all the occupiers were Jews. If a Gentile, or a Jew who did not recognize the law of *'erub*, shared the courtyard or street, the procedure was not possible (mErub. 6:1). For a commentary see W. Nowack, *'Erubin* (1926), pp. 56–59.

9. Cf. S. Krauss, *Sanhedrin–Makkot* (1933), pp. 320–4.

10. Cf. G. Mayer, *Para* (1964), p. 51.

11. Cf. W. Bauer, *Dammai* (1931), pp. 20–3. On keeping sheep and goats, see S. Krauss, REJ 53 (1907), pp. 14–55; J. Feliks, החקלאות בארץ ישראל בתקופת המשנה והתלמוד (1963), pp. 112–15.

mDem. 6:9: 'If a *ḥaver* and an *'am-ha'areẓ* inherit from their father who was an *'am-ha'areẓ*, each can say: You take the wheat in this place, I the wheat in that; you take the wine from this place, I the wine from that. But he may not say to him: You take the wheat, I the barley; you the fresh fruit, I the dried.'[12]

mDem. 6:12: 'If an *'am-ha'areẓ* says to a *ḥaver*, Buy me a bundle of vegetables, buy me a fine loaf,[13] the latter may buy without special remark and is free from tithe obligation. But if he has added, I buy this for myself and that for my friend, and has mingled them, he must pay the tithe of all of it, even if the latter is a hundred (i.e. a hundred times more than his own).'

mSheb. 5:9 =mGit. 5:9: 'A woman may lend to another who is suspected on account of *shebi'ith* (consuming the fruits of the seventh year) a flour-sieve, a corn-sieve, a hand-mill and an oven, but she may not help her to glean or to grind. The wife of a *ḥaver* may lend to the wife of an *'am-ha'areẓ* a flour-sieve and a corn-sieve and help her to glean and to grind. But once they have poured water onto the flour she must touch it no more with her, for the transgressor may not be assisted. All these things have been permitted only for the sake of peace, in the same way that it is permitted to wish good fortune to Gentiles (working in the field) in the seventh year, but not to Israelites, etc.'

mBik. 2:12: 'R. Judah says: The first-fruits may only be given to a (priest who is a) *ḥaver* and as a favour.'

mToh. 7:4: 'If the wife of a *ḥaver* leaves the wife of an *'am-ha'areẓ* milling at the mill in her house, if the mill stops, the house is unclean; if she continues to mill, only that is unclean which she can touch by stretching out her hand. If two such women are there, then, according to R. Meir, everything is unclean, for while one of them mills, the other can touch everything. But the sages say: Only that which each can touch by stretching out her hand.'

mToh. 8:5: 'If the wife of an *'am-ha'areẓ* enters the house of a *ḥaver* to fetch his son or daughter or cattle, the house remains clean because she has no permission (to linger there).

12. Cf. S. Krauss, *Talmudische Archäologie* I (1911), p. 105.
13. Cf. D. Correns, *Schebiit* (1960), p. 103.

The priests and Torah scholars or 'scribes'[14] were the two leading influences which determined Israel's internal development after the exile. In Ezra's time they were still essentially identical. During the Greek period they grew further and further apart. At about the time of the Maccabaean wars, they evolved into two parties sharply opposed to one another. From the priestly circles emerged the Sadducean party, and from those of the Torah scholars came the party of the Pharisees, the lay experts in religious matters.[15] Both groups are known, in particular from the evidence of Josephus and the New Testament, to have been mutually hostile, but to assume that their antagonism was one of ideas is to prejudice any understanding of their true character from the outset. The Pharisees were essentially concerned with strict legality.[16] The Sadducees were at first simply aristocrats persuaded by historical development into opposing Pharisaic legalism, but this conflict was by no means fundamental to their nature. A distorted picture is therefore obtained if the differences between them are compared point by point. It is rather that the Pharisee characteristics proceeded from their legal orientation, whereas those of the Sadducees derived from their inherited social standing.

I. The Pharisees

According to Josephus, the Pharisees concerned themselves with the strict interpretation and observance of the Torah, and spared themselves no efforts to fulfil the law in every detail. 'They are reckoned to interpret the laws exactly.'[17] 'They pride themselves on the exact interpretation

14. The mention of 'scribes' as such implies that we are dealing with the period preceding the formation of Pharisees and Sadducees, both of whom had their own scribes or legal experts.

15. 'Political animosity between Sadducees and Pharisees could rise to a high pitch, and at times lead to open civil war. Sharp economic and social differences added to the political controversies. The Sadducees, representatives of the priest and lay aristocracy, had every reason to resist customs and belief evolved by the masses under the leadership of middle class and "plebeian" intellectuals.' S. W. Baron, *A Social and Religious History of the Jews* II (^{2}1952), p. 35.

16. One of the main achievements of J. Neusner's work is that it demonstrates an evolutionary trend in rabbinic traditions regarding the Pharisees. In his opinion, the Pharisees of the last seventy or eighty years before the destruction of the Temple 'were (whatever else they were) primarily a society for table-fellowship, the high point of their life as a group' (*Pharisees* III, p. 318). Their emphasis on the importance of dietary laws and other purity regulations was based on their desire to raise the status of every Jew to equal that of the priests and to consider their table as similar to the table of God in the Jerusalem temple. *The Idea of Purity in Ancient Judaism* (1973), pp. 65–6. For an identification of the Pharisees as the 'scholar class', see E. Rivkin, HUCA 40–1 (1969–70), pp. 205–49.

17. *B.J.* ii 8, 14 (162); *Vita* 38 (191). See Act. 22:3; 26:5; Phil. 3:5.

of the law of the fathers.'[18] 'They make no concession to luxury.'[19] They were in other words men who sought earnestly and consistently to put into practice the ideal propounded by the Torah scholars of a life lived in conformity with the Torah; which is to say that they were the classic representatives of the course adopted by Judaism in its inner development during the post-exilic epoch. Whatever applies to this in general, does so in particular to the Pharisees. Their party was the nucleus of the nation, distinguishable from the rest only by their greater strictness and consistency. The basis of their endeavour was the Torah in all the complexity given it by centuries of work on the part of the Torah scholars. Its punctilious realization was the beginning and end of their efforts.[20] Hence a characterization of Pharisaism must include everything mentioned above (§ 25.III) concerning the development of Jewish religious law by the Torah scholars, and in addition, all that still remains to be discussed concerning the nature of Jewish life itself (§ 28).

The outstanding prominence accredited to the Pharisees in the ancient sources may no doubt in part be attributed to the fact that rabbinic traditions exclusively represent and uphold a basically Pharisaic point of view, and also that Josephus was one of their number. Nevertheless, it can scarcely be a coincidence that once a Pharisaic party as such came into existence, most of the more memorable Torah scholars proceeded from its ranks. There must also have been

18. *Ant.* xvii 2, 4 (41).

19. *Ant.* xviii 1, 3 (12).

20. The position of the Pharisees as an important and highly influential minority group within the body of Palestinian Jewry has been outlined with clarity and emphasis by Morton Smith in 'Palestinian Judaism in the First Century', *Israel: Its Role in Civilization*, ed. M. Davis (1956), pp. 67–81. His conclusion is aptly summarized by J. Neusner: 'The Pharisees were a small group within Palestinian Judaism. They claimed the right to rule all the Jews by virtue of their possessing the "Oral Torah" of Moses. They referred to a list of masters extending back to Moses. . . . In their own setting, however, the Pharisees were much like any other Hellenistic philosophical school or sect.' (*From Politics to Piety* (1973), p. 11.) Rabbinic tradition, and that branch of modern scholarship which has never entirely freed itself from the mould of tradition, have tended to imply that post-exilic Judaism, Pharisaism and rabbinic Judaism are three synonyms. Such a portrait is based on hindsight, i.e. on a view of the past evolution formulated after the triumph of the Pharisaic school of thought at Yavneh and Usha. During the existence of the Second Temple, the Pharisees were prominent, but not identical with the community. This being stated, it is proper to conclude that 'Judaism as it is now known begins with the Pharisees of the two centuries before the destruction of Jerusalem and the Temple in 70 A.D.' (Neusner, *From Politics to Piety*, p. 11). For a recent re-assertion of the traditional Jewish view that Pharisaism represents 'normative Judaism' even though the Pharisaic party numbered only 6,000 heads of families', see H. D. Mantel, 'The Sadducees and the Pharisees', *World History of the Jewish People* VIII, p. 117.

Sadducee scribes, but their work has left no mark on history. The Essenes, too, excelled in learning, but their leaders are mostly anonymous and their influence vanished after A.D. 70. On the few occasions, in any case, that Josephus and the New Testament refer to the party allegiance of Torah scholars, they are all regularly described as Pharisees.[21]

Needless to say, according to the Pharisaic outlook not only the written Torah was binding, but also the exegesis and supplementation, known as the 'oral Torah', provided by the scribes. The latter was regarded as the correct interpretation and further development of the written Torah, and zeal for the one entailed zeal for the other. As Josephus states explicitly: 'The Pharisees have imposed on the people many laws from the tradition of the fathers (ἐκ πατέρων διαδοχῆς) not written in the Law of Moses'.[22] When John Hyrcanus defected from the Pharisees, he annulled the rulings introduced by them κατὰ τὴν πατρῴαν παράδοσιν, but they were reintroduced at the restoration under Alexandra.[23] The New Testament also testifies to the value placed by the Pharisees on παράδοσις τῶν πρεσβυτέρων (Mk. 7:3; Mt. 15:2). That the whole of rabbinic Judaism held the same opinion in respect of παράδοσις has already been demonstrated (p. 341). Halakhah, or traditional law as it was developed and established by the Torah scholars, was by the turn of the first century A.D. pronounced as binding as the written Torah. 'R. Eleazar of Modiim said: Whoever expounds Scripture not in conformity with halakhah (שלא כהלכה) has no share in the world to come.'[24] One of the reasons given for the outbreaks of wars over the land is, 'People who expound the Torah not in conformity with halakhah'.[25] Thus traditional interpretation and traditional law were declared authoritative and, as is only consistent, departure from them was judged as blameworthy as departure from the written Torah. 'It is more culpable to teach against the ordinances of the scribes than against the Torah itself'.[26] If the traditional inter-

21. *Ant.* xv, 11 (3): 'Pollion the Pharisee and his disciple Samaias'. Cf. xv 10, 3 (370). Act. 5:34: 'One in the council, a Pharisee named Gamaliel'. *Vita* 38 (191): 'This Simeon was a native of Jerusalem, of a very illustrious family, and of the sect of the Pharisees'.

22. *Ant.* xiii 10, 6 (297).

23. *Ant.* xiii 16, 3 (408).

24. mAb. 3:12.

25. mAb. 5:8.

26. mSanh. 11:3. Whereas it is correct to say that among Pharisees and Essenes the traditional interpretation of biblical laws was the final rule (cf. Vermes, *PBJS*, p. 40), it would be a misunderstanding to assume that mSanh. 11:3 actually asserts that tradition is above Scripture. Its import seems to be that the denial of an obvious and basic scriptural teaching is less serious than rejecting that of the Scribes, for if it were claimed that there is no law regarding phylacteries, everyone would know that this is not so; but if it were argued that the form of

pretation is binding, it is in fact the final authority, and not the written Torah. This is the principle alluded to by Josephus's statement that the Pharisees never contradict the teaching of those who are older in years.[27]

As in its attitude towards biblical law, so in its religious and doctrinal views Pharisaism essentially represented the standpoint of later rabbinic Judaism. In this respect, the following points taken from Josephus and the New Testament are characteristic of the Pharisees as distinguished from the Sadducees.

1. The Pharisees taught that 'every soul . . . is imperishable but only the souls of the good pass into another body; those of the wicked suffer eternal punishment';[28] or as it is expressed in another passage, 'They believe that souls possess an immortal power and that under the earth there are rewards and punishments for those who in life have given themselves over to virtue or vice, and that eternal imprisonment is destined to some, but to others an easy passage to a new life'.[29] The Sadducees, by contrast, refused to accept resurrection (*μὴ εἶναι ἀνάστασιν*, Mt. 22:23; Mk. 12:18; Lk. 20:27; Act. 23:8; cf. 4:1, 2): 'They deny the continued existence of the soul and the punishments and rewards in the underworld.'[30] 'According to their teaching, souls perish together with bodies.'[31]

The Pharisee teaching described here by Josephus is simply the doctrine of retribution and resurrection first attested as a basic feature of Judaism in the Book of Daniel (Dan. 12:2), and after the triumph of Pharisaism, throughout all subsequent Jewish literature, including the New Testament. The righteous will rise to eternal life in the glory of the messianic kingdom, but the wicked will be punished with eternal torment. The kernel of this belief is, moreover, not merely a philosophical opinion concerning immortality; the directly religious interest of personal salvation depends on it, a salvation that appears to be guaranteed only on the assumption of bodily resurrection. The stress laid on the latter is in consequence so great that the Mishnah reads: 'Whoever says there is no resurrection of the dead [prescribed in the

---

the phylacteries approved by the teachers is incorrect and should be replaced by an earlier one, the authority of the currently binding tradition would be undermined. Cf. mHor. 1:3.

27. *Ant.* xviii 1, 3 (12).

28. *B.J.* ii 8, 14 (163). The passage that follows proves that Josephus does not ascribe to the Pharisees the doctrine of the transmigration of souls.

29. *Ant.* xviii 1, 3 (14).

30. *B.J.* ii 8, 14 (165).

31. *Ant.* xviii 1, 4 (16).

Torah] has no share in the world to come'.[32] By denying resurrection and immortality in general, the Sadducees rejected simultaneously the entire messianic hope, in the form at least in which later Judaism, built on Pharisaic foundations, expressed it.

2. The Pharisees are said to have believed in the existence of angels and spirits, whilst the Sadducees denied them. Although the statement to this effect in Act. 23:8 is not attested elsewhere, it accords with the image of the two parties obtained from other sources. (For the relevant Qumran doctrine, see below, pp. 581–3.) It is unnecessary to demonstrate that on this point also the Pharisees represented the outlook of later ages.

3. Differences of belief in regard to divine providence and human free will are also ascribed to Pharisees and Sadducees by Josephus. The Pharisees 'make everything dependent on destiny and on God, and teach that the doing and causing of the good is mostly the business of men but that destiny co-operates in every action'.[33] 'They maintain that all is brought about by destiny. Yet they do not thereby deprive the human will of its own activity, it having pleased God that there should be a mixture, and that the human will, with its virtue or baseness, should be joined to the will of destiny'.[34] 'They say that some things, but not all, are the work of destiny; some things depend on man himself, whether they happen or do not happen'.[35]

The Sadducees 'deny destiny wholly and entirely, and place God beyond the possibility of doing or planning evil. They say that good and evil are at man's choice and that the doing of the one or the other is according to his discretion'.[36] 'They deny destiny, maintaining that it is nothing, and that human things do not come about by its means. They ascribe all things to ourselves, inasmuch as we are ourselves the cause of prosperity and that we incur misfortune through our own folly.'[37]

It seems strange at first to find such philosophical notions among the religious parties of Palestine, and the suspicion arises that Josephus not only gave a philosophical colouring to the religious views of his fellow-

32. mSanh. 10:1. The words, 'prescribed in the Torah', are missing from some of the best codices, including MSS Kaufmann, de Rossi 138, Berlin 568, and the Mishnah of the Palestinian Talmud. This would imply that the denial of resurrection as such, and not merely its scriptural demonstrability, is envisaged here.

33. *B.J.* ii 8, 14 (163).

34. *Ant.* xviii 1, 3 (13).

35. *Ant.* xiii 5, 9 (172).

36. *B.J.* ii 8, 14 (164). The word ἐφορᾶν is a Greek technical term for the divine surveillance of the world, not only in the sense of *inspicere* but also in that of *prospicere, providere*. The corresponding Hebrew word, used in the saying of Akiba quoted, is צפה.

37. *Ant.* xiii 5, 9 (173).

countrymen to suit himself, but that he imputed to them actual philosophical theories, a suspicion which increases when his observations concerning the Essenes are taken into account. All in all, the pattern emerges that the Essenes taught that destiny is absolute, the Sadducees denied destiny entirely, and the Pharisees steered a middle course between the two. And to strengthen this same suspicion even further, Josephus explicitly asserts elsewhere that the Pharisees are to be compared to the Stoics, and the Essenes to the Pythagoreans.[38] In fact, the very expression εἱμαρμένη, which is quite impossible to reconcile with Judaism, proves that we have at least to deal with a strongly Hellenized presentation of Jewish views. But it is in effect only the garb that is borrowed from Greece. The substance itself is authentically Jewish. For basically, once the Greek form is removed Josephus is saying merely this: according to Pharisaic teaching, everything that happens comes about through God's providence; therefore it must be assumed that he also co-operates in human actions both good and bad. But this is a genuinely biblical view. On the one hand, a strict formulation of the notion of divine omnipotence leads to the concept that human action, good and bad, is brought about by God. On the other, the Old Testament emphasizes man's moral responsibility; he incurs guilt and punishment when he does wrong, and gains merit and reward for his goodness. Similarly, for later Judaism the idea of man's moral independence was fundamental, a basic presupposition underlying its zeal for the Torah and hope for the future. Both lines of thought are therefore authentically Jewish. Attention was also paid to the problem which they pose. Jesus ben Sira lays strong and conspicuous stress on free will, obviously in a conscious polemic against the assertion that God himself is the cause of sin. Yet the same ben Sira also says that God forms man according to his pleasure as the potter forms the clay.[39] Parallel short sayings are found in the Psalms of Solomon.[40] Thus the problem of divine providence and human freedom was a subject of reflection for Judaism in general.[41] This is of course not to say that the three

38. *Vita* 2 (12); *Ant.* xv 10, 4 (371). Cf. G. Vermes, *Discovery in the Judean Desert* (1956), p. 60; *DSS*, p. 129.

39. See Ecclus. 15:1–20 (free will); 36:10–15 (God's own pleasure). In spite of his emphasis on free will, Ben Sira still prays for protection from sin (Ecclus. 22:27–23:6).

40. Ps. Sol. 9:4: 'Our works are subject to our own choice and power (ἐν ἐκλογῇ καὶ ἐξουσίᾳ τῆς ψυχῆς ἡμῶν) to do right or wrong by the works of our hands'. By contrast, in 5:4 we read: 'For man and his portion are before You in the balance; He cannot add to, so as to enlarge, what has been prescribed by You' (παρὰ τὸ κρίμα σου).

41. See G. F. Moore, *Judaism* I, pp. 454–8; M. Kadushin, *The Rabbinic Mind* ([2]1965), pp. 53–5; E. E. Urbach, 'Studies in Rabbinic Views concerning Divine Providence', *Yehezkel Kaufmann Jubilee Volume* (1960), pp. 122–48 (Hebrew Section); *idem*, *The Sages*, pp. 227–54.

possible standpoints—(1) absolute fate, (2) absolute freedom, (3) an intermediate opinion—were represented as systematically as Josephus alleges by the three parties of Essenes, Sadducees and Pharisees. This systematization is certainly the weakest point in Josephus's argument. But even here there may be something true. It is possible that for the Essenes the divine factor, and for the Sadducees the human, occupied the foreground. The Pharisees in any case adhered to both lines of thought with equal determination: to divine omnipotence and providence, and to human freedom and responsibility. That the one exists side by side, and in spite of the others, is emphasized explicitly in a saying by Akiba: **הכל צפוי והרשות נתונה**, 'All is (fore)seen (by God), but freedom is given (to man)'.[42] Here too, therefore, the Pharisees represented not a sectarian viewpoint but the main outlook of Judaism.

In regard to politics, the Pharisaic view was also a genuinely Jewish one, namely that political questions are to be treated not from a secular but from a religious standpoint. The Pharisees were not a political party at all, or not essentially so. Their aims were not political but religious: the rigorous fulfilment of the Torah. Insofar as these were not obstructed, they could be content with any government. It was only when the secular power interfered with their observance of the law that they gathered together to oppose it, and then became, in a certain sense at any rate, a political party countering external power with external resistance. This happened not only in pre-Pharisaic times during the oppression by Antiochus Epiphanes, but also particularly under the Jewish princes John Hyrcanus and Alexander Jannaeus when, from their Sadducean stand, the latter opposed the Pharisaic rulings. On the other hand, under Alexandra, who left everything in their hands, the Pharisees held a leading position in the government which they nevertheless exploited only in the interests of their religious demands. To politics as such they were always relatively indifferent. It must however be acknowledged that there were two different religious viewpoints from which the political situation could be judged, especially at a time when the Jews were under Gentile government or one friendly to the Gentiles, viewpoints which could lead to quite contrary attitudes. One approach could be based on the idea of divine providence, in which case the domination of the Jews by the Gentiles would be thought of as desired by God. God gave power to the Gentiles over his people in order to punish them for their transgressions. It would therefore last only for as long as he wished. Consequently, it was above all necessary to submit willingly to this divine chastisement, to endure even a Gentile and harsh ruler, as long as the observance of the Torah was not thereby impeded.

42. mAb. 3:15.

It was from this standpoint that, for example, the Pharisees Pollio and Sameas exhorted their fellow citizens to accept the rule of Herod.[43] Again, at the time of the first war against the Romans, leading Pharisees such as Simeon son of Gamaliel were at the head of the mediators who only took part in the uprising because they were obliged to, but who in their heart of hearts were opposed to it.[44] If, on the other hand, the predominating influence was belief in the election of Israel, then the subjugation of the people of God by Gentiles would appear as an enormity to be purged. Israel was to acknowledge no other king but God alone, and the ruler anointed by him from the house of David. Gentile domination was contrary to Scripture. From this point of view it was doubtful, not so much whether the people should obey the Gentile authorities and pay tribute to them, but whether it was lawful to do so (Mt. 22:17 ff.; Mk. 12:14 ff.; Lk. 20:22 ff.). It appears also to have been the reason why the mass of the Pharisees refused to take the oath to Herod,[45] though they may equally have been motivated by a reluctance to swear any oath at all.[46] It may be presumed to have been the popular viewpoint, among the people as well as among the Pharisees. Indeed, it must have been, for every non-Pharisaic government, even when it did not hinder the practice of the law, always brought with it a certain threat to the free observance of the Torah. Hence, it was also a Pharisee, Zadok, who in company with Judas the Galilean founded the revolutionary party in A.D. 6.[47] Thus, however indifferent to politics Pharisaism was to begin with, the revolutionary trend which gained increasing ground among the Jews in the first century A.D. is to be attributed, indirectly at least, to its influence.[48]

No peculiarity emerges from this characterization of Pharisaism which might distinguish it from Judaism in general during the period of the Second Temple. Regarded as a spiritual orientation, it was simply identical with the trend adopted by the main body and the

43. *Ant.* xiv 9, 4 (174); xv i, 1 (3).

44. On Simeon, see *B.J.* iv 3, 9 (159). On the position of pro-Roman Jews in office at that time, see above, pp. 311–3. On Yohanan ben Zakkai, see J. Neusner, *A Life of Yohanan ben Zakkai* ([2]1970), pp. 157–71; E. M. Smallwood, *The Jews under Roman Rule* (1976), pp. 289–90, 304–5.

45. *Ant.* xv 10, 4 (370); xvii 2, 4 (42).

46. According to *Ant.* xv 10, 4 (370–1), Pharisees and Essenes were excused from taking the oath of loyalty. In the case of the Essenes, Josephus states, *B.J.* ii 8, 6 (135), that they refused to swear on principle. Cf. Vermes, *DSS*, pp. 100, 126, 129.

47. *Ant.* xviii 1, 1 (4). See further pp. 599–600 below.

48. The two attitudes outlined above could also exist side by side in so far as a Gentile government could be regarded both as willed by God and an outrage. See in particular 4 Ezr.

classical representatives of post-exilic Jewry. Nevertheless, the Pharisees formed a party within the nation, an *ecclesiola in ecclesia*. In one of the two passages in which Josephus, or rather his source Nicolaus of Damascus, mentions the Pharisees' refusal to take the oath of loyalty, he describes them as a 'group of Jews', and gives their number as six-thousand.[49] In the New Testament and in Josephus they appear quite plainly as a small body within the nation. Even their name points to this. In Hebrew it is פרושים,[50] פרישין and in Aramaic פרישיא, whence the Greek, *Φαρισαῖοι*, meaning 'the separated'. The only question is, to what does this term refer? Were they men who set themselves apart from all uncleanness and unlawfulness, or from certain persons? It might be an argument for the first alternative that in rabbinic Hebrew the nouns פרישה and פרישות also occur with the meaning 'separation', viz. from all uncleanness.[51] But if separation from uncleanness alone were intended, with no reference to persons, other positive descriptions such as 'the Pure', 'the Just', 'the Pious', etc., would have been more apposite. Entirely decisive however is the fact that a separation from uncleanness is always a simultaneous separation from unclean persons. The first without the second—in the Levitical concept of purity—is not possible, since impurity adheres to persons.[52] The observance of Jewish dietary laws also leads necessarily to an ἀφορίζεσθαι of persons, as in the example of Peter in Antioch (Gal. 2:12). If, therefore, a reference to persons must also be taken into account, it would seem obvious to derive the name from the 'separation' that took place in the time of Zerubbabel, and again under Ezra, when the élite of the returned exiles set themselves apart from the Gentiles and half-Jews living in the land and from their uncleanness (Ezr. 6:21, 9:1; 10:11; Neh. 9:2; 10:29). But as J. Wellhausen rightly noted, this separation was not characteristically Pharisaic. All Israel was subjected to this separation at that time.[53] The Pharisees must have obtained their name from a separation in which the main body of the people did not participate, in other

49. *Ant.* xvii 2, 4 (42).

50. See mYad. 4:6–8; mHag. 2:7; mSot. 3:4.

51. mZab. 5:1: לאחר פרישתו ממטמאין, 'After his separation from what had rendered him unclean'. mToh. 4:12: טהרת פרישות, 'The cleanness of the separate life'; mSot. 9:15: 'When Rabban Gamaliel the Elder died . . . purity and abstinence disappeared, טהרה ופרישות. mAb. 3:14: 'R. Akiba said, . . . Vows are a fence around פרישות. See also A. Büchler, *Der galiläische Am-haareṣ des zweiten Jahrhunderts* (1906), p. 167; R. Meyer, *Tradition und Neuschöpfung im antiken Judentum* (1965), pp. 12–15. E. Rivkin, 'Defining the Pharisees: the Tannaitic Sources', HUCA 40–1 (1969–70), pp. 205–49; A. Michel-J. Le Moyne, 'Pharisiens', DB Supp. VII, cols. 1055–6.

52. Even ethically both hang together. In the interests of moral purity Paul warns the Corinthians to avoid association with immoral people (2 Cor. 6:17; cf. Isa. 52:11).

53. Wellhausen, *Pharisäer und Sadducäer*, pp. 76 ff.

words, from having set themselves apart, by virtue of their stricter understanding of the concept of purity, not only from the uncleanness of the Gentiles and half-Jews but also from that uncleanness which, in their opinion, adhered to a great part of the people itself. It is in this sense that they were called the 'separated' or 'self-separating'. The description can have been meant as either praise or censure. They can have named themselves in this way, because they kept themselves, as far as was possible, from all uncleanness, and consequently from contact with the unclean nation. They can also have been so named in a pejorative sense by their adversaries, as 'separatists' who in the interests of their own particular purity set themselves apart from the mass of the people.[54] This must have been the original significance of the name, for it is not likely that they gave it to themselves. Other more positive self-appellations would have occurred to them, and in fact they first appear in history as חסידים (see below).[55] Their opponents,

54. The pejorative interpretation, as may be expected, dominates patristic literature. See Clement, *Homil.* ix 28: *οἵ εἰσιν ἀφορισμένοι καὶ τὰ νόμιμα ὡς γραμματεῖς τῶν ἄλλων πλεῖον εἰδότες.* Pseudo-Tertullian, *Adv. Haer* 1: 'Pharisaeos, qui additamenta quaedam legis adstruendo a Iudaeis divisi sunt, unde etiam hoc accipere ipsum quod habent nomen digni fuerunt'. Origen, *In Mt.* 23:2 (ed. Lommatzsch IV, p. 194): 'Qui autem maius aliquid profitentes dividunt se ipsos quasi meliores a multis, secundum hoc Pharisaei dicuntur, qui interpretantur divisi et segregati. Phares enim divisio appellatur'. *In Mt.* 23:23 f. (ed. Lommatzsch IV, pp. 219–20): 'Similiter Pharisaei sunt omnes, qui iustificant semetipsos, et dividunt se a caeteris dicentes: noli mihi appropriare, quoniam mundus sum. Interpretantur autem Pharisaei, secundum nomen Phares, divisi, qui se ipsos a caeteris diviserunt. Phares autem dicitur hebraica lingua divisio'. *In Mt.* 23:29: (ed. Lommatzsch IV, pp. 233 ff.): 'recte Pharisaei sunt appelati, id est praecisi, qui spiritualia prophetarum a corporali historia praeciderunt'. *In Ioh.* (ed. Lommatzsch I, p. 210): *οἱ δὲ Φαρισαῖοι ἅτε κατὰ τὸ ὄνομα ὄντες διῃρημένοι τινὲς καὶ στασιώδεις.* *In Ioh.* (ed. Lommatzsch I, p. 113): *Φαρισαίων δὲ τῶν ἀποδιῃρημένων καὶ τὴν θείαν ἑνότητα ἀπολωλεκότων· Φαρισαῖοι γὰρ ἑρμηνεύονται οἱ διῃρημένοι.* Epiphanius, *Haer.* 16, 1: *ἐλέγοντο δὲ Φαρισαῖοι διὰ τὸ ἀφορισμένους εἶναι αὐτοὺς ἀπὸ τῶν ἄλλων, διὰ τὴν ἐλελοπερισσοθρησκείαν τὴν παρ' αὐτοῖς νενομισμένην· Φάρες γὰρ κατὰ τὴν Ἑβραΐδα ἑρμηνεύεται ἀφορισμός.* Jerome, *Contra Luciferianos* 23 (Migne, PL XXIII, col. 178): 'Pharisaei a Iudaeis divisi propter quasdem observationes superfluas nomen quoque a dissidio susceperunt (cf. Ps.-Tertullian, p. 408 below). *In Mt.* 22:23 (CCL lxxvii, p. 204): 'Pharisaei traditionum et observationum, quas illi δευτερώσεις vocant, iustitiam praeferebant, unde et divisi vocabuntur a populo; Sadducaei autem, quod interpretantur iusti, et ipsi vendicabant sibi quod non erant'. Nathan b. Yeḥiel declares in the '*Arukh*: 'A *Parush* is one who separates himself from all uncleanness, and from unclean food, and from the people of the land who are not careful about food'.

55. Cf. Meyer, *op. cit.* p. 14. The designation of a self-contained group by non-members usually differs from the official nomenclature. A propos of the Essenes, see Vermes, *PBJS*, pp. 8–9. The title 'Christians' was also originally a nickname given in Antioch (Act. 11:26). On the parallelism between קדוש ('saint') and פרוש ('separated one'), see J. Jeremias, *Jerusalem*, p. 249, n. 13. Among themselves, the Pharisees may have preferred the names of חבר (companion), סופר (scribe), or חכם (sage). Cf. below.

however, knew them as 'separatists'. This explains why the name appears in only three passages of the Mishnah, and in the most important of these issues from the mouth of a Sadducee.[56] But the rabbinic terminology would also suggest that once it had come into use, the Pharisees themselves accepted it, which they could very well do because from their standpoint 'separation' was pleasing to God.[57]

If the name 'Pharisees' shows that they set themselves apart from the rest of the people, the term which they applied to themselves, **חברים**, 'companions', indicates that they formed a close-knit community. In the language of the Mishnah and of ancient rabbinic literature in general, this term is synonymous with 'Pharisees'. It is clear from the passages quoted above (pp. 484–7), that a **חבר** was one who punctiliously observed the law, particularly in respect of Levitical purity and priestly dues. This term, furthermore, comprised all who acted thus, not only the professional scholars. For it was not the uneducated who were their formal opposites,[58] but the **עם הארץ**, of whom a strict observance of the law could not be expected.[59] Hence

56. The main passage is mYad. 4:6–8. See also mHag. 2:7; mSot. 3:4.

57. It has been suggested that the Pharisees saw a pun between **פרש**, to separate, and **פרש**, to distinguish, i.e. to interpret, **פרוש**, interpretation. Cf. Moore, *Judaism* I, p. 62, Michel-Le Moyne, *art. cit.*, DB Supp. VII, col. 1955; A. Schalit, *König Herodes* (1969), pp. 737–8.

58. The uneducated as opposed to the scholar is known as **הדיוט**, ἰδιώτης mR.Sh. 2:8.

59. The term **עם הארץ** figures frequently in the Bible, particularly in Jeremiah, Ezekiel and 2 Kings (with parallels in Chronicles). It is also found occasionally in other books (Jer. 1:18; 34:19; 37:2; 44:21; 52:6, 25; Ezek. 7:27; 12:19; 22:29; 33:2; 39:13; 46:3, 9; 2 Kgs. 11:14, 18, 19, 20; 15:5; 16:15; 21:24; 23:30, 35; 24:14; 25:3, 19; 2 Chron. 23:12, 20, 21; 26:21; 32:25; 37:1). In most of these texts, it characterizes the people in general as distinguished from the king and the authorities. The priests also belonged to the elite from which the people were distinguished (Jer. 1:18; 34:19). Yet the expression does not denote only the humbler levels of society, for these are called **דלת עם הארץ**, 'the poorest of the people of the land' (2 Kgs. 24:14; see also 25:12 and Jer. 40:7; 52:15, 16). In Ezra and Nehemiah, 'the peoples of the lands' are the Gentiles (Ezr. 9:1; Neh. 9:30) whose descendants dwelt in Palestine in the time of Ezra and Nehemiah and intermarried with Israelites. This is why there is mention not only of 'the peoples of the lands' **עמי הארצות** (Ezr. 3:3; 9:1–2, 11; Neh. 9:30; 10:29), but also of 'the peoples of the land', **עמי הארץ** (Ezr. 10:2, 11; Neh. 10:31, 32). These were non-Jews living in the Jewish land. The later rabbinic terminology is related partly to the older canonical books, and partly to Ezra and Nehemiah; to the former, in so far as there is mention, not of the 'peoples', but of the 'people' of the land (**עם הארץ**); to the latter, in so far as the phrase alludes to those not living by the Torah as opposed to those who do. They are the people dwelling in the land as opposed to the narrower community of the strictly observant. The collective singular, **עם** is however also used of an individual. Thus 'an *'am ha-'arez'* is one of the 'people of the land'. See in general mDem. 1:2, 3; 2:2, 3; 3:4; 6:9, 12; mSheb. 5:9; mM.Sh. 3:3; 4:6; mHag. 2:7; mGit. 5:9; mEdu. 1:14; mAb. 2:5; 3:10: mHor. 3:8; mKin. 13:6; mToh. 4:5; 7:1, 2, 4, 5; 8:1, 2, 3, 5; mMaksh. 6:3; mTeb. 4:5. Cf. A. Geiger,

the terminology of a later date, according to which a חבר is a 'colleague' of the rabbis, a scholar, must not be read into these Mishnah passages.[60] Here, a *ḥaver* is one who observes the Torah, including the *παραδόσεις τῶν πρεσβυτέρων*, and is therefore identical with a Pharisee.[61] But this affords a deep insight into the Pharisees' estimate of themselves. As distinguished from the common people, and a fortiori from the members of other religious parties, the Pharisees were the *ḥaverim*, the brothers of the Covenant, who represented the true community of Israel. Whereas in the Old Testament every Israelite is a *ḥaver* of the other, the Pharisees recognized as *ḥaver* proper only the strict observer of the Torah.[62]

Urschrift, p. 151; A. Büchler, *Das galiläische Am ha-Areṣ* (1906); L. Finkelstein, *The Pharisees* (³1962) II, pp. 754–61; R. Meyer, *op. cit.*, pp. 31–3; A. Oppenheimer, ''Am ha-Areẓ', Enc. Jud. 2, cols. 833–6; J. P. Weinberg, 'Der *'am hā'āreṣ* des 6.–4. Jh. v. u.Z.', Klio 56 (1974), pp. 325–35. The designation of the uneducated as country people, i.e. as 'boors', 'peasants', 'pagani', etc., is a well-attested linguistic usage. This implies that the Pharisees were no doubt essentially town-dwellers. Cf. also A. Oppenheimer, *The 'Am Ha-'Aretz. A Study in the Social History of the Jewish People* (1977).

60. Already in rabbinic literature of the third and fourth centuries A.D. the term 'companions', חברייא frequently means the young men assembled round a noted teacher of the Torah, and is therefore synonymous with תלמידים (see W. Bacher, 'Zur Geschichte der Schulen Palästinas im 3. und 4. Jahrhundert, MGWJ (1899), pp. 345–60). So at that time חבר was equivalent to 'scholar' (see JE VI, pp. 121–4). In the Mishnah and the baraitas, חבר can be used to denote the colleague of a scholar or a judge (e.g. mEdu. 5:7; mSanh. 11:2), but where it is used as a *terminus technicus*, it is different from תלמיד חכם, and indicates a wider circle; for example in bShab. 11a, 'with a Gentile and not with a חבר; with a חבר and not with a תלמיד חכם'. bBekh. 30b, 'Whoever takes on himself the statutes of the חבירות must do so in the presence of three חברים; even if he is a תלמיד חכם, he must do so in the presence of three חברים. Cf. Bacher, *op. cit.*, pp. 345, 357–9. Cf. J. Neusner, 'The Fellowship (Haburah) in the Second Jewish Commonwealth', HThR 53 (1960), pp. 125–42; R. Meyer, *op. cit.*, pp. 24–8. Neusner, *The Idea of Purity*, pp. 67–9. For possible parallels between the *ḥaburah* and the Qumran community, cf. S. Lieberman, 'The Discipline in the so-called Dead Sea Manual of Discipline', JBL 71 (1951), pp. 199–206 [=*Texts and Studies* (1974), pp. 200–7]; G. Vermes, *Discovery*, pp. 48–52; *DSS*, pp. 120–2, 132; C. Rabin, *Qumran Studies* (1957), pp. 11–21, 31–3.

61. The identification of פרוש with חבר results from a comparison of mHag. 2:7 with mDem. 2:3 (see above pp. 385, 386). In the first passage, עם הארץ and פרוש are contrasted, and in the latter, עם הארץ and חבר. In both places, the עם הארץ is the unclean person by whose garments the פרוש and חבר are defiled. So Nathan ben Yehiel of Rome in the *'Arukh* (see פרוש, and the citation of mHag. 2:7) rightly gives to פרושים the explanation, 'they are the חברים who eat ordinary food in a state of cleanness'. Cf. J. Levy, *Chaldäisches Wörterbuch*, s.v. חברא and s.v. חבר in *Neuhebräisches Wörterbuch*; S. Krauss, *Synagogale Altertümer* (1922), pp. 19–23; R. Meyer, *op. cit.*, pp. 23–8; Enc. Jud. 7, cols. 1489–92. For a different view, see E. Rivkin, HUCA 40–1 (1969/70), pp. 205–49.

62. חבר in the Mishnah is the equivalent of the biblical רע. In general, it denotes a 'companion', a person belonging to a similar category. The *ḥaver* of a

That the Pharisees in fact, as their name signifies, kept themselves apart from the rest of the people, is attested in various passages of the Mishnah. 'The garments of the " *'am ha-areẓ*" are *midras* (unclean) for the Pharisees'.[63] 'A *ḥaver* does not enter the house of an *'am ha-'areẓ* and does not accept him as a guest if the latter wears his own garments'.[64] 'If the wife of a *ḥaver* leaves the wife of an *'am ha-'areẓ* milling at the mill in her house, if the mill stops, the house is unclean; if she continues to mill, only that is unclean which she can touch by stretching out her hand', etc.[65] Thus the Gospel accounts of Pharisaic criticism of Jesus because of his free intercourse with 'publicans and sinners' (Mk. 2:14–17; Mt. 9:9–13; Lk. 5:27–32) corresponds exactly to the viewpoint here described.[66]

This exclusiveness of Pharisaism justifies in any case its description as a sect, *αἵρεσις*, the term applied to it in the New Testament (Act. 15:5; 25:5) and also by Josephus. But at the same time, it was the legitimate and typical representative of post-exilic Judaism. It merely drew the conclusions from its principles that the only true Israel are those who punctiliously observe the Torah, and since the Pharisees alone do this, they are the only true Israel.

Now that these general features of Pharisaism have been established, the question of its origin can be raised and its history outlined. Essentially, it is as old as so-called 'legal' Judaism itself. Once every-day life is organized as a continuous fulfilment of the Torah, and obedience to the Torah is regarded as the basis of religious conduct, Pharisaism already exists in principle. Its first appearance as a 'sect', however, as a party within the Jewish nation, cannot be traced further back than to the time of the Maccabaean revolt. The Hasidim, the Pious, *οἱ 'Ασιδαῖοι*, took part in this struggle, in the earlier stages in any case (1 Mac. 2:42; 7:12 ff.). They fought at the side of Judas for the religion of their fathers, but were not identical with the Maccabaean party.[67] It would

---

rabbi is a rabbi, the *ḥaver* of a priest is a priest, the *ḥaver* of an Israelite is an Israelite. Where no specific meaning is given, a *ḥaver* is simply a Jew. So e.g. mHul. 11:2, where it is the opposite of נכרי, 'stranger'; also in the passages mentioned in n. 59 above, where it stands midway between גוי and תלמיד חכם. For the Qumran Community's claim to be the true Israel, see G. Vermes, *DSSE*, pp. 16–68; *PBJS*, pp. 38–40; *DSS*, pp. 88, 98, 214; J. Neusner, *The Idea of Purity in Ancient Judaism* (1973), pp. 32–71.

63. mHag. 2:7.

64. mDem. 2:31.

65. mToh. 7:4. Cf. the passages quoted in n. 59.

66. On the peculiarity of the attitude of Jesus, cf. Vermes, *Jesus the Jew*, p.224.

67. See vol. I, pp. 157, 169; J. Maier, *Geschichte der jüdischen Religion* (1972), pp. 51–3. For a somewhat different theory, see P. R. Davies, 'Ḥasidim in the Maccabean Period', JJS 28 (1977), pp. 127–40.

appear that during the Greek period, when the chief priests and the rulers of the people displayed an increasingly lax attitude to the Torah, these Hasidim formed themselves into a community of people who took it upon themselves to fulfil the Torah in every detail. Hence when the Maccabees raised the standard of revolt in defence of the faith of their fathers, the Hasidim joined them, but only for as long as the struggle really was for the Torah and religion. When this was no longer the case, and the purpose of the war became increasingly one of national independence, they appear to have withdrawn. Josephus first mentions them as an independent group, preceding the Sadducees and the Essenes, under Jonathan,[68] but it is not until the time of John Hyrcanus I that they appear not as allies but opponents of the Maccabees.

In the course of time, the Maccabees founded a political dynasty. The ancient High-Priestly family was ousted and the Maccabees or Hasmonaeans entered into their political inheritance. But with this, tasks which were essentially political devolved on them. Their central concern was no longer with the fulfilment of the Torah but with the preservation and extension of their political power. The pursuit of such political aims necessarily divided them more and more from their former friends, the Hasidim or '*Perushim*'.[69] It was not that the Hasmonaeans fell away from the Torah, but a secular policy was in itself hardly compatible with the Scripture-centredness of Pharisaism. It was inevitable that a breach would occur sooner or later, and it did so under John Hyrcanus. For whereas he adhered to the Pharisees at the beginning of his rule, he later dissociated himself from them and turned to the Sadducees. The cause of the breach is related by Josephus rather in the style of a legend,[70] but the fact itself, that the change took place under Hyrcanus, is entirely credible. From then on, the Pharisees appear as opponents of the Hasmonaeans not only under Hyrcanus I and his son Aristobulus, but especially under Alexander Jannaeus. Under this fierce warrior-king who cared little for religious matters, the opposition flared into open revolt. For six years Jannaeus with his mercenaries was at war with the Jews led by the Pharisees.[71] All that he finally obtained was the outward intimidation, but not the real subjection, of his adversaries. For with their emphasis on religious interests, the Pharisees had the mass of the people on their side. Thus it is not surprising that Alexandra, for the sake of peace with the people,

68. *Ant.* xiii 5, 9 (171).

69. For the theory that the Hasidim evolved into the Essene community led by the priestly aristocracy of the sons of Zadok, as well as into the lay movement of the Pharisees, see below, pp. 586–7.

70. *Ant.* xiii 10, 5–6 (288–96).

71. *Ant.* xiii 13, 5 (376).

and also because of a personal preference for the Pharisees, handed over power to them. The victory was now complete; the whole conduct of internal affairs was in their hands. All the Pharisaic decrees abolished by John Hyrcanus were reintroduced; the Pharisees largely dominated Jewish public life.[72]

During the ages that followed, amid all the changes of government, under the Romans and the Herodians, the Pharisees maintained their leadership in spiritual matters, especially in urban circles.[73] It is true that the Sadducean High Priests stood at the head of Sanhedrin. But in fact it was the Pharisees, and not the Sadducees, who made the greatest impact on the ordinary people, as Josephus states again and again.[74] The Pharisees had the masses for their allies,[75] the women being especially devoted to them.[76] They held the greatest authority over the congregations, so that everything to do with worship, prayer, and sacrifice took place according to their instructions.[77] Their popularity is said to have been so high that they were listened to even when they criticized the king or the High Priest.[78] They were in consequence best able to restrain the king.[79] For the same reason, also, the Sadducees in their official functions complied with the Pharisaic requirements because otherwise the people would not have tolerated them.[80]

This great authority which the Pharisees exercised was but the counterpart of the exclusive position which they adopted. With the disappearance of Sadducean authority after the destruction of the Temple, the failure of the Zealots and the dissolution of the Essene brotherhood, the survivors of the Pharisaic movement became the only dominant force in the life of the Palestinian Jewish community, and

72. *Ant.* xiii 16, 2 (408).

73. *Ant.* xiii 1, 3 (15). *Ant.* xviii, 1, 3 (15) '. . . they are . . . extremely influential among the town-dwellers. . . . This is the great tribute that the inhabitants of the cities . . . have paid to the excellence of the Pharisees'. Pharisaic learning would naturally be city-centred. Note that the title, 'village scribes' is used sarcastically by Josephus in *B.J.* i 24, 3 (679); *Ant.* xvi 7, 3 (203).

74. It is worth noting that the supremacy of Pharisaic influence is stressed by Josephus in *Antiquities* and not in *B.J.* This is probably the result of the change in politico-religious power at the end of the first century A.D., by which time Pharisee leadership had imposed itself on Palestinian Jewry and been accepted by the Romans; cf. in particular M. Smith, 'Palestinian Judaism in the First Century', *Israel: Its Role in Civilization*, ed. M. Davies (1956), pp. 67–81.

75. *Ant.* xiii 10, 6 (298).

76. *Ant.* xvii 2, 4 (41).

77. *Ant.* xviii 1, 3 (15).

78. *Ant.* xvii 10, 5 (288).

79. *Ant.* xvii 2, 4 (41).

80. *Ant.* xviii 1, 4 (17).

were solely responsible for the revival and recodification of the ancestral traditions in the form of rabbinic Judaism.[81]

81. The identification of the Pharisees with the Damascus/Qumran Community is a minority view among scholars. Its chief exponents are L. Ginzberg in connexion with the Zadokite Fragments, *Eine unbekannte jüdische Sekte* (1922); E. T. *An Unknown Jewish Sect* (1976), and C. Rabin in regard to the Dead Sea Scrolls, *Qumran Studies* (1957). For a critical assessment, see Vermes, *DSS*, pp. 119–22. Among the more numerous writers who identify the community, with or without reservations, as the sect of the Essenes, cryptic names such as 'the seekers of smooth things' (CD 1:18; 1QH 2:15, 32; 4:10–11; 4QpNah. 1:2, 7; 2:2, 4; 3:3, 6), or the 'builders of the wall' (CD 4:19; 8:13, 18), designating the doctrinal opponents of the Qumran group, are often seen as alluding to the Pharisees; cf. e.g. A. Dupont-Sommer, *The Essene Writings from Qumran* (1961), p. 269, n. 2; 'Observations sur le Commentaire de Nahum découvert près de la Mer Morte', Journal des Savants (1963), pp. 210–14; R. Meyer, *Tradition und Neuschöpfung im antiken Judentum* (1965), pp. 58–66; Vermes, *DSSE*, pp. 59, 65, etc.; *DSS*, pp. 144–5, 152.

II. The Sadducees

The nature of the Sadducees does not stand out as sharply as that of the Pharisees. The scanty statements supplied by the sources cannot easily be unified. The reason for this seems to be that the Sadducees themselves were not a consistent phenomenon like the Pharisees, but a complex one, requiring to be considered from various angles.

Their most salient characteristic is that they were aristocrats. Josephus repeatedly describes them as such: 'They win over only the wealthy; they have not the people on their side'.[1] 'This teaching has reached but few, but these are men of the highest standing.'[2] When Josephus speaks of this 'teaching' arriving at only a few, it is all of a piece with his whole way of depicting Pharisaism and Sadduceeism as philosophical trends. Once this veneer is removed, the actual information given is that the Sadducees were aristocrats, wealthy (*εὔποροι*) and persons of rank (*πρῶτοι τοῖς ἀξιώμασιν*); which is to say that they mostly belonged to, or were associated with, the priesthood. For from the beginning of the Greek and even the Persian period, it was the priests and their aristocratic lay allies who ruled the Jewish state.[3] The New Testament and Josephus testify more than sufficiently to the fact that the High-Priestly families belonged to the Sadducean party.[4] This is not however to say that the Sadducees were exclusively a party of priests. The contrast between Sadducees and Pharisees is not one of a priestly party versus a party of the religiously observant, but of a clerical and lay aristocracy vis-à-vis an essentially lay group which derived its authority from learning. The Pharisees were by no means hostile to the priests as such. On the contrary, they interpreted the laws on the priestly revenues generously in the priests' favour, awarding them their first-fruits, heave-offering, tithes, first-born, etc., in fullest measure.[5] They also acknowledged the greater holiness and higher rank of the priests in the theocracy.[6] The priests for their part were also not

1. *Ant.* xiii 10, 6 (298).

2. *Ant.* xviii 1, 4. Cf. J. Jeremias, *Jerusalem*, pp. 229–30; J. Le Moyne, *Les Sadducéens*, pp. 349–50.

3. *Vita* 1 (1).

4. Act. 5:17. *Ant.* xx 9, 1 (199). Cf. Le Moyne, *op. cit.*, pp. 229–31.

5. Cf. in the Mishnah the tractates Demai, Terumoth, Ma'aseroth, Hallah, Bikkurim, and Bekhoroth.

6. mHag. 2:7: 'For them that eat heave-offering (i.e. the priests), the clothes of Pharisees count as *midras* (unclean)'. mHor. 3:8: 'A priest precedes a Levite, a

altogether hostile to Pharisaism. In the last decades preceding the destruction of the Temple and the first decades following it, there were a number of priests who themselves belonged to the Pharisees.[7] Their opponents were accordingly not the priests as such, but only the chief priests and the patrician laity, those who by virtue of their wealth and office held an influential position in civil life.

In view of these facts, it is reasonable to suppose that the Sadducees derived their name צדוקים,[8] *Σαδδουκαῖοι*,[9] from the priest Zadok whose descendants had held the priestly office in Jerusalem since Solomon's time. At all events, it may be considered certain that the name does not spring, as was often thought, from the adjective צדיק.[10] Instead, most scholars now prefer to connect it with the proper name צדוק.[11] For in the first derivation the change from 'i' to 'u' remains unexplained,[12] whereas the pronunciation of the proper name Zadok as Zadduk (*Σαδδούκ*, צדוק) is vouched for by the common testimony of the

---

Levite an Israelite'. Precedence was also given to priests in the reading of Scripture in the synagogue (mGit. 5:8).

7. It is attested already of Yose b. Yoezer that he was a חסיד in the priesthood (mHag. 2:7). A certain Yoezer, who was a Temple official and a priest, belonged to the school of Shammai (mOrl. 2:12). In Josephus we find a *Ἰώαζαρος (Γοζαρος) ἱερατικοῦ γένους, Φαριζαῖος καὶ αὐτός, Vita* 39 (197); cf. 63 (324). Josephus himself was a priest and a Pharisee, *Vita* 1 (2). There is also mention of a R. Judah ha-Kohen (mEdu. 8:2) and a R. Yose ha-Kohen (mEdu. 8:2; mAb. 2:8). Most renowned among the priestly Torah scholars are Hananiah (see above p. 371) and R. Eleazar ben Azariah (see p. 375). R. Ishmael and R. Tarphon are also said to have been priests (see pp. 376, 378).

8. On this designation see mYad. 4:6–7; mErub. 6:2; mMak. 1:6; mPar. 3:7; mNid. 4:2. The singular is in mErub. 6:2.

9. Cf. Josephus and the N.T.

10. Thus many of the Church Fathers, e.g. Epiphanius, *Haer*. 14, 2: *ἐπονομάζουσι δὲ οὗτοι ἑαυτοὺς Σαδδουκαίους, δῆθεν ἀπὸ δικαιοσύνης τῆς ἐπικλήσεως ὁρμωμένης. Σεδὲκ γὰρ ἑρμηνεύεται δικαιοσύνη*. Jerome, *In Mt*. 22:23 (CCL lxxvii, p. 205): 'Sadducaei autem, quod interpretantur iusti'. The derivation from צדיק was advocated by Derenbourg, *Essai*, p. 78.

11. See the fully documented statement of the *status quaestionis* in Le Moyne, pp. 157–63, and on the history of the hypothesis, L. Finkelstein, *The Pharisees* II, p. 663, n. 20. The suggestion of T. W. Manson that the origin of the name is to be sought in the Greek *σύνδικοι*, appearing in a bilingual Palmyrene inscription as סדקיא ('Sadducees and Pharisees: the Origin and Significance of the Names', BJRL 22 (1938), pp. 1–18), is classified by Le Moyne among the 'solutions fantaisistes' (*op. cit.*, p. 159) on the grounds that it does not satisfactorily account for either consonants or vowels of the New Testament or Josephan form.

12. Cf. however, R. North, 'The Qumran "Sadducees" ', CBQ 17 (1955), pp. 165–6 who, on the basis of Accadian *ṣaduk* ('right', 'just'), interprets 'Sadducee' of a person 'administering justice'. See also Le Moyne, *op. cit.* p. 162. The explanation still fails to account for the doubling of the daleth. See further n. 13 below.

Septuagint,[13] Josephus,[14] and a vocalized manuscript of the Mishnah.[15] Thus the party named צדוקים is related to צדוק as ביתסים is to Boethus and אפיקורוסים to Epicurus. Less sure is the identity of the Zadok from whom the Sadducees took their name. A legend in Aboth de R. Nathan traces them to a Zadok, disciple of Antigonus,[16] but the account is historically unreliable, (1) because Aboth de R. Nathan is of late origin; (2) because its information on the Boethusians is wrong (see n. 16); and (3) because the legend is based not on tradition but on scholarly deduction: i.e., that the Sadducees, who denied the immortality of the soul, arrived at their heresy through misunderstanding a saying of

13. The name Zadok occurs in the Old Testament fifty-three times. Among these ten passages in Ezekiel, Ezra, and Nehemiah (Ezek. 40:46; 43:19; 44:15; 48:11; Ezr. 7:2; Neh. 2:4, 29; 10:21; 11:11; 13:13) where the LXX has the form *Σαδδούκ*. The Lucianic recension has almost always *Σαδδούκ* in the other passages; cf. also the Greek text of the Ascension of Isaiah 2:5 (Amherst Papyri, ed. Grenfell and Hunt (1908), p. 4), though the editor wrongly corrected the *Σαδδούκ* of the MS. to *Σαδώκ*. Cf. similar statistics from Hatch-Redpath, and see Le Moyne, p. 158, n. 2: the spelling *Σαδώκ(χ)* (which one would expect for צדוק) does appear to be the rare exception, e.g., 1 Chron. 29:22 *Σαδωχ* (Luc. *Σαδδουκ*). T. W. Manson argues (*op. cit.*, p. 145, n. 4) that the Greek form of the name has been influenced by the form of *Σαδδουκαῖοι*. Cf. also Le Moyne, p. 158 and n. 9.

14. A Pharisee, *Σάδδουκος* (Niese: *Σαδδωκος*) is mentioned in *Ant.* xviii 1, 1 (4). See also *'Ανανίας Σαδδουκί* in *B.J.* ii 17, 10 (451); 21, 7 (628), where *Σαδδουκί* cannot mean 'Sadducee', the person in question according to *Vita* 39 (197) being a Pharisee. Cf. G. R. Driver, *The Judaean Scrolls* (1965), pp. 229 ff.

15. In the Cod. de Rossi 138, the name of Rabbi Zadok is pointed in only a minority of passages, and where it is, usually reads *Ẓaddūḳ* or *Ẓaddūḳ*. See also mPea. 2:4; mTer. 10:9; mShab. 24:5; mPes. 3:6; 7:2; 10:3. See however, Le Moyne, *op. cit.*, pp. 157–8. The Albeck-Yalon edition of the Mishnah always points the name as *Ẓādōḳ*.

16. Aboth de-Rabbi Nathan (ed. Schechter, p. 26): 'Antigonus of Sokho took over from Simeon the Righteous. He used to say: Be not like slaves that serve their master for the sake of reward; be rather like slaves who serve their master with no thought of reward; and let the fear of heaven be upon you, so that your reward may be doubled in the world to come. Antigonus of Sokho had two disciples who used to study his words. They taught them to their disciples, and their disciples to their disciples. These latter scrutinized the words and said, "What were our fathers thinking of that they spoke thus? Is it possible that a labourer should work all day and not take his reward in the evening? If our fathers had known that there is another world and a resurrection of the dead, they would not have spoken in this manner". Then they arose and broke away from the Torah and split into two sects, the Sadducees and the Boethusians: the Sadducees after the name of Zadok, the Boethusians after the name of Boethus.' For an annotated translation, see A. J. Saldarini, *The Fathers according to Rabbi Nathan* (1975), pp. 85–6. See also A. Geiger, *Urschrift*, p. 105; J. Wellhausen, *Pharisäer und Sadducäer*, p. 46; C. Taylor, *Sayings of the Jewish Fathers*, 1877, p. 126. The Boethusians, ביתסים, who are also mentioned once in the Mishnah (mMen. 10:3), derived their name from the High-Priestly family of Boethus in the time of Herod (see above, p. 234). Thus they are in any case related to the Sadducees. See also however, Le Moyne, *op. cit.*, pp. 113–15, 160–2.

Antigonus of Sokho, viz. that man should do good without regard to future reward.[17] Accordingly, the only remaining choice is either to derive the name Sadducee from some unknown Zadok who at some unknown time founded the party of aristocrats, or to trace it back to the priestly line of the Zadokites. The former is possible but the latter more probable.[18] The descendants of Zadok performed the priestly duties in the Temple at Jerusalem from the time of Solomon. Since the Deuteronomic reform, which forbade all sacrifice outside Jerusalem, only the rites performed there were lawful. Hence Ezekiel, in his ideal image of a theocracy, grants the privilege to the 'Zadokites' (בני צדוק) alone to officiate as priests in the Temple at Jerusalem (Ezek. 40:46; 43:19; 44:15; 48:11). When worship was restored after the exile, Ezekiel's demand was not wholly carried out inasmuch as some of the other priestly clans were able to uphold their rights.[19] The Zadokites nevertheless formed the nucleus and main body of the priesthood in the post-exilic age. This is most clearly to be seen from the fact that the Chronicler in his genealogy traces back the house of Zadok to Eleazar, the elder son of Aaron, thereby implying that the Zadokites had, if not the only, at any rate the first and nearest claim to the priesthood (1 Chron. 5:30–41). This procedure of the Chronicler proves at the same time that the name of the ancestor of this clan was still vividly remembered in the epoch of Chronicles, in the fourth century B.C. Jesus ben Sira also praises God that he 'has chosen the sons of Zadok to be priest': הודו לבוחר בבני צדוק לכהן (Ecclus. 51:12, line 9 of a hymn missing from the Greek and Syriac).[20] A party associated with the chief priests could therefore well be called Zadokite or Sadducean. For although these priests constituted but a fraction of the בני צדוק, they were nevertheless their authoritative representatives. Their orientation was Zadokite.[21]

In addition to their aristocratic status, a further distinctive characteristic of the Sadducees is that they acknowledged only the written

17. Cf. Wellhausen, *op. cit.*, p. 46. For the saying of Antigonus of Sokho, see mAb. 1:3. See above, p. 357.

18. Cf. Le Moyne, *op. cit.*, p. 163.

19. This may be inferred from the fact that in Chronicles, in addition to the line of Eleazar (i.e. the Zadokites), that of Ithamar appears authorized to perform the priestly offices (1 Chron. 24). See above, p. 252, n. 56.

20. S. Schechter, *The Wisdom of Ben Sira* (1899), pp. (22) and li; H. L. Strack, *Die Sprüche Jesus', des Sohnes Sirachs* (1903), p. 55; *The Book of Ben Sira*, edited by the Academy of the Hebrew Language (1973), p. 65.

21. Cf. especially Wellhausen, *Pharisäer und Sadducäer*, pp. 47–50; Leszynsky, *op. cit.*, pp. 96 ff.; Le Moyne, *op. cit.*, pp. 350 ff. The structure of the Qumran community provides a convincing parallel. It consists of 'the sons of Zadok; the Priests . . . and the multitude of the men of the community' (1QS 5:2–3; 1QSa 1:2). Cf. G. Vermes, *Discovery in the Judean Desert* (1956), pp. 74–76; *DSSE*, pp. 16–33; *DSS*, pp. 87–115.

Torah as binding, and rejected the entire body of traditional interpretation and further development formed during the course of the centuries by the Torah scholars. 'The Sadducaean group say that only the written regulations are to be esteemed as lawful, and that those which derive from the tradition of the fathers are not to be observed.'[22] So remote were they from the Pharisee principle of absolute authority that they actually believed it commendable to contradict their teachers.[23] It was a question, as is evident, of rejecting the *παραδόσις τῶν πρεσβυτέρων*, the whole accumulation of legal rulings developed by the Pharisaic Torah scholars in their supplementation and classification of the written law. The opinion of many of the Church Fathers that the Sadducees acknowledged only the Pentateuch but rejected the Prophets,[24] has no support in Josephus and is therefore regarded as erroneous by most modern scholars.[25] A real rejection of the Prophets

22. *Ant.* xiii 10, 6 (297), cf. xviii 1, 4 (16). Commenting on the latter passage in the Loeb edition, L. H. Feldman points out that the Sadducees nevertheless had their own traditions. But these were decrees or *gezeroth* (cf. mMak. 1:6), proclaimed by virtue of priestly authority, and not presented as an oral Torah revealed by God to Moses and transmitted via an uninterrupted chain of tradition.

23. *Ant.* xviii 1, 4 (16). Daube has suggested that the Sadducees took over this method of argumentation from the Hellenistic schools of philosophy ('Rabbinic Methods of Interpretation and Hellenistic Rhetoric', HUCA 22 (1949), p. 243, but Feldman, *loc. cit.* (above, n. 22) notes that there is no evidence of contact between the Sadducees and Hellenistic schools.

24. Origen, *Contra Celsum* i 49 (ed. Lommatzsch XVIII, p. 93): *οἱ μόνου δὲ Μωσέως παραδεχόμενοι τὰς βίβλους Σαμαρεῖς ἢ Σαδδουκαῖοι. Idem, In Mt.* 22:29 (Lommatzsch IV, 166): *τοῖς Σαδδουκαίοις μὴ προσιεμένοις ἄλλην γραφὴν ἢ τὴν νομικήν . . . τοὺς Σαδδουκαίους ὁτὶ μὴ προσιέμενοι τὰς ἑξῆς τῷ νόμῳ γραφὰς πλανῶνται. Ibid.* vol. xvii, ch. 36 (on Mt. 22:31–32). (Lommatzsch IV, p. 169): *καὶ εἰς τοῦτο δὲ φήσομεν ὅτι μύρια δυνάμενος περὶ τοῦ ὑπάρχειν τὴν μέλλουσαν ζωὴν τοῖς ἀνθρώποις παραθέσθαι ἀπὸ προφητῶν ὁ Σωτήρ· τοῦτο οὐ πεποίηκεν διὰ τὸ τοὺς Σαδδουκαίους μόνην προσίεσθαι τὴν Μωσέυς γραφὴν ἀφ' ἧς ἐβουλήθη αὐτοὺς συλλογισμῷ δυσωπῆσαι.* Jerome, *In Mt.* 22:31–2: 'Hi quinque tantum libros Moysis recipiebant, prophetarum vaticinia respuentes. Stultum ergo erat inde proferre testimonia, cuius auctoritatem non sequebantur'. Hippolytus, *Adv. Haer.* ix 29: *προφήταις δὲ οὐ προσέχουσιν ἀλλ' οὐδὲ ἑτέροις τισὶ σοφοῖς. Πλὴν μόνῳ τῷ διὰ Μωσέως νόμῳ, μηδὲν ἑρμηνεύοντες.* Ps.-Tertullian, *De praescriptione haereticorum* (Migne, PL II, col. 61): 'taceo enim Iudaismi haereticos, Dositheum inquam Samaritanum, qui primus ausus est prophetas quasi non in spiritu sancto locutus repudiare, taceo Sadducaeos, qui ex huius erroris radice surgentes ausi sunt ad hanc haeresim etiam resurrectionem carnis negare'. The Pseudo-Tertullian tractate, in addition to the genuine *De praescriptione haereticorum*, probably belongs to the first half of the third century, see B. Altaner, *Patrology*, p. 172. Cf. S. J. Isser, *The Dositheans* (1976), pp. 33–8. Jerome has the same, almost word for word, in his *Contra Luciferianos* 23 (Migne, PL XXIII, col. 178): 'taceo de Iudaismi haereticis, qui ante adventum Christi legem traditam dissiparunt: quod Dosithaeus Samaritanorum princeps prophetas repudiavit: quod Sadducaei ex illius radice nascentes etiam resurrectionem carnis negaverunt'.

25. Cf. Le Moyne, *op. cit.*, pp. 358–9; the Prophets and Writings may have been regarded as less authoritative than the Torah by Sadducees and Pharisees alike. Leszynsky (*op. cit.*, p. 165) argues that this exclusive acceptance of the Torah

is unthinkable, but it is quite possible that the Sadducees considered only the Pentateuch as canonical in the strict sense of the word.[26]

In the face of the opposition of principles which the Sadducees raised against the whole Pharisaic tradition, the individual legal differences between the two parties possess but a secondary interest. A number are mentioned in rabbinic literature,[27] but the relevant notices cannot in the main be accepted as wholly historical, especially the statements contained in the medieval commentary on Megillath Taanith. But as far as they are trustworthy, they are so scattered and disconnected that it is impossible to discern in them any unifying principle, such as the defence of priestly intersts by the Sadducees. In penal legislation the Sadducees were more severe and the Pharisees more mild, according to Josephus.[28] This may have been due to the Sadducees' strict adherence to the letter of the law, while the Pharisees did all in their power to mitigate its severity by interpretation and adaptation. In one of the points mentioned by the Mishnah, the Sadducees went even beyond the demands of the Torah: they required compensation not only for injury caused by a man's ox or ass (as in Exod. 21:32, 35 f.), but also by his manservant or maidservant.[29] On the other hand, they insisted that false witnesses should be put to death only when the accused, as a result of their testimony, had already been executed (Dt. 19:19–21), whereas the Pharisees asked for this to be done even if only judgement had been pronounced.[30] In this case, therefore, the Pharisees were more severe. These differences were obviously not really differences of principle. Similarly, in questions of ritual it is possible to speak of a difference of principle only in so far as the Sadducees did not regard as binding the Pharisaic rulings on, for example, cleanness and uncleanness. They derided their Pharisaic opponents because of the oddities and inconsistencies that resulted

---

can have been confined only to certain 'Sadducean' sects who shared this attitude with the Samaritans. On the Church Fathers' confusion of Sadducees and Samaritans, cf. Le Moyne, *op. cit.*, p. 151.

26. So K. Budde, *Der Kanon des Alten Testaments* (1900), pp. 42–3. Cf. Le Moyne, *op. cit.*, pp. 357–9.

27. A. Geiger, *Urschrift*, pp. 134 ff.; J. Derenbourg, *Essai*, pp. 132 ff.; J. Wellhausen, *Pharisäer*, pp. 56–75; J. Z. Lauterbach, *art. cit.*, HUCA 6 (1929), pp. 69–139; the material is collected in Str.-B., IV, pp. 344 ff.; the rabbinic sources are discussed by Leszynsky, *op. cit.*, pp. 36–141, and Le Moyne, *op. cit.*, pp. 167–239. See also S. Zeitlin, *Studies in the Early History of Judaism* II (1974), pp. 259–91.

28. *Ant.* xx 9, 1 (199); cf. xiii 10, 6 (294).

29. mYad. 4:7. Cf. pp. 384 f. above.

30. mMak. 1:6. On juridical differences, see G. Hölscher, *Der Sadduzäismus*, pp. 22–4 and 30–2, where the Sadducean view is attributed to Roman influence. Cf. also Le Moyne, *op. cit.*, pp. 227–9.

from their laws of purity.[31] The Pharisees in their turn declared all Sadducee women unclean, 'if they follow after the ways of their fathers'.[32] Yet it is evident that the Sadducees were far from renouncing the principle of Levitical purity in itself, since they demanded an even higher degree of purity than did the Pharisees for priests who burned the Red Heifer.[33] This is at the same time the only point on which a definite priestly concern is apparent, namely, that of priestly ritual cleanness. With regard to festival laws, it is mentioned that the 'Boethusians' (who appear to have been a branch of the Sadducees) held that the sheaf of first-fruits at the Passover should not be offered on the second day of the feast, but on the day following the Sabbath in the festival week,[34] and that the Feast of Weeks falling seven weeks later (Lev. 23:11) should correspondingly always be celebrated on the day following the Sabbath.[35] This difference, however, is so purely technical that it merely gives expression to the exegetical outlook of the

31. The attacks of the Sadducees on the Pharisees mentioned in mYad. 4:6, 7 can only have been intended as mockery, for the Sadducees would surely not agree that 'heretical books' soiled the hands (mYad. 4:6), or that the 'stream' should be declared unclean when poured from a clean vessel to an unclean (mYad. 4:7). But they wished to ridicule the peculiarities of the Pharisees. See Le Moyne, *op. cit.*, pp. 209 ff., 212 ff.

32. mNid. 4:2.

33. mPar. 3:7. The Torah lays down that the priest should take a bath of purification after the burning of the Heifer; he then remained unclean until the evening (Num. 19:3–8). The Sadducees wished him to burn the Heifer after he had become clean at sunset. Their view was therefore more demanding. Cf. Le Moyne, *op. cit.*, pp 266 ff.

34. mMen. 10:3. That is, they understood by the שבת (Lev. 23:11), not the first day of the feast, but the weekly Sabbath. The traditional interpretation which takes it to be the first day of the feast, and 'the morrow of the Sabbath' to be the second day, is attested by the LXX (τῇ ἐπαύριον τῆς πρώτης), Philo, *Spec. Leg.* ii 29 (162), and Josephus, *Ant.* iii 10, 5 (248). On the history of the interpretation, and especially on Sadducaean opinion, see Wellhausen, *op. cit.*, pp. 59 f. and 67; D. Chowlson, *Das letzte Passahmahl Christi* (1892), pp. 60–7; G. Hölscher, *Der Sadduzäismus*, pp. 24–6; Leszynsky, *op. cit.*, pp. 57 ff.; Str.-B., pp. 850 ff.; Finkelstein, *Pharisees* II, pp. 641–54; Le Moyne, *op. cit.*, pp. 177–90. According to the Book of Jubilees 15:1; 16:13; 44:4–5, the Festival of Harvest (identical with the Feast of Weeks, see 6:21; 22:1) must have been celebrated 'in the middle' of the third month. This dating follows neither the Pharisaic nor Sadducean exposition of Lev. 23:11 and 15, but is based on a solar calendar, adopted also in the Qumran community (cf. vol. I, pp. 596–601), in which Passover (15 Nisan) is always celebrated on a Wednesday. If the count of the fifty days begins on 'the morrow of the Sabbath', i.e. a Sunday, in the week following Passover (that is on 26 Nisan), the Feast of Weeks falls on Sunday 15 Sivan, in 'the middle' of the third month, instead of on 6 Sivan of the traditional Jewish calendar. Cf. A. Jaubert, *La date de la Cène* (1957), pp. 20–4; J. van Goudoever, *Biblical Calendars* (^{2}1961), pp. 15–29.

35. mHag. 2:4. The words עצרת אחר השבת 'The Feast of Weeks falls on the day after the Sabbath', are given in mHag. 2:4 as an erroneous view attributed in mMen. 10:3 to the Sadducees (Boethusians).

Sadducees with its non-acceptance of tradition. It is not an issue of principle. The one difference that mattered in the law of festivals, particularly in the interpretation of the Sabbath commandment, was that the Sadducees did not acknowledge the Pharisaic rules as binding.[36] Thus the difference in principle between the two parties is confined to this general denial by the Sadducees of the body of tradition held by the Pharisees to be compulsory. All the rest are differences which necessarily arise when one school of thought refuses to acknowledge as an obligation the exegetical tradition of the other. Moreover, it should not be concluded that the Sadducees rejected every tradition held by the Pharisees. Quite apart from the fact that from the time of Alexandra they were no longer the exclusive leaders, they agreed in theory with some, perhaps with much, of the Pharisaic tradition. They denied only its general authority, and reserved the right to their own opinion.

In this rejection of the Pharisaic legal tradition, the Sadducees represented an older viewpoint: they stood by the written Torah. For them, none of the subsequent development was binding. Their religious outlook was similarly very conservative. Its essential features have already been discussed (cf. pp. 391–4 above). (1) They rejected belief in bodily resurrection and in reward in a life to come, and indeed in any kind of personal survival whatever. (2) They also denied the existence of angels and spirits. (3) They maintained finally 'that good and evil are in the choice of man and he can do the one or the other as he wishes'; that God therefore exercises no influence upon human actions and that man is himself the cause of his own fortune and misfortune.[37]

There is no doubt that in regard to the first two points the Sadducees represented the original doctrine of the Old Testament as distinct from that of later Judaism. For with the exception of the Book of Daniel, the Old Testament knows little of the resurrection of the body or of retribution in a future life, of personal salvation of the individual or future punishment for the sins of this life, but only of a shadowy continuation of existence in Sheol. Likewise, belief in angels and demons in the form in which it later developed is foreign to the Old Testament. The Sadducees were thus faithful to the earlier outlook in both these respects.

The Sadducees laid an emphasis on human freedom in which, if the

36. From mErub. 6:2, it might be thought that the Sadducees also observed certain Pharisaic decrees regarding the Sabbath. In fact, however, the context shows that the Sadducees 'did not acknowledge (the law of) 'erub' (mErub. 6:1). The Sadducee's intention can therefore only have been to annoy his Pharisee neighbour. Cf. Le Moyne, *op. cit.*, p. 204.

37. J. Halévy, 'Traces d'aggadot saddučéennes dans le Talmud', REJ 8 (1884), pp. 38–56.

relevant statements of Josephus are to be believed, it is possible to catch sight of a lessening of the religious motive. They wished to think of man as relying on himself and rejected the idea that God also played a part in human affairs.

These last remarks may in part indicate how the aristocracy came to adopt the course known as 'Sadducean'. To understand the origin of this school of thought, it is necessary to proceed from the fact that already in the Persian, but particularly in the Greek period, the priestly upper classes were in charge of the conduct of political affairs. The High Priest was the head of state; leading priests without doubt directed the *Gerousia* (the subsequent Sanhedrin). The duties of the priestly aristocracy were therefore as much political as religious. As a result, political issues and interests radically affected their whole attitude. But the more these took precedence, the more those of religion fell behind. This seems to have been particularly true in the Hellenistic period, the reason being that political interests were linked to the interests of Greek culture. Whoever wished to achieve something politically in the world of that time had to be on a more or less friendly footing with Hellenism. So Hellenism gained increasing ground even among the leading priests in Jerusalem. And in a corresponding measure the latter became estranged from Jewish religious interests.[38] It is therefore understandable that it was precisely in these circles that Antiochus Epiphanes found readiest acceptance. Some of the high-ranking priests were even prepared without further ado to exchange Jewish rites for Greek. This full-scale Hellenization was admittedly not of long duration; the Maccabaean rising quickly put an end to it. But the tendencies of the priestly aristocracy nevertheless remained essentially the same. Though there was no more talk of a pagan cult, and though the professed Hellenizers were either expelled or silenced, there was still among the priestly aristocracy the same wordly-mindedness and the same comparative laxity in matters of religion.[39] The Maccabaean rising, however, resulted in a revival and strengthening of traditional religious life. The tendency of the Hasidim towards strict observance of the Torah gained more and more influence. And with it, their claims also mounted. He alone was a true Israelite who observed the law in accordance with the interpretation given by the Torah scholars. But the more pressing these demands became, the more decisively did the aristocracy reject them. It therefore appears that it

38. Cf. M. Hengel, *Judaism and Hellenism* I (1974), pp. 47–57.

39. For the Hellenization of the Maccabaean-Hasmonaean priestly dynasty, see Hengel, *op. cit.* I, p. 76; II, p. 150, n. 753. Concerning the secularization of the ruling priestly autocracy according to the Qumran community, see in particular 1QpHab. 8:8–13; 9:4–7.

was the religious revival itself of the Maccabaean period that led to a consolidation of the parties. A largely lay section of the Hasidim followed their principles to their conclusion and became 'Pharisees'. The ruling priestly aristocracy and leading laity refused to be bound by the achievements of the previous few centuries in regard to both the interpretation of the Torah and the development of religious views. They saw in the *παραδόσις τῶν πρεσβυτέρων* an unnecessary limitation of their hereditary, judicial and doctrinal authority. Their conservative and autocratic tendencies on the one hand, and their secular culture on the other, inclined them to hold as either superfluous or unacceptable the progressive religious ideas of the Pharisees. As many of the leaders of this party belonged to the ancient priestly family of Zadokites, they and their whole following were known as Sadducees.[40]

A second group of Hasidim under the priestly leadership of other 'sons of Zadok' distinct from and opposed to the Hasmonaean dynasty is thought to have founded the Essene/Qumran community. These appear to have combined the 'Sadducean' concept of priestly supremacy with the Pharisaic emphasis on doctrinal and legal renewal and re-adaptation by means of biblical exegesis.[41]

Under the first Maccabees (Judas, Jonathan and Simon), the allied 'Zadokite' aristocracy retreated of necessity into the background. The ancient pontifical family, some of whose members at least were pro-Greek, was dismissed. The office of High Priest remained vacant for a time. Then in 153/152 B.C., Jonathan Maccabaeus was appointed High Priest and thereby founded a new High-Priestly dynasty, that of the Hasmonaeans, whose whole past inclined them at first to support the Assidaean/Pharisaic party. Nevertheless, under Jonathan and Simon, the Sadducees were not totally ousted from the scene. The old aristocracy was certainly purged of its extreme phil-Hellenic elements but it did not disappear once and for all. The newly risen Hasmonaeans therefore had to come to some sort of understanding with it and to concede to it at least some of the seats in the *Gerousia*. Such was the situation until the time of John Hyrcanus. From then on, however, the Sadducees became once more the real ruling party. John Hyrcanus, Aristobulus I and Alexander Jannaeus all depended on them (see above, pp. 401–2). The reaction under Alexandra saw a return to power of the Pharisees, but politically their domination did not last long. Despite the growth of Pharisee spiritual authority, in politics the Sadducaean aristocracy was able to retain their hold, and that notwithstanding the fall of the Hasmonaeans and notwithstanding Herod's proscription of the old pro-Hasmonaean nobility. In the Herodian-Roman period, some

40. Cf. Le Moyne, *op. cit.*, pp. 381 ff.

41. Cf. G. Vermes, *Discovery*, pp. 73–6; *DSSE*, pp. 61–5; *DSS*, pp. 150–6; M. Hengel, *op. cit.*, I, pp. 224–7. For fuller details, see below, pp. 579–87.

of the High Priestly families belonged to the Sadducean party. This is clearly attested of the Roman period at least.[42] The price which the Sadducees had to pay to ensure their supremacy in this later period was admittedly a high one: in the performance of their official functions they had to accommodate themselves to popular Pharisaic views.[43]

With the downfall of the Jewish state, the Sadducees vanished from history. Political leadership was their main function, and when national independence came to an end, so did they. Whereas the Pharisees were not only unaffected by the collapse of political affairs but profited from the new situation to establish themselves as exclusive leaders of the Jewish people, the ground on which the Sadducees were able to exist disappeared from under them. It is consequently not surprising that their true identity was no longer known. A few authentic traditions concerning them are preserved in the Mishnah, but their image in the subsequent stages of rabbinic literature becomes increasingly nebulous and distorted.

42. Act. 5:17; *Ant.* xx 9, 1 (199).
43. *Ant.* xviii 1, 4 (17). See above, p. 402.

§ 27. SCHOOL AND SYNAGOGUE

It was the fundamental belief of post-exilic Judaism that a knowledge of the Torah was the highest good in life, and the acquisition of such knowledge, worthy of the greatest effort. On all sides, the admonition sounded to attend to this task.

'Yose ben Yoezer of Zeredah said: Let your house be a meeting-house for the sages (חכמים). Become dusty with the dust of their feet and drink in their words thirstily.'[1]

'Joshua ben Perahiah said: Provide yourself with a teacher (רב).'[2]

'Shammai said: Make the (study of the) Torah a regular occupation (קבע).'[3]

'Rabban Gamaliel said: Provide yourself with a teacher and you thus avoid the doubtful.'[4]

'Hillel said: An ignorant man cannot be pious (לא עם הארץ חסיד).'[5]

Moreover he used to say: 'The more Torah study, the more life; the more schooling, the more wisdom; the more counsel, the more reasonable behaviour . . . Whoever acquires knowledge of the Torah, acquires life in the world to come.'[6]

'R. Yose ha-Kohen said: Take trouble to learn the Torah for it is not obtained by inheritance.'[7]

'R. Eleazar ben Arakh said: Be zealous in the study of the Torah.'[8]

'R. Hananiah ben Teradion said: If two sit together and do not converse on the Torah, they are a gathering of scoffers, of whom it is written, *Sit not where scoffers sit*. But if two sit together and converse on the Torah then the Shekhinah is present among them.'[9]

'R. Simeon said: If three eat together at one table and do not converse on the Torah, it is as though they partake of offerings of the dead. . . . But if three eat together at one table and converse on the Torah, it is as though they eat at the table of God.'[10]

1. mAb. 1:4.
2. mAb. 1:6.
3. mAb. 1:15.
4. mAb. 1:16.
5. mAb. 2:6.
6. mAb. 2:7.
7. mAb. 2:12.
8. mAb. 2:14.
9. mAb. 3:2; cf. 3:6.
10. mAb. 3:3.

'R. Jacob said: Whoever whilst walking repeats to himself the Torah but interrupts to call out, "What a beautiful tree! What a beautiful field!", Scripture charges it to his account as though he forfeits his life.'[11]

'R. Nehorai said: Travel always to a place where there is Torah teaching and do not say that it will follow after you or that your companions will obtain it for you. And do not rely on your own sagacity.'[12]

'R. Nehorai also said: I disregard all business in the world and teach my son only the Torah, for its profit is enjoyed in this world and its capital (הקרן) remains for the world to come.'[13]

'The following things have no measure: Peah, first-fruits, the festal offerings, acts of charity and study of the Torah. The following are things the interest (פירות) on which is enjoyed in this world while the capital (הקרן) remains for the world to come: the honouring of father and mother, deeds of loving-kindness, making peace between fellow-men, and more than all this, the study of the Torah.'[14]

'The bastard (ממזר) who knows the Torah (תלמיד חכם) precedes the High Priest in rank if he is an ignorant man (עם הארץ).'[15]

An esteem such as this for the Torah necessarily prompted the employment of every means to bestow if possible on the whole nation the benefit of a thorough knowledge and practice of the Bible. The law of Israel determined by the Pharisaic Torah scholars in their schools had to become the common possession of the entire people, theoretically as well as practically. For it was a question of both: of knowing and of doing the Torah. Josephus praises this as a virtue of the nation of Israel, that among them neither the one nor the other was preferred, unlike the case of the Lacedaemonians and Cretans, where education was solely practical and entailed no verbal instruction (*ἔθεσιν ἐπαίδευον οὐ λόγοις*), or that of the Athenians or other Greeks, who contented themselves with theoretical learning but neglected practice. 'Our lawgiver, however, combined the two with great care. For he left neither the practice of morals silent nor the teaching of the Law unperformed.'[16] The instruction which constituted the prerequisite of practice began in early youth and carried on throughout the whole of life. Its foundations were laid by the school and the family. Its continuation rested with the synagogue.

11. mAb. 3:7.
12. mAb. 4:14.
13. mKid. 4:14.
14. mPea. 1:1.
15. mHor. 3:8. Cf. in general on the necessity and value of Torah study: Moore, *Judaism* II, pp. 239–47; J. Maier, *Geschichte der jüdischen Religion* (1972), pp. 106–13; Urbach, *The Sages*, pp. 603–20.
16. *C.Ap.* ii 16–17 (172–3).

I. School

Bibliography

Wiesen, J., *Geschichte und Methodik des Schulwesens im talmudischen Altertum* (1892).

Stein, S., *Schulverhältnisse, Erziehungslehre und Unterrichtsmethoden im Talmud* (1901).

Bacher, W., 'Das altjüdische Schulwesen', JJGL 6 (1903), pp. 48–82.

Stern, J., *Die talmudische Pädagogik* (1915).

Swift, F. H., *Education in Ancient Israel from Earliest Times to 70 A.D.* (1919).

Gollancz, H., *Pedagogics of the Talmud and that of Modern Times* (1924).

Moore, G. F., *Judaism* I (1927), pp. 308–22.

Fischel, W., *Die jüdische Pädagogik in der tannaitischen Literatur* (1928).

Morris, N., *The Jewish School from the Earliest Times to the Year 500* (1937).

Schwabe, M., על בתי הספר היהודים והיוניים־רומיים בתקופת המשנה והתלמוד, Tarbiz 21 (1949/50), pp. 112–23.

Baron, S. W., *A Social and Religious History of the Jews* II (²1952), pp. 274–9.

Ebner, E., *Elementary Education in Ancient Israel during the Tannaitic Period* (10–200 C.E.) (1956).

Morris, N., תולדות החנוך של עם ישראל I (1960).

Berman, A., תולדות החנוך בישראל ובעמים (²1968).

Aberbach, M., 'Educational Problems and Institutions in the Talmudic Age', HUCA 37 (1968), pp. 107–20.

Safrai, S., 'Elementary Education, its Religious and Social Significance in the Talmudic Period', *Jewish Society throughout the Ages*, ed. H. H. Ben Sasson and S. Ettinger (1971), pp. 148–69.

Maier, J., *Geschichte der jüdischen Religion* (1972), pp. 111–13.

Demsky, A., Moriel, Y., 'Education', Enc. Jud. 6, cols. 381–403.

Hengel, M., *Judaism and Hellenism* I (1974), pp. 65–83.

Goldman, I. M., *Lifelong Learning among Jews* (1975), pp. 11–68.

Goodblatt, D. M., *Rabbinic Instruction in Sasanian Babylonia* (1975).

Safrai, S., 'Education and Study of the Torah', JPFC II (1977), pp. 945–69.

Moses, according to Josephus, laid down that boys should 'begin by learning the laws (τοὺς νόμους), most beautiful of lessons and a source of felicity'.[17] He commanded that children should be instructed in the rudiments of knowledge (reading and writing) and that they should be taught to know the laws and the deeds of the forefathers: the latter, that they might imitate them; the former, that growing up with them they might not transgress them, or have the excuse of ignorance.[18] Josephus repeatedly extols the zeal with which the instruction of the young was carried out:

'We take most trouble of all over the education of children, and

17. *Ant.* iv 8, 12 (211).

18. *C.Ap.* ii 25 (204). On γράμματα = the elements of knowledge (reading and writing), see Bauer-Arndt-Gingrich, *A Greek-English Lexicon of the N.T.*, p. 164.

regard observance of the laws and the acts of piety based on it to be the most important concern of our whole life.'[19]

'If one of us should be questioned about the laws, he would recite them all more easily than his own name. Since we acquire them from our earliest consciousness, we have them as it were engraved in our souls. And a transgressor is rare, but evasion from punishment impossible.'[20]

Philo expresses himself similarly:

'Since the Jews consider their laws to be divine revelations and are instructed in them from their earliest youth, they bear the image of the law in their souls.'[21] 'Even before any instruction in the holy laws and unwritten customs, they are taught, so to speak, from their swaddling-clothes by parents, teachers and educators to believe in God, the one Father and Creator of the world.'[22]

Speaking of himself, Josephus boasts that in his fourteenth year he was already so well versed in the Torah that the High Priest and leading men of Jerusalem came to him 'for precise information on some particular point in our ordinances.'[23] In view of all this, there can be no doubt, therefore, that in the circles of traditional Judaism a boy was familiarized with the demands of the Torah from earliest childhood.[24]

Obviously, this education was primarily the duty and task of parents. But it seems that already by the time of Jesus the community also provided for the instruction of the young by establishing schools. A later legend to the effect that Simeon ben Shetah prescribed that children (תינוקות) should attend elementary school (בית הספר) is of little significance.[25] For Simeon is the subject of a large number of stories, and his role in the institution of primary education cannot be proved. It may nevertheless be assumed that elementary schools did exist in the time of the Mishnah, i.e., in the second century A.D. There are, for example, legal rulings in respect of the חזן (minister of the congregation) teaching the children to read on the Sabbath.[26] It is also decreed that an unmarried man must not teach children (לא ילמוד אדם רוק סופרים).[27]

19. *C.Ap.* i 12 (60).
20. *C.Ap.* ii 18 (178).
21. *Legat.* 31 (210).
22. *Legat.* 16 (115). The phrase *πολὺ πρότερον τῶν ἱερῶν νόμων* may also be rendered, according to F. H. Colson (Loeb, *in h.l.*, note *c*), as 'long before' (the sacred laws). Cf. also E. M. Smallwood, *Philonis Alexandrini Legatio ad Gaium* (1970), pp. 207–8.
23. *Vita* 2 (9).
24. Cf. also Test. of Levi 13:2; Ps.-Philo, LAB 22:5–6. In Jub. 11:16 (Abraham) and 19:14 (Jacob), knowledge of writing is associated with correct religious attitudes. In Christian communities, too, children were instructed in the Scriptures. Cf. 2 Tim. 3:15: *ἀπὸ βρέφους ἱερὰ γράμματα οἶδας*.
25. yKet. 32c. Cf. Moore, *Judaism* III, p. 104, n. 92.
26. mShab. 1:3.
27. mKid. 4:13.

Elsewhere we are told that in certain cases the testimony of an adult is valid in regard to what he once saw as a child (קטן) in the primary school.[28] It is consequently not impossible to believe a later tradition that Joshua ben Gamla (= Jesus the son of Gamaliel) ordered school-teachers (מלמדי תינוקות) to be appointed in every province and in every town, and children to be brought to them from the age of six or seven.[29] The only Jesus son of Gamaliel known to history is the High Priest of that name, who flourished in about A.D. 63–5 (see above, p. 232). This information must therefore refer to him. As his enactment presupposes that boys' schools had already existed for some time, it is reasonable to envisage them as operating in the age of Jesus, though perhaps not yet as a general and well-established institution.[30]

Instruction, as is clear from the above-mentioned passages in Philo and Josephus, was almost exclusively concerned with the Torah. For all this zeal in the upbringing of the young was aimed at impressing the Torah on their minds and not at providing them with a general education. Thus their first lessons were in reading and memorizing the Scriptural text. The primary school was therefore known simply as בית הספר because its subject was the 'book' of the Torah, or as is once specifically stated, the text of the Bible (מקרא), in contrast to the בית מדרש which was devoted to further 'study'.[31] Hence it was basically only interest in the Torah that caused the teaching of reading to be

28. mKet. 2:10.

29. bB.B. 21a: 'Rab Judah said in the name of Rabbi: Truly may it be remembered to this man's credit! Joshua ben Gamla is his name. Had he not lived, the Torah would have been forgotten in Israel. For at first, whoever had a father was taught the Torah by him; whoever had none, did not learn the Torah. . . . Afterwards, it was ordained that teachers of boys should be appointed in Jerusalem. . . . But only whoever had a father was sent to school by him; whoever had none, did not go. Then it was ordained that teachers be appointed in every province, and that boys of the age of sixteen and seventeen be sent to them. But he whose teacher was angry with him ran away, until Joshua ben Gamla came and decreed that teachers be appointed in every province and every town (בכל מדינה ומדינה ובכל עיר ועיר), and children of six or seven years be brought to them.' Cf. S. Safrai, 'Elementary Education, its Religious and Social Significance in the Talmudic Period', *Jewish Society throughout the Ages*, ed. H. H. Ben-Sasson and S. Ettinger (1971), pp. 149–50. On the duty of a father to teach his son Hebrew and Torah from the moment he begins to speak, see Sifre-Dt. 11:19 (46), ed. Finkelstein, p. 104.

30. Maimonides gives exact instructions on the subject of schools and assumes them to be a necessary institution for Judaism, *Hilkhoth Talmud Torah*, Chap. 2, ed. M. Hyamson, *Mishneh Torah: The Book of Knowledge* (1962), pp. 589–99.

31. yMeg. 73d: 'R. Pinḥas said in the name of R. Hoshaiah: There were 480 synagogues in Jerusalem and each had a *beth-sepher* and a *beth-talmud*, the former for the *miḳra* (Scripture), the latter for the *mishnah* (the oral Torah).' Cf. Str.-B. II, p. 150. The phrases בית המדרש and ישיבה indicating schools appear already in Ecclus. 51:23, 29. Cf. M. Hengel, *Judaism and Hellenism* (1974) I, p. 79; II, p. 54, n. 165.

fairly widespread. For since in the case of written Scripture (as distinct from oral tradition) great importance was attached to the actual reading of the text (see below on the rules relating to public worship), the elementary teaching of the Torah was of necessity bound up with lessons in reading. A knowledge of reading must therefore have existed wherever there was a somewhat more thorough knowledge of the Torah. Thus already in pre-Christian times mention is made of privately owned copies of the Bible.[32] The rather more difficult art of writing was less general.[33]

Hand in hand with theoretical instruction went training in religious practice. For although children were not obliged to fulfil the Torah, they were nevertheless habituated to it from their earliest years. It was for example the duty of adults to make their children keep to the Sabbath rest.[34] They were gradually accustomed to a strict fast on the Day of Atonement by taking part in it one or two years before it became obligatory.[35] Certain matters were compulsory even for children. For instance, whilst they were not asked to read the *Shema*ʻ or to put on *tefillin*, they were required to recite the *Shemoneh ʻEsreh* and grace at table.[36] Young boys were expected to attend in the Temple on the great festivals.[37] In particular, they were bound to observe the Feast of

32. Cf. 1 Mac. 1:56 f. In mYeb. 16:7, the story is told of a Levite who died at an inn while on a journey, leaving behind a stick, a travelling bag and a book of the Torah. On the spread of private ownership of copies of Scripture see L. Blau, *Studien zum althebräischen Buchwesen* (1902), pp. 84–97. For the substantial amount of biblical MSS. found in the Judaean Desert (Qumran, Masada, etc.), see Vermes, *DSS*, pp. 15–16, 20, 200–1.

33. An ostracon, bearing a complete alphabet, found in the ruins of Qumran, is identified as 'the exercise of a pupil-scribe' by R. de Vaux, *Archaeology and the Dead Sea Scrolls* (1973), p. 103. A letter addressed to two of Simeon ben Kosiba's lieutenants, requesting the delivery of palm branches and ethrogs, was written in Greek, 'as we have no-one who knows Hebrew'. Cf. Y. Yadin, *Bar Kokhba* (1966), p. 130 and p. 28, n. 118 above. The most likely meaning is that no one able to write in Hebrew was present and the despatch of the message was urgent 'because of the feast'. For an alternative, but improbable, reading, see p. 79, n. 279.

34. mShab. 16:6.

35. mYom. 8:4.

36. mBer. 3:3: 'Women and slaves and minors are exempt from reciting the *Shema*ʻ and from wearing phylacteries, but they are not exempt from the *tefillah* (the *Shemoneh ʻEsreh*), from the *Mezuzah*, or from saying grace at table.'

37. mHag. 1:1: 'All are subject to the command *to appear* (*before the Lord*) excepting a deaf-mute, an imbecile, a child, one of doubtful sex, one of dual sex, women, slaves that have not been freed, a man that is lame or blind or sick or aged, and one that cannot go up (to Jerusalem) on his feet. Who is deemed a child (קטן)? Any that cannot ride on his father's shoulders and go up from Jerusalem to the Temple Mount. So the school of Shammai. And the school of Hillel says: Any that cannot hold his father's hand and go up (on his feet) from Jerusalem to the Temple Mount, as it is written, Three *regalim* (three times on foot).' From

Tabernacles.[38] But as soon as the first signs of manhood became apparent, the Israelite adolescent was obliged to fulfil the entire Torah.[39] He therewith entered into all the rights and duties of an adult, and was from then on a בר מצוה.[40] Later, the age for this change was fixed, and the young Jew attained legal majority on his thirteenth birthday.[41]

Lk. 2:42 reporting Jesus' first pilgrimage, it may be inferred that as a rule young men living outside the city took part in pilgrimages from their twelfth year. Cf. S. Safrai, 'Pilgrimage to Jerusalem at the End of the Second Temple Period', *Studies on the Jewish Background of the New Testament*, ed. O. Michel *et al.* (1969), pp. 12–21; JPFC II, pp. 898–904.

38. mSuk. 2:8: 'Women, slaves and minors are exempt from (the law of) *sukkah*; but a minor who no longer needs his mother must fulfil the law of *sukkah*. The daughter-in-law of Shammai the Elder once bore a child (during the Feast) and he broke away some of the roof-plaster and made a *sukkah*, roofing-over the bed for the sake of the child.' mSuk. 3:15: 'If a boy who is not of age knows how to shake it, he must carry the *lulab*'.

39. mNid. 6:11: 'If a boy has grown two hairs, he is subject to all the commands prescribed in the Torah.' The same applies to girls, except that women share neither all the rights nor all the legal duties of men. Cf. also mSanh. 8:1.

40. The expression *bar-mizwah* is found already in the Talmud (bBM 96a). See K. Kohler, 'Bar Mizwah', JE II, pp. 509–10.

41. Thus in an appendix to the tractate Aboth, mAb. 5:21: 'At five years old (one comes) to the study of Scripture; at ten years, to the Mishnah; at thirteen years (בן שלש עשרה) to the fulfilment of the commandments; at fifteen years to the Talmud; at eighteen years to the bride-chamber,' etc. Jesus at the age of twelve years, is said to have displayed remarkable learning (Lk. 2:41–52). On one special point, namely the validity of oaths, the attainment of the thirteenth year is demanded by the Mishnah, see mNid. 5:6: 'If a boy is twelve years and one day old, his vows must be examined; if he is thirteen years and one day old, his vows are valid.' There is some talmudic evidence to indicate that schooling continued until the age of twelve or thirteen years (bKid. 30a; bKet. 50a), without stating however that such a rule applied already at the beginning of the first century A.D. Cf. Safrai, 'Elementary Education' (cf. above n. 29), p. 152; 'Education', JPFC II, pp. 952–3. The 'Messianic Rule' from Qumran (1QSa) includes valuable evidence relative to school ages and subjects of intruction. 'From [his y]outh they shall instruct him in the Book of Meditation (ספר ההגו) and shall teach him, according to his age, the precepts of the Covenant (בחוקי הברית). He [shall be educated] in their statutes (במשפטיהמה) for ten years. . . . At the age of twenty years [he shall be] enrolled. . . .' (1QSa 1:6–9; *DSSE*, p. 119.) This text appears to imply that the teaching of the 'precepts of the Covenant' and the 'statutes' of the Community took place between the ages of ten and twenty years. It was preceded by an initial instruction in the 'Book of Meditation'. For an identification of the latter it is to be borne in mind that in addition to its employment as the first text-book, familiarity with this book is a basic qualification for the office of judge (CD 10:6) or priestly leader of a group of ten men (CD 13:2). This dual use of the same document (employed for rudimentary teaching and highest authority) seems to point to the Bible, and more particularly to the Torah. Cf. *DSSE*, p. 19; *DSS*, p. 113. See also Jos. 1:8. It is worth noting that according to mAb. 5:21, 'post-biblical' instruction begins at the age of ten and ends at eighteen, at which age a young man is expected to marry. In 1QSa, marriage is postponed to the age of twenty years (*ibid.* 1:10), 'higher' education takes place during the previous ten

years and the teaching of the ספר ההגו from the loosely-defined moment of 'youth', נעורים. Although Jewish education founded on the Torah was intended to be exclusive, it had to compete with the influence of Hellenistic civilization. See in particular, M. Hengel, 'Greek Education and Culture and Palestinian Judaism' and 'Greek Literature and Philosophy in Palestine', in *Judaism and Hellenism* I, pp. 65–78, 83–99. Cf. also S. Lieberman, *Hellenism in Jewish Palestine* (1950). For the knowledge of the Greek language, see pp. 74–80 above.

II. Synagogue

Bibliography

(a) *General works:*

Löw, L., 'Der synagogale Ritus', *Gesammelte Schriften* IV (1898), pp. 1–71.

Bacher, W., 'Synagogue', HDB IV (1902), pp. 636–43. 'Synagogue', JE XI (1905), pp. 619–28.

Juster, J., *Les Juifs dans l'empire romain* I (1914), pp. 456–72.

Krauss, S., *Synagogale Altertümer* (1922) (still the fundamental work on the subject). 'Synagoge', RE IVA (1932), cols. 1284–1316.

Sonne, I., 'Synagogue', IDB (1962) IV, pp. 476–91.

Levy, I., *The Synagogue: Its History and Function* (1963).

Schrage, W., 'Synagoge', TDNT VII (1971), pp. 798–841.

Hruby, K., *Die Synagoge* (1971).

Hengel, M., 'Proseuche und Synagoge', *Tradition und Glaube, Festschr. K. G. Kuhn* (1971), pp. 157–84.

Gutmann, J. (ed.), *The Synagogue: Studies in Origins, Archaeology and Architecture*, with a Prolegomenon (1975).

Heinemann, J. and J. J. Petuchowski, *Literature of the Synagogue* (1975).

Safrai, S., 'The Synagogue', JPFC II (1976), pp. 908–44.

(b) *Origin of the Synagogue:*

Finkelstein, L., 'The Origin of the Synagogue', PAAJR 1 (1928/9), 7–59 [=*Pharisaism in the Making* (1972), pp. 1–11].

Zeitlin, S., 'The Origin of the Synagogue', *ibid.* 2 (1930/1), pp. 69–81.

Moore, G. F., *Judaism* III (1930), pp. 88–92.

Weingreen, J., 'The Origin of the Synagogue', Hermathena 98 (1964), pp. 68–84 [≠*From Bible to Mishna* (1976), pp. 115–31].

Gutmann, J., 'The Origin of the Synagogue. The Current State of Research', Archäologischer Anzeiger 87 (1972), pp. 36–40 [=*The Synagogue*, ed. J. Gutmann (1975), pp. 72–6].

(c) *Archaeology:*

Krauss, S., *Talmudische Archäologie* I–III (1910–12).

Kohl, H., Watzinger, C., *Antike Synagogen in Galiläa* (1916).

Krauss, S., 'Die galiläischen Synagogenruinen und die Halakha', MGWJ 65 (1921), pp. 211–20.

Sukenik, E. L., *Ancient Synagogues in Palestine and Greece* (1934).
'The Present State of Ancient Synagogue Studies', Bulletin of the L. M. Rabinowitz Fund for the Exploration of Ancient Synagogues 1 (1949), pp. 8–23.

Goodenough, E. R., *Jewish Symbols in the Greco-Roman Period* I–XIII (1953–69).

Kanael, B., *Die Kunst der antiken Synagogue* (1961).

Lifshitz, B., *Donateurs et fondateurs dans les synagogues juives* (1967). (Greek inscriptions concerning the foundation and rebuilding of synagogues.)

Baumgarten, J. M., 'Art in the Synagogue: Some Talmudic Views', Judaism 19 (1970), pp. 196–206.

Avi-Yonah, M., 'Synagogue Architecture in the Late Classical Period', *Jewish Art*, ed. C. Roth (1971), pp. 65–82.
'Synagogue-Architecture', Enc. Jud. 15 (1971), cols. 595–600; 'Ancient Synagogues', Ariel 32 (1973), pp. 29–43 [=*The Synagogue*, ed. J. Gutmann (1975), pp. 95–109].
Saller, S. J., *Second Revised Catalogue of the Ancient Synagogues of the Holy Land* (1972).
Meyer, E. M., 'Synagogue Architecture', IDBS (1976), pp. 842–4.
Hüttenmeister, F., Reeg, G., *Die antiken Synagogen in Israel*. I. *Die jüdischen Synagogen, Lehrhäuser und Gerichtshöfe*. II. *Die samaritanischen Synagogen* (1977) [a comprehensive collection of archaeological, epigraphical and literary material from the first to the seventh century].

For recent archaeological work, see the bulletins in RB and IEJ.

The third century A.D. synagogue of Dura Europos has occasioned a rich yield of literature:

Rostovtzeff, M. I., *Dura Europos and its Art* (1938).
du Mesnil du Buisson, R., *Les peintures de la synagogue de Dura Europos* (1939).
Sukenik, E. L., בית הכנסת של דורא אירופוס וצייוריו (1947).
Wischnitzer, R., *The Messianic Theme in the Paintings of the Dura Synagogue* (1948).
Noth, M., 'Dura Europos und seine Synagoge', ZDPV 75 (1959), pp. 164–81.
Kraeling, C. H., *The Synagogue* (*The Excavations at Dura-Europos . . . Final Report* VIII/1) (1956).
Bickerman, E. J., 'Symbolism in the Dura Synagogue', HThR 58 (1965), pp. 127–51.
Goodenough, E. R., *Jewish Symbols* IX–XI (1964).
Nock, A. D., 'The Synagogue Murals of Dura Europos', *H. A. Wolfson Jubilee Volume* (1965), pp. 631–9.
Goodenough, E. R., Avi-Yonah, M., 'Dura-Europos', Enc. Jud. 6, cols. 275–98.
Gutmann, J. (ed.), *The Dura-Europos Synagogue* (1973).
Perkins, A., *The Art of Dura-Europos* (1973).

Deep and expert knowledge of the Torah could be obtained only from the Torah scholars in the *beth ha-midrash* (see above, § 25). Inevitably, no more than a very few could attain to such a level. For the mass of the people it was already a great gain that an elementary familiarity with Scripture became and remained common. But this too could only be done by means of an institution through which the Torah would be woven into the experience of each individual throughout his whole life. Such an institution was created by post-exilic Judaism in the custom of Sabbath readings of Scripture in the synagogue. For it should above all be borne in mind that the main object of these Sabbath meetings was not religious worship in the narrower sense, but religious teaching, i.e. instruction in the Torah. Josephus correctly explains the issue in this sense. 'He (our law-giver) made the Law to be an excellent and necessary subject of instruction in that it is not to be heard but once or twice or frequently, but he ordained that every week the people should set aside their other occupations and gather together to listen to the Law and learn it accurately.'[1] Philo is therefore not far wrong when he calls the synagogues schools (διδασκαλεῖα) where 'the ancestral philosophy' (τὴν πάτριον φιλοσοφίαν) was cultivated and every kind of virtue taught.[2] In the New Testament, too, διδάσκειν constantly figures as the main activity in the synagogues.[3] Further evidence is furnished by the Theodotus inscription, dating to the beginning of the first century A.D. and discovered on the Ophel in Jerusalem in 1913/14 which describes the synagogue founded by Theodotus as a place built for 'the reading of the Law and the teaching of the precepts'.[4] The origin of these Sabbath meetings in buildings specially constructed for the purpose is not known. The earliest documentary evidence relates to Egyptian Judaism: the oldest Graeco-Jewish documents mentioning synagogues (προσευχαί) date to the time of Ptolemy III (Euergetes), 247–21 B.C., and from the beginning of the first century B.C. the term προσευχή is also attested in an inscription from the surviving remains of the synagogue on Delos.[5] In the Old

1. *C.Ap.* ii 17 (175) = Euseb. *Praep. ev.* viii 8, 11: *Κάλλιστον καὶ ἀναγκαιότατον ἀπέδειξε παίδευμα τὸν νόμον οὐκ εἰσάπαξ ἀκροασομένοις οὐδὲ δὶς ἢ πολλάκις ἀλλ' ἑκάστης ἑβδομάδος τῶν ἄλλων ἔργων ἀφεμένους ἐπὶ τὴν ἀκρόασιν ἐκέλευσε τοῦ νόμου συλλέγεσθαι καὶ τοῦτον ἀκριβῶς ἐκμανθάνειν. Ant.* xvi 2, 4 (43)—words of Nicolaus of Damascus: *τήν τε ἑβδόμην τῶν ἡμερῶν ἀνίεμεν τῇ μαθήσαι τῶν ἡμετέρων ἐθῶν καὶ νόμου.*

2. *Vit. Mos.* ii 39 (216): *'Αφ' οὗ καὶ εἰσέτι νῦν φιλοσοφοῦσι ταῖς ἑβδόμαις 'Ιουδαῖοι τὴν πάτριον φιλοσοφίαν, τὸν χρόνον ἐκεῖνον ἀναθέντες ἐπιστήμῃ καὶ θεωρίᾳ τὸν περὶ φύσιν. Τὰ γὰρ κατὰ πόλεις προσευκτήρια τί ἕτερόν ἐστιν ἢ διδασκαλεῖα φρονήσεως καὶ ἀνδρίας καὶ σωφροσύνης καὶ δικαιοσύνης, εὐσεβείας τε καὶ ὁσιότητος καὶ συμπάσης ἀρετῆς, ᾗ κατανοεῖται καὶ κατορθοῦται τά τε ἀνθρώπεια καὶ θεῖα.* Cf. *Legat.* 23 (156): *'Ηπίστατο οὖν καὶ προσευχὰς ἔχοντας καὶ συνιόντας εἰς αὐτάς, καὶ μάλιστα ταῖς ἱεραῖς ἑβδόμαις, ὅτε δημοσίᾳ τὴν πάτριον παιδεύονται φιλοσοφίαν.*

3. Mt. 4:23; Mk. 1:21; 6:2; Lk. 4:15, 31; 6:6; 13:10; Jn. 6:59; 18:20.

4. 'Theodotus son of Vettenus, priest *(ἱερεύς)* and archisynagogue, son of an archisynagogue, grandson of an archisynagogue, constructed the synagogue for the reading of the law and the teaching of the precepts *(ᾠκοδόμησε τὴν συναγωγὴν εἰς ἀν[άγν]ωσ[ιν] νόμου καὶ εἰς [δ]ιδαχ[ὴ]ν ἐντολῶν).* Cf. Frey, CIJ II, no. 1404 (pp. 332–35); B. Lifshitz, *Donateurs et fondateurs dans les synagogues juives* (1967), no. 79, pp. 70–71.

5. The following pre-Christian inscriptions or papyri from Egypt and Delos mention Jewish *προσευχαί*. See also CPJ I, p. 8, and P. M. Fraser, *Ptolemaic Alexandria* (1972), ch. 2, n. 316 and 5, n. 766.

(a) Inscription from Schedia south of Alexandria from the time of Ptolemy III (Euergetes, 247–221 B.C.): *ὑπὲρ βασιλέως Πτολεμαίου καὶ βασιλίσσης Βερενίκης ἀδελφῆς καὶ γυναικὸς καὶ τῶν τέκνων τὴν προσευχὴν οἱ 'Ιουδαῖοι*, OGIS 726; S. Krauss, RE IVA, col. 1306; SB 8922; Frey, CIJ II, no. 1440, pp. 366–7; CPJ III, p. 141, no. 1440 (Appendix I: the Jewish Inscriptions of Egypt).

(b) Inscription of the dedication of the synagogue at Arsinoe-Crocodilopolis in the reign of Ptolemy III Euergetes: *ὑπὲρ βασιλέως Πτολεμαίου τοῦ Πτολεμάιου καὶ βασιλίσσης Βερενίκης τῆς γυναικὸς καὶ ἀδελφῆς καὶ τῶν τέκνων οἱ ἐν Κροκ[ο]δίλων πόλει 'Ιου[δαῖ]οι τὴν προ[σ]ε[υχήν]* A. Vogliano, Riv. filol. 67 (1939), pp. 247–51; SB 8939; CPJ III, p. 164, no. 1532A.

Testament they are first encountered in Ps. 74:8 under the name of מועדי אל. Their origin may go back to the age of Ezra, or even to that of the exile.[6] By Jesus' time, in any case, 'teaching in the synagogue on

---

(c) Inscription from Lower Egypt, now in the Berlin Museum, a repetition of an older inscription probably also from the time of Ptolemy III = Euergetes I (but possibly from that of Ptolemy VIII Euergetes II, who ruled at various periods between 170 and 116 B.C.). For the earlier date see L. Mitteis, U. Wilcken, *Grundzüge und Chrestomathie der Papyruskunde* I.2 (1912), p. 78, no. 54: *Βασιλεὺς Πτολεμαῖος Εὐεργέτης τὴν προσευχὴν ἄσυλον*. CIL III 6583; OGIS 129; SB 8880; Frey, CIJ II, no. 1449 (pp. 374–76); CPJ III, p. 144, no. 1449.

(d) Papyrus from Fayûm in Middle Egypt, and dating to 11 May 218, a petition from a woman to the king on account of the theft of a cloak which the thief would not return, in which appear the words *ἐν τῇ προσευχῇ τῶν Ἰου[δαίων]* (the thief seems to have deposited the cloak with the 'servant of the proseuche'). Text, translation and bibliography in CPJ I, no. 129.

(e) Two inscriptions at Athribis, probably from the time of Ptolemy VI Philometor: (1) *ὑπὲρ βασιλέως Πτολεμαίου καὶ βασιλίσσης Κλεοπάτρας Πτολεμαῖος Ἐπικύδου ὁ ἐπιστάτης τῶν φυλακιτῶν καὶ οἱ ἐν Ἀθρίβει Ἰουδαῖοι τὴν προσευχὴν Θεῷ ὑψίστῳ*. (2) *ὑπὲρ βασιλέως Πτολεμαίου καὶ βασιλίσσης Κλεοπάτρας καὶ τῶν τέκνων Ἑρμίας καὶ Φιλοτέρα ἡ γυνὴ καὶ τὰ παιδία τήνδε ἐξέδραν τῇ προσευχῇ*. OGIS 96, 101; Krauss, RE IVA, cols 1306–7; SB 8872; 8875; Frey, CIJ II, nos. 1443–4 (pp. 370–1); CPJ III, pp. 142–3, nos. 1443–4.

(f) Inscription from Nitriai, in the south-west of the Delta, dating to between 143 and 117 B.C.: *ὑπὲρ βασιλέως Πτολεμαίου καὶ βασιλίσσης Κλεοπάτρας τῆς ἀδελφῆς καὶ βασιλίσσης Κλεοπάτρας τῆς γυναικὸς Εὐεργετῶν οἱ ἐν Νιτρίαις Ἰουδαῖοι τὴν προσευχὴν καὶ τὰ συγκύροντα*. SEG VIII 366; CIJ II, no. 1422; SB 7454; CPJ III, p. 142, no. 1442.

(g) Inscription from Xenephyris near Damanhur, also dating to between 143 and 117 B.C. (similar dedication): *οἱ ἀπὸ Ξενεφύρεος Ἰουδαῖοι τὸν πυλῶνα τῆς προσευχῆς*. SB 5862; CIJ II, no. 1441; CPJ III, p. 141, no. 1441.

(h) Inscription from Alexandria, second century B.C.: *[θ]εῷ ὑψίστῳ [ἐπήκοῳ τ]ὸν ἱερὸν [περίβολον καὶ] τὴν προσ[ευχὴν καὶ τὰ συγ]κύροντα*. SB 589; CIJ II, no. 1433; CPJ III, p. 139, no. 1433.

(i) Papyrus from Arsinoe in the Fayûm, late second century B.C., P. Tebtunis 86. In this list of properties, a *προσευχὴ Ἰουδαίων* is twice mentioned (ll. 18 and 29) which owned a piece of land known as 'holy garden-land' *(ἱερὰ παράδεισος)*. See CPJ I, no. 134.

(j) Inscription at Alexandria (Gabbary), date uncertain, but probably 36 B.C.: *ὑπὲρ βασ[ιλίσση]ς καὶ β[ασιλ]έως θεῷ [με]γάλῳ ἐ[πηκό]ῳ Ἄλυπ[ος τὴν] προσε[υχὴν] ἐπόιει [. . .] (ἔτους) ιε' Με[χειρ . . .]*, Bulletin de la Societé archéol. d'Alexandrie 4 (1902), p. 86; SAB 1902, p. 1094 = Archiv für Papyrusforschung 2 (1902), p. 559; OGIS 742; SB 8934; CIJ II, no. 1432 (p. 360); CPJ III, p. 139, no. 1432.

(k) Fragmentary papyrus of unknown provenance from the second half of the first century B.C. mentioning a resolution passed 'at the session held in the proseuche', *ἐπὶ τῆς γ[ε]νηθείσης συναγωγῆς ἐν τῇ προσευχῇ*. CPJ I, no. 138.

(l) Inscription from Delos. CIJ I, no. 726: *Ἀγαθοκλῆς καὶ Λυσίμαχος ἐπὶ προσευχῇ*. For the synagogue see A. Plassart, 'La Synagogue juive de Délos', *Mélanges Holleaux* (1913), pp. 201–15; RB 11 (1914), pp. 523–34; E. R. Goodenough, *Jewish Symbols* II, pp. 71–5; Ph. Bruneau, *Recherches sur les cultes de Délos* (1970), pp. 480–93 (the most authoritative modern discussion). See further vol. III, § 31.1.

6. J. Bright, *A History of Israel* ([2]1972), p. 439. On the origin of the synagogue, cf. Bibliography, Section (b).

the Sabbath' was already an established institution (Mk. 1:21; 6:2; Lk. 4:16, 31; 6:6; 13:10; Act. 13:14, 27, 42, 44; 15:21; 16:13; 17:2; 18:4).

According to Act. 15:21, Moses had from early generations 'in every city those who preach him, for he is read every Sabbath in the synagogues'. Josephus and Philo, and later Judaism in general, trace the whole system back to Moses himself.[7] This of course is of interest only in so far as it shows that post-biblical Judaism regarded it as an essential part of its religious institutions. There can be no question of any real pre-exilic origin.

1. Community Organization

The pre-requisite of the whole system is above all the existence of a religious community. And here the question arises as to whether in the cities and localities of Palestine in the time of Jesus the civic and religious communities were so separate that the latter possessed an independent organization. In considering this point it should firstly be noted that political circumstances were themselves not uniform throughout Palestine. As has already been demonstrated (p. 183), three different circumstances were possible, and in fact existed, in this respect. Jews could be excluded from civic rights; Jews and non-Jews could enjoy equal rights; or civic rights could be extended to Jews alone. The first two cases were possible in cities with a predominantly Greek or very mixed population. In both, the Jews were instructed to organize themselves into an independent religious community for the fulfilment of their religious needs. For whether they collaborated in the conduct of civic affairs or not, they still needed an independent organization for their religious affairs. In both these instances, then, the question asked may be answered in the affirmative. Accordingly, the position of the synagogal communities in these cities was the same as that of the cities of the Diaspora. Very different, however, was the situation in cities and localities with a population wholly or predominantly Jewish. Here the local authorities were certainly all Jews, and the few non-Jews present were excluded from the council of elders or the city council. This was certainly true of Jerusalem, for example. Since the local authorities had in any case a great deal to do with religious affairs (Jewish law recognizes no separation between the

7. Cf. in addition to Josephus, *C.Ap.* ii 17 (195) and Philo, *Vit. Mos.* ii 39 (216), Philo in *Praep. Ev.* viii 7, 12–13, and *Spec. Leg.* ii 15 (62), Tg. Ps-Jonathan on Exod. 18:20 attributes to Moses the composition of the prayer to be recited in the synagogues (בבית כנישתהון). In conformity with the tendency to assign all the pious institutions of the Mosaic period to the patriarchal age, the בית אולפנא and the בית מדרשא were already in existence in the days of Jacob. He ministered in the former and himself built a בית מדרשא. Cf. Ps.Jon. on Gen. 25:27 and 33:17. Cf. Neof. Gen. 25:27 (Jacob dwelt in the בתי מדרשא).

religious and the rest), it would seem a priori highly probable that the synagogues came under their jurisdiction as well. Or would a special council of elders have been appointed for that particular purpose? This would have been very unnatural in small places. But even in larger cities with several synagogues there was no occasion for it. It was enough that the authorities appointed to each synagogue the officials (an almoner, an *archisynagogus* and a minister) necessary for the maintenance of its own affairs. There was at least no urgent reason for forming a council of elders for each separate synagogue. But the meagreness of our material obliges us to concede that this may possibly have happened. Indeed, in one instance it is even probable: the Hellenized Jews in Jerusalem—the Libertines, Cyrenians, Alexandrians, Cilicians and Asiatics—quite clearly formed special 'congregations' (Act. 6:9).[8] But these were, in effect, special circumstances: the difference of nationality necessitated a special organization. For the simpler circumstances of the smaller localities in Palestine, a separation of political and religious communities would have been quite artificial. It would have been altogether contrary to the nature of post-exilic Judaism, which recognizes the political community only in the form of the religious. But there is no lack of positive evidence to the effect that the civic community as such also conducted the affairs of the synagogue. In the Mishnah for example, it is taken entirely for granted that the synagogue, the sacred ark and the sacred books are as much the property of the city, that is of the civic community, as the streets and public baths.[9] The inhabitants of the city (בני העיר) had as much right of disposal over the former as over the latter.[10] When R. Eleazar ben Azariah says that the musaph prayer is to be recited only in a city community (חבר העיר), the inference is that the city community, the civic commune as such, concerned itself with synagogue worship.[11]

8. The *Λιβερτῖνοι* are probably Roman 'freedmen' or their descendants, hence descendants of the Jews whom Pompey sent as prisoners to Rome and who were soon freed by their masters, Philo, *Legat.* 23 (155). Many may later have returned to Jerusalem and formed a separate community there. Similarly, the numerous Hellenistic Jews living in Jerusalem, from Cyrene, Alexandria, Cilicia and Asia, also formed special communities. For the conjectural reading, Lybians (*Λιβύων*, *Λιβυστίνων*, cf. the Armenian version), see E. Haenchen, *The Acts of the Apostles*, *in loc.*

9. mNed. 5:5: 'Which things belong to the (people of that) town? The public place, the bath-house, the synagogue, the ark (of the law) and the books (of Scripture).'

10. mMeg. 3:1: 'If the people of a town sell their open space, they must buy a synagogue with the price; if a synagogue, then an ark; if an ark, then (scroll) wrappings; if wrappings, then books; if books, then the Torah.'

11. mBer. 4:7: 'R. Eleazar b. Azariah says, The *musaph* (i.e. additional prayer for Sabbaths and feast-days) may be recited only in a city congregation. The sages say, In a city congregation and outside a city congregation. R. Judah says in his

It seems likely, therefore, that synagogue congregations existed independently side by side with the political community only in cities with a mixed population. In purely Jewish districts, the elders of the locality will also have been elders of the synagogue.

In so far as the community is regarded as religious, it is known as a כנסת (congregation, *συναγωγή*, Aram. כנישתא), and its members as בני הכנסת.[12] The expression *συναγωγή* also occurs in the context of Greek

---

own name, Wherever there is a city congregation the individual is exempt from reciting the *musaph*'. The unusual expression is variously explained. But since a community is meant, and since a religious community is otherwise known not as חבר but as כנסת, חבר must be taken to allude to a civic community, which agrees admirably with bMeg. 27b. On חבר עיר, cf. also Semaḥoth 11–12; A. Büchler, *Der galiläische Am-ha-Areṣ des 2. Jahrhunderts* (1906), pp. 210–12; S. Krauss, *Synagogale Altertümer* (1922), pp. 19–23; R. Meyer, *Tradition und Neuschöpfung im antiken Judentum* (1965), p. 26; S. Safrai, 'Jewish Self-government', JPFC I (1974), pp. 415–16.

12. mBekh. 5:5; mZab. 3:2. The community of Israel as a whole is also known as כנסת ישראל, W. Bacher, *Die exegetische Terminologie der jüdischen Traditionsliteratur* (1905) I, p. 85; II, pp. 87 f. On the formation of the word, see Bacher, HDB IV, p. 636. The Greek *συναγωγή* is used, e.g. in Act. 6:9; 9:2, with the meaning 'congregation'. Inscription from Phocea (CIJ II, no. 738): *ἡ συναγωγὴ ἐ[τείμη]σεν τῶν Ἰουδαίων*; inscription from Acmonia in Phrygia, no. 766 (better text in MAMA VI, 624): *ἡ συναγωγὴ ἐτίμησεν* etc.: inscription from Panticapaeum on the Cimmerian Bosphorus, A.D. 81, Latyschev, IOSPE II (1890), no. 52; IGR I 881; CIJ I, no. 683; CIRB no. 70: *συνε[πιτ]ροπευούσης δὲ καὶ τῆ[ς] συναγωγῆ[ς] τῶν Ἰουδαίων* (so also Latyschev no. 53; CIJ no. 684; CIRB, no. 73). Note also CIRB, no. 72; and 71: *ἐπιτροπευούσης τῆς συναγωγῆς τῶν Ιουδαίων καὶ Θεὸν σεβῶν*, cf. H. Bellen, JAC 8/9 (1965/6), pp. 171–6. Frequently in Roman-Jewish epitaphs, cf. vol. III, § 31, ii. The use of *συναγωγή* to mean 'congregation' or 'assembly' is particularly clear in the three Jewish decrees from Berenice (Benghazi), CIG 5631–2, republished by J. and G. Roux, REG 62 (1949), pp. 281–96; G. Caputo, Parola del Passato 12 (1957), pp. 132–4 = SEG XVII, no. 823. That in later Judaism it was the usual word for 'congregation' is evident, in particular, from the language of the Church Fathers, who use *συναγωγή* of both Jews and Christians in the sense of a group of persons assembled for worship, while applying *ἐκκλησία* only to the Christian church, see G. W. H. Lampe, *A Patristic Greek Lexicon, s.vv.* The Ebionites employed *συναγωγή* for their own Christian congregation as well (Epiphanius, *Haer.* 30, 18: *συναγωγὴν δὲ οὗτοι καλοῦσι τὴν ἑαυτῶν ἐκκλησίαν καὶ οὐχὶ ἐκκλησίαν*. In Christian Palestinian Aramaic, כנישתא, which corresponds to the Greek *συναγωγή*, seems to have been the usual word for 'church', see F. Schulthess, *Lexicon Syro-Palaestinum* (1903), p. 95 s.v. However, in the Christian sphere *ἐκκλησία* has retained its supremacy since the time of Paul. At first glance, this contrast between Jewish and Christian usage is surprising, since in the Old Testament no essential distinction is made between *συναγωγή* and *ἐκκλησία*. The LXX has *συναγωγή* for עדה, and usually *ἐκκλησία* for קהל; equally, the Targums have כנישתא for עדה, and קהלא generally for קהל. The former is chiefly used in the books of Exodus, Leviticus, Numbers and Joshua, and the latter in Deuteronomy, 1 and 2 Chronicles, Ezra and Nehemiah, both very frequently, and both without any real difference, to denote 'the congregation of Israel'. But later Judaism seems to have made a distinction in the use of the two concepts so that *συναγωγή*

cultic societies. There, it is equivalent to *σύνοδος* and (in accordance with the original meaning) mainly refers, not to the society, but to its periodically recurrent festive 'congregation' or meeting.[13] Nevertheless,

---

describes the congregation more from the point of view of its empirical reality, and *ἐκκλησία* more from that of its ideal significance: *συναγωγή* is a community established in some place or other; *ἐκκλησία* is the congregation of those called to salvation by God as the קהל, the ideal community of Israel (on קהל cf. mYeb. 8:2; mKid. 4:3; mHor. 1:4–5; mYad. 4:4). *συναγωγή* simply expresses an empirical fact; *ἐκκλησία* contains a religious value-judgement. This differentiation between the two notions, one that appears to have prevailed already in Judaism, explains how in Christian usage the latter expression is employed almost exclusively. In passing, it should finally be noted that the expression צבור is used frequently in the Mishnah. It in no way refers to the congregation as a community, but as a totality as distinguished from an individual; thus e.g. in the expression שליח צבור to be discussed later, in mBer. 5:5; mR.Sh. 4:9. In sacrificial language, public sacrifices offered in the name of the whole of Israel are called קרבנות צבור; mShek. 4:1, 6; mSuk. 5:7; mZeb. 14:10; mMen. 2:2; 8:1; 9:6, 7, 9; mTer. 2:1; mKer. 1:6; mPar. 2:1: cf. also חטאת צבור in mYom. 6:1; mZeb. 5:3, and elsewhere; זבחי שלמי צבור; mPes. 7:4; mZeb. 5:5 and elsewhere. A public fast is referred to as one ordained על הצבור; mTaan. 1:5–6; 2:9–10. צבור is therefore not the community but the totality. In Qumran terminology, עדה and קהל are largely synonymous and denote the whole congregation of Israel. The Community itself is known as יחד, and its governing body as the 'Council of the Community', עצת היחד. Cf. *DSS*, pp. 88–92; see also P. Wernberg-Møller, 'The Nature of the YAḤAD according to Manual of Discipline and related Documents', *Dead Sea Scroll Studies* 1969, ALUOS 6 (1969), pp. 56–81, cf. W. Schrage, TDNT VII (1971), pp. 809–10.

13. So especially in the Testament of Epicteta, *c.* 200 B.C., from Thera, IG XII 3, no. 330; cf. also Th. Ziebarth, *Das griechische Vereinswesen* (1896), pp. 7 f. Epicteta organized a hero-cult for her dead husband and for two dead sons, which must have been observed by the male members of the family. (1) The association, whose 25 members had to devote themselves to this aim, was not however called *συναγωγή* but *τὸ κοινὸν τοῦ ἀνδρείου τῶν συγγενῶν*. Only in respect of the yearly meetings of the association were the formulae used: *ὥστε γίνεσθαι τᾶν συναγωγὰν ἐπ' ἁμέρας τρεῖς ἐν τῷ μουσείῳ* (ll. 118–19), or *τὰν δὲ συναγωγὰν τοῦ ἀνδρείου τῶν συγγενῶν γίνεσθαι ἐμ μῆνι Δελφινίῳ* (131–3). (2) The word has the same meaning in an honorific degree of the *politeuma* of the Idumaeans near Memphis (second century B.C.): *ἐπὶ συναγωγῆς τῆς γενηθείσης ἐν τῷ ἄνω Ἀπολλωνιείῳ*, OGIS 737. (3) In the honorific decree of a *thiasos* (of uncertain provenance, probably from Bithynia, second century B.C.) for a priestess of Cybele and Apollo, said to have been crowned *ἐν τῇ τοῦ Διὸς συναγωγῇ*, A. Conze, *Reise auf der Insel Lesbos* (1865), pp. 61–4, plate xix = P. Foucart, *Des associations religieuses chez les Grecs*, p. 238, no. 65. For *συναγωγή* meaning 'meeting', see also Syll.[3] 734, l. 10; 735, l. 49 (Messenian law on mysteries at Andania) etc. (4) On the inscriptions on the tomb which King Antiochus of Commagene constructed for himself, OGIS 383; IGLS I, no. 1, he orders a yearly celebration of his birthday and accession to the throne and assigned the inhabitants of his kingdom, classified according to towns and cities, each to their nearest holy places, *εἰς συναγωγὰς καὶ πανηγύρεις καὶ θυσίας ταύτας* (ll. 93–5; cf. also l. 151). See H. Dörrie, *Der Königskult des Antiochos von Kommagene im Lichte neuer Inschriften-Funde* (1964), pp. 67, 77, 128, 166–7. Assemblies for the purpose of feasting—with or without a cultic character—could also be called *συναγωγαί*, Athenaeus 192B; 362E. Cf. OGIS 748 (a list of gifts

individual examples are attested in which συναγωγή describes the society itself.[14]

The powers of the elders of the congregation in religious matters must be envisaged as analogous to their authority in civic affairs. Thus as the city administration and jurisdiction lay entirely in their hands, so presumably did the direction of religious matters. There is in any case no trace in Jewish congregations of anything resembling the way in which the full assembly of the Christian church at Corinth (1 Cor. 5), or the Qumran community (1QS 8:25–9:2), itself discussed and decided on individual cases of discipline and administration. Instead this was done by the appropriate bodies, i.e. the elders of the congregation. It is highly likely that it was, in particular, within their competence to exercise the most weighty of all religious disciplinary acts: the pronouncement of excommunication or exclusion from the congregation. The strict infliction of this punishment was nothing less than vital to post-exilic Judaism. In continuous contact with a Gentile environment, the Jewish communities could only preserve themselves by constantly and carefully eliminating alien elements. As the more rigid organization of the post-exilic community initially decreed that whoever did not submit to the new order should be expelled from the congregation (Ezr. 10:8), similarly care had to be taken to eliminate opposing elements by way of community discipline. That this institution existed in the time of Jesus may be inferred from the New Testament (Lk. 6:22); Jn. 9:22; 12:42; 16:2). According to Josephus, excommunication was also practised by the Essenes,[15] and detailed rules relating to this form of punishment survive among the Qumran scrolls.[16] The one uncertainty is whether expulsion was of various kinds. Elias Levita (d. 1549) in his *Tishbi*[17] distinguishes three, namely *nidduy*, *ḥerem* and *shammatta*. Of these, the third may be omitted straight away since in

---

which a certain Philetairos distributed for public purposes, in the third century B.C.): *εἰς ἔλαιον καὶ συναγω[γὰς] τῶν νέων ἀργυρίου τάλαντα Ἀλεξάνδρεια εἴκοσιν ἕξ*. Considering the large sum, the word should be completed as *συναγωγάς*, not *συναγωγήν*, as Dittenberger suggested). Similarly *συναγώγιον*, see n. 62.

14. When the decree of the *κοινὸν τῶν Ἀτταλιστῶν* (second century B.C.), OGIS 326, l. 12, says that the kings behaved kindly to *τὴν ἡμετέραν αἵρεσιν καὶ συναγωγήν*, the *συναγωγή* there is at least in transition to the meaning 'association'. This is already evident in the description of a guild of barbers near Heraclea Pontica as *συναγωγὴ τῶν κουρέων*, with an *ἀρχισυνάγ[ωγ]ος* (probably early first century A.D.), Archäol.-epigr. Mittheilungen aus Österreich-Ungarn 19 (1896), p. 67. Like *συναγωγή*, the more frequent *σύνοδος* is also (1) a meeting; (2) an association.

15. *B.J.* ii 8, 8 (143–4).

16. Cf. *DSSE*, pp. 27-8; *DSS*, pp. 92–3. For details, see below.

17. This is a dictionary completed in 1541 intended to supplement Nathan ben Yeḥiel's *'Arukh*. Cf. G. E. Weil, *Elie Lévita* (1963), pp. 135–41.

the Talmud נדוי and שמתא are used synonymously.[18] The only traditional distinction is between נדוי, temporary exclusion, and חרם, permanent excommunication. How old this distinction is, is nevertheless difficult to say. Only the *ἀφορίζειν* (Lk. 6:22) or *ἀποσυνάγωγον ποιεῖν* or *γίνεσθαι* (Jn. 9:22; 12:42; 16:2), is directly attested in the New Testament, i.e. only the custom of expulsion as such. Of the two phrases used in 1 Cor. 5, *παραδοῦναι τῷ Σατανᾷ* (5:5) and *αἴρειν ἐκ μέσου* (5:2), it is unsure whether the latter represents a stricter form of punishment. The Mishnah also mentions only expulsion (נדוי), thereby implying the possibility of readmission.[19] On the other hand, the Old Testament already recognizes the concept of חרם, an irrevocable ban or curse, and that this was current in later Judaism, at least as a dogmatic idea (in the sense of a curse), is evident from the repeated New Testament use of the terms *ἀνάθεμα* and *ἀναθεματίζειν* (Rom. 9:3; 1 Cor. 12:3; 16:22; Gal. 1:8, 9; Mk. 14:71, Act. 23:12, 14, 21). Actual anathematization in the synagogues from the second century A.D. must underlie the claim made by Justin and Epiphanius that the Jews cursed the Christians in their daily prayers.[20] In short, the New Testament evidence, together with that of the Dead Sea Scrolls, suggests that already in the time of Jesus exclusion from the synagogue could take place, with or without the *ἀνάθεμα*.[21]

Additional important information also emerges from the Qumran writings. According to the penal code of 1QS 6–7, minor infringements of the Community Rule were punished by various penances (נענש), though except for one instance, when it is specified that a man is to be deprived of one quarter of his food (6:25), it is unclear what offenders were required to do. The duration of these sentences ranged in any case from three months for 'speaking foolishly' (7:9), to sixty days for being unable to repair inadvertent damage (7:8), or one month for falling asleep during a meeting (7:10), or a minimum of ten days for interrupting a speaker (7:9–10) or gesticulating with the left hand (7:15). Expulsion could be temporary or permanent. Temporary

18. Cf. J. Levy, *Chaldäisches Wörterbuch* s.v. חרם.

19. mTaan. 3:8; mM.K. 3:1–2; mEdu. 5:6; mMid. 2:2.

20. Justin, *Dial. c. Tryph.* 16. Epiphanius, *Pan.* 29, 9. Further particulars in the appendix on the *Shemoneh 'Esreh*, ברכת המינים.

21. Cf. on excommunication in general, K. Kohler, 'Anathema', JE I, pp. 559–62; J. Juster, *Les Juifs dans l'empire romain* II (1914), pp. 159–61; H. Mantel, *Studies in the History of the Sanhedrin* (1961), pp. 225–7; 'Herem', Enc. Jud. 8, cols. 344–55; W. Schrage, TDNT VII, pp. 848–52; M. Delcor, 'Les tribunaux de l'église de Corinthe et les tribunaux de Qumrân', *Studiorum Paulinorum Congressus Catholicus 1961* (1963), pp. 535–48 [= *Paul and Qumran*, ed. J. Murphy-O'Connor (1968), pp. 69–84]; G. Forkman, *The Limits of the Religious Community. Expulsion from the Religious Community within the Qumran Sect, within Rabbinic Judaism, and within Primitive Christianity* (1972).

expulsion in the form of exclusion from table fellowship could last for one or two years. One year of exclusion was imposed for lying in matters of property (6:24–5), for disobeying superiors (6:25–27), for speaking in anger against a priest (7:2–3), for deliberately insulting a companion (7:4–5) and for slandering a fellow sectary (7:15–16); and two years' exclusion—the first from 'purity' (טהרה), the second from the 'Drink' (משקה)—was imposed on a former member before he could be re-instated (7:18–20). For the graver offences of uttering the Name of God (6:27–7:2), slandering the Congregation (7:16–17), murmuring against the authority of the Congregation (7:17), leaving the community after having been a member for ten years (7:22–24) and sharing food or property with an excommunicated person (7:24–25), the sentence was permanent excommunication. In a separate list dealing with members of the Council of the Community or Council or Holiness, permanent excommunication is also the penalty for any deliberate breach of the law of Moses (1QS 8:21–3); inadvertent transgressors are sentenced here to two years of exclusion from communal activity (8:24–9:2). There is no doubt, therefore, that the two kinds of excommunication are part of the legal system represented by the Dead Sea Scrolls.

The imposition of these disciplinary measures in main-stream Judaism was very likely the responsibility of the elders of the congregation. For in the post-exilic period the mass of the people as such—so far as is known—nowhere exercised jurisdiction; it should in consequence not be supposed that they did so in respect of excommunication. In fact it is clear from, for example, Jn. 9:22 that it was imposed by the 'Jews', i.e. (in the language of the Gospels), by the Judaean authorities of the nation. This is indirectly confirmed by the fact that at the time of the Mishnah, when the Jewish political organization was dissolved and the rabbis began to take over more and more of the powers of the local authorities, it was the 'sages' (חכמים) who imposed and lifted the ban of excommunication.[22] In Talmudic and post-Talmudic times also, it lay in the hands of competent congregation authorities.[23]

2. Officers

Besides the elders in charge of the affairs of the congregation in general, special officers were appointed for particular purposes. Strangely

22. See especially mM.K. 3:1–2.

23. Justinian's *Novella* 146, ed. R. Schoell and G. Kroll, *Corpus Iuris Civilis* III ([3]1904), pp. 714–18, where the Greek text of the Bible is permitted to be read in Jewish synagogues, and the Jewish authorities are instructed not to obstruct this by imposing a ban, reads in the latter respect: *Οὐδὲ ἄδειαν ἕξουσιν οἱ παρ' αὐτοῖς ἀρχιφερεκῖται ἢ πρεσβύτεροι τυχὸν ἢ διδάσκαλοι προσαγορευόμενοι περινοίας τισὶν ἢ ἀναθεματισμοῖς τοῦτο κωλύειν*. For an English translation see P. Kahle, *The Cairo Geniza* ([2]1959), pp. 315–17.

enough, no one was nominated to conduct worship proper: the reading of the Scriptures, preaching and public prayer. In the first century A.D., these were still performed by the members of the congregations themselves, which accounts for Jesus (and Paul) being able to speak in various synagogues (see below on the order of divine service). But although there were no special readers, preachers or ministers, an officer was needed to supervise the arrangements of divine worship and the business of the synagogue as a whole. This was the *archisynagogus* or president.[24] Such ἀρχισυνάγωγοι are found throughout the Jewish world, not only in Palestine, as attested in the New Testament[25] and in inscriptions,[26] but also in Asia Minor,[27] Greece,[28] Italy,[29] Africa,[30] and the Roman empire in general.[31] From the Jews, the office and title passed to the Judaeo-Christian communities of Palestine.[32] The Hebrew title ראש הכנסת[33] is without doubt synonymous with it. That this office

24. E. Schürer, *Die Gemeindeverfassung der Juden in Rom in der Kaiserzeit* (1897), pp. 25–8; J. Juster, *Les Juifs* I, pp. 450–53; S. Krauss, *Synagogale Altertümer* (1922), pp. 114–21; Frey, CIJ I, pp. xcvii–ix; B. Lifshitz, 'Fonctions et titres honorifiques dans le communautés juives', RB 67 (1960), pp. 58–64; *idem*, *Donateurs et fondateurs dans les synagogues juives* (1967), Index s.v.; W. Schrage, TDNT VII, pp. 844–7; U. Rappaport, 'Archisynagogos', Enc. Jud. 3, cols. 335–6.

25. Mk. 5:22, 35, 36, 38; Lk. 8:49; 13:14.

26. CIJ II, no. 991; 1404 (Theodotus inscr.).

27. Act. 13:15 (Pisidian Antioch). Epiphanius, *Haer.* 30, 11 (Cilicia). Inscriptions from Smyrna: CIJ II, no. 741; Acmonia in Phrygia: 766 (cf. MAMA VI, no. 264): ὁ διὰ βίου ἀρχισυνάγωγος and another [ἀρχισυνά]γωγος; Myndus in Caria, 756; Synnada in Lycia: 759.

28. Act. 18:8, 17 (Corinth). IG IV 190=CIJ I, no. 722 (Aegina).

29. CIJ I, nos. 265, 336, 383, 504 (Rome). See H. J. Leon, *The Jews of Ancient Rome* (1960), pp. 171–3. CIL X, 3905=CIJ I, no. 533; CIJ I, nos. 584, 587, 596; CIL IX, 6201=CIJ I, no. 587; 6205=CIJ I, no. 584 (Venusia); IG XIV, 2304=CIJ I, no. 638 (Brescia). Note the *archisynagogus* now attested from Ostia, R. Meiggs, *Roman Ostia* ([2]1973), p. 588.

30. Synagogue of Naro at Hammam-Lif, not far from Carthage (discovered in 1883). The inscription in an ante-room: 'Asterius filius Rustici arcosinagogi, M(a)rgarita Riddei (?) partem portici tesselavit'. On the floor of the synagogue itself was found a mosaic with figures of birds, animals and fish. The menorah appears twice in the mosaic and a third time at the end of an inscription, CIL VIII, 12457; Krauss, *Synagogale Altertümer*, p. 226. See Goodenough, *Jewish Symbols* II, pp. 89–92.

31. *Cod. Theod.* xvi 8, 4, 13, 14. Cf. also Justin, *Dial. c. Tryph.* 137.

32. Epiphanius, *Pan.* 30, 18: πρεσβυτέρους γὰρ οὗτοι ἔχουσι καὶ ἀρχισυναγώγους.

33. mSot. 7:7–8. 'The blessings of the High Priest on the Day of Atonement shall proceed thus: The minister of the synagogue (*ḥazzan ha-keneseth*) takes a Torah scroll and gives it to the president of the synagogue (*rosh ha-keneseth*), and the president of the synagogue gives it to chief of the priests, and chief of the priests gives it to the High Priest. The High Priest receives it standing and reads it standing. . . . (8) The reading by the king on the first day of Tabernacles in the sabbatical year shall proceed thus: A wooden platform (βῆμα) is erected for the king in the forecourt and he takes his seat upon it. . . . The minister of the synagogue takes a Torah scroll and gives it to the president of the synagogue,

differed from that of an elder of the congregation is clear from the appearance side by side of the titles *πρεσβύτεροι* and *ἀρχισυνάγωγοι*.[34] But even more telling is the evidence of inscriptions, which show that one and the same person could hold the office of *ἄρχων* and of *ἀρχισυνάγωγος*.[35] In the Diaspora, the *ἄρχοντες* were the 'chiefs' of the congregations and responsible for their direction in general (note especially the inscriptions from Cyrenaica in n. 12 above). The office of *archisynagogus* was therefore different from theirs. But he cannot have been the chief of the *ἄρχοντες* either, for that person is known as *γερουσιάρχης* (see vol. III, § 31, on the Diaspora). He had accordingly nothing whatever to do with the direction of the congregation in general. Instead, his special responsibility was to attend to public worship. He is called *archisynagogus* not as chief of the congregation, but as leader of its meetings for worship. As a rule, he was probably chosen from among the elders. It is said in particular of his functions that he had, for example, to decide who should read the Bible and the prayer,[36] and to summon suitable persons to preach.[37] He had, generally speaking, to ensure that nothing improper took place in the synagogue (Lk. 13:14), and probably also had charge of the synagogue building.[38] Ordinarily, there would have been only one president to each synagogue (cf. Lk. 13:14). But sometimes several are referred to; thus Act. 13:15 (*ἀπέστειλαν οἱ ἀρχισυνάγωγοι πρὸς αὐτούς*), while the less definite *εἷς τῶν ἀρχισυναγώγων* in Mk. 5:22 may be explained as 'one from the class of presidents'. In later times, the style *ἀρχισυνάγωγος* seems also to have been applied just as a title even to children and women.[39] It is worth

---

and the president of the synagogue gives it to the chief of the priests, and the chief of the priests gives it to the High Priest, and the High Priest gives it to the king, and the king receives it standing and reads it sitting. . . .' For the first half of this passage see also mYom. 7:1.

34. Epiphanius, *Haer.* 30, 11; 18; *Cod. Theod.* xvi 8, 13; cf. *Acta Pilati* (ed. Tischendorf), p. 221. On *πρεσβύτεροι* see L. Robert, Rev. Phil. 32 (1958), pp. 41–2,

35. Leon, *Jews of Ancient Rome*, no. 265: 'Stafylo archonti et archisynagogo'. CIL X 3905=CIJ no. 833. 'Alfius Juda arcon, arcosynagogus'. Cf. also CIJ. no. 504=Leon, no. 504: *Ἰουλιανὸς ἱερεὺς ἄρχων . . . υἱὸς Ἰουλιανοῦ ἀρχισυναγώγου*. Act. 14:2 (D) reads: *οἱ δὲ ἀρχισυνάγωγοι τῶν Ἰουδαίων καὶ οἱ ἄρχοντες τῆς συναγωγῆς ἐπήγαγον αὐτοῖς διωγμὸν κατὰ τῶν δικαίων*. The author of this text thus recognized that *ἀρχισυνάγωγοι* and *ἄρχοντες* are different. For *ἄρχων* in inscriptions, L. Robert, Rev. Phil. 32 (1958), p. 40.

36. See Rashi and Bartenora on mYom. 7:1 and mSot. 7:7.

37. Act. 13:15. In Pisidian Antioch, Paul and Barnabas were invited by the archisynagogus to speak if they had a *λόγος παρακαλήσεως*.

38. CIJ II, no. 722: the *archisynagogus* Theodorus in Aegina directs the building of a synagogue (*ἐκ θεμελίων τὴν συναγ[ωγὴν] οἰκοδόμησα*). Cf. B. Lifshitz, *Donateurs et fondateurs*, pp.13–14.

39. CIL IX, 6201=CIJ I, no. 587: *τάφος Καλλίστου ν<η>πίου ἀρχοσσιναγωγοῦ* (sic), *ἐτῶ γ[. . . μη]νων γ'*. IGR IV, IH 52=CIJ (Smyrna): *Ῥουφεῖνα Ἰουδαία ἀρχισυνάγωγος*.

noting that *archisynagogoi* appear in Gentile cults also. But whether the expression is of Jewish or Gentile origin is not as yet known.[40]

CIJ II, no. 756: [Θ]εοπέμπτης [ἀρ]χισυν(αγώγου) Myndos in Caria, beginning of the Byzantine era. See. L. Robert, *Hellenica* I (1940), pp. 26–7. Note also Σοφία Γορτυνία πρεσβυτέρα κὲ (sic) ἀρχισυναγωγίσσα Κισάμου (in Crete), A. C. Bandy, Hesperia 32 (1963), pp. 227–9; cf. BE 1963, no. 413. The juvenile ἄρχοντες, on the Jewish epitaphs in Rome (Leon, no. 88, 120), are analagous (see vol. III § 31, ii); see also γραμμα[τεὺς] νήπιος, six years old (CIJ I, no. 146=Leon, no. 146). On a Christian Latin inscription in Africa there appears a lector of five years (CIL VIII, no. 453). For *lectores infantuli* see Victor Vitensis III, 34 (CSEL VII). According to mMeg. 4:5–6 minors were permitted to read the Scripture but not the Prayer (התפלה). For the titles 'father' or 'mother' of the synagogue see M. Hengel, ZNW 57 (1966), pp. 176–8, and add AE 1969/70, no. 748 (Volubilis, Mauretania): πατὴρ τῆς συναγωγῆς. On the bestowal of honorific titles on women, see vol. III, § 31, ii.

40. For non-Jewish uses, note Eusebius *HE* vii 10, 4 mentioning an ἀρχισυνάγωγος τῶν ἐν ἀπ' Αἰγύπτου μάγων (where the usage is non-technical, and probably merely abusive). On an inscription from Olynthos, CIG II, p. 994, add. no. 2007 f.=L. Duchesne and C. Bayet, *Mission au mont Athos* (1876, no. 119), there appears an Αἰλιανὸς Νείκων ὁ ἀρχισυνάγωγος θεοῦ ἥρωος. On an inscription in Chios (CIG II, p. 1031 add., 221c) five [ἀρχισυ]νάγωγοι οἱ ἄρξαντες. An inscription in Thessalonica (IG XII. 2 (1), no. 288, cf. no. 289), giving a decree by an association for the worship of Heracles for a member of the community, is dated from the year A.D. 154, mentions ἀρχισυναγωγοῦντος Κώτυος Εἰρήνης. For the inscription from near Heraclea Pontica mentioning an association of barbers with an ἀρχισυνάγωγος, see n. 14. Lastly when Severus Alexander was allegedly called a 'Syrus Archisynagogus' (*SHA*, *Vita Sev. Alex.* 28) it is probable but not absolutely certain that the phrase alludes to a Jewish rather than heathen *archisynagogus*. See A. D. Momigliano, 'Severo Alessandro Archisynagogus. Una Conferma alla Historia Augusta', Athenaeum N.S. 12 (1934), pp. 151–3=*Quarto Contributo* (1969), pp. 531–3. The allied title συναγωγός is frequently attested in the cult associations of the Black Sea, in particular in Panticapeum on the Cimmerian Bosphorus, Latyschev, IOSPE II (1890), nos. 19, 60–4; IV (1901), nos. 207, 208, 210, 211, 212, 469; F. Ziebarth, Rhein. Mus. 55 (1900), p. 513; also at Gorgippia on the Cimmerian Bosphorus, Latyschev IV, no. 434; Ziebarth, p. 514. See CIRB, p. 837 s.v. The same office is found at Chios, G. Dunst, Archiv. f. Pap. 16 (1958), pp. 172–7; cf. BE 1959, no. 312. The communities at Tanais observed the cult of θεὸς ὕψιστος and were evidently influenced by Judaism; see E. Schürer, SAB 1897, pp. 20–225; for a recent discussion see M. Hengel, 'Proseuche und Synagoge', *Festgabe K. G. Kuhn* (1971), pp. 157–84. On the other hand the title συναγωγεύς is attested elsewhere: in Delos, BCH 11 (1887), p. 256: συναγωγέως διὰ βίου Αὔλου Καλουίνου; in the neighbourhood of Elausa in western Cilicia, OGIS 573, a decree of the Σαββατίσται, who among other things voted to στεφανοῦσθαι . . . τὸν συναγωγέα; in Tomi on the Black Sea, Archäol.-epigr. Mittheilungen aus Österreich 6 (1882), pp. 19–20; here among the officers of a cult-association is named in the first place the συναγωγεύς or συναγωγός—the reading of the last syllable is doubtful; cf. also Bull. Inst. Arch. Bulg. 25 (1962), p. 214, no. 20. Also at Istros, SEG I, no. 330. Lucian says of his Peregrinus Proteus (*Peregr.* 2) that as a pupil of the Christians he had soon outstripped these, so that they were only children in relation to him: προφήτης καὶ θιασάρχης καὶ ξυναγωγεὺς καὶ πάντα μόνος αὐτὸς ὤν. Constructions with ἀρχι, such as ἀρχερανιστής, ἀρχιθιασίτης, ἀρχιμύστης, appear frequently in Greek cult-associations. See material in F. Ziebarth, *Das griechische Vereinswesen* (1896), p. 219 (word index, s.v.).

In addition to the *archisynagogus*, there was a receiver of alms, the גבאי צדקה.[41] These officers were of course not concerned with worship as such, and where the religious and civic communities were not separate, are rather to be considered as civic officials. They must nevertheless be named here since it was in the synagogues that the collection of alms took place.[42] A distinction was made between the weekly money-chest (קופה=*cupa*), from which the local poor were supported regularly once a week, and the 'plate' (תמחוי), from which any needy person (especially strangers) could obtain a daily portion.[43] Whoever had food for two meals was to take nothing from the תמחוי, and whoever had food for fourteen meals, nothing from the קופה.[44] Collection for the קופה was to be made by at least two, and the distribution by at least three, persons.[45]

41. mDem. 3:1; mKid. 4:5. The latter passage states that the descendants of גבאי צדקה are even without special investigation to be accounted Israelites of pure descent whom members of the priestly class may marry. It is clear therefore that they were officers. For the office itself, see S. Krauss, *Talmudische Archäologie* III (1912), p. 67; *Synagogale Altertümer* (1922), p. 127.

42. Mt. 6:2. Cf. Str.-B. I, pp. 387–91.

43. tPea. 4:9. Cf. S. Lieberman, *ad loc.* (1955), p. 57. On קופה (=cupa) in general, see above p. 72. On קופה and תחמוי, cf. S. Krauss, *Griechische und lateinische Lehnwörter in Talmud, Midrasch und Targum* II (1899), pp. 516, 590–1; *Talmudische Archäologie*, Index, s.v. The קופה is as a rule a basket, e.g. for fruit (mShab. 10:2), vegetables (mDem, 2:5; mKel. 17:1), horse-beans (mMak. 4:6), fish (mMak. 6:3), straw (mShab. 18:1; mBez. 4:1; mKel. 17:1; mOhal. 6:2); also for carrying large sums of money (mShek. 5:3: the didrachmae collected in the treasury were taken from it in *kuppoth*, each of which held three סאה [one *seah*= 1½ Roman *modii*=cca 24 pints, see *Ant.* ix 4, 5 (85); Jerome, *Comm in Matth.* 13:33, PL XXVI, col. 92; CCL lxxvii, p. 110. But the later distinction, that money was collected in the קופה and gifts in kind in the תמחוי (thus Maimonides, *loc. cit.*), is hardly valid for Mishnaic times. The size of the vessels suggests that to begin with they were both used for gifts in kind; but money also became involved in both cases: 'A poor man, who gives a *perutha* for the קופה and a *perutha* for the תמחוי' (tPea. 4:10). At Passover, the poor were also to receive four cups of wine from the תמחוי (mPes. 10:1).

44. mPea. 8:7.

45. mPea. 8:7. On the distribution of alms in Talmudic and post-Talmudic times, see S. Krauss, *Talmudische Archäologie* III (1912), pp. 66–74. In regard to almsgiving among the Essenes, Josephus asserts that each member was free to help the needy at his own discretion, i.e. the care of the poor was not entrusted to an official. See *B.J.* ii 8, 6 (134). In the Damascus Rule, on the other hand, a special monthly levy was administered by the Guardian (מבקר) and the judges: 'They shall place the earnings of at least two days out of every month into the hands of the Guardian and the judges, and from it they shall give to the fatherless, and from it they shall succour the poor and the needy, the aged sick and the homeless, the captives taken by a foreign people, the virgin with no near kin, and the ma[iden for] whom no man cares. . . .' (CD 14:12–16). Cf. Vermes, *DSS*, p. 105. For officers charged by the primitive church with the care of the poor (διακονεῖν τραπέζαις), see Act. 6:1–5.

The third office was that of minister, the חזן הכנסת,[46] *ὑπηρέτης*[47] or *διάκονος*.[48] His task was to bring out the holy writings for the services and afterwards to replace them;[49] he was charged with announcing the beginning and the end of the Sabbath by blowing a trumpet.[50] He was in every respect the servant of the congregation; he had for example to execute punishment on those condemned to be scourged;[51] but he also taught the children to read.[52] On a papyrus from the third century B.C. found in Middle Egypt, a *νακόρος* (=*νεωκόρος*) appears in connexion with a *προσευχὴ τῶν Ἰουδαίων*.[53] Since *νεωκόροι* are otherwise (in a Jewish context) Temple servants,[54] the *νακόρος* is obviously a synagogue servant or minister.

The שליח צבור who recited the prayer during the service in the name of the congregation is usually regarded as one of its officers.[55] In fact, however, the prayer was not said by a permament officer, but by any member of the congregation in turn (see below, p. 449). The שליח צבור was therefore the authorized representative of the congregation, i.e. anyone who recited the prayer in its name.[56]

Still less to be considered as officers of the congregation are the ten workless men (עשרה בטלנים) charged against payment of money, especially in post-Talmudic Judaism, with attending services in the synagogue so that the מנין of ten members required for a religious assembly should always be present. The arrangement is totally foreign to the age of the Mishnah. Admittedly, the expression itself occurs

46. mSot. 7:7–8; mYom. 7:1; mMak. 3:12; mShab. 1:3 (חזן); tSuk. 4:6,11; tTaan. 1:14. Aramaic חזנא in mSot. 9:15. Cf. Epiphanius, *Pan.* 30 11: *Ἀζανιτῶν τῶν παρ' αὐτοῖς διακόνων ἑρμενευομένων ἢ ὑπερετῶν*. חזנים also occur in the Temple, mSuk. 4:4; mTam. 5:3. See S. Safrai, *op. cit.*, JPFC II, pp. 935–6, 940–2.

47. Lk. 4:20. Such a minister is presumably also meant in a Jewish epitaph from Rome: *Φλάβιος Ἰουλιανὸς ὑπηρέτης. Φλαβία Ἰουλιανὴ θυγάτηρ πατρί. Ἐν εἰρήνῃ ἡ κοίμησίς σου*, CIJ, no. 172; Leon, no. 172. Note CIJ II, no. 805 = IGLS IV, no. 1321 (Apamea, Syria): *ἐπὶ Νεμία ἀζζάνα*.

48. Cf. Frey, CIJ I, no. 805.

49. mSot. 7:7–8; mYom. 7:1; Lk. 4:20.

50. tSuk. 4:11; cf. n. 93 below.

51. mMak. 3:12.

52. mShab. 1:3. Later, the חזן became a prayer-leader. For his various functions, see W. Bacher, HDB IV, pp. 640–1; S. Krauss, *Synagogale Altertümer* (1922), pp. 127–31; J. Juster, *Les juifs dans l'empire romain* I (1914), p. 454.

53. BCH 27 (1903), p. 200. Cf. Th. Reinach, *Mélanges Nicole* (1905), pp. 451–9; RE IVA, col. 1307; CPJ I, no. 129.

54. In Philo, *νεωκόροι* = Levites, *Spec. Leg.* i 32 (156). Note also the *φροντιστής* or curator, attested at Side, Rome, Joppa and Aegina, L. Robert, Rev. Phil. 32 (1958), pp. 38–9. His precise functions are unknown. A reader (*ἀναγνωστής*) is also mentioned in various synagogues, see L. Robert, *Hellenica* XI/XII (1960), pp. 395–7.

55. mBer. 5:5; mR.Sh. 4:9. Cf. S. Krauss, *Synagogale Altertümer*, p. 131; J. Maier, *Geschichte der jüdischen Religion* (1972), p. 114.

56. Cf. JE XI, p. 261; S. Krauss, *Synagogale Altertümer*, pp. 131–7.

there.[57] But originally it must have described men not kept by their work from attending synagogue, even on weekdays. For on the Sabbath, everyone was workless; idleness would not have been the distinctive mark of a few individuals. It can therefore not apply to the ordinary Sabbath services; and still less is it said that ten workless men must be present in *every* congregation. On the contrary, it is specified, solely as the characteristic of a great city, that even on weekdays a sufficient number of synagogue visitors can always be found without any difficulty. It was not until considerably later that this arrangement was made and the concept thereby given another connotation.

3. Buildings

The building in which the congregation met for worship was the בית הכנסת;[58] in Aramaic, בי[ת] כנישתא; or simply כנישתא,[59] *συναγωγή*[60] or *προσευχή*[61] in Greek. In the older linguistic usage of the Diaspora,

57. mMeg. 1:3: 'What is known as a large city? Any in which there are ten workless men. If there are fewer, it is known as a village'. Cf. Krauss, *Synagogale Altertümer*, pp. 99, 103–4.

58. mBer. 7:3; *mTer. 11:10; mBik. 1:4; mErub. 10:10; *mPes. 4:4; mSuk. 3:13; mR.Sh. 3:7; mMeg. 1:3; mNed. 5:5; 9:2; mSheb. 4:10; mNeg. 13:12. In the passages marked *, the plural form בתי כניסיות occurs. Cf. S. Krauss, *Synagogale Altertümer*, pp. 7–9. CD 11:22 has בית השתחות, house of worship (the Temple?).

59. J. Levy, *Chaldäisches Wörterbuch* and *Neuhebräisches Wörterbuch*, s.v. W. Bacher, HDB IV, p. 636; S. Krauss, *Synagogale Altertümer*, Index, s.v.

60. Cf. Krauss, *Synagogale Altertümer*, pp. 11–17. Frequently in the New Testament. In Josephus three times only: *Ant.* xix 6, 3 (300); *B.J.* ii 14, 4–5 (285–9); vii 3, 3 (44). In Philo, *Quod omnis probus* 12 (81) [on the Essenes]: *εἰς ἱεροὺς ἀφικνούμενοι τόπους οἳ καλοῦνται συναγωγαί*. Frequently too in later literature; e.g. *Cod. Theod.* xvi 8, *passim*. Cf. also CIG 9894=IGR IV 190=CIJ I, no. 722; (Aegina), BCH 21 (1897), p. 47=CIJ II, no. 861 (Greek inscription at Tofas in Batanaea) and the mosaic inscriptions in the synagogue of Naro (Hammam-Lif) in North Africa (see above n. 29). This last reads: 'Sancta sinagoga Naron(itanam) pro salutem suam (*sic*) ancilla tua Iuliana p(uella) de suo propium (*sic*) teselavit'. Cf. CIL VIII 12457; Krauss, *Syn. Altertümer*, p. 266. The use of the term *συναγωγή* to denote a Christian (Marcionite) place of worship is only once authenticated, on an inscription from A.D. 319 at Deir-Ali, some three miles south of Damascus: *συναγωγὴ Μαρκιονιστῶν κώμ(ης) Λεβάβων* (Le Bas and Waddington, *Inscriptions grecques et latines* III, n. 2558=OGIS 608. Cf. also Harnack, ZWTh 1876, p. 103).

61. So especially on the inscriptions and papyri of Egypt mentioned on pp. 425f. above (third to first century B.C.); further see Philo, *In Flacc.* 6 (41); 7 (45, 47–9, 53); 14 (122). *Legat.* 20 (132, 134, 137, 138); 22 (148); 23 (152, 156, 157); 25 (165); 29 (191); 43 (346); 46 (371). 3 Mac. 7:20. Act. 16:13: *ἔξω τῆς πύλης παρὰ ποταμὸν οὗ ἐνομίζομεν προσευχὴν εἶναι.* Josephus, *Vita* 54 (277): *συνάγονται πάντες εἰς τὴν προσευχήν, μέγιστον οἴκημα πολὺν ὄχλον ἐπιδέξασθαι δυνάμενον.* CIG II, pp. 1004 f., Add. no. 2114bb=Latyschev, IOSPE II, nos. 52–3=CIJ I, nos. 683–4; CIRB, nos. 70–1 (inscriptions from Panticapaeum on the Cimmerian Bosphorus). Cleomedes, *De motu circulari corporum caelestium* (ed. Ziegler, 1891) II 1, 91 ('Epicurus uses absurd expressions, so that one might think they are derived *ἀπὸ μέσης τῆς προσευχῆς, Ἰουδαϊκά τινα καὶ παρακεχαραγμένα*). Juvenal, *Sat.* iii, 296: 'Ede, ubi consistas, in

συναγωγή does not yet have this meaning. Where it appears at all, it signifies 'the congregation', while the regular expression for the meeting-house is *προσευχή*. Both terms are still distinguished in this way in the inscriptions of Panticapaeum (first century A.D.; see above, p. 429, and the full text in vol. III, § 31). For *συναγωγή*=congregation, see also the (admittedly later) inscriptions of Phocea and Acmonia (above, p. 429; in both, the building is called simply *ὁ οἶκος*) and those of the Roman catacombs; for *προσευχή*=meeting house, see Egyptian inscriptions from the third to the first century B.C., and in general the evidence quoted in n. 61. The transfer of the expression *συναγωγή* to 'meeting house' appears to have occurred first in Palestine, and not to have passed into the language of the Diaspora until the first century A.D. On the one occasion that Philo uses *συναγωγή*, he is speaking of the Essenes in Palestine, and it is clear that he is not familiar with the term. The rest of the evidence quoted in n. 60 is either Palestinian or very late. The Acts of the Apostles, which employs *συναγωγή* also for meeting-houses in the Diaspora (Act. 13:5, 14; 14:1; 17:1, 10, 17: 18:4, 7, 19, 26; 19:8, only in 16:13, 16 *προσευχή*) therefore follows the Palestianian usage. The terms *προσευκτήριον*[62] and *σαββατεῖον*[63] are found in isolated instances. On the other hand, it is a mistake to assume that *συναγώγιον* appears in this sense. In the passages referred to, it denotes, not the building, but the 'coming together' or congregation.[64]

The preference was to build synagogues outside the cities in the

---

qua te quaero proseucha?'—CIL VI 9281=CIJ I, no. 531 (Rome): 'Dis M.P. Corfidio Signino pomario de aggere a proseucha' etc. ('Corfidius of Signia, fruit seller at the wall near the proseucha'). The word also occurs in Gentile worship to denote a place of prayer. See CIG 2079=Latyshev I², no. 176 (inscription from Olbia). Cf. Juster, *Les Juifs* I, pp. 456ᵇ–7; Krauss, *Syn. Altertümer*, pp. 9–17. Epiphanius, *Haer.* 80 1, on the Gentile Messalians or *'Ευχῖται* (see n. 75 below). On Messalianism see M. Kmosko. *Liber Graduum, Patrologia Syriaca* III (1926), pp. clxxi–ccxciii. However there may be Jewish influence here, as there certainly is on the inscription from Gorgippia, Latyshev II, no. 400=CIJ I, no. 690.

62. Philo, *Vit. Mos.* ii 39 (216).

63. *Ant.* xvi 6, 2 (164) (in an edict of Augustus). Here too, there possibly belongs CIG 3509=IGR IV 1281=CIJ II, no. 752: *Φάβιος Ζώσιμος κατασκευάσας σορόν, ἔθετο ἐπὶ τόπου καθαροῦ ὄντος πρὸ τῆς πόλεως πρὸς τῷ Σαμβαθείῳ ἐν τῷ Χαλδαίου περιβόλῳ*. This *Σαμβαθεῖον* was perhaps a shrine of the Chaldaic sibyl. See V. Tscherikover, 'The Sambathions', Scrip. Hierosol. I (1954), pp. 78–98, on pp. 83–4. Cf. vol. III § 33, the chapter on the Sibylline oracles. בית שבתא דיהודיי=synagogue occurs in Syriac.

64. Philo, *Legat.* 40 (311): *ἵνα ἐπιτρέπωσι τοῖς 'Ιουδαίοις μόνοις εἰς τὰ συναγώγια συνέρχεσθαι. Μὴ γὰρ εἶναι ταῦτα συνόδους ἐκ μέθης* etc. *De somniis* ii, 18 (127) (speech of a governor, probably Flaccus): *καὶ καθεδεῖσθε ἐν τοῖς συναγωγίοις ὑμῶν τὸν εἰωθότα θίασον ἀγείροντες*, etc. For the explanation cf. Athenaeus viii, p. 365c: *ἔλεγον δὲ . . . καὶ συναγώγιον τὸ συμπόσιον*. The word has the meaning 'community' in CIG no. 9908 =CIJ I, no. 508=Leon, no. 508 (Rome): *πατὴρ συναγωγίων*.

neighbourhood of rivers or by the sea-shore, so that all could perform the necessary ablutions before taking part in worship.[65]

Size and architectural style were naturally very varied.[66] The earliest ruins discovered in the fortresses of Herodium and Masada may give some idea of the synagogue architecture in vogue in Palestine at the time of Jesus.[67] The remains preserved in many places in Galilee do not

[*Text continues on p. 443*

65. See especially Act. 16:13 and Josephus, *Ant.* xiv 10, 23 (258): The people of Halicarnassus decree that the Jews 'may build places of prayer near the sea in accordance with their native customs' (*τὰς προσευχὰς ποιεῖσθαι πρὸς τῇ θαλάττῃ κατὰ τὸ πάτριον ἔθος*). The *προσευχή* mentioned on p. 426, n. 5 (i), according to P. Tebtunis 86=CPJ I, no. 134, lay close to the water. Cf. also n. 74 below and TDNT VII, p. 814 and n. 99. There is admittedly no trace of this in rabbinic literature; instead, it is laid down that synagogues should be built on the highest point of the town (tMeg. 4:23). But it is at least probable that the neighbourhood of water (if such was available) was sought, for there is no doubt of the obligation to wash the hands before prayer. Cf. on this, Aristeas (ed. Wendland, 305–6) on the seventy interpreters: *ὡς δ'ἔθος ἐστὶ πᾶσι τοῖς 'Ιουδαίοις ἀπονιψάμενοι τῇ θαλάσσῃ τὰς χεῖρας, ὡς ἂν εὔξονται πρὸς τὸν θεόν*. Judith 12:7; Clement of Alexandria, *Strom.* iv 22, 142; Sibyll. 3:591–3. E. L. Sukenik, *Ancient Synagogues in Palestine and Greece* (1934), pp. 49–50, argues that the siting of synagogues near to water was a Hellenistic Jewish custom. But the synagogue of Capernaum is on the shores of Lake Galilee, and in the upper Galilean town of Gischala (Gush Ḥalav), one synagogue was built on the top of a hill and another at its foot near a spring. Cf. M. Avi Yonah, Enc. Jud. 7, col. 589.

66. See in general, M. Avi-Yonah, 'Synagogue Architecture in the Late Classical Period', *Jewish Art*, ed. C. Roth (1971), pp. 64–82; Enc. Jud. 15, cols. 595–600; 'Ancient Synagogues', in *The Synagogue* (ed. J. Gutmann), pp. 95–109; A. Seager, 'The Architecture of the Dura and Sardis Synagogues', *ibid.*, pp. 149–93.

67. For the study of the architecture of Palestinian synagogues, see the Bibliography at the head of this section. The most important surveys are H. Kohl and C. Watzinger, *Antike Synagogen in Galiläa* (1916); E. L. Sukenik, *Ancient Synagogues in Palestine and Greece* (1934); E. R. Goodenough, *Jewish Symbols in the Greco-Roman World* I (1953), pp. 181–264. For a valuable brief outline, see M. Avi-Yonah, 'Synagogue—Architecture', Enc. Jud. 15, cols. 595–600. See also W. Schrage, TDNT VII, pp. 814–18. The only two Palestinian synagogues which definitely belong to the age of Jesus are those discovered in the Herodian fortresses of Masada and Herodium. The synagogue of Masada passed through two stages. In its original form it consisted of a rectangular building (15 × 12m) with two rows of columns. The floor was of grey plaster. The entrance was in the eastern wall, leading through an ante-room into the main hall. The Zealots introduced various structural alterations. They removed two pillars from the western row and constructed a cell in the north-western corner. They also dismantled the wall dividing the ante-room from the main room, and replaced them by two columns, and they installed stepped and plastered stone benches along the walls. Cf. Y. Yadin, 'The Excavation of Masada 1963/64—Preliminary Report', IEJ 15 (1965), pp. 76–9; *Masada* (1966), pp. 181–91, with illustrations on pp. 180–5. Yadin (*Masada*, p. 185) and Avi-Yonah (Enc. Jud. 15, col. 595) note that the plan of the Herodian building is reminiscent of several early synagogues in Galilee. The synagogue found in Herodium is of a similar type. Nevertheless, since it is a converted dining-room of the Herodian palace—occupants of the fortress during the first Jewish revolt installed stepped benches along the walls and constructed a

ritual bath in the proximity—this discovery appears to be less significant than that in Masada, where the hall in question was probably built originally for a religious purpose. Cf. V. Corbo, RB 75 (1968), p. 427. For illustrations see Qadmoniot 1 (1968), p. 133; RB 77 (1970), pl. xxa. It is also doubtful whether two of the assembly rooms of Qumran—locus 4 with a low bench around it, possibly a council chamber, and locus 77 which served also as dining room—may properly be described as synagogues. Cf. R. de Vaux, *Archaeology and the Dead Sea Scrolls* (1973), pp. 10–11, 26–7. Cf. Schrage, TDNT VII, p. 818, n. 124.

Two main architectural patterns separated by a transitional style may be distinguished among the Palestinian synagogues. The first is represented by the earlier Galilean synagogues, normally dating from the late second to the fourth century A.D. (e.g., Capernaum, Chorazin, etc.). They are rectangular stone buildings with a stone pavement. Inside is a gallery of three rows of columns, two running lengthwise and one across. Stone benches are built against two or three of the walls. (Both these characteristics appear already in Masada.) The seat of honour, no doubt that of the president of the synagogue, was known as the 'seat' or 'chair of Moses' (*ἡ Μωϋσέως καθέδρα*, Mt. 23:2; קתדרא דמשה, PRK, ed. Buber, p. 12). Several such seats have been discovered, e.g. at Chorazin, at Hammath near Tiberias, and at Delos (cf. Sukenik, *Ancient Synagogues*, pp. 57–61). The 'chair of Moses' from Chorazin bears an Aramaic inscription commemorating one of the benefactors (cf. Frey, CIJ II, no. 981, pp. 166–7). For the 'chair of Moses', see W. Bacher, 'Le siège de Moïse', REJ 34 (1897), pp. 299–301; I. Renov, 'The Seat of Moses', IEJ 5 (1955), pp. 262–7 [=*The Synagogue* (ed. J. Gutmann), pp. 233–9]. For the unlikely theory that the 'chair' was the receptacle of the Torah scroll, see C. Roth, 'The "Chair of Moses" and its Survivals', PEQ 81 (1949), pp. 100–10. In general, these synagogues resemble Graeco-Roman basilicas. Their façade looks southwards, i.e. facing Jerusalem, but they have no fixed place for the Ark of the Torah. The chief peculiarity of the transitional type, which first appeared in the second half of the third century A.D. (e.g. Arbel, Beth Shearim, Hammath, Eshtemoa, etc.), is a visible orientation of worship towards Jerusalem by the construction of a niche in the wall facing the Holy City, no doubt to serve as a receptacle for the Torah. The final stage of development, which began in the fifth century A.D. (e.g. Beth Alpha, Gerasa, Jericho, Maon, etc.), is marked by the adoption of the elongated basilica-shape of churches, with the apse pointing to Jerusalem and containing the Ark of the Torah (as well as a place reserved for a genizah or depository of sacred texts no longer fit for use). The entrance is in the wall opposite Jerusalem. Two rows of columns divide the interior into a central nave and two aisles. For further detail, see M. Avi-Yonah's article in Enc. Jud. 15, cols. 595–8. It should be noted that the traditional chronology adopted here has been challenged by the archaeologists responsible for the excavations at Capernaum between 1968 and 1972. Cf. V. Corbo, S. Loffreda, A. Spijkerman, *La Sinagoga di Cafarnao dopo scavi del 1969* (1970); S. Loffreda, 'The Synagogue of Capernaum. Archaeological Evidence for its Late Chronology', LASBF 22 (1972), pp. 5–29; V. Corbo, 'La Sinagoga di Cafarnao dopo gli scavi del 1972', *ibid.*, pp. 204–35. These archaeologists place the construction of the synagogue between the last decade of the fourth and the middle of the fifth century A.D. Cf. S. Loffreda, 'The Late Chronology of the Synagogue of Capernaum', IEJ (1973), pp. 37–42. Against this view, see G. Foerster, 'Notes on Recent Excavations at Capernaum', IEJ 21 (1971), pp. 207–11; M. Avi-Yonah, IEJ 23 (1973), pp. 43–5. On the vast literature on the synagogue of Dura-Europos, see the Bibliography at the head of this section and n. 73 below. Note that the synagogue discovered at Ostia is thought to go back to the first century A.D. See R. Meiggs, *Roman Ostia* ([2]1973), pp. 586–7. For Herodium, Capernaum and Masada, cf. now F. Hüttenmeister, *Die antiken Synagogen in Israel* I (1977), pp. 173–4, 260–70, antedate the third century A.D. The great synagogue of Alexandria is said to have been in the form of a basilica.[68] In Greek inscriptions, there is occasional mention of parts of synagogue buildings: an *ἐξέδρα* in Athribis, a *πρόναος* in Mantinea, a *περίβολος τοῦ ὑπαίθρου* in Phocea, a fountain and a courtyard at Side, a dining-room and quadriportico at Stobi in Macedonia.[69] In the *περίβολοι* dedicatory inscriptions and votive offerings were erected, as in the forecourt of the Temple at Jerusalem.[70]

In the rich ornamentation of the synagogue ruins in Palestine may be distinguished, in addition to Jewish religious symbols proper (*menorah*, *shofar*, *lulab* and *ethrog* and the *maggen David*), figures from the animal world, such as lions, lambs and eagles, as well as signs of the zodiac (in the mosaic floors at Beth Alpha and Hammath), and even pagan themes such as a griffon and capricorn (Capernaum), and a Hercules, a centaur and a Medusa (Chorazin).[71] At a later stage, biblical scenes were depicted in mosaics, viz., the Binding of Isaac at Beth Alpha, Noah's Ark at Gerasa, and Daniel in the Lion's Den at Naaran. In the *Akedah* mosaic, God is symbolized by a hand.[72] But neither these, nor the famous biblical frescoes from the third century synagogue of Dura Europos on the Euphrates,[73] are likely to reflect the customs prevalent in Palestine in the first half of the first century A.D.[74]

314–15. Cf. also G. Foerster, 'The Synagogues at Masada and Herodion', Journ. of Jewish Art 3–4 (1977), pp. 6–11.

68. tSuk. 4:6; ySuk. 55ab. Philo also mentions among the Alexandrian synagogues one which was *μεγίστη καὶ περισημοτάτη*, *Legat.* 20 (134).

69. *ἐξέδρα* at Athribis, Egypt: OGIS 101 = CIJ II, no. 1444 = CPJ III, p. 143, no. 1444; *πρόναος* at Mantinea (CIJ I, no. 720); *οἶκος* and *περίβολος τοῦ ὑπαίθρου*, at Phocea on the Ionic coast of Asia Minor, fountain and courtyard at Side, L. Robert, Rev. Phil. 32 (1958), pp. 36–47; *τὸ τρίκλεινον σὺν τῷ τετραστόῳ* at Stobi, CIJ I, no. 694, see M. Hengel, 'Die Synagogeninschrift von Stobi', ZNW 57 (1966), pp. 145–83. For the surviving synagogue from Delos, see n. 5. For that of Sardis, in use as a synagogue by the second half of the third century A.D., see A. R. Seager, 'The Building History of the Sardis Synagogue', AJA 76 (1972), pp. 425–35.

70. Philo, *In Flacc.* 7 (48–9); cf. *Legat.* 20 (133). In respect of the Temple at Jerusalem, see *Ant.* xv 11, 3 (395); also 1 Mac. 11:37; 14:26, 48 (Public records).

71. See Sukenik, *Ancient Synagogues*, pp. 11, 24; Avi-Yonah, Enc. Jud. 15, col. 597.

72. Cf. Sukenik, *Ancient Synagogues*, pp. 33–4.

73. M. I. Rostovtzeff, *Dura Europos and its Art* (1938); R. du Mesnil du Buisson, *Les peintures de la synagogue de Dura Europos* (1938); E. L. Sukenik, בית הכנסת של דורא אירופוס וציוריו (1947); C. H. Kraeling, *The Synagogue: The Excavations at Dura Europos—Final Report* VIII, 1 (1956); E. R. Goodenough, *Jewish Symbols* IX–XI (1964); J. Gutmann (ed.), *The Dura Europos Synagogue* (1973); A. Perkins, *The Art of Dura Europos* (1973).

74. On the strict ban on figurative representation in the first century A.D., see Vermes, *PBJS*, pp. 76–7. The first distinction between cultic and decorative purposes is attributed to Gamaliel II (*cca* A.D. 100), and assent to mural paintings

That there were in addition religious meeting-houses built like theatres without a roof is impossible to prove. This is attested only of the Samaritans.[75] It is certainly true that on fast-days the Jews prayed publicly, not in the synagogue, but in an open space, for instance by the sea-shore.[76] But these were real open spaces and there is no indication of the existence of unroofed buildings. Even less likely is it that it was these buildings, as distinct from synagogues proper, that were called *προσευχαί* in the narrower sense of the word. For the testimony of Epiphanius, the supposed chief authority, offers no evidence for this.[77] The Acts of the Apostles seem rather to argue a

---

and mosaics, to R. Yoḥanan and R. Abin in the second half of the third century. Cf. *ibid.* p. 77. See also Tg.Ps.-Jon. on Lev. 26:1: 'You may lay upon the ground of your sanctuaries a mosaic pavement engraved with images and likenesses (סטיו חקיק בציורין ודיוקנין תשוון בארעית מקדשיכון), but not to worship it'. See also J. Gutmann, 'The Second Commandment and the Image of God', HUCA 32 (1961), pp. 161–74; E. R. Goodenough, 'The Rabbis and Jewish Art in the Greco-Roman Period', *ibid.*, pp. 269–79; J. M. Baumgarten, 'Art in the Synagogne: Some Talmudic Views', Judaism 19 (1970), pp. 196–206 [= *The Synagogue*, ed. J. Gutmann (1975), pp. 79–89].

75. Epiphanius, *Pan.* 80, 1.

76. mTaan. 2:1: 'How did they order the matter on the (last seven) days of fasting? They brought out the ark (of the Torah) into the open space in the town and put wood-ashes on the ark and on the heads of the president (נשיא) and the father of the court (אב בית דין); and each took (of the ashes) and put them on his head. The eldest among them uttered before them words of admonition. . . .' (further liturgical directions follow). Tertullian, *De ieiunio* 16: 'Iudaicum certe ieiunium ubique celebratur, cum omissis templis per omne litus quocumque in aperto aliquando iam precem ad caelum mittunt'. *Idem, Ad nationes* i 13: 'Iudaici ritus lucernarum et ieiunia cum azymis et orationes litorales'. *Ant.* xiv 10, 23 (258): *καὶ τὰς προσευχὰς ποιεῖσθαι πρὸς τῇ θαλάσσῃ κατὰ τὸ πάτριον ἔθος* (concerning *προσευχάς* or *δεήσεις ποιεῖσθαι* = to perform one's devotions', cf. 1 Tim. 2:1; Lk. 5:33, Phil. 1:4. It therefore does not mean, 'to build proseuchae', as many have understood it). Cf. also Philo, *In Flacc.* 14 (121–4).

77. Epiphanius, *Pan.* 80, 1 (on the Messalians): *Τινὰς δὲ οἴκους ἑαυτοῖς κατασκευάσαντες ἢ τόπους πλατεῖς, φόρων δίκην, προσευχὰς ταύτας ἐκάλουν. Καὶ ἦσαν μὲν τὸ παλαιὸν προσευχῶν τόποι ἔν τε τοῖς Ἰουδαίοις ἔξω πόλεως καὶ ἐν τοῖς Σαμαρείταις, ὡς καὶ ἐν ταῖς Πράξεσι τῶν ἀποστόλων ηὕρομεν* (here follows the quotation of Act. 16:13). *Ἀλλὰ καὶ προσευχῆς τόπος ἐν Σικίμοις, ἐν τῇ νυνὶ καλουμένῃ Νεαπόλει ἔξω τῆς πόλεως, ἐν τῇ πεδιάδι, ὡς ἀπὸ σημείων δύο, θεατροειδὴς, οὕτως ἐν ἀέρι καὶ αἰθρίῳ τόπῳ ἐστὶ κατασκευασθεὶς ὑπὸ τῶν Σαμαρειτῶν πάντα τὰ τῶν Ἰουδαίων μιμουμένων.* In explanation it should be noted, firstly, that what Epiphanius says of the Gentile Messalians is naturally not applicable to Jewish circumstances. Nevertheless they employed the word *προσευχή* for both kinds of places of prayer, the *οἶκοι* and the *τόποι πλατεῖς*. Secondly, in the learned remark that follows, Epiphanius presumably wishes to say that the Jews and Samaritans also have places of prayer in the open air known as *προσευχαί*. But he has independent knowledge of this only in respect of the Samaritans. In the case of the Jews, he knows nothing more (cf. the praeter. *ἦσαν τὸ παλαιόν*) and rests his assertion only on Act. 16:13. And even if he were right, this would in no way prove that these places of prayer, as distinct from the synagogues, were called *proseuchae*.

distinction between *προσευχή* and *συναγωγή*, since Act. 16:13 and 16 speaks of a *προσευχή* in Philippi, and immediately afterwards, in 17:1, of a *συναγωγή* in Thessalonica. But if there was any difference at all, it can only have been that the *προσευχή* was appointed solely for prayer and the *συναγωγή* for other cultic activities. But even this is untenable for Act. 16:13 and 16:16, where *προσευχή* is obviously the ordinary place of Sabbath meeting at which Paul also preached. Furthermore, since Philo certainly uses the word in relation to the synagogue proper, no realistic distinction can be established between the two expressions.[78]

In view of the importance attached to these Sabbath meetings, it must be assumed that at least one synagogue stood in every town of Palestine, even in the smaller places.[79] In the larger cities their number was considerable, as for example in Jerusalem,[80] Alexandria[81] and Rome.[82] Special emblems seem sometimes to have characterized the various synagogues of the same locality: if, that is to say, the interpretation is accepted that in Sepphoris there was a 'synagogue of the vine' (כנישתא דגופנא)[83] and in Rome a 'synagogue of the olive tree' (*συναγωγὴ ἐλαίας*).[84]

78. On the identity of the two, see S. Krauss, RE IVA, cols. 1287–88; Bauer, Arndt and Gingrich, *A Greek-English Lexicon of the NT*, p. 720; M. Hengel, 'Proseuche und Synagogue', *Festgabe K. G. Kuhn* (1971), pp. 157–84 = *The Synagogue* (ed. J. Gutmann), pp. 27–54.

79. They were for instance synagogues in Nazareth (Mt. 13:54; Mk. 5:2; Lk. 4:16) and Capernaum (Mk. 1:21; Lk. 7:5; Jn. 6:59). Cf. Act. 15:21: *κατὰ πόλιν*. Philo, *Spec. Leg.* ii 15 (62): *Ἀναπέπταται γοῦν ταῖς ἑβδόμαις μυρία κατὰ πᾶσαν πόλιν διδασκαλεῖα φρονήσεως καὶ σοφροσύνης καὶ ἀνδρείας καὶ δικαιοσύνης καὶ τῶν ἄλλων ἀρετῶν.* W. Bacher, HDB IV, p. 637, gives rabbinic references. For a detailed list, see Krauss, *Synagogole Altertümer*, pp. 199–267; 'Synagoge' RE IVA, cols. 1294–1308.

80. Act. 6:9; 24:12. A synagogue of the Alexandrians in Jerusalem also in tMeg. 3:6; yMeg. 73d. See § 22 (p. 76) on the variant of the Babylonian Talmud. The Talmudic story that there were 480 synagogues in Jerusalem (see p. 419, n. 31) is hardly to be taken literally. Christian sources speak of seven synagogues in Zion. Thus the Bordeaux Pilgrim of A.D. 333, *Itinera Hierosolymitana* (ed. Geyer, p. 22; CCL clxxv, p. 16); 'ex septem synagogis, quae illic fuerant, una tantum remansit'. Optatus of Milevis iii 2 (CSEL XXVI, p. 70): 'in illa monte Sion . . . in cuius vertice . . . fuerant septem synagogae'; and Epiphanius, *De mens.* 14: *καὶ ἑπτὰ συναγωγαί, αἳ ἐν τῇ Σιὼν μόναι ἑστήκεσαν ὡς καλύβαι, ἐξ ὧν μία περιελείφθη ἕως χρόνου Μαξιμωνᾶ τοῦ ἐπισκόπου καὶ Κονσταντίνου τοῦ βασιλέως ὡς σκηνὴ ἐν ἀμπελῶνι κατὰ τὸ γεγραμμένον.* Maximonas was bishop from about A.D. 335–48.

81. Philo, *Legat.* 20 (132): *πολλαὶ δέ εἰσι καθ' ἕκαστον τμῆμα τῆς πόλεως.*

82. Philo, *Legat.* 23 (156) speaks of *προσευχαί* in Rome in the plural. For further details on Roman synagogues see H. J. Leon, *The Jews of Ancient Rome* (1960), pp. 135–66 and vol. III, § 31.

83. yNaz. 56a. Cf. however, Krauss, *Synagogale Altertümer*, p. 210 (synagogue of the Gophnites).

84. Leon, *op. cit.*, no. 281 (p. 305), no. 509 (p. 340). On other interpretations, see *ibid.* pp. 145–7.

The fittings of the early synagogues were fairly simple.[85] The principal object was the ark (תיבה or ארון) in which the Torah scrolls and other sacred books were kept.[86] These were wrapped in linen cloths (מטפחות)[87] and lay in a case (תיק = θήκη).[88]

For the readers and preachers there was, in later ages in any case, a raised area (בימה = βῆμα, tribune) on which stood the reading desk.[89] Both are mentioned in the Jerusalem Talmud[90] and presumably existed in New Testament times. Other fittings mentioned are the lamps.[91]

Finally there were the horns (שופרות) and the trumpets (חצוצרות), instruments indispensable to worship. The horns were blown on the first day of the New Year, and the trumpets on fast-days.[92] The beginning

85. Cf. Krauss, *Synagogale Altertümer*, pp. 364–92.

86. The תיבה is mentioned in mMeg. 3:1; mNed. 5:5; mTaan, 2:1–2 (according to this passage it was portable); cf. also the frequently recurring phase, לפני עבר התיבה (see below, p. 450). The full phrase is תיבה של ספרים: tYad. 2:12; cf. Str.-B. IV, pp. 126–39. Chrysostom, *Orat. adv. Iudaeos* vi 7 (PG XLVIII, col. 914): *"Αλλως δὲ, ποία κιβωτὸς νῦν παρὰ 'Ιουδαίοις, ὅπου ἱλαστήριον οὐκ ἔστιν; ὅπου οὐ χρησμὸς, οὐ διαθήκης πλάκες . . . 'Εμοὶ τῶν ὑπὸ τῆς ἀγορᾶς πωλουμένων κιβωτίων οὐδὲν ἄμεινον αὕτη ἡ κιβωτὸς διακεῖσθαι δοκεῖ, ἀλλὰ καὶ πολλῷ χεῖρον.* Regarding sacred books kept in synagogues, see Josephus, *Ant.* xvi 6, 2 (164). Chrysostom, *Orat. adv. Iudaeos* i 5 (PG XLVIII, col. 850): *'Επειδὴ δέ εἰσί τινες, οἵ καὶ τὴν συναγωγὴν σεμνὸν εἶναι τόπον νομίζουσιν, ἀναγκαῖον καὶ πρὸς τούτους ὀλίγα εἰπεῖν . . . 'Ο νόμος ἀπόκειται, φησὶν, ἐν αὐτῷ καὶ βιβλία προφητικά. Καὶ τί τοῦτο; Μὴ γὰρ ἔνθα, ἂν ᾖ βιβλία τοιαῦτα, καὶ ὁ τόπος ἅγιος ἔσται; Οὐ πάντως.* Similarly *Orat.* vi 6–7 (PG XLVIII, cols. 711–16). Cf. W. Bacher, HDB IV, p. 639; JE II, pp. 107–11; TDNT VII, p. 819. For figurative representations, see Leon, *op. cit.*, pp. 196, 200–1, 208–9, 220–3; E. R. Goodenough, *Jewish Symbols* IV, pp. 99–144.

87. mKil. 9:3; mShab. 9:6; mMeg. 3:1; mKel. 28: 4; mNeg. 11:11. Cf. Krauss, *Synogogale Altertümer*, pp. 381–4.

88. תיק הספר in mShab. 16:1. תיק הספרים in tYad. 2:12. The word תיק alone in mKel. 16:7–8; cf. Krauss, *Griechische und lateinische Lehnwörter* II, p. 588; *Synagogale Altertümer*, pp. 382–4; L. Blau, *Studien zum althebräischen Buchwesen* (1902), pp. 173–80. On the use of book-cases in classical antiquity see RE III, col. 970; Th. Birt, *Kritik und Hermeneutik: nebst Abriss des antiken Buchwesens* (1913), pp. 332–4.

89. Cf. mSot. 7:8; 2 Esd. 18:4. For a βῆμα with inscription from Syracuse, see Frey, CIJ I, no. 653. For a *podium* from Byzantine times referred to as ἄμβων, cf. CIJ II, no. 781, pp. 38–9. In general see JE I, pp. 430–1; X, pp. 267–8. Krauss, *Synagogale Altertümer*, pp. 384–5; TDNT VII, pp. 819–20.

90. yMeg. 73d. Here the reading-desk is called אנלגין, ἀναλογεῖον. This is how it should be read following *Aruch*, instead of אנגלין as given by the editions. The same word is also in mKel. 16:7. See Levy, *Neuhebr Wörterb.* s.v.; Krauss, *Griech. und lat. Lehnwörter* II, p. 73 (אנלגין); *Synagogale Altertümer*, pp. 388–9.

91. mTer. 11:10; mPes. 4:4. Krauss, *Synagogale Altertümer*, pp. 390–1. On the stone candlestick intended to contain seven earthenware lamps discovered in the synagogue of Ḥammath, see Sukenik, *Ancient Synagogues*, p. 55, and plate XIIa.

92. mR.Sh. 3:4; mTaan. 2:3. Cf. Str.-B. IV, pp. 140–2. In Philo the feast of-New Year is called the feast of *σάλπιγγες*, *Spec. Leg.* i 35 (186); ii 31 (188); cf. Krauss, *Talmudische Archäologie* III, pp. 96–7; *Synagogale Altertümer*, p. 410; G. Friedrich, TDNT VII, p. 83.

and the end of the Sabbath were also announced by the minister of the synagogue with blasts on the trumpet so that the people would know when to stop work and when to resume.[93]

As meeting-houses of the congregation, the synagogues were not used exclusively for religious purposes. A political meeting was once held in the great *προσευχή* at Tiberias.[94] There is frequent reference in the New Testament to correction being administered in synagogues (Mt. 10:17; 23:34; Mk. 13:9; cf. Act. 22:19; 26:11).[95] Eating and drinking were on the whole forbidden in them,[96] but there is mention in rabbinic literature of meals taken there.[97] Their real purpose, however, was to serve as places where the people could meet for instruction and prayer.

4. Worship

The order of service was already considerably developed and established in New Testament times. The seating was arranged in a certain order, with the more distinguished members of the congregation in the front places and the younger ones behind. Men and women were presumably segregated.[98] On the orientation of the seating, see n. 106.

93. tSuk. 4:11; mHul. 1:7; yShab. 16a; bShab. 35b. Cf. J. Levy, *Neuhebräisches Wörterbuch*, חצוצרות. In the Temple at Jerusalem this was done by the priests, *B.J.* iv 9, 12 (582); mSuk. 5:5. On the horns and trumpets at Qumran, see Y. Yadin, *The Scroll of the War of the Sons of the Light against the Sons of Darkness* (1962), pp. 87–113.

94. Josephus, *Vita* 54 (280).

95. Cf. W. Schrage, TDNT VII, p. 831. According to mMak. 3:12, scourging was administered by the minister of the synagogue (חזן הכנסת), but it is not specified where the sentence was carried out. Cf. Krauss, *Synagogale Altertümer*, p. 186.

96. bMeg. 28a.

97. yShab. 3a: 'R. Mishah and R. Samuel b. R. Yizḥak sat and ate in one of the upper synagogues (בחדא מן כנישתא עילייתא) of Tiberias'. So also yBer. 5d. See in general on the use of synagogues for purposes other than worship, W. Bacher, HDB IV, pp. 642 f.

98. On the *πρωτοκαθεδρία* of the scribes and Pharisees, see Mt. 23:6; Mk. 12:39; Lk. 11:43; 20:46. Philo says of the Essenes that they sat in order of age, the younger 'below' (i.e. behind) the older men. *Quod omnis probus* 12 (81): *καθ' ἡλικίας ἐν τάξεσιν ὑπὸ πρεσβυτέροις νέοι καθέζονται*. A similar hierarchical seating order is established in the Qumran rules for the assembly and the solemn meal. 'This is the rule for the Assembly of the Congregation: Each man shall sit in his place (בתכונו). The Priest shall sit first, and the elders second, and all the rest of the people according to their rank' (1QS 6:8–9). 'And [when] they shall gather for the common [tab]le to eat . . . the Priest . . . shall bless the first-fruits of bread and wine, and shall be the first [to extend] his hand over the bread. Thereafter the Messiah of Israel shall extend his hand over the bread, [and] all the Congregation of the Community [shall utter a] blessing, [each man in the order] of his dignity (כבודו). It is according to this statute that they shall proceed at every me[al] at which] at least ten men are gathered together.' (1QSa 2:17–22). In the Diaspora deserving

In the great synagogue at Alexandria, the men are said to have been separated according to their trades (אומנות).[99] If there was a leper in the congregation, a special compartment was erected for him.[100] For a normal meeting for worship, at least ten persons were required to be present.

As principal parts of the service, the Mishnah mentions the recitation of the *Shema*ʻ, the Prayer, the reading of the Torah, the reading of the prophets, the priestly blessing.[101] To this was added the translation of the portions of Scripture read aloud, which is also assumed in the Mishnah (see below), and its exposition by means of an elevating discourse, which in Philo appears as almost the most important part of the proceedings.[102]

---

men or women were given the προεδρία by a communal decree after the Greek fashion; see the inscription at Phocea, CIJ II, no. 738. The segregation of the sexes must be taken for granted, even though it is not mentioned in any of the older sources for Philo's assertion in *De vita contemplativa* 9 (69), concerning the banquet of the Therapeutae, that the men reclined 'by themselves on the right and women by themselves on the left', cannot be used here. Nor is a special compartment for women mentioned in the Talmud, see Löw, *Gesammelte Schriften* IV, pp. 55–71. Yet galleries supposedly intended for women have been found in some of the ancient synagogues in Galilee. Cf. Krauss, *Synagogale Altertümer*, p. 356; E. L. Sukenik, *Ancient Synagogues*, pp. 47–8; Goodenough, *Jewish Symbols* I, pp. 182, 193.

99. ySuk. 55ab.

100. mNeg. 13:12.

101. mMeg. 4:3.

102. Philo gives three summary descriptions of synagogue worship: (1) Eusebius, *Praep. evang.* viii 7, 12–13 from the first book of the *Hypothetica*: *Τί οὖν ἐποίησε [scil. ὁ νομοθέτης] ταῖς ἑβδόμαις ταύταις ἡμέραις; Αὐτοὺς εἰς ταυτὸν ἠξίου συνάγεσθαι, καὶ καθεζομένους μετ' ἀλλήλων σὺν αἰδοῖ καὶ κόσμῳ τῶν νόμων ἀκροᾶσθαι τοῦ μηδένα ἀγνοῆσαι χάριν. Καὶ δῆτα συνέρχονται μὲν ἀεί, καὶ συνεδρεύουσι μετ' ἀλλήλων· οἱ μὲν πολλοὶ σιωπῇ, πλὴν εἴ τι προσεπιφημίσαι τοῖς ἀναγινωσκομένοις νομίζεται· τῶν ἱερέων δέ τις ὁ παρὼν ἢ τῶν γερόντων εἷς ἀναγινώσκει τοὺς ἱεροὺς νόμους αὐτοῖς, καὶ καθ' ἕκαστον ἐξηγεῖται μέχρι σχεδὸν δείλης ὀψίας.* (2) *Spec. Leg.* ii 15 (62): *Ἀναπέπταται γοῦν ταῖς ἑβδόμαις μυρία κατὰ πᾶσαν πόλιν διδασκαλεῖα φρονήσεως καὶ σωφροσύνης καὶ ἀνδρείας καὶ δικαιοσύνης καὶ τῶν ἄλλων ἀρετῶν. Ἐν οἷς οἱ μὲν ἐν κόσμῳ καθέζονται, σὺν ἡσυχίᾳ τὰ ὦτα ἀνωρθωκότες, μετὰ προσοχῆς πάσης, ἕνεκα τοῦ διψῆν λόγων ποτίμων. Ἀναστὰς δέ τις τῶν ἐμπειροτάτων ὑφηγεῖται τἄριστα καὶ συνοίσοντα, οἷς ἅπας ὁ βίος ἐπιδώσει πρὸς τὸ βέλτιον.* (3) On the Essenes, *Quod omnis probus* 12 (82): *Ὁ μὲν τὰς βίβλους ἀναγινώσκει λαβών, ἕτερος δὲ τῶν ἐμπειροτάτων, ὅσα μὴ γνώριμα παρελθὼν ἀναδιδάσκει.* To these observations should be added (4) the address by an Egyptian governor, probably Flaccus, to the Jews in *Somn.* ii 18, (127): *καθεδεῖσθε ἐν τοῖς συναγωγίοις ὑμῶν, τὸν εἰωθότα θίασον ἀγείροντες καὶ ἀσφαλῶς τὰς ἱερὰς βίβλους ἀναγινώσκοντες κἂν εἴ τι μὴ τρανὲς εἴη διαπτύσσοντες καὶ τῇ πατρίῳ φιλοσοφίᾳ διὰ μακρηγορίας ἐνευκαιροῦντές τε καὶ ἐνσχολάζοντες.* The post-Talmudic tractate *Soferim* c. 10–21 (ed. M. Higger) gives a series of detailed directions for synagogue worship. Cf. L. Blau, 'Liturgy'. JE VIII, pp. 132–40; I. Elbogen, *Der jüdische Gottesdienst in seiner geschichtlichen Entwicklung* (^{3}1931); A. Z. Idelsohn, *Jewish Liturgy and its Development* (1932); J. Heinemann, *Prayer in the Period of the Tannaim and the Amora'im* (1964), pp. 138–57 (in Hebrew) [E.T. *Prayer in the*

The *Shema'*, so called from the opening words שמע ישראל, consists of Deut. 6:4–9, 11:13–21 and Num. 15:37–41, preceded and followed by one or two benedictions (see the Appendix). It is always distinguished from the Prayer proper and is more in the nature of a confession of faith. Hence the *Shema'* is not 'prayed' but 'recited' (קריאת שמע). As it undoubtedly belongs to the time of the Second Temple, certain fixed prayers must also by then have been customary in public worship. It is nevertheless very difficult to determine how much of the considerable liturgy of post-Talmudic Judaism reaches back to that earlier age.[103] The formula calling on the people to pray, ברכו את יהוה, is explicitly mentioned in the Mishnah.[104] Another custom reaching back to the period of the Mishnah is that of uttering the first and last three benedictions of the *Shemoneh 'Esreh* (for details, see the Appendix) at services on Sabbaths and feast-days.[105]

The people prayed standing with their faces turned towards the Holy of Holies,[106] towards Jerusalem. Presumably, they also faced in the same direction when sitting.[107] Prayer was not uttered by the whole congregation, but by the person called on to do so (שליח צבור) by the

---

Talmud. Forms and Patterns (1977), pp. 218–50]; L. Jacobs, 'Liturgy', Enc. Jud. 11, cols. 392–404; J. Heinemann-J. J. Petuchowski, *Literature of the Synagogue* (1975) [prayers, sermons, poetry].

103. Cf. Elbogen, *op. cit.*, pp. 14–106; Idelsohn, *op. cit.* pp. 23–33.

104. mBer. 7:3.

105. mR.Sh. 4:5 shows that the custom goes back to the time of the Mishnah. Cf. also mTam. 5:1 describing the Temple service.

106. On standing for prayer, see Mt. 6:5; Mk. 11:25; Lk. 18:11; mBer. 5:1; mTaan. 2:2. On turning towards the Holy of Holies, i.e. towards Jerusalem: Ezek. 8:16; 1 Kgs. 8:48; Dan. 6:11; mBer. 4:5–6; tBer. 3:16; Jerome, *Comment. in Ezech., ad. loc.* (CCL lxxv, pp. 100–1); L. Ginzberg, 'Adoration', JE I, pp. 208–11. On the orientation of synagogues, see above n. 67. Cf. also H. Rosenau, 'A Note on Synagogue Orientation', JPOS 16 (1936), pp. 33–6; F. Landsberger, 'The Sacred Direction in Synagogue and Church', HUCA 28 (1957), pp. 181–203 [=*The Synagogue* (ed. J. Gutmann), pp. 239–61].

107. tMeg. 4:21: 'The elders sit with their face to the people and their back to the sanctuary. The ark (תיבה) stands with its front to the people and its back to the sanctuary. When the priests confer the blessing, they stand with their face to the people and their back to the sanctuary. The synagogue minister (חזן, here as prayer-leader) stands with his face to the sanctuary, and likewise all the people are turned to the sanctuary'. For the evidence of Galilean synagogues, cf. above n. 67. Cf. Schrage, TDNT VII, p. 815–16. The Tosefta, at variance with the orientation of surviving synagogue ruins, prescribes that an entrance must always be to the east, in conformity with the Temple of Jerusalem (tMeg. 4:22). For the eastern entrance to the synagogue of Masada, see above n. 67. The synagogue of Caesarea is oriented towards the south, with its entrance to the east. Cf. M. Avi-Yonah and A. Negev, IEJ 13 (1963), p. 147. The Judaean synagogue of Eshtemoa, south-west of Jerusalem, has the niche for the ark of the Torah in the middle of the long wall facing the Holy City, whereas the three entrances are in the short wall facing east. Cf. M. Avi-Yonah, Enc. Jud. 15, col. 597 and Plan 2.

archisynagogus; the congregation made only certain responses, in particular the *Amen*.[108] The prayer-leader stepped before the case containing the Torah scrolls, hence עבר לפני התיבה as the usual expression for 'to lead in prayer'.[109] Every member was entitled to do this except minors.[110] The person who recited the Prayer could do the same with the *Shema*' and read the lesson from the Prophets, and if he was a priest, pronounce the blessing.[111]

The Scripture readings (the Pentateuch as well as the Prophets) could equally be undertaken by any member of the congregation, even by a minor.[112] The latter were excluded only from reading the book of Esther on the Feast of Purim.[113] If priests and Levites were present, they took precedence in reading.[114] It was customary for the reader to stand.[115] In the case of the book of Esther, standing and sitting were both allowed;[116] and the king was permitted to sit when he read his portion of the Torah at the Feast of Tabernacles during a sabbatical year.[117]

The Torah reading was so ordered that the whole of the Pentateuch was read consecutively in a three-yearly cycle.[118] The Masoretic

108. On the call to prayer by the *archisynagogus*, see above p. 435; on the שליח צבור, see p. 438. אמן as a response is found already in Dt. 27:15 ff.; Neh. 5:13; 8:6; 1 Chron. 16:36; Tob. 8:8. See also 1QS 1:20; 2:10, 18; mBer. 5:4; 8:8; mTaan. 2:5. For Christian worship, 1 Cor. 14:16; Justin, *I Apol*. 65, 67. The LXX translates *Amen* in the Pentateuch, Prophets and Psalms into Greek; so also Judith 13:20 (γένοιτο). Against this, ἀμήν figures in Neh. 5:13; 8:6; 1 Chron. 16:36; 1 Ezr. 9:47; frequently in Symmachus (see Hatch and Redpath, *Concordance*), Theodotion Dt. 27:15. See W. H. Hogg, 'Amen, Notes on its Significance and Use in Biblical and Post-biblical Times', JQR 9 (1897), pp. 1–23; L. Ginzberg, JE I, pp. 491 f., Elbogen, *Der jüdische Gottesdienst*, pp. 495–7. On the Christian use, F. Cabrol; 'Amen' *Dict. d'arch. chr*. I (1907), cols. 1554–73; H. Schlier, TDNT I, pp. 335–8.

109. mBer. 5:3–4; mErub. 3:9; mR.Sh. 4:7; mTaan. 1:2, 2:5; mMeg. 4:3, 5, 6, 8. Cf. also mTaan. 2:1. Cf. Elbogen, *op. cit*., pp. 27, 497–98.

110. mMeg. 4:6. In Christian congregations also prayer was said by a member of the congregation. See 1 Cor. 11:4.

111. mMeg. 4:5.

112. mMeg. 4:5–6. That the reading of the Torah was not the task of a permanent officer is evident from Philo *ap*. Eusebius, *Praep. ev*. viii 7, 13 (for the wording see above p. 448).

113. mMeg. 2:4.

114. mGit. 5:8: 'The following things are ordained for the sake of peace: The priest reads first, after him the Levite, after him the Israelite, for the sake of peace'. Philo also suggests a priestly precedence, but he assumes that there was always only one reader; *Praep. ev*. viii 7, 13: τῶν ἱερέων δέ τις ὁ παρὼν ἢ τῶν γερόντων εἷς.

115. Cf. mYom. 7:1; mSot. 7:7 (p. 434 above). See also Lk.4:16 (ἀνέστη ἀναγνῶναι) and Str.-B. *in h.l.*

116. mMeg. 4:1.

117. mSot. 7:8.

118. bMeg. 29b. As the existence of the triennial cycle is nowhere attested in Tannaitic literature, its currency in the age of Jesus is merely conjectural.

arrangement of the Pentateuch into one hundred and fifty-four sections probably traces back to this three-yearly cycle. But there are also calculations of one hundred and sixty-one, one hundred and sixty-seven and one hundred and seventy-five sections.[119] The arrangement varied therefore. The count of one hundred and seventy-five sections may point to a three and a half yearly cycle (twice in seven years).[120] Several members of the congregation were invited by an officer[121]—originally the *archisynagogus* no doubt—to take part in the reading, at least seven at the Sabbath services (not so on week-days), of whom the first and last were to pronounce a benediction (ברכה) at the beginning and the end.[122] Each had to read at least three verses of the Torah,[123] and was not to repeat them from memory.[124] This in any case is the order prescribed by the Mishnah, which was of course observed only in Palestinian synagogues. The Talmud asserts explicitly of non-

119. See especially L. Zunz, *Die gottesdienstlichen Vorträge der Juden* ([2]1892), pp. 3–4; J. Theodor, 'Die Midraschim zum Pentateuch und der dreijährige palästinensische Cyklus', MGWJ 1885–7; A. Büchler, 'The Reading of the Law and Prophets in a Triennial Cycle', JQR 5 (1893), pp. 420–68; 6 (1894), pp. 1–73; K. Kohler, 'Law, Reading from the' JE VII, pp. 747–8; J. Jacobs, 'Triennial cycle' JE XII, pp. 254–7; J. Mann, *The Bible as Read and Preached in the Old Synagogue* I–II (1940–66); J. Heinemann, 'The Triennial lectionary Cycle', JJS 19 (1968), pp. 41–8; N. Fried, 'List of the Sedarim for Numbers', Textus 7 (1969), pp. 103–13; 'Triennial Cycle', Enc. Jud. 15, cols. 1386–9; C. Perrot, *La lecture de la Bible dans la Synagogue. Les anciennes lectures palestiniennes du Shabbat et des fêtes* (1973).

120. For attempts to reconstruct the triennial cycle in detail, see 'Sidra', JE XI, pp. 328 f.; 'Triennial cycle', JE XII, pp. 254–7; Enc. Jud. 15, cols. 1387–8. While the triennial cycle was customary in Palestine and Egypt until the twelfth century (cf. *The Itinerary of Benjamin of Tudela*, ed. M. N. Adler (1907), p. 70), in Babylonia the whole Pentateuch was read each year in 54 sections. This usage was later adopted by Judaism generally. On the 54 divisions in a year see 'Sidra' JE XI, pp. 328 f., 'Torah, Reading of', Enc. Jud. 15, cols. 1246–55. Since the publication by A. Guilding of *The Fourth Gospel and Jewish Worship* (1960), the relationship between synagogal Scripture reading and the composition of the Gospels has been the subject of lively, though largely inconclusive, debate. Cf. J. R. Porter, 'The Pentateuch and the Triennial Lectionary Cycle', *Promise and Fulfilment*, ed. F. F. Bruce (1963), pp. 163–74; L. Morris, *The New Testament and the Jewish Lectionaries* (1964); L. Crockett, 'Luke 4:16–30 and the Jewish Lectionary Cycle', JJS 17 (1966), pp. 13–46; J. Heinemann, 'The Triennial Lectionary Cycle', JJS 19 (1968), pp. 41–9; C. Perrot, 'Luc 4, 16–20 et la lecture biblique dans l'ancienne synagogue', *Exégèse biblique et judaïsme*, ed. J. E. Mesnard (1973), pp. 170–86, with detailed bibliography on p. 185, n. 8; M. D. Goulder, *Midrash and Lection in Matthew* (1974).

121. On the invitation to read the Torah, cf. Krauss, *Synagogale Altertümer*, p. 172. In the age of Jesus, this was probably the privilege of the archisynagogue.

122. mMeg. 4:2. Cf. Elbogen, *Gottesdienst*, pp. 171–2.

123. mMeg. 4:4.

124. Cf. mMeg. 2:1 (in regard to the book of Esther)' mTaan. 4:3 (where reciting from memory is mentioned as an exception).

Palestinian Jews that among them the whole *parashah* was read by one person alone;[125] and Philo agrees with this, for he clearly assumes that the Torah reading was undertaken by one man (see p. 448).

Already in New Testament times the reading from the Torah was joined by a section from the Prophets (i.e. the נביאים of the Hebrew canon), as may be seen from Lk. 4:17, where Jesus reads a section from Isaiah, and from Act. 13:15 (ἀνάγνωσις τοῦ νόμου καὶ τῶν προφητῶν), as also from the Mishnah, where readings from the Prophets are mentioned.[126] Since these concluded the service, the congregation being therewith dismissed, the recitation from the Prophets was named the recitation of 'dismissal' (הפטרה or אפטרה); for which reason the prophetic sections themselves were called *haftaroth*.[127] No *lectio continua* was required for them,[128] and they were read by one person alone.[129] Moreover, they were read only at principal services on the Sabbath, and not at services during the week or on Sabbath afternoons.[130]

As the language in which Scripture was read was no longer familiar to the whole people, a translation had to be provided. The reading was therefore accompanied by a *targum*, a continuous rendering into

125. yMeg. 75a (on the ruling in the Mishnah that on the Sabbath seven persons should always be called upon to read the Torah): 'Jews speaking a foreign language (הלעוזות) have not this custom, but one person reads the whole *parashah*'. See J. Levy, *Neuhebr. Wörterb.* II, p. 515a: לעוז.

126. mMeg. 4:1–5. A Büchler, 'The Reading of the Law and Prophets in a Triennial Cycle', JQR 6 (1894), pp. 1–73. E. N. Adler, 'MS of Haftaras of the Triennial Cycle, sec. xi/xii', JQR 8 (1896), pp. 528 f.; A. Büchler, 'Haftarah', JE VI, pp. 135–7; J. Jacobs, 'Triennial cycle', JE XII, pp. 254–57; Elbogen, *Gottesdienst*, pp. 174–84; J. Mann, *The Bible, passim*; N. Fried, 'The Haftarot of T.S. B. 17, 25', Textus 3 (1963), pp. 128–9; 'Some further Notes on Haftarot Scrolls', Textus 6 (1968), pp. 18–26; Enc. Jud. 16 cols. 1342–5.

127. See W. Bacher, *Die exegetische Terminologie der jüdischen Traditionsliteratur* II (1905), p. 14. Against this interpretation, Elbogen remarks that there is no evidence to indicate that the Prophetic reading ever terminated the service and argues that הפטיר בנביא (mMeg. 4:1–5) means not 'to dismiss the congregation with the Prophet', but 'to end the reading of Scripture with the Prophet'. Cf. *Gottesdienst*, p. 175.

128. mMeg. 4:4. Whether in the first century A.D. the choice of the prophetic passage was left to the reader cannot be proved or disproved. Cf. Lk. 4:17 ff. In post-Mishnaic times, the *haftarah*, too, was fixed (see on this the literature cited in n. 126). On feast-days and certain special sabbaths this was already the case in the Tannaitic age according to tMeg. 4.

129. mMeg. 4:5.

130. mMeg. 4:1–2. Of the *ketubim*, only the five *megilloth* were used in the synagogue service, and these only on particular occasions in the year: namely, the Song of Songs at Passover, Ruth at the Feast of Weeks, Lamentations on 9 Ab, Ecclesiastes at the Feast of Tabernacles, and Esther at Purim. See L. Blau, 'Megilloth', JE VIII, pp. 429 f. The reading of Esther at Purim is attested as established tradition in mMeg. For the liturgical reading of the other *megilloth*, the earliest reference is post-Talmudic (*Soferim* 14:3). Cf. Elbogen, *Gottesdienst*, p. 185.

Aramaic. In the absence of definite evidence, it is not possible to determine whether the interpreter (מתורגמן, תרגמן) was a permanent officer, or whether competent members of the congregation (even a minor, mMeg. 4:6) took it in turns to fulfil this role. The text of the Torah was read and translated verse by verse, but in the case of the Prophets, three verses could be read at a time; though if any formed a separate section, it too had to be read singly.[131] It may be taken for granted that the translation was conveyed only orally. Not until the fourth century A.D. is there an isolated reference to the translation being read from a written *targum*.[132]

The reading from the Bible was followed by an address or sermon (דרשה) in which the portion read was expounded and given practical application. That such commentaries were frequent is apparent from the διδάσκειν ἐν ταῖς συναγωγαῖς[133] so often mentioned in the New Testament, as well as from Lk. 4:20 ff., and from the explicit testimony of Philo (see p. 448). On whether the sermon preceded or followed the reading from the Prophets, see p. 452 above. The preacher (דרשן)[134] sat on a raised place (Lk. 4:20: ἐκάθισεν).[135] Preaching, too, was not restricted to particular persons, but as appears especially from Philo, was open to any competent member of the congregation.[136]

A blessing pronounced by a priest (Num. 6:22 ff.) and answered by the congregation with 'Amen', ended the service.[137] If there was no

131. Cf. especially mMeg. 4:4, 6, 10. See Zunz, p. 8; JE VIII, 521 f.; W. Bacher, *Die exegetische Terminologie der jüd. Traditionsliteratur* I–II (1905), תרגם and תרגום. See also R. le Déaut, *Introduction a la littérature targumique* (1966), pp. 23–51. On the theory that Greek versions of Scripture are Greek Targums, see P. Kahle, *The Cairo Geniza* ([2]1959), pp. 213–14; but see J. W. Wevers, 'Proto-Septuagint Studies', *In the Seed of Wisdom* (Festschrift T. J. Meeks) (1954), pp. 58–77. It is worth noting that in Scythopolis in the time of Diocletian, 'the Greek reading was translated into Aramaic' during the Christian service; see Eusebius, *De mart, Pal.* according to the long, Syriac, recension, B. Violet, TU XIV, 4 (1896), p. 4. In Jerusalem, the same happened in about A.D. 385–8. See *Pereg. Egeriae* 47, 3–4 (CCL clxxvi, p. 89). Epiphanius, *De fide* 21, lists among officers of the Christian congregation the ἑρμηνευταὶ γλώσσης εἰς γλῶσσαν ἢ ἐν ταῖς ἀναγνώσεσιν ἢ ἐν ταῖς προσομιλίαις. See Zahn, *Gesch. des neutest. Kanons* I, p. 43.

132. yMeg. 74d. See W. Bacher, JE XII, pp. 57–8.

133. Mt. 4:23; Mk. 1:21; 6:2; Lk. 4:15; 6:6; 13:10; Jn. 6:59; 18:20.

134. Ben Zoma was a celebrated *darshan* (mSot. 9:15).

135. Elbogen, *Gottesdienst*, pp. 194–8.

136. Elbogen, *op. cit.*, p. 197.

137. mBer. 5:4; mMeg. 4:3, 5, 6, 7. On the blessing ritual, see mSot. 7:6 (= mTam. 7:2): 'How is the priestly blessing uttered? In the provinces it is pronounced in three parts; in the Temple, in one part. In the Temple, the Name is pronounced as it is written (יהוה), but in the provinces a substitute is used (אדוני). In the provinces, the priests raise their hands only to the height of the shoulder; in the Temple, above the head, except for the High Priest who may not raise his hands above the diadem (attached to his turban). R. Judah says: The High Priest also raised his hand above the diadem'. According to bR.Sh. 31b;

priest in the congregation, the blessing was not given. Instead, the words of benediction were recited by the *ḥazzan*.[138]

Such was the order of service for the Sabbath morning. But the people re-assembled in the synagogue in the afternoon at the time of the *minḥah* offering. Thus Philo's remark that these Sabbath meetings lasted μέχρι σχεδὸν δείλης ὀψίας is not unfounded considering their length. At the afternoon service there was no reading from the Prophets but only from the Torah. And only three members took part in the reading, no more and no less.[139]

The same order was observed in the week-day services held regularly on the second and fifth days of the week (Monday and Thursday).[140]

The people also met to read the Torah at the New Moon. On that occasion four members of the congregation shared in the *parashah*.[141] In fact, every festival during the year was marked by worship and readings from the Torah. The selection prescribed for each feast-day is set out in the Mishnah.[142]

APPENDIX

The Shema' and the Shemoneh 'Esreh

Because of their antiquity and the importance attached to them in Jewish worship, the *Shema'* and the *Shemoneh 'Esreh* need to be examined more closely.

I. The *Shema'*[143] consists of three texts, Dt. 6:4–9, Dt. 11:13–21 and

---

bSot. 40b, Yohanan ben Zakkai decreed that after the destruction of the Temple the priests should pronounce the blessing barefoot (J. Neusner, *A Life of Yohanan ben Zakkai* (²1970), pp. 211–2). In general, see Num. R. on Num. 6: 22 ff. (Soncino, pp. 407 ff.); Elbogen, *Gottesdienst*, pp. 67–72; Enc. Jud. 13, cols. 1060–3. On the priestly blessing at Qumran, see 1QS 2:1–4.

138. See Elgoben, *Gottesdienst*, p. 71; Idelsohn, *Jewish Liturgy*, p. 194.

139. mMeg. 3:6; 4:1.

140. mMeg. 3:6; 4:1. Cf. 1:2, 3.

141. mMeg. 4:2.

142. mMeg. 3:5–6.

143. See in general Zunz, pp. 382–4; L. Blau, 'Origine et histoire de la lecture du Schema et des formules de bénédiction qui l'accompagnent', REJ 31 (1895), pp. 179–201; JE XI, 266 f.; I. Elbogen, 'Studies in the Jewish Liturgy', JQR 18 (1906), pp. 587–99; 19 (1907), pp. 229–49; O. Holtzmann, *Die Mischna-Berakot* (1912), pp. 1–10; Elbogen, *Gottesdienst*, pp. 16–26; A. Z. Idelsohn, *Jewish Liturgy* (1932), pp. 88–92; L. J. Liebreich, 'The Benediction immediately preceding and following the Shema' ', REJ 125 (1965), pp. 151–65, L. Jacobs, 'Shema, Reading of', Enc. Jud. 14, cols. 1370–4; J. Heinemann and J. J. Petuchowski, *Literature of the Synagogue* (1975), pp. 15–28.

Num. 15:37–41: those Torah passages, therefore, which proclaim mainly that YHWH alone is the God of Israel and ordain certain memorials for the constant remembrance of him. The three passages are named in the Mishnah after the words with which they begin, (a) שמע, (b) והיה אם שמע and (c) ויאמר.[144] The opening and closing benedictions (*berakhoth*) are arranged around this nucleus; the Mishnah lays down that the morning *Shema'* is to be preceded by two benedictions and followed by one, and that the evening *Shema'* is to be preceded by two and followed by two.[145] The first words of the closing benediction are cited in the Mishnah exactly as they are used today: אמת ויציב.[146] Accordingly, although the wording of the blessings was later considerably expanded, they nevertheless belong basically to the Mishnaic period.[147]

This prayer, or more correctly, confession of faith, is required to be uttered twice a day, morning and evening, by every adult male Israelite.[148] Women, slaves and children are exempt.[149] It need not be said in Hebrew, but can be recited in any language.[150]

The antiquity of the custom of reciting the *Shema'* is already apparent from the fact that such detailed directions are given in the Mishnah.[151] But the Mishnah also mentions that the prayer is said by the priests in the Temple, which presupposes that it was in use at least before A.D. 70.[152] In fact, Josephus regards its origin as so remote that he sees it as having been laid down by Moses himself.[153]

II. The *Shemoneh 'Esreh*[154] though somewhat more recent than the *Shema'*, is fundamentally still very old. The chief prayer of Judaism,

144. mBer. 2:2; mTam. 5:1.

145. mBer. 1:4.

146. mBer. 2:2; mTam. 5:1.

147. For an analysis of the present text, see Elbogen, *Gottesdienst*, pp. 16–26.

148. mBer. 1:1–4.

149. mBer. 3:3.

150. mSot. 7:1; tSot. 7:7. The recital of the Shema' in Greek at Caesarea is mentioned in ySot. 21b.

151. Cf. also mPes. 4:8; mTaan. 4:3. mSot. 5:4; mAb. 2:13.

152. mTam. 4:3; 5:1.

153. *Ant.* iv 8, 13 (212): *Δὶς δ' ἑκάστης ἡμέρας, ἀρχομένης τε αὐτῆς καὶ ὁπότε πρὸς ὕπνον ὥρα τρέπεσθαι, μαρτυρεῖν τῷ θεῷ τὰς δωρεὰς ἃς ἀπαλλαγεῖσιν αὐτοῖς ἐκ τῆς Αἰγυπτίων γῆς παρέσχε, δικαίας οὔσης φύσει τῆς εὐχαριστίας καὶ γενομένης ἐπ' ἀμοιβῇ μὲν τῶν ἤδη γεγονότων ἐπὶ δὲ προτροπῇ τῶν ἐσομένων*. There can be no doubt that Josephus means by this the custom of reciting the *Shema'*.

154. See in general Zunz, pp. 380–2; I. Loeb, 'Les dix-huit bénédictions' REJ 19 (1889), pp. 17–40; I. Lévi, 'Les dix-huit bénédictions et les psaumes de Salomon' REJ 32 (1896), pp. 161–78; 33 (1896), pp. 142–3; S. Schechter, 'Genizah Specimens' JQR 10 (1898), pp. 656–7; I. Elbogen, 'Geschichte des Achtzehngebets', MGWJ 46 (1902), pp. 330–57, 427–39, 513–30; 'Shemoneh Esreh', JE XI, pp. 270–82; P. Fiebig, *Berachoth, der Mischnatraktat 'Segensprüche'* (1906), pp. 26–9; O. Holtzmann, *Die Mischna-Berakot* (1914), pp. 10–27 (contains both the Babylonian and the Palestinian recensions with a German translation); K.

every Israelite, including women, slaves and children, is required to recite it three times a day, in the morning, the afternoon (at the time of the *minḥah* offering) and the evening.[155] So much is it the prayer of prayers that it is known simply as התפלה, 'the Prayer'. In its later form in the Babylonian recension, it consists not of eighteen *berakhoth*, as its name שמונה עשרה suggests, but nineteen:

1. Blessed art thou, Lord our God and God of our fathers, God of Abraham, God of Isaac and God of Jacob, great, mighty and fearful God, most high God, who bestowest abundant grace and createst all things and rememberest the promises of grace to the fathers and bringest a Redeemer to their children's children for thy Name's sake out of love. O King, who bringest help and salvation and who art a shield. *Blessed art thou, Lord, shield of Abraham.*

2. Lord, thou art almighty for ever, who makest the dead alive. Thou art mighty to help, thou who sustainest the living out of grace, makest the dead alive out of great mercy, supportest those who fall, healest the sick, freest the captive, and keepest thy word faithfully to them who sleep in the dust. And who is like thee, Lord of mighty deeds, and who is comparable to thee, King, who makest dead and alive and causest help to spring forth. And thou art faithful to make the dead alive. *Blessed art thou, Lord, who makest the dead alive.*

3. Thou art holy and thy Name is holy and the holy praise thee every day. *Blessed art thou, Lord, holy God.*

4. Thou grantest knowledge to mankind and teachest men understanding. Grant us the knowledge, understanding and discernment (which come) from thee. *Blessed art thou, Lord, who grantest knowledge.*

Kohler, 'The Origin and Composition of the Eighteen Benedictions', HUCA I (1924), pp. 387–425; L. Finkelstein, 'The Development of the Amida', JQR 16 (1925–6), pp. 1–43, 127–69 [= *Pharisaism in the Making* (1974), pp. 245–331]; I. Elbogen, *Gottesdienst*, pp. 27–60, 515–20, 582–6; A. Z. Idelsohn, *Jewish Liturgy*, pp. 92–110; K. G. Kuhn, *Achtzehngebet und Vaterunser und der Reim* (1951); D. Hedegård (ed.), *Seder R. Amram Gaon* I (1951), (contains the earliest form of the Babylonian recension with an English translation). L. J. Liebreich, HUCA 34 (1963), pp. 125–76; J. Heinemann, *Prayer in the Period of the Tannaim and the Amoraim* (²1966), pp. 138–57 (in Hebrew) [E.T., *Prayer in the Talmud* (1977), pp. 218–50]; 'Amidah', Enc. Jud. 2, cols. 838–46; Heinemann-Petuchowski, *Literature of the Synagogue*, pp. 29–45.

155. mBer. 3:3, 4:1.

5. Lead us back, our Father, to thy Torah; and bring us, our King, to thy service, and cause us to return in perfect repentance to thy presence. *Blessed art thou, Lord, who delightest in repentance.*

6. Forgive us, our Father, for we have sinned; pardon us, our King, for we have transgressed. For thou forgivest and pardonest. *Blessed art thou, Lord, gracious, rich in forgiveness.*

7. Look on our affliction and plead our cause, and redeem us speedily for thy Name's sake; for thou art a mighty redeemer. *Blessed art thou, Lord, redeemer of Israel.*

8. Heal us, O Lord, and we shall be healed, save us and we shall be saved; for thou art our praise. And bring perfect healing to all our wounds. For thou art a God and King who heals, faithful and merciful. *Blessed art thou, Lord, who healest the sick of thy people Israel.*

9. Bless this year for us, Lord our God, and cause all its produce to prosper; and bless the land; and satisfy us with goodness; and bless our year as the good years. *Blessed art thou, Lord, who blessest the years.*

10. Proclaim our liberation with the great trumpet, and raise a banner to gather together our dispersed, and assemble us from the four corners of the earth. *Blessed art thou, Lord, who gatherest the banished of thy people Israel.*

11. Restore our judges as in former times and our counsellors as in the beginning; and take from us sorrow and sighing; and reign over us, thou Lord alone, in grace and mercy; and justify us in judgement. *Blessed art Thou, Lord, King, who lovest justice and judgement.*

12. And for informers let there be no hope; and let all who do wickedness quickly perish; and let them all be speedily destroyed; and uproot and crush and hurl down and humble the insolent, speedily in our days. *Blessed art thou, Lord, who crushest enemies and humblest the insolent.*

13. Over the righteous and over the pious; and over the elders of thy people of the house of Israel; and over the remnant of their Torah scholars; and over the righteous proselytes; and over us, may thy mercy shower down, Lord our God. And give a rich reward to all who faithfully trust in thy Name. And cause our portion to be with them for ever, that we may not be put to shame. For we have trusted in thee. *Blessed art thou, Lord, support and trust of the righteous.*

14. And to Jerusalem, thy city, return with mercy and dwell in its midst as thou hast spoken; and build it soon in our days to be an everlasting building; and raise up quickly in its midst the throne of David. *Blessed art thou, Lord, who buildest Jerusalem.*

15. Cause the shoot of David to shoot forth quickly, and raise up his horn by thy salvation. For we wait on thy salvation all the day. *Blessed art thou, Lord, who causest the horn of salvation to shoot forth.*

16. Hear our voice, Lord our God; spare us and have mercy on us, and accept our prayer with mercy and pleasure. For thou art a God who hearest prayers and supplications; and let us not return empty, our King, from before thy Face. For thou hearest the prayer of thy people Israel with mercy. *Blessed art thou, Lord, who hearest prayer.*

17. Be pleased, Lord our God, with thy people Israel and with their prayer. Bring back the worship into the Holy of Holies of thy house and accept in love and pleasure the sacrifices of Israel and her prayer. And may the worship offered by Israel thy people be pleasing to thee always. O that our eyes might see thy return with mercy to Zion. *Blessed art thou, Lord, who causest thy presence* (שכינה) *to return to Zion.*

18. We praise thee, for thou art the Lord our God and the God of our fathers for ever and ever, the rock of our life, the shield of our salvation from generation to generation. We praise thee and recount thy praise, for our life that is given into thy hand and for our souls which are in thy charge; and for thy wonders to us every day; and for thy marvels; and for thy deeds of goodness at every time, at evening and morning and midday. All-Good, of whose mercy there is no end, Merciful One, whose grace increases, we wait on thee forever. And for all this be praised and thy Name be exalted, our King, forever in all eternity. And may all that lives praise thee, *selah*, and praise thy Name in truth, thou God, our salvation and our help, *selah. Blessed art thou, Lord, All-Good is thy Name, and it is fitting to praise thee.*

19. Bring peace, goodness and blessing, grace and favour and mercy over us and over all Israel, thy people. Bless us our Father, all of us together, with the light of thy Face. For by the light of thy Face thou hast given us Lord our God, the Torah of life and loving kindness and righteousness and blessing and mercy and life and peace. And may it be good in thine eyes to bless thy people Israel at all times and in every hour with thy

peace. *Blessed art thou, Lord, who blessest thy people Israel with peace. Amen.*

Of these nineteen *berakhoth*, the first three praise God's omnipotence and grace, and the last two (18 and 19) thank him for his goodness and beg his blessing in general. In between are supplications proper: nos. 4–9 ask for knowledge, repentance, forgiveness, deliverance from evil, health and a fruitful land; nos. 10–17 pray for the reunion of the dispersed, the restoration of national supremacy, the destruction of the godless, the reward of the just, the rebuilding of Jerusalem, the sending of the Messiah, the hearing of prayer and the reinstitution of sacrificial worship.

From its content it is evident that the Prayer did not reach its final form until after the destruction of Jerusalem in A.D. 70, for nos. 14 and 17 presuppose the fall of the city and the cessation of sacrifice. On the other hand, it is already cited in the Mishnah under the name **שמונה עשרה**,[156] which mentions in addition that Rabban Gamaliel II, R. Joshua, R. Akiba and R. Eliezer, all authorities from the beginning of the second century, deliberated on whether all eighteen benedictions were to be said daily or only an excerpt from them,[157] as well as on how the additions during the rainy season and on the Sabbath were to be interpolated, and in what form to pray on New Year's day.[158] Accordingly, it must have been given the form of eighteen benedictions in around A.D. 70–100; but the underlying foundation of the Prayer is certainly much older.[159]

The wording of the Prayer of around A.D. 70–100 can no longer be reconstructed in detail, but of the known recensions, the text found in the Cairo Geniza and published by S. Schechter in 1898 presumably comes closest to it. In this, the individual benedictions are frequently shorter than in the Babylonian versions. The structure of the whole, however, is almost exactly the same. In particular, the doxologies with

156. mBer. 4:3; mTaan. 2:2.

157. mBer. 4:3.

158. mBer. 5:2; mR.Sh. 4:5; mTaan. 1:1–2. At the close of the Sabbath the so-called **הבדלה** was interpolated, i.e. the 'separation', by means of which the Sabbath was separated from the week-day. See mBer. 5:2; mHul. 1:7. Cf. 'Habdala' JE VI, pp. 118–21; Elbogen, *Gottesdienst*, pp. 120–2.

159. The prayer contained in the Hebrew text of Ben Sira following Ecclus. 51:12 displays remarkable parallels with the *Shemoneh 'Esreh*: God as 'shield of Abraham' (Ecclus. 51:12, 10=*Shemoneh 'Esreh* 1); as 'redeemer of Israel' (Ecclus. 51:12, 5=*Sh. 'E.* 8); as 'gatherer of the dispersed of Israel' (Ecclus. 51:12, 5= *Sh. 'E.* 10); as 'builder of his city and his sanctuary' (Ecclus. 51:12, 7=*Sh. 'E.* 14); as he 'who makes a horn to spring from the house of David' (Ecclus. 51:12, 8= *Sh. 'E.* 15). Cf. JE XI, pp. 280–1; Elbogen, *Gottesdienst*, p. 29.

which each benediction ends agree almost word for word with those of the common version and reveal the framework which undoubtedly originated during the last three decades of the first century A.D.

The Palestinian Recension

1. Blessed art thou, Lord, God of our fathers, God of Abraham, God of Isaac and God of Jacob, great, mighty and fearful God, most high God who createst heaven and earth, our shield and the shield of our fathers, our trust in every generation. *Blessed art thou, Lord, shield of Abraham.*

2. Thou art mighty, humbling the proud; strong, and judging the violent; thou livest for ever and raisest the dead; thou blowest the wind and bringest down the dew; thou providest for the living and makest the dead alive; in an instant thou causest our salvation to spring forth. *Blessed art thou, Lord, who makest the dead alive.*

3. Thou art holy and thy Name is awesome, and beside thee there is no God. *Blessed art thou Lord, the holy God.*

4. Grant us, our Father, the knowledge (which comes) from thee, and understanding and discernment (which come) from thy Torah. *Blessed art thou Lord, who grantest knowledge.*

5. Lead us back, Lord, to thee and we shall repent. Renew our days as of old. *Blessed art thou who delightest in repentance.*

6. Forgive us, our Father, for we have sinned against thee. Wipe out and remove our evil deeds from before thine eyes. For thy mercies are many. *Blessed art thou, Lord, rich in forgiveness.*

7. Look on our affliction and plead our cause and redeem us for thy Name's sake. *Blessed art thou, Lord, redeemer of Israel.*

8. Heal us, Lord our God, of the pain of our heart; remove from us sorrow and grief and raise up healing for our wounds. *Blessed art thou who healest the sick of thy people Israel.*

9. Bless this year for us, Lord our God, and cause all its produce to prosper. Bring quickly the year of our final redemption; and give dew and rain to the land; and satisfy the world from the treasuries of thy goodness; and bless the work of our hands. *Blessed art thou, Lord, who blessest the years.*

10. Proclaim our liberation with the great trumpet and raise a banner to gather together our dispersed. *Blessed art thou, Lord, who gatherest the banished of thy people Israel.*

11. Restore our judges as in former times and our counsellors as in the beginning; and reign over us, thou alone. *Blessed art thou, Lord, who lovest judgement.*

12. And for apostates let there be no hope; and may the insolent kingdom be quickly uprooted, in our days. And may the Nazarenes and the heretics perish quickly; and may they be erased from the Book of Life; and may they not be inscribed with the righteous. *Blessed art thou, Lord, who humblest the insolent.*

13. May thy mercies be showered over righteous proselytes; and give us a rich reward, together with those who do thy pleasure. *Blessed art thou, Lord, trust of the righteous.*

14. Be merciful, Lord our God, with thy great mercies, to Israel thy people and to Jerusalem thy city; and to Zion, the dwelling-place of the glory; and to thy Temple and thy habitation; and to the kingship of the house of David, thy righteous Messiah. *Blessed art thou, Lord, God of David, who buildest Jerusalem.*

15. Hear, Lord our God, the voice of our prayer, and be merciful to us; for thou art a gracious and merciful God. *Blessed art thou, Lord, who hearest prayer.*

16. Be pleased, Lord our God, and dwell in Zion; and may thy servants serve thee in Jerusalem. *Blessed art thou, Lord, whom we worship in awe.*

17. We praise thee, Lord, our God, and the God of our fathers, on account of all the goodness and grace and mercies which thou hast granted to us, and hast done to us and to our fathers before us. And if we say our feet are slipping, thy grace, O Lord, succours us. *Blessed art thou, Lord, the All-Good, thou art to be praised.*

18. Bring thy peace over Israel, thy people, and over thy city and over thine inheritance; and bless all of us together. *Blessed art thou, Lord who makest peace.*

The most important variant of the Palestinian recension is the absence of a separate benediction—the 15th in the Babylonian text—praying for the coming of the Messiah; its contents are expressed in a shorter form, in the 14th benediction.[160] Thus the Palestinian version has actually eighteen *berakhoth.* But whereas this feature appears to speak for the originality of this text, others cast doubt on it. The

160. The wording neither implies nor excludes the actual destruction of the Temple. The exclusive reference to proselytes in the 13th benediction may be seen as a sign of antiquity.

specific allusion to the coming of the Messiah can scarcely be omitted from a prayer which otherwise comprises all aspects of future hope; its combination with the prayer for the building of Jerusalem appears to be clumsy. There is, moreover a definite tradition that the figure of nineteen *berakhoth* arose from the interpolation of the '*berakhah* against heretics' (ברכת המינים), i.e. no. 12; not, that is to say, from dividing no. 14 in two. 'Simeon the cotton merchant arranged the eighteen benedictions according to their order in the time of Rabban Gamaliel at Yavneh. Rabban Gamaliel said to the sages: Is there anyone among you who can formulate the *berakhah* against heretics? Samuel the Small then rose and formulated it.'[161] If this is a reliable tradition, the Palestinian text should be regarded as approximately the oldest, but not as the Prayer dating back to the beginning of the second century A.D. It is to be noted also that other Geniza fragments containing significant variants show that the textual tradition continued to be elastic.[162]

No definite argument is to be built on the mention of Christians in the *berakhah* against heretics in regard to a first century A.D. date of the Palestinian recension. On the one hand, the textual tradition is uncertain.[163] On the other, the patristic evidence of the cursing of Christians by Jews is of a later date.[164] The inclusion of נצרים

161. bBer. 28b: שמעון הפקולי הסדיר שמונה עשרה ברכות לפני רבן גמליאל על הסדר ביבנה. אמר להם רבן גמליאל לחכמים, כלום יש אדם שיודע לתקן ברכת המינים? עמד שמואל הקטן ותקנה. This follows the question why there should be 19 instead of 18 *berakhoth*.

162. See Schechter, *art. cit.* and Finkelstein, *art. cit.*, pp. 142–69. The combination of the 14th and 15th benedictions may be due to an attempt to safeguard the total of 18 benedictions after the insertion of a new *berakhah*.

163. The *berakhah* is directed against various categories of enemies of Jewry. In the Babylonian recension there are 'slanderers' (מלשינים), 'all who do wickedness', 'enemies' and the 'insolent' (זדים). The מינים do not appear here at all but are mentioned in other recensions. On the *birkath ha-minim*, cf. I. Elbogen, *Geschichte des Achtzehngebets* (1903), pp. 30–6, 57 f.; A. T. Herford, *Christianity in Talmud and Midrash* (1903), pp. 125–37; JE XI, p. 281, Finkelstein, JQR 16 (1925/26), pp. 156–7.

164. Cf. Epiphanius, *Pan.* 29, 9: *Οὐ μόνον γὰρ οἱ τῶν Ἰουδαίων παῖδες πρὸς τούτους κέκτηνται μῖσος, ἀλλὰ καὶ ἀνιστάμενοι ἕωθεν καὶ μέσης ἡμέρας, ὅτι εὐχὰς ἐπιτελοῦσιν ἑαυτοῖς ἐν ταῖς συναγωγαῖς, ἐπαρῶνται αὐτοῖς, καὶ ἀναθηματίζουσι τρὶς τῆς ἡμέρας φάσκοντες ὅτι Ἐπικαταράσαι ὁ θεὸς τοὺς Ναζωραίους.* Jerome, *In Esaiam* 5: 18–19 (CCL lxxvii, p. 76). '(Iudaei) usque hodie perseverant in blasphemiis et ter per singulos dies in omnibus synagogis sub nomine Nazarenorum anathematizant vocabulum Christianum'. *In Esaiam* 49:7 (CCL lxxiiia, p. 538): '(Iudaei Christo) ter per singulos dies sub nomine Nazarenorum maledicunt in synagogis suis'. *In Esaiam* 52:4 ff. (*ibid.*, p. 578): '(Iudaei) diebus ac noctibus blasphemant Salvatorem et sub nomine, ut saepe dixi, Nazarenorum ter in die in Christianos congerunt maledicta'. Justin is less decided, *Dialog. c. Tryph.* 16: *Καταρώμενοι ἐν ταῖς συναγωγαῖς ὑμῶν τοὺς πιστεύοντας ἐπὶ τὸν Χριστόν.* Justin frequently expresses himself in a similar way (ch. 47, 93, 95, 96, 108, 117, 133). Ch. 137 is characteristic: *Συμφάμενοι οὖν μὴ λοιδορῆτε ἐπὶ τὸν υἱὸν τοῦ θεοῦ, μηδὲ Φαρισαίοις πειθόμενοι διδασκάλοις τὸν βασιλέα τοῦ Ἰσραὴλ ἐπισκώψητέ ποτε, ὁποῖα διδάσκουσιν οἱ ἀρχισυνάγωγοι ὑμῶν, μετὰ τὴν προσευχήν.*

(Nazarenes or Judaeo-Christians) in the Geniza version is unique in the textual tradition of the *Shemoneh 'Esreh*. נצרים is the narrower concept, מינים (=heretics, apostates in general) the broader, and probably the older.[165]

This passage refers not to cursing Christians, but to mocking (ἐπισκώπτειν) Christ, and so the *birkath ha-minim* is out of the question. This last of course was not said 'after the prayer' (μετὰ τὴν προσευχήν) but in the middle of it.

165. M. Friedländer, 'Encore un mot sur Minim, Minout et Guilionim dans le Talmud', REJ 38 (1898), pp. 194–203. For a discussion of the meaning of מינים, see W. Bacher, 'Le mot "Minim" désigne-t-il quelquefois des chrétiens?', REJ 38 (1899), pp. 37–45; I. Lévi, 'Le mot "Minim" désigne-t-il jamais une sect juive de gnostiques antinomistes ayant exercé son action en Judée avant la destruction du Temple?', *ibid.*, pp. 204–10; A. Marmorstein, 'The Background of Haggadah', HUCA 6 (1929), pp. 141–203 [*Studies in Jewish Theology* (1950), pp. 25–71]; A. Büchler, 'The Minim of Sepphoris and Tiberias in the Second and Third Centuries', *Studies in Jewish History* (1956), pp. 245–74; K. G. Kuhn, 'Giljonim and sifre minim', *Judentum, Urchristentum, Kirche* (*Jeremias Festschrift*) (1960), pp. 24–61; M. Simon, *Verus Israel* ([2]1964), pp. 215–38, 500–3; G. Vermes, 'The Decalogue and the Minim', *In Memoriam P. Kahle* (1968), pp. 232–40 [*PBJS*, pp. 169–77]; Enc. Jud. 12, cols. 1–3.

§ 28. LIFE AND THE LAW[1]

I. General Remarks

The whole purpose of education in family, school and synagogue was to transform the Jewish people into 'disciples of the Lord'. The ordinary man was to know, and do, what the Torah asked of him. His whole life was to conform to the precepts and commandments of the 'Instruction' (תורה) or 'Enlightenment' (אורייתא).[2] Obedience to these rules, which were firmly believed to have been laid down by God himself, was seen by Torah scholars, Pharisees and rabbis alike as the only way to put into practice the heavenly command, 'You shall be for me a kingdom of priests and a holy nation' (Exod. 19:5). In fact, by the first century A.D. submission to the Torah had become such an essential part of Judaism that Josephus could declare: 'Nowadays . . . violation of the laws has with most nations become a fine art. Not so with us. Robbed though we be of wealth, of cities, of all good things, our Law at least remains immortal; and there is not a Jew so distant from his country, so much in awe of a cruel despot, but has more fear of the Law than of him'.[3] Elsewhere he writes: 'Time and again before now the sight has been witnessed of prisoners enduring tortures and death in every form in the theatres rather than utter a single word against the laws and allied documents'.[4]

But how did this enthusiasm for the Torah obtain such a hold?

1. This section on 'Life and the Law', itself a reformulation of Schürer's own title, *Das Leben under dem Gesetz*, presents the reviser with a new kind of problem. He is faced here not so much with an antiquated account or a faulty historical reconstruction, as with questionable value judgements. It has been decided therefore not to reproduce § 28 unchanged, as a period piece: readers concerned with a late nineteenth century ideology can read the German original or the previous English translation. On the other hand, since to delete the chapter completely would be to deprive the revised volume of a great deal of interesting information, the subject has been treated in this new version from a historical rather than a theological vantage point. Moreover, the purpose of the Pharisees and their rabbinic heirs is obviously no longer represented as a trivialization of religion, but identified as an attempt to elevate everyday Jewish life as a whole, and in its minute details, to the sphere of cultic worship. It should also be noted that although in the historical survey that follows, Jewish observances and customs are referred to in the past tense, the laws on which they are based are still valid and practised by traditional Judaism.

2. Cf. above, p. 321, n. 22.

3. *C.Ap.* ii 38 (276–7).

4. *C.Ap.* i 8 (43); cf. i 22 (191); ii 30 (219). See also *B.J.* ii 8, 10 (152–3); bBer. 61b.

Briefly, because of a conviction that unquestioning compliance with God's commandments is the essence of religion, but also because of an expectation of divine reward or retribution. The prophetic idea of the Covenant concluded by God with his people was understood to mean that the people were to observe the Torah strictly and conscientiously, and God in return would pay the promised recompense, both to the nation and the individual Jew, for their good deeds and offences.[5] Again and again, certain sins or virtues are associated with definite forms of punishment or reward, and divine justice is conceived of forensically, as paying the appropriate retribution for man's lawful and unlawful actions.

> 'Seven kinds of retribution come upon the world for seven chief transgressions. (1) If a part of the people pays tithe on their produce, and a part does not, famine arises from drought so that a part suffers hunger and a part has enough. (2) And if none pay tithes, famine arises from war, disturbances and drought. (3) And if no dough-offering has been set apart, all-destroying famine arises. (4) Pestilence comes upon the world when such crimes prevail as are punished with death in the Torah but are not brought before the court, as also because of crimes in connection with the seventh-year produce. (5) The sword comes upon the world because of delay in pronouncing justice, because of the perverting of justice, and because of not expounding the Torah in accordance with *halakhah*. (6) Rapacious beasts come upon the world because of perjury and because of desecration of the divine Name. (7) Exile comes upon the world because of idolatry, incest, murder and (neglect of) the year of release.'[6]

Recompense for obedience to the Torah was also firmly believed.

> 'If a man performs but a single commandment, it shall be well with him; he shall have length of days and shall inherit the land.'[7]

> 'According to the labour so also shall be the reward.'[8]

> 'Know that all is brought into account.'[9]

Every fulfilment of the Law therefore brings with it a corresponding reward, and the only reason why God gave Israel so many command-

5. Cf. A. Marmorstein, *The Doctrine of Merits in Old Rabbinical Literature* (1920). See also the excellent chapter on 'Motives of Moral Conduct' in G. F. Moore, *Judaism* II, pp. 89–111. Cf. E. E. Urbach, *The Sages*, pp. 436–71, 879–94.

6. mAb. 5:8–9. Similarly e.g. mShab. 2:6. The Old Testament bases for this are the promises or threats of blessings and curses in Lev. 26 and Dt. 28.

7. mKid. 1:10.

8. mAb. 5:23.

9. mAb. 4:22.

ments and precepts was that his people should have ample opportunities to acquire merit.[10]

Both punishment and reward are meted out to men in this present life, but full retribution is delayed until the 'world to come' (העולם הבא). Then, all apparent injustices will be put right. The righteous who have suffered in this world will receive compensation accordingly. But even apart from this, complete recompense is reserved for the world to come. For then Israel as a nation and individual Jews will be rewarded for their faithfulness with a life of bliss. Good works such as honour of father and mother, charitable deeds, peace-making, and especially Torah study, are therefore to be compared to capital, the interest on which is enjoyed already in this life, but which itself remains for the world to come.[11] Yet although on the popular level this expectation of a future reward contributed powerfully to a zealous observance of the commandments, on the more elevated plane it was always believed that the Torah was to be obeyed 'for its own sake' (לשמה)[12] or 'for the sake of Heaven' (לשם שמים).[13] The saying of Antigonus of Sokho, 'Be not like servants who serve their master for the sake of reward, but be like those who do service without consideration of reward',[14] foreshadows many similar counsels preserved in rabbinic literature.[15] As G. F. Moore aptly remarks, 'There is a certain irony in the fact that the first recorded word of a Pharisee should be a repudiation of the supposed 'Pharisaic' wage-theory of righteousness'.[16]

On the other hand, there is no denying that though traditional Jews could regard the mass of commandments—six hundred and thirteen in all (תריג=613), consisting in three hundred and sixty-five prohibitions and two hundred and forty-eight positive precepts—as a means provided by God of acquiring merit, they could also arouse a misguided zeal for external observance alone. Thus Paul writes: *ζῆλον θεοῦ ἔχουσιν ἀλλ' οὐ κατ' ἐπίγνωσιν* (Rom. 10:2). Foreseeing or reacting to this criticism, Jewish teachers sought to reduce the laws to a smaller number and ended with a single rule incorporating them all. The Ten Commandments are presented by Philo as 'summaries (*κεφάλαια*) of all the special laws',[17] and a tradition, preserved in the name of R. Simlai, a third century A.D. Palestinian Amora, traces in the Bible itself the movement from six hundred and thirteen to one.

10. mMak. 3:16.
11. mPea. 1:1; cf. mKid. 4:14.
12. mAb. 6:1; Sifre Deut. 306; bTaan. 7a.
13. mAb. 2:2, 12; 4:11; 5:17.
14. mAb. 1:3.
15. Cf. Moore, *Judaism* II, pp. 45–108.
16. *Ibid.*, p. 96.
17. *Decal.* 29 (154).

'Moses revealed six hundred and thirteen commandments: three hundred and sixty-five prohibitions according to the number of days in a solar year, and two hundred and forty-eight positive precepts corresponding to the number of the parts of the human body (cf. mOhal. 1:8). Then came David and chose eleven (cf. Ps. 15). Then came Isaiah and chose six (cf. Isa. 33:15). Then came Micah and chose three (cf. Mic. 6:8). Then came Isaiah again and chose two (Isa. 56:1). Finally Amos came and chose one: "Seek me and you shall live" (Am. 5:4).'[18]

The most famous epitome of the Torah is associated with the name of Hillel. When requested by a Gentile to teach him the whole of the Torah quickly, he is said to have replied: 'Do nothing to your fellow that you would hate to be done to you! This is the entire Torah; all the rest is merely interpretation'.[19] The same reduction of the 'Law and the Prophets' to a single golden rule, formulated positively, appears also in the Gospels: 'All that you would wish that men should do to you, do also to them!' (Mt. 7:12; Lk. 6:31).[20]

II. Sabbath Observance

General rules may be the staple of philosophical speculation but for regulating the practical life of a whole community they are insufficient and inappropriate. Following the pattern already manifest in the Bible, the body of Jewish religious law contained in the Mishnah, developed and codified by Torah scholars, Pharisees and rabbis, evolved not unexpectedly in the direction of an increasingly precise case-law corresponding to, and reflecting, the conditions and needs of Palestinian Jewish society in the first two centuries A.D.[21] In this respect, one of the most important subjects, both in regard to its extent and significance

18. Cf. bMak. 23b, see W. Bacher, *Agada der palästinensischen Amoräer* I, pp. 558–9. On the 613 commandments, see J. Bloch, 'Les 613 lois', REJ 1 (1880), pp. 197–211; 2 (1882), pp. 27–40. Cf. 'Commandments, 613', Enc. Jud. 5, cols. 760–83.

19. bShab. 31a. See W. Bacher, *Agada der Tannaiten* I, pp. 4–5; E. E. Urbach, *The Sages*, p. 589. The saying seems to have been proverbial: cf. Tob. 4:15, καὶ ὃ μισεῖς μηδενὶ ποιήσῃς.

20. Cf. Moore, *Judaism* II, p. 87.

21. The authorities quoted in the Mishnah belong mostly to the period between A.D. 70–170, but it may reasonably be assumed that mishnaic law does not differ *essentially* from the legislation prevailing in the earlier decades of the first century in matters not affected by the destruction of the Temple and of Jewish state institutions.

was the law regulating the Sabbath observance.[22] The short pentateuchal ban on work on the Sabbath day, which enters into almost no detail (Ex. 16:23–30; 20:8–11; 23:12; 31:12–17; 34:21; 35:1–3; Lev. 23:3; Num. 15:32–6; Dt. 5:12–15. Cf. Isa. 58:13; Jer. 17:21–4; Ezek. 22:8; Am. 8:5; Neh. 10:32; 13:15–22), grew in the course of time into a lengthy Mishnah tractate.[23] For the rabbis, feeling it necessary to be more exact, specified the following thirty-nine activities as forbidden on the Sabbath: (1) sowing, (2) ploughing, (3) reaping, (4) binding sheaves, (5) threshing, (6) winnowing, (7) cleaning crops, (8) grinding, (9) sifting, (10) kneading, (11) baking, (12) shearing wool, (13) washing wool, (14) beating, (15) dyeing, (16) spinning, (17) making the warp, (18) making two bind-cords, (19) weaving two threads, (20) separating two threads, (21) making a knot, (22) untying a knot, (23) sewing two stitches, (24) tearing in order to sew two stitches, (25) hunting a deer, (26) killing it, (27) skinning it, (28) salting it, (29) preparing its hide, (30) scraping off the hair, (31) cutting it up, (32) writing two letters, (33) erasing in order to write two letters, (34) building, (35) pulling down, (36) extinguishing fire, (37) lighting fire, (38) striking with a hammer, (39) carrying from one area to another.[24]

Each of these main regulations required further debate on their meaning and extent, and it is here that the casuistry proper begins. According to Ex. 34:21, ploughing and reaping are forbidden. But by the time of the Mishnah, even the gathering of a few ears of corn was regarded as reaping.[25] Thus when the disciples of Jesus once did this on the Sabbath they were taken to task by some Pharisees, not for the plucking itself (which according to Dt. 23:26 is permitted), but for reaping on the Sabbath day (Mt. 12:1–2; Mk. 2:23–4; Lk. 6:1–2). In a different domain, it was necessary to know which knots were affected by the prohibition of work on the Sabbath and which were permitted (nos. 21–2).

> 'These are knots for which they (who tie them on the Sabbath) are held guilty: camel-drivers' knots and sailors' knots; and as a man becomes guilty for tying them, so does he become guilty for untying them. R. Meir says: No guilt is incurred in respect of a knot which

22. Cf. in the Mishnah the tractates Shabbath, Erubin and Beẓah: the Book of Jubilees 2:25–33 and 50. See also HDB IV, pp. 317–23; JE, pp. 587–602, Moore, *Judaism* II, pp. 21–39; J. Z. Lauterbach, *Rabbinic Essays* (1951), pp. 437–70; L. Jacobs, 'Sabbath', Enc. Jud. 14, cols. 562–7.

23. Earlier stages of the evolution are represented in Jub. 2:25–33; 50 and in CD 10:14–11:23.

24. mShab. 7:2. Cf. also Jub. 50 and CD, *loc. cit.*

25. Philo, *Vit. Mos.* ii 4 (22): 'For it is not permitted to cut any shoot or branch, or even a leaf, or to pluck any fruit whatsoever.' Cf. yShab. 9c. Cf. Str.-B. on Mt. 12:2, I, pp. 615–18.

can be untied with one hand. There are knots on account of which, unlike the camel-drivers' knots and sailors' knots, no guilt is incurred. A woman may tie up a tear in her shift, and also the bands of a cap, those of a belt, the straps of shoes and sandals, skins with wine and oil, and a pot with meat.'[26]

And when knots in the belt were permitted, it was also ruled that a bucket could be tied over a well with a belt, though not with a rope.[27]

The interdiction on writing on the Sabbath (no. 32) is defined as follows:

'Whoever writes two letters (of the alphabet), whether with his right hand or with his left, whether they are of one kind or two, or whether two symbols,[28] or in different languages, is guilty. Whoever forgetfully writes two letters, is guilty whether he writes with ink, or with paint, with red chalk, with gum, with copperas, or with anything that leaves a lasting mark. And whoever writes on two walls forming a corner, or on two tablets of an account-book, so that they (the two letters) may be read together, is guilty. Whoever writes on his body is guilty. . . . If a man writes in dark fluids, in fruit-juice, or in the dust of the road, in dry sand, or in anything in which the writing does not stay, he is free. If a man writes with the wrong side of his hand, or with his foot, or with his mouth, or with his elbow; or if a man adds a letter to other writing, or if he covers other writing (a palimpest); or if a man intends to write a *ḥeth* (ח) and writes two *zains* (זז), or (if he writes) one letter on the floor and another on the ceiling, or on two walls of a house, or on two pages of a book so that they cannot be read together, he is free. . . . If on two occasions a man writes two letters forgetfully, one in the morning and another towards evening, Rabban Gamaliel declares him guilty, but the sages pronounce him free.'[29]

Ex. 16:23 forbids baking and boiling on the Sabbath, so hot meals had to be prepared before Sabbath began and kept warm. In doing so, however, care had to be taken not to increase the heat for this would constitute 'boiling'. Accordingly, certain materials were recommended for the purpose and certain others banned.

'Food may not be placed in peat, in dung, in salt, in lime or in sand, whether wet or dry; nor in straw, in grape-skins, in flock, in herbs that are still wet, but only if they are dried. But it may be placed in

26. mShab. 15:1–2.
27. mShab. 15:2.
28. סמיונות according to the best texts, cf. W. Nowack, *Schabbat* (1924), p. 144. The printed editions read סממניות (different inks): see ed. Albeck-Yalon II, p. 47.
29. mShab. 12:3–6.

garments, under corn, under dove's feathers, under shavings and under combed flax. R. Judah forbids fine combed flax but permits the coarse.'[30]

According to Ex. 35:3 it is forbidden to light fire on the Sabbath. The ban on extinguishing fire was added later. But it was asked in regard to this latter precept what should be done if a non-Jew came to a conflagration.

'If a foreigner comes to extinguish the fire, he is neither to be told, Put it out! nor, Do not put it out! since one is not bound to hold him to his rest.'[31]

The prohibition naturally included lights and lamps.

'Whoever extinguishes a lamp for fear of Gentiles, robbers, or an evil spirit, or for the sake of a sick man that he may sleep, he is free. But if it should be done to spare the lamp, the oil, or the wick, he is guilty. R. Yose pronounces him free, except in regard to the wick, since he thereby prepares charcoal.'[32]

'A man may set a vessel under the lamp to catch the sparks, but he may not fill it with water, since he would thereby extinguish.'[33]

The last of the thirty-nine main prohibitions, i.e., the ban on carrying anything from one domain to another, המוציא מרשות לרשות (a precept inspired by Jer. 17:21–4), provided much material for debate because of the elasticity of the idea רשות (cf. already Jub. 2:29–30; 50:8). The quantity not to be carried was precisely defined. It was determined, for example, that it was a desecration of the Sabbath to carry food equal in weight to a dried fig,[34] or wine enough to mix in a

30. mShab. 4:1. Cf. Scholion to Juvenal vi, l. 542: 'ideo dixit foenoque supellectile, quod his pulmentaria sua et calidam aquam die sabbati servare consuerunt'; Scholion to iii, l. 13: 'uno die ante sabbatum in cofinis edulia sua calida ponebant involventes in feno post involutionem linteaminum et mapparum, ut sabbato calido haberent'. See H. Rönsch, *Collectanea philologa* (1891), pp. 249–54. It was important to store food for the Sabbath because for the Jews as for antiquity in general a feast-day was celebrated worthily with a good meal (Neh. 8:10; Tob. 2:1). For this reason too it was a duty to enjoy the Sabbath, and fasting was forbidden (Jud. 8:6; Jub. 50:10, 12). The meal described in Persius, *Sat.* v 179–84 = Stern, GLAJJ I, no. 190, is in no way a Lenten meal but a proletarian feast-day meal. Cf. Str.-B. I, pp. 611–15 (on Mt. 12:1); II, pp. 202–3 (on Lk. 14:1). Greek and Roman writers are mistaken when they regard the Sabbath as a fast-day: Strabo xvi 2, 40 (763); Suetonius, *Div. Aug.* 76; Justin xxxvi 2, 14; Petronius, Fr. 37 ed. Bucheler. See Stern, GLAJJ I, nos. 115 (Strabo), 137 (Justin), 195 (Petronius).

31. mShab. 16:6.

32. mShab. 2:5.

33. mShab. 3:6.

34. mShab. 7:4.

cup, or milk enough for one swallow, or honey enough to put on a wound, or oil enough to anoint a small limb, or water enough to moisten an eye-salve,[35] or a piece of papyrus large enough to write a tax receipt,[36] or parchment enough to write the shortest section of the tefillin (the *Shema' Yisrael*), or ink enough to write two letters,[37] or reed enough to make a pen,[38] etc. It was also forbidden to wear articles of clothing that were not garments proper. A soldier was not to go out with armour, helmet, greaves, sword, bow, shield or spear.[39] 'A legless man may go out with his wooden stump. So R. Meir. But R. Yose forbids it'.[40] Only in the case of an outbreak of fire was the interdict on carrying burdens suspended:

> 'All the Holy Scriptures may be rescued from fire. The case of the book may be rescued together with the book, that of the *tefillin* together with the *tefillin*, even though there is money in them. Food for the three meals may be rescued. If fire breaks out in the evening of the Sabbath, they may rescue food for three meals; if in the morning, they may rescue for two meals; if in the afternoon, only for one meal. And a basketful of loaves may be rescued, even though it be enough for a hundred meals, a cake of figs and a jar of wine.'[41]

In addition to these prohibitions, certain precautionary measures aimed at avoiding actions which might possibly lead to a desecration of the Sabbath.

> 'A tailor is not to go out with his needles as evening falls, for he might forget and go out with it (after Sabbath has begun); nor a scribe with his pen.'[42]

> 'Meat, onions and eggs may not be roasted if there is not time to roast them during the day. Bread is not to be put into the oven at

35. mShab. 8:1. Cf. bShab. 76a. See also Nowack, *Schabbat*, pp. 70–1, and Danby, *op. cit.*, p. 107, n. 3–4.
36. mShab. 8:2.
37. mShab. 8:3.
38. mShab. 8:5.
39. mShab. 6:2, 4. The ban in mShab. 6:2 on wearing sandals punched with nails was known also to Origen (*De principiis* iv 17): 'Sed et quod ait: "non levare onus in die sabbati" impossibile mihi videtur. Ex his enim ad fabulas infinitas, sicut sanctus apostolus dicit, Iudaeorum doctores devoluti sunt, dicentes non reputari onus, si calceamenta quis habeat sine clavis, onus vero esse, si caligulas quis cum clavis habuerit.' The Greek according to the *Philocalia* reads: *φάσκοντες βαστάγμα μὲν εἶναι τὸ τοιόνδε ὑπόδημα οὐ μὴν καί τὸ τοιόνδε, καὶ τὸ ἥλους ἔχον σανδάλιον οὐ μὴν καὶ τὸ ἀνήλωτον*. Cf. N. R. M. de Lange, *Origen and the Jews* (1976), p. 40.
40. mShab. 6:8.
41. mShab. 16:1–3.
42. mShab. 1:3.

dusk, nor cakes to be set on the coals if their surface cannot harden during the day. R. Eliezer says: If there is time only for the bottom surface to harden.'[43]

Circumspection extended even further in, for example, the interdict on reading or on ridding clothes of vermin by lamplight on the Sabbath. Both being occupations that require a particularly bright light, there might be a temptation to tilt the lamp to bring more oil to the wick. The schoolmaster was nevertheless permitted to supervise children reading with the help of a light, though he himself might not do so.[44]

In addition to the thirty-nine principal forms of work there were other forbidden tasks and activities not covered by them. Some are listed in the following regulation for feast-days (when the rest was less strict):

> 'Everything on account of which a man becomes guilty on the Sabbath whether because of violation of the rest, or because of acts performed out of free choice, or because of acts ordained by commandments, is also not permitted on a feast-day. The following with respect to the rest: they may not climb a tree, ride an animal, swim in water, clap the hands, slap the thighs, or dance. The following with respect to acts performed out of free choice: they may not sit in judgement, be betrothed to a wife, perform the taking off of the shoe (*ḥaliẓah*) or enter into a levirate marriage. The following with respect to acts ordained by commandments: they may consecrate nothing, offer nothing for valuation, dedicate nothing to be anathema, and set nothing apart for heave-offering or tithe. All this is declared forbidden on a feast-day, let alone on the Sabbath.'[45]

To the same category belongs in particular the regulation that on the Sabbath a Jew may not go more than two thousand cubits from his place of domicile (at the onset of Sabbath).[46] This was called the 'Sabbath limit', תחום השבת, and a stretch of two thousand cubits, a 'Sabbath journey' (Act. 1:12, *σαββάτου ὁδός*).[47] This rule, founded on

43. mShab. 1:10.

44. mShab. 1:3.

45. mBez. 5:2.

46. mErub. 5:5. On the distance of 2,000 cubits (according to Num. 5:1–8), cf. mErub. 4:3, 7; 5:7. CD 10:21 limits the distance for walking outside the town (חוץ לעירו) to 1,000 cubits, but allows a man to follow his cattle as far as 2,000 cubits 'to pasture if outside his town'. The figure of 1,000 cubits appears in Num. 35:4; 2,000 in 35:5. Cf. C. Rabin, *The Zadokite Documents* (1954), p. 53; L. H. Schiffman, *The Halakhah at Qumran* (1975), pp. 91–8. Origen, *De Principiis* iv 17 (Greek of the Philocalia: *ὥσπερ καὶ περὶ τοῦ σαββάτου, φάσκοντες τόπον ἑκάστῳ εἶναι δισχιλίους πήχεις*). Jerome, *Epist.* 121 *ad Algasiam*, quaest. 10: 'solent respondere et dicere: Barachibas et Simeon et Hellel magistri nostri tradiderunt nobis ut bis mille pedes ambulemus in sabbato'.

47. Cf. Str.-B. II, pp. 590–4; Moore, *Judaism* II, p. 32.

Ex. 16:29, together with the prohibition on carrying burdens from one place to another, was progressively relaxed in legislation relating to ערובין, as will be seen presently.

Despite the very strict obligation to keep the Sabbath holy, some exceptions were introduced either for humanitarian reasons or because of a commandment still more sacred. In the latter respect, the requirements of Temple worship came into consideration. The daily burnt-offering was to be offered on the Sabbath also; indeed, a special sacrifice was prescribed for that day (Num. 28:9–10). Therefore, all the operations necessary for it were permitted (Mt. 12:51: 'On the Sabbath day, the priests in the Temple profane the Sabbath and are guiltless').[48] The arrangements connected with the Passover sacrifices were also allowed on the Sabbath; but in this case it was very carefully stipulated which transactions were or were not lawful.[49] Circumcision belonged to the same category. Everything necessary might be done on the Sabbath as long as it could not be performed on the previous day. For whatever could be done then in preparation, was forbidden on the Sabbath itself.[50] In the interests of humanity, it was permitted to assist a woman at her confinement on the Sabbath,[51] and it was laid down as a general rule that all danger to life took precedence over the Sabbath כל ספק נפשות דוחה את השבת.[52]

> 'If a building falls on a man, and there is doubt whether he is underneath it or not, or whether he is alive or dead, or whether he is a Gentile or an Israelite, they may clear the rubble from over him on the Sabbath. If they find him alive they may clear more of it away; but if he is dead, they may let him lie.'[53]

A physician might attend to a patient on the Sabbath if his life was in danger. R. Mattithiah ben Heresh even allowed medicine to be

48. Cf. Jub. 50:10–11.

49. mPes. 6:1–2. The decree that Passover takes precedence over the Sabbath is attributed to Hillel: tPes. 4:13; yPes. 33a; bPes. 66a; cf. Neusner, *The Pharisees* I, pp. 231–35, 245–51, 254–57. See G. F. Moore, *Judaism* I, pp. 78–9. For other exceptions from the Sabbath commandment in favour of Temple worship, see also mErub. 10:11–15. CD 11:17–18 maintains the superiority of the Sabbath over any other feast, thus probably reflecting the cultic law prior to the innovation inspired by Hillel: 'No man on the Sabbath shall offer anything on the altar except the Sabbath burnt-offering'. Cf. Rabin, *Zadokite Documents*, p. 58. L. H. Schiffman, *The Halakhah at Qumran* (1975), pp. 128–9, argues, however, that this law is directed against the offering of the *tamid* on the Sabbath, and not of the Passover sacrifice.

50. mShab. 19:1–5. Jn. 7:22–3. See C. K. Barrett, *The Gospel according to St. John* (1955), pp. 264–5.

51. mShab. 18:3.

52. mYom. 8:6. Cf. Mekh. R. Ishmael on Ex. 31:17 (ed. Lauterbach III, pp. 197–8); bYom. 85a. See Moore, *Judaism* II, pp. 30–1.

53. mYom. 8:7.

dropped into a man's mouth on the Sabbath if he had a pain in his throat, since there might be danger to his life.[54] But this was the opinion of one master and by no means generally valid. On the whole, intervention by the physician was permitted only when life was at risk.

> 'They may not . . . set a broken limb. Whoever has sprained a hand or foot may not pour cold water over it.'[55]

> 'The priest serving in the Temple may replace on the Sabbath a wound plaster removed during the service; elsewhere it is not permitted; nowhere may they put one on themselves for the first time. . . . If a priest injures his finger, he may bind it with rushes in the sanctuary during the service on the Sabbath; elsewhere it is not permitted; everywhere it is forbidden to press out blood.'[56]

The basic rule that the saving of life takes precedence over the Sabbath was defined and universally accepted at the beginning of the Maccabaean uprising after a group of Asidaeans, attacked by Gentiles, had given themselves up to massacre rather than fight on the Sabbath.[57] From then on it was resolved to take up the sword for defence, though not for attack, on the Sabbath also.[58] But although adopted,[59] this rule was carried out only in cases of extreme distress, so that in later times it still happened that the enemy was able to turn the Sabbath to their own advantage.[60]

How strict the adherence of Jewish soldiers was to the law of the Sabbath rest is apparent from the fact that even a man like Josephus took it for granted,[61] and that the Romans felt obliged to exempt Jews

54. mYom. 8:6.

55. mShab. 22:6.

56. mErub. 10:13–14. See Nowack, *Erubin*, pp. 97, 99. When there is danger to life, Rabbinic law declares medical treatment permissible on the Sabbath (mShab. 2:5; mYom. 8:6: 'Whenever there is doubt that life may be in danger, this overrides the Sabbath'). The conflict described in the Gospels between the Pharisees and Jesus concerning his cures on the Sabbath day may be attributable to a stringent interpretation of the principle, viz. that healing is to be postponed when there is no danger to life (Mt. 12:9–13; Mk. 3:1–5; Lk. 6:6–10; 13:10–17; 14:1–6; Jn. 5:1–16; 9:14–16). See JE X, p. 597; G. Vermes, *Jesus the Jew*, pp. 25, 231. Note that the Mishnah places certain restrictions on the treatment of minor illnesses without forbidding it completely (mShab. 14:4; 22:6).

57. 1 Mac. 2:34–8; *Ant.* xii 6, 2 (274).

58. 1 Mac. 2:39–42; *Ant.* xii 6, 2 (277).

59. *Ant.* xiii 1, 3 (12); xiv 4, 2 (63); xviii 9, 2 (319).

60. *Ant.* xiii 12, 4 (337); xiv 4, 2 (63); Cass. Dio xxxvii 16; xlix 22; lxvi 7. Cf. also *Ant.* xii 1, 1 (4); *C. Ap.* i 22 (209–10) (Ptolemy I son of Lagus took Jerusalem on the Sabbath); Jub. 50:12.

61. *B.J.* ii 21, 8 (634) = *Vita* 32 (159).

from military duties because the Jewish Sabbath and Roman discipline were irreconcilably opposed.[62]

III. Purity Laws

Even deeper than the impact of the Sabbath laws was the effect on daily life of the extensive regulations concerned with cleanness and uncleanness.[63] A great number of detailed ordinances on these points appear already in the Bible (Lev. 11:15, Num. 5:1–4 and especially Num. 19), which declares as unclean and causing uncleanness certain sexual matters, as well as certain symptoms in persons and objects included under the general heading of leprosy, and finally the corpses of both men and animals. But it also provides instruction on the removal of uncleanness by means of sacrifice or ablutions which vary

62. *Ant.* xiv 10, 11–14 (223–32); 10, 16 (234); 10, 18–19 (236–40). Under the Ptolemies the Jews were still liable for military service, *Ant.* xii 1, 1 (8); 2, 4 (34); Aristeas (ed. Wendland, 36–7); they served also under the Seleucids, 1 Mac. 10: 36–7; 11:44; 13:40, *Ant.* xiii 8, 411 (249). Cf. also *Ant.* xi 8, 5 (339); xiv 8, 1 (128); *B.J.* i 9, 3 (187); *Ant.* xvii 2, 1–3 (23–31). Cf. J. Juster, *Les Juifs dans l'emprie romain* II (1914), pp. 255–79.

63. Cf. 'Clean and Unclean', EB, I pp. 836–48. 'Uncleanness' HDB IV, pp. 825–34; IDB I, pp. 641–8; W. Brandt, *Die jüdische Reinheitslehre und ihre Beschreibung in der Evangelien* (1910); J. Neusner, 'First cleanse the Inside', NTSt 22 (1976), pp. 486–95. For a correct insight into the meaning of cleanness and uncleanness and the importance attached to them by post-biblical Judaism, it has to be borne in mind that in late biblical legislation, that of the priestly school, the context of purity and impurity was mainly cultic. To enter the Temple, perform acts of worship and partake of a sacrificial meal, the Jew had to be in a state of cleanness. If not, he was excluded from the Sanctuary and its activities. The various religious parties which came into being between the Maccabaean revolt and the first war against Rome adopted their own particular stand on this point. The Sadducees no doubt carried on the biblical tradition which perfectly suited their interests. The Essenes transferred to their community, considered temporarily at least as the one valid Temple, the prerogatives of the Jerusalem Sanctuary. The Christians likewise recognized their own fellowship as a new Sanctuary requiring a special form of spiritual purity. As for the Pharisees, and rabbinic Judaism in their wake, their intention was to elevate their own homes to the dignity of a sanctuary. They consequently centred the laws of purity on the table, with the idea of eating their everyday meals in the same state of purity as that required of the priests in the Temple. This undoubtedly carried with it the risk that instead of achieving the ideal of 'a kingdom of priests and a holy people', the ordinary Jew would confuse the means with the end, and the learned scholar overlook the larger spiritual issues because of his preoccupation with legal minutiae. Nevertheless, the fundamental inspiration of Pharisaism cannot be perceived without a sympathetic understanding of its central outlook. For a full discussion of the problem see J. Neusner, *The Idea of Purity*, pp. 32–71 and especially *idem*, *History of the Mishnaic Law of Purities* I–XXII (1974–77).

according to the nature and degree of the uncleanness. In the Mishnah, all twelve tractates of Seder Tohoroth are devoted to the further development of these regulations. The basis of the discussions is the enumeration given at the beginning of Kelim (1:1–4) of the main kinds of impurity (the 'fathers of uncleanness', אבות הטמאות), themselves mostly derived from scriptural commandments (Lev. 11–15; Num. 19). Each is subjected to questioning concerning the circumstances in which it may be contracted, how and to what extent it may be transmitted to others, the utensils and objects capable and incapable of becoming unclean, and finally, the means and rituals required for purification. The following outline of the laws relating to utensils liable to contract and transmit uncleanness, and to those unable to do so, will provide some idea of the problems involved. The biblical sources are Num. 19:14–15 and 31:20–4. One question concerns the material out of which the utensils are made; another relates to their shape (whether hollow or flat).

In respect of hollow earthenware vessels it was decided that their (inner) airspace contracts and transmits uncleanness, and also the hollow of the base, but not their outer surface. They may be purified only by being broken.[64] But what is to be understood by 'broken'? A fragment still counts as a vessel (and therefore capable of contracting uncleanness) 'if as much remains of one (originally) containing a *log* that it can hold enough to anoint the little toe (of a day-old child), and of a vessel containing from one *log* to one *seah*, room for a quarter-*log*; from one *seah* to two *seahs*, room for a half-*log*; and of from two or three *seahs* to five, room for one *log*.'[65] But whilst hollow earthenware vessels may contract uncleanness from the inside but not the outside, the following were judged impervious to uncleanness altogether: a flat tray without a rim, an open coal shovel, a perforated grid-iron for corn, brick conduits whether or not they are curved and hollowed, etc.[66] Liable to contract impurity, by contrast, are a tray with a rim, an unbroken coal shovel, a tray full of dishes, an earthenware spice-box, an ink-stand with several containers.[67] Utensils of wood, leather, bone and glass contract no uncleanness if they are flat; but if they are of any depth, they do so not only in their air-space, like those of earthenware, but also on their outer surface. They become clean when broken, but if other vessels are made from the pieces, they become unclean once more.[68] When are they considered broken?

64. mKel. 2:1. Cf. Neusner, *Purities* I, pp. 46–55.
65. mKel. 2:2. Cf. Neusner, *ibid.* pp. 55–62.
66. mKel. 2:3. Cf. Neusner, *ibid.* pp. 62–7.
67. mKel. 2:7. Cf. Neusner, *ibid.* pp. 73–5.
68. mKel. 2:1. Cf. Neusner, *ibid.* pp. 46–8; II, pp. 50–5.

'In all household utensils the measure (of a hole affecting purity) is the pomegranate. R. Eliezer says: The measure depends on the size of the vessel.'[69]

'By pomegranates is to be understood: of such a kind that three sit side by side. The pomegranate defined as a measure is one that is not too large, but of medium size.'[70]

'If a chest, a box or a cupboard has lost a foot, then even if they can still contain something, they are pure. R. Yose holds that all those which can admit the measure, even though not in the right position, are susceptible to uncleanness.'[71]

To the decrees concerning uncleanness must be added others relating to the removal of impurity by sacrifice and ablutions. On the latter subject the principal issue was to determine what sort of water was needed for sprinkling over the hands, for washing utensils and for the purificatory bath. Six types of water-supply are distinguished in the Mishnah. (1) A pond, and water in ditches, cisterns or pits, and also mountain water that no longer flows, and collected water amounting to less than forty *seahs*. All this, if it has not been defiled, is suitable for (the preparation of) *ḥallah*[72] and for ritual hand-washing. (2) Flowing mountain water. This may be used for the heave-offering (*terumah*) and for hand-washing. (3) Collected water containing forty *seahs*. In this people can immerse themselves (a purificatory bath) and their utensils. (4) A spring with little water, into which more drawn water has been poured. It is similar to the previous type in that in the place where it is collected (i.e. without flowing) it cleanses as a purificatory bath, and similar to pure spring water in that it cleanses vessels even if the water is scarce. (5) 'Smitten' water, i.e. water arising from mineral or warm springs. This purifies only while flowing. (6) Pure spring water. This serves as a purificatory bath for those with running sores, to sprinkle lepers, and is fit to be mixed with the ashes of the sin-offering.'[73]

These general maxims form the basis for further casuistic legislation. Discussion turns on the conditions and requirements rendering the 'collected water' mentioned in (3)—i.e. such rain, spring or river water as is not drawn but conducted directly through gutters or pipes into a container—fit for bathing or for cleansing utensils. The chief concern

69. mKel. 17:1. Cf. Neusner, *Purities* II, pp. 87–9, giving the various interpretations.

70. mKel. 17:4–5. Cf. Neusner, *ibid.* pp. 95–9.

71. mKel. 18:3. Cf. Neusner, *ibid.* pp. 126–8.

72. The dough for the heave-offering which is to be separated during the baking.

73. mMikw. 1:1–8. For the brief Qumran laws see CD 10:10–13. Cf. Vermes, *DSS*, pp. 179–80, 192.

here is that no 'drawn water' should be included in it. The following examples will serve as an illustration.

'R. Eliezer says: A quarter-*log* of drawn water in the beginning renders the water which afterwards falls into it unfit for a purificatory bath; but three *logs*, when water was there already. The sages say: in the beginning, as well as with the supplement of three *logs*.'[74]

'If a man places vessels under the water-spout (running into the bath), they render the bath unfit (because it then counts as drawn water). According to the school of Shammai, it is one and the same whether they have been placed there or forgotten; according to the school of Hillel, if they have merely been forgotten they do not make it unfit.'[75]

'If drawn water has mingled with rain-water in the courtyard, or in a hollow, or on the steps of the bath pit, then the bath, if the greater part of it is fit, is fit; if the greater part is unfit, or both are equal, it is unfit. But this only if they have mingled before reaching the pool. If each flows into the bath, then if it is known for certain that forty *seahs* of fit water had entered before three *logs* of drawn water fell into it, it is fit, otherwise it is not.'[76]

It is disputed also whether snow, hail, frost, ice and the like are suitable for filling a bath.[77]

The regulations concerning the washing of hands, or more precisely the pouring of water over the hands, are also detailed. In particular, water is always to be poured over the hands before eating (immersion being necessary only in the case of sacred meals, i.e. sacrificial food). It is also debated which vessels are to be used for the pouring, which kind of water is suitable, who should pour, and how much of the hands should be covered with water.[78]

The Gospel references to cups, pots and dishes (Mt. 15:2; Mk. 7:2–5; Mt. 23:25–6; Lk. 11:38–9) have to be set against the Mishnah ordinances to become fully intelligible.[79]

74. mMikw. 2:4.

75. mMikw. 4:1.

76. mMikw. 4:4. For the *mikveh* discovered at Masada, see Y. Yadin, Enc. Jud. 11, col. 1089; *Masada* (1966), pp. 164–8 with illustrations. For the two baths identified in the Qumran ruins, see R. de Vaux, *Archaeology and the Dead Sea Scrolls* (1973), pp. 9–10, 131–2.

77. mMikw. 7:1.

78. mBer. 8:2–4; mHag. 2:5–6; mEdu. 3:2; mYad. 1:1–5; 2:3. For the Essene ritual baths before meals, see below, p. 569.

79. Cf. Str.-B. I, pp. 695–704; 934–6; II, pp. 13–14, 188; A. Finkel, *The Pharisees and the Teacher of Nazareth* ([2]1974), pp. 140–1; J. Neusner, *The Idea of Purity*, pp. 61–3; NTSt 22 (1976), pp. 486–95.

IV. Ritualism

Highly characteristic of this powerful trend towards ritualism are also the three symbols intended to remind every observant Jew of his duties to God: the *ẓiẓith*, the *mezuzah* and the *tefillin*. (1) The *ẓiẓith* (ציצית, plur. ציציות; κράσπεδα in LXX and the New Testament, כרוספדין in Targum Onkelos, τὸ κόκκινον ῥάμμα in Justin Martyr, and simply ציצין or ציצייתא in the Palestinian Targums)[80] are the tassels or fringes of blue or white wool prescribed by Num. 15:37 ff. and Dt. 22:12 to be worn by every Israelite at the four corners of his garment. As the passage from Numbers specifies, the purpose of the tassel is that you may look on it, and remember all the commandments of the Lord, and do them.'[81] (2) The *mezuzah* (מזוזה) is an oblong box fixed to the right-hand door-post of the house and each room, containing a little scroll of parchment on which are written (according to Dt. 6:9 and 11:20) in twenty-two lines the two sections of Dt. 6:4–9 and 11:13–21.[82] It is

80. Justin, *Dial. c. Tryph.* 46–7 (ed. Otto II, p. 154). The editions have τὸ κόκκινον βάμμα (dye) but this does not make sense. For the correct reading of ῥάμμα (threads), see Hesychius, *Lexicon*, s.v. κράσπεδα· τὰ ἐν τῷ ἄκρῳ τοῦ ἱματίου κεκλωσμένα ῥάμματα καὶ τὸ ἄκρον αὐτοῦ.

81. Cf. Aristeas (ed. Wendland, 158); Mt. 9:20; 14:36; 23:5; Mk. 6:56; Lk. 8:44. Cf. LXX and Targums on Num. 15:38 and Dt. 22:12. mM.K. 3:4; mEdu. 4:10; mMen. 3:7; 4:1. For the rabbinic rules, see M. Higger, *Seven Minor Tractates* (*Ẓiẓith*) (1930) and A. Cohen (ed.), *The Minor Tractates of the Talmud* II (1965), pp. 655–7. Cf. Str.-B. IV/1, pp. 277–92; IBD II, pp. 325–6; TDNT *s.v.* κράσπεδον; Enc. Jud. 16, cols. 1187–8. The colour of the *zizith* is now white, but originally it was hyacinth blue (for details, see Enc. Jud. 15, cols. 913–14 s.v. *Tekhelet*). mMen. 4:1 already assumes that both colours are allowed. Concerning a dispute between Moses and Korah, whether the *ẓiẓith* should be white with an interwoven filament of blue, or whether it should be blue altogether, see Ps.-Jon. on Num. 16:2, and G. Vermes, *PBJS*, pp. 172–3. They are no longer worn, as the Pentateuch directs, and as was still customary at the time of Jesus, on the over-garment (טלית, ἱμάτιον), but on the two square woollen shawls, one of which is always worn on the body, while the other is thrown over the head only during prayer. These shawls are of course also called *tallith*, the one worn on the body being the טלית קטן or ארבע כנפות, and the other the טלית גדול . Cf. JE II, pp. 75–6; Enc. Jud. 15, cols. 743–5.

82. Cf. Aristeas (ed. Wendland, 158); Josephus, *Ant.* iv 8, 13 (213); mBer. 3:3; mShab. 8:3; mMeg. 1:8; mM.K. 3:4; mGit. 4:6; mMen. 3:7; mKel. 16:7; 17:6. For the rabbinic rules, see Higger, *op. cit.* (in n. 81 above) *Mezuzah* and *Minor Tractates of the Talmud* II, pp. 659–63; Enc. Jud. 11, cols. 1474–7. In Qumran Cave 8, 42 fragmentary lines of Dt. 10:12–11:21, originally probably belonging to a pre-rabbinic *mezuzah*, have been found. The *Shema'* is missing. Cf. M. Baillet, DJD III (1962), pp. 158–61 and Pl. XXXIV. Fragments belonging to seven *mezuzoth* from Cave 4 have been published by J. T. Milik in DJD VI (1977), nos. 149–55. *Mezuzah* A (no. 149) contains the Decalogue (Ex. 20:7–12/Dt. 5:11–16); *mezuzah* B (no. 150) Dt. 6:5–6; 10:14–11:2; *mezuzah* C (no. 151) Dt. 5:27–6:9; 10:12–20; *mezuzah* D (no. 152), Dt. 6:5–7; *mezuzah* E (no. 153), Dt. 11:17–18; *mezuzah* F (no. 154), Ex. 13:1–4 and *mezuzah* G (no. 155), Ex. 13:11–16.

meant not only to turn the thoughts in thanksgiving to God, but is also believed to prevent evil spirits from entering.[83] (3) The *tefillin* or prayer-straps which every male Jew is required to put on at morning prayer (except on the Sabbath and holy days), are known in the Bible as טוטפרת (bracelets and head-bands), in rabbinic literature as תפלין (from תפלה, prayer), and in the New Testament as φυλακτήρια (prophylactery, amulet). Their use is based on Ex. 13:9, 16 and Dt. 6:8; 11:18. There are two *tefillin*: (a) the תפלה של יד (hand *tefillah*)[84] or תפלה של זרוע (arm *tefillah*),[85] a small cup-shaped hollow case made of parchment, containing a small parchment scroll on which are written Ex. 13:1–10; 11–16 and Dt. 6:4–9; 11:13–21, and fastened to the left upper arm by means of a strap; (b) the תפלה של ראש (head *tefillah*), with a similar case, but differing from the former in that it is divided into four compartments containing the biblical passages written on four parchment scrolls,[86] attached by a strap to the middle of the forehead just below the hairline.[87] The Greek designation of *tefillin* as φυλακτήρια (amulets) is evidence that their significance was seen chiefly to lie in their ability to drive away evil spirits during prayer.[88]

Of these three symbolic reminders, the *zizith* is definitely based on the Pentateuch but this is probably true of the other two also. The

83. Enc. Jud. 11, col. 1476.

84. Cf. mMen. 4:1.

85. Cf. mMikw. 10:3.

86. Cf. Barthélemy-J. T. Milik, DJD I (1955), pp. 72–8 and Pl. XIV; K. G. Kuhn, *Phylakterien aus Höhle 4 von Qumran* (1957); M. Baillet, DJD III (1962), pp. 149–57; J. T. Milik, 'Fragments . . . d'un phylactère dans la grotte 4 de Qumrân', RB 73 (1966), pp. 94–106; Y. Yadin, *Tefillin from Qumran* (1969); J. T. Milik, DJD VI (1977), nos. 128–48, has published the remains of twenty-one *tephillin* from Cave 4. They mostly contain the deuteronomic version of the Ten Commandments. The maximum extent of the Qumran excerpts are: Ex. 12:43–13:16; Dt. 5:1–6:9 10:12–11:21. There are, however, four phylacteries (C–F, nos. 130–3) representing the choice of texts of the rabbinic tradition. On the exclusion of the Decalogue from the *tefillin* due to controversies with *minim*, cf. A. M. Habermann, על התפילין בימי קדם, Eretz Israel 3 (1954), pp. 174–7; G. Vermes, 'Pre-Mishnaic Jewish Worship and the Phylacteries from the Dead Sea', VT 9 (1959), pp. 65–72; 'The Decalogue and the Minim', *In Memoriam Paul Kahle* (1968), pp. 252–40 (=*PBJS*, pp. 169–77).

87. Aristeas (ed. Wendland, 159); Mt. 23:5; *Ant.* iv, 8, 13 (213); Justin, *Dial. c. Tryph.* ch. 46 f. (ed. Otto 11, p. 154). Origen on Mt. 23:5 (ed. Lommatzsch IV, p. 201); mBer. 3:1, 3; mShab. 6:2; 8:3; 16:1; mErub. 10:1–2; mShek. 3:2; mMeg. 1:8; m.M.K. 3:4; mNed. 2:2; mGit. 4:6; mSanh. 11:3; mSheb. 3:8, 11; mMen. 3:7; 4:1; mArak. 6:3–4; mKel. 16:7; 18:8; 23:1; mMikw. 10:2–4; mYad. 3:3. Cf. M. Higger, *op. cit.* [in n. 81 above] (*Teflllin*), and *Minor Tractates of the Talmud* II, pp. 647–54; Str.-B. IV/1, pp. 250–76. Cf. L. Blau, JE X, pp. 21–8; IDB III, pp. 808–9; Enc. Jud. 15, cols. 898–904.

88. See M. L. Rodkinson, *History of Amulets, Charms and Talismans* (1893); L. Blau, *Altjüdisches Zauberwesen* (1898), p. 152; JE X, p. 27; T. Reik, *Pagan Rites in Judaism* (1964), pp. 103–52; E. E. Urbach, *The Sages*, pp. 126–9.

importance attached to them, however, and the care with which everything is ordered down to the smallest detail (the number of threads and knots required in the *ẓiẓith*, the method of writing out the texts for the *mezuzah* and the *tefillin*, etc.), was characteristic of post-biblical Judaism. Reverence for the *tefillin* was almost as great as that shown for the Bible itself, and like the latter, they were to be rescued in the event of a fire on the Sabbath.[89] Even the straps were said to render the hands unclean,[90] and the case containing the *tefillin* had the same status as those holding the Scriptural scrolls.[91]

A preoccupation with ritual is apparent in the Mishnaic treatment of formal prayer. Whether its rubrics were already as specific and universally binding in the age of Jesus is uncertain, but it may safely be assumed that at least some of them were in use before the final system was formulated at Yavneh.[92]

The *Shema'*, which is not so much a prayer as a confession of faith in God, and the *Shemoneh 'Esreh*, the Prayer *par excellence*, both of them recited at morning and in the evening (for particulars, see § 27, Appendix), are regulated down to the smallest particulars in the rabbinic sources. In order to apply definitely to the age of Jesus, the present remarks are confined to the *Shema'*, since it is possible that the Eighteen Benedictions did not reach their final form until the end of the first century.[93] Firstly the time-limits are fixed within which the evening and morning *Shema'* are to be said. According to the Mishnah, the moment to begin the evening *Shema'* is 'when the priests re-enter to partake of their heave-offering'; the moment to end is, according to R. Eliezer ben Hyrcanus, at the end of the first night-watch, according to common opinion, midnight, and according to Rabban Gamaliel, the first light of dawn.[94] The morning *Shema'* may be recited 'as soon as blue can be distinguished from white. R. Eliezer says, blue from green'. It should end when 'the sun shines forth, R. Joshua says, at the third hour (9 a.m.), for such is the custom of the children of princes, to rise only at the third hour.'[95] As the major part of the *Shema'* consists of biblical texts, the question arose whether a person had fulfilled his

89. mShab. 16:1.
90. mYad. 3:3.
91. mShab. 16:1.
92. The Yavnean origin of the systematic rabbinic legislation is argued in detail in J. Neusner, *Pharisees* I–III. In regard to prayers, it is especially important to remember that the cessation of Temple worship invested synagogal and private prayer with a greater ritual significance. On the cultic recitation of the *Shema'* in the Temple, see mTam. 5:1.
93. Cf. Str.-B. IV/1, pp. 189–207; Enc. Jud. 14, cols. 1370–4.
94. mBer. 1:1. Cf. J. Neusner, *Eliezer ben Hyrcanus* I (1973), pp. 18–22.
95. mBer. 1:2. Cf. Neusner, *ibid.*

Shema' duty who had been reading the relevant passages at the time of the *Shema'* prayer. The answer given is: If he did so with intention (אם כון לבו), he fulfilled the duty; otherwise not.[96] Again, the Mishnah considers the circumstances in which a person reciting the *Shema'* in the street should greet passers-by or return greetings. Three cases are taken into consideration: (1) greetings inspired by fear; (2) greetings inspired by respect; (3) greetings to all and sundry. R. Meir permitted greetings of respect (מפני הכבוד), and replies to greetings, to be made at the natural breaks in the *Shema'*; but in the middle, only greetings and replies to greetings inspired by fear (מפני יראה). R. Judah ben Elai went a step further and allowed a return of respectful greetings in the middle of the *Shema'*, and in the natural breaks, a return of greetings to all and sundry.[97] By contrast, it was pointed out in connection with the Eighteen Benedictions that the ancient *ḥasidim* refused to interrupt their prayers to return even the king's greetings (or even if they discovered a snake wound round their leg).[98]

One beautiful custom was never to eat or drink without giving thanks to God (in accordance with the precept Dt. 8:10). *Berakhoth* were recited by everyone, including women, children and slaves, both before and after meals.[99] But here too the sages were concerned that the correct prayer should be uttered at the correct time and in the correct manner.[100]

> 'If the blessing has been said over the wine before the meal, the wine after the meal is exempt. If the blessing has been said over the lesser dishes before the meal, the lesser dishes after the meal are exempt. If the blessing is said over the bread, the lesser dishes are exempt.'[101]

> 'If salted food is brought first, and bread afterwards, the blessing is said over the salted food and the bread is exempt.'[102]

96. mBer. 2:1.
97. mBer. 2:1–2.
98. mBer. 5:1. Cf. G. Vermes, 'Hanina ben Dosa', JJS 23 (1972), pp. 34–6 (=*PBJS*, pp. 183–6).
99. mBer. 3:3–4. On the blessing of the bread and new wine at Qumran, see 1QS 6:4–5; 1QSa 2:17–21. In the first instance, grace is recited by the presiding priest; in the second, by the Priest-Messiah followed by the whole congregation. Cf. also Sibyl. 4:25–6. Jesus also always said grace (Mt. 14:19; 15:36; 26:26 and par.) and Christians did so from the beginning (Rom. 14:6; 1 Cor. 10:30; 1 Tim. 4:4). Cf. Str.-B. IV/2, pp. 627–36; J. Heinemann, 'Birkhath ha-Zimmun and Havurah-Meals', JJS 13 (1962), pp. 23–9; L. Finkelstein, *Pharisaism in the Making* (1972), pp. 333–84 ['The Birkat ha-Mazon' (JQR 19 (1929), pp. 211–62)]; Enc. Jud. 7, cols. 838–41; J. Heinemann, *Prayer in the Talmud* (1977), pp. 115–22.
100. mBer. 6:1–3.
101. mBer. 6:5.
102. mBer. 6:7.

'If a man has eaten grapes, figs and pomegranates, he says three blessings afterwards. This is the opinion of Rabban Gamaliel. The sages say: One blessing, three-fold in content.'[103]

'How much food entitles a man to recite the common grace? (Food) the size of an olive. R. Judah says: Of an egg.'[104]

'If a man has eaten and has forgotten to say grace, he must, according to the school of Shammai, return to his place and say the blessing. The school of Hillel permits him to say the blessing wherever he remembers it. Until when is a man obliged to say the blessing? Until the food is digested in the stomach.'[105]

It cannot be denied that the evidence in general points to a great emphasis on external observance in prayer as elsewhere. Yet Jesus was not alone in criticizing the abuses to which it tended to lead.[106] For R. Eliezer ben Hyrcanus, himself an important contributor to the body of rites and rituals, is said to have declared:

'Whoever makes of his prayer a fixed form, his prayer is no supplication.'[107]

One final aspect of post-biblical religious life remains to be considered, that of fasting.[108] That the Pharisees fasted frequently and valued this religious practice is mentioned in the New Testament (cf. Mt. 9:14; Mk. 2:18; Lk. 5:33). In fact, there were few public fasts fixed by the calendar. But from time to time, extraordinary fast-days were added because of some general calamity, such as the failure of rain in the autumn. These fast-days were always deferred to the second and the fifth days of the week (Monday and Thursday), and in such a way that they began on the second day; thus a three-day fast would fall on a Monday, Thursday and the following Monday.[109] But in addition to

103. mBer. 6:8.

104. mBer. 7:2.

105. mBer. 8:7.

106. Cf. Mt. 6:5; 15:7–8; Mk. 7:6; 12:40; Lk. 20:47.

107. mBer. 4:4. Cf. mAb. 2:13. See J. Neusner, *Eliezer ben Hyrcanus* I (1973), pp. 23, 26; II, pp. 352, 356.

108. Cf. JE V, pp. 247–9; Enc. Jud. 6, cols. 1189–96. See also Str.-B. IV, pp. 77–114; S. Lowy, 'The Motivation of Fasting in Talmudic Literature', JJS 9 (1958), pp. 19–38; E. E. Urbach, *Sefer Yovel Y. Baer* (1960), pp. 148–68; S. Safrai, JPFC II, pp. 814–16; H. A. Brongers, Oudtest. Stud. 20 (1977), pp. 1–21.

109. mTaan. 2:9. Cf. *Didache* 8:1: *Αἱ δὲ νηστεῖαι ὑμῶν μὴ ἔστωσαν μετὰ τῶν ὑποκριτῶν· νηστεύουσι γὰρ δευτέρᾳ σαββάτων καὶ πέμπτῃ· ὑμεῖς δὲ νηστεύσατε τετράδα καὶ παρασκευήν*. Cf. *Const. apost.* vii 23; Epiphanius, *Pan.* 16, 1: *ἐνήστευον δὶς τοῦ σαββάτου, δευτέραν καὶ πέμπτην*. Fasting was forbidden not only on the Sabbath but also on the day preceding it (Judith 8:6). On the duty of eating well on the Sabbath, see above, p. 470, n. 30. On prayers for fast-days, see I. Lévi, REJ 47 (1903), pp. 161–7; I. Elbogen, *Gottesdienst*, pp. 235–9.

these general fasts, there was also a great deal of voluntary individual fasting; some strict ascetics, for instance, fasted on Monday and Thursday all the year through.[110]

Fasts varied in their strictness. On less important occasions, people continued to wash and anoint themselves. In severer fasts, they did neither. And during fasts intended to be exceptionally rigorous, they withheld from all pleasurable activities, even the exchange of greetings. The longer the rains delayed in the autumn, the sharper was the fast. If the 17th of Marḥeshvan came without rain having fallen, some began to hold fasts of three days. If the new moon of Kislev came without rain having fallen, three days of general fasting was ordered. At this stage, some food and drink might be taken after nightfall; people could wash and anoint themselves, wear sandals and have sexual intercourse. If after this still no rain fell, three more fast-days were decreed, entailing abstinence from food after nightfall, and also from washing and anointing, work and sexual intercourse. If rain was further delayed, seven general fast-days followed; the *shofar* was blown and the shops were closed for part of the day. If the drought continued, it was laid down that 'they must give themselves but little to business, building or planting, betrothals or marriages or mutual greetings, as becomes men who suffer God's displeasure'.[111]

V. Social Changes and the Law

Due to changes in social, political, economic and religious circumstances, a religion such as post-biblical Judaism, founded on a canonical corpus of sacred writings intended to offer guidance in all of life's aspects, was sooner or later bound to encounter issues unforeseen in biblical legislation or rules which had become obsolete. Whilst the canon of Scripture remained open, dilemmas of this kind could be resolved by new enactments. But once it was closed, legislation had to be replaced by interpretation. Often the required adaptation was straightforward. But again and again, the commentator was obliged to depart in some secondary area from the original purpose of a commandment so that his contemporaries could remain faithful to the essence of the law and the ordinary conduct of their lives still be possible. The legal fiction known as *'erub* provides an excellent illustration of this.

110. Lk. 18:12; cf. bTaan. 12a: 'One who takes it on himself to fast on the second, the fifth and the second day throughout the whole year': יחיד שקיבל עליו שני וחמישי ושני של כל שנה. There is no reference to special fasting in the Qumran writings. For the ascetic customs of the Therapeutae, see below, p. 592.

111. mTaan. 1:4–7; cf. Mt. 6:16–18. See also Dan. 10:3; mYom. 8:1. Cf. Str.-B. IV/1, pp. 77–114. On Jewish views on the value of fasting, see L. Löw, *Gesammelte Schriften* I (1889), pp. 107 ff.; cf. also Lowy, *art. cit.* in n. 108, above.

It was, as has been seen earlier, forbidden to carry anything on the Sabbath from one domain (רשות) to another. This would have had the inconvenient effect of preventing almost all freedom of movement on the Sabbath since the term רשות (or more precisely, רשות היחיד, the private domain) is a narrow one. The concept of the 'domain' was therefore extended. The first measure adopted to achieve this end was the so-called mingling of the courtyards (ערוב חצרות), i.e., the combination of several houses in a courtyard (each of which formed a רשות היחיד) into a single רשות היחיד. Such a combination was effected by all the inhabitants depositing food in a particular place before the Sabbath or feast-day, to demonstrate that they regarded the whole courtyard with all its houses as one whole. By doing so, they were permitted to carry objects in and out of this domain on a holy day.[112] The nature and amount of the food constituting the *'erub* is described at great length in the Mishnah.[113]

However, not much was gained by this mingling of the courtyards. Another way was therefore found of supplementing it, namely the 'mingling of the entrance'(ערוב מבוי), i.e., the closing of a narrow lane, or a space surrounded on three sides, by means of a beam, a wire or a string, so that both became רשות היחיד.[114]

It will also be recalled, that it was forbidden to walk more than two thousand cubits on the Sabbath. This rule too was made less onerous by a similar means, the 'mingling of the boundaries' (ערוב תחומין). Whoever, that is to say, wished to travel further than two thousand cubits, deposited food for two meals somewhere within the boundary (towards its end). He thereby declared that that would be his place of residence and was able to proceed another two thousand cubits beyond it.[115]

In the more serious question of divorce, the law promulgated in Deut. 24:1–4—that a man may be rid of his wife if he finds something shameful (ערות דבר) in her—was again interpreted leniently by some of the rabbis. The more rigorous house of Shammai expounded the vague ערות דבר as דבר ערוה (literally a 'thing of nakedness'), i.e., some form of immorality.[116] But the general understanding was that any kind of marriage breakdown qualified a husband to divorce his wife.[117] (There was, and still is, no question in Jewish law of a woman divorcing her husband). The school of Hillel even went so far as to define a spoiled

112. Cf. JE V, pp. 203–4; Moore, *Judaism* II, pp. 31–3; Enc. Jud. 6, cols. 849–50.

113. mErub. 6–7.

114. mErub. 1:1–10; 7:6–11.

115. mErub. 3–4, 8.

116. mGit. 9:10; cf. Mt. 19:3.

117. Cf. Josephus, *Ant.* iv 8, 23 (253); *Vita* 76 (426) concerning his own divorce.

dinner as ערות דבר (i.e. improper). And R. Akiba taught that a man was justified in putting away his wife if he had found another prettier woman.[118] In fact, divorce was relatively easy in those days and the Pharisees and rabbis intended to keep it so.[119]

In regard to filial obligations, the New Testament (Mk. 7:11–12; Mt. 15:5)[120] accuses the Pharisees of giving priority over the commandment, 'Honour your father and your mother', to the religious obligation to consecrate certain things to God as *ḳorban* (offering). Conflict between the duties owed to religion and to parents without doubt exercised the minds of the rabbis and led sometimes to the former taking precedence over the latter. Yet it is not without interest that in this specific context of sacred vows, the strict Qumran ruling, 'And no man shall consecrate the food of his house[121] to God',[122] echoes the New Testament teaching. Furthermore, the same point of view, given in the name of R. Eliezer ben Hyrcanus, is propagated in the Mishnah itself as being the common opinion, namely that 'a vow may be annulled on account of the honour due to father and mother'.[123]

The religious life of Palestinian Judaism outlined in these pages aimed at the sanctification of the individual and the nation. In practice, however, the great accumulation of commandments and obligations could lead also to pettiness, formalism, and an emphasis on outward observance rather than true integrity. Even though rhetorically exaggerated and representing the standpoint of a Galilean charismatic,[124] a number of the sayings attributed to Jesus by Matthew and Luke undoubtedly expose the excesses and abuses to which a legally motivated religion tended to lead: to straining the gnat and swallowing the camel (Mt. 23:24); to cleansing the outside but not the inside of a cup (Mt. 23:25; Lk. 11:19); to whitewashing the sepulchre (Mt. 23:27–8; Lk. 11:11). A similar criticism from a Hellenistic-Jewish point of view led Paul to write, 'They have a zeal for God, but it is not enlightened' (Rom. 10:2).

118. mGit. 9:10.

119. Cf. Vermes, *PBJS*, pp. 65–7; J. A. Fitzmyer, Theol. Studies 37 (1976), pp. 197–226; Eretz-Israel 14 (1978), pp. 103*–10*.

120. For Mishnaic parallels, see Str.-B. I, pp. 711–17.

121. Reading [בי]תו.

122. CD 16:14–15.

123. mNed. 9:1. For an Aramaic *ḳorban* inscription, see J. T. Milik, SBFLA (1956–7), pp. 232–9; J. A. Fitzmyer, 'The Aramaic Qorbān Inscription from Jebel Hallet eṭ-Ṭûri and Mk 7:11/Mt. 15:5', JBL 78 (1959), pp. 60–5 (=*Essays on the Semitic Background of the New Testament* (1971), pp. 93–100). For further bibliography, see *ibid.*, p. 100, n. 15.

124. On the theory of a clash between Judaean and Galilean religious outlook, and between charismatic Judaism and the Pharisees, see G. Vermes, *Jesus the Jew*, pp. 54–7, 80–2; cf. also D. Flusser, *Jesus* (1969), p. 56.

At the same time, it should not be forgotten that Jewish religious life in the age of Jesus, like all organized religion throughout the centuries, was compounded of light as well as of darkness, and that if its rites and observances were often matters of social conformity, they were also animated, to varying degrees, by inward spirituality. Indeed, one of the remarkable phenomena of that time is that the very same sages who, as legal experts, were responsible for many hair-splitting judgements and decisions on subjects which to an outside observer of today may seem trivial, were also capable of profound spiritual counsel. 'Judge not your fellow until you are in his place', said Hillel.[125] R. Yose the Priest: 'Let your fellow's property be as dear to you as your own . . . and do all your deeds for the sake of Heaven.'[126] R. Eliezer ben Hyrcanus taught: 'Let the honour of your fellow be as dear to you as your own.'[127] 'And when you pray, know before whom you stand; for through this you will gain the life of the world to come.'[128] He also commented: 'He who has something to eat today and says, What shall I eat tomorrow, lo, such is one of those of little faith, as it is written, "A day's portion every day" (Exod. 16:4). He who created the day, created its sustenance.'[129] And R. Judah ben Tema said: 'Be strong as a leopard, light as an eagle, quick as a gazelle, brave as a lion, to do the will of your Father in heaven'.[130]

125. mAb. 2:4.
126. mAb. 2:12.
127. mAb. 2:10.
128. bBer. 28b.
129. Mekh. de-R. Simeon on Exod. 16:4 (ed. Epstein-Melamed, p. 106).
130. mAb. 5:20. Str.-B. offers a substantial amount of rabbinic parallels to the sayings of Jesus. They should, however, be treated as raw material requiring a historico-critical evaluation before they can be used for comparative purposes.

§ 29. MESSIANISM

Bibliography

Drummond, J., *The Jewish Messiah* (1877).

Weber, F., *System der altsynagogalen palästinischen Theologie aus Targum, Midrasch und Talmud dargestellt* (1880, 1897).

Edersheim, A., *The Life and Times of Jesus the Messiah* ([2]1884).

Hühn, E., *Die messianischen Weissagungen des israelitisch-jüdischen Volkes bis zu den Targumim* I (1899).

Baldensperger, B., *Die messianischen-apokalyptischen Hoffnungen des Judentums* ([3]1903).

Marmorstein, A., 'Les signes du Messie', REJ 51 (1906), pp. 176–86.

Greenstone, J. H., *The Messianic Idea in Jewish History* (1906).

Rabinsohn, M., *Le Messianisme dans le Talmud et les Midraschim* (1907).

Oesterley, W. O. E., *The Evolution of the Messianic Idea* (1908).

Lagrange, M.-J., *Le Messianisme chez les Juifs* (1909).

Humbert, P., *Le Messie dans le Targum des Prophètes* (1911).

Elbogen, I., 'Die messianische Idee in den altjüdischen Gebeten', *H. Cohen Festschrift* (1912), pp. 669–79.

Messel, N., *Der Menschensohn in den Bilderreden des Henoch* (1922).

König, E., *Die messianischen Weissagungen des Alten Testaments* (1923).

Dürr, L., *Ursprung und Ausbau der israelitisch-jüdischer Heilandserwartung* (1925).

Carlebach, J., 'Pessimismus und Messiashoffnung', Jeschurun 14 (1927), pp. 105–23.

Moore, G. F., *Judaism* II (1927), pp. 323–76.

Case, S. J., 'The Rise of Christian Messianism', *Studies in Early Christianity* (1928), pp. 313–32.

Str.-B. IV (1928): 29. Exkurs: 'Diese Welt, die Tage des Messias und die zukünftige Welt', pp. 799–1015.

Dennefeld, L., *Le Messianisme* (1929).

Gressmann, H., *Der Messias* (1929).

Godard, A., *Le Messianisme* (1929).

Stauffer, E., 'Die Messiasfrage im Judentum und Christentum', ZThK 12 (1931), pp. 165–91.

Jeremias, A., *Die biblische Erlösererwartung* (1931).

Marmorstein, A., 'The Age of R. Joḥanan and the Signs of the Messiah', Tarbiz 3 (1931–2), pp. 161–80 (Hebrew).

Guillaume, A., 'The Messiah in Judaism and Christianity', ET 43 (1931–2), pp. 406–11.

Sarachek, J., *The Doctrine of the Messiah in Mediaeval Jewish Literature* (1932).

Kroening, G., *The Messiah in the Old Testament* (1932).

Cooper, D. L., *The Messiah. His Nature and Person* (1933).

Frey, J. B., 'Le conflit entre le messianisme de Jésus et le messianisme des juifs de son temps', Biblica 14 (1933), pp. 133–49, 269–93.

Volz, P., *Die Eschatologie der jüdischen Gemeinde im neutestamentlichen Zeitalter* ([2]1934).

Brierre-Narbonne, J., *Les prophéties messianiques de l'Ancien Testament* (1933).
Exégèse talmudique des prophéties messianiques (1934).
Exégèse targumique des prophéties messianiques (1935).

Exégèse midrašique des prophéties messianiques (1935)
Exégèse apocryphe des prophéties messianiques (1936).
Exégèse zoharique des prophéties messianiques (1938).
Le Messie souffrant dans la littérature rabbinique (1940).

Buber, M., *Königtum Gottes* (²1936, ³1967). E.T. *Kingship of God* (1967).

Zobel, M., *Gottesgesalbter. Der Messias und die messianische Zeit in Talmud und Midrasch* (1938).

Jansen, H. L., *Die Henochgestalt: Eine vergleichende religionsgeschichtliche Untersuchung* (1939).

Vischer, W., *Das Christuszeugnis des Alten Testaments. Teil 2, Die Propheten. Hälfte 1. Die Frühen Propheten* (1942).

Sjöberg, E., *Der Menschensohn im äthiopischen Henochbuch* (1946).

Campbell, J. Y., 'The Origin and Meaning of the Term Son of Man', JThSt 48 (1947), pp. 147 ff.

Wischnitzer, R., *The Messianic Theme in the Paintings of the Dura Synagogue* (1948).

Bentzen, A., *King and Messiah* (1954).

Sjöberg, E., *Der verborgene Menschensohn in den Evangelien* (1955).

Roth, C., 'Messianic Symbols in Palestinian Archaeology', PEQ 87 (1955), pp. 151–64.

Klausner, J., *The Messianic Idea in Israel* (1956).

Ringgren, H., *The Messiah in the Old Testament.* [Studies in Biblical Theology, 18] (1956).

Mowinckel, S., *He that Cometh: The Messiah Concept in the Old Testament and Later Judaism* (1956).

Fohrer, G. (ed.), *Messiasfrage und Bibelverständnis* (1957).

Teeple, H. M., *The Mosaic Eschatological Prophet* [JBL Monograph 10] (1957).

Chevallier, M. A., *L'esprit du Messie dans le bas-judaïsme et le Nouveau Testament* (1958).

Hurwitz, S., *Die Gestalt des sterbenden Messias* (1958).

Hengel, M., *Die Zeloten* (1961, ²1976).

van der Woude, A. S., *Die messianischen Vorstellungen der Gemeinde von Qumran* (1962).

Massaux, E., *Le venue du Messie: Messianisme et eschatologie*, eds. E. Massaux, P. Grelot *et al.* [Recherches Bibliques VI] (1962).

Carmignac, J., *Christ and the Teacher of Righteousness* (1962).

Michel, O., Betz, O., 'Von Gott bezeugt', *Judentum-Urchristentun-Kirche, Festschrift J. Jeremias* (1964), pp. 3–23.

Grelot, P., 'Le Messie dans les apocryphes de l'Ancien Testament', *La venue du Messie*, eds. E. Massaux, *et al.* [Recherches Bibliques VI] (1962).

Black, M., *The Scrolls and Christian Origins* (1962), pp. 145–63.

Lohse, E., 'Der König aus Davidsgeschlecht: Bemerkungen zur messianischen Erwartung der Synagoge', *Abraham unser Vater: Festschrift Otto Michel* (1963), pp. 337–45.

Coppens, J., 'L'espérance messianique. Ses origines et son développement', RSR 37 (1963), pp. 113–49.

Jeremias, G., *Der Lehrer der Gerechtigkeit* (1963).

Hruby, K., 'Die rabbinische Exegese messianischer Schriftstellen', Judaica 21 (1965), pp. 100–22.

Hruby, K., 'Die Messiaserwartung in der talmudischen Zeit', Judaica 20 (1964), pp. 6–22.

Hruby, K., 'Anzeichen für das Kommen der messianischen Zeit', Judaica 20 (1964), pp. 73–90.

Tödt, H. E., *The Son of Man in the Synoptic Tradition* (1965).

Bousset, W., *Die Religion des Judentums im neutestamentlichen Zeitalter* ([4]1966), pp. 222–68.
Kramer, W., *Christ, Lord, Son of God* (1966).
Hruby, K., 'Messianisme et eschatologie dans la tradition rabbinique', Lex Orandi 40 (1967), pp. 43–63.
Borsch, F. H., *The Son of Man in Myth and History* (1967).
Higgins, A. J. B., 'Jewish Messianic Belief in Justin Martyr's "Dialogue with Tryphon" ', NT 9 (1967), pp. 298–305.
Werblowsky, R. J. Z., 'Messianism in Jewish History', Cahiers d'Histoire Mondiale 11, 1–2 (1968), pp. 30–45 [=*Jewish Society through the Ages*, ed. H. H. Ben Sasson and S. Ettinger (1971)].
Coppens, J., *Le Messianisme Royal* (1968).
Liver, J., משיח, Enẓ. Miḳra'it 5 (1968), pp. 507–26.
Grelot, P., 'Messias, Messiaserwartung', Sacramentum mundi 3 (1969), pp. 439–44, 4 (1969), pp. 14–16.
Rehm, M., *Der königliche Messias im Licht der Immanuel-Weissagungen des Buches Jesaja* (1968).
Scholem, G., *The Messianic Idea in Judaism, and other Essays on Jewish Spirituality* (1971).
Fitzmyer, J. A., *Essays in the Semitic Background of the New Testament* (1971), pp. 128–60.
Maier, J., *Geschichte der jüdischen Religion* (1972), pp. 178–82.
Vermes, G., *Jesus the Jew* (1973), pp. 129–59, 250–6.
Levey, S. H., *The Messiah: An Aramaic Interpretation—The Messianic Exegesis of the Targum* (1974).
Coppens, J., *Le messianisme et sa relève prophétique* (1974).
Urbach, Ephraim E., *The Sages: their Concepts and Beliefs* (1975), pp. 649–92, 990–1009.
Vermes, G., *The Dead Sea Scrolls in English* ([2]1975), pp. 47–51.
Vermes, G., *The Dead Sea Scrolls: Qumran in Perspective* (1977), pp. 184–6, 194–6.

See also the following dictionaries and encyclopaedias:

A. Gelin, art. 'Messianisme', DB Supp. V (1955), col. 1165–212.
L. Dennefeld, art. 'Messianisme', DThC X, 2 1929, col. 1511–26.
H. L. Ginsberg, D. Flusser *et al.*, art. 'Messiah', Enc. Jud., 11, cols 1407–27.
W. Grundmann, F. Hesse, M. de Jonge, A. S. van der Woude, *χρίω, χριστός*, etc., TDNT 9 (1974), pp. 493–580.
E. Rivkin, art. 'Messiah, Jewish', IDBS (1976), pp. 588–91.

Concerning the periodical literature since the discovery of the Qumran scrolls, see the bibliographies in RQ and Biblica. Cf. also B. Jongeling, *A Classified Bibliography of the Finds in the Desert of Judah* 1958–69 (1971), and J. A. Fitzmyer, *The Dead Sea Scrolls, Major Publications and Tools for Study* (1975), pp. 114–18.

The following list includes the more important articles:

Burrows, M., 'The Messiahs of Aaron and Israel', Angl. ThR 34 (1952), p. 204.
Priest, J. F., 'The Messiah and the Meal in IQSa', JBL 82 (1953), pp. 95–100.
Kuhn, K. G., 'Die beiden Messias Aarons und Israel', NRSt 1 (1954–5), pp. 168–79 (revised English version, 'The Two Messiahs of Aaron and Israel', in *The Scrolls and the New Testament*, ed. K. Stendahl (1957), pp. 54–64).
Brown, R. E., 'The Messianism of Qumran', CBQ 19 (1959), pp. 53–82.
Ehrlich, E. L., 'Ein Beitrag zur Messiaslehre der Qumransekte', ZAW 68 (1956), pp. 234–43.

Schubert, K., 'Die Messiaslehre in den Texten von Khirbet-Qumran', BZ 1 (1957) pp. 177–97.

Kuhn, H. W., 'Die beiden Messiase in den Qumrantexten und die Messiasvorstellung in der rabbinischen Literatur', ZAW 70 (1958), pp. 200–8.

Liver, J., 'The Doctrine of the Two Messiahs in Sectarian Literature in the Time of the Second Commonwealth', HThR 52 (1959), pp. 149–85.

van der Woude, A. S., 'Le Maître de justice et les deux Messies de la communauté de Qumrân', *La Secte de Qumrân et les origines du christianisme* (1959), pp. 121–34.

Gnilka, J., 'Die Erwartung des messianischen Hohenpriesters in den Schriften von Qumran und im Neuen Testament', RQ 2 (1959–60), pp. 395–426.

Prigent, P., 'Quelques testimonia messianiques. Leur histoire littéraire de Qumrân aux pères de l'église', ThZ 15 (1959), pp. 419–30.

Hinson, G., 'Hodayoth 3:6–18: In What Sense Messianic?', RQ 2, (1959–60), pp. 183–203.

Héring, Jean, 'Analecta Qumraniana, Section 2: Encore le messianisme dans les écrits de Qumrân', RHPhR 41 (1961), pp. 160–2.

Weiss, C., 'Messianismus in Qumran und im Neuen Testament', *Qumran-Probleme: Vorträge des Leipziger Symposiums über Qumran-Probleme* (1961), pp. 353–68.

LaSor, W. S., 'The Messianic Idea in Qumran', in *Studies and Essays in Honour of A. Neuman* (1962), pp. 343–64.

Priest, J. F., 'Mebaqqer Paqidh and the Messiah', JBL 81 (1962), pp. 51–61.

Fritsch, C. T., 'The so-called priestly Messiah of the Essenes', Ex Oriente Lux 17 (1963), pp. 242–8.

Huppenbauer, H. W., 'Zur Eschatologie der Damaskusschrift', RQ 4 (1963), pp. 567–73.

Stefaniak, L., 'Messianische oder eschatologische Erwartungen in der Qumransekte?', *Neutestamentliche Aufsätze* (Festschrift J. Schmid) (1963), pp. 294–302.

Starcky, J., 'Les quatre étapes du messianisme à Qumrân', RB 70 (1963), pp. 481–505.

Laurin, R. B., 'The Problem of the Two Messiahs in the Qumran Scrolls', RQ 4 (1963), pp. 39–52.

Starcky, J., 'Un texte messianique araméen de la grotte IV de Qumrân', *Mémorial du Cinquentenaire de l'École des Langues Orientales Anciennes de l'Institut Catholique de Paris, 1914–1964* (1964), pp. 51–66.

van der Woude, A. S., 'Melchisedek als himmlische Erlösergestalt in den neugefundenen eschatologischen Midrashim aus Qumran Höhle 11', Oudtestamentliche Studien 14 (1965), pp. 354–75.

Higgins, A. J. B., 'The Priestly Messiah', NTSt 12 (1965–6), pp. 211–39.

Brown, R. E., 'J. Starcky's Theory of Qumran Messianic Development', CBQ 28 (1966), pp. 51–7.

Caquot, A., 'Ben Sira et le messianism', Semitica 16 (1966), pp. 43–68.

Deichgräber, R., 'Zur Messiaserwartung der Damaskusschrift', ZAW 78, (1966) pp. 133–43.

de Jonge, M., 'The Use of the Word "Anointed" in the Time of Jesus', NT 8 (1966), pp. 132–48.

Browne, R. E., 'The Teacher of Righteousness and the Messiah(s)', *The Scrolls and Christianity*, ed. M. Black (1969), pp. 37–44.

de Jonge, M., 'The Role of Intermediaries in God's Final Intervention in the Future according to the Qumran Scrolls', *Studies on the Jewish Background of the New Testament*, ed. O. Michel *et al.* (1969), pp. 44–63.

Villalón, J. R., 'Sources vétéro-testamentaires de la doctrine qumrânienne des deux Messies', RQ 8 (1972), pp. 53–63.

Milik, J. T., 'Milkî-ṣedeq et Milkî-resha' dans les anciens écrits juifs et chrétiens', JJS 23 (1972), pp. 95–144.

de Jonge, M., 'Jewish Expectations about the "Messiah" according to the Fourth Gospel', NTSt 19 (1972–3), pp. 248–70.

Two main groups are to be distinguished in the sphere of religious ideas prevalent among the Jewish people during the period under discussion: general religious ideas on the relationship of man and the world to God, and specifically Israelite ideas on the relationship of the Jewish people to the God of Israel. Of these the latter predominate; they form the nucleus round which the others are grouped and to which they are linked. In later times, however, these specifically Israelite ideas again acquired their special colouring through the legal concept of the relationship between God and Israel. To the belief that God chose this one nation for himself and therefore bestowed his benefits on them exclusively, was added the further thought that he also gave them a law and thereby bound himself to grant his blessings provided that that law was obeyed. The Torah was to be observed for its own sake (לשמה) and the fulfilment of its commandments brought its own reward (in acts of obedience and loving-kindness); nevertheless it was also expected that Israel's faithfulness would be suitably rewarded in the life both of the nation and of the individual.[1] Yet it was obvious that in actual experience the reward came neither to the people as a whole, nor to individuals, in the proportion anticipated. Accordingly, the more deeply this awareness penetrated into the mind of the nation and the individual, the more they were forced to turn their eyes to the future; and of course, the worse their present state, the more lively their hope. It may therefore be said that in later eras religious consciousness was concentrated upon hope for the future. A perfect age to come was the goal to which all other religious ideas were teleologically related. As the conduct of the Israelite was essentially observance of the Torah, so his faith was centred on awaiting God's kingdom. It was around these two poles, as has been noted earlier (p. 466), that the religious life of the Jews revolved at this time. They were zealous for the Torah so that one day they might have a share in the 'world to come'.

I. Relation to the Older Messianic Hope

Expectation of the better future was already a basic element of the religious consciousness of the Old Testament prophets. It was never entirely lost by the people, even though it was not always as vigorous as it became after the Maccabaean uprising. In the course of time,

1. mMak. 3:16; cf. above § 28, p. 466.

however, this hope underwent many changes. Indeed, there was far more freedom of movement in the sphere of belief than in that of conduct. Whereas legal precepts were binding in their smallest detail and were to be handed down unchanged from one generation to another, a relatively greater latitude was permitted in respect of religious thought; as long as certain fundamentals were adhered to, individual requirements were allowed far freer play (see above, pp. 339–55, *Halakhah and Haggadah*). In consequence, hope of the future also developed in a variety of ways. Nevertheless, certain common basic points may be observed which on average distinguish the later messianic hope from the earlier. The earlier expectation moved within the setting of the present world and was simply directed towards a better future for the nation. The hope of the pre-exilic prophets was that the community would be morally purified and cleansed of all its bad elements; that it would flourish unmolested and respected in the midst of the Gentile world, its enemies either destroyed or forced to acknowledge Israel and its God; that it would be ruled by a just, wise and powerful king of the house of David, so that internal justice, peace and joy would prevail; and even that all natural evils would be annihilated and a condition of unclouded bliss come into being. This vision was however substantially modified in later ages, partly during the time of the later prophets, but particularly in the post-biblical period.

1. Above all else, the prospect widened and lengthened to embrace the world: it was not only the future of the nation that mattered but also that of the universe. Whereas the Gentiles had been considered only in so far as they were related in some way to Israel, the expectation of later times extended ever more positively to the fate of all mankind. Originally judgement was one which would purify Israel or, alternatively, destroy its enemies. Later, it developed into a judgement of the world by God or by his Anointed, the messianic King of Israel, which would decide the fate of all men and all nations. The earlier ideal kingdom of the future did not reach beyond the actual boundaries of the holy land; the later kingdom of God was seen to contain all those who, willingly or by force, were united within one kingdom of the world under the sceptre of Israel. The Messiah was therefore to be judge and ruler of the world. Even the animals and heaven and earth—i.e. the whole universe in the strict sense—were to be transformed; the old creation was to be destroyed and replaced by the new and lovely.

This enlargement of the concept of the future was already partly brought about by the extension of the political horizon. The more the small individual states were engulfed by the great world powers, the easier it became to imagine the ideal kingdom of the future as a world power. After the downfall of the last Gentile kingdom of the world,

God himself would take the sceptre into his hand and found a kingdom in which he, the heavenly King, would rule through his people. But still more important than the widening of the political horizon in the development of the messianic idea was the expansion of the notion of God himself and of the world in general. At first, YHWH was God and King of Israel alone. Later, he was envisaged ever more precisely and clearly as God and King of the world; and with this, an idea of the 'world' took shape as of a unified whole comprising all that exists. It was essentially this extension of religious consciousness in general which gave rise to the growing universalism of the expectation of a future age of blessedness.

2. This extension and enlargement of hope for the future was related, on the other hand, much more specifically to the individual. Again, this was associated with the development of religious consciousness in general. Originally, YHWH was the God of the nation, one who controlled the fortunes and misfortunes of his people. The fate of the individual was scarcely considered. But with the deepening of religious awareness, he came increasingly to feel himself to be the object of God's care. Each knew that his destiny was in God's hand and was sure that God would not forsake him. The strengthening of this individual belief in Providence gradually gave an individual shape also to hope for the future, though admittedly not until relatively late: there is no definite evidence of it before Daniel. The form in which it was first expressed was in belief in resurrection. Since the just Israelite was certain that his personal, and indeed his enduring and eternal salvation was desired by God, he expected that he, together with every other just man, would participate in the future glory of the nation. Therefore, whoever was overtaken by death before this came to pass, especially the martyr, might hope that one day God would re-awaken him and take him to the kingdom of glory. The object of resurrection was participation in the nation's glorious future; and the basis of belief in resurrection was an increasing interest in personal salvation.

It was however not interest in salvation alone that assumed a personal form; increasingly, attention in general was turned to the future destiny of the individual, *in malam partem* as well. God—it was thought—keeps account in heaven of the deeds of every man, of every Israelite at least. And judgement will be pronounced on the basis of these heavenly ledgers; reward and punishment will be measured out exactly in accord with each one's merits. Thus the expected resurrection also came to be seen differently as affecting all men; not only the righteous but also the unrighteous would rise again to receive judgement. But this idea was never commonly accepted; many continued to look only for a resurrection of the just.

In the end, interest in the salvation of the individual was no longer content even with resurrection for the purpose of participating in the messianic kingdom. This was regarded no more as the final and supreme bliss. After it a still higher, everlasting heavenly beatitude was awaited: namely an absolute transfiguration in heaven for the good and for the godless not merely exclusion from the kingdom but eternal agony and torment in hell.

3. These last factors, combined with the failure of political messianism in A.D. 70 and 135, are associated with a further characteristic distinguishing the later expectation from that of earlier ages: it became more transcendent, more and more transposed into the supernatural, the ultramundane. The older hope remained within the framework of the present world. The enemies of Israel would be destroyed; the people would be purified; their future would be glorious. However imaginary the representation of this future blessedness, it nevertheless stayed within the context of idealized present circumstances. In the later approach, present and future became more and more sharply opposed, the gulf between them grew ever deeper, the concept increasingly dualistic. Entry into the messianic age was to be the start of a new world, a new עולם. But this world to come (עולם הבא) was to be in every respect entirely the opposite of the present world (עולם הזה) ruled by the ungodly powers of Satan and his angels and therefore submerged in sin and evil. The future world was to be under the dominion of God (and his Anointed); therefore only righteousness and blessedness would prevail there. There was scarcely any connection between them. By a miraculous act of God, the one would be destroyed and the other called into existence.

Although this approach is greatly dependent on the earlier idea, the opposition between present and future is far more sharply drawn. The earlier concept sees much more of God's gracious rule in the present time as well. According to later thought, it might almost appear as though God had surrendered the government of the present to the Satanic forces and reserved the full exercise of his dominion for the world to come. Accordingly, future salvation was also increasingly regarded as purely transcendent. All the good things of the new world are to proceed from above, from heaven, where they have pre-existed for all eternity. They are reserved there for the saints as an 'inheritance' which will one day be apportioned to them. In particular, the perfect new Jerusalem is already there, the city which will descend on earth in place of the old one at the consummation of time. Equally there already, in the company of God, is the perfect King of Israel chosen by God from eternity, the Messiah. Henceforward, all goodness and perfection can in fact only come from above, because everything earthly in its present condition is the exact reverse of the divine. So in the end, hope of the future reached beyond earthly existence altogether. Final redemption would not be found even in a kingdom of glory on an earth made new, but in a condition of absolute transfiguration in heaven.

With the concept of salvation itself, so also the idea of the way in which it was to be realized became more and more transcendent. Judgement was to be a forensic act in which, with no intervention by earthly powers, man's fate was to be decided by God or his Anointed; and the execution of this sentence was to take place only through supernatural powers, through a miraculous act of God which would destroy the old and call into existence a new order of things.

It is possible that Iranian influences may have affected this development of Jewish expectation, bearing in mind that the Jewish people were subject to Persian rule for two hundred years. These influences are unmistakable in angelology; in eschatology they are not so evident, but to some extent nevertheless probable. The doctrine of an individual reward after death and a strong transcendentalism are characteristic of Persian eschatology. But these are the very points which distinguish the later Jewish from the older Israelite eschatology. All in all, therefore, one may well speak of the probability of Persian influences. But they are only of a general nature. As soon as the details are considered, the parallels vanish; or where they are stronger, the antiquity of the Persian views may be in doubt. The Jewish concepts remain special throughout, and are to be explained as modifications or supplementations of Old Testament ideas. Iranian religion therefore enters into consideration only as an incidental factor which furthered the development in some way, not as one that dominated it.

4. Finally, messianic hope acquired an essentially new colouring in later times from its increasing systematization in the work of the Torah scholars and rabbis. The freedom of religious imagination was replaced by learned research into the writings of the prophets which determined doctrinally the details of the messianic picture of the future. The task of the Torah scholars was primarily, of course, the establishment and elaboration of the law. But following the same methods, they then developed and defined the religious ideas themselves, including the messianic expectations. Thus, not only were the relevant details collected and arranged by them, but by means of combining one text with another, after the fashion of haggadic midrash, new details emerged (see above, § 25.III). To acquire fresh information, the most diverse passages were ingeniously related to one another, and the messianic ideals ever more precisely and comprehensively determined. This learned doctrine was nevertheless fluid. For unlike the detail of halakhah, it never became really binding. The individual was therefore

free to accept as much or little of it as he wished, and to fashion it according to his own opinion, so that the messianic hope was in a state of flux and is encountered in different forms especially during the first century A.D.

Above all, it is to be noted that the characteristics mentioned here of the later messianic expectation were by no means everywhere the same. But the essential ancient hope of a glorious future for Israel predominated in later times also.

But did this hope remain constantly alive among the people? In its general form as it affected the future for the nation, messianic expectation did not die with the disappearance of prophecy. In the last pre-Christian centuries, and especially in the first century A.D., it became once more very lively, as the Pseudepigrapha, Qumran, Josephus and the Gospels show so decisively. But in addition to manifesting itself as an expectation of final national prosperity, it expressed in particular the hope of a Messiah, or of several messianic figures. This will become clear in the following pages where the historical development of messianism will be outlined, followed by a systematic survey of messianic concepts.

II. Historical Survey

The visions of the book of Daniel (about 167 to 165 B.C.) exercised a profound influence on the formation of the messianic idea. In the age of distress (עת צרה, Dan. 12:1) which had broken upon Israel in consequence of the wicked actions of Antiochus Epiphanes, the author foretells a coming deliverance. God himself will sit in judgement on the kingdoms of this world and will take away from them power and dominion and will uproot and wipe them out for ever. But 'the saints of the Most High' will receive the kingdom and possess it for evermore. All peoples and nations and tongues will serve them, and their kingdom will never be destroyed (7:9–27; 2:44). The just who have fallen asleep will also have their share in it; they will rise from the dust to everlasting life, whereas the ungodly will awaken to everlasting shame (12:2). Whether Daniel visualized a messianic King at the head of his kingdom of saints of the Most High is not clear. He makes no mention of such a person in any case. For he who appears in the form of a man (כבר אנש, 7:13) is in no way the personal Messiah but, as the author clearly and expressly says in his interpretation, the people of the saints of the Most High (7:18, 22, 27).[2] As the kingdoms of the world are

2. Nevertheless, from very early times the Danielic figure has been identified with the Messiah. See below on 1 En. 37–71 and 4 Ezr. 13, pp. 505, 511 f. Cf. G. Dalman, *Words of Jesus*, pp. 241 f.; H. Gressmann, *Der Messias* (1929), pp. 343–73; W. O. E. Oesterley, *The Jews and Judaism during the Greek Period* (1941),

represented by beasts which ascend from the sea, so the kingdom of the saints is symbolized by a human form which travels with the clouds. The kernel of Daniel's messianic hope is therefore the universal dominion of the devout (see especially 2:44; 7:14, 27). Moreover, the author does not think of this as brought about simply by a judgement of God, as might appear from ch. 7. He says rather in 2:44 that the kingdom of the saints shall 'break in pieces and consume' the ungodly, i.e. conquer them by force of arms, though admittedly with God's support and in accordance with his will. It is further worth noting that in this book the hope of a bodily resurrection is plainly and firmly expressed (12:2).

Accordingly, here as earlier, the messianic hope is for a glorious future for the nation, but with a dual modification: namely that the future kingdom of Israel is envisaged as a kingdom of the world, and that all the dead saints will also participate in it.

In the apocryphal books of the Old Testament,[3] messianic hope is not very prominent, a characteristic due only in part to the predominantly historical or didactic contents of these writings. Indeed, most of them are evidence that at the time that Daniel revived it, messianic expectation had in general greatly weakened. It is not possible to say for certain how Ecclesiasticus stands in regard to some points. It is clear that the author not only pleads, but really hopes, for the destruction of Israel's enemies and a glorious future for the nation corresponding to God's promises. Of particular importance is the confident prayer, 36:11–17:

> Gather all the tribes of Jacob,
> that they may receive their inheritance as of old.
> Have mercy on the people called by thy Name,
> Israel, whom thou didst surname Firstborn.
> Have mercy on thy holy city,
> Jerusalem, the place of thy dwelling.

---

p. 152; H. H. Rowley, *Darius the Mede* (1935), pp. 62 f., especially p. 62, n. 2; A. Feuillet, 'Le Fils de l'homme de Daniel et la tradition biblique', in RB 60 (1953), pp. 183 f.; J. Coppens-L. Dequeker, 'Le Fils de l'homme et les Saints du Très-Haut en Daniel 7, dans les Apocryphes et dans le Nouveau Testament', Anal. Lovan. Bibl. & Or. III, 23 (1961); L. Dequeker, 'The "Saints of the Most High" in Qumran and Daniel', Oudtest. St. 18 (1973), pp. 108–87. On the whole issue see Vermes, *Jesus the Jew* (1973), pp. 169–76, 257–9.

3. Cf. on this Drummond, *The Jewish Messiah*, pp. 196 f. See also now, P. Grelot, 'Le Messie dans les Apocryphes de l'Ancien Testament', in E. Massaux, P. Grelot, *et. al.*, *La venue du Messie: messianisme et eschatologie* [Recherches Bibliques VI] (1962), pp. 18–50 (Bibliography, p. 21, n. 1: this study includes the Pseudepigrapha as well as the Apocrypha); M.-J. Lagrange, *Le Messianisme chez les Juifs* (1909), pp. 210 ff.; J. Klausner, *Messianic Idea*, pp. 246 ff.

Fill Zion with thy majesty,
and thy temple with thy glory.
Testify to the first of thy works,
and confirm the vision spoken in thy Name.
Give reward to them who wait on thee,
that thy prophets may be found trustworthy.
Thou wilt hear the prayer of thy servants,
in accordance with thy benevolence towards thy people,
that all the ends of the earth may know
that thou art the everlasting God.

The glory prayed for is thought of as one of limitless time.[4] But it is characteristic that the expression of prayer and hope is conveyed in very general terms; in particular, despite the reference to the promises of the prophets there is no mention of a messianic King. There may be allusions to such a person in two other passages, but in both, the interpretation is uncertain.[5] If the author hoped for a messianic King on the ground of prophetic visions, this expectation arose more from the study of Scripture than from a real religious need. He was much more concerned about the everlasting continuance of the priesthood of the house of Phinehas than about the renewal of the Davidic dynasty (45:24 f.). That the beginnings of a scholarly messianism were already present is shown by the expectation of the reappearance of Elijah (48:10–11).

A more lively picture would of course emerge if the passage following 51:12 in the Hebrew text (it is missing in the Greek and Syriac) were genuine in its entirety. Here, God is extolled not only as the redeemer of Israel and as the gatherer of the dispersed (vv. 5–6), but also as he who 'builds his city and his holy place' and who 'causes a horn to sprout from the house of David'. These phrases are found word for word in the

4. No appeal should be made here to 44:13, with its statement in Greek that 'the seed' of the Fathers (σπέρμα αὐτῶν) remains for ever, since from the Hebrew and Syriac it appears that this should read, 'his memorial' (as is confirmed by parallelisms). Note, however, that the Masada Ecclesiasticus reads with the Greek; cf. Y. Yadin, *The Ben Sira Scroll from Masada* (1965), p. 37. This is, nevertheless, clearly a corruption in Hebrew, followed by the Greek: a dittograph of זרעם in the previous line replacing the true reading זכרם). But 37:25 certainly reads, 'the life of Israel (Jeshurun) continues for days without count'. The verse is preserved in two Geniza fragments (B and D): cf. *The Book of Ben Sira: The Historical Dictionary of the Hebrew Language* (1973), p. 38.

5. Ecclus. 47:11 says of David that God has exalted his horn 'for ever' (לעולם), but this vague expression does not necessarily mean a dynasty without end. Ch. 47:22 is translated by Box and Oesterley: 'and he will give to Jacob a remnant, and to the house of David a root from him'. Cf. Charles, *Apocrypha* I, p. 499. But a future interpretation of ויתן is not demanded by the context. The Greek translation has ἔδωκεν. Cf. further Th. Middendorf, *Die Stellung Jesu Ben Siras zwischen Judentum und Hellenismus* (1973), p. 67.

Shemoneh 'Esreh (see above, p. 461) and were possibly—though not very probably—introduced from there into the text of the Hebrew Ben Sira.

Expectation of a messianic King is in any case far from the thoughts of the author of 1 Maccabees, who for his part sees the guarantee of Israel's greatness to lie in the dynasty of the Hasmoneans.[6] Otherwise, the Apocrypha reveal, for instance, the expectation that God will judge the Gentiles (Jdt. 16:4) and will reassemble the dispersed people of Israel into one nation (2 Mac. 2:18; Bar. 2:27–35; 4:36–7, 5:5–9); that the nation will be established for ever (2 Mac. 14:15). The author of Tobit hopes not only that the just will be assembled and the people of Israel raised up and Jerusalem magnificently rebuilt with gold and precious stones (Tob. 13:12–18; 14:7), but also, in common with some of the Old Testament prophets, that all the Gentiles will turn to the God of Israel (Tob. 13:11; 14:6–7).

In the Hellenistic Wisdom of Solomon, the nationalistic element becomes unimportant; indeed owing to his Platonizing anthropology, the author cannot expect true salvation for his soul until after death. For him therefore, the essential is that the righteous who have died shall one day sit in judgement over the Gentiles (Wis. 3:8; 5:1; cf. 2 Cor. 6:2 f.).[7]

One important feature distinguishing the religious expectation of the earlier apocryphal books (Ecclus., Jdt., Tob., 1 Mac.) from the messianic hope of later times is the absence of hope of resurrection.[8] In this respect, the books mentioned adopt the ancient Israelite position: the dead have no more than a shadowy existence in Sheol; there is no blissful after-life.[9] The expectation of resurrection attested in the book

6. The words attributed to the dying Mattathias in 1 Mac. 2:57, *Δαυὶδ . . . ἐκληρονόμησε θρόνον βασιλείας εἰς αἰῶνα αἰῶνος*, or according to a better reading, *εἰς αἰῶνας*, ascribe only a long duration to the dynasty of David, not an everlasting one. Cf. M. Black, *The Scrolls and Christian Origins*, p. 139, n. 2.

7. Cf. C. Larcher, *Études sur le livre de la Sagesse* (1969), pp. 310 f. (Larcher scarcely does justice to this rôle of 'the righteous' in Wisdom.) Cf. also C. H. Dodd, *According to the Scriptures* (1952), p. 68, who sees in 1 Cor. 6:2 f. a reference to Dan. 7:22. But the idea also appears in 1 En. 1:9, 38; cf. also Jub. 24:29; Mt. 19:28; Lk. 22:30; Rev. 20:4. See also C. K. Barrett, *First Epistle to the Corinthians* (1968), p. 136. For the rôle of Enoch as the representative 'righteous man', M. Black, 'The Eschatology of the Similitudes of Enoch', JThS 3 (1952), pp. 1–10. Larcher explains the singular in Wisd. 4:13 f., 5:1 f. as representing a group, and to be understood collectively (*ibid.*, p. 128).

8. See W. Bousset, *Religion*,[4] pp. 269, n. 1, Volz, *Eschatologie*, pp. 229 ff. Moore, *Judaism* II, pp. 292 ff. See further below, p. 539.

9. Cf. in particular Ecclus. 7:17; 10:9–11; 14:17–19; 17:28; 22:11; 38:21; 41:1–4. Here, death is regarded simply as the end of life; there is no hint of another new existence. Survival rests only in the memory of those who come after (44:8–15). In the kingdom of death there is repose (28:21; 30:17). There is no delight there

of Daniel had therefore not become generally accepted in the second century B.C. and indeed never penetrated certain circles (e.g. the Sadducees). It figures clearly only in Maccabees (2 Mac. 7:9, 14, 23, 29, 36; 12:43–4). The Wisdom of Solomon has instead the expectation of a blessed after-life (3:1–9; 4:7; 5:16; 6:20).[10]

In the oldest Jewish Sibylline Oracles of around 140 B.C., the flow of messianic prophecy is rich and abundant. Sibyl. 3:286 f. must not of course be referred to here (καὶ τότε δὴ θεὸς οὐρανόθεν [Geffcken: οὐράνιος] πέμψει βασιλῆα, Κρινεῖ δ' ἄνδρα ἕκαστον ἐν αἵματι καὶ πυρὸς αὐγῇ), as this alludes to Cyrus.[11] Nor can υἱὸς θεοῖο, 3:775 be cited, if according to a persuasive conjecture of C. Alexandre (*Oracula Sibyllina* [²1869], *ad loc.*), νηόν is to be read instead of υἱόν.[12] And finally, it is erroneous to interpret the κόρη, in whom according to Sibyl. 3:784–6 God will dwell, as the mother of the Messiah.[13] For the κόρη, Hebr. בתולה, is none other than Jerusalem. But even allowing for all these passages, it nevertheless remains true that the whole section Sibyl. 3:652–795 is almost exclusively messianic in content, despite the fact that there is but one brief mention of the messianic King at the beginning. God will send a King from the east (ἀπ' ἠελίοιο), the text reads, who will put an end to all war upon earth, destroying some, and fulfilling the promises made to the others. And he will not do this independently, but in obedience to God's commands.[14] At his appearance (for this is no doubt the author's

---

(תענוג, τρυφή) to pursue (14:16), and God can no longer be praised (17:27 f.). If 11:26 is concerned with reward ἐν ἡμέρᾳ τελευτῆς, then this is surely an inexact translation for 'at the end of his days', i.e., at the end of his life.

10. See Larcher, *Études sur le livre de la Sagesse* (1969), pp. 237 f.

11. This is disputed by H. N. Bate, *The Sibylline Oracles*, Books III–IV (Translations of Early Christian Documents, Series II, Hellenistic Jewish Texts, 1918). Bate identifies the figure in question with the 'Messiah, King and Judge'. (Introduction, p. 31, p. 58 note *ad loc.*) On the Sibyllines, RE, Zweite Reihe II (1923), col. 2073 ff. and 2117 ff. (Jewish and Christian); V. Nikiprowetzky, *La troisième Sibylle* (1970). (No comment on 3:286 f.) Note, however, that in the form in which this work has been transmitted, it cannot be earlier than the Augustan period. See vol. III, § 33.

12. This emendation is much closer to the context than the hypothesis that the whole verse is a Christian interpolation (Gfrörer, Hilgenfeld, Geffcken). Bate revives the theory of a Christian interpolation (*op. cit. ad loc.*). Cf. RE, col. 2129; Nikiprowetzky, *op. cit.*, pp. 329, 353.

13. Cf. O. Betz, 'Die Geburt der Gemeinde durch den Lehrer', NTSt 3 (1956–7), pp. 314 ff.

14. Sibyl. 3: 652–6: 'And then from the sunrise God shall send a king, Who shall give every land relief from the bane of war. Some he shall slay, and to others he shall consummate faithful vows. He shall not do all these things by his own will, but in obedience to the good ordinances of the mighty God.' Cf. Bousset, *Religion*,[4] pp. 222, 226, 260–1.

meaning) the Gentile kings will gather once more for an attack on God's Temple and the holy land. They will offer their idolatrous sacrifices around Jerusalem. But God will speak to them with a mighty voice, and they will all perish by the hand of the Immortal One. The earth will quake, the mountains and hills will collapse, and Erebus will appear. The Gentiles will die by war, sword and fire because they raised their spears against the Temple (663–97). The children of God will then live in peace and tranquillity, for the hand of the Holy One will protect them (698–709). And the Gentile nations seeing this, will encourage one another to bless and praise God and to send gifts to his Temple and accept his law, for it is the most just law on earth (710–26). Peace will then prevail among all the kings of the earth (744–61). And God will establish an everlasting kingdom over all men. From all the corners of the earth men will bring offerings to his Temple. And God's prophets will lay down the sword, for they will be judges of men and just kings. And God will dwell on Zion and universal peace will prevail on earth (767–95).

As may be seen, the chief emphasis falls on the eventual recognition and acknowledgement of the law of God by the nations on earth. Yet the author does not look for this alone, but also for the establishment of an everlasting kingdom over all mankind (767–8: *βασιλήϊον εἰς αἰῶνας πάντας ἐπ' ἀνθρώπους*) with Jerusalem as its theocratic centre. It is true that he mentions the King sent by God as his instrument in the restoration of universal world peace only in the preamble (652–6). But the King is undoubtedly to be thought of as the intervening cause when it is said in v. 689 that God will destroy the attacking Gentiles by battle and the sword (*πολέμῳ ἠδὲ μαχαίρῃ*). And if in the kingdom of peace only the prophets of God in general (*θεοῦ μεγάλοιο προφῆται*, i.e. no doubt the Israëlites, 'the saints of the Most High' as Daniel names them) are described as judges and kings (781–2), at least the author's words do not exclude that a theocratic King stood at their head. It is worth noting in any case that in his image of the future even this writer, often believed to be an Alexandrian, cannot dispense with a God-sent king.

Relatively little messianic material is to be found in the oldest sections of the Book of Enoch (dating to the second century B.C.).[15] It is the end of the vision of history that is especially considered here

15. Cf. O. Eissfeldt, *Introduction* (1965), p. 619. On the 4Q Aramaic fragments of this part of 1 Enoch, see J. T. Milik, 'Problèmes de la littérature hénochique à la lumière des fragments araméens de Qumrân', HThR 64 (1971), pp. 354 ff. and especially, *The Books of Enoch. Aramaic Fragments of Qumran Cave* 4 (1976). Milik dates the Book of Dreams (1 En. 83–90) to 164 B.C. (p. 44).

(90:16–38). The author expects first of all a final powerful attack by the Gentiles (i.e. mainly the Syrians), which will however be defeated by God's miraculous intervention (vv. 16–19). A throne will then be erected in the lovely land and God will sit in judgement. First, the fallen angels and the apostate Israelites will be cast into the fiery depths (vv. 20–7). Then the old Jerusalem (for the 'house' is Jerusalem) will be done away with and God will bring in a new Jerusalem and erect it in place of the old one (vv. 28–9). In this new Jerusalem will live the pious Israelites, and the Gentiles will pay homage to them (v. 30). At this point, the Messiah will appear (in the form of a white bullock) and all the Gentiles will entreat him and be converted to God the Lord (vv. 37–8).[15a]

The transcendental character of the later messianic idea is manifest here: the new Jerusalem has nothing in common with the old, but is brought miraculously down from heaven. The Messiah appears, but not until God has sat in judgement; he himself therefore takes no part in it.

It should further be noted that in the first section of Enoch there is also no expectation of everlasting life for the individual, but only of a long and happy life in this world (1:8; 5-7–9; 10:9–11:2; chs. 24–5). The religious hopes for individuals consequently follow the same lines as in Ecclesiasticus.

The figure of the messianic King is encountered in fuller colour and sharper outline in the Psalms of Solomon, composed most likely in the time of Pompey (63–48 B.C.).[16] These psalms are instructive if only because their author emphasizes both that God himself is Israel's King (17:1), and also that the kingdom of the house of David will never fail before God (17:5). Where the first is the case it must therefore not to be assumed without further ado that the second is impossible. The poet's longing for the Davidic king is particularly vivid because Jerusalem in his time had fallen under the Gentile rule of the Romans and no future expectation could be built on the Sadducee-minded dynasty of the Hasmonaeans. He therefore hopes that God will raise up a King from the line of David to rule over Israel and crush its enemies and cleanse Jerusalem of the Gentiles (17:23–7). This King will gather a holy people together and will judge the tribes of the nation and not allow unrighteousness to remain among them, and will distribute them throughout the land according to their tribes, and no stranger will dwell among them (17:28–31). And the Gentile nations will serve him, and will come to Jerusalem to see the glory of the Lord, bringing as

15a. However, see now J. T. Milik, *The Books of Enoch* (1976), p. 45.

16. For bibliographical material see Eissfeldt, *Introduction*, pp. 610, 773; A.-M. Denis, *Introduction aux pseudépigraphes grecs d'Ancien Testament* (1970), pp. 60 ff. Full details in volume III.

gifts the children of Israel 'who had fainted'. And he will be a righteous King, taught by God (17:32–5). And there will be no unrighteousness in those days. For all will be saints. And their King will be the Anointed of the Lord.[17] He will not put his trust in horse or rider. For the Lord himself will be his King. And he will smite the earth with the word of his mouth for ever (17:36–9). He will bless the people of his Lord with wisdom. And he will be pure from sin. And he will rule over a great nation and not be weak. For God will make him strong through his holy spirit. He will lead them all in holiness and there will be no pride among them (17:40–6). This will be the beauty of the King of Israel. Blessed are they who will be born in those days (17:47–51).

The writer appears to hope, not for God-fearing kings in general of the house of David, but for a single Messiah endowed by God with miraculous powers, holy and free from sin (17:41, 46), one made mighty and wise by God through the holy spirit (17:42), who will therefore smite his enemies not with external weapons but by the word of his mouth (17:39 after Isa. 11:4). Despite this idealization he is nevertheless presented as a worldly ruler, a real King of Israel. To the evidence of Ps. 17 should be added Ps. 18:6–10, and especially Ps. 11 (gathering of the dispersed) and 3:16; 14:2 ff. (resurrection of the righteous).

As the Psalms of Solomon appear to have been occasioned by the oppression of the Pompeian period, so a more recent Sibylline piece (Sibyl. 3:36–92) was a response to the despotism of Antonius and Cleopatra in Egypt. At that time when Rome had acquired dominion over Egypt also, the Sibyl awaited the beginning of the kingdom of God on earth and the coming of a holy King who would reign for ever over every land. The relevant passage (3:46–50) reads:

Αὐτὰρ ἐπεὶ Ῥώμη καὶ Αἰγύπτου βασιλεύσει,
Εἰς ἕν ἰθύνουσα,[18] *τότε δὴ βασιλεία μεγίστη*

17. *Χριστὸς κύριος* (17:36) is probably an incorrect translation of משיח יהוה; cf. Lam. 4:20. In 18:8, *Χριστοῦ κυρίου* is to be interpreted according to the preceding *Χριστοῦ αὐτοῦ* (18:6), *κυρίου* being therefore dependent on *Χριστοῦ* (J. Wellhausen, *Die Pharisäer und die Sadducäer*, p. 132). In Lk. both occur (2:11, *Χριστὸς κύριος*; 2:26 *τὸν Χριστὸν κυρίου*). For alternative explanations of *Χριστὸς κύριος*, see especially H. Schürmann, *Das Lukasevangelium* (1969), p. 111. According to Schürmann, the *Χριστὸς κύριος* in Lk. 2:11 may be a Lucan redaction, interpreting the *Χριστός* title (cf. Lk. 23:2 where it is interpreted by *βασιλεύς*). Similarly, Psalms of Solomon 17:36, Lam. 4:20, may be a 'free translation' of משיח יהוה. It could also be a Hellenistic 'messianic' interpretation, Jewish or Christian; if the former, then it prepared the way for the application of the title *κύριος* to the Messiah.

18. One manuscript has *εἰς ἕν δηθύνουσα.* Geffcken conjectures on this: *εἰσέτι δηθύνουσα,* 'still Rome hesitates'. (The Sibyl is pretending to live at an earlier period when the dominion of Rome over Egypt still did not exist.) Nikiprowetzky reads with MS. *Ψ, εἰς ἕν ἰθύνουσα,* and renders: ['Mais lorsque Rome sur l'Égypte aussi étendra son empire] *la soumettant à un gouvernement unique* (alors le très grand Royaume du Roi immortel brillera sur les hommes . . .').

Ἀθανάτου βασιλῆος ἐπ' ἀνθρώποισι φανεῖται.
Ἥξει δ' ἁγνὸς ἄναξ πάσης γῆς σκῆπτρα κρατήσων
Εἰς αἰῶνας πάντας ἐπειγομένοιο χρόνοιο.

The immortal King whose kingdom will appear among men is of course God himself. On the other hand, the ἁγνὸς ἄναξ who will hold the sceptre in every land for ever can be none other than the Messiah. Thus here too, as in the Psalm of Solomon, the personal Messiah and the idea of the kingdom of God appear side by side.

If already in the Psalms of Solomon the form of the messianic King towers over the ordinary human dimension, this is even more conspicuous in the Parables (chs. 37–71) of the book of Enoch. Here the messianic image chiefly follows the book of Daniel; the expression 'son of man' is applied to the person of the Messiah, and the coming from heaven is understood literally, whereby pre-existence is ascribed to him. However, in the light of the Qumran evidence, no early, i.e. pre-A.D. 70, date for the Parables is likely; in consequence, they cannot be included in the present historical sketch,[19] and will be used only in the systematic survey.

Evidence of the existence of messianic expectation in the time of Herod is provided by Josephus's narrative, *Ant.* xvii 2, 4 (43 ff.). The Pharisees are said to have promised Pheroras, Herod's brother, that the rule of Herod and his family would end and pass to Pheroras and his children. At the same time, however, the Pharisees are reported as having promised a eunuch called Bagoas that he would be named father and benefactor in a pronouncement made by the future king who, since all would lie in his hands, would grant him the ability to marry and to father children of his own.[20] This future king who will restore fertility to the eunuch is naturally not Pheroras, but the Messiah (see Isa. 56:3: 'Neither let the eunuch say, Behold, I am a dry tree'). Therefore, either Pheroras wrongly applied to himself the Pharisees' words concerning the approaching downfall of the rule of Herod and the coming king, or Herod, when these remarks reached his ears, merely assumed that he did.[21]

19. See J. T. Milik, 'Problèmes de la littérature hénochique à la lumière des fragments araméens de Qumrân', HThR 64 (1971), pp. 373–8; *The Books of Enoch* (1976), p. 96, dating the composition of the Parables to *ca* A.D. 270. Cf. however Vermes, *Jesus the Jew*, p. 176. Below, pp. 520 f.

20. *Ant.* xvii 2, 4 (45): ἦρτο δὲ ὁ Βαγώας ὑπ' αὐτῶν ὡς πατήρ τε καὶ εὐεργέτης ὀνομασθησόμενος τοῦ ἐπικατασταθησομένου προρρήσει βασιλέως, κατὰ χεῖρα γὰρ ἐκείνῳ τὰ πάντ' εἶναι, παρέξοντος αὐτῷ γάμου τε ἰσχὺν καὶ παιδώσεως τέκνων γνησίων. Translators of Josephus render προρρήσει wrongly, advancing the nonsense that Bagoas is to be called the father of the king who restores to him his ability to beget children!

21. Cf. J. Wellhausen, *Die Pharisäer und die Sadducäer*, p. 25; A. Schalit, *König Herodes*, pp. 630–1.

The Assumption of Moses,[22] dating from around the beginning of the Christian era, prophesies in beautiful and spirited language the advent of the kingdom of God. After foreseeing a period of hardship such as that suffered under Antiochus Epiphanes, the author continues in chapter 10:

> 'And then His kingdom shall appear among all creatures. And then Satan shall be no more and sorrow shall depart with him. . . . For the Heavenly One shall arise from the throne of his kingdom, and he shall go forth from his holy dwelling-place with indignation and wrath for his children's sake. And the earth shall tremble; to its ends shall it be shaken; and the high mountains shall be brought low and the hills fall. The sun shall give no light and the moon . . . shall change into blood (cf. Joel 3:4) and the circle of the stars shall fall into disorder. And the sea shall recede into the abyss, and the springs shall fail, and the rivers dry up. Then shall God arise, the Most High, the only Everlasting One, and shall step forth, and shall scourge the nations and destroy all their idols. Then shall you be happy, Israel, and shall climb upon the eagle's back and wings (see below p. 531) . . . And God shall lift you up and cause you to soar to the starry heaven. And you shall see from on high your adversaries on earth, and shall know them, and shall rejoice, and shall give thanks, and shall acknowledge your Creator.'

With this expectation of Israel's elevation into heaven the picture of the future is concluded. Of a messianic kingdom in the accepted sense there is no mention at all.

The Book of Jubilees depicts in broad outline the age of joy and delight which will enter in for Israel when she turns to God (Jub. 23:27–31).[23]

> 'And the days shall begin to grow many and to increase amongst those children of men, from generation to generation and from day to day, until their lifetime approaches one thousand years. And there shall be no aged or weary of life, but they shall all become as children and young lads, and shall complete all their days and live in peace and

22. Cf. Eissfeldt, *Introduction*, pp. 623–4, 774; A.-M. Denis, *Introduction aux pseudépigraphes grecs d'Ancien Testament*, pp. 1–14; R. H. Charles, *The Assumption of Moses* (1897) (dated A.D. 7–30; cf. pp. lv–lviii). See further, vol. III; E.-M. Laperrousaz, *Le Testament de Moïse (généralement appelé 'Assomption de Moïse')*, Semitica 19 (1970); G. W. E. Nickelsburg, *Studies in the Testament of Moses* (1973).

23. R. H. Charles, *Apocrypha and Pseudepigrapha of the Old Testament* II, pp. 1–82; Eissfeldt, *Introduction*, pp. 606–8, 773; A.-M. Denis, *Introduction aux pseudépigraphes grecs d'Ancien Testament* (1970), pp. 150–62. See further, vol. III.

joy, inasmuch as there shall be no Satan nor any evil destroyer, but all their days shall be days of blessing and healing. At that time the Lord shall heal his servants; and they shall rise up and see deep peace, and shall drive out their enemies, and the righteous shall watch and give thanks and rejoice with joy for ever. And they shall see all their judgements on their enemies and all their curses. And their bones shall indeed rest in the earth, but their spirits shall have much joy; and they shall know that it is God who sits in judgement and exercises mercy towards hundreds and thousands and towards all who love him.'

Whilst it is only said in general here that the servants of the Lord 'shall drive out their adversaries', in another passage world dominion is promised to the seed of Jacob (32:18–19).[24] God said to Jacob:

> 'I am the God who created heaven and earth. I shall increase you, and multiply you exceedingly; and kings shall come from you and shall rule wherever the foot of the sons of man has trodden. I shall give to your seed all the earth which is under heaven, and they shall rule over all the nations according to their desire; and afterwards they shall draw the whole earth to themselves and shall inherit it for ever'.

This world dominion of the posterity of Jacob will however be brought about by the tribe of Judah. Isaac said to Judah (31:18–20):[25]

> 'God give you strength and power to trample upon all who hate you! Be a prince, you and one of your sons, over the sons of Jacob! May your name and the name of your sons go out and extend over the whole earth and in [all] lands! Then shall the Gentiles fear before your face and all the nations shall be dismayed. In you shall be the help of Jacob, and in you the salvation of Israel. And when you sit on the throne of the renown of your righteousness, deep peace shall rule over all the seed of the children of the beloved (i.e. Abraham).'

The words 'you and one of your sons' seem to point to the coming Messiah.

The intensity of messianic hope in the age of Jesus is attested very characteristically by the fact that even a philosopher such as Philo depicts the awaited happiness of the just and virtuous within the

24. Charles, *op. cit.*, p. 62.

25. Charles, *op. cit.*, p. 61. Charles compares Test. Levi 18, Test. Reub. 6, and 1 En. 90, and suggests that here the Messiah ('one of thy sons') has no active part to play, as in 1 Enoch 90. He also thinks that 'this seems to be the earliest instance of the presence of a Messiah in a temporary Messianic kingdom; cf. 23:30'.

framework and in the colouring of Jewish national expectation.[26] Two passages in particular of his work, 'On the reward of the good and the punishment of the wicked', *Praem.* 29 (164–5, 168) and 25 (85)–20 (126), are involved here. In the first he expresses the hope that all Israelites, or rather, all those who return to the law of God (for he is concerned with this, and not with natural descent from Abraham) will assemble in the holy land.

> 'For though they dwell at the ends of the earth as slaves among their enemies who have led them away captive, yet shall they at a given signal one day all be freed, because their sudden turning to virtue shall astonish their masters. For they will release them because they will be ashamed of ruling over better men. When this unexpected freedom is bestowed on them who were previously dispersed in Hellas and in barbarian lands, on islands and on the mainland, they shall on one impulse hurry from all quarters to a place indicated to them, led by a divine superhuman apparition which, invisible to all others, is visible only to the saved. . . .[27] When they then have arrived, the ruined cities shall be rebuilt, and the deserts reinhabited, and the unfruitful land shall be changed into fruitfulness.'

In the second passage Philo describes the age of happiness and peace which will enter in when men turn back to God. Above all, they will be safe from wild beasts.

> 'Bears and lions and panthers and Indian elephants and tigers, and all animals of invincible strength and vigour shall turn from living

26. Cf. on the Messianic idea in Philo, A. Gfrörer, *Philo und die alexandrinische Theosophie* (1831) I, pp. 495–534. Whether there is anything more than an implicit messianism in Philo is debatable. E. R. Goodenough, *An Introduction to Philo Judaeus* (1962), p. 78, states that Philo 'kept his messianism to himself'. At the same time, he argues that *Praem.* 29 (165) affords 'a glimpse of a still higher type of King for whom he (Philo) was looking, that figure which is usually called the Messiah, an ideal Warrior and King' (*The Politics of Philo Judaeus*, p. 115). Drummond [*The Jewish Messiah* (1871), *Philo Judaeus or the Jewish Alexandrian Philosophy* (1888)], failed to find any Messiah in Philo. More recent scholars tend to agree with Goodenough's view: e.g., G. Bertram, 'Philo als politisch-theologischer Propagandist des spätantiken Judentums', ThLZ 64 (1939), pp. 193–9, F. Grégoire, 'Le Messie chez Philon d'Alexandre', Ephem. Theol. Lovan. 12 (1935), pp. 28–50; J. de Savignac, 'Le messianisme de Philon d'Alexandrie', NT 4 (1960), pp. 319–27. By contrast, Annie Jaubert, relying mainly on *Praem.* 15 (87)–16 (95), continues to maintain that Philo presented a 'discreet Messianism', cf. *La notion de l'alliance dans le Judaïsme* (1963), pp. 383–5. For the messianic interpretation of Num. 24:7, the basis of Philo's exegesis in *Praem.* 16 (95) (cf. also *V.M.* i 290), see Vermes, *Scripture and Tradition* ([2]1973), pp. 159–61.

27. *ξεναγούμενοι πρός τινος θειοτέρας ἢ κατὰ φύσιν ἀνθρωπίνην* [*v.l.* *ἀνθρωπίνης*] *ὄψεως, ἀδήλου μὲν ἑτέροις, μόνοις δὲ τοῖς ἀνασωζομένοις ἐμφανοῦς*. The allusion concerns a phenomenon similar to the pillar of fire guiding the Israelites through the wilderness after the exodus from Egypt rather than the Messiah.

solitarily to living together, and from intercourse with few, after the manner of herd animals, shall become accustomed to the sight of man, who shall not, as previously, be attacked by them, but feared as their master; and they shall revere him as their natural lord. Some, emulating tame animals, shall like lapdogs even offer him homage by wagging their tails. The genus of scorpions and snakes and other reptiles shall then no longer possess any harmful venom.' *Praem.* 15 (89–90).

A further blessing of this age will be peace among men. For they will be ashamed to be more savage than unreasoning beasts. And whoever attempts to disturb the peace will be destroyed.

'For a man shall come forth, says the prophecy (Num. 24:7), who taking to the field and waging war shall conquer great and populous nations, God himself sending help to his saints. This consists in imperturbable boldness of the soul and invincible strength of the body, of which qualities each is in itself terrible to enemies, but against which, when they are united, no resistance is possible. But some of the enemies shall, as the prophecy says, not even be worthy to perish by human hands. Against them, he shall set swarms of wasps which shall fight for an ignominious overthrow for the saints. But these (*τοῦτον* should probably read *τούτους*, i.e. the saints) shall not only have certain victory in battle without the shedding of blood, but also invincible power of government for the welfare of the subjected, who subject themselves out of love or fear or respect. For they possess three qualities, which are the greatest, and which found an indestructible government: holiness and mighty power and benevolence (*σεμνότητα καὶ δεινότητα καὶ εὐεργεσίαν*), the first of which engenders reverence, the second fear, the third love. But if they are harmoniously unified in the soul, they engender subjects who are obedient to the rulers.' *Praem.* 16 95–7.[28]

For the period after Jesus there is more than enough evidence of the liveliness of messianic hope. The many politico-religious movements in the time of the procurators (A.D. 44–66) show with what feverish suspense God's miraculous intervention in history and the beginning of his kingdom on earth were expected. How else could people such as Theudas and the Egyptian have found hundreds and thousands to believe in their promises? Even Josephus admits that the messianic

28. A similar figure, the Messiah of Israel or the Prince of the Congregation, appears in the Qumran documents (e.g. 1QSa 2:14; CD 7:20): Numbers 24:17, the Star and Sceptre in the Balaam prophecy, is messianically interpreted along the same lines as Philo's use of Numbers 24:7 (LXX) (CD *loc. cit.*, 4QTest.) and his rôle is also that of the conquering Messiah (e.g. 1QSb v. 27). See further pp. 550–1.

expectation was one of the most powerful levers in the great rebellion against Rome. He himself was not ashamed to apply messianic prophecies to Vespasian, as did also Yohanan ben Zakkai, and this found a reflection in Tacitus and Suetonius.[29]

On the position of messianic hope after the destruction of the Temple, in the last decades of the first century A.D., copious information is provided by the Apocalypses of Baruch and Ezra. Baruch[30] describes the last things as follows. First, there will be a period of general and terrible confusion. Men will hate each other and fight with one another. The dishonourable will rule over men of high repute, the base over the illustrious, the godless over heroes. And nations prepared by God beforehand for the purpose will come and fight against the remaining princes. And it will come to pass that whoever escapes the war will succumb to earthquake; and whoever escapes this, to fire; and he who escapes fire, to famine. And whoever is saved from all these evils shall be delivered into the hands of the Messiah (70:2–10). For he will be made manifest, and will destroy the hosts of the final kingdom of the world. And the last prince still remaining shall be chained and brought to Zion; and the Messiah shall convict him of godlessness and slay him (39:7–40:2). The Messiah shall then assemble the nations and shall grant life to some but wipe out the others with the sword. He shall grant life to those who submit to the seed of Jacob. But those who have oppressed Israel shall be wiped out (72:2–6). He shall then sit on the

29. *B.J.* vi 5, 4 (312): *Τὸ δὲ ἐπᾶραν αὐτοὺς μάλιστα πρὸς τὸν πόλεμον ἦν χρησμὸς ἀμφίβολος ὁμοίως ἐν τοῖς ἱεροῖς εὑρημένος γράμμασιν, ὡς κατὰ τὸν καιρὸν ἐκεῖνον ἀπὸ τῆς χώρας τις αὐτῶν ἄρξει τῆς οἰκουμένης. Τοῦτο οἱ μὲν ὡς οἰκεῖον ἐξέλαβον, καὶ πολλοὶ τῶν σοφῶν ἐπλανήθησαν περὶ τὴν κρίσιν· ἐδήλου δ'ἄρα τὴν Οὐεσπασιανοῦ τὸ λόγιον ἡγεμονίαν, ἀποδειχθέντος ἐπὶ 'Ιουδαίας αὐτοκράτορος.* Cf. Tacitus, *Hist.* v 13: 'Pluribus persuasio inerat, antiquis sacerdotum literis contineri, eo ipso tempore fore ut valesceret oriens profectique Iudaea rerum potirentur. Quae ambages Vespasianum ac Titum praedixerant; sed volgus more humanae cupidinis sibi tantam fatorum magnitudinem interpretati ne adversis quidem ad vera mutabantur.' Suetonius, *Vesp.* 4: 'Percrebuerat oriente toto vetus et constans opinio, esse in fatis, ut eo tempore Iudaea profecti rerum potirentur. Id de imperatore Romano, quantum postea eventu paruit, praedictum Iudei ad se trahentes rebellarunt.' See A. von Harnack, 'Der jüdische Geschichtsschreiber Josephus und Jesus Christus', Internationale Monatschrift 7 (1913), pp. 1013–67; E. Norden, 'Josephus und Tacitus über Jesus Christus und eine messianische Prophetie', Neue Jahrb. für das klassische Altertum 31 (1913), pp. 637–66; R. Eisler, *ΙΗΣΟΥΣ ΒΑΣΙΛΕΥΣ* I, p. 343, n. 8; II, pp. 603–4; G. Ricciotti, *Flavio Guiseppe* IV, p. 189, n. on *B.J.* vi 5, 4 (312); P. Corssen, 'Die Zeugnisse des Tacitus und Pseudo-Josephus über Christus', ZNW 15 (1914), pp. 114–40; O. Michel-O. Bauernfeind, *de bello judaico*, II.2, Exkurs XV, 'Der *Χρήσμος ἀμφίβολος* und seine Deutung', pp. 190–2; S. G. F. Brandon, *Jesus and the Zealots* (1967), pp. 335, n. 3, p. 362. Cf. also vol. I, p. 494 and n. 41.

30. Charles, *Apocrypha and Pseudepigrapha*, I, pp. 569–95; Eissfeldt, *Introduction*, pp. 627–30, 775; A.-M. Denis, *Introduction aux pseudépigraphes grecs d'Ancien Testament*, pp. 182 ff. See vol. III, § 32.

throne of his kingdom for ever;[31] and peace shall appear, and sorrow and tribulation shall depart from men, and joy shall reign over the whole earth. And the wild beasts shall come and serve men; and vipers and dragons shall submit to young children. And reapers shall not be exhausted nor builders be weary (73–74; cf. 40:2–3). And the earth shall yield her fruits ten-thousandfold. And on every vine there shall be a thousand branches, and on every branch a thousand clusters, and on every cluster a thousand grapes, and one grape shall yield one *kor* of wine.[32] And manna shall again fall from heaven and men shall again eat it in those days (29:5–8). And at the end of that time, all the dead shall arise, the just and the unjust, in the same shape and bodily form which they had previously. But after the judgement the resurrected shall be changed. The bodies of the just shall be changed into radiant light, but the godless shall wither and become uglier than before. And they shall be given up to torment. But the just shall see the invisible world and dwell in the heights of that world. And Paradise shall spread before them, and they shall see the hosts of angels standing before the throne of God. And their glory shall be greater than that of the angels (30; 50–1, cf. 44:15).

The eschatological expectations of the writer of the Fourth Book of Ezra agree in all essential points with those of Baruch.[33] He too predicts a preliminary dreadful famine and distress (5:1–13; 6:8–28; 9:1–12; 13:29–31). After this, the Messiah, the son of God, shall be revealed. And it shall come to pass that when the nations hear his voice they shall forget the war among themselves and shall gather together in countless multitudes to attack the Anointed. But he shall stand on Mount Zion and shall convict them of their ungodliness and shall destroy them by the Torah, without battle and without weapons of war (13:25–8, 32–8; cf. 12:31–3). Then shall the hidden city (i.e. the heavenly Jerusalem) appear (7:26); and the ten tribes shall return to the holy land (13:39–47). And the Anointed shall protect and gladden God's people in the holy land and shall show them many wonders for four hundred years (7:27–8; 12:34; 13:48–50; cf. 9:8). And after this time, the Anointed and all men who have breath shall die. And the world shall return to the silence of death for seven days, as in the beginning. And after seven days a world shall be awakened which now sleeps, and the corrupt

31. 2 Bar. 73:1: '. . . When he has . . . sat down in peace for ever on the throne of His kingdom'. 40:3: 'And his principate shall stand for ever, until the world of corruption is at an end (Charles' translation). From this last passage it is clear that the rule of the Messiah is not to last strictly 'for ever' but only until the end of this present world.

32. Cf. Papias in Irenaeus, *Haer.* v 33, 3–4.

33. R. H. Charles, *Apocrypha and Pseudepigrapha* II, pp. 542–624. Eissfeldt, *Introduction*, pp. 624–7; A.-M. Denis, *Introduction aux pseudépigraphes grecs d'Ancien Testament*, pp. 194 ff. See further vol. III, § 32.

world shall disappear. And the earth shall give up those who sleep within her, and the receptacles shall give back the souls entrusted to them (7:29–32). And the Most High shall appear on the judgement seat and patience shall have an end; only judgement shall remain; and the reward shall come to light (7:33–5). And the place of torment shall be revealed, and opposite it, the place of rest; the abyss of hell, and opposite it, Paradise. And the Most High shall say to the risen: Look on him whom you denied and did not honour, whose commands you did not obey. Here is joy and bliss, and there is fire and torment. And the duration of the day of judgement shall be a week of years (7:36–43; cf. 7:84 and 95–8).

Such are the messianic expectations of the two Apocalypses. That they are not isolated but form an essential part of Jewish religious thought is apparent from the *Shemoneh 'Esreh*, the daily prayer of the Jews revised in about A.D. 100. As this prayer has already been fully discussed (pp. 455–63), it is enough at this point to recall that the tenth benediction prays for the gathering of the dispersed; the eleventh, for the reinstatement of national authority; the fourteen, for the rebuilding of Jerusalem; the fifteenth, for the sending of the Son of David and the establishment of his kingdom; and finally the seventeenth for the restoration of sacrificial worship in Jerusalem. In the shorter Palestinian recension, the fifteenth *berakhah* is missing. The prayer for the coming of the Son of David is merely indicated in conjunction with the fourteenth *berakhah*.[34]

Because of their composite character, and the difficulty in dating their constitutive elements, this survey has purposely passed over the Targums, where 'the King Messiah' frequently appears.[35] For whereas a number of Targumic traditions are no doubt pre-Christian, the surviving compositions probably belong to the second to the fourth century A.D. The situation here, therefore, is the same as that affecting other rabbinical writings (Mishnah, Talmud, Midrash): although based on older material, in their present form they do not belong to the period under discussion.

The essential features of Jewish messianic hope of this later time (around the beginning of the third century A.D.) are very well summarized by Hippolytus:

34. The prayer for the re-building of Jerusalem and restoration of the '*abodah* (sacrificial worship) occurs also in the Passover Liturgy. See mPes. 10:6.

35. A list of messianic passages in the Targums may be found in J. Buxtorf, *Lexicon Chaldaicum* (1639), cols. 1268–73. Cf. R. Le Déaut, *La Nuit Pascale: Essai sur la signification de la Pâque juive à partir du Targum d'Exode xii.42* (1963), especially pp. 279–303. See also M. McNamara, *The New Testament and the Palestinian Targum to the Pentateuch* (1966), pp. 238–52; J. Bowker, *The Targums and Rabbinic Literature* (1969), pp. 278 ff., 290, etc.; S. H. Levey, *The Messiah: An Aramaic Interpretation—The Messianic Exegesis of the Targum* (1974).

'For they say that his generation will be of the stock of David, but not from a virgin and the holy spirit, but from a woman and a man, according as it is natural for all to be procreated from seed. And they allege that he will be king over them, a warlike and powerful man, who, when he has gathered together the entire people of the Jews, and when he has done battle with all the nations, will restore for them Jerusalem the royal city. Into this city he will bring together the entire race, and will once again reinstate them in the ancient circumstances as a nation exercising royal and priestly functions, and dwelling in security for a long time. Then, when they are gathered together, war will be waged against them, and in this war Christ will fall by the sword. Then, after a short time, the end and conflagration of the universe will follow. In this way, their opinions concerning the resurrection will be fulfilled, and a recompense be rendered to each man according to his works.'[36]

Of messianic expectation among the Samaritans at the time of Jesus nothing precise is known since the sources on Samaritan theology belong to a later era. In these, the Messiah is called *Taheb* (he who returns or who converts?), and is represented above all as a prophet who restores everywhere the true doctrine (cf. Jn. 4:25), but also as priest and king.[37]

For Qumran messianism, see Appendix B below.

36. *Ref. omn. haer.* ix 30: *Γένεσιν μὲν γὰρ αὐτοῦ [scil. τοῦ Χριστοῦ] ἐσομένην λέγουσιν ἐκ γένους Δαβίδ, ἀλλ' οὐκ ἐκ παρθένου καὶ ἁγίου πνεύματος, ἀλλ' ἐκ γυναικὸς καὶ ἀνδρός, ὡς πᾶσιν ὅρος γεννᾶσθαι ἐκ σπέρματος, φάσκοντες τοῦτον ἐσόμενον βασιλέα ἐπ' αὐτούς, ἄνδρα πολεμιστὴν καὶ δυνατόν, ὅς ἐπισυνάξας τὸ πᾶν ἔθνος 'Ιουδαίων, πάντα τὰ ἔθνη πολεμήσας, ἀναστήσει αὐτοῖς τὴν 'Ιερουσαλὴμ πόλιν βασιλίδα, εἰς ἣν ἐπισυνάξει ἅπαν τὸ ἔθνος καὶ πάλιν ἐπὶ τὰ ἀρχαῖα ἔθη ἀποκαταστήσει βασιλεῦον καὶ ἱερατεῦον καὶ κατοικοῦν ἐν πεποιθήσει ἐν χρόνοις ἱκανοῖς· ἔπειτα ἐπαναστῆναι κατ' αὐτῶν πόλεμον ἐπισυναχθέντων· ἐν ἐκείνῳ τῷ πολέμῳ πεσεῖν τὸν Χριστὸν ἐν μαχαίρῃ, ἔπειτα μετ' οὐ πολὺ τὴν συντέλειαν καὶ ἐκπύρωσιν τοῦ παντὸς ἐπιστῆναι, καὶ οὕτως τὰ περὶ τὴν ἀνάστασιν δοξαζόμενα ἐπιτελεσθῆναι, τάς τε ἀμοιβὰς ἑκάστῳ κατὰ τὰ πεπραγμένα ἀποδοθῆναι.* There is much material in Jerome on the Jewish messianism in his time. See the summary by S. Krauss, JQR 6 (1894), pp. 240–5.

37. A. Cowley, 'The Samaritan doctrine of the Messiah', Expositor (1895), pp. 161–74. J. A. Montgomery, *The Samaritans* (1907), pp. 243–50. See further, A. Merx, 'Der Messiah oder Ta'eb der Samaritaner', BZAW, 17 (1909); J. Macdonald, *The Theology of the Samaritans* (1964), especially, pp. 362 ff. M. Black, *Scrolls*, pp. 158 ff.

III. A Systematic Presentation

To supplement this historical survey, the following pages provide a systematic outline of messianism based on all the inter-Testamental sources, including the Dead Sea Scrolls, but presented according to the pattern emerging from the Apocalypses of Baruch and Ezra since it is in these two late compositions that eschatological expectation is most fully developed.

1. *The final ordeal and confusion*[1]

Reference to the last things is almost always accompanied by the notion, recurring in various forms, that a period of special distress and affliction must precede the dawn of salvation. It was of course reasonable to suppose that the way to happiness should lie through affliction. This is also explicitly predicted in the Old Testament (Hos. 13:13; Dan. 12:1 and elsewhere). In rabbinic teaching, the doctrine therefore developed of the חבלי המשיח,[2] the birth pangs of the Messiah which must precede his appearance (the expression is from Hos. 13:13; cf. Mt. 24:8: πάντα δὲ ταῦτα ἀρχὴ ὠδίνων; Mk. 13:8: ἀρχὴ ὠδίνων ταῦτα).[3] The threatening calamity will be heralded by omens of all kinds. Sun and moon will be darkened. Swords will appear in heaven. Columns of foot-soldiers and cavalry will advance through the clouds (Sibyl. 3:795–807; cf. 2 Mac. 5:2–3; 1QM 12:9; 19:1–2; *B.J.* vi 5,3 (289, 299); Tacitus *Hist.* v 13). Everything in nature will fall into tumult and disorder. The sun will shine by night, the moon by day. Blood will drip from wood, the voices of stones will ring out, in sweet water salt will be found (4 Ezr. 5:1–13). Sown ground will appear as though unsown, full barns will be discovered empty, springs will cease to flow (4 Ezr. 6:17–28). Among

1. Str.-B. I, p. 950; IV, pp. 977 f.; Moore, *Judaism* II, p. 361; Volz, *Eschatologie*, p. 147; J. Schniewind, *Das Evangelium des Markus* (1947) ad Mk. 13:8; A. Schlatter, *Der Evangelist Matthaeus* (1948), pp. 698 f.; S. Mowinckel, *He that Cometh*, p. 272 f.; J. Klausner, *The Messianic Idea* (1956), pp. 440–50; G. R. Beasley Murray, *A Commentary on Mark Thirteen* (1957), p. 36 f.; Bousset, *Religion*,[4] p. 250 f.

2. See Str.-B. I, p. 950: apart from one doubtful example, the expression occurs only in the singular חבלו של משיח, Aramaic, חבליה דמשיח; J. Klausner, *The Messianic Idea*, p. 440, n. 1.

3. For the Qumran doctrine on the final pre-messianic upheaval, see 1QM 1, especially lines 11–12: 'And it shall be a time of (great) tribulation (צרה) for the people which God shall redeem; of all of its tribulations none shall be as this, from its sudden beginning until its end in eternal redemption.' Cf. 1QH 3:6–18.

mankind, too, all the restraints of order will be loosened. Sin and godlessness will rule on earth. As though in the grip of madness, people will fight against each other. Friend will be against friend, son against father, daughter against mother. Nations will rise against nations. And to war will be added earthquake, fire and famine to carry men off (Bar. 70:2–8; 4 Ezr. 6:24; 9:1–12; 13:29–31; mSot. 9:15).[4] Cf. also Mt. 24:7–12, 21; Mk. 13:19; Lk. 21:23; 1 Cor. 7:26. Tim. 3:1, and 1QM (passim).

2. *Elijah as precursor*[5]

On the basis of Malachi 3:23–4, the prophet Elijah was expected to return to prepare the way of the Messiah. This is already presumed in Ecclesiasticus (43:10–11). In the New Testament, of course, there is frequent allusion to Elijah's coming (see especially Mt. 17:10; Mk. 9:11; also Mt. 11:14; 16:14, Mk. 6:15; 8:28; Lk. 9:8, 19. Jn. 1:21). Belief in it even passed into later Christian literature.[6] The aim of Elijah's mission, according to Mal. 3:24, will be mainly to establish peace on earth and in general change disorder into order (Mt. 17:11: ἀποκαταστήσει πάντα; Mk. 9:12: ἀποκαθιστάνει πάντα). The principal text in the Mishnah reads:[7]

4. mSot. 9:15: 'As marks of the near Messiah wantonness increases; ambition shoots up; the vine yields fruit yet wine is costly. Government turns to heresy and there is no rebuke. The house of assembly (the synagogue) is dedicated to lewdness. Galilee is destroyed; Gablan is laid waste. The inhabitants of a region pass from city to city without finding pity. The learning of the sages becomes foolish; those who fear sin are despised; truth is banished. Youths humiliate the aged; the aged stand before children. The son demeans the father; the daughter rebels against the mother; the daughter-in-law against the mother-in-law; the members of a man's household are his enemies (cf. Mic. 7:6, Mt 10:35–6, Lk. 12:53). The face of this generation is as that of a dog, so that the son is not ashamed before his father'. Cf. H. Bietenhard, *Soṭa* (1956), *in loc.*

5. W. Bousset, *Der Antichrist in der Überlieferung des Judenthums des neuen Testaments und der alten Kirche* (1895); E.T. *The Antichrist Legend: A Chapter in Christian and Jewish Folklore* (1896); G. Steindorff, *Die Apokalypse des Elias, Eine unbekannte Apokalypse* T.U. XVII, 3 (1899); Str.-B. IV (2), Excurs 28 (I, II); TDNT s.v. Ἠλ(ε)ίας; Volz, *Eschatologie*, pp. 193 f.; J. Klausner, *The Messianic Idea*, pp. 451–7; Bousset, *Religion*,[4] pp. 232–3; J. Ernst, *Die eschatologischen Gegenspieler in den Schriften des Neuen Testaments, Biblische Untersuchungen* III (1967), pp. 129 ff.; A.-M. Denis, *Introduction aux pseudepigraphes grecs d'Ancien Testament* (1970), p. 168; J.-M. Rosenstiehl, *L'Apokalypse d'Élie, Textes et Études pour servir à l'histoire de judaïsme intertestamentaire* I (1972); G. Vermes, *Jesus the Jew*, pp. 94–7, 244–5; M. Black, 'The "Two Witnesses" of Rev. 11.3 f. in Jewish and Christian Apocalyptic Tradition', C. K. Barrett *et al.* (eds.), *Donum Gentilicium: New Testament Studies in honour of David Daube* (1978), pp. 227–37.

6. Commodian, *Carmen apologet.* ll. 826 f.; Sibyl. 2, 187–90 (of Christian origin): **Καὶ τόθ' ὁ Θεσβίτης γε, ἀπ' οὐρανοῦ ἅρμα τιταίνων/Οὐράνιων, γαίῃ δ'ἐπιβὰς, τότε σήματα τρισσὰ/Κόσμῳ ὅλῳ δείξει τε ἀπολλυμένου βιότοιο.**

7. mEdu. 8:7. Cf. J. Neusner, *A Life of Yohanan ben Zakkai* ([2]1970), pp. 87–8; *Development of a Legend* (1970), p. 201.

'R. Joshua said: I have received the tradition from Rabban Yohanan ben Zakkai, who heard it from his teacher, and his teacher from his teacher, as a tradition of Moses from Sinai, that Elijah will not come to declare families unclean or clean, to exclude or to admit, but only to exclude those who have been brought in by force and to admit those who have been excluded by force. A family named Beth Zerepha was in the land beyond Jordan and was excluded by force by a certain Ben Zion. And yet another (family) was there (of unclean blood) which was brought in by Ben Zion by force. Elijah will come to declare such as these to be unclean or clean, to exclude or to admit. R. Judah says: Only to admit but not to exclude. R. Simeon says: His mission is merely to settle disputes. The sages say: Neither to exclude nor to admit, but his coming is merely to establish peace in the world. For it is written, *I will send you Elijah the prophet who will turn the heart of the fathers to the children and the heart of the children to the fathers* (Mal. 4:5)'.

The settlement of disputes being part of the task of one who introduces order and establishes peace, the Mishnah lays down that whenever the ownership of money and property is in dispute, or whenever the ownership of something found is unknown, this must be left 'until Elijah comes'.[8]

Very occasionally the opinion is also expressed that Elijah is to anoint the Messiah,[9] and that he will reawaken the dead.[10]

Besides Elijah, many looked for the prophet like Moses promised in Dt. 18:15 (1QS 9:11; 4QTest 5–8; Jn. 1:21; 6:14; 7:40; Act. 3:22; 8:37),[11] though others interpreted this passage as applying to the Messiah himself. The New Testament hints at other prophets, too, as precursors of the Messiah, such as Jeremiah (Mt. 16:14). There is also mention in Christian sources of the return of Enoch (Evang. Nicodemi 25, and the patristic commentators on Rev. 11:3).[12]

8. mB.M. 3:4–5; 1:8; 2:8. Cf. mShek. 2:5.

9. Justin, *Dial c. Tryph*. 8: *Χριστὸς δὲ εἰ καὶ ἔστι που, ἄγνωστός ἐστι καὶ οὐδὲ αὐτός πω ἑαυτὸν ἐπίσταται οὐδὲ ἔχει δύναμίν τινα, μέχρις ἂν ἐλθὼν Ἠλίας χρίσῃ αὐτὸν καὶ φανερὸν πᾶσι ποιήσῃ*. *Ibid*. 49: *Καὶ γὰρ πάντες ἡμεῖς τὸν Χριστὸν ἄνθρωπον ἐξ ἀνθρώπων προσδοκῶμεν γενήσεσθαι καὶ τὸν Ἠλίαν χρίσαι αὐτὸν ἐλθόντα*. Cf. Klausner, *The Messianic Idea*, p. 455; Vermes, *Jesus the Jew*, p. 138. Cf. also Jn. 1:31.

10. mSot. 9:15: 'The resurrection of the dead shall come through Elijah of blessed memory.' Cf. Klausner, *Messianic Idea*, p. 456. This expectation is based on the biblical representation of Elijah as an awakener of the dead.

11. Cf. Vermes, *Jesus the Jew*, pp. 95–7, 245, below p. 553.

12. Cf. E. Hennecke, *New Testament Apocrypha* (1963/4) I, p. 475 (Gospel of Nicodemus), II, p. 669 (Apocalypse of Peter). Cf. also II, p. 153 (Pseudo-Titus Epistle) and commentaries on Rev. 11:3. See also M. Black, *op. cit.* (above, n. 5).

3. *The coming of the Messiah*

After these preparations the Messiah will appear. It is in no way correct that pre-Christian Judaism expected the Messiah's coming to follow the judgement, and that the idea of the Messiah sitting in judgement on his enemies was due to Christian influence. Not only in Baruch and Ezra, the Parables of Enoch (which may have been affected by Christian thought) and in the Targums, but also in the oldest Sibylline Oracles 3:652–6, in the Psalms of Solomon, 17:24, 26, 27, 31, 38, 39, 41 and in Philo, *De praemiis et poenis* 16 (91–7)—in documents therefore that antedate Christianity—the Messiah appears to conquer the ungodly powers.[13] The opposing view that he will manifest himself only after the judgement is found once only, namely in 1 Enoch, 90:16–38.[13a]

As far as his names are concerned, as the King of Israel appointed and anointed by God he is mostly known as the Anointed, the Messiah (1 En. 48:10; 52:4; Bar. 29:3; 30:1; 39:8; 40:1; 70:9; 72:2; 4 Ezr. 7:28–9, where the Latin translation is interpolated; 4 Ezr. 12:32: *Unctus*), Greek *Χριστὸς κύριος* (Ps. Sol. 17:36; 18:6, 8), Hebrew **המשיח** (1QSa 2:12; mBer. 1:5), **משיח ישראל** (1QSa 2:14), **משיח (מן) אהרון וישראל** (CD 12:23, 14:19, 19:10, 20:1 [[מאהרון]]),[14] Aramaic **משיחא** (mSot. 9:15) or **מלכא משיחא** (both frequently found in the Targums);[15] in the New Testament, *Μεσσίας* (Jn. 1:42; 4:25).[16] Because *Χριστός* had become a Christian term, Greek-speaking Jews of the Christian era preferred the expression *'Ηλειμμένος* introduced by Aquila's translation of the Bible.[17] Further,

13. The appearance of the 'Messiah of Israel' with his 'chiefs of thousands' in 1QSa 2:11–12 envisages a similar conquest of the ungodly powers. Cf. also 1QSb 5:27, and below, p. 550. The ultimate overthrow of the 'Sons of Darkness' under the 'Angel of Darkness' in the forty years War Scroll also presupposes a final Armaggedon, but it is debated whether the Messiah is to play a rôle in this last conflict. Cf. M. Black, *Scrolls and Christian Origins*, p. 155 f.

13a. Cf. above p. 503, n. 15a.

14. Cf. 1QS 9:11, **משיחי אהרון וישראל**, 'the *Messiahs* (plur.) of Aaron and Israel'. On the messianism of Qumran see below, Appendix B.

15. Cf. in general on the title 'Messiah', Dalman, *Words of Jesus*, pp. 237–45; Moore, *Judaism* II, p. 330 n., Volz, *Eschatologie*, p. 173 f.; Klausner, *Messianic Idea*, p. 7 f.; Bousset, *Religion*, pp. 227–8.

16. *Μεσσίας* is the better attested form, not *Μεσιάς*, as many MSS. have it. Since according to all analogous cases an Aramaic, and not Hebrew, form is to be assumed, *Μεσσίας* is not **משיח** but **משיחא**. Cf. above, p. 22, and Dalman, *Grammatik des jüdisch-palästinischen Aramäisch* ([2]1905), p. 157, n. 3.

17. See Origen on Jn. 4:25 (ed. Lommatzsch II, p. 48): *Μεσσίας μέντοι γε 'Εβραϊστὶ καλεῖται, ὅπερ οἱ μὲν 'Εβδομήκοντα Χριστὸς ἡρμήνευσαν, ὁ δὲ 'Ακύλας 'Ηλειμμένος*. Origen's observation is confirmed by the remains of Aquila's translation of Dan. 9:26 (= Eusebius, *Dem. Ev.* viii 2:90, p. 397), Ps. 2:2 (*Syr. Hexapl.* and Philastr. *Haer.* 142, CSEL xxxvii; Aquila, 'adversum Unctum eius'), Ps. 84:10; 89:39; 1 Sam. 2:35 (= Eusebius, *Dem. ev.* iv 16, 45, p. 191); 2 Sam. 1:21 (Saul's shield). See Origen, *Hexapla* (ed. Field). Jerome, *Com. in Esaiam* 27:13: 'Iudaei cassa sibi vota promittunt, quod in consummatione mundi, quando [Antichristus, ut dicitur] *ἠλειμμένος* suus venerit' (the bracketted words are missing in some MSS. and

like the theocratic king of the Old Testament, he is sometimes designated 'son of God' (1 En. 105:2; 4 Ezr. 7:28–9; 13:32, 37, 52; 14:9; cf. 4QFlor 1:10–12). Also, as it was generally acknowledged on the basis of Old Testament prophecy[18] that the Messiah would come from the family of David (Ps. Sol. 17:5, 23; Mt. 22:42; Mk. 12:35; Lk. 20:41; Jn. 7:42; 4 Ezr. 12:32;[19] Targ. Jonathan on Isa. 11:1; Jer. 23:5; 33:15), 'son of David' is a customary title for the Messiah (often in the New Testament *υἱὸς Δαυείδ*; in Targ. Jonathan on Hos. 3:5 בר דוד; in Qumran pIsa 11:1–3,[20] and in the 15th *berakhah* of the *Shemoneh 'Esreh*, צמח דוד).[21] As one of David's line, he must be born in David's town of Bethlehem (Mic. 5:1 and Targum; Mt. 2:5; Jn. 7:41–2).

Pre-Christian Judaism—in so far as its messianic expectations can be conclusively documented—regarded the Messiah as a fully human

---

should certainly be omitted). *Id. Com. in Zach.* 14:15 (CCL lxxviA): 'haec Iudaei sub ἠλειμμένῳ suo carnaliter explenda contendunt'. *Id. Com. in Mal.* 3:1 (CCL lxxviA): 'Iudaei hoc . . . referunt ad ἠλειμμένον hoc est Christum suum'; *In Mal.* 4 end) (CCL lxxviA): 'Iudaei et Iudaizantes haeretici ante ἠλειμμένον suum Eliam putant esse venturum'. In the *Διδασκαλία Ἰακώβου νεοβαπτίστου* (see N. Bonwetsch, NGG (1899), pp. 411–40), the Messiah throughout is called ὁ ἠλειμμένος (pp. 418, 432, 435); similarly in F. Cumont, 'Une formule grecque de renonciation au judaïsme', Wiener Studien (1902), pp. 468–9. Sophocles, Greek Lexicon s.v. *Ἠλειμμένος* refers to Cyril of Jerusalem, *Cateches.* xv 11 (PG 33, col. 885A) and Cosmas Indicopleustes vi 25 (ed. Sources Chrétiennes 197, III, p. 41). Cf. also *Onomastica Sacra* (ed. Lagarde), p. 177, 59; 195, 80.

18. Is. 11:1, 10, Jer. 23:5, 30:9, 33:15, 17, 22; Ezek. 34:23 f., 37:24 f.; Hos. 3:5; Amos. 9:11; Mic. 5:1; Zech. 12:8. See Gressmann, *Der Messias*, pp. 193; S. Mowinckel, *He that Cometh*, p. 160.

19. Here the words, 'qui orietur ex semine David', are certainly missing from the Latin translation, but the unanimous testimony of the oriental versions shows that they must be considered original. See A. M. Ceriani, *Monumenta Sacra* V, p. 96. Cf. B.-M. Pelaia, 'Eschatologia messianica IV libri Esdrae', Verbum Domini 11 (1931), pp. 244–9, 310–18.

20. For rabbinical material on the 'Son of David', see Dalman, *Words of Jesus*, pp. 316–9. For the Davidic tradition in the Qumran writings, see A. S. van der Woude, *Die messianischen Vorstellungen der Gemeinde von Qumran* (1957), pp. 185–9; Black, *The Scrolls and Christian Origins* (1961), pp. 145–63; J. Starcky, 'Les quatre étapes du messianisme à Qumrân', RB 70 (1963), pp. 481 f. See further E. Lohmeyer, *Gottesknecht und Davidsohn*, in *Forschungen zur Religion und Literatur des Alten und Neuen Testaments*, N.F. 43 (1953), especially p. 64 f.; F. Hahn, *The Titles of Jesus in Christology* (1969), pp. 240–58; G. Schneider, 'Die Davidsohnfrage, Mk. 12, 35–37', Biblica 53 (1972), pp. 65–90; Vermes, *Jesus the Jew*, pp. 130–9, 251; F. Neugebauer, 'Die Davidsohnfrage (Mk. xii 35–7) und der Menschensohn', NTSt 21 (1974), pp. 81–90.

21. Cf. on Jewish views in general concerning the person of the Messiah, Moore, *Judaism* II, especially pp. 324, 330–1, 347; Str.-B. I, p. 11; Volz, *Eschatologie*, pp. 173–4; Klausner, *Messianic Idea*, pp. 519–31; Mowinckel, *He that Cometh*, pp. 159–60; Bousset, *Religion*,[4] pp. 222–32, 242–68; Vermes, *Jesus the Jew*, p. 130 f.

individual, a royal figure descended from the house of David.[22] This is no less true of the priestly Messiah expected, along with the royal Messiah or Prince of the Congregation, by the Qumran sect, as well as of the other messianic figure of the Prophet. (See further below, p. 553.) At the same time, messianic speculation,[23] some of which may well have formed the expectations of individuals or groups, especially in certain esoteric circles, tended with the growth of apocalyptic fantasy in the direction of a supra-mundane messianism; the more exceptional the position allotted to the Messiah, the more his person outstrips the bounds of common humanity. In the freedom of movement which existed in the field of religious ideas, this happened in very different ways. Yet in general, the Messiah was thought of as an earthly king and ruler, but as one endowed by God with special gifts and powers. This is particularly clear in the Psalms of Solomon. He appears here as an entirely human king (17:23, 47), righteous and learned (17:35), free from sin and holy (17:41, 46), and endowed by the holy spirit with power, wisdom and righteousness (17:42). Sibyl. 3:49 expresses the same view, only more briefly, in calling him ἁγνὸς ἄναξ. By contrast, in 4 Ezra[24] and the Parables of Enoch, his appearance is raised to the level of the supernatural and he is credited with pre-existence.[25] This is especially evident in 4 Ezr. 12:32, 'Hic est unctus, quem reservavit Altissimus in finem', and 13:26, 'Ipse est, quem conservat Altissimus multis temporibus'. As pre-existence is explicitly taught here, so is it assumed in the promise to Ezra (14:9) that after his assumption into heaven, Ezra himself would return with the Messiah ('tu enim recipieris ab hominibus et converteris residuum cum filio meo et cum similibus tuis, usque quo finiantur tempora'). Pre-existence is described as a state of concealment in God, 14:52: 'Sicut non potest hoc vel scrutinare vel

22. The promise of a king from the house of David 'for ever' means merely that the dynasty is not to die out. Thus, Simon Maccabaeus was chosen by the people as Prince and High Priest 'for ever' (εἰς τὸν αἰῶνα, 1 Mac. 14:41), i.e. the titles of Prince and High Priest are declared hereditary in his family. According to the Qumran Blessings of Jacob (4QPBless), 'whenever Israel rules there shall [not] fail to be a descendent of David upon the throne' (cf. J. M. Allegro, JBL 75 (1956), pp. 174–6).

23. G. Vermes, *Jesus the Jew*, pp. 130 f. and especially p. 134.

24. On the messianism of 4 Ezra, see G. H. Box, *The Ezra Apocalypse* (1912); Klausner, *Messianic Idea*, pp. 349–65.

25. Cf. on the concept of the pre-existence of the Messiah, G. A. Barton, 'On the Jewish-Christian Doctrine of the Pre-existence of the Messiah', JBL 21 (1902), pp. 78–91; Str.-B. II, p. 334; Moore, *Judaism* II, p. 343 f.; E. Sjöberg, *Menschensohn*, pp. 90–1; T. W. Manson, *Studies in the Gospels and Epistles* (1962), pp. 135–6; H. E. Tödt, *The Son of Man in the Synoptic Tradition* (1965), p. 28; M. D. Hooker, *The Son of Man in Mark* (1967), p. 42, n. 5; Volz, *Eschatologie*, p. 206; Bousset, *Religion*,[4] pp. 262–8; Dalman, *Words of Jesus*, pp. 299–303; Vermes, *Jesus the Jew*, pp. 138–9; Urbach, *The Sages*, pp. 684–5, 994.

scire quis, quid sit in profundo maris, sic non poterit quisquam super terram videre filium meum, vel eos qui cum eo sunt, nisi in tempore diei.'

A similar form of speculation to that in 4 Ezra occurs in the Parables of Enoch (1 En. 37–71).[26] The particular phrase connected with the Messiah in this work is 'Son of Man' (1 En. 46:1–6; 48:2–7; 62:5–9, 14; 63:11; 69:26–9; 70:1; 71:17),[27] a designation springing from the direct

26. Until the Qumran discoveries, the Parables of Enoch, found only in the Ethiopic version of that work, have been regarded as furnishing evidence for a (pre-Christian) supernatural Messiah. Their absence from 4Q Aramaic Enoch, and related considerations, probably require this work to be placed at the earliest in the late first century A.D. The editor of the Aramaic fragments dates the Parables to 'A.D. 270 or shortly afterwards', J. T. Milik, *The Books of Enoch. Aramaic Fragments of Qumrān Cave 4* (1976), p. 96. It is subject to debate whether it is to be classed as 'Jewish' evidence or as a 'Christianized' apocalypse. See M. Black, 'The Eschatology of the Similitudes of Enoch', JThSt 3 (1952), pp. 1–10, and especially Milik, *op, cit.*, pp. 89–98. For 1 Enoch, see vol. III, § 32. Cf. also J. C. Hindley, 'Towards a Date for the Similitudes of Enoch', NTSt 14 (1967–8), pp. 551–65; G. Widengren, 'Iran and Israel in Parthian Times with Special Regard to the Ethiopic Book of Enoch', Temenos 2 (1966), pp. 139–77; M. Black, 'The Fragments of the Aramaic Enoch from Qumran', W. C. van Unnik (ed.), *La littérature juive entre Tenach et Mischna, quelques problèmes, Recherches Bibliques* IX (1974), pp. 15–28. For the Ethiopic evidence, see E. Ullendorff, 'An Aramaic "Vorlage" of the Ethiopic Text of Enoch', *Atti del Convegno internazionale di Studi Etiopici*, Accademia Nazionale dei Lincei 357 (1960), pp. 259–68; *Ethiopia and the Bible* (1968), p. 61. Note in particular *The Ethiopic Book of Enoch. A New Edition in the Light of the Aramaic Dead Sea Fragments* by M. A. Knibb in consultation with Edward Ullendorff (1978).

27. How on the basis of the Daniel passages the expression 'son of man' came in Enoch to be 'individualised', and to refer to the transcendental figure of a heavenly Messiah, may be illustrated by the following passages (in the translation of R. H. Charles): 1 En. 46: 1–4: 'And there I saw One who had a head of days . . . and with Him was another being whose countenance had the appearance of a man . . . and I asked the angel . . . concerning that Son of Man . . . and he answered and said unto me: This is the Son of Man who hath righteousness, with whom dwelleth righteousness . . . And this Son of Man whom thou hast seen shall raise up the kings and the mighty from their seats, etc.' 48:2: 'And at that hour that Son of Man was named in the presence of the Lord of spirits, and his name before the Head of Days.' 62:5–9: 'And pain shall seize them, when they see that Son of Man sitting on the throne of his glory . . . for from the beginning the Son of Man was hidden, and the Most High preserved him . . . and all the kings and the mighty . . . shall . . . set their hope upon that Son of Man.' 62:14: 'And with that Son of Man shall they eat.' 63:11: 'And after that their faces shall be filled with darkness and shame before that Son of Man.' 69:26–9: 'And there was great joy amongst them, . . . because the name of that Son of Man had been revealed unto them . . . and the sum of judgement was given unto the Son of Man . . . and from henceforth there shall be nothing corruptible, for that Son of Man has appeared . . . and the word of that Son of Man shall go forth and be strong before the Lord of spirits.' 70:1: 'And it came to pass after this that his name (i.e. Enoch) during his lifetime was raised aloft to that Son of Man and to the Lord of

application of Daniel's image (7:13) to a heavenly messianic or quasi-messianic figure. Inasmuch as he is represented as the chosen instrument of God, he is also called 'the Elect' (1 En. 39:6 f.; 40:5; 45:3–5; 49:2–4; 51:3, 5; 52:6–9; 53:6; 55:4; 61:5, 8, 10; 62:1 f.).

The pre-existence of the Messiah is assumed; his name was uttered before the Lord of the Spirits before the sun and the signs were created, before the stars of the heaven were made (48:3). He was chosen and hidden by God from the beginning and the Most High preserved him (48:6; 62:7). Thus when Enoch was guided by the angel through the heavenly regions, he saw 'the Elect' and 'his dwelling-place under the pinions of the Lord of the spirits', and 'all the righteous and elect shone

---

spirits. . . .' 71:14: 'And he (the angel) came to me . . . and said . . . Thou art the Son of Man who is born unto righteousness. . . .' 71:17: 'And so there shall be length of days with that Son of man. . . .'—H. Lietzmann, *Der Menschensohn* (1896), pp. 42–8, and J. Wellhausen, *Skizzen und Vorarbeiten* VI (1899), p. 199, are correct when they emphasize that the term, 'son of man' in Enoch is nowhere a title or a name if 'title' or 'name' are understood in a narrower sense, for with the pronoun 'that' it is almost uniformly referred back to the original description in ch. 46. But it has been argued that, through the constant use of this reference in passages already remote from ch. 46, the expression developed into a fixed 'designation', indeed it almost becomes a title or name, as is shown by two passages quoted (62:7 and 69:27) where 'the son of man' is used instead of 'that son of man'. Note however that in both instances 'the son of man' is preceded by the phrase, 'that son of man' (62:5 and 69:26). See further, N. Messel, *Der Menschensohn in den Bilderreden des Henoch* (1922), p. 3; Vermes, *Jesus the Jew*, p. 175. On 48:2, the Messiah whose name is named forever, cf. Targ. Jon. on Zech. 4:7; Dalman, *The Words of Jesus*, p. 301; Klausner, *The Messianic Idea*, pp. 460–1. See further J. M. Creed 'The Heavenly Man', JThS 26 (1925), pp. 113–36; N. Messel, *Der Menschensohn in den Bilderreden des Henoch* (1922); Volz, *Eschatologie*, pp. 186 f.; H. L. Jansen, *Die Henochgestalt. Eine vergleichende religionsgeschichtliche Untersuchung* (1939); E. Sjöberg, *Der Menschensohn im äthiopischen Henochbuch* (1946); J. Y. Campbell, 'The Origin and Meaning of the Term Son of Man', JThSt 48 (1947), pp. 145–55; M. Black, 'The Eschatology of the Similitudes of Enoch', JThSt 3 (1952), pp. 1–10; G. Iber, *Überlieferungsgeschichtliche Untersuchungen zum Begriff des Menschensohns im Neuen Testament* (1953); S. Mowinckel, *He that Cometh* (1956), pp. 354–5; A. J. B. Higgins, 'Son of Man-Forschung since "The Teaching of Jesus"', *New Testament Essays: Studies in Memory of T. W. Manson* (1959), pp. 119–35; T. W. Manson, 'The Son of Man in Daniel, Enoch and the Gospels', *Studies in the Gospels and Epistles* (ed. M. Black, 1963); H. E. Tödt, *The Son of Man in the Synoptic Tradition* (1956), pp. 27–30; Bousset, *Religion*, pp. 262–8; M. D. Hooker, *The Son of Man in St. Mark* (1967), pp. 33–47; F. H. Borsch, *The Son of Man in Myth and History* (1967), pp. 145–56; F. Hahn, *The Titles of Jesus in Christology* (1969), pp. 15–67; C. Colpe, TDNT VIII (1969), pp. 400–77; R. Leivestad, 'Exit the Apocalyptic Son of Man', NTSt 18 (1972), pp. 243–67; B. Lindars, 'Re-enter the Apocalyptic Son of Man', NTSt 21 (1975), pp. 52–72; G. Vermes, *PBJS*, pp. 147–65 (=Appendix E in M. Black, *An Aramaic Approach to the Gospels and Acts*, [3]1967, pp. 310–30); J. Bowker, 'The Son of Man', JThSt 28 (1977), pp. 19–48; C. F. D. Moule, *The Origin of Christology* (1977), pp. 11–22; G. Vermes, 'The Present State of the Son of Man Debate', JJS 29 (1978), pp. 124–35.

before him as fiery lights' (39:6–7).[28] Enoch describes once again, 46:1–4, how 'that son of man' was shown to him. His countenance is full of graciousness like one of the holy angels (46:1). He it is who has righteousness, in whom righteousness dwells, and who reveals all the treasures of that which is hidden, because the Lord of the Spirits has chosen him, whose lot has surpassed all things before the Lord of Spirits in uprightness for ever (46:3). His glory is for ever and ever and his might from generation to generation. The spirit of wisdom dwells in him, and the spirit of insight, and the spirit of understanding and of power, and the spirit of those who have fallen asleep in righteousness. And he shall judge the secret things, and no man shall be able to speak a lying word before him, for he is chosen before the Lord of spirits, according to his pleasure (49:2–4).

It is not surprising that there have been many attempts to trace this entire line of thought to Christian influence, and it is doubtful if such influences can be altogether excluded, since this work can now scarcely be dated to the age of the Second Temple. At the same time, such ideas are fully comprehensible from Old Testament premises.[29] Statements such as that in Mic. 5:1, that the origins of the Messiah are from ages past, from the beginning of days (מקדם מימי עולם), may easily be taken in the sense of pre-existence from eternity. And Dan. 7:13–14 needs only to be understood to refer to the person of the Messiah, and his travel on the clouds as a descent from heaven, and the doctrine of pre-existence reveals itself.[30] This interpretation was encouraged by the whole development which tended to assert that everything truly valuable pre-existed in heaven.[31]

28. On the identification of Enoch with the Son of Man in ch. 71, see further Sjöberg, *Menschensohn*, pp. 147–89; Janzen, *Henochgestalt*, p. 124 f.; Mowinckel, *He that Cometh*, p. 386–7; F. H. Borsch, *The Son of Man in Myth and History*, 1967, p. 151–2; Black, *Eschatology*, pp. 4–5; R. Otto, *The Kingdom of God and the Son of Man*, pp. 201–8; Vermes, *Jesus the Jew*, pp. 174–5, 259.

29. The line of development from 4 Ezra to the New Testament is traced by G. Ellwein, 'Die Apocalypse des IV Esdras und das urchristliche Zeugnis von Jesus dem Christos', in *Heim-Festgabe* (1934), pp. 29–47.

30. That there is any thought of the Daniel Son of Man 'coming down' from heaven in Dan. 7:13 is denied by modern exegetes: the imagery in Daniel represents one 'like a son of man' as simply 'coming to' the Ancient of Days, but nothing is said or implied by Daniel about whence he comes. See especially the work of T. F. Glasson, *The Second Advent: the Origin of the New Testament Doctrine* ([3]1963); J. A. T. Robinson, *Jesus and His Coming: the Emergence of a Doctrine* (1957); Vermes, *Jesus the Jew*, pp. 169, 186–8, 257, 261. For a full discussion of the rôle of the cloud, see J. Luzarraga, *Las tradiciones de la nube en la Biblia y en el Judaismo primitivo* (1973).

31. See above, p. 495, and Harnack on Hermas, *Vis.* ii, 4, 1 (according to Hermas the Christian church is 'pre-existent'). See especially Harnack, *History of Dogma* I (1894), pp. 102 f. A heavenly model of the Tent of Revelation and its vessels is presupposed already in the Old Testament, Ex. 25:9; 26:30; 27:8; Num.

The idea of a pre-existent Messiah continued in post-Christian Judaism in the form of the pre-existence of his name (see n. 25), and this was in harmony with the Jewish emphasis on the humanity of the Messiah echoed in Justin's *Dialogue with Trypho*, 49: *πάντες ἡμεῖς τὸν Χριστὸν ἄνθρωπον ἐξ ἀνθρώπου προσδοκῶμεν γενήσεσθαι*. It has been argued that a Talmudic passage, yTaan 65b, is relevant here: 'R. Abbahu said: If a man says to you, "I am God", he lies; "I am a son of man (בן אדם)", he will in the end regret it; "I will ascend to heaven", he says so but will not fulfil it'; but this is questionable.[32]

In regard to the time of the Messiah's appearance, the later rabbis made all kinds of ingenious calculations.[33] A fairly general view seems to have been that the present world would endure for six thousand years, corresponding to the six days of creation, since for God one day is as a thousand years.[34] Yet even on this assumption the moment of his coming was again reckoned variously, according to whether the days of the Messiah were identified with the future עולם or the present one (cf. below, no. 9). According to the first interpretation, contained in patristic sources, the Messianic age would dawn after the expiration of the sixth thousand-year period (thus Barnabas, Irenaeus, Hippolytus

---

8:4. Cf. Heb. 8:1–7. On the heavenly Jerusalem ('the Jerusalem above'), cf. Gal. 4:26, Str.-B. III, p. 573, Bousset, *Religion*,[4] pp. 38, 489, etc.; TDNT VII, pp. 324, 336; for the Qumran evidence, cf. especially DJD III, pp. 184–93, and Vermes, *DSS*, p. 72. On 'worship' in heaven, see Moore, *Judaism* I, p. 404; for the Qumran evidence, see Vermes, *DSS*, pp. 125–9, 182.

32. On this passage see H. Lietzmann, *Der Menschensohn* (1896), pp. 49–50, and Vermes, *Jesus the Jew*, p. 258 (n. 40), both denying that there is any connection with Daniel. 'Wir haben vielmehr eine rabbinische Auslegung von Num. 23:19 vor uns: "Gott ist nicht ein Mann, dass er lüge und ein Menschensohn dass er bereue: ein solcher spricht und thut es nicht und redet und hält es nicht." Das erklärt nun Rabbi Abahû so: 'Wenn zu dir ein Mensch sagt: "Gott bin ich", so lügt er. "Ein Sohn Adam's bin ich", sein Ende [wird sein] es zu bereuen, denn "ich werde emporsteigen zum Himmel" sagt er [wohl] aber er halt es nicht.' (Lietzmann). 'The contrast between God and the *son of man* derives from *Numbers*, and is interpreted by Abbahu as expressing the difference between the divine and the human. . . . The rabbi from Caesarea seems to attack the Patristic claim that *son of man* describes the humanity of Jesus as opposed to the divinity expressed by *son of God*' (Vermes).

33. bSanh. 96b–97a. Cf. Moore, *Judaism* II, pp. 352 ff.; Klausner, *Messianic Idea*, pp. 420–1.

34. Barnabas, 15; Irenaeus, *Haer*. v 28, 3; Hippolytus, *Com. in Dan*. 4:32 (ed. Bonwetsch), pp. 242–5. In the Slavonic Enoch 32:2–33:2 the world's existence is said to extend over 7,000 years. Charles, *Apocrypha and Pseudepigrapha* II, p. 451; A. Vaillant, *Le Livre des secrets d'Hénoch: Texte slave et traduction française* (1952), p. 105, n. 7; Klausner, *Messianic Idea*, pp. 421 ff. On the question of the end, in general, see Volz, *Eschatologie*, pp. 72, 143–4. Bousset, *Religion*,[4] pp. 247 ff.

and others). According to the second (that the days of Messiah belonged to the present עולם), the current duration of the world is divided in the Talmud into three periods: two thousand years without the Torah, two thousand years under the Torah and two thousand years of messianic time. The age appointed for the Messiah had therefore already started; but he could not come yet because of the people's transgressions.[35]

The latter was the view generally held, in rabbinic circles in any case, namely that the Messiah could only come if the people did penance and fulfilled the Torah perfectly. 'If Israel repents, they will be redeemed'. 'If Israel were to keep two Sabbaths according to the rules, they would immediately be redeemed'.[36]

The manner of the coming of the Messiah is represented as sudden: all at once he is there and he appears as a victorious ruler. On the other hand, since it was supposed that he would be born as a child in Bethlehem, the two views are unified by the hypothesis that he will first live in concealment and then suddenly emerge.[37] Therefore the Jews say in Jn. 7:27: *ὁ Χριστὸς ὅταν ἔρχηται, οὐδεὶς γινώσκει πόθεν ἐστίν*. And it is for this reason that in Justin's *Dialogue with Trypho* the representative of Jewish opinion leaves open the possibility that the Messiah might already have been born but simply not yet revealed.[38] The Jerusalem Talmud relates that the Messiah was born in Bethlehem on the day the Temple was destroyed, but that a short time afterwards he was carried off from his mother by a tempest.[39] It is assumed also in the Targum Jonathan on Micah 4:8 that he is already present, but is still concealed because of the sins of the people.[40] Rabbinic traditions

35. Cf. bSanh. 97a; bAZ 9a. See Moore, *Judaism* II, pp. 352, 357; Klausner, *Messianic Idea*, pp. 408–19.

36. bSanh. 97a; bShab. 118b. Cf. I. Lévi, 'La discussion de R. Josué et de R. Eliézer sur les conditions de l'avènement du Messie', REJ 35 (1897), pp. 282–5; Klausner, *Messianic Idea*, pp. 422 ff., 427 f.; *Jesus of Nazareth* (1925), pp. 245–7; Urbach, *The Sages*, pp. 668–72.

37. Cf. J. Lightfoot, *Horae Hebraicae*, on Jn 7:27. N. Messel, 'Die Einheitlichkeit der jüdischen Eschatologie', BZAW 30 (1909); Str.-B. I, pp. 160 f., 481, 960, 1018; II, pp. 339, 340; III, p. 315; IV, p. 488, p. 766; H. Gressmann, *Der Messias* (1929), pp. 447–58; E. Sjöberg, *Der verborgene Menschensohn in den Evangelien* (1955); E. Stauffer, 'Agnostos Christos', *The Background of the New Testament and its Eschatology*, ed. W. D. Davies and D. Daube, in honour of C. H. Dodd (1956), pp. 281–99; S. Mowinckel, *He that Cometh* (1959), pp. 304–8; T. W. Manson, *Studies in the Gospels and Epistles* (1962), p. 136–7; Tödt, *The Son of Man in the Synoptic Tradition* (1965), Excursus 1, pp. 297–302; R. E. Brown, *The Gospel according to John* (1966), p. 53; Vermes, *Jesus the Jew*, pp. 137–8, 252–3.

38. *Dial. c. Tryph.* 8 (for the Greek text, see n. 9 above). *Ibid.* 110: εἰ δὲ καὶ ἐληλυθένα λέγουσιν οὐ γινώσκεται ὅς ἐστιν, ἀλλ' ὅταν ἐμφανὴς καὶ ἔνδοξος γένηται, τότε γνωσθήσεται ὅς ἐστι, φασί.

39. For the text, see yBer. 5a and Ekha R. 1:51; cf. G. Dalman, *Aramäische Dialektproben* ([2]1926), p. 14. See also Vermes, *Jesus the Jew*, p. 138.

40. Cf. S. H. Levey, *The Messiah: An Aramaic Interpretation* (1974), p. 92.

opine that he will come from Rome.[41] According to the Gospels, the belief was general, however, that when he comes he will prove his identity by means of miracles (Mt. 11:4 ff.; Lk. 7:22 ff.; Jn. 7:31).[42]

4. *The last assault of the hostile powers*[43]

After the Messiah has appeared, the Gentile powers will gather for a final assault against him. This expectation, too, is suggested by Old Testament passages, notably Daniel 11 and Psalm 2. It is expressed most clearly in Sibyl. 3:663 ff. and 4 Ezr. 13:33 ff., also in 1 En. 90:16, and 1 QM 15–19, except that here there is question not of an attack against the Messiah but against the community of God.

It is frequently assumed that this last assault will be under the leadership of a chief adversary of the Messiah, an 'Antichrist' (the name appears in the New Testament, in the Johannine Epistles 1 Jn. 2:18, 22; 4:3; 2 Jn. 7; the issue in 2 Bar. ch. 40; 2 Thes. 2; Rev. 13).[44] In later rabbinic sources the name of this principal adversary of the people of Israel is given as Armilus (ארמילוס/ארמלגוס), i.e. Romulus,[45] the Greek

41. Pal. Targums on Ex. 12:42, and bSanh. 88a. G. Dalman, *Der leidende und sterbende Messias* (1888), p. 41; Str.-B. II, p. 340; A. von Gall, *Βασιλεία τοῦ Θεοῦ. Eine religionsgeschichtliche Studie zur vorkirchlichen Eschatologie* (1926), p. 400. On the Targums to Ex. 12:42, see Vermes, *Scripture and Tradition* (1961, [2]1973), p. 217; R. Le Déaut, *La nuit pascale* (1963), pp. 271–2, 359–69; M. McNamara, *The New Testament and the Palestinian Targum of the Pentateuch* (1966), pp. 210–11; Black, *Aramaic Approach* ([3]1967), pp. 237–8; Vermes, *PBJS*, pp. 223–4. On bSanh. 98a, see Vermes, *Jesus the Jew*, p. 116.

42. This view is absent from the rabbinic texts. '. . . *the Messiah . . . is never mentioned anywhere in the Tannaitic literature as a wonder-worker* per se' (Klausner, *Messianic Idea*, p. 506). For the anti-charismatic tendency of the rabbis, see Vermes, *Jesus the Jew*, pp. 80–2; D. Daube, 'Enfant terrible', HThR 68 (1975), pp. 370–6, especially p. 375.

43. See Str.-B. IV, pp. 981 ff.; S. Mowinckel, *He that Cometh*, pp. 313 ff. For the Qumran evidence, see especially 1QM, and Y. Yadin, *The Scroll of the War of the Sons of Light against the Sons of Darkness* (1962).

44. M. Friedländer, 'L'Anti-Messie', REJ 38 (1899), pp. 14–37; *Der Antichrist in den vorchristlichen jüdischen Quellen* (1901); R. H. Charles, *The Ascension of Isaiah* (1900), pp. li–lxxiii; L. Ginzberg, 'Antichrist', JE I, pp. 625–7; W. Bousset, *The Anti-Christ Legend: A Chapter in Christian and Jewish Folklore* (1896); B. Rigaux, *L'Antichrist et l'opposition au royaume messianique dans l'Ancien et le Nouveau Testament* (1932); Volz, *Eschatologie*, p. 282; H. A. Guy, *The New Testament Doctrine of the Last Things* (1948), pp. 146–9; J. Schmid, 'Der Antichrist und die hemmende Macht', Theol. Quartalschrift 129 (1949), pp. 323–343; G. Vos, *The Pauline Eschatology* (1953), pp. 114–15; Klausner, *Messianic Idea*, pp. 373–4; Bousset, *Religion*[4], pp. 254–6; J. Ernst, *Die eschatologischen Gegenspieler in den Schriften des Neuen Testaments* (1967); C. H. Giblin, *The Threat to Faith: An Exegetical and Theological Examination of 2 Thessalonians 2* (Analecta Biblica 31) (1967), pp. 66–7.

45. Cf. Tg. Ps.-Jon. Deut. 34:3, Isa. 11:4; A. Jellinek, *Bet ha-Midrasch* III, pp. 124–5; Dalman, *Der leidende und der sterbende Messias der Synagogue* (1888), pp. 13–14; Bousset, *The Anti-Christ Legend*, pp. 53, 186; Krauss, *Griechische und*

corruption being *'Ερμόλαος*.[46] The reappearance of Gog and Magog is also awaited on the basis of Ezekiel 38–9 as a last manifestation of the demonic powers (Rev. 20:8–9).[47]

In several of the Qumran scrolls a certain Milkireša', 'King of Evil', occupies a position resembling that of the Antichrist.[48] Appearing as a satanic being, or even as Satan himself, at the end-time, he is the antitype of Milkiẓedeḳ, 'King of Righteousness'.[49]

5. *Destruction of hostile powers*[50]

The destruction of the hostile powers will follow, according to Old Testament prophecy, from a mighty vengeance inflicted by God himself on his adversaries.[51] The most faithful portrayal of this view is given in the Assumption of Moses, in which chapter 10 recalls in many respects Joel 3–4. Closely related to it is the description provided in 1 Enoch in so far as it too represents God himself as annihilating the power of the Gentile nations (90:18–19), and as then sitting in judgement, one in which nevertheless only the fallen and disobedient angels and the apostate Israelites (the blinded sheep) are condemned (90:20–7), whereas the remaining Gentiles submit to the community of God (90:30). The Messiah, who is entirely absent from the Assumption of Moses, does not appear here until after the judgement (90:37). Common to both, therefore, is the concept of God himself pronouncing judgement. But the customary notion was that the Messiah would destroy the hostile powers. Already in the oldest Sibylline Oracles (3:622 ff.) he comes to 'put an end to all war upon earth, killing some and fulfilling

---

lateinische Lehnwörter I, pp. 241–3; II, p. 132; Ginzberg, *art.* 'Armilus', JE II, pp. 118–20. See also Mowinckel, *He that Cometh*, p. 290; F. F. Hvidberg, *Menigheden av den nye Pagt I Damascus* (1928), p. 277, n. 1; Klausner, *Messianic Idea*, pp. 373, 407, 496; Enc. Jud. 2, cols. 476–7.

46. Thus e.g. in the *Διδασκαλία 'Ιακώβου νεοβαπτίστου*, ed. Bonwetsch, NGGW, phil.-hist. Kl. (1899), pp. 418, 431, 439.

47. Cf. Sibyl. 3:319 f., 512 f., mEdu. 2:10. Cf. Klausner, *Messianic Idea*, pp. 127 f., 483 f.; Volz, *Eschatologie*, pp. 150 f.; Bousset, *Religion*,[4] pp. 219–20. See also 1QM 11:16: '. . . when Thou chastisest Gog and all his assembly gathered about him . . .'

48. See J. T. Milik, 'Milkî-ṣedeq et Milkî-reša' dans les anciens écrits juifs et chrétiens', JJS 24 (1972), pp. 95–144; Vermes, *DSSE*[2], pp. 253–4, 280–1. See below, pp. 553–4.

49. Milik, *op. cit.*, p. 125. The angelic Redeemer, Melkizedek, is also primarily described as a judge in 11QMelch. Cf. below, p. 553.

50. See Volz, *Eschatologie*, pp. 151 ff.; Mowinckel, *He that Cometh*, p. 269; Bousset, *Religion*[4], pp. 218 ff.; *L'Assomption de Moïse*, ed. Laperousaz, ad 10:8.

51. See W. Cossmann, *Die Entwicklung des Gerichtsgedankens bei den alttestamentlichen Propheten*, BZAW 29 (1915); Mowinckel, *He that Cometh*, p. 273; Bousset, *Religion*[4], pp. 202 f.; M. Hengel, *Judaism and Hellenism* I, pp. 200 f.

the promises given to others'. Philo, *Praem.* 16 (95), mentions that he 'shall lead his host to war and shall subdue great and populous nations'. In the Psalms of Solomon he is depicted even more clearly as conqueror of the Gentile adversaries of the people of God, and it is especially noteworthy that in this work he overthrows his enemies (17, 27, 39) by the word of his mouth (ἐν λόγῳ στόματος αὐτοῦ, according to Isa. 11:4).[52] The representation, especially in the Apocalypse of Baruch and 4 Ezra (Bar. 39:7–40:2; 70:2–6; 4 Ezr. 12:32–3; 13:27–8, 35–8), of the primary work of the Messiah once he appears as being the destruction of the Gentile world-powers, is thus in accord with these older prototypes. The difference nevertheless is that according to 4 Ezra this annihilation results exclusively from the judgement pronounced by God's Anointed (13:28: 'non tenebat frameam neque vas bellicosum'; 13:38: 'perdet eos sine labore per legem'), whilst in the Apocalypse of Baruch there is mention of judicial processes but also of weapons of war (the first, 40:1–2; the second, 72:6).

In the Parables of Enoch, the judgement of the Messiah on the ungodly world is portrayed even more definitely than in 4 Ezra as a purely judicial affair. This is consistent with the concept of the messianic nature predominating in these Apocalypses. The Messiah is not a warrior, but a supernatural being descended from heaven. He therefore executes punishment on the enemies of the people of God not as a general, but as a judge appointed by God. Admittedly, warlike overtones are heard here too. In 1 Enoch 46:4–6, it is said of 'the Son of Man' that he startles the kings and the mighty from their camps, loosens the bridles of the powerful, crushes the teeth of the sinners and casts down kings from their thrones and kingdoms; and in 1 Enoch 52:4–9, that nothing on earth can resist his power. 'There shall be no iron for war, nor material for a breastplate; bronze shall be of no service, and tin [shall be of no service] and of no worth, and lead shall not be desired'. But from these very words it is apparent that there is question here not of a battle but of the destruction of the enemy by a higher power. Thus throughout, the function of the Messiah is described as that of a sovereign judge. His competence is that of one who possesses the spirit of wisdom and understanding; he shall judge that which is hidden and no man shall be able to utter idle words before him (49:3–4). He, the Elect, shall sit on the throne of his glory upon which God has placed him, to pronounce judgement on men and angels (45:3; 52:3; 55:4; 61:8–10). The most detailed accounts are those of chapters 62 and 69. The Lord of spirits seats him (this emendation is no doubt preferable to 'sat' attested by the manuscripts) on the throne of his glory. And the word of his mouth slays all sinners and all the unrighteous shall be destroyed from before

52. Cf. below, pp. 550–2 for Qumran parallels.

his face (62:2). And the kings and the mighty of the earth, when they see him, shall be smitten with fear and terror and shall bless and glorify and extol him and entreat him for mercy (62:4–9). But the Lord of spirits shall press them so that they flee hurriedly from his presence; and their faces shall be filled with shame, and darkness heaped upon them. And the avenging angels shall receive them, to execute vengeance on them for having maltreated his children and elect (62:10–11). According to the other account (ch. 69), he sits on the throne of his glory and the totality of judgement is given to him, 'that Son of Man', and he causes sin to vanish and to be obliterated from the face of the earth, together with those who have led the world astray. They shall be bound with chains and confined in their place of assembly doomed to destruction, and all their works shall vanish from the face of the earth. And from henceforth nothing corrupt shall exist (69:27–9).

In the Targums, the Messiah is again depicted as a mighty warrior who conquers his enemies in battle. Thus in the Targum on Isaiah 10:27, 'The nations shall be crushed by the Messiah', and particularly in the Palestinian Targums (Ps.-Jon., Fragm. Tg. and Neof.) on Genesis 49:11: 'How beautiful is King Messiah who shall arise from the house of Judah, He girds his loins and goes forth to battle against them that hate him, and he slays kings and rulers'. (The translation follows the Neofiti recension.) One sees, in effect, that the idea common to them all of a destruction of the ungodly powers by the Messiah varies greatly in its details.[53]

The messianic age could not begin until the godless were destroyed. For 'as long as transgressors are in the world, so long does God's anger

53. There is mention in a *baraita* (bSuk. 52a) of a 'Messiah son of Joseph' of whom it is said merely that he will be put to death whereas life will be promised to the Messiah son of David. In the same place (bSuk. 52a), Zech. 12:10 is also applied to him without any reference to the cause and manner of his death. Other sources assign to this subordinate Messiah, also called 'Messiah son of Ephraim', the duty of conquering the principal enemies of the people of God. The origin of this whole concept is obscure. It may derive from the dual nature and dual mission of the Messiah, being divided between two persons: the one fights and falls in battle, the other, brings only salvation. Whilst the latter is of Davidic descent, the former is made to spring from the tribe of Joseph or Ephraim (thus Klausner). Dalman considers Dt. 33:17 to be the source of the concept. He is nowhere described as the Messiah of the ten tribes; neither is his death envisaged as expiatory. Cf. in general: Klausner, *Messianic Idea*, pp. 483 f.; Mowinckel, *He that Cometh*, p. 285 f., 290 f., 314 f., 325 f.; V. Sadek, 'Der Mythos vom Messias dem Sohn Josefs', Archiv Orientalni 43 (1965), pp. 27–43. The slain Messiah is thought to have been conceived after the pattern of Simeon ben Kosiba and it is worth noting that in Ps.-Jon. on Ex. 40:11 no idea of defeat and death is linked to the Ephraimite Messiah, cf. Vermes, *Jesus the Jew*, pp. 139–40, 253. See also J. Heinemann, 'The Messiah of Ephraim and the premature Exodus of the Tribe of Ephraim', HThR 68 (1975), pp. 1–15.

continue; but as soon as they vanish from the earth, so soon does God's anger also turn from the world'.[54]

6. *The renewal of Jerusalem*[55]

As the messianic kingdom was to be established in the holy land (cf. e.g. 4 Ezr. 9:8), Jerusalem itself must first of all be renewed. This, however, was envisaged in differing ways. The expectation in its simplest form was of a cleansing of the holy city, in particular of 'the Gentiles who now tread it underfoot' (Ps. Sol. 17:25, 33),[56] a hope which took the form, after the destruction of Jerusalem, of a foreseen reconstruction of the city 'as an everlasting building' (*Shemoneh 'Esreh*, 14th *berakhah*). But in addition, it was also thought that a much more beautiful Jerusalem already existed with God in heaven in the pre-messianic age, and that when the messianic period began it would descend upon earth. The biblical foundation for this idea is especially Ezekiel 40–8, but also Isaiah 54: 11 ff., 60, Haggai 2:7–9, and Zechariah 2:6–17, in that the new Jerusalem described in these passages is conceived of as already existing in heaven.[57] For the Qumran evidence see n. 55. In the New Testament too there is frequent mention of this *ἄνω Ἰερουσαλήμ* (Gal. 4:26), *Ἰερουσαλὴμ ἐπουράνιος* (Hebr. 12:22), *καινὴ Ἰερουσαλήμ* (Rev. 3:12; 21-2; 10); cf. also the Testament of Dan. 5:12, *ἡ νέα Ἰερουσαλήμ*. According to the Apocalypse of Baruch, the heavenly Jerusalem stood in Paradise before Adam sinned. But when he transgressed the command of God, it was taken from him and preserved in heaven, as was Paradise. Later, it was shown to Abraham in a vision at night, as well as to Moses on Mount Sinai (2 Bar. 4:2–6). Ezra also saw it in a vision (4 Ezr. 10:44–59). This new and glorious Jerusalem

54. mSanh. 10:6.

55. See R. H. Charles, *Revelation* II, p. 150 ff., especially pp. 158–61; Str.-B. IV, pp. 883–5, 919–31; Moore, *Judaism* II, pp. 341–3; Volz, *Eschatologie*, pp. 372 ff.; G. von Rad, 'Die Stadt auf dem Berge', Ev. Theol. 8 (1948–49), p. 439–47; H. Bietenhard, *Die himmlische Welt im Urchristentum und Spätjudentum* (1951), pp. 192–204. For the idea of a 'new Jerusalem' (whether a heavenly or a future earthly Jerusalem), cf. Klausner, *Messianic Idea*, pp. 287, 346, 361–2; TDNT VII s.v. *Σιών*; Bousset, *Religion*^{4}, pp. 239–40; R. J. McKelvey, *The New Temple: The Church in the New Testament* (1969), pp. 1–40, 141–4; Enc. Jud. 9, cols. 1559–60. For the Qumran material, see J. T. Milik, DJD I, pp. 134–5; DJD III, pp. 184–93; M. Baillet, *ibid.*, pp. 84–90; B. Jongeling, 'Publication provisoire d'un fragment provenant de la grotte 11 de Qumrân', JSJ 1 (1970), pp. 58–64, 185–6; cf. Vermes, *DSSE*^{2}, pp. 262–4; *DSS*, p. 72.

56. See the preceding note. Cf. also Black, *Scrolls and Christian Origins*, p. 110. A similar purification of Jerusalem is no doubt implied in the Qumran War Scroll (1QM 2:1–6) which describes the restoration of the Temple cult in the 7th year of the final war, when Jerusalem will be reconquered and taken from the Sons of Darkness.

57. A similar picture is contained in several Qumran fragments also. For references see n. 55.

shall thus appear on earth in place of the old, and in its magnificence and beauty shall far outstrip it (1 En. 53:6; 90:28–9; 4 Ezr. 7:26. Cf. also 2 Bar. 32:4). The continuance of this hope is also attested by Jerome, who for his part attacked it vigorously as a Jewish and Judaeo-Christian idea.[58]

7. *The gathering of the dispersed*[59]

That the dispersed of Israel would participate in the messianic kingdom and return for this purpose to the Holy Land was so self-evident that this hope would have been cherished even without the Old Testament prophecies. Jesus ben Sira himself prays: 'Gather all the tribes of Jacob together, that they may receive their inheritance as in the days of old' (36:11). On the passage found only in Hebrew praising God as he 'who gathers together the dispersed of Israel' (51:12, 6), see above p. 499. The Psalms of Solomon (Ps. 11) describe how from evening to morning, from the north and from the isles, the dispersed of Israel assemble and travel to Jerusalem. The Greek Book of Baruch concurs with this, in part word for word (4:36–7; 5:5–9. Philo sees the dispersed journeying from every quarter to Jerusalem under the leadership of a divine apparition, *Praem.* 28 (164)–29 (165). Also, the prophecy of Isaiah, that the Gentile nations themselves shall bring the dispersed as an offering to the Temple (Isa. 49:22; 60:4, 9; 66:20), reappears in the Psalms of Solomon 17:34, whilst the assembly is at the same time represented as the work of the Messiah (Ps. Sol. 17:28, Tg. Jon. to Jer. 33:13). According to 4 Ezra, the ten tribes move into a land hitherto uninhabited called Arzareth (the Latin version) or Arzaph ('finis mundi', the Syriac version), to observe their laws there.[60] They will return from this place when the messianic age dawns, and the Most High will dry up the sources of the Euphrates to enable them to pass over (4 Ezr. 13:39–47). Indeed, given the universality of this hope for the gathering of the dispersed, it is remarkable that the return of the

58. Jerome, *Com. in Esaiam* 49:14: 'Ierusalem, quam Iudaei et nostri Iudaizantes iuxta apocalypsim Ioannis, quam non intelligunt, putant auream atque gemmatam de coelestibus ponendam, cuius terminos et infinitam latitudinem etiam in Ezechielis ultima parte describi'. Similarly *Com. in Ezech.* 36; *Com. in Ioel* 3:16.

59. Cf. Moore, *Judaism* II, pp. 366–9; Volz, *Eschatologie*, pp. 341–3; A. Oepke, *Das neue Gottesvolk* (1950), p. 57 f.; S. Aalen, *Die Begriffe 'Licht' und 'Finsternis'* (1951), pp. 204 f., 209, 212 f., 228, 311 f.; Klausner, *Messianic Idea*, p. 470–82; J. Jeremias, *Jesus' Promise to the Nations* (1958), p. 55 ff.; Bousset, *Religion*,[4] pp. 236–8.

60. *Arzareth*, ארץ אחרת, 'terra alia' (4 Ezr. 13:45); the Hebrew expression is in Dt. 29:27, the passage applied in mSanh. 10:3 to the ten tribes (see next note). Cf. Charles, *Apocrypha and Pseudepigrapha* II, p. 69, Bousset, *Religion*,[4] p. 237. For the Syriac see A. M. Ceriani, *Monumenta Sacra et profana* V, p. 102: 'Arzaph, the end of the world'. This seems to be an interpretation of Arzaph = ארץ סוף, with an allusion to the סוף (ים) 'the reed (sea)'.

ten tribes was questioned at all by individuals.[61] But from the daily prayer of the *Shemoneh 'Esreh* (10th *berakhah*), 'Raise a banner to gather our dispersed, and gather us from the four ends of the earth', it is clear that such doubts were sporadic.[62]

8. *The kingdom of glory in the Holy Land*

The messianic kingdom will have at its head the messianic King. Nevertheless, its supreme Ruler will be God himself. Cf. e.g. Sibyl. 3:704–6, 717, 756–9. Ps. Sol. 17:1, 38, 51; 1QM *passim*; *Shemoneh 'Esreh*, 11th *berakhah*; *B.J.* ii 8, 1 (118). Therefore, with the establishment of this kingdom the idea of God's sovereignty over Israel will acquire full reality and truth. God is of course already King of Israel. But he does not exercise his sovereignty to its full extent; it is rather that he has surrendered his people temporarily to Gentile powers to chastise them for their sins. But in the glorious kingdom of the future, he will take back its government into his own hands. For this reason it will be called, in contrast to the Gentile kingdoms, the kingdom of God (*βασιλεία τοῦ θεοῦ* in the New Testament, especially in Mark and Luke; Sibyl. 3:47–8: *βασιλεία μεγίστη ἀθανάτου βασιλῆος*. Cf. Ps. Sol. 17:4. Ass. Mos. 10:1, 3).[63] The expression used by Matthew, *βασιλεία τῶν οὐρανῶν*, 'kingdom of heaven', [64] has a similar meaning. For in line with a well-

61. mSanh. 10:3: 'The ten tribes shall never return. for it is written of them (Dt. 29:27), *And he will cast them into another land like this day*. Thus as this day goes and returns not, so shall they also go and not return. Thus R. Akiba. But R. Eliezer says: As the day darkens and becomes light once more, so for the ten tribes for whom it became dark shall there be light once more.' Tradition varies moreover in regard to the authorities represented by these sayings. In ARN A, ch. 36 (ed. Schechter, p. 108), the second (favourable) opinion is accredited to R. Akiba, the unfavourable one to R. Simon b. Judah. Others vary again. See details in W. Bacher, *Die Agada der Tannaiten* I², pp. 137 f. Cf. II, pp. 145, 472; J. Neusner, *Eliezer ben Hyrcanus* I (1973), pp. 453–4.

62. For later times cf. Jerome, *Com. in Ioel* 3:7: 'Promittunt ergo sibi Iudaei immo somniant, quod in ultimo tempore congregentur a Domino et reducantur in Ierusalem. Nec hac felicitate contenti, ipsum Deum suis manibus Romanorum filios et filias asserunt traditurum, ut vendant eos Iudaei non Persis et Aethiopibus et caeteris nationibus quae vicinae sunt, sed Sabaeis, genti longissimae'.

63. Moore, *Judaism* II, pp. 371–5; G. Gloege, *Reich Gottes und Kirche im Neuen Testament* (1929); see also s.v. *βασιλεία*, TDNT I, pp. 569–76; Volz, *Eschatologie*, pp. 167 f.; T. W. Manson, *The Teaching of Jesus* (²1935), pp. 116 ff.; C. H. Dodd, *Parables of the Kingdom* (1935); K. L. Schmidt *et al.*, *Basileia* (1957); Sverre Aalen, ' "Reign" and "House" in the Kingdom of God in the Gospels', NTSt 8 (1962), pp. 215–40; G. Lundström, *The Kingdom of God in the Teaching of Jesus* (1963) (Bibliography, pp. 279–96); N. Perrin, *The Kingdom of God in the Teaching of Jesus* (1963); G. E. Ladd, *Jesus and the Kingdom: The Eschatology of Biblical Realism* (1966) (comprehensive bibliography, pp. 337–67); Bousset, *Religion*,⁴ pp. 213–18.

64. Cf. on this expression in general, Str.-B. I, pp. 172–84 (on Mt. 3:2); G. Dalman, *Words of Jesus*, pp. 91 f.; Ass. Mos., ch. 10; Ps. Sol. 17:4; 2 Bar. 73; 1QSb 3:5.

known Jewish idiom, 'heaven' is here synonymous with 'God'. It is a kingdom that will be governed not by earthly powers, but by heaven.[65]

The Holy Land will be the centre of this kingdom. 'To inherit the land' is therefore equivalent to participating in the messianic realm.[66] Such an identification indicates how decisively the ancient prophetic expectations determined later hopes for the future: the perfect kingdom of God is now also a national kingdom of the people of Israel.[67] Yet it was not to be restricted to the boundaries of Palestine; on the contrary, it is usually conceived of as embracing the whole world.[68] Indeed, it is prophesied already in the Old Testament that the Gentile nations shall also acknowledge the God of Israel as the supreme Judge (Isa. 2:2 ff.; Mic. 4:1 ff.; 7:16 f.) and be converted to him (Isa. 42:1–6; 49:6; 51:4–5. Jer. 3:17; 16:19 f.; Zeph. 2:11; 3:9. Zech. 8:20 ff.), and shall consequently be admitted into the theocracy (Isa. 55:5; 56:1 ff. Jer. 12:14 ff.; Zech. 2:15) so that Israel's God shall be King over all the earth (Zech. 14:9) and the Messiah be an ensign for all the peoples (Isa. 11:10).[69] Daniel

65. The formula מלכות שמים occurs frequently, though not as a rule with the meaning 'kingdom of heaven', but in the abstract sense of the sovereignty or government of heaven, i.e., the dominion of God (e.g. mBer. 2:2, 5). In this particular passage, however, there can be no doubt that שמים stands metonymically for God. It is all the more strange to dispute the correctness of this formulation where *βασιλεία* occurs in the concrete sense of 'kingdom'; for the genitive *τῶν οὐρανῶν* remains the same whether *βασιλεία* means 'the kingship' or 'the kingdom'. Should the expression מלכות שמים occur by chance in rabbinic literature and *not* mean the 'kingdom of heaven', this would easily be explained by the fact that the rabbis in general seldom speak of 'the kingdom of God'. For this they use instead the expressions, 'the days of Messiah', or 'the עולם to come', or some such phrase. It seems however that the expression does occur with this meaning; thus especially Pes. R. (ed. Buber), p. 51a: הגיע זמנה של מלכות הרשע שתעקר מן העולם הגיע זמנה של מלכות שמים שתגלה. 'The time has come for the ungodly kingdom, that it be uprooted from the world; the time has come for the kingdom of heaven, that it be revealed'. See J. Levy, *Neuhebr. Wörterb.* s.v. מלכות. Cf. Urbach, *The Sages*, pp. 400–1.

66. mKid. 1:10. Cf. Mt. 5:5; 1 En. 5:7 (*τὴν γῆν κληρονομεῖν*); Ps. of Sol. 14:6 (*ζωὴν κληρονομεῖν*). See also Volz, *Eschatologie*, p. 411. On the biblical idea of 'inheritance', TDNT s.v. *κληρονομία*, III, p. 767 (Foerster). W. D. Davies, *The Gospel and the Land: Early Christianity and Jewish Territorial Doctrine* (1972), especially pp. 366–7. Cf. 1QM 12:11; 19:4 ('Fill Thy land with glory and Thine inheritance with blessing'.)

67. Cf. on the national character, Volz, *Eschatologie*, pp. 368 f.; Bousset, *Religion*⁴, pp. 213–42.

68. See Volz, *Eschatologie*, pp. 379 f.; Klausner, *Messianic Idea*, pp. 502 f.; Bousset, *Religion*⁴, p. 215. According to 1QM 2:10–14, after regaining Palestine the Sons of Light will subjugate all the sons of Shem, Ham and Japheth, including among the latter the Kittim-Romans, the former masters of mankind.

69. Cf. on universalism in the Bible: J. Wellhausen, *Israelitische und jüdische Geschichte* (²1901), pp. 224–6; A. Bertholet, *Die Stellung der Israeliten und der Juden zu dem Fremden* (1896), pp. 91–122, 191–5; M. Weinfeld, 'Universalism and Particularism in the Period of Exile and Restoration', Tarbiz 33 (1963–4),

promises most emphatically that power over all the kingdoms of the world shall lie with the saints of the Most High (Dan. 2:44; 7:14, 27). This hope was maintained by later Judaism, but in a different way. According to the Sibylline Oracles, when the Gentiles become aware of the peace and quiet of the people of God, they will see reason and give praise and honour the one true God, and send gifts to his Temple and walk in accordance with his laws (Sibyl. 3:698–726). God will then establish a kingdom over all mankind, one in which the prophets of God shall be judges and upright kings (3:766–83). According to Philo, the pious and the virtuous will rule the world because they possess the three qualities which pre-eminently qualify men to do so, i.e. *σεμνότης*, *δεινότης* and *εὐεργεσία*. And the rest will submit to them out of *αἰδώς* or *φόβος* or *εὔνοια*, *Praem.* 16 (97). Elsewhere, the universal dominion of the pious appears to be founded on power. The Gentiles will pay homage to the Messiah because they will recognize that God has given him power (1 En. 90:30, 37; Parables of En. 48:5; 53:1; Ps. Sol. 17:32–5. Sibyl. 3:49: *ἁγνὸς ἄναξ πάσης γῆς σκῆπτρα κρατήσων*; 2 Bar. 72:5; Tg. on Zech. 4:7: the Messiah will rule over all kingdoms).[70] According to Jubilees 32:18–19, it was promised already to Jacob that kings would descend from him who would rule wherever the children of men had set foot. 'And I will give to your seed all the earth which is under heaven and they shall rule over all the nations according to their desire; and afterwards they shall draw the whole earth to themselves and inherit it for ever'.[71]

For the rest, the messianic age is described, mostly on the basis of Old Testament texts, as one of untroubled joy and gladness.[72] The Parables of Enoch emphasize as a crowning bliss that the Messiah will

---

pp. 228–42; Bousset, *Religion*[4], pp. 77–84; G. Fohrer, *Studien zur alttestamentlichen Theologie und Geschichte* (1969), pp. 13–22; *History of Israelite Religion* (1973), pp. 343–4.

70. Cf. S. H. Levey, *The Messiah: An Aramaic Interpretation* (1974), p. 98. Many have interpreted Ass. Mos. 10:8 as referring to an overthrow of the Romans by the Jews: 'Tunc felix eris tu Israhel et ascendes supra cervices et alas aquilae'. But from the following it seems rather that the idea is that Israel is to be lifted to heaven on the wings of an eagle ('et altabit te deus et faciet te haerere caelo stellorum . . . et conspicies a summo et videbis inimicos tuos in terra'). This passage probably recalls Dt. 32:11 (LXX: *ὡς ἀετὸς . . . διεὶς τὰς πτέγυρας αὐτοῦ ἐδέξατο αὐτούς, καὶ ἀνέλαβεν αὐτοὺς ἐπὶ τῶν μεταφρένων αὐτοῦ*. *Alae* = *πτέγυρες* and *cervices* = *μεταφρένα*). See *Le Testament de Moïse*, ed. E.-M. Laperrousaz, ad 10:8.

71. Note also the sixth century A.D. writer, Cosmas Indicopleustes, *Topographia Christiana* vi 25 (ed. Sources Chrét. III, p. 41): *αὐτοὶ δῆθεν τὸν ἐρχόμενον προσδοκῶσιν, ὅν καὶ Ἠλειμμένον καλοῦσιν, βασιλεύειν ἐπὶ γῆς αὐτῶν ἐλπίζουσιν καὶ ὑποτάσσειν αὐτοῖς πάντα τὰ ἔθνη*.

72. Str.-B. IV, pp. 880 ff.; S. Mowinckel, *He that Cometh*, p. 319; Volz, *Eschatologie*, pp. 359–68; Klausner, *The Messianic Idea*, pp. 506–17.

then dwell among men. 'On that day I will cause my Elect to dwell among them. . . . And I will transform the earth and will make it into a blessing' (1 En. 45:4–5). 'And the Lord of spirits shall dwell over them, and they shall eat with that Son of Man and lie down and rise up for ever and ever' (62:14). All war, strife, discord and quarrelling will come to an end, and peace, righteousness, love and faithfulness rule on earth (Sibyl. 3:371–80; 751–60; Philo, *Praem.* 16 (91); 2 Bar. 73:4–5). Even the wild animals will cease to be hostile and will serve men (Sibyl. 3:787–94; Philo, *Praem.* 15 (88); 2 Bar. 73:6; Tg. on Isa. 11:6). Nature will be unusually fruitful (Sibyl. 3:620; 23; 743; 50; 1 En. 10:18–19; 2 Bar. 29:5–8). Wealth and prosperity will prevail among men: Philo, *Praem.* 17 (98)–18 (105). The span of life will once more approach a thousand years, yet men will not grow old or weary but will be like babes and young children (Jub. 23:27–30). All will enjoy bodily strength and health. Women will bear children without pain and the reaper will not tire as he works (Philo, *Praem.* 20 (118–26); 2 Bar. 73:2–3, 7; 74:1).[73]

These external blessings are, however, not the only benefits. They merely follow from the fact that the messianic community is a holy nation sanctified by God and governed by the Messiah in righteousness. He suffers no unrighteousness to remain among them and there is not a man among them who knows wickedness. There is no wickedness in

73. Cf. 1QS 4:2–8. Sometimes this glory to come is also represented as a feast (סעודה) prepared by God for the righteous. Already in the Syriac Baruch Apocalypse (and subsequently often) there is mention that Behemoth and Leviathan are to be consumed on this occasion (2 Bar. 29:4). The defective text of 1 En. 60: 7–10 and 24b should possibly also be completed in this way. For rabbinic descriptions of this סעודה, cf. bPes. 119b, bB.B. 75a; cf. also A. Jellinek, *Bet ha-Midrasch* III, pp. 75–6; V, pp. 45–6; VI, pp. 150–1; Rufinus, *Apologia in Hieronymum* i 7: 'Est enim Iudaeorum vere de resurrectione talis opinio, quod resurgent quidem, sed ut carnalibus deliciis et luxuriis caeterisque voluptatibus corporis perfruantur.' Jerome on Isa. 59:5 (ed. Vallarsi IV, p. 705): 'Qui igitur audiens traditiones Iudaicas ad escas se mille annorum voluerit praeparare'. 'Une Formule grecque de Renonciation au Judaïsme', ed. F. Cumont, *Wiener Studien* (1902), p. 468: *Ἔτι ἀναθεματίζω πάντας τοὺς τὴν τοῦ Ἠλειμμένου μᾶλλον δὲ τὴν τοῦ ἀντιχρίστου προσδοκῶντας ἔλευσιν, ὅν καὶ τράπεζαν αὐτοῖς ἑτοιμάσειν ἐλπίζουσι μεγίστην καὶ προθήσειν εἰς ἑστίασιν τὸν Ζίζ, πτηνόν τι ζῷον, τὸν δὲ Βεχεμὼθ τετράπουν, τὸν δὲ Λεβιαθὰν ἐνάλιον, οὕτω μέγιστα καὶ πλήθοντα ταῖς σαρξὶν ὡς ἀρκείν εἰς τροφὴν ἕκαστον μυριάσιν ἀπείροις.* Cf. J. Wellhausen, *Skizzen und Vorarbeiten* VI (1899), p. 232 (use of Behemoth and Leviathan arising from Ps. 74:14). The age of this concept is attested in the New Testament passages: Mt. 8:11 = Lk. 13:29; Lk. 14:15; Mt. 26:29 = Mk. 14:25 = Lk. 22:18; Lk. 22:30. Cf. also Hippolytus, *Works* I, ed. Achelis ([2]1897), p. 247; L. Ginzberg, *Legends of the Jews* I, pp. 27–9; V, pp. 41; 46; RGG IV, cols. 337–8; G. Dalman, *Words of Jesus*, pp. 110–13; H. Gunkel, *Schöpfung und Chaos* ([2]1921), pp. 315–18; Moore, *Judaism* II, pp. 363–4; Volz, *Eschatologie*, pp. 389, 404; J. C. L. Gibson, *Canaanite Myths and Legends* (1978), pp. 14 ff., 68 ff.; O. Kaiser, *Die mythische Bedeutung des Meeres in Agypten, Ugarit und Israel*, BZAW 78 (1959), pp. 144 f.; I. Jacobs, 'Elements of Near-Eastern Mythology in Rabbinic Aggadah', JJS 28 (1977), pp. 1–11.

their midst because they are all holy (Ps. Sol. 17:28, 29, 36, 48, 49; 18:9, 10). Life in the messianic kingdom is a continual λατρεύειν θεῷ ἐν ὁσιότητι καὶ δικαιοσύνῃ ἐνώπιον αὐτοῦ (Lk. 1:74–5). And the Messiah's dominion over the world of the Gentiles is by no means envisaged as resting on power alone; he is frequently thought of as a light to the nations (Isa. 42:6; 49:6; 51:4; Enoch 48:4; Lk. 2:32; cf. especially the passages mentioned earlier, Sibyl. 3:710–26).

Since an Israelite was conditioned to imagine a λατρεύειν θεῷ in the forms of Temple worship and observance of the Torah, it goes without saying that these too will not cease in the messianic kingdom. This is in any case the prevailing view.[74] Even the Qumran sect, which had temporarily withdrawn from the Temple for political reasons, believed that cultic worship would be restored in the seventh year of the War (1QM 2:1–6).[75] In Jubilees, the eternal validity of the laws is enjoined with particular emphasis.[76] Thus even after the destruction of the

74. For further particulars see Volz, *Eschatologie*, pp. 376–8; W. D. Davies, *Torah in the Messianic Age and in the Age to Come* (1952), pp. 51–2; Klausner, *Messianic Idea*, pp. 513 f.; B. Gärtner, *The Temple and the Community in Qumran and the New Testament* (1965), ch. 1, 'The Priesthood and the Jerusalem Temple', pp. 1, 3; R. J. McKelvey, *The New Temple* (1969), pp. 1; 22 (select bibliography), pp. 207–29); G. Schrenk, ἱερόν, TDNT III, pp. 230–47. For Qumran in general, see Vermes, *DSS*, pp. 163–97.

75. See Y. Yadin, *The Scroll of the War of the Sons of Light against the Sons of Darkness*, pp. 262 f.; Vermes, *DSSE*, pp. 124–5; P. R. Davies, *IQM, the War Scroll from Qumran* (1977), pp. 26–8.

76. See the summary by Charles, *Apocrypha and Pseudepigrapha* II, p. 91. The main passages read as follows. Jub. 2:33: 'This law and testimony (of the Sabbath) was given to the children of Israel as an everlasting law for ever for their generations'. 6:14: 'And for this law (against eating blood) there is no end of days, for it is valid for ever' (in general, 6:11–14). 13:25–6: 'And the Lord ordained it (tithing) as an ordinance for ever, that they should give it to the priests who serve before Him, that they should receive it for ever. And this law has no limitation of days, but he has commanded it for everlasting generations. . . .' 15:25: 'This law (circumcision) is valid for all generations for ever, and there is no circumcision of days, . . . but it is an everlasting ordinance. . . .' 15:28–9: 'But do you command the children of Israel that they preserve the sign of this covenant for their generations as an everlasting ordinance. . . . For the commandment is ordained for the covenant, that they should preserve it for ever over all the children of Israel'. 16:29–30: (the law of tabernacles) '. . . a law for ever according to their generations. . . . And this has no limitation of days but is ordained for ever over Israel. . . .' 30:10: 'And for this law (against marrying Gentiles), there is no limitation of days and no forgiveness and no pardon. . . .' 32:10: 'And for this law (the second tithe) there is no limitation of days for ever'. 33:16–17: '. . . In your days it (the law against incest) is as a law of the time and of the days, and an everlasting law for the everlasting generations. And for this law there is no consummation of days. . . .' 49:8 '(The Passover law) is an everlasting ordinance . . . and there is there no limit of days, for it is established for ever'.

Temple, the Jew goes on to pray daily for the restoration of the sacrificial cult (עבודה).[77]

In this glorious kingdom of the future, not only Israelites living in the messianic age will participate, but also all those who have died. They will emerge from their graves to enjoy with their compatriots of the final generation the bliss of the kingdom. (For details see below no. 10).[78]

For many, eschatological expectations culminate in this hope of a kingdom of glory in Palestine whose duration is imagined as being without end. As biblical prophecy promises the people of Israel that they will dwell for ever in their land (Jer. 24:5; Ezek. 37:25; Joel. 4:20), that the throne of David will never stand unoccupied (Jer. 33:17, 22) and that David will be Prince of Israel for ever (Ezek. 37:25), and as in particular Daniel describes the kingdom of the saints of the Most High as eternal (מלכות עלם; Dan. 7:27), so too, later writers frequently attribute eternal duration to the messianic kingdom (Sibyl. 3:766; Ps. Sol. 17:4; Sibyl. 3:49; 50; 1 En. 62:14). The same view is expressed in the Fourth Gospel by 'the Jews' (Jn. 12:34, *Ἡμεῖς ἠκούσαμεν ἐκ τοῦ νόμου ὅτι ὁ Χριστὸς μένει εἰς τὸν αἰῶνα*), which shows that this concept was current also in first century A.D. Jewish thought.[79] Life in the messianic kingdom is, in effect, represented as the condition of highest blessedness imaginable. The blessings of heaven have descended upon earth. The earth has itself become a part of heaven.[80]

Often, however, the glory of the messianic kingdom is not regarded as final and supreme. An even higher heavenly bliss is looked for, with the result that only a limited duration is ascribed to the rule of the Messiah,[81] the length of which is fully debated in the Talmud.[82] Among the more ancient written records, this view is most clearly expressed in the Apocalypse of Baruch and 4 Ezra. The former admittedly says of the Messiah (73:1) that he will sit 'for ever on the throne of his kingdom'. But the meaning appears from another passage (40:3): 'And his reign

77. *Shemoneh 'Esreh*, 17th *berakhah* (see above p. 458). Cf. also the Passover liturgy in mPes. 10:6.

78. Cf. Dan. 12:2; Ps. Sol. 3:16; 1 En. 51:1–5. See further below, p. 539, n. 90 (literature on resurrection).

79. Cf. Str.-B. II, p. 552.

80. In the Qumran texts, members of the community associate with the angels (the 'Sons of Light') in worship and in war. See Black, *Scrolls and Christian Origins*, p. 139–40; Vermes, *DSS*, pp. 175–84.

81. Cf. Str.-B. III, pp. 823–7; IV, pp. 799–1015; Moore, *Judaism* II, pp. 375–6; H. Bietenhard, *Das tausendjährige Reich* (1955); Klausner, *Messianic Idea*, pp. 420–6; Mowinckel, *He that Cometh*, pp. 277, 321, 324 f., 367 f., 403 f.; Bousset, *Religion* , pp. 248 f.; J. Massingberd Ford, *Revelation* (Anchor Bible, 1975), pp. 350 f. (includes patristic references).

82. bSanh. 99a; cf. Klausner, *Messianic Idea*, pp. 420.

shall endure for ever, until the world of corruption comes to an end.' The Messiah's dominion is therefore to last only as long as this transitory world. Similarly, in 4 Ezra (12:34) it is said that he will redeem and refresh the people of God 'quoadusque veniat finis, dies iudicii'. A still more detailed explanation appears in the main text (7:28–9): 'Iocundabuntur (*al.* iocundabit), qui relicti sunt, annis quadringentis. Et erit post annos hos, et morietur filius meus Christus et omnes qui spiramentum habent hominis' (*al.* 'homines').[83] The calculation that the messianic kingdom is to endure for four hundred years is to be found in the above-mentioned Talmudic passage (bSan. 99a), which discloses also that this reckoning rests on Gen. 15:13 (the bondage in Egypt lasted for four hundred years); cf. Ps. 90:15: 'Gladden us again according to the days wherein thou hast humiliated us, according to the years wherein we have seen evil.' The age of joy is therefore to endure for as long as that of distress. Another calculation is presupposed in Revelation (20:4–6), inasmuch as the duration is stated to be one thousand years in accordance with the words of the psalm that one thousand years is for God as one day. This reckoning, too, is mentioned in the Talmud.[84]

It appears, then, that wherever the messianic kingdom is envisaged as one of temporary duration, the end of this time is expected to be marked by another renewal of the world and the last judgement.

9. *The renewal of the world*[85]

The hope of a new heaven and new earth is founded chiefly on Isa. 65:17 and 66:22 (cf. too Mt. 19:28; Rev. 21:1; 2 Pet. 3:13). Accordingly, a distinction was made between a present and future world, העולם הזה and העולם הבא,[86] in the New Testament frequently: *ὁ αἰὼν οὗτος* and *ὁ αἰὼν ὁ μέλλων* or *ὁ ἐρχόμενος* (e.g. Mt. 12:32; Mk. 10:30; Lk. 18:30; Eph. 1:21). A difference of conception nevertheless existed in so far as the new world was thought of as beginning either with the start of the messianic age or after it had ended. The former view is reflected, for

83. The Latin translation and one Arabic version have the number 400 (the second Arabic version has 1,000): the Syriac has 30; in the Ethiopic and Armenian it is missing altogether.

84. bSanh. 97a. Cf. Klausner, *Messianic Idea*, pp. 420–6.

85. Cf. Mt. 19:28: *παλιγγενεσία*. See Dalman, *Words of Jesus*, p. 177–9; Str.-B. III, pp. 840–7 (on Rev. 21:1); Volz, *Eschatologie*, pp. 338–40; S. Mowinckel, *He that Cometh*, p. 275; Black, *Scrolls*, p. 134 ff.; Bousset, *Religion*[4], pp. 280–2. For the concept at Qumran (ועשות חדשה), see 1QS 4:25; cf. below, p. 554.

86. mBer. 1:5; mPeah 1:1; mKid. 4:14; mB.M. 2:11; mSanh. 10:1–4; mAb. 2:7; 4:1, 16, 17; 5:19; 2 Bar. 44:15; 48:50; 73:5; 4Ezr. 6:9; 7:12–13, 42–3; 8:1; Dalman, *Words of Jesus*, pp. 147–58; Moore, *Judaism* II, pp. 377–95; Volz, *Eschatologie*, pp. 64–6; Klausner, *Messianic Idea*, pp. 488–91; Mowinckel, *He that Cometh*, pp. 263 f.; Bousset, *Religion*[4], pp. 243–6; J. Maier, *Geschichte der jüdischen Religion* (1972), pp. 180–1; TDNT s.v. *αἰών*; Enc. Jud. 6, col. 874–80; 12, cols. 1355–7.

example, in the Parables of Enoch, 45:4–5: 'And on that day I will cause my Elect to dwell among them, and will transform heaven and make it to be a blessing and light for ever. And I will transform the earth and make it into a blessing, and will cause my Elect to dwell on it' (cf. also 91:16). The second belief is expressed in 4 Ezra which foresees, after the messianic age has run its course, a deathly seven-day silence falling on the earth, followed by the dawn of the new world and the setting of the old (7:30–1). In accordance with these different conceptions the messianic age is either identified with the future world or reckoned as already existent. For example, the Targum on 1 Kings 4:33 alludes to 'The future world of the Messiah' (**עלמא דאתי דמשיחא**), and the Mishnah (mBer. 1:5) contrasts the present world (**העולם הזה**) with the days of Messiah (**ימות המשיח**), the latter being identified as **העולם הבא**. In 4 Ezra, on the other hand, the age of the Messiah is counted as belonging to the present world, and the future world as not beginning until the last judgement, i.e. after the close of the messianic era (see especially 7:42–3, with which 6:9 is admittedly not easily reconcilable). The Tannaitic midrash Sifre also distinguishes between 'the days of the Messiah' and 'the world to come'.[87] The New Testament, and apparently also the Qumran texts, identify the **עולם** to come with the age of the Messiah. It was not until a higher heavenly bliss was looked for after the close of the messianic kingdom that the messianic age came to be reckoned as belonging to the present **עולם**, and the renewal of the world as not taking place until after the end of that age. In rabbinic theology, this idea became the prevailing one (see the literature mentioned in n. 86). Occasionally, the messianic age is assigned a position between this world and the world to come. Thus already in the Apocalyse of Baruch (74:2–3): 'For that age (the messianic era) is the end of that which is corruptible and the beginning of that which is not corruptible. . . . Therefore it is far from evil and near to those things which do not die.'

The manner in which the destruction of the old world is to occur is, in the main, not worked out in detail. In Hellenistic and Palestinian Judaism it was expected to be an annihilation by fire, this idea having in part biblical connections, and in part an association with Stoic teaching on *ἐκπύρωσις*.[88]

87. Sifre on Dt. 11:21 (47), ed. Finkelstein, p. 104: 'That your days may be multiplied בעולם הזה and the days of your children לימות המשיח, as long as the heavens are above the earth לעולם הבא.'

88. Biblical points of contact are: (1) the idea that God is surrounded by fire when he comes to judge, Dan. 7:9–10; cf. 1 Cor. 3:13; 2 Thes. 1:8; (2) the prophetic image of the melting of the heavenly powers and earthly creatures before the wrath of God (Isa. 34:4: ונמקו כל צבא השמים; 64:1–2, LXX). But the concept of a real destruction of the world by fire outdoes both of these: Pseudo-Sophocles in Justin, *De Monarchia* 3, and Clement of Alexandria, *Stromateis* VI 4,

10. *A general resurrection*[89]

The last judgement is to be preceded by a general resurrection of the dead. On this point, however, there are so many opinions in Jewish religious thought that it is not feasible to enter into them all at the present time.[90] On the whole, belief in a resurrection or re-animation of

---

121–2 = Eusebius, *Praep. ev.* xii 13, 48; *Sibyl.* 4:172–7; Hystapes in Justin, *Apol.* i 20; Hippolytus, *Philosophoumena* ix 30, employs the term ἐκπύρωσις. In Christian sources: 2 Pet. 3:10–12; the passages from the Christian Sibyllines, E. Fehr, *Studia in Oracula Sibyllina* (1893), pp. 72–3. Celsus regards the teaching on ἐκπύρωσις as a dominant one among Christians, Origen, *C. Cels.* iv 11. Cf. also W. Bousset, *The Anti-Christ*, pp. 238–9; Volz, *Eschatologie*, pp. 318 ff.; Bousset, *Religion*[4], pp. 281–2, 512, 517. The Judaeo-Christian teaching on ἐκπύρωσις differs from the Stoic one. On the history of the latter cf. the Philonic writing, *De aeternitate mundi*, where the Stoic teaching is disputed from a peripatetic standpoint. Cf. R. Arnaldez's introduction to *De aeternitate mundi* in *Les oeuvres de Philon d'Alexandrie*, vol. 30 (1969). Cf. also Josephus, *Ant.* i 2, 3 (70); Life of Adam and Eve, 49:3; 1QH 3:29–32; Vermes, 'La secte juive de la Nouvelle Alliance d'après ses Hymnes récemment découverts', Cahiers Sioniens 4 (1950), pp. 192–5; R. Mayer, *Die biblische Vorstellung von Weltenbrand: eine Untersuchung über die Beziehungen zwischen Parsismus und Judentum* (1956); Black, *Scrolls and Christian Origins*, pp. 136–7; *Scrolls and Christian Doctrine*, pp. 19–20; M. Hengel, *Judaism and Hellenism* II (1974), p. 135.

89. According to 4 Ezr. 7:31–4, the order is (1) renewal of the world; (2) general resurrection; (3) last judgement.

90. Moore, *Judaism* II, pp. 378–9; Volz, *Eschatologie*, pp. 229–56; A. T. Nikolainen, *Der Auferstehungsglaube in der Bibel und ihrer Umwelt* (1944); H. Riesenfeld, *The Resurrection in Ezekiel xxxvii and in the Dura-Europos Paintings* (1948); A. Marmorstein, *Studies in Jewish Theology* (1950), pp. 145–78; G. Molin, 'Entwicklung und Motive der Auferstehungshoffnung vom Alten Testament bis zur rabbinischen Zeit', Judaica 9 (1953), pp. 225–39; R. Martin-Achard, *De la mort à la resurrection d'après l'Ancien Testament* (1956); S. Mowinckel, *He that Cometh* (1956), especially pp. 234 f., 273 f.; H. Bardtke, *Der Erweckungsgedanke in der exilisch-nachexilischen Literatur des Alten Testaments*, BZAW 77 (1958); K. Schubert, 'Die Entwicklung der Auferstehungslehre von den nach-exilischen bis zur frührabbinischen Zeit', BZ 6 (1962), pp. 177–214; M. Black, *Scrolls and Christian Origins*, pp. 141 f.; S. Lieberman, 'Some Aspects of After Life in Early Rabbinic Literature', *H. A. Wolfson Jubilee Volume* (1965), pp. 495–532; Bousset, *Religion*,[4] especially pp. 169 f., 270 f.; G. W. E. Nickelsburg, *Resurrection, Immortality and Eternal Life in Intertestamental Judaism* (1972); H. C. C. Cavallin, *Life after Death: Paul's Argument for the Resurrection of the Dead in 1 Cor. 15. Part I: An Enquiry into the Jewish Background* (1974) (Bibliography, pp. 217–43). The nature of Qumran belief in an after-life is disputed. Some hold that the view of immortality depicted in the Scrolls is identical with that of Lk. 20:35 ff., where in the (general?) resurrection men and women become 'like the angels'. Cf. F. Nötscher, *Zur theologischen Terminologie der Qumran-Texte* (1956), pp. 149–57; R. E. Laurin, 'The Question of Immortality in the Qumran Hodayot', JSS 3 (1958), pp. 344–55. (Laurin denies that the Essenes had any doctrine of resurrection.) M. Black, *Scrolls and Christian Origins*, p. 139 ff.; J. van den Ploeg, 'The Belief in Immortality in the Writings of Qumran', Bibliotheca Orientalis XVIII, 1–2 (1961), pp. 118–24; Vermes, *DSSE*, p. 51; *DSS*, pp. 186–8, 196–7; cf. also Enc. Jud. 14, cols. 96–103.

the dead (תחית המתים),[91] first formulated, after many earlier statements, clearly and precisely in Daniel (12:2), was already firmly established in the time of Jesus. (Cf. e.g. 2 Mac. 7:9, 14, 23, 36; 12:43–4; Ps. Sol. 3:16; 14:22 ff.; *Ant.* xviii 1, 3 (14); *B.J.* ii 8, 14 (163); 2 Bar. 30:1–5; 50:1; 51:6; 4 Ezr. 7:32; 1 En. 51:1; Test. Judah 25:1; Test. Benjamin 10:6–8; *Shemoneh 'Esreh*, 2nd *berakhah*; mSanh. 10:1; mAb. 4:22; cf. also mBer. 5:2; mSot. 9:15.) This remark is valid in any case of the spheres influenced by Pharisaism, which constituted the majority by far. Only the Sadducees denied resurrection,[92] and Hellenistic Judaism substituted for it the immortality of the soul.[93]

For the interval between death and resurrection,[94] a separation was in the main assumed of the just from the unjust, a preliminary state of blessedness being ordained for the former, and for the latter, a preliminary condition of torment (see especially 1 En. 22, 4 Ezr. 7:75–107). According to 1 En. 22:2, the place for departed souls is divided into four parts, three of them dark and one light (*τρεῖς αὐτῶν σκοτεινοὶ καὶ εἷς φωτεινός*), the dark being reserved for sinners and the light for the righteous. But they remain in these places only until the great day of

91. This term figures in e.g., mBer. 5:2. mSot. 9:15. mSanh. 10:1.

92. *Ant.* xviii 1, 4 (16); *B.J.* ii 10, 14 (165); Act. 23:8. Cf. above, p. 411.

93. Wisd. 3:1–9; 4:7; 5:15 f.; 6:19 f. Cf. C. Larcher, *Études sur le livre de la Sagesse*, pp. 237 f. With regard to Philo, cf. E. R. Goodenough, 'Philo on Immortality', HThR 39 (1946), pp. 85, 108; H. C. C. Cavallin, *Life after Death* (1974), pp. 135 f.; 4 Mac. 9:8; 13:16; 15:2; 17:5, 18; 18:23. According to Josephus, the Essenes did not teach resurrection but immortality of the soul; see *Ant.* viii 1, 5 (18), *B.J.* ii 7, 11 (154). Cf. Black, *Scrolls and Christian Origins*, pp. 187–91. Cf. also Jub. 23:31 ('And their bones shall rest in the earth and their spirits shall have much joy'). Cf. 1 En. 103:2–4: 'I know this mystery . . . that all goodness and joy and glory are prepared for them and are written down for the spirits of those that have died in righteousness, and that manifold good will be given to you in recompense for your labours. . . . And your spirits, (the spirits) of you who die in righteousness, will live and rejoice and be glad, and their spirits will not perish, but their memorial will be before the face of the Great One unto all the generations of the world. . . .' Cf. also Tob. 3:6–10. See R. H. Charles, *A Critical History of the Doctrine of the Future Life in Israel, in Judaism, and in Christianity* (1899); N. Söderblom, *La vie future d'après le Mazdéisme à la lumière des croyances parallèles dans les autres religions: Étude d'eschatologie comparée* (1901); N. Messel, *Die Einheitichkeit der jüdischen Eschatologie*, BZAW 30 (1915); H. Bietenhard, *Die himmlische Welt im Urchristentum und Spätjudentum* (1951), pp. 183–4; J. van den Ploeg, 'L'immortalité de l'homme d'après les textes de la Mer Morte', VT 2 (1952), pp. 171–5; 3 (1953), pp. 191–2; O. Cullmann, *Immortality of the Soul or Resurrection of the Dead* (1958); R. E. Laurin, *op. cit.* in n. 90 above; Cavallin, *op. cit.*, especially sections on 1 Enoch, pp. 40 f., Psalms of Solomon, pp. 57 f., Philo, pp. 135 f., Jubilees, pp. 36 f., Early Rabbinic Tradition, pp. 171 f.; G. W. E. Nickelsburg, *op. cit.* in n. 90 above, pp. 174 ff.

94. Cf. on this, Moore, *Judaism* II, pp. 301–3; Volz, *Eschatologie*, pp. 256 ff. Bousset, *Religion*[4], pp. 295–6. On patristic and New Testament views on an intermediate state, see the literature in nn. 96 and 101.

judgement (22:11: μέχρι τῆς μεγάλης ἡμέρας τῆς κρίσεως).[95] Thus whereas according to the older concept the lot of all the departed is alike in Sheol, it is now thought that they face a preliminary tribunal immediately after death. This expectation is at the basis of the parable of the rich man and Lazarus (Lk. 16:22 ff.). For the place where Lazarus finds himself is not heaven but a compartment of the underworld; and it is not said that Lazarus and the rich man are to remain eternally where the parable shows them to be. Their fate has indeed been decided for ever; but this does not prevent the stage described by the parable from being regarded as a temporary and preliminary one, as the related description in 1 En. 22 bears out.[96] Josephus too gives it as Pharisaic teaching that prior to resurrection the lot of departed souls in the underworld varies, *Ant.* xviii 1, 3 (14): *ἀθάνατόν τε ἰσχὺν ταῖς ψυχαῖς πίστις αὐτοῖς εἶναι, καὶ ὑπὸ χθονὸς δικαιώσεις τε καὶ τιμὰς αἷς ἀρετῆς ἢ κακίας ἐπιτήδευσις ἐν τῷ βίῳ γέγονε, καὶ ταῖς μὲν εἱργμὸν ἀΐδιον προτίθεσθαι, ταῖς δὲ ῥᾳστώνην τοῦ ἀναβιοῦν*. In the Apocalypse of Baruch and 4 Ezra, there is frequent mention of receptacles (*promptuaria*) in which the souls of the righteous are accommodated after death (2 Bar. 30:2; 4 Ezr. 4:35, 41; 7:32, 80, 95, 101). In Maccabees it is presumed that the dead participate in the destiny of the living: Jeremiah and Onias make intercession for their people (2 Mac. 15:12–16). The tendency in general is to intensify the representation of this preliminary bliss of the pious dead so that the difference between it and permanent blessedness grows gradually less. In later rabbinic Judaism, the dominant view is that the souls of the just (not their bodies) are removed to 'Paradise' (the גן עדן) immediately after death;[97] and this Paradise is increasingly regarded as heavenly. The Parables of Enoch move in an analogous direction but their statements appear sometimes to disagree; the blessedness of the just is sometimes in heaven and sometimes in a distant 'garden' somewhere on earth, and in addition, it is not always

95. 1 En. 22:13 evidently supposes that the righteous rise again. Here, as in general eschatology, the passage in ch. 22 does not accord with the bulk of chs. 1–36. Cf. on the eschatology in chs. 1–36, p. 503 above. Cf. Bietenhard, *Die himmlische Welt*, p. 70 f.

96. This interpretation of the parable in Lk. 16 is advocated very emphatically by the earlier church fathers, who throughout emphasize that the pious dead are *not* instantly taken up to heaven. They sometimes name the place 'Paradise' to which the just repair after death, but do not consider this to be a place in heaven. The main texts are: Justin, *Dial. c. Tryph.* 5 (ed. Otto, p. 24); also ch. 80 (ed. Otto, p. 290); Irenaeus, *Haer.* ii 34, 1; v 5, 1; v 31, 1-2. Tertullian, *De anima*, 55, 58; *De resurrectione*, 43. Particularly detailed is Hippolytus in the fragment *Περὶ τοῦ παντός*, ed. K. Holl, *Fragmente vornicänischer Kirchenväter* from *Sacra parallela* (1899), pp. 137–43; J. N. Sevenster, *Leven en dood in de Evangeliën* (1952), p. 127; K. Hanhart, *The Intermediate State in the New Testament* (1966), pp. 16–42, pp. 80 f.; pp. 190 f.; H. Bietenhard, *Die himmlische Welt*, pp. 161 f.

97. Cf. the previous note.

clear whether a preliminary or permanent blessedness is meant (1 En. 39:3–12; 60:8, 23; 61:12; 70:3–4; 71:16–17).[98] In the age of Jesus, the evidence, though slight, suggests that the Jewish view was that only specific, privileged men of God such as Enoch, Moses and Elijah, as well as Ezra and others like him, would be admitted into a condition of glory in heaven immediately after death (4 Ezr. 14:9: 'tu enim recipieris ab hominibus et converteris residuum cum filio meo et cum similibus tuis, usquequo finiantur tempora'; 2 Mac. 15:12–16 should probably also be understood in this sense). On the other hand, the expectation that all the righteous dead are taken into heavenly bliss immediately after death is primarily a characteristic of Hellenistic Judaism. It replaces belief in resurrection and is only artificially compatible with it.[99] Indeed, because it excludes belief in the resurrection as it was originally intended, it was condemned as heretical by the early Church Fathers.[100] The idea, expressed in a Christian section of the Ascension of Isaiah (9:7–8), that all the righteous dead since Adam are now in the seventh heaven, was therefore by no means generally current.

The New Testament displays a diversity similar to that of the Jewish sources. The expectation of an immediate transfer of the just to heaven seems to exist: Lk. 23:43; 2 Cor. 5:8; Phil. 1:23; Act. 7:59; Rev. 6:9 ff.; 7:9 ff. But it is open to question whether 'Paradise' in Lk. 23:43 is to be envisaged as a place in heaven; and it should be considered whether the other passages are not concerned with a privilege granted to martyrs

98. Cf. P. Grelot, 'La géographie mythique d'Hénoch et ses sources orientales', RB 65 (1958), pp. 33–69; J. T. Milik, 'Hénoch au pays des aromates', RB 65 (1958), pp. 70–7; *The Books of Enoch* (1976), pp. 37–41.

99. Cf. the works listed in n. 93. The statements in 4 Mac. are especially noteworthy since this book is otherwise very close to the Pharisaic views. This renders it all the more remarkable that it removes the hope of resurrection so prominent in its prototype, 2 Mac. 7:9, and replaces it with the expectation that the pious will be taken to God in heaven; they will be *παρὰ θεῷ* (9:8); Abraham, Isaac and Jacob receive them (13:16); they come *εἰς αἰώνιον ζωὴν κατὰ θεόν* (15:2); they stand beside God *ἐν οὐρανῷ* (17:5); *τῷ θείῳ νῦν παρεστήκασι θρόνῳ καὶ τὸν μακάριον βιοῦσιν αἰῶνα* (17:18). Cf. F.-M.. Abel, *Les Livres des Maccabées* (1949), p. 373; 18:23: they are gathered into the company of the fathers. Cf. R. B. Townsend in Charles, *Apocrypha and Pseudepigrapha* II, p. 662 ('apparently there is no resurrection of the body'); so also M. Hadas, *The Third and Fourth Books of Maccabees* (1953), p. 121. This type of belief in immortality seems identical with that favoured by the Qumran sectaries; cf. Black, *Scrolls and Christian Origins*, pp. 138 f.; and above, p. 539, n. 90. Cf. also Str.-B. II, pp. 266–7; IV, pp. 1139–40. Bietenhard, *Die himmlische Welt*, pp. 180 ff.

100. Justin, *Dial. c. Tryph.*, 80 (ed. Otto, p. 290, ed. 3): *οἱ καὶ λέγουσι μὴ εἶναι νεκρῶν ἀνάστασιν, ἄλλα ἅμα τῷ ἀποθνήσκειν τὰς ψυχὰς αὐτῶν ἀναλαμβάνεσθαι εἰς τὸν οὐρανόν, μὴ ὑπολάβητε αὐτοὺς χριστιανούς*. Cf. also ch. 5, ed. Otto, p. 24. Irenaeus, *Haer*. v 31, 1–2 firmly rejects as heretical the teaching of those who say that on leaving the body the 'inner man' 'in supercoelestem ascendere locum' (v 31, 2). Similarly Hippolytus in the exhaustive debate in the fragment on *Περὶ τοῦ πάντος* (K. Holl, *Fragmente vornicänischer Kirchenväter*, pp. 137–43).

who die in the service of Christ. Only Rev. 7:9 ff. will not fit in with this theory.[101] It is in any case incorrect to say that according to the New Testament all believers are conveyed to a heavenly paradise immediately they die.[102] No firmly fixed and generally valid views developed on this point.

The new corporeality of the resurrected is discussed extensively in the Apocalypse of Baruch 50:1–51:6; cf. also 4 Ezr. 7:97.

An important difference in the doctrine of resurrection consisted in the expectation either that there would be only a resurrection of the just for the purpose of participating in the messianic kingdom, or that there would be a general resurrection (of the just and the godless) for judgement, shortly before the dawn of the messianic era and shortly after its end. The first form is no doubt the older of the two. It appears for example in the Psalms of Solomon (3:16; 14:2 ff.), but is also mentioned by Josephus as the average Pharisaic opinion, *Ant.* xviii 1, 3 (14); *B.J.* ii 8, 14 (163).[103] The expectation of a general resurrection for judgment is an extension of this earliest resurrection hope. Thus Daniel, Enoch, the Apocalypse of Baruch, 4 Ezra, the Testaments of the Twelve Patriarchs and the Mishnah, in the passages quoted above.[104]

101. On New Testament doctrine, cf. especially TDNT, s.v. ᾅδης, I, pp. 146–50; s.v. παράδεισος, V, pp. 763 f.; O. Michel, *Der Mensch zwischen Tod und Gericht, Theol. Gegenwartsfragen* (1940), pp. 6–28; J. Jeremias, 'Zwischen Karfreitag und Ostern', ZNW 42 (1949), pp. 194–201, especially p. 200; E. Lohmeyer, *Philipper-Kolosser-Philemon-Briefe* ([13]1964), on Phil. 1:23 and 3:10, pp. 63 f., 138 f.; see also the literature cited above in n. 96, especially K. Hanhart, *op. cit.*, p. 104 f., 181. Tertullian states expressly that only martyrs come to Christ immediately after death, *De resurr.* 43: 'Nemo enim peregrinatus a corpore statim immoratur penes dominum nisi ex martyrii praerogativa'.

102. Cf. TDNT s.v. παράδεισος, V, p. 769. See also V. Hanhart, *op. cit.*, pp. 205 f.

103. *Ant.* xviii 1, 3 (14) says nothing specifically about resurrection, but simply that 'souls have power to survive death', but at *B.J.* ii 8, 14 (163) it is stated that '. . . Every soul . . . is imperishable but the soul of the good alone passes into another body (while the souls of the wicked suffer eternal punishment).' This has been interpreted as containing a reference to metempsychosis by Thackeray, *Selections from Josephus* (1919), p. 159, who compares *B.J.* iii 8, 5 (374): '. . . their souls (the souls of the righteous) . . . are allotted the most holy place in heaven, whence, in the revolution of the ages, they return to find in chaste bodies a new habitation.' However, L. H. Feldman, in Loeb note to *Ant.* xviii 1, 3 (14), rightly interprets this as belief in resurrection, since metempsychosis does not seem to have been a Pharisaic doctrine. But there may have been some accommodation in all these passages in Josephus to current Greek ideas about the immortality of the soul. Cf. also G. Maier, 'Die jüdischen Lehrer bei Josephus', *Josephus-Studien* (*Festschrift für O. Michel*), ed. O. Betz *et al.* (1974), pp. 264–5.

104. In the Mishnah cf. especially mAb. 4:22: 'They who are born destined to die; the dead, to be re-awakened; the re-awakened to stand before judgement; that men may learn, teach and be persuaded that he is the Almighty etc.' mSanh. 10:3 also assumes that the resurrection is to be a general one in that it says only exceptionally, of individual prominent sinners who have received their judgement already in their lifetime, that they shall not be resurrected for judgement.

In this connection there is again the difference that resurrection and judgement were expected either before the opening of the messianic age or after its end. The first view, represented by Daniel (12:2), is no doubt the older, for the probable original purpose of the judgement was to inaugurate the messianic era. It was not until the messianic beatitude was no longer regarded as final and supreme that judgment, as the decision pronounced on man's final destiny, was moved to the conclusion of messianic time. Thus in particular the Apocalypse of Baruch and 4 Ezra. In the New Testament's Book of Revelation, expectation of a resurrection of the pious before the establishment of the messianic kingdom is combined with the hope of a general resurrection after its close.

The awakening itself is set in train by the sounding of the divine trumpets (1 Cor. 15:52, 1 Thes. 4:16; cf. Mt. 24:31; 4 Ezr. 6:23).[105]

11. *The last judgement. eternal bliss and damnation*[106]

There can only be question of a last judgement after the messianic age has ended if a limitation is set to its duration. Of the older authorities, therefore, only the Apocalypse of Baruch and 4 Ezra are involved here. The rest represent judgement as coinciding with the destruction of the hostile powers, an event that occurs before the onset of the messianic era (see above, no. 5). In the Apocalypse of Baruch, the last judgement is only briefly mentioned (50:4). 4 Ezra is somewhat more expansive (7:33–44; 6:1–17 according to the Ethiopic version). It discloses, in particular, that it is God himself who will sit in judgement. In addition, there can be no doubt that according to both these Apocalypses sentence is to be passed not only on the people of Israel, but on the whole of mankind (2 Bar. 51:4–5; 4 Ezr. 7:37). The general principle is that all Israelites are to share in the world to come (mSanh. 10:1: **כל ישראל יש להם חלק לעולם הבא**). But needless to say, all sinners in Israel (painstakingly classified in mSanh. 1:1–4) are to be excluded from it. Since the sentence on each individual is to conform exactly to his works, his deeds are inscribed in heavenly books already during his lifetime (1 En. 98:7–8; 104:7; also ch. 89–90. Jub. 30:19–23; 36; 10 and

105. On this 'eschatological' trumpet-blast, see Bousset, *The Anti-Christ Legend*, pp. 247–8; Moore, *Judaism* II, pp. 63–4; G. Friedrich, TDNT VII, pp. 71–88; Vermes, *Scripture and Tradition*, pp. 213–14. Cf. also commentaries on 1 Cor. 15:52 and 1 Thes. 4:16.

106. C. H. Toy, *Judaism and Christianity* (1890), pp. 372–414; R. H. Charles, *Eschatology, Hebrew Jewish and Christian* (1899), pp. 196 f.; Moore, *Judaism* II, pp. 292 f.; Volz, *Eschatologie*, pp. 272–331, 359–408; S. Mowinckel, *He that Cometh*, pp. 273 f.; F. Nötscher, *Zur theologischen Terminologie der Qumran-Texte* (1956), pp. 158 f.; Bousset, *Religion*[4], pp. 202–30; S. G. F. Brandon, *The Judgment of the Dead* (1967), pp. 67–75; G. W. E. Nickelsburg, *Resurrection, Immortality and Eternal Life in Intertestamental Judaism* (1972), pp. 39–43.

elsewhere; Test. of Asher 7:5; CD 20:18–20 [B 2:18–20] (ספר זכרון); cf. 1QH 1:23–4 (חרת זכרון); mAb. 2:1; Lk. 10:20. Phil. 4:3; Rev. 3:5; 13:8; 20:15; Hermas, Vis. i 3, 2).[107] The wicked will be cast into the fire of Gehinnom (2 Bar. 44:15; 51:1–2, 4; 6. 4 Ezr. 7:36–8 and 84).[108] This damnation is usually regarded as eternal.[109] Nevertheless, the opinion is also expressed that the pains of hell will continue for a limited time only and that Gehinnom will cease to exist in the world to come.[110] The just and the pious will be received into Paradise and will dwell in the

107. Cf. on these heavenly books especially A. von Harnack's note on Hermas, *Vis.* i 3, 2; Charles, *The Book of Enoch* (1912), pp. 91–2; Bousset, *Religion*[4], p. 158.

108. The Hebrew גיהנום: mKid. 4:14; mEdu. 2:10; mAb. 1:5; 5:19, 20. Frequently in the Targums and Talmud. In the New Testament γέεvα: Mt 5:22, 29 f.; 10:28; 18:9; 23:15, 33. Mk. 9:43, 45, 47. Lk. 12:5; Jas. 3:6; *Gê-hinnom* (Valley of Hinnom) is a valley near Jerusalem where the Israelites sacrificed to Moloch: Jer. 32:34–55, cf. 2 Kgs. 21:4–5; see G. Fohrer, *History of Israelite Religion* (1973), p. 53. Jeremiah therefore prophesied that that very same place would be the site of doom, of a terrible blood-bath in which the Israelites would be slaughtered (Jer. 7:31 f.; 19:5 f.). In 1 Enoch (26–7) the expectation is then formulated that all the wicked will be gathered together in this valley for judgement to be executed on them. The name Gehinnom is not mentioned, but it is clearly described as the valley between Zion and the Mount of Olives. It is therefore still a real valley near Jerusalem. Cf. Milik, *The Books of Enoch*, pp. 44–5. Eventually, however, Gehinnom is thought of as a place of punishment in the underworld into which the godless will be cast. For late rabbinic descriptions of Gehinnom see A. Jellinek, *Bet ha-Midrasch* I, pp. 147–9; II, pp. 48–51; V, pp. 48 f. Cf. further R. H. Charles, *Eschatology, Hebrew, Jewish and Christian* (1899), pp. 156 f., 188, 225, 237 f., 251 f.; 286, 302; Moore, *Judaism* II, pp. 301 f., 339, 387, 391 f.; Volz, *Eschatologie*, pp. 327 f.; A. Schlatter, *Der Evangelist Matthäus* (1948), p. 171; H. Bietenhard, *Die himmlische Welt*, pp. 205 f.; F. Nötscher, *Zur theologischen Terminologie der Qumran-Texte*, pp. 160 f.; Str.-B. IV, pp. 1016–1165; RE VI, cols. 418 f.; TDNT, γέεvα, I, pp. 655–6; Enc. Jud. 12, cols. 996–8. Otherwise Hades and its darkness are also described as the future lot of the ungodly: e.g., Ps. Sol. 14:6, 15:11, 16:2. Cf. TDNT, s.v. ᾅδης I, pp. 146–50.

109. Isa. 66:24; Dan. 12:2; Mt. 3:12; 25:46; Lk. 3:17; Test. Zeb. 10; Ash. 7:5; Reub. 5:5; 1QS 4:12–13; Josephus, *B.J.* ii 8, 14 (163): ἀϊδίῳ τιμωρίᾳ; *Ant.* xviii 1, 6 (14): εἱργμὸν ἀΐδιον (both passages are cited above in their context, pp. 382 f.). Str.-B. IV, pp. 1022 f.; cf. A. Schlatter, *Der Evangelist Matthäus*, ad Mt. 25:46, p. 728; TDNT s.v. κόλασις, III, p. 817. Cf. also Mart. Polycarp. 2:3; 2 Clem. 6:7; Diognetus 10:7.

110. mEdu. 2:10: 'R. Akiba said: "... the punishment of Gog and Magog which is to come shall endure for twelve months; and the punishment of the unrighteous in Gehenna shall endure for twelve months". But this no doubt applies only to the sinners of Israel. As a rule, punishment in hell is forever. See D. Castelli, 'The Future Life in Rabbinical Literature', JQR 1 (1880), p. 345. Cf. tSanh. 13:4 (the wicked of Israel and of the nations are annihilated at the end of twelve months). According to the school of Shammai (tSanh. 13:3), those in whom good and evil are equally balanced shall descend to Gehinnom and return to be healed (cf. also bB.M. 58b). Others held that damnation is temporal: 'There is no Gehinnom in the world to come' (bNed. 8b). The Qumran view is unclear as the punishment of the wicked is described there both as total destruction and eternal suffering. Cf. especially 1QS 4:11–14.

high places of that world and behold the majesty of God and his holy angels. Their countenances will shine like the sun and they will live for ever (Dan. 12:3; 2 Bar. 51:3, 7; 14; 4 Ezr. 7:36–8; 95–8. Cf. also Ass. Mos. 10:9–10).[111]

Religious individualism has no close links with the older prophetic expectation, which always has in mind the nation as such. The final destiny of the individual is not necessarily determined by that of the nation and vice versa. There is a connection only as long as individual hope exists in the simplest form of belief in resurrection, that the good will be reawakened to participate in the messianic kingdom. But once this expectation assumes a more transcendent form and somehow extends to a blessed life in a supernatural world, a tension develops between the two spheres of belief; they cannot be combined except artificially. The variety of ways in which this was done led to the great diversity, and even inconsistency, of concepts of the future. This is seen most clearly in the Hellenized form of expectation, namely that the soul will pass after death to a supernatural, heavenly existence. There is no room here for life in the messianic kingdom. But Palestinian eschatology also moved in the same direction. What was formerly seen as the privilege of individual men of God—elevation to a heavenly existence—increasingly became the hope of the good in general. Accordingly, the ancient national expectation had either to be annulled or to be combined with it in appearance only. In the Apocalypses of Baruch and Ezra, and in Qumran literature, the latter course is taken. But this additive method shows clearly that two disparate elements are welded together here. In point of fact, the tendency was to replace the national kingdom of the Messiah by a 'kingdom of heaven', one in which the difference between heaven and earth is abolished.

111. In rabbinic Hebrew, Paradise is usually given as גן עדן (e.g., mAb. 5:20), or פרדס, the latter more rarely (in the Mishnah it means only a 'park' in the natural sense, mSanh. 10:6; mHul. 12:1; mArak. 13:2). In the Testaments of the Twelve Patriarchs both occur (*'Εδέμ* Test. Dan 5; *παράδεισος* Test. Levi 18). In the New Testament *παράδεισος* Lk. 23:43; 2 Cor. 12:4; Rev. 2:7. The Syriac translations of the New Testament render *παράδεισος* sometimes as 'garden of Eden', sometimes by the Greek word itself. Paradise as a place of permanent beatitude is to be thought of as in heaven; according to 1 En. 32, it lies in a far part of the earth. Late rabbinic descriptions in Jellinek, *Bet ha-Midrasch* II, pp. 48–51, 52 f.; III, pp. 131–40, 194–8; V, pp. 42–8; VI, pp. 151–2. See in general New Testament commentaries on Lk. 23:43; 2 Cor. 12:4; Rev. 2:7. E. Klostermann, *Das Lukasevangelium* (1919), pp. 530–1 (ad Lk. 16:22) and p. 597 (ad Lk. 23:43); H. Windisch, *Der zweite Korintherbrief* (1924), and C. K. Barrett, *The Second Epistle to the Corinthians* (1973), ad 2 Cor. 12:4; G. R. Beasley-Murray, *The Book of Revelation* (1974), pp. 79 f.; J. Massyngberde Ford, *Revelation* (1975), p. 358; Str.-B. ad Lk. 23:43, II, pp. 264–9; Moore, *Judaism* II, pp. 303 f., pp. 390 f.; Bietenhard, *Die himmlische Welt*, pp. 170 ff.; TDNT, s.v. *Παράδεισος* (J. Jeremias), V, pp. 763–71; P. Grelot, *op. cit.* and J. T. Milik, *op. cit.* in n. 98 above; Enc. Jud. 13, cols. 77–85.

Thus whereas religious individualism was disparate from the national expectation, it was in complete harmony with religious universalism. Indeed, one form of it also concurred with the national hope. The judgement was to be of all the enemies of the Jews, and the messianic kingdom was to embrace the whole world inasmuch as the Gentiles would submit to the Jewish nation or join them voluntarily. But in leaving the confines of this earthly world and ascending to the supernatural, this universal expectation clashed with that of the nation. If the last great judgement was to be a judgement of the world wherein all men must appear before the seat of God and the destiny of all would be decided in conformity with their deeds on earth, national differences must cease to be of importance. It would no longer primarily be a question of whether Jew or Gentile, but of whether good or bad. The ethical factor comes to the fore—the wicked Jew joins the ranks of the ungodly Gentiles—and the national factor to some extent recedes.

The emergence of an individual and universal cast of thought, and its elevation to the transcendental, resulted in an aspiration for the replacement of the politico-national hope by one that was essentially religious. But it amounted to no more than a powerful start in that direction. The national expectation still carried greater weight. It was modified in various ways; it was enriched with elements essentially different from its own; but it remained firm throughout the changes of the years. In cosmopolitan Christianity, it was superseded by a supranational vision. But even there, chiliasm, inherited from Jewish political messianism, governed religious thinking for another two hundred years.

Appendix A. The Suffering Messiah[112]

The question has been endlessly debated whether the idea of a suffering Messiah, and in particular one whose sufferings and death

112. Cf. A. Wünsche, יסורי המשיח or *Die Leiden des Messias* (1870); also the works by Neubauer and Driver mentioned in n. 123; G. Dalman, *Der leidende und der sterbende Messias der Synagoge im ersten nachchristlichen Jahrtausend* (1888); C. H. H. Wright, 'The Pre-Christian Jewish Interpretation of Is. LII, LIII', The Expositor 7 (1888), pp. 364–77, 401–20. Consult further Str.-B. I, pp. 481–5, II, pp. 273–99; Moore, *Judaism* I, pp. 551–2, III, p. 63, p. 166; J. Jeremias, *'Αμνὸς τοῦ θεοῦ—παῖς θεοῦ*, ZNW 34 (1935), pp. 115–23; P. Seidelin, 'Der Ebed Jahwe und die Messiasgestalt in Jesajatargum', ZNW 35 (1936), pp. 194–231; J. J. Brierre-Narbonne, *Le Messie souffrant dans la littérature rabbinique* (1940); E. Lohmeyer, *Gottesknecht und Davidsohn* (1945); C. C. Torrey, 'The Messiah Son of Ephraim', JBL 66 (1947), pp. 253–77; I. Engnell, 'The 'Ebed Yahweh Songs and the Suffering Messiah in "Deutero-Isaiah" ', BJRL 31 (1948), pp. 54–93; C. R. North, *The Suffering Servant in Deutero-Isaiah* (1948); H. H. Rowley, *The Suffering Servant and the Davidic Messiah* (1950); W. H. Wolff, *Jesaia 53 im Urchristentum* (1950); J. Jeremias, 'Zum Problem der Deutung von Jes. 53 im palästinischen Spätjudentum', in *Aux Sources de la Tradition Chrétienne*, Mélanges offerts à M. Goguel

could have atoning value, is to be found in pre-Christian and rabbinical Judaism. In later Judaism, passages certainly exist that are familiar with the thought of the burdens and afflictions of the Messiah: from the word והריחו in Isa. 11:3 the conclusion is drawn that God has loaded the Messiah with commands and sufferings, like mill-stones (במצות ויסורין כרחים).[113] In another text, the Messiah is described as seated at the gates of Rome binding and unbinding his wounds.[114] In 4 Ezra it is predicted that the Messiah shall die after a reign of four hundred years. But such ideas have nothing to do with atonement and death, and in any case such evidence is late and post-Christian. The nub of the problem is whether the Isaianic Servant of the Lord, and in particular his atoning sufferings as predicted in Isa. 53, admitted of a messianic interpretation in pre-Christian and rabbinic Judaism.

Despite the confident affirmation of some theologians,[115] the evidence adduced for a Jewish messianic understanding of Isaiah 53 and related Servant passages is less than convincing; the Testament of Benjamin 3:8 (Armenian) may be a Christian interpolation, and it may be necessary to rule the Parables of Enoch altogether out of court. It is doubtful if even the faintest echoes of such an interpretation are to be found in the Septuagint, Aquila, Symmachus and the Targum (which expressly repudiates the suffering and humiliation, while interpreting messianically the exaltation aspects of Isaiah 53).[116] Claims for a soteriological meaning for the sufferings of the Qumran Teacher of Righteousness have also been rightly rejected.[117] It is true that Trypho in Justin Martyr's *Dialogue* (68, 89) is represented as conceding, more than once, that the Messiah is παθητός according to Scripture (with explicit references to Isa. 53); but care must be taken not to give too much weight to the evidence of a Christian apologist.

On the other hand, sundry rabbinic passages, in agreement with Isa. 53:4 ff., turn on suffering for the sins of men. Thus the Messiah is once given the name חוליא, Sick One (or according to another reading, חיורא, Leper), this being justified by an appeal to Isa. 53:4: 'Surely he

(1950), pp. 113–19; M. Black, 'Servant of the Lord and Son of Man', Scot. Journ. Theol. (1953), pp. 1–11; H. Hegermann, *Jesaja 53 in Hexapla, Targum und Peschitta* (1954); TDNT. s.v. *Παῖς θεοῦ*, V, pp. 653 ff.; E. Lohse, *Märtyrer und Gottesknecht* (1955); M. D. Hooker, *Jesus and the Servant* (1955); Klausner, *Messianic Idea*, p. 407; Mowinckel, *He that Cometh*, pp. 300, 325 f., 410 f.; E. E. Urbach, *The Sages*, pp. 687–8.

113. bSanh. 93b. Cf. Dalman, *op. cit.*, pp. 38–9.

114. bSanh. 98b. Cf. Wünsche, pp. 57 f.; Dalman, pp. 39 f.

115. E.g. Jeremias in TDNT, s.v. *Παῖς θεοῦ*.

116. Cf. Lohse, *op. cit.* (in n. 112), p. 108, n. 4, on Hegermann, *op. cit.* (in n. 112).

117. Cf. J. T. Milik, *Ten Years of Discovery in the Wilderness of Judaea* (1959), p. 80; but cf. M. Black, *The Dead Sea Scrolls and Christian Doctrine* (1966), pp. 14 f. (The author of the Hodayoth does apply Isa. 53 to his sufferings.)

has borne our griefs and carried our sorrows: but we esteemed him stricken and smitten of God and afflicted'.[118] According to a passage cited by Raymundus Martini from Sifre, R. Yose the Galilean says: 'The King Messiah has been humbled and made small on account of the unfaithful; as it is written, 'He was pierced for our transgressions etc.' (Isa. 53:5). How much more then will he make satisfaction for all generations; as it is written, 'And the Lord made him bear the guilt of us all' (Isa. 53:6).[119] As this passage does not occur in the traditional text of Sifre, it is open to question whether it has been abridged or whether Raymundus Martini possessed an interpolated copy.[120] It is also uncertain whether the saying did in fact originate from R. Yose the Galilean, who was a contemporary of Akiba (see above, p. 380). But it is not in itself improbable that at about that time individual scholars interpreted Isa. 53:4 ff. as referring to the Messiah. This is borne out in particular by the words of Trypho in Justin's *Dialogue with Trypho* (ch. 90):[121] *Παθεῖν μὲν γὰρ καὶ ὡς πρόβατον ἀχθήσεσθαι οἴδαμεν· εἰ δὲ καὶ σταυρωθῆναι κ.τ.λ.* It was an idea relating to the Messiah quite familiar to rabbinic Judaism, namely that the perfectly just man not only fulfils all the commandments, but also atones through suffering for past sins, and that the excessive suffering of the just is for the benefit of others.[122] But however much the idea of a suffering Messiah is, from these premises, conceivable within Judaism, it did not become a dominant notion. The 'official' Targum Jonathan certainly leaves intact the relation of Isaiah 53 to the Messiah, but it interprets the very verses which deal with the sufferings of the Servant of God as *not* referring to the Messiah.[123] In none of the many works discussed here is there the slightest allusion to an expiatory suffering of the Messiah. How alien these ideas were to Judaism is also attested by the behaviour of both the disciples and the opponents of Jesus (Mt. 16:22; Lk. 18:34; 24:21; Jn. 12:34).[124]

118. bSanh. 98b. Cf. Wünsche, pp. 62–3; Dalman, pp. 36–7.

119. מלך המשיח המתענה והמצטער בעד הפושעים שנ׳ והוא מחולל מפשעינו וגו׳ על אחת כמה וכמה שיזכה לכל הדורות כלן הה״ד ויהוה הפגיע בו את עון כלנו. Cf. Raymundi Martini . . . *Pugio Fidei adversus Mauros et Judaeos* (repr. 1967), p. 175.

120. See Dalman, pp. 43 f.

121. On the relationship between Trypho and R. Tarphon, see above, p. 379.

122. See Moore, *Judaism* I, pp. 546–52; Lohse, *op. cit.* pp. 9–10; Vermes, *Scripture and Tradition*, pp. 202–4.

123. On the history of the interpretation of Isa. 53 by the Jews, cf. Origen *C. Cels.* i 55, and especially A. Neubauer and S. R. Driver, *The fifty-third chapter of Isaiah according to the Jewish Interpreters* I: Texts; II: Translations (1876–7); J. Jeremias, *'Αμνὸς θεοῦ—παῖς θεοῦ*, ZNW 34 (1935), pp. 115–23; *παῖς θεοῦ*, TDNT V, pp. 616–713.

124. Passages from later midrashim and other Jewish works see in Wünsche, *op. cit.*, pp. 66–108.

APPENDIX B. THE QUMRAN MESSIAHS AND MESSIANISM

In addition to sharing the classic concept of the Davidic King Messiah, Qumran introduced a less familiar idea into traditional Jewish messianism by its expectation of a Priest Messiah. It also shared the belief of the Maccabaean period in a coming Prophet who could be regarded as a messianic figure. (Prophets and charismatic leaders generally, as well as kings and priests, were all designated as 'anointed'.) It is its sacerdotal messianism, however, which is the most characteristic feature of Qumran messianic hopes, a not unexpected ideal for a sect with priestly origins, priestly leadership and a priestly organization (cf. below, pp. 575–6).

The earliest reference to the two Messiahs is probably at 1QS 9:11, where the author urges the keeping of the sect's laws 'until the coming of a (the) Prophet and the Messiahs of Aaron and Israel'.[125] The question of the Prophet set aside, this text implies a dual messiahship, a coming priestly Messiah of Aaron and a secular Messiah of Israel.[126] This messianic duumvirate is confirmed and elaborated in other key messianic texts: at 1QSa 2:11–22 a messianic banquet is described, to take place in the event of 'God begetting (?) the Messiah to be with them',[127] in which the presiding figures are the Priest and the Messiah of Israel, the latter a military leader, seated with his commanders, the Priest accompanied by his brethren, the sons of Aaron. The Priest takes precedence over the warrior Messiah in matters of ritual and doctrine. Two similar figures appear in other texts: 1QSb 5:20–8 contains blessings for the Priest (Messiah) and a blessing for the Prince of the Congregation, the latter the Davidic Warrior Messiah (1QSb 5:27 '. . . thou shalt tread down the Gentiles like mud in the streets'). The title Prince (נשיא) is Ezekiel's term for the Davidic Messiah.[128] The latter is also referred to as the 'branch of David' (צמח דויד) (cf. Jer. 23:5, 33:15; Zech. 3:8, 6:12), to appear accompanied

125. See further below, p. 551, n. 132.

126. Consult especially the works of A. Dupont-Sommer, K. G. Kuhn, J. Liver, R. E. Brown, A. S. van der Woude. (Above, Bibliog., pp. 490–1; see also Black, *Scrolls and Christian Origins*, pp. 145–63; Vermes, *DSSE*, pp. 47–51; *Jesus the Jew*, pp. 132–7; *DSS*, pp. 184–8, 194–6. For a detailed bibliography on Qumran Messianism, see J. A. Fitzmyer, *The Dead Sea Scrolls. Major Publications and Tools for Study* (1975), pp. 114–18.

127. Cf. Black, *Scrolls and Christian Origins*, p. 148 f. For the textual debate relating to the 'begetting' of the Messiah, Y. Yadin, 'A Crucial Passage in the Dead Sea Scrolls', JBL 78 (1959), pp. 240–1; O. Michel-O. Betz, 'Von Gott gezeugt', *Judentum, Urchristentum, Kirche* (J. Jeremias Festschrift), ed. W. Eltester (1960), pp. 11–12; see Vermes, *Jesus the Jew*, pp. 199, 262–3.

128. 1QSb 5:20; CD 7:20. The Book of Ezekiel was an important authority for the priestly Qumran sect: cf. CD 3:18–4:2.

by his priestly partner designated דורש התורה, 'the Interpreter of the Law' (1QFlor. 1:11; cf. CD 7:18 where the 'Star' is the 'Interpreter of the Law' and the 'Sceptre', the 'Prince of the (whole) congregation'.) This title suggests that the Priest Messiah, like the sect's founder who was also a priest (see below), was to be the supreme authority in all matters of interpretation of the Torah, as also the guide and instructor in Torah of his lay partner.[129]

This unique type of messiahship is clearly modelled on the Moses-Aaron, Joshua-Zerubbabel partnership, repeated in the Eleazar-Bar-Kokhba duumvirate of the Second Revolt.[130] Strikingly parallel examples of the same expectation are contained in the Testaments of the Twelve Patriarchs, e.g., in Levi 18 (the priestly Messiah; Reub. 6:8: *ἀρχιερεὺς Χριστός*), Judah 24 (the royal Messiah); cf. also Sim. 7:2; Levi 2:11, 8:11 f.; Dan 5:10; Gad 8:1. Judah 21:2–5 sums up: 'To me God has given kingship, to him (Levi) the priesthood; and he has subordinated the kingship to the priesthood.'[131]

While this messianic scheme is well attested for Qumran, there are indications that it did not emerge all at once, but that the final form in which it crystallized as a dual messiahship was preceded by more than a single stage of development.[132] The earliest form of Qumran messianic aspiration appears to have been the expectation of the Priest Messiah (perhaps heralded or accompanied by the Prophet). The founder of the sect, the so-called 'Teacher of Righteousness', was a priest: his full title is given in 4 QpPs 37 III 15 as 'the Priest (הכוהן), the [rightful] Teacher ([מורה ה[צדק)'.[133] His opponent, the Wicked Priest (הכוהן הרשע), was a

129. Cf. Vermes, *DSSE*, p. 49; *DSS*, p. 185.

130. Cf. R. E. Brown, 'The Teacher of Righteousness and the Messiahs', *The Scrolls and Christianity*, ed. M. Black (1969), p. 43. On Eleazar and Bar Kokhba, cf. vol. I, p. 544.

131. Cf. K. G. Kuhn, 'The Two Messiahs of Aaron and Israel', in *The Scrolls and the New Testament*, pp. 57 f.; K. Schubert, 'Die Messiaslehre in den Testamenten der 12 Patriarchen im Lichte der Texte von Chirbet Qumran', *Akten des 24 internat. Orientalisten-Kongress, München, 1957* (1959), pp. 197–8; P. Grelot, 'Le Messie dans les apocryphes de l'Ancient Testament', *La venue du Messie* (1962), pp. 19–50; A. R. C. Leaney, *The Rule of Qumran and its Meaning* (1966), pp. 226–7.

132. See J. Starcky, 'Les quatres étapes du messianisme à Qumrân', RB 70 (1963), pp. 481 ff.; cf. R. E. Brown, 'J. Starcky's Theory of Qumran Messianic Development', CBQ 28 (1966), pp. 51–7; Black, *The Scrolls and Christian Doctrine* pp. 5 f. On the basis of a second manuscript of 1QS which omits verse 11 (the, messianic prediction) Starcky argues that in the earliest Hellenistic period (*c.* 200–150 B.C.) (when 1QS circulated in this non-messianic form) there was a total eclipse of messianism at Qumran. It was re-awakened in the Hasmonaean period (*c.* 160–50 B.C.) with a doctrine of a sacerdotal and a secular Messiah.

133. The designation 'Teacher of Righteousness', though it has established itself in the terminology of the Scrolls, is a questionable translation of the Hebrew title. See A. M. Honeyman, 'Notes on a Teacher and a Book', JJS 4 (1953), p. 131: 'The term *ṣedeq* refers not to the moral content of his (the Teacher's) instruction,

reigning High Priest in Jerusalem, but one probably with no legitimate family claim to the pontificate, possibly one of the Hasmonaean usurpers of High-Priestly office.[134] The sect's priestly messianism stems from its expectations, after the demise of its founder, the first to be called מורה הצדק, of another legitimate High Priest 'at the end of the days'. CD 6:10–11 lays down that the sectarians are not to be instructed in any legal doctrines or rules other than those taught and enacted by their founder 'until there arise יורה הצדק[135] at the end of the days'. CD 19:35–20:1 contains a regulation about the exclusion of apostates from the sect's register of members, 'from the day of the gathering in of the Teacher of the Community until the coming of the Messiah out of Aaron and Israel'.[136] The original expectation was probably for the rise of the Priest Messiah at the end of a forty-year period of exile in the wilderness corresponding to the Sinai wanderings (CD 20:15).[137]

At what stage the dual messianism arose is not known, but it was probably in the Hasmonaean period that sacerdotal messianism coalesced with the traditional Davidic promise.[138] The Damascus Document consistently refers to the rise of 'the Messiah of Aaron and Israel' (12:23–13:1; 14:19; 20:1), a designation which may suggest the absorption in the concept of the Priest Messiah of the messianic prerogatives of his secular partner. This double title, which has been variously explained, possibly represents a development in the Roman period[139] or, conceivably, a priestly ideal inspired by resentment of secular messianic views. At the same time, despite the singular form of this title the Damascus Document also testifies to the doctrine of *two* Messiahs.[140]

---

but to the legitimacy of his status. . . .' Cf. also J. Weingreen, 'The Title *Moreh Ṣedeḳ*', JSS 6 (1961), pp. 162–74. By contrast, in favour of the phrase, 'Teacher of Righteousness', note the title δικαιοσύνης κῆρυξ given to Noah, preacher of repentance before the flood, in 2 Pet. 2:5; cf. Vermes, Cahiers Sioniens 4 (1950), p. 194. The status to which the Teacher laid claim can only have been that of legitimacy as either a deposed, exiled and persecuted High Priest, or a pretender to high-priestly office of the family of Zadok. See especially Black, *The Scrolls and Christian Doctrine* (1966), pp. 6 f. and for the identification of the Teacher and his opponent, the Wicked Priest, see below (n. 134).

134. For the identification of the *dramatis personae* of the Scrolls, see Vermes, *DSSE*, ch. 3, and especially pp. 57 f.; *DSS*, pp. 150–5, 160. The suggestion that the Wicked Priest (הכוהן הרשע) is a word-play on 'the Chief Priest' (כוהן הראש) has been made by several scholars; cf. Black, *Scrolls and Christian Doctrine*, p. 7, n. 6.

135. יורה is a variation of מורה.

136. For this expression, see below, p. 553.

137. Cf. G. Jeremias, *Der Lehrer der Gerechtigkeit* (1963), pp. 284 f.

138. Cf. J. Starcky, *op. cit.*

139. Starcky, *ibid.* Cf. Vermes, *Jesus the Jew*, pp. 136–7 and notes.

140. Above, p. 550.

The third messianic-type figure of the Qumran sect is 'the Prophet', mentioned explicitly once only at 1QS 9:11: '... they (the members of the Community) shall depart from none of the counsels of the Law ... until the coming of the Prophet and the Messiahs of Aaron and Israel (עד בוא נביא ומשיחי אהרון וישראל)'. This phrase recalls the role of Elijah as forerunner, and the stipulation in 1 Mac. 4:46 that the desecrated stones of the Temple were to be stored away 'until a Prophet should arise who could be consulted about them'. The reference would seem, however, to be more specifically to the prediction of the rise of the Moses-like Prophet of Deut. 18:18–19, as is clear from 4QTest. which cites first Deut. 5:28–9, 18:18–19, predicting the rise of an eschatological Prophet, followed by Numbers 24:15–17, the Star and the Sceptre, and Deut. 33:8–11, the blessing of Levi by Jacob. These last two scriptural passages refer to the King and Priest Messiahs, and the order suggests, as at 1QS 9:11, that the Moses-like Prophet should precede the coming of the Messiahs. The figure of the Prophet was one of the liveliest of popular deliverers in the New Testament period, among Samaritans as well as among Jews and Christians, as appears from the Fathers of the Church as well as from the New Testament itself (Jn. 1:31, 6:14; cf. 7:40; Act. 3:22–3, 7:37).[141] It has been argued that the Qumran sect at one time regarded its founder as the Prophet.[142]

The Qumran sect also knows of another High-Priestly, but in this case also angelic deliverer, viz., the heavenly Melkizedek, a figure which may have contributed substantially to New Testament christological ideas. The document in question[143] is a midrashic fragment, eschatological in content. The heavenly Melkizedek, identical with the archangel Michael, is the chief of the 'sons of heaven' and referred to as אלוהים and אל. The former term can be used of 'judges', and this would suit the context of judgement, but אל and probably also אלוהים imply heavenly beings (אלים, 1QM 1:10–11; 17:7, etc.). The heavenly judge and saviour is portrayed as presiding over the last judgement and condemnation of his adversary Belial or Satan, elsewhere also designated

141. Cf. H. M. Teeple, *The Mosaic Eschatological Prophet* (1957), especially pp. 49–73.

142. Cf. Vermes, *Discovery in the Judean Desert*, p. 221; *DSSE*, pp. 49–50; *Jesus the Jew*, pp. 94–6; *DSS*, pp. 185–6, 195; Teeple, *op. cit.*, pp. 51 f.; J. Jeremias, TDNT IV, pp. 863, 6. At Test. Levi 8:15 John Hyrcanus is assigned the role of 'a prophet of the Most High'; cf. Josephus, *B.J.* i 2, 8 (68).

143. For the text see A. S. van der Woude, 'Melchisedek als himmlische Erlösergestalt', Oudtestamentische Studien 14 (1965), pp. 354–73; M. de Jonge, A. S. van der Woude, '11Q Melchizedek and the New Testament', NTSt 12 (1966), pp. 301–26; J. T. Milik, 'Milkî-ṣedeq et Milkî-rešha' dans les anciens écrits juifs et chrétiens', JJS (1972), pp. 96–109. See also J. A. Fitzmyer, *Essays on the Semitic Background of the New Testament* (1971), pp. 221–67; Vermes, *DSSE*², pp. 265–8; *DSS*, pp. 82–3; F. L. Horton, *The Melchizedek Tradition* (1976), pp. 64–82.

Melkiresha'.[144] The final judgement is represented as a great liberation on the Day of Atonement at the end of the tenth Jubilee cycle. The fragment sheds valuable light on the Melkizedek figure in the Epistle to the Hebrews.[145]

If the messianism of Qumran originated in a political movement to restore a rightful High Priest to the pontifical throne, it developed in time into a full-blown messianic doctrine within the context of an apocalyptic eschatology having a transcendental as well as a historical dimension. The advent of the Messiahs was to be heralded and accompanied by tribulation and warfare in which Satan would do his utmost to lead the chosen people of God astray.[146] The exodus motif of forty years sojourn in the wilderness was further elaborated into a forty year period of Armageddon in a prolonged series of battles between the 'Sons of Light', angelic bands led by Michael, and allied to the chosen people (i.e. the Qumran community), and the 'Sons of Darkness', Belial and his hosts of evil spirits and ungodly men, the latter ultimately represented by the Kittim-Romans. Finally, an end would come to the period of wickedness, a divine purgation of mankind and a 'new creation' (ועשות חדשה, 1QS 4:25) when the elect would recover all the 'glory of Adam' (כבוד אדם, 1QS 4:23).[147] The Messianic Banquet where the two Messiahs preside and partake of the bread and the wine, may be interpreted in the light of Ezekiel 44:3–4, as the inauguration of the new worship in the eschatological Temple.[148]

144. See above, p. 526.

145. F. L. Horton, *op. cit.*, however denies any influence of the Qumran Melkizedek on the New Testament.

146. Cf. Vermes, *DSSE*, p. 49.

147. Cf. Black, *Dead Sea Scrolls and Christian Origins*, p. 135; A. R. C. Leaney, *The Rule of Qumran and its Meaning* (1966), pp. 160 f.

148. Black, *op. cit.*, pp. 109 f. It is not yet certain whether the so-called 'Son of God' text from the pseudo-Danielic collection from Cave 4 (4QpsDan A^a = 4Q243) should be dealt with here. In an unofficial preliminary edition, J. A. Fitzmyer suggests that the document is properly apocalyptic, but not messianic. For the Aramaic original and Fitzmyer's translation, see 'The Contribution of Qumran Aramaic to the Study of the New Testament', NTSt 20 (1974), p. 393. Cf. Vermes, *DSS*, pp. 73–4.

§ 30. THE ESSENES

Sources

Philo, *Quod omnis probus* 12 (75)–13 (91); *Hypothetica* in Eusebius, *Praeparatio evangelica* (ed. K. Mras, GCS 43) viii 11, 1–18; *De vita contemplativa*.

Josephus, *B.J.* ii 8, 2–13 (119–61); *Ant.* xiii 5, 9 (171–2); *Ant.* xviii 1, 2 (11, 18–22).

Pliny the Elder, *Naturalis Historia* v 15/73.

For a convenient edition of all the classical texts: Philo, Josephus, Pliny, Synesius, Hegesippus, Hippolytus, Epiphanius, *Constitutiones Apostolorum*, Jerome, Filastrius, Nilus, Isidore of Seville, Michael of Antioch, Solinus, Josippon, Albertus Magnus, see A. Adam and C. Burchard, *Antike Berichte über die Essener* (²1972).

For a comprehensive view of the research on Essenism from the late eighteenth to the beginning of the twentieth century see S. Wagner, *Die Essener in der wissenschaftlichen Discussion* (1960).

For the Qumran manuscripts, see Vol. I, pp. 119–21.

Bibliography

(a) Bibliographical works:

Adam, A., Burchard, C., *Antike Berichte über die Essener* (²1972), pp. 66–88.

Burchard, C., *Bibliographie zu den Handschriften vom Toten Meer* I–II (1957–65).

LaSor, W. S., *Bibliography of the Dead Sea Scrolls 1948–1957* (1958).

Jongeling, B., *A Classified Bibliography of the Finds of the Desert of Judah 1958–1969* (1971).

Fitzmyer, J. A., *The Dead Sea Scrolls, Major Publications and Tools for Study* (1975).

(b) Studies prior to Qumran:

Frankel, Z., 'Die Essäer nach talmudischen Quellen', MGWJ 2 (1853), pp. 30–40, 61–73.

Hilgenfeld, A., *Die jüdische Apokalyptik in ihrer geschichtlichen Entwicklung* (1857), pp. 243–86.

Hilgenfeld, A., *Ketzergeschichte des Urchristenthums* (1884), pp. 87–149. 'Noch einmal die Essäer', ZWTh 43 (1900), pp. 180–211.

Ginsburg, C. D., *The Essenes. Their History and Doctrines* (1864).

Lucius, P. E., *Der Essenismus in seinem Verhältniss zum Judenthum* (1881).

Friedländer, M., 'Les Esséniens', REJ 14 (1887), pp. 186–216. *Entstehungsgeschichte des Christenthums* (1894), pp. 98–142.

Friedländer, M., *Die religiösen Bewegungen innerhalb des Judenthums im Zeitalter Jesu* (1905), pp. 114–68.

Conybeare, F. C., *Philo about the Contemplative Life or the Fourth Book of the Treatise concerning Virtues* (1895).

Wendland, P., 'Die Therapeuten und die philonische Schrift vom beschaulichen Leben', Jahrb. f. class. Philol. Suppl. 22 (1896), pp. 695–772.

Lightfoot, J. B., *St. Paul's Epistles to the Colossians and to Philemon* (³1897), pp. 80–96, 347–417.

Zeller, E., 'Zur Vorgeschichte des Christenthums. Essener und Orphiker', ZWTh 42 (1899), pp. 195–269.

Zeller, E., *Die Philosophie der Griechen* (⁴1903), III, 2, pp. 307–84.

Kohler, K., art. 'Essenes', JE V, pp. 224–32.
Graetz, H., *Geschichte der Juden* III, 1 ([5]1905), pp. 90–8; III, 2 ([5]1906), pp. 698–705, 800–5.
Brandt, W., *Die jüdischen Baptismen oder das religiöse Baden im Judentum mit Einschluss des Judenchristentums* (1910), pp. 64–9, 143–4.
Bauer, W., art. 'Essener', RE Suppl. IV (1924), cols. 386–430.
Lightley, J. W., *Jewish Sects and Parties in the Time of Jesus* (1925), pp. 267–322.
Bousset, W., Gressmann, H., *Die Religion des Judentums im späthellenistischen Zeitalter* ([3]1926, [4]1966), pp. 456–68.
Lévy, I., *La légende de Pythagore de Grèce en Palestine* (1927), pp. 231–4, 264–93.
Cerfaux, L., 'Le baptême des Esséniens', RScR 19 (1929), pp. 248–65 [*Recueil L. Cerfaux* (1954), I, pp. 321–36].
Cumont, F., 'Esséniens et Pythagoriciens d'après un passage de Josèphe', CRAIBL (1930), pp. 99–112.
Lagrange, M.-J., *Le judaïsme avant Jésus-Christ* (1931), pp. 307–30, 581–6.
Marchal, L., art. 'Esséniens', DB Suppl. II (1934), cols. 1190–32.
Heinemann, I., art. 'Therapeutai', RE V[A] (1934), cols. 2321–46.
Thomas, J., *Le mouvement baptiste en Palestine et Syrie (150 av. J.-C.–300 ap. J.-C.)* (1935), pp. 4–32.

(c) Studies utilizing the Qumran material:
Dupont-Sommer, A., *Aperçus préliminaires sur les manuscrits de la Mer Morte* (1950).
Brownlee, W. H., 'A Comparison of the Covenanters of the Dead Sea Scrolls with pre-Christian Jewish Sects', BA 13 (1950), pp. 50–72.
Baumgarten, J. M., 'Sacrifice and Worship among the Jewish Sectarians of the Dead Sea (Qumrân) Scrolls', HThR 46 (1953), pp. 141–59.
Vermes, G., *Les manuscrits du désert de Juda* (1953, [2]1954), pp. 57–66.
Delcor, M., 'Contribution à l'étude de la législation des sectaires de Damas et de Qumrân', RB 61 (1954), pp. 533–53; 62 (1955), pp. 60–75.
Braun, F.-M., 'Essénisme et Hermétisme', RThom 54 (1954), pp. 523–58.
Marcus, R., 'Pharisees, Essenes and Gnostics', JBL 73 (1954), pp. 157–61.
Molin, G., 'Qumrân-Apokalyptik-Essenismus', Saeculum 6 (1955), pp. 244–81.
Black, M., 'The Account of the Essenes in Hippolytus and Josephus' in *The Background of the N.T. and its Eschatology in Honour of C. H. Dodd* (1956), pp. 172–5.
Michel, O., 'Der Schwur des Essener', ThLZ 81 (1956), cols. 189–90.
Philonenko, M., 'La notice du Josèphe slave sur les Esséniens', Semitica 6 (1956), pp. 69–73.
Roberts, B. J., 'The Qumran Scrolls and the Essenes', NTSt 3 (1956), pp. 58–65.
Rubinstein, A., 'The Essenes according to the Slavonic Version of Josephus' *Wars*', VT 6 (1956), pp. 307–8.
Vermes, G., *Discovery in the Judean Desert* (1956), pp. 52–61.
Ploeg, J. van der, 'The Meals of the Essenes', JSSt 2 (1957), pp. 163–75.
Rabin, C., 'Yaḥad, Ḥaburah and Essenes', *Sukenik Memorial* (1957), pp. 104–22 (Hebrew).
Rabin, C., *Qumran Studies* (1957).
Rubinstein, A., 'Observations on the Old Russian Version of Josephus' *Wars*', JSSt 2 (1957), pp. 329–48.
Carmignac, J., 'Conjecture sur un passage de Flavius Josèphe relatif aux Esséniens', VT 7 (1957), pp. 318–9.
Cross, F. M., *The Ancient Library of Qumran and Modern Biblical Studies* (1958, [2]1961), pp. 52–79.

Kuhn, K.-G., 'The Lord's Supper and the Communal Meal at Qumran', *The Scrolls and the N.T.*, ed. K. Stendahl (1958), pp. 65–93.
Kuhn, K.-G., art. 'Essener', RGG II (^{3}1958), cols. 701–3.
Smith, M., 'The Description of the Essenes in Josephus and the Philosophoumena', HUCA 29 (1958), pp. 273–313.
Grelot, P., 'L'eschatologie des Esséniens et le livre d'Hénoch', RQ 1 (1958), pp. 113–31.
Vaillant, A., 'Le Josèphe slave et les Esséniens', Semitica 8 (1958), pp. 39–40.
Medico, H. del, *Le mythe des Esséniens des origines à la fin du moyen âge* (1958).
Philonenko, M., 'Le Testament de Job et les Therapeutes', Semitica 8 (1958), pp. 41–53.
Roth, C., *The Historical Background of the Dead Sea Scrolls* (1958).
Strugnell, J., 'Flavius Josephus and the Essenes: Ant. xviii 18–22', JBL 77 (1958), pp. 106–15.
Black, M., 'The Patristic Accounts of Jewish Sectarianism', BJRL 41 (1959), pp. 285–303.
Roth, C., 'Why the Qumran Sect cannot have been Essenes', RQ 1 (1959), pp. 417–22.
Roth, C., 'Were the Qumran Sectaries Essenes?', JThSt 10 (1959), pp. 87–93.
Kosmala, H., *Hebräer-Essener-Christen* (1959).
Milik, J. T., *Ten Years of Discovery in the Wilderness of Judaea* (1959).
Vaux, R. de, 'Une hachette essénienne?', VT 9 (1959), pp. 399–407.
Zeitlin, S., 'The Account of the Essenes in Josephus and the Philosophoumena', JQR 49 (1959), pp. 292–9.
Geoltrain, P., 'La contemplation à Qumrân et chez les Thérapeutes', Semitica 9 (1959), pp. 49–57.
Geoltrain, P., 'Esséniens et Hellénistes', ThZ 15 (1959), pp. 241–54.
Geoltrain, P., 'Le Traité de la Vie Contemplative de Philon d'Alexandrie', Semitica 10 (1960), pp. 5–67.
Simon, M., *Les sectes juives au temps de Jésus* (1960), pp. 42–73, 105–13.
Vermes, G., 'Essenes—Therapeutai—Qumran', Durham Univ. Journ. 21 (1960), pp. 97–115.
Vermes, G., 'The Etymology of "Essenes"', RQ 2 (1960), pp. 427–43 [*PBJS*, pp. 8–29].
Audet, J.-P., 'Qumrân et la notice de Pline sur les Esséniens', RB 68 (1961), pp. 346–87.
Gnilka, J., 'Das Gemeinschaftmahl der Essener', BZ 5 (1961), pp. 39–55.
Gnilka, J., 'Die essenischen Tauchbäder und die Johannestaufe', RQ 3 (1961), pp. 185–207.
Moehring, H. R., 'Josephus on the Marriage Customs of the Essenes' in *Early Christian Origins, in honour of H. R. Willoughby*, ed. A. Wikgren (1961), pp. 120–7.
Dupont-Sommer, A., *The Essene Writings from Qumran* (1961).
Black, M., *The Essene Problem* (1961).
Black, M., *The Scrolls and Christian Origins* (1961).
Laperrousaz, E. M., 'Infra hos Engadda', RB 69 (1962), pp. 369–80.
Burchard, C., 'Pline et les Esséniens', RB 69 (1962), pp. 533–69.
Vermes, G., 'Essenes and Therapeutai', RQ 3 (1962), pp. 495–504 (*PBJS*, pp. 30–6].
Delcor, M., 'Un roman d'amour d'origine thérapeute: le livre de Joseph et Asénath', Bull. Litt. Eccl. 63 (1962), pp. 3–27.
Talmon, S., 'A further Link between the Judaean Covenanters and the Essenes', HThR 56 (1963), pp. 313–19.
Daumas, F.-Miquel, P., *De vita contemplativa, Les oeuvres de Philon d'Alexandrie* 29 (1963).

Jaubert, A., *La notion de l'alliance dans le judaïsme aux abords de l'ère chrétienne* (1963), pp. 477–82.
Nikiprowetzky, V., 'Les suppliants chez Philon d'Alexandrie', REJ 2 (1963), pp. 241–78.
Driver, G. R., *The Judaean Scrolls* (1965).
Black, M., 'The Tradition of the Hasidaean-Essene Ascetism', *Colloque de Strasbourg* (1965), pp. 19–32.
Rowley, H. H., 'The History of the Qumran Sect', BJRL 49 (1966), pp. 203–32.
Daumas, F., 'La "solitude" des Thérapeutes et les antécédents égyptiens du monachisme chrétien', *Philon d'Alexandrie. Lyon 11–15 septembre 1966* (1967), pp. 347–58.
Burchard, C., 'Solin et les Esséniens', *ibid.* 74 (1967), pp. 392–407.
Baumgarten, J. M., 'The Essene Avoidance of Oil and the Laws of Purity', RQ 6 (1967), pp. 183–92
Philonenko, M., *Joseph et Aséneth* (1968), pp. 99–109.
Black, M., 'The Dead Sea Scrolls and Christian Origins', *The Scrolls and Christianity*, ed. M. Black (1969), pp. 97–106.
Negoïtsa, A., 'Did the Essenes survive the 66–71 War?', RQ 6 (1969), pp. 517–30.
Braun, H., *Spätjüdisch-häretischer und frühchristlicher Radikalismus. Jesus von Nazareth und die essenische Qumransekte* ([2]1969), pp. 67–89.
Albright, W. F.-Mann, C. S., 'Qumran and the Essenes' in *The Scrolls and Christianity*, ed. M. Black (1969), pp. 11–25.
Guillaumont, A., 'A propos du célibat des Esséniens', in *Hommages à A. Dupont-Sommer* (1971), pp. 395–404.
Marx, A., 'Les racines du célibat essénien', RQ 7 (1971), pp. 323–42.
Murphy-O'Connor, J., 'The Essenes and their History', RB 81 (1974), pp. 215–44.
Hengel, M., *Judaism and Hellenism* I (1974), pp. 218–47.
Isser, S., 'The Conservative Essenes: A new Emendation of Antiquities XVIII 22', JSJ 7 (1976), pp. 177–80.
Baumgarten, J. M., '4Q Halakah[a]5, the Law of Ḥadash and the Pentecontad Calendar', JJS 27 (1976), pp. 36–46.
Vermes, G., 'The Impact of the Dead Sea Scrolls on the Study of the New Testament', JJS 27 (1976), pp. 107–16.
Vermes, G., *The Dead Sea Scrolls: Qumran in Perspective* (1977), pp. 125–62.
Murphy-O'Connor, J., 'The Essenes in Palestine', BA 40 (1977), pp. 106–24.
Delcor, M. (ed.), *Qumrân. Sa piété, sa théologie et son milieu* (1978).

Separate from the mainstream of Jewish life in Palestine in the age of Jesus, a religious community existed which, though it grew on Jewish soil, on many points differed strikingly from traditional Judaism, and which, though it exercised no determinative influence on the development of the nation, nevertheless deserves attention as a special problem in the history of the Jewish people in the inter-Testamental age. Following the example of Josephus, the usual custom is to place this community of Essenes or Essaeans with the Pharisees and the Sadducees as a third Jewish sect. As need hardly be said, however, this is a phenomenon of an entirely different kind. Whereas the Pharisees and the Sadducees were great politico-religious parties, the Essenes, despite their own partly political origins, were—in their fully evolved state—rather to be compared to a monastic order.

Much about them is puzzling. Their name, to begin with, is obscure. Josephus generally alludes to them as *'Εσσηνοί*,[1] but also as *'Εσσαῖοι*.[2] For Pliny they are *Esseni*, for Philo always *'Εσσαῖοι*. Though Philo maintains that their name is to be associated with *ὅσιοι*, this is really only a play on words.[3] It is commonly held that the term is of Semitic origin, but there is little agreement concerning its meaning.[4] The derivation most widely advanced is that from the Syriac, *hase*', 'pious' (the equivalent of the Hebrew חסיד).[5] According to this, *'Εσσηνοί* is thought to depend on the absolute plural חסין, *'Εσσαῖοι* on the emphatic plural חסיא;[6] but the weakness of this theory is that חסי is never attested in such a sense in Jewish Aramaic.

Since the Qumran discoveries, another etymology has been revived, אסיא = healers.[7] This is associated (1) with Josephus's positive statement concerning the Essenes' interest in medicinal substances 'with a view to the treatment of diseases';[8] (2) with Philo's exegesis of the term *θεραπευταί* not merely in the sense of 'worshippers' but also in that of spiritual 'healers' who cured both bodies and souls;[9] (3) with ideas

1. So 14 times in all: *Ant.* xiii 5, 9 (171, 172 twice); xiii 10, 6 (298); xiii 11, 2 (311); xv 10, 4 (372); xv 10, 5 (373, 378 twice); xviii 1, 2 (11); xviii 1, 5 (18); *Vita* 2 (10); *B.J.* ii 8, 2 (119); ii 8, 11 (158); ii 8, 13 (160); v 4, 2 (145).

2. So *Ant.* xv 10, 4 (371); xvii 13, 3 (346); *B.J.* i 3, 5 (78); ii 7, 3 (113); ii 20, 4 (567); iii 2, 1 (11).

3. *Quod omnis probus* 12 (75): διαλέκτου Ἑλληνικῆς παρώνυμοι ὁσιότητος. *Ibid.* 13 (91): τὸν λεχθέντα τῶν 'Εσσαίων ἢ ὁσίων ὅμιλον. Eusebius, *Praep. evang.* viii 11, 1 (ed. Mras): καλοῦνται μὲν 'Εσσαῖοι, παρὰ τὴν ὁσιότητα, μοὶ δοκῶ, τῆς προσηγορίας ἀξιωθέντες. It appears unlikely that Philo in these explanations was thinking of the Semitic *ḥase*. As the first passage shows, he really derives the name from the Greek ὁσιότης. Cf. M. Black, *The Essene Problem* (1961), p. 4, n. 2.

4. See the detailed survey by G. Vermes, 'The Etymology of "Essenes"', *PBJS* (1975), pp. 9–19.

5. Cf. e.g. F. M. Cross, *The Ancient Library of Qumran* (1958), p. 37, n. 1; J. T. Milik, *Ten Years of Discovery* (1959), p. 80, n. 1; M. Hengel, *Judaism and Hellenism* (1974) I, p. 175; II, p. 116, n. 455. See also Milik, DJD II, p. 164, interpreting the geographical term, מצד חסידין, 'Fortress of the Pious' in Mur. no. 45 as designating the establishment of the Essenes at Qumran.

6. The initial ח with the subsequent sibilant doubled can be transcribed in Greek *ἑσσ* or *ἀσσ*: e.g. *ἑσσήνης* = חשן, *Ant.* iii 7, 5 (163); iii 8, 9 (218); *'Ασσούρ* = חצר, 1 Kings 10:23 (LXX); *'Εσσεβών* = חשבון. Note that חסידים is spelt *'Ασιδαῖοι* with a single *σ*. Hellenistic Greek uses the endings *-ηνός* and *-αῖος* indiscriminately: hence appeal to an Aramaic absolute or emphatic state is not necessary for the explanation of *'Εσσηνός*/*'Εσσαῖος*. Nevertheless, the two Semitic forms may have exercised some influence on the Greek structure.

7. Vermes, *PBJS*, pp. 19–29. First published in RQ 2 (1960), pp. 427–43.

8. *B.J.* ii 8, 6 (136): σπουδάζουσι δ' ἐκτόπως περὶ τὰ τῶν παλαιῶν συντάγματα μάλιστα τὰ πρὸς ὠφέλειαν ψυχῆς καὶ σώματος ἐκλέγοντες· ἔνθεν αὐτοῖς πρὸς θεραπείαν παθῶν ῥίζαι τε ἀλεξητήριον καὶ λίθων ἰδιότητες ἀνερευνῶνται.

9. *Quod omnis probus* 12 (75): λέγονταί τινες παρ' αὐτοῖς ὄνομα 'Εσσαῖοι . . . κατ' ἐμὴν δόξαν, οὐκ ἀκριβεῖ διαλέκτου Ἑλληνικῆς, παρώνυμοι ὁσιότητος, ἐπειδὴ κἀν τοῖς μάλιστα θεραπευταὶ θεοῦ γεγόνασιν, οὐ ζῷα καταθύοντες, ἀλλ' ἱεροπρεπεῖς τὰς ἑαυτῶν διανοίας

relating to medicine in inter-Testamental Judaism, including the Dead Sea Scrolls and the New Testament.[10]

Even more obscure than their name is the origin of the Essenes themselves. Josephus first mentions them in the period of Jonathan Maccabaeus around 150 B.C.[11] He refers specifically to an Essene called Judas in the time of Aristobulus I (105–104 B.C.).[12] Accordingly, the origin of the order is presumably to be dated to the second century B.C. But it is still a matter of argument whether the sect was an entirely Jewish movement, or whether it was subject to foreign influences. The classical sources on Essenism, namely Philo[13], Josephus[14] and Pliny,[15]

κατασκευάζειν ἀξιοῦντες. *De vita contemplativa* 1 (2): θεραπευταὶ . . . ἐτύμως καλοῦνται, ἤτοι παρόσον ἰατρικὴν ἐπαγγέλονται κρείσσονα τῆς κατὰ πόλεις, ἡ μὲν γὰρ σώματα θεραπεύει μόνον, ἐκείνη δὲ καὶ ψυχὰς νόσοις κεκρατημένας χαλεπαῖς τε καὶ δυσιάτοις, ἃς ἐγκατέσκηψαν ἡδοναὶ καὶ ἐπιθυμίαι καὶ λῦπαι καὶ φόβοι πλεονεξίαι τε καὶ ἀφροσύναι καὶ ἀδικίαι καὶ τὸ τῶν ἄλλων παθῶν καὶ κακιῶν ἀνήνυτων πλῆθος, ἢ παρόσον ἐκ φύσεως καὶ τῶν ἱερῶν νόμων ἐπαιδεύθησαν θεραπεύειν τὸ ὄν, ὃ καὶ ἀγαθοῦ κρεῖττόν ἐστι καὶ ἑνὸς εἰλικρινέστερον καὶ μονάδος ἀρχεγονώτερον.

10. Vermes, *PBJS*, pp. 24–28; *Jesus the Jew*, pp. 59–63.

11. *Ant.* xiii 5, 9 (171).

12. *Ant.* xiii 11, 2 (311); *B.J.* i 3, 5 (78–80).

13. *Quod omnis probus* 12 (75)–13 (91), and the fragment from the *Pro Iudaeis defensio* or *Hypothetica* in Eusebius, *Praeparatio evangelica* viii 11, 1–18, ed. Mras, GCS 43, 1, pp. 455–7; Adam-Burchard, *Antike Berichte über die Essener* (Kleine Texte 182, 1972). The authenticity of both these reports and of Philo's *De vita contemplativa* is no longer questioned. See the literature cited in Adam-Burchard, pp. 7, 13, 75 f., and pp. 591–7 below. See also the bibliography on the Essenes and Therapeutae in H. L. Goodhart and E. R. Goodenough, *Politics of Philo Judaeus* (1938); S. Wagner, *Die Essener, Die Therapeutenfrage*, pp. 194–202; L. H. Feldman, *Scholarship on Philo and Josephus* (1937–62) in *Studies in Judaica*, p. 3; M. Petit, *Quod omnis probus liber sit* (*Les oeuvres de Philon*, 28) (1974), pp. 20–5; F. Daumas, *De vita contemplativa* (*ibid.* 29) (1963), pp. 11–25.

14. *B.J.* ii 8, 2–13 (119–61); *Ant.* xiii 5, 9 (171–3); xv 10, 4–5 (371–9); xviii 1, 5 (18–22). For Josephus's references to individual Essenes and other incidental notices, see Adam-Burchard, pp. 22–5.

15. *NH* v 15/73. The remaining sources, Filastrius, Nilus, Hippolytus, Synesius of Cyrene, Hegesippus, Epiphanius, Jerome, Solinus, etc. largely depend on Philo, Josephus and Pliny. See, in general, the introductory remarks in Adam-Burchard, *op. cit.* Cf. further Black, *The Scrolls and Christian Origins* (The Essenes in Hippolytus and Josephus), pp. 187–91; C. Burchard, 'Zur Nebenüberlieferung von Josephus' Bericht über die Essener Bell 2, 119–61 bei Hippolyt, Porphyrius, Josippus, Niketas Choniates und anderen', *Josephus-Studien* (O. Michel Festschr.), ed. O. Betz *et al.* (1974), pp. 77–96. Hippolytus and Porphyry reproduce Josephus's account in *B.J.* ii. Solinus (3rd c. or first half of 4th c. A.D.) draws on Pliny in an apparently garbled version (cf. Adam-Burchard, p. 68); his 'additional' information that the area of the Dead Sea was particularly favourable for the cultivation of the virtue of chastity seems his own invention. The Abbot Nilus (d. c. A.D. 430) mentions Jewish philosophers and ascetics who may have some connexion with the Essenes and whom he regards as the descendants of the Rechabites founded by Jehonadab (cf. 2 Kgs. 10:15–18, Jer. 35): see Adam-

provide basic information concerning the beginnings and nature of the group. But if, as will be advanced presently,[16] the Qumran scrolls represent the same religious community, a substantial amount of first-hand Hebrew and Aramaic evidence must be added to the source material on which research into Essenism is now to be based.

As the identity of the Essenes and the Qumran sectaries is no more than a hypothesis—however probable—the treatment of the subject will proceed in two stages. First, the data of the Graeco-Latin sources will be evaluated, with Qumran-parallels given in the footnotes. Second, the Dead Sea Scrolls will be examined systematically and their evidence compared to that obtained from Philo, Josephus and Pliny.

Burchard, p. 70; cf. H. J. Schoeps, *Theologie und Geschichte des Judenchristentums* (1949), pp. 252 f. See also M. Simon, 'Les sectes juives d'après les témoignages patristiques' in *Studia Patristica* I, TU 63 (1957), pp. 526 f.; Black, *The Scrolls and Christian Origins*, 'The Patristic Accounts of Jewish Sects', pp. 48–74. See also A. Schmidtke, *Judenchristliche Evangelien*, TU III, 7 (1911), p. 206.

In rabbinic literature the Essenes are never mentioned—not by name at any rate. For attempts at identifying rabbinic allusions, see Wagner, *Die Essener*, pp. 114–27; Vermes, *Discovery*, pp. 48–52.

16. See below, pp. 583–5.

I. The Essenes according to Philo, Josephus and Pliny

1. *Organization of the Community*: Philo and Josephus agree in estimating the number of Essenes in their time as amounting to more than four thousand.[1] As far as we know they lived only in Palestine; there is at least no definite evidence of their presence outside it, unless a total or partial indentification of Essenes and Therapeutae is accepted.[2] According to Philo, they lived chiefly in villages, avoiding cities because of the immorality of town-dwellers.[3] Yet elsewhere he says they also lived in many towns of Judaea.[4] According to Josephus,

1. Philo, *Quod omnis probus* 12 (75); Josephus, *Ant*. xviii 1, 5 (21). It has been argued that Josephus uses Philo here. In the detailed account given by Josephus himself, *B.J.* ii 8 (119–61), the following points are omitted: (1) the number 4,000; (2) rejection of animal sacrifice; (3) agriculture as the predominant occupation; (4) rejection of slavery. All these are mentioned by Philo, and by Josephus in the later report, *Ant*. xviii 1, 5 (18–22), possibly from their inclusion in the Philonic accounts. G. Hölscher, art. 'Josephus', RE IX, col. 1991, refutes the theory of Josephus's dependence on Philo. Cf. also Farmer, art. 'Essenes', IDB II (1962), p. 144, who suggests a common source. On J. Jeremias's related estimate of the total population of Palestine in the time of Jesus at 500,000–600,000, see *Jerusalem in the Time of Jesus* (1969), pp. 205, 252. Cf. A. von Harnack, *Die Mission und Ausbreitung des Christentums* I ([4]1924), p. 12.

2. Whether the Christian ascetics in Rome (Romans 14–15) and Colossae (Col. 2) were Christianized Essenes is very questionable. If in Philo's *Quod omnis probus* 12 (75) the reading of *ἡ Παλαιστίνη καὶ Συρία* were correct, the appearance of the Essenes would be attested only in Syria. But this should surely be read *ἡ Παλαιστίνη Συρία*. For (1) the best Philo MSS give it thus, see P. Wendland, *Archiv f. Gesch. der Philos*. V, p. 230; (2) Eusebius, who also cites the passage (*Praep. Ev*. viii 12, 1), reads *ἡ ἐν Παλαιστίνῃ Συρίᾳ*; (3) the expression *ἡ Παλαιστίνη Συρία* is used elsewhere by Philo, *Virt*. 40 (221), *Θάμαρ ἦν ἀπὸ τῆς Παλαιστίνης Συρίας*, and the same expression was altogether quite common since Herodotus (and accepted into official Roman parlance from the time of Antoninus Pius). See Herodot. i 105, 1: *ἐν τῇ Παλαιστίνῃ Συρίῃ*; ii 106, 1 the same: iii 5, 2: *Συρίων τῶν Παλαιστίνων καλεομένων*; iii 91, 1: *Συρίη ἡ Παλαιστίνη καλεομένη*. See Avi-Yonah, RE Supp. XIII, cols 322–3, s.v. 'Palastina'. Josephus, *Ant*. viii 10, 3 (260): *τὴν Παλαιστίνην Συρίαν* (from Herodotus). Polemon in Eusebius, *Praep. Ev*. x 10, 15: *ἐν τῇ Παλαιστίνῃ καλουμένῃ Συρίᾳ*. For the official Roman usage the oldest example is a military diploma of A.D. 139, CIL XVI, 87. The coins of Flavia Neapolis frequently have the legend *ΦΛ. ΝΕΑΠ. ΣΥΡΙΑΣ ΠΑΛΑΙΣΤΙΝΗΣ* (de Saulcy, *Numismatique*, pp. 248 f.; *BMC Palestine*, pp. xxv–vi). Cf. also Pape-Benseler, *Wörterb. der griech. Eigennamen*, s.v. *Παλαιστίνη*. Cf. Preisigke, *Wörterbuch der griechischen Papyrusurkunden* III (1931) and Supp. (1969–71), s.v. *Παλαιστίνη*.

3. Philo, *Quod omnis probus* 12 (75–6): *λέγονταί τινες παρ' αὐτοῖς ὄνομα Ἐσσαῖοι . . . Οὗτοι τὸ μὲν πρῶτον κωμηδὸν οἰκοῦσι, τὰς πόλεις ἐκτρεπόμενοι, διὰ τὰς τῶν πολιτευομένων χειροήθεις ἀνομίας*.

4. Philo, *Hypothetica* 11, 1: *οἰκοῦσι δὲ πολλὰς μὲν πολεῖς τῆς Ἰουδαίας, πολλὰς δὲ κώμας, καὶ πολυανθρώπους ὁμίλους*.

they were even to be found in every town (in Palestine).[5] It would accordingly be a mistake to be led by Pliny's description to look for them only in the desert somewhere between Jericho and Engedi by the Dead Sea.[6] It is rather that the settlement there was distinguished from the others as one of the largest. For their life in common they had

5. *B.J.* ii 8, 4 (124): *μία δ' οὐκ ἔστιν αὐτῶν πόλις, ἀλλ' ἐν ἑκάστῃ μετοικοῦσι πολλοί.* 'Every town' can only mean every town in Palestine, not every town of the sect, as Hilgenfeld argued, *Judenthum u. Judenchristenthum*, p. 25. There were certainly Essenes in Jerusalem also, where they appear many times in history: *Ant.* xiii 11, 2 (311–2); xv 10, 5 (373–8); xvii 13, 3 (346); *B.J.* ii 20, 4 (567); v 4, 2 (745): *ἐπὶ τὴν Ἐσσηνῶν πύλην*, possibly because the house of the Essene order was situated nearby. For a different hypothesis, see Y. Yadin, 'The Gate of the Essenes and the Temple Scroll', *Jerusalem Revealed* (1975), pp. 90–1. Cf. for Qumran, CD 10:21, 12:19, which imply communities in towns ('cities').

6. *NH* v 15/73: 'Ab occidente litora Esseni fugiunt usque qua nocent, gens sola et in toto orbe praeter ceteras mira, sine ulla femina, omni venere abdicata, sine pecunia, socia palmarum. In diem ex aequo convenarum turba renascitur, large frequentantibus quos vita fessos ad mores eorum fortuna fluctibus agit. Ita per saeculorum milia (incredible dictu) gens aeterna est, in qua nemo nascitur. Tam fecunda illis aliorum vitae paenitentia est. Infra hos Engada oppidum fuit' . . . See for editions Adam-Burchard, p. 67. For the identification of the Qumran community with the Essenes, here located by Pliny 'above', i.e. north of En-gedi, see especially A. Dupont-Sommer, *Aperçus préliminaires sur les manuscrits de la Mer Morte* (1950), p. 166, n. 3, and *The Dead Sea Scrolls* (1952), pp. 85 f. See also M. Burrows, *The Dead Sea Scrolls* (1955), p. 280; G. Vermes, *Discovery*, pp. 17 f.; J. T. Milik, *Ten Years of Discovery* (1959), p. 44 f.; J. Hubaux, *Les Esséniens de Pline* (1959); M. Black, *The Scrolls and Christian Origins* (1961), pp. 9 f.; R. de Vaux, *Archaeology*, pp. 133–7; Vermes, *DSS*, pp. 127, 135. Cf. also J.-P. Audet, 'Qumrân et la notice de Pline sur les Esséniens', RB 68 (1961), pp. 346–87, and G. R. Driver, *The Judaean Scrolls* (1965), pp. 400 f. The interpretation of Pliny, by Audet and Driver, placing the Essene settlement above En-gedi, not at Qumran, has not been corroborated by the excavations in the En-gedi area conducted by B. Mazar between 1961 and 1965: see B. Mazar, T. Dothan, I. Dunayevsky, *En-Gedi. The First and Second Seasons of Excavations, 1961–1962*, 'Atiqot, Engl. ser. V (1966); B. Mazar, I. Dunayevsky, IEJ 14 (1964), pp. 121–30; B. Mazar, *Archaeology and the Old Testament*, ed. D. Winton Thomas (1967), pp. 223–30. See also Chr. Burchard, 'Pline et les Esséniens', RB 69 (1962), pp. 533–69, and E. M. Laperrousaz, 'Infra hos Engadda', *RB* 69 (1962), pp. 369–80 (both against Audet). The exegesis of 'infra hos', i.e. further down as signifying further south, accords well with Pliny's general description of that corner of Judaea. The sites mentioned are: Jericho, the Essene settlement, En-gedi, Masada. That is to say, the three known places are listed from north to south. Hence the Essene settlement lies south of Jericho and north of En-gedi and the only location fitting this description is Qumran. Dio Chrysostom (end of the first century A.D.), according to the testimony of his biographer Synesius, also mentioned the Essenes as a community on the Dead Sea. Cf. K. Treu, *Synesius von Kyrene. Dion Chrysostomos oder vom Leben nach seinem Vorbild* (1959), p. 14 [=Adam-Burchard, p. 39]: *ἔτι καὶ τοὺς Ἐσσηνοὺς ἐπαινεῖ που, πόλιν ὅλην εὐδαίμονα τὴν παρὰ τὸ Νεκρὸν Ὕδωρ ἐν τῇ μεσογείᾳ τῆς Παλαιστίνης κειμένην παρ' αὐτά που τὰ Σόδομα.* Dio could have visited Palestine, though scarcely while Qumran still existed. More probably, he is following a source—according to many, Pliny. So Adam-Burchard, p. 39; but cf. C. Burchard, 'Pline et les Esséniens', RB 69 (1962), p. 558, n. 113.

houses where they dwelt together.[7] Their whole community was strictly and uniformly organized. At the head were superiors (ἐπιμεληταί) to whom the members were bound in unconditional obedience.[8] Whoever wished to enter the order was presented with three insignia: a small hatchet (ἀξινάριον),[9] an apron (περίζωμα) and a white robe (λευκὴ ἐσθώς).[10] He was not received immediately into the community, but had first to undergo a year of probation, after which he was admitted to the ritual ablutions. Then followed a further probationary period of two years.[11] Only after the end of this, and after he had sworn a formidable

7. Philo, *Hypothetica* 11, 5: *Οἰκοῦσι δ'ἐν ταὐτῷ, κατὰ θιάσους ἑταιρίας καὶ συσσίτια ποιούμενοι, καὶ πάνθ' ὑπὲρ τοῦ κοινωφελοῦς πραγματευόμενοι διατελοῦσιν.* Josephus, *B.J.* ii 8, 5 (129) records that for meals *εἰς ἰδίον οἴκημα συνίασιν, ἔνθα μηδενὶ τῶν ἑτεροδόξων ἐπιτέτραπται παρελθεῖν.* Cf. also Philo, *Quod omnis probus* 12 (85): *Οὐδενὸς οἰκία τίς ἐστιν ἰδία, ἣν οὐχὶ πάντων εἶναι συμβέβηκε. Πρὸς γὰρ τὸ κατὰ θιάσους συνοικεῖν, ἀναπέπταται καὶ τοῖς ἑτέρωθεν ἀφικνουμένοις τῶν ὁμοζήλων.*

8. *B.J.* ii 8, 6 (134). For the *ἐπιμεληταί*, and the Qumran מבקר or פקיד see below, p. 576, n. 7.

9. On the *ἀξινάρ(ιδ)ιον*, *B.J.* ii 8, 7 (137); 9 (148), cf. Deut. 23:13 and 1QM 7:6 f. The implement, a small *ἀξίνη*, was probably a *securis dolabrata*. For a description of these tools, see K. D. White, *Agricultural Implements of the Roman World* (1967), pp. 60–6. For the background to such customs (Pythagoraean, Zoroastrian and Hindu parallels), consult J. Bidez-F. Cumont, *Les mages hellénisés* II, pp. 297 f. See further, J. Carcopino, *Le mystère d'un symbole chrétien. L'ascia* (1955), pp. 53–6; R. de Vaux, 'Une hachette essénienne?', VT 9 (1959), pp. 399–407; Black, *The Scrolls and Christian Origins*, p. 30, n. 6; Vermes, *PBJS*, p. 11.

10. Cf. *B.J.* ii 8, 4 (123); 5 (129–31); 7 (137); Philo, *Vita contemp.* 8 (66). The 'white garment', described at *B.J.* ii 8, 5 (131) as resembling 'holy vestments' (*ὡς ἱερὰς . . . τὰς ἐσθῆτας*), betrays the priestly origins and character of the sect. Cf. Exod. 28:39–43; Ez. 44:17–19 and 1QM 7:10 f. (the ceremonial 'vestments of white byssus', בגדי שש לבן, of the 'sons of Aaron'). Although they are said by Josephus to be always 'clothed in white' (*λευχειμονεῖν*, 123) the 'white vestments' were probably only used on ceremonial occasions (cf. Philo, *l.c.*). They are to be distinguished from the linen loin-clothes worn before the ceremonial bath: *B.J.* ii 8, 5 (129) and below, p. 569, n. 48. On the priestly origins of the Qumran sect, see below, pp. 575–6.

11. Cf. *B.J.* ii 8, 3 (122) and 1QS 5:7–13; 6:13–23; 7:18–21; CD 13: 11–13, 15:5 f. The rites of initiation as described in 1QS were first compared with the Josephan account by Millar Burrows, 'The Discipline Manual of the Judaean Covenanters', in *Oudtest. Stud.*, 8 (1950), pp. 158 ff. One of the main differences is that, according to Josephus, the period of initiation is three years, whereas in 1QS it is two. See Driver, *The Judaean Scrolls*, p. 110 ff. However, the two years at Qumran were preceded by a first stage of instruction, the length of which is unspecified (1QS 6: 13–15), cf. A. Dupont-Sommer, 'Culpabilité et rites de purification dans la secte juive de Qumrân', Semitica 15 (1965), pp. 61–70. See also C. Rabin, *Qumran Studies* (1957), pp. 1–21; A. Penna, 'Il reclutamento nell' Essenismo e nell' antico monachesimo cristiano', RQ 1 (1959), pp. 345–64 [*B.J.* ii 8, 7 (137–42)]; Vermes, 'Essenes-Therapeutai-Qumran', Durham University Journal (1960), pp. 107–8; O. Betz, 'Die Proselytentaufe der Qumransekte und die Taufe im Neuen Testament', RQ 1 (1958), pp. 213–34; J. Gnilka, 'Die essenischen Tauchbäder und die Johannestaufe', RQ 3 (1960), pp. 185–207; Black, *The Scrolls and Christian Origins*, pp. 92 f.

oath, was he permitted to sit at the common table and enter fully into the order. By his oath he vowed himself to unconditional frankness toward the brethren, and equally to keeping the teachings of the order secret from non-members.[12] Only adult men were admitted.[13] Yet they also took in children to educate them in their principles.[14] When Josephus says that the Essenes were divided into four grades according to 'the duration of their discipline',[15] his statement is to be read in connection with the account of the admission to the order: the three lowest grades are the novices in their first, second and third years of probation, the final stage is that of becoming a full member of the community.[16] A court consisting of at least one hundred members pronounced judgement on offences.[17] Anyone who transgressed severely was expelled from the community.[18]

The strongest bond joining the members together was an absolute common ownership of property. 'Their community of goods is truly

12. *B.J.* ii 8, 7 (141). For the 'formidable oath' cf. 1QS 5:7 f.; CD 15:5 f.; 1QH 14:17 f. Cf. Black, *Scrolls*, p. 94 f.; Driver, *Judaean Scrolls*, especially p. 68 ff.; C. Rabin, *The Zadokite Documents* XIX, 1–5, and *Qumran Studies* (1957), pp. 5, 10, 17. Cf. O. Michel, 'Der Schwur der Essener', ThLZ, 81 (1956), cols. 189–90; E. Kutsch, 'Der Eid der Essener', *ibid.*, cols. 195–8.

13. Philo, *Hypothetica*, 11, 3; cf. Vermes, *PBJS*, p. 32; Black, *The Scrolls and Christian Origins*, p. 47.

14. Josephus, *B.J.* ii 8, 2 (120). Cf. 1QSa 1:4 ff.; CD 15: 5–6.

15. *B.J.* ii 8, 10 (150): διῄρηνται δὲ κατὰ χρόνον τῆς ἀσκήσεως εἰς μοίρας τέσσαρας. Cf. A. Dupont-Sommer, *The Essene Writings from Qumran* (1961), p. 32, n. 5. On the organization of the Qumran community see M. Burrows, *The Dead Sea Scrolls* (1955), pp. 234–5; *More Light on the Dead Sea Scrolls* (1958), pp. 355–62, especially p. 359; Driver, *The Judaean Scrolls*, pp. 521–2; Rabin, *Qumran Studies*, pp. 1–21 (The Novitiate); Milik, *Ten Years of Discovery*, pp. 99–101; S. H. Siedl, *Qumran: eine Mönchsgemeinde im alten Bund* (1963), pp. 221–317; Vermes, *DSSE*, pp. 25–9; *DSS*, pp. 87–115. Below, p. 577.

16. Josephus's account specifies a year's training in the sect's 'way of life' prescribed for the candidate outside the community; *B.J.* ii 8, 7 (137), followed by a period during which he is brought into closer contact with the sect, participating, for instance, in its ritual baths, *B.J.* ii 8, 7 (138); then follow a further two years before admission to full membership. Cf. 1QS 2:19–23; 5:2 f., 23 f.; 6:8 f.; 1QSa 2:11 f.; CD 14:3–6. The scrolls do not mention any probationary period for the novice outside the community but clearly mark the three stages of novitiate within it—the two separate years of preparation, and the final admission (1QS 6:16–23). Cf. A. Dupont-Sommer, *The Jewish Sect of Qumran and the Essenes*, pp. 89–92; M. Burrows, 'The Discipline Manual of the Judaean Covenanters', in Oudtestamentische Studien 8, p. 163; Black, *The Scrolls and Christian Origins*, pp. 92 f.; Vermes, *DSS*, pp. 95–6.

17. *B.J.* ii 8, 9 (145). Cf. 1QS 6:24 f.; 1QSa 1:25 f.; CD 14:3 f. No numbers are given for this court in 1QS, 1QSa. See below, p. 576.

18. *B.J.* ii 8, 8 (143). Cf. 1QS 7:1 f.; 16 f.; 22–5; 8:21–9:2. Cf. C.-H. Hunziger, 'Beobachtungen zur Entwicklung der Disziplinanordnung der Gemeinde von Qumran', in H. Bardtke (ed.), *Qumran-Probleme*, pp. 231–47. See further below, p. 577.

admirable; and no one is found possessing more than another. For there is a law that those who enter hand over their property to the order, so that neither abject poverty nor inordinate wealth is to be seen anywhere; the property of individuals joins the common stock and all enjoy a single patrimony like brothers.'[19] 'They neither buy nor sell anything among themselves, but each one gives what he has to any in need, and receives from him in exchange something useful to himself. And without making any return, they are permitted freely to take anything from any of their brothers.'[20] 'The overseers (*ἐπιμεληταί*) of the common property are elected and each without distinction is appointed in the manner of all to the various offices.'[21] 'To collect the revenues (*ἀποδέκτας τῶν προσόδων*) and the produce of the earth they select excellent men, and priests to prepare the bread and food.'[22] So Josephus. Philo observes similarly: 'None allows himself to possess anything of his own, neither a house, nor slave, nor field, nor flocks, nor anything that procures abundant wealth. But they place all things together and enjoy the common profits of them all.'[23] 'The wages which they earn through different trades are handed over to one person: the steward (*ταμίας*) elected by them. He receives them and at once buys what is necessary and provides ample food and whatever else human life requires.'[24] 'Not only their food, but also their clothing is held in common. For the winter, thick cloaks are available, and for the summer, light tunics so that each may use them according to his pleasure. For whatever one possesses is held to belong to all; and whatever they all possess, as belonging to each one.'[25] 'There is only one money-chest for all, and common disbursement and common garments and common food

19. *B.J.* ii 8, 3 (122); cf. *Quod omnis probus* 12 (85–7); 1QS 1:11–13; 6:17, 19 f.; 24 f.; 1QpHab. 12:9 f. See further below, p. 578.

20. *B.J.* ii 8, 4 (127). See further below, p. 578.

21. *B.J.* ii 8, 3 (123): *χειροτονητοὶ δ' οἱ τῶν κοινῶν ἐπιμεληταί, καὶ αἱρετοι πρὸς ἁπάντων εἰς τὰς χρείας ἕκαστοι.* If the reading *ἀδιαίρετοι* is adopted, the relevant section is to be translated: 'each of them will without distinction render service to them all'. *B.J.* ii 8, 6 (134). The overseers (*ἐπιμεληταί*), *B.J.* ii 8, 3; *ἀποδέκται τῶν προσόδων*, *Ant.* xviii 1, 5 (22); *ταμίαι* Philo, *Hypothetica* 11:10; *ἐπίτροποι*, *B.J.* ii 8, 6 (134) appear to have been, at the same time, presidents of the order, for the latter were also called *ἐπιμεληταί*, *B.J.* ii 8, 5, 6 (129, 134).

22. *Ant.* xviii 1, 5 (22): *ἀποδέκτας δὲ τῶν προσόδων χειροτονοῦντες καὶ ὁπόσα ἡ γῆ φέροι ἄνδρας ἀγαθούς, ἱερεῖς τε ἐπὶ ποιήσει σίτου τε καὶ βρωμάτων.* Cf. *B.J.* ii 8, 5 (131). See also 1QS 1:9 f.; 6:4 f.; 1QSa 2:11–22, etc., and pp. 575–6 below.

23. *Hypothetica* 11, 4. Cf. 1QS 1:11–13, 6:17, 19 f.; 1QpHab. 12:9 f. See below, p. 578.

24. *Hypothetica*, 11, 10: *'Εκ δὴ τῶν οὕτως διαφερόντων ἕκαστοι τὸν μισθὸν λαβόντες ἑνὶ διδόασι τῷ χειροτονηθέντι ταμίᾳ. Λαβὼν δ' ἐκεῖνος αὐτίκα τἀπιτήδεια ὠνεῖται, καὶ παρέχει τροφὰς ἀφθόνους, καὶ τἄλλα ὧν ὁ ἀνθρώπινος βίος χρειώδης.* This *ταμίας* (treasurer) appears to be identical with the האיש המבקר על מלאכת הרבים, 1QS 6:20. Cf. below, p. 578.

25. *Hypothetica*, 11, 12.

at common meals. For the sharing of roof, life and table is nowhere found so firmly established in actual practice. And this is as one would expect. For all the wages they earn in a day's work they keep not as their own, but they rather put it into the common stock and allow the benefit of their labours to be shared by those who wish to make use of it. The sick are not neglected on account of their inability to earn, since the common stock stands ready for their care, so that they can assuredly meet expenses out of the plentiful reserves.'[26]

As is indicated in the texts cited, it went without saying that in their strictly observed common life all those who needed help were cared for by the order. If a man was ill, he was nursed at the common expense. The elders enjoyed a happy old age in the care of the younger men, as though they had many excellent children around them.[27] Each had the right to support the needy from the common purse in accordance with his own judgment. It was necessary to obtain the consent of the procurators (ἐπίτροποι) only in a case of relatives.[28] Travelling members of the sect found an hospitable reception everywhere. Indeed, a special officer (κηδεμών) was appointed in every town to attend to the needs of travelling brethren.[29]

The daily work of the Essenes was strictly regulated. It began with prayer, after which they were sent off to work by the superiors. They reassembled for purifying ablutions, and then they sat down to a common meal. The meal finished, they returned to work, to reassemble once again in the evening for another meal.[30] The chief occupation was agriculture.[31] But they also pursued all sorts of trades. On the other hand, according to Philo, all commerce was forbidden because it stimulates greed, and equally the manufacture of weapons.[32]

2. *Ethics, Customs and Usages*: The Essenes are described by Philo as well as by Josephus as true masters of morality. Josephus calls them

26. *Quod omnis probus* 12 (86–7). From Qumran parallels, see n. 23 above, and pp. 577–8 below.

27. *Hypothetica* 11, 13. Cf. CD 18:1–5, and C. Rabin, *The Zadokite Document* (1954), p. 70; M. Black, *The Essene Problem*, p. 24 f.

28. *B.J.* ii 8, 6 (134).

29. *B.J.* ii 8, 4 (124–5). Cf. Mk. 6:6–8.

30. *B.J.* ii 8, 5 (129). Cf. Vermes, 'Essenes-Therapeutai-Qumran', Durham University Journal, p. 102. On the meal cf. *Quod omnis probus* 12 (86); *De vita contemplativa* 4 (36 f.); 8 (64); 11 (89); 1QS 6:4 f.; 1QSa 2:17–22. See below, p. 579.

31. *Ant.* xviii 1, 5 (19): τὸ πᾶν πονεῖν ἐπὶ γεωργίᾳ τετραμμένοι. *Hypothetica* 11, 8. Cf. R. de Vaux, *Archaeology and the Dead Sea Scrolls* (1973), pp. 28–9, 59–60, 73–4, 84–5.

32. *Hypothetica* 11, 8–9; *Quod omnis probus* 12 (78). For regulations about commercial dealings at Qumran, cf. 1QS 5:16–7; CD 12:8–10; 13:14–15 and below, p. 577.

βέλτιστοι δὲ ἄλλως (ἄνδρες) τὸν τρόπον,[33] and Philo competes with him in praising them.[34] Their life was abstemious, simple and without desires. 'They shun pleasures as a vice and consider moderation and control of the passions as the essence of virtue.'[35] They ate and drank only as much as was needed to appease hunger and thirst.[36] By abstaining from passionate emotion, they were 'righteous stewards of wrath'.[37] At their meals they were 'content with the same fare day after day, loving frugality and rejecting luxury as a disease of both soul and body.'[38] They cast off their clothing and shoes only when they had become totally unusable.[39] They did not amass treasures of gold and silver, or acquire them out of a desire to gain large estates, but only what was required for the necessities of life.[40]

In addition, however, to these general characteristics of simplicity and moderation, their ethical principles and customs and practices included a series of features peculiar to them. These will be simply enumerated here and explained later.

1. 'There is no slave among them, but all are free, inasmuch as they work for one another.'[41]
2. 'Everything they say is more certain than an oath. Indeed, swearing is rejected by them as being more evil than perjury. For anyone who does not merit belief without calling on God is already condemned.'[42]

33. *Ant.* xviii 1, 5 (19).

34. Cf. *Quod omnis probus* 12 (88–91) (ἀθληταὶ ἀρετῆς). Compare *ibid.* (80–5) with *B.J.* ii 8, 7 (139–42) listing the contents of the oath each had to vow on entrance. For Qumran parallels, see 1QS 5:7 f.; CD 15:5 f.; 1QH 14:17 f.

35. *B.J.* ii 8, 2 (120): τὰς μὲν ἡδονὰς ὡς κακίαν ἀποστέφονται, τὴν δὲ ἐγκράτειαν καὶ τὸ μὴ τοῖς πάθεσιν ὑποπίπτειν ἀρετὴν ὑπολαμβάνουσι. On Essene asceticism, see H. Strathmann, *Geschichte der frühchristlichen Askese* (1914), pp. 83–100; 148–157; Vermes, 'Essenes-Therapeutai-Qumran', Durham University Journal, pp. 97–8; G. Kretschmar, 'Beitrag zur Frage nach dem Ursprung frühchristlicher Askese', ZThK 61 (1964), pp. 27–67; M. Black, 'The Tradition of Hasidaean Essene Asceticism: Its Origins and Influence', in *Aspects du Judéo-Christianisme* (1965); A. Steiner, 'Warum lebten die Essener asketisch?', BZ 15 (1971), pp. 1–28.

36. *B.J.* ii 8, 5 (133): the cause of peace and quiet at meal-times is ἡ διηνεκὴς νῆψις, καὶ τὸ μετρεῖσθαι παρ' αὐτοῖς τροφὴν καὶ ποτὸν μέχρι κόρου.

37. *B.J.* ii 8, 6 (135): ὀργῆς ταμίαι δίκαιοι, θυμοῦ καθεκτικοί. The reference is clearly to self-control: cf. 1QS 5:25 f.; 6:25 f.; CD 9:1–8; Mt 5:21–6. 'Righteous stewards of wrath' might also refer to their just administration of punishment. Cf. K. Stendahl, 'Hate, Non-Retaliation and Love', HThR 55 (1962), pp. 343–55.

38. *Hypothetica* 11, 11.

39. *B.J.* ii 8, 4 (126).

40. *Quod omnis probus* 12 (76).

41. *Quod omnis probus* 12 (79): δοῦλός τε παρ' αὐτοῖς οὐδὲ εἷς ἐστιν, ἀλλ' ἐλεύθεροι πάντες, ἀνθυπεργοῦντες; cf. *Ant.* xviii 1, 5 (21): οὔτε δούλων ἐπιτηδεούσι κτῆσιν. Cf. J. Strugnell, 'Flavius Josephus and the Essenes', JBL 77 (1958), pp. 109 f.

42. *B.J.* ii 8, 6 (135): πᾶν μὲν τὸ ῥηθὲν ὑπ' αὐτῶν ἰσχυρότερον ὅρκου, τὸ δὲ ὀμνύειν αὐτοῖς περιίσταται, χεῖρόν τι τῆς ἐπιορκίας ὑπολαμβάνοντες· ἤδη γὰρ κατεγνῶσθαί

3. They reject anointing with oil. And if anyone has been anointed against his will, he wipes it off. 'For they hold a rough outward appearance as praiseworthy.'[43]
4. They bathe in cold water before each meal.[44] They do the same each time they attend to the duties of nature.[45] Contact with a non-member, and even with a sectary of a lower class, requires a purifying bath.[46]
5. They think it fitting to wear white clothing always,[47] which is why every new member is handed a white garment when he enters.[48]
6. They conduct themselves with particular modesty in attending to their natural functions. With the small hatchet (*σκαλίς, ἀξινάριον*) which every member receives, they dig a pit one foot deep, cover themselves with a cloak so as not to offend the radiance of God (*ὡς μὴ τὰς αὐγὰς ὑβρίζοιεν τοῦ θεοῦ*), relieve themselves in the pit, and then fill it once more with the excavated soil. For this they seek out isolated places, and afterwards bath themselves as the unclean are accustomed to do. On the Sabbath, however, they entirely abstain from relieving themselves.[49] But their modesty also manifests

---

φασιν τὸν ἀπιστούμενον δίχα θεοῦ. Cf. *Quod omnis probus* 12 (84), they teach *τὸ ἀνώμοτον, τὸ ἀψευδές* (abstinence from oaths, veracity). Cf. also *Ant.* xv 10, 4 (371), where Herod exempted Essenes from taking the oath of allegiance. A curious exception is the 'formidable oaths' sworn on admission to the order, *B.J.* ii 8, 7 (139). Cf. CD 9:1–8; 19:1 f. See below, p. 577. Cf. also Mt. 5:34; Jas. 5:12.

43. *B.J.* ii 8, 3 (123): *κηλῖδα δ' ὑπολαμβάνουσι τὸ ἔλαιον, κἂν ἀλειφθῇ τις ἄκων, σμήχεται τὸ σῶμα τὸ γὰρ αὐχμεῖν ἐν καλῷ τίθενται.* On this avoidance of oil, cf. Driver, *The Judaean Scrolls*, pp. 102–3, citing mYom. 8:1 (cf. bYom. 76b). On fast-days anointing oneself was considered a luxury. The Essenes may have also feared defilement. Cf. further G. W. Buchanan, 'The Role of Purity in the Structure of the Essene Sect', RQ 4 (1964), pp. 397–406; J. M. Baumgarten, 'The Essene Avoidance of Oil and the Laws of Purity', in RQ 6 (1967–9), pp. 183–92 (avoidance of oil is to be understood as resulting from Essene scruples concerning Levitical purity).

44. *B.J.* ii 8, 5 (129): *ἀπολούονται τὸ σῶμα ψυχροῖς ὕδασιν.* Cf. ii 8, 7 (138). The obligation to take a ritual bath, instead of merely washing the hands, implies that the Essene meal was endowed with a sacred character. Cf. mHag. 2:5: 'to eat ordinary food (חולין), second tithes or heave-offerings, only the hands need to be washed; to eat consecrated (or sacrificial) food (קדש), an immersion is necessary.' Cf. Mk. 7:3–4; Mt. 15:2; Lk. 11:38. For the Qumran ritual ablutions and baths cf. 1QS 3:8 f.; 5:13; 6:16 f.; 22, 25: 7:3, 16; CD 11:2 1f. and below, p. 582.

45. *B.J.* ii 8, 9 (149). In this case the whole procedure follows the directions given in Deut. 23:12–14, except for the final ablution. See G. W. Buchanan, *art. cit., l.c.*

46. *B.J.* ii 8, 10 (150); cf. G. W. Buchanan, *op. cit., l.c.* For a similar distinction of uncleanness, see mHag. 2:7 (p. 385 above) and Origen, *In Mt.* 23:23–4.

47. *B.J.* ii 8, 3 (123).

48. *B.J.* ii 8, 7 (137); cf. above, p. 564, n. 10.

49. *B.J.* ii 8, 9 (147).

itself in other ways. When they bath, they tie an apron round their loins.[50] They also avoid spitting into the middle or towards the right.[51]

7. According to Philo, Pliny and several passages of Josephus they totally reject marriage: Ἐσσαίων οὐδεὶς ἄγεται γυναῖκα;[52] Josephus however knows of a branch of Essenes who permitted marriage.[53] Both Philo and Josephus attribute the custom of celibacy to misogyny: women are wanton and incapable of fidelity,[54] but Josephus adds that the Essenes do not condemn marriage in principle.[55]
8. They send votive offerings to the Temple, but offer no animal sacrifice, considering their own sacrifices to be of more value. For this reason, they are excluded from the Temple at Jerusalem.[56]
9. Finally, one of the chief peculiarities of the Essenes was their custom of the common meal. The food was prepared by priests,[57] in accordance with certain purity rules special to the sect.[58] Josephus's account runs as follows: 'After the purificatory bath, they assemble in a special dwelling-place where no uninitiated person is admitted. Purified, they enter the refectory as into a sanctuary. And after

50. *B.J.* ii 8, 5 (129).

51. *B.J.* ii 8, 9 (147): τὸ πτύσαι δὲ εἰς μέσους ἢ τὸ δεξιὸν μέρος φυλάσσονται. The same expression 'to spit into the midst' (אל תוך) is used in 1QS 7:13, and Josephus, εἰς μέσους. The regulations in Josephus forbid spitting to the right-hand side (the side of good omen) and into the midst of a session of the company: 1QS forbids it at meetings of the community. For a similar prohibition in the synagogue, see yBer. 59b, 62b–63a, cf. Driver, *The Judaean Scrolls*, p. 113.

52. *Hypothetica* 11, 14–17; Pliny, *NH* v 73; Josephus, *B.J.* ii 8, 2 (120–1), *Ant.* xviii 1, 5 (21); for Qumran, see below, p. 578.

53. *B.J.* ii 8, 12 (160–1). See below, p. 578.

54. *B.J.* ii 8, 12 (161).

55. See Vermes, *Discovery*, pp. 211–2; H. R. Moehring, 'Josephus on the Marriage Customs of the Essenes', in *Early Christian Origins. Studies in Honor of H. R. Willoughby* (1961), pp. 120–7; Black, 'The Tradition of Hasidaean-Essene Asceticism', in *Aspects du Judéo-Christianisme* (1965), pp. 19–33; A. Marx, 'Les racines du célibat essénien', RQ 7 (1969–72), pp. 323–42; A. Guillaumont, 'À propos du célibat des Esséniens', *Hommages à André Dupont-Sommer* (1971), pp. 395–404; R. Murray, *Symbols of Church and Kingdom: A Study in Early Syriac Tradition* (1975), pp. 17 f. For Qumran, see below, p. 578.

56. *Quod omnis probus* 12 (75): οὐ ζῷα καταθύοντες, ἀλλ' ἱεροπρεπεῖς τὰς ἑαυτῶν διανοίας κατασκευάζειν ἀξιοῦντες. *Ant.* xviii 1, 5 (19): εἰς δὲ τὸ ἱερὸν ἀναθήματα στέλλοντες, θυσίας οὐκ ἐπιτελοῦσιν διαφορότητι ἁγνειῶν ἃς νομίζοειν, καὶ δι' αὐτὸ εἰργόμενοι τοῦ κοινοῦ τεμενίσματος ἐφ' αὑτῶν τὰς θυσίας ἐπιτελοῦσιν. The reading οὐκ ἐπιτελοῦσιν is based on the Epitome and the Latin version ('*non* celebrant'): 'They send offerings to the temple, but do *not* perform sacrifices, employing a different ritual of purification'. See the note by L. H. Feldman in Loeb *ad loc.* Cf. 1QS 9:3–5; CD 6:11–20; 11:17–21; 16:13 f. Cf. R. Marcus, 'Pharisees, Essenes and Gnostics', JBL 73 (1954), p. 158; J. Strugnell, 'Flavius Josephus and the Essenes, Antiquities xviii 18–22', JBL 70 (1958), p. 113 f. See further below, p. 582.

57. *Ant.* xviii 1, 5 (22). See above, p. 566, n. 22.

58. *B.J.* ii 8, 8 (143).

> they have sat down in silence, the baker serves the loaves in order, and the cook places before each one a plate containing a single dish. The priest prays before the meal, and no one may eat anything before the prayer. After the meal, he prays again. At the beginning and at the end they honour God as the bountiful giver of life. After which they lay aside their garments as sacred vestments, and go back to work until evening. On their return they eat again in the same manner.'[59]

The belief that the Essenes abstained from flesh and wine like the Egyptian Therapeutai, the Pythagoraeans or the Judaeo-Christian Ebionites, is based on a statement of Jerome which may have arisen through a misunderstanding of garbled reports attributed to Josephus.[60]

3. *Religious thought*: The Essene ideological standpoint was fundamentally Jewish. Although Josephus ascribes to them belief in an un-

59. *B.J.* ii 8, 5 (129–32). These sacred meals may be identical with the 'sacrifices' (θυσίαι) held by the Essenes to be more precious than those offered in Jerusalem, *Ant.* xviii 1, 5 (19). The ἱεραὶ ἐσθῆτες are the white ceremonial garments. See above, p. 564, n. 10.

60. Jerome, *Adv. Iovinianum* ii 14 (PL XXIII, cols. 316–17): 'Iosephus in secunda Iudaicae captivitatis historia et in octavo decimo antiquitatum libro et contra Appionem duobus voluminibus tria describit dogmata Iudaeorum: Pharisaeos, Sadducaeos, Essaenos. Quorum novissimos miris effert laudibus, quod et ab uxoribus et vino et carnibus semper abstinuerint, et quotidianum ieiunium verterent in naturam.' The opening of this passage shows that Jerome did not make use of Josephus at all but of Porphyry, who in his work *De abstinentia* iv 11–13 reproduces Josephus's account as follows: 'Ἰώσηπος . . . ἐν τῷ δευτέρῳ τῆς Ἰουδαϊκῆς ἱστορίας . . . καὶ ἐν τῷ ὀκτωκαιδεκάτῳ τῆς ἀρχαιολογίας . . . καὶ ἐν τῷ δευτέρῳ τῷ πρὸς τοὺς Ἕλληνας. . . The last statement is wrong: the sects are not mentioned in *Contra Apionem*. But neither Josephus nor Porphyry say anything about the Essenes abstaining from meat and wine. Porphyry himself, throughout his work, requires abstention from meat. He is, however, sufficiently accurate not to introduce anything alien into Josephus's account. It was Jerome who first thought of this addition, no doubt because he combined Josephus's account with Philo's description of the Therapeutae (cf. below, p. 597).

In regard to the use of meat and wine among the Essenes, there are at least two reasons for assuming this was probable: (1) according to *Hypothetica* 11, 8 they also kept cattle; (2) *B.J.* ii 8, 5 (132–3) explains the peace and quiet of their mealtimes as being due to their taking only enough food and drink (τροφὴν καὶ ποτόν) to appease their appetites, which makes sense only if they also drank wine. Cf. 1QSa 2:17–22 and below, p. 582. The 'wine' (תירוש) of 1QSa has been variously explained: it is a poetic term for ordinary wine (D. Barthélemy and J. T. Milik, DJD I, p. 118): 'new wine' (Vermes, Durham University Journal (1960), p. 112). J. M. Baumgarten argues that *tirosh* is less liable than ordinary wine to become contaminated ('The Essene Avoidance of Oil and the Laws of Purity', RQ 6 (1967–8), p. 191, n. 42). The use of unfermented wine is traced to the priestly origins of the sect, M. Delcor, 'Repas cultuels esséniens', RQ 6 (1967–8), pp. 414–5; Vermes, *DSS*, p. 111.

alterable destiny through which human free-will is eliminated,[61] this is without doubt to be understood only in the sense of an absolute belief in Providence.[62] And although he says that the Essenes make everything dependent on destiny and the Sadducees nothing, while the Pharisees adopt a middle position between the two, this may be true in so far that the belief in Providence shared by the Essenes with the Pharisees was adhered to by the former with particular conviction. As, on this point, the Essenes were merely exaggerated Pharisees, so were they in their reverence for the Law and the Lawgiver. 'After God they hold the name of the Lawgiver in greatest awe and whoever blasphemes against him is punished with death.'[63] 'They study ethics with extreme care, taking as teachers the ancestral laws, which no human mind could possibly have conceived without divine inspiration.'[64] In their services, the Torah was read and expounded exactly as among other Jews; and Philo notes that they showed a special preference for allegorical interpretation.[65]

They were extraordinarily strict in their observance of the Sabbath. On that day they would not risk moving a vessel from its place or even attend to their natural functions.[66] In other ways, also, they showed themselves to be loyal Jews. They sent their offerings (*ἀναθήματα*) to the Temple in spite of being excluded from it.[67] Furthermore, they

61. *Ant.* xiii 5, 9 (172). Cf. xviii 1, 5 (18): *Ἐσσηνοῖς δὲ ἐπὶ μὲν θεῷ καταλείπειν φιλεῖ τὰ πάντα ὁ λόγος* . . . Cf. 1QS 3:13–4:26.

62. Cf. the remarks concerning the Pharisees (p. 392).

63. Josephus, *B.J.* ii 8, 9 (145): *Σέβας δὲ μέγα παρ' αὐτοῖς μετὰ τὸν θεὸν τοὔνομα τοῦ νομοθέτου· κἂν βλασφημήσῃ τις εἰς τοῦτον, κολάζεται θανάτῳ.* G. R. Driver, *The Judaean Scrolls*, pp. 108, 113: reverence for Moses as national Lawgiver, like esteem of the Sabbath, is common to all Jews, but as Driver points out, there is nowhere any parallel to the Essene penalty for 'blaspheming' against Moses. The importance of Moses for Qumran may be judged from 1QS 5:8; 8:15, 22; 1QS 1:3 cf. 9:9. See also H. Braun, *Spätjüdisch-häretischer und frühchristlicher Radikalismus* I, p. 68, n. 3. A. Dupont-Sommer sees in the 'Lawgiver' not Moses, but the founder of the sect. Cf. *The Essene Writings*, p. 31, n. 3.

64. Philo, *Quod omnis probus* 12 (80): *τὸ ἠθικὸν εὖ μάλα διαπονοῦσιν, ἀλείπταις χρώμενοι τοῖς πατρίοις νόμοις, οὓς ἀμήχανον ἀνθρωπίνην ἐπινοῆσαι ψυχὴν ἄνευ κατακωχῆς ἐνθέου.* Cf. *B.J.* ii 8, 12 (159): *βίβλοις ἱεραῖς καὶ διαφόροις ἁγνείαις καὶ προφητῶν ἀποφθέγμασιν ἐμπαιδοτριβούμενοι.* It is questionable whether the Bible is to be understood under *συντάγματα* (al. *συγγράματα*) *τῶν παλαιῶν*, *B.J.* ii 8, 6 (136), since according to *B.J.* ii 8, 7 (142) the sect had its own literature also. The Qumran library has supplied many such books.

65. *Quod omnis probus* 12 (82). On Philo's own preference for allegorical exegesis, see J. Pépin, 'Remarques sur la théorie de l'exégèse allégorique chez Philon', *Philon d'Alexandrie*, Lyon 11–15 septembre 1966 (1967), pp. 131–67; I. Christiansen, *Die Technik der allegorischen Auslegungswissenschaft bei Philon von Alexandrien* (1969). On Bible interpretation at Qumran, see below, pp. 579–80.

66. *B.J.* ii 8, 9 (147). Cf. *Quod omnis probus* 12 (81). Cf. CD 10:14–11:18.

67. *Ant.* xviii 1, 5 (19). See above, p. 570, n. 56.

appear to have retained the priesthood of the house of Aaron.[68]

In view of this decisively and basically Jewish cast of mind, there can of course be no question of any sun-worship among the Essenes. Therefore, although Josephus asserts that before the sun is visible 'they direct towards it certain ancestral prayers as though entreating it to rise,' this cannot be meant in the sense of adoration but only of invocation.[69] It seems more likely that Josephus is describing here an Essene custom in a form intelligible to Hellenistic readers, rather than defining the meaning it had for the Jewish sect itself. The same remark may apply to the statement that modesty in the performance of natural functions is motivated by the desire of the Essenes not to insult the radiance of the sun.[70] It may perhaps be worth noting that from Talmudic times the recitation of the morning *Shema*' has been preceded by a benediction thanking God for the creation of light.[71]

It should furthermore be borne in mind that much in Essene teaching was peculiar to them. However, when Josephus maintains that a newly initiated sectary must swear not to pass on any of the teachings (δόγματα) otherwise than as he himself received them,[72] it is not sure whether he means by this special doctrines. Nevertheless, the sect possessed its own books which it was the duty of the members to preserve with great care.[73] From the writings of the ancients, they studied what might benefit soul and body, namely the healing powers

68. This is a question of the interpretation of *Ant.* xviii 1, 5 (22): ἀποδέκτας δὲ τῶν προσόδων χειροτονοῦντες καὶ ὁπόσα ἡ γῆ φέροι ἄνδρας ἀγαθούς, ἱερεῖς τε διὰ ποίησιν σίτου τε καὶ βρωμάτων. The meaning is equivocal. It can signify: 'To collect the revenues . . . they select excellent men (and they select them also as) priests to prepare the bread and food', meaning that priesthood was elected, not hereditary. If the phrase is divided, the final clause would imply that the Essenes chose their bakers and cooks from the ranks of the priests. See further above, p. 566, n. 22, and below, p. 576 on the priestly character of the officers at Qumran.

69. *B.J.* ii 8, 5 (128): πρὶν γὰρ ἀνασχεῖν τὸν ἥλιον οὐδὲν φθέγγονται τῶν βεβήλων, πατρίους δέ τινας εἰς αὐτὸν εὐχας, ὥσπερ ἱκετεύοντες ἀνατεῖλαι. Cf. Philo, *Vita cont.* 3 (27); 11 (89). See F. Perles, 'The Hebrew Names of the Essenes and Therapeutae', JQR 67 (1926/7), pp. 405 f.; J. Strugnell, 'Flavius Josephus and the Essenes', JBL 77 (1958), pp. 111 f.

70. *B.J.* ii 8, 9 (148): ὡς μὴ τὰς αὐγὰς ὑβρίζοιεν τοῦ θεοῦ. Cf., however, for an opposite point of view Test. of Benjamin 8: ὁ ἥλιος οὐ μιαίνεται προσέχων ἐπὶ κόπρον καὶ βόρβορον, ἀλλὰ μᾶλλον ἀμφότερα ψύχει καὶ ἀπελαύνει τὴν δυσωδίαν. See J. Bidez-F. Cumont, *Les mages hellénisés* (1938), p. 297 f. and above p. 569, n. 49.

71. Cf. I. Elbogen, *Der jüdische Gottesdienst* ([3]1931), pp. 16 f.

72. *B.J.* ii 8, 7 (142): μηδενὶ μὲν μεταδοῦναι τῶν δογμάτων ἑτέρως ἢ ὡς αὐτὸς μετέλαβεν. According to *B.J.* ii 8, 7 (141) the Essenes were bound by oath not to reveal anything, presumably of their secrets, to outsiders, under pain of death. Cf. 1QS 4:6; 5:15 f.; 9:16 f, 21 f.

73. *B.J.* ii 8, 7 (142): συντηρήσειν ὁμοίως τά τε τῆς αἱρέσεως αὐτῶν βιβλία. Of these the Qumran finds have yielded numerous examples.

of medicinal roots and the properties of stones.[74] They attached great importance to angelology; members on entering were required to swear to guard the angels' names.[75] On the basis of their study of the Bible and their purifications they claimed prophetic gifts. Josephus avers that they seldom erred in their predictions,[76] bearing out his statement with several examples of Essene prophecy fulfilled, such as one pronounced by a Judas in the time of Aristobulus I,[77] a Menahem in the time of Herod,[78] and a Simon in the time of Archelaus.[79] But the Essene teaching about which he has most to say is that of the soul and its immortality. If his report is to be trusted, they taught that bodies may be perishable but souls are immortal, and that, dwelling originally in subtlest ether, they are drawn down by the lure of sensual love and bound to bodies as to prisons, but once freed from the fetters of sensuality, they soar joyfully up as though redeemed from long-lasting slavery. To the good (souls), a life is destined beyond the ocean where they will be troubled by neither rain nor snow nor heat, but where a gentle zephyr will constantly blow. But to the wicked (souls), a darker and colder corner is allotted, full of unceasing torment.[80]

74. *B.J.* ii 8, 6 (136); cf. n. 8 above. See below, p. 592. For the Essene practice of healings, cf. Vermes, *PBJS*, pp. 24–7; *Jesus the Jew*, pp. 62–3.

75. *B.J.* ii 8, 7 (142): *συντηρήσειν . . . τὰ τῶν ἀγγέλων ὀνόματα.*

76. *B.J.* ii 8, 12 (159). Cf. *B.J.* ii 8, 7 (142). The Essenes taught their art of predicting the future to their disciples: *Ant.* xiii 11, 2 (311). A. Dupont-Sommer corrects *διαφόροις ἀγείαις* in *B.J.* ii 8, 12 (159) to *διαφόροις ἁγίαις* (sacred writings); cf. *Essene Writings*, p. 34, n. 3. This emendation is, however, unnecessary since purification and asceticism are part of the late Jewish concept of prophecy; cf. Vermes, *Jesus the Jew*, pp. 99–102.

77. *Ant.* xiii 11, 2 (311–3); *B.J.* i 3, 5 (70–80).

78. *Ant.* xv 10, 5 (373–8).

79. *Ant.* xvii 13, 3 (345–8); *B.J.* ii 7, 3 (113).

80. Cf. Vermes, *DSS*, p. 187. For another version, with important differences, see Hippolytus, *Refutatio omnium haeresium* ix 18–28, and Black, *The Scrolls and Christian Origins*, Appendix B: 'The Essenes in Hippolytus and Josephus'. Cf. 1QS 3:13–4:26; 1QH 1:21 f. etc.

II. The Qumran Community according to the Dead Sea Scrolls

As indicated earlier,[1] the analysis of the classical accounts of the Essenes is now to be followed by a systematic survey of the Dead Sea Scrolls with a view (1) to piecing together their information concerning the organization, doctrines and religious practices of the Qumran community; (2) to determining the relationship between the Essenes and the Judaean sectaries; and (3) to tracing Essene/Qumran origins and history.

1. *Organization of the Qumran Community:*[2] Study of the various codes (1QS, CD, 1QM and 1QSa) makes it possible to reconstruct the organization, government and life of the sect. To do this successfully, the scholar must bear in mind, however, that the Community Rule legislates for a kind of monastic society, whilst the statutes of the Damascus Rule are concerned with town communities leading a lay existence,[3] and that the various legal accounts are bound to reflect customs of successive periods. Moreover, some of them, viz. 1QM and 1QSa, although no doubt reflecting to some extent a contemporary state of affairs, appear to plan for a future age.

The Community (יחד)[4] of Qumran claimed, as sects generally do, to represent the genuine traditions of the religious body from which it had separated. Its members formed the true Israel, and like it, were divided into clergy—priests and Levites—and laity (e.g. 1QS 8: 5–9). They maintained the symbolical grouping into twelve tribes (e.g. 1QM 2: 1–3), and into the smaller units of thousands, hundreds, fifties and tens (e.g. 1QS 2:21–2).

Supreme authority lay in the hands of the priests. Although they governed the sect through a general assembly or the Council of the

1. Cf. above, p. 561.

2. For the latest survey, see Vermes, *DSS*, pp. 87–115. The Temple Scroll, published at the end of 1977, reached us too late for use in this volume. Its contents will be analysed in the literature section in vol. III. Meanwhile see Y. Yadin, *The Temple Scroll* (*Hebrew Edition*) I–III (1977).

3. For the towns, see above, p. 563, n. 5.

4. Cf. commentaries on 1QS in general. See also A. Dupont-Sommer, *The Essene Writings*, p. 44; P. Wernberg-Møller, 'The Nature of the YAḤAD according to the Manual of Discipline and related Documents', *Dead Sea Scroll Studies* 1969, ALUOS 6 (1969), pp. 56–81. Other principlal terms designating the sect are עדה, קהל, and עצה. The initiates are referred to as הרבים, 'the many', 'the multitude '(1 QS 6:1 ff., etc.).

Community, it was the 'sons of Zadok' (בני צדוק) or 'sons of Aaron' (בני אהרון) who pronounced the final word on matters of doctrine, justice and property (1 QS 5:2; 9:7).[5]

The smallest unit, the group of ten (עשרה אנשים), was expected to include a priest for the recitation of the blessing over meals (1QS 6:2–5; CD 12:2–3), for continuous Torah study,[6] and for the performance of legal functions traditionally reserved to members of the sacerdotal class, e.g. the administration of the leprosy laws (CD 13:4–7). The management of the community's affairs was entrusted to the guardian or overseer (מבקר), presumably a priest, who dealt with admissions, instruction and decision-making, and with determining the right conduct of every member of his unit. He was also in charge of practical matters and communal finance (1QS 6:13–23; CD 13:7–16).[7]

At the head of the sect as a whole stood a priest-president-general (הכוהן אשר יפקד א[ת] הרבים) and a guardian of all the camps (המבקר אשר לכל המחנות) (CD 14:6–12). Besides these, the Damascus Rule mentions ten judges elected for a specific term, four priests and Levites and six laymen (CD 10:4–10).[8] In the ultimate phase of the eschatological age, the sect was also to have a supreme lay leader, the נשיא or prince who was no doubt to be identical with the Messiah of Israel or the royal Messiah (1QM 5:1; 1QSa 2:14, 20).[9] A compulsory retiring age

5. Cf. above, p. 573, n. 68.

6. The איש דורש התורה (1QS 6:6) is no doubt identical with the priest-president. The sacerdotal quality of the messianic 'interpreter of the Law' is implied in CD 7:18 where he is mentioned in association with the 'Prince of the whole congregation' (נשיא כל העדה) and in 4QFlor 1:11 (דורש התורה – צמח דויד). For the Qumran expectation of a priestly and a royal Messiah, see above, pp. 550–2.

7. The various official titles within the sect are: (1) המבקר (1QS 6:12, 19; CD 9:19, 22; 13:5–7, 13, 15–16; 14; 10–12; 16:11). Whether the person described as האיש המבקר על מלאכת הרבים is identical with the overseer/guardian, or another functionary (bursar) is unclear. For a discussion of the various officers, see Vermes, *Discovery*, p. 45; B. Reicke, 'The Constitution of the Primitive Church in the Light of the Qumran Documents', in *The Scrolls and the New Testament* (1958), p. 150, 154 f.; L. Rost, 'Zur Struktur der Gemeinde des Neuen Bundes im Lande Damaskus', VT 9, 1959, pp. 393–8; G. Vermes, 'Essenes-Therapeutai-Qumran', Durham University Journal (1960), pp. 99–100; M. Black, *The Scrolls and Christian Origins* (1962), p. 115; J. F. Priest, 'Mebaqqer, Paqid, and the Messiah', JBL 81 (1962), pp. 55–61; P. Osten-Sacken, 'Bemerkungen zur Stellung des Mebaqqer in der Sektenschrift', ZNW 55 (1964), pp. 18–26; G. R. Driver, *The Judaean Scrolls* (1965), pp. 106–7; 521–3; Vermes, *DSS*, pp. 87–115.

8. Cf. Vermes, *DSS*, pp. 99–100, 113. The Essene tribunal of a hundred (cf. n. 17, p. 565 above) also reflects a decimal system, unlike the courts of three, twenty-three and seventy-one of the Mishnah (mSanh. 1:1, 4, 5). mSanh. 1:3 mentions cases to be dealt with by a tribunal of ten judges of whom one should be a priest. The 'Ordinances' from Cave 4 (4Q 159) allude to a tribunal of twelve, two priests and ten laymen. Cf. J. M. Baumgarten, 'The Duodecimal Courts of Qumran, Revelation and the Sanhedrin', JBL 95 (1976), pp. 59–78.

9. For the title נשיא borne by Simeon ben Kosiba, cf. vol. I, p. 544.

of fifty was laid down for the guardian of all the camps, and of sixty for holders of other offices (CD 14:7, 9; 10:6–10).

Admission to the community, as practised in the 'monastic' brotherhood described in 1QS, began with a ceremony called 'entry into the Covenant', i.e. an undertaking on oath that the postulants would obey all the laws of Moses according to the interpretation of the sect's priestly hierarchy (1QS 1:16 ff.; 5:1–11). They thus became 'members of the Covenant' (באי הברית, 1QS 2:18, etc.), synonymous with 'men of the community' (אנשי היחד, 1QS 5:1, etc.). A further period of unspecified length followed, during which the new recruit received instruction. He then appeared before the congregation, which confirmed him as a novice or dismissed him. If accepted, he was to undergo two years of special training, with a test at the end of each year. The final examination decided whether a man was to be declared a full member, with the right to take part actively in all the community's affairs, including voting at meetings and the sharing of property (1QS 6:13–23).[10]

Any deliberate transgression of the Torah barred the way to full membership. And an established member found guilty of an act of disobedience, committed wilfully or through negligence, was expelled and no further contact with him tolerated (1QS 8:20–4).[10a] Minor offences were punished with a penance entailing a reduction of the food ration, or with varying degrees of exclusion from the common life which could last from ten days to two years (1QS 6:24–7:25).

Judging by the differences in the rules, it would appear that Covenant members living in towns and villages—distinct from the Qumran-type communities—were expected to comply with the sect's strict discipline but not to own property in common. They were allowed to trade with non-members, even with Gentiles (CD 13:14–16; 12:9–11). Also, they appear not to have been permitted to accept anything from outsiders except against payment (1QS 5:16–17). In each of their settlements, a communal chest was maintained through regular contributions (two

10. In the first year of the novitiate, the candidate was not admitted to the Community's 'purity' (טהרה), probably ritually clean food and the vessels and utensils in which it was contained or cooked. He could not share, moreover, in the sect's property. In the second year, the ban on touching the pure things was limited to liquids (משקה), and he was to hand over his money and belongings to the 'Bursar', but they were set aside and not yet absorbed into community ownership. Cf. S. Lieberman, JBL 71 (1951), pp. 199–206 [=*Texts and Studies* (1974), pp. 200–7]; J. Licht, חומרת משקה הרבים מטהרת הרבים בסרך היחד, *Sefer Segal*, ed. J. M. Grintz (1964), pp. 300–9; Vermes, *DSS*, pp. 95–6, 111.

10a. Cf. M. Delcor, 'Les tribunaux de l'église de Corinthe et les tribunaux de Qumrân', *Studiorum Paulinorum Congressus Catholicus 1961* (1963), pp. 535–48; G. Forkman, *The Limits of the Religious Community. Expulsion from the Religious Community within the Qumran Sect, within Rabbinic Judaism and within Primitive Christianity* (1972).

days' wages per month) and served to finance charitable activities such as the support of widows, orphans, the sick, etc. (CD 14:12–16). Members of the monastic brotherhood, by contrast, undertook to hand over their property and earnings to the 'bursar' (1QS 6:19–20), who in turn provided everyone with his needs.[11]

The question of marriage among the sectaries is complex. The Damascus Rule (CD 7:6–7) and the Messianic Rule (1QSa 1:4) speak of married members and children. The War Rule does likewise, but stipulates that during the eschatological war no woman or child shall enter the camp of the sons of Light (1QM 7:4–5). Also, although only a small number of tombs have been opened, the secondary cemeteries of Qumran held the remains of women and children.[12] The Community Rule, on the other hand, is silent in regard to women and also positively enjoins 'not to follow a sinful heart and lustful eyes' (1:6). Moreover, the main Qumran cemetery has in fact yielded (with one exception) only male skeletons.[13] Recalling that Josephus mentions unmarried and married Essenes, it is in consequence reasonable to conclude that the Dead Sea Community likewise included members of both sexes, the married sectaries probably outnumbering their celibate brethren.[14]

11. For the rules followed in the lay communities, set out in CD and 1QSa, see Vermes, *DSS*, pp. 97–105. Regarding the bond between desert and town sectaries, cf. *ibid.*, pp. 105–9. The compulsory communism of the Qumran monastic group, identical to that of the Essenes (cf. above, pp. 566–7, nn. 23–6), may be compared to the optional common ownership of Act. 2:44–5; 4:32–5:2; cf. J. G. Greehy, 'Community of Goods—Qumran and Acts', Irish Theol. Quart. 32 (1965), pp. 230–40; J. A. Fitzmyer, 'Jewish Christianity in Acts in the Light of the Qumran Scrolls' in *Essays on the Semitic Background of the N.T.* (1971), pp. 271–303. A common purse administered by Judas is also implied in the group headed by Jesus in Jn. 12:6; 13:29. Cf. Vermes, *DSS*, pp. 216–17. It it is accepted that the economic regime of the members of the Covenant living in towns and villages was distinct from that of the monastic brotherhood, objections raised against the identification of the Qumran sect as Essene lose most of their force. Cf. C. Rabin, *Qumran Studies* (1957), p. 23; G. R. Driver, *The Judaean Scrolls* (1965), pp. 113–16.

12. The various cemeteries and their 1,200 tombs are described by de Vaux, *op. cit.*, pp. 45–8, 57–8, 88–9. Cf. also S. H. Steckoll, 'Preliminary Excavation Report in the Qumran Cemetery', RQ 6 (1968), pp. 323–44; N. Haas, H. Nathan, 'Anthropological Survey of the Human Skeletal Remains from Qumran', *ibid.*, pp. 345–52; E.-M. Laperrousaz, *Qoumrân. L'établissement essénien des bords de la Mer Morte. Histoire et archéologie du site* (1976), pp. 19–25.

13. Cf. R. de Vaux, *Archaeology and the Dead Sea Scrolls* (1973), pp. 128–9.

14. On the problem of celibacy, see above p. 570, n. 55. Cf. also Vermes, *Jesus the Jew*, pp. 99–102; *DSS*, pp. 181–2, 193. Two features of Qumran marriage laws are to be noted. (1) The age at which a man may take a wife is given as twenty (1QSa 1:10–11; cf. S. B. Hoenig, 'On the Age of Mature Responsibility in 1QSa', JQR 48 (1957), pp. 371–5; 'The Age of Twenty in Rabbinic Tradition and 1 QSa', JQR 49 (1958), pp. 209–14) against the age of eighteen recommended in the Mishnah (mAb. 5:21). Twenty is also the age required for 'enrolment', i.e. full membership (1QSa 1:8–9; CD 15:5–6). The Scrolls make no reference to the trial

All the members of the sect attended an annual general assembly at the Feast of the Renewal of the Covenant (or Pentecost, cf. below) when the order of precedence among the sectaries was reviewed (cf. 1QS 1–3; especially 2:19).[15] The monastic brethren met nightly for study and prayer (1QS 6:7). Some of the meetings were accompanied by a solemn meal, at which bread and *tirosh* were blessed by the presiding priest (1QS 6:4–5; 1QSa 2:17–21).[16]

The Community Rule mentions a tribunal or 'Court of Inquiry' (1QS 6:24) designed to try those who offended against community discipline. A detailed penal code defines the punishment attached to the various transgressions; for example, speaking out of turn in public incurred ten days' penance, whilst a deliberate breach of the Mosaic Law demanded irrevocable expulsion (1QS 6:24–7:25). The Damascus Rule refers to a court of ten judges, four of them priests and six Israelite lay-men (CD 10:4–10), and specifies rules applying to witnesses (CD 9:16–10:3). Imprisonment appears among the penalties (CD 12:4–6). Any sectary who willingly participated in a capital case before a Gentile court (CD 9:1), preached 'apostasy under the dominion of the spirits of Belial' (CD 12:2–3), or slandered the people of Israel or committed treason (11QTemple 67:6–13), was to die.[17]

2. *Doctrine and religious observances*: The members of the Qumran sect professed to belong to a 'new Covenant' (1QpHab. 2:3; CD 8:21, 35),

---

of betrothed women mentioned by Josephus, *B.J.* ii 8, 13 (161) connected apparently with the onset of puberty (cf. Dupont-Sommer, *Essene Writings*, p. 35, n. 3). (2) The sect condemns polygamy rather than divorce (CD 4:20–5:2) and marriage between uncle and niece (CD 5:8–11). Cf. Vermes, 'Sectarian Matrimonial Halakhah in the Damascus Rule', JJS 25 (1974), pp. 197–202 [=*PBJS*, pp. 50–6 giving a full bibliographical survey]; 'The Qumran Interpretation of Scripture in its Historical Setting', *PBJS*, pp. 40–1; J. A. Fitzmyer, 'The Matthean Divorce Texts and some new Palestinian Evidence', Theol. Studies 37 (1976), pp. 197–226.

15. Cf. Vermes, 'Essenes-Therapeutai-Qumran', Durham University Journal (1960), pp. 112–13; M. Weise, *Kultzeiten und kultischer Bundesschluss in der "Ordensregel" von Qumran* (1961); Vermes, *DSS*, pp. 107, 177–9, 192.

16. See above, p. 567, n. 30. Cf. K. G. Kuhn, 'The Lord's Supper and the Communal Meal at Qumran', *The Scrolls and the N.T.* (1958), pp. 65–93; Black, *The Scrolls and Christian Origins*, pp. 102–18; M. Delcor, 'Repas cultuels esséniens et thérapeutes. Thiases et Haburoth', RQ 6 (1968), pp. 401–25; Vermes, *DSS*, pp. 94, 111, 182, 193. For the meaning of תירוש as unfermented grape-juice, cf. tNed. 4:3; Sifre Deut. 42 and Vermes, *DSS*, p. 111.

17. For the problem of single witnesses, see B. Levine, RQ 8 (1973), pp. 195–6; J. Neusner, *ibid.*, pp. 197–217; L. H. Schiffman, *ibid.*, pp. 603–12; B. S. Jackson, *Essays in Jewish and Comparative Legal History* (1975), pp. 172–201; N. L. Rabinovitch, RQ 9 (1977), pp. 113–16. For the exegesis of CD 9:1; cf. P. Winter, 'Sadoqite Fragment IX, 1', RQ 6 (1967), pp. 131–6; Z. W. Falk, '*Behuqei hagoyim* in Damascus Document IX, 1', *ibid.* (1969), p. 569. For the literature on 'hanging/crucifixion', see Vermes, *DSS*, p. 114; M. Hengel, *Crucifixion* (1977), pp. 84–5.

based on the message of Moses and the prophets, but understood in the light of the preaching of the Teacher of Righteousness and of the authoritative exegesis given by the sons of Zadok, the priestly leaders of the Community.[18]

In biblical thinking, the notion of Covenant is inseparable from that of a chosen people: Israelite birth is synonymous with election.[19] By contrast, when an adult Jew joined the Qumran sect, he played a personal and active part in becoming one of God's chosen. His particular situation awakened in him an awareness of human frailty and of the all-

18. The various exegetical methods employed in the Scrolls may be outlined as follows:

1. Halakhic reinterpretation develops biblical law either (a) in a straight line or (b) completely transforms it by complex and sometimes tortuous reasoning. For (a) see CD 16:10–12 (the right conceded by Num. 30:9 to the husband to annul his wife's vows is limited to those which were improper in the first place). For (b) see CD 16:14–15 (duties towards parents and family override a man's obligation to bring gifts to the Temple, demonstrated by a punning exegesis of Mic. 7:2).

2. Pesher or the fulfilment interpretation of prophecv. This perhaps most typical form of exegesis attempts to identify biblical predictions with events relating to the history of the Community. In 1QpHab, the Chaldaeans of the time of Habakkuk become its final foe, the Kittim (i.e. the Romans); and the culprit criticized by the prophet become the Wicked Priest, the enemy of the Teacher of Righteousness, and his followers, etc.

3. Haggadic supplement may take the direct form of filling a gap in the biblical narrative; e.g., Abraham learns from a premonitory dream that his life will be in danger if it is known that Sarah is his wife: 1QapGen. 19:14–24. It may in addition employ symbolical exegesis for doctrinal ends; e.g., the Council of the Community is substituted for the Temple, alluded to as *Lebanon* (Hab. 2:17) in 1QpHab 12:3–4.

For a fuller exposition of Qumran exegesis, legal and doctrinal, see Vermes, art. 'Interpretation (History of) at Qumran and in the Targums', IDBS (1976), pp. 438–43. Cf. also F. F. Bruce, *Biblical Exegesis in the Qumran Texts* (1959); O. Betz, *Offenbarung und Schriftforschung in der Qumransekte* (1960); Vermes, *Scripture and Tradition* ([2]1973); 'The Qumran Interpretation of Scripture in its Historical Setting', *PBJS*, pp. 37–49; L. H. Schiffman, *The Halakhah at Qumran* (1975). See further Fitzmyer's bibliography, pp. 110–11.

19. For the theology of the Scrolls, see in addition to general works the Qumran bibliographies (Jongeling, pp. 78–93; Fitzmyer, pp. 112–13). Cf. in particular F. Nötscher, *Zur theologischen Terminologie der Qumran-Texte* (1956); *Gotteswege und Menschenwege in der Bibel und Qumran* (1958); H. W. Huppenbauer, *Der Mensch zwischen zwei Welten* (1959); M. Weise, *Kultzeiten und kultischer Bundeschluss in der "Ordensregel" vom Toten Meer* (1961); G. Jeremias, *Der Lehrer der Gerechtigkeit* (1963); A. Jaubert, *La notion de l'Alliance dans le judaïsme aux abords de l'ère chrétienne* (1963); J. Becker, *Das Heil Gottes* (1964); B. Gärtner, *The Temple and the Community in Qumran and the N.T.* (1965); H. Braun, *Qumran und das N.T.* II (1966); A.-M. Denis, *Les thèmes de la connaissance dans le Document de Damas* (1967); M. Black (ed.), *The Scrolls and Christianity* (1969); P. von Osten-Sacken, *Gott und Belial* (1969); G. Klinzing, *Die Umdeutung des Kultus in der Qumrangemeinde und im N.T.* (1971); E. H. Merrill, *Qumran and Predestination* (1975); E. P. Sanders, *Paul and Palestinian Judaism* (1977), pp. 239–321; Vermes, *DSS*, pp. 163–97.

pervading reality of divine grace, sentiments that transpire again and again in the Qumran hymns. Another of the specific themes in these poems is the recognition in salvation of a dual divine gift: the revealed knowledge of what is right and good, and the God-given power enabling the sectary to embrace truth and practise justice. Knowledge and grace were believed to lead the elect towards the way of holiness, to illuminate for them the secrets of heaven, and to allow them to contemplate even the most sacred of all visions, that of the *Merkabah*, the Chariot-Throne of God (4QŠirŠabb 2).[20]

The principal aim of the Qumran sectaries was to lead a life of continuous worship in which the Sons of Light on earth joined their voices to those of the celestial choirs of the angels. Cultic acts were to be performed in the correct manner, and at the divinely prescribed moments, in conformity with the unchangeable laws of time itself governing day and night, the weeks, the months, the four seasons and the years.[21]

The daily prayer was to be offered at the onset of light and of darkness, i.e. at dawn and dusk.[22] Time was measured according to a solar calendar following 'the laws of the great light of heaven' (1QH 12:5), the year being thus divided into 52 weeks and each season into 13 weeks, i.e. into three months of 30 days, with an additional day linking one season to another.[23] The result was absolute regularity: seasons and years always started on the same day of the week. Moreover, since according to the Bible the sun and the moon were created on the fourth day, every New Year in the Qumran reckoning fell on a Wednesday; so did also Passover. Similarly, the Day of Atonement fell always on a Friday. The festivals of the Dead Sea Community were in consequence celebrated on days which for other Jews were ordinary working days.[24]

20. Cf. Vermes, *DSSE*, pp. 34–41; *DSS*, pp. 169–75.

21. On times of worship, see A. Dupont-Sommer, 'Contribution à l'exégèse du Manuel de Discipline X, 1–8', VT 2 (1952), pp. 229–43; S. Talmon, 'The Order of Prayers of the Sect from the Judaean Desert,' Tarbiz 29 (1959), pp. 1–20 (Hebrew); M. Weise, *Kultzeiten und kultischer Bundesschluss* ... (1961); A. R. C. Leaney, *The Rule of Qumran and its Meaning* (1966), pp. 80–90; J. Licht, 'The Doctrine of "Times" according to the Sect of Qumran and other "Computers of Seasons" ', Eretz Israel 8 (1967), pp. 63–70 (Hebrew); Vermes, *DSSE*, p. 42; *DSS*, pp. 175–6, 192.

22. Cf. above, p. 573.

23. Cf. vol I, p. 592, n. 15; pp. 599–601. Cf. especially A. Jaubert, *La date de la Cène* (1957), pp. 13–30, 142–9; S. Talmon, 'The Calendar Reckoning of the Sect from the Judaean Desert', Scrip. Hier. 4 (1958), pp. 162–99; G. R. Driver, *The Judaean Scrolls* (1965), pp. 316–30; J. M. Baumgarten, '4Q Halakah[a] 5, the Law of Ḥadash and the Pentecontad Calendar', JSS 27 (1976), pp. 36–46; see also the bibliography in Fitzmyer, *op. cit.*, pp. 129–37.

24. Cf. 1QpHab. 11:6–8; S. Talmon, 'Yom hakkippurim in the Habakkuk Scroll', Biblica (1951), pp. 549–63; M. R. Lehmann, 'Yom Kippur in Qumran', RQ 3 (1961), pp. 117–24; Vermes, *DSS*, p. 177.

As the Community adhered to all the precepts of the Law of Moses, the sectaries observed all the biblical feasts; but they ascribed a very special importance to the Feast of Weeks or Pentecost. In traditional Judaism, this day marks the anniversary of the מתן תורה, the revelation of the Law on Sinai; for the sect, it became the yearly occasion for the renewal of the Covenant (1QS 1–3).[25]

The laws of cleanness and uncleanness played a significant part in the life of the Community, and the ordinances concerning purification by water are clearly set out in the Damascus Rule (CD 10:10–13), the War Rule (1QM 14:2–3), and the Community Rule (1QS 3:4–5; 5:13). The latter passages possibly allude to purification by means of a ritual bath in connection with entry into the Covenant.[26]

For the desert sectaries of Qumran, the Temple of Jerusalem was a place of abomination; its precincts were considered polluted, its priests wicked, and the liturgical calendar prevailing there, unlawful. The sect therefore offered spiritual worship until the time when the sacrificial cult, properly performed, could be restored in the seventh year of the eschatological war (1QM 2:5–6).[27]

The sacred meal of the sect (1QS 6:4–5) was no doubt a substitute for the sacrificial meals of the Temple. It would be celebrated again in the final age as an eschatological banquet attended by the priestly Messiah and the Messiah of Israel (1QSa 2:17–22).[28] The messianic doctrine of the Qumran sect has been discussed in § 29, pp. 550–4. Belief in the resurrection of the dead was not a central tenet of the Qumran faith. The occasional allusions to an awakening of those who 'lie in the dust'

25. Cf. Vermes, 'Essenes-Therapeutai-Qumran' Durham Univ. Journal 52 (1960), pp. 112–13; Black, *The Scrolls and Christian Origins* (1962), p. 92; B. Noack, 'The Day of Pentecost in Jubilees, Qumran and Acts', ASTI 1 (1962), pp. 73–95; M. Delcor, 'Das Bundesfest in Qumran und das Pfingstfest', Bibel und Leben 4 (1963), pp. 188–204; art. 'Pentecôte', DB Suppl. VII (1964), cols. 858–79; A. R. C. Leaney, *op. cit.* [in n. 21 above], pp. 95–107; Vermes, *DSS*, pp. 177–8, 192.

26. For the Essene ablutions, cf. p. 569. For the Qumran and Christian purification by water, cf. O. Betz, 'Die Proselytentaufe der Qumransekte und die Taufe im Neuen Testament', RQ 1 (1959), pp. 213–34; E. F. Sutcliffe, 'Baptism and Baptismal Rites at Qumran', Heythrop Journ. 1 (1960), pp. 69–101; J. Gnilka, 'Die essenische Tauchbäder und die Johannestaufe', RQ 3 (1961), pp. 185–207; A. Dupont-Sommer, 'Culpabilité et rites de purification dans la secte juive de Qoumrân', Semitica 15 (1965), pp. 61–70; H. Braun, *Qumran und das Neue Testament* II (1966), pp. 1–29; J. A. Fitzmyer, *Essays on the Semitic Background of The New Testament* (1971), pp. 469–73.

27. Cf. Vermes, *DSSE*, pp. 45–7; *PBJS*, pp. 83–5; *DSS*, pp. 180–1. Cf. especially, B. Gärtner, *The Temple and the Community in Qumran and the N.T.* (1965); G. Klinzing, *Die Umdeutung des Kultus in der Qumrangemeinde und im N.T.* (1971). Note, however, that CD 11:19–20 legislates on sacrifices and offerings in the Temple.

28. Cf. above, p. 579, n. 16.

or who are 'gnawed by worms' (1QH 6:34–5; 11:10–14) may be simply metaphorical. On the other hand, numerous references are made to eternal life granted to the Sons of Light in the company of the Sons of Heaven (e.g. 1QS 11:5–9; 1QH 11:10–14, etc.).[29]

3. *The Qumran Community and the Essenes*: Although a minority of scholars, whilst acknowledging a certain degree of relationship between the two movements, refuse to admit that they are the same,[30] the wide consensus of opinion favours an identification of the people of Qumran with the Essene sect.[31]

The main arguments in support of the Essene identity are:

1. Short of discovering another more appropriate site, the sectarian establishment of Khirbet Qumran would appear to be the principal Essene settlement[32] located by Pliny between Jericho and Engedi.[33]
2. Chronologically, the Essenes flourished, according to Josephus, between the rule of Jonathan and the first Jewish war.[34] The

29. Cf. Vermes, *Discovery*, pp. 118–19; R. B. Laurin, 'The Question of Immortality in the Qumran Hodayot', JSSt 3 (1958), pp. 344–55; K. Schubert, 'Das Problem der Auferstehungshoffnung in der Qumrantexten und in der frührabbinischen Literatur', WZKM 56 (1960), pp. 154–67; J. van der Ploeg, 'The Belief in Immortality in the Writings of Qumran', Bibliot. Orient. 18 (1961), pp. 118–24; Black, *The Scrolls and Christian Origins* (1961), pp. 136–42; G. W. E. Nickelsburg, *Resurrection, Immortality, and Eternal Life in Intertestamental Judaism* (1972), pp. 144–67; 'Future Life', IDBS, p. 350; Vermes, *DSS*, pp. 186–8, 196–7.

30. Cf. below, pp. 550–4.

31. Among the first to suggest a connection with Essenism was E. L. Sukenik, *Megillot genuzot* I (1948), p. 16, and A. Dupont-Sommer, *Aperçus préliminaires sur les manuscrits de la Mer Morte* (1950), pp. 105–17. R. de Vaux identified Khirbet Qumran with the Essene settlement of Pliny ('Fouille au Khirbet Qumran', RB 60 (1953), p. 105). The theory was further developed by A. Dupont-Sommer, *Essene Writings from Qumran* (1961). Cf. also J.-P. Audet, 'Qumran et la notice de Pline sur les Esséniens', RB 68 (1961), pp. 346–87; Chr. Burchard, 'Pline et les Esséniens. A propos d'un article récent', RB 69 (1962), pp. 533–69 (against Audet); 'Solin et les Esséniens. Remarques à propos d'une source negligée', RB 74 (1967), pp. 392–407; W. F. Albright and C. S. Mann, 'Qumran and the Essenes: Geography, Chronology and Identification of the Sect', in *The Scrolls and Christianity*, ed. M. Black (1969), pp. 11–25; M. Petit, *Quod omnis probus, Les oeuvres de Philon d'Alexandrie* 28 (1974), pp. 114–24; Vermes, *DSS*, pp. 125–30, 133–6. For a connexion with the Egyptian Therapeutai, see Vermes, 'Essenes-Therapeutai-Qumran', Durham University Journal (1960), pp. 97–115; Black, *The Scrolls and Christian Origins* (1962), pp. 45–7; V. Nikiprowetzky, 'Les suppliants chez Philon d'Alexandrie', REJ 122 (1963), pp. 67–78; M. Delcor, 'Repas culturels esséniens et thérapeutes', RQ 6 (1969), pp. 401–25. Cf. below, pp. 591–7.

32. Cf. R. de Vaux, *Archaeology and the Dead Sea Scrolls* (1973), pp. 133–8.

33. Cf. p. 563, n. 6 above.

34. *Ant.* xiii 5, 9 (171); *B.J.* ii 8, 10 (152); ii 20, 4 (567).

occupation of the Qumran site is dated by the archaeologists to approximately the same period.[35]

3. The organization of the common life described in the two sets of sources, as well as their rites, doctrines and customs, show so many and such striking similarities, that the hypothesis equating Qumran sectaries with Essenes appears to be endowed with the highest degree of probability.[36]

A number of differences admittedly exist, e.g. essential features of Essenism, common ownership of property and celibacy, do not seem to characterize every group depicted in the Scrolls, or alternatively, every stage of the sect's existence. Nevertheless, if the argument advanced in the previous section proves admissible, viz. that the town members of the Covenant and those of the monastic order followed different economic disciplines, the discrepancy will be less significant.[37] Other variations may be explained by the secrecy surrounding the sect's doctrines, a complete knowledge of which presupposed full initiation into the order. Pliny, as a Roman, by definition did not qualify for this, neither does Philo claim to have been in actual contact with the Essenes. As for Josephus, the best informed of the three, he may have had practical experience of Essene life, but he was not, and could not have been, a properly trained sectary.[38] Moreover, neither Pliny, Philo, nor Josephus were addressing themselves to an Essene audience; consequently, and to varying degrees, they had to tailor their accounts to suit the needs of their readers. The logic of Dupont-Sommer's conclusion is still strongly recommended: 'The accounts written by (Philo and Josephus) are essentially summary; they could not enter into all the complexities of situations and regulations, and necessarily tended to simplify, and also sometimes to colour, the facts according to their own taste. There may be vagueness and even some inaccuracy; are there not even a few divergences between Philo and Josephus themselves? It is quite inevitable that external evidence should fail to coincide absolutely rigorously with the documents themselves. . . . As far as the Qumran documents are concerned, it is necessary to add one further point. These writings are not all of the same age and can betray, from one document to the next, a certain evolution in institutions and beliefs. . . . Finally, it should be borne in mind that the Qumran sect,

35. Cf. R. de Vaux, *op. cit.*, pp. 5 f.

36. Cf. Dupont-Sommer, *The Essene Writings*, pp. 39–67; Vermes, *DSS*, pp. 127–30.

37. Cf. above, pp. 577–8.

38. Cf. *Vita* 2 (9–12). Josephus asserts that between the ages of sixteen and nineteen, he received training in the systems of the Pharisees, Sadducees and Essenes. He also spent three years with the hermit Bannus. At the end of all this he chose to become a Pharisee.

i.e. the Essene sect, was . . . esoteric. Consequently, those who spoke of it from the outside *cannot have known all*. Also they *may not have wished to say all*.'[39]

A further consideration may be added to support the Essenes = Qumran desert brotherhood theory. None of the other hypotheses appears to be as strong as the Essene case. Thus whilst the latter cannot be held as fully proven, it is to be preferred to theories linking Qumran with the Pharisees,[40] Sadducees,[41] Zealots,[42] Judaeo-Christians,[43] not to mention the medieval Karaites.[44]

III. The Origin and History of the Essenes

The classical sources yield no information relating to the rise of the Essene movement,[45] and provide only incidental references to its later history.

39. Cf. Dupont-Sommer, *The Essene Writings*, pp. 66–7. Cf. Vermes, *DSS*, pp. 128–30.

40. C. Rabin, *Qumran Studies* (1957), Ch. IV, The Sect and its Opponents, pp. 53–70; 'a diehard Pharisaic group' (p. 69). For criticism, see Dupont Sommer, *op. cit.*, pp. 403–8; Vermes, *DSS*, pp. 121–2.

41. R. North, 'The Qumran "Sadducees" ', CBQ 17 (1955), pp. 164–88. For criticism, see Vermes, *DSS*, pp. 118–19.

42. C. Roth, *The Historical Background of the Dead Sea Scrolls* (1958); 'Why the Qumran Sect cannot have been Essenes', RQ 1 (1959), pp. 417–22; 'Were the Qumran Sectaries Essenes?', JThSt 10 (1959), pp. 87–93, and especially G. R. Driver, *The Judaean Scrolls* (1965). For criticism, see Dupont-Sommer, *op. cit.*, pp. 397–403; R. de Vaux, 'Essenes or Zealots', NTSt 13 (1966), pp. 89–104; Vermes, *DSS*, pp. 124–5.

43. J. L. Teicher, 'The Dead Sea Scrolls—Documents of the Jewish-Christian Sect of the Ebionites', JJS 2 (1951), pp. 67–99. Cf. also *ibid.* 2 (1951), pp. 115–43; 3 (1952), pp. 53–5, 111–18, 128–32, 139–50; 4 (1953), pp. 1–13, 49–58, 93–103, 139–53; 5 (1954), pp. 47–59, 93–9, 139–47; VT 5 (1955), pp. 189–98; Y. Baer, '*Serekh ha-Yaḥad*—The Manual of Discipline. A Jewish-Christian Document from the Beginning of the Second Century C.E.', Zion 29 (1964), pp. 1–60 (Hebrew). For criticism, see Dupont-Sommer, *op. cit.*, pp. 395–7; Vermes, *DSS*, pp. 117, 131, 220–1. For the theory of New Testament fragments in Cave 7, see J. O'Callaghan, '¿Papiros neotestamentarios en la cueva 7 de Qumrân?', Biblica 53 (1972), pp. 91–100; *Los papiros griegos de la cueva 7 de Qumrân* (1974). Against O'Callaghan, cf. P. Benoit, RB 79 (1972), pp. 321–4; 80 (1973), pp. 5–12; M. Baillet, Biblica 53 (1972), pp. 508–16; 54 (1973), pp. 340–50; C. H. Roberts, JThSt 23 (1972), pp. 446–7. For a full bibliography, see J. A. Fitzmyer, *The Dead Sea Scrolls* . . ., pp. 119–23.

44. Cf. S. Zeitlin, *The Zadokite Fragments* (1952). For criticism see Dupont-Sommer, *op. cit.*, pp. 395–7; N. Wieder, *The Judean Scrolls and Karaism* (1956), p. 253: 'Did the Qumran documents emanate from Karaite circles? . . . The answer must be an emphatic 'No' ".

45. If Pliny were to be believed, Essenism would be seen as an eternal, 'meta-historical' phenomenon: 'Ita per saeculorum milia, incredibile dictu, gens aeterna est in qua nemo nascitur' (*NH* v 15/73).

In the light of the conclusion reached at the end of the previous section identifying the Essenes with the Qumran Community,[46] this very patchy picture can be filled in a little. Since the Qumran writings are notoriously alien to historiography proper—most of the relevant data derive from Bible interpretation of the *pesher* type[47]—it is thought preferable to limit the present reconstruction of Qumran/Essene history to the main outline without integrating into the picture the more speculative secondary traits elaborated by some scholars.[48]

Accepting the interpretation of archaeological discoveries which date the beginning of the Essene settlement at Qumran to between cca. 140–130 B.C.,[49] the events which gave rise to the sect belong to the earlier decades of the second century B.C.[50]

The original nucleus of the Essenes was born during the epoch of the Hellenistic crisis culminating in the persecution launched by Antiochus Epiphanes (CD 1:5).[51] It was the 'plant root' which God 'caused to spring . . . to inherit his land' (CD 1:7), i.e. the congregation of the

46. Cf. pp. 583 f. above.

47. Cf. above, p. 580.

48. One should in particular, be very careful in employing poetic allusions extracted from certain Hodayoth on the assumption that not only is the leader to whom they refer the Teacher of Righteousness but that the latter is the author of the poems in question. For the literary-historical theory, cf. G. Jeremias, *Der Lehrer der Gerechtigkeit* (1963). For the amalgamation of his data into a historical reconstruction, see H. Stegemann, *Die Entstehung der Qumrangemeinde* (Diss. Bonn 1965, privately published in 1971), and J. Murphy-O'Connor, 'The Essenes and Their History', RB 81 (1974), pp. 215–44. Cf. Vermes, *DSS*, pp. 145–6.

49. R. de Vaux, *Archaeology and the Dead Sea Scrolls* (1973), pp. 5, 18, etc.

50. The synthesis that is outlined here has been propounded with minor variations by the following: Vermes, *Discovery* (1956), pp. 66–97; *DSSE*, pp. 61–8; *DSS*, pp. 142–62; F. M. Cross, *The Ancient Library of Qumran* (1958, ²1961), pp. 135–53; 'The Early History of the Qumran Community', *New Directions in Biblical Archaeology*, ed. D. N. Freedman and J. C. Greenfield (1971), pp. 70–89; J. T. Milik, *Ten Years of Discovery* (1959), pp. 84–7; G. Jeremias, *Der Lehrer der Gerechtigkeit* (1963); R. de Vaux, *Archaeology* (1973), pp. 116–17; H. Stegemann, *Die Enstehung der Qumrangemeinde* (1971), pp. 200 ff.; M. Hengel, *Judaism and Hellenism* I (1974), pp. 224–7; J. Murphy-O'Connor, *art. cit.* [in n. 48], RB 81 (1974), pp. 215–44; 'Demetrius I and the Teacher of Righteousness', *ibid.* 83 (1976), pp. 400–20; H. Burgmann, 'The Wicked Woman: Der Makkabäer Simon', RQ 8 (1974), pp. 323–59; 'Gerichtsherr und Generalankläger: Jonathan und Simon', RQ 9 (1977), pp. 3–72. For alternative theories, cf. H. H. Rowley, 'The History of the Qumran Sect', BJRL 49 (1967), pp. 203–32 [pre-Maccabaean age]; J. Carmignac, *Les textes de Qumrân* II (1963), pp. 48–55 [age of Alexander Jannaeus]; A . Dupont-Sommer, *The Essene Writings* (1961), pp. 351–7 [age of Hyrcanus II]; C. Roth, *The Historical Background of the Dead Sea Scrolls* (1958) and G. R. Driver, *The Judaean Scrolls* (1965) [age of the first Jewish war].

51. Murphy-O'Connor, *art. cit.*, pp. 221–3, argues for a Babylonian pre-history of the sect before its return to Palestine. This is based on the questionable exegesis that Damascus is a symbol for Babylon. On the Damascus symbolism, see Vermes, *Scripture and Tradition* (²1973), pp. 43–9.

Hasidim.[52] Twenty years later the Teacher of Righteousness appeared (CD 1:10–11), the founder-organizer of the Qumran/Essene community, a priest (4QpPs 37 ii 19, iii 15) of no doubt high Zadokite lineage.[53] A conflict arose between him and Jonathan, who in 153/2 B.C. accepted the pontifical office and became the 'Wicked Priest'. It is noteworthy that the first mention of the Essenes by Josephus is placed during Jonathan's rule.[54] The Teacher and his followers were forced to withdraw to a place of exile, possibly Qumran, where their opponent visited them on their day of Atonement (1QpHab 11:4–8). Jonathan's downfall and execution by Tryphon in 143/2 B.C. was seen by the Essenes as a divine punishment (1QpHab 9:2, 9–12). In 4QTestimonia, he is cursed as one of two brothers, 'instruments of violence', the other being Simon Maccabaeus.[55]

Chronologically, the next reference to the Essenes comes from Josephus who mentions an Essene prophet, by the name of Judas, under the reign of Aristobulus I.[56] Reverting to the Qumran evidence, the later Hasmonaeans, in particular Alexander Jannaeus, 'the furious young lion' (4QpNah 1:5; cf. 4QpHos 2:2–3), continued to be held in intense hatred by the Essenes, who rejoiced in the defeat by Pompey of the Jewish rulers, 'the last priests of Jerusalem' (1QpHab 9:4–7).

Essene history covering the second half of the first century B.C. and the first half of the first century A.D. is attested only by the references in Josephus, and by the archaeological evidence from the Qumran site. According to Josephus the sect appears to have flourished under Herod, who dispensed them from the obligatory oath of allegiance,[57] no doubt on account of the prophecy of the Essene Menahem foretelling that Herod would become king of the Jews.[58] Whether the occupation of the Qumran site was discontinued for a time under Herod after the earthquake in 31 B.C. remains uncertain despite R. de Vaux's claim,[59] especially because of the discovery of at least ten Herodian coins among the ruins.[60]

There are two further Josephus testimonies regarding the period

52. Cf. vol. I, pp. 145, 157, etc.

53. Murphy-O'Connor conjecturally identifies him with the (anonymous and hypothetical) acting High Priest who functioned between Alcimus and Jonathan Maccabaeus. Cf. *art. cit.*, RB 81 (1974), pp. 229–30.

54. *Ant.* xiii 5, 9 (171).

55. F. M. Cross prefers to see Simon as the 'Wicked Priest'. Cf. *op. cit.* [in n. 15 above]. See also G. W. E. Nickelsburg, 'Simon—A Priest with a Reputation for Faithfulness', BASOR 223 (1976), pp. 67–8.

56. *Ant.* xiii 11, 2 (311–13).

57. *Ant.* xv 10, 4 (371–2).

58. *Ant.* xv 10, 5 (373–8).

59. Cf. *Archaeology*, pp. 20–4.

60. Cf. Vermes, *DSS*, pp. 33–4.

prior to the outbreak of the first revolution. Firstly, at the turn of the eras, Simon the Essene is reported to have interpreted a dream of the ethnarch Archelaus.[61] Secondly, in his Autobiography, Josephus reveals that in his youth, in mid-first century A.D., he experimented with the three religious schools of the Jews, those of the Sadducees, the Pharisees and the Essenes.[62]

Literary evidence from the War Rule indicates that the Essene attitude towards Rome, neutral at the time of Pompey, became hostile later and that the Kittim-Romans were seen as the final foe whose defeat by the Sons of Light would inaugurate the kingdom of God.

The mention by Josephus of John the Essene among the generals of the first anti-Roman war is the only direct allusion to active participation by an individual member of the sect in the rebellion.[63] Whether the group as a whole resisted the legionaries when the Qumran establishment was conquered by them, probably in A.D. 68,[64] is open to question: the Essenes may have evacuated the buildings, later seized by the Zealots, before the arrival of the Romans. Likewise the presence of a manuscript of the Angelic Liturgy (4QŠirŠabb) in the Zealot stronghold of Masada,[65] may be due either to a Zealot pillage of Qumran or to the embracement by an Essene group of the cause of the rebellion. Finally, if Josephus's notice of Essene bravery under Roman torture[66] is to be connected with the fall of Qumran, the disappearance of the sect from the scene of history can be attributed to the fatal blow that its central establishment suffered in the summer of A.D. 68.[67]

The combined evidence of the classical sources and the Dead Sea discoveries, both literary and archaeological, relative to Essenism provides a more comprehensive picture and deeper understanding of this curious historical and religious phenomenon than Josephus, Philo and Pliny were able to do. The priestly characteristics of the movement discernible in the Greek accounts become easily comprehensible when the Zadokite origin and leadership of the Community is borne in mind. Non-participation of the Qumran Essenes in the sacrificial worship of the Temple also takes on a new meaning when it is realized that priestly rivalry was involved, and that the replacement of the

61. *Ant.* xvii 13, 3 (345–8).
62. *Vita*, 2 (10–11).
63. *B.J.* ii 20, 4 (567). This John commanded the province of Thamna together with Lydda, Joppa and Emmaus.
64. Cf. de Vaux, *op. cit.*, pp. 36–41. For the numismatic evidence see p. 37.
65. Cf. Y. Yadin, *Masada* (1966), pp. 173–4.
66. *B.J.* ii 8, 10 (152–3). Cf. Vermes, *DSS*, pp. 155–6; see, however, Dupont-Sommer, *Essene Writings*, p. 33, n. 2.
67. Cf. Vermes, *Discovery*, p. 101; *DSS*, p. 156.

Jerusalem cultus by the Community ritual was intended to be temporary, until the reconquest of the Sanctuary by the sect during the eschatological war (1QM 2:1–6). In the circumstances, the issue of foreign influences which so greatly exercised pre-Qumran scholarship,[68] becomes quite secondary. Buddhist and Indian borrowings must now be considered most unlikely.[69] Persian impact on Essene dualism and angelology is probable but derives no doubt from Iranian influence on Judaism as such, rather than directly on the sect itself.[70] As for the adoption of Pythagoraean ideas, whereas knowledge of them among Hellenized Jews was probable, direct Essene dependence on Pythagoraean teachings and customs is difficult to conceive and impossible to prove.[71]

'If we consider the Essene community against its environment, the essential thing is not the supposed "Pythagoraean" influences, but the fact that the Hellenistic observers like Josephus—or Nicolaus of Damascus—could present them as Jewish "Pythagoraeans". . . . The ancient reporters like Philo, Pliny the Elder, Solinus, Porphyry and above all Dio Chrysostom presented the Essenes as a *community of*

68. Cf. S. Wagner, *Die Essener in der wissenschaftlichen Diskussion* (1960), pp. 133–76, 224–8.

69. Cf. Isidore Lévy, *Recherches esséniennes et pythagoriciennes* (1965), pp. 31–5; H. Kruse, 'Buddhist Influence on Essenism', *Proc. IXth Internat. Congr. for the Hist. of Rel.* (1960), pp. 123–8.

70. Cf. K. G. Kuhn, 'Die Sektenschrift und die iranische Religion', ZThK 49 (1952), pp. 296–316; A. Dupont-Sommer, *Nouveaux aperçus sur les manuscrits de la Mer Morte* (1953), pp. 157–72; G. Widengren, 'Quelques rapports entre juifs et iraniens à l'époque des parthes', VT Suppl. 4 (1957), pp. 197 ff.; H. W. Huppenbauer, *Der Mensch zwischen zwei Welten* (1959); D. Winston, 'The Iranian Component in the Bible, Apocrypha and Qumran: a Review of the Evidence', Hist. of Religions 5 (1966), pp. 183–216. It is interesting to note that in Philo's list of examples of virtue the Persian *Magi* come first, followed by the Indian *Gymnosophists* and the Jewish Essenes: *Quod omnis probus* 11 (74)–12 (75). Cf. on the Magi, J. Bidez-F. Cumont, *Les mages hellénisés* I–II (1938); on the Gymnosophists, M. Petit, *Les oeuvres de Philon d'Alexandrie* 28 (1974), pp. 93–9.

71. Josephus was the first to advance the view that the Essenes were Jewish Pythagoraeans: *οἱ παρ' ἡμῖν Ἐσσαῖοι γένος τοῦτ' ἔστιν διαίτῃ χρώμενον τῇ παρ' Ἕλλησιν ὑπὸ Πυθαγόρου καταδεδειγμένῃ*, *Ant.* xiii 10, 4 (371). For the thesis adopted here, see Hengel, *Judaism and Hellenism* I (1974), pp. 243–7. For earlier discussion, see E. Zeller, *Philosophie der Griechen* III, 2 ([4]1903), pp. 307–77; I. Lévy, *La légende de Pythagore de Grèce en Palestine* (1927), pp. 264–93, 573–84; *Recherches esséniennes et pythagoriciennes* (1965), pp. 57–63; A. Dupont-Sommer, *Nouveaux Aperçus*, pp. 155–6; P. Grelot, 'L'eschatologie des esséniens et le livre d'Hénoch', RQ 1 (1958), p. 127; M. Hadas, *Hellenistic Culture: Fusion and Diffusion* (1959), pp. 194–5; T. F. Glasson, *Greek Influence in Jewish Eschatology* (1961), pp. 49–50.

For the debate on Orphic tendencies, see J. A. Sanders, 'Ps. 151 in 11QPss', ZAW 75 (1963), pp. 73–86; I. Rabinowitz, 'The Alleged Orphism of 11QPss 28.3–12', ZAW 76 (1964), pp. 193–200; A. Dupont-Sommer, 'Le Psaume CLI dans 11QPsa et le problème de son origine essénienne', Semitica 14 (1964), pp. 25–62.

"*philosophers*", who led an ascetic life in the wilderness by the Dead Sea in the service of the knowledge of God, wisdom and the love of man.'[72]

But the aims and aspirations of the Essenes are best expressed in their own words:

'[The Master shall teach the sai]nts to live [according to] the Book of the Community Rule, that they may seek God with a whole heart and soul, and do what is good and right before Him as He commanded by the hand of Moses and all his servants the Prophets. . . .[73]

'They shall separate from the congregation of the men of falsehood and shall unite, with respect to the Law and possessions, under the authority of the sons of Zadok the Priests who keep the Covenant, and the multitude of the men of the Community who hold fast to the Covenant. Every decision concerning doctrine, property and justice shall be determined by them.

'They shall practice truth and humility in common, and justice and uprightness and charity and modesty in all their ways. No man shall walk in the stubbornness of his heart so that he strays after his heart and eyes and evil inclination, but he shall circumcise in the Community the foreskin of evil inclination, and of stiffness of neck that he may lay a foundation of truth for Israel, for the Community of the everlasting Covenant. They shall atone for all those in Aaron who have freely pledged themselves to holiness, and for those in Israel who have freely pledged themselves to the House of Truth, and for those who join them to live in community.'[74]

72. M. Hengel, *Judaism and Hellenism* I, p. 247.
73. 1QS 1:1–2.
74. 1QS 5:1–6.

Appendix A: The Therapeutae

I. Philo's Account

Whilst reserving the discussion of literary issues for § 34 in volume III, it seems appropriate to add to this chapter on Essenism a description of the Therapeutae whose life and customs are treated in Philo's *De vita contemplativa*.[1]

The Therapeutae[2] are said to have been widely dispersed, but especially numerous all over Egypt, particularly around Alexandria on the shores of the Mareotic Lake, 3 (21–2). They fled the cities and chose solitude, 2 (19–20). Their Mareotic settlement was surrounded by farms and villages, 3 (23). It consisted of a communal building and a group of simple private dwellings so spaced as to cater for privacy, but close enough to promote fellowship and provide protection against bandits, 3 (24). In each house was a sacred room known as a sanctuary (*σεμνόν*) or *μοναστήριον* (inner chamber?), to which only 'laws, prophetic oracles and psalms were taken, 3 (25).

The communal building or common sanctuary (*τὸ κοινὸν μοναστήριον*) served as place of worship and a refectory, 3 (32); 4 (36). Men and women occupied separate enclosures where they could hear, but not see, each other, 3 (32–3). They sat in rows, 8 (67); 10 (75), on wooden plank-beds 9 (69), on which they reclined during the banquets, 10 (81).

Before joining the order, candidates relinquished their property to their families or friends, 2 (13). Thereafter they devoted themselves wholly to contemplation without practising any secular craft, 3 (30).

Precedence among the Therapeutae was based on the number of years spent within the group, 3 (30); 8 (67). The Sabbath service was conducted by the 'senior member' (*ὁ πρεσβύτατος*) who was the chief doctrinal expert, 3 (31). The festal gatherings were directed by a president (*πρόεδρος*), 10 (79). Although both sexes were represented, 1 (2), male and female Therapeutae lived in celibacy—most of the women were elderly virgins (*γηραιαὶ παρθένοι*), 9 (68).

No specific initiation is mentioned. In their 'sanctuaries' the members

1. For the Philonic authenticity of the work, see especially F. C. Conybeare, *Philo about the Contemplative Life* (1895); P. Wendland, 'Die Therapeuten und die philonische Schrift vom beschaulichen Leben', Jahrbücher für Class. Philol. Suppl. 22 (1896), pp. 695–772; I. Heinemann, art. 'Therapeutai', RE V^A (1934), cols. 2321–46; P. Geoltrain, 'Le Traité de la Vie contemplative de Philon d'Alexandrie', Semitica 10 (1960), pp. 5–67; F. Daumas-P. Miquel, *De vita contemplativa—Les oeuvres de Philon d'Alexandrie* 29 (1963), pp. 11–25.

2. On the name, see above p. 559, n. 9.

taught themselves the mysteries of the holy life, 3 (25). Some of them adopted the contemplative existence from their early youth, 8 (67–8). They possessed one garment for summer use and one for winter, 4 (38). At their feasts they wore a white robe, 8 (66). In the 'common sanctuary' they sat silently and behaved decorously, 3 (30–1); 10 (75, 77).

They ate simple food and no more than was necessary to sustain them, 4 (37); they abstained from meat and wine, 9 (73–4). They took no food or drink before sunset, 4 (34). Some of them fasted for three, and even six days, 4 (34–5).

Their day began with prayer at dawn, 3 (27); 11 (89), and was spent in spiritual exercises, 3 (28). At sunset they prayed again, 3 (27) and took their single daily meal, 4 (34), probably in their private dwellings, 3 (30). On Sabbaths and feast-days they assembled in the 'common sanctuary', 3 (30, 32); 8 (66), attended religious service and ate together, 4 (36–7); 11 (73). Before certain festivals they kept vigil until sunrise, 11 (83, 89).

The Therapeutae were dedicated to the worship of God through self-healing and the contemplation of truth, 1 (2). At dawn they turned towards the rising sun asking God to fill their minds with divine light, 3 (27); 11 (89). During the day they studied the Bible, 3 (25), as is required of 'disciples of Moses' (*οἱ Μωυσέως γνώριμοι*), 7 (63), and looked for its hidden meanings by way of allegorical exegesis, a method learnt from the writings of the ancients, the founders of their philosophy, 3 (28–9). They also composed hymns and psalms to God in a variety of metres, 3 (29). They continued to contemplate even in their dreams and to 'give utterance to the glorious verities of their holy philosophy', 3 (26). During the formal Sabbath worship, the 'senior member' delivered a sermon, 3 (30–2).

On the vigil of the 'chief feast', 8 (65), i.e. the Feast of Weeks or Pentecost,[3] the seniors reclined in their places, with their young attendants beside them, 10 (75). The women also took up their positions on the other side of the enclosure. The president expounded a scriptural passage allegorically, 10 (75, 78), then rose and sang a hymn composed by himself, or by some other poet of the past, followed by each participant in turn, 10 (80). Supper came next. As they had no slaves, 9 (70–1), the attendants brought in the tables laid with the most holy food (*τὸν παναγέστατον σιτίον*) consisting of leavened bread seasoned with salt and hyssop, 10 (81). The Therapeutae were not priests and were of lower status, 10 (82); yet they emulated and outdid them in their continuous abstinence from wine, 9 (74), whereas the priests were forbidden to drink only when it was their turn to offer sacrifice (Lev.

3. Cf. above, p. 582, n. 25.

10:9; Ezek. 44:21). The feast continued until dawn with hymns sung by men and women separately and finally in a mixed choir, like Israel led by the prophet Moses and the prophetess Miriam by the Red Sea, 11 (83–7). At sunrise they stood facing the east, and prayed with outstretched hands before returning each to his own sanctuary and study of philosophy, 11 (89).

Citizens of heaven and of the world, 11 (90), the Therapeutae healed passions and blindness, 1 (2); 2 (10–11), raised self-mastery to the foundation of virtue, combined a love of solitude, 3 (30), with community life, 3 (24), and devoted their whole existence to contemplation, 'the best and most divine part of philosophy', 8 (67).

II. Therapeutae—Essenes—Qumran

(a) *Therapeutae and Essenes*

There are striking similarities as well as dissimilarities between *De vita contemplativa* and the notices on the Essenes in Philo and Josephus. The three sources agree that both groups ate in community (though among the Therapeutae, perhaps only on Sabbaths and feast days), rejected slavery, practiced moderation in eating, abstained from marriage, chose self-mastery and the spirit of fraternity as chief virtues, and showed utmost reverence for the Law of Moses. Moreover, if the etymology Essenes=אסיא=θεραπευταί is accepted,[4] the two communities bore the same name and shared the aims and ideals expressed in it.

Further parallels exist between Philo's respective portrayals: Therapeutae and Essenes fled from the cities, detested commerce, assembled in a community centre for worship and meals, celebrated the Sabbath, and interpreted the Bible allegorically. Each member possessed a summer and a winter garment and the junior sectaries displayed filial devotion towards their elders.

Other peculiarities of Philo's Therapeutae are attributed to the Essenes by Josephus. In both groups, young people were present, and a white robe was worn by those who entered the sacred refectory to partake in the solemn meal consisting of bread and one other course. Both communities recited their morning prayers facing the rising sun, possessed sacred writings other than the Bible, and practised bodily and spiritual healing. Furthermore, silence was characteristic of both; some members were endowed with prophetic gifts and were obliged to pass on the truth discovered. Both Therapeutae and Essenes defended themselves against robbers.

4. Cf. above, pp. 559–60.

On the other hand, several characteristics of the Therapeutae are without parallel in the accounts on the Essenes, such as their abstention from meat and wine, their chief feast and the vigil connected with it. Other features, again, appear to be in conflict. The Essenes were Palestinians, the Therapeutae lived mainly in Egypt; the latter's common life was on a smaller scale than that of the Essenes, and their daily fast until sunset contradicts the Essene rule of two daily meals. No mention is to be found in the Essene notices of women in the same celibate establishment. Finally, in contrast to the clearly defined economic regime of the Essenes, there is no hint of any common ownership of property among the Therapeutae, or for that matter of any source of subsistence. Moreover, according to Philo the Essenes embraced the active life, whereas the Therapeutae were contemplatives.

It should be noted that the geographical factor does not constitute an insuperable obstacle to an identification of the two groups, especially if it is remembered that Philo himself locates Therapeutae in 'many places of the world', 3 (21): *πολλαχοῦ τῆς οἰκουμένης*. The presence of male and female but unmarried Therapeutae does not strictly militate against the statement that the Essenes, apart from one of their branches, renounced marriage. The day-long fasting and the vegetarianism of the Therapeutae may be attributed to the smaller needs of sedentary contemplatives compared with those of the active Essenes. As for the differing economic regimes, the conflict must be due in part to Philo's inaccurate picture. If the Therapeutae abandoned all their possessions, possessed no money, owned no slaves, and did nothing to earn a living, how did they subsist? Were they supported by those who occupied the farms and villages around the Mareotic Lake? Is this a veiled allusion to a community of active ascetics, like the Essenes according to 1 (1), who took it on themselves to care for those who had chosen 'the better part'?

(b) *Therapeutae and Qumran*

The rules and customs reflected in the Qumran Scrolls show further resemblances to the Therapeutae which do not appear in the Essene notices of Philo and Josephus. To begin with, they testify to a form of contemplative life: 'the Interpreter of the Law' was to devote all his time to Torah study (1QS 6:6–7; 8:11–2). The 'common sanctuary' of the Therapeutae served as a place of worship and a refectory, and similarly at Qumran the largest room (loc. 77), measuring 22 m by 4.50 m, was a place of assembly and a dining-hall, the latter use being evident from the discovery there of fragments belonging to more than a thousand pots, plates, dishes, jugs, bowls, beakers, etc.[5]

5. R. de Vaux, *Archaeology and the Dead Sea Scrolls* (1973), pp. 11–2, 25–7, 110–1.

The service described by Philo in connection with the chief feast of the Therapeutae (Bible interpretation, hymns, meal, vigil) is not unlike the programme observed by the members of the Qumran brotherhood who, after their community supper, used one-third of every night 'to read the Book, study law and to pray together' (1QS 6:7–8).[6] Moreover, the Qumran Hodayoth, which are chiefly individual prayers, some of them expressing the concerns of a leader, would find a satisfactory *Sitz im Leben* in the context of a ceremony parallel to that of the Therapeutae during which the president and each member recited a hymn in succession.[7] Likewise, 1QSa 2:17–21 describes a meal at which, instead of a single grace, each participant in hierarchical order pronounced a blessing. Therapeutae etiquette demanded that they should gesticulate only with their right hand, 10 (77); the use of the left hand was also forbidden at Qumran (1QS 7:15).

However, perhaps the most significant parallel between Therapeutae and Qumran was their common adoption of the Pentecontad calendar, 8 (65),[8] and the fact that Pentecost was their 'chief feast'.[9] For, according to an unpublished document from Cave 4, the Qumran Essenes, like the Therapeutae, divided the year into seven fifty-day periods, each ending with an agricultural festival.[10] At Qumran, as in the neighbourhood of Alexandria, the greatest of these festivals was the Feast of Weeks or Renewal of the Covenant.[11]

By contrast, the Qumran sectaries differed from the Therapeutae insofar as they (possibly) drank wine at their meals (1QS 6:5; 1QSa 2:17–20), and ate meat, a fact proved by the deposits of animal bones, apparently ritually buried, discovered among the Qumran ruins.[12]

III. The Relationship between Therapeutae and Essenes

The doubts expressed in the nineteenth century about the Philonic authenticity of *De vita contemplativa* (cf. more fully volume III, § 34), and about the actual existence of a Jewish sect of Therapeutae in first

6. At first sight, the meaning of the rule appears to be that all the members of the group should participate in a study-prayer session for one-third of every night. Dupont-Sommer (*Essene Writings*, p. 85, n. 5) envisages a permanent vigil, held in rotation by one-third of the membership, thus echoing the practice of the Therapeutae described by Philo.

7. Cf. Vermes, *DSSE*, pp. 149–50.

8. Cf. vol. I, p. 600, n. 31. See also J. M. Baumgarten, '4Q Halakah[a] 5, the Law of Ḥadash and the Pentecontad Calendar', JJS 27 (1976), pp. 39–42.

9. Cf. above, p. 579.

10. Cf. J. T. Milik, *Ten Years of Discovery*, p. 92.

11. Cf. 1QS 1–3; 5:7–8; Jub. 6:11–21. See J. M. Baumgarten, *art. cit.*, p. 40; Vermes, *DSS*, pp. 177–8.

12. R. de Vaux, *Archaeology*, pp. 12–13, 111. For the meaning of *tirosh*, see above, p. 579, n. 16.

century A.D. Egypt, have now been largely dispelled as a result of the works of F. C. Conybeare, P. Wendland, I. Heinemann, P. Geoltrain and F. Daumas.[13] It is proper, therefore, at this juncture to attempt an assessment of the evidence with a view to determining whether Essenes and Therapeutae were two separate sects within the same movement, or the same sect described from differing points of view in the various sources.

The data listed in the previous pages appear to argue against a theory claiming full identity between Therapeutae and Essenes, and the common opinion of modern scholarship is, in fact, that the two sects, although originating from the same root,[14] or from the same spiritual need of pious Jews,[15] were nevertheless separate developments. Yet if it is borne in mind that our knowledge of the Therapeutae depends on a single ancient witness, Philo, and that his account is influenced by philosophical considerations—he wished to present the followers of the active and of the contemplative life as clearly distinguishable—some of the evidence usually cited to differentiate the two groups becomes somewhat less convincing.

In addition to the fresh information deriving from the Qumran Scrolls, the following points may be quoted in support of a closer bond between Therapeutae and Essenes.

The opening sentence of *De vita contemplativa* may be read with Scaliger as implying that the Therapeutae were contemplative Essenes: 'Quod Christiani non essent, sed mere Esseni, statim initio libri ostendit Philo.'[16]

The title of the work itself in the old Latin version identifies Therapeutae and Essenes: 'Philonis Iudaei liber de statu Essaeorum, id est Monachorum, qui temporibus Agrippae regis monasteria sibi fecerunt.' This is followed by the opening words: 'De statu Essaeorum disputaturus . . .'.[17] It may be worth noting that according to Scaliger the original Greek title of *De vita contemplativa* was *Περὶ θεωρετικοῦ βιοῦ τῶν Ἐσσαίων*.[18]

Whereas it is unthinkable that anyone today would give serious thought to Eusebius's theory that the Therapeutae were Egyptian

13. For the debate, see S. Wagner, *Die Essener* . . ., pp. 194–202. References to the authors listed are given in n. 1 above.

14. M. Simon, *Les sectes juives au temps de Jésus* (1960), pp. 105–13, especially 112–13.

15. F. Daumas, *op. cit.* [in n. 1 above], p. 57.

16. J. J. Scaliger, *Opus de emendatione temporum* (1629), p. xxii. Cf. Conybeare, *op. cit.* [in n. 1 above], p. 278; see also p. 192. The text of Philo reads: *Ἐσσαίων περὶ διαλεχθεὶς οἳ τὸν πρακτικὸν ἐζήλωσαν καὶ διεπόνησαν βίον . . . αὐτίκα καὶ περὶ τῶν θεωρίαν ἀσπασαμένων ἀκολουθίᾳ τῆς πραγματείας ἑπόμενοις τὰ προσήκοντα λέξω*, 1 (1).

17. Cf. Conybeare, *op. cit.*, p. 146.

18. *Op. cit.* [in n. 16], p. 538.

Christians (*HE* ii 16–17), it may not be without significance that Jerome and Epiphanius refer to them as 'Esseni' and *'Ιεσσαῖοι*.[19]

In the light of the ancient data, therefore, and the fresh support they have received from the Dead Sea discoveries, the hypothesis that the Therapeutae were members of an Egyptian branch of the Palestinian Essene movement deserves serious consideration.[20]

19. Jerome, *Adversus Iovinianum* ii 14 (PL 23, cols. 316–17): 'Iosephus . . . [Esseos] miris effert laudibus, quod et uxoribus et vino et carnibus semper abstinuerunt et cottidianum ieiunium verterint in naturam. Super quorum vita Philo, vir doctissimus, proprium volumen edidit.' Epiphanius, *Haer.* xxix 4, 9–10: *Καὶ πολλὰ ἔστι περὶ τούτου λέγειν, ἀλλ' ὅμως ἐπειδὴ εἰς τὸν τόπον ἐλήλυθα εἰπεῖν δι' ἣν αἰτίαν 'Ιεσσαῖοι ἐκαλοῦντο πρὶν τοῦ καλεῖσθαι Χριστιανοὶ οἱ εἰς Χριστὸν πεπιστευκότες, τούτου ἕνεκα ἔφημεν ὅτι 'Ιεσσαὶ πατὴρ γίνεται τοῦ Δαβὶδ, καὶ ἤτοι ἐξ ὑποθεσέως τούτου τοῦ 'Ιεσσαὶ ἤτοι ἐκ τοῦ ὀνόματος 'Ιησοῦ τοῦ κυρίου ἡμῶν ἐπεκλήθησαν 'Ιεσσαῖοι, διὰ τὸ ἐξ 'Ιησοῦ ὁρμᾶσθαι μαθηταὶ αὐτοῦ ὄντες, ἢ διὰ τὸ τῆς ἐτυμολογίας τοῦ ὀνόματος τοῦ κυρίου. 'Ιησοῦς γὰρ κατὰ τὴν 'Εβραϊκὴν διάλεκτον θεραπευτὴς καλεῖται, ἤτοι ἰατρὸς καὶ σωτήρ.*

20. Cf. Milik, *Ten Years of Discovery*, p. 92; Vermes, 'Essenes—Therapeutai—Qumran', Durham Univ. Journ. 21 (1960), pp. 97–115; 'Essenes and Therapeutai', RQ 3 (1962), pp. 495–504 [*PBJS*, pp. 30–6]; *DSS*, p. 136; Black, *The Scrolls and Christian Origins* (1961), p. 165. On the link between the Therapeutae and Christian monasticism in Egypt, see F. Daumas, *op. cit.* [in n. 1 above], pp. 58–66; 'La "solitude" des Thérapeutes et les antécédents égyptiens du monachisme chrétien', *Philon d'Alexandrie* (1967), pp. 347–58; A. Guillaumont, 'Philon et les origines du monachisme', *ibid.*, pp. 361–73.

Appendix B: The Fourth Philosophy: *Sicarii* and Zealots*

Sources

Josephus, *Ant.* xviii 1, 1 (4–10).

Ἰούδας δὲ Γαυλανίτης ἀνὴρ ἐκ πόλεως ὄνομα Γάμαλα Σάδδωκον Φαρισαῖον προσλαβόμενος ἠπείγετο ἐπὶ ἀποστάσει, τήν τε ἀποτίμησιν οὐδὲν ἄλλο ἢ ἄντικρυς δουλείαν ἐπιφέρειν λέγοντες καὶ τῆς ἐλευθερίας ἐπ' ἀντιλήψει παρακαλοῦντες τὸ ἔθνος· ὡς παρασχὸν μὲν κατορθοῦν εἰς τὸ εὔδαιμον ἀνακειμένης τῆς κτήσεως, σφαλεῖσιν δὲ τοῦ ταύτης περιόντος ἀγαθοῦ τιμὴν καὶ κλέος ποιήσεσθαι τοῦ μεγαλόφρονος, καὶ τὸ θεῖον οὐκ ἄλλως ἢ ἐπὶ συμπράξει τῶν βουλευμάτων εἰς τὸ κατορθοῦν συμπροθυμεῖσθαι μᾶλλον, ἂν μεγάλων ἐρασταὶ τῇ διανοίᾳ καθιστάμενοι μὴ ἐξαφίωνται πόνου τοῦ ἐπ' αὐτοῖς. καὶ ἡδονῇ γὰρ τὴν ἀκρόασιν ὧν λέγοιεν ἐδέχοντο οἱ ἄνθρωποι, προὔκοπτεν ἐπὶ μέγα ἡ ἐπιβολὴ τοῦ τολμήματος, κακόν τε οὐκ ἔστιν, οὗ μὴ φυέντος ἐκ τῶνδε τῶν ἀνδρῶν καὶ περαιτέρω τοῦ εἰπεῖν ἀνεπλήσθη τὸ ἔθνος· πολέμων τε ἐπαγωγαῖς οὐχ οἷον τὸ ἄπαυστον τὴν βίαν ἔχειν, καὶ ἀποστέρησιν φίλων, οἳ καὶ ἐπελαφρύνοιεν τὸν πόνον, λῃστηρίων τε μεγάλων ἐπιθέσεσιν καὶ διαφθοραῖς ἀνδρῶν τῶν πρώτων, δόξα μὲν τοῦ ὀρθουμένου τῶν κοινῶν, ἔργῳ δὲ οἰκείων κερδῶν ἐλπίσιν. ἐξ ὧν στάσεις τε ἐφύησαν δι' αὐτὰς καὶ φόνος πολιτικός, ὁ μὲν ἐμφυλίοις σφαγαῖς μανίᾳ τῶν ἀνθρώπων εἴς τε ἀλλήλους καὶ αὐτοὺς χρωμένων ἐπιθυμίᾳ τοῦ μὴ λείπεσθαι τῶν ἀντικαθεστηκότων, ὁ δὲ τῶν πολεμίων, λιμός τε εἰς ὑστάτην ἀνακείμενος ἀναισχυντίαν, καὶ πόλεων ἁλώσεις καὶ κατασκαφαί, μέχρι δὴ καὶ τὸ ἱερὸν τοῦ θεοῦ ἐνείματο πυρὶ τῶν πολεμίων ἥδε ἡ στάσις. οὕτως ἄρα ἡ τῶν πατρίων καίνισις καὶ μεταβολὴ μεγάλας ἔχει ῥοπὰς τοῦ ἀπολουμένου τοῖς συνελθοῦσιν, εἴ γε καὶ Ἰούδας καὶ Σάδδωκος τετάρτην φιλοσοφίαν ἐπείσακτον ἡμῖν ἐγείραντες καὶ ταύτης ἐραστῶν εὐπορηθέντες πρός τε τὸ παρὸν θορύβων τὴν πολιτείαν ἐνέπλησαν καὶ τῶν αὖθις κακῶν κατειληφότων ῥίζας ἐφυτεύσαντο τῷ ἀσυνήθει πρότερον φιλοσοφίας τοιᾶσδε· περὶ ἧς ὀλίγα βούλομαι διελθεῖν, ἄλλως τε ἐπεὶ καὶ τῷ κατ' αὐτῶν σπουδασθέντι τοῖς νεωτέροις ὁ φθόρος τοῖς πράγμασι συνέτυχε.

Ant. xviii 1, 6 (23–5).

Τῇ δὲ τετάρτῃ τῶν φιλοσοφιῶν ὁ Γαλιλαῖος Ἰούδας ἡγεμὼν κατέστη, τὰ μὲν λοιπὰ πάντα γνώμῃ τῶν Φαρισαίων ὁμολογούσῃ, δυσνίκητος δὲ τοῦ ἐλευθέρου ἔρως ἐστὶν αὐτοῖς μόνον ἡγεμόνα καὶ δεσπότην τὸν θεὸν ὑπειληφόσιν. θανάτων τε ἰδέας ὑπομένειν παρηλλαγμένας ἐν ὀλίγῳ τίθενται καὶ συγγενῶν τιμωρίας καὶ φίλων ὑπὲρ τοῦ μηδένα ἄνθρωπον προσαγορεύειν δεσπότην. ἑωρακόσιν δὲ τοῖς πολλοῖς τὸ ἀμετάλλακτον αὐτῶν τῆς ἐπὶ τοιούτοις ὑποστάσεως περαιτέρω διελθεῖν παρέλιπον· οὐ γὰρ δέδοικα μὴ εἰς ἀπιστίαν ὑποληφθῇ τι τῶν λεγομένων ἐπ' αὐτοῖς, τοὐναντίον δὲ μὴ ἐλασσόνως τοῦ ἐκείνων καταφρονήματος δεχομένου τὴν ταλαιπωρίαν τῆς ἀλγηδόνος ὁ λόγος ἀφηγῆται. ἀνοίᾳ τε τῇ ἐντεῦθεν ἤρξατο νοσεῖν τὸ ἔθνος Γεσσίου Φλώρου, ὃς ἡγεμὼν ἦν, τῇ ἐξουσίᾳ τοῦ ὑβρίζειν ἀπονοήσαντος αὐτοὺς ἀποστῆναι Ῥωμαίων. καὶ φιλοσοφεῖται μὲν Ἰουδαίοις τοσάδε.

Bibliography

Kohler, K., 'Wer waren die Zeloten oder Kannaim?', *Festschrift zu Ehren des Dr. A. Harkavy*, ed. D. von Günzburg and I. Markon (1908), pp. 1–17.

Kohler, K., art. 'Zealots', JE XII, pp. 639–42.

Jackson, F., and Lake, K., *The Beginnings of Christianity*, I, 1. *Prolegomena* (1920), pp. 421–5.

Kennard, J. S., 'Judas of Galilee and his Clan', JQR 36 (1945–6), pp. 281–6.

Farmer, W. R., *Maccabees, Zealots, and Josephus* (1956).

* Compiled by Dr. C. T. R. Hayward, Department of Religious Studies, University of Lancaster.

Roth, C., *The Historical Background of the Dead Sea Scrolls* (1958).
Roth, C., 'The Zealots in the War of 66–73', JSSt 4 (1959), pp. 332–55.
Roth, C., 'The Zealots—A Jewish Religious Sect', Judaism 8 (1959), pp. 33–40.
Hengel, M., *Die Zeloten* (1961, ²1976).
Zeitlin, S., 'Zealots and Sicarii', JBL 81 (1962), pp. 395–8.
Zeitlin, S., 'Masada and the Sicarii', JQR 55 (1964), pp. 299–317.
Driver, G. R., *The Judaean Scrolls* (1965).
Yadin, Y., *Masada: Herod's Fortress and the Zealots' Last Stand* (1966).
Brandon, S. G. F., *Jesus and the Zealots* (1967).
Brandon, S. G. F., art. 'Zealots', Enc. Jud. 16, cols. 947–50.
Brandon, S. G. F., art. 'Sicarii', Enc. Jud. 14, cols. 1491–2.
Applebaum, S., 'The Zealots: The Case for Revaluation', JRS 61 (1971), pp. 156–70.
Borg, M., 'The Currency of the Term "Zealot" ', JThSt 22 (1971), pp. 504–12.
Nikiprowetzky, V., 'La mort d'Eléazar fils de Jaïre et les courants apologétiques dans le *de bello Judaico* de Flavius Josèphe', *Hommages à André Dupont-Sommer* (1971), pp. 461–90.
Smith, M., 'Zealots and Sicarii: Their Origins and Relations', HThR 64 (1971), pp. 1–19.
Stern, M., art. 'Zealots', Enc. Jud. Yearbook (1973), pp. 132–52.
Black, M., 'Judas the Galilean and Josephus's "Fourth Philosophy" ', *Josephus-Studien* (O. Michel Festschrift), ed. by O. Betz *et al.* (1974), pp. 45–54.
Rhoads, D. M., *Israel in Revolution: 6–74 C.E. A Political History based on the Writings of Josephus* (1976).
Smallwood, E. M., *The Jews under Roman Rule* (1976), pp. 153–5, 312–69.
Stern, M., 'The Zealots', *A History of the Jewish People*, ed. H. H. Ben Sasson (1976), pp. 274–6.
Loftus, F., 'The Martyrdom of the Galilean Troglodytes', JQR 66 (1976), pp. 212–23.
Loftus, F., 'The Anti-Roman Revolts of the Jews and the Galileans', JQR 68 (1977), pp. 78–98.
Stern, M., 'Sicarii and Zealots', *World History of the Jewish People* VIII (1977), pp. 263–301.

Along with the three 'philosophical sects' of Pharisees, Sadducees and Essenes, Josephus lists a fourth unnamed philosophy founded by Judas of Gamala and Zaddok the Pharisee, somewhat inconsistently describing it as having nothing in common with the other three (*B.J.*),[1] yet agreeing in all things with the Pharisees, save that 'they have a passion for liberty that is almost unconquerable, since they are convinced that God alone is their leader and master (*Ant.*)'.[2] Judas and Zaddok announced their philosophy at the time of Quirinius's census,[3] inciting the Jews to rebel against Rome and insisting that the census was designed to reduce the people to slavery, an intolerable condition for a nation whose lord was God alone.[4]

1. *B.J.* ii 8, 1 (108).
2. *Ant.* xviii 1, 6 (23). English quotations are from the translation of H. St.J. Thackeray.
3. See vol. I, pp. 381–2. Zaddok the Pharisee is not included in the account of the philosophy's formation in *B.J.* ii 8, 1 (108).
4. *Ant.* xviii 1, 6 (23); cf. *B.J.* ii 8, 1 (108).

Josephus calls Judas σοφιστής[5] and ἡγεμών[6] of the fourth philosophy, which influenced all who took up arms against Rome and led finally to the war of A.D. 66.[7] Josephus's well-known bias in his writing of the history of the war[8] appears nowhere more plainly than in his description of the opponents of Roman authority as λῃσταί, 'brigands',[9] στασιασταί, 'rebels',[10] or νεωτερίζοντες,, 'revolutionaries'.[11] Judas's family was prominent among these freedom fighters. His father Ezekias[12] had opposed Herod's tyranny; his sons Simon and Jacob were crucified for anti-Roman activities under Tiberius Julius Alexander;[13] his descendant Menahem seized Masada at the beginning of the revolt in 66,[14] and was leader of the revolution in Jerusalem until his murder by Eleazar b.

5. *B.J.* ii 8, 1 (108). This description marks out Judas as a teacher with his own distinctive interpretation of the Torah: see below, pp. 603–4, and Hengel, *Zeloten*, pp. 85–9.

6. *Ant.* xviii 1, 6 (23).

7. In view of the distinctions which Josephus draws between the various groups of rebels, it is essential to recall that they all sprang from Judas' philosophy. Using the metaphor of seed-sowing and planting, Josephus declares that there was no sort of evil which was not *sowed* by these men, including under this heading the beginning of the war, the removal of those in favour of peace, brigand raids, and the assassination of the aristocracy, *Ant.* xviii 1, 1 (6). Then Judas' followers *sowed the seeds* which produced civil war among the revolutionaries (see vol. I, pp. 496–501), and *planted* the roots of the people's destruction, *Ant.* xviii 1, 1 (10).

8. Cf. Hengel, *Zeloten*, pp. 6–18; H. Lindner, *Die Geschichtsauffassung des Flavius Josephus im Bellum Judaicum* (1972); V. Nikiprowetzky, 'La mort d'Eléazar fils de Jaïre. . . .', pp. 461–90.

9. Cf. *B.J.* ii 12, 2 (228), a group of 'brigands' attacked Caesar's slave on the road to Beth-Horon; *B.J.* ii 13, 2 (253), Felix captures many of the 'brigands' led by Eleazar b. Deinaeus; *B.J.* ii 14, 1 (271), Festus deals with 'brigands'. The Sicarii active in the time of Felix, *B.J.* ii 13, 3 (254) are called 'brigands' in *Ant.* xx 8, 5 (160); the Zealots are similarly labelled 'brigands', *B.J.* iv 3, 12 (198). Hengel, *Zeloten*, pp. 26–35, discusses the offence of 'brigandage' in Roman Law and the various penalties meted out: cf. B. S. Jackson, *Theft in Early Jewish Law* (1972), pp. 36–7; and see also vol. I, p. 462, n. 29.

10. E.g. *B.J.* ii 17, 7; 17, 9 (431,441); the 'brigands' of *B.J.* ii 12, 2 (228) appear as 'seditious revolutionaries' in *Ant.* xx 5, 4 (113); Eleazar b. Deinaeus is presented as leader of a brigand band καὶ στασιώδους, *B.J.* ii 12, 4 (235). See also *B.J.* i 1, 4 (10); ii 15, 3 (320), 15, 4 (324), 17, 9 (441), this last referring to Zealots.

11. *B.J.* i 1, 2 (4), 10, 4 (202); ii 14, 1 (274), 17, 1 (407).

12. See vol. I, p. 275. Judas, son of Ezekias, attacked Herod's arsenal at Sepphoris, *B.J.* ii 4, 1 (56); *Ant.* xvii 10, 5 (271–2); cf. vol. I, p. 332. His identification with Judas the Galilean, as he is called in Acts 5:37, who opposed the census and started the fourth philosophy, is accepted by Derenbourg, *Essai*, p. 237; Graetz, *Geschichte* III, 1, pp. 250–8; Klausner, *Historyah* III, pp. 251–2; Hengel, *Zeloten*, pp. 337–8, where a bibliography is provided; J. S. Kennard, 'Judas of Galilee and his Clan', JQR 36 (1945–6), pp. 281–4. The identification is, however, considered unlikely by E. M. Smallwood, *The Jews under Roman Rule*, p. 153, n. 40.

13. Cf. vol. I, p. 457.

14. *B.J.* ii 17, 8 (433–4); vol. I, p. 486.

Simon's party;[15] and Menahem's nephew Eleazar b. Jair led the last stand of the freedom fighters at Masada.[16]

During the years A.D. 6 to 66 the fourth philosophy gained more and more adherents. Under Cumanus, brigands attacked Caesar's slave Stephanus,[17] and two of their leaders, Eleazar b. Deinaeus[18] and Alexander, wrought reprisals on the Samaritans for their murder of Galilean pilgrims.[19] Under Felix, the Sicarii, so called from the *sica* or curved dagger which they carried concealed in their garments to stab their unsuspecting victims, began their major political assassinations,[20] while under Albinus they carried on guerilla warfare, kidnapping high officials whom they would release in exchange for political prisoners, or bribing the procurator for the same end.[21] The outbreak of war found Menahem, son of Judas, in control of Masada,[22] whence he proceeded to Jerusalem. At first he led the revolution there, but was opposed and later murdered by the followers of Eleazar b. Simon.[23] After the collapse of resistance in Galilee, the war was concentrated in Jerusalem, where factions soon emerged within the revolutionary movement: Josephus lists, in order, the Sicarii, the followers of Simon b. Giora, the men of John of Gischala, and the Zealots.[24]

15. *B.J.* ii 17, 9 (445–9). He had appeared in Jerusalem as king, *σοβαρὸς γὰρ ἀναβεβήκει προσκυνήσων ἐσθῆτί τε βασιλικῇ κεκοσμημένος καὶ τοὺς ζηλωτὰς ἐνόπλους ἐφελκόμενος*, *B.J.* ii 17, 9 (444); cf. 17, 8 (433–4). Possibly bSanh. 98b has preserved a memory of Menahem's messianic pretensions in its statement that the Messiah's name is Menahem son of Hezekiah; cf. Lam.R. 1:16; yBer 5a; Kohler, 'Zealots', p. 641. Menahem's father Judas seems also to have set himself up as a messianic figure, *B.J.* ii 4, 1 (56); *Ant.* xvii 10, 5 (271–2), and his grandfaṭher would have been Ezekias. See also Hengel, *Zeloten*, pp. 296–307, and for the warrior Messiah in Palestinian tradition cf. Tg. Ps.-Jon on Gen. 49:11; Num. 24:7, 17, 24. Josephus, *B.J.* vi, 5, 4 (312–5) admits that Messianic speculation was known to the rebels; see also M. McNamara, *The New Testament and the Palestinian Targum to the Pentateuch* (1966), pp. 230–3.

16. *B.J.* vii 10, 1–11, 5 (410–end); vol. I, pp. 511–13.

17. *B.J.* ii 12, 2 (228); vol. I, pp. 458–9.

18. *B.J.* ii 12,4 (235); *Ant.* xx 6, 1 (121); vol. I, p. 459. He may be the ben Dinai of Rabbinic tradition, who, according to Song R. 2:7 (1) attempted to force the messianic redemption of Israel. See Kohler, 'Zealots', p. 642; 'Wer waren die Zeloten. . . .', p. 15, who includes with him the murderers, הרצחנים, Amram and Taḥina, because of whose atrocities Rabban Yohanan b. Zakkai declared that the rite of the עגלה ערופה had been abolished (mSotah 9:9; cf. Graetz, *Geschichte* III, 2, p. 432). He was eventually captured by Felix, *B.J.* ii 13, 2 (253); vol. I, p. 463.

19. *B.J.* ii 12, 4–5 (235–8); *Ant.* xx 5, 4–6, 2 (117–25).

20. See vol. I, p. 463.

21. See vol. I, pp. 468–9.

22. See vol. I, p. 486.

23. Almost certainly Zealots: see below, pp. 604–5, and M. Stern, 'Zealots', Enc. Jud. Yearbook (1973), p. 145, who sees opposition to monarchy as one of the distinguishing features of the Zealot party.

24. *B.J.* vii 8, 1 (262–70); vi 2, 6 (148).

Considerable discussion has surrounded Josephus's use of the terms Sicarii and Zealots, the relationship of these groups to one another, and their connection with the fourth philosophy of Judas.[25] Given that Josephus's accounts of these groups are not entirely consistent, and that his reports are not always complete, it is impossible to arrive at certainty about the exact significance of these denominations. The evidence, however, indicates that the terms Sicarii and Zealots were used in connection with two separate, even opposing groups; that the Sicarii were organized by Judas at the census,[26] and that they remained loyal to his descendants, who provided them with quasi-messianic leaders until the fall of Masada.[27] After Menahem's murder and his followers' flight from Jerusalem, they are never heard of again in the city, but confined their activities to Masada. The Zealots, by contrast, were active only in Jerusalem. They are not named as a separate group until after the outbreak of war, when they appear as already organized under the leadership of the priest Eleazar b. Simon.[28] After the arrival in Jerusalem of John of Gischala they split into two factions, the more extreme of which was led by him.[29] The connection of the Sicarii with Judas's philosophy seems clear; yet although the Zealots are a group separate from the Sicarii,[30] an association between them and Judas's ideas cannot be ruled out:[31] Josephus stresses that the fourth philosophy

25. See, e.g., M. Stern, 'Zealots', Enc. Jud. (1973), p. 144; M. Borg, 'The Currency of the Term Zealot', JThSt 22 (1971), pp. 504–12; S. Zeitlin, 'Masada and the Sicarii', JQR 55 (1964), pp. 299–317; 'Zealots and Sicarii', JBL 81 (1962), pp. 395–8; M. Smith, 'Zealots and Sicarii: Their Origins and Relations', HThR 64 (1971), pp. 1–19; S. Applebaum, 'The Zealots: The Case for Revaluation', JRS 61 (1971), pp. 156–70; F. Jackson and K. Lake, *The Beginnings of Christianity*, I 1, pp. 421–5; G. Vermes, *Jesus the Jew* (1973), pp. 46–8; cf. vol. I, pp. 381–2.

26. *B.J.* vii 8, 1 (254).

27. See vol. I, pp. 511–13; and above, p. 601.

28. *B.J.* ii 20, 3 (564). Josephus first uses the word 'zealot' at *B.J.* ii 17, 9 (444), describing Menahem as τοὺς ζηλωτὰς ἐνόπλους ἐφελκόμενος. The phrase is best translated, with Thackeray, as '. . . his zealous followers'; cf. M. Smith, 'Zealots and Sicarii. . . .', pp. 7–8; M. Stern, 'Zealots', Enc. Jud. Yearbook, p. 144.

29. See vol. I, pp. 496–7.

30. Josephus's evidence must be given its full weight. The fact that ARNb 7 reports that Sicarii burned all the provisions in Jerusalem, while ARNa 6 ascribes this to Zealots should not necessarily be construed as evidence that Sicari and Zealots are the same: ARN is a late compilation which cannot overturn Josephus's first-hand testimony. See M. Smith, 'Zealots and Sicarii . . .', p. 9. The same observations are valid for the garbled account of Hippolytus (*Haer.* ix 26) quoted first by Kohler, 'Wer waren die Zeloten oder Kannaim', *Festschrift Harkavy* (1908), p. 8. This Church father also appears to equate Zealots and Sicarii as factions of the Essenes, but he cannot be accepted as a primary source for our knowledge of first century revolutionary movements; see M. Borg, 'The Currency of the Term Zealot', JThSt 22 (1971), pp. 504–12.

31. See E. M. Smallwood, *The Jews under Roman Rule* (1976), p. 154; M. Stern, 'Zealots', Enc. Jud. Yearbook, p. 144.

was responsible for the ruin of the Jewish cause,[32] and if that philosophy were confined to the Sicarii it is hard to see how such can have been so.[33]

Judas's philosophy, therefore, was probably the common property of all the revolutionary groups. Its first distinguishing mark was its desire for freedom, ἐλευθερία; even the legend on the coins minted during the war of A.D. 66–70 reads חרות ציון, 'Freedom of Zion'.[34] The Holy City and Temple were to be free so that pure worship could be offered: they could then proclaim on other coins לגאלת ציון, 'Of the Redemption of Zion'.[35] Judas and Zaddok asserted that the census should be regarded as slavery, and called on loyal Jews to begin the process of redemption which could not be accomplished without their active assistance.[36] The Bible explicitly states that Israel should not be numbered:[37] further, the census was a preliminary to taxation, and all adult male Israelites would be required to pay tribute to Caesar with coins bearing Caesar's image. This, in the eyes of Judas, constituted a breach of the Torah, which forbids images, idolatry, and the worship of other gods. This 'sharpening'[38] of the Torah's demands is evident also in the second tenet of the fourth philosophy, the affirmation that God alone is leader and master, a biblical commonplace which those who fought against Rome were to take *au pied de la lettre*.[39] God is Israel's lord (אדון); by proclaiming his uniqueness in reciting *Shema*', the Jews take upon themselves 'the yoke of the Kingdom of Heaven'.[40] Thus radically interpreting

32. *Ant.* xviii 1, 1 (6–10); cf. Hengel, *Zeloten*, pp. 61–78.

33. So M. Stern, *op. cit.*, p. 144.

34. For the evidence of the coins, see Y. Yadin, IEJ 15 (1965), pp. 1–120; *Masada: Herod's Fortress and the Zealots' last Stand* (1966), pp. 97–8, 108–9, 168–71; and above, vol. I, Appendix IV 'Hebrew Coins', p. 605.

35. Legends of a similar sort appear on coins of the Bar Kokhba rebellion: see vol. I, p. 606. For the notion of גאלה, cf. Hengel, *Zeloten*, pp. 122, 124.

36. *Ant.* xviii 1, 1 (5). Human co-operation with God was also a tenet of Pharisaic beliefs, *Ant.* xviii 1, 3 (13); *B.J.* ii 8, 14 (163), and explains partly Josephus's statement that the Fourth Philosophy agreed with the Pharisees in all save the points mentioned. Certain Pharisees, particularly those of Beth Shammai, had activistic tendencies, and may have sympathized with Judas' movement: see J. Klausner, *Historyah* IV, p. 200; Graetz, *Geschichte* III, 1, p. 255; Hengel, *Zeloten*, pp. 91–3; M. Stern, 'Zealots', p. 144. This active violence took no account of Israel's repentance, which, according to main stream rabbinic Judaism, had merited the Exodus from Egypt, Ex.R. 1:36; Tg.Ps.-Jon. on Ex. 2:25; cf. also Mk. 1:4; Mt. 1:15; 3:1 ff.; 4:17. For the view that Jesus and his disciples were sympathetic to the Zealots, see S. G. F. Brandon, *Jesus and the Zealots* (1967).

37. Cf. Hengel, *Zeloten*, pp. 134–5.

38. Cf. Hengel, *op. cit.*, pp. 232–3.

39. Biblical texts asserting divine lordship over Israel were expounded in an eschatological sense. It has been suggested that the title σοφιστής given to Judas *B.J.* ii 8, 1 (108) and to Menahem, *B.J.* ii 17, 8 (433) implies that they were skilled exponents of the Torah: see Hengel, *Zeloten*, pp. 229–34.

40. See Str.-B. I, pp. 172–7; I. Elbogen, *Der jüdische Gottesdienst*, pp. 24, 236–8, 242; Hengel, *Zeloten*, pp. 95–8.

God's sovereignty, Judas set out to establish the Kingdom of God on earth: for this reason neither his followers nor their successors called any man master (δεσποτής); indeed, they were prepared to put their opponents to death, and submit to death themselves, rather than acknowledge human lordship. But Josephus brands these ideas as 'folly',[41] and blames them for the ills which befell the nation: for the historian, Judas's philosophy constituted an 'innovation and reform in ancestral traditions', and was an intrusion into Jewish life.[42]

The Sicarii of Masada remained faithful to Judas to the end: the speech of Eleazar b. Jair made before the survivors decided to commit suicide rather than fall into Roman hands is proof of this. Eleazar says that they had determined to serve none save God, who alone is the true and just master of men; they had refused to become slaves, and would not do so now that their defeat was inevitable. Death would liberate their souls.[43]

Josephus presents the formation of the Zealot party as a coalition of 'brigands' from the city and the country based on a group led by the priest Eleazar b. Simon.[44] *Ζηλωταί*, it seems, was the party's name for itself. This Greek word represents the Hebrew קנאים, Aramaic קנאי,[45] and has a distinguished theological pedigree. Phinehas, grandson of Aaron, and Elijah, are singled out by the Bible for special praise on account of their zeal: Phinehas slew the apostate Zimri as he consorted with the heathen Midianitess, and thus turned God's wrath from Israel by making atonement for the apostasy.[46] Elijah was very zealous, withstood Ahab and Jezebel, and slew the heathen prophets.[47] When Antiochus IV Epiphanes attempted to abolish the faith of Israel and profaned the Sanctuary, Judas Maccabaeus resisted him, purified the Temple, and rededicated it, thus laying the foundations for the independent Hasmonaean state.[48] The Hasmonaeans traced their ancestry from Phinehas;[49] like him they were zealous for God's law by ridding the land and Temple of apostates.[50] They were an example, and

41. *Ant.* xviii 1, 6 (23).
42. *Ant.* xviii i, 1 (9); *B.J.* ii 8, 1 (108).
43. *B.J.* vii 8, 6 ff. (323 ff.). Their belief in the after-life compares with that of the Pharisees, *Ant.* xviii 1, 3 (14); *B.J.* ii 8, 10 (151). The excavations of Masada indicate the fidelity of the Sicarii to the Torah: see Y. Yadin, *Masada* (1966). The Sicarii figure occasionally in Rabbinic writings: see mMaksh. 1:6; Lam.R. to Lam. 4:4, 7; Eccl.R. to Eccl. 7:12; mKel. 17:12; Hengel, *Zeloten*, pp. 51–7.
44. *B.J.* iv 3, 1–9 (121–59); ii 20, 3 (564). In the opinion of Zeitlin, 'Judaism as a Religion', JQR 34 (1943–4), p. 351, n. 364, the Zealots were a priestly group.
45. See vol. I, p. 382, n. 128.
46. Num. 25:1–15.
47. 1 Kgs. 18; 19:10, 14.
48. See vol. I, pp. 138–63.
49. 1 Mac. 2:54.
50. 1 Mac. 2:19–28.

individual Jews would strive, even at the risk of their lives, to emulate the zeal of these heroes.[51] The Zealot party drew on such traditions, but Josephus accuses them of lawlessness and of subverting ancestral laws.[52] Thus they would put to death without the Sanhedrin's confirmation actual or potential collaborators with Rome;[53] they elected a High Priest by lot,[54] fortified the Temple,[55] abolished the sacrifice on behalf of Caesar,[56] and used the wine and oil stored in the Temple for their own support.[57] This zeal for God and his house may be seen as ushering in the last Day, before which, however, the 'woes' of the end-time were to be endured. The burning of supplies and food by the Zealots was apparently intended to increase these 'woes'; indeed, all their sufferings and martyrdoms were sacrifices for the Law and the people, and would hasten the coming of the age when God alone would rule.[58]

In their concern for the end, the Zealots were joined by prophets, whom Josephus scathingly calls γόητες.[59] They had been active for many years before the war, but with the Temple under siege their

51. On the relationships between the zeal of the Hasmoneans and the later Zealots, see W. R. Farmer, *Maccabees, Zealots, and Josephus* (1956), pp. 47–83. Individual 'zealots' are most likely spoken of in mSanh. 9:6, הגונב את הקסוה והמקלל בקוסם והבועל ארמית קנאים פוגעין בהן: The Gemara (bSanh. 82a) relates this mishnah to the Hasmoneans. Kohler, 'Zealots', p. 639, notes that these acts are not cases for criminal procedure, but are comparable to Phinehas's zealous act. Phinehas is singled out as an individual zealot, 4 Mac. 18:12; see M. Smith, 'Zealots and Sicarii . . .', p. 6. The Apostle Paul's zeal for the Law is of the same order, Gal. 1:14; Phil. 3:6; Acts 21:20; Hengel, *Zeloten*, pp. 184–6. The disciple of Jesus, Simon the Zealot (see vol. I, p. 382, n. 128) was most likely also an individual who took the Law 'into his own hands'; cf. M. Borg, 'The Currency of the Term Zealot', p. 508, but see also M. Stern, 'Zealots', p. 144.

52. *B.J.* vii 8, 1 (268); iv 5, 5 (348).

53. E.g. *B.J.* iv 3, 4 (138–46); 3, 10 (170); 6, 1 (357). For the necessity of confirmation of such sentences by the Sanhedrin, see *Ant.* xiv 9, 3 (165–7). Phinehas, prototype of the Zealots, had similarly acted unilaterally: his action called for comment on the part of the Sages. Thus he is approved because the Sanhedrin had forgotten the *halakhah* (Num.R. 20:6; Tg.Ps.-Jon. on Num. 25:7), or because Moses had become weak (Num.R. 20:25; Tg.Ps.-Jon. on Num. 25:6), or because the Pharisees allowed his deed (Sifre to Num. 131). For later rabbinic censure of Phinehas, see Hengel, *Zeloten*, pp. 172–5.

54. *B.J.* iv 3, 6 (147–50); 3, 8 (155–7). Zealot concern with the abolition of the priestly oligarchy appears to mark off that party from the Sicarii: so M. Stern, 'Zealots', p. 145.

55. *B.J.* iv 3, 10 (173).

56. *B.J.* ii 17, 2 (410).

57. *B.J.* v 13, 6 (563–6).

58. *B.J.* vi 7, 2 (364): 'Indeed, when they beheld the city burning, they declared with beaming faces that they cheerfully awaited the end . . .'. See Hengel, *Zeloten*, pp. 251–2; for the 'woes', see mSotah 9:15; bSanh. 97a, 98b; bShab. 118a; Volz, *Eschatologie*, p. 176; Moore, *Judaism* II, pp. 360–2.

59. *B.J.* vi 5, 2 (286). For the place of prophecy in Zealot thought, see Hengel, *Zeloten*, pp. 235–50.

prophesyings grew more intense.[60] They urged the people into the desert to await a new act of redemption, a 'second Exodus';[61] and in the days immediately preceding the destruction of the Sanctuary, they called on them to watch for the 'tokens of their deliverance'.[62]

With the capture of the Sanctuary, the Zealots requested Titus that they might retire to the desert, presumably to expect redemption.[63] Titus forbade this. Only the Sicarii at Masada held out now, but at length they fell by their own hands. Some escaped to Egypt and Cyrene, to be destroyed by the Romans whose claims they had sworn to deny and whose power they had so valiantly opposed.[64]

60. Any attack on the Temple seems to have produced outbursts of ecstatic utterances, as when Herod attacked Antigonus there, *B.J.* i 18, 1 (347).
61. *Ant.* xx 8, 6 (167–8).
62. *B.J.* vi 5, 2 (285).
63. *B.J.* vi 6, 3–4 (253–4); 8, 6–7 (323–61).
64. See vol. I, pp. 508–13.